The Broadview Anthology of

BRITISH LITERATURE

Volume 1
The Medieval Period

The Broadview Anthology of British Literature

The Broadview Anthology of

BRITISH LITERATURE

Volume 1
The Medieval Period

GENERAL EDITORS

Joseph Black, University of Massachusetts
Leonard Conolly, Trent University
Kate Flint, Rutgers University
Isobel Grundy, University of Alberta
Don LePan, Broadview Press
Roy Liuzza, University of Tennessee
Jerome J. McGann, University of Virginia
Anne Lake Prescott, Barnard College
Barry V. Qualls, Rutgers University
Claire Waters, University of California, Davis

broadview press

LIBRARY AND ARCHIVES CANADA CATALOGUING IN PUBLICATION

The Broadview Anthology of British Literature / general editors, Joseph Black ... [et al].

Includes bibliographical references and index.
Contents: v. 1. The Medieval period.
ISBN 1-55111-609-X (v. 1)

1. English literature. I. Black, Joseph Laurence, 1962–

PR1109.B77   2006   820.8   C2006-900091-3

Broadview Press is an independent, international publishing house, incorporated in 1985. Broadview believes in shared ownership, both with its employees and with the general public; since the year 2000 Broadview shares have traded publicly on the Toronto Venture Exchange under the symbol BDP.

We welcome comments and suggestions regarding any aspect of our publications—please feel free to contact us at the addresses below or at broadview@broadviewpress.com.

North America
PO Box 1243,
Peterborough, Ontario
Canada K9J 7H5

3576 California Road,
Orchard Park, NY, USA 14127
Tel: (705) 743-8990;
Fax: (705) 743-8353
email: customerservice@broadviewpress.com

UK, Ireland, and continental Europe
NBN International
Estover Road
Plymouth
UK PL6 7PY
Tel: +44 (0) 1752 202301;
Fax: +44 (0) 1752 202331;
Fax Order Line: +44 (0) 1752 202333;
Cust Ser: enquiries@nbninternational.com
Orders: orders@nbninternational.com

Australia and New Zealand
UNIREPS,
University of New South Wales
Sydney, NSW, 2052
Australia
Tel: 61 2 9664 0999;
Fax: 61 2 9664 5420
email: info.press@unsw.edu.au

www. broadviewpress.com

Broadview Press gratefully acknowledges the financial support of the Government of Canada through the Book Publishing Industry Development Program for our publishing activities.

Cover design by Lisa Brawn

PRINTED IN CANADA

Contributing Editors and Writers

Managing Editor   Don LePan
Editorial Coordinator   Jennifer McCue
General Academic and Textual Editor   Colleen Franklin
Design Coordinator   Kathryn Brownsey

Contributing Editors

Sandra Bell	Stephen Glosecki	Anne Lake Prescott
Emily Bernhard Jackson	Amanda Goldrick-Jones	Joyce Rappaport
Joseph Black	Michael Keefer	Herbert Rosengarten
Robert Boenig	Don LePan	Janice Schroeder
Laura Cardiff	Roy Liuzza	Andrew Taylor
Noel Chevalier	Marie Loughlin	Peggy Thompson
Mita Choudhury	D.L. Macdonald	Craig Walker
Thomas J. Collins	Anne McWhir	Claire Waters
Leonard Conolly	David Oakleaf	James Winny
Dianne Dugaw	Jude Polsky	

Contributing Writers

Laura Cardiff	Jane Grove	Nicole Shukin
Jude Polsky	Camille Isaacs	James Soderholm
Jane Beal	Erik Isford	Anne Sorbie
Rachel Bennett	Don LePan	Jenna Stook
Emily Bernhard Jackson	John McIntyre	Candace Taylor
Rebecca Blasco	Kenna Olsen	David van Belle
Julie Brennan	Kendra O'Neal Smith	Shari Watling
Andrew Bretz	Laura Pellerine	bj Wray
Emily Cargan	Jason Rudy	Nicole Zylstra
Wendy Eberle-Sinatra	Anne Salo	
Peter Enman	Janice Schroeder	

Layout and Typesetting

Kathryn Brownsey   Susan Chamberlain

Illustration Formatting and Assistance

Cheryl Baldwin   Lisa Brawn

PRODUCTION COORDINATORS

Barbara Conolly   Leonard Conolly   Judith Earnshaw

PERMISSIONS COORDINATORS

Emily Cargan   Jennifer Elsayed   Amy Nimegeer

PROOFREADERS

Jennifer Bingham   Anne Hodgetts
Martin Boyne   Amy Neufeld
Lucy Conolly   Lynn Neufeld
Lynn Fraser

EDITORIAL ADVISORS

Rachel Ablow, University of Rochester
Rita Bode, Trent University
Susan Brown, University of Guelph
Catherine Burroughs, Wells College
Elizabeth Campbell, Oregon State University
Nancy Cirillo, University of Illinois, Chicago
David Cowart, University of South Carolina
Alex Dick, University of British Columbia
Len Diepeveen, Dalhousie University
Daniel Fischlin, University of Guelph
Robert Forman, St. John's University
Barbara Gates, University of Delaware
Chris Gordon-Craig, University of Alberta
Stephen Guy-Bray, University of British Columbia
Elizabeth Hodgson, University of British Columbia
Michael Keefer, University of Guelph
Gordon Kipling, University of California, Los Angeles
William Liston, Ball State University
Peter Mallios, University of Maryland
Rod Michell, Thompson Rivers University
Byron Nelson, West Virginia University
Michael North, University of California, Los Angeles
John Pollock, San Jose State University
Carol Senf, Georgia Tech
Sharon Smulders, Mount Royal College
Goran Stanivukovic, St. Mary's University
Julian Yates, University of Delaware

CONTENTS

Preface

A Fresh Approach

To those with some awareness of the abundance of fresh material and lively debate in the field of English Studies in recent generations, it may seem surprising that this abundance has not been more fully reflected in the number of available anthologies. Thirty years ago there were two comprehensive anthologies designed for courses surveying British Literature: *The Norton Anthology of English Literature* and one alternative. In recent years there have been still two choices available—the *Norton* and one alternative. Over that time span *The Longman Anthology of British Literature* replaced *The Oxford Anthology of English Literature* in the role of "alternative," but there has been no expansion in range of available choices to match the expansion of content and of approach that has characterized the discipline itself. The number of available handbooks and guides to writing has multiplied steadily (to the point where there are literally hundreds of available choices), while the number of comprehensive anthologies of British literature has remained at two.

For those of us who have been working for the past three years on *The Broadview Anthology of British Literature*, it is not difficult to understand why. The very expansion of the discipline has made the task of assembling and editing an anthology that fully and vibrantly reflects the ways in which the British literary tradition is studied and taught an extraordinarily daunting one. The sheer amount of work involved is enormous, but so too is the amount of expertise that needs to be called on. With that background very much in mind, we have charted a new course in the preparation of *The Broadview Anthology of British Literature*. Rather than dividing up the work among a relatively small number of academics, and asking each of them to handle on their own the work of choosing, annotating, and preparing introductions to texts in their own areas of specialization, we have involved a large number of contributors in the process (as the pages following the

title page to this volume attest), and encouraged a high degree of collaboration at every level. First and foremost have been the distinguished academics who have served as our General Editors for the project, but in all there have literally been hundreds of people involved at various stages in researching, drafting headnotes or annotations, reviewing material, editing material, and finally carrying out the work of designing and typesetting the texts and other materials. That approach has allowed us to draw on a diverse range of talent, and to prepare a large anthology with unusual speed. It has also facilitated the maintenance of a high degree of consistency. Material has been reviewed and revised in-house at Broadview, by outside editors (chief among them Colleen Franklin, an academic with a wide-ranging background and also a superb copy editor), by a variety of academics with an extraordinarily diverse range of backgrounds and academic specialities, and by our team of General Editors for the project as a whole. The aim has been not only to ensure accuracy but also to make sure that the same standards are applied throughout the anthology to matters such as extent and coverage in author introductions, level of annotation, tone of writing, and student accessibility.

Our General Editors have throughout taken the lead in the process of making selections for the anthology. Along the way we have been guided by several core principles. We have endeavored to provide a selection that is broadly representative, while also being mindful of the importance of choosing texts that have the capacity to engage readers' interest today. We have for the most part made it a policy to include long works in their entirety or not at all; readers will find complete in these pages works such as *Utopia*, *Confessions of an English Opium Eater*, *In Memoriam* and *A Room of One's Own* that are often excerpted in other anthologies. Where inexpensive editions of works are available in our series of paperback Broadview Editions, we have often decided to omit them here, on the grounds that those wishing to teach one or more such works may easily order them in a combination package with the anthology; on these grounds we have decided against including *Frankenstein*, *Pride and Prejudice*, or *Heart of Darkness*. (For both Mary Shelley and Jane Austen we have made exceptions to our general policy regarding excerpts, however, including selections from *The Last Man* to represent Shelley and the first four chapters of *Pride and Prejudice*, together with a complete shorter work, *Lady Susan*, to represent Austen.)

Any discussion of what is distinctive about *The Broadview Anthology of British Literature* must focus above all on the contents. In every volume of the anthology there is material that is distinctive and fresh–including not only selections by lesser-known writers but also less familiar selections from canonical writers. The anthology takes a fresh approach too to a great many canonical texts. The first volume of the anthology includes not only Roy Liuzza's translation of *Beowulf* (widely acclaimed as the most engaging and reliable translation available), but also new translations by Liuzza of many other works of Old English poetry and prose. Also included in the first volume of the anthology are a new verse translation of *Judith* by Stephen Glosecki, and new translations by Claire Waters of several of the *Lais* of Marie de France. The second volume includes *King Lear* not only in the full Folio version but also with three key scenes from the Quarto version; readers are thus invited to engage first-hand with the question of how textual issues may substantially affect larger issues of meaning. And so on through all six volumes.

In a number of these cases the distinctive form of the anthology facilitates the presentation of content in an engaging and practical fashion. Notably, the adoption of a two-column format allows for some translations (the Marie de France *Lais*, the James Winny translation of *Sir Gawain and the Green Knight*) to be presented in parallel column format alongside the original texts, allowing readers to experience something of the flavor of the original, while providing convenient access to an accessible translation. Similarly, scenes from the Quarto version of *King Lear* are presented alongside the comparable sections of the Folio text, and passages from four translations of the Bible are laid out parallel to each other for ready comparison.

The large trim-size, two-column format also allows for greater flexibility in the presentation of visual materials. Throughout we have aimed to make this an anthology that is fully alive to the connections between literary and visual culture, from the discussion of the CHI-RHO page of the Lindisfarne Gospels in the first volume of the anthology (and the accompanying color illustration) to the inclusion in Volume 6 of a number of selections (including Graham Greene's "The Basement Room," Hanif Kureishi's "My Son the Fanatic," Tom Stoppard's "Professional Foul," and several skits from "Monty Python's Flying Circus") that may be discussed in connection with film or television versions. Along the way appear several full-page illustrations from the Ellesmere manuscript of Chaucer's *Canterbury Tales* and illustrations to a wide variety of other works, from *Robinson Crusoe* and *Gulliver's Travels* to *A Christmas Carol* and *The Road to Wigan Pier*.

CONTEXTUAL MATERIALS

Visual materials are also an important component of the background materials that form an important part of the anthology. These materials are presented in two ways. Several "Contexts" sections on particular topics or themes appear in each volume of the anthology, presented independent of any particular text or author. These include broadly based groupings of material on such topics as "Religion and Spiritual Life," "Print Culture," "India and the Orient," "The Abolition of Slavery," "The New Art of Photography," and "The End of Empire." The groups of "In Context" materials each relate to a particular text or author. They range from the genealogical tables provided as a supplement to *Beowulf*; to materials on "The Eighteenth-Century Sexual Imagination" (presented in conjunction with Haywood's *Fantomina*); to a selection of materials relating to the Peterloo massacre (presented in conjunction with Percy Shelley's "The Mask of Anarchy"); to materials on "'The Vilest Scramble for Loot' in Central Africa" (presented in conjunction with Conrad's "An Outpost of Progress"). For the most part these contextual materials are, as the word suggests, included with a view to setting texts in their broader literary, historical, and cultural contexts; in some cases, however, the materials included in "Contexts" sections are themselves literary works of a high order. The autobiographical account by Eliza M. of nineteenth-century life in Cape Town, for example (included in the section in Volume 5 on "Race and Empire"), is as remarkable for its literary qualities as it is for the light it sheds on the realities of colonial life. In the inclusion of texts such as these, as well as in other ways, the anthology aims to encourage readers to explore the boundaries of the literary and the non-literary, and the issue of what constitutes a "literary text."

WOMEN'S PLACE

A central element of the broadening of the canon of British literature in recent generations has of course been a great increase in the attention paid to texts by women writers. As one might expect from a publisher that has played an important role in making neglected works by women writers widely available, this anthology reflects the broadening of the canon quantitatively, by including a substantially larger number of women writers than have earlier anthologies of British literature. But it also reflects this broadening in other ways. In many anthologies of literature (anthologies of British literature, to be sure, but also anthologies of literature of a variety of other sorts) women writers are set somewhat apart, referenced in introductions and headnotes only in relation to issues of gender, and treated as important only for the fact of their being women writers. *The Broadview Anthology* strenuously resists such segregation; while women writers are of course discussed in relation to gender issues, their texts are also presented and discussed alongside those by men in a wide variety of other contexts, including seventeenth-century religious and political controversies, the abolitionist movement and World War I pacifism. Texts by women writers are front and center in the discussion of the development of realism in nineteenth-century fiction. And when it comes to the twentieth century, both Virginia Woolf and Dorothy Richardson are included alongside James Joyce as practitioners of groundbreaking modernist narrative techniques.

"BRITISH," "ENGLISH," "IRISH," "SCOTTISH," "WELSH," "OTHER"

The broadening of English Studies, in conjunction with the expansion and subsequent contraction of British power and influence around the world, has considerably complicated the issue of exactly how inclusive anthologies should be. In several respects this anthology (like its two main competitors) is significantly more inclusive than its title suggests, including a number of non-British writers whose works connect in important ways with the traditions of British literature. We have endeavored first of all to portray the fluid and multilingual reality of the medieval period through the inclusion not only of works in Old and Middle English but also, where other cultures interacted with the nascent "English" language and "British" culture, works in Latin, in French, and in Welsh. In later periods the word "British" becomes deeply problematic in different respects, but on balance we have preferred it to the only obvious alternative, "English." There are several objections to the latter in this context. Perhaps most obviously, "English" excludes authors or texts not only from Ireland but also from Scotland and from Wales, both of which retain to this day cultures quite distinct from that of the English. "English literature," of course, may also be taken to mean "literature written in English," but since the anthology does not cover *all* literature written in English (most obviously in excluding American literature), the ambiguity would not in this case be helpful.

The inclusion of Irish writers presents a related but even more tangled set of issues. At the beginning of the period covered by the six volumes of this anthology we find works, such as the *Book of Kells*, that may have been created in what is now England, in what is now Scotland, in what is now Ireland—or in some combination of these. Through most of the seventeenth, eighteenth, and nineteenth centuries almost the whole of Ireland was under British control—but for the most part unwillingly. In the period covered in the last of the six volumes Ireland was partitioned, with Northern Ireland becoming a part of the United Kingdom and the

Republic of Ireland declared independent of Britain on 6 December 1921. Less than two months earlier, James Joyce had completed *Ulysses*, which was first published as a complete work the following year (in Paris, not in Britain). It would be obviously absurd to regard Joyce as a British writer up to just before the publication of *Ulysses*, and an Irish writer thereafter. And arguably he and other Irish writers should never be regarded as British, whatever the politics of the day. If on no other grounds than their overwhelming influence on and connection to the body of literature written in the British Isles, however, we have included Irish writers—among them Swift, Sheridan, Wilde, Shaw, Beckett, Bowen, Muldoon, and Heaney as well as Joyce —throughout this anthology. We have also endeavored to give a real sense in the introductions to the six volumes of the anthology, in the headnotes to individual authors, and in the annotations to the texts themselves, of the ways in which the histories and the cultures of England, Ireland, Scotland and Wales, much as they interact with one another, are also distinct.

Also included in this anthology are texts by writers from areas that are far removed geographically from the British Isles but that are or have been British possessions. Writers such as Mary Rowlandson, Olaudah Equiano, and Phillis Wheatley are included, as they spent all or most of their lives living in what were then British colonial possessions. Writers who came of age in an independent United States, on the other hand, are not included, unless (like T.S. Eliot) they subsequently put down roots in Britain and became important British literary figures. Substantial grey areas, of course, surround such issues. One might well argue, for example, that Henry James merits inclusion in an anthology of British literature, or that W.H. Auden and Thom Gunn are more American poets than British ones. But the chosen subject matter of James's work has traditionally been considered to mark him as having remained an American writer, despite having spent almost two-thirds of his life in England. And both Auden and Gunn so clearly made a mark in Britain before crossing the Atlantic that it would seem odd to exclude them from these pages on the grounds of their having lived the greater part of their adult lives in America. One of our competitors includes Sylvia Plath in their anthology of

British literature; Plath lived in England for only five of her thirty years, though, and her poetry is generally agreed to have more in common with the traditions of Lowell, Merwin and Sexton than with the currents of British poetry in the 1950s and '60s.

As a broad principle, we have been open to the inclusion of twentieth and twenty-first century work in English not only by writers from the British Isles but also by writers from British possessions overseas, and by writers from countries that were once British possessions and have remained a part of the British Commonwealth. In such cases we have often chosen selections that relate in one way or another to the tradition of British literature and the British colonial legacy. Of the Judith Wright poems included here, several relate to her coming to terms with the British colonial legacy in Australia; similarly, both the Margaret Atwood and the Alice Munro selections include work in which these Canadian authors attempt to recreate imaginatively the experience of British emigrants to Canada in the nineteenth century; the Chinua Achebe story in the anthology concerns the divide between British colonial culture and traditional Nigerian culture; and so on. For convenience we have also grouped most of the post-World War II non-British authors together, following the "Contexts: The End of Empire" section. (Other than that, the table of contents for the anthology is arranged chronologically according to the birthdate of each author.)

THE HISTORY OF LANGUAGE, AND OF PRINT CULTURE

Among the liveliest discussions we had at meetings of our General Editors were those concerning the issue of whether or not to bring spelling and punctuation into accord with present-day practice. We finally decided that, in the interests of making the anthology accessible to the introductory student, we should *in most cases* bring spelling and punctuation in line with present-day practice. An important exception has been made for works in which modernizing spelling and punctuation would alter the meaning or the aural and metrical qualities. In practice this means that works before the late sixteenth century tend to be presented either in their original form or in translation, whereas later texts tend to have spelling and punctuation modernized. But where spelling and punctuation choices in later texts are known (or believed on reliable authority) to represent conscious choice on the part of the author rather than simply the common practice of the time, we have in those cases, too, made an exception and retained the original spelling and punctuation. (Among these are texts by Edmund Spenser, by William Cowper, by William Blake, John Clare, and several other poets of the Romantic era, by George Bernard Shaw, and by contemporary figures such as Linton Kwesi Johnson.)

Beyond this, we all agreed that we should provide for readers a real sense of the development of the language and of print culture. To that end we have included in each volume examples of texts in their original form—in some cases through the use of pages shown in facsimile, in others by providing short passages in which spelling and punctuation have not been modernized. A list of these appears near the beginning of each volume of the anthology.

We have also included a section of the history of the language as part of the introduction to each volume. And throughout the anthology we include materials—visual as well as textual—relating to the history of print culture.

A DYNAMIC AND FLEXIBLE ANTHOLOGY

Almost all major book publishing projects nowadays are accompanied by an adjunct website, and most large-scale anthologies are accompanied by websites that provide additional background materials in electronic form. The website component of this anthology, on the other hand, is precisely that—a *component* of the anthology itself. The notion of a website of this sort grew organically out of the process of trying to winnow down the contents of the anthology to a manageable level—the point at which all the material to be included would fit within the covers of bound books that would not be overwhelmingly heavy. And we simply could not do it. After we had made a very substantial round of cuts we were still faced with a table of contents in which each volume was at least 200 or 300 pages longer than our agreed-upon maximum. Our solution was not to try to cut anything more, but rather to select a range of material to be made available in a website component of the anthology. This material is in every way produced according to the same high standards of the material in the bound books; the editorial standards, the procedures for annotation, the author introductions, and the page design and layout—all are the same. The texts on the web, in short, are not "extra" materials; they are an integral part of the full anthology. In accordance with that principle, we have been careful to include a wide range of texts by lesser-known writers within the bound books, and a number of texts by canonical writers within the web component of the anthology.

The latter may be used in a variety of ways. Most obviously, readings from the web component are available to any purchaser of the book. Instructors who adopt *The Broadview Anthology of British Literature* as a course text are also granted permission to reproduce any web material for which Broadview holds copyright in a supplementary coursepack. An alternative for instructors who want to "create their own" anthology is to provide the publisher with a list of desired table of contents; Broadview will then make available to students through their university bookstore a custom-made coursepack with precisely those materials included. Other options are available too. Volumes of the anthology itself may of course be shrink-wrapped together at special prices in any desired combination. They may also (for a modest additional charge) be combined in a shrink-wrapped package with one or more of the over 200 volumes in the Broadview Editions series.

We anticipate that over the years the web-based component of the anthology will continue to grow—every year there will be a greater choice of web-based texts in the anthology. And every year too we anticipate additional web "extras" (discussed below). But we never foresee a day when the web will be the only option; we expect physical books always to remain central to Broadview's approach to publishing.

THE BROADVIEW LIST

One of the reasons we have been able to bring a project of this sort to fruition in such a relatively short time is that we have been able to draw on the resources of the full Broadview list: the many titles in the Broadview Editions series, and also the considerable range of other Broadview anthologies. As the contributors' pages and the permissions acknowledgments pages indicate, a number of Broadview authors have acted as contributing editors to this volume, providing material from other volumes that has been adapted to suit the needs of the present anthology; we gratefully acknowledge their contribution.

As it has turned out, the number of cases where we have been able to draw on the resources of the Broadview list in the full sense, using in these pages texts and annotations in very much the same form in which they appear elsewhere, has been relatively small; whether because of an issue such as the level of textual modernization or one of style of annotation, we have more often than not ended up deciding that the requirements of this anthology were such that we could not use material from another Broadview source as-is. But even in these cases we often owe a debt of gratitude to the many academics who have edited outstanding editions and anthologies for Broadview. For even where we have not drawn directly from them, we have often been inspired by them—inspired to think of a wider range of texts as possibilities than we might otherwise have done, inspired to think of contextual materials in places where we might otherwise not have looked, inspired by the freshness of approach that so many of these titles exemplify.

EDITORIAL PROCEDURES AND CONVENTIONS, APPARATUS

The in-house set of editorial guidelines for *The Broadview Anthology of British Literature* now runs to over 40 pages, covering everything from conventions for the spacing of marginal notes, to the use of small caps for the abbreviations CE and BCE, to the approach we have adopted to references in author headnotes to name changes. Perhaps the most important core principle in the introductions to the various volumes, in the headnotes for each author, in the introductions in "Contexts" sections, and in annotations throughout the anthology, is to endeavor to provide a sufficient amount of information to enable students to read and interpret these texts, but without making evaluative judgements or imposing particular interpretations. In practice that is all a good deal more challenging than it sounds; it is often extremely difficult to describe why a particular author is considered to be important without using language that verges on the interpretive or the evaluative. But it is fine line that we have all agreed is worth trying to walk; we hope that readers will find that the anthology achieves an appropriate balance.

ANNOTATION: It is also often difficult to make judgments as to where it is appropriate to provide an explanatory annotation for a word or phrase. Our policy as been to annotate where we feel it likely that most first- or second-year students are likely to have difficulty understanding the denotative meaning. (We have made it a practice not to provide notes discussing connotative meanings.) But in practice the vocabularies and levels of verbal facility of first- and second-year students may vary enormously, both from institution to institution and within any given college or university class. On the whole, we provide somewhat more annotation than our competitors, and somewhat less interpretation. Again, we hope that readers will find that the anthology has struck an appropriate balance.

THE ETHICS AND POLITICS OF ANNOTATION: On one issue regarding annotation we have felt that principles are involved that go beyond the pedagogical. Most anthologies of British literature allow many words or phrases of a racist, sexist, anti-Semitic, or homophobic nature either to pass entirely without comment, or to be glossed with apologist comments that leave the impression that such comments were excusable in the past, and may even be unobjectionable in the present. Where derogatory comments about Jewish people and money-lending are concerned, for example, anthologies often leave the impression that money-lending was a pretty unsavory practice that Jewish people entered by choice; it has been all too rare to provide readers with any sense of the degree to which English society consistently discriminated against Jews, expelling them entirely for several centuries, requiring them to wear physical marks identifying their Jewish status, prohibiting them from entering most professions, and so on. *The Broadview Anthology* endeavors in such cases, first of all, not to allow such words and phrases to pass without comment; and second, to gloss without glossing over.

DATES: We make it a practice to include the date when a work was first made public, whether publication in print or, in the case of dramatic works, made public through the first performance of the play. Where that date is known to differ substantially from the date of composition, a note to this effect is included in parentheses. With medieval works, where there is no equivalent to the "publication" of later eras, where texts often vary greatly from one manuscript copy to another, and where knowledge as to date of original composition is usually imprecise, the date that appears at the end of each work is an estimate of the date of the work's origin in the written form included in the anthology. Earlier oral or written versions are of course in some cases real possibilities.

TEXTS: Where translations appear in this anthology, a note at the bottom of the first page indicates what translation is being used. Similar notes also address overall textual issues where choice of copy text is particularly significant. Reliable editions of all works are listed in the bibliography for the anthology, which is included as part of the website component rather than in the bound books, to facilitate ready revision. (In addition to information as to reliable editions, the bibliography provides for each author and for each of the six periods a select lists of important or useful historical and critical works.) Copyright information for texts not in the public domain, however, is provided within the bound books in a section listing Permissions Acknowledgments.

INTRODUCTIONS: In addition to the introductory headnotes for each author included in the anthology, each "Contexts" section includes a substantial introduction, and each volume includes an introduction to the period as a whole. These introductions to the six volumes of the anthology endeavor to provide a sense not only of the broad picture of literary developments in the period, but also of the historical, social, and political background, and of the cultural climate. Readers should be cautioned that, while there is inevitably some overlap between information presented here and information presented in the author headnotes, an effort has been made to avoid such repetition as much as possible; the general introduction to each period should thus be read in conjunction with the author headnotes. The general introductions aim not only to provide an overview of ways in which texts and authors included in these pages may connect with one another, but also to give readers a sense of connection with a range of other writers and texts of the period.

READING POETRY: For much of the glossary and for the "Reading Poetry" section that appears as part of the appendices to each volume we have drawn on the superb material prepared by Herbert Rosengarten and Amanda Goldrick-Jones for *The Broadview Anthology of Poetry*; this section provides a concise but comprehensive introduction to the study of poetry. It includes discussions of diction, imagery, poetic figures, and various poetic forms, as well as offering an introduction to prosody.

MAPS: Also appearing within each of the bound books are maps especially prepared for this anthology, including, for each volume, a map of Britain showing towns and features of relevance during the pertinent period; a map showing the counties of Britain and of Ireland; maps both of the London area and of the inner city; and world maps indicating the locations of some of the significant places referenced in the anthology, and for later volumes showing the extent of Britain's overseas territories.

GLOSSARY: Some other anthologies of British literature include both glossaries of terms and essays introducing students to various political and religious categories in British history. Similar information is included in *The Broadview Anthology of British Literature*, but we have adopted a more integrated approach, including political and religious terms along with literary ones in a convenient general glossary. While we recognize that "googling" for information of this sort is often the student's first resort (and we recognize too the value of searching the web for the wealth of background reference information available there), we also recognize that information culled from the Internet is often far from reliable; it is our intent, through this glossary, through our introductions and headnotes, and through the wealth of accessible annotation in the anthology, to provide as part of the anthology a reliable core of information in the most convenient and accessible form possible.

OTHER MATERIALS: A chart of Monarchs and Prime Ministers is also provided within these pages. A range of other adjunct materials may be accessed through *The*

Broadview Anthology of British Literature website. "Texts and Contexts" charts for each volume provide a convenient parallel reference guide to the dates of literary texts and historical developments. "Money in Britain" provides a thumbnail sketch of the world of pounds, shillings, and pence, together with a handy guide to estimating the current equivalents of monetary values from earlier eras. And the website offers too a variety of aids for the student and the instructor. An up-to-date list of these appears on the site.

Acknowledgments

The names of those on the Editorial Board that shaped this anthology appear on the title page, and those of the many who contributed directly to the writing, editing, and production of the project on the following two pages. Special acknowledgment should go to Jennifer McCue, who as Editorial Coordinator has been instrumental in tying together all the vast threads of this project and in making it a reality; to Laura Cardiff and Jude Polsky, who have carried larger loads than any others in drafting introductory materials and annotations, and who have done so with great skill and unfailing grace; to Kathryn Brownsey, who has been responsible for design and typesetting, and has continued to do a superb job and to maintain her good spirits even when faced with near-impossible demands; to Colleen Franklin, for the range of her scholarship as well as for her keen eye as our primary copy editor for the entire project; to Emily Cargan, Jennifer Elsayed and Amy Nimegeer who have together done superb work on the vast job of clearing permissions for the anthology; and to Michelle Lobkowicz and Anna Del Col, who have ably and enthusiastically taken the lead with marketing matters.

The academic members of the Advisory Editorial Board and all of us in-house at Broadview owe an enormous debt of gratitude to the hundreds of academics who have offered assistance at various stages of this project. In particular we would like to express our appreciation and our thanks to the following:

Rachel Ablow, University of Rochester

Bryan Alexander, Middlebury College

James Allard, Brock University

Sharon Alker, Whitman College

Laurel Amtower, San Diego State University

Rob Anderson, Oakland University

Christopher Armitage, University of North Carolina, Chapel Hill

Clinton Atchley, Henderson State University

John Baird, University of Toronto

William Baker, Northern Illinois University

Karen Bamford, Mount Allison University

John Batchelor, University of Newcastle

Lynn Batten, University of California, Los Angeles

Alexandra Bennett, Northern Illinois University

John Beynon, California State University, Fresno

Robert E. Bjork, Arizona State University

Rita Bode, Trent University

Robert Boenig, Texas A & M University

Rick Bowers, University of Alberta

David Brewer, Ohio State University

William Brewer, Appalachian State University

Susan Brown, University of Guelph

Sylvia Brown, University of Alberta

Sheila Burgar, University of Victoria

Catherine Burroughs, Wells College

Rebecca Bushnell, University of Pennsylvania

Elizabeth Campbell, Oregon State University

Cynthia Caywood, University of San Diego

Jane Chance, Rice University

Ranita Chatterjee, California State University, Northridge

Nancy Cirillo, University of Illinois, Chicago

Eric Clarke, University of Pittsburgh

Jeanne Clegg, University of Aquila, Italy

Thomas J. Collins, University of Western Ontario

Kevin Cope, Louisiana State University

David Cowart, University of South Carolina

Catherine Craft-Fairchild, University of St. Thomas

Carol Davison, University of Windsor

Alex Dick, University of British Columbia

Len Diepeveen, Dalhousie University

Mary Dockray-Miller, Lesley College
Frank Donoghue, Ohio State University
Chris Downs, Saint James School
Julie Early, University of Alabama, Huntsville
Siân Echard, University of British Columbia
Garrett Epp, University of Alberta
Daniel Fischlin, University of Guelph
Verlyn Flieger, University of Maryland
Robert Forman, St. John's University
Roberta Frank, Yale University
Jeff Franklin, University of Colorado, Denver
Maria Frawley, George Washington University
Mark Fulk, Buffalo State College
Andrew Galloway, Cornell University
Michael Gamer, University of Pennsylvania
Barbara Gates, University of Delaware
Daniel Gonzalez, University of New Orleans
Jan Gorak, University of Denver
Chris Gordon-Craig, University of Alberta
Ann-Barbara Graff, Georgia Tech University
Michael Griffin, formerly of Southern Illinois
    University
Elisabeth Gruner, University of Richmond
Stephen Guy-Bray, University of British Columbia
Ruth Haber, Worcester State College
Margaret Hadley, University of Calgary
Robert Hampson, Royal Holloway University of
    London
Michael Hanly, Washington State University
Lila Harper, Central Washington State University
Joseph Harris, Harvard University
Anthony Harrison, North Carolina State University
Douglas Hayes, Winona State University
Jennifer Hellwarth, Allegheny University
Peter Herman, San Diego State University
Kathy Hickock, Iowa State University
John Hill, US Naval Academy
Thomas Hill, Cornell University
Elizabeth Hodgson, University of British Columbia
Joseph Hornsby, University of Alabama
Scott Howard, University of Denver
Tara Hyland-Russell, St. Mary's College
Catherine Innes-Parker, University of Prince Edward
    Island
Jacqueline Jenkins, University of Calgary

John Johansen, University of Alberta
Richard Juang, Susquehanna University
Michael Keefer, University of Guelph
Sarah Keefer, Trent University
Jon Kertzer, University of Calgary
Helen Killoran, Ohio University
Gordon Kipling, University of California, Los Angeles
Anne Klinck, University of New Brunswick
Elizabeth Kraft, University of Georgia
Mary Kramer, University of Massachusetts, Lowell
Linda Leeds, Bellevue Community College
Mary Elizabeth Leighton, University of Victoria
William Liston, Ball State University
Sharon Locy, Loyola Marymount University
Peter Mallios, University of Maryland
Arnold Markley, Penn State University
Pamela McCallum, University of Calgary
Kristen McDermott, Central Michigan University
John McGowan, University of North Carolina
Thomas McLean, University of Otago, New Zealand
Rod Michell, Thompson Rivers University
Kitty Millett, San Francisco State University
Richard Moll, University of Western Ontario
Monique Morgan, McGill University
Lucy Morrison, Salisbury University
Byron Nelson, West Virginia University
Carolyn Nelson, West Virginia University
Claudia Nelson, Southwest Texas State University
Holly Faith Nelson, Trinity Western University
John Niles, University of Wisconsin, Madison
Michael North, University of California, Los Angeles
Mary Anne Nunn, Central Connecticut State University
David Oakleaf, University of Calgary
Tamara O'Callaghan, Northern Kentucky University
Karen Odden, Assistant Editor for *Victorian Literature
    and Culture* (formerly of University of Wisconsin,
    Milwaukee)
Erika Olbricht, Pepperdine University
Patrick O'Malley, Georgetown University
Patricia O'Neill, Hamilton College
Delilah Orr, Fort Lewis College
Cynthia Patton, Emporia State University
Russell Perkin, St. Mary's University
Marjorie G. Perloff, Stanford University
John Peters, University of North Texas

Alexander Pettit, University of North Texas

Jennifer Phegley, The University of Missouri, Kansas City

John Pollock, San Jose State University

Mary Poovey, New York University

Gautam Premnath, University of Massachusetts, Boston

Regina Psaki, University of Oregon

Katherine Quinsey, University of Windsor

Geoff Rector, University of Ottawa

Margaret Reeves, Atkinson College, York University

Cedric Reverand, University of Wyoming

Gerry Richman, Suffolk University

David Robinson, University of Arizona

Laura Rotunno, Pennsylvania State University, Altoona

Nicholas Ruddick, University of Regina

Jason Rudy, University of Maryland

Donelle Ruwe, Northern Arizona University

Michelle Sauer, Minot State University

SueAnn Schatz, Lock Haven University of Pennsylvania

Dan Schierenbeck, Central Missouri State University

Norbert Schürer, California State University, Long Beach

David Seed, University of Liverpool

Carol Senf, Georgia Tech University

Judith Slagle, East Tennessee State University

Sharon Smulders, Mount Royal College

Malinda Snow, Georgia State University

Goran Stanivukovic, St. Mary's University

Richard Stein, University of Oregon

Eric Sterling, Auburn University Montgomery

James Stokes, University of Wisconsin, Stevens Point

Mary-Ann Stouck, Simon Fraser University

Nathaniel Strout, Hamilton College

Lisa Surridge, University of Victoria

Beth Sutton-Ramspeck, Ohio State University

Nanora Sweet, University of Missouri, St. Louis

Dana Symons, Simon Fraser University

Andrew Taylor, University of Ottawa

Elizabeth Teare, University of Dayton

Doug Thorpe, University of Saskatchewan

Jane Toswell, University of Western Ontario

Herbert Tucker, University of Virginia

John Tucker, University of Victoria

Mark Turner, King's College, University of London

Eleanor Ty, Wilfrid Laurier University

Deborah Tyler-Bennett, Loughborough University

Kirsten Uszkalo, University of Alberta

Lisa Vargo, University of Saskatchewan

Gina Luria Walker, The New School, New York City

Kim Walker, Victoria University of Wellington

Miriam Wallace, New College of Florida

Hayden Ward, West Virginia State University

Ruth Wehlau, Queen's University

Lynn Wells, University of Regina

Chris Willis, Birkbeck University of London

Lisa Wilson, SUNY College at Potsdam

Anne Windholz, Augustana College

Susan Wolfson, Princeton University

Kenneth Womack, Pennsylvania State University

Carolyn Woodward, University of New Mexico

Julia Wright, Wilfrid Laurier University

Julian Yates, University of Delaware

Arlene Young, University of Manitoba

Lisa Zeitz, University of Western Ontario

THE MEDIEVAL PERIOD

From a medieval perspective, the very title of this collection is interestingly problematic. The implication of deliberate choice in the term "anthology" (as opposed, for example, to a "miscellany") reminds us that in any such collection decisions have been made about what does and does not "fit," about lines of influence between works, and about defining the boundaries of a literary tradition. Medieval literature written in England, for instance, was by no means entirely, nor indeed mostly, written in English; works in Latin, Anglo-Norman French, Middle Welsh and Old Irish all survive alongside works in the languages now known to us as Old and Middle English. Many of these non-English texts had a profound influence on the literary tradition in English; to the extent that we have had to omit such works here, we have created gaps in the story this anthology tries to tell.

The anthology's designation of its literature as "British," moreover, raises a terminological difficulty that is almost as old as the Middle Ages itself. "British" and "English" are by no means interchangeable terms in the medieval period, and the uses of these terms as labels for a language and literary tradition have always been entwined with political realities and national identities. Broadly speaking, the word "British" derives from the Roman name for early Celtic settlers in what we now call the British Isles; "English" refers to the Germanic invaders and settlers who began arriving in the fifth century, pushed the Celtic inhabitants to the west and the north (now Wales and Scotland) and eventually ruled the central part of the island. For many centuries, the English defined themselves by their difference from the British, and *vice versa*. At the same time those who attempted to claim legitimate rulership of England made strategic use of the "British" tradition, perhaps most obviously in the ongoing traditions surrounding King Arthur, whose origins lie deep in British legendary history. But the intercultural appropriation between "British" and "English" has often worked both ways, and continues to do so: the Anglo-Irish poet Seamus Heaney laces his modern translation of *Beowulf*, a decidedly "English" poem, with idiosyncratic Ulsterisms and Celtic turns of phrase.

Finally, the very word "literature" (deriving from the Latin *litterae*, "letters") implies an existence in writing, but a great deal of what remains in written form from the Middle Ages had a prior existence as, or owes enormous debts to, oral forms. Most of what we now read as literature, from romances to lyrics to sermons, was written to be heard, not read. Texts of vernacular works in the Middle Ages are by no means as solidly fixed—as "textual"—as works of modern literature, or of medieval works in Latin, for that matter; the circumstances of their creation and reception are, at least ostensibly, performative and communal, not silent and solitary like a modern student reading this book. Modern literary culture tends to regard the written text, fixed and inert, as the primary or "real" form of a literary work; for some medieval works, especially those from the earlier Middle Ages, the written text seems to be almost an afterthought, little more than an aid to the memory of the reader/performer who recreates the "real" work by voicing the text out loud.

At the same time, however, the concept of a collection that gathers the authoritative examples of a cultural tradition would have been very familiar to medieval readers, who made extensive use of such collections. Medieval manuscripts that contain multiple works may be anything from carefully planned volumes presented to a patron, to somewhat haphazard gatherings of texts, to collections composed by an individual for his or her own use; our current knowledge of medieval literary culture could rightly be said to rest on medieval anthologies. Thus a reader who first encounters these texts in an anthologized form will encounter them in a format not so unlike their original manuscript context. The single-text "monograph"—one work between two covers—is by no means the most common mode of transmission for medieval texts, and the effort to determine the relationships between texts in medieval manuscripts, the intentions of the creators of such compilations and their effect upon readers, is one of the most interesting and important areas of contemporary medieval literary studies.

The drawing of artificial lines, whether geographical or temporal, is a profound limitation on one's understanding of the history of western literature. At the same time, we cannot simply ignore the geographical facts—which are historical and political facts as well, insofar as the unity of the island of Britain was imagined and achieved—or the differences between one age and another, although the borders (both of historical periods and of kingdoms) may always be contested. This collection likewise relies on distinctions—sometimes arbitrary, sometimes necessary, some obvious and some obscure—to give it shape and contour, form and structure. In English literary history one of the most obvious divisions lies between the literature of the Anglo-Saxons—the English before the Norman Conquest (1066)—and that of the English after the Conquest. Within these two broadly drawn periods further divisions can be made: early Old English literature, as far as we can reconstruct it, differs markedly from literature after the reign of Alfred the Great (d. 899), who sought to begin a program of vernacular literacy and bestowed a certain royal authority on English as a quasi-official written language.

After the Conquest, although English manuscripts were produced and read in somewhat reduced numbers, Norman French was the language of courtly culture in England. In the absence of schools and pedagogical traditions, English began to manifest the changes that characterize "Middle" English. After this period of "early" Middle English—roughly from the century after the Conquest until the beginning of the fourteenth century—English began to take its place alongside the culturally more prestigious Latin (the language of the church) and French (the language of the court, of law, and of administration); authors increasingly chose to write literary texts in English for aristocratic readers. The fifteenth century saw a gradual re-development of a written "standard" English, and an outpouring of literary works (particularly of a devotional nature) that fostered and responded to rising literacy rates. With the advent of printing in the latter fifteenth century, books became ever more widely available and the language increasingly standardized; in the sixteenth century, with the wider spread of printing in England, the standard became more and more fixed, even as the language was rapidly changing again, into what linguists call early Modern English.

HISTORY, NARRATIVE, CULTURE

Even a set of very broad periodizations like these raises questions about the relation between historical events and literary developments, or more generally speaking between culture and the imagination. Can we understand these literary works better by learning more about their historical context? Or can these works of the imagination shed light on that context and help us fill in its blank spaces? Which partner in the inseparable pairing of text and context will serve as the solid ground from which we can survey the other—which one is beyond interpretation? Has the human imagination changed so much that we only have access to it historically, and not immediately? On the other hand, what can we really *know* about the past, except what is said about it?

These questions vexed the minds of many medieval authors as well. Most modern scholars, like their medieval predecessors such as Isidore of Seville (a Spanish bishop who lived c. 560–636), are careful to note that history is not simply "what happened" in the past, but the *stories we tell* about what happened in the past. Events, objects, even stories, do not speak for themselves; they have to be arranged and explained, looked at and looked into, and gradually placed in a context constructed from our interpretations of other objects, events and stories. In this sense, no matter how great our respect for objectivity or how carefully balanced our analysis may be, our study of the past says as much about us as it does about the past we try to study. And texts help us understand their context as much as contexts help us understand texts.

In his poem *Ars Poetica* the modern author Archibald MacLeish insisted that "A poem should not mean / But be," but readers of literature from the distant past cannot indulge in the soothing luxury of that misconception. A rock can simply "be"; the remains of a stone wall, however, must "mean" something—they mark a boundary, claim a space, indicate a settlement. A rough diamond lying underground might "be"; but when it has been mined, cut, polished, weighed, set, valued, bought, and worn as jewelry, it is no longer "palpable and mute / as a globed fruit"; it has entered the noisy world of meaning. Similarly, a poem like *Beowulf* or *Sir Gawain and the Green Knight* does not simply exist as a self-evident story; like any work of the human imagination, it responds to and acts on the world in which it was created. Objects and events—the Sutton Hoo ship burial, Durham Cathedral, the Magna Carta, the Black Death of the fourteenth century— positively hum with meaning and intention and human consequences; they are inextricably caught in the web of signification and interpretation. Nothing goes without saying. Even a thing of astonishing beauty which we may enjoy simply for the æsthetic pleasure it gives us is not a self-contained object; it had a function in the society that made it, and part of its meaning—even the meaning of its beauty—lies in that function, which might range from the deepest of spiritual blessings to the purest gaudy display of its owner's ability to possess and appreciate expensive objects. To ignore the cultures that surrounded, created, and consumed these objects—whether they are artifacts in a museum or texts in a book— would be a fundamental mistake.

The famous CHI-RHO page of the early eighth-century Lindisfarne Gospels (London, British Library, MS Cotton Nero D.iv, a color illustration of which appears elsewhere in this volume), offers one example of the kinds of context we might consider when looking at a medieval artifact. We may begin by admiring its beauty, enjoying its exotic strangeness or Celtic "alterity," and marveling at the skill of its creators (whose names, as it happens, are recorded in the manuscript). Such an image could have a number of different effects on its viewers: it might impress those who can't read with the beauty and value of God's Word; it might attest to the devotion of the artists who made such a complex design, as well as their sophistication and expertise as craftsmen; it might display a religious house's capability for such 'conspicuous consumption' in the service of God. As we consider it more closely, we may find ourselves puzzled by the presence of a Greek monogram in a Latin text,

decorated in a distinctively "Insular" style in Northumbria c. 700. At least three cultures are on display here. The page insists on the intersection of English, Irish and Latin cultures—as intricately woven together as the knotty patterns of its own design. Looking more closely, we can see an English interlinear gloss to the Latin text, written in much smaller script, added some 200 years later. Its presence creates yet another layer of meaning and raises further questions. Who would write in such a rich and beautiful book? Is the gloss a necessary addition, suggesting that the Latin text was not sufficiently accessible to those using the book? What might its presence tell us about the status of Latin as a learned language, or a sacred one, in medieval England? The questions arising from this single page of a manuscript remind us that it is not simply a work of remarkable beauty, but a complex artifact of cultural history.

Saint Luke, Lindisfarne Gospels.
This page and a decorative "carpet page" precede the text of the gospel itself.

First text page, Gospel of Saint Luke, Lindisfarne Gospels. The text reads as follows: "Quoniam quidem multi conati sunt ordinare narrationem," "Since many have undertaken to put in narrative order …"

Note: A reproduction of the CHI-RHO page from the Lindisfarne Gospels appears in the section of color illustrations.

The CHI-RHO page embodies, in a particularly striking way, the reciprocal relationship of text and context; while it has much to tell us about the world of its creators, what we know about their world must also be brought to bear on our understanding of the manuscript. To take another example, the poem *Beowulf* has been used to explain other texts (or objects, in the case of the early East Saxon ship-burial at Sutton Hoo; the poem was introduced as evidence in the inquest which determined the ownership and disposition of the priceless objects unearthed from that site in 1939); conversely, other texts and objects can be brought to bear on the obscurities of the text of *Beowulf* and used as explanatory tools. And of course the poem has a place in a series of cultural moments—the unknown moment of its creation, the moment of its transcription into the manuscript in which it survives, the moment of its rediscovery and publication, the modern moment in which it is studied today. Each of these contributes, in some way, to the 'meaning' of *Beowulf*, and however tempting it may be to give priority to the more distant (and hence less familiar) contexts, no one of these cultural moments, strictly speaking, has a greater claim on the poem than another. We may wish to regard material objects as somehow more 'real' than stories, but from the distant perspective from which we observe them now, they are not: these bright objects on a blank background are as mute and as meaningful, as mysterious and as communicative, as the anonymous stories surviving in single manuscripts by unknown hands.

So the questions we might ask as we approach these texts involve less what they "are" than what they "do", what they might mean not only to their imagined original audience(s) but to us, and how that meaning might change as our knowledge develops. What draws us to these old tales? What do we derive from them? Can we understand them in anything like their original form, with our inevitably modern minds? To what extent can we negotiate the difference between the present and the past? This is a constant problem, a challenge for any reader of early literature. A reader of a contemporary novel is seldom aware of the complex web of cultural assumptions that sustains the narrative; these assumptions are transparent and automatic. For readers of early literature the assumptions are solid, opaque, at times impenetrable—but this awareness of the alterity of the reader to the text is, we think, a very healthy thing. It is always good to be reminded that meanings are not simply "there" in the text, waiting for the reader to stumble over them; they are kindled by the friction between the reader, the story and the world they both inhabit. Medieval texts force this awareness upon us, but it serves us well as readers of any literary work.

The cultures of the Middle Ages are as varied as they are numerous, and diverse as well in the ways in which they interacted with one another. Moreover, the medieval period was one of continual change. Such change tended to occur at a slower pace than it does in our own time, but the medieval era saw vast and violent upheavals, and great cultural and social developments. From long habit, however, we refer to the millennium following the collapse of the Roman Empire in the fifth century CE as one period, the Middle Ages (or, using the Latinized form of the same phrase, the medieval period). At the end of this long expanse of time falls what we still sometimes call the Renaissance (or "rebirth"). This term reflects Renaissance writers' and thinkers' view of their own time. Many modern historians and literary scholars see the Renaissance of the fourteenth to sixteenth centuries as representing the final flowering of medieval culture rather than a dramatic break with the past; where historians *in* the Renaissance saw difference and division, historians *of* the period tend to see continuity and development.

Even so, many readers coming to the study of medieval literature or culture for the first time will be struck by a sense of strangeness in much of what they encounter. They will enter worlds in which nature is malevolent, not benign; in which Christ fights as a warrior; in which the walls of an ancient city are said to have been broken by fate; in which it is possible to have one's head sliced off and carry it around before putting it back on; in which doubtful legal claims may be decided by the judgment of God through trial by ordeal or by battle; in which water may be thought to flow upward; and in which the middle of a literary text can be said to be inherently better from a moral point of view than the beginning or the end. Much as this introduction aims to convey, and offer a context for, the complexity and sophistication that often characterize medieval texts, it will also recognize that it is difficult —and perhaps even undesirable—for modern readers to lose entirely their sense of strangeness and even wonder in experiencing the products of medieval literature and medieval culture.

Just as the literature of the Middle Ages may seem unusual to us, many modern readers may be surprised by the marginal political status of England and the English language in the Middle Ages. Britain was geographically on the edge of the world, and at the periphery of the political life of the continent; England was for many centuries the object rather than the subject of imperial ambitions. The status of English varied considerably from one century to another, but it was never at any time the dominant global force it is today. The ways in which an extraordinarily diverse cultural and linguistic mix began, over the course of the Middle Ages, to produce the works presented here—as well as, ultimately, the language of this introduction—will be a major theme of these pages.

ENGLAND BEFORE THE NORMAN CONQUEST

ROMAN AND CELTIC BRITAIN

We know little or nothing of the inhabitants of Britain before 500 BCE, when groups of people that we now call the Celts began to migrate from continental Europe to Britain and Ireland. We have come to think of these peoples as a unified group in large part because the artistic and literary heritage of Celtic culture that has come down to us displays considerable unity in the characteristics of its narratives, in the bold decorative style of its visual arts, and in the close ties among Celtic languages. But the Celts, who had spread throughout much of Europe in the centuries before they began to inhabit Britain, were very much a loose grouping of societies, often at odds with one another, with no overarching administrative authority or social coherence.

The Romans invaded and conquered Celtic Britain in the first century CE. Britain lay at the edge of the Roman Empire; the Romans never managed to conquer Ireland or what is now Scotland, then largely inhabited by a Celtic or possibly pre-Celtic people of particularly fierce reputation known as the Picts. (In the early second century CE the Romans constructed the rampart known as "Hadrian's Wall" across the island as a defense against them.) Throughout most of what is now England and Wales, however, the Romans were successful in establishing administrative structures that made *Britannia* a province of the Roman Empire. Though far from the heart of the Empire, Britain was clearly a rich and valuable province, and much of the population, at least in the centers of the island, was thoroughly Romanized. It is now thought that the island was densely populated; it enjoyed a thriving money economy and commerce, with a number of large urban centers including a settlement on the banks of the Thames River named *Londinium*, a network of roads, large villas in the Roman style, heated baths, water and sewage service in some areas, and sturdy traditions of Roman administration, education, and literacy. When Christianity spread throughout the Roman empire, it spread in Britain as well—Christian mosaics have been discovered on the site of a large fourth-century villa, and in 314 three British bishops attended a council in Arles, France. In the early years of the fifth century Saint Patrick, a Roman Briton, traveled through Ireland as a missionary bishop, spearheading the conversion of that island. In many respects Britain in the fourth century had a prosperity it would not see again until the fourteenth century.

Roman Britain was highly fortified and well defended from its hostile neighbors, but at the turn of the fifth century the Roman legions stationed in Britain were withdrawn for deployment in the heart of the Empire, in part to defend Rome from the various barbarian tribes pouring across its eastern frontiers. Soon afterwards, the Scots and the Picts began to encroach upon the territories of the Romanized British. It is unclear who ruled the island during these years or how it was defended; the Britons were left to their own devices, and tradition portrays them as hapless and virtually helpless. The traditional story, told among other places in the writing of a sixth-century Briton named Gildas, tells how the Britons turned to the Germanic peoples of continental Europe for assistance. The Angles, Saxons, and Jutes, Germanic tribes who occupied the coastal areas of what is now northwestern Germany and Denmark, were quite willing to work as soldiers for hire, but once they had established themselves in Britain as allies of the Britons, they began to demand land of their own, seized power from their employers, slaughtered and dispossessed them, and soon established themselves in the eastern parts of the island.

Contemporary archaeological evidence suggests, however, that the Germanic migrations actually took place in numerous waves from the later fourth century on. Relations between these Germanic invaders, who were probably not numerous, and the British are hard to reconstruct, but it appears that British culture was eventually supplanted not simply because the British were driven out, but because many of them intermingled with their Germanic conquerors and adopted the dress, language and culture of their new ruling class so that whatever their cultural heritage, they became, to later archaeologists and historians, indistinguishable from the Germanic Angles and Saxons. When the Romans had ruled, the Britons were Romanized; when the Saxons ruled, they were Saxonized. On the other hand, there are few words of British origin in Old English, the language of the Germanic invaders, and it is certainly significant that the Old English word *wealh* means both 'slave' and 'Welshman'. But whatever the reasons for its erosion, by around 600 CE a distinctively British culture was largely confined to Wales and Cornwall. On the continent a parallel series of events occurred, with groups of Franks pushing the Celtic peoples of Gaul to the geographical margin of Brittany. Although they had been marginalized geographically and politically, however, the Celtic peoples continued to exert a powerful shaping influence on what would become English literature, which persisted even after the Norman Conquest, in the retelling of Irish and Welsh legends, in the survival of the genre of story known as the "Breton lay," and in the fragmentary memories of British kings and warlords who led a temporarily successful resistance against the Saxon invaders—stories which formed the kernel of truth at the heart of the legends of King Arthur, arguably the great political myth of the Middle Ages.

MIGRATION AND CONVERSION

The culture of the Angles, Saxons and Jutes was quite different from that of the Romanized Britons. Though there is some evidence for continuing populations in Roman cities, the Germanic migrants were largely rural rather than urban, and built primarily in wood rather than stone—most of the great buildings of the Romans fell into ruin or were plundered for building materials. Their society were apparently organized, at least during the migration period, around a male leader and warrior band rather than the hearth and family, or the city or state. If the characterization of the first century CE Roman historian Tacitus is to be believed, the continental Germanic tribes were a notably warlike culture: "they are not so easily persuaded to plow the earth and to wait for the year's produce as they are to challenge an enemy and earn the honor of wounds," Tacitus comments. "They actually think it tame and stupid to acquire by the sweat of toil what they might win by their blood." Certainly later centuries regarded the Germanic tribes as particularly fierce. The Angles and Saxons had a writing system—runic carvings—but no culture of literacy in which it might be put to more than the simplest uses. Their economy was based on barter and gift-exchange, not money. Perhaps most importantly, the Angles and Saxons were pagan, worshipping a pantheon of northern gods such as Woden and Thor, and as they came to dominate Britain so the influence of Christianity moved (with the Britons themselves) to the margins.

But Christianity did not disappear as Britain became England (from *engla-land*, the land of the Angles). When Pope Gregory the Great sent Augustine (now known as Augustine of Canterbury, not to be confused with the more famous Augustine, bishop of Hippo in north Africa) on a mission to convert the English in 597, he met with extraordinary early success, in part no doubt because Christianity already had a strong presence in Britain. King Æthelberht of Kent, for example, who was Augustine's first notable convert, was married to a Frankish Christian named Bertha. The expansion of English power over the west and southwest of the island undoubted brought many British Christians under English rule. Apart from its spiritual benefits, conversion to Christianity offered the appeal of new political alliances with other Christian kings, and the considerable power of Latin literacy, law, science, philosophy, and education. Nonetheless conversion was a significant cultural change, and the momentum of conversion wavered back and forth for a century or so, with large areas of resistance and a good deal of back-sliding; Christianized England was not everywhere peaceful and prosperous or even thoroughly converted. By the beginning of the eighth century, however, the English were Christian enough to send missionaries like St. Boniface to preach the gospel to the pagan Saxons in Germany.

Alongside the Franks, the native British Christians, and the Roman missionaries, the Irish were busy in this period establishing monasteries in northern England. St. Columba founded the important monastery of Iona in Scotland in the mid-sixth century. This early insular monastic culture produced an extraordinary flourishing of Christian decorative art that finds its greatest expression in the Book of Kells. Tensions between the churches of the Roman mission and the idiosyncratic and relatively independent Irish churches were often high, but many of the most enduring Christian documents from the first centuries following the conversion of Britain, even those made in Northumbrian monasteries after the official rejection of the 'Irish' model of Christianity at the Synod of Whitby (664), are manuscripts in the Celtic tradition.

One of the most remarkable of these is the Lindisfarne Gospels, mentioned above, dating from around 700 (of which illustrations appear elsewhere in this volume). Like the Book of Kells, this manuscript of the gospels is remarkable for the profusion and richness of its detailed illustrations; the motifs of intertwined lions of different colors, the zoomorphic shapes, and the sheer density of intricate detail of these gospel manuscripts make them central documents in the history both of Christian and of Celtic art. It would be misleading to mention the visually impressive Lindisfarne Gospels, however, without placing it in context with other manuscripts such as the Codex Amiatinus, a massive (75 lbs) copy of the Bible now in Florence. This manuscript, though visually more sedate than the Lindisfarne Gospels, contains a biblical text so closely similar to the original Latin translation of St. Jerome (known as the Vulgate Bible) that today it forms the basis for the scholarly reconstruction of Jerome's text. The Codex Amiatinus was made at the same time as the Lindisfarne Gospels, in the monastery of Wearmouth-Jarrow; while the Lindisfarne Gospels are a strong testimony to the Irish influence on Christian culture in England, the Codex Amiatinus it is a powerful statement of Northumbrian monasticism's aspirations to pure *romanitas* as opposed to the provincial practices of the Irish and British. Between the shifting forces of these various traditions—the ideals of Roman orthodoxy, the influence of the Irish

Page from the Gospel of St. Mark, Book of Kells (ninth century). The page size of the original is 9 ½ inches by 12 ½ inches. Like many early Insular manuscripts, the provenance of this book is uncertain. The monastery at Kells in County Meath, Ireland, was established at the time of the Viking invasions early in the ninth century by monks from the large monastery at Iona, off the coast of Scotland. Among the many hypotheses as to the book's origin are theories that the monks brought the book with them from Iona in its present (unfinished) state; that some work was done at Iona, some at Kells; and even that the book originated at Lindisfarne in the north-east of England. This uncertainty indicates the high degree of interaction among the monasteries of Ireland, Scotland, and northern England during this period.

monasteries, the political pull of the Frankish world, and the remnants, however tattered, of the native British church—England became a Christian nation.

When the Northumbrian historian Bede wrote his *Ecclesiastical History of the English People* around 725, in fact, religion was the only unity the English had; political unity had to grow out of this unity of religious practice. Near the beginning of his history, Bede states that "At the present time [i.e., the early 700s], there are five languages in Britain, the English, British, Irish, Pictish, and Latin, just as the divine law is written in five books, each in its own own way devoted to seeking out and setting forth one and the same knowledge of sublime truth and true sublimity. The Latin tongue, through the study of the Scriptures, has become common to all the rest." By "English" Bede refers to what we now call Old English; by "British" he means the Celtic language of the Britons, ancestor of modern Welsh. The fact that Bede counts Latin, the learned language of religion and science, among the languages of Britain, however, suggests that he is not speaking of cultures or ethnic divisions in the modern sense. His point is not so much anthropological as it is spiritual—Britain was the fortunate recipient of the unifying force of Latin Christianity—but it does remind us of the linguistic, cultural and intellectual diversity to be found in Anglo-Saxon England.

The story that Bede recounts of the period from 597 to 700 is in some respects parallel to the story of Britain under Roman rule. As it had under the Romans, the island became an outpost at the edge of an empire—in this case, however, an empire founded on religion rather than on secular power. Just as Roman administrators in Britain had reported to their superiors in Rome, so too the archbishops of Canterbury and of York (the two pre-eminent centers of Christianity in Britain, as ordained by Pope Gregory the Great) derived their authority from the pope in Rome; the Roman church had inherited many of the bureaucratic systems, and some of the universalizing aspirations, of the Roman Empire, and the Pope assumed the role and name of *pontifex maximus* (from which he retains the modern title "Pontiff"), the sacerdotal aspect of imperial power. England's was, to be sure, a missionary church, not always willing or able to follow the Roman church in all

respects; the English church developed in a relationship, with varying degrees of tension and accommodation, between Christian conversion and secular Germanic culture, and from an early date the English church displayed distinctively local features. As a purely practical matter, too, communication was an enormous challenge in an era when a courier traveling across Europe on horseback could typically cover little more than thirty miles (fifty kilometers) per day. To send a message from London to Rome and receive a reply could thus be expected to take the better part of two months. And yet many people made the journey, and were expected to make it—the roads between England and Rome were familiar to bishops, pilgrims, penitents, monks, messengers, and merchants. Within Britain, too, transportation and communication—and thus any form of centralized control—were made problematic by purely logistical considerations.

It was also in accordance with the church's own inclinations to make some effort to preserve traditional culture and customs, reinvesting existing practices with a Christian meaning. Bede's *Ecclesiastical History* preserves a letter written by Pope Gregory to the Abbot Mellitus in 601, as the latter was going to join Augustine's mission in Britain; Gregory instructs him to tell Augustine that

> the temples of the idols in that nation ought not to be destroyed; but let the idols that are in them be destroyed; let holy water be made and sprinkled in the said temples, let altars be erected, and relics placed. For if those temples are well built, it is requisite that they be converted from the worship of devils to the service of the true God; that the nation, seeing that their temples are not destroyed, may remove error from their hearts, and knowing and adoring the true God, may the more familiarly resort to the places to which they have been accustomed. And because they have been used to slaughter many oxen in the sacrifices to devils, some solemnity must be exchanged for them on this account, as that on the day of the dedication, or the nativities of the holy martyrs, whose relics are there deposited, they may build themselves huts of the boughs of trees, about those churches which have been turned to that use from temples, and celebrate

the solemnity with religious feasting, and no more offer beasts to the Devil, but kill cattle to the praise of God in their eating, and return thanks to the Giver of all things for their sustenance; to the end that, whilst some gratifications are outwardly permitted them, they may the more easily consent to the inward consolations of the grace of God.

Gregory may not be entirely clear on the precise nature of English paganism—he seems to imagine England to be like Rome, with temples and priesthoods—but his strategy permits many sorts of accommodations of Christian practice to English culture, and *vice versa*. Doubtless this hastened the process of conversion; Bede himself, writing barely a century after the beginning of the Roman mission to England, does not seem to regard lingering paganism among the English as a contemporary problem worth mentioning. The old pagan gods of the north were abandoned along with pagan temples and rituals—though remnants of their importance persisted, as they do today in our days of the week: *Wednesday* is 'Woden's day', *Thursday* is 'Thor's Day', and so on. But the Anglo-Saxons managed to adopt the civilization offered by Christianity and at the same time adapt it to their own Germanic heritage. From the perspective of literary history, this policy of "cleansing the temples" fostered an amazing interpenetration of Germanic and Christian ideas; each is re-thought and revised in terms of the other, and it is impossible as well as inappropriate to separate 'Christian' from 'pagan' elements in the literature of the Anglo-Saxons. A longing for the heavenly home could be expressed in the tones of traditional elegy, Christ could be portrayed as a mighty warrior and his crucifixion as a heroic battle, and the pagan past could be depicted with regretful admiration and poignant sadness in a long poem like *Beowulf.*

Throughout this period monasteries were the most important outposts of Christian culture in England. The institutions of monasticism had their roots in the ascetic tradition of early Christianity, the belief that one could serve God best by living apart from the world in a state of constant prayer and self-denial. A monastery, as the concept developed in the third and fourth centuries CE, was a place where ascetically minded Christians could live together, supporting one another in prayer and penitential practice while mitigating some of the harsher aspects of the solitary life. As monastic communities grew various rules were devised, some no more than collections of observations and advice. In the sixth century the *Rule* of St. Benedict outlined a clear and codified plan for the communal life, a plan that is still followed today in monastic communties around the world. The Benedictine rule—which, however rigorous it might seem to a modern reader, was meant to curb some of the ascetic extremes seen in Benedict's own time—was the foundation on which the great monastic establishments were built, where work, communal prayer, and study comprised the *Opus Dei* or 'work of God', and which spread what Jean LeClercq has called "the love of learning and the desire for God" throughout early medieval Europe.

Many different rules and monastic orders developed throughout the Middle Ages; their practices differed from one order to another and one house to the next, but the general principles were constant. Monks were not usually ordained as priests, and had no pastoral responsibilities to minister to a congregation (though monasteries often did, especially in the early Middle Ages, provide pastoral care in areas without an established system of parishes). Monks were obliged to give up worldly wealth, their position in society, and their connections with family and friends so as to live in a community of individuals devoted to the same goals; at the same time, however, abbots were often from the same families as the secular rulers, and became powerful rulers and possessors of great wealth. Monastic communities always observed, at least in theory, a strict separation of the sexes, but the monastic life was open to women as much as to men; the English practice in the century before Bede was to have double monastic houses of monks and nuns, in almost all cases headed by an abbess such as the famous and noble Hild of Whitby. The monasteries, as the most important locus for intellectual activity and for the preservation and creation of cultural artifacts, became essential to the continuance of Latin culture, the practices of literacy, and the texts both of the church fathers and of classical authors, which were copied and read even as they were sometimes regarded with suspicion. Monastic culture flourished so vigorously in the north of England that one scholar has described Northumbria in the genera tions around 700 as a "veritable monastic Riviera."

INVASION AND UNIFICATION

This came to a dramatic end in the 790s with the first waves of invasions by the various Scandinavian peoples known to history as 'Vikings', and organized monastic life in England seems to have fallen into a state of more or less complete disrepair in the course of the ninth century. (It would be restored in the later tenth century by the reformers Oswald, Dunstan, and Æthelwold; by this time, however, the centers of monastic culture were in Canterbury, Winchester and Glastonbury rather than the far north, which was thoroughly Danish and in some places re-paganized.) Among the first targets of Viking attack were the holy island of Lindisfarne, which fell in 793, and Bede's monastery at Jarrow, which was destroyed in 794; the raids would continue on and off for two centuries. The Vikings were in many ways an extraordinary group of peoples. Whereas previous invaders such as the Angles, Saxons, and Jutes traveled relatively short distances, the Vikings constructed longships that proved capable of crossing the Atlantic; the remains of a Viking settlement at L'anse Aux Meadows in Newfoundland, dating from about 1000, are evidence that they even traveled to the New World. They established settlements in Iceland and Greenland, and settled in Ireland, Scotland, and Normandy as well as in England (the territory of Normandy takes its name from the 'northmen'). The popular image of the Vikings is one of raiders who would arrive, plunder, and return to their homeland; in fact, Viking raids were followed in most areas by invasion and settlement, and gradually Viking groups were absorbed into local populations. For most of the tenth century Viking raids ceased; the former raiders had become farmers, and had begun to intermarry with Anglo-Saxons in a process of cultural and linguistic assimilation that continued through the eleventh century.

The ruins at Lindisfarne.

The Viking presence contributed significantly to the unification of the Anglo-Saxon kingdoms and the first stirrings of what might be called, for lack of a better term, national feeling, both in Scotland and in England. The centers of political power shifted southward, to Mercia in the eighth century and Wessex in the ninth; smaller kingdoms formed alliances and larger ones expanded their rule, until most of England was united under King Alfred the Great of Wessex, who reigned from 871 to 899. Alfred was able to raise a substantial army and stop the Vikings militarily; while the Vikings maintained control over the north and northeast of England, Alfred and his successors controlled most of the remainder of the country.

With peace secured, Alfred began promoting education and literary culture—what is of incalculable importance for the history of English literature is that he proposed to encourage the translation of Latin works into English and the cultivation of vernacular literacy. Alfred surrounded himself with a learned circle of advisors after the manner of the Frankish emperor Charlemagne (d. 814), and was himself literate in Latin—he translated several works from Latin, including Boethius's *Consolation of Philosophy*, though probably with a great deal of assistance from his advisors. He sets out the reasoning behind his policy of

English translation in the Preface to his translation of Gregory the Great's *Pastoral Care*—and it is significant that he announces his program of education and translation in a book on how to rule and govern:

> I recalled how the law was first composed in the Hebrew language, and thereafter, when the Greeks learned it, they translated it all into their own language, and all other books as well. And so too the Romans, after they had mastered them, translated them all through myriad interpreters into their own language.... Therefore it seemed better to me ... that we too should turn certain books which are the most necessary for all men to know into a language that we can all understand.

Alfred's educational program was designed primarily to help him govern, but one of its legacies is the relatively large quantity of literary, historical, legal, spiritual, and political writing in English (about 30,000 lines of poetry and about ten times as much prose) that has survived, almost all of it in manuscripts from the tenth and eleventh centuries. Under Alfred the *Anglo-Saxon Chronicle* was probably begun; to this year-by-year historical record we owe a great deal of our knowledge of the period.

The authority of even the most capable and ambitious rulers in the early Middle Ages was seldom able to survive long after their deaths. More often than not family feuding would undo much of what had been accomplished, as happened when fighting among Charlemagne's three sons led to the tripartite division of the Carolingian empire. Alfred had rather better luck with his descendants, who were able to consolidate his accomplishments and even extend them somewhat; his descendant Edgar (r. 959–75) commanded the allegiance of all of the most important English lords, had ties to the most important families on the Continent, and had in his control all senior church appointments. Under the weaker leadership of the next generation, however, in particular Æthelred II (r. 978-1016), and in the face of a renewed series of Viking attacks (dramatically depicted in the poetic *Battle of Maldon*, written some time after the actual battle in 991), the allegiance of the great lords and landholders to the King loosened, and the shameful decline of the English

nobility described in the *Anglo-Saxon Chronicle* culminated in the Danish King Cnut (r. 1016–35) taking the English throne.

The end of the tenth century was by no means entirely a period of decline, however; it was also a time of such literary figures as the homilist and grammarian Ælfric, the archbishop Wulfstan, and the scholar Byrhtferth of Ramsey; during these years a number of *de luxe* decorated manuscripts were produced, and important works such as the *Rule* of St. Benedict and the Gospels were translated into English. It is also perhaps a tribute to the strength of Alfred's reforms that much of the administrative, military, and church structures he had put into place survived the conquest of England by a Danish king—as, indeed, they would in part survive the conquest fifty years later by the Normans. That these conquests did not cause more destruction than they did must also be attributed in part to the fact that these invading cultures were far from alien to English culture. In the centuries between the early Viking invasions and the reign of Cnut, Christianity had reached Scandinavia; whereas the early Vikings had raided and destroyed monasteries, Cnut was a Christian who continued to support the monasteries much as Alfred and his descendants had done. Similarly, while the Vikings had conquered Normandy in the early tenth century, by the time the Normans invaded Britain in 1066, the Viking culture there had largely been assimilated to that of Christian France.

ENGLAND AFTER THE NORMAN CONQUEST

THE NORMANS AND FEUDALISM

The Norman Conquest of England in 1066 was the next in the long series of invasions and migrations—Celts, Romans, Angles, Saxons, Jutes, and Vikings—that have shaped English culture. That it has held a special place as a focal point in English history is no doubt partly due to its timing, almost exactly at the point where many scholars see larger forces creating a dividing line between the early and the later Middle Ages. French language and culture never threatened to extinguish the existing Anglo-Saxon culture and English language, although they did exert enormous and lasting influence on them. The contrast with the Anglo-Saxon migrations is striking: these effectively and permanently imposed an English culture on Britain, while conquest by the Normans never permanently imposed French culture on England. But the Norman invasion helped to change Britain in fundamental ways—most obviously in language, but also in social and economic structure.

From the Bayeux Tapestry (late eleventh century). This object is actually an embroidered banner, around 20 inches high and 230 feet long, rather than a woven tapestry. It was probably created by English embroiderers, who were particularly skilled in this kind of work. This section of the tapestry shows the Norman ships landing at Pevensy, Sussex, 28 September; several ships have already landed on the beach, and horses are being unloaded from another ship that has just arrived. The text of the tapestry at this point (translated from the Latin) reads as follows: Here the horses are getting out of the ships. And here the soldiers [hurry to Hastings to seize supplies].

For all its far-reaching consequences, the invasion itself was a relatively modest affair. When Harold was crowned as king following the death of King Edward, the succession was disputed by William, Duke of Normandy, who settled the matter militarily; with a force probably numbering no more than 8,000, he crossed the channel, and had soon defeated and killed Harold in a day-long battle just outside Hastings. His victory brought England under the rule of a French-speaking king with substantial territorial claims in France, a situation that would persist for roughly the next three hundred years. Despite this obvious shift, and despite the triumphant narrative of the Bayeux tapestry, probably made within a generation of the battle for a Norman patron, the effects of the Conquest, particularly as it was viewed at close range rather than years later, apparently did not always loom so large. In this connection it is interesting to compare the five different accounts in different manuscripts of the *Anglo-Saxon Chronicle* that have come down to us. At one extreme is the remarkably brief account of a scribe writing at Winchester in the manuscript known as the Parker MS: "In this year King Edward died and Earl Harold succeeded to the kingdom, and held it forty weeks and one day; and in this year William came and conquered England. And in this year Christ Church was built and a comet appeared on 18 April." By contrast, a scribe writing a generation or more later in Peterborough presents a much fuller account of how Harold was forced to fight a Norse invader in the north of the country before meeting William at Hastings, and conveys more of the immediate effects of William's conquest. Yet even here one has the sense that the death of a local abbot is regarded as being of almost as much importance as the Norman invasion:

And King Harold was informed [of the victory of a Norse King near the town of York], and he came with a very great force of English men and met him at Stamford Bridge, and killed him and Earl Tostig and valiantly overcame all the invaders. Meanwhile

Count William landed at Hastings on Michaelmas Day, and Harold came from the north and fought with him before all of the army had come and there he fell and his two brothers Gyrth and Leofwine; and William conquered this country, and came to Westminster, and Archbishop Aldred consecrated him king, and people paid taxes to him, and gave him hostages and afterwards bought their land. And Leofric, Abbot of Peterborough, was at that campaign and fell ill there, and came home and died soon after, on the Eve of All Saints. God have mercy on his soul. In his day there was every happiness and every good at Peterborough, and he was beloved by everyone, so that the King gave to Saint Peter and him the Abbacy of Burton and that of Coventry which Earl Leofric, who was his uncle, had built, and that of Crowland and that of Thorne. And he did much for the benefit of the monastery of Peterborough with gold and silver and vestments and land, more indeed than any before or after him.

Significant here is the mention of people paying taxes to William and "buying" their lands. William exacted tribute from the conquered both in the immediate aftermath of his invasion and on an ongoing basis, keeping as much as a fifth of English lands for himself and dividing much of the rest among members of his family and the barons who had supported him, who in turn maintained their own followers. While neither the lords nor the peasants of Anglo-Saxon England had held legal title to their land in quite the way that we conceive of it today, they had in practice exercised rights over that land similar to those that we would describe as the rights of ownership. Under the Normans, by contrast, nobles held the land that they occupied not on any permanent basis but as part of a system of exchange. The king granted land to a nobleman as a *fief*; in return for the right to its use the nobleman was obliged to perform services for the king, including making payments at various times and providing armed knights whenever the king might demand them. The nobleman, in his turn, would grant land—again, as a fief—to a knight, who in return would owe to the nobleman military service and other dues. The knight would typically retain a substantial portion of this land, and then divide the rest among the peasantry. There were

obligations in the other direction, as well: knights were obliged to provide protection for the peasantry, nobles for the knights, and the king for the nobles. The relationship at each level was, in theory at least, entirely voluntary and often publicly proclaimed, with the "vassal" (or holder of the fief) kneeling and promising homage and fealty to his lord, and a kiss between the two then sealing their mutual obligation.

The institution of this new system was marked in a unique way by William through the compilation of the Domesday Book (so-called in reference to the "Day of Judgment" at the end of the world), an extraordinary survey on a county-by-county basis of all the lands held by the king and by his vassals, recording all the obligations of the land holders. Without the sort of commitment to record keeping and enforcement that the Domesday Book represented (a commitment made possible, it must be said, by the underlying social order inherited from the Anglo-Saxons), the Normans might not have succeeded to such a great degree in imposing a new network of obligation on the conquered people. It must be noted, however, that the Domesday book was seldom used to settle disputes or clarify ownership—the two functions for which, one might suppose, such a comprehensive census would be undertaken—in the first century of its existence. The eleventh-century ability to make records outpaced the development of a system in which to exploit them, and it would take some time before the mechanisms of government could make efficient use of such burdensome archives of documents. It has been argued that the Domesday Book, for all the impressive bureaucracy that brought it about, reflects a mistaken idea of the nature of written obligations: William may have imagined that the island of Britain could be granted to him by a written charter, like any other piece of land, and that recording the disposition of property and population would somehow fix them permanently in that state. But even if Domesday was more symbolic than useful, the imposition of feudal obligations was fairly thorough in England; the Anglo-Saxon nobles were quickly assimilated, dispossessed or killed, leaving William in effective control of England. The Norman conquests of Wales and Scotland, however, were much slower and more piecemeal, and the Anglo-Norman kings never exercised very much

Ornamental belt buckle (early 7th century CE) from the Sutton Hoo burial site. Twentieth century excavations at Sutton Hoo in southeast England uncovered a remarkable collection of artifacts from an Anglo-Saxon ship-burial. In addition to this buckle, 40 other gold objects were discovered in the burial mound, together with human remains, the bones of horses, weaponry, silverware, and the remains of large open ships.

CHI-RHO page from the Lindisfarne Gospels (c. 698 CE). See the introduction for a discussion of this page.

Nave, Durham Cathedral (1093–1133). One of the largest and most imposing of English cathedrals, Durham was built by Norman bishops over a remarkably short period. A shrine for Saint Cuthbert, it also houses the bones of the Venerable Bede.

"Annunciation to the Shepherds," stained glass (later 14th century), Victoria and Albert Museum.

"Virgin and Child," stained glass (14th century), Eaton Bishop Church, Herefordshire.

"Sir James Berners" (late 14th century), stained glass, St. Mary's Church, West Horseley, Surrey. This knight, who was beheaded in 1388, is shown here wearing armor typical of the period.

Opening page of the Prologue to *The Wife of Bath's Tale*, Ellesmere manuscript.
(This item is reproduced by permission of the *Huntington Library*, San Marino, California. EL26C9F72r.)

control over Ireland.

The late eleventh century in England saw the arrival of the Jews as well as the French invaders. Christian disdain for moneylending—although there were certainly Christian usurers—and the exclusion of Jews from some other professions meant that they tended to become strongly associated with, and very important in, the financial workings of the kingdom. In the twelfth and thirteenth centuries, until their expulsion in 1290, they served at times as a financial last resort for the king, because their relatively unprotected status as non-Christians made them vulnerable to much more severe forms of taxation and the abrogation of debts incurred by Christians but never repaid. Another important development of the later eleventh century, which would become much more central to civic life in the late Middle Ages, was the rise of guilds—initially merchant guilds that exercised a monopoly over the trade in a particular area, but later craft guilds that established regulations allowing them to control who could practice a given craft and that offered social and financial support to their members, as well as regulating the quality of production. While guilds and confraternities of some description, often purely religious in orientation, had existed since perhaps the seventh century, they became increasingly important in the course of the twelfth and thirteenth centuries, particularly in England, and their rise coincided with the growth of urban centers and of new forms of religious devotion.

HENRY II AND AN INTERNATIONAL CULTURE

If William was the key figure in establishing Norman and feudal rule in England, his great-grandson Henry II (r. 1154–89) was the key figure in its preservation and extension through the later Middle Ages. Henry's coming to the throne in 1154 brought to an end almost twenty years of civil war under the disputed kingship of Stephen, in the course of which barons and church leaders had taken advantage of the collapse of royal authority to expand local powers. Many of them began to encroach on land claimed by the crown, and to build private castles to protect their domains. Henry put a stop to these practices, taking back the lands, tearing down the castles, and reorganizing royal authority in a fashion that was increasingly supported by standardized records and documents. Central authority over legal matters, which had previously been largely restricted to capital cases, was now extended to legal matters of all sorts; the first legal textbook was composed in Henry's reign. The expansion of the crown's legal control came in part at the expense of the church, and provoked one of the most famous incidents of Henry's reign, his clash with Thomas Becket (1118–70), Archbishop of Canterbury, who wanted the clergy to retain their right to be tried in church courts independent of the secular legal system. The Archbishop was subsequently murdered, allegedly on the orders of Henry, an event that exercised a tremendous hold on the contemporary imagination. As John of Salisbury tells the story (in the earliest surviving account of the murder, written in 1171), Becket was standing before the altar when the knights who had come in pursuit of him arrived and told him that it was his time to die. John writes:

> Steadfast in speech as in spirit, he replied: "I am prepared to die for my God, to preserve justice and my church's liberty. But if you seek my head, I forbid you on behalf of God almighty and on pain of anathema to do any hurt to any other man, monk, clerk or layman, of high or low degree.... I embrace death readily, so long as peace and liberty for the Church follow from the shedding of my blood." ...
> He spoke, and saw that the assassins had drawn their swords; and bowed his head like one in prayer. His last words were "To God and St. Mary and the saints who protect and defend this church, and to the blessed Denis, I commend myself and the church's cause." ... A son's affection forbids me to describe each blow the savage assassins struck, spurning all fear of God, forgetful of all fealty and any human feeling. They defiled the cathedral and the holy season with a bishop's blood and with slaughter.

It remains unclear whether or not Henry ordered Becket's murder. What is clear is that the outcry was so great that Henry was forced to perform public penance—and to accept that the church would, to some extent, remain outside the realm of royal authority. Becket's martyrdom created the Canterbury shrine that was the goal of Chaucer's pilgrims, among many others.

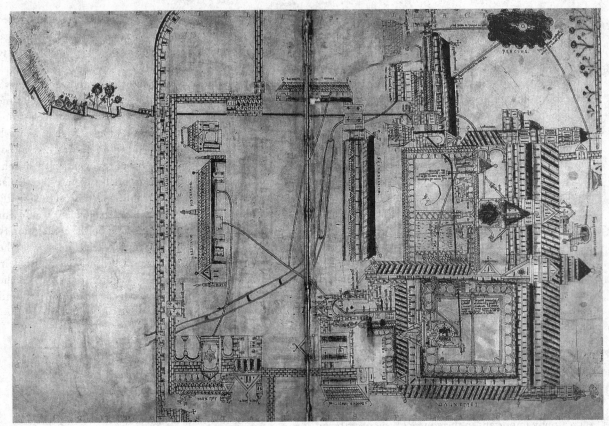

Plan for Canterbury Cathedral, c. 1160.

Canterbury Cathedral, the seat of the Archbishop of Canterbury, head of the English Church, is a kind of time capsule of Christianity in Britain since Anglo-Saxon times. The earliest church known to have stood on this site was that of St Augustine of Canterbury, who arrived as a missionary in 597 CE; traces of this building are believed to lie beneath the current structure. An Anglo-Saxon church was built over that of Augustine in the ninth or tenth century; it was destroyed by fire in 1067 and rebuilt by the Normans shortly afterward, and this construction still forms the basic fabric of the existing church, although it was modified and decorated further in the succeeding centuries. The plan shows the extensive monastic buildings as well as the cathedral itself. The lines shown connecting the buildings represent the plumbing system. At the top left the vineyard and orchard are indicated. The murder of St. Thomas Becket, then Archbishop, on the Cathedral's altar, made Canterbury a major pilgrimage shrine.

Durham Cathedral, begun in 1093, is regarded as one of the finest examples of Norman architecture in Europe; this style, a form of the Romanesque, is characterized by round arches (as here, along the sides of the nave) and vast but relatively spare interiors. Durham also displays some features (such as the pointed vaulting) that came to characterize the Gothic style of many later cathedrals.

Lincoln Cathedral, Galilee Porch.

Begun in 1072 and substantially rebuilt in the late twelfth and early thirteenth centuries, Lincoln Cathedral shows some of the classic features of both Romanesque and Gothic architecture. The Gothic Galilee Porch dates from c. 1230.

Salisbury cathedral (thirteenth century). With a spire of 404 feet, this was until the 1960s the tallest building in England. It is a classic example of the high Gothic style, with its pointed arches, flying buttresses to support a higher vault, and greater intricacy of design, including decorative features such as exterior sculpture and stained glass windows.

If Henry's extensions of the power of the English throne throughout the realm were unprecedented—though not, as the example of Becket suggests, entirely unopposed—so too was his extension of that power beyond the British Isles. Like previous Anglo-Norman monarchs, Henry controlled much of what is now northern France as well as England. With his marriage to Eleanor of Aquitaine in 1152 he had acquired control of much of southern France; he also exerted control over most of Scotland and Wales and in 1171 he invaded and took control of Ireland, where he quickly imposed the same feudal structures and judicial system on the

Irish people as he had on the English. Despite England's political control over Ireland—which itself was of varying strength over the next centuries —there was relatively little cultural assimilation, and the English nobles ruling in Ireland formed to a large extent a self-contained enclave. Like Scotland and Wales, with which it formed intermittent alliances, Ireland throughout this period pursued its own political strategies in the British Isles and on the Continent. And despite the efforts of Henry and the kings who followed him, the English presence in France was far less enduring than its presence in Ireland. By 1453, at the close of the Hundred Years' War between France and England, the port town of Calais was the only remnant of English control over France.

Henry II and Eleanor of Aquitaine sailing across the English Channel. Detail of illustration from Matthew Paris, *Historia Major* (c. 1240). The king and queen made the crossing many times as they traveled between their French and English kingdoms.

The period around the Norman Conquest also coincided with important developments in learned culture. England had produced outstanding scholars at various points in the early Middle Ages—among them Bede, the Latin poet Aldhelm, Ælfric, Byrhtferth, and most famously Alcuin of York, a monk of York who became master of Charlemagne's palace school—and in the eleventh century was home to the illustrious Anselm of Bec (1033–1109), one of the founders of scholastic thought, whose career demonstrates the international culture of the church and the schools, both of which used Latin an international language. Born in Italy, Anselm became abbot of a monastery in Normandy, and was eventually appointed Archbishop of Canterbury —the leading church position in England. His development of the ontological argument for the existence of God in his *Why God Became Man* (excerpted in this volume) is a good example of scholastic ways of thinking, proceeding on the basis of deductive logic to new theological conclusions. While there were outstanding individual thinkers at this time, however, the universities were still in their infancy; in most of Europe, schools had existed for the most part only in association with cathedrals or monasteries and their chief purpose was to provide training for clerics. In the wake of monastic and ecclesiastical reform in the tenth and eleventh centuries, these schools began to expand their curricula to provide a more highly educated clergy at all levels. Already by the end of the eleventh century there was some form of instruction taking place at Oxford, and by the end of the twelfth century it was a substantial enough center of learning to have attracted its first foreign student, and to benefit when Henry II forbade English scholars to study at the university of Paris. The university of Bologna was also already in existence at this time, and these three were soon followed by others across Europe.

The British Isles in the twelfth century also saw the rise of new modes of historical writing, including works such as William of Malmesbury's *Gesta Regum Anglorum* or "Deeds of the English Kings," Henry of Huntingdon's *Chronicle,* and Geoffrey of Monmouth's *Historia Regum Britanniae* or "History of the Kings of Britain." These writers' approach to history emphasized, as their titles suggest, the deeds of kings and the rise and fall of nations; in this they departed from predecessors more interested in depicting the Christian framework of history. The period also illustrates the political uses of literature. While Henry II—unlike, for example, King Alfred—is not particularly remembered for his own literary activities, numerous works in Anglo-Norman are associated with him as a patron or dedicatee, and his desire to solidify and extend his claims on both French and English lands was one of the things that made him an important figure for literary history. Henry and his descendants are known as the Angevin (or Plantagenet) kings, a reference to Henry's father, Geoffrey "Plantagenet" of Anjou, and this designation accurately represents their ongoing political and cultural interest in France. Henry's reign saw the production and wide dissemination of numerous literary and historical works that proved foundational for British literature, especially the development of the Arthurian legend.

Geoffrey of Monmouth's *History*, completed around 1139, offers an account of the history of the realm going back to its mythical Trojan founder, Brutus (from whom the name Britain supposedly derived), and provided the foundation for the Arthurian stories of the later Middle Ages. Henry II, the descendant of Normans who, like the mythical British under Arthur, had battled the Saxons for control of Britain, was only the first in a long line of kings to find this legend, with its potential to offer an authoritative and legitimizing history, an appealing subject; Arthur's imperial ambitions, as told in this version of the tale, also offered a supposed historical precedent for English claims to rule on the continent.[1] Geoffrey's *History* was popular throughout Europe, however, and in the British Isles alone was translated into Middle Welsh, Anglo-Norman, and Middle English. The Anglo-Norman version *Brut*, by the poet Wace, was dedicated to Henry's queen, Eleanor of Aquitaine, a further suggestion of the story's royal allure. Later in the century, French authors—most notably Chrétien de Troyes (c. 1150–90)—inserted into the legendary history of Arthur episodes that focused on the individual achievements of knights and on romantic (sometimes adulterous) love, creating a considerably greater role for female characters. Their works took their name from the language in which they were written, *roman* as opposed to Latin (French, from which we derive the modern literary term *romance* as well as the name for the *romance* languages), a choice that reflected the growing audience for vernacular poetry in the European courts.

A form closely related to the romance, and also written in the vernacular, was the Breton lay, a short narrative with, usually, a significant element of the marvelous and a central emphasis on a romantic relationship rather than large-scale political or military events. The lays' emphasis on the supernatural, which is often attributed to their origin in the Celtic culture of Brittany, is reminiscent at times of the early-twelfth-century prose tales of the *Mabinogi* from medieval Wales—which also, however, show notable chivalric and courtly features. By far the most famous medieval lays are those by an Anglo-Norman author who calls herself simply "Marie" and who apparently wrote in England in Henry's time; her twelve short tales—two of which are set in the world of Arthurian legend—offer a particularly careful attention to women's role in the conflicts of loyalty that often characterize romance narratives, and are one of the relatively few medieval works by a named female author, though the Marie who wrote the lays is usually identified with the "Marie de France" who composed a collection of fables and an account of a knight's visionary journey to purgatory. Romance and the lays took some time to make their way into English; Layamon translated Wace's *Brut* into English around the turn of the thirteenth century, but most Middle English romances date from the late-thirteenth and fourteenth centuries, probably reflecting the linguistic tendencies of their primary audience, the French-speaking nobility, before the fourteenth century.

As had happened centuries earlier in the wake of Alfred's rule, royal authority was scaled back under Henry's successors, who included two of his sons: first Richard I (the Lionheart), who ruled from 1189 to 1199, and then John, who ruled until 1216. In order to raise money in his struggle against Phillip II of France for territory on the continent, John imposed extraordinary taxes on English barons and other nobles; the

---

[1] Although the Normans may have liked to associate themselves with the British side in the Arthurian legends, Welsh poets of the time, whose culture was the more direct descendant of the early British, cast the Normans in the role of the despised English.

barons rebelled and forced the king to sign a document setting out the rights and obligations both of the nobles and of the king himself, and making explicit that the king was not to contravene these customary arrangements without consulting the barons. The document also reaffirmed the freedom of the English church, particularly the freedom from royal interference in the election of bishops or other officeholders. Under this "great charter" or Magna Carta, the power of the king was for the first time limited by the terms of a written document.

The Thirteenth Century

1215 was a momentous year in medieval Europe. In addition to the signing of Magna Carta—whose ultimately far-reaching effects were at the time felt only in England—this year witnessed the Fourth Lateran Council, a major gathering of church leaders under the guidance of the energetic Pope Innocent III. Lateran IV represented an extraordinarily far-reaching attempt to unify Christian practice and raise standards of Christian observance. The Canons of the Council covered almost all aspects of Christian life, and their effects on both religious practice and religious instruction resounded through the rest of the Middle Ages. Christians from now on were required to confess their sins formally and receive Communion at least once a year, and the sacrament of the altar was officially declared to involve transubstantiation, meaning that the body and blood of Christ were actually present in, rather than merely represented by, the bread and wine consecrated at the Mass (a doctrine that became a matter of serious dispute, however, in later medieval England). A new network of regulation was put into place to govern marriages, with secret marriages prohibited and marriage itself declared a sacrament.

Associated with the increased emphasis on the importance of priests administering sacraments to the faithful were increased efforts to ensure that members of the clergy were educated and competent; one of the canons involved the maintenance of cathedral schools free to clerics. Bishops were required to preach in their dioceses or ensure that there were others who could do so in their stead, and clergy were forcefully reminded of

the requirement of clerical celibacy. Individual Christians, for their part, were expected to be able to recite a small number of prayers, but there was no thought of encouraging widespread education of a sort that would enable the populace to read the word of God on their own. On the contrary, it was considered important to keep the Bible at a remove from the common people so that it could be safely interpreted to them through church intermediaries. The controversy that later developed over this issue would extend over several centuries and become a crucial concern for the Lollard or Wycliffite sect in fourteenth- and fifteenth-century England, as well as central distinguishing point between the Roman Catholic Church and the various Protestant faiths in the Reformation.

As this suggests, the reforms of the Fourth Lateran Council aimed to strengthen the Christian community, but with this came a new emphasis on differentiating, excluding, and penalizing unorthodox believers and non-Christians. The canons include extensive commentary on the need to control and excommunicate heretics; they require Jews and "Saracens" (Muslims) to wear distinctive clothing lest they be mistaken for Christians; they prohibit Jews from holding public office and make provisions to encourage crusading against Muslim control of the Holy Land. The English joined wholeheartedly in the Crusades and the restrictions placed on Jews. There had been massacres of Jews, particularly at York, already in the late twelfth century; expulsions from various cities by the local lords became widespread as early as the 1230s; and in 1290 Edward I expelled all Jews from England. It is not surprising, in view of this, that anti-Jewish miracle stories became popular across Europe during this period; Chaucer's *Prioress's Tale* is a later example of this genre. Heresy remained a concern throughout Europe, although in this period the persecutions were more severe in France and other parts of the continent than in England.

The Fourth Lateran Council was in part a response to increased lay devotion and interest in religion, which offered a challenge to the sometimes inadequate pastoral care provided by the clergy. In the early thirteenth century, for example, the records of the Bishop of Winchester show numerous priests being forced to declare that they will learn the Creed, the Ten

Commandments, the Seven Deadly Sins, and various other basic Christian doctrines within the space of a year, or pay a fine of forty shillings, a far from unusual instance that suggests that their preparation was not all that could have been wished. We may note, however, that some of the greatest works of Middle English religious literature survive in a closely related group of texts from around this same time: the *Ancrene Riwle* (Rule for Anchoresses) and the saints' lives and other spiritual-guidance texts that accompany it in the manuscripts testify to the presence of learned and committed religious men and women in early thirteenth-century England.

The new religious movements that arose in the course of the twelfth and thirteenth centuries— movements often instigated by the laity—were in some cases accepted by the church, though others were declared heretical; the growth in such movements was so great that the Council decreed that no new religious orders could be instituted after 1215, a decree that was largely observed. Among the new groups, the most significant, particularly for literary history, were the fraternal orders or friars (terms that derive from the Latin and French words for "brother"): the Augustinian hermits, Carmelites, and, especially, Dominicans and Franciscans. Like the monks of the early church, the members of these new movements embraced poverty and learning. Unlike previous monks of any era, however, they devoted themselves to carrying religion directly to the people, rather than living an enclosed life; their aim was to pursue the "vita apostolica," the way of life of the Apostles. Founded in the first part of the thirteenth century, they spread with great rapidity, and had a substantial presence in the British Isles by around 1250.

The friars' considerable success and speedy growth derived in no small part from their practice of preaching and establishing foundations in urban centers. The tremendous growth in the European economy from the eleventh century onward had fostered the development of ever-larger towns and cities that made possible an increasing specialization of labor that is reflected in the rise of craft guilds and, in another sense, in the friars themselves. The religious and civic cultures that each represented were deeply entwined. Guilds, which by this time were at the center of civic life, had patron saints and made religious fellowship a central part of their collective identities; their later sponsorship of the great cycle plays of the fourteenth to sixteenth centuries was a natural outgrowth of this melding. And although St Francis, the founder of the Franciscans, had entirely rejected his merchant background upon his conversion, the preachers of his order and the others found the towns, with their concentrated populations and alleged moral turpitude, an ideal place for their work.

Builders at work. Detail of illustration to Matthew Paris, *Historia Major* (c. 1240).

Matthew Paris, a monk at the famous Benedictine Abbey of St. Alban's, near London, took over the chronicle kept by his abbey in 1235 and continued it until his death in 1259. He is one of the liveliest sources for all kinds of information on the mid-thirteenth century, and was among those who commented (with some disapproval) on the spread of the friars and, among other things, their extensive building projects as their orders grew ever larger.

In the British Isles as elsewhere, the friars proved popular and controversial in almost equal measure; a fierce critique of them by the Irish bishop Richard FitzRalph (c. 1299–1360) survives in over seventy manuscripts from every part of Europe, and their influence at the University of Paris in the mid-thirteenth century so infuriated the other clerics there that the pope had to intervene. Their preaching was widely admired, however, perhaps especially by lay audiences, and while they quickly became part of the church and university hierarchies, they also claimed a particular affinity for pastoral work. Their mission thus promoted the translation and dissemination of religious teaching among the laity, and their energy in this activity made their writings an important influence on the development of literature in the vernacular languages of Europe, including England. Their emergence and quick expansion both coincided with and furthered the rise of lay involvement in religious life, whether this took the form of pilgrimage, of spiritual reading or writing, of attendance at sermons and church services, or of devotion to saints' cults, particularly that of the Virgin Mary. Nor were the friars the only force for increased religious education; English churchmen were particularly active in their response to the canons of the Fourth Lateran Council, and many works of spiritual instruction for the clergy or the laity, in Latin, Anglo-Norman, or English, attempted to disseminate the basic tenets of the faith. The *Speculum Confessionis* usually attributed to the learned Robert Grosseteste (c. 1170–1253), bishop of Lincoln, is one example of the new works that responded to the requirement of yearly confession; another is the Anglo-Norman *Manuel des Pechiez* (c. 1270), the source for Robert Mannyng's *Handlyng Synne* (1303), which aimed to give laypeople the knowledge they needed to live in accordance with Christian teaching. Just as the influence of the French aristocracy after the Norman Conquest brought French language and literature into the realm of English literary history, so the broader emphasis on basic Christian instruction in the thirteenth century and beyond made Latin works and church teachings increasingly available to vernacular audiences.

The growing lay participation in religion is reflected in the growth of certain characteristic literary genres.

The *exemplum,* or illustrative short story, most famously characteristic of medieval sermons, often provided a narrative argument for avoiding particular sins or emulating certain virtues; the closely related form of the *miraculum,* or miracle story, aimed to impress the reader or hearer with a sense of wonder. In the later Middle Ages *exempla* and other short narrative forms were often especially associated with the preaching of the friars, because they were thought to be appealing to laypeople, who might need help with the fine points of doctrine and would find narrative more accessible. These tales were sometimes criticized for being more entertaining than instructive, and indeed are not always very different from the genres of fable or fabliau—the latter being a "funny short story in verse," often dealing with sexual or economic deception and valuing cleverness over morality. Popular in French, fabliaux are essentially non-existent in (written) English until Chaucer, whose *Miller's, Reeve's,* and *Shipman's Tales,* among others, are based on this genre.

Saints' lives, another widely popular literary form, are also one of the oldest genres in English literature; the Old English *Martyrology* of the ninth century is a particularly thorough example, but some of the earliest texts in Middle English are the lives of three virgin martyrs Juliana, Katherine, and Margaret, all dating from the early thirteenth century. Intriguingly, lives of women martyrs of the early church were extremely popular in late-medieval England; Chaucer's *Second Nun's Tale,* which recounts the life of St. Cecilia, is another well-known (later) example. As with the Bible, even texts that do not center on the life or deeds of a saint may invoke the saints or briefly recount their miracles; they were part of the common knowledge of the time, and widely represented in art. Saints were regarded as protectors and intercessors, and the retelling of their lives was part of the effort to promote their cults and gain their assistance; their stories could provide points of contact with the sacred, particularly since they came from many walks of life.

The growing attention to pastoral care further stimulated the need for clerical education, and the worldly duties of the clergy—from the care of souls (including the writing of sermons) to administration of lands or finances—made studies in logic, rhetoric, and other subjects beyond theology or canon law an important part of their training. At the same time, contact with Arab scholars made both Arabic learning and the writings of classical philosophers—Aristotle most influential among them—newly available in Western Europe. The need to assimilate these traditions and bring them into accord with Christian teaching fostered the development of the scholastic method, or scholasticism, which gathered the evidence of various authorities and worked to synthesize it, usually by means of a debate form, into a single coherent authority. The structure of university study was quite different from its modern descendant, though not unrecognizably so. A student would first study the seven liberal arts, around which higher education was organized throughout the later Middle Ages: grammar, rhetoric, and logic (or dialectic), collectively known as the trivium, and arithmetic, music, astronomy and geometry, called the quadrivium. Students who wished to continue could pursue further studies in theology, medicine, or law—roughly the equivalent of modern graduate schools.

Despite the intellectual flowering of the eleventh to thirteenth centuries, education remained in essence a luxury good for most of the population. Not only laborers, but many of the nobility and even some of the clergy never learned to read, although the widespread practice of reading or reciting aloud—both secular and religious works—and of course of hearing sermons meant that they were not cut off from literate culture. Our own inevitable focus on the written sources that survive should not blind us to the ways in which those who could not themselves read or write still had considerable access to the great narratives and images of their culture.

THE ENGLISH MONARCHY

The religious and cultural energy of the thirteenth century in England was not particularly reflected in its monarchs; the period's important political developments tended to arise, as we have seen in the case of John and Magna Carta, from limitations on the king's power rather than, as with William the Conqueror or Henry II, his exercise of that power. The reign of John's son

Henry III (1216–72) was long but not particularly successful; he came to the throne as a child and by the end of his reign his son held effective power. Under his rule the monarchy lost ground to both external and internal forces. The French dauphin Louis controlled the southern part of England upon Henry's accession, but was expelled in 1217; later in the century, however, Henry had to sell most of his French possessions to pay war debts, and the English barons continually challenged the king's authority, culminating in his effective deposition in 1264–65 by the forces led by the baron Simon de Montfort, who as regent convened a kind of proto-Parliament. Simon's death in 1265 at the hands of Henry's troops made him a martyr to many of the English, and both praise-poems and laments in his honor survive from the period. The most significant legacy of the barons' increased power was the consolidation of the principle of the king's limited rulership and the idea that the people of the realm (primarily the nobility) should take some part in its governance. The losses of French territory had contributed to a growing tendency for the ruling inhabitants of England to regard themselves as *English* (rather than Norman, Angevin, French, and so on); the broader participation in government in the course of the century may have solidified this tendency. By the early fourteenth century language could be seen as a unifying force in the nation: "both the learned and unlearned man who were born in England can understand English," asserts one commentator of the period.

Henry's son Edward I, a much more successful ruler than his father, managed to mend the relationship between monarchy and people, in part by strengthening administrative structures related to law (Chancery), finances (the Exchequer), and governance (the Council); in this he built on the legacy of Henry II and the achievements of the baronial challenge, and the meetings of his Council were the first to bear the name of Parliaments. He also conquered Wales, which never fully regained its independence, although resistance to English rule continued. Like other English monarchs, however, he was unable to gain much control over Ireland, and despite diplomatic and military attempts, he never managed to conquer Scotland, which remained officially independent of England until the eighteenth century. A significant outcome of the ongoing English-Scots conflict was the growth of a sense of national identity among the Scots at least as marked as that among the English; we see this in the declaration of Arbroath (1320), sent to the pope by the nobles of Scotland as a group, in which they declared that they were speaking for "the community of the realm" and that "for so long as one hundred men remain alive, we shall never under any conditions submit to the domination of the English." Edward's attempts to subdue Scotland demonstrated once more the political usefulness of legendary history: in putting forward the English claim on Scottish territory, he made reference to the historical assertions of Layamon's *Brut*, the Middle English translation of the legends gathered in Geoffrey of Monmouth's *History of the Kings of Britain*.

The strong, if sometimes brutal, kingship of Edward I contrasts sharply with the troubled rule of his son Edward II (1307–27), who was frequently at odds with his nobles and eventually was deposed by his French queen, Isabella, and her lover, Roger Mortimer, an English baron. Edward was succeeded by his son Edward III (1327–77), whose long reign provided a certain stability but involved considerable losses for England. Edward III forcefully reasserted his claims to French territory through his French mother, and began the long-lasting conflict that came to be known as the Hundred Years' War (1337–1453). This conflict displayed the ongoing contradictoriness of medieval English attitudes toward France: Edward's embrace of a French-derived chivalric culture and claim to the French throne tended to link the nobility of both countries, who exchanged hostages and diplomatic missions, while at the same time the battles provided a focus for anti-French sentiment as old as the Norman Conquest and for renewed claims for English as a valued national language. This was not, of course, a sudden development; already in the thirteenth century a writer could assert that "common men know no French, among a hundred scarcely one," and similar claims become increasingly common in the fourteenth century. Despite considerable early success in the war, meanwhile, England's French holdings dwindled almost to nothing by the time of Edward III's death, and his continuing demand for funds to pursue his military projects put considerable strain on the economy, already weakened by the northern European famine of 1315–18.

Even more significant than the famine was the great plague of 1348–49, the "Black Death," which had a lasting impact on the demography, the economy, and ultimately the culture of Britain and Europe more generally. It is believed that roughly one-third of western Europe's population died in the plague, though not evenly across all areas; the population of London is estimated to have fallen by almost half, from perhaps 70,000 to about 40,000. In the wake of the plague, there was—not surprisingly—a severe labor shortage; this enabled a certain amount of social mobility as people were able to take higher-paying work, and the countryside suffered further depopulation as laborers left for the towns. Some employers competed for scarce labor by improving wages or conditions of labor, but the Statute of Laborers of 1351 officially restricted both wages and labor mobility, a cause of long-standing friction between the working population of England and its large landholders. Some of that tension found violent expression early in the reign of Edward's successor, his grandson Richard II (r. 1377–99) who inherited the throne at the age of only ten; his father, the Black Prince, had died in 1376. Severe taxation and limits on wages imposed in the wake of the Black Death caused considerable distress among the general populace, and helped to spark the Rising of 1381 (at which time the kingdom was still under the regency of John of Gaunt, Richard's uncle), in which groups from all over the country challenged the legislative and fiscal policies of the nobility, although they declared their allegiance to King Richard. While this uprising was easily quelled, it was a tremendous shock to the political and cultural establishment and foreshadowed the struggles for legitimacy that continued throughout the early fifteenth century; it also left behind an unusually rich record of non-nobles' views on the political economy of their day. Beyond the general unrest, Richard's autocratic style and struggles with his nobles for control of the country made the last quarter of the fourteenth century a politically fragile time in England. The king's preference for his own favorites over other, more powerful lords led these "Lords Appellant," as they called themselves, to challenge his authority and, eventually, to succeed in severely circumscribing his power as well as executing several of his closest advisors in 1388. A major source of the conflict between these lords and the King was Richard's desire to make peace with France; the King did eventually succeed in instituting a truce in 1396 through his marriage to the French princess Isabella (his beloved first wife, Anne of Bohemia, had died in 1394). In his later years he regained much of his control, in part through the help of his uncle John of Gaunt, but became increasingly despotic and took harsh revenge on the lords who had threatened his power. The contest culminated in the usurpation of the throne in 1399 by the Lancastrian Henry Bolingbroke (Henry IV), who had earlier been banished from the kingdom; Henry took advantage of Richard's absence in Ireland, where he was continuing the fruitless attempts to bring it under English control. Richard was later murdered in prison, echoing the fate of his deposed great-grandfather, Edward II.

CULTURAL EXPRESSION IN THE FOURTEENTH CENTURY

Richard's rulership may not have been a great success, but he is known, like Henry II, for his deep interest in artistic and cultural production and for the extraordinary literary output that took place under his reign —which was, unlike Henry's, as likely to be in English as in French. The writers of the period, some of the best-known figures of medieval English literature, include John Gower, Geoffrey Chaucer, the *Gawain*-poet, and William Langland; they are sometimes referred to as the "Ricardian poets" because of their activity under Richard II. While this contemporaneity signals the literary activity of the time, however, their writings by no means reflect a unified literary culture; while there are certainly overlaps and, in the case of Chaucer and Gower, even mutual references between some of their works, the main thing they have in common apart from historical era is that they all wrote in English. As this introduction has tried to suggest, this in itself is a striking fact; only at the end of the fourteenth century do we begin to see the major works of later-medieval English literature participating, often deliberately, in the project of making English a literary language worthy to take its place alongside Latin and the

illustrious continental vernaculars, particularly French and Italian, and raising it to a position of renewed prominence and respect in its native country after a perceived period of neglect. At the same time, these authors were anything but removed from non-English influences. Gower composed works in Latin and French as well as English; Chaucer translated French and Italian works, and borrowings from continental and Latin traditions shape all his poetry; Langland's *Piers Plowman* contains numerous lines in Latin and is strongly influenced by monastic Latin literary forms, while its use of personification allegory echoes a popular pan-European mode also seen in the hugely influential French *Romance of the Rose*; in *Sir Gawain and the Green Knight*, the legendary history of Arthur is blended with borrowings from Celtic sources and Christian chivalric culture.

This brings us to an important point about medieval writers—one that applies to all the works in this volume, but that is usefully demonstrated by the Ricardian poets: they did not regard originality in the modern sense as an essential component of a literary work's value. While a medieval poet or preacher or chronicler certainly aimed to tell his story or convey his message in the best possible way, he or she would willingly draw on, borrow from, translate, compile, and rework previous authors or storytellers. (The same could, of course, be said of Shakespeare.) Indeed, a link to authoritative sources—which could be written or oral—is often a crucial component of a medieval composition's own claims to authority. The increasing availability of Latin works, through preaching or written translation into the vernacular, or French ones, through performance or translation into English, along with Welsh, Breton, and Irish story material and works in other continental vernaculars, thus provided a rich trove from which Middle English authors constructed their writings.

The tendency of the "big four" Ricardian poets to draw all the attention in the fourteenth century can overshadow their debts to, and continuity with, the century that preceded them. *Sir Gawain* is part of a substantial tradition of Middle English romance—Arthurian and other—that includes *Sir Orfeo*, *Sir Launfal*, and the *Alliterative* and *Stanzaic Morte Arthure*, among many others. These vary in form but show the tendency of romance, too, to draw on a wide range of traditions for its subject matter. The lay *Sir Orfeo*, for example, reworks the story of Orpheus and Eurydice into a form with both Celtic and chivalric aspects: the classical underworld of Hades becomes a fairy land ruled by a powerful lord. The *Alliterative* and the *Stanzaic Morte Arthure*, meanwhile, each recount the fall of Arthur's kingdom, but with very different emphases—the Alliterative *Morte* sees imperial ambition and family treachery as essential elements, while the *Stanzaic* focuses on the adulterous love of Lancelot and Guinevere and the clash of blood brotherhood with the fraternal ties of the Round Table. Chaucer mocks traditional romance forms in his parodic *Tale of Sir Thopas* from the *Canterbury Tales*, and was all too aware of the challenges posed to idealized chivalry by the military realities of the fourteenth century. But as a member of the royal court, he could appreciate the virtues of what has rightly been called "the principal secular literature of entertainment" of the later Middle Ages, and the appeal to an idealized past or a magic-laden landscape, the conflicts of loyalties or contests for love that characterize many romances help to structure works as otherwise diverse as the *Franklin's, Wife of Bath's, Knight's* and *Merchant's Tales*.

Religious belief and practice are another crucial context for much late-fourteenth-century writing. Early in the century, the poet and canon Robert Mannyng (fl. 1288–1338) translated a handbook on basic Christian teachings from Anglo-Norman to English, titling it *Handlyng Synne* (1303) and illustrating it lavishly with *exempla*; the work indicates the growing audience for such spiritual "self-help" works in the English vernacular, and it has been suggested as a possible influence on many later works, including Gower's *Confessio Amantis*, Chaucer's *Canterbury Tales*, and Langland's *Piers Plowman*. Whether or not Mannyng's work formed part of their background, they were all able to draw on extensive knowledge of biblical material and Christian history, as well as on the wealth of exemplary narratives that characterized many works designed for religious instruction in the vernacular.

The late fourteenth century also sees the first records of the biblical drama of late medieval England. Though little is certain regarding the origins of such drama, we do know that in the late fourteenth century substantial groups of plays presenting biblical subject matter began to be performed in several English towns, often in conjunction with festival days of late spring or summer such as Whitsun ("White Sunday," or Pentecost, the seventh Sunday after Easter) and the Feast of Corpus Christi (a celebration of the Eucharist, held eleven days later); such plays continued to be performed until their suppression in the late sixteenth century. We know too that the presentation of the plays (which have variously been termed "miracle plays," "mystery plays," and "cycle plays"—designations that are all problematic in one way or another as blanket terms) varied. The texts that survive from the northern towns of York and Chester consist of more-or-less unified sequences of short plays—often called "pageants," like the wagons in which they were performed—that present the full sweep of biblical history. The sequence of plays from Coventry is in some respects similar, but includes only New Testament material. Two much more disparate manuscript collections of plays exist, known as "the N-Town plays" and "the Towneley plays." No firm evidence suggests that either group of plays was ever performed as a sequence—or, indeed, that there was ever any intention to perform the collected plays as a sequence. The N-Town collection contains what was once a separate play on the childhood of Mary as well as a two-part Passion Play. The Towneley collection is of particular interest for a small group of remarkable plays traditionally ascribed to the "Wakefield Master." (Three of these plays contain textual allusions to the area of Wakefield.)

Individual biblical plays, particularly in the northern sequences, were generally produced by particular craft guilds, representing a large outlay of time and money; in addition to providing religious instruction and entertainment, the plays reflected and emphasized the guilds' central importance to civic life at this time, as well as the growth of lay power in the governance of many towns. But production of biblical drama was not restricted to annual guild-sponsored performances in towns; some plays were produced by local parishes and some plays performed in the halls of great houses, often by troupes of traveling players.

The scope of late medieval English drama is similarly diverse. The body of surviving religious drama deriving from some other areas, such as East Anglia, includes not only biblical plays but also a large number of plays depicting the lives of saints or the performance of miracles. Passion plays and Christmas plays were also frequently performed in the late medieval period, as were interludes (typically, short comic sketches, intended for performance at court); mummings (dumb shows with masked performers); folk plays (featuring music and dance as well as dialogue, typically depicting the death and revival of a legendary hero); and Robin Hood plays.

A fifteenth- and sixteenth-century form that has attracted particular interest is the genre conventionally referred to as the "morality play." Plays in this genre (such as *Mankind* and *The Castle of Perseverance*) depict in allegorical form the struggles of a universal human figure; vices and virtues are personified as characters and participate fully in the action of the play. Morality plays were clearly intended to encourage devout individuals to consider their own moral position and to maintain a keen awareness of the state of their souls. But morality plays could also offer a broad range of entertainment —as the humor and energy of *Mankind* amply demonstrate.

The continuing growth of lay participation in spiritual matters that we see reflected in a work like *Handlyng Synne* or in the biblical dramas became, in other contexts, one of the most contentious issues in fourteenth and fifteenth century England. The critiques of the clergy, and particularly of monks and friars, that had accompanied ecclesiastical reform movements from the tenth century onward were strongly endorsed in the works of the Oxford theologian John Wyclif (c. 1324-84). In the course of a long and influential writing career, he attacked the church for its enormous wealth and criticized clerics for their moral failings, questioned the doctrine of transubstantiation, and moved toward a view that all laypeople should have direct access to the Bible and could communicate directly with God, needing no priestly intermediation (although he was in many cases sympathetic to parish priests). His views, some of which were declared heretical by the Archbishop of Canterbury's council in 1382, were nonetheless widely shared, including by some of the nobility at Richard II's court. Wyclif provided much of the intellectual foundation for the English sect known as

Wycliffites or Lollards, and had an enormous influence on the religious, literary, and political culture of late-medieval England. Many of the issues that aroused his wrath are addressed also in Langland's *Piers Plowman*, a text highly critical of clerical and ecclesiastical shortcomings, although unlike the writings of Wyclif and his followers it was not generally regarded as heretical.

Yet another aspect of fourteenth-century spirituality is evident in the *Showings* of the anchoress Julian of Norwich, one of the most important visionary texts of the Middle Ages. Julian's theologically complex and deeply learned account of her experience forms part of both a long tradition of women's visionary literature in medieval Europe (going back at least to the twelfth-century German abbess Hildegard of Bingen) and of a flowering of vernacular religious writing in late fourteenth-century England that also includes authors like Richard Rolle and Walter Hilton. And to set Julian's image of the created world as a hazelnut in the palm of God's hand alongside *Sir Gawain and the Green Knight*'s richly detailed hunting scenes or the mysterious John Mandeville's accounts of satyrs, the phoenix, and the exotic kingdoms of the east is to be reminded of the enormous diversity of the literature of late-medieval England. As we noted at the beginning of this introduction, moreover, medieval manuscripts would in many cases have kept this diversity immediately present to readers, recording texts of very different genre alongside one another: saints' lives with confessional manuals, fabliaux with satirical poetry, romances with recipes. Such compilations are reflected in miniature, as it were, by "compilation poems" like the *Canterbury Tales*, which place stories from varied genres and traditions within a unifying frame, or *Piers Plowman*, which blends social critique, personification allegory, and anticlerical satire into a visionary autobiography.

FIFTEENTH-CENTURY TRANSITIONS

Writers in fifteenth-century England were deeply aware of the rich and authoritative literary tradition that immediately preceded them, drawing on and praising the works of their predecessors even as they devised a distinctive tradition of their own. In political and religious terms as well, the fifteenth century reaped the whirlwind of the late fourteenth, beginning with a crisis of royal authority as the "usurper" Henry IV tried to solidify his claims to the throne and to contain a major nationalist rebellion in Wales led by Owain Glyndwr (Owen Glendower). Religious legitimacy was also at issue, as ongoing Wycliffite (or Lollard) challenges to current church practices caused aggressive responses on the part of the ecclesiastical and secular hierarchies— most notably the royal decree *De heretico comburendo* of 1401, ordering that recalcitrant heretics were to be burnt at the stake (the first institution of such punishment in England), and the famous *Constitutions* (1407–09) of Thomas Arundel, Archbishop of Canterbury, which declared that the making or owning of Bibles in English was forbidden and set strict limits on acceptable religious composition in the vernacular. William Thorpe's testimony during his trial for heresy before Archbishop Arundel, an excerpt from which appears on the website to this volume, demonstrates the depth of commitment and the high level of religious understanding that the Lollards brought to this struggle, which both sides regarded as a matter of eternal life and death as well as immediate political importance. The religious and political threats came together in the short-lived rebellion led by Sir John Oldcastle in 1413, in which he and other Londoners tried to depose the new King Henry V; the fact that Oldcastle had at this time already been convicted of heresy (as a Lollard) solidified the link many secular and church lords made between religious and worldly sedition. While Henry V's military success in France—most famously at the battle of Agincourt in 1415—and his strength as a ruler eased some of the strain, anxiety about the monarchy's legitimacy and about composition in the vernacular are evident in much of the literary production of the century.

One of the modes in which these anxieties were expressed, however, was an outpouring of carefully orthodox religious literature in English, often in forms such as saints' lives, visionary narratives, or meditations on the life of the Virgin or on Christ's Passion. The great religious foundations of Henry V, Sheen Charterhouse and Syon Abbey, were important centers for both the dissemination of fourteenth-century writings and the creation of new works (many of which were transla-

tions from Latin or French); when Henry VI came to the throne after his father's early death, his own devout tendencies reinforced the link between the Lancastrian court and monastic spirituality. Religious devotion was far from limited to the elite, however; probably the most famous English text of the first half of the fifteenth century is the *Book of Margery Kempe*, composed by a laywoman living in the world as an account of her spiritual experiences, visions, pilgrimages, and trials for heresy. Margery's frequent conversations with divine and saintly personages show her to be simultaneously extraordinary in and typical of her time; fifteenth-century devotion, particularly in the vernacular, often emphasized emotional connection to and a sense of familiarity with the figures of salvation history.

The intense spirituality of figures such as Margery Kempe contrasts sharply in tone with many of the historical events of the later part of the century. The civil war between the Lancastrian and Yorkist factions— known to us as the Wars of the Roses from the two groups' emblems—pitted descendants of Edward III against one another as claimants to the throne. Begun under the weak kingship of Henry VI, who was deposed by the Yorkist faction in 1460, returned briefly to the throne in 1470, and was executed in 1471, the struggle went on until 1485 when Henry Tudor, a Lancastrian descendant (on his mother's side) of Edward III, defeated Richard III of the house of York and united the warring houses by marrying Elizabeth, daughter of the Yorkist king Edward IV (1461–70, 1471–83). Henry's direct descent, on his father's side, from the twelfth-century Welsh prince Rhys made his rulership the apparent fulfillment of longstanding Welsh prophecies that a Briton would rule England once more.

The chaos and disillusionment that attended the period of civil war echo through the *Morte Darthur* of Thomas Malory, who drew on Middle English and French works to create his massive cycle of Arthurian romances. This text, a kind of summation of the Arthurian obsessions of later-medieval England, became one of the first printed books in England when William Caxton published it in 1485. In his preface, Caxton— who gave Malory's work the title by which we know it—described the *Morte Darthur* as recounting "noble chivalry, courtesy, humanity, friendliness, hardiness, love, friendship, cowardice, murder, hate, virtue and sin," a catalogue whose ending echoes the often dark tone of Malory's work. The *Morte Darthur* seems to reflect and perhaps comment upon the decline of the chivalric world that Malory, a knight who apparently fought on both sides in the Wars of the Roses, would have known well, and its account of the competing loyalties that eventually destroy Arthur and his kingdom would surely have resonated with contemporary events.

The printing of Malory's work by Caxton was only one small piece of the latter's enormous output. Between about 1475 and his death in 1491, he published almost a hundred different works, many of them his own translations; the most famous of the latter is his *Golden Legend*, an English version of a monumentally influential thirteenth-century Latin compendium of saints' lives. He is probably best known, however, for his awareness of and influence on the canon of British literature; works by Chaucer, Lydgate and Gower were among his most important productions, with Malory joining them not long after. His attention to the ever-growing market for vernacular literature and his admiration of the great authors of the past made his professional life one of the great shaping forces on the development of the British tradition, as well as, of course, the instrument of England's entry into the world of printed books. Caxton's (numerous) early readers included members of the Paston family, a wealthy Norfolk clan. Their extensive surviving letters, which range in date from 1422 to 1529, deal not with legendary heroism or magical encounters, but with the minutiae of everyday

Table of contents and woodcut illustration from *The Game and Play of Chesse*, printed by William Caxton (2nd edition 1481).

life: bills, quarrels with neighbors, marriages, deaths, political gossip. Like the Tudor dynasty, the civic dramas, and the early print culture of England, they carry us forward into the sixteenth century, and offer a glimpse of the kinds of everyday events and concerns that formed the original contexts for all the works presented here.

Advertisement issued by William Caxton (c. 1477).

LANGUAGE AND PROSODY

Old English is sufficiently distant from modern English that it must be studied and learned as a different language; for this reason works in Old English in this anthology are presented in modern English translation (though a few passages in Old English are provided). All poetry in Old English had roughly the same formal structure, only the outlines of which are reproduced in the translations. Each line has four stresses, with a pause (or *caesura*) breaking the line into halves of two stresses each. The verse is *accentual* rather than metrical, with no fixed number of unstressed syllables in a line; lines follow one of several different patterns of alternation of stressed and unstressed syllables. Lines are held together by *alliteration* (repetition of initial sounds; all vowels were considered to alliterate) rather than rhyme; the third stressed syllable of each line must alliterate with at least one of the first two stressed syllables, but there are no rules for the linking of lines, and generally no formal stanzaic structures. The closing lines of *Beowulf* (3178–82) illustrate these principles; stressed syllables are in bold type, and alliterating syllables are underlined (the letters þ and ð are pronounced like the *th* in *thin* and *then*; æ is pronounced like *a* in *hat*; diphthongs are one sound, but final *-e* is pronounced, so that the half-line *Geat-a leod-e* has four syllables):

Swa be**gnor**nodon   **Geat**a **leod**e
so lamented   the Geatish people

hlafordes **hryr**e,   **heorð**-gen**eat**as,
the lord's downfall, hearth-companions,

cwædon þæt he **wær**e   **wyr**uld-**cyn**inga
said that he was   of world-kings

manna **mild**ust   ond **mon**-ð**wær**ust,
of men the mildest   and most gentle,

leodum **lið**ost ond **lof**-**georn**ost.
to people the kindest, and most eager for fame.

The linguistic beginnings of the transition to Middle English predate the Norman invasion of 1066, but the changes in the language are seldom manifest in writing before the twelfth century. Among the latest surviving works deemed by scholars to have been written in Old English are a section of the *Anglo-Saxon Chronicle* added in Peterborough around 1154, and some late twelfth-century copies of eleventh-century homilies and gospel translations.

The linguistic changes that characterize the transition from Old to Middle English are as much a reflection of the changing cultural situation of English as they are of changing grammar or phonology. By 1100 the leaders of the church, the government, and the aristocracy (that is, practically anyone who could read or write) either spoke French as a native language or had learned French. The English language survived, however; Norman knights who settled in England married English women, had their children raised by English nurses, and worked with the English-speaking peasants and overseers on their farms. The total number of French speakers in England at any time was relatively small and bilingualism was probably common on all but the highest and lowest levels of society. For almost two centuries, however, this small number of French speakers included all officials, nobles, and high-ranking churchmen in the country. English was by no means the prestige language it had been among the Anglo-Saxons. There was little support for English literature among the literate classes, and no formal system of education or book-production to encourage writing in English; for more than a century after the Conquest, English had no place in the political, intellectual, or economic life of the country.

We may think of this situation as parallel, at least in linguistic terms, to the colonial settlements of India, Africa, and the Caribbean, in which a dominant language-culture influences the subject language-culture and *vice versa*; in such environments, to speak one language or another can be a highly charged and socially conscious act. In the early Middle English period one finds English poetry like *The Owl and the Nightingale* written in the French style (with rhymed meter rather than alliterative stressed lines), expressing French literary values, and borrowing French words and forms. French remained the language of the nobility (and thus of Parliament and the royal courts of law) until the late fourteenth century, and the English language borrowed widely from French as it expanded to deal with a more diverse and complex society, and with the growing literary ambitions of English authors. Both languages, meanwhile, continued to interact in complex ways with the language of unquestioned intellectual prestige, Latin.

The borrowings of French words into the English vocabulary are many, and generally seem to have been culturally motivated; thus, English borrows words for government (*peace, justice, court, judge, sentence*—though *gallows* is an English word) and culture (*noble, dame, gentle, honor, courtesy, polite, manners*). One effect of all this borrowing is that English has a great flexibility in its synonyms; we can express things in several different ways using words from different origins: we can *ask* or *question* someone, and get an *answer* or a *response*, which may make us *glad* or *pleased*, or it may make us *mad* or *angry*, and lead to a *fight* or *dispute* (or even an *altercation*). Often the English and French words for the same thing have come to differ in meaning: it has long been observed, for example, that animals used for meat are called by their English names when they are in the field—*cow, calf, pig, sheep, deer*—and by their French names on the table—*beef, veal, pork, mutton, venison*. This linguistic development reflects the social situation of post-Conquest England, in which the lower-class English raised the animals and the upper-class French ate them; it may also have something to do with the superiority of French over English cooking, which was recognized even a thousand years ago.

Alongside this generous borrowing of vocabulary and literary forms, one of the most important changes in Middle English was the wearing-away of the complex inflectional system of Old English, which had already begun to disappear by the end of the tenth century in some dialects, and the concomitant fixing of word-order into something more like its modern form. Another was the representation of many different regional dialects in written Middle English; Old English had regional varieties, but by far the majority of surviving manuscripts are written in some approximation of the standard West Saxon of the late tenth century. In the absence of a strong educational system teaching a standard for English spelling, regional dialects were much more fully represented in written Middle English. The differences between Old and Middle English can be seen in the following two passages, each translating the opening verses of Psalm 23; the former is from the Old English "Paris Psalter" of the ninth century, the latter from the Wycliffite translation of the Bible in the later

fourteenth century (the same verses from the modern Douay-Rheims Bible, also translated from the Latin Vulgate, appear after the two passages):

> Drihten me ræt, ne byð me nanes godes wan, and he me geset on swyðe good feohland. And fedde me be wætera staðum, and min mod gehwyrfde of unrotnesse on gefean. He me gelædde ofer þa wegas rihtwisnesse, for his naman.

> The Lord gouerneth me, and no thing schal faile to me; in the place of pasture there he hath set me. He nurschide me on the watir of refreischyng; he conuertide my soule. He ledde me forth on the pathis of rigtfulnesse; for his name.

> *The LORD ruleth me; and I shall want nothing. He hath set me in a place of pasture: he hath brought me up, on the water of refreshment. He hath converted my soul. He hath led me on the paths of justice, for his own name's sake.*

Even in these few lines the differences are notable: considerable developments in vocabulary (*Drihten > Lord, ræt > gouerneth, feohland > the place of pasture, mod > soule, gehwyrfde > conuertide, wegas > pathis*), changes in word order (*Drihten me ræt > The Lord gouerneth me, he me geset > he hath set me, min mod gehwyrfde > he conuertide my soule*) and the erosion of inflectional endings (*be wætera staðum > on the watir of refreischyng, for his naman > for his name*) all indicate the movement of English towards its present state. The Middle English passage is nearly identical to the early Modern English of the Douay-Rheims version. To understand something of the dialect diversity in written Middle English, however, one should compare the Wycliffe version to the same passage in two other Middle English texts, the *West Midlands Psalter* and the Yorkshire version of Richard Rolle, both written around the middle of the fourteenth century:

> (*West Midlands Psalter*) Our Lord gouerneþ me, and noþyng shal defailen to me; in þe stede of pasture he sett me þer. He norissed me vp water of fyllyng; he turned my soule fram þe fende. He lad me vp þe bistiges of rigtfulnes for his name.

(*Richard Rolle Psalter*) Lord gouerns me and naþyng sall me want; in sted of pasture þare he me sett. On þe watere of rehetynge forþ he me broght; my saule he turnyd. He led me on þe stretis of rightwisnes; for his name.

By the end of the thirteenth century English began to appear once again as a language of official documents and public occasions. In 1337 a lawyer addressed the Parliament in English for the first time, as a chronicle says, "so that he might be better understood by all"; in 1362 Parliament ordered all lawsuits to be conducted in English. There is some indication that at the beginning of the fourteenth century the nobility had to be taught French—the language still held prestige, but it was by no means the native tongue of those born on English soil. Not surprisingly, it is in the same period, the fourteenth century, that English literary output becomes significant again, but the language that emerged was strongly altered by two centuries of 'underground' existence and the shaping pressure from the dominant French language and literary culture. It is thought that the use of alliterative verse in the Old English style may have persisted through the twelfth and thirteenth centuries, though evidence of this is scarce and ambiguous. In the fourteenth century alliterative verse reappears in written form throughout much of England, and is used for subjects as varied as Arthurian legendary history (the Alliterative *Morte Arthure*), Christian dream vision (*Pearl*), and satiric commentary (Langland's *Piers Plowman*), among others. Rhymed, metrical, non-alliterative poetry like that of Chaucer and Gower was largely inspired by French traditions.

The literary flowering of the second half of the fourteenth century was by no means restricted to one region. Chaucer wrote in the dialect of London and the east Midlands which, more than any other, is the ancestor of modern English; the author of *Sir Gawain and the Green Knight*, on the other hand, wrote in a dialect of the northwest midlands. As Chaucer himself put it, there was great "diversitee in English and in writing of our tonge." With the coming of the printing press in the fifteenth century, however, the printed language began to take on more and more common characteristics, though it would be not until the late

eighteenth and early nineteenth centuries that grammar, spelling, and punctuation were standardized.

In reading Old and Middle English (in whatever dialect) it is important to be aware of the major ways in which the language differs from our own. For any historical period of English the reconstruction of pronunciation is only approximate, but a careful study of sound changes, spelling, cognate languages and word histories allows scholars to make highly educated guesses about the way Old and Middle English sounded. Old English used some letters not found in the Latin alphabet, including [*thorn* (þ), *eth* (ð), and *yogh* (ȝ); the first two survived into Middle English, where thorn gradually came to be written much like the letter *y* (giving rise to the common misreading of 'ye' for 'the' in faux-antique signs like 'yᵉ olde shoppe'). Some Old English consonant clusters were pronounced in unusual ways; *sc* was pronounced like *sh* and *cg* like *dg*, so that OE *scip* and *ecg* sounded much like their modern descendants *ship* and *edge*. The consonants *c* and *g* were pronounced differently depending on their position in a word; the Old English words *gold* and *camb* were pronounced much as in Modern English *gold* and *comb*, but *geat* was pronounced with a *y* as if it were roughly *yat*, and *ciric* was pronounced with *ch* sounds as in its modern descendent *church*.

One way in which Old and Middle English are dramatically different from Modern English is in sounding all consonants, including those in combinations such as *kn, gn, lk,* and *wr* that have become largely or entirely silent in modern English. The word "knight," for example, is pronounced something like "k-ni*cht*" (with the *i* short). Final unstressed *e* in words is always sounded in Old English, and sounded far more frequently in Middle English than is the case in modern English—though during the late medieval period the sounding of the final *e* was beginning to die out, and scholars continue to dispute how frequently the final *e* should be sounded in Chaucerian English. Vowels are pronounced roughly as in French or Spanish —the modern English values are the result of a "Great Vowel Shift" which began in the fifteenth century. The long *a* in words such as "made," for example, was pronounced like the *a* in "father"; the long *e* in words such as "sweete" was sounded like the *a* in "mate"; the long *i* (or *y*) in words such as "lif" and "myn" was pronounced in the same way we sound the *i* in "machine"; the long *o* in words such as "do" and "spoon" was sounded as we pronounce the *o* in "note"; and the long *u* (or *ou* or *ow*) in words such as "flowr" was sounded as we would pronounce the *oo* in "boot."

While Middle English is far less inflected than Old English, meaning that fewer grammatical differences are signaled in the form of words, matters are, as noted above, complicated by dialect. Third person singular formations of verbs, for example, tend to end in *-s* or *-ys* in northern dialects, and in *-th* or *-ith* (later *-eth*) in southern dialects. "She has" is thus a form deriving from northern Middle English dialects, and "she hath" from southern English forms (cf. Richard Rolle's "Lord gouerns me" where the Wycliffite version has "The Lord gouerneth me"). When the sheep thief Mak in *The Second Shepherds' Play* pretends to be from southern England he says "ich be" instead of "I am" as northerners then (and all English speakers nowadays) would say. Word order in Middle English is often substantially different from modern practice, with the verb often coming later in the sentence than is our custom in statements, but coming at the beginning at the sentence in questions, as is the practice in many Romance languages. Many Middle English words are of course unfamiliar to the modern reader, but there are also many "false friends"–words that look identical or very similar to modern English words but carry significantly different denotations. *Lewd,* which in Old English means "secular, not relating to the clergy," comes in Middle English to mean "unlearned," but without any suggestion of a sexual character. *Sely,* though the ancestor of the modern "silly," can mean "poor," "miserable," or "innocent" as well as "strange" or "foolish." Even at the level of a single word, one might say, we can see the peculiar and provocative mixture of strangeness and familiarity, the haunting family resemblances and the disconcerting dissonances, that make the study of medieval literary culture so compelling and rewarding. We hope that in this collection of works you will come to know its powerful appeal.

History of the Language and of Print Culture

In an effort to provide for readers a direct sense of the development of the language and of print culture, examples of texts in their original form have been provided in each volume. A list of these within the present volume appears below.

Bede

c. 673 – 735

Bede "the Venerable," the most learned writer of the Anglo-Saxon period, was born in Northumbria around 673. At the age of seven he entered the twin monastery of Wearmouth-Jarrow and remained there, except for a few short excursions, until his death. Under the Abbot Ceolfrith, Bede received a thorough education in grammar, rhetoric, mathematics, music, natural science and the study of Scripture; he was ordained a deacon at 19 and a priest at 30. In a brief autobiographical note appended to his *Ecclesiastical History* he describes himself in this manner: "Amid the observance of the discipline of the Rule [of St. Benedict] and the daily task of singing in the church, it has always been my delight to learn or to teach or to write." Over the course of his life Bede produced a body of writing that remains impressive for its clarity, intelligence, range and devotion. His works, which survive in hundreds of manuscripts, were deeply influential and widely copied throughout the Middle Ages. Apart from a brief and enigmatic Old English poem and a lost translation of the Gospel of John he is said to have composed on his deathbed, all Bede's works were written in Latin, then the international language of scholarship and of the Church.

The founder of Jarrow monastery, Benedict Biscop, had traveled extensively and assembled an impressive library; during Bede's lifetime this remote outpost on the northeastern coast of England—founded about the year Bede was born, and scarcely 50 years after the rulers of Northumbria had converted to Christianity—was perhaps the most learned monastic center in all of Europe. Bede's writings include numerous works of Scriptural commentary, many homilies, works on meter and orthography, lives of several saints, books of poetry and hymns, and several treatises on cosmology and timekeeping. He was deeply interested in time and its measurement, a matter of some urgency in his lifetime because the Irish and Roman churches had different methods for calculating the date of Easter. In some years the two churches celebrated the feast on different days, which to Bede was a shocking sign of disunity. In his works promoting the Roman method of reckoning Easter he also helped establish the foundations of medieval astronomy and chronology; Bede is primarily responsible for popularizing the western "BC" and "AD" system of reckoning dates using the *anno domini* or "year of (the birth of) our Lord" as the dividing principle.

It is Bede's historical works, however, that are best known today. His *Historia Ecclesiastica Gentis Anglorum* (*Ecclesiastical History of the English People*), completed in 731, is an extensive history of England which takes as its theme the conversion of the Anglo-Saxon invaders who had displaced the native Britons. The *Ecclesiastical History* imagines an "English" people united not so much by culture or language or geography as by faith, the Roman Christianity brought to the island by Augustine of Canterbury and other missionaries sent by Pope Gregory the Great in 597. This work still provides the foundation for much of our knowledge of England in the fourth, fifth, and sixth centuries. Bede's talent as a historian was his ability to take multiple sources—documents, other histories, local oral traditions and legends—and weave them together into a coherent narrative. Though Bede was not fully a historian in the modern sense, his approach is far less foreign to the modern historical sensibility than that of most medieval chroniclers; unlike many writers of the time, for example, he makes frequent reference to the sources for the material he is recounting. In Bede's narrative, written very much from the Northumbrian point of view, the English are gradually and inevitably brought into the happy embrace of the Roman church, triumphing against the bitterness and treachery of the native Britons, the well-meaning but deluded zeal of the Irish missionaries, and the temporizing and backsliding of one pagan king after another. It is a tribute to Bede's great literary talent that in many ways the story he constructs from whatever meager evidence was available to him is still regarded as a fundamentally accurate account.

The following selections give some of the flavor of Bede's work: a geographical prologue describing the island of Britain; a lively narrative of the coming of the Angles and Saxons derived largely from the early sixth-century Briton Gildas's *De excidio Britonum* ("The Ruin of Britain"), a passionate work of moral exhortation written from a stridently anti-English perspective; a detailed psychological portrait of the Northumbrian king Edwin's slow movement towards conversion; and an account of two remarkable figures from the monastery of Whitby, the abbess Hild and the lay brother Cædmon. Cædmon's story is far more widely read today. According to Bede, Cædmon receives a miraculous talent for poetic composition and becomes a great composer of religious verse; Cædmon's *Hymn* (which Bede records in Latin, not English) is sometimes treated as the first English Christian poetic work. Bede's account of the life and miracles of the abbess Hild, however, plays a role of equal importance in his larger history; it is included here to suggest that the paired lives of a learned aristocratic woman and an illiterate peasant can tell us a great deal about the boundaries of Bede's narrative and the kinds of material it excludes, about the relationship between history and hagiography, and about the ways in which the cultural roles prescribed by one's gender and class affect the shape of one's spiritual journey.

from *Ecclesiastical History of the English People*[1]

1. A DESCRIPTION OF THE ISLAND OF BRITAIN AND ITS INHABITANTS (I.1)

Britain, an island in the ocean, formerly called Albion, is situated in the northwest, opposite the coasts of Germany, France, and Spain, which form the greatest part of Europe, though at a considerable distance from them. It extends 800 miles to the north and is 200 miles broad, except where several promontories extend further in breadth, which makes the circuit of its coastline 3600 miles. To the south lies Belgic Gaul, from which the closest port for travelers is the city of *Rutubi Portus*, corrupted by the English into "Reptacestir."[2] The distance from there across the sea to *Gessoriacum*,[3] the closest point in the land of the Morini, is fifty miles, or as some writers say, 450 *stadia*. Behind the island, where it opens upon the boundless ocean, are the Orkney Islands.

Britain is rich in grain and trees, and is well adapted for feeding cattle and beasts of burden. It also produces vines in some places, and has plenty of land and waterfowls of various kinds; it is remarkable also for its rivers, abounding in fish, particularly salmon and eels, and plentiful springs. Seals and dolphins are frequently taken, and even whales; besides many sorts of shellfish

[1] *Ecclesiastical History of the English People*   The standard edition of the *Historia Ecclesiastica*, with a modern English translation, is Bertram Colgrave and R.A.B. Mynors, eds., *Bede's Ecclesiastical History of the English People* (Oxford, 1969). The present translation by R.M. Liuzza, relies heavily on that work, as well as the earlier work of L.C. Jane (London: J.M. Dent; New York: E.P. Dutton, 1910) and J.M. Wallace-Hadrill's *Bede's Ecclesiastical History of the English People: A Historical Commentary* (Oxford: Clarendon Press, 1991).

[2] *Reptacestir* Richborough.

[3] *Gessoriacum* Boulogne.

such as mussels, in which are often found excellent pearls of all colors, red, purple, violet, and green, but mostly white. There is also a great abundance of cockles, from which a scarlet dye is made, a most beautiful color which never fades from the heat of the sun nor exposure to the rain; but the older it is, the more beautiful it becomes. Britain has salt springs and hot springs, and from them flow rivers which furnish hot baths, suitable for all ages and sexes, arranged for each separately. For water, as St. Basil says,[1] receives the quality of heat when it passes through certain metals, so that it becomes not only hot but scalding. Britain has also many veins of metals, copper, iron, lead, and silver; it produces much excellent jet, which is black and sparkling, burns in fire, and when heated drives away serpents; when it is warmed by rubbing it attracts whatever is applied to it, like amber. The island was once famous for its twenty-eight noble cities, besides innumerable castles which were all strongly secured with walls, towers, gates, and locks.

Because Britain lies almost under the North Pole, the nights are light in summer, so that at midnight it is difficult for those who are watching to tell whether the evening twilight still lingers, or the dawn of morning is coming, since the sun at night returns to the east through the northern regions without passing far below the horizon. For this reason the summer days are extremely long; on the other hand the winter nights are also of great length, namely eighteen hours, for the sun then withdraws into the regions of Africa. In summer too the nights are extraordinarily short, as are the days in winter, each containing only six equinoctial hours,[2] while in Armenia, Macedonia, Italy, and other countries in the same latitude, the longest day or night extends to fifteen hours, and the shortest to nine.

At the present time, there are five languages in Britain, the English, British,[3] Irish, Pictish, and Latin,

just as the divine law is written in five books, each in its own way devoted to seeking out and setting forth one and the same knowledge of sublime truth and true sublimity. The Latin tongue, through the study of the Scriptures, has become common to all the rest. At first this island had no other inhabitants than the Britons, from whom it derived its name, and who, coming over into Britain, so it is said, from Armorica,[4] took possession of the southern parts of it. When they had made themselves masters of the greatest part of the island, beginning from the south, it is said that the Pictish race from Scythia,[5] putting to sea in a few long ships, were driven by the winds beyond the shores of Britain and arrived on the northern coast of Ireland. There they found the Irish race and asked to be allowed to settle among them, but their request was refused. Ireland is the largest island next to Britain, and lies to the west of it; but though it is shorter than Britain to the north, yet it runs out far beyond it to the south, opposite to the northern parts of Spain, though a wide sea lies between them. The Picts came to this island, as has been said, by sea and asked that a place be granted them where they might settle. The Irish answered that the island could not hold them both; but they said, "We can give you some good advice as to what to do. We know of another island not far from ours, to the east, which we often see in the distance on a clear day. If you will go there, you can make settlements; but if anyone should oppose you, you shall have our help." And so the Picts, sailing over into Britain, began to occupy the northern parts of the island, because the Britons had seized the southern parts. Now the Picts had no wives, so they asked the Irish for some; they consented to give them women only on condition that, when any difficulty should arise, they should choose a king from the female line rather than the male; this custom, as is well known, has been observed among the Picts to this day. In the course of time Britain received a third nation in addition to the Britons and the Picts, namely the Irish, who came from Ireland under their leader Reuda, and won lands from

---

[1] *St. Basil says* In his *Hexaemeron*, a treatise on the six days of creation.

[2] *equinoctial hours* As Bede explains in his *De temporum ratione* (*The Reckoning of Time*), these hours are those which divide the day evenly into twenty-four parts (i.e., like a modern day); "common" hours divide day and night into twelve hours each of uneven length, so that summer hours are long during the day and short at night, and winter hours are just the reverse.

[3] *British* I.e., Welsh.

---

[4] *Armorica* Area along the northwest coast of France somewhat larger than modern Brittany.

[5] *Scythia* Irish tradition reports that the Picts come from Thrace; Bede may be following this here, or using "Scythia" to mean the farthest northern regions of the world, Ultima Thule.

the Picts either by fair means or by force of arms. They still possess these lands. They are to this day called *Dalreudini* after their commander—in their language, *Dal* signifies a part.[1]

Ireland far surpasses Britain in breadth and in wholesomeness and serenity of climate, for the snow rarely lies there above three days. No man makes hay in the summer for winter use, or builds stables for his beasts of burden. No reptiles are found there, and no snake can live there; for although serpents have often been carried to Ireland from Britain, as soon as the ship comes near the shore and the scent of the air reaches them, they die. In fact almost everything in the island is good against poison. We have seen how, for example, when people have been bitten by serpents, the leaves of manuscripts from Ireland were scraped, and the scrapings put in water and given to them to drink. These scrapings immediately expelled the spreading poison, and eased the swelling. The island abounds in milk and honey, nor is there any lack of vines, fish, or fowl; and it is noted for deer and goats. It is properly the native land of the Irish; they migrated from there, as has been said, and formed the third nation in Britain in addition to the Britons and the Picts. There is a very wide arm of the sea, which originally divided the nation of the Picts from the Britons; it runs from the west very far into the land, where, to this day, stands the strong city of the Britons, called Alcluith.[2] The Irish settled on the north side of this bay and made their home there.

2. THE COMING OF THE ENGLISH TO BRITAIN

[After the Goths attack Rome in 410, the Roman legions in Britain withdraw, leaving the British defenseless, "utterly ignorant of the arts of war." They are immediately attacked by the Irish from the west and the Picts from the north. Bede's source for this section is the British historian Gildas, whose *De excidio Britonum* ("On the Ruin of Britain") is a stern and prophetic work upbraiding the British for their sins and lamenting the punishments they suffered at the hands of the Saxon invaders. Bede's

allegiances are different, of course, but the harsh tone of Gildas's polemic, and his assertion that the coming of the English was ordained by God, is put to good use in Bede's excoriation of the British (Bede's deep dislike of the British arose, ostensibly at least, from their refusal to convert their conquerors to Christianity).]

In the year of our Lord 423, Theodosius the younger became emperor after Honorius, the forty-fifth from Augustus, and governed the Roman empire twenty-six years. In the eighth year of his reign Palladius was sent by Celestinus, the Roman pontiff, to the Irish who believed in Christ, to be their first bishop.[3] In the twenty-third year of his reign Aetius, a man of high rank and a patrician, held his third consulship with Symmachus. The wretched remnants of the Britons sent him a letter which began: "To Aetius, thrice Consul, the groans of the Britons." In the course of the letter they expressed their sorrows: "The barbarians drive us to the sea; the sea drives us back to the barbarians: between them we face two sorts of death—we are either slaughtered or drowned." Yet all this could not procure any assistance from him, because he was engaged in a deadly war with Blædla and Attila, kings of the Huns. And even though Blædla had been murdered the year before this by the treachery of his brother Attila, nevertheless Attila himself remained so dangerous an enemy to the state that he devastated almost all of Europe, attacking and destroying cities and castles. At the same time there was a famine in Constantinople, which was followed shortly afterwards by the plague, and a great part of the walls of that city fell to the ground, along with fifty-seven towers. Many cities also fell into ruins, and the famine and pestilential stench which filled the air destroyed thousands of men and cattle.

Meanwhile this famine afflicted the Britons more and more, leaving a lasting memory of its malice to posterity. It forced many of them to submit themselves to their predatory enemies; others still held out, trusting in divine assistance when none was to be had from men. These continually made raids from the mountains,

---

[1]   *part* Irish *dal* actually means "meadow," "valley"; it is in Old English that the word *dæl* means "part."

[2]   *Alcluith* Dumbarton.

[3]   *Palladius was sent ... bishop* Nothing much is known of Palladius beyond what Bede reports; Bede never mentions St. Patrick, who is generally remembered as the "Apostle to the Irish."

caves, and forests, and at last they began to inflict severe losses on the enemy who had been plundering their land for so many years. The shameless Irish robbers then returned home, intending to come back before long; the Picts, from that time on, remained quiet in the farthest part of the island, though they did not cease to plunder and harass the Britons from time to time.

When the ravages of the enemy finally ceased, there was such an abundance of grain in the island as had never been known before. With abundance came an increase in luxury, which was immediately followed by every sort of crime; in particular, cruelty and hatred of truth and love of falsehood increased so much that if anyone among them happened to be milder than the rest and somewhat inclined to truth, all the rest heaped hatred and missiles upon him, as if he had been the enemy of Britain. Not only were laymen guilty of these things, but even our Lord's own flock and their pastors too; they cast off the light yoke of Christ[1] and thrust their necks under the burden of drunkenness, hatred, argument, strife, envy, and other crimes of this sort. In the meantime a severe plague suddenly fell upon that corrupt generation, and soon destroyed so many of them that there were scarcely enough people left alive to bury the dead: yet those who survived could not be awakened from the spiritual death which their sins had brought upon them, either by the death of their friends or by the fear of their own death. For this reason, a still more severe retribution soon afterwards fell upon this sinful nation for their horrible wickedness. They consulted as to what should be done, and where they should seek help to prevent or repel the very frequent attacks of the northern nations, and they all agreed with their King Vortigern[2] that they should call the Saxons to their aid from across the sea. As events clearly showed, this was ordained by the will of our Lord Himself so that evil might fall upon them for their wicked deeds.

In the year of our Lord 449 Marcian became emperor with Valentinian, the forty-sixth emperor from Augustus, and ruled for seven years. At this time the nation of the Angles or Saxons, being invited by Vortigern, came to Britain in three long ships; they were granted a place to settle in the eastern part of the island so that they might appear to be fighting for their country, but their real intention was to enslave it. Accordingly they first fought against the enemy who attacked from the north, and won the victory. When this became known at home in their own country, and also the fertility of the country and the cowardice of the Britons, a much larger fleet was quickly sent over with a greater number of men; this, added to the troop already there, made an invincible army. The newcomers received a grant of land from the Britons, on condition that they wage war against their enemies for the peace and safety of the country, and the Britons agreed to pay them.

Those who came over were from three powerful tribes in Germany—the Saxons, Angles, and Jutes. From the Jutes are descended the people of Kent and of the Isle of Wight, and that part of the kingdom of the West Saxons just opposite the Isle of Wight, which is still today called the nation of the Jutes. From the country of the Saxons, that is, the region which is now known as Old Saxony, came the East Saxons, the South Saxons, and the West Saxons. From the country of the Angles—that is, the region between the provinces of the Jutes and the Saxons which is called *Angulus*, and which is said to remain deserted from that day to this—came the East Angles, the Middle Angles, the Mercians, and all the Northumbrian race (that is, those people that dwell north of the river Humber), and the other Anglian tribes.[3] Their first commanders are said to have been two brothers, Hengest and Horsa. Horsa was afterwards killed in battle by the Britons, and was buried in the eastern part of Kent, where there is still a monument bearing his name. They were the sons of Wihtgils, son of Witta, son of Woden, from whose stock the royal

---

[1] *Not only ... of Christ* See Matthew 11.29.

[2] *King Vortigern* Bede expands on his source Gildas here to supply the name of the king Vortigern (which means "chief lord"—Gildas calls him only *superbus tyrannus*, which basically means the same thing) and the names of the Saxons Hengest and Horsa (both names mean "horse"). Vortigern later has a prominent (though ignominious) role in the Arthurian legends as shaped by Geoffrey of Monmouth's *History of the Kings of Britain*.

[3] *Anglian tribes* Or "English people." In the title of his work, and in its text as well, Bede refers to all the invading tribes as the *gens Anglorum* or "English people."

families of many kingdoms claim their descent.[1]

In a short time hordes of these peoples flooded into the island, and their numbers increased so much that they became a terror to the natives who had invited them. Then suddenly they joined forces with the Picts, whom they had by this time driven far away by the force of their arms, and began to turn their weapons against their allies. First they made them supply a greater quantity of food; then, seeking an occasion to quarrel, they insisted that unless more plentiful supplies were brought to them, they would break the alliance and ravage the whole island. Nor were they slow in carrying out their threats—to make a long story short, the fire kindled by the hands of these pagans executed God's just revenge on the nation for its crimes, not unlike the fire once kindled by the Chaldeans which consumed the walls and city of Jerusalem.[2] Likewise here in Britain the just Judge ordained that the fire of these brutal conquerors should ravage all the neighboring cities and countryside from the east to the western sea, without opposition, until it covered almost every part of the doomed island. Public and private buildings fell into ruins; priests were everywhere slain before the altars; the prelates and people alike were destroyed with fire and sword regardless of their rank; and there was no one left to bury those who had died in such a cruel slaughter. Some of the miserable remnant were captured in the mountains and butchered in heaps; others, exhausted by hunger, came forward and submitted themselves to the enemy, ready to accept perpetual slavery for the sake of food, if only they were not killed on the spot. Some fled sorrowfully beyond the sea, while others remained in their own land and led a miserable life among the forests, crags, and mountains, always expecting every moment to be their last.

When the victorious army had destroyed and dispersed the native peoples, and returned home to their own settlements,[3] the Britons slowly began to gather strength and courage. They emerged from their hiding places and unanimously prayed for divine assistance that they might not be utterly destroyed. Their leader at that time was Ambrosius Aurelius,[4] a modest man who was, by chance, the sole member of the Roman nation to survive the storm in which his parents, who were of a royal and famous family, had perished. Under his leadership the Britons regained their strength, challenged their victors to battle and, by the help of God, won the victory. From that time on, sometimes the natives, and sometimes their enemies, prevailed, until the year of the siege of Mount Badon, when the Britons made no small slaughter of their enemies, about forty-four years after their arrival in England. But more of this hereafter.

3. The Life and Conversion of Edwin, King of Northumbria; the Faith of the East Angles

[The conversion of Edwin is in many ways the central event in Bede's long history—it sets England firmly on the road to Christianity and represents the crowning achievement of the mission of Augustine of Canterbury, sent by Pope Gregory the Great to convert the island. Bede probably relied on local knowledge and memories for his story; he therefore has to explain why Edwin's conversion is significantly delayed and accomplished with much foot-dragging.

According to Bede's account, Edwin secured his kingship in Northumbria with the help of Rædwald, the king of East Anglia, in 616; later he married Æthelburh, daughter of the Christian king Æthelberht of Kent, in 625. One of the conditions of the marriage was that he put no obstacles in the way of Christian worship in his kingdom, and promise to consider becoming a Christian himself. Æthelburh arrives in Northumbria accompanied by the bishop Paulinus; though Paulinus works diligently to convert Edwin, he is unsuccessful for a long time.

---

[1] *They were the ... their descent*   Bede is apparently not troubled by the fact that Woden is a Germanic god, suggesting that by his day active worship of Woden was not widespread. In medieval historical writing, the various classical and Germanic gods (when they are not written off as demons masquerading to lead men astray) are usually explained as ancient heroes whose exploits and stature were inflated over time until they were worshipped as gods.

[2] *not unlike ... Jerusalem*   See 2 Kings 25.8–10.

[3] *settlements*   I.e., in Britain, not Germany.

[4] *Ambrosius Aurelius*   Bede's information comes from Gildas; no earlier or more reliable source is known for Ambrosius Aurelius, later transformed into King Arthur. The battle of Mount Badon, if it occurred at all, probably took place around 500 CE.

When Edwin survives an assassination attempt by the West Saxons on the same day he celebrates the birth of his daughter (whom he allows to be baptized), he promises to convert if God will grant him victory over his enemies. After his campaign against the West Saxons is successful, however, he delays fulfilling his promise for a long time, despite the instruction of Paulinus, the prayers of his wife, and the entreaties of the Pope (Boniface) himself.

Bede's account of Edwin's conversion is sometimes caught between its contradictory impulses towards hagiography (in which conversion is described as a personal journey to faith, punctuated by miracles) and political history (in which conversion is seen as an act of royal policy). But it is marked by a lively sense of scene and character, and vividly conveys the fragile and sometimes dangerous nature of early Anglo-Saxon kingship, the power of the "heroic" code as an ideal of behavior, and the complex implications of conversion; Bede's report (or invention) of the council at which Edwin hears the opinions of his advisors—the unnamed philosophical nobleman, the opportunistic high priest Coifi—is a classic scene, a Christian writer's lyrical, almost elegiac imagination of the pagan heart.]

Such was the letter that Pope Boniface wrote for the salvation of King Edwin and his nation. But a heavenly vision, which God in His mercy had once chosen to reveal to Edwin when he was in exile at the court of Rædwald, king of the Angles, was of greater use in urging him to understand and embrace the counsels of salvation. Paulinus saw how difficult it was for the king's proud mind to bow to the humility of the way of salvation and accept the mystery of the life-giving cross, but at the same time he continued to use both exhortation with men and prayer to God for his and his subjects' salvation. At length, as we may suppose, he was shown in spirit the nature of the vision that had once been revealed to the king. Nor did he lose any time in warning the king to fulfill the vow he had made when he saw the vision, which he had promised to undertake if he should be delivered from the trouble he was in at that time, and ascend to the throne.

His vision was this: when his predecessor Æthelfrith was persecuting him, he wandered secretly for many years through several places and kingdoms, and at last came to Rædwald, asking him for protection against the plots of his powerful persecutor. Rædwald gladly received him, and promised to do what he asked. But when Æthelfrith learned that he had been seen in that kingdom, and had been hospitably entertained by the king and his retainers, he sent messengers to offer Rædwald a great sum of money to kill Edwin. But this had no effect; he sent a second and a third time, offering more and more each time, and threatening to make war on him if he refused. Rædwald, either terrified by his threats or corrupted by his bribes, yielded to his request and promised either to kill Edwin or to give him up to the messengers. A trusty friend of Edwin's found this out, and went into his chamber when he was going to bed, for it was the first hour of the night. He called him outside, told him what the king had promised to do with him, adding, "If you are willing, I will take you from this kingdom right now, and lead you to a place where neither Rædwald nor Æthelfrith will ever find you." Edwin answered, "I thank you for your goodwill, but I cannot do what you suggest, lest I be the first to break the compact I have made with this great king; he has done me no wrong, nor shown me any enmity. If I must die, let it rather be by his hand than by that of some meaner person. For where should I now fly, when I have for so many years been a vagabond through all the kingdoms of Britain, trying to escape the snares of my enemies?" His friend went away, and Edwin remained alone outside; sitting with a heavy heart in front of the palace, he began to be overwhelmed with many thoughts, not knowing what to do or which way to turn.

He remained a long time in silent anguish, brooding over his misfortunes, when suddenly in the dead of night he saw a man approach him whose face and dress were equally strange. He was more than a little frightened at this unexpected sight. The stranger came close, saluted him, and asked why he sat there alone and melancholy on a stone at that time, when everyone else was resting, and fast asleep. Edwin asked in reply what concern it was to him whether he spent the night indoors or out. The stranger replied, "Do not think that I am unaware of the cause of your grief, your sleeplessness, and your sitting alone outside. For I know who you are, and why you grieve, and the evils which you fear will fall upon you. But tell me, what reward would you give the man who would free you from this anguish, and persuade Rædwald neither to harm you himself, nor to give you up to be murdered by your enemies?" Edwin replied that he would give that person all that he was able in return for such a favor. The other continued, "What if he also assured you that you will overcome your enemies, and be a king who surpasses in power not only all your ancestors, but also all who have reigned before you over the English?" Edwin, encouraged by these questions, did not hesitate to promise that he would make a suitable return to anyone who should offer him such great benefits. Then the man said, "If the one who truly foretold so many good things could also give you better and more useful advice for your life and salvation than any of your ancestors or kindred ever heard of, would you consent to obey him, and to follow his saving counsel?" Edwin did not hesitate to promise that he would follow in every detail the directions of the one who could rescue him from so many troubles and raise him to the throne. At this answer the man who was speaking to him laid his hand on his head saying, "When this sign shall come to you, remember this conversation that has passed between us, and do not hesitate to fulfill what you have now promised." Having uttered these words, it is said that he immediately disappeared, so that the king might realize that it was not a man but a spirit that had appeared to him.

The young prince sat there alone for a time, rejoicing in the consolation he had received but deeply troubled and anxiously wondering who it was that had talked to him in that way, or where he had come from. Meanwhile the friend mentioned earlier returned, greeted him pleasantly and said, "Rise, go inside, and let yourself sleep without fear! The king has changed his mind and intends to do you no harm but rather to keep the promise he made you; when he secretly revealed to the queen the plan I told you before, she talked him out of it, warning that was unworthy of so great a king to sell his good friend for gold when he was in such distress, and to sacrifice his own honor, more precious than any ornament, for the love of money." In short, the king did as he had said, and not only refused to betray the banished man to his enemy's messengers, but helped Edwin to recover his kingdom. As soon as the messen-

gers had returned home, he raised a mighty army to overthrow Æthelfrith. Rædwald did not give him time to gather all his forces; he attacked him with a much larger army and killed him on the borders of the kingdom of Mercia, on the east bank of the river Idle. In this battle Rædwald's son Regenhere was killed. And thus Edwin, in accordance with the vision he had received, not only escaped the snares of the king his enemy, but after his death succeeded him on the throne.

King Edwin hesitated to accept the word of God preached by Paulinus, and for some time, as we have said, used to sit alone for several hours at a time, earnestly debating within himself what he ought to do and what religion he should follow. One day the man of God[1] came to him, laid his right hand on the king's head, and asked him if he recognized this sign. The king, trembling, was about to fall down at his feet but Paulinus raised him up and said in a voice that seemed familiar, "Behold, with God's help you have escaped the hands of the enemies you feared; behold, you have obtained by His gift the kingdom you desired; take heed not to delay what you promised to do—receive the faith and keep the commandments of Him who rescued you from earthly adversity and has raised you to the honor of an earthly kingdom. If, from this time forward, you are willing to follow his will, which is made known to you through me, He will not only deliver you from the everlasting torments of the wicked, but also make you a partaker with Him of His eternal kingdom in heaven."

When the king heard these words, he answered that he was both willing and bound to accept the faith which Paulinus taught, but that he would confer about it with his chief men and counselors so that, if they agreed with him, they might all together be cleansed in Christ, the Fountain of Life. Paulinus agreed, and the king did as he said: holding a meeting with his council of wise men, he asked each one in turn what he thought of this new doctrine, and the new worship of God that had been proclaimed.

Coifi, chief of his own priests, immediately answered, "Consider, O king, this new doctrine that is being preached to us. For I say to you truly that as far as I can tell, the religion we have practiced until now has no virtue in it. None of your people has devoted himself

---

[1] *man of God* I.e., Paulinus.

more diligently to the worship of our gods than I, and yet there are many who receive greater favors and greater honor from you than I do, and are more prosperous in all their undertakings. If the gods had any power they would have helped me more readily, since I have been more careful to serve them. It follows, therefore, that if on examination those new doctrines which are now preached to us are found to be better and more effective, we should accept them immediately and without delay."

Another of the king's chief men agreed with his words and his advice, and then added: "This is how the present life of man, O king, seems to me in comparison with that time which is unknown to us: as if you are sitting in your feasting-hall with your ealdormen and thanes[1] in wintertime, with a good fire burning in the middle of the hall and all inside is warm, while outside the winter storms of rain and snow are raging; and a sparrow flies swiftly through the hall, entering in at one door and quickly flying out at another. While he is within the winter storms cannot touch him; but after the briefest moment of calm he immediately vanishes out of your sight, out of the winter and back into it again. So this life of man appears just for a moment—of what went before, or what is to follow, we know nothing at all. If this new doctrine contains anything more certain, it seems right that we should follow it." The other elders and counselors spoke in the same way, by divine inspiration.

Coifi added that he wanted to listen more attentively to what Paulinus had to say about the God he preached. The king ordered Paulinus to speak and Coifi, hearing his words, cried out, "I have long realized that our religion is worthless—the the more diligently I sought the truth in our worship, the less I found it. But now I freely confess that such truth shines forth clearly in this preaching, which can bestow on us the gift of life, salvation, and eternal happiness. Therefore I advise, O king, that we instantly abandon and set fire to those temples and altars which we have consecrated without reaping any benefit from them." What more is there to say? The king publicly accepted the gospel which Paulinus preached, renouncing idolatry, and confessed his faith in Christ; and when he asked the high priest who should be the first to profane the altars and temples

of their idols, together with the enclosures around them, Coifi answered, "I will; for who can more properly than myself destroy those things which I once worshipped in ignorance, through the wisdom which has been given me by the true God, and set an example for others?" And immediately, casting aside his former superstitions, he asked the king to furnish him with arms and a stallion, and mounting it he set out to destroy the idols. Now the high priest was not allowed to carry arms or to ride on any horse but a mare; but with a sword girded about him and a spear in his hand, he mounted the king's stallion and set off for the idols.[2] The common people, seeing this, thought he was mad; but wasting no time, as soon as he drew near the temple he profaned it by casting into it the spear which he held, and rejoicing in the knowledge of the worship of the true God, he ordered his companions to destroy and set fire to the temple and all its enclosures. This place where the idols once stood is still shown, a short distance east of York beyond the river Derwent. Today it is called Goodmanham, the place where the high priest, by the inspiration of the true God, profaned and destroyed the altars which he had himself consecrated.

So King Edwin and all the nobles of his nation, and a large number of the common people, received the faith and regeneration by holy baptism in the eleventh year of his reign, that is in the year of our Lord 627, and about 180 years after the coming of the English into Britain. He was baptized at York on Easter day, the 12th of April, in the church of St. Peter the Apostle which he himself had built of timber, while he was a catechumen[3] and receiving instruction in order to receive baptism. In the same city he established an episcopal see for his instructor and bishop Paulinus. As soon as he was baptized he began, under the direction of Paulinus, to build a larger and more noble church of stone in the same place, in the midst of which the chapel which he had built first would be enclosed. The foundations were laid and he began to build the church square, surrounding the former chapel, but before the walls were raised

1 *ealdormen and thanes* Noblemen.

2 *Now the high priest ... idols* Bede is our only authority for this custom, or for the existence of "high priests" in Anglo-Saxon pagan religion.

3 *catechumen* Person preparing to be baptized into the Catholic faith.

to their proper height, the king was cruelly slain[1] and the work was left to his successor Oswald. Paulinus continued to preach the word of the Lord in the kingdom for six years, that is, until the end of the king's reign, with his consent and favor, and all who were predestined for eternal life believed and were baptized. Among these were Osfrid and Eadfrid, King Edwin's sons, who were born to him while he was in exile; their mother was Cwenburh, daughter of Ceorl, king of the Mercians.

Other children of his by Queen Æthelburh were baptized later, namely Æthelhun and a daughter Æthelthryth and a second son Uscfrea; the first two were snatched from this life while still in their white garments,[2] and buried in the church at York. Yffi, son of Osfrith, was also baptized, and many more nobles and members of the royal family. It is said that the fervor of the faith and the longing for the washing of salvation was so great among the Northumbrians that once when Paulinus came to the king and queen in their royal palace called *Ad gefrin*,[3] he spent thirty-six days there fully occupied in catechising and baptizing, and during these days, from morning till night, he did nothing but instruct the people who came from every village and region in Christ's saving word. When they were instructed, he washed them with the water of absolution in the river Glen, which is nearby. This palace was abandoned by the kings who followed Edwin and another built instead, at the place called *Mælmin*.[4]

All this happened in the kingdom of Bernicia; but in the kingdom of Deira also, where Paulinus used to stay frequently with the king, he baptized in the river Swale, which runs by the village of Catterick, for in the earliest days of the church there they could not build chapels or baptistries. But in *Campodonum*,[5] where there was also a royal dwelling, he built a church which afterwards was burned down, together with all the buildings, by the pagans who killed King Edwin. In its place later kings built a dwelling for themselves in the region called *Loidis*.[6] The altar, which was made of stone, escaped the fire and is still preserved in the monastery of the most reverend abbot and priest Thrythwulf, which is in the forest of Elmet.

Edwin was so devoted to the true worship that he also persuaded Eorpwald, son of Rædwald and king of the East Saxons, to abandon his idolatrous superstitions and, with his whole kingdom, to accept the Christian faith and sacraments. Indeed his father Rædwald had long before been initiated into the mysteries of the Christian faith in Kent, but in vain; for on his return home, he was seduced by his wife and by certain perverse teachers, and turned back from the sincerity of the faith, so that his last state was worse than his first.[7] Like the ancient Samaritans, he seemed at the same time to serve Christ and the gods whom he had previously served, and in the same temple he had one altar for Christian sacrifice and another small one to offer victims to devils. Ealdwulf, ruler of that kingdom up to our own time, testified that the temple had stood until his time, and that he had seen it when he was a boy. King Rædwald, noble by birth but ignoble in his actions, was the son of Tytil, whose father was Wuffa, from whom the kings of the East Angles are called Wuffings.[8]

Eorpwald, not long after he had embraced the Christian faith, was killed by a heathen called Ricberht; and afterwards the kingdom remained in error for three years, until Eorpwald's brother Sigeberht came to the

---

[1]   *The king was cruelly slain*   In battle against Cædwalla, king of the Britons, and Penda, King of the Mercians.

[2]   *white garments*   I.e., still wearing the white robe given to those who are newly baptized and worn every day for the first week after the sacrament.

[3]   *Ad gefrin*   Present-day Yeavering, Northumberland. Archaeologists have excavated the site of Edwin's hall, an impressive complex of large buildings and outdoor spaces on the site of a Neolithic hill fort.

[4]   *Mælmin*   Near present-day Millfield, Northumberland.

[5]   *Campodonum*   Roman site near Dewsbury, Yorkshire.

[6]   *Loidis*   Leeds.

[7]   *so that his ... his first*   See Luke 11.26.

[8]   *King Rædwald ... Wuffings*   Bede's account of Rædwald's incomplete conversion and excessive ecumenism contrasts sharply with that of Edwin's deep, thoughtful and fervent faith; moreover, since he is a Northumbrian, Bede's center of gravity is in the north, not least because his sources of information were probably richer. But the treacherous and backsliding East Saxons should not be underrated: Rædwald is widely thought to be the king honored by the elaborate and richly decorated ship-burial at Sutton Hoo, and the *Wuffings* may or may not be the same as the Swedish *Wylfings* mentioned in *Beowulf*.

throne. Sigeberht was a devout Christian and a learned man; he was in exile during his brother's life and went to live in Gaul, where he was admitted to the sacraments of the Christian faith. As soon as he came to the throne he made it his business to see that the whole kingdom shared his faith. His efforts were strongly supported by Bishop Felix. The bishop had been born and ordained in Burgundy; when he came to Archbishop Honorius and expressed his desires, the archbishop sent him to preach the word of life to this nation of the Angles. Nor were his wishes in vain, for the devoted sower reaped an abundant harvest of believers in this spiritual field— indeed, as his name signified,[1] he delivered all of that kingdom from longstanding evil and unhappiness, brought it to the faith and to the works of righteousness, and gave it the gift of everlasting felicity. He received the see of his bishopric in the city of *Dommoc*,[2] and when he had ruled as bishop over the kingdom for seventeen years, he ended his days there in peace.

Paulinus also preached the word to the kingdom of Lindsey, the first land on the south bank of the river Humber, bordering on the sea. He first converted the prefect of the city of Lincoln, whose name was Blæcca, and his whole family. In this city he also built a stone church of beautiful workmanship; its roof has now either fallen through age or been thrown down by enemies, but the walls are still standing, and every year some miraculous cures are wrought in that place for the benefit of those who seek them in faith. When Justus departed to Christ, in his place Paulinus consecrated Honorius as bishop in that church, as we will later tell in its proper place.

An abbot and priest of the monastery of Partney, a most truthful man whose name was Deda, told me this about the faith of this kingdom: an old man had told him that he himself had been baptized at noon by Bishop Paulinus, in the presence of King Edwin, with a great number of people, in the river Trent, near the city which in English is called *Tiowulfingacæstir*.[3] He also used to describe the appearance of Paulinus: he was tall, a little stooping, with black hair, a thin face, a slender

and aquiline nose, and an aspect both venerable and majestic. In his ministry he also had with him a deacon named James, a man of zeal and great reputation in Christ's Church, who survived right up to our days.

It is reported that there was such perfect peace in Britain, wherever the dominion of King Edwin extended, that, as the proverb still says, a woman with a new-born child could walk throughout the island from sea to sea without receiving any harm. The king cared so much for the good of his nation that in various places where he had noticed clear springs near the highways, he had stakes set up with bronze drinking-cups hanging from them, for the convenience of travelers. No one dared to touch them for any other purpose than the one they were designed for, because they feared the king and loved him dearly. His dignity was so great throughout his realm that not only were banners carried before him in battle, but even in time of peace, when he rode about his cities, estates, or regions with his thegns, a standard-bearer always used to go before him, and when he walked along the roads, there used to be carried before him the type of standard which the Romans call a *tufa* and the English a *thuf*.

4. ABBESS HILD OF WHITBY; THE MIRACULOUS POET CÆDMON

In the year of our Lord 680 Hild, the most devout servant of Christ, abbess of the monastery that is called Whitby,[4] departed on the 17th of November after having performed many heavenly works on earth, to receive the rewards of the heavenly life, at the age of sixty-six. She spent her first thirty-three years living most nobly in the secular habit, and more nobly dedicated the remaining half to our Lord in the monastic life. She was of noble birth, being the daughter of Hereric, nephew to King Edwin; in Edwin's company she received the faith and mysteries of Christ at the preaching of Paulinus of blessed memory, the first bishop of the Northumbrians, and she preserved her faith undefiled until she was rewarded with the sight of Him in heaven.

---

[1]   *as his name signified*   Felix means "fortunate" or "happy" in Latin.

[2]   *Dommoc*   Dunwich.

[3]   *Tiowulfingacæstir*   Littleborough.

[4]   *Whitby*   Bede uses the Old English name "Streaneshalch."

Resolving to give up the secular habit and serve Him alone, she withdrew to the kingdom of the East Angles, for she was related to the king there; she intended to pass over from there into Gaul, leaving her native land and all that she had to live as a stranger for our Lord's sake in the monastery of Chelles, so that she might more easily reach her eternal home in heaven. Her sister Hereswith, mother of Ealdwulf, king of the East Angles, was at that time living in the same monastery under the discipline of the monastic Rule, waiting for her heavenly crown. Inspired by her example, Hild continued a whole year in the kingdom of the East Angles with the intention of going abroad; Bishop Aidan called her home, however, and gave her enough land to support herself on the north side of the river Wear, where she lived in the monastic life for a year, with a small group of companions.

After this she was made abbess in the monastery called *Heruteu*,[1] which had been founded not long before by Heiu, a devoted handmaid of Christ, who is said to have been the first woman in the kingdom of Northumbria to take the habit and vows of a nun, having been ordained by Bishop Aidan. But soon after she had founded that monastery, Heiu went away to the town of *Calcaria*, which the English call *Kælcacæstir*,[2] and there made her dwelling. Hild, the handmaid of Christ, was appointed to rule over that monastery, and immediately began to establish a rule of life there in all things, as she had been taught by many learned men; for Bishop Aidan and other devout men who knew her visited her frequently, instructed her diligently, and loved her dearly for her innate wisdom and devotion to the service of God.

When she had ruled over this monastery for some years, wholly intent upon establishing a rule of life there, it happened that she also undertook either to found or to reform a monastery in the place called *Streaneshalch*, which she carried out with great industry. She established the same rule in this monastery as in the other, and she taught there the strict observance of justice, piety, chastity, and other virtues, above all peace and charity. After the example of the primitive church, no one there was rich, and no one was poor, for all things were common to all, and none had any private property. Her wisdom was so great that not only ordinary people, but even kings and princes sometimes asked for and received her advice; she obliged those who were under her direction to devote so much time to the study of the Holy Scriptures, and to exercise themselves so much in works of justice, that there might be no difficulty in finding many there who were fit for ecclesiastical duties, that is for the service of the altar.

In fact we have seen five men from that monastery become bishops, all of them men of singular merit and sanctity: Bosa, Ætla, Oftfor, John, and Wilfrid. The first of them, as we related elsewhere, was consecrated bishop of York; of the second, it may be observed that he was appointed bishop of Dorchester. Of the two last we shall later relate that John was consecrated bishop of Hexham and Wilfrid, bishop of York; of Oftfor we will here note that after he applied himself to the reading and observance of the Scriptures in both of Hild's monasteries, being anxious to attain to greater perfection, he went to Kent to join Archbishop Theodore, of blessed memory. After he had spent more time in sacred studies there, he resolved to go to Rome, which in those days was considered to be an act of great merit. After his return to Britain, he went to the province of the Hwicce, where King Osric then ruled, and remained there a long time, preaching the word of faith and setting an example of holy life to all who saw and heard him. At that time Bosel, the bishop of that kingdom, suffered such weakness of body that he could not carry out his episcopal duties; so Oftfor was appointed bishop in his place by universal consent, and was consecrated at King Æthelred's command by Bishop Wilfrid, of blessed memory, who was at that time bishop of the Middle Angles because Archbishop Theodore was dead, and no other bishop had been ordained in his place. Before Bosel, a most learned and industrious man of excellent ability named Tatfrid had been chosen bishop there, also from Hild's monastery, but he had been snatched away by an untimely death before his consecration.

All who knew Abbess Hild, the handmaid of Christ, called her Mother because of her outstanding piety and grace. She was not only an example of holy life to those who lived in her monastery, but provided an opportunity for repentance and salvation to many who lived far

---

[1] *Heruteu* Hartlepool.

[2] *Kælcacæstir* Uncertain; possibly Tadcaster.

away who heard the happy news of her diligence and virtue. This was bound to happen so that the dream which her mother Breguswith had during Hild's infancy should be fulfilled. When her husband Hereric lived in exile under the British king Cerdic, where he was later poisoned, Breguswith dreamed that she was looking for him most carefully, and could find no sign of him anywhere; but suddenly, after having tried with all her might to find him, she found a most precious necklace under her garment, and as she was gazing at it very attentively, it cast such a blaze of light that it spread throughout all Britain. This dream came true in her daughter Hild, whose life was a bright example, not only to herself, but to many who desired to live well.

After she had governed this monastery many years, it pleased Him who has made such merciful provision for our salvation to subject her holy soul to the trial of a long sickness so that, like the apostle, her strength might be made perfect in weakness.

She was struck by a fever and fell into a violent heat, and for six years was afflicted continually; during all which time she never failed to give thanks to her Maker or to instruct the flock entrusted to her care both in public and in private. From her own experience she admonished everyone to serve the Lord dutifully in health and always to return thanks to Him in adversity or bodily illness. In the seventh year of her illness, she began to suffer internally and approached her last day. Around cock-crow, having received the viaticum of Holy Communion,[1] she called together the handmaids of Christ who were in the monastery, and admonished them to preserve the Gospel peace among themselves and towards all others; and as she was exhorting them she joyfully saw death approaching or, to use the words of our Lord, she passed from death into life.

That same night it pleased Almighty God by a vision to reveal her death in another monastery at some distance from hers called Hackness, which she had built that same year. In that monastery was a nun called Begu, who for thirty years or more had dedicated her virginity to God and served Him in the monastic life. While she was in the dormitory of the sisters, she suddenly heard in the air the familiar sound of the bell which used to awaken the sisters and call them to prayers when any one of them had been taken out of this world. Opening her eyes, she seemed to see the top of the house open, and a strong light pour in from above; looking intently at that light, she saw the soul of the handmaid of the Lord borne into heaven in the midst of that light, attended by angels. Then awaking and seeing the other sisters lying around her, she realized that what she had seen was either a dream or a vision; greatly frightened, she rose immediately and ran to a maiden named Frigyth, who was then presiding over the monastery in place of the abbess. With many tears and sighs, Begu told her that the Abbess Hild, mother of them all, had departed this life, and that she had seen her ascend with a great light, and with angels conducting her, into eternal bliss and the company of the inhabitants of heaven. When Frigyth heard this, she awoke all the sisters, and called them to the church; she ordered them to pray and sing psalms for Hild's soul, which they did for the rest of the night. At break of day, the brothers came from the place she had died with news of her death. They answered that they already knew it, and when they told how and when they had heard it, it was found that her death had been revealed to them in a vision in the very same hour that the brothers said she had died. Thus it was happily ordained by Heaven that when some watched her departure out of this world, others watched her entrance into the eternal life of the spirit. These monasteries are about thirteen miles distant from each other.

It is also reported that her death was made known in a vision the same night to one of the holy maidens who loved her most passionately, in the same monastery where this servant of God died. She saw Hild's soul ascend to heaven in the company of angels; and she declared this, the very same hour it happened, to those servants of Christ who were with her, and awakened them to pray for her soul, even before the rest of the congregation had heard of her death, for it was only made known to the whole monastery the next morning. This same nun was at that time with some other servants of Christ in the remotest part of the monastery, where the women who had recently entered the monas-

1   *viaticum ... Communion*   Communion received by someone who is possibly near death.

tery used to spend their time of probation until they were instructed in the Rule and admitted to the society of the community.

In Hild's monastery was a certain brother specially marked by the grace of God, who used to make pious and religious verses, so that whatever he learned from the holy Scriptures through interpreters, he soon afterwards turned into poetry of great sweetness and humility, in English, which was his native language. By his verses the minds of many were often inspired to despise the world and to long for the heavenly life. After him other Englishmen tried to compose religious poems, but none could ever compare with him, for he did not learn the art of poetry from men or through a man,[1] but received the gift of song freely by divine grace. For this reason he never could compose any trivial or foolish poem, but only those which were concerned with devotion and were fitting for his pious tongue to utter.

He had lived in the secular life until he was well advanced in years, and had never learned any verses; therefore sometimes at feasts, when it was agreed for the sake of entertainment that all present should take a turn singing, when he saw the harp coming towards him, he would rise up from the table in the middle of the feast, go out, and return home. On one occasion when he did this, he left the house of feasting and went to the stable, where it was his turn to take care of the animals that night. In due time he stretched out to rest; a person appeared to him in his sleep, saluted him by name, and said, "Cædmon, sing me something." Cædmon answered, "I cannot sing; that is why I left the feast and came here, because I could not sing." The man who was talking to him replied, "Nevertheless, you must sing to me."

"What shall I sing?" he asked. "Sing about the beginning of created things," he replied. At that, Cædmon immediately began to sing verses which he had never heard before in praise of God, whose general sense is this: "We ought now to praise the Maker of the heavenly kingdom, the power of the Creator and his counsel, the deeds of the Father of glory and how He, since He is the eternal God, was the author of all marvels and first, as almighty Guardian of the human race, created heaven as a roof for the sons of men, and then the earth."[2] This is the sense but not the actual order of the words he sang in his sleep, for poetry, no matter how well composed, cannot be literally translated from one language into another without losing much of its beauty and dignity. Awaking from his sleep, Cædmon remembered all that he had sung in his dream, and soon added more verses in the same manner, praising God in a worthy style.

In the morning he went to the steward, his master, and told him of the gift he had received; the steward led him to the abbess, who ordered him, in the presence of many learned men, to recount his dream and repeat his poem, so that they might all decide what it was and where it had come from. It was clear to all of them he had received a gift of heavenly grace from our Lord. Then they explained to him a passage of sacred history or doctrine, and ordered him, if he could, to turn it into verse. He undertook this task and went away; when he returned the next morning he repeated it to them, composed in excellent verse. At this the abbess, recognizing the grace of God in this man, instructed him to renounce the secular habit and take up the monastic life; when this was done she joined him to the rest of the brethren in her monastery and ordered that he should be taught the whole course of sacred history. He learned all that he could by listening, and turned it over in his mind like a clean beast chewing the cud,[3] turned it into the most harmonious verse, and recited it so sweetly that his teachers became in turn his audience. He sang of the creation of the world, the origin of the human race, and all the history of Genesis; and made many verses on the departure of the children of Israel from Egypt, and their entry into the Promised Land, and many other stories from the holy Scriptures; of the Incarnation, Passion, and Resurrection of our Lord, and of His Ascension into heaven, of the coming of the Holy Spirit and the teaching of the apostles, also of the terror of future

---

[1] *from men or through a man*   See Galatians 1.1.

[2] *We ought now … the earth*   See below for Cædmon's *Hymn* in Old English. Bede gives only this paraphrase; in two manuscripts of Bede's Latin *Historia* a poem in the Northumbrian dialect of Old English is added in the margins. When Bede's work was translated into Old English at the end of the ninth century, the translators substituted a version of this poem for Bede's paraphrase, and omitted the disclaimer that follows it.

[3] *He learned … the cud*   See Leviticus 11.3; Deuteronomy 14.6.

judgment, the horror of the pains of hell, and the joys of the kingdom of heaven, and many more songs about the divine mercies and judgments by which he tried to turn all men away from the love of vice and to inspire in them the love and practice of good works. He was a very devout man, humbly submissive to the discipline of the monastic rule, but full of zeal against those who behaved otherwise; for this reason his life had a lovely ending.

When the hour of his departure drew near, for fourteen days he was afflicted with a bodily weakness which seemed to prepare the way, yet mild enough that he could talk and walk the whole time. Nearby was the house to which the sick and dying were carried. As evening fell on the night he was going to depart this life, he asked his attendant[1] to prepare a place for him there so he could take his rest. The attendant wondered why he should desire that, because there seemed to be no sign of his dying soon, but did what he had asked. They went there and were talking pleasantly and joyfully with the people who were already in the house; when it was past midnight he asked them whether they had the Eucharist there. They answered, "What need do you have of the Eucharist? You are not likely to die, since you talk so merrily with us, just as though you were in perfect health." "Nevertheless," he said, "bring me the Eucharist." When he had taken it into his hand he asked whether they were all in charity with him, without any complaint or quarrel. They answered that they were all in perfect charity, and free from anger; and likewise asked him whether he felt the same towards them. He answered at once, "My sons, I am in charity with all the servants of God." Then strengthening himself with the heavenly viaticum, he prepared for his entrance into the next life; he asked how near it was to the time when the brothers had to awaken to sing their nightly praise of our Lord. They answered, "It is not far off." He said, "Good; let us wait until then," and signing himself with the sign of the holy cross, he laid his head on the pillow and fell into a slumber, and so ended his life quietly. Thus it came to pass that, just as he had served God with a simple and pure mind and quiet devotion, so now he departed into His presence and left the world by a quiet death, and his tongue, which had composed so many holy words in praise of the Creator, uttered its last words while he was in the act of signing himself with the cross, and commending his spirit into God's hands; and from what has been said, it seems he had foreknowledge of his death.

5. CÆDMON'S HYMN IN OLD AND MODERN ENGLISH

Nu sculon herian   heofonrices weard,
Metodes meahta   ond his modgeþanc,
weorc wuldorfæder,   swa he wundra gehwæs,
ece Drihten,   or astealde.
He ærest scop   ielda bearnum
heofon to hrofe,   halig Scieppend;
þa middangeard   manncynnes weard,
ece Drihten,   æfter teode,
firum foldan   Frea ælmihtig.

Now (we) ought to praise Heaven-kingdom's guardian,
the Maker's might and his mind's thoughts,
the work of the glory-father, as he of each of wonders,
eternal Lord, established a beginning.[2]
He first shaped for men's sons
Heaven as a roof, the holy Creator;
then middle-earth mankind's guardian,
eternal Lord, afterwards prepared
the earth for men, the Lord almighty.

—C. 731

---

[1] *his attendant*   Older monks were attended by young novices who took care of them.

[2] *Lord … beginning* I.e., He established the beginning of every wonder.

EXETER BOOK ELEGIES

Most of the Old English poetry that has survived is contained in only four manuscripts. The richest and most diverse of these is Exeter Cathedral Library MS 3501, a large anthology of secular and religious poems. The Exeter Book was given to the Cathedral library by the bishop Leofric some time before 1072 CE (and has remained there ever since), but it was written probably a century earlier, somewhere in the south of England. Because some pages have been lost from the manuscript, we cannot say how many poems it originally contained, and we do not know the impulse behind its compilation. But the Exeter Book is a fascinating miscellany, ranging from serious religious poetry on the Advent and Ascension of Christ, to verse lives of St. Guthlac and Juliana, to a translation of a Latin poem on the Phoenix, to a collection of almost 100 verse riddles which are sometimes comical or obscene. The poems are probably by many different authors; a poet named Cynewulf encoded his own name (in runes) in two poems, *Juliana* and *Christ II*, but all others are anonymous and untitled.

The Exeter Book includes a group of short philosophical poems, differing in style and outlook but similar in tone, which have come to be known as "elegies": among these are *The Wanderer*, *The Seafarer*, *The Wife's Lament*, *The Ruin*, *Wulf and Eadwacer*, and *The Husband's Message*. The label "elegy" here is potentially misleading. In Greek and Latin literature the term refers to a particular metrical form, and since the sixteenth century the word has been used in English literature to describe a poem of lament or mourning (the most famous English elegies include Milton's *Lycidas*, Shelley's *Adonais*, and Tennyson's *In Memoriam*). But the term "elegy" is sometimes used more loosely to describe any serious meditative poem, and it is in this sense that these Old English poems should be considered elegies. The poems share certain themes and concerns—the passage of time and the transience of earthly things, the pain of exile and separation, the ache of absence and longing—as well as certain images and scenes such as ruined or abandoned buildings, desolate landscapes, storms at sea, darkness, night and the chill of winter. These themes, and the traditional language in which they are presented, are also found in other Old English poems; certain passages of *Beowulf* may be called elegiac, and the contemplation of earthly instability sometimes seems to pervade Old English literature. The tone and language of elegy may have roots deep in the traditions of Germanic poetry, but it is also influenced by late classical works such as Boethius's *Consolation of Philosophy*; the recognition that the "world under the heavens" is a place of tragic impermanence would probably be regarded as equally good Christian doctrine and pagan wisdom. Both *The Wanderer* and *The Ruin* also appear to borrow from the Latin convention of posing "ubi sunt?" questions—in literal translation, "Where are they" or "Where are these things?"

Most of the Old English elegies are monologues spoken by an unidentified character whose situation is unclear but who seems to be cut off from human society and the comforts of home and friendship. But even though they share the poetic language of exile and longing, each poem has its own shape and purpose, and each makes its own statement about the problems and possibilities of earthly life. *The Wanderer* is initially concerned with a wandering warrior who has lost his Lord; the focus of the second half of the poem opens up to lament the passing of a whole way of life, the heroic world of the warrior's hall. *The Wife's Lament* (one of only two poems in the Exeter Book to be written from a woman's point of view) is a poem of intense personal longing for an absent husband or lover. *The Seafarer*, like *The Wanderer*, divides into two parts. The opening lines of the poem consist of a first-person narrative describing the hardships of going to sea, and contrasting them with the comforts of staying at home on land; around line 65 the poem shifts from a narrative to a spiritual meditation that is at times explicitly and even aggressively homiletic and Christian. *The Ruin* describes the remains of an ancient city—most probably an ancient Roman city in Britain, such as Bath, which had been abandoned centuries before the writing of this poem. The poem is detached and dispassionate about the scene it describes, and—in contrast to *The Seafarer*—whatever moral judgments it makes are implicit and indirect.

Each of the four poems presented below has some structural and interpretive difficulties. *The Wanderer* is a dramatic monologue with a prologue and epilogue, but the beginnings and endings of speeches are not indicated in the manuscript and can only be guessed at. *The Seafarer* switches tone so radically that many readers (including Ezra Pound, who translated the poem) have simply rejected the second, more homiletic half. *The Wife's Lament* is obscure more by virtue of its language than its structure—a number of the poem's key terms are ambivalent or uncertain. And the pages of the Exeter Book containing *The Ruin* have been so damaged that the poem is itself a ruin, crumbling into incoherence. The poems develop philosophical arguments and present evidence and conclusions, but Old English poetic language is not necessarily congenial to the demands of precise reasoning; sentence boundaries and relationships between clauses are often uncertain. And yet despite these interpretive problems, the Exeter Book "elegies" are among the most moving and powerful poems in Old English; their vision of life as both infinitely precious and inevitably transitory still strikes a responsive chord in the hearts of many readers.

⌘ ⌘ ⌘

The Wanderer [1]

Always the one alone longs for mercy,
the Maker's mildness, though, troubled in mind,
across the ocean-ways he has long been forced
to stir with his hands the frost-cold sea,
5 and walk in exile's paths. *Wyrd* [2] is fully fixed!
Thus spoke the Wanderer, mindful of troubles,
of cruel slaughters and the fall of dear kinsmen: [3]
"Often alone, every first light of dawn,
I have lamented my sorrows. There is no one living
10 to whom I would dare to reveal clearly
my heart's thoughts. I know it is true

that it is in the lordly nature of a nobleman
to closely bind his spirit's coffer,
hold his treasure-hoard, whatever he may think.
15 The weary mind cannot withstand *wyrd*,
the troubled heart can offer no help,
and so those eager for fame often bind fast
in their breast-coffers a sorrowing soul,
just as I have had to take my own heart—
20 often wretched, cut off from my homeland,
far from dear kinsmen—and bind it in fetters,
ever since long ago I hid my gold-giving friend
in the darkness of earth, and went wretched,
winter-sad, over the ice-locked waves,
25 sought, hall-sick, a treasure-giver,
wherever I might find, far or near,
someone in a meadhall who knew of my people,
or who'd want to comfort me, friendless,
accustom me to joy. He who has come to know
30 how cruel a companion is sorrow
to one who has few dear protectors, will understand this:
the path of exile claims him, not patterned gold,
a winter-bound spirit, not the wealth of earth.
He remembers hall-holders and treasure-taking,
35 how in his youth his gold-giving lord
accustomed him to the feast—that joy has all faded.

---

[1] *The Wanderer* The present text has been translated for *The Broadview Anthology of British Literature* by R.M. Liuzza.

[2] *Wyrd* A powerful but not quite personified force; the closest parallel in modern English is "Fate." It is related to the verb "weorthan," meaning roughly "to occur." Its meanings range from a neutral "event" to a prescribed "destiny" to a personified "Fate"; it is useful to think of "wyrd" as "what happens," usually in a negative sense.

[3] *Thus spoke ... kinsmen* The manuscript in which the poem survives does not have quotation marks, or clear indications of where speeches begin and end in this poem; we are not sure whether lines 1–5 are spoken by the same character who speaks the following lines, or whether they are the narrator's opinion on the general situation of the Wanderer.

And so he who has long been forced to forego
his dear lord's beloved words of counsel will understand:
when sorrow and sleep both together
40 often bind up the wretched exile,
it seems in his mind that he clasps and kisses
his lord of men, and on his knee lays
hands and head, as he sometimes long ago
in earlier days enjoyed the gift-throne.[1]
45 But when the friendless man awakens again
and sees before him the fallow waves,
seabirds bathing, spreading their feathers,
frost falling and snow, mingled with hail,
then the heart's wounds are that much heavier,
50 longing for his loved one. Sorrow is renewed
when the memory of kinsmen flies through the mind;
he greets them with great joy, greedily surveys
hall-companions—they always swim away;
the floating spirits bring too few
55 well-known voices. Cares are renewed
for one who must send, over and over,
a weary heart across the binding of the waves.[2]

And so I cannot imagine for all this world
why my spirit should not grow dark
60 when I think through all this life of men,
how they suddenly gave up the hall-floor,
mighty young retainers. Thus this middle-earth
droops and decays every single day;
and so a man cannot become wise, before he has
      weathered
65 his share of winters in this world. A wise man
      must be patient,
neither too hot-hearted nor too hasty with words,
nor too weak in war nor too unwise in thoughts,
neither fretting nor fawning nor greedy for wealth,
never eager for boasting before he truly understands;
70 a man must wait, when he makes a boast,
until the brave spirit understands truly
whither the thoughts of his heart will turn.

The wise man must realize how ghastly it will be
when all the wealth of this world stands waste,

75 as now here and there throughout this middle-earth
walls stand blasted by wind,
beaten by frost, the buildings crumbling.
The wine halls topple, their rulers lie
deprived of all joys; the proud old troops
80 all fell by the wall. War carried off some,
sent them on the way, one a bird carried off
over the high seas, one the gray wolf
shared with death—and one a sad-faced man
covered in an earthen grave. The Creator
85 of men thus wrecked this enclosure,
until the old works of giants[3] stood empty,
without the sounds of their former citizens.

He who deeply considers, with wise thoughts,
this foundation and this dark life,
90 old in spirit, often remembers
so many ancient slaughters, and says these words:
'Where has the horse gone? where is the rider? where
      is the giver of gold?
Where are the seats of the feast? where are the joys
      of the hall?
O the bright cup! O the brave warrior!
95 O the glory of princes! How the time passed away,
slipped into nightfall as if it had never been!'
There still stands in the path of the dear warriors
a wall wondrously high, with serpentine stains.
A storm of spears took away the warriors,
100 bloodthirsty weapons, *wyrd* the mighty,
and storms batter these stone walls,
frost falling binds up the earth,
the howl of winter, when blackness comes,
night's shadow looms, sends down from the north
105 harsh hailstones in hatred of men.
All is toilsome in the earthly kingdom,
the working of *wyrd* changes the world under heaven.
Here wealth is fleeting, here friends are fleeting,
here man is fleeting, here woman is fleeting,
110 all the framework of this earth will stand empty."

So said the wise one in his mind, sitting apart
      in meditation.

---

[1] *it seems ... gift-throne* The description seems to be of some sort
of ceremony of loyalty, charged with intense regret and longing.

[2] *Cares are ... waves* The grammar and reference of this intense,
almost hallucinatory scene are not entirely clear; the translation
reflects one commonly proposed reading.

[3] *works of giants* Ruined buildings are called "the work of giants"
(*enta geweorc*) in several places in Old English literature.

He is good who keeps his word,[1] and the man who
    never too quickly
shows the anger in his breast, unless he already
    knows the remedy
115 a noble man can bravely bring about. It will be
    well for one who seeks mercy,
consolation from the Father in heaven, where for
    us all stability stands.

The Seafarer [2]

I sing a true song of myself,
  tell of my journeys, how in days of toil
I've often suffered troubled times,
hard heartache, come to know
5 on the keel of a ship many of care's dwellings,
terrible tossing of the waves, where the anxious
night-watch often held me at the ship's stem
when it knocks against the cliffs. Pinched with cold
were my feet, bound by frost
10 in cold fetters, while cares seethed
hot around my heart, hunger tore from within
my sea-weary mind. That man does not know,
he whose lot is fairest on land,
how I, wretched with care, dwelt all winter
15 on the ice-cold sea in the paths of exile,
deprived of dear kinsmen,
hung with icicles of frost while hail flew in showers.
I heard nothing there but the noise of the sea,
the ice-cold waves; the wild swan's song
20 sometimes served as my music, the gannet's call
and the curlew's[3] cry for the laughter of men,
the seagull's singing for mead-drink.
Storms beat the stone cliffs where the tern answered
    them,
icy-feathered; often the eagle screamed,
25 dewy-feathered—no sheltering family
could bring consolation to my desolate soul.

And so[4] he who has tasted life's joy in towns,
suffered few sad journeys, scarcely believes,
proud and puffed up with wine, what I, weary,
30 have often had to endure in my seafaring.
The night-shadow darkened; snow came from the
    north,
frost bound the ground, hail fell on earth,
coldest of grains. And so[5] they compel me now,
my heart-thoughts, to try for myself
35 the high seas, the tossing salt streams;
my heart's desire urges my spirit
time and again to travel, so that I might seek
far from here a foreign land.
    And so no man on earth is so proud in spirit,
40 nor so gifted in grace or so keen in youth,
nor so bold in deeds, nor so beloved of his lord,
that he never has sorrow over his seafaring,
when he sees what the Lord might have in store for
    him.
He has no thought of the harp or the taking of rings,
45 nor the pleasures of woman or joy in the world,
nor anything else but the tumbling waves—
he always has longing who hastens to sea.
The groves take blossom, the cities grow fair,
the fields brighten, the world rushes on;
50 all these urge the eager-hearted
spirit to travel, when one has a mind
to journey far over the flood-ways.
Even the cuckoo urges with its sad voice,
summer's guardian announces sorrow
55 bitter in the breast-hoard. He does not know,

---

[1] *who keeps his word* Or "keeps faith." These last lines offer an answer to the Wanderer's unresolved melancholia—the wisdom of self-control and the hope of Christian salvation.

[2] *The Seafarer* The present text has been translated for *The Broadview Anthology of British Literature* by R.M. Liuzza.

[3] *gannet ... curlew* Seabirds.

[4] *And so* The repeated connecting word "forthon" is notoriously difficult in this poem—it points forwards and/or backwards, meaning either "therefore" or "thus" or "because." In a poem in which a logical progression is by no means clear or easy to follow this is a significant source of ambiguity. Rendering it with the vague "and so," preserves some of the interpretive difficulty found in the original.

[5] *And so* The disjunction between what has come before and what come after this line is so great that it has been proposed that a second speaker is introduced here (there are no quotation marks in Old English that might clarify this ambiguity). Though this "two-speaker" theory is no longer widely accepted, it reflects the difficulty many critics have reconciling the conflicting attitudes presented in the poem—sea voyage as terrible suffering, sea voyage as longed-for escape, sea-voyage as metaphor for spiritual pilgrimage, or even for life itself.

the man blessed with ease, what those endure
who walk most widely in the paths of exile.

    And so now my thought flies out from my breast,
my spirit moves with the sea-flood,
60 roams widely over the whale's home,
to the corners of the earth, and comes back to me
greedy and hungry; the lone flier cries out,
incites my heart irresistibly to the whale's path
over the open sea—because hotter to me
65 are the joys of the Lord than this dead life,
loaned, on land.[1] I will never believe
that earthly goods will endure forever.
Always, for everyone, one of three things
hangs in the balance before its due time:
70 illness or age or attack by the sword
wrests life away from one doomed to die.
And so for every man the praise of posterity,
those coming after, is the best eulogy—
that before he must be on his way, he act
75 bravely on earth against the enemies' malice,
do bold deeds to beat the devil,
so the sons of men will salute him afterwards,
and his praise thereafter live with the angels
forever and ever, in the joy of eternal life,
80 delight among heaven's host. The days are lost,
and all the pomp of this earthly kingdom;
there are now neither kings nor emperors
nor gold-givers as there once were,
when they did the greatest glorious deeds
85 and lived in most lordly fame.
All this noble host is fallen, their happiness lost,
the weaker ones remain and rule the world,
get what they can with toil. Joy is laid low,
the earth's nobility grows old and withers,
90 just like every man throughout middle-earth.
Old age overtakes him, his face grows pale,
the graybeard grieves; he knows his old friends,
offspring of princes, have been given up to the earth.

When life fails him, his fleshly cloak will neither
95 taste the sweet nor touch the sore,
nor move a hand nor think with his mind.
Though a brother may wish to strew his brother's
grave with gold, bury him among the dead
with myriad treasures to take with him,
100 that gold will be useless before the terror of God
for the soul that is full of sin,
the gold he had hidden while he lived here on earth.

    Great is the terror of God, the earth trembles
       before it;
He established the sturdy foundations,
105 the earth's solid surface and the high heavens.
Foolish is he who dreads not the Lord; death will
       find him unprepared.
Blessed is he who lives humbly; that mercy comes
       to him from heaven,
the Maker strengthens his spirit, for he believes in
       His might.
A man must steer a strong mind and keep it stable,
110 steadfast in its promises, pure in its ways;
every man must hold in moderation
his love for a friend and his hatred for a foe,
though he may wish him full of fire …
… or his friend consumed
115 on a funeral pyre.[2] Fate is greater,
the Maker mightier than any man's thoughts.

    Let us consider where we should have our home,
and then think how we may come there,
and let us also strive to reach that place
120 of eternal blessedness,
where life is found in the love of the Lord,
hope in Heaven. Thanks be to the Holy One
that He has so honored us, Ruler of Glory,
Eternal Lord, throughout all time. Amen.[3]

---

[1] *And so … on land* At this point the sea-voyage is revealed to be a journey of spiritual discovery. The hermit-monks of Ireland had a particular penchant for taking to small boats and trusting in God for their safety. Some reached Iceland, some are rumored to have reached the Americas; many others, no doubt, found rest at the bottom of the sea.

[2] *full of fire … funeral pyre* Something is missing from the manuscript here; the translation is conjectural and makes as little sense as the original.

[3] *Let us consider … Amen* The tone of these last lines, different in many respects from the rest of the poem, seems to place the poem finally in a homiletic setting—the exhortation of a preacher rather than the confession of a weathered mariner.

The Wife's Lament [1]

I make this song of myself, deeply sorrowing,
my own life's journey. I am able to tell
all the hardships I've suffered since I grew up,
but new or old, never worse than now—
5 ever I suffer the torment of my exile.

First my lord left his people
over the tumbling waves; I worried at dawn
where on earth my leader of men might be.
When I set out myself in my sorrow,
10 a friendless exile, to find his retainers,
that man's kinsmen began to think
in secret that they would separate us,
so we would live far apart in the world,
most miserably, and longing seized me.

15 My lord commanded me to live here; [2]
I had few loved ones or loyal friends
in this country, which causes me grief.
Then I found that my most fitting man
was unfortunate, filled with grief,
20 concealing his mind, plotting murder
with a smiling face. So often we swore
that only death could ever divide us,
nothing else—all that is changed now;
it is now as if it had never been,
25 our friendship. Far and near, I must
endure the hatred of my dearest one.

They forced me to live in a forest grove,
under an oak tree in an earthen cave. [3]
This earth-hall is old, and I ache with longing;
30 the dales are dark, the hills too high,
harsh hedges overhung with briars,
a home without joy. Here my lord's leaving
often fiercely seized me. There are friends on earth,
lovers living who lie in their bed,
35 while I walk alone in the first light of dawn
under the oak-tree and through this earth-cave,
where I must sit the summer-long day;

there I can weep for all my exiles,
my many troubles; and so I can never
40 escape from the cares of my sorrowful mind,
nor all the longings that seize me in this life.

May the young man always be sad-minded
with hard heart-thoughts, yet let him have
a smiling face along with his heartache,
45 a crowd of constant sorrows. Let to himself
all his worldly joys belong! let him be outlawed
in a far distant land, so my friend sits
under stone cliffs chilled by storms,
weary-minded, surrounded by water
50 in a sad dreary hall! My beloved will suffer
the cares of a sorrowful mind; he will remember
too often a happier home. Woe to the one
who must wait with longing for a loved one. [4]

The Ruin [5]

Wondrous is this foundation—the fates have broken
and shattered this city; the work of giants
     crumbles.
The roofs are ruined, the towers toppled,
frost in the mortar has broken the gate,
5 torn and worn and shorn by the storm,
eaten through with age. The earth's grasp
holds the builders, rotten, forgotten,
the hard grip of the ground, until a hundred
generations of men are gone. This wall, rust-stained
10 and covered with moss, has seen one kingdom after
     another,
stood in the storm, steep and tall, then tumbled.
The foundation remains, felled by the weather,
it fell .... [6]
grimly ground up ....

---

[1] *The Wife's Lament*   The present text bas been translated for *The Broadview Anthology of British Literature* by R.M. Liuzza.

[2] *My lord ... to live here*   Or, "take up a dwelling in a grove" or "live in a (pagan) shrine." The precise meaning of the line, like the general meaning of the poem, is a matter of dispute and conjecture.

[3] *earthen cave*   Or "an earthen grave" or barrow.

[4] *May the young man ... loved one*   These difficult lines have been read as a particular reflection, imagining the mental state of her distant beloved, or as a general reflection on the double-faced nature of the world; here, following the reading of some critics, they are taken as a kind of curse.

[5] *The Ruin*   The present text has been translated for *The Broadview Anthology of British Literature* by R.M. Liuzza.

[6] *it fell....*   Several lines are lost here; the translation tries to make sense of a few surviving words.

15 …… cleverly created ….
…… a crust of mud surrounded …
….. put together a swift
and subtle system of rings; one of great wisdom
wondrously bound the braces together with wires.

20   Bright were the buildings, with many bath-houses,
high noble gables and a great noise of armies,
many a meadhall filled with men's joys,
until mighty fate made an end to all that.
The slain fell on all sides, plague-days came,
25 and death destroyed all the brave swordsmen;
the seats of their idols became empty wasteland,
the city crumbled, its re-builders collapsed
beside their shrines. So now these courts are empty,
and the rich vaults of the vermilion[1] roofs
30 shed their tiles. The ruins toppled to the ground,
broken into rubble, where once many a man
glad-minded, gold-bright, bedecked in splendor,
proud, full of wine, shone in his war-gear,

gazed on treasure, on silver, on sparkling gems,
35 on wealth, on possessions, on the precious stone,[2]
on this bright capital of a broad kingdom.
    Stone buildings stood, the wide-flowing stream
threw off its heat; a wall held it all
in its bright bosom where the baths were,
40 hot in its core, a great convenience.
They let them gush forth …..
the hot streams over the great stones,
under…
until the circular pool …. hot …
45 ….. where the baths were.
Then ….
….. that is a noble thing,
how …. the city ….[3]
—? IOTH CENTURY

---

[1] *vermilion* Shade of red.

[2] *precious stone* The singular form here is unexpected, but may be nothing more than a collective noun.

[3] *the city*…. The poem, appropriately, trails off into decay.

THE DREAM OF THE ROOD

The devotional and visionary poem known as *The Dream of the Rood* survives in a manuscript called the Vercelli Book; the manuscript was written in the southeast of England in the later tenth century but was left in the northern Italian town of Vercelli (an important stop on the pilgrimage route from England to Rome) by the end of the eleventh century. The Vercelli Book contains twenty-three prose homilies and six poems; as with most Old English literature, its origins, authorship and audience are not known.

Although the Vercelli book was copied in the tenth century, *The Dream of the Rood* may be considerably older. Several lines from the poem are carved in runic characters on a large stone monument known as the Ruthwell Cross, found in a small church in Dumfriesshire (on the western border of England and Scotland). The Cross, which has been dated to the early eighth century, is elaborately carved with scenes from the Gospels and lives of the saints, antiphons in Latin, and decorative scroll-work; if the runic inscriptions were part of the original monument (and not a later addition), then portions of *The Dream of the Rood* are among the earliest written Old English poems.

The Dream of the Rood tells the story of the Crucifixion of Christ from the point of view of the Cross, which appears to the narrator in a dream and recounts its experiences. Christ is presented as a heroic warrior, eagerly leaping on the Cross to do battle with Death; the Cross is a loyal retainer who is painfully and paradoxically forced to participate in his lord's execution. The narrator who witnesses all then shares his vision, describes the virtues of devotion to the Cross, and looks forward to the time when the righteous, protected by the Cross, will be taken up into the banquet-halls of heaven. The blending of Christian themes and heroic conventions is a striking example of how the Anglo-Saxons vigorously re-imagined Christianity even as they embraced it. *The Dream of the Rood* interweaves biblical, liturgical, and devotional material with the language of heroic poetry and elegy, and something of the ambiguity and wordplay of the *Riddles*; its complex structure of echoes, allusions, repetitions, and verbal parallels makes it one of the most carefully constructed poems in Old English.

⌘ ⌘ ⌘

The Dream of the Rood [1]

Listen! I will speak of the sweetest dream,
   what came to me in the middle of the night,
when speech-bearers slept in their rest.
It seemed that I saw a most wondrous tree
5 raised on high, circled round with light,
the brightest of beams. All that beacon was
   covered in gold; gems stood
fair at the earth's corners, and five there were

up on the cross-beam. All the angels of the lord
   looked on,
fair through all eternity;[2] that was no felon's gallows,
10 but holy spirits beheld him there,
men over the earth and all this glorious creation.
   Wondrous was the victory-tree, and I was fouled
      by sins,
wounded with guilt; I saw the tree of glory
honored in garments, shining with joys,

---

[1] *The Dream of the*   Translated by R.M. Liuzza for *The Broadview Anthology of British Literature.*

[2] *All the … eternity* These lines are difficult and much debated; another possible translation is "All creation, eternally fair / beheld the Lord's angel there," the Lord's angel presumably being the Cross itself, God's messenger to earth.

15 bedecked with gold; gems had
covered worthily the creator's tree.
And yet beneath that gold I began to see
an ancient wretched struggle, for it first began
to bleed on the right side. I was all beset with sorrows,
20 fearful for that fair vision; I saw that eager beacon
change garments and colors—now it was drenched,
stained with blood, now bedecked with treasure.
     And yet, lying there a long while,
I beheld in sorrow the savior's tree,
25 until I heard it utter a sound;
that best of woods began to speak words:
"It was so long ago—I remember it still—
that I was felled from the forest's edge,
ripped up from my roots. Strong enemies seized me
     there,
30 made me their spectacle, made me bear their criminals;
they bore me on their shoulders and then set me on a
     hill,
enemies enough fixed me fast. Then I saw the lord of
     mankind
hasten eagerly when he wanted to ascend onto me.
There I dared not bow down or break,
35 against the lord's word, when I saw
the ends of the earth tremble. Easily I might
have felled all those enemies, and yet I stood fast.
Then the young hero made ready—that was God
     almighty—
strong and resolute; he ascended on the high gallows,
40 brave in the sight of many, when he wanted to
     ransom mankind.
I trembled when he embraced me, but I dared not
     bow to the ground,
or fall to the earth's corners—I had to stand fast.
I was reared as a cross: I raised up the mighty king,
the lord of heaven; I dared not lie down.
45 They drove dark nails through me; the scars are
     still visible,
open wounds of hate; I dared not harm any of them.
They mocked us both together; I was all drenched
     with blood
flowing from that man's side after he had sent
     forth his spirit.
     Much have I endured on that hill
50 of hostile fates: I saw the God of hosts

cruelly stretched out. Darkness had covered
with its clouds the ruler's corpse,
that shining radiance. Shadows spread
grey under the clouds; all creation wept,
55 mourned the king's fall: Christ on the cross.
And yet from afar men came hastening
to that noble one; I watched it all.
I was all beset with sorrow, yet I sank into their hands,
humbly, eagerly. There they took almighty God,
60 lifted him from his heavy torment; the warriors then
     left me
standing drenched in blood, all shot through with arrows.
They laid him down, bone-weary, and stood by
     his body's head;
they watched the lord of heaven there, who
     rested a while,
weary from his mighty battle. They began to build a
     tomb for him
65 in the sight of his slayer; they carved it from bright
     stone,
and set within the lord of victories. They began to
     sing a dirge for him,
wretched at evening, when they wished to travel hence,
weary, from the glorious lord—he rested there
     with little company.[1]
And as we stood there, weeping, a long while
70 fixed in our station, the song ascended
from those warriors. The corpse grew cold,
the fair life-house. Then they began to fell us
all to the earth—a terrible fate!
They dug for us a deep pit, yet the lord's thanes,
75 friends found me there …
adorned me with gold and silver.[2]
     Now you can hear, my dear hero,
that I have endured the work of evil-doers,
harsh sorrows. Now the time has come
80 that far and wide they honor me,
men over the earth and all this glorious creation,

---

[1] *with little company* I.e., utterly alone.

[2] *silver* There is no gap in the manuscript here, but something is obviously missing—the story of the Finding of the True Cross, told (among other places) in the Old English poem *Elene*. The Cross is buried, hidden, forgotten, then recovered by Helen, mother of the emperor Constantine; its authenticity is established and it becomes an object of veneration and sign of victory.

and pray to this sign. On me the son of God
suffered for a time; and so, glorious now
I rise up under the heavens, and am able to heal
85 each of those who is in awe of me.
Once I was made into the worst of torments,
most hateful to all people, before I opened
the true way of life for speech-bearers.
Lo! the Kkng of glory, guardian of heaven's kingdom
90 honored me over all the trees of the forest,
just as he has also, almighty God, honored
his mother, Mary herself,
above all womankind for the sake of all men.
    Now I bid you, my beloved hero,
95 that you reveal this vision to men,
tell them in words that it is the tree of glory
on which almighty God suffered
for mankind's many sins
and Adam's ancient deeds.
100 Death he tasted there, yet the Lord rose again
with his great might to help mankind.
He ascended into heaven. He will come again
to this middle-earth to seek mankind,
on doomsday, almighty God,
105 the lord himself and his angels with him,
and he will judge—he has the power of judgment—
each one of them as they have earned
beforehand here in this loaned life.
No one there may be unafraid
110 at the words which the ruler will speak:
he will ask before the multitude where the man
        might be
who for the lord's name would taste
bitter death, as he did earlier on that tree.
But they will tremble then, and little think
115 what they might even begin to say to Christ.
But no one there need be very afraid
who has borne in his breast the best of beacons;
but through the cross shall seek the kingdom
every soul from this earthly way,
120 whoever thinks to rest with the ruler."
    Then I prayed to the tree with a happy heart,
eagerly, there where I was alone

with little company. My spirit longed to start
the journey forth; it has felt
125 so much of longing. It is now my life's hope
that I may seek the tree of victory
alone, more often than all men,
and honor it well. I wish for that
with all my heart, and my hope of protection is
130 fixed on the cross. I have few wealthy friends
on earth; they all have gone forth,
fled from worldly joys and sought the king of glory;
they live now in heaven with the high father,
and dwell in glory, and each day I look forward
135 to the time when the cross of the lord,
on which I have looked while here on this earth,
will fetch me from this loaned life,
and bring me where there is great bliss,
joy in heaven, where the lord's host
140 is seated at the feast, with ceaseless bliss;
and then set me where I may afterwards
dwell in glory, share joy
fully with the saints. May the lord be my friend,
he who here on earth once suffered
145 on the hanging-tree for human sin;
he ransomed us and gave us life,
a heavenly home. Hope was renewed
with cheer and bliss for those who were burning there.[1]
The son was successful in that journey,
150 mighty and victorious, when he came with a multitude,
a great host of souls, into God's kingdom,
the one ruler almighty, the angels rejoicing
and all the saints already in heaven
dwelling in glory, when almighty God,
155 their ruler, returned to his rightful home.
—IOTH CENTURY

---

[1] A well-known Christian tradition known as the "Harrowing of Hell" tells how Jesus, after His death on the Cross, descended into Hell and broke open its gates, releasing the souls of those unjustly imprisoned by Satan since the creation of human beings. Jesus conveyed them to Heaven, then returned to earth for His resurrection.

rume reþe fyr nebid snottor reaþo cristes fysle
paþeþ uton to þam beacne utþe cunnon hyran þyhtan
þæt þe lhupony leoht uppe mid englum agan moton
gesum to geoce þonne god pile eorðan lyfet brðege
þyrcan:⁊

Hwæt ic swefna cyst secgan wylle hæt me gemætte
to midre nihte syðþan reord bærend reste wunedon.
þuhte me þæt ic gesawe syllicre treow onlyft
lædan leohte be wunden beama beorhtost eall þæt
beacen wæs begoten mid golde gimmas stodon fægere
æt foldan sceatum swylce þær fife wæron uppe
on þam eaxle gespanne be heoldon þær engel dryht
nes ealle fægere þurh forð gesceaft ne wæs ðær huru
fracodes gealga. Achine þær be heoldon halige gastas
men ofer moldan ⁊eall þeos mære gesceaft:⁊
Syllic wæs se sige beam ⁊ic synnum fah forwunded
mid wommum geseah ic wuldres treow. wædum ge weor
ðode wynnum scinan gegyred mid golde gimmas hæfdon
be wrigene weorðlice wealdes treow ⁊hwæðre ic
þurh þæt gold ongytan meahte earmra ærgewin
þæt hit ærest ongan swætan on þa swiðran healfe
eallic wæs mid sorgum gedrefed. forht ic wæs for
þære fægran ge sylhðe ge seah ic þæt fuse beacen.

o

Lines 1-21 of the Vercelli Book.

The Ruthwell Cross.

THE COTTON MAXIMS

This collection of proverbs is found in an eleventh-century manuscript now in the British Library, BL Cotton Tiberius B.i, commonly known as the Cotton Manuscript after its one-time owner Sir Robert Cotton (1571–1631). It is copied there between a poetic list of liturgical feasts called the *Menologium* and a version of the *Anglo-Saxon Chronicle*; the arrangement creates a fitting progression from the cycle of the Christian year, to the eternal truths of nature and society, to the flow of historical events.

The loosely-linked collection of proverbial observations is a poetic genre as old as Hesiod's *Works and Days* and the Biblical book of Proverbs. Post-medieval Western culture has tended to look down on clichés (in Shakespeare's *Hamlet*, Polonius's stream of proverbial advice to Laertes is one sign of his foolishness), but such "wisdom literature" was well respected in the ancient and medieval world, and survived well into the modern age in such works as Benjamin Franklin's *Poor Richard's Almanac*. Maxims point to universal facts of life ("fish gotta swim, birds gotta fly," as Jerome Kern and Oscar Hammerstein II would write in *Showboat*) or norms of behavior (e.g., the fish "shall be" in the water spawning, and the king in his hall giving out rings—the implication being that a king in his hall is as natural as a fish in water, and ring-giving generates life as abundantly as a fish spawns fry). In Old English literature proverbial statements are often recognized by their use of the world *sceal* —"shall"—which in this context implies a general tendency (usually translated here as "must" or "belongs," or with the simple present tense, as in the first line).

The Cotton Maxims are also sometimes referred to as the *Cotton Gnomes* (a "gnome" is a short, pithy statement of a truth) and as the *Maxims II*; a similar, longer collection of maxims or "gnomic verses" appears in the *Exeter Book*. Though *The Cotton Maxims* may seem like—and in places may actually be—a disorganized jumble of random observations, some common threads can be perceived, and if the reader lets go of the demand for paragraph-style unity he or she can appreciate instead the concatenation of associations, similitudes and contrasts that make up the poetic structure. Reading in this spirit, one can also notice a number of recurring motifs, themes that would be perfectly at home in much more widely-appreciated literary works like *The Wanderer*: delight in the manifold and various harmonies in the diversity of the world, acknowledgment of God's power and mystery in establishing and ordaining the world, and recognition of the need for wisdom to balance the destructive forces of human desire.

⌘ ⌘ ⌘

Maxims II (The Cotton Maxims)[1]

A king controls his realm. Cities are clear from afar,
ancient ingenious giant-works on the earth,
wondrous foundations of stone. In the sky wind is
swiftest,
thunder loudest in its time. Great are the glories of Christ,

5   *wyrd*[2] is most powerful. Winter is coldest,
Lent most frosty, cold for the longest time,
summer most sun-lovely, its sunshine hottest,
autumn most bountiful, and brings to men

---

[1] The text is taken from E.V.K. Dobbie, *Anglo-Saxon Minor Poems* (New York, 1942), with minor corrections.

[2] *wyrd* A powerful but not quite personified force; the closest parallel in modern English is "Fate." It is related to the verb "weorthan," meaning roughly "to occur." Its meanings range from a neutral "event" to a prescribed "destiny" to a personified "Fate"; it is useful to think of "wyrd" as "what happens," usually in a negative sense.

the fruits of the seasons, sent from God.
10   Truth is trickiest, and treasure, gold, most costly
to every man; and old folks are wisest,
having known many years and endured much—
woe is wondrously clinging, but the clouds glide past.
Good comrades encourage a young nobleman
15   in battle and in bestowing rings.
In the nobleman, courage; the blade endures combat
against the helmet. The hawk belongs on the glove,
though wild; the wolf belongs in his den,
a wretched loner; in the woods the boar,
20   strong with great tusks; a good man belongs at home,
striving for fame. The spear belongs in the hand,
decorated with gold, and jewels in a ring,
standing broad and high. Streams belong in the waves,
mingling with the flood; the mast on a ship,
25   the sailyard hanging heavy. The sword belongs in
        the lap,
a lordly iron; the dragon belongs in his barrow,
old, proud of his finery; the fish in the water,
spawning his own kind, the king in his hall,
handing out rings. The bear belongs on the heath,
30   old and frightening; down from the hills flows
a river, sea-grey. An army sticks together,
a troop firm in glory; trust must be in a nobleman,
wisdom in a man. The woods on the earth
must blossom with leaves, a barrow must stand
35   green on the ground, and God in His Heaven,
judging our deeds. The door belongs in the hall,
broad building-mouth; the boss on the shield,
firm finger-protector. The bird belongs above,
sailing on the wind, the salmon in the water,
40   gliding with the trout. Tempests from the heavens
come into this world, churned by the wind.
A thief goes out in murky weather; a monster
        dwells in the fens[1]
alone in the land; a lady, a woman, must visit her lover
with secret cunning, if she does not want to make
        people think

45   she can be bought with rings.[2] The waves surge salty,
misty clouds and ocean flood flow around every land,
and mountain streams; cattle must breed
and multiply on the earth; the star must shine
bright in the heavens, just as the Maker commanded.
50   Good against evil, youth against age,
life against death, light against darkness,
army against army, enemies against each other,
foe against foe—all must fight to gain ground,
accuse the other of sin. A wise man must always
        consider
55   the contentiousness of the world—the criminal hangs,
rightly pays for the crime he has committed
against mankind. The Maker alone knows
where his soul must travel afterwards;
and all those spirits who travel to God
60   after their death-day await judgment
in the Father's embrace. The shape of the future
is hidden and secret; the Lord alone knows,
the Redeeming Father. No one returns
here under the firmament who will truly
65   say to men what sort of thing God's creation is,
the thrones of the triumphant, where He himself dwells.
—? 10TH CENTURY

---

[1]   *fens* Swamps, marshes.

[2]   *she can be bought with rings* I.e., if she does not want it to be
rumored that she is a prostitute. This reading, offered by Joseph A.
Dane, "*On folce gepeon*: Note on the Old English *Maxims II* Lines
43–5," *Neuphilologische Mitteilungen* 85 (1984): 61–64, is only one
possible interpretation of a difficult passage which apparently alludes
to social norms we no longer understand. The idea of "buying with
rings" may refer to the custom of giving a "bride-price" as part of a
marriage; the woman's "secret cunning" (*dyrne cræft*) may be an
allusion to the alleged affinity of women and magical charms and
spells. The implication may be that a woman must seek out her own
lover by magical means if she wants to have any control over her
marriage plans at all. Another possible translation is "a lady, a
woman, must find a lover by secret means so that she may be
married, if she does not have a good reputation among her people."
See Audrey L. Meaney, "The *ides* of the Cotton Gnomes," *Medium
Ævum* 48 (1979): 23–39.

Exeter Book Riddles

The Exeter Book manuscript of Old English poetry ends with two sections of short verse riddles. The manuscript is damaged and it is impossible to know how many riddles were in the original collection, but it is likely that there were 100, following the model of the popular Latin *Enigmata* ("Riddles") of Aldhelm and Symphosius. But apart from this, there are few similarities between the Latin and English versions of this popular poetic genre. The *Enigmata* of Aldhelm were apparently used as classroom examples of the principles of Latin versification, but it is unlikely that the English Riddles would have served such a purpose for apprentice English poets. Moreover, very few of the English Riddles depend on the sort of deliberate obscurity common in the *Enigmata*—no. 82 below is an example, but it is closely modeled on one of the Latin Riddles of Symphosius.

Many of the Exeter Book Riddles echo one another's language, especially in the repeated closing line *saga hwæt ic hatte* "say what I am called," but it is unlikely that the whole collection was written by one person. Apart from one Riddle which is found in an earlier version, there is little evidence for the origins and audience of the Riddles, either individually or collectively. A number of the Riddles seem to come from a bookish milieu, probably monastic (see nos. 24 and 45), and others are somewhat philosophical in tone (no. 41), but the presence of about a dozen riddles with obscene double meanings (see nos. 42 and 43 below) still raises a few eyebrows. Unlike the Latin riddles, which give away their solutions in their titles, some of the Old English riddles are apparently meant to be genuinely puzzling and difficult to solve—in fact a few (such as no. 91 below) continue to baffle readers to this day. In many cases, however, the pleasure of the Riddles seems to lie not in obscurity but in observation—they are in essence short lyric poems which show the world at a slightly odd angle, and bring the material and the natural world to new life through metaphor, analogy, wordplay, and misdirection. In the Riddles creatures speak, things express their point of view, everyday objects perform heroic deeds, and innocent household items become obscene projections of human desire. The playful language of the Riddles is a kind of lens through which the wonder, poignancy and wild energy of the created world are brought into focus. Whether they were written for education, inspiration, or amusement, the delight of the Riddles lies in their gift for seeing familiar things with fresh eyes, and compressing these insights in a few short lines which draw the listener into sharing the process of that perception; they help remind us that the poetic landscape of Old English literature was not as gloomy, as pious, or as bloody as is sometimes thought.

⌘ ⌘ ⌘

Riddle 5 [1]

My gown is silent as I thread the seas,
Haunt old buildings or tread the land.

---

[1]   The following riddles are from Craig Williamson's *A Feast of Creatures: Anglo-Saxon Riddle Songs* (Philadelphia: U of Pennsylvania Press, 1982). The Old English text is edited by Craig Williamson, *The Old English Riddles of the "Exeter Book"* (Chapel Hill, NC: University of North Carolina Press, 1977). The numbers are those of Williamson's edition and translation.

Sometimes my song-coat and the supple wind
Cradle me high over the homes of men,
5   And the power of clouds carries me
Windward over cities. Then my bright silks
Start to sing, whistle, roar,
Resound and ring, while I
Sail on untouched by earth and sea,
10   A spirit, ghost and guest, on wing.

Riddle 12

Once I was a plain warrior's weapon—
    Now a stripling prince wraps my body
With bright twists of silver and gold.
Sometimes men kiss me, or carry me to battle
5 Where I call my lord's companions to wage war.
Bright with jewels, I am borne by a horse
Over hard plains, sometimes by the sea-stallion
Over storm waves. Sometimes a woman,
Ring-adorned, fills my breast for the table—
10 Later I lie stripped of sweet treasure,
Hard and headless on the long boards.
Clothed in gold, I may grace the wall
Where men sit drinking, a soldier's gem.
Wound with silver, I sometimes ride
15 A warrior's horse, swallowing soldier's breath,
Blasting battle-song. Sometimes I bring
Bold men to wine, sometimes I sing caution
—Or rescue thieves' catch or scatter foes
For my lord. Say what I am called.

Riddle 23

I am a wonderful help to women,
    The hope of something to come. I harm
No citizen except my slayer.
Rooted I stand on a high bed.
5 I am shaggy below. Sometimes the beautiful
Peasant's daughter, an eager-armed,
Proud woman grabs my body,
Rushes my red skin, holds me hard,
Claims my head. The curly-haired
10 Woman who catches me fast will feel
Our meeting. Her eye will be wet.

Riddle 24

A life-thief stole my world-strength,
    Ripped off flesh and left me skin,
Dipped me in water and drew me out,

Stretched me bare in the tight sun;
5 The hard blade, clean steel, cut,
Scraped-fingers folded, shaped me.
Now the bird's once wind-stiff joy
Darts often to the horn's dark rim,
Sucks wood-stain, steps back again
10 With a quick scratch of power, tracks
Black on my body, points trails.
Shield-boards clothe me and stretched hide,
A skin laced with gold. The bright song
Of smiths glistens on me in filigree tones.
15 Now decorative gold and crimson dye,
Cloisoned jewels and a coat of glory
Proclaim the world's protector far and wide—
Let no fool fault these treasured claims.
If the children of men make use of me,
20 They will be safer and surer of heaven,
Bolder in heart, more blessed in mind,
Wiser in soul: they will find friends,
Companions and kinsmen, more loyal and true,
Nobler and better, brought to new faith—
25 So men shall know grace, honor, glory,
Fortune, and the kind clasp of friends.
Say who I am—glorious, useful to men,
Holy and helpful from beginning to end.

Riddle 41

A noble guest of great lineage dwells
    In the house of man. Grim hunger
Cannot harm him, nor feverish thirst,
Nor age, nor illness. If the servant
5 Of the guest who rules, serves well
On the journey, they will find together
Bliss and well-being, a feast of fate;
If the slave will not as a brother be ruled
By a lord he should fear and follow
10 Then both will suffer and sire a family
Of sorrows when, springing from the world,
They leave the bright bosom of one kinswoman,
Mother and sister, who nourished them.
Let the man who knows noble words
15 Say what the guest and servant are called.

Riddle 42

A small miracle hangs near a man's thigh,
Full under folds. It is stiff, strong,
Bold, brassy, and pierced in front.
When a young lord lifts his tunic
5 Over his knees, he wants to greet
With the hard head of this hanging creature
The hole it has long come to fill.

Riddle 43

I heard of something rising in a corner,
Swelling and standing up, lifting its cover.
The proud-hearted bride grabbed at that boneless
Wonder with her hands; the prince's daughter
5 Covered that swelling thing with a swirl of cloth.

Riddle 45

A moth ate songs—wolfed words!
That seemed a weird dish—that a worm
Should swallow, dumb thief in the dark,
The songs of a man, his chants of glory,
5 Their place of strength. That thief-guest
Was no wiser for having swallowed words.

Riddle 81

S hunning silence, my house is loud
While I am quiet: we are movement bound
By the Shaper's will. I am swifter,
Sometimes stronger—he is longer lasting,
5 Harder running. Sometimes I rest
While he rolls on. He is the house
That holds me living—alone I die.

Riddle 82

A weird creature came to a meeting of men,
Hauled itself in to the high commerce
Of the wise. It lurched with one eye,
Two feet, twelve hundred heads,
5 A back and belly—two hands, arms,
Shoulders—one neck, two sides.
Untwist your mind and say what I mean.

Riddle 91

I am noble, known to rest in the quiet
Keeping of many men, humble and high born.
The plunderers' joy, hauled far from friends,
Rides richly on me, shines signifying power,
5 Whether I proclaim the grandeur of halls,
The wealth of cities, or the glory of God.
Now wise men love most my strange way
Of offering wisdom to many without voice.
Though the children of earth eagerly seek
10 To trace my trail, sometimes my tracks are dim.
—10TH CENTURY

Solutions: 5, swan; 12, horn (for drinking or hunting); 23, penis or onion; 24, manuscript book (Bible), made of parchment; 41, soul and body; 42, key; 43, dough; 45, book-moth; 81, fish and river; 82, a one-eyed seller of garlic; 91 unsolved.

Old English Metrical Charms

Modern scholars often give the name "charm" to a sort of language, usually in verse, that is used for magical purposes. Most Old English charms were accompanied by some form of physical action, whether a significant gesture, writing words on an object, or the preparation of a medical compound. The precise relation between the words and the action are debatable and probably indefinable. The "charms" below are all intended to do good—settle a swarm of bees or cure a disease—but presumably charms and other magical practices could be used for evil purposes as well, though no examples have survived.

The cultural place of such texts, and their role in the medical theory and practice of the Anglo-Saxons, have generated a great deal of controversy. Hundreds of pages of medical literature have survived from Anglo-Saxon England, most of them containing translations from late-classical sources in Latin (which in turn were translated from medical works in Greek). Manuscripts collecting and organizing medical recipes attest to the sophistication and professionalization of the practice of medicine among the Anglo-Saxons. Only a few works appear to preserve native Germanic practices and beliefs; these have attracted a great deal of attention for the information they might reveal about the religion of the pre-Christian Anglo-Saxons. They represent only a small fraction of the medical literature of the period, but they have a great deal to tell us about the way health and sickness were imagined in the early Middle Ages.

These texts are complicated from any perspective, medical or spiritual, and their cultural significance is easily mistaken. Although some charms—and many prose medical remedies in Old English—involve the use of plants which have been shown to have some therapeutic value, it should be emphasized that the plants in a given remedy were probably not recommended for their chemical properties but because of other qualities, such as those evident in the "Nine Herbs Charm." Modern herbal remedies, though sometimes outside the mainstream of modern medicine, are used within the theoretical frameworks supplied by chemistry, physiology, and pharmacology; Old English charms are not. And although the charms retain traces of pre-Christian thought and belief, such as the mention of the god Woden in the "Nine Herbs Charm," it should not be thought that they are "pagan" or antithetical to Christianity. The efficacy of the "dwarf" charm, for example, depends upon the ready availability of communion wafers, and calls upon the power of the Seven Sleepers of Ephesus, a group of early Christian saints. Many other charms involve Latin prayers and Christian sacramental practices such as the sign of the Cross or the saying of Mass; the "Nine Herbs Charm" invokes the power of Christ more often than that of Woden.

⌘ ⌘ ⌘

The Old English Bee Charm[1]

Against a swarm of bees[2] take earth, cast it with your right hand under your right foot, and say:

I seize it under foot: I've found it now.
Lo! earth has might over all creatures
and against malice and over mindlessness
and over the mighty man with his mighty tongue.

And thereupon, when they swarm, throw gravel over them and say:

Victory-wives! sit:[3] sink to earth now!
Never to the woodland wild may you fly!
Be as mindful of my fortune
As folks all are of food and home.

Against a Dwarf

Against a dwarf[4] take seven little wafers like those one offers [at Mass], and write these names on each wafer: Maximianus, Malchus, Johannes, Martimianus, Dionisius, Constantinus, Serafion.[5] Then one should

sing the charm follows here, first in the left ear, then in the right ear, then over the person's crown. And then have a virgin go in and hang it around his neck; and do so for three days, and he will soon be well.

Spider creature came right in here—
had his harness in hand: you're his horse, he claimed!
and to your neck tied reins! Then they began
  to rise from the land.
As they left the land their limbs grew cool.
Then in she dashed— the dwarf's sister![6]
Then she ended it all and oaths she swore:
no hurt would come to harm the sick
nor whoever gets the lore and learns this charm
and knows how to chant this charm as well.
  Amen. Fiat.[7]

For a Sudden Stitch

For a sudden stitch,[8] feverfew and the red nettle that grows in the grain, and plantain; boil in butter.

Loud were they—real loud![9] when they rode
  down mound;

---

[1] *The Old English Bee Charm* The present translations, by Stephen O. Glosecki: for *The Broadview Anthology of British Literature*, are based upon texts as found in E.V.K. Dobbie's *The Anglo-Saxon Minor Poems*.

[2] *Against a swarm of bees* Presumably to make a swarm of bees settle into a *skep* or manmade hive.

[3] *Victory-wives! sit* The meaning of this line is much debated. It may be that the word(s) translated "victory-wives" is actually a verb of command, and the Old English line *sitte ge sige wif sigað to eorþan* actually means "sit you down, settle, women, sink to the earth."

[4] *Against a dwarf* Originally, perhaps, a night demon of some sort; in Old English prose texts translated from Latin medical treatises, however, the word seems to mean nothing more than "fever" (Latin *febrem*), and it is not certain that the word signified much more than a particular kind of disease, just as modern doctors speak of "malaria" and "influenza" without believing that these are caused by bad air or the malign influence of the stars. The vivid poem that accompanies this charm, however, certainly suggests some sort of personified agent of illness, in which the patient is the steed and the evil dwarf—the "spider-creature"—is the rider.

[5] *take seven ... Serafion* Since the dwarf attacks sleeping victims, the charm opens with sympathetic appeal to the Seven Sleepers of Ephesus, an early Christian legend similar to the Rip van Winkle story. Seven young Christian men of Ephesus, fleeing persecution by

the Emperor Decius (249–251), took refuge in a cave, where they were walled in while sleeping. Nearly two hundred years later, after the Roman Empire had officially converted to Christianity, the cave was opened and the Sleepers awoke. Thinking they had been asleep only one night, they went into the city of Ephesus, causing much confusion; eventually the miraculous truth was revealed, whereupon the young men died, praising God. The Seven Sleepers were often invoked in medieval prayers against insomnia and fever.

[6] *the dwarf's sister* The manuscript reads "the animal's sister"—i.e., the spider's?

[7] *Fiat* Latin: so be it.

[8] *For a sudden stitch* The Old English word *færstice* appears only here; considering the seriousness of the invocations, "stabbing pain" might be a better translation. The charm protects against a pain visualized as being caused by a "little spear" (l. 6) shot either by "gods" (OE *esa*, whose meaning is not entirely certain), "elves" (OE *ylfa*) or "witches" (OE *hægtessan*; in German lumbago is still called *Hexenschuss*). Elves were thought to cause pains in humans and cattle by shooting projectiles at them; they were often equated with devils and lesser demons in Christian thought.

[9] *Loud were ... real loud* It is not clear who "they" are, elves or devils or the "mighty women" of l. 8 (who may or may not be the same as the witches mentioned later in the charm), or where the

resolute they were   when over land they rode.
5 Shield yourself now: you can shake this attack.
Out! little spear!   if inside here!
Under linden[1] I stood,   under lambent shield
where those mighty women   wielded power:
and screaming spears   they sent our way!
10 Now I'll send them   another one back—
flying arrow   forth against them!
Out! little spear,   if inside here!
Sat that smith[2] there,   smacked little knife,
[world's best iron][3]   with wonder-punch.[4]
15 Out! little spear,   if inside here!
Six smiths sat there,   slaughter-spear forging.
Out, spear!   Not in, spear!
If within here be   an iron bit—
wicked witch-work,   away must it melt!
20 If you were shot in skin   or shot in flesh
or shot in blood   [or shot in bone]
or shot in limb: never let your life be harmed.
If it were old gods' shot   or elfin shot
or hag-witch shot,   I'll help you now.
25 This your cure for old gods' shot!   This your cure
       for elfin shot!
This your cure for hag-witch shot!   I'll help for sure!
[Fly off, dart-point!]   far to cliff-head!
May God help you.   Health be with you.

Then take the knife; put it in the potion.[5]

"mound" (OE *hlæw*, which usually denotes a pre-Christian burial mound) is.

[1] *linden* Shield (of lime-wood).

[2] *Sat that smith* In many cultures smiths are perceived as ambivalent, often malevolent or half-magical figures; it is not known who this smith (or the "six smiths" mentioned in l. 16) is supposed to be.

[3] *[world's best iron]* Here and in other half-lines in brackets, there is no gap in the manuscript to indicate a loss, but something seems missing in the meter or sense of the poem. The lines supplied are conjectural.

[4] *with wonder-punch* Or "powerful in wounding."

[5] *potion* Presumably the buttery stew of feverfew, nettle and plantain prescribed at the beginning of the text. It is also possible, however, that the terse instructions (in OE, *ado on wætan*) mean that the knife is to be smeared with the salve and then placed on the part of the body afflicted by the pain.

The Nine Herbs Charm[6]

Mind you, mugwort,   how much you showed,
what you arranged   at Rainmelding.[7]
Eldest of herbs,   "Una"[8] we call you.
You have might against three,   might against thirty,
5 might against all venom   and against onfliers;[9]
you have might against the foe   who fares
       through the land.
And you, plantain,   plant-tribes' mother,
eastward open,   inward mighty:
over you carts clattered;   over you queans[10] rode;
10 over you brides clamored;   over you bulls snorted:
all this you withstood   and struck against,
just as you withstand them all: onfliers, venom,
and the loathsome foe   who fares through the land.
This herb's called "Stunner,"   on stone well grown:
15 she stands against poison;   she'll stun your pain.
"Valiant" we call her—   venom she allays;
she casts out venom,   overcomes evil.
This is the plant   that pummeled the worm:
she has might against all venom,   she has might
       against onfliers,
20 she has might against the foe   who fares through
       the land.
Launch them now, cock's-spur: lesser lash bigger;
bigger lash lesser   till both be healed.
Mind you, mayweed,[11]   how much you showed:
the end you achieved   at Alorford:

---

[6] *The Nine Herbs Charm* This translation has been adapted from Stephen Glosecki, "'Blow these vipers from me': Mythic Magic in *The Nine Herbs Charm*," in L.C. Gruber, ed., *Essays On Old, Middle, Modern English and Old Icelandic: In Honor of Raymond P. Tripp, Jr.* (Lewiston, NY: Mellen, 2000), 117–19. The text of the charm is corrupt, its context obscure, and its meaning unclear. The recitation of charms over herbs was expressly condemned in some Anglo-Saxon homilies and law codes; Christian prayers were recommended instead. Such prayers and blessings over plants are not uncommon in Anglo-Saxon medicine, but the botanical animism of this charm is otherwise unknown.

[7] *what you … Rainmelding* Or, "what you brought about at the Great Proclamation."

[8] *Una* Latin: one.

[9] *onfliers* Flying or airborne diseases.

[10] *queans* Women.

[11] *mayweed* Mayweed is presumably synonymous with chamomile.

25　never will airborne illness　　end a lifetime
　　if one make a meal　　from mayweed now.
　　Known as nettle,　　the next herb here—
　　a seal sent it　　over sea ridges
　　to undo anger　　and other venom.
30　These nine have might　　against nine venoms.
　　+ Snake came stealing—　　he stung someone![1]
　　Then Woden grabbed　　nine glory-twigs,
　　knocked that adder　　into nine pieces!
　　There it ended:　　apple and venom:
35　never would it slither　　inside a house!
　　+ Chervil and fennel,　　both full of might:
　　herbs created　　by the all-wise Lord,
　　holy in heaven,　　while hanging there;[2]
　　He set them and sent them　　into seven worlds
40　to remedy all,　　the wretched and the blest.
　　They stand against pain,　　they strike against venom,
　　They have might against three,　　might against thirty,
　　against fiendish fist　　and fast attack,
　　against vile creatures'　　vicious witchcraft.
45　+ Now these nine herbs have might　　against nine
　　　　magic sendings,[3]
　　against nine venoms　　and against nine fliers—
　　against the red venom,[4]　　against the reeking venom,

　　against the white venom,　　against venom in blue,
　　against the yellow venom,　　against venom in green,
50　against the black venom,　　against the blue venom,
　　against the brown venom,　　against venom purplish,
　　against worm-blister,　　against water-blister,
　　against thorn-blister,　　against troll-blister,
　　against ice-blister,　　against venom-blister—
55　if there fly in from the east　　any oncoming venom
　　or in from the north　　flying in here now
　　or any from the west　　over the world of man.
　　+ Christ stood over old ones—　　each and every
　　　　kind.[5]
　　I alone fathom　　a fast river
60　where the nine adders　　are all watching.
　　Let all plants now　　spring up from their roots!
　　Let the seas divide—　　all salt water—
　　when I blow this poison　　right past you now.

Mugwort, plantain that is open to the east, lamb's cress, cock's-spur grass, mayweed, nettle, crabapple, chervil and fennel, old soap. Work the herbs into a powder, mix with the soap and with the pulp of an apple.[6] Make a paste from water and ashes; take fennel, boil it in the paste, and bathe with beaten egg[7] when the salve is applied, both before and after. Sing the charm over each of the herbs, thrice before they are ground up, and also over the apple; and sing the same charm into the man's mouth and into both ears and over the wound before he applies the salve.

---

[1] *someone* The manuscript reads "no-one" (OE *nan*). Along with the *Sudden Stitch* charm, this is the only reference to non-Christian gods in Anglo-Saxon medical literature, and the only reference anywhere to Woden battling a serpent. Our knowledge of pre-Christian Anglo-Saxon religion is exceptionally sparse, and for all we know this passage may owe as much to the story of Moses and the serpent in the wilderness (Numbers 21.4–9) as to any actual Germanic belief.

[2] *Then Woden … hanging there* Woden gives way to Christ or is somehow identified with him (or has "Christ" been substituted for an earlier reference to Woden?) whose death on the cross gives rise to healing plants; folk beliefs of several cultures still hold that Good Friday—the day of Christ's crucifixion—is a good day for planting. It may also be relevant here that in Old Norse legend Odin also experienced hanging on Yggdrasil, the "World Tree."

[3] *nine magic sendings* Another possible translation of this line is that the nine herbs have might against "nine of those who fled from glory," i.e., nine demons.

[4] *red venom* Presumably the various venoms and blisters listed refer to different diseases, but none of them can be identified.

[5] *Christ stood … every kind* The meaning is unknown; other possible translations are "Christ, whose nature was unique, overcame disease" and "Christ stood against every type of illness."

[6] *Mugwort … an apple* The dazzling and surreal poetry of the charm is followed by a rather prosaic list of ingredients and instructions. But it would be as wrong to discard the "superstition" of the charm in favor of the "rational" recipe as it would be to remove the practical elements of the cure from the "poetic" invocation that accompanies it. Both were presumably important to the readers and users of this text.

[7] *boil it … beaten egg* Or "boil with the mixture"?

BEOWULF

Only one copy of the poem that modern editors call *Beowulf* has survived, and it probably survived only by accident. A manuscript containing *Beowulf* and a small collection of other texts—a poetic treatment of the Old Testament story of Judith, a prose life of St. Christopher, and two treatises of fantastical geography known as *The Wonders of the East* and *Alexander's Letter to Aristotle*—was copied by two scribes, probably in the decade after 1000, in a monastic center somewhere in the south of England; it lay disregarded for centuries, narrowly escaped destruction by fire in 1731, and is now preserved in the British Library under the shelfmark Cotton Vitellius A.xv.

Beowulf is the longest surviving poem in Old English, consisting of 3,182 extant lines of alliterative verse divided into forty-four sections. Its language is allusive and embellished and its narrative digressive and complex, but its relatively straightforward plot follows the outlines of a folktale: a young hero who fights in isolation from friends and family engages in fabulous battles against monstrous foes, faces three challenges in ascending order of difficulty, and in the end wins glory and fame. The fabulous outlines of the story equally recall the deep undertones of myth: the mighty Beowulf may be a distant cousin of Thor, and his death may contain a hint of Ragnarok, the northern apocalypse.

But whatever its underlying structural patterns, *Beowulf* is neither myth nor folktale; its stories of dragon-slaying and night-battles are set against a complex background of legendary history. The action of the poem unfolds in a recognizable version of Scandinavia: Hrothgar's hall Heorot has been plausibly placed in the village of Lejre on the Danish island of Zealand; Beowulf's tribe of Geats may be the historical Gautar of Southern Sweden; and a number of the poem's characters (Heremod, Hrothgar, Ingeld, and Hygelac) are mentioned in other sources as if they were figures of history rather than fable. Moreover, *Beowulf* is an intensely political poem; the poet seems as intrigued by Danish diplomacy and the bitter feud between the Geats and Swedes as he is by the hero's monster-slaying. Kingdoms and successions, alliances and truces, loyalties and the tragically transient stability of heroic society are the poem's somber subtext, a theme traced less in the clashes of the battlefield than in the patterns of marriage and kin, in stories remembered and retold, in allusion and digression and pointed foreshadowing.

Despite the poem's historical interests, we cannot read *Beowulf* with any modern expectation of historical accuracy. Like many medieval works, *Beowulf* is frustratingly ambivalent—not quite mythical enough to be read apart from the history it purports to contain, nor historical enough to furnish clear evidence for the past it poetically recreates. The action of the poem is set in a somewhat vague heroic *geardagum* ("bygone days"), an age not meant to be counted on a calendar, nor its kingdoms and tribes marked on a map. Nor, undoubtedly, were the monstrous races of Grendels and dragons so clearly distinct in the poet's mind from the real dangers of the real world just beyond the margins of the known. While medieval authors certainly made distinctions between *historia* and *fabula*, the boundaries between these terms are not nearly as impermeable as those of our modern categories "history" and "fable."

Both the ultimate and the immediate origins of *Beowulf* are unknown. Most scholars assume that the single surviving manuscript, written around 1000–20, is a copy of an earlier text, and probably the last in a long chain of copies. But it may be impossible to determine when that chain of texts began, or what cultural and literary milieu gave birth to the poem; proposed dates have ranged from 700 to 1000, and most years in between. The poem seems to arise from a world in which such stories were common, and it presupposes our own position in this world. The poem begins with the assumption that we are hearing a well-known story, or a least a story from a familiar milieu: "We have heard of the glory … of the folk-kings of the spear-Danes," the poet asserts, and the way he tosses out cryptic allusions throughout the poem suggests that his audience was already familiar with songs and stories of other kings and heroes. But at what time in the history of the Anglo-Saxons did such a world exist? And can we trust the narrator as a faithful reporter of this world, or should we view him as a vivid creator of the illusion of antiquity?

The question of the origin of *Beowulf* is not just philological pedantry: the poem will yield very different meanings if it is imagined to have been produced in the time of Bede (c. 725, just a generation or two after the conversion of the English) or of Alfred (c. 880, a time of nation-building and political centralization) or of Ælfric (c. 1000, after half a century of monastic reform and a decade which saw the demoralizing collapse of national security). The earlier we think the poem to be, the more potentially authentic its historical material; the later we imagine it, the more openly fictional and nostalgic it seems. Moreover, the more closely we try to assign a date and place of origin to the poem, the more closely we read it as a text, the intention of a single author or a reflection of a particular ideology, rather than a product of a poetic art whose composition may have been oral and communal and whose traditional roots are beyond discovery.

Most critics agree that the heroic action of the poem is thoroughly accommodated to a world in which the truths of Christianity are accepted without question; they disagree, often sharply, on the meaning and purpose of that accommodation. Some scholars have argued that *Beowulf* is a type of Christ, because he gives his life for his people; others have read the poem as a condemnation of pagan pride, greed and violence. These two extreme positions capture the poem's deliberate ambivalence: *Beowulf* is a secular Christian poem about pagans which avoids the easy alternatives of automatic condemnation or enthusiastic anachronism. The person responsible for putting *Beowulf* in its final form was certainly a Christian: the technology of writing in the Anglo-Saxon period was almost entirely a monopoly of the church. The manuscript in which *Beowulf* survives contains a saint's legend and a versified Bible story, and the poet indicates a clear familiarity with the Bible and expects the same from his audience. Though the paganism of *Beowulf*'s world is downplayed, however, it is not denied; his age is connected to that of the audience but separated by the gulf of conversion and the seas of migration.

More recent work, rather than trying to define a single source for the poem's complex and peculiar texture (whether that source is pure Germanic paganism or orthodox Augustinian Christianity), recognizes that *Beowulf*, like the culture of the Anglo-Saxons themselves, reflects a variety of interdependent and competing influences and attitudes, even a certain tension inherent in the combination of biblical, patristic, secular Latin, and popular Germanic material. The search for a single unified "audience" of *Beowulf*, and with it a sense of a single meaning, has given way to a recognition that there were many readers in Anglo-Saxon England, often with competing and conflicting interests.

⌘⌘⌘

Beowulf, lines 1–21
(British Library, Ms Cotton Vitellius A.xv, fol. 129r).

Beowulf

PROLOGUE

Listen!
We have heard of the glory in bygone days
of the folk-kings of the spear-Danes,[1]
how those noble lords did lofty deeds.

    Often Scyld Scefing[2] seized the mead-benches
5 from many tribes, troops of enemies,
struck fear into earls. Though he first was
found a waif, he awaited solace for that—
he grew under heaven and prospered in honor
until every one of the encircling nations
10 over the whale's-riding[3] had to obey him,
grant him tribute. That was a good king!
A boy was later born to him,
young in the courts, whom God sent
as a solace to the people—He saw their need,
15 the dire distress they had endured, lordless,
for such a long time. The Lord of Life,
Wielder of Glory, gave him worldly honor;
Beowulf,[4] the son of Scyld, was renowned,
his fame spread wide in Scandinavian lands.
20 Thus should a young man bring about good
with pious gifts from his father's possessions,
so that later in life loyal comrades
will stand beside him when war comes,
the people will support him—with praiseworthy deeds
25 a man will prosper among any people.

    Scyld passed away at his appointed hour,
the mighty lord went into the Lord's keeping;
they bore him down to the brimming sea,
his dear comrades, as he himself had commanded

30 while the friend of the Scyldings[5] wielded speech—
that dear land-ruler had long held power.
In the harbor stood a ring-prowed ship,
icy, outbound, a nobleman's vessel;
there they laid down their dear lord,
35 dispenser of rings, in the bosom of the ship,
glorious, by the mast. There were many treasures
loaded there, adornments from distant lands;
I have never heard of a more lovely ship
bedecked with battle-weapons and war-gear,
40 blades and byrnies;[6] in its bosom lay
many treasures, which were to travel
far with him into the keeping of the flood.
With no fewer gifts did they furnish him there,
the wealth of nations, than those did who
45 at his beginning first sent him forth
alone over the waves while still a small child.[7]
Then they set a golden ensign
high over his head, and let the waves have him,
gave him to the Deep with grieving spirits,
50 mournful in mind. Men do not know
how to say truly—not trusted counselors,
nor heroes under the heavens—who received that cargo.

1

    Then Beowulf Scylding, beloved king,
was famous in the strongholds of his folk
55 for a long while—his father having passed away,
a lord from earth—until after him arose
the great Healfdene, who held the glorious Scyldings
all his life, ancient and fierce in battle.
Four children, all counted up,
60 were born to that bold leader of hosts:
Heorogar, Hrothgar, and Halga the Good,
I heard that ...[8] was Onela's queen,
dear bedfellow of the Battle-Scylfing.

---

[1] *spear-Danes* The Danes are described by many different epithets in the poem.

[2] *Scyld Scefing* The name means "Shield, Son of Sheaf" (i.e., of grain). The mysterious origins of Scyld, who seems to arrive providentially from nowhere and is returned to the sea after his death, have occasioned much critical speculation.

[3] *whale's-riding* A condensed descriptive image of the sea—the riding-place of whales. Elsewhere the sea is the "gannet's bath" and the "swan's riding."

[4] *Beowulf* Not the monster-slaying hero of the title, but an early Danish king. Many scholars argue that the original name was *Beow*.

[5] *Scyldings* The Danes, "sons of Scyld."

[6] *byrnie* Coat of ring-mail.

[7] *With no fewer ... small child* Scyld was found destitute—this statement is an example of *litotes*, or ironic understatement, not uncommon in Anglo-Saxon poetry.

[8] A name is missing from the manuscript here; it has been conjectured from parallel sources that is should be Yrse, or Ursula. The Swedish ("Scylfing") king Onela appears later in the story, causing much distress to Beowulf's nation.

Then success in war was given to Hrothgar,
65   honor in battle, so that his beloved kinsmen
eagerly served him, until the young soldiers grew
into a mighty troop of men. It came to his mind
that he should order a hall-building,
have men make a great mead-house
70   which the sons of men should remember forever,[1]
and there inside he would share everything
with young and old that God had given him,
except for the common land and the lives of men.
Then the work, as I've heard, was widely proclaimed
75   to many nations throughout this middle-earth,
to come adorn the folk-stead. It came to pass
swiftly among men, and it was soon ready,
the greatest of halls; he gave it the name "Heorot,"[2]
he who ruled widely with his words.
80   He remembered his boast; he gave out rings,
treasure at table. The hall towered
high and horn-gabled—it awaited hostile fires,
the surges of war; the time was not yet near
that the sword-hate of sworn in-laws
85   should arise after ruthless violence.[3]
    A bold demon who waited in darkness
wretchedly suffered all the while,
for every day he heard the joyful din
loud in the hall, with the harp's sound,
90   the clear song of the scop.[4] He said
who was able to tell of the origin of men
that the Almighty created the earth,
a bright and shining plain, by seas embraced,
and set, triumphantly, the sun and moon
95   to light their beams for those who dwell on land,
adorned the distant corners of the world
with leaves and branches, and made life also,
all manner of creatures that live and move.
— Thus this lordly people lived in joy,

100   blessedly, until one began
to work his foul crimes—a fiend from Hell.
This grim spirit was called Grendel,
mighty stalker of the marches, who held
the moors and fens; this miserable man
105   lived for a time in the land of giants,
after the Creator had condemned him
among Cain's race—when he killed Abel
the eternal Lord avenged that death.[5]
No joy in that feud—the Maker forced him
110   far from mankind for his foul crime.
From thence arose all misbegotten things,
trolls and elves and the living dead,
and also the giants who strove against God
for a long while—He gave them their reward for that.

2

115   When night descended he went to seek out
the high house, to see how the Ring-Danes
had bedded down after their beer-drinking.
He found therein a troop of nobles
asleep after the feast; they knew no sorrow
120   or human misery. The unholy creature,
grim and ravenous, was ready at once,
ruthless and cruel, and took from their rest
thirty thanes;[6] thence he went
rejoicing in his booty, back to his home,
125   to seek out his abode with his fill of slaughter.
When in the dim twilight just before dawn
Grendel's warfare was made known to men,
then lamentation was lifted up after the feasting,
a great mourning-sound. Unhappy sat
130   the mighty lord, long-good nobleman,
suffered greatly, grieved for his thanes,
once they beheld that hostile one's tracks,
the accursed spirit; that strife was too strong,
loathsome and long.
                    It was not longer
135   than the next night until he committed
a greater murder, mourned not at all
for his feuds and sins—he was too fixed in them.
Then it was easy to find a thane

---

[1] Or "a greater meadhall / than the sons of men had ever heard of."
The reading adopted here is that of Mitchell and Robinson.

[2] *Heorot* "Hart." An object recovered from the burial-mound at
Sutton Hoo, perhaps a royal insignia, is surmounted by the image of
a hart.

[3] The hall Heorot is apparently fated to be destroyed in a battle
between Hrothgar and his son-in-law Ingeld the Heathobard, a
conflict predicted by Beowulf at 2024–69. The battle itself happens
outside the action of the poem.

[4] *scop* Poet-singer.

[5] *Cain … Abel* See Genesis 4.1–16.

[6] *thanes* Companions of a king.

who sought his rest elsewhere, farther away,
140 a bed in the outbuildings,[1] when was pointed out—
truly announced with clear tokens—
that hall-thane's hate; he kept himself afterwards
farther and safer, who escaped the fiend.
So he ruled, and strove against right,
145 one against all, until empty stood
the best of houses. And so for a great while—
for twelve long winters the lord of the Scyldings
suffered his grief, every sort of woe,
great sorrow, for to the sons of men
150 it became known, and carried abroad
in sad tales, that Grendel strove
long with Hrothgar, bore his hatred,
sins and feuds, for many seasons,
perpetual conflict; he wanted no peace
155 with any man of the Danish army,
nor ceased his deadly hatred, nor settled with money,
nor did any of the counselors need to expect
bright compensation from the killer's hands,[2]
for the great ravager relentlessly stalked,
160 a dark death-shadow, lurked and struck
old and young alike, in perpetual night
held the misty moors. Men do not know
whither such whispering demons wander about.
     Thus the foe of mankind, fearsome and solitary,
165 often committed his many crimes,
cruel humiliations; he occupied Heorot,
the jewel-adorned hall, in the dark nights—
he saw no need to salute the throne,
he scorned the treasures; he did not know their love.[3]
170 That was deep misery to the lord of the Danes,
a breaking of spirit. Many a strong man sat
in secret counsel, considered advice,

what would be best for the brave at heart
to save themselves from the sudden attacks.
175 At times they offered honor to idols
at pagan temples, prayed aloud
that the soul-slayer[4] might offer assistance
in the country's distress. Such was their custom,
the hope of heathens—they remembered Hell
180 in their minds, they did not know the Maker,
the Judge of deeds, they did not know the Lord God,
or even how to praise the heavenly Protector,
Wielder of glory. Woe unto him
who must thrust his soul through wicked force
185 in the fire's embrace, expect no comfort,
no way to change at all! It shall be well for him
who can seek the Lord after his deathday
and find security in the Father's embrace.

3

With the sorrows of that time the son of Healfdene[5]
190 seethed constantly; nor could the wise hero
turn aside his woe—too great was the strife,
long and loathsome, which befell that nation,
violent, grim, cruel, greatest of night-evils.
     Then from his home the thane of Hygelac,[6]
195 a good man among the Geats, heard of Grendel's deeds—
he was of mankind the strongest of might
in those days of this life,
noble and mighty. He commanded to be made
a good wave-crosser, said that that war-king
200 he would seek out over the swan's-riding,
the renowned prince, when he was in need of men.
Wise men did not dissuade him at all
from that journey, though he was dear to them;
they encouraged his bold spirit, inspected the omens.
205 From the Geatish nation that good man
had chosen the boldest champions, the best
he could find; one of fifteen,
he sought the sea-wood. A wise sailor
showed the way to the edge of the shore.
210 The time came—the craft was on the waves,
moored under the cliffs. Eager men

---

[1] *outbuildings* Hrothgar's hall is apparently surrounded by smaller buildings, including the women's quarters (see lines 662–5, 920–4). Under normal circumstances the men sleep together in the hall, ready for battle (1239–50).

[2] *bright compensation* Germanic and Anglo-Saxon law allowed that a murderer could make peace with the family of his victim by paying compensation, or *wergild*. The amount of compensation varied with the rank of the victim.

[3] This is a much-disputed passage; my reading follows a suggestion made by Fred C. Robinson in "Why is Grendel's Not Greeting the *gifstol a wræc micel?*" and repeated in Mitchell and Robinson's *Beowulf*.

[4] *soul-slayer* The Devil.

[5] *son of Healfdene* I.e., Hrothgar.

[6] *thane of Hygelac* I.e., Beowulf.

climbed on the prow—the currents eddied,
sea against sand—the soldiers bore
into the bosom of the ship their bright gear,
215 fine polished armor; the men pushed off
on their wished-for journey in that wooden vessel.
Over the billowing waves, urged by the wind,
the foamy-necked floater flew like a bird,
until in due time on the second day
220 the curved-prowed vessel had come so far
that the seafarers sighted land,
shining shore-cliffs, steep mountains,
wide headlands—then the waves were crossed,
the journey at an end. Thence up quickly
225 the people of the Weders[1] climbed onto the plain,
moored their ship, shook out their mail-shirts,
their battle-garments; they thanked God
that the sea-paths had been smooth for them.
    When from the wall the Scyldings' watchman,
230 whose duty it was to watch the sea-cliffs,
saw them bear down the gangplank bright shields,
ready battle-gear, he was bursting with curiosity
in his mind to know who these men were.
This thane of Hrothgar rode his horse
235 down to the shore, and shook mightily
his strong spear, and spoke a challenge:
"What are you, warriors in armor, wearing
coats of mail, who have come thus sailing
over the sea-road in a tall ship,
240 hither over the waves? Long have I been
the coast-warden, and kept sea-watch
so that no enemies with fleets and armies
should ever attack the land of the Danes.
Never more openly have there ever come
245 shield-bearers here, nor have you heard
any word of leave from our warriors
or consent of kinsmen. I have never seen
a greater earl on earth than that one among you,
a man in war-gear; that is no mere courtier,
250 honored only in weapons—unless his looks belie him,
his noble appearance! Now I must know
your lineage, lest you go hence
as false spies, travel further
into Danish territory. Now, you sea-travelers
255 from a far-off land, listen to my

simple thought—the sooner the better,
you must make clear from whence you have come."

4

    The eldest one answered him,
leader of the troop, unlocked his word-hoard:
260 "We are men of the Geatish nation
and Hygelac's hearth-companions.
My father was well-known among men,
a noble commander named Ecgtheow;
he saw many winters before he passed away,
265 ancient, from the court; nearly everyone
throughout the world remembers him well.
With a friendly heart have we come
seeking your lord, the son of Healfdene,
guardian of his people; be of good counsel to us!
270 We have a great mission to that famous man,
ruler of the Danes; nor should any of it be
hidden, I think. You know, if things are
as we have truly heard tell,
that among the Scyldings some sort of enemy,
275 hidden evildoer, in the dark nights
manifests his terrible and mysterious violence,
shame and slaughter. With a generous spirit
I can counsel Hrothgar, advise him how,
wise old king, he may overcome this fiend—
280 if a change should ever come for him,
a remedy for the evil of his afflictions,
and his seething cares turn cooler;
or forever afterwards a time of anguish
he shall suffer, his sad necessity, while there stands
285 in its high place the best of houses."
    The watchman spoke, as he sat on his horse,
a fearless officer: "A sharp shield-warrior
must be a judge of both things,
words and deeds, if he would think well.
290 I understand that to the Scylding lord
you are a friendly force. Go forth, and bear
weapons and armor—I shall guide your way;
and I will command my young companions
to guard honorably against all enemies
295 your ship, newly-tarred, upon the sand,
to watch it until the curved-necked wood
bears hence across the ocean-streams
a beloved man to the borders of the Weders—

---

[1] *Weders* I.e., Geats.

and such of these good men as will be granted
300 that they survive the storm of battle."
They set off—their vessel stood still,
the roomy ship rested in its riggings,
fast at anchor. Boar-figures shone
over gold-plated cheek-guards,[1]
305 gleaming, fire-hardened; they guarded the lives
of the grim battle-minded. The men hastened,
marched together, until they could make out
the timbered hall, splendid and gold-adorned—
the most famous building among men
310 under the heavens—where the high king waited;
its light shone over many lands.
Their brave guide showed them the bright court
of the mighty ones, so that they might go
straight to it; that fine soldier
315 wheeled his horse and spoke these words:
"Time for me to go. The almighty Father
guard you in his grace,
safe in your journeys! I must to the sea,
and hold my watch against hostile hordes."

5

320 The road was stone-paved, the path led
the men together. Their mail coats shone
hard, hand-linked, bright rings of iron
rang out on their gear, when right to the hall
they went trooping in their terrible armor.
325 Sea-weary, they set their broad shields,
wondrously-hard boards, against the building's wall;
they sat on a bench—their byrnies rang out,
their soldiers' war-gear; their spears stood,
the gear of the seamen all together,
330 a gray forest of ash. That iron troop
was worthy of its weapons.
                    Then a proud warrior[2]
asked those soldiers about their ancestry:

"From whence do you carry those covered shields,
gray coats of mail and grim helmets,
335 this troop of spears? I am herald and servant
to Hrothgar; never have I seen
so many foreign men so fearless and bold.
For your pride, I expect, not for exile,
and for greatness of heart you have sought out Hrothgar."
340 The courageous one answered him,
proud prince of the Weders, spoke words
hardy in his helmet: "We are Hygelac's
board-companions—Beowulf is my name.
I wish to explain my errand
345 to the son of Healfdene, famous prince,
your lord, if he will allow us,
in his goodness, to greet him."
Wulfgar spoke—a prince of the Wendels,
his noble character was known to many,
350 his valor and wisdom: "I will convey
to the friend of the Danes, lord of the Scyldings,
giver of rings, what you have requested,
tell the famous prince of your travels,
and then quickly announce to you the answer
355 which that good man sees fit to give me."

He hastily returned to where Hrothgar sat
old and gray-haired, with his band of earls;
he boldly went, stood by the shoulder
of the Danish king—he knew the noble custom.
360 Wulfgar spoke to his friend and lord:
"There have arrived here over the sea's expanse,
come from afar, men of the Geats;
the oldest among them, the fighting men
call Beowulf. They have requested
365 that they, my lord, might be allowed
to exchange words with you—do not refuse them
your reply, gracious Hrothgar!
In their war-trappings they seem worthy
of noble esteem; notable indeed is that chief
370 who has shown these soldiers the way hither."

6

Hrothgar spoke, protector of the Scyldings:
"I knew him when he was nothing but a boy—
his old father was called Ecgtheow,

---

[1] *Boar-figures … cheek-guards* The boar was a sacred animal in
Germanic mythology; in his *Germania* the Roman historian Tacitus
mentions warriors wearing boar-images into battle (ch. 45). Images
of boars may have been placed on helmets to protect the wearer from
the "bite" of a sword, which was often quasi-personified as a serpent.
Archaeologists have unearthed several Anglo-Saxon helmets with
various kinds of boar-images on them.

[2] *proud warrior* I.e., Wulfgar.

to whom Hrethel the Geat[1] gave in marriage
375   his only daughter; now his daring son
has come here, sought a loyal friend.
Seafarers, in truth, have said to me,
those who brought to the Geats gifts and money
as thanks, that he has thirty
380   men's strength, strong in battle,
in his handgrip. Holy God
in His grace has guided him to us,
to the West-Danes, as I would hope,
against Grendel's terror. To this good man
385   I shall offer treasures for his true daring.
Be hasty now, bid them enter
to see this troop of kinsmen all assembled;
and tell them in your words that they are welcome
to the Danish people."
390   He announced from within:[2]
"My conquering lord commands me to tell you,
ruler of the East-Danes, that he knows your ancestry,
and you are to him, hardy spirits,
welcome hither from across the rolling waves.
395   Now you may go in your war-gear
under your helmets to see Hrothgar,
but let your battle-shields and deadly spears
await here the result of your words."
      The mighty one arose, and many a man with him,
400   powerful thanes; a few waited there,
guarded their battle-dress as the bold man bid them.
They hastened together as the man led them,
under Heorot's roof; [the warrior went][3]
hardy in his helmet, until he stood on the hearth.
405   Beowulf spoke—his byrnie gleamed on him,
war-net sewn by the skill of a smith—:
"Be well, Hrothgar! I am Hygelac's kinsman
and young retainer; in my youth I have done
many a glorious deed. This business with Grendel
410   was made known to me on my native soil;
seafarers say that this building stands,

most excellent of halls, idle and useless
to every man, after evening's light
is hidden under heaven's gleaming dome.
415   Then my own people advised me,
the best warriors and the wisest men,
that I should, lord Hrothgar, seek you out,
because they knew the might of my strength;
they themselves had seen me, bloodstained from battle,
420   come from the fight, when I captured five,
slew a tribe of giants, and on the salt waves
fought sea-monsters by night, survived that tight spot,
avenged the Weders' affliction—they asked for trouble!—
and crushed those grim foes; and now with Grendel,
425   that monstrous beast, I shall by myself have
a word or two with that giant. From you now I wish,
ruler of the Bright-Danes, to request,
protector of the Scyldings, a single favor,
that you not refuse me, having come this far,
430   protector of warriors, noble friend to his people—
that I might alone, O my own band of earls
and this hardy troop, cleanse Heorot.
I have also heard that this evil beast
in his wildness does not care for weapons,
435   so I too will scorn—so that Hygelac,
my liege-lord, may be glad of me—
to bear a sword or a broad shield,
a yellow battle-board, but with my grip
I shall grapple with the fiend and fight for life,
440   foe against foe. Let him put his faith
in the Lord's judgment, whom death takes!
I expect that he will, if he is allowed to win,
eat unafraid the folk of the Geats
in that war-hall, as he has often done,
445   the host of the Hrethmen.[4] You'll have no need
to cover my head—he will have done so,
gory, bloodstained, if death bears me away;
he will take his kill, think to taste me,
will dine alone without remorse,
450   stain his lair in the moor; no need to linger
in sorrow over disposing of my body!
Send on to Hygelac, if battle should take me,
the best battledress, which my breast wears,
finest of garments; it is Hrethel's heirloom,

---

[1] *Hrethel the Geat* Father of Hygelac and grandfather of Beowulf.

[2] There is no gap in the manuscript, but the two halves of the line do not alliterate, and something is probably missing from the text at this point. Most editors add two half-lines with the sense "Then Wulfgar went to the door."

[3] A half-line is missing; the translation follows the most innocuous conjecture.

[4] *Hrethmen* I.e., Geats.

455 the work of Weland.[1] *Wyrd* always goes as it must!"[2]

7

Hrothgar spoke, protector of the Scyldings:
"For past favors, my friend Beowulf,
and for old deeds, you have sought us out.
Your father struck up the greatest of feuds,
460 when he killed Heatholaf by his own hand
among the Wylfings. When the Weder tribe
would not harbor him for fear of war,
thence he sought the South-Dane people
over the billowing seas, the Honor-Scyldings;
465 then I first ruled the Danish folk
and held in my youth this grand kingdom,
city of treasure and heroes—then Heorogar
was dead, my older brother unliving,
Healfdene's firstborn—he was better than I!
470 Later I settled that feud with fee-money;
I sent to the Wylfings over the crest of the waves
ancient treasures; he swore oaths to me.[3]
It is a sorrow to my very soul to say
to any man what Grendel has done to me—
475 humiliated Heorot with his hateful thoughts,
his sudden attacks. My hall-troop,
my warriors, are decimated; *wyrd* has swept them away
into Grendel's terror. God might easily
put an end to the deeds of this mad enemy!
480 Often men have boasted, drunk with beer,
officers over their cups of ale,
that they would abide in the beerhall
Grendel's attack with a rush of sword-terror.
Then in the morning this meadhall,
485 lordly dwelling, was drenched with blood,
when daylight gleamed, the benches gory,

the hall spattered and befouled; I had fewer
dear warriors when death took them away.
Now sit down at my feast, drink mead in my hall,[4]
490 men's reward of victory, as your mood urges."
Then a bench was cleared in the beerhall
for the men of the Geats all together;
the strong-minded men went to sit down,
proud in their strength. A thane did his service,
495 bore in his hands the gold-bright ale-cup,
poured the clear sweet drink. The scop sang
brightly in Heorot—there was the joy of heroes,
no small gathering of Danes and Geats.

8

Unferth[5] spoke, son of Ecglaf,
500 who sat at the feet of the Scylding lord,
unbound his battle-runes[6]—Beowulf's journey,
that brave seafarer, sorely vexed him,
for he did not wish that any other man
on this middle-earth should care for glory
505 under the heavens, more than he himself:
"Are you the Beowulf who strove with Breca
in a swimming contest on the open sea,
where in your pride you tried the waves
and for a foolish boast risked your life
510 in the deep water? No man, whether
friend or foe, could dissuade you two
from that sad venture, when you swam in the sea;
there you seized in your arms the ocean-streams,
measured the sea-ways, flailed your hands
515 and glided over the waves—the water roiled,
wintry surges. In the keeping of the water
you toiled for seven nights, and he outswam you,
and had more strength. Then in the morning
the swells bore him to the Heathoream shore;
520 from thence he sought his own sweet land,
beloved by his people, the land of the Brondings,
the fair fortress, where he had his folk,

---

[1] *Weland* Legendary blacksmith of the Norse gods. The antiquity of weapons and armor added to their value.

[2] *Wyrd* The Old English word for "fate" is sometimes quasi-personified, though apparently not to the extent that the goddess *Fortuna* was in Roman poetic mythology. The word survives, via Shakespeare's *Macbeth*, as the Modern English word "weird."

[3] Hrothgar pays the *wergild* for the man Ecgtheow killed, and Ecgtheow swears an oath of loyalty and support. It is this oath, passed on to the next generation, that Beowulf is fulfilling (at least this is Hrothgar's public sentiment; his thoughts in the privacy of his council are somewhat different).

---

[4] The meaning of this line in Old English is disputed.

[5] *Unferth* Unferth's name, which may be significant, means either "un-peace" or "un-reason." In the manuscript it is always spelled "Hunferth," though it alliterates with a vowel. His position at Hrothgar's feet appears to be one of honor.

[6] *unbound his battle-runes* Or "unleashed his hostile secret thoughts." *Run* in Old English often means "secret."

his castle and treasure. He truly fulfilled,
the son of Beanstan, his boast against you.
525 So I expect a worse outcome from you—
though you may have survived the storm of battle,
some grim combats—if for Grendel you dare
to lie in wait the whole night long."
  Beowulf spoke, son of Ecgtheow:
530 "What a great deal, Unferth my friend,
drunk with beer, you have said about Breca,
told his adventures! I will tell the truth—
I had greater strength on the sea,
more ordeals on the waves than any other man.
535 When we were just boys we two agreed
and boasted—we were both still
in our youth—that out on the great ocean
we would risk our lives, and we did just that.
We had bare swords, when we swam in the sea,
540 hard in our hands; we thought to protect
ourselves from whales. Not for anything
could he swim far from me on the sea-waves,
more swiftly on the water, nor would I go from him.
We two were together on the sea
545 for five nights, until the flood drove us apart,
surging waves, coldest of weathers,
darkening night, and a northern wind,
knife-sharp, pushed against us. The seas were choppy;
the fishes of the sea were stirred up by it.
550 There my coat of armor offered help,
hard, hand-locked, against those hostile ones,
my woven battle-dress lay on my breast
adorned with gold. Down to the ocean floor
a grisly foe dragged me, gripped me fast
555 in his grim grasp, yet it was given to me
to stab that monster with the point of my sword,
my war-blade; the storm of battle took away
that mighty sea-beast, through my own hand.

9

"Time and again those terrible enemies
560 sorely threatened me. I served them well
with my dear sword, as they deserved.
They got no joy from their gluttony,
those wicked maneaters, when they tasted me,
sat down to their feast on the ocean floor—
565 but in the morning, wounded by my blade,

they were washed ashore by the ocean waves,
dazed by sword-blows, and since that day
they never hindered the passage of any
sea-voyager. Light shone from the east,
570 God's bright beacon; the waves grew calm,
so that I could see the sea-cliffs,
the windswept capes. *Wyrd* often spares
an undoomed man, when his courage endures!
And so it came about that I was able to kill
575 nine of these sea-monsters. I have never heard
of a harder night-battle under heaven's vault,
nor a more wretched man on the water's stream;
yet I escaped alive from the clutches of my enemies,
weary from my journey. Then the sea washed me up,
580 the currents of the flood, in the land of the Finns,
the welling waters. I have never heard a word
about any such contest concerning you,
such sword-panic. In the play of battle
Breca has never—nor you either—
585 done a deed so bold and daring
with his decorated blade—I would never boast of it!—
though you became your brothers' killer,
your next of kin; for that you needs must suffer
punishment in Hell, no matter how clever you are.[1]
590 I will say it truly, son of Ecglaf,
that never would Grendel have worked such terror,
that gruesome beast, against your lord,
or shames in Heorot, if your courage and spirit
were as fierce as you yourself fancy they are;
595 but he has found that he need fear no feud,
no storm of swords from the Victory-Scyldings,
no resistance at all from your nation;
he takes his toll, spares no one
in the Danish nation, but indulges himself,
600 hacks and butchers and expects no battle
from the Spear-Danes. But I will show him
soon enough the strength and courage
of the Geats in war. Afterwards, let him who will

---

[1] Unferth's fratricide brings the general theme of kin-slaying, represented by Grendel's descent from Cain, inside Hrothgar's hall. In reality—at least in the reality of the heroic world depicted in poetry—it may not have been unthinkable for kinsmen to find themselves on opposite sides of a battle; loyalty to one's lord was supposed to outweigh the claims of blood-relation. The word "Hell" is not in the manuscript, but it is attested by one of the early transcriptions. Some scholars read *healle*, i.e., "hall."

go bravely to mead, when the morning light
605 of a new day, the sun clothed in glory
shines from the south on the sons of men!"
    Then the giver of treasure was greatly pleased,
gray-haired and battle-bold; the Bright-Danes' chief
had faith in his helper; that shepherd of his folk
610 recognized Beowulf's firm resolution.
There was man's laughter, lovely sounds
and winsome words. Wealhtheow went forth,
Hrothgar's queen, mindful of customs;
adorned with gold, she greeted the men in the hall,
615 then that courteous wife offered the full cup
first to the guardian of the East-Danes' kingdom,
bid him be merry at his beer-drinking,
beloved by his people; with pleasure he received
the feast and cup, victorious king.
620 The lady of the Helmings then went about
to young and old, gave each his portion
of the precious cup, until the moment came
when the ring-adorned queen, of excellent heart,
bore the mead-cup to Beowulf;
625 she greeted the Geatish prince, thanked God
with wise words that her wish had come to pass,
that she could rely on any earl for relief
from those crimes. He took the cup,
the fierce warrior, from Wealhtheow,
630 and then eager for battle he made his announcement.
Beowulf spoke, son of Ecgtheow:
"I resolved when I set out over the waves,
sat down in my ship with my troop of soldiers,
that I would entirely fulfill the wishes
635 of your people, or fall slain,
fast in the grip of my foe. I shall perform
a deed of manly courage, or in this meadhall
I will await the end of my days!"
These words well pleased that woman,
640 the boasting of the Geat; she went, the gold-adorned
and courteous folk-queen, to sit beside her lord.
    Then, as before, there in that hall were
strong words spoken, the people happy,
the sounds of a victorious nation, until shortly
645 the son of Healfdene wished to seek
his evening rest; he knew that the wretched beast
had been planning to do battle in the high building
from the time they could first see the sunrise

until night fell darkening over all,
650 and creatures of shadow came creeping about
pale under the clouds. The company arose.
One warrior greeted another there,
Hrothgar to Beowulf, and wished him luck,
gave him control of the wine-hall in these words:
655 "I have never entrusted to any man,
ever since I could hold and hoist a shield,
the great hall of the Danes—except to you now.
Have it and hold it, protect this best of houses,
be mindful of glory, show your mighty valor,
660 watch for your enemies! You will have all you desire,
if you emerge from this brave undertaking alive."

10

    Then Hrothgar and his troop of heroes,
protector of the Scyldings, departed from the hall;
the war-chief wished to seek Wealhtheow,
665 his queen's bedchamber. The glorious king[1]
had set against Grendel a hall-guardian
— as men had heard said—who did special service
for the king of the Danes, kept a giant-watch.
Surely the Geatish prince greatly trusted
670 his mighty strength, the Maker's favor,
when he took off his iron byrnie,
undid his helmet, and gave his decorated iron,
best of swords, to his servant
and bid him hold his battle-gear.
675 The good man, Beowulf the Geat,
spoke a few boasting words before he lay down:
"I consider myself no poorer in strength
and battle-deeds than Grendel does himself;
and so I will not kill him with a sword,
680 put an end to his life, though I easily might;
he knows no arts of war, no way to strike back,
hack at my shield-boss, though he be brave
in his wicked deeds; but tonight we two will
forgo our swords, if he dare to seek out
685 a war without weapons—and then let the wise Lord
grant the judgment of glory, the holy God,
to whichever hand seems proper to Him."
    He lay down, battle-brave; the bolster took
the earl's cheek, and around him many

---

[1] *The glorious king* Or "King of Glory," i.e., God?

690 a bold seafarer sank to his hall-rest.
None of them thought that he should thence
ever again seek his own dear homeland,
his tribe or the town in which he was raised,
for they had heard it said that savage death
695 had swept away far too many of the Danish folk
in that wine-hall. But the Lord gave them
a web of victory, the people of the Weders,
comfort and support, so that they completely,
through one man's craft, overcame their enemy,
700 by his own might. It is a well-known truth
that mighty God has ruled mankind
always and forever.

        In the dark night he came
creeping, the shadow-goer. The bowmen slept
who were to hold that horned hall—
705 all but one. It was well-known to men
that the demon foe could not drag them under
the dark shadows if the Maker did not wish it;
but he, wakeful, keeping watch for his enemy,
awaited, enraged, the outcome of battle.

II

710 Then from the moor, in a blanket of mist,
Grendel came stalking—he bore God's anger;
the evil marauder meant to ensnare
some of human-kind in that high hall.
Under the clouds he came until he clearly knew
715 he was near the wine-hall, men's golden house,
finely adorned. It was not the first time
he had sought out the home of Hrothgar,
but never in his life, early or late,
did he find harder luck or a hardier hall-thane.
720 To the hall came that warrior on his journey,
bereft of joys. The door burst open,
fast in its forged bands, when his fingers touched it;
bloody-minded, swollen with rage, he swung open
the hall's mouth, and immediately afterwards
725 the fiend strode across the paved floor,
went angrily; in his eyes stood
a light not fair, glowing like fire.
He saw in the hall many a soldier,
a peaceful troop sleeping all together,
730 a large company of thanes—and he laughed inside;
he meant to divide, before day came,

this loathsome creature, the life of each
man from his body, when there befell him
the hope of a feast. But it was not his fate
735 to taste any more of the race of mankind
after that night. The kinsman of Hygelac,
mighty one, beheld how that maneater
planned to proceed with his sudden assault.
Not that the monster[1] meant to delay—
740 he seized at once at his first pass
a sleeping man, slit him open suddenly,
bit into his joints, drank the blood from his veins,
gobbled his flesh in gobbets, and soon
had completely devoured that dead man,
745 feet and fingertips. He stepped further,
and took in his hands the strong-hearted
man in his bed; the monster reached out
towards him with his hands—he quickly grabbed him
with evil intent, and sat up against his arm.
750 As soon as that shepherd of sins discovered
that he had never met on middle-earth,
in any region of the world, another man
with a greater handgrip, in his heart he was
afraid for his life, but none the sooner could he flee.
755 His mind was eager to escape to the darkness,
seek out a host of devils—his habit there
was nothing like he had ever met before.
The good kinsman of Hygelac remembered then
his evening speech, and stood upright
760 and seized him fast. His fingers burst;
the giant turned outward, the earl stepped inward.
The notorious one meant—if he might—
to turn away further and flee, away
to his lair in the fen; he knew his fingers
765 were held in a hostile grip. That was an unhappy journey
that the harm-doer took to Heorot!
The great hall resounded; to the Danes it seemed,
the city's inhabitants, and every brave earl,
like a wild ale-sharing.[2] Both were angry,

---

[1] *monster* The OE word *æglæca*, which literally means "awesome one"
or "terror," is elsewhere applied to the dragon-slaying Sigemund (line
892, where it is translated "fierce creature") and to Beowulf himself. Its
translation here is admittedly tendentious. The word appears elsewhere,
variously translated, in lines 159, 433, 732, 556, etc.

[2] *wild ale-sharing* The general sense of the OE word *ealuscerwen* is
"panic" or "terror," but its precise meaning (probably "a dispensing
of ale") is unclear; did the Danes think a wild party was going on? Or

770　fierce house-wardens—the hall echoed.
It was a great wonder that the wine-hall
withstood their fighting and did not fall to the ground,
that fair building—but it was fastened
inside and out with iron bands,
775　forged with skill. From the floor there flew
many a mead-bench, as men have told me,
gold-adorned, where those grim foes fought.
The Scylding elders had never expected
that any man, by any ordinary means,
780　could break it apart, beautiful, bone-adorned,
or destroy it with guile, unless the embrace of fire
might swallow it in flames. The noise swelled
new and stark—among the North-Danes was
horrible terror, in each of them
785　who heard through the wall the wailing cry—
God's adversary shrieked a grisly song
of horror, defeated, the captive of Hell
bewailed his pain. He pinned him fast,
he who among men was the strongest of might
790　in those days of this life.

12

That protector of earls would not for anything
let that murderous visitor escape alive—
he did not consider his days on earth
of any use at all. Many an earl
795　in Beowulf's troop drew his old blade,
longed to protect the life of his liege-lord,
the famous captain, however they could.
But they did not know as they entered the fight,
those stern-minded men of battle,
800　and thought to strike from all sides
and seek his soul, that no sword,
not the best iron anywhere in the world,
could even touch that evil sinner,
for he had worked a curse on weapons,
805　every sort of blade. His separation from the world
in those days of this life
would have to be miserable, and that alien spirit
would travel far into the keeping of fiends.
Then he discovered, who had done before

---

were they dismayed by the loss of their mead-hall? Or does OE *ealu*
mean "luck"?

810　so much harm to the race of mankind,
so many crimes—he was marked by God—
that his body could bear it no longer,
but the courageous kinsman of Hygelac
had him in hand—hateful to each
815　was the life of the other. The loathsome creature felt
great bodily pain; a gaping wound opened
in his shoulder-joint, his sinews sprang apart,
his joints burst asunder. Beowulf was given
glory in battle—Grendel was forced
820　to flee, mortally wounded, into the fen-slopes,
seek a sorry abode; he knew quite surely
that the end of his life had arrived,
the sum of his days. The will of the Danes
was entirely fulfilled in that bloody onslaught!
825　He who had come from afar had cleansed,
wise and stout-hearted, the hall of Hrothgar,
warded off attack. He rejoiced in his night-work,
his great courage. That man of the Geats
had fulfilled his boast to the East-Danes,
830　and entirely remedied all their distress,
the insidious sorrows they had suffered
and had to endure from sad necessity,
no small affliction. It was a clear sign,
when the battle-brave one laid down the hand,
835　arm and shoulder—there all together
was Grendel's claw—under the curved roof.

13

Then in the morning was many a warrior,
as I have heard, around that gift-hall,
leaders of the folk came from far and near
840　throughout the wide land to see that wonder,
the loathsome one's tracks. His parting from life
hardly seemed sad to any man
who examined the trail of that inglorious one,
how he went on his weary way,
845　defeated by force, to a pool of sea-monsters,
doomed, put to flight, and left a fatal trail.
The water was welling with blood there—
the terrible swirling waves, all mingled together
with hot gore, heaved with the blood of battle,
850　concealed that doomed one when, deprived of joys,
he laid down his life in his lair in the fen,
his heathen soul—and Hell took him.

Then the old retainers returned from there,
and many a youth on the joyful journey,
855   bravely rode their horses back from the mere,
men on their steeds. There they celebrated
Beowulf's glory: it was often said
that south or north, between the two seas,[1]
across the wide world, there was none
860   better under the sky's expanse
among shield-warriors, nor more worthy to rule—
though they found no fault with their own friendly lord,
gracious Hrothgar, but said he was a good king.
At times the proud warriors let their horses prance,
865   their fallow mares fare in a contest,
wherever the footpaths seemed fair to them,
the way tried and true. At times the king's thane,
full of grand stories, mindful of songs,
who remembered much, a great many
870   of the old tales, found other words
truly bound together; he began again
to recite with skill the adventure of Beowulf,
adeptly tell an apt tale,
and weave his words. He said nearly all
875   that he had heard said of Sigemund's
stirring deeds,[2] many strange things,
the Volsung's strife, his distant voyages
obscure, unknown to all the sons of men,
his feuds and crimes—except for Fitela,
880   when of such things he wished to speak to him,
uncle to nephew[3]—for always they were,

in every combat, companions at need;
a great many of the race of giants
they slaughtered with their swords. For Sigemund
885   no small fame grew after his final day,
after that hardened soldier, prince's son,
had killed a dragon, keeper of a hoard;
alone, he dared to go under gray stones,
a bold deed—nor was Fitela by his side;
890   yet so it befell him that his sword pierced
the wondrous serpent, stood fixed in the wall,
the manly iron; the dragon met his death.
That fierce creature had gone forth in courage
so that he could possess that store of rings
895   and use them at his will; the son of Wæls
loaded his sea-boat, bore the bright treasure
to the ship's hold. The serpent melted in its own heat.

He was the most famous of exiles, far and wide,
among all people, protector of warriors,
900   for his noble deeds—he had prospered for them—
since the struggles of Heremod had ceased,
his might and valor. Among the Eotens[4]
he was betrayed into his enemies' hands,
quickly dispatched. The surging of cares
905   had crippled him too long; he became a deadly burden
to his own people, to all noblemen;
for many a wise man had mourned
in earlier times over his headstrong ways
who had looked to him for relief from affliction,
910   hoped that that prince's son would prosper,
receive his father's rank, rule his people,
hoard and fortress, a kingdom of heroes,
the Scylding homeland. The kinsman of Hygelac
became to all of the race of mankind
915   a more pleasant friend; sin possessed him.[5]
Sometimes, competing, the fallow paths
they measured on horseback. When morning's light
raced on and hastened away, many a retainer,
stout-hearted, went to see the high hall
920   to see the strange wonder; the king himself,
guard of the treasure-hoard, strode glorious
from the woman's chambers with a great entourage,

---

[1]   *between the two seas* A conventional expression like Modern
English "coast to coast"; probably it originally referred to the North
and Baltic seas.

[2]   Beowulf is praised indirectly, by being compared first to Sigemund, another famous monster-slayer (a different version of whose
story is told in the Old Norse *Volsungasaga* and the Middle High
German *Nibelungenlied*; there the dragon-slaying is attributed to
Sigemund's son Siegfried); and then contrasted to Heremod, an
earlier king of the Danes who descended into tyranny (it is sometimes assumed that the disastrous ending of Heremod's reign is the
cause of the Danes' lordlessness and distress mentioned at the
beginning of the poem). The implication is that Beowulf's deeds
place him in the ranks of other exemplary figures. The method of
narration is allusive and indirect, as though the audience were
expected to know the details of the story and appreciate an elliptical
reference to them.

[3]   *uncle to nephew* Fitela is actually Sigemund's son by his own
sister—either the poet is being discreet, or his version of the story
differs from the Norse.

---

[4]   *Eotens* Perhaps "Jutes." The word literally means "giants" and
may be a tribal name, or an epithet, or may in fact refer to an actual
race of giants.

[5]   *sin possessed him* I.e., Heremod.

a chosen retinue, and his royal queen with him
measured the meadhall-path with a troop of maidens.

14

925   Hrothgar spoke—he went to the hall,
stood on the steps, beheld the steep roof
plated with gold, and Grendel's hand:
"For this sight let us swiftly offer thanks
to the Almighty! Much have I endured
930 of dire grief from Grendel, but God may always
work, Shepherd of glory, wonder upon wonder.
It was not long ago that I did not expect
ever in my life to experience relief
from any of my woes, when, stained with blood,
935 this best of houses stood dripping, gory,
a widespread woe to all wise men
who did not expect that they might ever
defend the people's fortress from its foes,
devils and demons. Now a retainer has done
940 the very deed, through the might of God,
which we all could not contrive to do
with all our cleverness. Lo, that woman could say,
whosoever has borne such a son
into the race of men, if she still lives,
945 that the God of Old was good to her
in childbearing. Now I will cherish you,
Beowulf, best of men, like a son
in my heart; hold well henceforth
your new kinship. You shall have no lack
950 of the worldly goods which I can bestow.
Often have I offered rewards for less,
honored with gifts a humbler man,
weaker in battle. Now by yourself
you have done such deeds that your fame will endure
955 always and forever—may the Almighty
reward you with good, as He has already done!"
     Beowulf spoke, son of Ecgtheow:
"Freely and gladly have we fought this fight,
done this deed of courage, daringly faced
960 this unknown power. I would much prefer
that you might have seen the foe himself
decked in his finery,[1] fallen and exhausted!

With a hard grip I hoped to bind him
quickly and keenly on the killing floor,
965 so that for my handgrasp he would have to
lie squirming for life, unless he might slip away;
I could not—the Creator did not wish it—
hinder his going, no matter how hard I held
that deadly enemy; too overwhelming was
970 that fiend's flight. Yet he forfeited his hand,
his arm and shoulder, to save his life,
to guard his tracks—though he got thereby,
pathetic creature, little comfort;
the loathsome destroyer will live no longer,
975 rotten with sin, but pain has seized him,
grabbed him tightly in its fierce grip,
its baleful bonds—and there he shall abide,
guilty of his crimes, the greater judgment,
how the shining Maker wishes to sentence him."
980   Then the son of Ecglaf[2] was more silent
in boasting words about his battle-works
after the noblemen, through the earl's skill,
looked on the hand over the high roof,
the enemy's fingers; at the end of each nail
985 was a sharp tip, most like steel,
heathen talons, the terrible spikes
of that awful warrior; each of them agreed
that not even the hardest of ancient and honorable
irons could touch him, or injure at all
990 the bloody battle-paw of that baleful creature.

15

     Then it was quickly commanded that Heorot
be adorned by hands inside; many there,
men and women, prepared that wine-hall,
the guest-house. Gold-dyed tapestries
995 shone on the walls, many wonderful sights
to any man who might look on them.
That shining building was nearly shattered
inside, entirely, fast in its iron bands,
its hinges sprung; the roof alone survived
1000 unharmed, when that horrible creature,
stained with foul deeds, turned in his flight,
despairing of life. Death is not an easy
thing to escape—try it who will—

---

[1] *in his finery* Literally "in his adornments," a peculiar phrase since
Grendel is notoriously not armed and unadorned. Perhaps Beowulf
means "covered in a garment of blood"?

[2] *son of Ecglaf* I.e., Unferth.

but compelled by necessity all must come
1005 to that place set aside for soul-bearers,
children of men, dwellers on earth,
where the body, fast on its bed of death,
sleeps after the feast.
                          Then was the set time
that the son of Healfdene went to the hall;
1010 the king himself wished to share in the feast.
I have never heard of a greater host
who bore themselves better before their treasure-giver.
Those men in their glory moved to their benches,
rejoiced in the feast; fairly those kinsmen
1015 took many a full mead-cup,
stouthearted in the high hall,
Hrothgar and Hrothulf. Heorot within was
filled with friends—no false treacheries
did the people of the Scyldings plot at that time.[1]
1020 He gave to Beowulf the blade of Healfdene,[2]
a golden war-standard as a reward for victory,
the bright banner, a helmet and byrnie,
a great treasure-sword—many saw them
borne before that man. Beowulf received
1025 the full cup in the hall, he felt no shame
at that gift-giving before his bowmen;
never have I heard tell of four treasures
given more graciously, gold-adorned,
from one man to another on the ale-benches.
1030 On the crown of the helmet as a head-protector
a ridge, wound with wire, stood without,
so that the file-sharp swords might not terribly
harm him, shower-hard, when shield-fighters
had to go against hostile forces.
1035 The protector of earls ordered eight horses
with ornamented bridles led into the building,
in under the eaves; on one sat
a saddle, skillfully tooled, set with gemstones;
that was the warseat of the high-king
1040 when the son of Healfdene sought to perform
his swordplay—the widely-known warrior
never failed at the front, when the slain fell about him.
And the lord of the Ingwines[3] gave ownership
of both of them to Beowulf,
1045 the horses and weapons, bid him use them well.
So manfully did the mighty prince,
hoard-guard of warriors, reward the storm of battle
with such steeds and treasures that none who will speak
the truth rightfully could ever reproach them.

16

1050   Then the lord of earls, to each of those
on the meadbenches who had made with Beowulf
a sea-journey, gave jeweled treasures,
antique heirlooms, and then ordered
that gold be paid for the man whom Grendel
1055 had wickedly slain—he would have done more,
if wise God and one man's courage
had not prevented that fate. The Maker ruled all
of the race of mankind, as He still does.
Therefore understanding is always best,
1060 spiritual foresight—he must face much,
both love and hate, who long here
endures this world in these days of strife.
    Noise and music mingled together
before the leader of Healfdene's forces,
1065 the harp was touched, tales often told,
when Hrothgar's scop was set to recite
among the mead-tables his hall-entertainment
about the sons of Finn, surprised in ambush,
when the hero of the Half-Danes, Hnæf the Scylding
1070 had to fall in a Frisian slaughter.[4]

---

[1] Implicit in this statement is the idea that, at some later time, the people of the Scyldings did plot false treacheries; from other sources it is possible to infer that after the death of Hrothgar, his nephew Hrothulf ruled rather than Hrethric, Hrothgar's son. Many scholars assume that the story of some sort of treacherous usurpation was known to the audience; this gives a special urgency to much of what happens in these scenes of feasting, especially the speeches of Wealhtheow.

[2] The translation follows the reading of Mitchell and Robinson, and see Bruce Mitchell, "Beowulf, line 1020b: *brand* or *bearn*?" The manuscript is usually emended to mean "The son of Healfdene gave to Beowulf."

[3] *Ingwines* I.e., Danes.

[4] *the sons of Finn … Frisian slaughter* The story is obscure; the survival of a fragment of another poem ("The Fisht at Finnshurs") telling the same story helps clarify the action somewhat. Hnæf, prince of the Danes, is visiting his sister Hildeburh at the home of her husband Finn, king of the Frisians. While there, the Danish party is treacherously attacked (perhaps by a Jutish contingent among Finn's troops, unless the "Jutes" and Frisians are one and the same people); after five days of fighting Hnæf lies dead, along with many casualties on either side. Hnæf's retainer Hengest is left to lead the remnant of Danish survivors.

Hildeburh, indeed, had no need to praise
the good faith of the Jutes.[1] Guiltless, she was
deprived of her dear ones in that shieldplay,
her sons and brothers—sent forth to their fate,
1075 dispatched by spears; she was a sad lady!
Not without cause did she mourn fate's decrees,
the daughter of Hoc, after daybreak came
and she could see the slaughter of her kin
under the very skies where once she held
1080 the greatest worldly joys. War took away
all of the thanes of Finn, except a few,
so that he could not continue at all
a fight with Hengest on the battlefield,
nor could that woeful remnant drive away
1085 the prince's thane—so they offered them terms:[2]
they would clear out another hall for them,
a house and high-seat, of which they should have
half the control with the sons of the Jutes,
and Folcwalda's son,[3] with feasting and gifts,
1090 should honor the Danes each and every day,
gladden the troops of Hengest with gold rings
and ancient treasures, ornamented gold,
just as often as he would encourage
the hosts of the Frisians in the beerhall.
1095 They swore their pledges then on either side,
a firm compact of peace. With unfeigned zeal
Finn swore his oaths to Hengest, pledged that he,
with the consent of his counselors, would
support with honor those sad survivors,
1100 and that none should break their pact in word or deed,
nor through malice should ever make mention,
though they should serve their ring-giver's slayer,
without a lord, as they were led by need—
and if, provoking, any Frisian spoke
1105 reminding them of all their murderous hate,
then with the sword's edge they should settle it.
The oath[4] was made ready, and ancient gold

was brought from the hoard; the Battle-Scyldings'
best fighting-man was ready for the fire.
1110 It was easy to see upon that pyre
the bloodstained battle-shirt, the gilded swine,
iron-hard boar-images, the noblemen
with fatal wounds—so many felled by war!
Then Hildeburh commanded at Hnæf's pyre
1115 that her own son be consigned to the flames
to be burnt, flesh and bone, placed on the pyre
at his uncle's shoulder; the lady sang
a sad lament. The warrior ascended;
to the clouds coiled the mighty funeral fire,
1120 and roared before their mound; their heads melted,
their gashes burst open and spurted blood,
the deadly body-bites. The flame devoured,
most greedy spirit, those whom war destroyed
of both peoples—their glory departed.

17

1125 The warriors left to seek their native lands,
bereft of friends, to behold Frisia,
their homes and high fortresses. Hengest still
stayed there with Finn that slaughter-stained winter,
unwilling, desolate. He dreamt of home,
1130 though on the frozen sea he could not[5] steer
his ring-prowed ship—the ocean raged with storms,
strove with the wind, and winter locked the waves
in icy bonds, until there came another
year to the courtyard—as it yet does,
1135 always observing its seasons and times,
bright glorious weather. Gone was the winter,
and fair the bosom of earth; the exile burned
to take leave of that court, yet more he thought
of stern vengeance than of sea-voyages,
1140 how he might arrange a hostile meeting,
remind the Jutish sons of his iron sword.
So he did not refuse the world's custom
when the son of Hunlaf[6] placed a glinting sword,

---

[1] *Jutes* I.e., Frisians.

[2] *them terms* The referent of this pronoun in not entirely clear—who offers what to whom? The terms of the truce are unthinkable—no hero could honorably follow the killer of his lord. In the following line "they" refers to the Frisians, "them" to the Danes.

[3] *Folcwalda's son* I.e., Finn.

[4] *oath* Some editors emend to *ad*, "pyre."

---

[5] *not* OE *ne* "not" is not in the manuscript; most editors and translators add it to make better sense of the passage and of Hengest's character.

[6] *the son of Hunlaf* It is not clear who this is: perhaps Guthlaf or Oslaf (mentioned a few lines later), perhaps not; apparently some retainers remained with Hengest in Finn's hall, nursing their resentment throughout the winter. Some scholars take the OE word

the best of battle-flames, upon his lap;
1145   its edge was not unknown among the Jutes.
And so, in turn, to the bold-minded Finn
befell cruel sword-evil in his own home,
when Guthlaf and Oslaf spoke of their grief,
the fierce attack after their sea voyage,
1150   and cursed their wretched lot—the restless heart
could not restrain itself. The hall was stained
with the lifeblood of foes, and Finn was slain,
the king among his host; the queen was seized.
The Scylding bowmen carried to their ships
1155   all the house property of that earth-king,
whatever they could find in Finn's homestead,
brooches and bright gems. On their sea journey
they bore that noble queen back to the Danes
and led her to her people.
                                        The lay was sung,
1160   the entertainer's song. Glad sounds rose again,
the bench-noise glittered, cupbearers gave
wine from wondrous vessels. Wealhtheow came forth
in her golden crown to where the good two
sat, nephew and uncle; their peace was still whole then,
1165   each true to the other. Likewise Unferth, spokesman,[1]
sat at the foot of the Scylding lord; everyone trusted
      his spirit,
that he had great courage, though to his kinsmen he
      had not been
merciful in sword-play. Then the lady of the Scyldings
      spoke:
      "Take this cup, my noble courteous lord,
1170   giver of treasure! Be truly joyful,
gold-friend of men, and speak to the Geats
in mild words, as a man should do!
Be gracious to the Geats, mindful of the gifts
which you now have from near and far.
1175   I have been told that you would take this warrior
for your son. Heorot is cleansed,
the bright ring-hall—use your many rewards
while you can, and leave to your kinsmen
the folk and kingdom, when you must go forth

1180   to face the Maker's decree. I know that my own
dear gracious Hrothulf will hold in honors
these youths, if you should give up the world
before him, friend of the Scyldings;
I expect that he would wish to repay
1185   both our sons kindly, if he recalls all
the pleasures and honors that we have shown him,
in our kindness, since he was a child."
She turned to the bench where her boys sat,
Hrethric and Hrothmund, and the hero's son,
1190   all the youths together; the good man,
Beowulf the Geat, sat between the brothers.

18

The flagon was borne to him, a friendly greeting
conveyed with words, and wound gold
offered with good will, two armlets,
1195   garments and rings, and the greatest neck-collar
ever heard of anywhere on earth.
Under heaven I have not heard tell of a better
hoard-treasure of heroes, since Hama carried off
to the bright city the Brosinga necklace,[2]
1200   the gem and its treasures; he fled the treachery
of Eormanric, chose eternal counsel.
      Hygelac the Geat on his last journey
had that neck-ring,[3] nephew of Swerting,
when under the banner he defended his booty,
1205   the spoils of slaughter. Fate struck him down
when in his pride he went looking for woe,
a feud with the Frisians. He wore that finery,
those precious stones, over the cup of the sea,
that powerful lord, and collapsed under his shield.
1210   Into Frankish hands came the life of that king,
his breast-garments, and the great collar too;
a lesser warrior looted the corpses
mown down in battle; Geatish men

---

hunlafing as the name of a sword.

[1] _spokesman_ The Old English word _thyle_ has been variously interpreted, from "court jester" to "official speechmaker." The present translation grants Unferth a measure of dignity and position to which, perhaps, he is not entitled.

[2] _Brosinga necklace_ The Brosinga necklace had apparently been worn by the Norse goddess Freya. Nothing much is known of Hama, who apparently stole the necklace from Eormanric, famous king of the Goths. The "bright city" and "eternal counsel" may refer to his retreat into a monastery and Christianity (a story told in the Old Norse _Thidrekssaga_), though this is not entirely certain.

[3] _Hygelac ... neck-ring_ The first of several mentions of Hygelac's ill-fated raid against the Frisians. Later we are told that Beowulf gives the necklace to Hygd, Hygelac's wife; she apparently let him borrow it when he went on his piratical raid.

held that killing field.
                        The hall swallowed the noise.
215 Wealhtheow stood before the company and spoke:
"Beowulf, beloved warrior, wear this neck-ring
in good health, and enjoy this war-garment,
treasure of a people, and prosper well,
be bold and clever, and to these boys be
220 mild in counsel—I will remember you for that.
You have made it so that men will praise you
far and near, forever and ever,
as wide as the seas, home of the winds,
surround the shores of earth. Be while you live
225 blessed, o nobleman! I wish you well
with these bright treasures. Be to my sons
kind in your deeds, keeping them in joys!
Here each earl is true to the other,
mild in his heart, loyal to his liege-lord,
230 the thanes united, the nation alert;
the troop, having drunk at my table, will do as I bid."

    She went to her seat. The best of feasts it was—
the men drank wine, and did not know *wyrd*,
the cruel fate which would come to pass
235 for many an earl once evening came,
and Hrothgar departed to his own dwelling,
the mighty one to his rest. Countless men
guarded that hall, as they often had before.
They cleared away bench-planks, spread cushions
240 and bedding on the floor. One of those beer-drinkers
lay down to his rest fated, ripe for death.
They set at their heads their round battle-shields,
bright boards; there on the bench was
easily seen over the noblemen
245 the high battle-helmet, the ringed byrnie,
the mighty wooden spear. It was their custom
to be always ready, armed for battle,
at home or in the field, every one of them,
on whatever occasion their overlord
250 had need of them; that was a good troop.

19

    They sank into sleep—one paid sorely
for his evening rest, as had often happened
when Grendel guarded that gold-hall,
committed his wrongs until he came to his end,
255 died for his sins. It was clearly seen,

obvious to all men, that an avenger still
lived on after that enemy for a long time
after that grim battle—Grendel's mother,
monster-woman, remembered her misery,
1260 she who dwelt in those dreadful waters,
the cold streams, ever since Cain
killed with his blade his only brother,
his father's kin; he fled bloodstained,
marked for murder, left the joys of men,
1265 dwelled in the wasteland. From him awoke
many a fateful spirit—Grendel among them,
hateful accursed foe, who found at Heorot
a wakeful warrior waiting for battle.
There the great beast began to seize him,
1270 but he remembered his mighty strength,
the ample gifts which God had given him,
and trusted the Almighty for mercy,
favor and support; thus he overcame the fiend,
subdued the hellish spirit. He went away wretched,
1275 deprived of joy, to find his place of death,
mankind's foe. But his mother still
greedy, grim-minded, wanted to go
on her sorrowful journey to avenge her son's death.

    She reached Heorot, where the Ring-Danes
1280 slept throughout the building; sudden turnabout
came to men, when Grendel's mother
broke into the hall. The horror was less
by as much as a maiden's strength,
a woman's warfare, is less than an armed man's
1285 when a bloodstained blade, its edges strong,
hammer-forged sword, slices through
the boar-image on a helmet opposite.[1]
Then in the hall was the hard edge drawn,
swords over seats, many a broad shield
1290 raised in hands—none remembered his helmet
or broad mail-shirt when that terror seized them.
She came in haste and meant to hurry out,
save her life, when she was surprised there,
but she had quickly seized, fast in her clutches,
1295 one nobleman when she went to the fens.
He was the dearest of heroes to Hrothgar
among his comrades between the two seas,
mighty shield-warrior, whom she snatched from his rest,

---

[1] In fact Grendel's mother is a much more dangerous opponent for Beowulf; the point of these lines is not clear.

a glorious thane. Beowulf was not there,
but another place had been appointed
for the famous Geat after the treasure-giving.
Heorot was in an uproar—she took the famous hand,
covered in gore; care was renewed,
come again to the dwellings. That was no good exchange,
that those on both sides should have to bargain
with the lives of friends.

Then the wise old king,
gray-bearded warrior, was grieved at heart
when he learned that he no longer lived—
the dearest of men, his chief thane, was dead.
Quickly Beowulf was fetched to the chambers,
victory-blessed man. Just before dawn
that noble champion came with his companions,
went with his men to where the old king waited
wondering whether the Almighty would ever
work a change after his tidings of woe.
Across the floor walked the worthy warrior
with his small troop—the hall-wood resounded—
and with his words he addressed the wise one,
lord of the Ingwines, asked him whether
the night had been agreeable, after his urgent summons.

20

Hrothgar spoke, protector of the Scyldings:
"Ask not of joys! Sorrow is renewed
for the Danish people. Æschere is dead,
elder brother of Yrmenlaf,
my confidant and my counselor,
my shoulder-companion in every conflict
when we defended our heads when the footsoldiers
    clashed
and struck boar-helmets. As a nobleman should be,
always excellent, so Æschere was!
In Heorot he was slain by the hand
of a restless death-spirit; I do not know
where that ghoul went, gloating with its carcass,
rejoicing in its feast. She avenged that feud
in which you killed Grendel yesterday evening
in your violent way with a crushing vice-grip,
for he had diminished and destroyed my people
for far too long. He fell in battle,
it cost him his life, and now has come another

mighty evil marauder who means to avenge
her kin, and too far has carried out her revenge,
as it may seem to many a thane
whose spirit groans for his treasure-giver,
a hard heart's distress—now that hand lies dead
which was wont to give you all good things.

I have heard countrymen and hall-counselors
among my people report this:
they have seen two such creatures,
great march-stalkers holding the moors,
alien spirits. The second of them,
as far as they could discern most clearly,
had the shape of a woman; the other, misshapen,
marched the exile's path in the form of a man,
except that he was larger than any other;
in bygone days he was called 'Grendel'
by the local folk. They knew no father,
whether before him had been begotten
any more mysterious spirits. That murky land
they hold, wolf-haunted slopes, windy headlands,
awful fenpaths, where the upland torrents
plunge downward under the dark crags,
the flood underground. It is not far hence
—measured in miles—that the mere stands;
over it hangs a grove hoar-frosted,
a firm-rooted wood looming over the water.
Every night one can see there an awesome wonder,
fire on the water. There lives none so wise
or bold that he can fathom its abyss.
Though the heath-stepper beset by hounds,
the strong-horned hart, might seek the forest,
pursued from afar, he will sooner lose
his life on the shore than save his head
and go in the lake—it is no good place!
The clashing waves climb up from there
dark to the clouds, when the wind drives
the violent storms, until the sky itself droops,
the heavens groan. Now once again all help
depends on you alone. You do not yet know
this fearful place, where you might find
the sinful creature—seek it if you dare!
I will reward you with ancient riches
for that feud, as I did before,
with twisted gold, if you return alive."

21

Beowulf spoke, son of Ecgtheow:
"Sorrow not, wise one! It is always better
385 to avenge one's friend than to mourn overmuch.
Each of us shall abide the end
of this world's life; let him who can
bring about fame before death—that is best
for the unliving man after he is gone.
390 Arise, kingdom's guard, let us quickly go
and inspect the path of Grendel's kin.
I promise you this: he[1] will find no protection—
not in the belly of the earth nor the bottom of the sea,
nor the mountain groves—let him go where he will!
395 For today, you must endure patiently
all your woes, as I expect you will."
The old man leapt up, thanked the Lord,
the mighty God, for that man's speech.
Then for Hrothgar a horse was bridled
400 with plaited mane. The wise prince
rode in full array; footsoldiers marched
with shields at the ready. The tracks were seen
far and wide on the forest paths,
a trail through the woods, where she went forth
405 over the murky moor, bore the young man's
lifeless body, the best of all those
who had held watch over Hrothgar's home.
The son of nobles crossed over
the steep stone cliffs, the constricted climb,
410 a narrow solitary path, a course unknown,
the towering headlands, home of sea-monsters.
He went before with just a few
wise men to see the way,
until suddenly he saw mountain-trees,
1415 stunted and leaning over gray stone,
a joyless wood; the water went under,
turbid and dreary. To all the Danes,
the men of the Scyldings, many a thane,
it was a sore pain at heart to suffer,
1420 a grief to every earl, when on the seacliff
they came upon the head of Æschere.
The flood boiled with blood—the folk gazed on—
and hot gore. At times a horn sang

its eager war-song. The footsoldiers sat down.
1425 They saw in the water many kinds of serpents,
strange sea-creatures testing the currents,
and on the sloping shores lay such monsters
as often attend in early morning
a sorrowful journey on the sail-road,
1430 dragons and wild beasts. They rushed away
bitter, enraged; they heard the bright noise,
the sound of the battle-horn. A Geatish bowman
cut short the life of one of those swimmers
with a bow and arrow, so that in his body stood
1435 the hard war-shaft; he was a slower swimmer
on the waves, when death took him away.
At once in the water he was assailed
with the barbed hooks of boar-pikes,
violently attacked and dragged ashore,
1440 the strange wave-roamer; the men inspected
this grisly visitor.
Beowulf geared up
in his warrior's clothing, cared not for his life.
The broad war-shirt, woven by hand,
cunningly made, had to test the mere—
1445 it knew well how to protect his bone-house
so that a battle-grip might not hurt his breast
nor an angry malicious clutch touch his life.
The shining helmet protected his head,
set to stir up the sea's depths,
1450 seek that troubled water, decorated with treasure,
encircled with a splendid band, as a weapon-smith
in days of old had crafted it with wonders,
set boar-images, so that afterwards
no blade or battle-sword might ever bite it.
1455 Not the smallest of powerful supports was that
which Hrothgar's spokesman lent him at need;
that hilted sword was named Hrunting,
unique among ancient treasures—
its edge was iron, etched with poison-stripes,
1460 hardened with the blood of war; it had never failed
any man who grasped it in his hands in battle,
who dared to undertake a dreadful journey
into the very home of the foe—it was not the first time
that it had to perform a work of high courage.
1465 Truly, the son of Ecglaf, crafty in strength,
did not remember what he had said before,
drunk with wine, when he lent that weapon

---

[1] *he* I.e., Grendel's mother. The hero does not note carefully enough the gender of Grendel's mother, or else the pronoun *he* refers to OE *magan* "kinsman," a masculine noun.

to a better swordsman; he himself did not dare
to risk his life under the rushing waves,
1470   perform a lordly act; for that he lost honor,
his fame for courage. Not so with the other,
when he had geared himself up for battle.

22

Beowulf spoke, son of Ecgtheow:
"Consider now, famous kinsman of Healfdene,
1475   wise prince, now that I am eager to depart,
gold-friend to men, what we spoke of before:
if ever in your service I should
lose my life, that you would always be
in a father's place to me when I have passed away.
1480   Be a protector to my band of men,
my boon-companions, if battle should take me,
and send on to Hygelac, beloved Hrothgar,
the gifts of treasure which you have given me.
The lord of the Geats will understand by that gold,
1485   the son of Hrethel will see by that treasure,
that I found a ring-giver who was good
in ancient customs and, while I could, enjoyed it.
And let Unferth have that ancient heirloom,
that well-known man have my wave-patterned sword,
1490   hard-edged, splendid; with Hrunting I shall
win honor and fame, or death will take me!"
After these words the Weder-Geat man
hastened boldly, by no means wished to
stay for an answer; the surging sea received
1495   the brave soldier. It was the space of a day[1]
before he could perceive the bottom.
Right away she who held that expanse of water,
bloodthirsty and fierce, for a hundred half-years,
grim and greedy, perceived that some man
1500   was exploring from above that alien land.
She snatched at him, seized the warrior
in her savage clutches, but none the sooner
injured his sound body—the ring-mail encircled him,
so that she could not pierce that war-dress,
1505   the locked coat of mail, with her hostile claws.
Then that she-wolf of the sea swam to the bottom,
and bore the prince of rings into her abode,
so that he might not—no matter how strong—

wield his weapons, but so many wonders
1510   set upon him in the water, many a sea-beast
with battle-tusks tearing at his war-shirt,
monsters pursuing him.[2]
                    Then the earl perceived
that he was in some sort of battle-hall
where no water could harm him in any way,
1515   and, for the hall's roof, he could not be reached
by the flood's sudden rush—he saw a fire-light,
a glowing blaze shining brightly.
Then the worthy man saw that water-witch,
a great mere-wife; he gave a mighty blow
1520   with his battle-sword—he did not temper that stroke—
so that the ring-etched blade rang out on her head
a greedy battle-song. The guest discovered then
that the battle-flame would not bite,
or wound her fatally—but the edge failed
1525   the man in his need; it had endured many
hand-to-hand meetings, often sheared through helmets,
fated war-garments. It was the first time
that the fame of that precious treasure had fallen.
Again he was stalwart, not slow of zeal,
1530   mindful of glory, that kinsman of Hygelac—
the angry challenger threw away that etched blade,
wrapped and ornamented, so that it lay on the earth,
strong, steel-edged. He trusted his strength,
the might of his handgrip—as a man should do
1535   if by his warfare he thinks to win
long-lasting praise: he cares nothing for his life.
The man of the War-Geats grabbed by the shoulder
Grendel's mother—he had no regret for that feud;
battle-hardened, enraged, he swung her around,
1540   his deadly foe, so she fell to the ground.
Quickly she gave him requital for that
with a grim grasp, and grappled him to her—
weary, he stumbled, strongest of warriors,
of foot-soldiers, and took a fall.
1545   She set upon her hall-guest and drew her knife,
broad, bright-edged; she would avenge her boy,
her only offspring. On his shoulders lay
the linked corselet; it defended his life,
prevented the entrance of point and blade.
1550   There the son of Ecgtheow would have ended his life

---

[1]   *It was the space of a day* Or "it was daylight."

[2]   *pursuing him* Or "attacked their adversary." The Old English word *æglæcan* may refer here to Beowulf or to the sea-monsters.

under the wide ground, the Geatish champion,
had not his armored shirt offered him help,
the hard battle-net, and holy God
brought about war-victory—the wise Lord,
555   Ruler of the heavens, decided it rightly,
easily, once he stood up again.

23

He saw among the armor a victorious blade,
ancient giant-sword strong in its edges,
an honor in battle; it was the best of weapons,
560   except that it was greater than any other man
might even bear into the play of battle,
good, adorned, the work of giants.[1]
The Scyldings' champion seized its linked hilt,
fierce and ferocious, drew the ring-marked sword
565   despairing of his life, struck in fury
so that it caught her hard in the neck,
broke her bone-rings; the blade cut through
the doomed flesh—she fell to the floor,
the sword was bloody, the soldier rejoiced.
570   The flames gleamed, a light glowed within
even as from heaven clearly shines
the firmament's candle. He looked around the chamber,
passed by the wall, hefted the weapon
hard by its hilt, that thane of Hygelac,
575   angry and resolute—nor was the edge useless
to that warrior, but he quickly wished
to pay back Grendel for the many battle-storms
which he had wrought on the West-Danes
much more often than on one occasion,
580   when Hrothgar's hall-companions
he slew in their beds, devoured sleeping
fifteen men of the Danish folk,
and made off with as many more,
a loathsome booty. He paid him back for that,
585   the fierce champion, for on a couch he saw
Grendel lying lifeless,
battle-weary from the wound he received
in the combat at Heorot. His corpse burst open
when he was dealt a blow after death,
590   a hard sword-stroke, and his head chopped off.

Soon the wise men saw it,
those who kept watch on the water with Hrothgar—
all turbid were the waves, and troubled,
the sea stained with blood. The graybearded
1595   elders spoke together about the good one,
said they did not expect that nobleman
would return, triumphant, to seek
the mighty prince; to many it seemed
that the sea-wolf had destroyed him.
1600   The ninth hour came; the noble Scyldings
abandoned the headland, and home went
the gold-friend of men. The guests[2] sat
sick at heart, and stared into the mere;
they wished, but did not hope, that they would
1605   see their lord himself.
                                Then the sword began,
that blade, to waste away into battle-icicles
from the war-blood; it was a great wonder
that it melted entirely, just like ice
when the Father loosens the frost's fetters,
1610   unwraps the water's bonds—He wields power
over times and seasons; that is the true Maker.
The man of the Geats took no more precious treasures
from that place—though he saw many there—
than the head, and the hilt as well,
1615   bright with gems; the blade had melted,
the ornamented sword burned up; so hot was the blood
of the poisonous alien spirit who died in there.
Soon he was swimming who had survived in battle
the downfall of his enemies, dove up through the water;
1620   the sea-currents were entirely cleansed,
the spacious regions, when that alien spirit
gave up life-days and this loaned world.
        The defender of seafarers came to land,
swam stout-hearted; he rejoiced in his sea-booty,
1625   the great burden which he brought with him.
That splendid troop of thanes went towards him,
thanked God, rejoiced in their prince,
that they might see him safe and sound.
Then from that bold man helmet and byrnie
1630   were quickly unstrapped. Under the clouds
the mere stewed, stained with gore.
They went forth, followed the trail,
rejoicing in their hearts; they marched along the road,

---

1   *the work of giants* Old, highly-praised weapons are often called
"the work of giants"—whether this reference is meant to connect the
sword to the giants "who fought against God" is not clear.

2   *guests* I.e., the Geats who had come to Heorot with Beowulf.

the familiar path; proud as kings
1635 they carried the head from the sea-cliff
with great trouble, even for two pairs
of stout-hearted men; four of them had to
bear, with some strain, on a battle-pole
Grendel's head to the gold-hall,
1640 until presently fourteen proud
and battle-hardy Geats came to the hall,
warriors marching; the lord of those men,
mighty in the throng, trod the meadhall-plain.
Then the ruler of thanes entered there,
1645 daring in actions, honored in fame,
battle-brave hero, to greet Hrothgar.
Then, where men were drinking, they dragged by its hair
Grendel's head across the hall-floor,
a grisly spectacle for the men and the queen.
1650 Everyone stared at that amazing sight.

24

Beowulf spoke, son of Ecgtheow:
"Look! son of Healfdene, prince of the Scyldings,
we have brought you gladly these gifts from the sea
which you gaze on here, a token of glory.
1655 Not easily did I escape with my life
that undersea battle, did my brave deed
with difficulty—indeed, the battle would have been
over at once, if God had not guarded me.
Nor could I achieve anything at that battle
1660 with Hrunting, though that weapon is good;
but the Ruler of Men granted to me
that I might see on the wall a gigantic old sword,
hanging glittering—He has always guided
the friendless one—so I drew that weapon.
1665 In that conflict, when I had the chance, I slew
the shepherds of that house. Then that battle-sword
burned up with its ornaments, as the blood shot out,
hottest battle-sweat. I have brought the hilt
back from the enemy; I avenged the old deeds,
1670 the slaughter of Danes, as seemed only right.
Now you have my word that you may in Heorot
sleep without care with your company of men,
and every thane, young and old,
in your nation; you need fear nothing,
1675 prince of the Scyldings, from that side,
no deadly manslaughters, as you did before."

Then the golden hilt was placed in the hand
of the gray-haired war-chief, wise old leader,
that old work of giants; it came to the keeping
1680 of the Danish lord after the fall of demons,
a work of wonder-smiths; and when that evil-hearted man,
God's adversary, gave up the world,
guilty of murders—and his mother too—
it passed to the possession of the best
1685 of world-kings between the two seas,
of all those that dealt out treasures in Danish lands.
Hrothgar spoke—he studied the hilt
of the old heirloom, where was written[1] the origin
of ancient strife, when the flood slew,
1690 rushing seas, the race of giants—
they suffered awfully. That was a people alien
to the eternal Lord; a last reward
the Ruler gave them through the raging waters.
Also, on the sword-guard of bright gold
1695 was rightly marked in rune-letters,
set down and said for whom that sword,
best of irons, had first been made,
with scrollery and serpentine patterns. Then spoke
the wise son of Healfdene—all fell silent:
1700 "One may, indeed, say, if he acts in truth
and right for the people, remembers all,
old guardian of his homeland, that this earl was
born a better man! My friend Beowulf,
your glory is exalted throughout the world,
1705 over every people; you hold it all with patient care,
and temper strength with wisdom. To you I shall fulfill
our friendship, as we have said. You shall become a comfort
everlasting to your own people,
and a help to heroes.
                                        Not so was Heremod
1710 to the sons of Ecgwala,[2] the Honor-Scyldings;[3]
he grew not for their delight, but for their destruction
and the murder of Danish men.
Enraged, he cut down his table-companions,
comrades-in-arms, until he turned away alone
1715 from the pleasures of men, that famous prince;
though mighty God exalted him in the joys

---

[1] *written* Or "carved." It is not clear whether the scene is visual or textual, depicted or written in (presumably runic) characters.

[2] *Ecgwala* A king of Danes.

[3] *Honor-Scyldings* I.e., Danes.

of strength and force, advanced him far
over all men, yet in his heart he nursed
a blood-ravenous breast-hoard. No rings did he give
1720 to the Danes for their honor; he endured, joyless,
to suffer the pains of that strife,
a long-lasting harm to his people. Learn from him,
understand virtue! For your sake I have told this,
in the wisdom of my winters.

      It is a wonder to say
1725 how mighty God in His great spirit
allots wisdom, land and lordship
to mankind; He has control of everything.
At times He permits the thoughts of a man
in a mighty race to move in delights,
1730 gives him to hold in his homeland
the sweet joys of earth, a stronghold of men,
grants him such power over his portion of the world,
a great kingdom, that he himself cannot
imagine an end to it, in his folly.
1735 He dwells in plenty; in no way plague him
illness or old age, nor do evil thoughts
darken his spirit, nor any strife
or sword-hate shows itself, but all the world
turns to his will; he knows nothing worse.

25

1740   "At last his portion of pride within him
grows and flourishes, while the guardian sleeps,
the soul's shepherd—that sleep is too sound,
bound with cares, the slayer too close
who, sinful and wicked, shoots from his bow.[1]
1745 Then he is struck in his heart, under his helmet
with a bitter dart—he knows no defense—
the strange, dark demands of evil spirits.
What he has long held seems too little;
angry and greedy, he gives no golden rings
1750 for vaunting boasts, and his final destiny
he neglects and forgets, since God, Ruler of glories,
has given him a portion of honors.
In the end it finally comes about
that the loaned life-dwelling starts to decay
1755 and falls, fated to die; another follows him

---

[1] The slayer is sin or vice; the soul's guardian is reason, conscience
or prudence.

who doles out his riches without regret,
the earl's ancient treasure; he heeds no terror.
Defend yourself from wickedness, dear Beowulf,
best of men, and choose the better,
1760 eternal counsel; care not for pride,
great champion! The glory of your might
is but a little while; soon it will be
that sickness or the sword will shatter your strength,
or the grip of fire, or the surging flood,
1765 or the cut of a sword, or the flight of a spear,
or terrible old age—or the light of your eyes
will fail and flicker out; in one fell swoop
death, o warrior, will overwhelm you.

 "Thus, a hundred half-years I held the Ring-Danes
1770 under the skies, and kept them safe from war
from many tribes throughout this middle-earth,
from spears and swords, so that I considered none
under the expanse of heaven my enemy.
Look! Turnabout came in my own homeland,
1775 grief after gladness, when Grendel became
my invader, ancient adversary;
for that persecution I bore perpetually
the greatest heart-cares. Thanks be to the Creator,
eternal Lord, that I have lived long enough
1780 to see that head, stained with blood,
with my own eyes, after all this strife!
Go to your seat, enjoy the feast,
honored in battle; between us shall be shared
a great many treasures, when morning comes."

1785   Glad-hearted, the Geat went at once
to take his seat, as the wise one told him.
Then again as before, a feast was prepared
for the brave ones who occupied the hall
on this new occasion. The dark helm of night
1790 overshadowed the troop. The soldiers arose;
the gray-haired ruler was ready for bed,
the aged Scylding. Immeasurably well
did rest please the Geat, proud shield-warrior;
at once a chamberlain led him forth,
1795 weary from his adventure, come from afar,
he who attended to all the needs
of that thane, for courtesy, as in those days
all battle-voyagers used to have.

 The great-hearted one rested; the hall towered
1800 vaulted and gold-adorned; the guest slept within

until the black[1] raven, blithe-hearted, announced
the joy of heaven. Then light came hurrying
[bright over shadows;] the soldiers hastened,
the noblemen were eager to travel
1805 back to their people; the bold-spirited visitor
wished to seek his far-off ship.

  The hardy one ordered Hrunting to be borne
to the son of Ecglaf,[2] bid him take his sword,
lordly iron; he thanked him for the loan,
1810 and said that he regarded it as a good war-friend,
skillful in battle, and the sword's edges
he did not disparage; he was a noble man.
And when the warriors were eager for their way,
equipped in their war-gear, the nobleman went,
1815 the Danes' honor, to the high seat where the other was:
the hero, brave in battle, saluted Hrothgar.

26

  Beowulf spoke, son of Ecgtheow:
"Now we seafarers, come from afar,
wish to say that we desire
1820 to seek Hygelac. Here we were honorably
entertained with delights; you have treated us well.
If ever on earth I can do any thing
to earn more of your affection,
than the battle-deeds I have done already,
1825 ruler of men, I will be ready at once.
If ever I hear over the sea's expanse
that your neighbors threaten you with terror
as your enemies used to do,
I will bring you a thousand thanes,
1830 heroes to help you. I have faith in Hygelac—
the lord of the Geats, though he be young,
shepherd of his people, will support me
with words and deeds, that I might honor you well
and bring to your side a forest of spears,
1835 the support of my might, whenever you need men.
If ever Hrethric decides, son of a prince,
to come to the Geatish court, he will find
many friends there; far-off lands

are better sought by one who is himself good."

1840   Hrothgar spoke in answer to him:
"The wise Lord has sent those words
into your heart; I have never heard
a shrewder speech from such a young man.
You are strong in might and sound in mind,
1845 prudent in speech! I expect it is likely
that if it should ever happen that the spear
or the horrors of war take Hrethel's son,[3]
or sickness or sword strike the shepherd of his people,
your lord, and you still live,
1850 that the sea-Geats could not select
a better choice anywhere for king,
hoard-guard of heroes, if you will hold
the realm of your kinsmen. Your character pleases me
better and better, beloved Beowulf.
1855 You have brought it about that between our peoples,
the Geatish nation and the spear-Danes,
there shall be peace, and strife shall rest,
the malicious deeds that they endured before,
as long as I shall rule this wide realm,
1860 and treasures together; many shall greet
another with gifts across the gannet's bath;[4]
the ring-necked ship shall bring over the sea
tribute and tokens of love. I know these nations
will be made fast against friend and foe,
1865 blameless in everything, in the old way."

  The protector of heroes, kinsman of Healfdene,
gave him twelve great treasures in the hall;
bid him seek his own dear people in safety
with those gifts, and quickly come again.
1870 Then the good king, of noble kin, kissed
that best of thanes and embraced his neck,
the Scylding prince; tears were shed
by that gray-haired man. He was of two minds—
but in his old wisdom knew it was more likely
1875 that never again would they see one another,
brave in their meeting-place. The man was so dear to him
that he could not hold back the flood in his breast,
but in his heart, fast in the bonds of his thought,
a deep-felt longing for the dear man
1880 burned in his blood. Beowulf from thence,
gold-proud warrior, trod the grassy lawn,

---

[1] *black* Either OE *blac* "shining" or *blæc* "black"; the translation
prefers the irony of the image of the black raven, not otherwise
known as a harbinger of joy, announcing the surprising good news
of a dawn without slaughter.

[2] *Son of Ecglaf* I.e., Unferth.

[3] *Hrethel's son* I.e., Hygelac.

[4] *gannet's bath* I.e., the sea.

exulting in treasure; the sea-goer awaited
its lord and owner, where it rode at anchor.
As they were going, the gift of Hrothgar
1885 was often praised; that king was peerless,
blameless in everything, until old age took from him
—it has injured so many—the joy of his strength.

27

Those men of high courage then came to the sea,
that troop of young retainers, bore their ring-mail,
1890 locked shirts of armor. The coast-guard observed
the return of those earls, as he had once before;
he did not greet those guests with insults
on the clifftop, but he rode towards them,
said that the warriors in their shining armor
1895 would be welcome in their ships to the people of the
Weders.
The sea-curved prow, the ring-necked ship,
as it lay on the sand was laden with war-gear,
with horses and treasures; the mast towered high
over Hrothgar's hoard-gifts.
1900 To the ship's guardian he[1] gave a sword,
bound with gold, so that on the mead-benches
he was afterwards more honored by that heirloom,
that old treasure. Onward they went, the ship
sliced through deep water, gave up the Danish coast.
1905 The sail by the mast was rigged fast with ropes,
a great sea-cloth; the timbers creaked,
the wind over the sea did not hinder at all
the wave-floater on its way; the sea-goer sped on,
floated foamy-necked, forth upon the waves,
1910 the bound prow over the briny streams,
until they could make out the cliffs of Geatland,
familiar capes; the keel drove forward
thrust by the wind, and came to rest on land.
Right away the harbor-guard was ready at the shore,
1915 who for a long time had gazed far
over the currents, eager for the beloved men;
he moored the broad-beamed ship on the beach
fast with anchor-ropes, lest the force of the waves
should drive away the handsome wooden vessel.
1920 He bade that the nobleman's wealth be borne ashore,
armor and plated gold; they had not far to go

to seek their dispenser of treasure,
Hygelac son of Hrethel, where he dwelt at home
with his companions, near the sea-wall.
1925   The building was splendid, the king quite bold,
high in his hall, Hygd[2] very young,
wise, well-mannered, though few winters
had the daughter of Hæreth passed within
the palace walls—yet not poor for that,
1930 nor stingy of gifts to the Geatish people,
of great treasures. She considered Thryth's pride,[3]
famous folk-queen, and her terrible crimes;
no man so bold among her own retainers
dared to approach her, except as her prince,[4]
1935 or dared to look into her eyes by day;
for he knew that deadly bonds, braided by hand,
were waiting for him—first the hand-grip,
and quickly after a blade appointed,
so that a patterned sword had to settle things,
1940 proclaim the execution. That is no queenly custom
for a lady to perform—no matter how lovely—
that a peace-weaver[5] should deprive of life
a friendly man after a pretended affront.
The kinsman of Hemming[6] put a halt to that:
1945 then ale-drinkers told another tale,
said she caused less calamity to the people,
less malicious evil, after she was
given gold-adorned to the young champion,
fair to that nobleman, when to Offa's floor
1950 she sought a journey over the fallow sea
at her father's wish, where she afterwards

---

[1] *he* I.e., Beowulf.

[2] *Hygd* Hygelac's queen.

[3] These lines are difficult. Some editions and translations read the name as "Modthryth"; the reading adopted here smoothes out a transition that is otherwise abrupt even by the standards of this poem. This "digression" on the character of a queen, with some elements of a folktale, is the counterpoint to the story of Heremod in earlier sections.

[4] *her prince* I.e., as her husband or her father.

[5] *peace-weaver* This epithet reflects the common practice, whose sometimes-tragic consequences are explored at length elsewhere in the poem, of settling intertribal feuds with a marriage between the daughter of one lord and the son of another.

[6] *kinsman of Hemming* Offa I, fourth-century king of the continental Angles, not Offa II, the eighth-century king of Mercia. The elaborate praise offered to Offa I has been taken to suggest that the poem may have been written or circulated in the court of Offa II, but there is otherwise no evidence for this.

on the throne, famous for good things,
used well her life while she had it,
held high love with that chief of heroes,
1955 of all mankind, as men have told me,
the best between the two seas
of all the races of men; therefore Offa,
in gifts and battle, spear-bold man,
was widely honored, and held in wisdom
1960 his own homeland. From him arose Eomer
as a help to heroes, kinsman of Hemming,
grandson of Garmund, skilled in violence.

28

The hardy man[1] with his hand-picked troop
went across the sand, trod the sea-plain,
1965 the wide shore. The world's candle shone,
hastening from the south. They had survived their journey,
went boldly to where they knew
the protector of earls, slayer of Ongentheow,[2]
good young battle-king, gave out rings
1970 in his fortress. To Hygelac
the arrival of Beowulf was quickly reported,
that to the enclosures his battle-companion,
protector of warriors, came walking alive
back to his court, safe from his battle-play.
1975 Quickly, as the powerful one commanded,
the hall was cleared out inside for the foot-guests.
     He sat down with him, who had survived the fight,
kinsmen together, after he greeted
his friend and liege-lord with a formal speech,
1980 with courteous words and cups of mead.
The daughter of Hæreth[3] passed through the hall,
cared for the people, bore the cup
to the hand of the hero.[4] Hygelac began
to question his companion courteously
1985 in the high hall—curiosity pressed him
to know how the sea-Geats' adventures were:
     "How did you fare, beloved Beowulf,

---

[1] *The hardy man* I.e., Beowulf.

[2] *slayer of Ongentheow* Hygelac. The death of the Swedish king Ongentheow (at the hands of Wulf and Eofor, retainers of Hygelac) is told below, section 40.

[3] *daughter of Hæreth* I.e., Hygd.

[4] *to the hand of the hero* The manuscript reads "to the hands of heathens," which makes sense, but is usually emended.

in your journey, when you suddenly resolved
to seek a far-off strife over the salt sea,
1990 a battle in Heorot? Did you better at all
the well-known woe of Hrothgar,
the famous prince? For that I seethed
with heart-care and distress, mistrusted the adventure
of my beloved man; long I implored
1995 that you not seek that slaughter-spirit at all,
let the south-Danes themselves make
war against Grendel. I say thanks to God
that I might see you again safe and sound."
     Beowulf spoke, son of Ecgtheow:
2000 "It is no mystery to many men,
my lord Hygelac—the great meeting,
what a time of great struggle Grendel and I
had in that place where he made so many
sorrows for the victory-Scyldings,
2005 life-long misery—I avenged them all,
so that none of Grendel's tribe needs to boast
anywhere on earth of that uproar at dawn,
whoever lives longest of that loathsome kind,
enveloped in foul evil. First I came there
2010 to the ring-hall to greet Hrothgar;
quickly the famous kinsman of Healfdene,
once he knew of my intentions,
assigned me a seat with his own sons.
That troop was in delight; never in my life
2015 have I seen among hall-sitters, under heaven's vault,
a more joyous feast. At times the famous queen,
bond of peace to nations, passed through the hall,
urged on her young sons; often she gave
twisted rings before she took her seat.
2020 At times before the hall-thanes the daughter of Hrothgar
bore the ale-cup to the earls in the back—
Freawaru, I heard the men in the hall
call her, when the studded treasure-cup
was passed among them. She is promised,
2025 young, gold-adorned, to the gracious son of Froda;[5]
the ruler of the Scyldings has arranged this,
the kingdom's shepherd, and approves the counsel
that he should settle his share of feud and slaughter

---

[5] *the gracious son of Froda* Ingeld, prince of the Heathobards. His attack on the Danes, alluded to earlier in the poem (80–5), was apparently unsuccessful; another Old English poem, *Widsith*, reports that "Hrothulf and Hrothgar … humbled Ingeld's battle-array."

with this young woman. But seldom anywhere
after the death of a prince does the deadly spear rest
for even a brief while, though the bride be good!

"It may, perhaps, displease the Heathobards' prince,
and every retainer among his tribe,
when across the floor, following that woman, goes
a noble son of the Danes, received with honors;
on him glitters an ancestral heirloom,
hard, ring-adorned, once a Heathobard treasure
as long as they were able to wield their weapons.

29

"And then in that deadly shield-play they undid
their beloved comrades and their own lives.
Then an old spear-bearer[1] speaks over his beer,
who sees that ring-hilt and remembers all
the spear-deaths of men—his spirit is grim—
begins, sad-minded, to test the mettle
of a young thane with his innermost thoughts,
to awaken war, and says these words:

'Can you, my friend, recognize that sword,
which your father bore into battle
in his final adventure beneath the helmet,
that dear iron, when the Danes struck him,
ruled the field of slaughter after the rout of heroes,
when Withergyld[2] fell—those valiant Scyldings?
Now here some son or other of his slayer
walks across this floor, struts in his finery,
brags of the murder and bears that treasure
which ought, by right, to belong to you.'

He urges and reminds him on every occasion
with cruel words, until the time comes
that Freawaru's thane, for his father's deeds,
sleeps, bloodstained from the bite of a sword,
forfeits his life; from there the other
escapes alive, for he knows the land well.
Then on both sides the sworn oaths of earls
will be broken, once bitter violent hate
wells up in Ingeld, and his wife-love

grows cooler after his surging cares.
Thus I expect that the Heathobards' part
in the Danish alliance is not without deceit,
nor their friendship fast.

I will speak further
concerning Grendel, so that you might certainly know,
giver of treasure, how it turned out,
the heroic wrestling-match. When heaven's gem
slipped under the ground, the angry spirit came,
horrible, evening-grim, sought us out
where, unharmed, we guarded the hall.
The attack came first against Hondscio[3] there,
deadly to that doomed man—he fell first,
a girded champion; Grendel was
that famous young retainer's devourer,
gobbled up the body of that beloved man.
None the sooner did that slayer, blood in his teeth,
mindful of misery, mean to leave
that gold-hall empty-handed,
but in his mighty strength he tested me,
grabbed with a ready hand. A glove[4] hung
huge, grotesque, fast with cunning clasps;
it was all embroidered with evil skill,
with the devil's craft and dragons' skins.
Inside there, though I was innocent,
that proud evil-doer wanted to put me,
one of many; but it was not to be,
once I angrily stood upright.

30[5]

"It is too long to tell how I handed back payment
to the people's enemy for all his evils—
there, my prince, I did honor to your people
with my actions. He escaped away,
enjoyed his life a little while longer;
yet behind him, guarding his path, was his right

---

1 *an old spear-bearer* Of the Heathobards, outraged by the presence of his former enemies, the Danes. In heroic poetry when a warrior falls, his killer is often awarded his armor; the sword is a vivid reminder of the fate of its former owner and the duty of revenge which is passed on to the next generation.

2 *Withergyld* Apparently a famous Heathobard warrior.

3 *Hondscio* We finally learn the name of the retainer killed in section 11. The name, as in modern German (Handschuh), means "glove."

4 *glove* It is not clear what this is; apparently a pouch of some kind. It is characteristic of a troll in Norse legend. In any case it does not figure in the narrator's own description of Grendel's attack, and is but one of several discrepancies between the two tellings of the story.

5 The placement of this section is conjectural; the sectional divisions of the manuscript are confused at this point.

2100 hand in Heorot, and wretched, he went hence,
sad at heart, and sank to the sea-floor.
      For that bloody onslaught the friend of the Scyldings
repaid me greatly with plated gold,
many treasures, when morning came,
and we had gathered together to the feast again.
2105 There was song and joy; the aged Scylding,[1]
widely learned, told of far-off times;
at times the brave warrior touched the song-wood,
delight of the harp, at times made lays
both true and sad, at times strange stories
2110 he recounted rightly. That great-hearted king,
gray-bearded old warrior wrapped in his years,
at times began to speak of his youth again,
his battle-strength; his heart surged within him
when, old in winters, he remembered so much.
2115 And so there inside we took our ease
all day long, until night descended
again upon men. There, quickly ready
with revenge for her griefs, Grendel's mother
journeyed sorrowful; death took her son,
2120 the war-hate of the Weders. That monstrous woman
avenged her son, killed a soldier
boldly at once—there the life of Æschere,
wise old counselor, came to its end.
And when morning came the men of the Danes
2125 were not able to burn his body, death-weary,
with flames, nor place him on a funeral pyre,
beloved man; she bore away his corpse
in her evil embrace under the upland streams.
That, to Hrothgar, was the most wrenching distress
2130 of all those that had befallen that folk-leader.
Then the prince—by your life—implored me,
his mind wracked, that in the roaring waves
I should do a noble deed, put my life in danger,
perform glorious things—he promised me reward.
2135 In the waves I found, as is widely known,
a grim, horrible guardian of the abyss.
There, for a while, we fought hand-to-hand;
the sea foamed with blood, and I severed the head
of Grendel's mother with a mighty sword

2140 in that [battle-]hall;[2] I barely managed
to get away with my life—I wasn't doomed yet—
and the protector of earls once again gave me
many treasures, that kinsman of Healfdene.

31

      "So that nation's king followed good customs;
2145 in no wise have I lost those rewards,
the prize for my strength, but the son of Healfdene
offered me treasures at my own choice,
which I wish to bring to you, o war-king,
to show good will. Still all my joys
2150 are fixed on you alone; I have few
close kinsmen, my Hygelac, except for you."
      He ordered to be borne in the boar standard,
the helmet towering in battle, the gray byrnie,
the decorated sword, and told this story:
2155 "Hrothgar gave me this battle-gear,
wise prince, and commanded particularly
that first I should tell you the story of his gift—
he said that Heorogar the king[3] first had it,
lord of the Scyldings, for a long while;
2160 none the sooner would he give to his own son,
the valiant Heoroward—loyal though he was—
that breast-armor. Use all well!"
Then, as I've heard, four swift horses,
fallow as apples, well-matched, followed
2165 that war-gear; he gave him as a gift
the horses and harness—as kinsman should behave,
never knitting a net of malice for another
with secret plots, preparing death
for his hand-picked comrades. Hygelac's nephew
2170 was loyal to him, hardy in the fight,
and each man to the other mindful of benefits.—
I heard that he gave the necklace to Hygd,
the wondrous ornamented treasure which Wealhtheow
      had given him,
to that lord's daughter, along with three horses
2175 graceful and saddle-bright; her breast was adorned
the more graciously after that ring-giving.
      So the son of Ecgtheow showed himself brave,

---

[1] *the aged Scylding* It is not clear whether this is Hrothgar or not, or how many storytellers and singers are at this banquet.

[2] *[battle-]hall* A word is missing; other editors and translators supply different words, such as *grund* or "earth."

[3] *Heorogar the king* Eldest brother of Hrothgar.

renowned for battles and noble deeds,
pursued honor, by no means slew, drunken,
180   his hearth-companions; he had no savage heart,
but the great gift which God had given him,
the greatest might of all mankind, he held,
brave in battle. He had been long despised,
as the sons of the Geats considered him no good,
185   nor did the lord of the Weders wish to bestow
many good things upon him on the meadbenches,
for they assumed that he was slothful,
a cowardly nobleman. Reversal came
to the glorious man for all his griefs.
190   The protector of earls, battle-proud king,
ordered the heirloom of Hrethel[1] brought in,
adorned with gold; among the Geats there was
no finer treasure in the form of a sword.
He laid the sword in Beowulf's lap,
195   and gave him seven thousand hides of land,[2]
a hall and a princely throne. Both of them held
inherited land in that nation, a home
and native rights, but the wider rule
was reserved to the one who was higher in rank.
200   Then it came to pass amid the crash of battle
in later days, after Hygelac lay dead,
and for Heardred[3] the swords of battle held
deadly slaughter under the shield-wall,
when the Battle-Scylfings sought him out,
205   those hardy soldiers, and savagely struck down
the nephew of Hereric[4] in his victorious nation—
then came the broad kingdom
into Beowulf's hands; he held it well
for fifty winters—he was then a wise king,
210   old guardian of his homeland—until
in the dark nights a dragon began his reign,
who guarded his hoard in the high heaths
and the steep stone barrows; the path below
lay unknown to men. Some sort of man
215   went inside there, found his way to

---

1 *Hrethel* Father of Hygelac.

2 *hides* Units of land, originally the amount of land which could support a peasant and his family; its actual size varied from one region to another. Seven thousand hides is by any measure a very generous area.

3 *Heardred* Son of Hygelac.

4 *nephew of Hereric* I.e., Heardred.

the heathen hoard—his hand …[5]
inlaid with jewels. He[6] got no profit there,
though he had been trapped in his sleep
by a thief's trickery: the whole nation knew,
2220 and all the people around them, that he was enraged.

32

Not for his own sake did he who sorely harmed him
break into that worm-hoard,[7] or by his own will,
but in sad desperation some sort of [slave][8]
of a warrior's son fled the savage lash,
2225 the servitude of a house, and slipped in there,
a man beset by sins. Soon he gazed around
and felt the terror from that evil spirit;
yet …
       …made…
2230   … when the terror seized him
he snatched a jeweled cup.[9]
              There were many such
antique riches in that earth-hall,
for in ancient days an unknown man
had thought to hide them carefully there,
2235 the rich legacy of a noble race,
precious treasures. In earlier times
death had seized them all, and he who still survived
alone from that nation's army lingered there,
a mournful sentry, expected the same,
2240 that he might enjoy those ancient treasures
for just a little while. A waiting barrow
stood in an open field near the ocean waves,
new on the cape, safe with crafty narrow entrances;
he bore within the noble wealth,
2245 the plated gold, that guardian of rings,
a share worthy of a hoard, and spoke few words:
    "Hold now, o thou earth, for heroes cannot,

---

5 The manuscript is damaged here and some text is unreadable. Among many conjectural restorations one thing is clear—a cup is taken from the dragon's hoard.

6 *He* The thief; "he" in the following line refers to the dragon. These lines are nearly illegible and other readings have been proposed.

7 *worm-hoard* Dragon's treasure.

8 *slave* The word is illegible in the manuscript; the translation follows most editions.

9 *yet … cup* The manuscript is unreadable at this point.

the wealth of men—lo, from you long ago
those good ones first obtained it! Death in war
2250 and awful deadly harm have swept away
all of my people who have passed from life,
and left the joyful hall. Now have I none
to bear the sword or burnish the bright cup,
the precious vessel—all that host has fled.
2255 Now must the hardened helm of hammered gold
be stripped of all its trim; the stewards sleep
who should have tended to this battle-mask.
So too this warrior's coat, which waited once
the bite of iron over the crack of boards,
2260 molders like its owner. The coat of mail
cannot travel widely with the war-chief,
beside the heroes. Harp-joy have I none,
no happy song; nor does the well-schooled hawk
soar high throughout the hall, nor the swift horse
2265 stamp in the courtyards. Savage butchery
has sent forth many of the race of men!"

So, grieving, he mourned his sorrow,
alone after all. Unhappy sped
both days and nights, until the flood of death
2270 broke upon his heart. An old beast of the dawn
found that shining hoard standing open—
he who, burning, seeks the barrows,
a fierce and naked dragon, who flies by night
in a pillar of fire; people on earth
2275 fear him greatly. It is his nature to find
a hoard in the earth, where, ancient and proud,
he guards heathen gold, though it does him no good.[1]

Three hundred winters that threat to the people
held in the ground his great treasury,
2280 wondrously powerful, until one man
made him boil with fury; he[2] bore to his liege-lord
the plated cup, begged for peace
from his lord. Then the hoard was looted,
the hoard of rings fewer, a favor was granted
2285 the forlorn man; for the first time
his lord looked on that ancient work of men.

When the dragon stirred, strife was renewed;
he slithered along the stones, stark-hearted he found
his enemy's footprint—he had stepped too far

2290 in his stealthy skill, too close to the serpent's head.
Thus can an undoomed man easily survive
wrack and ruin, if he holds to the Ruler's
grace and protection![3] The hoard-guardian
searched along the ground, greedy to find
2295 the man who had sorely harmed him while he slept;
hot, half-mad, he kept circling his cave
all around the outside, but no one was there
in that wilderness to welcome his warfare
and the business of battle. Soon he returned to his barrow,
2300 sought his treasure; he soon discovered
that some man had disturbed his gold,
his great wealth. The hoard-guardian waited
impatiently until evening came;
the barrow's shepherd was swollen with rage,
2305 the loathsome foe would repay with fire
his precious drinking-cup. Then day was departed
to the delight of that worm; he did not linger
on the barrow wall, but took off burning
in a burst of flames. The beginning was terror
2310 to the people on land, and to their ring-giving lord
the ending soon would be sore indeed.

33

Then that strange visitor began to spew flames
and burn the bright courts; his burning gleams
struck horror in men. That hostile flier
2315 would leave nothing alive.
The worm's warfare was widely seen,
his ferocious hostility, near and far,
how the destroyer hated and harmed
the Geatish people, then hastened to his hoard,
2320 his dark and hidden hall, before the break of day.
He had surrounded the people of that region with fire,
flames and cinders; he took shelter in his barrow,
his walls and warfare—but that trust failed him.

To Beowulf the news was quickly brought
2325 of that horror—that his own home,
best of buildings, had burned in waves of fire,
the gift-throne of the Geats. To the good man that was
painful in spirit, greatest of sorrows;
the wise one believed he had bitterly offended
2330 the Ruler of all, the eternal Lord,

---

[1] The association of dragons and hoarded treasure is ancient and proverbial.

[2] *he* I.e., the thief.

[3] This is the narrator's version of Beowulf's comment at lines 572–73.

against the old law; his breast within groaned
with dark thoughts—that was not his custom.
The fire-dragon had found the stronghold of that folk,
that fortress, and had razed it with flames
2335 entirely and from without; for that the war-king,
prince of the Weders, devised revenge.
Then the lord of men bade them make,
protector of warriors, a wondrous war-shield,
all covered with iron; he understood well
2340 that wood from the forest would not help him,
linden against flames. The long-good nobleman
had to endure the end of his loaned days,
this world's life—and so did the worm,
though he had held for so long his hoarded wealth.

2345   Then that prince of rings scorned to seek out
the far-flung flier with his full force of men,
a large army; he did not dread that attack,
nor did he worry much about the dragon's warfare,
his strength or valor, because he had survived
2350 many battles, barely escaping alive
in the crash of war, after he had cleansed,
triumphant hero, the hall of Hrothgar,
and at battle crushed Grendel and his kin,
that loathsome race.

        It was not the least
2355 of hand-to-hand combats when Hygelac was slain,
when the king of the Geats, in the chaos of battle,
the lord of his people, in the land of the Frisians,
the son of Hrethel, died sword-drunk,
beaten by blades. Beowulf escaped from there
2360 through his own strength, took a long swim;
he had in his arms the battle-armor
of thirty men, when he climbed to the cliffs.
By no means did the Hetware[1] need to exult
in that fight, when they marched on foot to him,
2365 bore their linden shields; few came back
from that brave soldier to seek their homes.
The son of Ecgtheow crossed the vast sea,
wretched, solitary, returned to his people,
where Hygd offered him the hoard and kingdom,
2370 rings and royal throne; she did not trust
that her son could hold the ancestral seat
against foreign hosts, now that Hygelac was dead.
But despite their misery, by no means

could they prevail upon that prince at all
2375 that he should become lord over Heardred,
or choose to rule the kingdom.
Yet he upheld him[2] in the folk with friendly counsel,
good will and honors, until he was older,
and ruled the Weder-Geats.

                Wretched exiles,
2380 the sons of Ohthere,[3] sought him out across the seas;
they had rebelled against the Scylfings' ruler,[4]
the best of all the sea-kings
who dispensed treasure in the Swedish lands,
a famous king. That cost him[5] his life:
2385 for his hospitality he took a mortal hurt
with the stroke of a sword, that son of Hygelac;
and the son of Ongentheow afterwards went
to seek out his home, once Heardred lay dead,
and let Beowulf hold the high throne
2390 and rule the Geats—that was a good king.

34

In later days he[6] did not forget
that prince's fall, and befriended Eadgils
the wretched exile; across the open sea
he gave support to the son of Ohthere
2395 with warriors and weapons. He[7] wreaked his revenge
with cold sad journeys, and took the king's life.
    And so the son of Ecgtheow had survived
every struggle, every terrible onslaught,
with brave deeds, until that one day
2400 when he had to take his stand against the serpent.

---

[2] *upheld him*   Beowulf upheld Heardred, as champion and in effect a kind of regent.

[3] *sons of Ohthere*   I.e., Eanmund and Eadgils.

[4] *Scylfing's ruler*   Onela, son of Ongentheow. Ohthere had succeeded his father Ongentheow, but after his death his brother Onela apparently seized the throne and drove the two young men Eanmund and Eadgils into exile. They take refuge at the Geatish court, for which Heardred is attacked and killed by Onela. Later Eanmund is killed by Weohstan (see section 36 below) but Eadgils, with the help of Beowulf, becomes king (section 34).

[5] *him*   I.e., Heardred.

[6] *he*   I.e., Beowulf, whose revenge for the death of his lord Heardred takes a curiously indirect form—he supports Eadgils' return to Sweden, where Onela is killed.

[7] *He*   I.e., Eadgils.

---

[1] *Hetware*   A Frankish tribe apparently on the side of the Frisians.

Grim and enraged, the lord of the Geats
took a dozen men[1] to seek out the dragon;
he had found out by then how the feud arose,
the baleful violence; the precious vessel
2405 had come to him through the thief's hands.
He was the thirteenth man among that troop,
who had brought about the beginning of that strife,
a sad-minded captive—wretched and despised
he led the way to that plain. He went against his will
2410 to where he alone knew the earth-hall stood,
an underground cave near the crashing waves,
the surging sea; inside it was full
of gems and metal bands. A monstrous guardian,
eager for combat, kept his gold treasures
2415 ancient under the ground; getting them
was no easy bargain for any man.

     The battle-hardened king sat down on the cape,
then wished good health to his hearth-companions,
the gold-friend of the Geats. His heart was grieving,
2420 restless and ripe for death—the doom was
       immeasurably near
that was coming to meet that old man,
seek his soul's treasure, split asunder
his life and his body; not for long was
the spirit of that noble king enclosed in its flesh.
2425   Beowulf spoke, the son of Ecgtheow:
"In my youth I survived many storms of battle,
times of strife—I still remember them all.
I was seven years old when the prince of treasures,
friend to his people, took me from my father;[2]
2430 Hrethel the king held me and kept me,
gave me gems and feasts, remembered our kinship.
I was no more hated to him while he lived
— a man in his stronghold—than any of his sons,
Herebeald and Hæthcyn and my own Hygelac.
2435 For the eldest,[3] undeservedly,
a death-bed was made by the deeds of a kinsman,
after Hæthcyn with his horn bow
struck down his own dear lord with an arrow—
he missed his mark and murdered his kinsman,

2440 one brother to the other with a bloody shaft.
That was a fight beyond settling, a sinful crime,
shattering the heart; yet it had to be
that a nobleman lost his life unavenged.
     "So it is sad for an old man
2445 to live to see his young son
ride on the gallows[4]—then let him recount a story,
a sorry song, when his son hangs
of comfort only to the ravens, and he cannot,
though old and wise, offer him any help.
2450 Each and every morning calls to mind
his son's passing away; he will not care
to wait for any other heir or offspring
in his fortress, when the first one has
tasted evil deeds and fell death.
2455 He looks sorrowfully on his son's dwelling,
the deserted wine-hall, the windswept home,
bereft of joy—the riders sleep,
heroes in their graves; there is no harp-music,
no laughter in the court, as there had been long before.

35

2460 "He takes to his couch and keens a lament
all alone for his lost one; all too vast to him
seem the fields and townships.
          So the protector of the Weders[5]
bore surging in his breast heartfelt sorrows
for Herebeald. He could not in any way
2465 make amends for the feud with his murderer,
but neither could he hate that warrior
for his hostile deeds, though he was not dear to him.
Then with the sorrow which befell him too sorely,
he gave up man's joys, chose God's light;[6]
2470 he left to his children his land and strongholds
     —as a blessed man does—when he departed this life.

---

[4] It is usually suggested that this is a kind of epic simile, comparing Hrethel's grief over his son's death—a death beyond the scope of vengeance—to the grief of a criminal's father, who cannot claim compensation for the execution of his son. Mitchell and Robinson suggest that this is rather a reference to a pagan practice, part of the cult of Odin (also known as "Woden"), in which the body of a man who did not die in battle was ritually hanged on a gallows. If this interpretation is correct, the "old man" is Hrethel himself.

[5] *the protector of … Weders* I.e., Hrethel.

[6] *God's light* I.e., he died.

---

[1] *a dozen men* Literally "one of twelve"—Beowulf, Wiglaf, and ten others. The thief who leads the way is the thirteenth man.

[2] *took me … father* Beowulf was brought up as a noble foster-child in the royal court.

[3] *eldest* I.e., Herebeald.

Then there was strife between Swedes and Geats,[1]
a quarrel in common across the wide water,
hard hostility after Hrethel died,
until the sons of Ongentheow[2]
were bold and warlike, wanted no peace
over the sea, but around the Hill of Sorrows[3]
they carried out a terrible and devious campaign.
My friends and kinsmen got revenge for those
feuds and evils[4]—as it is said—
although one of them paid for it with his own life,
a hard bargain; that battle was fatal
for Hæthcyn, king of the Geats.
Then, I've heard, the next morning, one kinsman
avenged the other with the sword's edge,[5]
when Ongentheow attacked Eofor;
his battle-helm slipped, the old Scylfing
staggered, corpse-pale; Eofor's hand recalled
his fill of feuds, and did not withhold the fatal blow.
          "I have paid in battle for the precious treasures
he[6] gave me, as was granted to me,
with a gleaming sword; he gave me land,
a joyous home. He had no need
to have to go seeking among the Gifthas
or the Spear-Danes or the Swedes
for a worse warrior, or buy one with his wealth;
always on foot I would go before him,
alone in the front line—and all my life
I will wage war, while this sword endures,
which before and since has served me well,
since I slew Dæghrefn, champion of the Hugas,[7]
with my bare hands in front of the whole army.
He could not carry off to the Frisian king

that battle-armor and that breast-adornment,[8]
but there in the field the standard-bearer fell,
a nobleman in his strength; no blade was his slayer,
but my warlike grip broke his beating heart,
cracked his bone-house. Now the blade's edge,
hand and hard sword, shall fight for the hoard."
          Beowulf spoke, said boasting words
for the very last time: "I have survived
many battles in my youth; I will yet
seek out, an old folk-guardian, a feud
and do a glorious deed, if only that evildoer
will come out to me from his earth-hall."
Then for the last time he saluted
each of the soldiers, his own dear comrades,
brave in their helmets: "I would not bear a sword
or weapon to this serpent, if I knew any other way
I could grapple with this great beast[9]
after my boast, as I once did with Grendel;
but I expect the heat of battle-flames there,
steam and venom; therefore shield and byrnie
will I have on me. From the hoard's warden
I will not flee a single foot, but for us
it shall be at the wall as *wyrd* decrees,
the Ruler of every man. My mind is firm—
I will forgo boasting against this flying foe.
Wait on the barrow, protected in your byrnies,
men in war-gear, to see which of the two of us
after the bloody onslaught can better
bear his wounds. It is not your way,
nor proper for any man except me alone,
that he should match his strength against this monster,
do heroic deeds. With daring I shall
get that gold—or grim death
and fatal battle will bear away your lord!"
          Then that brave challenger stood up by his shield,
stern under his helmet, bore his battle-shirt
under the stone-cliffs, trusted the strength
of a single man—such is not the coward's way.
He saw then by the wall—he who had survived
a great many conflicts, good in manly virtues,
the crash of battles when footsoldiers clashed—
stone arches standing, and a stream

---

[1] *strife … Geats* This refers to a time a generation before the conflicts of Heardred, Eanmund and Eadgils; the Swedish-Geatish feud is longstanding.

[2] *sons of Ongentheow* I.e., Ohthere and Onela.

[3] *Hill of Sorrows* A hill in Geatland, in OE *Hreosnabeorh*.

[4] The scene of this revenge is apparently Sweden, in a place called "Ravenswood"; this battle is described again in sections 40 and 41.

[5] *one kinsman … sword's edge* Hygelac avenged the death of Hæthcyn on his slayer Ongentheow—not directly but through his man Eofor.

[6] *he* I.e., Hygelac.

[7] *Hugas* Frankish tribes allied to the Frisians; the battle in question may be the same as Hygelac's fatal raid.

[8] *breast-adornment* Possibly the same as the necklace described in 1195–1214.

[9] *great beast* The OE word *æglæcan* is here used of the dragon.

shooting forth from the barrow; its surge
was hot with deadly flames, and near the hoard
he could not survive for very long
unburnt, for the dragon's flaming breath.
2550 Enraged, the ruler of the Weder-Geats
let a word burst forth from his breast,
shouted starkly; the sound entered
and resounded battle-clear under the gray stone.
Hate was stirred up—the hoard-warden recognized
2555 the voice of a man; there was no more time
to sue for peace. First there issued
the steam of that great creature out of the stone,
hot battle-sweat; the earth bellowed.
The warrior in the barrow turned his shield-board
2560 against the grisly stranger, lord of the Geats,
when the writhing beast's heart was roused
to seek combat. The good war-king
had drawn his sword, its edges undulled,
an ancient heirloom; each of the two
2565 hostile ones was horrified by the other.
He stood stouthearted behind his steep shield,
that friend and commander, when the worm coiled itself
swiftly together—he waited in his war-gear.
Then coiled, burning, slithering he came,
2570 rushing to his fate. The shield defended well
the life and limb of the famous lord
for less time than he might have liked;
there on that day for the first time
he faced the outcome,[1] and *wyrd* did not
2575 grant victory in battle. The lord of the Geats
raised his hand, struck that mottled horror
with his ancient sword, so that that edge failed
bright against the bony scales, bit less strongly
than the king of that nation needed it to do,
2580 hard-pressed in battle. Then the barrow-warden
was more savage after that battle-stroke,
and spit out gruesome fire; wide sprang
the battle-flames. The gold-friend of the Geats
did not boast of his glorious victories; his bare sword
2585 failed at need, as it should never have done,
that ancient good iron. It was no easy journey
for the famous son of Ecgtheow to agree
to give up his ground in that place;

he was forced, against his will, to find
2590 a place of rest elsewhere—just as every one of us
must give up these loaned days.
                              It was not long
until those two great creatures[2] came together again.
The hoard-guard took heart, his breast swelled with breath
once again; he[3] suffered anguish,
2595 trapped by flames, he who had once ruled his folk.
His comrades, hand-chosen, sons of noblemen,
did not take their stand in a troop around him,
with warlike valor—they fled to the woods
and saved their lives. The spirit rose up in sorrow
2600 in the heart of one of them; nothing can overrule
kinship at all, in one who thinks well.

36

He was called Wiglaf, Weohstan's son,
a worthy shield-warrior, a prince of the Scylfings,[4]
kinsman of Ælfhere. He saw his liege-lord
2605 suffer heat under his war-helmet;
he recalled the honors he had received from him,
the wealthy homestead of the Waegmundings,
every folk-right that his father had possessed;
he could not hold back—his hand seized
2610 the pale linden shield, and he drew his old sword.
It was known among men as the heirloom of Eanmund,
son of Ohthere; that friendless exile
was slain in battle with the edge of a sword
by Weohstan, who brought to his kinsman
2615 the burnished helmet, the ringed byrnie,
the old giant-work sword; Onela gave to him
the war-equipment of his young kinsman,
the shining armor—he never spoke of a feud,
though he had slain his brother's son.[5]

---

[1] *for the first time ... outcome*   Or "if he could have controlled the outcome for the first time."

[2] *creatures*   OE *æglæcan* again, here referring to Beowulf and the dragon together.

[3] *he*   I.e., Beowulf.

[4] *a prince of the Scylfings*   Wiglaf's nationality is in question—he is both a Swede and a Wægmunding (like Beowulf; see lines 2813–14). His father fought on the Swedish side in their feuds with the Geats. Tribal allegiance is more fluid than modern nationality.

[5] *he never ... brother's son*   Onela never spoke of a feud, though Weohstan had killed Onela's brother's son, for he wished him dead. As elsewhere in the poem, a sword is the reminder of both victory and vengeance.

He[1] kept that war-gear for a great many years,
the blade and byrnie, until his boy could
perform brave deeds like his father before him;
he gave him among the Geats that battle-gear,
every piece of it, when, old, he departed this life
2625 and went forth. That was the first time
that the young warrior had to weather
the storm of battle beside his noble lord.
His courage did not melt, nor did his kinsman's legacy
weaken in war; the worm discovered that,
2630 when they began to meet together.
        Wiglaf spoke, said to his companions
many true words—he was mournful at heart—
"I remember the time that we took mead together,
when we made promises to our prince
2635 in the beer-hall—he gave us these rings—
that we would pay him back for this battle-gear,
these helmets and hard swords, if such a need
as this ever befell him. For this he chose us from the army
for this adventure by his own will,
2640 thought us worthy of glory, and gave me these treasures—
for this he considered us good spear-warriors,
proud helmet-wearers, even though our prince,
shepherd of his people, intended to perform
this act of courage all alone,
2645 because he has gained the most glory among men,
reckless heroic deeds. Now the day has come
that our noble lord has need of the support
of good warriors; let us go to it,
help our warlord, despite the heat,
2650 grim fire-terror. God knows for my part
that I would much prefer that the flames should enfold
my body alongside my gold-giving lord.
It seems wrong to me that we should bear shields
back to our land, unless we first might
2655 finish off this foe, defend the life
of the prince of the Weders. I know full well
that he does not deserve to suffer
this torment all alone among the Geatish troop,
or fall in the struggle; now sword and helmet,
2660 byrnie and battle-dress, shall be ours together!"
        He hurried through the deadly fumes, bore his
                helmet
to the aid of his lord, spoke little:

"Dear Beowulf, do all well,
as in your youth you said you would,
2665 that you would never let in your whole life
your fame decline; now firm in deeds,
single-minded nobleman, with all your strength
you must protect your life—I will support you."
After these words the worm came angrily,
2670 terrible vicious creature, a second time,
scorched with surging flames, seeking out his enemies,
the hated men. The hot flames rolled in waves,
burned the shield to its rim; the byrnie was not
of any use to the young soldier,
2675 but he showed his courage under his kinsman's shield,
the young warrior, when his own was
charred to cinders. Still the battle-king
remembered his glory, and with his mighty strength
swung his warblade with savage force,
2680 so that it stuck in the skull. Nægling shattered—
the sword of Beowulf weakened at battle,
ancient and gray. It was not granted to him
that iron-edged weapons might ever
help him in battle; his hand was too strong,
2685 he who, I am told, overtaxed every blade
with his mighty blows, when he bore to battle
a wound-hardened[2] weapon—it was no help to him at all.
        Then that threat to the people for a third time,
fierce fire-dragon, remembering his feud,
2690 rushed on the brave man, hot and bloodthirsty,
when he saw the chance, seized him by the neck
in his bitter jaws; he was bloodied
by his mortal wounds—blood gushed in waves.

37

Then, I have heard, in his king's hour of need
2695 the earl[3] beside him showed his bravery,
the noble skill which was his nature.
He did not heed that head when he helped his kinsman;
that brave man's hand was burned, so that
he struck that savage foe a little lower down,
2700 the soldier in armor, so that his sword plunged in
bejeweled and bloody, so that the fire began
to subside afterwards. The king himself

---

[1] *he* I.e., Weohstan.

[2] *wound-hardened* Or "wondrously hard"; the OE text is unclear.

[3] *earl* I.e., Wiglaf.

still had his wits, drew the war-dagger,
bitter and battle-sharp, that he wore in his byrnie;
2705 the protector of the Weders carved through the
    worm's midsection.
They felled their foe—their force took his life—
and they both together had brought him down,
the two noble kinsmen; a thane at need,
as a man should be! But that, for the prince, was
2710 his last work of victory, by his own will,
of worldly adventures.
                When the wound
which the earth-dragon had worked on him
began to burn and swell, he soon realized
that in his breast, with an evil force,
2715 a poison welled; then the nobleman went,
still wise in thought, so that he sat
on a seat by the wall. On that work of giants he gazed,
saw how stone arches and sturdy pillars
held up the inside of that ancient earth-hall.
2720 Then with his hands the thane, immeasurably good,
bathed with water his beloved lord,
the great prince, spattered with gore,
sated with battle, and unstrapped his helmet.
Beowulf spoke—despite his wound,
2725 that deadly cut; he knew clearly
that his allotted life had run out,
and his joys in the earth; all gone
was his portion of days, death immeasurably near:
    "Now I should wish to give my war-gear
2730 to my son, if there had been such,
flesh of my flesh, if fate had granted me
any heir. I held this people
fifty winters; there was no folk-king,
not any of the neighboring tribes,
2735 who dared to face me with hostile forces
or threaten fear. The decrees of fate
I awaited on earth, held well what was mine;
I sought no intrigues, nor swore many
false or wrongful oaths. For all that I may
2740 have joy, though sick with mortal wounds,
because the Ruler of men need not reproach me
with the murder of kinsmen, when my life
quits my body. Now go quickly
to look at the hoard under the hoary stone,
2745 dear Wiglaf, now that the worm lies dead,

sleeps with his wounds, stripped of his treasure.
Hurry, so I might witness that ancient wealth,
those golden goods, might eagerly gaze on
the bright precious gems, and I might more gently,
2750 for that great wealth, give up my
life and lordship, which I have held so long."

<h2 style="text-align:center">38</h2>

Then swiftly, I have heard, the son of Weohstan
after these words obeyed his lord,
sick with wounds, wore his ring-net,
2755 the woven battle-shirt, under the barrow's roof.
As he went by the seat he saw there, triumphant,
the brave young warrior, many bright jewels,
glittering gold scattered on the ground,
wonders on the walls, and the lair of that worm,
2760 the old dawn-flier—flagons standing,
ancient serving-vessels without a steward,
their trappings all moldered; there was many a helmet
old and rusty, a number of arm-bands
with twisted ornaments.—Treasure may easily,
2765 gold in the ground, give the slip
to any one of us: let him hide it who will![1]—
Likewise he saw an ensign, all golden,
hanging high over the hoard, greatest hand-work,
linked together with skill; light gleamed from it
2770 so that he could see the cave's floor,
survey those strange artifacts. There was no sign
of the serpent there—a sword had finished him off.
Then the hoard in that barrow, as I've heard, was looted,
ancient work of giants, by one man alone;
2775 he piled in his arms cups and plates,
whatever he wanted; he took the ensign too,
brightest of beacons. His aged lord's blade
—its edge was iron— had earlier harmed
the one who was protector of those treasures
2780 for such a long time, who bore his fiery terror
flaming before the hoard, seething fiercely
in the darkest night, until he died a bloody death.
    The messenger rushed out, eager to return,
burdened with treasures; he was burning to know

---

[1] *give the slip ... who will* Or "can get the better of any man—
heed [these words] who will!" The OE is uncertain; the translation
follows Mitchell and Robinson.

2785 whether, stout-hearted, he would find still alive
the prince of the Weders, weakened by wounds,
in the place where he had left him on that plain.
Then with the treasures he found the famous prince,
his own lord, his life at an end,
2790 all bloody; he began once more
to sprinkle water on him, until the point of a word
escaped from his breast. [...]¹
Old, full of grief, he looked on the gold:

"For all these treasures, I offer thanks
2795 with these words to the eternal Lord,
King of Glory, for what I gaze upon here,
that I was able to acquire such wealth
for my people before my death-day.
Now that I have sold my old lifespan
2800 for this hoard of treasures, they will attend²
to the needs of the people; I can stay no longer.
The brave in battle will bid a tomb be built
shining over my pyre on the cliffs by the sea;
it will be as a monument to my people
2805 and tower high on Whale's Head,
so that seafarers afterwards shall call it
'Beowulf's Barrow,' when their broad ships
drive from afar over the darkness of the flood."

The boldminded nobleman took from his neck
2810 a golden circlet, and gave it to the thane,
the young spear-carrier, and the gold-covered helmet,
ring and byrnie, bid him use them well:
"You are the last survivor of our lineage,
the Wægmundings; fate has swept away
2815 all of my kinsmen, earls in their courage,
to their final destiny; I must follow them."
That was the last word of the old warrior,
his final thought before he chose the fire,
the hot surging flames—from his breast flew
2820 his soul to seek the judgment of the righteous.³

---

¹ Half a line (or more?) is missing from the manuscript at this point.

² *they will attend* Usually translated "you [Wiglaf] will attend ...";
the OE verb may be indicative or imperative, but it is unambigu-
ously plural, and the imperative plural is not used elsewhere in the
poem to address a single person.

³ *the judgment of the righteous* Literally "the *dom* (fame) of the
truth-fast," an ambiguous pronouncement. It is not clear whether
this means that Beowulf's soul will receive the sort of judgment that
a righteous soul ought to receive (and so go to Heaven), or that it
will be judged by those "fast in truth" (and so go to Hell as an

Then it came to pass with piercing sorrow
that the young warrior had to watch
his most precious lord fare so pitifully,
his life at an end. Likewise his slayer lay dead,
2825 the awesome earth-dragon deprived of his life,
overcome by force. The coiled serpent
could no longer rule his hoard of rings—
edges of iron did away with him,
the hard, battle-scarred shards of the smithy,
2830 so that the wide-flier, stilled by his wounds,
toppled to the ground near his treasure-house.
No more soaring about in the skies
at midnight, preening in his precious treasures,
showing his face—he fell to earth
2835 through that war-commander's handiwork.
Indeed, few men on earth, no matter how strong,
could succeed at that, as I have heard tell,
though he were daring in every deed,
could rush against the reek of that venomous foe,
2840 or rifle through that ring-hall with his hands,
if he should find a waking warden
waiting in that barrow. Beowulf's share
of that royal treasure was repaid by his death—
each of them had journeyed to the end
2845 of this loaned life.

It was not long before
the men late for battle left the woods,
ten of those weak traitors all together
who had not dared to hoist their spears
when their lord of men needed them most;
2850 now shamefaced, they carried their shields
and battledress to where the old man lay dead,
to stare at Wiglaf. He sat exhausted,
a foot-soldier at his lord's shoulder,
tried to rouse him with water—but it was no use.
2855 He could not, no matter how much he wanted,
keep the life in the body of his captain,
nor change any bit of the Ruler's decree;
the judgment of God would guide the deeds
of every man, as it still does today.
2860 Then it was easy to get a grim answer
from that youth to those who gave up courage.

---

unbaptized pagan).

Wiglaf spoke, son of Weohstan,
looked, sad-hearted, on those unloved:
2865   "He can say—o yes—who would speak the truth
that the liege-lord who gave you those gifts of treasures,
the military gear that you stand in there,
when on the ale-benches he often handed out
helmets and byrnies to the hall-sitters,
a lord to his followers, whatever he could find
2870   finest anywhere, far or near—
that all that battle-dress he absolutely
and entirely threw away, when war beset him.
Our nation's king had no need to boast
of his comrades-in-arms! But the Ruler of victories
2875   allowed that he, alone with his blade,
might avenge himself when he needed your valor.
Only a little life-protection could I offer
him in battle, but began nevertheless
to support my kinsman beyond my own strength;
2880   ever the worse was the deadly enemy
when I struck with my sword, a fire less severe
surging from his head. Too few supporters
thronged around our prince in his great peril.
Now the getting of treasure, the giving of swords,
2885   and all the happy joys of your homeland
shall end for your race; empty-handed
will go every man among your tribe,
deprived of his land-rights, when noblemen learn
far and wide of your flight,
2890   your inglorious deed. Death is better
for any earl than a life of dishonor!"

40

He bade that the battle-work be announced to
            the camp
up by the cliff's edge, where that troop of earls,
shield-bearers, sat sad-minded
2895   all the long morning, expecting either
the final day of their dear lord
or his homecoming. He who rode up to the cape
was not at all silent with his new tidings,
but he spoke truly in the hearing of all:
2900   "Now is the joy-giver of the Geatish people,
the lord of the Weders, laid on his deathbed,
holding a place of slaughter by the serpent's deeds;
beside him lies his life-enemy,

sick with knife-slashes; he could not with his sword
2905   make in the monstrous beast
any kind of wound. Wiglaf sits,
Weohstan's offspring, over Beowulf,
one earl over the other, now dead;
he holds with desperate heart the watch
2910   over friend and foe.
                    Now this folk may expect
a time of trouble, when this is manifest
to the Franks and Frisians, and the fall of our king
becomes widespread news. The strife was begun
hard with the Hugas, after Hygelac came
2915   travelling with his ships to the shores of Frisia,
where the Hetware attacked him in war,
advanced with valor and a vaster force,
so that the warrior in his byrnie had to bow down,
and fell amid the infantry; not at all did that lord
2920   give treasure to his troops. Ever after that
the Merovingians have not shown mercy to us.
    "Nor do I expect any peace or truce
from the Swedish nation, but it has been well-known
that Ongentheow ended the life
2925   of Hæthcyn, son of Hrethel, in Ravenswood,
when in their arrogant pride the Geatish people
first sought out the Battle-Scylfings.
Immediately the ancient father of Ohthere,
old and terrifying, returned the attack—
2930   the old warrior cut down the sea-captain,[1]
rescued his wife, bereft of her gold,
Onela's mother and Ohthere's;
and then hunted down his deadly enemies
until they escaped, with some difficulty,
2935   bereft of their lord, into Ravenswood.
With his standing army he besieged those sword-leavings,
weary, wounded; he kept threatening woe
to that wretched troop the whole night through—
in the morning, he said, with the edge of his sword
2940   he would gut them, and leave some on the gallows-tree
as sport for birds. But for those sad-hearted men
solace came along with the sunrise,
after they heard Hygelac's horn and trumpet
sounding the charge, when the good man came
2945   following the trail of that people's troop.

---

[1]   *old warrior ... sea-captain*   Ongentheow killed Hæthcyn. Hygelac
is not present at this battle, but arrives later.

41

"The bloody swath of the Swedes and Geats,
the slaughter of men, was easily seen,
how the folk had stirred up feud between them.
That good man[1] then departed, old, desperate,
2950 with a small band of kinsmen, sought his stronghold,
the earl Ongentheow turned farther away;
he had heard of proud Hygelac's prowess in battle,
his war-skill; he did not trust the resistance
he might muster against the seafarers' might
2955 to defend from the wave-borne warriors his treasure,
his women and children; he ran away from there,
old, into his fortress. Then the pursuit was offered
to the Swedish people, the standard of Hygelac
overran the place of refuge,
2960 after the Hrethlings thronged the enclosure.
There with the edge of a sword was Ongentheow,
old graybeard, brought to bay,
so that the king of that nation had to yield
to Eofor's will. Angrily he struck;
2965 Wulf the son of Wonred lashed at him with his weapon,
so that with his blow the blood sprang in streams
from under his hair. Yet the ancient Scylfing
was undaunted, and dealt back quickly
a worse exchange for that savage stroke,
2970 once the ruler of that people turned around.
The ready son of Wonred could not
give a stroke in return to the old soldier,
for he had cut through the helmet right on his head
so that he collapsed, covered in blood,
2975 fell to the ground—he was not yet fated to die,
but he recovered, though the cut hurt him.
The hardy thane of Hygelac[2] then let
his broad blade, as his brother lay there,
his ancient giant-made sword, shatter that gigantic helmet
2980 over the shield-wall; then the king stumbled,
shepherd of his people, mortally stricken.
    There were many there who bandaged his[3]
        kinsman,
quickly raised him up, when a way was clear for them,
so that they had control of that killing field.

---

[1] *good man* I.e., Ongentheow.

[2] *thane of Hygelac* I.e., Eofor, Wulf's brother.

[3] *his* I.e., Eofor's.

2985 Then one warrior plundered another,[4]
took from Ongentheow the iron byrnie,
his hard hilted sword and his helmet too,
and carried the old man's armor to Hygelac.
He[5] took that war-gear and promised him gifts
2990 among his people—and he kept that promise;
the king of the Geats repaid that carnage,
the offspring of Hrethel, when he made it home,
gave to Eofor and Wulf extravagant treasures,
gave them each lands and locked rings,
2995 worth a hundred thousand. Not a man in this world
    could
reproach those rewards, since they had won them
    with their deeds;
and to Eofor he gave his only daughter,
the pride of his home, as a pledge of his friendship.
    "That is the feud and the fierce enmity,
3000 savage hatred among men, that I expect now,
when the Swedish people seek us out
after they have learned that our lord
has perished, who had once protected
his hoard and kingdom against all hostility,
3005 after the fall of heroes, the valiant Scyldings,[6]
worked for the people's good, and what is more,
performed noble deeds. Now we must hurry
and look upon our people's king,
and go with him who gave us rings
3010 on the way to the pyre. No small part
of the hoard shall burn with that brave man,
but countless gold treasures, grimly purchased,
and rings, here at last with his own life
paid for; then the flames shall devour,
3015 the fire enfold—let no warrior wear
treasures for remembrance, nor no fair maiden
have a ring-ornament around her neck,
but sad in mind, stripped of gold, she must
walk a foreign path, not once but often,
3020 now that leader of our troop has laid aside laughter,

---

[4] *one ... another* Eofor plundered Ongentheow.

[5] *He* I.e., Hygelac.

[6] *Scyldings* The manuscript reading ("Scyldings" is a further object of "protected") is often emended to *Scylfingas*, i.e., Swedes, or *scildwigan*, "shield-warriors"; the present reading is that of Mitchell and Robinson. As it stands in the manuscript the Geatish herald is referring to Beowulf's earlier adventures against Grendel and his mother.

his mirth and joy. Thus many a cold morning
shall the spear be grasped in frozen fingers,
hefted by hands, nor shall the sound of the harp
rouse the warriors, but the dark raven,
3025 greedy for carrion, shall speak a great deal,
ask the eagle how he fared at his feast
when he plundered corpses with the wolf."[1]

    Thus that brave speaker was speaking
a most unlovely truth; he did not lie much
3030 in words or facts. The troop of warriors arose;
they went, unhappy, to the Cape of Eagles,
with welling tears to look at that wonder.
There on the sand they found the soulless body
of the one who gave them rings in earlier times
3035 laid out to rest; the last day
had come for the good man, when the war-king,
prince of the Weders, died a wondrous death.
But first they saw an even stranger creature,
a loathsome serpent lying on the plain
3040 directly across from him; grim with his colors
the fire-dragon was, and scorched with his flames.
He was fifty feet long, lying there
stretched out; once he had joy in the air
in the dark night, and then down he would go
3045 to seek his den, but now he was fast in death;
he had come to the end of his cave-dwelling.
Cups and vessels stood beside him,
plates lay there and precious swords,
eaten through with rust, as if in the bosom of the earth
3050 they had lain for a thousand winters;
all that inheritance was deeply enchanted,
the gold of the ancients was gripped in a spell
so that no man in the world would be able to touch
that ring-hall, unless God himself,
3055 the true King of Victories, Protector of men,
granted to whomever He wished to open the hoard,
to whatever person seemed proper to Him.[2]

Then it was plain that the journey did not profit
the one[3] who had wrongfully hidden under a wall
3060 that great treasure. The guardian had slain
that one and few others;[4] then that feud was
swiftly avenged. It is a wonder to say
where a valiant earl should meet the end
of his span of life, when he may no longer
3065 dwell in the meadhall, a man with his kinsmen.
So it was with Beowulf, when he sought the barrow's
    guardian
and a hostile fight; even he did not know
how his parting from life should come to pass,
since until doomsday mighty princes had deeply
3070 pronounced, when they placed it there,
that the man who plundered that place would be
harried by hostile demons, fast in hellish bonds,
grievously tortured, guilty of sins,
unless the Owner's grace had earlier
3075 more readily favored the one eager for gold.[5]
    Wiglaf spoke, son of Weohstan:
"Often many earls must suffer misery
through the will of one man, as we have now seen.
We could not persuade our dear prince,
3080 shepherd of a kingdom, with any counsel,
that he should not greet that gold-guardian,
let him lie there where he long had been,
inhabit the dwellings until the end of the world:
he held to his high destiny. The hoard is opened,
3085 grimly gotten; that fate was too great
which impelled the king of our people thither.
I was in there, and looked over it all,
the hall's ornaments, when a way was open to me;
by no means gently was a journey allowed
3090 in under that earth-wall. In eager haste I seized
in my hands a great mighty burden

---

[1] *the dark raven ... the wolf*   The eagle, wolf, and raven, the "beasts of battle," are a recurring motif in Old English poetry.

[2] *unless God himself ... proper to him*   The power of the pagan spell can be overruled by the will of the true God.

---

[3] *the one*   I.e., the dragon.

[4] *that one and few others*   Or "that one of a few," i.e., "a unique man" or "a man of rare greatness."

[5] *favored the one eager for gold*   The OE text is corrupt and the precise meaning of this passage is not certain; the present translation tries to incorporate several suggested interpretations. The general sense seems to be clear enough—the gold was cursed, and only God's special grace would enable anyone to remove it. What this implies about Beowulf's failure, and his moral status, is less clear.

of hoard-treasure, and bore it out hither
to my king. He was still conscious then,
thoughtful and alert; he spoke of many things,
3095 an old man in his sorrow, and ordered that I greet you;
he asked that you build a great high barrow
for your prince's deeds, in the place of his pyre,
mighty and glorious, since he was of men
the most worthy warrior throughout the wide world,
3100 while he could enjoy the wealth of a hall.
Let us now make haste for one more time
to see and seek out that store of cunning gems,
the wonder under the wall; I will direct you
so that you can inspect them up close,
3105 abundant rings and broad gold. Let the bier be ready,
quickly prepared, when we come out,
then let us bear our beloved lord,
that dear man, to where he must long
rest in the keeping of the Ruler."
3110   Then the son of Weohstan, brave battle-warrior,
let it be made known to many heroes
and householders that they should bring from afar
the wood for the pyre to that good one,[1]
the leader of his folk: "Now the flames must devour,
3115 the black blaze rise over the ruler of warriors,
who often awaited the showers of iron
when the storm of arrows hurled from bow-strings
shot over the wall, the shafts did their duty
swift on feather-wings, sent on the arrow-heads."
3120   Lo, then the wise son of Weohstan
summoned from that host some of the best
of the king's thanes, seven altogether;
he went, one of eight, under that evil roof;
one of the brave warriors bore in his hands
3125 a flaming torch, and went before them.
It was not chosen by lots who should loot that hoard,[2]
once the men saw it sitting in the hall,
every part of it unprotected,
lying there wasting; there was little lament
3130 that they should have to hurry out with
the precious treasures. They also pushed the dragon,
the worm, over the cliff-wall, let the waves take him,
the flood embrace the guard of that finery;

then the twisted gold, an uncountable treasure,
3135 was loaded in a wagon, and the noble one was carried,
the gray-haired warrior, to the Cape of Whales.

43

    The people of the Geats then prepared for him
a splendid pyre upon the earth,
hung with battle-shields and helmets
3140 and bright byrnies, as he had bidden;
there in the middle they laid the mighty prince,
the heroes lamenting their dear lord.
Then the warriors kindled there on the cliff
the greatest of funeral pyres; dark over the flames
3145 the woodsmoke rose, the roaring fire
mingled with weeping—the wind lay still—
until it had broken that bone-house
hot at the heart. With heavy spirits
they mourned their despair, the death of their lord;
3150 and a sorrowful song sang the Geatish woman,[3]
with hair bound up, for Beowulf the king,
with sad cares, earnestly said
that she dreaded the hard days ahead,
the times of slaughter, the host's terror,
3155 harm and captivity. Heaven swallowed the smoke.
    Then the Weder people wrought for him
a barrow on the headland; it was high and broad,
visible from afar to sea-voyagers,
and in ten days they built the beacon
3160 of that battle-brave one; the ashes of the flames
they enclosed with a wall, as worthily
as the most clever of men could devise it.
In the barrow they placed rings and bright jewels,
all the trappings that those reckless men
3165 had seized from the hoard before,
let the earth hold the treasures of earls,
gold in the ground, where it yet remains,
just as useless to men as it was before.
Then round the mound rode the battle-brave men,
3170 offspring of noblemen, twelve in all;
they wished to voice their cares and mourn their king,

---

[1] *that good one* I.e., the dead Beowulf.

[2] *It was not chosen ... hoard* I.e., everybody had a share; there was
enough for all.

[3] *Geatish woman* The manuscript is damaged throughout this
section and the readings in this passage are conjectural; it is not clear
who the "Geatish woman" is, though her advanced age is indicated
by her bound-up hair. Typically, in Germanic poetry, it is women
(and poets) who mourn.

utter sad songs and speak of that man;
they praised his lordship and his proud deeds,
judged well his prowess. As it is proper
3175   that one should praise his lord with words,
should love him in his heart when the fatal hour comes,
when he must from his body be led forth,
so the men of the Geats lamented

the fall of their prince, those hearth-companions;
3180   they said that he was of all the kings of the world
the mildest of men and the most gentle,
the kindest to his folk and the most eager for fame.

In Context

Glossary of Proper Names

Abel	slain by his brother **Cain**; the story is told in Genesis 4.1–16
Ælfhere	kinsman of **Wiglaf**
Æschere	a prominent Dane, advisor to **Hrothgar**; slain by Grendel's mother
Battle-Scyldings	see **Scyldings**
Battle-Scylfings	see **Scylfings**
Beanstan	father of **Breca**
Beowulf	(prologue) Danish king, son of **Scyld**
Breca	engaged in a youthful swimming contest with Beowulf
Bright-Danes	see **Danes**
Brondings	the people of **Breca**
Brosinga	makers of the magical necklace of Freya in Norse myth, to which a necklace in the story is compared
Cain	slayer of **Abel** in Genesis 4.1–16; father of the race of monsters
Dæghrefn	a warrior of the **Hugas** slain by Beowulf in hand-to-hand combat during Hygelac's ill-fated raid on **Frisia**
Danes	**Hrothgar's** people; the **Scyldings**; also called Bright-, Half-, Ring-, Spear-, East-, West-, North-, and South-Danes
Eadgils	son of **Ohthere**, brother of **Eanmund**
Eanmund	son of **Ohthere**, brother of **Eadgils**; slain by **Weohstan**
East-Danes	see **Danes**
Ecglaf	father of **Unferth**
Ecgtheow	father of Beowulf
Ecgwala	a Danish king; the "sons of Ecgwala" are the **Danes**
Eofor	a warrior of the **Geats**; brother of **Wulf**; slayer of **Ongentheow**
Eomer	son of **Offa**
Eormanric	king of the Ostrogoths
Eotens	unclear: perhaps the **Jutes**, perhaps the **Frisians**, perhaps "giants" (the literal meaning of the word) as a nickname for one group or the other
Finn	king of the **Frisians**, husband of **Hildeburh**; killed by **Hengest**
Finns	the people of Finland; the Lapps
Fitela	legendary companion, nephew (and son) of **Sigemund**
Folcwalda	father of **Finn**
Franks	a Germanic tribe; see **Hetware**, **Hugas**, **Merovingians**

Freawaru	daughter of **Hrothgar**, betrothed to **Ingeld**
Frisians	a Germanic tribe; **Finn**'s people
Froda	chief of the **Heathobards**, father of **Ingeld**
Garmund	father of **Offa**
Geats	**Hygelac**'s people and Beowulf's; a Germanic tribe; also called War-Geats, Hrethmen, Hrethlings, Weders
Gifthas	an East-Germanic tribe
Grendel	descendent of **Cain**; monstrous marauder of the **Danes**
Guthlaf	a Danish warrior, companion of **Hengest**
Hæreth	father of **Hygd**
Hæthcyn	Geatish prince, second son of **Hrethel**
Half-Danes	see **Danes**
Halga	Danish prince, younger brother of **Hrothgar**
Hama	legendary Goth; stole **Brosinga** necklace
Healfdene	king of the **Danes**, father of **Hrothgar**
Heardred	king of the **Geats**, son of **Hygelac**
Heathobards	**Ingeld**'s people; a Germanic tribe
Heatholaf	a **Wylfing** slain by **Ecgtheow**
Heathoream	a Scandinavian tribe; Norwegians, more or less
Helmings	the family of **Wealhtheow**
Hemming	kinsman of **Offa** and **Eomer**
Hengest	leader of the **Danes**; killed **Finn** in **Frisia**
Heorogar	Dane, eldest brother of **Hrothgar**
Heorot	the great hall of **Hrothgar**
Heoroweard	Dane; son of **Heorogar**
Herebeald	Geatish prince, eldest son of **Hrethel**; killed by his brother **Hæthcyn**
Heremod	king of the **Danes** in the poem's distant past, before the **Scylding** dynasty
Hereric	brother of **Hygd**, uncle of **Heardred**
Hetware	a Frankish tribe, allied with the **Frisians**; fought against **Hygelac**
Hildeburh	sister of the Danish **Hnæf**, wife of the Frisian **Finn**
Hnæf	chief of the **Half-Danes**, brother of **Hildeburh**; killed by **Finn**
Hoc	Dane, father of **Hildeburh** and **Hnæf**
Hondscio	Geatish warrior, comrade of Beowulf; slain by **Grendel**
Honor-Scyldings	see **Scyldings**
Hrethel	king of the **Geats**, father of **Hygelac**, grandfather of Beowulf
Hrethlings	sons of **Hrethel**, i.e., the **Geats**
Hrethmen	the **Geats**
Hrethric	Dane, son of **Hrothgar**
Hrothgar	aged king of the **Danes** beset by **Grendel**; helped by Beowulf
Hrothmund	Dane, son of **Hrothgar**
Hrothulf	Dane, son of **Halga**, nephew of **Hrothgar**; not to be trusted
Hrunting	the sword of **Unferth**
Hugas	the **Franks**, allies of the **Frisians**
Hunlaf	father of one of the warriors in **Hengest**'s troop
Hygd	queen of the **Geats**, wife of **Hygelac**, daughter of **Hæreth**
Hygelac	king of the **Geats**, uncle of Beowulf
Ingeld	prince of the **Heathobards**, son of **Froda**, betrothed to **Freawaru**; after the events narrated in the poem he burns down the great hall of **Heorot**

Ingwines	the "friends of Ing": the Danes
Jutes	allies of the Frisians; see Eotens
Merovingians	the Franks
Nægling	Beowulf's sword
North-Danes	see Danes
Offa	king of the Angles, husband of Thryth
Ohthere	Swede, son of Ongentheow
Onela	Swede, son of Ongentheow; usurped throne
Ongentheow	Swedish king; killed by Wulf and Eofor
Oslaf	a Danish warrior, companion of Hengest
Ring-Danes	see Danes
Scyld Scefing	legendary founder of the Danish royal family
Scyldings	the Danes; also called Battle-, Honor-, Victory-Scyldings
Scylfings	the Swedes
Sigemund	legendary Germanic hero, son of Wæls
South-Danes	see Danes
Spear-Danes	see Danes
Swerting	uncle of Hygelac
Thryth	(often construed as Modthryth) wife of Offa
Unferth	Danish spokesman ("thyle") and courtier of Hrothgar
Victory-Scyldings	see Scyldings
Volsung	another name for Sigemund, son of Wæls
Wægmundings	the family of Weohstan, Wiglaf, and Beowulf
Wæls	father of Sigemund
War-Geats	see Geats
Wealhtheow	Danish queen, wife of Hrothgar
Weders	the Geats
Weland	legendary Germanic smith
Wendels	a Germanic tribe; perhaps the Vandals, perhaps not
Weohstan	father of Wiglaf; killed Eanmund
West-Danes	see Danes
Wiglaf	son of Weohstan, young retainer of Beowulf
Withergyld	a dead Heathobard
Wonred	a Geat, father of Wulf and Eofor
Wulf	a warrior of the Geats, brother of Eofor; assisted in killing Ongentheow
Wulfgar	a warrior of the Danes; herald at the court of Hrothgar
Wylfings	a Germanic tribe of which Heatholaf was a member, until Ecgtheow killed him
Yrmenlaf	a Dane, younger brother of Æschere

Genealogies

1. The Danes (Scyldings)

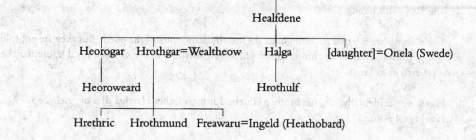

```
                    (Heremod)

                   Scyld Scefing

                     Beowulf

                    Healfdene

Heorogar   Hrothgar=Wealtheow   Halga   [daughter]=Onela (Swede)

Heoroweard                      Hrothulf

   Hrethric   Hrothmund   Freawaru=Ingeld (Heathobard)
```

2. The Geats

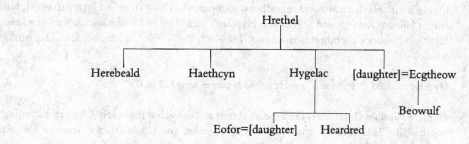

```
                    Hrethel

Herebeald   Haethcyn   Hygelac   [daughter]=Ecgtheow

                                             Beowulf

          Eofor=[daughter]   Heardred
```

3. The Swedes (Scylfings)

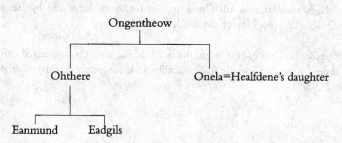

```
                   Ongentheow

        Ohthere          Onela=Healfdene's daughter

   Eanmund    Eadgils
```

The Geatish-Swedish Wars

When the story of Beowulf's fight with the dragon begins, the narrator leaps over fifty years in one brief passage. It is a tumultuous condensation of a complex chain of events (2200–08):

> Then it came to pass amid the crash of battle
> in later days, after Hygelac lay dead,
> and for Heardred the swords of battle held
> deadly slaughter under the shield-wall,
> when the Battle-Scylfings sought him out,
> those hardy soldiers, and savagely struck down
> the nephew of Hereric in his victorious nation—
> then came the broad kingdom
> into Beowulf's hands …

These events are referred to throughout the last thousand lines of the poem, but they are not told in a straightforward way or in chronological order. The fortunes of the Geatish royal house may be reconstructed as follows:

1. Hæthcyn accidentally kills his brother Herebeald; their father Hrethel dies of grief (2432–71). Hæthcyn becomes king.

2. After the death of Hrethel, Ohthere and Onela, the sons of the Swedish king Ongentheow, attack the Geats (2472–78).

3. In retaliation, Hæthcyn attacks Ongentheow in Sweden (2479–84); at first he is successful, but later is killed at Ravenswood (2922–41). Hygelac's men Wulf and Eofor kill Ongentheow, and Hygelac (Hæthcyn's brother) is victorious (2484–89, 2942–99). Ohthere becomes king of the Swedes.

4. Hygelac is killed in Frisia; his son Heardred becomes king (2354–78).

5. Ohthere's brother Onela seizes the Swedish throne and drives out the sons of Ohthere, Eanmund and Eadgils (2379–84). Heardred takes in these exiles, and Onela attacks Heardred for this hospitality and kills him. Onela allows Beowulf to rule the Geats (2385–90).

6. Around this time Weohstan, father of Wiglaf, kills Eanmund on behalf of Onela (2611–19).

7. Eadgils escapes later to kill Onela in Sweden, with help sent by Beowulf (2391–96); he presumably becomes king of the Swedes.

8. During Beowulf's fifty-year reign, the death of Eanmund is unavenged. After Beowulf's death, Eanmund's brother Eadgils will probably seek vengeance against Wiglaf, son of Weohstan (2999–3005).

JUDITH

This Old English poem survives in the manuscript that also contains the poem *Beowulf* (London, British Library, Cotton Vitellius A.xv). As with most Old English poems, its author is unknown, and the poem is untitled in the manuscript. It is commonly referred to as *Judith* because it takes its subject from the Book of Judith, a text found in the Greek and Latin versions of the Bible and accepted as canonical in Catholic traditions, but placed among the Apocrypha in the Protestant Bible. The book and the poem tell the story of a pious Hebrew widow, Judith, who rescues the people of the besieged city of Bethulia by beheading the Assyrian general Holofernes as he attempts to seduce her.

The beginning of the poem has been lost, and the story begins in mid-sentence just before the raucous banquet in which Holofernes orders Judith to be brought to his tent. It is not known how much is missing prior to the first surviving line of the poem. Although the first numbered section is X—implying that nine previous sections (perhaps some thousand lines) have been lost—some have suggested that this is misleading, and the surviving poem is nearly complete. Like other Old English Biblical poems, they argue, *Judith* is a heroic ode that focuses on the most crucial episode of the story, the slaying of Holofernes and the rout of the Assyrian army.

Judith is metrically unusual, especially in contrast to the metrical precision of its manuscript neighbor *Beowulf*. The poem abounds in hypermetric lines (lines with more than the four stresses normally found in lines of Old English poetry), in irregular alliteration, and in rhyme, a very rare feature in Old English poetry. This relatively unusual meter has suggested to some scholars that the poem was composed fairly late in the Anglo-Saxon period, but the relationship between metrical strictness and date of composition has not been established with any certainty.

Poetically *Judith* blurs the distinctions between ancient and contemporary, Biblical and Germanic, a characteristic of many other Old English poems such as *Exodus*—Hebrew warriors rage into battle clad in helmets and byrnies (coats of mail), carrying linden shield and ancient swords, while around them circle the traditional Germanic "beasts of battle," the wolf, raven and eagle. Accuracy of historical details mattered less to Anglo-Saxon poets than fidelity to the spirit of the story and the dramatic deployment of their traditional poetic motifs. In contrast to *Exodus*, however, the poem focuses on heroic action rather than complex allegorical interpretation. The choice of a female character as the subject of a heroic poem indicates the relatively high status of women within Anglo-Saxon nobility prior to the Norman invasion of 1066; the poem subtly alters its source to stress the heroine's wisdom and courage rather than the allure of her beauty or the cunning of her plot to seduce Holofernes. Judith is portrayed as a woman of power, and may have been seen by audiences not only as a figure from the Biblical past, but also as a contemporary hero; the homilist Ælfric, who wrote his own prose paraphrase of the Biblical Book of Judith, sees a connection between her time and his own. At the time Ælfric was writing, the Danes were carrying out frequent raids along the English coast; in Ælfric's retelling Judith is not only a Hebrew fighting against the Assyrians but also a saintly Christian queen defending her homeland against pagan invaders. We should therefore not be surprised that, although the poem is set in pre-Christian Israel, Judith prays to the Trinity of Father, Son and Holy Spirit to give her strength to assassinate Holofernes, nor that many of the poem's most dramatic moments seem drawn as much from Christian hagiography as from Old Testament history.

⌘⌘⌘

Judith[1]

... nor ever upon earth's broad surface[2]   could she be brought to doubt
the grace of God   who gave favor—
renowned Ruler—   when she needed it most:
protection came from the primal Power   against pure terror,
5   help from the highest Judge   when our heavenly Father
in glory bestowed   an outstanding gift,
thanks to her full belief,   her faith in the Almighty forever.
I've heard that Holofernes   then heartily called
for a wine-swilling   with wonders served
10   to senior thanes,°   each sweet delight;   *noblemen*
and the master of men   commanded them come.
Shield-fighters rushed   to their ruling prince—
all his folk-leaders.   That was the fourth day then
since she'd first arrived—   since the radiant lady,
15   elf-lovely[3] Judith,   ingenious had come.

Then to the feast they fared   and found their seats.
Wine-drinkers reveled,   wretched henchmen
in byrnies° bold.   Time after time were bowls so deep   *coats of mail*
down benches borne   brimful to hall-guests,
20   shield-warriors keen.   Likewise were cups and jugs
for the fated filled,   though their fell° ruler,   *cruel*
the fierce warlord,   didn't know fate was near.
Old Holofernes,   heroes' gold-friend,
sunk in wine-joy,   screamed with laughter,

[1] *Judith* The poem has been newly translated for this anthology by Stephen O. Glosecki. The translator has asked that the following note be included: "I am grateful to Roy Liuzza and Broadview's four anonymous readers, whose suggestions vastly improved this translation. As far as possible, I follow Classical Germanic rules of prosody (rules equally apparent in Old English, Old Norse, Old Saxon, and Old High German heroic verse). I discuss my alliterative approach in "Skalded Epic (Make It Old)" in Beowulf *in Our Time: Teaching* Beowulf *in Translation*, ed. Mary K. Ramsey, *OEN Subsidia* 31 (Kalamazoo: Medieval Institute Publications, 2002). I rely upon the original as edited in E.V.K. Dobbie's *Beowulf and Judith* (Anglo-Saxon Poetic Records IV. New York: Columbia University Press, 1953). Dobbie's introduction cites the poem's numerous hypermetric halflines. Though unable to preserve their original distribution, I include some long lines to suggest the poem's remarkably ornate versification. But I have simplified its equally ornate syntax. This is unavoidable, since, for instance, verb-final periods, though still grammatical in German, disappeared from English centuries ago (along with a powerful suspended effect, a sort of semantic "crack the whip" when the closing verb clinches the action and the preceding phrases fall into place). The original also includes a surprising amount of end rhyme (a feature Dobbie notes, with line references; this flourish suggests a late date of composition). I therefore take my own liberties with the rhyme, using it to mark pivotal passages in a translation dedicated to my wife Karen Anne Reynolds, *idese alf-scinre minre*."

[2] *... nor ever upon earth's broad surface* The opening of the poem is imperfect, and the translation is conjectural. The manuscript reading is "... doubted the gifts in this wide world."

[3] *elf-lovely* The Old English compound *ælf-scinu* may mean "wonderfully bright"; *Ælf-* is a common element in Old English names, so it presumably had a positive connotation.

25 roared and ranted,   raged and chanted,
    so no man afar   could fail to hear
    him storm with pride   while plunged in mead,
    demanding brave war-deeds   from bench-sitters.
    Treacherous schemer!   For the entire day he
30 drenched his band   with drafts of wine,
    arrogant ring-breaker,   until his band all swooned
    as drunk as death—   doughty veterans
    drained of virtue.   So he kept the drink flowing,
    poured for hall-thanes,   prince of warriors,
35 till dark of night   dropped down on men.
    Festering with evil,   he ordered her fetched—
    brought to his bedstead—   blessed maiden,
    in circlets rich   all ring-adorned.

    The appointed thanes   as their prince ordered—
40 byrnie-troops' chief—   charged off boisterous
    and grabbed Judith   from the guest-house there.
    Then with the wise lady   they went promptly,
    linden-shield° troops   leading her forth—   *shield made of lime-tree wood*
    the bright maiden—   to the mighty tent,[1]
45 towering pavilion   where the tyrant slept
    inside at night   by our Savior loathed—
    old Holofernes.   There flowed round his bed
    a fair curtain,   fly-net all golden,
    wrought so fine that the folk-leader—   fiercely lethal
50 prince of warriors—   could peer through it
    to see whomever   therein might come—
    whichever heroes' sons;   but at him not a one
    from the tribe of men   might take a look
    unless that arrogant lord   should issue commands
55 for counselors to come   from his keen warband.[2]

    Straight to his bed they brought   the brilliant lady.
    Sturdy warriors   strode to tell him
    they'd brought the holy maid   to the high tent then.
    The famous fort-prince   felt fiendish glee:
60 with filth and vice he'd ravish   the radiant lady!
    But the Guardian of Hosts,   glorious Judge,
    our Lord on high   wouldn't allow this thing:

---

[1] *tent* The poet uses the unusual word *træf* for "tent" rather than the more common *geteld*, perhaps because the latter could also mean "tabernacle" and had a more positive connotation.

[2] *There flowed … keen warband* The Biblical source only mentions that Holofernes's bed had a *canopeum*; the poet adds the apparently original detail that it functioned as a sort of see-though mirror, an appropriately sinister detail that aptly reflects the paranoia of those who wield the power of evil.

He stopped outrage;   He restrained evil.
Spawn of devils,   his spirit lustful,

65 he strode toward the bed   with his band of men.
Before that night elapsed   he'd lose honor,
reach the unhappy end   he'd earned before.
Evil-doer!   On earth he'd dwelt
a cruel prince,   oppressing men

70 under the clouds' rooftops.   Then the king collapsed
in midst of bed so drunk on wine   that his wit-locker
was of sense empty.   Off went his soldiers,
wine-glutted troops,   once they'd led that troth-breaker—
loathsome tyrant—   to his last resting.

75 Then the Savior's handmaid,   hearty and strong,
astutely sought   the most certain way
to end that besotted life   before the sinner woke.
Her locks entwined,   she took a sword—[1]
razor-sharp blade,   battle-hardened:

80 the Shaper's maid   from its sheath drew it
with her right hand then.   Heaven's Defender
she addressed by name—   Redeemer of all
in this world dwelling—   and these words then spoke:
"Source of all, great God on high,   and Spirit of holy help,

85 Son of the Almighty: mercy I need now,
Trinitarian strength!   Intensely now
is my heart inflamed: Lord, fierce sorrow
oppresses my soul.   Prince of heaven:
give me triumph and true belief;   let me take this sword

90 and cleave this murder-monger!   Mankind's Ruler,
grant me health and grace: I've never had greater need
for your mercy before.   Almighty Lord,
bright-minded Glory-Giver,   grant me vengeance;
let my mind's fury   inflame my heart!"[2]

95 Then supreme Justice   promptly filled her
with strength and zeal,   as He still will do
for everyone who dwells down here   seeking help for himself
with true faith and much counsel.   Thus her mind was filled
with hope renewed.   She took that heathen man

100 by the hair fast then   and with her fists tugging
stretched him deftly   in deep disgrace,

---

[1] *she took a sword* As in the climactic dragon-fight in *Beowulf,* there is a considerable gap between the drawing of the sword and its use.

[2] *Source of all … inflame my heart* Judith's prayer to the Trinity makes her more like a Christian saint than a Hebrew heroine, but her prayer for vengeance and courage in battle makes her a warrior rather than a martyr.

wielding control   of the wicked man,
that hapless wretch.   Then with her hair knotted
she hacked fearsome foe   with fateful blade,
105   carved halfway through   his hateful neck,
so that he lay in a drunken swoon   with a deadly wound
though as yet unslain,   with his soul elsewhere.
So she swung the sword   a second time then—
the brave lady   lashed in earnest,
110   and that heathen hound's   whole head unwound—
rolled forth on the floor,   leaving the foul carcass
empty behind it.   Elsewhere the soul went:
under the cliff of death   cast down below,
ever thereafter in torment tied,   to torture bound,
115   with worms wound round   rank under ground:
leashed in hellfire!   lost in darkness!
Never a hope of leaving hell—   hall of serpents!
Throughout endless time   eternally slow
his soul shall stay   enslaved below
120   in that darkest home   no joy to know!

Thus she won foremost fame   as a fighter there:
God gave Judith   glory at war—
the sky's Chieftain   let her achieve triumph.
Into her bag at once   the brilliant maid
125   put the army-hunter's   head all bloody—
in the supply pouch that   her companion had brought
with food for both   when they'd first set out—
fair-faced maiden,   filled with virtue
and astute judgment.   Judith gave her
130   the bloody head   to bear homeward.
She and her young helper—   high-born ladies,
boldly daring,   brave in spirit,
blessed with triumph—   both left quickly,
steadfast maidens,   to steal right through
135   the hostile camp   till they could clearly see
the gleaming walls   of the gorgeous town,
Bethulia indeed!   Adorned with rings,
they hastened forth   on the footpath then,
until, glad-minded,   they made it through
140   to the wall's gateway.   Warriors sat there
holding watch then,   wakeful guardsmen
at the mighty fort—   just as, with mournful heart
but good judgment,   Judith had ordered
before setting forth   filled with courage.
145   Lady so brave!—   back at last now,

famed for valor,   to her folk so dear:
at once the clear-minded woman   called for someone
to come towards her   from the tall fortress
to help them in   with utmost haste

150   through the wall's gateway;   and these words she spoke
to the victory-folk: "I can confirm for you
something to make us all grateful   and end grieving:
mourn no longer: the Measurer exults!
Toward you the Wonder-Prince   is well-disposed:

155   over the whole wide world   it's well-known now:
to you is glory given   and great honor
instead of the dire torment   you've endured so long."
All those city-dwellers   knew sudden bliss then,
once they'd heard her speak,   the holy maid,

160   over the high wall there.   The host rejoiced.
To the fortress-gate   all the folk hastened,
men with women   in multitudes.
The host in hordes   all hurried and thronged,
by the thousands pressed   toward the Prince's maid—

165   the young and old,   each uplifted—
all their minds hopeful   in that happy city
where they rejoiced to hear   of Judith's return
to her own homeland.   Humble, reverent,
with utmost haste   they helped her in.

170   Then the deep-minded maid   adorned with gold
bade her servant—   resourceful companion—
to unveil the man-hunter's   head before them—
show the bloody trophy   to the townspeople
so all could see   her success at war.

175   Then spoke the fine lady   to the folk-gathering:
"Victory-famed troops,   valiant commanders:
here you can see   the heathen warrior's
head before you.   Yes, Holofernes
now lies lifeless.   Our most loathsome foe,

180   who committed more murder   than any man on earth,
caused us grievous pain   and had plotted more
grief than before,   but God refused
him longer life—   didn't let him commit
more atrocity: for I took his life

185   with the help of God.   Now, each good man here
in this town dwelling: I tell you all,
shield-bearing men: you must make haste now
and gird for war.   When our glorious King,
God the Creator,   from the east sends high

190   His shining light,   then bear linden shields forth,

       boards before breasts   and byrnie-jackets
       under gleaming helms   to the host of the foe!
       With flashing swords   fell folk-leaders,
       their doomed chieftains.   Death is allotted
195   to all your foes   and honor to you,
       glory in battle,   as God in his might
       through this hand of mine   has made clear now."

       Then the eager host   became all ready
       to contend bravely.   Thence bold as kings
200   veteran companions   bore victory-flags
       forth to the fight—   forth for the right!
       Heroes under helmets   left the holy town
       at dawn of day   to din of shields
       loudly resounding.   And so the lean one rejoiced,
205   the wolf in the woods,   with the wan raven,
       corpse-hungry bird.   The beasts both knew
       the local troops   would allot them the fated,
       let them feast their fill.   There flew in their tracks,
       all prey-driven,   the dew-feathered
210   brown-coated eagle,   who sang battle songs
       through horn-hooked beak.[1]   The host advanced,
       bear-troops[2] to battle   by boards covered,
       by the curved linden—   those who not long before
       had suffered outlanders'   lashings of scorn,
215   heathen insults.   But that was all repaid—
       and repaid fiercely!—   when play of spears
       found the Assyrian host   once the Hebrews came
       to wage battle   under war-banners
       in the invaders' camp.   Keenly they launched
220   arrow-showers   shooting forward
       from horn-curved bows—   battle-adders,
       stout-headed darts!   Storming loudly
       furious warriors   flung forth spears then
       into the hardy throng.   Heroes went raging:
225   against that loathsome tribe,   the land-dwellers
       stepped stern-minded,   stout in spirit,
       unsoft to wake up   old opponents,
       all mead-weary.   With mighty hands
       thanes pulled from sheath   the patterned sword
230   with sturdy edge   to strike and slay

---

[1] *Then the eager host ... horn-hooked beak* The "beasts of battle" (the raven, wolf, and eagle) are a traditional motif in Old English poetry, signaling the beginning of a scene of slaughter.

[2] *bear-troops* Literally *beornas* or "warriors," but the animal imagery is not inappropriate here.

Assyrian foes,   fearsome warriors.
Their spirits frenzied,   they spared no one
in that army's ranks,   neither rich nor poor,
no man alive   they might subdue.

235   And so in those morning hours   the mighty thanes
fiercely assailed   the foreign troops
until the chief leaders   of that large army
were forced to find   fury drove them!
They showed their strength   with stout sword-swings,

240   Hebrew fighters.   Their foe brought word
to the eldest ranks   of ruling thanes:
to their flag-bearers   they brought fierce tidings:
they woke warlords   with wild stories—
told the mead-weary   of the morning kill,

245   deadly swordplay.   Then soon I'm told
death-fated troops   tossed aside sleep,
and, heavy-hearted,   they huddled round
the mighty tent   of their murderous prince,
old Holofernes.   They'd hoped quickly

250   to warn their lord   that war was near
before the attack itself   brought terror down
with all the armed Hebrews.   They all still thought
the bear-troops' chief   and the bright maiden
in the lovely tent   still lay together—

255   Judith the regal   and their corrupt leader
wickedly lusting.   But of his lords not one
would dare to wake   the war-chief there
or try to find   how the flag-warrior
had behaved himself   with the holy woman,

260   with God's handmaid.   The host approached,
Hebrew folk all   fighting briskly
with their hard weapons,   with haft requiting
old offenses   when the flashing sword
answered old slander.   Assyria watched

265   glory's downfall   in the day's work there—
her pride toppled!   But troops still stood
round the lord's tent then,   intensely alarmed,
their spirits darkening.   Drawn together
they began to murmur, moan,[1]   lament aloud,

270   and grind and gnash: they showed no virtue,
gnashing teeth in fear.   Thus did they forfeit honor,
glory and valor.   They wanted to go waken

---

[1]   *murmer, moan*   More comically, "cough," "clear their throats." The Old English word *cohhetan* appears only here
and its meaning is not known. The hesitation of the retainers is presumably meant to be ironic and bitterly comical.

their beloved leader—   which would do little good!
Sooner or later   someone would have to.
275   So a ring-warrior went   right to the tent—
undaunted enough   when need drove him.
On the bed he found—   blanched, sprawling—
his gold-giver: gone his spirit—
his life taken.   Then he tumbled flat—
280   to the earth frozen;   with frantic mind
he ripped his hair,   rent his garments,
and wailed out words   to warriors around,
unhappy all,   outside waiting:
"Here it's plain to see   ourselves all doomed:
285   we have clear token   our time has come,
evil upon us: now we all must lose,
assailed by strife: here lies sword-stricken—
our lord!—beheaded!"   Thus heavy-minded
they cast down weapons   and went with weary hearts
290   in flight trembling.   But they were attacked from behind
by the mighty host   until most who ran
with that force all lay   felled in battle
on the victory-field,   hacked flat by swords
as wolves would wish   and war-birds too,
295   all corpse-hungry.   Yet they kept fleeing,
shield-foe survivors.   Vying in foot-tracks
came the Hebrew force,   flushed with triumph,
honored with glory: God the Ruler,
our almighty Friend   gave His full support.
300   With bloody swords   they boldly went:
headstrong heroes   hacked a pathway
through the thronging foe.   They thrashed linden;
they slashed shield-wall—   those soldiers raged
with war's frenzy—   furious Hebrews.
305   Those thanes lusted   with a long thirst then
for the spear-thrusting.   There lay spent in dust,
by head-tally,   a high number
of slain nobles,   Assyrian lords,
the chief liege-men   of the loathsome tribe.
310   Few survived to go home!

                        Valiant as kings then
the warriors returned,   tearing through carnage,
reeking corpses.   They found room to loot—
land-dwellers there—   their most loathsome foe,
315   their old enemies,   all unliving.
They took bright booty,   bloody trappings,

board and broadsword,   burnished helmet,
much precious wealth.   Thus they won glory
on the battlefield   when they beat enemies,
320 the land-guardians: they'd laid to sleep
old foes with swords.   In swaths they sprawled,
those whom they loathed the most   among living tribes.
Then the whole nation   of noble clans—
foremost families—   took a full month there,
325 proud, hair-knotted,   to hoist and cart
to Bethulia the bright   beautiful city
helm and hip-sword,   hoary byrnies,
men's war-trappings   all tooled with gold:
they took more treasure   than any man living,
330 no matter how clever,   could recount fully—
all taken by troops   with true valor,
brave under banners,   battling in strife,
thanks to the wise counsel   of the keen Judith,
bold-minded maid.   From their mighty quest
335 spear-brave they gave   gifts of esteem
in her high honor: old Holofernes'
gory helm and broadsword   beside his byrnie so wide,
arrayed in gold so red,   with goods that the ring-warriors' prince
in pride and power had owned: his heirlooms and riches and gems,
340 all his glittering wealth and his rings: this to the radiant lady,
to the one so ingenious they gave.   And Judith devoted it all
to the glorious God of high hosts   who'd given her honor on earth,
renown in the worldly realm,   with reward in heaven to come,
triumph in splendor on high,   thanks to her true belief,
345 her faith in the Almighty forever.   In the end there could be no doubt
about the reward she'd cherished so long.   For this to our Lord so dear
be there glory forever arrayed.   Air and the lofty wind He made,
rolling sky and roomy ground,   rushing streams all tumbling down,
and, through His bounty of merciful love,   bliss in His heaven above.

—LATE 9TH OR EARLY 10TH CENTURY

THE BATTLE OF MALDON

During the reign of King Æthelred "the Unready" (978–1016), England experienced a renewed campaign of Viking attacks, which increased in strength and effect until the Danish King Cnut became King of England in 1016. Æthelred apparently lacked the resources, financial and otherwise, to repel the Vikings, and sources such as the *Anglo-Saxon Chronicle* depict his nobles and advisors as a treacherous, fragmented, and demoralized gang (the King's nickname, which may be a later invention, is in Old English *Un-ræd*, "no counsel," a pun on the name *Æthel-ræd* "noble counsel").

Though the last decade of the tenth century was a period of remarkable literary production by writers such as Ælfric, Wulfstan, and Byrhtferth of Ramsey, and saw the creation of many *de luxe* manuscripts and works of art, it is better remembered for the abysmal failure of Æthelred's policy of Viking appeasement. This began with a payment of £10,000 in 991, followed by £16,000 in 994, £24,000 in 1002, £36,000 in 1007, and £48,000 in 1012; finally, in 1013, the king was forced into exile in Normandy. The idea of buying off the Vikings with "Danegeld" was apparently inspired by the arrival in August of 991 of a fleet of 93 Viking ships; according to the *Anglo-Saxon Chronicle* the Viking army sacked Ipswich, sailed up the river Blackwater (Panta) to Maldon in Essex, and defeated the English army led by Byrhtnoth, ealdorman of Essex. Whether or not this battle was in fact the turning-point in Anglo-Danish relations, a poem was composed to commemorate the battle and the leader of the English army.

The manuscript of *The Battle of Maldon* was apparently already missing its beginning and end before the remaining pages were destroyed in a fire which devastated a portion of the British Library's manuscripts in 1731. Fortunately a transcript had been made before the fire, and this transcript is the only source for the poem. Only 325 lines of the poem survive, and while we do not know how much has been lost, the main action of the battle is complete and fairly clear. The Vikings have beached their boats on a spit of land that is cut off from the shore when the tide is in, but accessible via a causeway at low tide. The English army, ranged on the shore opposite the Vikings, is depicted as being composed of Byrhtnoth's own troops—his "retainers"—and a more or less trained local militia drawn from all ranks of society; a Viking messenger cannily tries to exploit potential differences in class or status among the troops, but the narrator portrays them as united by loyalty to their leader and a desire for honor.

The poem's attitude towards its hero, however, is not entirely celebratory; Byrhtnoth is praised for his bravery and strength, but his decision to allow the Vikings passage across the causeway (so that they might have more room to fight) is said to arise from his *ofermod*, a word which can mean either "pride" or "great courage." Byrhtnoth's loyalty to his king, Æthelred, and his ringing refusal to pay tribute to the Vikings must have had provocative resonance in the last years of the King's reign, assuming the poem was written shortly after the battle. Byrhtnoth fights well but dies quickly, with a desperate prayer on his lips; upon his death the treacherous retainer Godric leaps on Byrhtnoth's horse and gallops away. The men further away from Byrhtnoth assume that it is he who is fleeing, so they do the same, and the army falls apart; the rest of the poem depicts the brave speeches and noble deaths of the men who remain.

The Battle of Maldon is not a news report but a reflection on the complex relation between military victory and moral triumph; it draws on the conventions of heroic poetry to give motive and meaning to the historical facts, and turns the humiliation of Byrhtnoth's death and defeat into a celebration of other virtues such as courage and steadfastness. The poem may idealize the voices and actions of ordinary soldiers facing certain death, but it does not glorify their leaders or their cause; though the Vikings are by no means depicted as heroic, or even for the most part as individuals, the poem's moral absolutes are not arranged as an English "us" against a Viking "them," but as a stark personal choice between courage and cowardice, truth and treachery, which is only made clearer by the impossibility of victory.

⌘ ⌘ ⌘

The Battle of Maldon[1]

... was broken.
Then he ordered every young soldier to send off his
    horse,
drive it far off and go forward,
pay heed to hands and high courage.
5 When the kinsman of Offa first discovered
that the earl would not suffer slackness,
he let fly from his hands his favorite hawk
off to the woods, and advanced to the battle;
by that you knew that the young warrior
10 would not weaken at battle, when he took up weapons.
Likewise Eadric wished to support his leader,
the lord in the fight; forward he went
with his spear to battle. He had a stout heart
as long as he might hold in his hands
15 board and broad sword; he fulfilled his boast
when he had to fight before his lord.
    Then Byrhtnoth began to array the troops,
ordered, instructed, and showed the soldiers
how they should stand and hold the field,
20 told them to hold their shields securely,
firm in their fists, and never be afraid.
When he had properly organized all those men,
he dismounted among the men where he most wanted
to be, where he knew his retinue most loyal and brave.
25   Then on the riverbank, stoutly shouting,
stood a Viking messenger who made a speech,
broadcast the boast of the seafarers
to the earl where he stood on the shore:
"Bold seamen have sent me to thee,
30 commanded me to say that thou must quickly
send us rings for protection; and it is better for you
to buy off this spear-storm with tribute

than for us to share such a hard battle.[2]
We needn't ruin one another, if you're rich enough;
35 we'll call a truce in exchange for gold.
If thou, the richest here, agree to this,
that thou wilt ransom thy people,
give to the seamen all the money they want
in exchange for peace, and take a truce with us,
40 we'll go back to our ships with your gold coins,
sail off on the sea, and hold you in peace."
    Byrhtnoth spoke out, raised his shield,
shook his slender spear and made a speech,
angry and resolute, he gave this answer:
45 "Do you hear, seafarer, what this people says?
they will give you spears for your tribute,
poisoned points and ancient swords,
the heriot that will not help you in battle.
Messenger of the sailors, take back a message,
50 tell your people much more hateful news:
here stands an undisgraced earl with his army,
who will defend this homeland,
the land of Æthelred, my own lord,
the folk and the fields. Fated are heathens
55 to fall in battle—it seems too shameful to me
to let you go with our gold to your ships
without a fight, now that you have come
this far into our country.
You shall not get your treasure so easily;
60 points and blades will settle this business,
grim war-play, before we pay tribute."
    Then he commanded his men to carry their shields
until they all stood on the river's edge.
The water kept each troop from the other
65 when the flood came flowing after the ebb,

---

1 *The Battle of Maldon* Translated by R.M. Liuzza for *The Broadview Anthology of British Literature.*

2 *Bold seamen ... hard battle* The translation preserves the use of singular (*thou, thee*) and plural (*you*) pronouns in the original, which may be a deliberate device to indicate that the messenger is trying to drive a wedge between Byrhtnoth and his army.

locking the water-streams.[1] It seemed too long
until they could bring their spears together.
They stood arrayed on the shores of the Panta,
the East-Saxon vanguard and the Viking army;
70 neither side could strike at the other,
unless one might fall from an arrow's flight.
The tide receded; the sailors stood ready,
a great many Vikings eager for battle.
The protector of heroes[2] ordered a hardened warrior
75 to hold the causeway; he was called Wulfstan,
the son of Ceol, brave among his kinsmen;
he shot with his Frankish spear the first man
who stepped most boldly across the bridge.
Beside Wulfstan stood fearless warriors,
80 Ælfere and Maccus, two valiant men
who would not take flight at the ford,
but stoutly defended themselves against the foe
as long as they might wield weapons.
When they perceived this, and clearly saw
85 that they would meet bitter bridge-wardens there,
the hateful visitors hatched a plot—
they asked if they could have access
to lead their footsoldiers across the ford.
    Then the earl in his overconfidence[3] began
90 to allow too much land to that hateful people.
Over the cold water he called out then,
the son of Byrhthelm, while the soldiers listened:
"Here's room enough—now come quickly to us,
bring on the battle; God alone knows

95 who will hold this place of slaughter."
On came the slaughter-wolves, not minding the water,
the Viking troop went west over the Panta,
carried their shields over the shining water,
the seamen bore their linden shields[4] to land.
100   Against the attackers Byrhtnoth and his men
stood ready; he ordered them to raise
the battle-wall with their shields, and stand
fast against the foe. The fight was near,
glory in combat; the time had come
105 when fated men should fall.
The cry was raised, ravens circled,
the eagle longed for prey, and panic was on earth.
They let fly the file-hard spears,
grimly ground spearheads from their grip;
110 the bows were busy, the shield-boards took the arrows.
The attack was bitter, on either hand
warriors fell, young men lay dead.
Wulfmar was wounded, chose his bed of slaughter;
the kinsman of Byrhtnoth, savagely cut
115 to pieces with swords, his sister's son.
Payback was brought to the Vikings for that:
I heard that Edward struck one fiercely
with his sword—not stingy with strokes—
until at his feet fell the doomed soldier;
120 his leader gave thanks for that
to his attendant when he had the chance.
    And so they stood their ground, stouthearted
young men at war, eagerly worked
to see who might be the first to win
125 the life of a doomed man with his spear,
soldiers with weapons; slaughter fell on earth.
They stood steadfast; Byrhtnoth encouraged them,
ordered each young warrior to give thought to war
if he hoped to earn fame from the Danes in the fight.
130   Then came a tough warrior, weapon raised,
his shield for protection, and stepped toward him.[5]
Just as firmly went the earl to the churl;[6]
each of them thought to harm the other.
The sailor sent off his southern spear
135 so that the lord of warriors was wounded;

---

[1] *locking the water-streams* The Blackwater (OE Panta) is a tidal
river; when the tide came in the island on which the Vikings have
landed was cut off from the shore. Later, at low tide, a stone
causeway connects it to the shore.

[2] *The protector of heroes* Byrhtnoth.

[3] *overconfidence* The Old English word "ofermod" is notoriously
ambiguous in this passage—literally it means "too much *mod*"
(spirit, courage), implying a degree of reckless excess in what might
still be an admirable quality, but in later Old English prose it often
translates Latin *superbia* "pride," a deadly sin. It is difficult to argue
that the hero of the poem—if that is what Byrhtnoth is—is guilty of
a deadly sin in deciding to engage the Vikings in battle where they
stood; but part of the poem's enduring interest is its undertone,
which qualifies the moral absolutes in which battles are usually
recounted. Whatever the precise meaning of the word "ofermod,"
and whatever the military necessities under which Byrhtnoth reaches
his decision, his act proves to be a fatal error, as even he seems to
recognize.

---

[4] *linden shields* Shields of lime-tree wood.

[5] *him* I.e., Byrhtnoth.

[6] *churl* Man without noble rank.

he shoved with his shield so that the shaft broke in two,
and sprung out the spear when the point sprang back.
The warrior was furious—he stabbed with his spear
the proud Viking who gave him that wound.
140 The battle-leader was bold—he let his spear go forth,
his hand threaded it through the young man's neck
and he took the life of his attacker.
Then without waiting he stabbed another
so his armor burst; he was wounded in the breast
145 through his ring-mail, a deadly point
stood at his heart. The earl was the happier;
he laughed, brave man, and thanked his Maker
for the day's work the Lord had allowed him.
          Then one of the Vikings threw a spear from his
                    hand,
150 let it fly from his fingers so it went too far,
through the noble thane of Æthelred.[1]
By his side stood a half-grown young warrior,
a boy in the battle, who very boldly
drew out the blood-drenched spear from the man—
155 Wulfstan's son, Wulfmar the young—
and sent the hard spear flying back again;
the point went in, so he lay on the earth,
the one who had grievously wounded his lord.
Then an armored man went to the earl,
160 he wanted to plunder the warrior's gear,
his robes and rings and decorated sword.
Byrhtnoth drew his sword, broad, bright-edged,
from its sheath, and swung at his mail-coat.
Too soon one of the seafarers stopped him
165 with a wound in the earl's arm.
The gold-hilted sword fell to the ground;
he could no longer hold the hardened blade,
or wield a weapon. But still the old warrior
said what he could, encouraged the young men
170 and bade them go forth as good companions.
He could no longer stand steady on his feet;
he gazed up to heaven:
          "I give thee thanks, O Lord of Nations,
for all the joys I have had in this world.
175 Now, gracious Maker, I have most desperate need
that Thou grant grace to my spirit,
so that my soul may journey to Thee
into Thy keeping, King of Angels,

and depart in peace. I implore Thee
180 that the fiends of Hell may not harm it."
Then the heathen savages hacked him up,
and both the men who stood beside him,
Ælfnoth and Wulmar, both lay dead,
and gave up their lives with their lord.
185   Then some unwilling ones bowed out of the battle:
the sons of Odda were the first in the flight,
Godric left the battle, and abandoned the good man
who had often given him many horses;
he leapt on the horse that belonged to his lord,
190 in his riding gear—which was not right!—
and his brothers with him both ran away,
Godwine and Godweg didn't care for battle,
but turned from the war and took to the woods,
fled to safety and saved their lives,
195 and many more beyond any good measure,
if they had remembered all the rewards
he had given them for their services.
So Offa had said, earlier that day
in the assembly, when he held a meeting,
200 that many a man spoke bravely there
who later would not stand firm at need.
          Then the people's leader lay fallen,
Æthelred's earl; all the house-troops
saw that their lord lay dead.[2]
205 Then forward pressed the proud thanes,
uncowardly men hastened eagerly;
they all wanted one of two things—
to give up their lives or avenge their dear lord.
          So the son of Ælfric urged them forward,
210 a warrior young in years spoke his words,
Ælfwine spoke, and bravely said:
"I remember the speeches we made over mead
when we raised our boasts on the benches,
heroes in the hall, about hard struggle;
215 now he who is bold has to prove it.
I will make known my noble descent to all:
I come from a famous family among the Mercians,
my ancestor was called Ealhelm,
a wise nobleman, and prosperous in the world.
220 Thanes will not mock me among my people,

---

[1] *thane of Æthelred* Nobleman, i.e., Byrhtnoth.

[2] *all the … lay dead* I.e., the troops closest to Byrhtnoth (cf. 23–25) see that he is dead; those further away mistake the fleeing Godric for their lord (236–41).

that I would go away from this army,
seek my homeland, now that my lord lies
cut down in battle. Mine is the greatest grief:
he was both my kinsman and my master."
225 He went forth, remembering revenge,
until with the point of his spear he struck one
of the seamen so that he lay dead on the ground,
cut down by his weapon. He urged his comrades,
friends and companions, to go forth.
230   Offa spoke, shook his ashen spear:
"Indeed, Ælfwine, you have reminded all
the thanes at need, now that our lord lies dead,
the earl on the earth. Each of us
needs to encourage every other
235 warrior to war, as long as his weapon
he can have and hold, the hard blade,
the spear and the good sword. Godric,
wretched son of Odda, has betrayed us all.
When he rode off on that horse, that proud steed,
240 too many men thought that it was our lord;
and so our forces were divided on this field,
the shield-wall broken. Shame on his deed,
by which he caused so many men to flee!"
    Leofsunu spoke and raised his shield,
245 his board for protection, and replied to him:
"I hereby promise that from hence I will not
flee the space of a single foot, but will go further,
avenge in the battle my beloved lord.
The steadfast men of Sturmer need not
250 mock me, now that my lord has fallen,
saying I would go home without my lord,
turn away from war—instead weapons shall take me,
point and iron." Full of ire he went forth,
fought tenaciously; he scorned flight.
255   Dunnere then spoke, shook his spear,
a humble churl, cried out over all,
urged each man to avenge Byrhtnoth:
"He must never weaken, who hopes to revenge
his lord on this people, nor care for his life!"
260 Then they went forth, not fearing for their lives;
the retainers set about fighting fiercely,
the grim spear-bearers, and asked God
that they might avenge their dear lord

and bring about the downfall of their foe.
265 The hostage began to help them eagerly;
he was from a strong family of Northumbrians,
the son of Ecglaf—his name was Æscferth.
He never weakened at the war-play,
but he shot forth arrows ceaselessly;
270 sometimes he struck a shield, sometimes a man,
again and again he gave one a wound,
as long as he was able to wield weapons.
    Still in the front stood Edward the Long,
brave and eager, spoke boastful words
275 that he would not flee a single foot's space,
or turn back now that his better lay dead.
He broke through the shield-wall and did battle
with the seamen, until he had worthily avenged
his treasure-giver, then took his place among the slain.
280 Likewise Ætheric, excellent comrade,
eager, death-ready, fought earnestly.
Sibyrht's brother and many another
split banded shields,[1] boldly defended themselves—
the shield-rim burst, and the byrnie[2] sang
285 its grim horrible song. Then Offa struck
a seafarer in the fight[3] so that he fell to the earth,
and there Gadd's kinsman sought the ground.
In the heat of battle Offa was hacked up,
but he had lived up to his promise to his lord—
290 he had boasted before his ring-giver
that they would ride together into the stronghold,
get home safely, or fall in the slaughter,
die of wounds on the field of war:
he lay like a thane at his lord's side.
295   Then shields were shattered, the sailors advanced,
enraged by battle; spears broke open
many a doomed man's life-house. Then Wistan went
    forth,
Thurstan's son, and fought with them;
he was the killer of three in that crowd,

---

[1] *banded shields* The precise meaning of the OE adjective "cellod,"
which appears only here, is not known.

[2] *byrnie* Coat of mail.

[3] *Then Offa … fight* The Old English specifically says "*the*
seafarer," as if some particular opponent had already been pointed
out; there may be a line or two missing, indicating that Offa stepped
forward, fought against an attacker, etc.

300 before Wigelin's son lay down in the slaughter.[1]
There was keen conflict; the men stood
firm in the struggle, warriors fell,
weary with wounds. Slaughter fell on earth.
Oswold and Eadwold all the while,
305 two brothers, exhorted the troops,
bade their band of brothers with their words
that they had to stand steady there at need,
use their weapons without weakness.
    Byrhtwold spoke, raised his shield—
310 he was an old retainer—and shook his ash-spear;
he most boldly gave the men a lesson:
"Spirits must be the harder, hearts the keener,
courage the greater, as our strength grows less.

Here lies our lord all hacked to pieces,
315 a good man in the dust. He will mourn evermore
who thinks to turn back from this war-play now.
I'm an old man; I will not leave,
but by the side of my lord—by such
a beloved man—I intend to lie."
320   So also the son of Æthelgar urged them all,
Godric, to the battle. Often he let go a spear,
sent a slaughter-shaft whirling to the Vikings,
as he advanced foremost among the folk,
hacked and laid low, until he fell on the field.
325 That was not the Godric who turned away from
    the battle …
—C. 1000

---

[1] *Wigelin's son … slaughter* It is not clear how Wistan is both the
son of Thurstan and of Wigelin, unless Wigelin is his mother.
"Matronymic" epithets are rare in Old English, but this may be an
instance of one.

Exodus

The poem now called *Exodus* survives in a manuscript in the Bodleian Library at Oxford (Bodl. Lib. MS Junius 11). The Junius Manuscript contains four Old English poems on Biblical themes (*Genesis A* and *B*, *Exodus*, *Daniel*, and *Christ and Satan*), separately composed but deliberately compiled in a volume that is unique among Old English poetic manuscripts for containing a series of illustrations (though the series was not completed). Together the poems of the Junius Manuscript offer a poetic retelling of redemption history from Satan's fall to the Last Judgment. The subject-matter of this manuscript is remarkably similar to the body of work which Bede ascribes to the poet Cædmon; early readers attributed the whole collection to Cædmon, but it is now generally agreed that the four poems are so different in style that they could not have been written by the same person.

The focus of *Exodus* is on one episode from the Biblical story of Moses, the crossing of the Red Sea, but the poet emphasizes the story's typological associations with the Harrowing of Hell and with baptism; its themes and structure have been plausibly connected to the Easter Vigil liturgy. In this way the poem manages to be both more and less than the Biblical Book of Exodus. It is also a poem of strenuous energy and sweeping action, very much a representative of the heroic style. Drawing on the traditional language of heroic poetry, the poem depicts the Israelites who fled with Moses from the wrath of Pharaoh as a proud triumphant army ready to march into battle. When Pharaoh's army is drowned in the sea, the sea itself is described as a warrior, fighting a divine battle against the enemies of God. At other times the Israelites in the desert are described as sailors and seafarers—appropriately enough, for they will soon be crossing the sea to a new land. In these ways, perhaps, the Anglo-Saxons found a mirror of their own experience, since they too were seafarers and migrants, conquerors of a new land across the ocean. In this sense the poem is a kind of self-portrait of its English audience.

Exodus contains some of the most dazzlingly inventive language of any Old English poem. It is full of metaphoric energy, exuberant wordplay and sound patterns; its syntax is in some places lively to the point of incoherence. It is a notoriously difficult poem, apparently not well preserved—there are gaps in the text, and some passages may be out of sequence—and the same energy that makes the poem's language so exciting and inventive and its narrative so powerful and surprising occasionally makes it difficult to recognize errors in the text, let alone correct them. The present translation is fairly loose in some passages where the text does not make perfect sense; in a few places the translation reflects the obscurity of the original.

⌘ ⌘ ⌘

Exodus[1]

Listen! far and wide throughout the world
      we have learned how the laws of Moses,
a marvelous code, were proclaimed to men—
a happy reward in heaven above
5 for every blessed soul's hard struggle,
a lasting counsel for all the living,
heavenly life—let him hear who will!
      He was exalted in the wilderness, where
the Lord of Hosts, the righteous King,
10 endowed him with His own power
and put mighty deeds into his hands.
Beloved of God, lord of his people,
canny and wise, commander of armies,
famous leader—Pharaoh, God's enemy,
15 he bound with a rod, and all his race.
There the God of triumph entrusted and gave
the lives of his kinsmen to that brave leader,
and a habitation in their homeland to Abraham's sons.
Great was the reward, and loyal the Lord,
20 who gave strength to his arms against the enemies' terror;
he conquered many a kingdom on the battlefield
and took dominion over many tribes.[2] In that first time[3]
that the God of Hosts addressed him,
He told him in words many wonderful truths,
25 how the wise Lord wrought the world,
the orb of the earth and the sky above,
established them in glory—and His own name too,
which the sons of men had never known,
wise Patriarchs, though they knew many things.
30   Afterwards, when he had strengthened and exalted
the prince of his people with true powers,
Pharaoh's enemy, for his exodus,

then that nation's army was soon drenched
in death, ancient plagues, and the overthrow
35 of too many of those treasure-hoarders—
their lamentation arose, their hall-joys slaughtered,
their wealth plundered.[4] Those wicked oppressors
He annihilated at midnight, many first-born sons,
the city-guards slain. A killer stalked widely,
40 choked the land with the corpses of the dead,
hostile persecutor of the people—and the host went
      forth.
There was widespread weeping, few worldly joys,
the laughter-smiths' hands were locked shut
when the people were allowed to depart on their
45 harsh journey,[5] the fiend and his hellish host
were despoiled—Heaven descended,
and their demon idols fell. A most famous day
across the earth it was, when that multitude set out,
so they suffered captivity for many years,
50 the accursed people of Egypt,
because they imagined they could ever hold back
the people of Moses, if the Maker had allowed them,
from their beloved and long-awaited journey.
      The army was eager, and bold their leader,
55 a brave commander of that nation of kinsmen.
He passed with his people through many desert lands,
the habitations of hostile men,
narrow passes, unknown paths,
until they bore their arms among the fierce borderers
60 whose lands lay shrouded in a cover of clouds,[6]
their high mountain dwellings. Moses led
his army past these, through many border-lands.

---

[1] *Exodus* The present translation is by R.M. Liuzza and has been
prepared especially for *The Broadview Anthology of British Literature*.
The translation is based on the text edited by P.J. Lucas, *Exodus* (U
of Exeter Press, 1977; 2nd ed. 1994), though considerable freedom
has been exercised with regard to Lucas's punctuation, emendations
and proposed translations. For advice and assistance the translator
expresses gratitude to J.R. Hall, Anne Klinck and Eileen Joy.

[2] *he conquered ... tribes* This refers perhaps to a future time when
the Hebrews settled in the land of Canaan and displaced the
inhabitants.

[3] *In that first time* In the wilderness, in the form of a burning bush
(see Exodus 3).

[4] *Afterwards ... plundered* A complex and multivalent passage;
"treasure," "hall-joys," and "wealth" all refer to the first-born sons of
the Egyptians, but they give the impression that the Hebrews
somehow conquered them in battle and took possession of their
wealth as well.

[5] *He annihilated ... journey* The blurring of the Egyptians' death
and the Israelites' exodus throughout this passage is a complex
double entendre, referring both to the Hebrews, reluctantly set free,
and to the first-born children, sent to their death. The description
recalls the legends of Christ's Harrowing of Hell (undertaken
between the Crucifixion and the Resurrection to rescue the souls of
the righteous from their imprisonment in Hell).

[6] *shrouded ... clouds* Though geographically imprecise, this is
probably a reference to the Nubians, whose name was thought to
derive from the Latin *nubes* (clouds).

Then two nights after they had escaped their enemies,
He commanded that glorious hero[1] to encamp
65   with all their host around the fortress of Etham,
with great clamor and resounding noise,
a mighty force among those borderlands.
Danger pushed their path northward—
to the south, they knew, lay the Sun-dwellers' land,[2]
70   the sunburnt hillsides of a people browned
by the hot coals of heaven. There Holy God
shielded the people from the scorching heat:
spread a canopy over the searing sky,
hung a holy veil in the burning air.[3]
75   A cloud spread broad across the sky
evenly divided earth and heaven,
went before that company, and heaven's bright fires
were quenched in its heat. The host, most happy people,
marveled at it. The sheltering day-shield
80   glided across the heavens; wise God
unfurled a sail across the course of the sun
whose halyards none could know
nor could the sailyard be seen
by any earth-dweller, no matter how skilled,
85   how that greatest of tabernacles was tied,
when he had honored with glory
those faithful people. The third encampment
was a comfort to them; the army observed
how those holy sails billowed above,
90   radiant miracle aloft; the multitude of Israel,
that people, saw in that place how the Lord,
the Lord of Hosts himself, had come to make camp.
Before them headed the fire and cloud
in the bright sky, twin beams,
95   each of them equally shared
in the high service of the Holy Spirit,
by day and night on the daring journey.
     Then, as I've heard, the next morning,
that bold-hearted people raised their brave trumpets,
100   heralds of glory. The group all arose,

a mighty army eager to set out
as Moses, their great leader, commanded them,
the people of God. Going before them they saw
their life-guide lay out the path of life;
105   the sky set the course, the sailors followed
on the sea-path.[4] The people were joyful,
loud the army's clamor. Each evening arose
a heavenly beacon, second marvelous sign,
wondrously held the setting sun's place
110   and blazed with light above the people,
a gleaming beam. Bright rays
stood blazing above the soldiers,
a shining shield-cover—shadows vanished,
and the deep shades of night could scarcely
115   stay hidden in their dens. Heaven's candle burned,
the new night-watchman had great need
to guard the host, lest the desert horror,
grey heath-stalker, should sever their lives
with the sudden clutch of violent storms.
120   Their forerunner had fiery locks,
bright beams, threatening to burn up
those desert troops with flaming terror,
a blaze of fire on that army, unless
they were brave in heart and obeyed Moses.
125   The bright troops shone, their shields gleamed,
the shield-bearers kept sight of the true path,
the sign above, until the barrier of the sea
at land's end prevented their progress,
their eager advance. Exhausted, they pitched
130   their camp, refreshed themselves with food
served by noble stewards, and restored their strength.
When the trumpets sang, the sailors spread
their field-tents in the hills; this was the fourth camp,
the shield-bearers' rest by the Red Sea.
135   Then terrible news arose among the army—
inland pursuit. Fear of slaughter
spread among the troops, those exiles awaited
their hostile pursuers, who had long punished
those homeless people with harsh affliction
140   and woeful oppression. They ignored their pledge,

---

[1]   *glorious hero*   I.e., God commanded Moses.

[2]   *Sun-dwellers' land*   Old English *sigelwara*, usually applied to the Ethiopians, though they are not mentioned in the Biblical story of Exodus.

[3]   *spread a canopy ... burning air*   This is the pillar of cloud described throughout Exodus. The cloud accompanies the Israelites by day, and a pillar of fire accompanies them by night (lines 93–97).

[4]   *Going before ... sea-path*   The "life-guide" is the pillar of cloud; the nautical imagery is a somewhat disconcerting way of describing the desert passage of the Hebrews from Egypt, but resonates powerfully in traditional Old English poetry—and will, of course, become more appropriate when the travelers reach the Red Sea.

the promise given by the elder Pharaoh …[1]

Then he became the custodian of the treasure
of all the Egyptians, and he greatly prospered.
But they forgot all that; the Egyptian nation
145 grew grim and hostile, did not hesitate at all,
carried out crimes against his kinsmen,
stirred up strife and devoured their pledges.
Seething desires surged in their hearts,
mighty passions; they wanted to repay
150 that good with evil, lies and treachery,
so the people of Moses would have paid in blood
for that day's work, if Almighty God
had granted success to their mission of destruction.
        The men's spirits began to despair
155 when they saw surging up from the south
the army of Pharaoh advancing forward,
a great forest moving, the cavalry gleaming,
with spears ready, the battle swarming,
shields shining, trumpets sounding,
160 banners aloft, an army marching across the border.
Black birds of prey croaked for carrion, greedy for
        slaughter
and a feast of corpses, dewy-feathered
dark Furies.[2] The wolves howled
a grim evening-song, eager for prey,
165 pitiless beasts, bold scavengers, followed
in their tracks, waiting the warriors' fall.
These border-stalkers bayed in the black of night,
doomed souls grew faint as the people despaired.
        At times proud thanes° from the host   noblemen
170 measured the miles with their galloping horses;
there the proud king, prince of men,
rode before the border-troop brandishing the standard;

the warriors' warlord fastened his helmet,
strapped on his chinguard as the standard gleamed,
175 ready for battle, he rattled his war-coat,
commanded his chosen troops to stand fast
and hold their formation. The friends[3] watched
the approach of that land-host with eyes full of hate.
        Around him[4] roved fearless warriors,
180 grey sword-wolves who welcomed battle
with a lust for combat, loyal to their leader.
For the host, he himself had chosen
from that nation two thousand most noble,
and all were kings and royal kinsmen
185 in the old order, esteemed for their ancestry:
each of them in turn had led forth
each and every male soldier
he was able to find on that occasion.
All the kings of that country were there
190 together in formation; the well-known trumpet
announced among the throng where the young men,
a horde of warriors, should bear their weapons.
        And so those dark legions surged forward,
foe upon foe, a vast multitude of the nation's might,
195 thousands at a time, eager to advance.
They meant with their mighty troops to attack
the people of Israel at the first light of day,
destroy them with swords in revenge for their brothers.
And so there was weeping and wailing in the camps,
200 a grim song at evening, terror spreading;
they put on their war-coats when panic seized them,
and fled the fearful tidings. The enemy was united,
the army war-bright, until the mighty angel
who protected the multitude repelled those proud ones,
205 so that those two enemies were no longer able
to see one another: their ways were separated.
        The exiles experienced a night-long reprieve,
though enemies loomed on either side—
the army or the sea, and no other way out.
210 Giving up hope for their homeland,
they sat among the sloping hills in somber clothing,
expecting sorrow. Watchful, they awaited,
all that company of kinsmen together,
the greater forces, until in the first light of dawn
215 Moses bade the heralds with brass trumpets

---

[1] *Pharaoh …*   There is a gap of perhaps four pages in the manuscript here; the missing lines apparently recounted how an earlier
Pharaoh had given Joseph authority over all Egypt (Genesis 41), but
when a new Pharaoh arose who knew nothing of Joseph, the
oppression of the Israelites began (Exodus 1). Dramatically the
passage, emphasizing the treachery of the Egyptians, is a delaying
device between the first mention of their pursuit and their visible
approach.

[2] *dark Furies*   The meter is defective here but no proposed solution
is entirely satisfactory. The word translated here as "Furies" is
wælceasega, "chooser of the slain," a word cognate with the "Valky-
rie" of Norse mythology but also used in Old English to gloss
classical figures like the Fates and Furies.

[3] *The friends*   I.e., the Israelites.

[4] *him*   I.e., the Pharaoh.

to assemble the people, and soldiers to arise,
put on their mail coats and consider their courage,
bear the bright armor, and with banners summon
the war-band to the shore. Swiftly the defenders
220 heeded the battle-call, the host was alerted;
they heard the trumpets, and the sailors hurried
over the hills from their tents, a troop in haste.
Then they assigned twelve troops to stand
against the vicious attack of the advancing enemy,
225 brave-spirited men whose courage was stirred.
In each one, fifty companies were chosen
from the most noble families among the nations,
assembled in battalions to bear arms;
and each hand-picked company of that famous host
230 was composed of ten hundred spear-carriers
and fighting men, gloriously favored—
a warlike host! The army's commanders
did not welcome the weak among their ranks,
the young who were not yet able
235 to defend themselves against the treacherous foe
in the shelter of a shield and a mail-shirt,
or those who had not known a sharp wound
over the edge of a shield, or bore battle-scars
from boasting spear-play. Nor could the old,
240 greybearded warriors, hold their own in battle
if their might had diminished among the brave men.
Instead, they selected battalions by their stature,
how their courage would endure honorably
among the people, and how powerfully
245 their skilled hands could grasp a spear.
When the stalwart army was assembled,
eager to advance, the ensign° rode on high,[1]   *flag*
brightest of beams; there they abided
until their guide, glittering above their shields,
250 burst through the gates of the air by the sea.
       Then the herald leapt up before that host,
bold battle-crier, raised up his shield
and ordered the commanders to quiet the army
so all could listen to their leader's speech.
255 That kingdom's guardian wanted to counsel
the hand-picked troops. With his holy voice,
the leader of that host spoke with worthy words:
"Do not be afraid, even though Pharaoh

has brought a vast army of sword-warriors,
260 countless men. The almighty Lord
intends today, through my hand,
to pay them back for their past deeds,
so that they shall no longer survive
to keep the people of Israel in misery.
265 You will not fear those dead foot-soldiers
in their doomed bodies—their brief lease on life
has come to an end. God's counsel
has fled your heart; I have a better way:
that you should always praise the Prince of Glory,
270 pray for the grace of the Lord of Life
and the salvation of victory as you set forth.
It is the eternal God of Abraham,
the Lord of Creation, lofty and powerful,
who guards this host with his Almighty Hand."
275   Then the lord of the living lifted up his voice
and spoke before the army to all the nation:
"Behold! most beloved of people, now you see
with your own eyes a most awesome wonder,
now with this green rod[2] in my right hand
280 I myself have struck the depths of the sea:
the waves ascend, and swiftly the waters
form a sturdy wall. The ways are dry,
a glistening road, the deep has revealed
its ancient foundations, where no man before,
285 as I have heard tell, has ever traveled,
mottled plains which always remain
forever hidden by the foaming waves.
A south wind, breath of the ocean, has unsealed
the sea's depths, the waves are split,
290 the surf churns out sand. Well I know
that Almighty God has shown mercy to you,
happy as in days of old. Now hurry,
that you may escape the embrace of your enemies,
now that the Ruler has raised up
295 red sea-streams as a sheltering rampart.
The retaining walls of this wondrous wave-road
are fairly raised to the roof of the heavens."
       With these words, all the host arose,
a courageous force. The sea lay calm;

---

1 *the ensign rode on high* I.e., the pillar, which at this point is "of
fire and of the cloud" (Exodus 14.24).

2 *green rod* The Old English phrase is *grene tacn*, literally "green (*or*
living) sign," which has occasioned much comment. The phrase may
simply be an error for *grene tane* "green rod" (corresponding to the
Latin *virga* [rod], the staff of Moses mentioned in Exodus 14.16).

300 upon the sand the hand-picked troops raised
their banners and bright shields. The sea-wall
stood upright alongside the Israelites
for an entire day.[1]

    That troop of earls was of one mind,
305 kept their covenant in close embrace—
they did not despise their dear lord's
holy teaching, when his sweet words were still
and his voice silent by their path through the sea.[2]

    The fourth tribe was the first to lead them,
310 an army of men marching through the waves
upon the green sea bed.[3] The soldiers of Judah
hastened alone down that unknown path
before all their brothers. And so Almighty God
gave them a great reward for that day's work—
315 glorious deeds of victory were granted to them,
so that later they might have lordship
over kingdoms, and rule their kinsmen.
When they entered the sea they raised their ensign,
a battle-standard high above their shields,
320 among the mass of spears those most lordly men
lifted up a golden lion, bravest of beasts.
With it, those warriors would not long suffer
insult or injury from any lord living,
as long as they could lift a spear in battle
325 against any nation. Ahead lay the attack,
hard hand-play, young men brave
in the carnage of weapons, fearless warriors,
bloody wounds and the rush of battle,
the grim grinding of helmets, when Judah advanced.

330   After that army the sailor followed boldly,
the son of Reuben; those sea-dwellers[4]
bore their shields over the salty marsh,

a multitude of men, a mighty legion
went forth fearlessly. In sinful deeds
335 he[5] squandered his lordship, and so he marched
in his beloved's footsteps—his brother had taken
his natural rights as first-born of that nation,
his wealth and status—yet still he was no coward.

    After them, among the throng of peoples,
340 the sons of Simeon advanced in troops,
the third tribe. Their banners waving,
the battalion pressed on, spear-points flashing
and shafts gleaming. The glimmer of day
came over the crest of the sea, God's bright beacon,
345 the glorious morning. The multitude went forth
there while one family followed after another,
in iron-clad armies—one man led these,
greatest in might, for which he became famous
on their march—beneath the pillar of cloud,
350 kin after kin; each one observed
the rights of each tribe and the rank of earls,
as Moses instructed them. They had one father,
a beloved prince, dear to his people,
ancient and wise, who held the land-right;
355 that great patriarch begat a line
of brave noblemen, a holy nation,
the race of Israel, righteous before the Lord.
This is how ancient writers in their wisdom
tell it, who know most about these tribes,
360 each one's lineage, origin and ancestry:

    Over new seas Noah[6] sailed,[7]
glorious prince, together with his three sons,
over the deepest of drenching floods
that had ever come over the earth.
365 He had in his heart a holy faith,
and so he steered over the ocean streams

---

[1] *entire day* A half-line is apparently missing here (or after the following line?); various suggestions, none compellingly plausible, have been made to fill the gap, but none is adopted here.

[2] *sea* The original is obscure here; this is a guess at its probable meaning.

[3] *green sea bed* The description of the sea floor as "green" has occasioned much debate; elsewhere in Old English poetry the road to Paradise is described as "green," and the poem may be pointing towards the moment's typological or allegorical significance.

[4] *sea-dwellers* Literally, "sea-vikings." It is by no means certain that the word had any of its later connotations in this passage, and a more neutral translation (reflecting Old English *wic* "dwelling") is given here.

---

[5] *he* I.e., Reuben.

[6] *Noah* The story of Noah and the ark is found in Genesis 5–9.

[7] *Over new ... sailed* Many readers and editors have felt the transition to be abrupt, and assumed that this passage originally belonged somewhere else. But the overarching nautical imagery connects it to the action described in the rest of the poem, and the typological connections found in the Easter Vigil liturgy make the linkage of Noah, Abraham, and Moses less peculiar to an early medieval reader than it might be to a modern one. The sense of narrative unity found here might be thought of as "liturgical" rather than "dramatic," and sequence less important than significance.

the greatest treasure-chest[1] I have ever heard tell of.
The wise sea-prince, to save the lives
of all who dwell upon on earth,
370 had reckoned up a lasting remnant,
a first generation, father and mother
of all who bear offspring, more diverse
than men can imagine. Likewise the heroes brought
into the bosom of the ship every kind of seed
375 for which men have use beneath the heavens.
   And so the words of wise men tell us
that the ninth in lineage from Noah
was Abraham's father among that folk.
This is the Abraham[2] to whom the God of angels
380 gave a new name; and near and far
entrusted the holy tribes into his keeping,
and lordship over nations. He lived in exile.
Later, he led the most beloved of creatures
at the Lord's behest; into the highlands
385 climbed the two kinsmen, up to Mount Sion.
They found the Covenant there, gazed on God's glory,
the holy pledge, as men have heard tell.
   In that same place the wise son of David,[3]
glorious king, through the counsel of the prophet
390 later built the temple of the Lord,
a holy shrine, highest and holiest—
the wisest among the world's kingdoms
of all earthly rulers, most renowned among men—
the greatest and most glorious that the sons of men
395 in all nations on earth ever made with their hands.[4]
   To the appointed meeting-place he led his son,
Abraham took Isaac; up blazed the pyre,
most deadly slayer—but he was not doomed to die[5]—
he intended to offer his offspring to the flames,
400 his best of children to the blazing pyre,
his sweet son as a sacrifice for victory,
his only heir upon the earth,
his life's consolation, which he had long awaited,
his lasting hope for the nation's legacy.

405 He made it clear, when he took the child
fast in his hands, and the famous man drew
his ancient heirloom (its edge rasping),
that he did not hold his son's life dearer
than his obedience to the King of Heaven.
410 Up he rose,[6]
ready to slay his only son,
still a boy, with his bloody blade,
put his child to the sword, if God had not stopped him;
the Bright Father would not take the boy
415 as a holy sacrifice, but laid His hands upon him.[7]
Then to restrain him came a voice from the heavens,
a sound of glory, and spoke these words:
"Abraham! do not slay your own child,
your son, with a sword. The truth is known,
420 now that the King of all Creation has tested you,
that you have kept your covenant with God,
a firm faith, which shall be a protector
for you all the days of your life
forever and ever, unfailing.
425 Why should the Son of Man need a stronger pledge?
Heaven and earth cannot confine
the words of His glory, wider and broader
than all the ends of the earth can enfold,
the orb of the world and the firmament above,
430 the depths of the sea and the yearning sky.[8]
The King of Angels, God of Hosts,
Ruler of destinies, righteous in victory,
swears you an oath by His own life,
that men across the earth, in all their wisdom,
435 will never know how to count the number
of all your tribe and offspring,
shield-bearing warriors, nor say it truly
unless someone might grow so wise in spirit
that he alone might reckon the number
440 of stones on the earth, stars in the heavens,
the sands of the sea-swell's salty waves;

---

[1] *treasure-chest* I.e., the ark and its contents, usually identified with the Church in medieval readings of Genesis.

[2] *Abraham* See Genesis 17 and forward.

[3] *wise son of David* I.e., Solomon.

[4] *temple ... hands* See 1 Kings 6.

[5] *most deadly ... to die* Or "the foremost life-slayer (i.e., Satan) was no happier for that."

[6] *Up he rose* A half-line is usually assumed to be missing here, but (as at line 304) the text makes sense as it stands, so nothing has been invented to fill the "gap."

[7] *Bright Father ... him* "Father" and "His" refer equally to Moses and to God.

[8] *yearning sky* It is not clear why the sky is described as *geomre* (sad or dreary) at this particular moment—the phrase, which is much better suited to the North Sea than the Middle East, may be traditional, but it does not occur elsewhere in Old English poetry.

But your people, most noble of nations,
free-born of their father, will occupy
the land of Canaan, between the two seas
445   even unto the borders of Egypt."...[1]
    All that folk[2] fell into a panic; fear of the flood
filled their wretched hearts, and the sea wreaked death.
The steep sea-slopes were soaked with blood,
the sea spewed gore, chaos was in the waves,
450   the water full of weapons, a death-mist arose.
The Egyptians were thrown into retreat:
they fled terrified, felt the sudden terror,
cowards, deserters, they sought out their homes—
their boasts were milder. The wild tossing waves
455   darkened over them again: none of that army
came home again, but fate cut off their retreat
and locked them in the waves. Where a road lay before,
the ocean raged, that host was overwhelmed,
the sea flowed forth. A storm arose[3]
460   up to high heaven, a great outcry of despair,
the enemies shrieked, the sky grew dark
with doomed voices, the flood was blood-muddy.
The shield-walls were shattered, and the greatest of
        sea-deaths
lashed the sky; those proud kings and their legions
465   were slain. Their screams grew silent,
the waves at an end; war-shields gleamed.
High above those heroes rushed a wall of water,
a mighty sea-stream. That multitude was caught
fast in death's fetters, deprived of escape,
470   snagged in their armor. The sands awaited
their ordained fate, when the flowing waves,
the ice-cold sea, the salty billows,
bare bringer of doom, driven from its course
might come seeking again its ancient bed,
475   an angry wandering spirit smiting his enemies.
With blood was the blue air defiled,

the flood threatened bloody terror wild
on the seafarers' march, while the true Maker
revealed his fury through the hand of Moses.
480   Ravaging, seething, the surging flood swept them away
in its deadly clutches; doomed men dropped,
the sea fell upon the land, the sky was shaken.
The ramparts gave way, the waves burst,
the sea-columns melted, when the Mighty One,
485   Heavenly Guardian, struck with His holy Hand
those wretched warriors of a proud nation[4]—
no restraining the course of the saving waters,
the might of the sea-streams; He wrecked the multitudes
in shrieking terror. The raging ocean
490   towered high, glided over them, terror mounted,
murderous waves gushed, and God's handiwork,
foamy-bosomed, fell upon the battle-path
from the heights of heaven; the flood's Guardian
struck the unprotected way with an ancient sword,
495   so that at the death-blow the legions slept,
a sinful throng, fast shut in,
lost their lives, an army flood-pale,
when they were buried under the brown water,
the proud and mighty waves.[5] The force all fell,
500   the afflicting ones, the legions of Egypt,
Pharaoh and all his army. God's adversary
quickly found as he sank to the sea-floor
that the Guardian of the waves was stronger than he—
angry and enraged, he had intended to settle
505   the battle in a deadly embrace. For that day's work
the Egyptians received an overwhelming reward,
for none of that army, vast beyond number,
ever survived to return home again
to tell of his fate, or proclaim in the cities
510   the worst tidings to the wives of those warriors,
the fall of their treasure's protectors,
but a mighty sea-death swallowed their legions
and their heralds with them. He who has power
drained the boasts of men—they fought against God.

---

[1]   *Egypt ...*   A page is missing in the manuscript here; it probably
would have told the story found in Exodus 14.23–26: the people of
Israel cross the Red Sea; the Egyptians pursue them; when Moses
stretches out his hands the sea returns to its former place and the
army of Pharaoh is destroyed.

[2]   *that folk*   I.e., Egyptians.

[3]   *A storm arose*   Some critics have interpreted these lines differently,
but it seems best to read the passage as an example (by no means the
only one in Old English poetry) of synaesthesia—the uproar of the
drowning army is described as a storm which darkens the sky.

---

[4]   *The ramparts ... nation*   These lines are difficult and no single
solution is entirely satisfactory; the translation is fairly loose. The
vivid impressionistic style of the passage seems almost to have gone
out of control, and the chaos of the scene described has shaken the
syntax of the description itself.

[5]   *fast shut in ... waves*   These lines are difficult and this translation
is conjectural.

515   Then Moses, man of noble virtue,
gave a holy speech on the shore of the sea,
spoke eternal wisdom to the Israelites
and deep counsel. Even now the nations speak
of that day's work, discover in Scripture
520 every law which the Lord, in words of truth,
ordained for them on that journey.
If the interpreter of Life will unlock,
the body's Guardian radiant in the breast,
these expansive blessings with the keys of the spirit,
525 the mysteries will be clear and good counsel will emerge,
for it has words of wisdom in its keeping,
and earnestly seeks to instruct our heart
so we will not lack for fellowship with God,
the Maker's mercy. He will enlighten us even more;
530 for now, scholars inform us of the better
and more lasting joys of Heaven. Here pleasure fades,
cursed with sin, allotted to exiles,
a wretched time of waiting. Homeless,
we anxiously inhabit this guest-house,
535 mourning in spirit, mindful of the house of pain
fast under the earth, a place of fire and worms,
the den of every kind of evil ever open,
while here those arch-thieves divide up their domain,
old age and early death. The day of reckoning draws near,
540 greatest of all glories, upon the earth,
a day marked by deeds: in the meeting-place
the Lord Himself will judge the multitude,
when He will lead into Heaven above
the souls of the righteous, blessed spirits,
545 where there is light and life and the joy of bliss.[1]
In delight that troop will praise the Lord,
King of Glory, God of Hosts, for all eternity.
    And so he spoke, mindful of wise counsel,
mildest of men made strong in might,
550 in a loud voice—awaiting their leader's will
the army stood silent, perceived that wonder,
his brave words of salvation. He said to the multitude:
"Mighty is this multitude, great our Commander,
the strongest of Supports who guides our journey.

555 He has given over to us the tribes of Canaan,
their cities and treasures and spacious kingdoms;
He will now fulfill what He long ago promised
with sworn oaths, the Lord of Angels,
to our fathers' generations in ancient days,
560 if you will only hold His holy precepts,
that you will overcome each of your enemies
and hold, rich in victory, the feast-halls of heroes
between the two seas: great will be your glory."
    At these words the whole host was glad,
565 trumpets of victory sounded, standards were raised
to the lovely sound. The folk had reached land;
the pillar of glory had guided the host,
the holy troop, under God's protection.
The shield-warriors exulted that they had escaped alive
570 from the power of their enemies, though they had
    passed boldly
under the roof of the waves, and seen the walls standing;
the sea through which they had borne their armor
    seemed brimming blood.
They rejoiced with war-songs when they escaped
    that army;
the battalions and legions lifted up a loud voice,
575 gave praise to God, raised a song of glory
for that day's work. The women opposite them,
greatest of gatherings, chanted a battle anthem
with voiced raised, sang of all these many wonders.
Then it was easy to see the African woman,[2]
580 adorned with gold at the edge of the sea,
her hands grasping neck-adornments;
they rejoiced, seeing their reward,
received the spoils of war[3]—their bondage was released.
They divided up the sea's leavings, ancient treasures,
585 along the shore by each tribe's ensign,
robes and shields; they divided rightly
gold and good cloth, the treasures of Joseph,
glorious possessions of men, whose guardians lay,
greatest of armies, fast in the arms of death.
—?8TH CENTURY

---

[1] *Then Moses, man of ... joy of bliss* Lines 515–48 have struck many critics as a later addition to the poem; they interrupt the speech of Moses (which resumes at 553) and may well be misplaced here, but no compelling alternative to the existing text has been proposed.

[2] *African woman* Perhaps Zipporah, Moses's Ethiopian wife (Numbers 12.1), who figures in medieval exegesis as an image of the Christian Church.

[3] *spoils of war* I.e., the armor and jewels of the drowned Egyptian army, washed up on the shores of the Red Sea.

THE ANGLO-SAXON CHRONICLE

The Anglo-Saxon Chronicle is not a single work, but a group of interrelated manuscripts. It is presumed to have originated during the reign of Alfred the Great, whose court scholars compiled a year-by-year record of important events from the birth of Christ to their own day. Their compilation was based on Bede's *Ecclesiastical History*, other written sources, some local traditions, and the annotations (called "annals") made in monastic Easter tables to record the most memorable events of each year—the death of an abbot, the appearance of a comet, a notably bad famine. From these unpromising bits and pieces the authors of the *Chronicle* assembled an essentially coherent narrative which tells a story of England from the time of the Romans to that of the heroic struggles of Alfred himself against the terror of the Viking raids. In this sense *The Chronicle* is a work of propaganda, designed to inspire the English to resist the Viking invasions.

The completed record was sent to various places across England around 892. Each copy was supplemented, interpolated into, and continued, sometimes annually as events were unfolding, and each represents the interests and narrow views of the place in which it was written. Some copies include records of local events, often no more than a line or two; others have lengthy continuations and elaborate histories of the monasteries in which they were kept. Scholars have discerned several different threads of continuations, interwoven in various ways (surviving manuscripts are often copies of copies of the originals, and a great deal of cross-borrowing and collating has taken place in the history of the *Chronicle* texts). A version from Peterborough was continued by two different scribes well into the twelfth century, providing an invaluable witness not only to the period of transition from English to Norman rule but also to the gradual shift of the English language from Old to Middle English.

It would be unwise to take every word of the *Chronicle* as a reliable or unbiased historical account, but it remains the most important source for our knowledge of Anglo-Saxon history. Among its sometimes bare annals are some sparks of political wisdom, narrative flair, historical insight, and even authorial wit; it offers not only a sturdy context in which to read Old English literature but a fascinating literary experience in itself.

⌘⌘⌘

from *The Anglo-Saxon Chronicles*[1]

A. THE COMING OF THE ANGLES AND SAXONS TO BRITAIN (449–495)

449.[2] Here[3] Martianus and Valentinian succeeded to the empire, and reigned seven winters. In their days Hengest and Horsa,[4] invited by Vortigern, king of the Britons, landed in Britain in a place that is called

---

[1] *The Anglo-Saxon Chronicles*   The present text, prepared by R.M. Liuzza for this volume, draws on various manuscripts; most entries follow the text of the Peterborough Chronicle (known as E to scholars) or the Winchester text (A). The translation draws heavily on those by James Ingram (1823) and J.A. Giles (1847); the translation of Michael Swanton (2000) has also been consulted.

[2] *449*   This story of the arrival of the Angles and Saxons is mostly from Bede's *Ecclesiastical History* with a few added details presumably from popular legend or local tradition.

[3] *Here*   Each year's entry begins with the word "here," i.e., "in this place on the page," reflecting the origins of the work as a series of annotations in annals.

[4] *Hengest and Horsa*   Both names mean "horse" in Old English and are probably not their given names.

Ipwin's-fleet;[1] first of all to support the Britons, but they later fought against them. The king directed them to fight against the Picts, and they did so, winning victory wherever they went. They then sent word to Angeln[2] asking them to send more assistance; they described the worthlessness of the Britons and the richness of the land. They then sent them greater support—the men came from three powers of Germany: the Old Saxons, the Angles, and the Jutes. From the Jutes are descended the men of Kent, the Wightware—that is, the tribe that now lives in the Isle of Wight—and that race in Wessex that is still called the race of the Jutes. From the Old Saxons came the East Saxons and the South Saxons and the West Saxons. From Angeln, which has remained a wasteland ever since between the Jutes and the Saxons, came the East Angles, the Middle Angles, the Mercians, and all of those north of the Humber. Their war-leaders were two brothers, Hengest and Horsa, the sons of Wihtgils; Wihtgils was the son of Witta, Witta the son of Wecta, Wecta the son of Woden.[3] From this Woden arose all our royal kindred, and that of the Southumbrians also.

455.   Here Hengest and Horsa fought with Vortigern the king on the spot that is called Aylesford, and his brother Horsa was killed there. Hengest afterwards succeeded to the kingdom with his son Æsc.

457.   Here Hengest and Æsc fought with the Britons in the place that is called Crayford, and there killed four thousand men. The Britons then abandoned the land of Kent, and in great terror fled to London.

465.   Here Hengest and Æsc fought with the Welsh near Wipped's-fleet; and there killed twelve Welsh chieftains. On Hengest's side a thane[4] whose name was Wipped was killed there.

---

[1]   *Ipwin's-fleet*   Modern Ebbsfleet in Kent.

[2]   *Angeln*   Narrow land between modern Germany and Denmark, roughly modern Schleswig.

[3]   *Their war-leaders ... Woden*   Most Anglo-Saxon royal genealogies trace the king's family back to a god, presumably as a way of emphasizing the king's status and power; later the genealogy of the West Saxon kings will incorporate Biblical figures as well.

[4]   *thane*   Like a knight.

473.   Here Hengest and Æsc fought with the Welsh, and took countless spoils. and the Welsh fled from the English like fire.

477.   Here came Ælla to Britain with his three sons, Cymen, and Wlencing, and Cissa, in three ships. They landed at a place that is called Cymen's Shore, and there slew many Welsh and drove some in flight into the wood that is called Andredsley.[5]

485.   Here Ælla fought with the Welsh near Mearcred's Burn.

488.   Here Æsc succeeded to the kingdom, and was king of the men of Kent twenty-four winters.[6]

490.   Here Ælla and Cissa besieged the city of Andred,[7] and killed everyone who lived there—not one Briton was left there afterwards.

495.   Here came two leaders into Britain, Cerdic and his son Cynric, with five ships, at a place that is called Cerdic's Shore, and they fought with the Welsh that same day.[8]

B. THE STORY OF CYNEWULF AND CYNEHEARD (755)

755.[9]   Here Cynewulf, with the consent of the West-Saxon council, deprived his relative Sigebriht of his kingdom, except Hampshire, because of his unrighteous deeds; and he retained Hampshire until he slew the ealdorman[10] who remained the longest with him. Then

---

[5]   *Andredsley*   The Weald.

[6]   *twenty-four winters*   One manuscript reads "xxx.iiii." rather than "xx.iiii."

[7]   *Andred*   Roman coastal fort near Pevensey, Sussex.

[8]   *Here came ... same day*   Cerdic is the leader of the West Saxons and ancestor of Alfred the Great.

[9]   *755*   This entry, whose source is unknown, suggests that long before their history was officially transcribed, prose tales of notable events circulated as part of Anglo-Saxon popular tradition. The story, whose chronology is unlike that of most other annals, is a finely-wrought and tightly-narrated saga in miniature, portraying conflicts between loyalty and power in desperate circumstances.

[10]   *ealdorman*   High-ranking nobleman.

Cynewulf drove him to the forest of Andred, and he remained there until a swineherd stabbed him by the stream at Privett—and the swineherd revenged the Ealdorman Cumbra.[1] The same Cynewulf fought many hard battles with the Welsh; and, about thirty-one winters after he had the kingdom, he wanted to expel a prince called Cyneheard, who was the brother of Sigebriht. And then he[2] learned that the king was gone with a small troop to visit a woman at Merton, and he rode after him, and surrounded the chamber from outside before the men who were with the king were aware of him.

When the king realized this, he went out the door and defended himself bravely until his eyes fell on the nobleman, and then he rushed out upon him and wounded him severely. Then they were all fighting against the king until they killed him. And then from the woman's screams the king's men became aware of the disturbance, and they ran to the spot, as quickly as they could get ready. The nobleman immediately offered each of them life and rewards, and none of them would accept it, but continued fighting until they all lay dead except for one British hostage, and he was severely wounded.

In the morning, the king's men who had been left behind heard that the king was slain. Then they rode to the spot—Osric his Ealdorman, and Wiferth his thane, and the men that he had left behind; and they met the nobleman at the enclosure[3] where the king lay dead. They had locked the gates against them, and they went up to them. He[4] promised them as much money and land as they wanted, if they would grant him the kingdom; and let them know that their kinsmen were already with him, who would never desert him. And then they said that no kinsman could be dearer to them than their lord, and they would never follow his murderer. Then they asked their kinsmen to depart from

him, safe and sound, and they replied that the same offer had been made to their companions who were with the king. They said that they would pay no more attention to that "than your companions did who were killed beside the king."[5] And they were fighting at the gates until they forced their way in and killed the nobleman and all the men who were with him, except one, who was the godson of the ealdorman,[6] and he spared his life, though he was often wounded.

This Cynewulf reigned thirty-one winters. His body lies at Winchester, and that of the nobleman at Axminster. Their paternal ancestry goes directly back to Cerdic.

C. KING ALFRED'S EARLY YEARS (871–78)

871. Here the army[7] came to Reading in Wessex; and three nights afterwards two jarls[8] rode up; they were met by Ealdorman Æthelwulf at Englefield and fought with them, and obtained the victory. There one of them was slain, whose name was Sidroc. About four nights after this, King Æthelred and Alfred his brother led their main army to Reading, where they fought with the enemy; and there was much slaughter on either hand, Ealdorman Æthelwulf being among the slain; and the Danes held possession of the field. And about four nights after this, King Æthelred and Alfred his brother fought with all the army on Ashdown, and the Danes were overcome. They had two heathen kings, Bagsecg and Halfdan, and many jarls; and they were in two divisions, in one of which were Bagsecg and Halfdan, the heathen kings, and in the other were the jarls. King Æthelred fought with the troops of the kings, and King Bagsecg was killed; Alfred his brother fought with the troops of the jarls, and there Jarl Sidroc the Ealdorman, Jarl Sidroc the younger, Jarl Osbern, Jarl Frene, and Jarl Harold were killed. They put both troops to flight; there

---

[1] *Ealdorman Cumbra* I.e., the one whom Sigebriht had killed in Hampshire.

[2] *he* I.e., Cyneheard.

[3] *enclosure* The scene should be imagined as a small building (a *burh*) surrounded by a wall (a *byrig*). The king's fight took place inside the enclosure; the king's men ride up to the outside of it and fight there.

[4] *He* I.e., Cyneheard.

[5] *They said … the king* The dramatic shift from indirect to direct discourse is striking; it may well be a mark of the story's origins in oral tradition.

[6] *ealdorman* I.e., Osric.

[7] *Here the army* In *The Chronicle* "the army" (Old English *here*) almost always means the Vikings.

[8] *jarls* This spelling has been preferred to the modern English "earl" as a way of indicating its use within the *Chronicle*.

were many thousands killed, and they kept fighting until nightfall. Within two weeks, King Æthelred and Alfred his brother fought with the army at Basing, and there the Danes had the victory. About two months after this, King Æthelred and Alfred his brother fought with the army at Merton. They were in two bands, and they put them both to flight, and had the victory for most of the day; and there was much slaughter on either hand, but the Danes became masters of the field; and there Bishop Heahmund was killed, along with many other good men. After this fight came a vast army in the summer to Reading. And after the Easter of this year King Æthelred died. He reigned five years, and his body lies at Wimborne Minster.

Then Alfred, his brother, the son of Æthelwulf, became king of Wessex. And within a month of this, King Alfred fought against all the army with a small force at Wilton, and long pursued them during the day; but the Danes got possession of the field. In this year there were nine general battles fought with the army in the kingdom south of the Thames, besides those skirmishes in which Alfred the king's brother, and every single ealdorman, and the thanes of the king often rode against them, which were not counted. Here also were slain nine jarls, and one king; and the same year the West-Saxons made peace with the army.

872. Here the army went to London from Reading, and there chose their winter-quarters. Then the Mercians made peace with the army.

873. Here the army went against the Northumbrians, and fixed their winter quarters at Torksey in Lindsey. And the Mercians again made peace with the army.

874. Here the army went from Lindsey to Repton, and there took winter quarters, and drove the king, Burhred, across the sea, when he had reigned about twenty-two winters, and subdued all that land. He then went to Rome, and there remained to the end of his life. And his body lies in the church of St. Mary, in the English Quarter. And the same year they gave Ceolwulf, a foolish king's thane, the kingdom of Mercia to hold; and he swore oaths to them, and gave hostages, that it should be ready for them whenever they wanted it, and

he would be ready with himself, and with all those that would remain with him, at the service of the army.

875. Here the army went from Repton; and Halfdan advanced with some of the army against the Northumbrians, and fixed his winter-quarters by the river Tine. The army then subdued that land, and often raided among the Picts and the Britons of Strathclyde. Meanwhile the three kings, Guthrum, Oscytel, and Anwind, went from Repton to Cambridge with a vast army, and settled there for one year. And that summer King Alfred went out to sea with an armed fleet, and fought against seven ships, and captured one of them and dispersed the others.

876. Here the army stole into Wareham, a fort of the West-Saxons. The king afterwards made peace with them; and they gave him as hostages those who were worthiest in the army; and swore with oaths on the holy bracelet, which they had never done before to any nation, that they would quickly go from his kingdom. Then, under cover of this, their cavalry stole by night into Exeter. The same year Halfdan divided the land of the Northumbrians, so that they were ploughing and providing for themselves.

877. Here the Danish army came into Exeter from Wareham, while the navy sailed west until they met with a great storm at sea, and 120 ships were lost at Swanage. Meanwhile King Alfred with his army rode after the cavalry as far as Exeter; but he could not overtake them before their arrival in the fortress, where they could not be attacked. There they gave him as many hostages as he required, swearing with solemn oaths to hold the strictest peace. In the fall the army entered Mercia, and divided some of it among themselves, and gave some to Ceolwulf.

878. Here about mid-winter, after twelfth-night, the Danish army stole out to Chippenham, and rode over the land of the West-Saxons and occupied it, driving many of the people over sea; and the greatest part of the others they rode down and subdued to their will, except for Alfred the king, who went with a little band with great difficulty into the woods and fastnesses of the

moors. And in the winter of this same year a brother of Ivar and Halfdan landed in Wessex, in Devonshire, with twenty-three ships, and was killed there, and eight hundred men with him, and forty of his army. There also was taken the banner which they called "The Raven." In the Easter of this year King Alfred with his little force raised a stronghold at Athelney, from which he assailed the army, assisted by that part of Somersetshire which was nearest to it. Then, in the seventh week after Easter, he rode to Brixton by the eastern side of Selwood, and there came out to meet him all the people of Somerset, and Wiltshire, and that part of Hampshire which is on this side of the sea; and they were very glad to see him. Then within one night he went from this retreat to Hey; and within one night after he proceeded to Heddington; and there fought with all the army and put them to flight, riding after them as far as the fortress, where he remained a fortnight. Then the army gave him hostages, and swore with many oaths that they would go out of his kingdom. They told him also that their king would receive baptism, and they fulfilled that promise. Three weeks later King Guthrum, attended by some thirty of the worthiest men in his army, came to the king at Aller, which is near Athelney, and there the king became his sponsor in baptism; and his chrism-loosing[1] was at Wedmore. He was there twelve nights with the king, who honored him and his companions with many gifts.

D. KING ÆTHELRED'S TROUBLES (980–93)

980. In this year on the 2nd of May Æthelgar was consecrated bishop for the bishopric of Selsey; and in the same year Southampton was plundered by a raiding ship-army, and most of the population slain or imprisoned. And the same year the Isle of Thanet was overrun, and the county of Chester was plundered by the raiding ship-army of the North.

981. In this year St. Petroc's-stow was plundered; and in the same year much harm was done everywhere along the sea-coast, both in Devonshire and Cornwall.

982. In this year three ships of Vikings came up in Dorsetshire and plundered in Portland. The same year London was burned. And in the same year died two ealdormen, Æthelmær in Hampshire and Edwin in Sussex. Æthelmær's body lies in the New Minster at Winchester, and Edwin's in the monastery at Abingdon. …

987. Here the port of Watchet was plundered.

988. Here Goda, the thane of Devonshire, was slain, and a great number with him; and Dunstan, the holy archbishop, departed this life, and sought a heavenly one. Bishop Æthelgar succeeded him in the archbishopric; but he lived only a little while after, one year and three months.

989. Here Abbot Edwin died, and Abbot Wulfgar succeeded to the abbacy. Sigeric was ordained archbishop this year, and went to Rome to receive his pallium.[2]

991. Here Ipswich was plundered; and very soon afterwards Ealdorman Byrhtnoth was slain at Maldon. In this same year it was decided that tribute should be given for the first time to the Danes, because of the great terror they caused along the sea-coast. That was at first 10,000 pounds. Archbishop Sigeric first advised this measure.

992. Here the blessed Archbishop Oswald departed this life, and sought a heavenly one; and in the same year died Ealdorman Æthelwin. Then the king and all his council resolved that all the ships that were of any account should be gathered together at London; and the king placed the army under the command of Ealdorman Ælfric, and Earl Thorod, and Bishop Ælfstan, and Bishop Æscwig, and told them that they should try to find a way to entrap the enemy. Then Ealdorman Ælfric sent and gave warning to the enemy; and on the night preceding the day of battle he scuttled away from the army, to his great disgrace. The enemy then escaped, except for the crew of one ship, who were slain on the

---

[1]   *chrism-loosing*   Ceremony which takes place a week after baptism.

[2]   *pallium*   Vestment, like a stole, bestowed by the pope on an archbishop as a sign of his office.

spot. Then the enemy met the ships from East Anglia and from London; and a great slaughter was made there, and they took the ship, all armed and rigged, that held the ealdorman. Then after the death of Archbishop Oswald, Ealdwulf, Abbot of Peterborough, succeeded to the sees[1] of York and of Worcester; and Cenwulf to the abbacy of Peterborough.

993.   Here in this year Bamburgh was destroyed, and much plunder was there taken. Afterwards the army came to the mouth of the Humber, and did much evil both in Lindsey and in Northumbria. Then a very great army was gathered, but when the armies should have come together, the generals were the first to set the example of flight; namely, Fræne and Godwin and Frithugist. In this same year the king ordered Ælfgar, son of Ealdorman Ælfric, to be blinded.

994.   Here in this year Olaf and Swein came to London, on the feast of the Nativity of St. Mary, with ninety-four ships, and they closely besieged the city, and they also wanted to set it on fire; but there they suffered more harm and evil than they ever supposed any citizens could inflict on them. The Holy Mother of God on that day showed her mercy to the citizens, and rescued them from their enemies. They went from there and wrought the greatest evil that ever any army could do, in burning and plundering and manslaughter, not only on the sea-coast in Essex, but in Kent and in Sussex and in Hampshire. Next they took themselves horses, and rode as widely as they wanted, and committed unspeakable evil. Then the king and his council resolved to send to them and offer them tribute and provision if they would stop their plunder. They accepted the terms, and the whole army came to Southampton, and there set up their winter quarters; they were fed by all the subjects of the West-Saxon kingdom, and were paid 16,000 pounds. Then the king sent Bishop Ælfeah and Ealdorman Æthelweard after king Olaf, and left hostages with the ships; they led Olaf with great pomp to the king at Andover. And King Æthelred received him at the bishops' hands, and honored him with royal gifts. In return Olaf promised—and he fulfilled that promise—that he would never come back to England in a hostile manner.

E. The Life and Death of William the Conqueror (1086)

1086.   One thousand and eighty-seven winters after the birth of our Lord and Savior Jesus Christ, in the twenty-first year after William began to govern and direct England, as God granted him, there was a very heavy and pestilent season in this land. Such a sickness came on men that nearly every other man had the worst disorder, that is, a fever, and so dreadfully that many men died from it. Afterwards, through the bad weather we mentioned, came so great a famine over all England that many hundreds of men died a miserable death through hunger. Alas! how wretched and how rueful a time was there! When poor wretches lay nearly driven to premature death, and then came sharp hunger to dispatch them completely! Who will not be pierced with grief at such a season? or who is so hardhearted as not to weep at such misfortune? Yet such things happen for the sins of the people, who will not love God and righteousness. So it was in those days, that little righteousness was in this land among any men except the monks alone, wherever they fared well. The king and the powerful men loved much, and too much, covetousness in gold and in silver; and did not care how sinfully it was obtained, provided it came to them. The king leased his land at the highest rate he possibly could; then came some other person, and offered more than the former, and the king leased it to the man that offered him more. Then came a third, and offered even more, and the king leased it to whomever offered most of all; and he did not care how very sinfully the stewards got it from wretched men, nor how many unlawful deeds they did; but the more men talked about just law, the more unjustly they acted. They raised unjust tolls, and many other unjust things they did, that are difficult to reckon.

Also in the same year, before harvest, the holy minster[2] of St. Paul, the episcopal see in London, was completely burned, with many other minsters, and the greatest and richest part of the whole city. So also, about the same time, almost every chief port in England was

---

[1] *sees* Cities in which bishops or archbishops reside and have authority.

[2] *minster* Church.

entirely burned. Alas! rueful and woeful was the fate of the year that brought forth so many misfortunes. In the same year also, before the Feast of the Assumption, King William went from Normandy into France with an army, and made war upon his own lord King Philip, and killed many of his men, and burned the town of Mante, and all the holy minsters that were in the town; and two holy men that served God, living in anchorite's[1] cells, were burned there. This being done, King William returned to Normandy. He did a pitiful thing, but an even more pitiful thing befell him. How more pitiful? He fell sick and was severely afflicted.

What shall I say? Sharp death, that spares neither rich men nor poor, seized him also. He died in Normandy, the day after the Nativity of St. Mary, and he was buried at Caen in St. Stephen's minster, which he had formerly raised, and afterwards endowed with many gifts. Alas! how false and how uncertain is this world's fortune! He that was before a rich king, and lord of many lands, then had no more land than a space of seven feet! and he that was once enshrouded in gold and gems lay there covered with dirt! He left behind him three sons: the eldest, called Robert, who was earl in Normandy after him; the second, called William, who wore the crown after him in England; and the third, called Henry, to whom his father bequeathed immense treasure.

If any person wants to know what kind of man he was, or what honor he had, or of how many lands he was lord, then we will write about him as well as we understand him: we who often looked upon him, and once lived in his court. This King William we speak of was a very wise man, and very rich; more splendid and powerful than any before him. He was mild to the good men that loved God, and harsh beyond all measure to men that opposed his will. On that same spot where God granted that he should gain England, he raised a mighty minster, and set monks therein, and endowed it well. In his days the great monastery in Canterbury was built, and also very many others over all England. This land was moreover well filled with monks, who modeled

their lives after the rule of St. Benedict,[2] and such was the state of Christianity in his time that each man who wanted to followed what pertained to his order.

He was also very dignified. Three times each year he wore his crown, as often as he was in England. At Easter he wore it in Winchester, at Pentecost in Westminster, at midwinter in Gloucester. And then with him were all the rich men over all England, archbishops and bishops, abbots and earls, thanes and knights. He was also a very stern man, and very hot-tempered, such that no man dared do anything against his will. He had earls in his bonds who acted against his will; bishops he threw from their bishoprics, and abbots from their abbeys, and thanes into prison. At length he did not spare his own brother Odo, who was a very rich bishop in Normandy. His bishopric was at Bayeux, and he was the foremost man of all next to the king. He had an earldom in England, and when the king was in Normandy, he was the mightiest man in this land: William confined him to prison. But among other things it should not be forgotten that he made good peace in this land, so that a man who was of any status might travel all over his kingdom, even with his pockets full of gold, unharmed. No man dared to slay another, no matter how much evil he had done to the other, and if any churl[3] lay with a woman against her will, he soon lost the same limb that he played with.

William truly reigned over England, and in his astuteness so thoroughly surveyed it that there was not a hide of land in England that he did not know who owned it, or what it was worth, and afterwards set it down in his book. The land of the Britons was in his power; and he built castles within it; and controlled that nation. So also he subdued Scotland by his great strength. Normandy was his native land, but he ruled also over the earldom of Maine; and if he might have lived two years more, he would have won Ireland by his shrewdness without any weapons. Assuredly in his time had men much distress, and very many sorrows.

---

[1] *anchorite* Hermit.

[2] *rule of St. Benedict* Monastic rule, i.e., for the ordering of monastic life, composed by St. Benedict (480–543), founder of the monastic Order of St. Benedict.

[3] *churl* Man without noble rank; at this time, a serf (following the Conquest).

Castles he had built, and crushed the poor.
The king himself was very stark,
and seized from his subjects many marks
of gold, and many hundred pounds of silver;
which he took of his people, for little need, justly and
    unjustly.
He was fallen into avarice, and loved greed above all.
He made many deer-parks, and set laws for them;
so that whosoever slew a hart, or a hind,[1]
should be blinded.
He forbade hunting of harts, and also of boars;
and he loved the tall deer as if he were their father.
Likewise he decreed that the hares should go free.
His rich men bemoaned it, and the poor men
    complained of it.
But he was so stern that he cared nothing about the
    hatred of them all;
for they must follow the king's will,
if they wanted to live, or have land,
or possessions, or even his peace.
Alas! that any man should presume to puff himself up so,
and boast over all men.
May the Almighty God have mercy on his soul,
and grant him forgiveness of his sins!

We have written these things concerning him, both good and evil, so that men may choose the good after their goodness, and flee from the evil entirely, and go in the way that leads us to the kingdom of heaven.

We could write many things that were done in this same year. So it was in Denmark that the Danes, a nation that was formerly accounted the truest of all, were turned aside to the greatest untruth, and to the greatest treachery that ever could be. They chose and submitted to King Cnut, and swore him oaths, and afterwards basely killed him in a church. It happened also in Spain that the heathens went and made inroads upon the Christians, and reduced much of the country to their dominion. But the king of the Christians, who was called Alfonso, sent everywhere into each land asking for assistance. And they came to his support from every Christian land, and killed or drove out all the heathen folk, and won their land again, with God's assistance. In this land also, in the same year, many rich men died: Stigand, Bishop of Chichester, and the Abbot of St. Augustine, and the Abbot of Bath, and the Abbot of Pershore, and the lord of them all, William, King of England, that we spoke of before. After his death his son, also called William, took to the kingdom, and was consecrated king by Archbishop Lanfranc at Westminster three days before Michaelmas. And all the men in England submitted to him, and swore oaths to him. When this was done the king went to Winchester, and inspected the treasury and the treasures that his father had gathered: gold, and silver, and vases, and purple cloth, and gems, and many other valuable things that are difficult to enumerate. Then the king did as his father asked him before his death, and distributed treasures for his father's soul to each monastery that was in England; to some he gave ten marks of gold, to some six, to each country church sixty pence. And into each shire were sent a hundred pounds of money to distribute to the poor, for William's soul. And before he died he commanded that they should release all the men that were in prison under his power. And the king was in London that midwinter.

—9TH–11TH CENTURIES

---

[1] *hart, or a hind* Male or female deer, stag or doe.

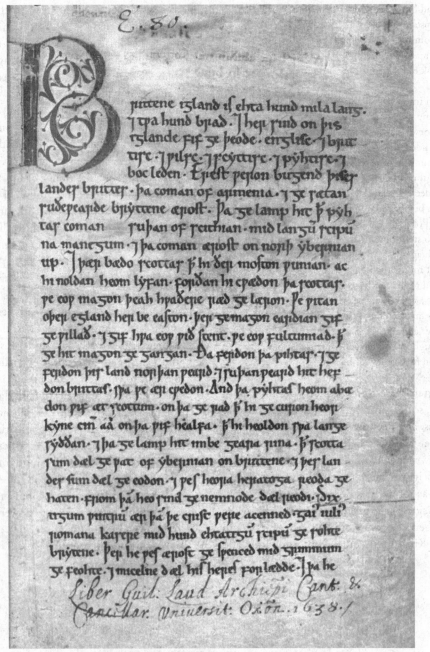

Preface to a manuscript of the *Anglo-Saxon Chronicle*
England, Peterborough Abbey, c. 1121 (Bodleian, Ms. Laud 636).

ALFRED THE GREAT, KING OF WESSEX
849 – 899

When Alfred became ruler of the West Saxons (871–99) his kingdom had been reduced and threatened by wave upon wave of Viking attacks; at one point he was forced to hide in the Somerset marshes to avoid capture. He ended his reign as a wealthy and successful "King of the Anglo-Saxons"—first by negotiating peace with his enemies and arranging the baptism of the Viking leader Guthrum, and then by strengthening the system of garrisons and military service, and building up the English naval forces. Alfred also extended his power beyond the boundaries of his own West Saxon kingdom into Mercia and the southeast, gaining control of neighboring kingdoms through a series of alliances and military coalitions. For keeping England from being placed entirely under Viking control, and for his wise and clever use of the powers of church and state to secure, strengthen and expand his kingdom, Alfred has long been called "The Great."

Part of his reputation rests on his support of learning and the arts. Most kings are presumed to have had scribes for writing documents and singer/poets for entertainment; in Alfred's court literary and artistic activity was far more extensive. Somewhat in the manner of Charlemagne, Alfred gathered to his court an assembly of international scholars and clerics who worked with him to promote English as a language of learning, teaching, religion and government. It is remarkable to consider (as Alfred himself does in some of his writings) that the ruler of a busy and often threatened kingdom would often spend whatever spare moments he had with a tutor, laboriously reading and translating Latin. But his biographer Asser testifies to Alfred's lifelong practices of prayer and study, and he undoubtedly recognized the need to rebuild the intellectual foundations of England after nearly a century of decline. Education in English was, he argued, both necessary (due to the dismal condition of Latin learning in England) and useful for promoting new values and ideas to a broader audience. It is generally agreed that Alfred himself translated Boethius's *Consolation of Philosophy*, St. Augustine's *Soliloquies*, and the first fifty Psalms; in each of these works he presumably relied on the advice of a circle of scholars and assistants, but each bears his distinctive, somewhat discursive style and characteristic vocabulary. It is likely that Alfred commissioned the translation of other works, including Bede's *Ecclesiastical History*, Orosius's *Historiae adversus paganos* (a work of world history showing how God's Providence has guided the fates of nations), and the *Dialogues* of Gregory the Great (a collection of stories of the miracles of the saints). Alfred was also undoubtedly responsible for initiating the *Anglo-Saxon Chronicle* and for commissioning his own biography.

For Alfred, as of course for most people in his day, there was no "separation of church and state"—a well-run kingdom was built upon Christian principles, and the public good depended on the ruler's piety. Alfred's law code was founded on the Biblical Ten Commandments, and when he announced his policy of promoting translation of important works of learning—what he calls "those books most necessary for all men to know"—into English, he began with Pope Gregory the Great's *Regula Pastoralis* ("Pastoral Care"), a handbook for bishops and priests. For Alfred, the work was a "how-to" manual for those in power, a compelling vision of how the social and moral diversity of society might be put in order by wise rulers and by a conflation of duty and devotion that would make spiritual development almost a civic obligation and "pastoral care" a model of political organization. In the prefatory letter attached to this translation Alfred justifies and explains his policy on vernacular education: bishops were expected to require their priests to be more learned, and royal officials were required to learn to read, or they would lose their positions.

King Alfred is responsible as much as any single person could be for the development of English into a language that could be used for literary and public documents, a language that soon came to be perceived as a worthy companion to Latin. If Bede imagined the "English People" united by their common faith, Alfred worked to build a "Kingdom of the English" around their common language. The policy set out in Alfred's "Preface" to the *Pastoral Care* was apparently somewhat unevenly applied during his own lifetime, but it laid the groundwork for a great flowering of learning—much of it created or preserved in English—in the next century.

⌘ ⌘ ⌘

Alfred's "Preface" to the Old English Version of Gregory the Great's *Pastoral Care*

King Alfred bids Bishop Wærferth to be greeted with his loving and friendly words;[1] and bids you know that it has come very often to my mind what wise men there once were throughout England,[2] both in the sacred and the secular orders; and how happy the times were then throughout England; and how the kings who had power over the people in those days were obedient to God and His ministers; and they maintained their peace, morality and power within their borders, and also enlarged their kingdom abroad; and how they prospered both in war and in wisdom; and also the sacred orders, how zealous they were about teaching, learning, and all the services that they should do for God; and how men from abroad sought wisdom and learning in this land, and how we now have had to acquire them from abroad if we would have them at all. It[3] was so completely decayed in England that there were very few on this side of the Humber[4] who could understand their services in English,[5] or even translate a letter from Latin into English; and I think that there were not many beyond the Humber. There were so few of them that I cannot think of even a single one south of the Thames when I

first came to the throne. Thanks be to Almighty God that we now have any supply of teachers. Therefore I command you to do, as I believe you wish to do, that you empty yourself of worldly affairs as often as you can, so that wherever you can apply the wisdom that God gave you, you eagerly apply it. Consider what punishments befell us in this world when we neither loved it[6] ourselves, nor left it to others; we loved only the name of Christians, and very few of the practices.

Then when I remembered all this, then I also remembered how I saw, before it had all been ravaged and burnt,[7] how the churches throughout all England stood filled with treasures and books, and also a great many of God's servants; and they had very little benefit from those books, because they could not understand anything in them, because they were not written in their own language. It is as if they had said, "Our elders, who formerly held these places, loved wisdom, and through it they obtained riches and left it to us. Here we can still see their tracks, but we cannot follow after them." And therefore we have now lost both the wealth and the wisdom, because we would not bend down to their tracks with our minds. Then when I remembered all this, then I wondered greatly at the good wise men who were once throughout England, and who had completely learned all those books, that they would not translate any part of them into their own language. But I answered myself at once and said: "They did not think that men would ever become so careless and learning so decayed: they deliberately avoided it, and intended that

---

[1] *King Alfred ... words* The letter begins formally in the third person but shifts quickly to a more personal voice.

[2] *England* Alfred consistently calls his kingdom *angelcynn*, "the race of the Angles," though he himself was a Saxon.

[3] *It* I.e., Wisdom.

[4] *Humber* River in northern England.

[5] *who ... English* Either the mass or the monastic Liturgy of the Hours, both said in Latin throughout the Middle Ages (and well into the modern age).

[6] *it* I.e., Wisdom.

[7] *it had all ... burnt* By the Vikings, whose attacks began in 793 and continued in waves of increasing frequency and ferocity to Alfred's own day.

the more languages we knew, the more wisdom would be here in this land."

Then I remembered how the law[1] was first established in the Hebrew language, and afterwards, when the Greeks learned it, they turned it all into their own language, and also all other books;[2] and later likewise the Romans, when they had learned them, turned all of them through wise translators into their own language. And also all other Christian peoples turned some part of them into their own language. Therefore it seems better to me, if it seems so to you, that we also turn certain books which are most necessary for all people to know into that language that we all can understand, and bring it about, as we very easily may with God's help (if we have peace), that all the youth of free men now in England who have the means to apply themselves to it, be set to learning, as long as they cannot be set to any other use, until the time when they know well how to read English writing. One may further teach in Latin those whom one wishes to teach further, and wants to promote to a higher order.[3]

Then when I remembered before this time how the knowledge of the Latin language was decayed through-out England, and yet many knew how to read English writing, I began among the other various and manifold duties of this kingdom to turn into English the book that is called in Latin *Pastoralis*, and in English *Shepherd's Book*, sometimes word for word, sometimes sense for sense, just as I had learned it from Plegmund my archbishop and from Asser my bishop and from Grimbold my masspriest and from John my masspriest. After I had learned it, I translated it into English, just as I understood it and as I could most meaningfully construe it. And I wish to send one to each bishopric in my kingdom, and in each will be an *æstel*[4] worth fifty mancuses. And I command in God's name that no one take the *æstel* from the book nor the book from the church; it is unknown how long there may be such learned bishops as now, thanks be to God, are nearly everywhere. Therefore I would like it always to be in that place, unless the bishop wishes to have it with him, or it is loaned out somewhere, or someone is making a copy of it.

—LATE 9TH CENTURY

---

[1] *law* I.e., the Law of Moses, the *Torah* or first five books of the Bible.

[2] *all other books* I.e., the other books of the Bible. Like many medieval writers, Alfred is not consistent in referring to the Bible as singular or plural. The Bible was both one book and many.

[3] *higher order* I.e., the religious life of the priesthood or monastery.

[4] *æstel* Usually thought to be a kind of pointer used to keep one's place while reading a book. A pointer worth fifty mancuses (one mancus was worth 30 silver pennies) would be very valuable. The intricately inlaid piece known as the Alfred Jewel in the Ashmolean Museum in Oxford may be the surviving knob of such an "æstel," with the shaft of its wooden pointer now lost.

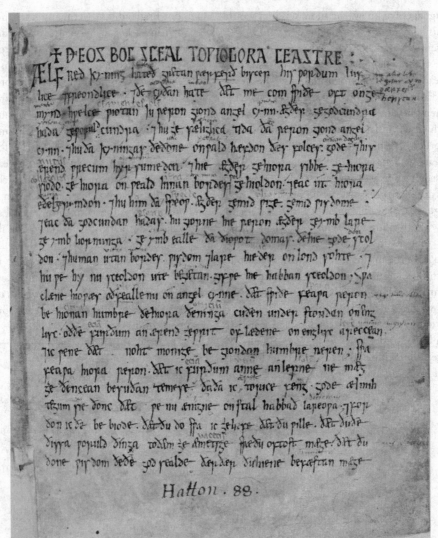

The beginning of Alfred's "Preface" to the translation of *Pastoral Care*
(Ms. [Manuscript] Hatton 20, folio 1r).

ÆLFRIC OF EYNSHAM
c. 945 – ca. 1010

Ælfric, monk of Cerne Abbas in Dorset and later abbot of the monastery of Eynsham in Oxfordshire, was a prolific writer of homilies, sermons, and saints' lives. He was born around 945, just at the beginning of a tenth-century monastic reform movement that fostered a renaissance in arts and letters in later Anglo-Saxon England. Inspired by developments on the Continent, the Benedictine reformers in England founded new monasteries and rebuilt and reorganized old ones; a close alliance between the king and the clergy, and a period of relative peace and national unity, created an environment rich in material and intellectual wealth. It was during this period, roughly the second half of the tenth century, that the manuscripts containing most of the surviving Old English poetry were copied, and many works translated from Latin into English including the *Rule of St. Benedict* and several books of the Bible. Ælfric was educated at the Cathedral school of Winchester under Abbot Æthelwold, one of the leaders of the reform movement; his prodigious literary output reflects the high standards of pastoral care, doctrinal accuracy, scholarship and stylistic fluency that he learned there.

In the last decade of the tenth century, however, England entered a period of decline. King Æthelred suffered military defeats during a new wave of Danish invasions, treachery among his demoralized advisors, and a loss of support from rich landowners and noblemen. Unlike his contemporary Wulfstan, Ælfric was not really active in the royal centers of power; instead he spent his career in relatively isolated monasteries which had been founded by his patrons, the nobleman Æthelweard and his son Æthelmær. Before his death sometime around 1010 Ælfric wrote many works, most of them in connection with his monastic and pastoral duties as teacher and preacher: two long series of homilies to be read on Sundays and major feasts throughout the year, many lives of saints for liturgical and private reading, translations of parts of the Bible, a Latin grammar in English, a *Colloquy* or conversational exercise for teaching Latin, and other pedagogical and pastoral works. But it would be wrong to imagine that Ælfric was unaware of or untroubled by the political decline that was evident around the turn of the millennium. Often, as in the saint's life translated below, his works deal with urgent issues of war and peace, violence and sanctity, heroism and right government—questions that must have been on many minds as Æthelred's kingship gradually crumbled into ruin.

Ælfric's *Life of St. Edmund* commemorates a king of the East Angles who was killed by the Danes in 869 and whose martyrdom was celebrated on 20 November. Ælfric's source is the Latin *Passio Sancti Edmundi* by Abbo of Fleury (c. 945–1004), reworked by Ælfric in an elaborate rhythmical prose style as an expression of a Christian ideal of kingship. Ælfric is careful to anchor the saint's legend in plausible historical report, tracing the story back to its source or relying on common consensus to justify his extraordinary claims for Edmund's power. The story is evenly divided between accounts of the saint's death and tales of his miraculous power after death; the miracles of the saints, signs of God's favor, were regarded as a proof of the truth of Christianity as opposed to the violent paganism of the Vikings and what Ælfric regarded as the stubbornness of the Jews. (Though it is not likely that there were any actual Jews in England during Ælfric's time, they served as a powerful metaphor for those who could accept Christianity but refused to do so.)

As Ælfric tells it, Edmund's story reminds his audience that even among the English, and even in the secular world, there are figures of ideal holiness worthy of remembrance, just as there are ideal figures like Beowulf to represent the highest values of the heroic life. Edmund's paradoxically heroic act of refusing to fight his enemies placed him in the company of other great saints—and, of course, for any Christian, the greatest exemplary figure of all, Jesus Christ. In a country threatened by war, and a culture rooted in ideals of violent, heroic self-assertion, this image of kingship as (literal) sacrifice may have offered a puzzling but powerful alternative to the political realities of the day.

⌘ ⌘ ⌘

The Passion of Saint Edmund, King and Martyr[1]

A certain very learned monk came from the south over the sea from St. Benedict's place, in the days of King Æthelred, to Archbishop Dunstan three years before he died; the monk was named Abbo. They were in conversation, Dunstan related the story of St. Edmund, just as Edmund's sword-bearer had related it to King Athelstan when Dunstan was a young man and the sword-bearer was a very old man. Then the monk set down that whole narrative in a book, and afterward, when the book came to us a few years later, we translated it into English, just as appears below. Within two years, the monk Abbo returned home to his monastery, and was quickly appointed abbot of the same monastery.

The blessed Edmund, King of the East Angles, was wise and honorable, and always honored Almighty God with noble customs. He was humble and virtuous, and remained so steadfast that he would not turn to shameful sins, nor turn away on either side from his good practices, but was always mindful of that true teaching, "You are appointed ruler? do not exalt yourself, but be among men as one of them."[2] He was generous to the poor and widows like a father, and with benevolence always guided his people to righteousness, restrained the violent, and lived blessedly in the true faith.

It eventually happened that the Danish people came with their fleet, pillaging and killing throughout the land, as is their custom. The principal leaders of the fleet were Ivar and Ubbi, united by the devil, and they landed in Northumbria with warships, and laid waste the land and killed the people. Then Ivar turned eastwards with his ships, and Ubbi remained in Northumbria, having won the victory with his savagery. Then Ivar came sailing to the East Angles in the year when

Prince Alfred, who later became the famous king of the West Saxons, was twenty-one. Ivar violently prowled about the land like a wolf, and slew the people, men and women and innocent children, and shamefully tormented the innocent Christians.

He then immediately sent the King a boastful message that he must submit to his service, if he cared for his life. The messenger came to King Edmund and quickly announced Ivar's message: "Ivar our King, brave and victorious on sea and land, has command of many people, and has now suddenly landed here with an army so that he might have winter quarters here with his troops. He now commands you to share your hidden treasures and your ancestral wealth with him without delay, and be his under-king, if you wish to live, for you do not have the power to resist him."

Then, indeed, King Edmund summoned a bishop who was nearby and considered with him how he should answer the fierce Ivar. The bishop was afraid for the King's life in this sudden turn of events, and said that it seemed advisable to him that he should submit to what Ivar demanded of him. Then the King fell silent and looked at the ground, and then said regally to him: "Alas, Bishop! the wretched people of this land are treated shamefully, and I would rather fall in battle, so long as my people could enjoy their native land." And the bishop said, "Alas, dear King! your people lie slain, and you do not have the forces to be able to fight, and these pirates will come and bind you alive, unless you save your life by fleeing, or save yourself by submitting to them." Then King Edmund said, very brave as he was: "I desire and wish in my heart that I alone should not survive after my dear thanes, who have been violently slain in their beds with their children and wives by these pirates. It has never been my custom to flee, but I would rather die, if I must, for my own land, and the Almighty God knows that I will never turn away from his service nor from his true love, whether I live or die."

After these words he turned to the messenger whom Ivar had sent to him and said to him, undaunted:

---

[1]   The Passion of Saint Edmund King and Martyr   Translated by R.M. Liuzza for The Broadview Anthology of British Literature.

[2]   You are ... them   See Ecclesiasticus 32.1.

"Indeed you would be now worthy of death, but I will not defile my clean hands with your foul blood, because I follow Christ, who gave us such an example; and I will gladly be slain by you if God so decrees it. Go now very quickly and tell your fierce lord, 'Edmund will never in his life submit to Ivar, a heathen chieftain, unless he first submit with faith to Christ the Savior in this land.'"

Then the messenger went away quickly and met the bloodthirsty Ivar along the way, hastening to Edmund with all his band, and told the dishonorable man how he had been answered. Then Ivar boldly commanded the army that they should seize only the King, who had despised his commands, and bind him quickly. And then, indeed, King Edmund, when Ivar came, stood within his hall, mindful of the Savior, and threw away his weapons; he wished to imitate the example of Christ, who forbade Peter to fight with weapons against the bloodthirsty Jews.[1] And then, indeed, these dishonorable men bound Edmund and insulted him shamefully and beat him with cudgels, and afterwards led the faithful King to a tree set fast in the earth and tied him to it with strong bonds, and again lashed him with whips for a long time; and he constantly cried out, between the strokes, with true faith to Christ the Savior. And then the heathens, because of his faith, became furiously angry, because he called on Christ to help him. They shot at him with spears, as if for their sport, until he was entirely covered by their shots like the bristles of a hedgehog, just as Sebastian was.[2]

When Ivar, the wicked pirate, saw that the noble King would not forsake Christ, but with steadfast faith continually cried out to Him, he commanded him to be beheaded, and the heathens did so. While he was still calling out to Christ, the heathens dragged the holy man to his death, and struck off his head with one blow, and his soul went blessed to Christ. There was a certain man nearby, kept hidden from the heathens by God, who overheard all this and afterwards told it, just as we tell it here.

Then, indeed, the pirates went back to their ship,

and hid the head of holy Edmund in thick brambles, so that it would not be buried. Then after a while, when they had gone away, the people of that land—those who were left—came to the place where their lord's headless body lay, and they were very sorry in their hearts for his death, and more so because they did not have the head for the body. Then the eyewitness who had seen it said that the pirates took the head with them, and it seemed to him, as indeed was very true, that they had hidden the head somewhere in the woods.

Then they all went together into the woods, searching everywhere through bushes and brambles, to see if they could find the head anywhere. It was also a great wonder that a wolf was sent by the guidance of God to guard the head day and night against other wild beasts. Then they went searching and continually crying out, as people who often go into the woods always do, "Where are you now, companion?" and the head answered them: "Here, here, here!" And so it called out frequently, answering them all whenever any of them called, until by means of that shouting they all came to it. There lay the gray wolf that watched over the head, and between his two paws he clasped the head, greedy and hungry, and did not dare, for God's sake, to taste the head, but guarded it against wild beasts. They were amazed at the wolf's care, and carried the holy head home with them, thanking the Almighty for all His wonders. But the wolf followed along with the head until they came to the village, as if he were tame, and then he turned back to the woods. The people of the land afterwards laid the head beside the holy body and buried it as best they could in such haste, and immediately built a church above it.

Eventually, many years later, when the pillaging stopped and peace was granted to the afflicted people, they banded together and built a church worthy of the saint, because miracles had frequently taken place at his grave in the chapel where he was buried. They wished to transport the holy body with public ceremony and lay it inside the church. It was great wonder then that he was just as whole as if he were alive, with an uncorrupted body, and his neck was healed which had been severed, and there was something like a red silken thread around his neck, to show people how he had been slain. Likewise the wounds which the bloodthirsty heathens had

---

[1] *And then ... Jews*   See John 18.10–11.

[2] *They shot ... Sebastian was*   St. Sebastian, whose feast is celebrated on 20 January, was a Roman soldier who was martyred under the Emperor Diocletian. According to legend he was riddled with arrows by a team of archers—but he recovered from this ordeal and returned to the Emperor, who then ordered him to be beaten to death with cudgels.

made on his body with their repeated shots had been healed by the Heavenly God; and he lies uncorrupted like this until this present day, awaiting the resurrection and eternal glory. His body, which lies undecayed, shows us that he lived here in the world without fornication, and journeyed to Christ with a pure life. A certain widow named Oswyn dwelt at the saint's tomb in prayers and fasting for many years afterwards; she would cut the saint's hair every year and pare his nails carefully with devotion, and keep them in a shrine as relics on the altar. So the people of that region venerated the saint with true faith, and Bishop Theodred richly endowed the church with gifts of gold and silver, in honor of the saint.

There came at a certain time eight unlucky thieves one night to the reverend saint, wishing to steal the treasures people had brought there, and craftily conniving how they might get in. One struck the hasps hard with a sledgehammer, one of them filed around them with a rasp, one even dug under the door with a spade, one of them with a ladder tried to unlock the window, but they toiled in vain and fared miserably, because the holy man miraculously bound them, each one as he stood there struggling with his tool, so that none of them could commit his crime, nor escape, but they stood in that manner until morning. People were amazed at how the criminals were hanging—one on a ladder, one bending down to dig, each bound fast in his labor. Then they were all brought to the bishop, who commanded that they should all hang on a high gallows; but he was not mindful how the merciful God spoke through his prophet these words that stand here, *Eos qui ducuntur ad mortem eruere ne cesses,* "always release those who are led to death";[1] and also the holy canons forbid those in holy orders, both bishops and priests, to concern themselves with thieves, for it is not fitting that those who are chosen to serve God should have a hand in any man's death, if they are the Lord's servants. Later, when Bishop Theodred had examined his books, he repented with lamentation that he had passed such a cruel sentence on the unfortunate thieves, and he always regretted it until the end of his life, and earnestly asked the people if they would fast with him for three whole days, asking the Almighty to have mercy on him.

In that region was a certain man named Leofstan,

powerful in the world and foolish before God, who rode to the saint's shrine with great arrogance, and very insolently commanded them to show him the holy saint to see if he was undecayed; but as soon as he saw the saint's body, he immediately went mad and roared savagely, and wretchedly ended with an evil death. This is similar to what the faithful Pope Gregory said in his narrative about Saint Lawrence, who lies in the city of Rome—that men, both good and evil, were always wanting to examine how he lay, but God restrained them, so that once seven men died there together when they were looking at him, and then others stopped examining the martyr with their human foolishness.

We have heard many miracles in popular report concerning the holy Edmund, which we will not set down in writing, but everyone knows them. By this saint and by others like him, it is clear that Almighty God is able to raise man again on Judgment Day uncorrupted from the earth, He who keeps Edmund whole in his body until that great day, though he came from the earth. Because of that worthy saint the place is worthy, that men should honor it and provide it well with pure servants of God in the service of Christ, because the saint is greater than men can conceive.

The English nation is not lacking in the Lord's saints, when in England there lie such saints as this holy King, and the blessed Cuthbert, and Æthelthryth in Ely, and also her sister, sound in body as a confirmation of the faith. There are also many other saints in the English nation who perform many miracles, as is widely known, for the praise of the Almighty in whom they believed. Christ reveals to mankind through His famous saints that He is Almighty God who does such miracles, though the wretched Jews completely rejected him, wherefore they are accursed, just as they wished upon themselves.[2] No miracles are performed at their tombs, because they do not believe in the living Christ, but Christ reveals to mankind where the true faith is, when He works such miracles through His saints widely throughout this earth. Wherefore to Him be glory forever with His Heavenly Father and the Holy Ghost. Amen.

—C. EARLY 11TH CENTURY

---

[1]   *always release ... death*   See Proverbs 24.11.

[2]   *though the wretched ... themselves*   See Matthew 27.25.

WULFSTAN
c. 960 – 1023

Wulfstan the Homilist (so called to avoid confusion with others of that name: an earlier Archbishop of York, a saintly Bishop of Worcester, and a monk of Winchester known as "Wulfstan the Cantor" for his musical accomplishments) was probably born in the East Midlands, became Bishop of London in 996, and simultaneously Bishop of Worcester and Archbishop of York in 1002. He died in 1023. As a bishop rather than an abbot he was directly involved in secular politics during an intensely troubled period in English history, but he still found time to write a great number of works, all in a powerfully distinctive style. The exact number of his sermons is not known—at least 23 English works and a number of Latin ones are acknowledged as his—but fragments and revisions abound, all of which can be attributed to him because of his idiosyncratic style. Wulfstan also wrote a guide to secular and clerical government (*The Institutes of Polity*), a set of canons for secular clergy, and treatises on the management of large landholdings and estates, and he had a hand in the law codes of Æthelred and of Cnut. According to one report (in the twelfth-century *Liber Eliensis*), "he was loved as a brother and honored as a father, and frequently summoned to the highest affairs of the realm" by these kings, and his position as well as his personality placed him in the center of political life.

Wulfstan's work, unlike the homilies and textbooks of the more scholarly Ælfric, often addresses practical and political matters, speaks directly to contemporary conditions, and is deeply concerned with the organization and right governance of the state. But, like Ælfric, Wulfstan was first and foremost a pastor, and in his homilies one can see how his political and civil interests are woven into his spiritual concerns. Also like Ælfric, Wulfstan was a deliberate stylist of English prose who exploited all the resources of vernacular poetry— alliteration, rhythm, variation, balance—and of hortatory rhetoric to bring his audience into his theme. The vigorous *Sermo Lupi ad Anglos* (signed with the Latin name *Lupus*, "wolf," a play on his English name) is written in strongly rhythmical prose. In it Wulfstan considers the Viking attacks as divine retribution for the sins of the English; he adopts the historical attitude of the sixth-century British writer Gildas, whose *De excidio Britanum* similarly lamented the arrival of the English as a retribution upon the British. In doing so Wulfstan places contemporary events into a Biblical historiography which sees the rise and fall of nations as a reflection of their moral status. Even pagans may be instruments of God's justice, as the pagan English were to the Christian Britons: Wulfstan rebukes the English, now Christian, with the observation that pagans practice their religion more faithfully and with more morality than Christians do. His eloquently savage portrait of his age is presumably meant to rouse his audience to repentance rather than despair; his answer to the terrors and moral collapse of his nation combines spiritual and political perspectives—do justice, obey the law, keep faith, and remember the waiting torments of Hell.

⌘ ⌘ ⌘

Sermo Lupi ad Anglos[1]

The Sermon of "Wolf" to the English, when the Danes were greatly persecuting them, which was in the 1014th year after the Incarnation of our Lord Jesus Christ.

Dear people, recognize what is true: this world is in haste and it draws near its end. And therefore in this world things get worse and worse, and so it needs must be that because of the people's sins things will get very much worse before the coming of the Antichrist; and then it will indeed be terrible and grim widely throughout the world. Understand well, too, that the Devil has led this nation too far astray for many years, and there has been little loyalty among men, though they might speak well, and too many wrongs have ruled this land, and there were never many men who sought the remedy as eagerly as they should, but every day they added one evil to another, and raised up wrong and injustice too widely throughout this entire land.

And therefore we have also suffered many injuries and insults, and if we are to expect any remedy then we must deserve better of God than we have done previously. For with great demerit we have earned the miseries that oppress us, and with very great merits we must obtain the remedy from God, if things are to improve henceforth. Indeed, we know full well that a great breach requires a great remedy, and a great fire needs no little water, if one is to quench that fire at all. And the necessity is great for every man henceforth diligently to heed God's law, and pay God's dues justly. Among heathen peoples no one dares withhold little or much of that which is pledged to the worship of false gods, and everywhere we withhold God's dues all too often. And among heathen people no one dares diminish, inside the temple or out, anything brought to the false gods and given over as an offering; and we have completely stripped the houses of God, inside and out, and the servants of God are everywhere deprived of respect and protection. And among heathen people no one dare abuse the servants of the false gods in any way, just as is now done too widely to the servants of God, where Christians ought to observe God's laws and protect God's servants.

But what I say is true: there is need of a remedy, because God's dues have decreased for too long in this land in every region, and the laws of the people have deteriorated all too much, and sanctuaries are commonly violated, and the houses of God are entirely stripped of ancient dues and are despoiled within of everything decent. And widows are wrongfully forced to take a husband, and too many are reduced to poverty and greatly humiliated; and poor men are sorely betrayed and cruelly defrauded, and widely sold out of this land into the power of foreigners, even though they are completely innocent; and with cruel injustice children in the cradle are enslaved for petty theft commonly throughout this nation; and the rights of freemen are taken away and the rights of slaves restricted, and the right to alms curtailed, and to speak briefly, the laws of God are hated and His teaching scorned; therefore through God's anger we all are frequently put to shame, let him know it who can. And although one might not imagine it, the harm will become common to all this nation, unless God protects us.

For it is clear and evident in us all that we have hitherto more often transgressed than we have amended, and therefore many things have fallen upon this nation. For a long time now, nothing has prospered either at home or abroad, but there has been plunder and famine, burning and bloodshed in every region time and again. And stealing and slaughter, plague and pestilence, murrain[2] and disease, slander and hatred, and the thievery of robbers has harmed us severely. And excessive taxes have greatly afflicted us, and bad weather has often caused crop failures, for there have been in this land, so it seems, many years now of injustices and unstable loyalties among men everywhere. Now very often a kinsman will not protect a kinsman any more than a foreigner, nor the father his children, nor sometimes the child his own father, nor one brother the other. Nor has any of us ordered his life as he should, neither the cleric according to the rule nor the layman according to the law. But all too frequently we have made lust into law for us, and have kept neither the teachings nor the laws of God or men as we should.

---

[1] *Sermo Lupi ad Anglos* The present text is translated by R.M. Liuzza for *The Broadview Anthology of British Literature.*

[2] *murrain* Disease afflicting domestic animals such as sheep and cattle.

Neither has anyone had loyal intentions toward others as justly as he should, but almost all men have betrayed and injured others by word and deed; and indeed almost everyone unjustly stabs the other in the back with shameful assaults, and worse, if he can.

For there are here in this land great disloyalties towards God and towards the state, and there are also in this country many who betray their lords in various ways, and the greatest of all betrayals of one's lord in the world is that a man betrays his lord's soul. And it is also a great betrayal of one's lord in the world when a man plots against his lord's life, or, living, drives him from the land, and both have happened in this country. They plotted against Edward and then killed, and afterwards burned him; and Æthelred was driven out of his country. And too many godparents and godchildren have been destroyed widely throughout this nation, and likewise too many other innocent people have been too commonly slain. And also far too many holy places have fallen down because previously certain men have been placed in them who ought not to have been, if one wished to show respect to God's sanctuary. And too many Christian people have been sold out of this land, all the time now, and all this is hateful to God, let him believe it who will. And it is shameful to speak of what happens too commonly, and dreadful to know what too many often do, who practice a wretched deed: they pool their money together and buy a woman in common as a joint purchase, and with the one woman commit foul sin, one after another and each after the other, just like dogs who do not care about filth, and then for a price they sell out of the land into the hands of the enemy this creature of God, His own purchase that He bought so dearly.

Also we know well where the crime has occurred that a father has sold his son for a price, and a son his mother, and one brother has sold another into the hands of foreigners; and all those are serious and terrible deeds, let him understand it who will. And yet that which is injuring this nation is still greater and more manifold: many are forsworn and greatly perjured, and vows are broken time and again, and it is evident in this nation that God's anger violently oppresses us, let him know it who can.

And indeed, how can greater shame befall men through the wrath of God than frequently does us for our own deeds? Though a slave should escape from his lord and, leaving Christendom become a Viking, and it afterwards happens that armed combat takes place between thane and slave, if the slave should slay the thane,[1] he will lie without payment to any of his family; but if the thane kills the slave that he had previously owned, he must pay the price of a thane. Utterly shameful laws and disgraceful tributes are common among us, because of God's anger, let him understand it who is able; and many misfortunes befall this nation time and again. For a long time now nothing has prospered at home or abroad, but there has been devastation and hatred in every region time and again, and for a long time now the English have been entirely without victory and too much disheartened through God's wrath, and the pirates so strong through God's consent that often in battle one drives away ten, sometimes less and sometimes more, all because of our sins. And often ten or twelve, one after the other, will disgracefully put to shame a thane's wife, and sometimes his daughter or close kinswomen, while he looks on, he who considered himself brave and strong and good enough before that happened. And often a slave will bind fast the thane who had been his lord, and make him a slave through God's anger. Alas the misery, and alas the public shame that the English now suffer, all because of God's anger! Often two seamen, or sometimes three, will drive the droves of Christian men all through this nation from sea to sea, huddled together as a public shame for us all, if we could in earnest properly feel any. But all the disgrace we often suffer we repay with honour to those who shame us: we pay them continually, and they humiliate us daily. They ravage and they burn, plunder and rob and carry off to the ship; and indeed, what else is there in all these events than the wrath of God on this nation, clear and evident?

It is no wonder that misfortune should befall us, because we know full well that for many years now men have not cared what they did in word or deed. Rather it seems this nation has become thoroughly corrupted through manifold sins and many misdeeds: through acts of murder and evil, through avarice and greed, through theft and thievery, through slavery and pagan abuses, through treachery and trickery, through the breach of

---

[1] *thane* Nobleman.

law and order, through mayhem upon kinsmen and manslaughter, through crimes against clergy and adulteries, through incest and various fornications. And everywhere, as we said before, by the breaking of oaths and by various lies many more than should be are lost and betrayed, and breaches of feasts and fasts are widely and frequently committed. And here in this land also there are far too many degenerate apostates, hostile enemies of the Church, and cruel tyrants, and widespread scorners of divine law and Christian custom, and everywhere in the nation foolish mockers, most often of those things that the messengers of God command, and especially those things which always by right belong to God's law. And therefore it has now come far and wide to such an evil state that men are nowadays more ashamed of good deeds than of misdeeds; because too often good deeds are dismissed with derision and God-fearing men are reviled all too much, and especially mocked and treated with contempt are those who love justice and fear God to any extent. And because men behave thus, blaming all that they should praise and hating too much all that they ought to love, they bring all too many to evil intentions and wicked deeds, so that they are never ashamed even though they sin greatly and commit wrongs against God himself. But because of idle assaults they are ashamed to atone for their misdeeds as the books teach, like those fools who for pride will not guard themselves against injury, until they cannot do so even though they wish to.

Here, so it seems, too many in this country are sorely injured by the stains of sin. Here there are slayers of men and slayers of kinsmen, and murderers of priests and enemies of monasteries, and here are perjurers and murderers, and here there are whores and child-killers and many foul fornicating adulterers, and here there are wizards and sorceresses,[1] and here there are robbers and thieves and plunderers, and, to be brief, countless numbers of crimes and misdeeds. And we are not ashamed of it at all, but we are greatly ashamed to begin the remedy as the books teach us, and that is obvious in this wretched and sinful nation. Alas, many could easily

call to mind much more in addition, which one man could not hastily devise, how wretchedly things have gone all the time now widely throughout this nation. And indeed let each one examine himself well, and not delay it all too long.

But lo! in God's name, let us do what is necessary for us, defend ourselves as best we may, lest we all perish together. There was a historian in the time of the Britons named Gildas, who wrote about their misdeeds, how they with their sins angered God so exceedingly that He finally allowed the army of the English to conquer their land and completely destroy the nobility of the Britons.[2] And this came about, he said, through robbery by the powerful and the coveting of ill-gotten gains, through the people's lawlessness and evil judgements, through the slackness of bishops and the abject cowardice of God's heralds, who too often kept silent from the truth and mumbled in their jaws when they should have cried out. Likewise, through the foul excesses of the people and through gluttony and manifold sins they destroyed their nation and themselves perished. But let us do what is needful—warn ourselves by such things; and what I say is true, we know of worse deeds among the English than we have ever heard of among the Britons. And therefore it is very necessary that we consider ourselves and earnestly plead with God Himself. And let us do what is necessary for us—bow to justice, and in some measure abandon injustice, and repair carefully what we have broken; and let us love God and follow God's laws, and earnestly practice what we promised when we received baptism, or those who were our sponsors at baptism; and let us arrange our words and deeds rightly, and cleanse our conscience thoroughly, and carefully keep our oaths and pledges, and have some faith between ourselves without deceit. And let us frequently consider the great judgment to which we all must come, and eagerly defend ourselves against the surging fires of the torments of hell, and earn for ourselves the glories and delights which God has prepared for those who do His will in the world. May God help us. Amen.

—1014

---

[1] *sorceresses* Wulfstan uses the word "wæl-cyrian," literally "choosers of the slain," related to the Norse Valkyries. But the word does not seem to have much mythological resonance here: as the context indicates, he apparently means only "female sorcerers" or "witches."

[2] *Britons* I.e., the Welsh, the Romano-Celtic Christian inhabitants of the island whom the Angles and Saxons displaced.

The first page of the manuscript text of *Sermo Lupi ad Anglos* (MS Cotton Nero Ai, fol. 110).

BLICKLING HOMILIES

The *Blickling Homilies* are a collection of English vernacular sermons from the end of the tenth century, surviving in a manuscript now in the Scheide Library in Princeton, New Jersey. These nineteen sermons cover many of the most important days in the liturgical calendar—Lent, Palm Sunday, Easter, Rogation Days (the three days of prayer and fasting before Ascension Thursday), the Ascension, the Annunciation and the Assumption of Mary. Other items cover the lives of saints such as John the Baptist, Peter and Paul, and Andrew. In the manuscript that has come down to us the texts are arranged in order of the liturgical year, but this may not be the original order of the items.

The collection is anonymous. Its contents are often unfavorably compared to the more polished and learned work of Ælfric or the rhetorical energy of Wulfstan; it is generally thought that the *Blickling Homilies* reflect the state of English preaching in the generation before Ælfric—more colloquial and anecdotal, more hortatory and sensational, less exegetical and scriptural. They are not necessarily less learned—the homily below draws on sermons of Caesarius of Arles and Gregory the Great for some passages—but they are, broadly speaking, more general, and seem to have been designed for a wider audience. These early homilies are primarily for reading aloud; their style and structure are more aural than textual, designed for listening rather than study and meditation.

Homily 10, probably intended for the third of the three Rogation Days before the feast of the Ascension, combines two powerful and popular themes: the decay of society, which signals the approaching end of the world, and the decay of the body which demonstrates the worthlessness of worldly things. It is apocalyptic only in a general sense, however, and bears few traces of the panic that is alleged to have gripped Christian Europe in the years surrounding 1000. It is really best thought of as a catechetical work, encouraging faith and fidelity to true doctrine and promising mercy to those who repent and put their lives in order. The sermon is particularly notable for its powerful theme of death and decay—the appeal of which can hardly be understated in this period—and for its use of the elegiac *ubi sunt* (Latin: "where they") motif as it laments the lost world of the past, a rhetorical flourish found also in the poem *The Wanderer*.

⌘ ⌘ ⌘

Blickling Homily 10[1]

Beloved men, listen! I now admonish and instruct every person, both men and women, both young and old, both wise and foolish, both the rich and the poor, that everyone should examine and understand himself, and whatever great sins or small he has committed, he should turn immediately to better things and to the true medicine; then we may have God Almighty merciful to us, because the Lord desires all men should be healthy and sound, and turn to the true knowledge, as David said, "Humble and fearing and trembling and quaking hearts, and those fearing their Creator, God will never despise nor disregard, but He hears their prayers when they cry to Him and ask Him for mercy."[2]

We can now see and recognize and very easily understand that the end of this world is very near; and many calamities have appeared and men's crimes and woes are greatly multiplied; and from one day to another we hear of monstrous torments and unnatural deaths that have come upon men throughout the country, and we often perceive that nation arises against nation, and unfortunate fighting gives rise to evil deeds;

---

[1] *Blickling Homily 10* The present translation, prepared for this volume by R.M. Liuzza, is adapted from that of R. Morris.

[2] *Humble ... for mercy* See Psalms 51.17.

and we often and frequently hear tell of the death of powerful men whose life was dear to men, and whose life seemed fair and beautiful and pleasant. And we are also informed of various diseases in many places of the world, and of growing famine. And we hear of many evils becoming more common and flourishing here in this life, and no good abides here, and all worldly things are very sinful, and too greatly cools the love that we ought to have for Our Lord, and we abandon those good works that we should undertake for our souls' health.

These tokens I have just described of this world's tribulations and perils are just as Christ Himself said to His disciples, that all these things should happen before the end of this world.[1] Let us now strive with all the might of good works and be eager for God's mercy, now that we can perceive that the time of the world's destruction is approaching, and therefore I admonish and warn everyone to consider carefully his own deeds, so that here in the world he may live rightly, before God and in the sight of the highest King. We should be generous to poor men, and charitable to the poor, as God Himself commanded us, to observe true peace and have concord among ourselves. And let those who have children instruct them in right discipline and teach them the way of life and the right way to Heaven. And if they in any way live their life wickedly, let them then at once be converted from their wickednesses and turn from their unrighteousness, that we thereby may all please God, as it stands required of all believing people, and not just of those who have subjected themselves to God in exalted positions—bishops and kings, and mass-priests, and archdeacons, but is also indeed required of subdeacons and monks.

And to all men it is necessary and profitable that they observe well their baptismal vows. Let no man here in this worldly kingdom be too proud in his thoughts, nor too strong in his body, nor too eager for malice, nor too bold in wickedness, nor too full of tricks, nor too fond of guile, neither given to making accusations nor to laying snares. Nor should anyone think that his body can or will make up for the burdens of sin in the grave; but there he will rot into dust and there await his fate, when the Almighty God will bring about an end to this world, and when He will draw His fiery sword and strike through all this world, and pierce through the bodies, and cut apart this middle-earth; and the dead will rise up, then shall the fleshly garment be as transparent as glass, and no trace of unrighteousness can be concealed at all.

Therefore it is needful for us that we not pursue foolish works too long, but we must make our peace with God and men, and establish firmly the right belief in our hearts, that it may and can dwell there, and there grow and bloom; and we must confess the true belief in the Lord God and our Savior Jesus Christ, His only-begotten Son, and in the Holy Ghost, who is co-eternal with the Father and Son. And we must trust in God's holy Church, and in those that have right belief; and we must believe in the forgiveness of sins and the resurrection of the body on the Day of Judgment, and we must believe in the everlasting life, and in the heavenly kingdom that is promised to all that are now workers of good. This is the right faith, which it behooves every man well to hold and perform, for no worker may perform good works before God without love and belief. And it is very necessary that we ourselves consider and bear this in mind, and then most diligently when we hear God's books explained and read to us, and the gospel declared, and His glories made known to men. Let us then diligently strive to be afterwards the better and the happier for the teaching that we have often heard.

Oh, beloved men, listen! we must take care not to love too greatly what we ought to leave behind, nor yet to give up too quickly what we ought to hold eternally. Let us now notice very carefully that no man in the world has such wealth, nor such magnificent riches here in the world, that he will not come to an end in a brief interval; and he shall leave behind all that was pleasant to him before in this world and most dear to possess and to hold; and no man is so dear to his kinsmen and his friends in the world, nor none of them loves him so greatly that he shall not immediately afterwards shrink from him, when the body and the spirit are separated, and his fellowship will seem loathsome and foul to him. That is no marvel; for, behold! what else is the flesh after the eternal portion, that is the soul, is removed? Lo! what else remains but the food of worms? Where then

---

[1] *These tokens ... world* See Luke 21.9.

shall be his riches and his feasts? Where then shall be his pride and his arrogance? Where then shall be his vain garments? Where then shall be the ornaments and the grand attire with which he previously adorned his body? Where then shall be his desire and his sinful lusts which he followed here in the world? Behold, then he must with his soul alone atone to God Almighty for all that he here in this world wickedly committed.

Let us now hear related a story[1] of a certain rich and powerful man: he possessed in this world great wealth and very splendid and manifold treasures, and lived in comfort. Then it happened that his life ended, and there came to him a sudden end of this transitory life. There was then a certain one of his kinsmen and earthly friends that loved him more than any other man; on account of the longing and sorrow caused by the other's death he could no longer stay in that country, but, with a sorrowful mind, he departed from his native land and from his dwelling-place, and dwelt in that land many years; and his longing never diminished, but greatly oppressed and afflicted him. Then after a time he began to long for his native land again, for he wished to see and examine the tomb again, to see what he was like whom formerly he had often seen beautiful in face and stature….[2] The bones of the dead man called to him, and thus said, "Why have you come hither to look at us? Now you may see here a portion of dust, and the leavings of worms, where before you saw a beautiful garment interwoven with gold. Behold now dust and dry bones, where before you saw, after the nature of flesh, limbs fair to look upon. Oh, my friend and kinsman, be mindful of this, and convince yourself that you are now what I once was, and after a time you will be what I now am. Remember this, and know that my riches that I once had are all vanished and decayed, and my dwellings have crumbled and perished. But turn to yourself and incline your heart to good counsel, and deserve that your prayers be acceptable to God Al-

mighty." Then, so sad and grieving, he departed from this spectacle of dust and turned himself away from all the affairs of this world; and he began to learn the praise of God and to teach it, and to love spiritual virtues, and thereby earned for himself the grace of the Holy Spirit; and he delivered also the other's soul from punishment and released him from torments.

Let us, then, beloved men, keep this in mind, and set this example in our hearts, that we should not love the adornments of the world too greatly, nor this middle-earth itself; because the world is all corruptible, and perishable, and subject to decay, and unstable; and this world is all transitory. Let us then carefully consider and know in regard to the beginning of this world, that when it was first formed it was full of all beauty, and was blooming in itself with many and various pleasures; and in that time it was pleasant to men upon earth, and healthful, and complete serenity was upon the earth, and an abundance of peace, and excellent progeny; and in that time this world was so fair and so delightful that it drew men to it by its beauty and pleasantness, away from Almighty God. And when it was thus fair and thus pleasant, it withered away in the hearts of Christ's holy people, and is now blooming in our hearts, as is fit. Now there is lamentation and weeping on all sides; now there is mourning everywhere, and breach of peace; now there is evil and slaughter everywhere; and everywhere this middle-earth flees from us with great bitterness, and we follow it as it flies from us, and love it as it passes away.

Listen! we may perceive by this that this world is fleeting and transitory. Let us then be mindful of this while we may and can, so that we may gladly submit to God. Let us obey Our Lord readily, and give thanks to Him for all His gifts and all his mercies, and for all His kindness and benefits that He has always shown to us, the Heavenly King that lives and reigns forever and ever, world without end, in eternity. Amen.

—LATE 10TH CENTURY

---

[1] *a story*   What follows is an *exemplum* or example, a narrative that illustrates the sermon's lesson.

[2] *stature …*   A line is missing here, apparently telling how the traveler returned home and saw the decaying corpse of his deceased friend.

GEOFFREY OF MONMOUTH

c. 1100 – c. 1154

Geoffrey of Monmouth was born at Monmouth and died at Llandaff. He may have been a Benedictine monk. After arriving in Llandaff in 1140, he became Archdeacon of St. Teilo's, and he was ordained a priest in 1151–52. He was elected Bishop of St. Asaph and consecrated at Lambeth by the Archbishop of Canterbury, but he died before he could enter his diocese. Geoffrey of Monmouth is best known for his chronicle, *The History of the Kings of Britain* (*Historia regum britanniae*), which he composed in Latin for an educated audience. His *Historia* appeared before 1139, but the chronicler continued to revise, reissuing his completed work in 1147. He also wrote a version of the *Prophecies of Merlin* and perhaps a life of Merlin (*Vita Merlini*) as well.

In his *Historia*, Geoffrey aimed to recount the history of the kings of Britain from before the time of Christ to the time of Cadwallader (689 CE). His version of the myth of the origins of his island nation begins with Brutus, the great-grandson of Aeneas, who ostensibly arrives in Albion in the late twelfth century BCE. With his Trojan followers, Brutus defeats the giants inhabiting the land, and his compatriots rename the island "Britain" in his honor. After this, Geoffrey follows the line of British kings up to the time of Julius Caesar and the Roman invasions. By the fifth century, after Rome has departed from Britain (c. 410 BCE), Geoffrey is ready to introduce Arthur, to whom he devotes approximately one-quarter of his *Historia*.

Geoffrey depicts Arthur as the son of Uther Pendragon and Ygerna, the wife of Gorlois, Duke of Cornwall. According to the *Historia*, Uther fell in love with Ygerna and wanted her for himself. In order to obtain her, Uther brought his army to attack the Duke, her husband. While Gorlois fought, Merlin cast a spell over Uther so that he would look exactly like Gorlois and thus be able to enter Tintagel, Gorlois's stronghold, and sleep with his wife. It was on this occasion that Arthur was conceived. Meanwhile, Gorlois died fighting against Uther's army, so Uther was soon able to resume his natural appearance and marry Ygerna.

With such a magical beginning, it is no surprise that Geoffrey's Arthur turns out to do extraordinary things. He becomes king as a young man and engages in a series of successful battles, defeating the Saxons, the Picts, and the Scots (with the help of his sword Caliburn), and conquering Ireland and Iceland as well. He marries Guinevere, a lady of Roman descent, and establishes an internationally famous order of knighthood which includes such men as Kay, Bedivere, and Gawain. After years of peace, he attacks and conquers Norway, Denmark, and much of Gaul. He holds court at Caerleon in Wales. But when Lucius, the western Emperor of Rome, demands tribute and the return of conquered lands, Arthur goes back to the continent to fight the Romans and defeats them in Burgundy. He might have continued his conquests except that news reaches him that his nephew Mordred has declared himself king, seduced the Queen, and made a pact with the Saxons. So Arthur returns to do battle with Mordred and routs him near the River Camel in Cornwall. Unluckily, Arthur is badly wounded in the fray. He is taken to the Isle of Avalon to recover from his wounds, but he transfers his crown to his cousin Constantine before his departure. Geoffrey does not record Arthur's death, leaving room for the belief in the future return of Arthur as King of Britain.

Geoffrey certainly used more than one source to create his fabulous *Historia*. He himself claimed that his chronicle was a translation of "a certain very ancient book written in the British language" that had been given to him by Walter, the Archdeacon of Oxford, but this book does not appear to have survived (and some doubt that it ever existed). Geoffrey's other sources include such historians as Gildas, Bede, and Nennius, and his account of Arthur also may have had a Welsh source.

Geoffrey's own imagination must be given credit, too, for his *Historia* reflects creative, if not always historically accurate, thinking.

Geoffrey's imagination and his status as a historian has been the subject of much debate. In his chronicle of 1151, Alfred of Beverly questioned why other historians do not acknowledge the deeds of the Britons celebrated by Geoffrey of Monmouth. In 1198, the historian William of Newburgh concluded that the Arthur and Merlin who appear in Geoffrey's *Historia* are fictitious characters, not historical ones, and he condemned Geoffrey as the "father of lies." William of Malmesbury, perhaps thinking of Geoffrey of Monmouth, complained that Arthur was the one about whom the Welsh tell "deceitful fables," and Ranulf Higden, the fourteenth-century compiler of the Latin *Polychronicon*, dismissed Geoffrey's portrayal of Arthur as improbable. Ranulf explained Geoffrey's glorification of Arthur by saying that each people likes to have its own hero and to praise him excessively; the Greeks have Alexander, for example, and the French have Charlemagne. Modern historians, beginning with the Renaissance historian Polydore Vergil, an Italian living in England who authored the *Anglica historia* (1534), have confirmed that Geoffrey of Monmouth departed from historical truth more often than he stuck to it. Nevertheless, Geoffrey's *Historia* exercised a tremendous influence not only on historical accounts of Britain, but also on romance narratives in medieval England and France.

Vernacular translations of Geoffrey's *Historia* abounded in the Middle Ages. Gaimar and Wace translated the work into Anglo-Norman, while Layamon and Robert of Gloucester translated it into English. Once translated into French, Geoffrey's *Historia* influenced French romance traditions dealing with the "Matter of Britain," including, perhaps most significantly, the works of Chrétien de Troyes. Geoffrey's *Historia* influenced both historical chronicles (the "Brut" tradition) and romance narratives such as the fourteenth-century alliterative poem *Morte Arthure* and the stanzaic *Le Morte Arthur* as well. In later centuries, it also helped to shape such works as Sir Thomas Malory's *Morte d'Arthur*, Tennyson's "Idylls of the King," and numerous modern novels that retell Arthurian legends.

⌘ ⌘ ⌘

from *A History of the Kings of Britain*[1]

Britain, best of islands, lieth in the Western Ocean betwixt Gaul[2] and Ireland, and containeth eight hundred miles in length and two hundred in breadth. Whatsoever is fitting for the use of mortal men the island doth afford in unfailing plenty. For she aboundeth in metals of every kind; fields hath she, stretching far and wide, and hillsides meet for tillage[3] of the best, whereon, by reason of the fruitfulness of the soil, the diverse crops in their season do yield their harvests. Forests also hath she filled with every manner of wild deer, in the glades whereof[4] groweth grass that the cattle may find therein meet change of pasture, and flowers of many colours that do proffer their honey unto the bees that flit ever busily about them. Meadows hath she, set in pleasant places, green at the foot of misty mountains, wherein be sparkling well-springs clear and bright, flowing forth with a gentle whispering ripple in shining streams that sing sweet lullaby unto them that lie upon their banks. Watered is she, moreover, by lakes and rivers wherein is much fish, and, besides the narrow sea of the Southern coast whereby men make voyage unto Gaul,[5] by three noble rivers, Thames, to wit, Severn and Humber,[6] the which she stretcheth forth as it were three

---

[1]   *A History of the Kings of Britain*   The translation from the Latin is by Ernest Rhys.

[2]   *Gaul*   France.

[3]   *meet*   Suitable; *tillage*   Land cultivation.

[4]   *glades*   Open spaces in forests; *whereof*   Of which.

[5]   *unto Gaul*   I.e., the English Channel.

[6]   *Thames*   England's chief commercial waterway, which passes through London; *Severn*   Longest river in England; *Humber* River in north-central England, large enough for seagoing vessels.

arms whereby she taketh in the traffic from oversea brought hither[1] from every land in her fleets. By twice ten cities, moreover, and twice four, was she graced in days of old, whereof some with shattered walls in desolate places be now fallen into decay, whilst some, still whole, do contain churches of the saints with towers builded wondrous fair on high, wherein companies of religious, both men and women, do their service unto God after the traditions of the Christian faith. Lastly, it is inhabited of five peoples, Romans, to wit, Britons, Saxons, Picts, and Scots.[2] Of these the Britons did first settle them[3] therein from sea to sea before the others, until, by reason of their pride, divine vengeance did overtake them, and they yielded them unto the Picts and Saxons. Remaineth[4] now for me to tell from whence[5] they came and in what wise[6] they did land upon our shores, as by way of foretaste of that which shall hereafter be related more at large.

After the Trojan War, Æneas, fleeing from the desolation of the city, came with Ascanius[7] by ship unto Italy. There, for that[8] Æneas was worshipfully[9] received by King Latinus,[10] Turnus, King of the Rutulians,[11] did wax[12] envious and made war against him. When they met in battle, Æneas had the upper hand, and after that Turnus was slain, obtained the kingdom of Italy and Lavinia the daughter of Latinus. Later, when his own last day had come, Ascanius, now king in his stead,[13] founded Alba on Tiber,[14] and begat a son whose name was Silvius. Silvius, unknown to his father, had fallen in love with and privily[15] taken to wife a certain niece of Lavinia, who was now about to become a mother. When this came to the knowledge of his father Ascanius, he commanded his wizards to discover whether the damsel should be brought to bed of[16] a boy or a girl. When they had made sure of the matter by art magic, they told him that the child would be a boy that should slay his father and his mother, and after much travel in many lands, should, albeit[17] an exile, be exalted unto the highest honours. Nor were the wizards out in their forecast, for when the day came that she should be delivered of a child, the mother bore a son, but herself died in his birth. Howbeit,[18] the child was given in charge unto a nurse, and was named Brute. At last, after thrice five years had gone by, the lad, bearing his father company out a-hunting, slew him by striking him unwittingly with an arrow. For when the verderers[19] drove the deer in front of them, Brute thinking to take aim at them, smote[20] his own father under the breast. Upon the death of his father he was driven out of Italy, his kinsfolk being wroth[21] with him for having wrought a deed so dreadful. ...

[Brutus wanders, collecting followers and showing his prowess as a leader, eventually reaching Albion.[22]]

---

[1] *hither* Here.

[2] *Britons* Celtic inhabitants of Great Britain at the time of the Roman invasions; *Saxons* West Germanic groups that invaded Great Britain sporadically in the fifth and sixth centuries; *Picts* Ancient Celtic people, early inhabitants of what is now Scotland.

[3] *them* Themselves.

[4] *Remaineth* It remains.

[5] *from whence* From where.

[6] *wise* Way.

[7] *Trojan War* Ten-year war between the Trojans and Greeks, caused by Paris's abduction of Helen, and ending in the destruction of Troy; *Æneas* Trojan hero who escaped the city's fall, and who wandered for seven years before founding Rome; *Ascanius* Æneas's son.

[8] *for that* Because.

[9] *worshipfully* Honorably.

[10] *King Latinus* King of Latium, a pre-Roman city in Italy.

[11] *Rutulians* Peoples of competing Italian tribes.

[12] *wax* Grow.

[13] *stead* Place.

[14] *Alba* Alba Longa, ancient pre-Roman city destroyed in the twelfth century BCE, shortly after Troy; *Tiber* Principal river of central Italy flowing through Rome.

[15] *privily* Secretly.

[16] *brought ... of* Give birth to.

[17] *albeit* Although.

[18] *Howbeit* Nevertheless.

[19] *verderers* Stewards of the forest.

[20] *smote* Struck.

[21] *wroth* Intensely angry.

[22] *Albion* England.

At that time the name of the island was Albion, and of none was it inhabited save only of a few giants. Nonetheless the pleasant aspect of the land, with the abundance of fish in the rivers and deer in the choice forests thereof did fill Brute and his companions with no small desire that they should dwell therein. Wherefore,[1] after exploring certain districts of the land, they drove the giants they found to take refuge in the caverns of the mountains, and divided the country among them by lot[2] according as the Duke made grant thereof. They began to till the fields, and to build them houses in such sort that after a brief space ye might have thought it had been inhabited from time immemorial. Then, at last, Brute calleth the island Britain, and his companions Britons, after his own name, for he was minded that his memory should be perpetuated in the derivation of the name. Whence afterward the country speech, which was aforetime called Trojan or crooked Greek, was called British. But Corineus called that share of the kingdom which had fallen unto him by lot Cornwall,[3] after the manner of his own name, and the people Cornishmen, therein following the Duke's example. For albeit that he might have had the choice of a province before all the others that had come thither, yet was he minded rather to have that share of the land which is now called Cornwall, whether from being, as it is, the *cornu* or horn of Britain, or from a corruption of the said name Corineus. For nought[4] gave him greater pleasure than to wrestle with the giants, of whom was greater plenty there than in any of the provinces that had been shared amongst his comrades. Among others was a certain hateful one by name Goemagot, twelve cubits[5] in height, who was of such lustihood[6] that when he had once uprooted it, he would wield an oak tree as lightly as it were a wand of hazel. On a certain day when Brute

was holding high festival to the gods in the port whereat[7] he had first landed, this one, along with a score of other giants, fell upon him and did passing[8] cruel slaughter on the British. Howbeit, at the last, the Britons collecting together from all quarters prevailed against them and slew them all, save Goemagot only. Him Brute had commanded to be kept alive, as he was minded to see a wrestling bout betwixt him and Corineus, who was beyond measure keen to match himself against such monsters. So Corineus, overjoyed at the prospect, girt[9] himself for the encounter, and flinging away his arms,[10] challenged him to a bout at wrestling. At the start, on the one side stands Corineus, on the other the giant, each hugging the other tight in the shackles of their arms, both making the very air quake with their breathless gasping. It was not long before Goemagot, grasping Corineus with all his force, broke him three of his ribs, two on the right side and one on the left. Roused thereby to fury, Corineus gathered up all his strength, heaved him up on his shoulders and ran with his burden as fast as he could for the weight to the seashore nighest at hand. Mounting up to the top of a high cliff, and disengaging himself, he hurled the deadly monster he had carried on his shoulder into the sea, where, falling on the sharp rocks, he was mangled all to pieces and dyed the waves with his blood, so that ever thereafter that place from the flinging down of the giant hath been known as Lamgoemagot, to wit, "Goemagot's Leap," and is called by that name unto this present day.

After that he had seen his kingdom, Brute was minded to build him a chief city, and following out his intention, he went round the whole circuit of the land in search of a fitting site. When he came to the river Thames, he walked along the banks till he found the very spot best fitted to his purpose. He therefore founded his city there and called it New Troy, and by this name was it known for many ages thereafter, until at last, by corruption of the word, it came to be called

---

[1] *Wherefore* For which reason.

[2] *by lot* Choosing lots was a method of making decisions. Objects bearing the marks of competitors would be placed in a receptacle and the first one to fall out or be taken out by an uninterested person would win.

[3] *Cornwall* Peninsular region in the far southwest of England.

[4] *nought* Nothing.

[5] *cubit* Unit of measurement equal to the distance between the elbow and the fingertips.

[6] *lustihood* Physical vigor.

[7] *whereat* Where.

[8] *passing* Surpassingly, exceptional.

[9] *girt* Prepared.

[10] *arms* Weapons.

Trinovantum. But afterward, Lud, the brother of Cassibelaunus, who fought with Julius Caesar,[1] possessed him of the helm of the kingdom, and surrounded the city with right noble walls, as well as with towers builded with marvellous art,[2] commanding that it should be called Kaerlud, that is, the City of Lud, after his own name. Whence afterward a contention arose betwixt him and his brother Nennius, who took it ill that he should be minded to do away the name of Troy in his own country. But since Gildas,[3] the historian, hath treated of this contention at sufficient length, I have chosen the rather to pass it over, lest that which so great a writer hath already set forth in so eloquent a style, I should only seem to besmirch[4] in mine own homelier[5] manner of speech.

Accordingly, when the aforesaid Duke founded the said city, he granted it as of right unto the citizens that should dwell therein, and gave them a law under which they should be peacefully entreated. At that time Eli[6] the priest reigned in Judaea,[7] and the Ark of the Covenant[8] was taken by the Philistines.[9] The sons of Hector[10] reigned in Troy, having driven out the descendants of Antenor.[11] In Italy reigned Sylvius Æneas, the son of Æneas and uncle of Brute, he being the third of the Latin kings. …

[There follows the genealogy and history of the many kings of Britain, including the following, whose story appears here in rather different form than in Shakespeare's play.]

When Bladud was thus given over to the destinies,[12] his son Lear was next raised to the kingdom, and ruled the country after manly fashion for three-score[13] years. He it was that builded the city on the river Soar,[14] that in the British is called Kaerleir, but in the Saxon, Leicester.[15] Male issue[16] was denied unto him, his only children being three daughters named Goneril, Regan, and Cordelia, whom all he did love with marvellous affection, but most of all the youngest born, to wit, Cordelia. And when that he began to be upon the verge of eld,[17] he thought to divide his kingdom amongst them, and to marry them unto such husbands as were worthy to have them along with their share of the kingdom. But that he might know which of them was most worthy of the largest share, he went unto them to make inquiry of each as to which of them did most love himself. When, accordingly, he asked of Goneril how much she loved him, she first called all the gods of heaven to witness that her father was dearer to her heart than the very soul that dwelt within her body. Unto whom saith her father: "For this, that thou hast set mine old age before thine own life, thee, my dearest daughter, will I marry unto whatsoever youth shall be thy choice, together with the third part of Britain." Next, Regan, that was second, fain[18] to take ensample[19] of her sister and to wheedle her father into doing her an equal kindness, made answer with a solemn oath that she

---

[1] *Julius Caesar* Roman general, emperor and historian (100–44 BCE) who invaded Britain in the first century BCE, and who was famously murdered by political enemies.

[2] *art* Skill, artifice.

[3] *Gildas* Anglo-Saxon historian (504–570 CE) who wrote *The Ruin of Britain*, a work portraying the nobles and the king as immoral plunderers. Gildas's work also contains an account of King Arthur's defeat of the Saxons.

[4] *besmirch* Stain the reputation of.

[5] *homelier* Less elevated, scholarly; simpler.

[6] *Eli* Biblical high priest and judge, effectively ruling Judaea.

[7] *Judaea* Ancient kingdom comprised of modern-day southern Israel and southwestern Jordan.

[8] *Ark … Covenant* Sacred chest in which the ancient Hebrews stored the stone tablets containing the Ten Commandments.

[9] *Philistines* Ancient people who inhabited Canaan when the Israelites arrived.

[10] *Hector* Heroic prince of Troy killed by Achilles in Homer's *Iliad*.

[11] *Antenor* Counselor of King Priam of Troy, spared by the Greeks during the city's destruction.

[12] *given … destinies* Died.

[13] *three-score* Sixty.

[14] *Soar* River in east English Midlands.

[15] *Leicester* Region of central England northeast of Birmingham, built on the site of a Roman settlement.

[16] *issue* Offspring.

[17] *eld* Old age.

[18] *fain* Glad.

[19] *ensample* Example.

could no otherwise express her thought than by saying that she loved him better than all the world beside. The credulous father thereupon promised to marry her with the same dignity as her elder sister, with another third part of the kingdom for her share. But the last, Cordelia, when she saw how her father had been cajoled by the flatteries of her sisters who had already spoken and desiring to make trial of him otherwise,[1] went on to make answer unto him thus: "Father mine, is there a daughter anywhere that presumeth to love her father more than a father? None such, I trow,[2] there is that durst[3] confess as much, save[4] she were trying to hide the truth in words of jest. For myself, I have ever loved thee as a father, nor never from that love will I be turned aside. Albeit that thou art bent on wringing more from me, yet hearken[5] to the true measure of my love. Ask of me no more, but let this be mine answer: So much as thou hast, so much art thou worth, and so much do I love thee." Thereupon forthwith, her father, thinking that she had thus spoken out of the abundance of her heart, waxed mightily indignant, nor did he tarry[6] to make known what his answer would be. "For that thou hast so despised thy father's old age that thou hast disdained to love me even as well as these thy sisters love me, I also will disdain thee, nor never in my realm shalt thou have share with thy sisters. Howbeit, sith[7] that thou art my daughter, I say not but that I will marry thee upon terms of some kind unto some stranger that is of other land than mine, if so be that fortune shall offer such an one; only be sure of this, that never will I trouble me to marry thee with such honour as thy sisters, inasmuch as, whereas up to this time I have loved thee better than the others, it now seemeth that thou lovest me less than they."

Straightway thereupon, by counsel of the nobles of the realm, he giveth the twain[8] sisters unto two Dukes, of Cornwall, to wit, and Albany, together with one moiety[9] only of the island so long as he should live, but after his death he willed that they should have the whole of the kingdom of Britain. Now it so fell out about this time that Aganippus, King of the Franks,[10] hearing report of Cordelia's beauty, forthwith dispatched his envoys to the King, beseeching him that Cordelia might be entrusted to their charge as his bride whom he would marry with due rite of the wedding-torch. But her father, still persisting in his wrath, made answer that right willingly would he give her, but that needs must it be without land or fee,[11] seeing that he had shared his kingdom along with all his gold and silver betwixt Cordelia's sisters Goneril and Regan. When this word was brought unto Aganippus, for that he was on fire with love of the damsel, he sent again unto King Lear saying that enough had he of gold and silver and other possessions, for that one-third part of Gaul was his, and that he was fain to marry the damsel only that he might have sons by her to inherit his land. So at last the bargain was struck, and Cordelia was sent to Gaul to be married unto Aganippus.

Some long time after, when Lear began to wax more sluggish by reason of age, the foresaid Dukes, with whom and his two daughters he had divided Britain, rebelled against him and took away from him the realm and the kingly power which up to that time he had held right manfully and gloriously. Howbeit, concord was restored, and one of his sons-in-law, Maglaunus, Duke of Albany, agreed to maintain him with threescore knights, so that he should not be without some semblance of state.[12] But after that he had sojourned with his son-in-law two years, his daughter Goneril began to wax indignant at the number of his knights, who flung gibes at her servants for that their rations were not more plentiful. Whereupon, after speaking to her husband, she ordered her father to be content with a service of thirty knights and to dismiss the other thirty that he

---

[1] *make ... otherwise* Test him in another way.

[2] *trow* Believe.

[3] *durst* Dares.

[4] *save* Unless.

[5] *hearken* Listen.

[6] *tarry* Delay.

[7] *sith* Since.

[8] *twain* Two.

[9] *moiety* Half.

[10] *Franks* Germanic tribes who conquered Gaul, the area of modern-day France.

[11] *fee* Dowry, money or goods given from the bride's family to the husband's at the time of marriage.

[12] *state* Status, power.

had. The King, taking this in dudgeon,[1] left Maglaunus, and betook him to Henvin, Duke of Cornwall, unto whom he had married his other daughter. Here, at first, he was received with honour, but a year had not passed before discord again arose betwixt those of the King's household and those of the Duke's, insomuch as that Regan, waxing indignant, ordered her father to dismiss all his company save five knights only to do him service. Her father, beyond measure aggrieved thereat, returned once more to his eldest daughter, thinking to move her to pity and to persuade her to maintain himself and his retinue. Howbeit, she had never renounced her first indignation, but swore by all the gods of Heaven that never should he take up his abode with her save he contented himself with the service of a single knight and were quit of all the rest. Moreover, she upbraided[2] the old man for that, having nothing of his own to give away, he should be minded to go about with such a retinue; so that finding she would not give way to his wishes one single tittle, he at last obeyed and remained content with one knight only, leaving the rest to go their way. But when the remembrance of his former dignity came back unto him, bearing witness to the misery of the estate[3] to which he was now reduced, he began to bethink him of going to his youngest daughter oversea. Howbeit, he sore misdoubted that she would do nought for him, seeing that he had held her, as I have said, in such scanty honour in the matter of her marriage. Nonetheless, disdaining any longer to endure so mean[4] a life, he betook him across the Channel into Gaul. But when he found that two other princes were making the passage at the same time, and that he himself had been assigned but the third place, he broke forth into tears and sobbing, and cried aloud: "Ye destinies that do pursue your wonted[5] way marked out by irrevocable decree, wherefore was it your will ever to uplift me to happiness so fleeting? For a keener grief it is to call to mind that lost happiness than to suffer the presence of the unhappiness that cometh after. For the memory of the days when in the midst of hundreds of thousands of warriors I went to batter down the walls of cities and to lay waste the provinces of mine enemies is more grievous unto me than the calamity that hath overtaken me in the meanness[6] of mine estate, which hath incited them that but now were grovelling under my feet to desert my feebleness. O angry fortune! will the day ever come wherein I may requite the evil turn that hath thus driven forth the length of my days and my poverty? O Cordelia, my daughter, how true were the words wherein thou didst make answer unto me, when I did ask of thee how much thou didst love me! For thou saidst, 'So much as thou hast, so much art thou worth, and so much do I love thee.' So long, therefore, as I had that which was mine own to give, so long seemed I of worth unto them that were the lovers, not of myself but of my gifts. They loved me at times, but better loved they the presents I made unto them. Now that the presents are no longer forthcoming, they too have gone their ways. But with what face, O thou dearest of my children, shall I dare appear before thee? I who, wroth with thee for these thy words, was minded to marry thee less honourably than thy sisters, who, after all the kindnesses I have conferred upon them have allowed me to become an outcast and a beggar?"

Landing at last, his mind filled with these reflections and others of a like kind, he came to Karitia, where his daughter lived, and waiting without[7] the city, sent a messenger to tell her into what indigence he had fallen, and to beseech his daughter's compassion inasmuch as he had neither food nor clothing. On hearing the tidings, Cordelia was much moved and wept bitterly. When she made inquiry how many armed men he had with him, the messengers told her that he had none save a single knight, who was waiting with him without the city. Then took she as much gold and silver as was needful and gave it unto the messenger, bidding him take her father to another city, where he should bathe him, clothe him, and nurse him, feigning that he was a sick man. She commanded also that he should have a retinue of forty knights well appointed[8] and armed, and

---

[1] *in dudgeon* As offensive.

[2] *upbraided* Scolded.

[3] *estate* Condition.

[4] *mean* Common.

[5] *wonted* Accustomed.

[6] *meanness* Lowliness.

[7] *without* Outside.

[8] *appointed* Equipped.

that then he should duly announce his arrival to Aganippus and herself. The messenger accordingly forthwith attended King Lear into another city, and hid him there in secret until that he had fully accomplished all that Cordelia had borne him on hand[1] to do.

As soon therefore, as he was meetly arrayed[2] in kingly apparel and invested with the ensigns[3] of royalty and a train of retainers, he sent word unto Aganippus and his daughter that he had been driven out of the realm of Britain by his sons-in-law, and had come unto them in order that by their assistance he might be able to recover his kingdom. They accordingly, with the great counsellors and nobles, came forth to receive him with all honour, and placed in his hands the power over the whole of Gaul until such time as they had restored him unto his former dignity.

In the meanwhile, Aganippus sent envoys throughout the whole of Gaul to summon every knight bearing arms therein to spare no pains in coming to help him to recover the kingdom of Britain for his father-in-law, King Lear. When they had all made them ready, Lear led the assembled host together with Aganippus and his daughter into Britain, fought a battle with his sons-in-law, and won the victory, again bringing them all under his own dominion. In the third year thereafter he died, and Aganippus died also, and Cordelia, now mistress of the helm of state in Britain, buried her father in a certain underground chamber which she had bidden be made under the river Soar at Leicester. This underground chamber was founded in honour of the two-faced Janus,[4] and there, when the yearly celebration of the day came round, did all the workmen of the city set hand unto such work as they were about to be busied upon throughout the year. …

Now Vortigern,[5] when he saw that there was none his peer in the kingdom, set the crown thereof upon his own head and usurped precedence over all his fellow-princes. Howbeit, his treason at last being publicly known, the people of the neighbouring out-islands,[6] whom the Picts had led with them into Albany, raised an insurrection against him. For the Picts, indignant that their comrades-in-arms had been thus put to death on account of Constans,[7] were minded to revenge them upon Vortigern, who was thereby not only sore troubled in his mind, but suffered heavy loss amongst his fighting-men in battle. On the other hand, he was still more sorely troubled in his mind by his dread of Aurelius Ambrosius and his brother Uther Pendragon, who, as hath been said, had fled into Little Britain[8] for fear of him. For day after day was it noised[9] in his ears that they were now grown men, and had built a passing huge fleet, being minded to adventure[10] a return unto the kingdom that of right was their own.

In the meanwhile three brigantines, which we call "longboats," arrived on the coasts of Kent full of armed warriors and captained by the two brethren Horsus and Hengist. Vortigern was then at Dorobernia, which is now called Canterbury, his custom being to visit that city very often. When his messengers reported unto him that certain men unknown and big of stature had arrived, he took them into his peace,[11] and bade them be brought unto him. Presently, when they came before him, he fixed his eyes upon the two brethren, for that they did surpass the others both in dignity and in

---

[1] *borne … hand* Charged him with the responsibility.

[2] *arrayed* Dressed.

[3] *ensigns* Emblems.

[4] *Janus* In Roman mythology, God of doorways and gates, traditionally represented with two faces looking in opposite directions.

[5] *Vortigern* Fifth-century CE warlord who is traditionally said to have invited the Anglo-Saxons to settle in Britain to help defend the country against Viking invasions.

[6] *out-islands* The Hebrides islands, off the western and northwestern coast of Scotland.

[7] *Constans* In Geoffrey's history, son of King Constantine of Britain, brother of Aurelius Ambrosius and Uther Pendragon.

[8] *Little Britain* Brittany, region of northwestern France, settled in the fifth century by Britons who had been driven from England by the Anglo-Saxons.

[9] *noised* Rumored.

[10] *adventure* Risk.

[11] *peace* Protection.

comeliness.[1] And, when he had passed the rest of the company under review, he made inquiry as to the country of their birth and the cause of their coming into his kingdom. Unto whom Hengist, for that he was of riper[2] years and readier[3] wit than the others, thus began to make answer on behalf of them all:

"Most noble of all the Kings, the Saxon land is our birthplace, one of the countries of Germany, and the reason of our coming is to offer our services unto thee or unto some other prince. For we have been banished from our country, and this for none other reason than for that the custom of our country did so demand. For such is the custom in our country that whensoever they that dwell therein do multiply too thick upon the ground, the princes of the diverse provinces do meet together and bid the young men of the whole kingdom come before them. They do then cast lots and make choice of the likeliest and strongest to go forth and seek a livelihood in other lands, so as that their native country may be disburdened of its overgrown multitudes. Accordingly, owing to our country being thus over-stocked with men, the princes came together, and casting lots, did make choice of these young men that here thou seest before thee and bade them obey the custom that hath been ordained of time immemorial. They did appoint, moreover, us twain brethren, of whom I am named Hengist and this other Horsus, to be their captains, for that we were born of the family of the dukes. Wherefore, in obedience unto decrees ordained of yore, have we put to sea and under the guidance of Mercury[4] have sought out this thy kingdom."

At the name of Mercury the King lifted up his countenance and asked of what manner religion they were. Unto whom Hengist:[5]

"We do worship our country gods, Saturn, Jove[6] and the rest of them that do govern the world, but most of all Mercury, whom in our tongue we do call Woden.[7] Unto him have our forefathers dedicated the fourth day of the week that even unto this day hath borne the name of Wednesday after his name. Next unto him we do worship the goddess that is most powerful above all other goddesses, Frea[8] by name, unto whom they dedicated the sixth day, which we call Friday after her name." Saith Vortigern: "Right sore doth it grieve me of this your belief, the which may rather be called your unbelief, yet nonetheless, of your coming do I rejoice, for either God or some other hath brought ye hither to succour[9] me in mine hour of need. For mine enemies do oppress me on every side, and so[10] ye make common cause with me in the toils of fighting my battles, ye shall be worshipfully retained in my service within my realm, and right rich will I make ye in all manner of land and fee."

The barbarians forthwith agreed, and after the covenant had been duly confirmed, remained in the court. Presently thereupon, the Picts issuing from Albany, mustered a huge army and began to ravage the northern parts of the island. As soon as ever Vortigern had witting thereof, he called his men together and marched forth to meet them on the further side Humber.[11] When the men of the country came into close quarters with the enemy, both sides made a passing sharp onset; but little need had they of the country to do much of the fighting, for the Saxons that were there did battle in such gallant fashion as that the enemies that aforetime were ever wont to have the upper hand were put to flight, hot foot, without delay.

Vortigern accordingly, when he had won the victory by their means, increased his bounties upon them and gave unto their duke, Hengist, many lands in the district of Lindsey for the maintenance of himself and his fellow-soldiers. Hengist therefore, as a politic[12] man and a

---

[1] *comeliness* Attractiveness.

[2] *riper* Older.

[3] *readier* Sharper.

[4] *Mercury* Roman messenger god and patron of travelers.

[5] *Unto ... Hengist* Hengist answered.

[6] *Saturn* Roman god of agriculture; *Jove* Supreme deity of Roman pantheon, equivalent to Zeus.

[7] *Woden* Anglo-Saxon equivalent of Odin, supreme deity and god of wisdom, war and culture.

[8] *Frea* Scandinavian goddess of beauty and love.

[9] *succour* Help.

[10] *so* If.

[11] *further ... Humber* Far side of the Humber.

[12] *politic* Shrewd.

crafty, when that he found the King bore so great a friendship towards him, spoke unto him on this wise:[1]

"My lord, thy foemen do persecute thee on every side, and few be they of thine own folk that bear thee any love. They all do threaten thee and say that they will bring in hither thy brother Aurelius Ambrosius from the shores of Armorica,[2] that, after deposing thee, they may raise him to be King. May it therefore please thee that we send unto our own country and invite warriors thence so that the number of our fighting men may be increased. Yet is there one thing further that I would beseech of the discretion of thy clemency, were it not that I misdoubt me I might suffer a denial thereof." Upon this saith Vortigern: "Send therefore thine envoys unto Germany and invite whomsoever thou wilt, and, as for thyself, ask of me whatsoever thou wilt, and no denial thereof shalt thou suffer." Thereupon Hengist bowed his head before him and gave him thanks, saying: "Thou hast enriched me of large dwelling-houses and lands, yet withal[3] hast thou withheld such honour as may beseem a Duke, seeing that my forefathers were dukes in mine own land. Wherefore, methinketh amongst so much beside, some city or castle might have been given unto me, whereby I might have been held of greater account by the barons of thy realm. The rank of an Earl or a Prince might have been granted unto one born of a family that hath held both these titles of nobility." Saith Vortigern: "I am forbidden to grant any boon of this kind upon thee, for that ye be foreigner and heathen men, nor as yet have I learnt your manners and customs so as that I should make ye the equals of mine own folk; nor yet, were I to hold ye as mine own very countryfolk, could I set precedent of such a grant so the barons of the realm were against it." Whereunto Hengist: "Grant," saith he, "unto thy servant but so much only as may be compassed round about by a single thong within the land that thou hast given me, that so I may build me a high place therein whereunto if need be I may betake me. For loyal liegemen unto thee I have been and shall be, and in thy fealty[4] will I do all that it is within my mind to do." Whereupon the King, moved by his words, did grant him his petition, and bade him send his envoys into Germany forthwith, so that the warriors he invited thence might hasten at once unto his succour. Straightway, as soon as he had dispatched his envoys into Germany, Hengist took a bull's hide, and wrought the same into a single thong throughout. He then compassed round with his thong a stony place that he had right cunningly chosen, and within the space thus meted[5] out did begin to build the castle that was afterwards called in British, Kaercorrei, but in Saxon, Thongceaster, the which in the Latin speech is called *Castrum corrigiæ.*[6]

Meantime the envoys returned from Germany, bringing with them eighteen ships full of chosen warriors. They convoyed also the daughter of Hengist, Rowen by name, whose beauty was unparagoned of any. When they were arrived, Hengist invited King Vortigern into his house to look at the new building and the new warriors that had come into the land. The King accordingly came privily forthwith, and not only praised the work so swiftly wrought, but received the soldiers that had been invited into his retinue. And after that he had been entertained at a banquet royal, the damsel stepped forth of her chamber bearing a golden cup filled with wine, and coming next the King, bended her knee and spoke, saying: "Laverd King, wacht heil!"[7] But he, when he beheld the damsel's face, was all amazed at her beauty and his heart was enkindled of delight. Then he asked of his interpreter what it was that the damsel had said, whereupon the interpreter made answer: "She hath called thee 'Lord King,' and hath greeted thee by wishing thee health. But the answer that thou shouldst make unto her is 'Drinc heil.'"[8] Whereupon Vortigern made answer: "Drinc heil!" and bade the damsel drink. Then he took the cup from her hand and kissed her, and drank; and from that day unto this hath the custom held in Britain that he who drinketh at a feast saith unto another, "Wacht heil!" and he that receiveth the drink

---

[1] *on ... wise* In this manner.

[2] *Armorica* Brittany, or Little Britain.

[3] *withal* At the same time.

[4] *fealty* Service.

[5] *meted* Measured.

[6] *Castrum corrigiæ* Latin: Fortress of the thong.

[7] *wacht heil* Germanic version of wassail, traditional British salutation used when presenting a cup of wine to a guest.

[8] *Drinc heil* Drink-hail, customary response to wassail.

after him maketh answer, "Drinc heil!" Howbeit, Vortigern, drunken with the diverse kinds of liquor, Satan entering into his heart, did wax enamoured of the damsel, and demanded her of her father. Satan entering into his heart, I say, for that he, being a Christian, did desire to mate him with a heathen woman. Hengist, a crafty man and a prudent, herein discovering the inconstancy of the King's mind, forthwith held counsel with his brother Horsus and the rest of the aldermen[1] that were with him what were best to be done as touching the King's petition. But they all were of one counsel, that the damsel should be given unto the King, and that they should ask of him the province of Kent in return for her. So the matter was settled out of hand. The damsel was given unto Vortigern, and the province of Kent unto Hengist without the knowledge of Gorangon the Earl that of right was lord thereof. That very same night was the King wedded unto the heathen woman, with whom thenceforth was he beyond all measure well-pleased. Nonetheless, thereby full swiftly did he raise up enemies against him amongst the barons of the realm and amongst his own children. For aforetime had three sons been born unto him, whereof these were the names: Vortimer, Katigern, and Pascentius.

[Vortigern, unpopular because of his Saxon ties, is eventually challenged for the kingdom by his son Vortimer, who has the people's support, but after Vortimer is poisoned, Vortigern regains his throne. Ultimately, however, he is defeated by Ambrosius Aurelianus, who in this account is the brother of Uther Pendragon and the uncle of Arthur. He and Uther jointly fight off the Saxon hordes and their allies.]

… Whilst these things were being enacted at Winchester,[2] there appeared a star of marvellous bigness and brightness, stretching forth one ray whereon was a ball of fire spreading forth in the likeness of a dragon, and from the mouth of the dragon issued forth two rays, whereof the one was of such length as that it did seem to reach beyond the regions of Gaul, and the other, verging toward the Irish sea, did end in seven lesser rays.

At the appearance of this star all that did behold it were stricken with wonder and fear. Uther, also, the King's brother, who was leading a hostile army into Cambria,[3] was smitten[4] with no small dread, insomuch as that he betook him unto sundry[5] wizards to make known unto him what the star might portend. Amongst the rest, he bade call Merlin, for he also had come along with the army so that the business of the fighting might be dealt with according to his counsel. And when he was brought unto the King and stood before him, he was bidden declare what the star did betoken. Whereupon, bursting into tears and drawing a long breath, he cried aloud, saying:

"O, loss irreparable! O, orphaned people of Britain! O, departure of a most noble King! Dead is the renowned King of the Britons, Aurelius Ambrosius, in whose death shall we all also be dead, save God deign[6] to be our helper! Wherefore hasten, most noble Duke Uther, hasten and tarry not to do battle upon thine enemies! The victory shall be thine, and King thou shalt be of the whole of Britain! For this is what yon star doth betoken, and the fiery dragon that is under the star! The ray, moreover, that stretcheth forth toward the regions of Gaul, doth portend that a son shall be born unto thee that shall be of surpassing mighty dominion, whose power shall extend over all the realms that lie beneath the ray; and the other ray signifieth a daughter whose sons and grandsons shall hold the kingdom of Britain in succession."

But Uther, albeit misdoubting whether Merlin spoke true, continued the advance against the enemy, that he had already begun, for he was so nigh unto Menevia[7] as that not more than half a day's march had to be covered. And when his advance was reported unto Gilloman, Pascentius and the Saxons that were with them, they issued forth to meet him and do battle with him. So soon as the armies came in sight of one another, they both set them in fighting array, and coming to close

---

[1] *aldermen* High-ranking Anglo-Saxon nobles.

[2] *Winchester* City in southern England, once the capital of the Anglo-Saxon kingdom of Wessex.

[3] *Cambria* Wales.

[4] *smitten* Struck.

[5] *sundry* Various.

[6] *deign* Condescends.

[7] *Menevia* Region in southern Wales.

quarters, began a hand to hand engagement, soldiers being slain on the one side and the other as is wont in such cases. At last, when the day was far spent, Uther in the end prevailed and obtained the victory after Gilloman and Pascentius had been slain. The barbarians thereupon took to flight, and scampered off to their ships, pursued by the Britons who slew a number of them in their flight. The Duke's victory being thus by Christ's favour complete, he returned the swiftest he might after so sore travail unto Winchester. For messengers had arrived announcing the death of the King and bringing word that he was presently to be buried by the bishops of the land within the Giants' Dance,[1] nigh the convent of Ambrius,[2] according to the instructions he had given when alive. When they heard of his departure, the pontiffs and abbots and all the clergy of the province assembled in the city of Winchester, and honoured him with a funeral such as was befitting a King so mighty. And, for that in his lifetime he had commanded he should be buried in the graveyard he had enclosed, thither they bore his body and laid it in the ground with right royal ceremony.

But his brother Uther, calling together the clergy of the country, took upon him the crown of the island, and with universal assent was raised to be King. And, remembering in what wise Merlin had interpreted the meaning of the star aforementioned, bade two dragons be wrought in gold in the likeness of the dragon he had seen upon the ray of the star. And when that they had been wrought in marvellous cunning craftsmanship, he made offering of the one unto the chief church of the See[3] of Winton, but the other did he keep himself to carry about with him in the wars. From that day forth was he called Uther Pendragon, for thus do we call a dragon's head in the British tongue. And the reason wherefore this name was given unto him was that Merlin had prophesied he should be King by means of the dragon.

… And when the Easter festival drew nigh, he bade the barons of the realm assemble in that city that he might celebrate so high holiday with honour by assuming the crown thereon. All obeyed accordingly, and repairing[4] thither from the several cities, assembled together on the eve of the festival. The King, accordingly, celebrated the ceremony as he had proposed, and made merry along with his barons, all of whom did make great cheer for that the King had received them in such joyful wise. For all the nobles that were there had come with their wives and daughters as was meet on so glad a festival. Among the rest, Gorlois, Duke of Cornwall, was there, with his wife Igerne, that in beauty did surpass all the other dames of the whole of Britain. And when the King espied her amidst the others, he did suddenly wax so fain of[5] her love that, paying no heed[6] unto none of the others, he turned all his attention only upon her. Only unto her did he send dainty tit-bits from his own dish; only unto her did he send the golden cups with messages through his familiars.[7] Many a time did he smile upon her and spoke merrily unto her withal. But when her husband did perceive all this, straightway he waxed wroth and retired from the court without leave[8] taken. Nor was any that might recall him thither, for that he feared to lose the one thing that he loved better than all other. Uther, waxing wroth hereat, commanded him to return and appear in his court that he might take lawful satisfaction for the affront he had put upon him. And when Gorlois was not minded to obey the summons, the King was enraged beyond all measure and swore with an oath that he would ravage his demesnes so he hastened not to make him satisfaction.[9] Forthwith, the quarrel betwixt the two abiding unsettled, the King gathered a mighty army together and went his way into the province of Cornwall and set fire to the cities and castles therein. But Gorlois, not daring to meet him in the field for that he had not so many armed men, chose

---

1   *Giants' Dance* Stonehenge, the group of standing stones on Salisbury Plain, dating from 2000 BCE. Geoffrey recounts the legend that Merlin had them magically moved from Ireland.

2   *convent of Ambrius* Convent named for Aurelius Ambr(os)ius.

3   *See* Center of Church authority.

4   *repairing* Traveling.

5   *fain of* Eager for.

6   *heed* Notice.

7   *familiars* Household members.

8   *leave* Permission.

9   *demesnes* Lands granted in exchange for feudal service; *so … satisfaction* If he did not act swiftly to make amends.

rather to garrison[1] his own strong places until such time as he obtained the succour he had besought[2] from Ireland. And, for that he was more troubled upon his wife's account than upon his own, he placed her in the Castle of Tintagel on the seacoast, as holding it to be the safer refuge. Howbeit, he himself betook him into the Castle of Dimilioc, being afraid that in case disaster should befall him both might be caught in one trap. And when message of this was brought unto the King, he went unto the castle wherein Gorlois had ensconced him, and beleaguered[3] him and cut off all access unto him. At length, at the end of a week, mindful of his love for Igerne, he spoke unto one of his familiars named Ulfin of Ricaradoc: "I am consumed of love for Igerne, nor can I have no joy, nor do I look to escape peril of my body save I may have possession of her. Do thou therefore give me counsel in what wise I may fulfil my desire, for, and[4] I do not, of mine inward sorrow shall I die." Unto whom Ulfin: "And who shall give thee any counsel that may avail, seeing that there is no force that may prevail whereby to come unto her in the Castle of Tintagel? For it is situated on the sea, and is on every side encompassed thereby, nor none other entrance is there save such as a narrow rock doth furnish, the which three armed knights could hold against thee, albeit thou wert standing there with the whole realm of Britain beside thee. But, and if Merlin the prophet would take the matter in hand, I do verily[5] believe that by his counsel thou mightest compass thy heart's desire."

The King, therefore, believing him, bade Merlin be called, for he, too, had come unto the leaguer.[6] Merlin came forthwith accordingly, and when he stood in presence of the King, was bidden give counsel how the King's desire might be fulfilled. When he found how sore tribulation of mind the King was suffering, he was moved at beholding the effect of a love so exceeding great, and saith he: "The fulfilment of thy desire doth demand the practice of arts new and unheard of in this thy day. Yet know I how to give thee the semblance of Gorlois by my leechcrafts[7] in such sort as that thou shalt seem in all things to be his very self. If, therefore, thou art minded to obey me, I will make thee like unto him utterly, and Ulfin will I make like unto Jordan of Tintagel his familiar. I also will take upon me another figure and will be with ye as a third, and in such wise we may go safely unto the castle and have access unto Igerne." The King obeyed accordingly, and gave heed[8] strictly unto that which Merlin enjoined[9] him. At last, committing the siege into charge of his familiars, he did entrust himself unto the arts and medicaments of Merlin, and was transformed into the semblance of Gorlois. Ulfin was changed into Jordan, and Merlin into Bricel in such sort as that none could have told the one from the other. They then went their way toward Tintagel, and at dusk hour arrived at the castle. The porter, weening that the Duke had arrived, swiftly unmade[10] the doors, and the three were admitted. For what other[11] than Gorlois could it be, seeing that in all things it seemed as if Gorlois himself were there? So the King lay that night with Igerne, for as he had beguiled her by the false likeness he had taken upon him, so he beguiled her also by the feigned discourses wherewith he did full artfully entertain her. For he told her he had issued forth of the besieged city for naught save[12] to see to the safety of her dear self and the castle wherein she lay, in such sort that she believed him every word, and had no thought to deny him in aught[13] he might desire. And upon that same night was the most renowned Arthur conceived, that was not only famous in after years, but was well worthy of all the fame he did achieve by his surpassing prowess.

In the meantime, when the beleaguering army found that the King was not amongst them, they did unadvisedly make endeavour to breach the walls and challenge

---

1 *garrison* Supply with soldiers.

2 *besought* Earnestly requested.

3 *beleaguered* Laid siege to.

4 *and* If.

5 *verily* Truly.

6 *leaguer* Siege.

7 *leechcrafts* Magical arts.

8 *gave heed* Paid attention.

9 *enjoined* Ordered.

10 *unmade* Unlocked.

11 *what other* Who else.

12 *naught save* Nothing except.

13 *aught* Anything.

the besieged Duke to battle. Who, himself also acting unadvisedly, did straightway sally forth with his comrades in arms, weening that his handful of men were strong enough to make head[1] against so huge a host of armed warriors. But when they met face to face in battle, Gorlois was amongst the first that were slain, and all his companies were scattered. The castle, moreover, that they had besieged was taken, and the treasure that was found therein divided, albeit not by fair casting of lots, for whatsoever his luck or hardihood[2] might throw in his way did each man greedily clutch in his claws for his own. But by the time that this outrageous plundering had at last come to an end messengers had come unto Igerne to tell her of the Duke's death and the issue of the siege. But when they beheld the King in the likeness of the Duke sitting beside her, they blushed scarlet, and stared in amazement at finding that he whom they had just left dead at the leaguer had thus arrived hither safe and sound, for little they knew what the medicaments of Merlin had accomplished. The King therefore, smiling at the tidings, and embracing the countess, spoke saying: "Not slain, verily, am I, for lo, here thou seest me alive, yet, nonetheless, sore it irketh me of the destruction of my castle and the slaughter of my comrades, for that which next is to dread is lest the King should overtake us here and make us prisoners in this castle. First of all, therefore, will I go meet him and make my peace with him, lest a worst thing befall us." Issuing forth accordingly, he made his way unto his own army, and putting off the semblance of Gorlois again became Uther Pendragon. And when he understood how everything had fallen out, albeit that he was sore grieved at the death of Gorlois, yet could he not but be glad that Igerne was released from the bond of matrimony. Returning, therefore, to Tintagel, he took the castle, and not the castle only, but Igerne also therein, and on this wise fulfilled he his desire. Thereafter were they linked together in no little mutual love, and two children were born unto them, a son and a daughter, whereof the son was named Arthur and the daughter Anna.

… After the death of Uther Pendragon, the barons of Britain did come together from the diverse provinces unto the city of Silchester, and did bear on hand Dubricius, Archbishop of the City of Legions,[3] that he should crown as king Arthur, the late King's son. For sore was need upon them, seeing that when the Saxons heard of Uther's death they had invited their fellow-countrymen from Germany, and under their Duke Colgrin were bent upon exterminating the Britons. They had, moreover, entirely subdued all that part of the island which stretcheth from the river Humber, as far as the sea of Caithness.[4] Dubricius therefore, sorrowing over the calamities of the country, assembled the other prelates, and did invest Arthur with the crown of the realm. At that time Arthur was a youth of fifteen years, of a courage and generosity beyond compare, whereunto his inborn goodness did lend such grace as that he was beloved of well-nigh all the peoples in the land. After he had been invested with the ensigns of royalty, he abided by his ancient wont,[5] and was so prodigal[6] of his bounties as that he began to run short of wherewithal[7] to distribute amongst the huge multitude of knights that made repair unto him. But he that hath within him a bountiful nature along with prowess, albeit that he be lacking for a time, nonetheless in no wise shall poverty be his bane for ever. Wherefore did Arthur, for that in him did valour keep company with largesse,[8] make resolve to harry the Saxons, to the end that with their treasure he might make rich the retainers that were of his own household. And herein was he monished[9] of his own lawful right, seeing that of right ought he to hold the sovereignty of the whole island in virtue of his claim hereditary. …

[There follow a long series of battles in which Arthur defeats enemies foreign and domestic, ending with the Scots, who beg for mercy.]

---

[1] *make head*   Advance.

[2] *hardihood*   Physical robustness.

[3] *City of Legions*   Caerleon in York.

[4] *sea of Caithness*   North Sea.

[5] *wont*   Custom.

[6] *prodigal*   Rashly generous.

[7] *wherewithal*   Financial means.

[8] *largesse*   Generosity in giving gifts.

[9] *monished*   Counseled.

… At last, when he had re-established the state of the whole country in its ancient dignity, he took unto him a wife born of a noble Roman family, Guenevere, who, brought up and nurtured in the household of Duke Cador, did surpass in beauty all the other dames of the island.…

When the high festival of Whitsuntide began to draw nigh, Arthur, filled with exceeding great joy at having achieved so great success, was fain to hold high court, and to set the crown of the kingdom upon his head, to convene the Kings and Dukes that were his vassals[1] to the festival so that he might the more worshipfully celebrate the same, and renew his peace more firmly amongst his barons. Howbeit, when he made known his desire unto his familiars, he, by their counsel, made choice of the City of Legions wherein to fulfil his design. For, situated in a passing pleasant position on the river Usk[2] in Glamorgan,[3] not far from the Severn sea, and abounding in wealth above all other cities, it was the place most meet for so high a solemnity.[4] For on the one side thereof flowed the noble river aforesaid whereby the Kings and Princes that should come from oversea might be borne thither in their ships; and on the other side, girdled[5] about with meadows and woods, passing fair was the magnificence of the kingly palaces thereof with the gilded verges[6] of the roofs that imitated Rome. Howbeit, the chiefest glories thereof were the two churches, one raised in honour of the Martyr Julius,[7] that was right fair graced by a convent of virgins that had dedicated them unto God, and the second, founded in the name of the blessed Aaron,[8] his companion, the main pillars whereof were a brotherhood of canons regular,[9] and this was the cathedral church of the third Metropolitan[10] See of Britain. It had, moreover, a school of two hundred philosophers learned in astronomy and in the other arts, that did diligently observe the courses of the stars, and did by true inferences foretell the prodigies[11] which at that time were about to befall unto King Arthur. Such was the city, famed for such abundance of things delightsome, that was now busking her[12] for the festival that had been proclaimed. Messengers were sent forth into the diverse kingdoms, and all that owed allegiance throughout the Gauls and the neighbour islands were invited unto the court. … Not a single Prince of any price[13] on this side Spain remained at home and came not upon the proclamation. And no marvel, for Arthur's bounty was of common report throughout the whole wide world, and all men for his sake were fain to come.

When all at last were assembled in the city on the high day of the festival, the archbishops were conducted unto the palace to crown the King with the royal diadem.[14] Dubric, therefore, upon whom the charge fell, for that the court was held within his diocese, was ready to celebrate the service. As soon as the King had been invested with the ensigns of kingship, he was led in right comely[15] wise to the church of the Metropolitan See, two archbishops supporting him, the one upon his right hand side the other upon his left. Four Kings, moreover, to wit, those of Albany, Cornwall, and North and South Wales, went before him, bearing before him, as was their right, four golden swords. A company of clerics in holy orders of every degree went chanting music marvellous sweet in front. Of the other party, the archbishops and pontiffs led the Queen, crowned with laurel[16] and

---

1 *vassals* Feudal retainers.

2 *Usk* Welsh river.

3 *Glamorgan* Region in Wales.

4 *solemnity* Solemn occasion.

5 *girdled* Encircled.

6 *verges* Borders.

7 *Martyr Julius* Roman soldier martyred in Caerleon in 302 for his Christian beliefs.

8 *Aaron* Julius's companion, also martyred in Caerleon.

9 *canons regular* Members of a religious community living under a strict code of behavior.

10 *Metropolitan* Seat of an ecclesiastical province.

11 *prodigies* Marvelous events.

12 *busking her* Preparing itself.

13 *price* Worth.

14 *diadem* Crown.

15 *comely* Pleasing.

16 *laurel* Bay leaves, traditionally given in ancient times as a sign of honor.

wearing her own ensigns, unto the church of the virgins dedicate. The four Queens, moreover, of the four Kings already mentioned, did bear before her according to wont and custom four white doves, and the ladies that were present did follow after her rejoicing greatly. At last, when the procession was over, so manifold[1] was the music of the organs and so many were the hymns that were chanted in both churches, that the knights who were there scarce knew which church they should enter first for the exceeding sweetness of the harmonies in both. First into the one and then into the other they flocked in crowds, nor, had the whole day been given up to the celebration, would any have felt a moment's weariness thereof. And when the divine services had been celebrated in both churches, the King and Queen put off their crowns, and doing on lighter robes of state, went to meat,[2] he to his palace with the men, she to another palace with the women. For the Britons did observe the ancient custom of the Trojans, and were wont to celebrate their high festival days, the men with the men and the women with the women severally.[3] And when all were set at table according as the rank of each did demand, Kay the Seneschal,[4] in a doublet furred of ermines,[5] and a thousand youths of full high degree[6] in his company, all likewise clad in ermines, did serve the meats along with him. Of the other part, as many in doublets furred of vair[7] did follow Bedevere the Butler,[8] and along with him did serve the drinks from the diverse ewers[9] into the manifold-fashioned cups. In the palace of the Queen no less did numberless pages,

clad in diverse brave liveries,[10] offer their service each after his office,[11] the which were I to go about to describe I might draw out my history into an endless prolixity.[12] For at that time was Britain exalted unto so high a pitch of dignity as that it did surpass all other kingdoms in plenty of riches, in luxury of adornment, and in the courteous wit of them that dwelt therein. Whatsoever knight in the land was of renown for his prowess did wear his clothes and his arms all of one same colour. And the dames, no less witty, would apparel them in like manner in a single colour, nor would they deign have the love of none save he had thrice approved him[13] in the wars. Wherefore at that time did dames wax chaste and knights the nobler for their love.

Refreshed by their banqueting, they go forth into the fields without the city, and sundry among them fall to playing at sundry manner[14] games. Presently the knights engage in a game on horseback, making show of fighting a battle whilst the dames and damsels looking on from the top of the walls, for whose sake the courtly knights make believe to be fighting, do cheer them on for the sake of seeing the better sport. Others elsewhere spend the rest of the day in shooting arrows, some in tilting[15] with spears, some in flinging heavy stones, some in putting the weight; others again in playing at the dice or in a diversity of other games, but all without wrangling;[16] and whosoever had done best in his own game was presented by Arthur with a boon of price.[17] And after the first three days had been spent on this wise, upon the fourth day all they that had done service in virtue of the office they held were summoned, and unto each was made grant of the honour of the office he held,

---

[1] *manifold* Much and varied.

[2] *doing on* Putting on; *to meat* To dinner.

[3] *severally* Separately.

[4] *Kay the Seneschal* In later renditions of Arthurian legend, foster-brother to Arthur; in Geoffrey, Kay is one of Arthur's champions; Kay is named as Arthur's seneschal, or steward, in the vast majority of the legends.

[5] *doublet … ermines* Close-fitting jacket trimmed with costly furs from ermines, small weasel-like animals.

[6] *degree* Social position.

[7] *vair* Squirrel fur.

[8] *Bedevere the Butler* In most versions of the legends, Bedevere is Arthur's cup-bearer and a constable of the kingdom.

[9] *ewers* Decorative pitchers usually with an oval body and a flared pour spout.

[10] *brave* Fine; *liveries* Distinctive clothing worn by feudal retainers.

[11] *after … office* According to his duties.

[12] *prolixity* Boring wordiness.

[13] *approved him* Proven himself.

[14] *manner* Manner of.

[15] *tilting* Jousting.

[16] *wrangling* Quarreling noisily.

[17] *boon … price* Prize of great worth.

in possession, earldom, to wit, of city or castle, archbish-opric, bishopric, abbacy, or whatsoever else it might be.

[Into this happy scene come Roman ambassadors, demanding tribute from Arthur. He refuses and decides to conquer Rome instead, and gets together a fleet to sail across to the continent.]

… And whilst that he was thronged about with his numberless ships, and was cleaving the deep with a prosperous course and much rejoicing, a passing deep sleep as about the middle of the night did overtake him, and in his sleep he saw in dream a certain bear flying in the air, at the growling whereof all the shores did tremble. He saw, moreover, a dreadful dragon come flying from the West that did enlumine[1] the whole country with the flashing of his eyes. And when the one did meet the other there was a marvellous fight betwixt them, and presently the dragon leaping again and again upon the bear, did scorch him up with his fiery breath and cast down his shrivelled carcass to the earth. And thereby awakened, Arthur did relate his dream unto them that stood by, who expounded the same unto him saying that the dragon did betoken himself, but the bear some giant with whom he should encounter; that the fight did foretoken a battle that should be betwixt them, and that the dragon's victory should be his own. None-theless, Arthur did conjecture otherwise thereof, ween-ing that such vision as had befallen him was more like to have to do with himself and the Emperor. At last, when the night had finished her course and the dawn waxed red, they came to in the haven of Barfleur,[2] and pitching their tents thereby, did await the coming of the kings of the islands and the dukes of the neighbour provinces.

Meanwhile tidings are brought unto Arthur that a certain giant of marvellous bigness hath arrived out of the parts of Spain, and, moreover, that he hath seized Helena, niece of Duke Hoel,[3] out of the hands of them that had charge of her, and hath fled with her unto the

top of the mount that is now called of Michael,[4] whither the knights of the country had pursued him. Howbeit, nought might they prevail against him, neither by sea nor by land, for when they would attack him, either he would sink their ships with hugeous rocks, or slay the men with javelins or other weapons, and, moreover, devour many half-alive. Accordingly, in the following night at the second hour,[5] he took with him Kay the Seneschal and Bedevere the Butler, and issuing forth of the tents, unknown to the others, started on his way towards the mount. For of such puissance[6] was his own valour that he deigned not lead an army against such monsters, as holding himself singly enough for their destruction, and being minded to spirit up his men to follow his ensample. Now, when they came anigh[7] the mount, they espied a great fire of wood a-blazing thereupon, and another smaller fire upon a smaller mount not far away from the first. So, being in doubt which were the one whereupon the giant had his wone,[8] they sent Bedevere to spy out the certainty of the matter. He, therefore, finding a little boat, oared him first unto the smaller mount, for none otherwise might he attain thereunto,[9] seeing that it was set in the sea. And when he began to climb up towards the top he heard above him the ullaloo[10] of a woman wailing above him, and at first shuddered, for he misdoubted him the monster might be there. But quickly recovering his hardihood, he drew his sword from the scabbard and mounted to the very top, whereon nought found he save the fire of wood they had espied. But close thereby he saw a newly-made grave-mound, and beside it an old woman weeping and lamenting, who, so soon as she beheld him, stinted her tears forthwith and spoke unto him on this wise: "O, unhappy[11] man, what evil doom[12]

---

[1] *enlumine* Light up.

[2] *haven of Barfleur* Harbor of a port town in northwestern France, a frequent point of arrival for travelers from England during the Middle Ages.

[3] *Duke Hoel* Ruler of Brittany.

[4] *Michael* Mont St. Michel, rocky islet off the north coast of France, where an eleventh-century steepled church stands.

[5] *second hour* Early evening.

[6] *puissance* Strength.

[7] *anigh* Near.

[8] *wone* Dwelling place.

[9] *for … thereunto* For he might by no other way get there.

[10] *ullaloo* Sound of lamentation.

[11] *unhappy* Unfortunate.

[12] *doom* Fate.

hath brought thee unto this place? O, thou that must endure the pangs unspeakable of death, woe is me for thee! Woe is me that a monster so accurst must this night consume the flower of thine youth! For that most foul and impious giant of execrable name shall presently be here, that did carry hither unto this mount the niece of our Duke, whom I have but just now sithence buried in this grave, and me, her nurse, along with her. On what unheard of wise will he slay thee and tarry not? Alas for the sorrow and the doom! This most queenly foster-child of mine own, swooning with terror when this abhorred monster would fain have embraced her, breathed forth the life that now can never know the longer day that it deserved! Ochone[1] for mine other soul—mine other life—mine other sweetness of gladness! Flee thou, my beloved, flee, lest he find thee here, and rend thee limb from limb by a pitiable death!" But Bedevere, moved to the heart deeply as heart of man may be moved, soothed her with words of comfort, and promising her such cheer as speedy succour might bring, returned unto Arthur and told him the story of what he had found. Howbeit, Arthur, grieving over the damsel's hapless fate, bade them that they should allow him to attack the monster singly, but if need were should come unto his rescue and fall upon the giant like men. They made their way from thence unto the greater mount, and giving their horses in charge to their squires, began to climb the mount, Arthur going first. Just then that unnatural monster was by the fire, his chops all besmeared with the clotted blood of half-eaten swine, the residue whereof he was toasting on spits over the live embers. The moment he espied them, when nought was less in his thought, he hastened him to get hold of his club, which two young men could scarce have lifted from the ground. The King forthwith unsheathed his sword, and covering him with his shield, hurried as swiftly as hurry he might to be beforehand with[2] him, and prevent his getting hold of the club. But the giant, not unaware of his intention, had already clutched it and smote the King upon the cover of his shield with such a buffet[3] as that the sound of the stroke filled the whole shore, and did utterly deafen his ears. But Arthur,

thereupon blazing out into bitter wrath, lifted his sword and dealt him a wound upon his forehead, from whence the blood gushed forth over his face and eyes in such sort as well-nigh blinded his sight. Howbeit, the blow was not deadly, for he had warded[4] his forehead with his club in such wise as to scape[5] being killed outright. Nonetheless, blinded as he was with the blood welling forth, again he cometh on more fiercely than ever, and as a wild boar rusheth from his lay[6] upon a huntsman, so thrust he in within the sweep of Arthur's sword, gripped him by the loins, and forced him to his knees upon the ground. Howbeit, Arthur, nothing daunted,[7] soon slipped from out his clutches, and swiftly bestirring him with his sword, hacked the accursed monster first in one place and then in another, and gave him no respite[8] until at last he smote him a deadly buffet on the head, and buried the whole breadth of his sword in his brainpan. The abhorred beast roared aloud and dropped with a mighty crash like an oak torn up by the roots in the fury of the winds. Thereupon the King broke out on laughing, bidding Bedevere strike off his head and give it to one of the squires to carry to the camp as a raree show[9] for sightseers. Nonetheless, he bade that they who came to look upon it should keep their tongues quiet, inasmuch as never had he forgathered[10] with none other of so puissant hardihood since he slew the giant Ritho upon Mount Eryri, that had challenged him to fight with him. For this Ritho had fashioned him a furred cloak of the beards of the kings he had slain, and he had bidden Arthur heedfully to flay off his beard and send it unto him with the skin, in which case, seeing that Arthur did excel other kings, he would sew it in his honour above the other beards on his cloak. Howbeit, in case he refused, he challenged him to fight upon such covenant, that he which should prove the better man of the twain should have the other's beard as well as the

---

[1]   *Ochone* Alas!

[2]   *be … with* Forestall.

[3]   *buffet* Blow.

[4]   *warded* Protected.

[5]   *scape* Escape.

[6]   *lay* Lair.

[7]   *nothing daunted* Frightened by nothing.

[8]   *respite* Rest.

[9]   *raree show* Spectacular display.

[10]   *forgathered* Encountered.

furred cloak. So when it came to the scratch[1] Arthur had the best of it and carried off Ritho's beard and his cloak, and sithence[2] that time had never had to do with none so strong until he lighted upon this one, as he is above reported as asserting. After he had won this victory as I have said, they returned just after daybreak to their tents with the head; crowds coming running up to look upon it and praising the valour of the man that had delivered the country from so insatiable a man. But Hoel, grieving over the loss of his niece, bade build a church above her body upon the mount where she lay, the which was named after the damsel's grave, and is called the Tomb of Helena unto this day. ...

The victory complete, Arthur bade the bodies of his barons be separated from the carcasses of the enemy, and embalmed in kingly wise, and borne when embalmed into the abbeys of the province. ... But the body of Lucius he bade bear unto the Senate with a message to say that none other tribute was due from Britain. Then he abode[3] in those parts until after the following winter, and busied him with bringing the cities of the Allobroges[4] into his allegiance. But the summer coming on, at which time he designed to march unto Rome, he had begun to climb the passes of the mountains, when message was brought him that his nephew Mordred,[5] unto whom he had committed the charge of Britain, had tyrannously and traitorously set the crown of the kingdom upon his own head, and had linked him in unhallowed[6] union with Guenevere the Queen in despite of her former marriage.

Hereof, verily, most noble Earl,[7] will Geoffrey of Monmouth say nought. Nonetheless, according as he hath found it in the British discourse aforementioned,[8] and hath heard from Walter of Oxford,[9] a man of passing deep lore in many histories, in his own mean style will he briefly treat of the battles which that renowned King upon his return to Britain after this victory did fight with his nephew. So soon therefore as the infamy of the aforesaid crime did reach his ears, he forthwith deferred the expedition he had emprised[10] against Leo, the King of the Romans, and sending Hoel, Duke of the Armoricans, with the Gaulish army to restore peace in those parts, he straightway hastened back to Britain with none save the island kings and their armies. Now, that most detestable traitor Mordred had dispatched Cheldric, the Duke of the Saxons, into Germany, there to enlist any soever[11] that would join him, and hurry back again with them, such as they might be, the quickest sail he could make. He pledged himself, moreover, by covenant to give him that part of the island which stretcheth from the river Humber as far as Scotland, and whatsoever Horsus and Hengist had possessed in Kent in the time of Vortigern. Cheldric, accordingly, obeying his injunctions, had landed with eight hundred ships full of armed Paynims,[12] and doing homage unto this traitor did acknowledge him as his liege lord[13] and king. He had likewise gathered into his company the Scots, Picts, and Irish, and whomsoever else he knew bore hatred unto his uncle. All told, they numbered some eight hundred thousand Paynims and Christians, and in their company and relying on their assistance he came to meet Arthur on his arrival at Richborough haven,[14] and in the battle that ensued did inflict sore slaughter on his men when they were landed.

---

[1] *scratch* Skirmish.

[2] *sithence* Since.

[3] *abode* Lingered.

[4] *Allobroges* People from southern Gaul.

[5] *Mordred* In Geoffrey's version of the story, Arthur's nephew by Anna. In later versions, Arthur's illegitimate son by the incestuous union with Morgause, his half-sister. In all versions, England is left in Mordred's care while Arthur is away.

[6] *unhallowed* Unholy, wicked.

[7] *most ... Earl* Robert, Earl of Gloucester (d. 1147), son of Henry I of England and patron to whom Geoffrey dedicates his *History*.

[8] *British ... aforementioned* Unsubstantiated Welsh book supposedly loaned to Geoffrey, which he claims as a source for his work.

[9] *Walter of Oxford* Archbishop of Oxford, friend of Geoffrey and historian, who reputedly lent Geoffrey the Welsh book.

[10] *emprised* Undertaken.

[11] *soever* Whosoever.

[12] *Paynims* Pagans.

[13] *liege lord* Feudal superior.

[14] *Richborough haven* Port of Richborough in Kent.

For upon that day fell Angusel, King of Albany, and Gawain, the King's nephew, along with numberless other. Eventus, son of Urian his brother, succeeded Angusel in the kingdom, and did afterward win great renown for his prowesses in those wars. At last, when with sore travail they had gained possession of the coast, they revenged them on Mordred for this slaughter, and drove him fleeing before them. For inured[1] to arms as they had been in so many battles, they disposed[2] their companies right skilfully, distributing horse and foot[3] in parties, in such wise that in the fight itself, when the infantry were engaged in the attack or defence, the horse charging slantwise at full speed would strain every endeavour to break the enemies' ranks and compel them to take to flight. Howbeit, the Perjurer again collected his men together from all parts, and on the night following marched into Winchester.[4] When this was reported unto Queen Guenevere, she was forthwith smitten with despair, and fled from York unto Caerleon, where she purposed thenceforth to lead a chaste life amongst the nuns, and did take the veil of their order in the church of Julius the Martyr.

But Arthur, burning with yet hotter wrath for the loss of so many hundred comrades-in-arms, after first giving Christian burial to the slain, upon the third day marched upon that city and beleaguered the miscreant[5] that had ensconced him therein. Nonetheless, he was not minded to renounce his design, but encouraging his adherents by all the devices[6] he could, marched forth with his troops and arrayed[7] them to meet his uncle. At the first onset was exceeding great slaughter on either side, the which at last waxed heavier upon his side and compelled him to quit the field with shame. Then, little caring what burial were given unto his slain, "borne by the swift-oared ferryman of flight," he started in all haste on his march toward Cornwall. Arthur, torn by inward

anxiety for that he had so often escaped him, pursued him into that country as far as the river Camel,[8] where Mordred was awaiting his arrival. For Mordred, being, as he was, of all men the boldest and ever the swiftest to begin the attack, straightway marshalled his men in companies, preferring rather to conquer or to die than to be any longer continually on the flight in this wise. There still remained unto him out of the number of allies I have mentioned sixty thousand men, and these he divided into three battalions, in each of which were six thousand six hundred and sixty-six men-at-arms. Besides these, he made out of the rest that were over a single battalion, and appointing captains to each of the others, took command of this himself. When these were all posted in position, he spoke words of encouragement unto each in turn, promising them the lands and goods of their adversaries in case they fought out the battle to a victory. Arthur also marshalled his army over against them, which he divided into nine battalions of infantry formed in square with a right and left wing, and having appointed captains to each, exhorted[9] them to make an end utterly of these perjurers and thieves, who, brought from foreign lands into the island at the bidding of a traitor, were minded to reave[10] them of their holdings and their honours. He told them, moreover, that these motley[11] barbarians from diverse kingdoms were a pack of raw recruits that knew nought of the usages[12] of war, and were in no wise able to make stand against valiant men like themselves, seasoned in so many battles, if they fell upon them hardily and fought like men. And whilst the twain were still exhorting their men on the one side and the other, the battalions made a sudden rush each at other and began the battle, struggling as if to try which should deal their blows the quicker. Straight, such havoc is wrought upon both sides, such groaning is there of the dying, such fury in the onset, as it would be grievous and burdensome to describe. Everywhere are wounders and wounded, slayers and slain. And after much of the day had been spent on this wise, Arthur at

---

[1]   *inured*   Accustomed.

[2]   *disposed*   Commanded.

[3]   *foot*   Foot soldiers, infantry.

[4]   *Winchester*   Arthur's capital city.

[5]   *miscreant*   Villain.

[6]   *devices*   Schemes.

[7]   *arrayed*   Put into order.

---

[8]   *Camel*   River in Cornwall.

[9]   *exhorted*   Earnestly begged.

[10]   *reave*   Rob.

[11]   *motley*   Rag-tag.

[12]   *usages*   Practices.

last, with one battalion wherein were six thousand six hundred and sixty-six men, made a charge upon the company wherein he knew Mordred to be, and hewing a path with their swords, cut clean through it and inflicted a most grievous slaughter. For therein fell that accursed traitor and many thousands along with him. Nonetheless not for the loss of him did his troops take to flight, but rallying together from all parts of the field, struggle to stand their ground with the best hardihood they might. Right passing deadly is the strife betwixt the foes, for well-nigh all the captains that were in command on both sides rushed into the press with their companies and fell. On Mordred's side fell Cheldric, Elaf, Egbricht, Bunignus, that were Saxons, Gillapatric, Gillamor, Gislafel, Gillar, Irish. The Scots and Picts, with well-nigh all that they commanded, were cut off to a man. On Arthur's side, Olbricht, King of Norway, Aschil, King of Denmark, Cador, Limenic, Cassibelaunus, with many thousands of his lieges as well Britons as others that he had brought with him. Even the renowned King Arthur himself was wounded deadly, and was borne thence unto the island of Avalon[1] for the healing of his wounds, where he gave up the crown of Britain unto his kinsman, Constantine, son of Cador, Duke of Cornwall, in the year of the Incarnation of Our Lord five hundred and forty-two.

[Having recounted the fates of the kings who followed Arthur, Geoffrey turns to the subject of the Britons' decline and the fall of Cadwallader, the last British king.]

… He, therefore, as I began to tell ye, falling sick, the Britons begin to quarrel, and by their accursed discords destroy the wealth of the country. A second calamity, moreover, followeth on the first, for a deadly and memorable famine fell upon the foolish folk, insomuch as that every province was empty of all sustenance of food, save only such partial provision as the huntsman's art could supply. And upon the heels of this famine followed a pestilence[2] of death so grievous as that in a brief space so great was the multitude of people laid low,[3] the living were not enough to bury the dead. By reason whereof, the miserable remnant of the people forsaking their own country in flocks did make their way unto lands oversea, with mighty lamentation chanting under the folds of the sails: "Thou hast given us, O Lord, even as sheep unto the slaughter, and amongst the nations hast Thou scattered us."[4] Yea, even King Cadwallader himself, voyaging with his wretched fleet for Armorica, did make addition unto the lamentation on this wise: "Woe unto us, miserable sinners, for our grievous iniquities, wherewith we have never ceased to offend against God so long as space was granted unto us for repentance! Wherefore the vengeance of His might lieth thus heavy upon us, and doth uproot us from our native soil, albeit that never were the Romans of old nor after them the Scots nor the Picts nor even the crafty treasons of the Saxons able to exterminate our people. In vain have we so oft recovered our country from them, seeing that it was not God's will we should reign therein for ever. He, the true Judge, when He saw that in no wise were we minded to cease from our iniquities and that no man could drive us forth of the kingdom, willed Himself to chastise our folly, and hath now directed against us this visitation of His wrath whereby we are compelled to forsake our own country by multitudes at a time. Now, therefore, return ye Romans; ye Scots and Picts return; return, ye Ambrons[5] and Saxons! Behold, Britain lieth open unto ye! She that never might ye avail to dispeople, hath by the wrath of God been now left desolate! Not your valour driveth us forth, but the might of Him that is over all, the God whom never hath our people been slow to offend."

In the midst of these and other lamentations was Cadwallader borne forth unto the Armorican shore, and upon his landing, came with all his multitude unto King Alan, nephew of Solomon,[6] and by him was worthily received. Britain, therefore, deserted of all her people save some few whom death had spared in the parts of Wales for a space of eleven years together, became a

---

[1] *Avalon*   Magical island said to be located off the western shore of England.

[2] *pestilence*   Plague.

[3] *laid low*   Killed.

[4] *Thou … us*   See Psalms 44.11.

[5] *Ambrons*   Germanic tribes.

[6] *Solomon*   King of Israel (c. 1035 BCE) known for his great wisdom.

place abhorred even of the Britons themselves; nor, in sooth,[1] did the Saxons find it a home to be desired at that same time, for they, too, died therein without intermission.[2] But when the deadly plague had ceased, the remnant of them, true unto their ancient wont, sent word unto their fellow-countrymen in Germany, telling them that now the island of Britain was deserted of her own people they might lightly[3] take possession thereof, so only they would come together and dwell therein. So, when they understood these tidings, that accursed folk, collecting a countless host of men and women, landed in the parts of Northumbria and inhabited the desolated provinces from Albany even unto Cornwall. For none indweller was there to say them nay, save only the few and needy little remnants of the Britons that had survived and herded together in the forest fastnesses[4] of Wales. From that time the power of the Britons ceased in the island, and the English began to reign.

Then, after some brief space of time had elapsed and the Saxon people had thus been reinforced, Cadwallader, bethinking him that his kingdom was now purged from the contagion of the plague, besought help of Alan that he might be restored unto his former kingdom. But when the King had granted his petition, behold, even as he was fitting out his fleet, the Voice of an Angel spoke unto him in thunder, forbidding him to emprise the adventure, for that God had willed the Britons should no longer reign in Britain before that time should come whereof Merlin had prophesied unto Arthur. The Voice bade him, moreover, that he should go unto Pope Sergius at Rome, where, after due penance done, he should be numbered amongst the blessed. Yet, further the Voice told him that the people of the Britons should again possess the island by merit of their faith when the appointed time should come, but that this time should not be until the Britons had obtained his relics[5] and had translated[6] them from Rome into Britain. Then, when the relics had likewise been revealed of the other saints, which had been hidden away by reason of the invasion of the Paynims, they should recover the kingdom they had lost. And when this message had been spoken in the ears of the holy man, he went straightway unto King Alan and made known unto him that which had been revealed unto himself.

Then Alan took diverse books, as that of the prophecies of the Eagle that did prophecy at Shaftesbury, and of the songs of Sibyl and Merlin, and began to search all things that were therein to see whether Cadwallader's revelation did agree with the written oracles. And when he found no discrepancy therein, he did counsel Cadwallader to be obedient unto the divine dispensation, and foregoing all thought of recovering Britain, to perform that which the angelic monition[7] had bidden him. He counselled him, moreover, to send his son Ivor and his nephew Ini to rule over the remnant of the Britons in the island, lest the people born of their ancient race should lose their freedom by the invasion of the barbarians. Then Cadwallader, renouncing worldly things for the sake of God and His kingdom everlasting, came unto Rome, and was confirmed by Pope Sergius, and no long time after, being smitten of a sudden lethargy, upon the twelfth day of the Kalends[8] of May in the year of Our Lord's incarnation, six hundred and eighty-nine, was released from the contagion of the flesh and did enter into the hall of the kingdom of Heaven.

When Ivor and Ini had got ships together, they raised all the men they could, and made for the island, where for nine-and-forty years they harassed the English people, and did most cruelly raid their lands, but all to little avail. For the said pestilence and famine and customary dissensions had so caused this proud people to degenerate that they could no longer keep their foes at a distance. And, as barbarism crept in, they were no longer

---

[1]   *sooth*   Truth.

[2]   *intermission*   Pause.

[3]   *lightly*   Easily.

[4]   *fastnesses*   Strongholds.

[5]   *relics*   Piece of body or personal belonging of a saint, venerated as holy.

[6]   *translated*   Process by which relics are transferred from one location to another.

[7]   *monition*   Instruction.

[8]   *Kalends*   First day of the month in the Roman calendar.

called Britons but Welsh, a word derived either from Gualo, one of their Dukes, or from Guales, their Queen, or else from their being barbarians. But the Saxons did wiselier, kept peace and concord amongst themselves, tilled their fields and builded anew their cities and castles, and thus throwing off the sovereignty of the Britons, held the empire of all Loegria[1] under their Duke Athelstan, who was the first to wear a crown amongst them. But the Welsh, degenerating from the nobility of the Britons, never afterwards recovered the sovereignty of the island, but on the contrary, quarrelling at one time amongst themselves, and at another with the Saxons, never ceased to have bloodshed on hand either in public or private feud.

Howbeit, their Kings who from that time have succeeded in Wales I hand over in the matter of writing unto Karadoc of Lancarvan,[2] my contemporary, as do I those of the Saxons unto William of Malmesbury and Henry of Huntingdon,[3] whom I bid be silent as to the Kings of the Britons, seeing that they have not that book in the British speech which Walter, Archdeacon of Oxford, did convey hither out of Brittany, the which being truly issued in honour of the aforesaid princes, I have on this wise been at the pains of translating into the Latin speech.

---

[1] *Loegria* England.

[2] *Karadoc of Lancarvan* Caradoc of Llancarfan (d. 1124), Welsh historian.

[3] *William of Malmesbury* British historian (c. 1095–1143), author of *Deeds of the Kings of England*; *Henry of Huntingdon* British chronicler (c. 1085–c. 1155), author of *A History of England*.

MARIE DE FRANCE

c. 1155 – 1215

Although she is widely credited with being the earliest female poet in France, and was arguably the leading female writer of the Middle Ages, little is known about Marie de France; no surviving documents refer to her life outside of her literary activity. What has come down to us are three works, which vary widely in genre: the *Lais* (c. 1155–70), a collection of short romance narratives; the *Ysopet* or *Fables* (c. 1167–89), a collection commonly accepted as the earliest translation of Aesop into French; and the less-studied *Espurgatoire de Saint Patrice* (*Legend of the Purgatory of Saint Patrick*, c. 1189), a didactic tale in which Patrick, an Irish knight, makes a spiritual journey through Purgatory.

Her name is known from the self-identification she makes in each of her texts; this occurs most forcefully and descriptively in the epilogue of the *Ysopet*:

> I shall name myself so that it will be remembered;
> Marie is my name, I am of France.
> It may be that many clerks
> will take my labor on themselves.
> I don't want any of them to claim it.

"France" itself is a slippery designation here, since it had multiple possible meanings in this period; it may be intended to convey that she was from Continental Europe instead of England, for instance, or from northern France instead of the southern Languedoc. The Norman dialect in which her works are composed suggests that Marie was native to Normandy, and lived during the latter part of the 12th century. The "King Henry" to whom she dedicates her *Lais* is usually identified as Henry II, the Angevin French king of England from 1154–89, and Marie is thought to have been a member of his court, which spoke the form of Norman dialect in which her works come down to us. It has sometimes been suggested that she was Henry's illegitimate sister Marie, who became Abbess of Shaftesbury around 1181, and who died in 1216, but without any other corroborating documents, such theories are no more than intriguing speculation. It seems very likely, however, that she was attached to the court of Henry II and his wife, Eleanor of Aquitaine, and was of noble birth; her works reveal a level of education and culture that would not usually have been available to a layperson of lower rank during this time. It is clear that she was educated in Latin, as well as French, and perhaps even in the Breton language, since she claims to have translated her *Lais* from that tongue.

The *Lais* of Marie de France are brief narratives written in octosyllabic rhyming couplets, which was the conventional literary vehicle for French romance during this time. This collection is made up of twelve stories, each prefaced by a short prologue in which Marie reveals that she is translating into French for the first time a number of "Breton *lais*." The *lais* were Celtic tales of romance that often involved elements of the fantastic. The compressed space of the form requires Marie to handle her material with considerable finesse and she recounts her tales with an economy of words and a tight narrative control that lend the romances a down-to-earth precision without sacrificing meaning or nuance.

Many of the *lais* have a strongly female focus, and in this regard offer a certain contrast to the romances of Marie's contemporaries. The works of male romancers, while treating the subject of love, often emphasized the tension between love and chivalric pursuits, and the need to balance the two in order to fulfill both personal needs and social responsibilities. Marie is largely uninterested in such concerns, and focuses instead on the personal desires of her characters, especially those of her female characters. Her *lais* often depict intensely intimate love relationships set against a backdrop of a threatening society in which unfulfilling marriages, the arbitrary dictates of court life, and oppressive social practices hold sway.

Lanval and *Chevrefoil* are *lais* drawn from the larger literary universe of Arthurian legend. The former recounts the tale of a knight whose inherent worth is unrecognized by the Arthurian court, and who is able to escape this uncaring and arbitrary society through the love of an otherworldly fairy figure, while the latter presents an episode involving the doomed lovers Tristan and Isolde and explores frustrated love, the grief of separation, and the transcendence of artistic expression. The other two *lais* presented here, like Marie's *Fables*, implicitly use the animal world to approach human emotion and relationships. In *Laüstic*, the love affair between a knight and his neighbor's wife raises the issues of violent jealousy, marital betrayal, and loss. In *Bisclavret*, the title character makes a startling confession to his wife that leads us into an examination of the clash between his innate nobility and his dangerous appearance, and the ability of loyalty and generosity to resolve this conflict.

⌘ ⌘ ⌘

Bisclavret (The Werewolf)[1]

Quant de lais faire m'entremet,	Since I have undertaken to compose lais,
ne voil ublïer Bisclaveret.	I don't want to forget *Bisclavret*.
Bisclaveret ad nun en bretan,	*Bisclavret* is the name in Breton;
Garwaf l'apelent li Norman.	the Normans call it *Garwaf*.
5 Jadis le poeit hume oïr,	There was a time when one would hear,
e sovent suleit avenir,	and it often used to happen,
humes plusurs garual devindrent	that many people became werewolves
e es boscages meisun tindrent.	and kept house in the woods.[2]
Garualf, c'est beste salvage:	The werewolf is a wild beast:
10 tant cum il est en cele rage,	when it is in that frenzy,
hummes devure, grant mal fait,	it devours people and does great harm.
es granz fore[z] converse e vait.	It lives in and roams the great forests.
Cest afere les ore ester;	Now I let this matter be;
del bisclaveret [vus] voil cunter.	I want to tell you about the *bisclavret*.
15 En Bretaine maneit un ber,	In Brittany there lived a baron,
merveille l'ai oï loër;	whom I have heard marvelously praised;
beaus chevalers e bons esteit	he was a handsome, good knight

---

[1] *Bisclavret, Lanval, Laüstic,* and *Chevrefoil* have all been newly translated for this anthology by Claire M. Waters. The Anglo-Norman text is based on British Library MS Harley 978, and emendations are marked by square brackets.

[2] *Since ... woods*   When referring to werewolves generally in her opening lines, Marie uses the name she has identified as Norman: "garual/garwaf." After this, in talking about her protagonist, she uses the Breton "bisclaveret." This translation signals the change in terms at line 14, where she switches to "bisclaveret," but thereafter translates "bisclaveret" as "werewolf" when it is used with a definite article or seems to be a generic term, and as "Bisclavret" (a name) when it specifically designates the protagonist himself—which is usually at key moments in the story.

	e noblement se cunteneit.	and conducted himself nobly.
	De sun seinur esteit privez	He was dear to his lord
20	e de tuz ses veisins amez.	and beloved by all his neighbors.
	Femme ot espuse mut vailant	He had married a most noble wife
	e que mut feseit beu semblant.	who made him good cheer.
	Il amot li e ele lui,	He loved her and she him,
	mes d'une chose ert grant ennui:	but she was greatly troubled by one thing:
25	que en la semeine le deperdeit	each week she lost him
	treis jurs entiers, que ele ne saveit	for three whole days, when she did not know
	u deveneit në u alout,	what became of him nor where he went,
	ne nul des soens nïent n'e[n] sout.	nor did any of his people know anything about it.
	Une feiz esteit repeirez	One day he returned
30	a sa meisun joius e liez.	to his house joyful and happy.
	Demandé li ad e enquis:	She questioned him and made an inquiry:
	"Sire," fait ele, "beau duz amis,	"Lord," she said, "fair sweet beloved,
	une chose vus demandasse	I would very much like to ask you
	mut volenters, si jeo osasse;	one thing, if I dared;
35	mes jeo creim tant vostre curuz,	but I am so afraid of your anger
	que nule rien tant ne redut."	that nothing frightens me more."
	Quant il l'oï, [si] l'acola,	When he heard this, he embraced her,
	vers li la traist, si la beisa.	drew her toward him and kissed her.
	"Dame," fait il, "[or] demandez!	"Lady," he said, "go ahead and ask!
40	Ja cele chose ne [querrez],	There is nothing you can ask that,
	si jo la sai, ne la vus die."	if I know, I will not tell you."
	"Par fei," fet ele, "ore sui garie!	"By my faith," she said, "now I am cured!
	Sire, jeo sui en tel effrei	Lord, I am so anxious
	les jurs quant vus partez de mei,	on those days when you leave me,
45	el [quor] en ai mut grant dolur	I have such great sorrow in my heart
	e de vus perdre tel poür,	and such fear of losing you,
	si jeo n'en ai hastif cunfort,	that if I do not get reassurance shortly,
	bien tost en puis aver la mort.	very soon I may die of it.
	Kar me dites u vus alez,	So do tell me where you go,
50	u vus estes, u vus conversez!	where you are, where you live!
	Mun escïent que vus amez,	It is my belief you are in love,
	e si si est, vus meserrez."	and if it is so, you do wrong."
	"Dame," fet il, "pur Deu, merci!	"Lady," he said, "mercy, by God!
	Mal m'en vendra si jol vus di,	Trouble will come to me if I tell you,
55	kar de m'amur vus partirai	for I will divide you from my love
	e mei memes en perdirai."	and destroy myself in doing so."
	Quant la dame l'ad entendu,	When the lady heard him,
	ne l'ad neent en gab tenu.	she considered it no joke.
	Suventefeiz li demanda;	Many times she asked him;
60	tant le blandi e losenga	she cajoled and flattered him so much
	que s'aventure li cunta;	that he told her what happened to him;
	nule chose ne li cela.	he hid nothing from her.

"Dame, jeo devienc besclaveret:
en cele grant forest me met,
65 al plus espés de la gaudine,
s'i vif de preie e de ravine."
Quant il li aveit tut cunté,
enquis li ad e demaundé
se il se despuille u vet vestu.
70 "Dame," fet il, "jeo vois tut nu."
"Di mei, pur Deu, u sunt voz dras."
"Dame, ceo ne dirai jeo pas;
kar si jeo les eüsse perduz
e de ceo feusse aparceüz
75 bisclaveret sereie a tuz jurs;
jamés n'avereie mes sucurs,
de si k'il me fussent rendu.
Pur ceo ne voil k'il seit seü."
"Sire," la dame li respunt,
80 "Jeo vus eim plus que tut le mund:
nel me devez nïent celer,
ne [mei] de nule rien duter;
ne semblereit pas amisté.
Qu'ai jeo forfait? pur queil peché
85 me dutez vus de nule rien?
Dites [le] mei, si ferez bien!"
Tant l'anguissa, tant le suzprist,
ne pout el faire, si li dist.
"Dame," fet il, "[delez] cel bois,
90 lez le chemin par unt jeo vois,
une vielz chapele i esteit,
ke meintefeiz grant bien me feit:
la est la piere cruose e lee
suz un buissun, dedenz cavee;
95 mes dras i met suz le buissun,
tant que jeo revi[e]nc a meisun."
La dame oï cele merveille;
de poür fu tute vermeille.
De l'aventure se esfrea.
100 E[n] maint endreit se purpensa
cum ele s'en puïst partir;
ne voleit mes lez lui gisir.
Un chevaler de la cuntree,
que lungement l'aveit amee
105 e mut preié[e] e mut requise
e mut duné en sun servise—
ele ne l'aveit unc amé

"Lady, I become a werewolf:
I go into that great forest,
to the deepest part of the woods,
and live on prey and plunder."
When he had told her everything,
she inquired and asked him
whether he undressed or went clothed.
"Lady," he said, "I go quite naked."
"Tell me, by God, where your clothes are."
"Lady, that I will not tell;
for if I should lose them
and were discovered through this
I would be a werewolf always;
there would never again be hope for me,
until they were returned to me.
For this reason I don't want it known."
"Sir," the lady replied to him,
"I love you more than all the world:
you must hide nothing from me,
nor mistrust me in any way;
that would not seem like friendship.
What have I done wrong? For what misdeed
do you mistrust me in any way?
You will do well to tell me!"
She so tormented and nagged him
that he could not do otherwise, and so he told her.
"Lady," he said, "near this wood,
beside the path by which I travel,
there is an old chapel,
which many times has been a great help to me:
there is a broad, carved-out stone
which is hollow inside, below a bush;
I put my clothes under the bush
until I return home."
The lady heard this marvel;
she turned quite red with fear.
She was terrified by this adventure.
Many times she thought hard
about how she could get away;
she did not want to lie beside him any more.
A knight of that land,
who had loved her a long time
and greatly implored and courted her
and greatly devoted himself to her service—
she had never loved him

	ne de s'amur aseüré—	or promised him her love—
	celui manda par sun message,	she sent to this man by messenger
110	si li descoveri sun curage.	and revealed her feelings to him.
	"Amis," fet ele, "seez leéz!	"Friend," she said, "rejoice!
	Ceo dunt vus estes travaillez	That for which you have labored
	vus otri jeo sanz nul respit:	I grant you without delay:
	ja n'i averez nul cuntredit.	you will find no resistance.
115	M'amur e mun cors vus otrei:	I grant you my love and my body;
	vostre drue fetes de mei!"	take me as your lover!"
	Cil l'en mercie bonement	He thanks her warmly
	e la fiance de li prent;	and accepts her promise,
	e ele le met par serement.	and she binds him to her by oath.
120	Puis li cunta cumfaitement	Then she told him just how
	ses sires ala e k'il devint;	her lord went away and what became of him;
	tute la veie kë il tint	she taught him the whole path
	vers la forest l[i] enseigna;	he took to the forest;
	pur sa despuille l'enveia.	she sent him to the discarded clothes.
125	Issi fu Bisclaveret trahiz	Thus Bisclavret was betrayed
	e par sa femme maubailiz.	and brought to ruin by his wife.
	Pur ceo que hum le perdeit sovent,	Since men often had known him to be missing,
	quidouent tuz communalment	everyone generally believed
	que dunc s'en fust del tut alez.	that he had gone away for good.
130	Asez fu quis e demandez,	He was widely sought and asked after,
	mes n'en porent mie trover;	but they could not find him at all,
	si lur estuit lesser ester.	so they had to let it be.
	La dame ad cil dunc espusee,	The lady then married him
	que lungement aveit amee.	who had loved her for a long time.
135	Issi remist un an entier,	Things remained this way for a whole year,
	tant que li reis ala chacier;	until the king went hunting;
	a la forest ala tut dreit,	he went straight to the forest
	la u li bisclaveret esteit.	where the werewolf was.
	Quant li chiens furent descuplé,	When the hounds were unleashed,
140	le bisclaveret unt encuntré;	they found the werewolf;
	a lui cururent tutejur	the hounds and hunters
	e li chien e li veneür,	chased it all day,
	tant que pur poi ne l'eurent pris	so that they very nearly caught it
	e tut deciré e maumis,	and completely tore it to shreds and destroyed it,
145	de si qu'il ad le rei choisi;	until it saw the king;
	vers lui curut quere merci.	it ran to him to ask mercy.[1]
	Il l'aveit pris par sun estrié,	It took him by the stirrup,

---

1 Although the noun "bisclaveret" is masculine, here the werewolf is referred to in English as "it" when it is in wolf form; the human protagonist Bisclavret, who is of course the same "person," is "he." This both helps to distinguish the wolf from the king and other masculine characters and conveys his dual nature; it also helps to account for the term "beast," which is several times applied to the wolf, and which is feminine in Old French. Only at the end, when the wise counselor seems to assume that the werewolf is indeed also the man Bisclaveret, is the werewolf called "he" in the translation (ll. 283–92).

la jambe li baise e le pié.
Li reis le vit, grant poür ad;
150 ses cumpainuns tuz apelad.
"Seignurs," fet il, "avant venez!
Ceste merveillë esgardez,
cum ceste beste se humilie!
Ele ad sen de hume, merci crie.
155 Chacez mei tuz ces chiens arere,
si gardez quë hum ne la fiere!
Ceste beste ad entente e sen.
Espleitez vus! Alum nus en!
A la beste durrai ma pes;
160 kar jeo ne chacerai hui mes."
    Li reis s'en est turné atant.
Le bisclaveret li vet siwant;
mut se tint pres, n'en vout partir,
il n'ad cure de lui guerpir.
165 Li reis l'en meine en sun chastel;
mut en fu liez, mut li est bel,
kar unke mes tel n'ot veü.
A grant merveille l'ot tenu
e mut le tient a grant chierté.
170 A tuz les suens ad comaundé
que sur s'amur le gardent bien
e li ne mesfacent de rien,
ne par nul de eus ne seit feruz;
bien seit abevreiz e [peüz].
175 Cil le garderent volenters.
Tuz jurs entre les chevalers
e pres del rei se alout cuchier.
N'i ad celui que ne l'ad chier;
tant esteit franc e deboneire,
180 unc ne volt a rien mesfeire.
U ke li reis deüst errer,
il n'out cure de deseverer;
ensemble od li tuz jurs alout:
bien s'aparceit quë il l'amout.
185   Oëz aprés cument avint.
A une curt ke li rei tint
tuz les baruns aveit mandez,
ceus ke furent de li cha[s]ez,
pur aider sa feste a tenir
190 e lui plus beal faire servir.
Li chevaler i est alez,
richement e bien aturnez,

it kisses his leg and his foot.
The king sees this and is very much afraid;
he called all his companions.
"Lords," he said, "come here at once!
Look at this wonder,
how this beast humbles itself!
It has human understanding, it begs mercy.
Get all these dogs away from me,
make sure that no one strikes it!
This beast has intelligence and understanding.
Hurry up! Let's go!
I will extend my peace to the beast;
for I will hunt no more."
    The king turned back at once.
The werewolf went along following him;
it stayed very close, it would not leave,
it had no desire to part from him.
The king led it into his castle;
he was very happy with it, it delighted him,
for he had never seen such a thing.
He considered it a great wonder
and held it very dear.
He commanded all his people
to take good care of it for love of him
and not ill-treat it in any way,
nor should any of them strike it;
it should be well fed and watered.
They took care of it gladly.
Every day it went to sleep
among the knights and close to the king.
There was no one who did not hold it dear;
it was so noble and kind,
it never wished to do wrong in any way.
Wherever the king had to go
it did not care to be apart from him;
it always went along with him:
he could see well that it loved him.
    Listen to what happened afterwards.
One time when the king held court
he had sent for all his barons,
those who were his vassals,
to help him celebrate
and to serve him as pleasingly as possible.
The knight who had Bisclavret's wife
went along there,

ki la femme Bisclaveret ot.
Il ne saveit ne ne quidot
que il le deüst trover si pres.

Si tost cum il vint al paleis
e le bisclaveret le aparceut,
de plain esleis vers li curut;
as denz le prist, vers lui le trait.
Ja li eüst mut grant leid fait,
ne fust li reis ki l'apela,
de une verge le manaça.
Deus feiz le vout mordrë al jur.
Mut s'esmerveillent li plusur,
kar unkes tel semblant ne fist
vers nul hume k'il veïst.
Ceo dïent tut par la meisun
ke il nel fet mie sanz reisun:
mesfait li ad, coment que seit,
kar volenters se vengereit.
A cele feiz remist issi,
tant que la feste departi
e li barun unt pris cungé;
a lur meisun sunt repeiré.
Alez s'en est li chevaliers,
mien escïent tut as premers,
que le bisclaveret asailli;
n'est merveille s'il le haï.

Ne fu puis gueres lungement,
ceo m'est avis, si cum j'entent,
que a la forest ala li reis,
que tant fu sages e curteis
u li bisclaveret fu trovez;
e il i est od li alez.
La nuit quant il s'en repeira,
en la cuntree herberga.
La femme le bisclaveret le sot.
Avenantment se appareilot;
al demain vait al rei parler,
riche present li fait porter.
Quant Bisclaveret la veit venir,
nul hum nel poeit retenir;
vers li curut cum enragiez.
Oiez cum il est bien vengiez:
le neis li esracha del vis!
Quei li p[e]üst il faire pis?
De tutes parz l'unt manacié;

well and richly dressed.
He did not know nor imagine
that he would find Bisclavret so close.
As soon as he arrived at the palace
and the werewolf saw him,
it ran at him full tilt;
it grabbed him with its teeth and dragged him down.
It would have done him great injury,
were it not for the king, who called to it
and threatened it with a staff.
Twice that day it tried to bite him.
Everyone was astonished,
for it had never acted like this
toward anyone it saw.
Everyone in the household said
that surely it did this for a reason:
the knight had in some way done it wrong
and now it was eager to avenge itself.
Things went along this way
until the festivities broke up
and the barons took their leave;
they went back to their houses.
The knight the werewolf had attacked
went away, I believe,
among the first;
it's no wonder if it hated him.

It was not long after,
it seems to me, as I understand it,
that the king, who was so wise and courteous,
went to the forest
where the werewolf was found,
and it went with him.
That night, when he was returning from there,
he took lodging in the countryside.
The werewolf's wife found this out.
She dressed herself becomingly;
the next day she went to talk to the king,
she had rich gifts brought to him.
When Bisclavret sees her coming,
no one could hold him back;
he ran toward her as though he were mad.
Hear how well he avenged himself:
he tore the nose from her face!
What worse could he have done to her?
They threatened him from all sides;

ja l'eüssent tut depescié,
quant un sages hum dist al rei,
240 "Sire," fet il, "entent a mei!
Ceste beste ad esté od vus;
n'i ad ore celui de nus
que ne l'eit veü lungement
e pres de li alé sovent.
245 Unke mes humme ne tucha
ne felunie ne mustra,
fors a la dame que ici vei.
Par cele fei ke jeo vus dei,
aukun curuz ad il vers li,
250 e vers sun seignur autresi.
Ceo est la femme al chevaler
que taunt par suliez aveir chier,
que lung tens ad esté perduz;
ne s[e]ümes [qu']est devenuz.
255 Kar metez la dame en destreit,
se aucune chose vus direit,
pur quei ceste beste la heit;
fetes li dire se ele le seit!
Meinte merveille avum veü
260 quë en Bretaigne est avenu."
Li reis ad sun cunseil creü:
le chevaler ad retenu;
de l'autre part ad la dame prise
e en mut grant destresce mise.
265 Tant par destresce e par poür
tut li cunta de sun seignur:
coment ele l'aveit trahi
e sa despoille li toli,
l'aventure qu'il li cunta,
270 e quei devint e u ala.
Puis que ses dras li ot toluz,
ne fud en sun païs veüz.
Tresbien quidat e bien creeit
que la beste Bisclaveret seit.
275 Le reis demande la despoille;
u bel li seit u pas nel voille,
ariere la fet aporter,
al bisclaveret la fist doner.
Quant il les urent devant li mise,
280 Ne se prist garde en nule guise.
Li produme le rei apela,
cil ki primes le cunseilla:

they would have torn him all to pieces,
when a wise man said to the king,
"Sire," he said, "listen to me!
This beast has been living with you;
there is not one of us
who has not watched it for a long time
and often been near it.
It has never touched anyone
nor shown any wickedness,
except to the lady I see here.
By the faith I owe you,
he has some cause for anger against her,
and also against her husband.
This is the wife of the knight
whom you used to hold so dear,
who has been missing for a long time;
we never knew what became of him.
Put the lady under duress about this,
to see if she will tell you anything
about why this beast hates her;
make her tell it if she knows!
We have seen many a wonder
come to pass in Brittany."
The king had faith in his counsel:
he had the knight arrested;
moreover he had the lady taken
and put to severe torture.
On account of such torture and out of fear
she told him all about her lord:
how she had betrayed him
and taken his clothes away,
the adventure that he had told her,
and what he became and where he went.
Since she had taken away his clothes,
he had not been seen in his lands.
She fully believed and supposed
that this beast was Bisclavret.
The king demanded the clothes he had left;
whether she liked it or not,
she had them brought back
and given to the werewolf.
When they were put in front of it,
it would not take any notice at all.
The wise man, the one
who had first advised the king, addressed him:

"Sire, ne fetes mie bien:
cist nel fereit pur nule rien,
285   que devant vus ses dras reveste
ne mute la semblance de beste.
Ne savez mie que ceo munte:
mut durement en ad grant hunte.
En tes chambres le fai mener
290   e la despoille od li porter;
une grant piece l'i laissums.
S'il devient hum, bien le verums."
Li reis memes le mena
e tuz les hus sur li ferma.
295   Al chief de piece i est alez,
deuz baruns ad od li menez;
en la chambrë entrent tut trei.
Sur le demeine lit al rei
trova il dormant le chevaler.
300   Li reis le curut enbracier;
plus de cent feiz l'acole e baise.

Si tost cum il pot aver aise,
tute sa tere li rendi;
plus li duna ke jeo ne di.
305   La femme ad del païs ostee
e chacie hors de la cuntree.
Cil s'en alat ensemble od li,
pur ki sun seignur ot trahi.
Enfanz en ad asés eüz;
310   puis unt esté bien cuneüz
[e] del semblant e del visage:
plusurs [des] femmes del lignage,
c'est verité, senz nes sunt [nees]
e [si] viveient esnasees.
315   L'aventure ke avez oïe
veraie fu, n'en dutez mie.
De *Bisclaveret* fu fet li lais
pur remembrance a tutdis mais.

"Sire, you are not doing this right:
he wouldn't, for anything,
put his clothing back on in front of you
nor change his animal appearance.
You have no idea what this means for him:
he feels terrible shame about it.
Have him led into your rooms
and take the clothing with him;
we'll leave him there for a while.
We shall see if he becomes a man."
The king himself led him in
and closed all the doors behind him.
After a time he went there,
taking two barons with him;
all three of them entered the chamber.
On the king's own bed
he found the knight sleeping.
The king ran to embrace him;
more than a hundred times he embraces and
    kisses him.
As soon as he was able,
he returned all his lands to him;
he gave him more than I say.
He banished his wife from the land
and chased her out of the country.
The man for whom she had betrayed her lord
went along with her.
She had a number of children,
who were quite recognizable
in face and appearance:
most of the women of that line,
in truth, were born without noses
and lived noseless.
    The adventure you have heard
was true, have no doubt.
The lai of *Bisclavret* was made
to be remembered forevermore.

Lanval

L'aventure d'un autre lai,
cum ele avient, vus cunterai.
Fait fu d'un mut gentil vassal;
en bretans l'apelent Lanval.

I shall tell you the adventure
of another lay, just as it happened.
It was made about a very noble vassal;
in Breton they call him Lanval.

5   A Kardoel surjurnot li reis
     Artur, li pruz e li curteis,
     pur les Escoz e pur les Pis,
     que destrui[ei]ent le païs;
     en la tere de Loengre entroënt
10   e mut suvent la damagoënt.
     A la Pentecuste en esté
     i aveit li reis sujurné.
     Asez i duna riches duns
     e as cuntes e as baruns.
15   A ceus de la table runde—
     n'ot tant de teus en tut le munde—
     femmes e tere departi
     par tut, fors un ki l'ot servi:
     ceo fu Lanval, ne l'en sovient,
20   ne nul de[s] soens bien ne li tient.
     Pur sa valur, pur sa largesce,
     pur sa beauté, pur sa prüesce
     l'envioënt tut li plusur;
     tel li mustra semblant d'amur,
25   se al chevaler mesavenist,
     ja une feiz ne l'en pleinsist.
     Fiz a rei fu de haut parage,
     mes luin ert de sun heritage.
     De la meisné le rei fu.
30   Tut sun aveir ad despendu,
     kar li reis rien ne li dona
     ne Lanval rien ne li demanda.
     Ore est Lanval mut entrepris,
     mut est dolent e mut pensis.
35   Seignurs, ne vus esmerveillez:
     hume estrange descunseillez
     mut est dolent en autre tere,
     quant il ne seit u sucurs quere.
     Le chevaler dunt jeo vus di,
40   que tant aveit le rei servi,
     un jur munta sur sun destrer,
     si s'est alez esbaneer.
     Fors de la vilë est eissuz,
     tut sul est en un pre venuz;
45   sur une ewe curaunt descent—
     mes sis cheval tremble forment.
     Il le descengle, si s'en vait;
     en mi le pre vuiltrer le lait.

The king was staying at Cardoel—
Arthur, the valiant and courteous—
on account of the Scots and Picts
who were ravaging the country:
they came into the land of Logres[1]
and repeatedly caused destruction there.
At Pentecost, in the summer,
the king had taken up residence there.
He gave many rich gifts
both to counts and to noblemen.
To the members of the Round Table—
they had no equal in all the world—
he shared out wives and land
among all except one who had served him:
that was Lanval, whom he did not remember,
nor did any of his men favor him.
For his valor, his generosity,
his beauty, his prowess,
most people envied him;
many a one pretended to love him
who wouldn't have complained for a moment
if something bad had befallen the knight.
He was a king's son, of high lineage,
but he was far from his heritage.
He was part of the king's household.
He had spent all his wealth,
for the king gave him nothing,
nor did Lanval ask him for anything.
Now Lanval is very unhappy,
very sorrowful and anxious.
Lords, do not wonder:
a foreign man without support
is very sorrowful in another land
when he does not know where to seek help.
The knight of whom I'm telling you,
who had served the king so well,
got on his horse one day
and went off to enjoy himself.
He went out of the town
and came, all alone, to a meadow;
he got down beside running water—
but his horse trembled terribly.
He unsaddled it and went off;
he let it roll around in the middle of the meadow.

---

[1] *Logres* The Celtic word for England.

	Le pan de sun mantel plia	He folded the end of his mantle
50	desuz sun chief puis le cucha.	and lay down with it under his head.
	Mut est pensis pur sa mesaise;	He is very worried by his difficult situation;
	il ne veit chose ke li plaise.	he sees nothing that pleases him.
	La u il gist en teu maniere,	As he lay there like this,
	garda aval lez la riviere,	he looked down toward the bank
55	[si] vit venir deus dameiseles;	and saw two maidens coming;
	unc n'en ot veü[es] plus beles.	he had never seen any more beautiful.
	Vestues ierent richement,	They were richly dressed
	lacie[es] mut estreitement	and very tightly laced
	en deus blians de purpre bis;	in tunics of dark purple;
60	mut par aveient bel le vis.	they had exceedingly lovely faces.
	L'eisnee portout un[s] bacins,	The elder was carrying basins
	doré furent, bien faiz e fins;	of gold, fine and well made;
	le veir vus en dirai sans faile.	I shall tell you the truth without fail.
	L'autre portout une tuaile.	The other carried a towel.
65	Eles s'en sunt alees dreit	They went right along
	la u li chevaler giseit.	to where the knight was lying.
	Lanval, que mut fu enseigniez,	Lanval, who was very well bred,
	cuntre eles s'en levad en piez.	got to his feet to meet them.
	Celes l'unt primes salué,	They greeted him first
70	lur message li unt cunté:	and told him their message:
	"Sire Lanval, ma dameisele,	"Sir Lanval, my lady,
	que tant est pruz e sage e bele,	who is most noble, wise, and beautiful,
	ele nus enveit pur vus;	sent us for you;
	kar i venez ensemble od nus!	now come along with us!
75	Sauvement vus i cundurums:	We will convey you safely to her.
	veez, pres est li paveilluns!"	Look, the pavilion is right here!"
	Le chevalers od eles vait;	The knight goes with them;
	de sun cheval ne tient nul plait,	he takes no heed of his horse,
	que devant li pe[ssei]t al pre.	who was off grazing in the meadow.
80	Treskë al tref l'unt amené,	They led him up to the tent,
	que mut fu beaus e bien asis.	which was very beautiful and well situated.
	La reïne Semiramis,	Not Queen Semiramis,
	quant ele ot unkes plus aveir	when she was at her richest
	e plus pussaunce e plus saveir,	and most powerful and wisest,
85	ne l'emperere Octovïen	nor the emperor Octavian
	n'esligasent le destre pan.	could have bought the right flap.
	Un aigle d'or ot desus mis;	A golden eagle was set on top of it;
	de cel ne sai dire le pris,	I can't tell its value,
	ne des cordes ne des peissuns	nor of the cords or the stakes
90	que del tref tienent les giruns;	that held the sides of the tent;
	suz ciel n'ad rei ki[s] esligast	no king under heaven could buy them
	pur nul aver k'il i donast.	for any wealth he might offer.
	Dedenz cel tref fu la pucele:	Inside the tent was the maiden:

flur de lis [e] rose nuvele,

95   quant ele pert al tens d'esté,

      trespassot ele de beauté.

      Ele jut sur un lit mut bel—

      li drap valeient un chastel—

      en sa chemise senglement.

100   Mut ot le cors bien fait e gent.

      Un cher mantel de blanc hermine,

      covert de purpre alexandrine,

      ot pur le chaut sur li geté.

      Tut ot descovert le costé,

105   le vis, le col e la peitrine;

      plus ert blanche que flur d'espine.

          Le chevaler avant ala,

      e la pucele l'apela;

      il s'est devant le lit asis.

110   "Lanval," fet ele, "beus amis,

      pur vus vienc jeo fors de ma tere;

      de luinz vus sui venu[e] quere.

      Se vus estes pruz e curteis,

      emperere ne quens ne reis

115   n'ot unkes tant joie ne bien;

      kar jo vus aim sur tute rien."

      Il l'esgarda, si la vit bele;

      amurs le puint de l'estencele,

      que sun quor alume e esprent.

120   Il li respunt avenantment.

      "Bele," fet il, "si vus pleiseit

      e cele joie me aveneit

      que vus me vousissez amer,

      ja [ne savrïez] rien commander

125   que jeo ne face a mien poeir,

      turt a folie u a saveir.

      Jeo frai voz comandemenz;

      pur vus guerpirai tutes genz.

      Jamés ne queor de vus partir:

130   ceo est la rien que plus desir."

      Quant la meschine l' oï parler,

      celui que tant la peot amer,

      s'amur e sun cors li otreie.

      Ore est Lanval en dreite veie!

135   Un dun li ad duné aprés:

      ja cele rien ne vudra mes

      quë il nen ait a sun talent;

      doinst e despende largement,

her beauty surpassed

the lily and the new rose

when they bloom in summer.

She lay on a very beautiful bed—

the sheets were worth a castle—

in nothing but her shift.

Her body was very elegant and comely.

She had thrown on for warmth

a costly mantle of white ermine,

lined with alexandrine silk.

Her side was entirely uncovered,

her face, her neck, and her breast;

she was whiter than hawthorn blossom.

    The knight went forward,

and the maiden called to him;

he sat down in front of the bed.

"Lanval," she said, "handsome friend,

for you I have come out of my own land;

I have come from afar to look for you.

If you are valiant and courteous,

no emperor, count, or king

ever had such joy or good fortune;

for I love you more than anything."

He looked at her, and saw she was beautiful;

love stung him with a spark

that lit and inflamed his heart.

He responded fittingly.

"Beautiful one," he said, "if it pleased you

that such joy should come to me

as to have you consent to love me,

you could never command anything

that I would not do to the best of my power,

be it folly or wisdom.

I will do what you command;

for you I will give up everyone.

I never wish to part from you:

this is what I most desire."

When the maiden heard him speak,

he who could love her so well,

she granted him her love and her body.

Now Lanval is on the right path!

She gave him still one more gift:

he will never again want anything

without having as much of it as he likes;

let him give and spend generously,

ele li troverat asez.

she will provide him with enough.

140 Mut est Lanval bien herbergez:¹
cum plus despendra richement,
plus averat or e argent.
"Ami," fet ele, "ore vus chasti,
si vus comant e si vus pri,
145 ne vus descoverez a nul humme!
De ceo vus dirai ja la summe:
a tuz jurs m'avrïez perdue,
se ceste amur esteit seüe;
jamés ne me purriez veeir
150 ne de mun cors seisine aveir."
Il li respunt que bien tendra
ceo que ele li comaundera.
Delez li s'est al lit cuchiez:
ore est Lanval bien herbergez.
155 Ensemble od li la relevee
demurat tresque a l[a] vespree,
e plus i fust, së il poïst
e s'amie lui cunsentist.
"Amis," fet ele, "levez sus!
160 Vus n'i poëz demurer plus.
Alez vus en, jeo remeindrai;
mes un[e] chose vus dirai:
quant vus vodrez od mei parler,
ja ne saverez cel liu penser,
165 u nuls puïst aver sa amie
sanz reproece, sanz vileinie,
que jeo ne vus seie en present
a fere tut vostre talent;
nul humme fors vus ne me verra
170 ne ma parole nen orra."
Quant il l'oï, mut en fu liez;
il la baisa, puis s'est dresciez.
Celes quë al tref l'amenerent
de riches dras le cunreerent;
175 quant il fu vestu de nuvel,
suz ciel nen ot plus bel dancel.

N'esteit mie fous ne vileins.
L'ewe li donent a ses meins
e la tuaille a [es]suier;
180 puis li portent a manger.

Lanval is very well situated:
the more richly he spends,
the more gold and silver he will have.
"Friend," she said, "now I warn you,
I command and beg you,
tell no one about this!
I will tell you the whole truth:
you would lose me forever
if this love should be known;
you could never see me again
or have possession of my body."
He replies that he will certainly hold to
what she commands.
He lay down beside her on the bed:
now Lanval is well lodged.
All afternoon he stayed with her
until the evening,
and he would have stayed longer, if he could
and his beloved had consented.
"Friend," she said, "get up!
You can't stay here any more.
You go on, I will remain—
but one thing I will tell you:
when you want to talk with me,
there is no place you can think of
where one could have his beloved
without reproach or villainy
that I will not be with you at once
to do all your will;
no man but you will see me
or hear my words."
When he heard this, he was delighted;
he kissed her, then got up.
The maidens who had brought him to the tent
covered him with rich clothes;
when he was newly dressed,
there was no handsomer young man under
heaven.
He was not at all foolish or base.
They gave him water for his hands
and the towel to dry them;
then they brought him to the table.

---

¹ *Mut ... herbergez* Other manuscripts have here, "mut est Lnval bien *assenez*" (Lanval is very well provided for) and some editors prefer this reading, since the line as it stands is repeated below at l. 154.

Od s'amie prist le super:
ne feseit mie a refuser.
Mut fu servi curteisement,
e il a grant joie le prent.

185   Un entremés i ot plener,
que mut pleiseit al chevalier:
kar s'amie baisout sovent
e acolot estreitement.

      Quant del manger furent levé,
190   sun cheval li unt amené.
Bien li unt la sele mise;
mut ad trové riche servise.
Il prent cungé, si est muntez;
vers la cité s'en est alez.

195   Suvent esgarde ariere sei.
Mut est Lanval en grant esfrei;
de s'aventure vait pensaunt
e en sun curage d[o]taunt.
Esbaïz est, ne seit que creir,

200   il ne la quide mie a veir.
Il est a sun ostel venuz;
ses hummes treve bien vestuz.
Icele nuit bon estel tient;
mes nul ne sot dunt ceo li vient.

205   N'ot en la vile chevalier
ki de surjur ait grant mestier,
quë il ne face a lui venir
e richement e bien servir.
Lanval donout les riches duns,

210   Lanval aquitout les prisuns,
Lanval vesteit les jugleürs,
Lanval feseit les granz honurs:
n'i ot estrange ne privé
a ki Lanval nen ust doné.

215   Mut ot Lanval joie e deduit:
u seit par jur u seit par nuit,
s'amie peot veer sovent,
tut est a sun comandement.

      Ceo m'est avis, memes l'an,
220   aprés la feste seint Johan,
d'ici qu'a trente chevalier
si erent alé esbanïer
en un vergier desuz la tur
u la reïne ert a surjur.

He took supper with his beloved:
he by no means refused.
He was served very courteously,
and accepted it with great joy.
There was an excellent extra dish
that greatly pleased the knight,
for he often kissed his lady
and embraced her closely.

      When they had gotten up from the table,
they brought him his horse.
They have put its saddle on well;
it has been richly looked after.
He took his leave and mounted;
he went toward the city.
Several times he looks back.
Lanval is greatly troubled;
he goes along thinking about his adventure
and worrying to himself.
He is astonished, he doesn't know what to
                    think,
he doesn't believe he will see her again.
He arrives at his lodging;
he finds his men handsomely dressed.
That night he keeps a rich table,
but no one knew where he got this from.
There was no knight in the town
who greatly needed sustenance
whom Lanval does not have brought to him
and well and richly served.
Lanval gave rich gifts,
Lanval ransomed prisoners,
Lanval clothed minstrels,
Lanval did great honor:
there was no stranger or dear friend
to whom Lanval did not give.
Lanval had great joy and pleasure:
he can see his beloved often,
whether by day or by night;
she is entirely at his command.

      That same year, as I understand,
after the feast of St. John,
as many as thirty knights
were going out to enjoy themselves
in a garden below the tower
where the queen was staying.

225 Ensemble od eus [esteit] Walwains
e sis cusins, li beaus Ywains.
E dist Walwains, li francs, li pruz,
que tant se fist amer de tuz:
"Par Deu, seignurs, nus feimes mal
230 de nostre cumpainun Lanval,
que tant est larges e curteis,
e sis peres est riches reis,
que od nus ne l'avum amené."
Atant se sunt ariere turné;
235 a sun ostel rev[u]nt ariere,
Lanval ameinent par preere.

A une fenestre entaillie
s'esteit la reïne apuïe[e];
treis dames ot ensemble od li.
240 La maisné [le rei] choisi;
Lanval choisi e esgarda.
Une des dames apela;
par li manda ses dameiseles,
les plus quointes [e] les plus beles:
245 od li si irrunt esbaïnïer
la u cil sunt al vergier.
Trente en menat od li e plus;
par les degrez descendent jus.
Les chevalers encuntre vunt,
250 que pur eles grant joïë unt.
Il les unt prises par les mains;
cil [parlemenz] ni ert pas vilains.
Lanval s'en vait a une part,
mut luin des autres. Ceo li est tart
255 que s'amie puïst tenir,
baiser, acoler e sentir;
l'autrui joie prise petit,
si il n'ad le suen delit.
Quant la reïne sul le veit,
260 al chevaler en va tut dreit;
lunc lui s'asist, si l'apela,
tut sun curage li mustra:
"Lanval, mut vus ai honuré
e mut cheri e mut amé.
265 tute m'amur poëz aveir;
kar me dites vostre voleir!
Ma drüerie vus otrei;
mut devez estre lié de mei."
"Dame," fet il, "lessez m'ester!

Gawain was with them
and his cousin, the handsome Yvain.
Gawain, the noble, the valiant,
who made himself so beloved by everyone, said,
"By God, my lords, we have done wrong
not to have brought along with us
our companion Lanval,
who is so generous and courteous,
and whose father is a rich king."
They turned back at once;
they go back to his lodging
and persuades Lanval to accompany them.

   The queen was leaning
on a window ledge;
she had three ladies along with her.
She saw the king's household;
she saw Lanval and noticed him.
She called one of her ladies;
she got her to send for her maidens,
the most elegant and lovely:
they will go to enjoy themselves with her
there where the men are in the orchard.
She took thirty or more of them with her;
they go down by the stairs.
The knights, who are delighted to see them,
go to meet them.
They took the ladies by the hand;
the conversation was not unrefined.
Lanval wanders off by himself,
quite far from the others. It seems long to him
until he might have his beloved,
kiss, embrace, and touch her;
he values little anothers' joy
if he does not have what pleases him.
When the queen sees him alone,
she goes right to the knight;
she sat by him and spoke to him,
she showed him all her feelings:
"Lanval, I have honored you greatly
and loved you and held you very dear.
You can have all my love;
tell me your desire!
I am willing to be your lover;
you should be delighted with me."
"Lady," he said, "let me be!

270	Jeo n'ai cure de vus amer.
	Lungement ai servi le rei;
	ne li voil pas mentir ma fei.
	Ja pur vus ne pur vostre amur
	ne mesfrai a mun seignur."
275	La reïne s'en curuça;
	irie[e] fu, si mesparla.
	"Lanval," fet ele, "bien le quit,
	vuz n'amez gueres cel delit.
	Asez le m'ad humme dit sovent
280	que des femmez n'avez talent.
	Vallez avez bien afeitiez,
	ensemble od eus vus deduiez.
	Vileins cüarz, mauveis failliz,
	mut est mi sires maubailliz
285	que pres de lui vus ad suffert;
	mun escïent que Deus en pert!"
	Quant il l'oï, mut fu dolent;
	del respundre ne fu pas lent.
	Teu chose dist par maltalent
290	dunt il se repenti sovent.
	"Dame," dist il, "de cel mestier
	ne me sai jeo nïent aidier;
	mes jo aim, [e] si sui amis
	cele ke deit aver le pris
295	sur tutes celes que jeo sai.
	E une chose vus dirai,
	bien le sachez a descovert:
	une de celes ke la sert,
	tute la plus povre meschine,
300	vaut meuz de vus, dame reïne,
	de cors, de vis e de beauté,
	d'enseignement e de bunté."
	La reïne s'en par[t] atant,
	en sa chambrë en vait plurant.
305	Mut fu dolente e curuciee
	de ceo k'il [l']out [si] avilee.
	En sun lit malade cucha;
	jamés, ceo dit, ne levera,
	si li reis ne l'en feseit dreit
310	de ceo dunt ele se plein[d]reit.
	Li reis fu del bois repeiriez;
	mut out le jur esté haitiez.
	As chambres la reïne entra.
	Quant ele le vit, si se clamma;

	I have no interest in loving you.
	For a long time I have served the king;
	I don't want to betray my faith to him.
	Never for you or for your love
	shall I wrong my lord."
	The queen became furious at this;
	in her anger, she spoke wrongly.
	"Lanval," she said, "it's quite clear to me
	you have no interest in that pleasure.
	People have often told me
	that you're not interested in women.
	You have shapely young men
	and take your pleasure with them.
	Base coward, infamous wretch,
	my lord is very badly repaid
	for allowing you to remain in his presence;
	I believe that he will lose God by it!"
	When he heard this, he was very distressed;
	he was not slow to respond.
	Out of anger he said something
	that he would often regret.
	"Lady," he said, "I know nothing
	about that line of work;
	but I love, and am loved by,
	one who should be valued more highly
	than all the women I know.
	And I'll tell you one thing,
	know it well and openly:
	any one of her servants,
	even the poorest maid,
	is worth more than you, lady queen,
	in body, face, and beauty,
	in manners and goodness."
	The queen leaves at once
	and goes into her chamber, crying.
	She was very upset and angry
	that he had insulted her in this way.
	She took to her bed, sick;
	never, she said, would she get up
	if the king did not do the right thing
	about the complaint she would make to him.
	The king returned from the woods;
	he had had a very pleasant day.
	He went into the queen's rooms.
	When she saw him, she made her appeal;

315   as piez li chiet, merci crie,
       e dit que Lanval l'ad hunie.
       De drüerie la requist;
       pur ceo que ele l'en escundist,
       mut [la] laidi e avila.
320   De tele amie se vanta,
       que tant iert cuinte e noble e fiere
       que meuz valut sa chamberere,
       la plus povre que [la] serveit,
       que la reïne ne feseit.
325   Li reis s'en curuçat forment;
       juré en ad sun serement:
       si il ne s'en peot en curt defendre,
       il le ferat arder u pendre.
       Fors de la chambre eissi li reis,
330   de ses baruns apelat treis;
       il les enveit pur Lanval,
       qüe asez ad dolur e mal.
       A sun [o]stel fu revenuz;
       il s'est[eit] bien aparceüz
335   qu'il aveit perdue s'amie:
       descovert ot la drüerie.
       En une chambre fu tut suls,
       pensis esteit e anguissus;
       s'amie apele mut sovent,
340   mes ceo ne li valut neent.
       Il se pleigneit e suspirot,
       d'ures en autres se pasmot;
       puis li crie cent feiz merci
       que ele par[ol]t a sun ami.
345   Sun quor e sa buche maudit;
       ceo est merveille k'il ne s'ocit.
       Il ne seit tant crïer ne braire
       ne debatre ne sei detraire
       que ele en veulle merci aveir
350   sul tant que la puisse veeir.
       Oi las, cument se cuntendra?
          Cil ke li reis ci enveia,
       il sunt venu, si li unt dit
       que a la curt voise sanz respit:
355   li reis l'aveit par eus mandé,
       la reïne l'out encusé.
       Lanval i vait od sun grant doel;
       il l'eüssent ocis [sun] veoil.
       Il est devant le rei venu;

she falls at his feet and asks for mercy
and says that Lanval has shamed her.
He asked her to be his lover;
because she refused him,
he insulted her greatly and said ugly things.
He boasted of such a beloved,
one who was so elegant, noble, and proud,
that her chambermaid,
the poorest girl who served her,
was worth more than the queen.
The king got extremely angry;
he swore an oath that
if Lanval cannot defend himself in court,
he will have him burnt or hanged.
The king went out of the chamber
and called three of his nobles;
he sends them for Lanval,
who has sorrow and trouble enough.
He had gone back to his lodging;
it was quite evident to him
that he had lost his beloved:
he had revealed their love.
He went into a chamber by himself,
anxious and distraught;
he calls on his beloved over and over,
and it does him no good at all.
He lamented and sighed,
he fainted repeatedly;
then a hundred times he begs her to have pity
and appear to her beloved.
He cursed his heart and his mouth;
it's a wonder he does not kill himself.
He cannot cry out or wail
or reproach or torment himself
enough to make her take pity on him,
even enough that he might see her.
Alas, what will he do?
   Those the king sent there
arrived, and said to him
that he must go to the court without delay:
the king had sent the order through them,
the queen had accused him.
Lanval goes there in his great sorrow;
they could have killed him for all he cared.
He came before the king;

360	mut fu dolent, taisanz e mu,	he was very sorrowful, silent and unspeaking,
	de grant dolur mustre semblant.	showing the appearance of great sorrow.
	Li reis li dit par maltalant,	The king says to him angrily,
	"Vassal, vus me avez mut mesfait!	"Vassal, you have done me a great wrong!
	Trop començastes vilein plait	You began too base a suit
365	de mei hunir e aviler	to shame and revile me
	e la reïne lendengier.	and insult the queen.
	Vanté vus estes de folie:	You boasted foolishly:
	trop par est noble vostre amie,	your beloved is far too exalted
	quant plus est bele sa meschine	when her maid is more beautiful
370	e plus vaillante que la reïne."	and worthy than the queen."
	Lanval defent la deshonur	Lanval denies the dishonor
	e la hunte de sun seignur	and shame of his lord
	de mot en mot, si cum il dist,	word by word, just as he said it,
	que la reïne ne requist;	for he had not requested the queen's love;
375	mes de ceo dunt il ot parlé	but he acknowledged the truth
	reconut il la verité,	of what he had said
	de l'amur dunt il se vanta:	concerning the love about which he boasted:
	dolent en est, perdue l'a.	he is sorrowful, for he has lost her.
	De ceo lur dit qu'il en ferat	Concerning this he says that he will do
380	quanque la curt esgarderat.	whatever the court judges best.
	Li reis fu mut vers li irez;	The king was quite furious with him;
	tuz ses hummes ad enveiez	he sent for all his men
	pur dire dreit que il en deit faire,	to say rightly what he must do,
	que hum ne li puis[se] a mal retraire.	so that no one would speak ill of it.
385	Cil unt sun commandement fait,	They did what he ordered,
	u eus seit bel, u eus seit lait.	whether they liked it or not.
	Comunement i sunt alé	They all went off together
	e unt jugé e esgardé	and judged and decided
	que Lanval deit aveir un jur;	that Lanval should have his day in court;
390	mes plegges truisse a sun seignur	but he must provide guarantees for his lord
	qu'il atendra sun jugement	that he will await his judgment
	e revendra en sun present:	and return to his presence:
	si serat la curt esforcie[e],	a larger court will be gathered,
	kar n'i ot dunc fors la maisne[e].	for now there was no one there but the household.
395	Al rei revienent li barun,	The nobles return to the king
	si li mustrent la reisun.	and explain to him their judgment.
	Li reis ad plegges demandé.	The king demanded guarantees.
	Lanval fu sul e esgaré;	Lanval was alone and in great distress;
	n'i aveit parent në ami.	he had no family or friends.
400	Walwain i vait, ki l'a plevi,	Gawain goes to act as a guarantor for Lanval,
	e tuit si cumpainun aprés.	and all his companions after him.
	Li reis lur dit: "E jol vus les	The king says to them: "I commend him to you
	sur quanke vus tenez de mei,	on the basis of whatever you may hold of me,

teres e fieus, chescun par sei."

405 Quant plevi fu, dunc n'[i] ot el;

alez s'en est a sun ostel.
Li chevaler l'unt conveé;
mut l'unt blasmé e chastïé
k'il ne face si grant dolur,
410 e maudïent si fol'amur.
Chescun jur l'aloënt veer,
pur ceo k'il voleient saveir
u il beüst, u il mangast;
mut dotouent k'il s'afolast.

415 Al jur que cil orent numé
li barun furent asemblé.
Li reis e la reïne i fu,
e li plegge unt Lanval rendu.
Mut furent tuz pur li dolent:
420 jeo quid k'il en i ot teus cent
ki feïssent tut lur poeir
pur lui sanz pleit delivre aveir;
il iert retté a mut grant tort.
Li reis demande le recort
425 sulunc le cleim e les respuns;
ore est trestut sur les baruns.
Il sunt al jugement alé,
mut sunt pensifz e esgaré
del franc humme d'autre païs
430 që entre eus ert si entrepris.
Encumbrer le veulent plusur
pur la volenté sun seignur.
Ceo dist li quoens de Cornwaille:
"Ja endreit [nus] n'i avera faille;
435 kar ki que en plurt e ki que en chant,
le dreit estuet aler avant.
Li reis parla vers sun vassal,
que jeo vus oi numer Lanval;
de felunie le retta
440 e d'un mesfait l'acheisuna,

d'un'amur dunt il se vanta,
e ma dame s'en curuça.
Nuls ne l'apele fors le rei;
par cele fei ke jeo vus dei,
445 ki bien en veut dire le veir,

---

lands and fiefs, each one for himself."
Once the pledge was made, there was
        nothing more to do;
Lanval went off to his lodging.
The knights went along with him;
they greatly rebuked and counseled him
not to be in such sorrow,
and they cursed such mad love.
Every day they went to see him,
for they wanted to know
if he was drinking, if he was eating;
they greatly feared that he would do himself
        harm.
    On the day that they had named
the nobles gathered.
The king and queen were there,
and the guarantors brought Lanval.
Everyone was very sad for him:
I believe that there were some hundred there
who would have done anything in their power
to free him without a trial;
he was very wrongly accused.
The king demands the verdict
according to the charges and the defense;
now it is entirely up to the nobles.
They went to sit in judgment,
very anxious and dismayed
over the noble man from another country
who was in such trouble among them.
Many want to find him guilty
according to their lord's wishes.
The count of Cornwall said,
"We must not fall short,
for whoever may weep or sing,
the law must take precedence.
The king has spoken against his vassal,
whom I hear you call Lanval;
he accused him of a crime
and brought charges of wrongdoing against
        him,
concerning a love of which he boasted,
which made my lady angry.
No one accuses him but the king;
by the faith I owe you,
whoever wants to speak the truth,

ja n'i deüst respuns aveir,
si pur ceo nun que a sun seignur
deit [hum] par tut fairë honur.[1]
450 Un serement l'engagera,
e li reis le nus pardura.

E s'il peot aver sun guarant
e s'amie venist avant
e ceo fust veir k'il en deïst,
dunt la reïne se marist,
455 de ceo avera il bien merci,
quant pur vilté nel dist de li.
E s'il ne peot garant aveir,
ceo li devum faire saveir:
tut sun servise perde del rei,
460 e sil deit cungeer de sei."
Al chevaler unt enveé,
si li unt dit e nuntïé
que s'amie face venir
pur lui tencer e garentir.
465 Il lur dit qu'il ne poeit:
ja pur li sucurs nen avereit.
Cil s'en rev[un]t as jugeürs,
ki n'i atendent nul sucurs.
Li reis les hastot durement
470 pur la reïne kis atent.
        Quant il deveient departir,
deus puceles virent venir
sur deus beaus palefreiz amblanz.
Mut par esteient avenanz;
475 de cendal purpre sunt vestues
tut senglement a lur char nues.
Cil les esgardou volenters.
Walwain, od li treis chevalers,
vait a Lanval, si li cunta;
480 les deus puceles li mustra.
Mut fu haitié, forment li prie
qu'il li deïst si ceo ert [s]'amie.
Il lur ad dit ne seit ki sunt

ne dunt vienent ne u eles vunt.

485 Celes sunt alees avant

there would not even be a case
except that to the name of his lord
a man should do honor in everything.
Lanval can affirm this by oath,
and the king will turn him over to us for
        judgment.
And if he can have his guarantor—
if his lady should come forward
and what he said about her,
which made the queen angry, was true—
then he will certainly receive mercy,
since he did not say it out of baseness.
And if he cannot produce proof,
we must make him understand this:
he loses all his service to the king
and must take his leave of him."
They sent to the knight,
and they told him and announced
that he should make his beloved come
to defend and bear witness for him.
He told them that he could not:
he would never get help from her.
They go back to the judges,
who expect no help from that quarter.
The king urged them fiercely
for the sake of the queen who was waiting.
        Just as they were about to make their ruling,
they saw two maidens coming
on two beautiful brisk palfreys.
They were extremely lovely;
they were dressed in purple taffeta
down to their bare skin.
Everyone gazed at them eagerly.
Gawain, and three knights with him,
went to Lanval and told him;
he showed him the two maidens.
He was very happy, and begged him
to say whether this was his beloved.
Lanval tells them that he does not know who
        they are
or where they come from or where they are
        going.
The maidens went along

---

[1] Lines 441–49 appear in a different order in the manuscript: 443–48, 442, 441. This emendation is made by most editors.

tut a cheval; par tel semblant
descendirent devant le deis,
la u seeit Artur li reis.
Eles furent de grant beuté,
490   si unt curteisement parlé:
"Reis, fai tes chambers delivrer
e de pa[il]es encurtiner,
u ma dame puïst descendre
si ensemble od vus veut ostel prendre."
495   Il lur otria mut volenters,
si appela deus chevalers:
as chambres les menerent sus.
A cele feiz ne distrent plus.

   Li reis demande a ses baruns
500   le jugement e les respuns
e dit que mut l'unt curucié
de ceo que tant l'unt delaié.
"Sire," funt il, "nus departimes
pur les dames que nus veïmes;
505   [nus n'i avum] nul esgart fait.
Or recumencerum le plait."
Dunc assemblerent tut pensif;
asez i ot noise e estrif.
Quant il ierent en cel esfrei,
510   deus puceles de gent cunrei—
vestues de deus pa[il]es freis,
chevauchent deus muls espanneis—
virent venir la rue aval.
Grant joie en eurent li vassal;
515   entre eus dïent que ore est gariz
Lanval li pruz e li hardiz.
Yweins i est a lui alez,
ses cumpainuns i ad menez.
"Sire," fet il, "rehaitiez vus!
520   Pur amur Deu, parlez od nus!
Ici vienent deus dameiseles
mut acemees e mut beles:
ceo est vostre amie vereiment!"
Lanval respunt hastivement
525   e dit qu'il pas nes avuot
ne il nes cunut ne nes amot.
Atant furent celes venues,
devant le rei sunt descendues.
Mut les loërent li plusur
530   de cors, de vis e de colur;

on their horses; in this fashion
they got down in front of the dais
where King Arthur was sitting.
They were very beautiful
and spoke courteously:
"King, make your chambers ready
and spread out silks
where my lady can step
if she wants to take lodging with you."
He very willingly granted this to them,
and called two knights:
they led them up to the chambers.
At that time they said no more.

   The king asks his nobles
for the judgment and the verdict
and says that they have made him very angry
by delaying for so long.
"Sire," they say, "we broke off our discussion
on account of the ladies that we saw;
we have not made a decision.
Now we will resume the trial."
Then they gathered, quite concerned;
there was a great deal of noise and debate.
While they were in this disarray,
they saw coming down the road
two maidens of noble bearing,
dressed in cool silks,
riding two Spanish mules.
The vassals were delighted by this;
they say to each other that now Lanval,
the bold and strong, is cured.
Yvain went to him,
taking his companions with him.
"Sir," he said, "rejoice!
For the love of God, speak to us!
Here come two maidens,
very elegant and beautiful:
surely it is your beloved!"
Lanval answers hastily
and says that he neither claimed them
nor knew them nor loved them.
Just then the maidens arrived
and dismounted before the king.
Many people greatly praised
their bodies, faces and coloring;

	n'i ad cele meuz ne vausist
	que unkes la reïne ne fist.
	L'aisnee fu curteise e sage,
	avenantment dist sun message:
535	"Reis, kar nus fai chambres baillier
	a oés ma dame herbergier;
	ele vient ici a tei parler."
	Il les cumandë a mener
	od les autres quë ainceis viendrent.
540	Unkes des muls nul plai[t] ne tindrent.
	Quant il fu d'eles deliverez,
	puis ad tuz ses baruns mandez
	que le jugement seit renduz:
	trop ad le jur esté tenuz.
545	La reïne s'en curuceit,
	que si lunges les atendeit.
	Ja departissent a itant,
	quant par la vile vient errant
	tut a cheval une pucele:
550	en tut le secle n'ot plus bele.
	Un blanc palefrei chevachot,
	que bel e süef la portot.
	Mut ot bien fet e col e teste:
	suz ciel nen ot plus bele beste.
555	Riche atur ot al palefrei:
	suz ciel nen ad quens ne rei
	ki tut [le] p[e]üst eslegier
	sanz tere vendre u engagier.
	Ele iert vestue en itel guise:
560	de chainsil blanc e de chemise,
	que tuz les costez li pareient,
	que de deus parz laciez esteient.
	Le cors ot gent, basse la hanche,
	le col plus blanc que neif sur branche,
565	les oilz ot vairs e blanc le vis,
	bele buche, neis bien asis,
	les surcilz bruns e bel le frunt
	e le chef cresp e aukes blunt;
	fil d'or ne gette tel luur
570	cum sun chevel cuntre le jur.
	Sis manteus fu de purpre bis;
	les pans en ot entur li mis.
	Un espervier sur sun poin tient,
	e un leverer aprés lui vient.
575	Il n'ot al burc petit ne grant

both of them were certainly worth
more than the queen ever was.
The elder was courteous and wise;
she spoke her message becomingly:
"King, make ready rooms for us
to receive my lady;
she is coming here to speak to you."
He orders that they be taken
to the others who had arrived previously.
They need not worry about the mules.
　　When he had sent them off,
he ordered all his nobles
that the judgment be given:
too much of the day had been taken up.
The queen was getting angry
that she was kept waiting so long by them.
They were about to take a decision,
when through the town comes
a maiden riding on a horse:
there was no lady in the world more beautiful.
She was riding a white palfrey,
which carried her well and gently.
It had a well-shaped neck and head:
there was no more beautiful animal under heaven.
The palfrey was richly harnessed:
no count or king under heaven
could have afforded it all
without selling or mortgaging land.
She was dressed in this manner:
in a shift of white linen,
which let both her sides be seen,
as it was laced on either side.
She had a lovely body, a long waist,
a neck whiter than snow on a branch,
grey-green eyes and white skin,
a beautiful mouth, a well-formed nose,
dark eyebrows and a lovely forehead
and curling golden hair;
no golden thread casts such a gleam
as did her hair in the sun.
Her mantle was dark purple;
she had wrapped its ends around her.
She holds a falcon on her fist,
and a greyhound runs behind her.
There was no one in the town, great or small,

	ne li veillard ne li enfant
	que ne l'alassent esgarder.
	Si cum il la veent errer,
	de sa beauté n'iert mie gas.
580	Ele veneit meins que le pas.
	Li jugeür, que la veeient,
	a [grant] merveille le teneient;
	il n'ot un sul ki l'esgardast
	de dreite joie ne s'eschaufast.
585	Cil ki le chevaler amoënt
	a lui veneient, si li cuntouent
	de la pucele ki veneit,
	si Deu plest, que le delivereit:
	"Sire cumpain, ci en vient une,
590	mes ele n'est pas fave ne brune;
	ceo'st la plus bele del mund,
	de tutes celes kë i sunt."
	Lanval l'oï, sun chief dresça;
	bien la cunut, si suspira.
595	Li sanc li est munté al vis;
	de parler fu aukes hastifs.
	"Par fei," fet il, "ceo est m'amie!
	Or m'en est gueres ki m'ocie,
	si ele n'ad merci de mei;
600	kar gariz sui, quant jeo la vei."
	La damë entra al palais;
	unc si bele n'i vient mais.
	Devant le rei est descendue
	si que de tuz iert bien [veüe].
605	Sun mantel ad laissié ch[e]eir,
	que meuz la puïssent veer.
	Li reis, que mut fu enseigniez,
	il s'est encuntre lui dresciez,
	e tuit li autre l'enurerent,
610	de li servir se presenterent.
	Quant il l'orent bien esgardee
	e sa beauté forment loëe,
	ele parla en teu mesure,
	kar de demurer nen ot cure:
615	"Reis, jeo ai amé un tuen vassal:
	veez le ici, ceo est Lanval!
	Acheisuné fu en ta curt.
	Ne vuil mie que a mal li turt
	de ceo qu'il dist; ceo sachez tu

not the old men or the children,
who did not go to look at her.
As they saw her pass,
there was no joking about her beauty.
She came along quite slowly.
The judges, who saw her,
considered it a great marvel;
there was not one who looked at her
who did not grow warm with sheer joy.
Those who loved the knight
came to him, and told him
of the maiden who was coming,
who, if it pleased God, would set him free:
"Sir companion, here comes one
who is not tawny nor dark;
she is the loveliest in the world,
of all the women who live."
Lanval heard this, he lifted his head;
he knew her well, and sighed.
The blood rose to his face;
he was very quick to speak.
"In faith," he said, "it is my beloved!
Now I care little who may kill me,
if she does not take pity on me;
for I am cured when I see her."
The lady entered the palace;
such a beauty had never come there.
She dismounted before the king
so that she was quite visible to all.
She let her mantle fall
so that they could see her better.
The king, who was very well-bred,
got up to meet her,
and all the others honored her
and offered themselves to serve her.
When they had looked at her well
and greatly praised her beauty,
she spoke in this way,
for she did not wish to delay:
"King, I have fallen in love with one of your
vassals:
you see him here, it is Lanval!
He was accused in your court.
I do not wish it to be held against him,
concerning what he said; you should know

620	que la reïne ad tort eü:
	unc nul jur ne la requist.
	De la vantance kë il fist,
	si par me peot estre aquitez,
	par voz baruns seit deliverez!"
625	Ceo qu'il jugerunt par dreit
	li reis otrie ke issi seit.
	N'i ad un sul que n'ait jugié
	que Lanval ad tut desrainié.
	Deliverez est par lur esgart,
630	e la pucele s'en depart.
	Ne la peot li reis retenir;
	asez gent ot a li servir.
	Fors de la sale aveient mis
	un grant perrun de marbre bis,
635	u li pesant humme muntoënt,
	que de la curt le rei [aloënt]:
	Lanval esteit munté desus.
	Quant la pucele ist fors a l'us,
	sur le palefrei, detriers li,
640	de plain eslais Lanval sailli.
	Od li s'en vait en Avalun,
	ceo nus recuntent li Bretun,
	en un isle que mut est beaus;
	la fu ravi li dameiseaus.
645	Nul hum n'en oï plus parler,
	ne jeo n'en sai avant cunter.

that the queen was wrong:
he never asked for her love.
And concerning the boast he made,
if he can be acquitted by me,
let your nobles set him free!"
The king grants that it should be so,
that they should judge rightly.
There was not one who did not judge
that Lanval was completely exonerated.
He is freed by their judgment,
and the maiden takes her leave.
The king cannot detain her;
she had enough people to serve her.
Outside the hall was set
a great block of dark marble,
where heavy men mounted,
who were leaving the king's court:
Lanval got up on it.
When the maiden came through the gate,
with one leap Lanval
jumped on the palfrey, behind her.
With her he went to Avalon,
so the Bretons tell us,
to a very beautiful island;
the young man was carried off there.
No one ever heard another word of him,
and I can tell no more.

Laüstic (The Nightingale)

	Une aventure vus dirai
	dunt li Bretun firent un lai.
	Laüstic ad nun, ceo m'est avis—
	si l'apelent en lur païs;
5	ceo est "[russignol]" en franceis
	e "nihtegale" en dreit engleis.
	[En] Seint Mallo en la cuntree
	ot une vile renumee.
	Deus chevalers ilec manëent
10	e deus for[z] maisuns aveient.
	Pur la bunté des deus baruns
	fu de la vile bons li nuns.
	Li uns aveit femme espusee,
	sage, curteise, mut acemee;

I shall tell you an adventure
of which the Bretons made a lai.
Its name is Laüstic, I believe—
so they call it in their country;
that is "rossignol" in French
and "nightingale" in proper English.
In the region of St. Malo
there was a well-known town.
Two knights lived there,
and had two strong houses.
Because of the goodness of the two men
the town had a good name.
One of them had married a woman
who was wise, courteous, and very gracious;

15	a merveille se teneit chiere	she had a great deal of self-respect
	sulunc l'usage e la manere.	according to custom and usage.
	Li autres fu un bachelers	The other was a young knight,
	bien conu entre ses pers	well regarded among his peers
	de prüesce, de grant valur,	for prowess and great bravery,
20	e volenters feseit honur:	and he willingly behaved honorably:
	mut turnëot e despendeit	he went tourneying a great deal and spent a lot
	e bien donot ceo qu'il aveit.	and gave out generously what he had.
	La femme sun veisin ama.	The woman loved her neighbor.
	Tant la requist, tant la preia,	He had so often asked and implored her,
25	e tant par ot en lui grant bien	and there was such great good in him,
	que ele l'ama sur tute rien,	that she loved him above all things,
	tant pur le bien que ele oï,	partly for the good that she heard of him,
	tant pur ceo qu'il iert pres de li.	partly because he was near to her.
	Sagement e bien s'entreamerent,	They loved one another wisely and well,
30	mut se covrirent e esgarderent	they dissembled and took good care
	qu'il ne feussent aparceüz	not to be perceived
	ne desturbez ne mescreüz;	nor disturbed nor suspected;
	e eus le poeient bien fere,	and they could easily do this,
	kar pres esteient lur repere.	because they lived close to one another.
35	Preceines furent lur maisuns	Their houses were neighboring,
	e lur sales e lur dunguns;	both their halls and their keeps;
	n'i aveit bare ne devise	there was no obstacle or barrier
	fors un haut mur de piere bise.	except a high wall of grey stone.
	Des chambres u la dame jut	From the room where the lady slept,
40	quant a la fenestre s'estut,	when she was at the window,
	poeit parler a sun ami	she could talk to her beloved
	de l'autre part, e il a li,	on the other side, and he to her,
	e lur aveirs entrechangier	and they could exchange things
	e par geter e par lancier.	by tossing or throwing them.
45	N'unt gueres rien que lur despleise,	There was hardly anything that displeased them,
	mut esteient amdui a eise—	they were both very much at ease—
	fors tant k'il ne poënt venir	except that they could not be together
	del tut ensemble a lur pleisir,	entirely at their pleasure,
	kar la dame ert estrei[t] gardee	for the lady was closely guarded
50	quant cil esteit en la cuntree.	when her husband was at home.
	Mes de tant aveient retur,	But at least they had the consolation,
	u fust par nuit u fust par jur,	whether at night or during the day,
	que ensemble poeient parler.	of talking to one another.
	Nul nes poeit de ceo garder	No one could prevent them
55	que a la fenestre n'i venissent	from coming to the window
	e iloec s'entreveïssent.	and seeing one another there.
	Lungement se sunt entreamé,	They loved one another for a long time,
	tant que ceo vient a un esté,	until there came a summer
	que bruil e pré sunt rever[d]i	when the woods and meadow were all green

60	e li vergier ierent fluri;	and the orchards were flowering;
	cil oiselet par grant duçur	the little birds with great sweetness
	mainent lur joie en sum la flur.	expressed their joy among the flowers.
	Ki amur ad a sun talent,	It is no wonder if one who has a mind to love
	n'est merveille s'il i entent!	gives it his attention!
65	Del chevaler vus dirai veir:	I shall tell you truly about the knight:
	il i entent a sun poeir	he attended to it with all his might,
	e la dame de l'autre part,	and the lady did so on the other side,
	e de parler e de regart.	both with words and with looks.
	Les nuiz, quant la lune luseit	At night, when the moon shone
70	e ses sires cuché esteit,	and her husband was in bed,
	de juste li sovent levot	often she got up from beside him
	e de sun mantel se afublot;	and put on her mantle;
	a la fenestre ester veneit	she would go stand at the window
	pur sun ami qu'el i saveit	on account of her beloved, who, she knew,
75	que autreteu vie demenot:	led a similar life:
	le plus de la nuit veillot.	he was awake most of the night.
	Delit aveient al veer,	They delighted in seeing one another,
	quant plus ne poeient aver.	when they could have no more.
	Tant i estut, tant i leva,	She was there so much, she got up so often,
80	que ses sires s'en curuça	that her husband became angry
	e meintefeiz li demanda	and asked her many times
	pur quei levot e u ala.	why she got up and where she went.
	"Sire," la dame li respunt,	"Sir," the lady answered,
	"il nen ad joïe en cest mund	"he has no joy in this world
85	ki nen ot le laüstic chanter.	who does not hear the nightingale sing.
	Pur ceo me vois ici ester.	That is why you see me here.
	Tant ducement le oi la nuit	I hear him so sweetly here at night
	que mut me semble grant deduit;	that it seems a great pleasure to me;
	tant me delit[e] e tant le voil	it delights me so and I desire it so
90	que jeo ne puis dormir de l'oil."	that I cannot close my eyes in sleep."
	Quant li sires ot que ele dist,	When her husband heard what she said,
	de ire e maltalent en rist.	he laughed out of anger and ill will.
	De une chose se purpensa:	He fixed his thoughts on one thing:
	que le laüstic enginnera.	entrapping the nightingale.
95	Il n'ot vallet en sa meisun	There was no servant in his house
	ne face engin, reis u la[ç]un;	who did not make a trap, net or snare;
	puis les mettent par le vergier.	then they put them in the orchard.
	N'i ot codre ne chastainier	There was no hazel tree or chestnut
	u il ne mettent laz u glu,	where they did not put a snare or birdlime,
100	tant que pri[s] l'unt et retenu.	until they took and captured it.
	Quant le laüstic eurent pris,	When they had caught the nightingale alive,
	al seignur fu rendu tut vis.	they took it to the lord.
	Mut en fu liez, quant il le tient;	He was very happy when he had it;
	as chambres la dame vient.	he came to the lady's chamber.

105	"Dame," fet il, "u estes vus? Venez avant, parlez a nus! Jeo ai le laüstic englué pur quei vus avez tant veillé. Des ore poëz gisir en peis:	"Lady," he said, "where are you? Come here, talk to me! I have caught the nightingale for which you stayed awake so long. From now on you can rest in peace:
110	il ne vus esveillerat meis." Quant la dame l'ad entendu, dolente e cureçuse fu. A sun seignur l'ad demandé, e il l'ocist par engresté:	he will wake you no more." When the lady had heard this, she was sorrowful and angry. She asked her lord for it, and he killed it out of spite:
115	le col li rumpt a ses deus meins. De ceo fist il ke trop vileins. Sur la dame le cors geta, se que sun chainse ensanglanta un poi desur le piz devant;	he broke its neck with his two hands. In this he behaved most basely. He threw the body at the lady, so that her shift was bloodied a bit above the breast in front;
120	de la chambre s'en ist a tant. La dame prent le cors petit; durement plure e si maudit tuz ceus ki le laüstic traïrent, e les engins e les laçuns firent,	with that he left the room. The lady takes the little body; she weeps bitterly and curses all those who betrayed the nightingale by making traps and snares,
125	kar mut li unt toleit grant hait. "Lasse," fet ele, "mal m'estait! Ne purrai mes la nuit lever ne aler a la fenestre ester, u jeo suleie mun ami veer.	for they have taken a great happiness from her. "Alas," she said, "it goes ill with me! I can no longer get up at night nor go to stand by the window, where I was accustomed to see my beloved.
130	Une chose sai jeo de veir: il quidra ke jeo me feigne. De ceo m'estuet que cunseil preigne. Le laüstic li trameterai; l'aventure li manderai."	I know one thing for certain: he will think that I am deceiving him. I must give thought to this matter. I will convey the nightingale to him; I will let him know of the adventure."
135	En une piece de samit a or brusdé e tut escrit ad l'oiselet envolupé; un sun vatlet ad apelé, sun message li ad chargié,	In a piece of samite embroidered and inscribed all over with gold she wrapped the little bird; she called a servant of hers, charged him with her message,
140	a sun ami l'ad enveié. Cil est al chevalier venuz; de part sa dame li dist saluz, tut sun message li cunta, e le laüstic li presenta.	sent him to her beloved. He came to the knight; he greeted him on behalf of his lady, told him all her message, and presented him with the nightingale.
145	Quant tut li ad dit e mustré e il l'aveit bien escuté, de l'aventure esteit dolenz; mes ne fu pas vileins ne lenz. Un vasselet ad fet forgeer;	When he had told and shown everything and the knight had listened well, he was sorrowful over the adventure; but he was not ill-bred or slow. He had a small casket made;

150 unc n'i ot fer ne acer,
tut fu de or fin od bones pieres,
mut precïuses e mut cheres;
covercle i ot tres bien asis.
Le laüstic ad dedenz mis,
155 puis fist la chasse enseeler.
Tuz jurs l'ad fet[e] od li porter.

    Cele aventure fu cuntee,
ne pot estre lunges cele.
Un lai en firent li Bretun:
160 Le Laüstic l'apelent hum.

it contained not a bit of iron or steel,
it was made all of fine gold with valuable gems,
most precious and costly;
it had a very well-fitting cover.
He put the nightingale inside,
then had the coffer sealed.
He carried it with him always.

    This adventure was told;
it could not long be hidden.
The Bretons made a lai of it;
men call it Laüstic.

Chevrefoil (The Honeysuckle)

Asez me plest e bien le voil
del lai que humme nume Chevrefoil
que la verité vus en cunt,
pur quei il fu fet e dunt.
5 Plusurs le me unt cunté e dit
e jeo l'ai trové en escrit
de Tristram e de la reïne,
de lur amur que tant fu fine,
dunt il eurent meinte dolur,
10 puis mururent en un jur.

    Li reis Markes esteit curucié;
vers Tristram sun nevuz irié;
de sa tere le cungea
pur la reïne qu'il ama.
15 En sa cuntree en est alez.
En Suhtwales, u il fu nez,
un an demurat tut entier;
ne pot ariere repeirier.
Mes puis se mist en abandun
20 de mort e de destructïun.
Ne vus esmerveilliez neent,
kar ki eime mut lëalment
mut est dolenz e trespensez,
quant il nen ad ses volentez.
25 Tristram est dolent e trespensis:
pur ceo se met de sun païs.
En Cornwaille vait tut dreit,
la u la reïne maneit.
En la forest tut sul se mist;
30 ne voleit pas que hum le veïst.

It pleases me well and I truly wish
to tell you the truth of the lai
that men call Chevrefoil,
why it was made and how it originated.
Many have told and recounted it to me
and I have found it written
about Tristan and the queen,
and their love that was so true,
for which they had great sorrow
and then died the same day.

    King Mark was angry,
enraged against his nephew Tristan;
he sent him away from his land
on account of the queen, whom he loved.
Tristan went into his own lands.
In South Wales, where he was born,
he stayed a full year;
he could not go back again.
But then he gave up caring
about death and destruction.
Don't be astonished by this,
for he who loves most loyally
is most sorrowful and despondent
when he does not have his wishes.
Tristan is sorrowful and despondent;
for this reason he leaves his country.
He goes straight to Cornwall,
where the queen was staying.
He went into the forest quite alone;
he did not wish anyone to see him.

En la vespree s'en eisseit,	In the evening he went out
quant tens de herberger esteit;	when it was time to find lodging;
od païsanz, od povre gent	with peasants, with poor people,
perneit la nuit herbergement.	he took lodging that night.
35 Les noveles lur enquereit	He asked them for news
del rei, cum il se cunteneit.	of the king and how he was behaving.
Ceo li dïent qu'il unt oï	They said that they had heard
que li barun erent bani.	that the lords were banished.[1]
A Tintagel deivent venir;	They were to go to Tintagel;
40 li reis i veolt sa curt tenir,	the king wanted to hold court there,
a pentecuste i serunt tuit.	at Pentecost they would all be there.
Mut i avera joie e deduit,	There would be great joy and delight,
e la reïnë i sera.	and the queen would be there.
Tristram l'oï, mut se haita:	Tristan heard this and was very glad:
45 ele ne purrat mie aler	there was no way she could go
k'il ne la veie trespasser.	without him seeing her pass by.
Le jur que li rei fu meüz,	The day that the king had set out,
e Tristram est al bois venuz:	Tristan came to the wood:
sur le chemin qu'il saveit	beside the road that he knew
50 que la reine passer deveit,	the queen must pass along,
une codre trencha par mi,	he split a hazel tree along its length
tute quarreie la fendi.	and squared it off.
Quant il ad paré le bastun,	When he had prepared the staff,
de sun cutel escrit sun nun.	with his knife he wrote his name.
55 [S]e la reïne s'aparceit,	If the queen should notice it,
que mut grant gardë s'en perneit—	as she was keeping careful watch—
autre feiz li fu avenu	it had happened other times
que si l'aveit aparceü—	that she had seen it—
de sun ami bien conustra	she would surely recognize the staff
60 le bastun quant ele le verra.	of her beloved when she saw it.
Ceo fu la summe de l'escrit	This was the sum of the writing
qu'il li aveit mandé e dit:	that he had sent and said:
que lunges ot ilec esté	that he had been there a long time
e atendu e surjurné	and waited and sojourned
65 pur [espïer] e pur saver	to have a glimpse and to know
coment il la pust veer,	how he might see her,
kar ne pot nent vivre sanz li.	for he could not live without her.
D'euls deus fu il autresi	For the two of them it was just
cum del chevrefoil esteit	as it is with the honeysuckle
70 ki a la codre se perneit:	that holds to the hazel tree:
quant il est si laciez e pris	when it is entwined and attached in this way
e tut entur le fust s'est mis,	and has established itself all around,
ensemble po[ë]nt bien durer;	they can endure well together,
mes ki puis les volt desevrer,	but if someone then wishes to separate them,

---

[1] That is, the lords who had made accusations of adultery against Tristan and the queen.

75	li codres muert hastivement	the hazel tree dies quickly
	e li chevrefoil ensemblement.	and the honeysuckle along with it.
	"Bele amie, si est de nus:	"Sweet beloved, so it is with us:
	ne vus sanz mei, ne mei sanz vus."	neither you without me, nor me without you."
	La reïne vait chevachant;	The queen came riding along;
80	ele esgardat tut un pendant.	she looked all along the slope of the road.
	Le bastun vit, bien l'aparceut,	She spotted the staff, she saw it well,
	tutes les lettres i conut.	she recognized all the letters.
	Les chevalers que la menoënt,	The knights who attended her,
	quë ensemblë od li erroënt,	who were traveling with her,
85	cumanda tuz [a] arester:	she commanded to stop:
	descendre vot e resposer.	she wished to dismount and rest.
	Cil unt fait sun commandement.	They did as she commanded.
	Ele s'en vet luinz de sa gent;	She went far from her people;
	sa meschine apelat a sei,	she summoned her maid,
90	Brenguein, que mut fu de bone fei.	Brangain, who was truly faithful.
	Del chemin un poi s'esluina;	She went a little way from the road;
	dedenz le bois celui trova	in the wood she found him
	que plus l'amot que rien vivant.	who loved her more than any living thing.
	Entre eus meinent joie grant.	They had great joy together.
95	A lui parlat tut a leisir,	She spoke to him quite at leisure,
	e ele li dit sun pleisir;	and told him her pleasure;
	puis li mustre cumfaitement	then she showed him just how
	del rei avrat acordement,	he could be reconciled with the king,
	e que mut li aveit pesé	and said it had weighed on him greatly
100	de ceo qu'il [l]'ot si cungïé;	that he had sent Tristan away as he had;
	par encusement l'aveit fait.	he had done it because of the accusation.[1]
	Atant s'en part, sun ami lait,	Then she departed, left her beloved—
	mes quant ceo vient al desevrer,	but when it came time to separate,
	dunc comenc[er]ent a plurer.	they both began to weep.
105	Tristram a Wales s'en rala,	Tristan went back to Wales,
	tant que sis uncles le manda.	until his uncle should send for him.
	Pur la joie qu'il ot eüe	Because of the joy that he had had
	de s'amie qu'il ot veüe	from seeing his beloved,
	e pur ceo k'il aveit escrit—	and because of what he had written—
110	si cum la reïne l'ot dit,	just as the queen had told him,
	pur les paroles remembrer—	in order to remember the words—
	Tristram, ki bien saveit harper,	Tristan, who was a gifted harper,
	en aveit fet un nuvel lai;	made of it a new lai.
	Asez brevement le numerai:	I will name it very briefly:
115	*Gotelef* l'apelent en engleis,	they call it *Goat-leaf* in English,
	Chevrefoil le nument en franceis.	and in French it is named *Chevrefoil*.
	Dit vus en ai la verité	I have told you the truth
	del lai que j'ai ici cunté.	of the lai I have recounted here.

---

[1] That is, the accusation of adultery between Tristan and the queen that some of the lords had made.

MIDDLE ENGLISH LYRICS

The Middle English poems in this section are for the most part difficult to date with any precision. In some cases they draw on relatively sophisticated lyric traditions from continental sources, but very largely they seem to be rooted in popular traditions that were probably already old when the earliest surviving copies of these poems were made. Like most short medieval poems that have survived, they are anonymous. From the familiarity with medieval Latin exhibited in some of the poems and their survival in manuscripts containing Latin alongside English (and French) texts, we may infer that many were read and quite possibly written by clerics—though even in these cases the authors may well have been adapting existing popular materials. Such poems have by convention been referred to for centuries as "medieval lyrics," though the term has been thought by some to be both anachronistic (the earliest appearance of the word "lyric" in English is in 1581) and somewhat misleading; in tone and subject matter many of these poems have little in common with the poems we have become accustomed to think of as "lyrical."

The majority of medieval lyrics that have survived deal with religious subjects, the most common being devotion to Jesus or the Virgin Mary (or both), often with a focus on Christ's Passion as it is linked to the theme of salvation and sacrifice, or Mary's roles as intercessor and suffering mother ("Now skrinketh rose and lily-flour," "Stond well, moder, under Rode"). Other religious lyrics contemplate Adam's fall and the transitory nature of life ("Farewell this world, I take my leve forever," "To dy, to dy / What haue I"), or the importance of constancy in faith. A number of religious lyrics draw on the conventions of secular literature, employing the topoi of so-called courtly love. Such is the case, for example, in "I sing of a maiden," in which Christ appears as a lover-knight and Mary is depicted as an unblemished maiden who chooses Christ as her son in the way that a secular poem might depict a lady bestowing her favor on a lover.

Modern readers may find a more immediate appeal in the lyrics that deal with secular themes. Earthly love is a frequent subject of these poems, sometimes dwelling on the perceived virtue and attractiveness of the beloved ("Betwene Mersh and Averil"), sometimes employing lewd word play ("I have a gentil cock"), and often taking the form of a lover's lament or complaint about a beloved's absence ("My lefe is faren in a lond"). Satires against women (such as "Of all creatures women be best") are common; most authorities think it probable that these medieval lyrics were all (or almost all) written by men, even those written in a woman's voice (such as "I lovede a child of this cuntree").

The range of emotion and expression in the lyrics is remarkably wide. Some poems are light-hearted celebrations of the pleasures of the ale-house ("Bring us in good ale") or the simple joy of experiencing nature's abundance ("Sumer is icumen in"). There is a refreshing directness (and sometimes a refreshing crudity) to many of these poems. Yet even those lyrics that clearly aim at comic entertainment can employ sophisticated poetic devices, such as internal rhyme, wordplay and allegory. Some lyrics (such as "Foweles in the frith") are ambiguous and perhaps ambivalent in their content, capable of both secular and religious readings.

We do not know how many of these poems were set to music, but the practice was apparently common; several manuscripts have come down to us that provide music to accompany their lyrics.

Harley Manuscript 978, now in the British Museum, is a miscellany dating from the second half of the thirteenth century; it was compiled and transcribed by monks at Reading Abbey. The page shown here provides the music as well as the English words to "Sumer is icumen in," which remains perhaps the best known of all medieval lyrics. Between the lines alternative words in Latin (focused on the "celicus agricola," or heavenly farmer) are provided by the monks.

Sumer is icumen in

Sumer° is icumen° in   *summer / has come*
Sing, cuccu, nu.[1] Sing, cuccu.
Sing, cuccu. Sing, cuccu, nu.

Sumer is icumen in—
5 Lhude° sing, cuccu.   *loudly*
Groweth sed° and bloweth° med°   *seed / blooms / meadow*
And springth the wude° nu[2]—   *wood*
Sing, cuccu.

Awe° bleteth after lomb,   *ewe*
10 Lhouth after calve cu,[3]
Bulluc sterteth, bucke verteth,
Murie° sing,[4] cuccu.   *merry*
Cuccu, cuccu,
Well singes thu,° cuccu—   *thou*
15 Ne swik thu naver nu![5]
—EARLIER 13TH CENTURY

Now goth sonne under wod

Now goth sonne under wod:°   *wood (of the Cross)*
Me reweth,° Mary, thy faire rode.° *pity / face, complexion*
Now goth sonne under Tree:
Me reweth, Mary, thy sonne and thee.
—EARLIER 13TH CENTURY

Foweles in the frith

Foweles° in the frith,°   *birds / wood*
The fisses° in the flod,°   *fishes / river, stream*
And I mon waxe wod:[6]

---

5 Much sorw I walk with
For beste of bon and blod.[7]
—LATER 13TH CENTURY

Betwene Mersh and Averil

Betwene Mersh° and Averil,°   *March / April*
When spray beginneth to springe,[8]
The lutel° fowl hath hire will   *little*
On hire lud to singe.[9]
5 Ich libbe° in love-longinge   *I live*
For semlokest° of alle thinge—   *the most fair, seemly*
He° may me blisse bringe;   *she*
Ich am in hire baundoun.°   *power, control*

An hendy hap ich habbe ihent![10]
10 Ichot° from Hevene it is me sent. *I know*
From alle wimmen my love is lent,
And light on Alisoun.[11]

On hue hire hair is fair enough,
Hire browe browne, hire eye blake;
15 With lossum chere he° on me logh,[12] *she*
With middle small and well imake.° *fashioned*
Bote° he me wolle° to hire take,   *unless / will*
For to ben hire owen make,[13]
Longe to liven ichulle° forsake,   *I shall*
20 And feye fallen adoun.[14]

Nightes when I wende° and wake—   *twist, turn*
Forthy mine wonges waxeth won[15]—

---

[7] *For ... blod* For beast of bone and blood.
[8] *When ... springe* When twigs/shoots begin to grow.
[9] *The lutel ... singe* The little bird has her wish to sing in her language.
[10] *An hendy ... ihent* I have received a fair fortune!
[11] *From alle ... on Alisoun* My love is taken from all women, and falls upon Alisoun.
[12] *With lossum ... logh* With beautiful face she laughed at me.
[13] *For to ... make* To be her own lover/companion.
[14] *Longe ... adoun* I shall not live long, and fated to die, fall down.
[15] *Forthy ... won* Therefore my cheeks grow pale.

---

[1] *cuccu, nu* Cuckoo, now.
[2] *Groweth sed ... wude nu* Seed grows and meadow blooms, and the wood now brings forth growth.
[3] *Lhouth ... cu* The cow lows after the calf.
[4] *Bulluc ... sing* The bullock starts, the buck breaks wind, sing merrily!
[5] *Well singes ... naver nu* You sing well, cuckoo—now never cease!
[6] *mon ... wod* Must go mad.

Levedy,° all for thine sake,   *lady*
Longinge is ilent me on.[1]
25   In world nis non so witer mon
That all hire bounte tell con:[2]
Hire swire is whittore then the swon,[3]
And fairest may in toun.[4]

Ich am for wowing° all forwake,°   *wooing / exhausted*
30   Wery so water in wore,[5]
Lest eny reve me my make,
Ich habbe iyirned yore.[6]
Betere is tholien while sore
Then mournen evermore.[7]
35   Geynest° under gore,[8]   *fairest*
Herkne to my roun!°   *song, cry*
—LATER 13TH CENTURY–EARLY 14TH CENTURY

Now skrinketh rose and lily-flour

Now skrinketh° rose and lily-flour,°   *fade / lily-flower*
That whilen° ber° that swete savour,   *at one time / bore*
In somer,° that swete tide.°   *summer / time*
Ne is no quene so stark ne stour,
5   Ne no levedy so bright in bour,[9]
That Ded ne shall by glide.[10]
Whoso° wol flesh lust forgon   *whoever*

---

[1] *Longinge ... on* Longing has fallen on me.

[2] *In world ... con* In the world there is no man so wise that he could tell all her virtue.

[3] *Her swire ... swon* Her neck is whiter than the swan.

[4] *And ... in toun* And she is the fairest maiden in town.

[5] *Ich am ... in wore* I am all wearied from wooing, as weary as water on the shore.

[6] *Lest ... yore* Lest any deprive me of my beloved, whom I have yearned for for so long.

[7] *Betere ... evermore* It is better to suffer miserably for a while than to mourn forever.

[8] *Geynest under gore* Loveliest under clothing (a common expression meaning "most beautiful").

[9] *Ne is ... bour* There is no queen so severe and fierce, nor lady so bright in her chamber.

[10] *That ... glide* That Death shall not come to her.

And Hevene blis abide,[11]
On Jesu be his thoght anon,°   *at once*
10   That therled° was his side.   *pierced*

From Petresbourgh in o morewening,°   *morning*
As I me wende o° my pleying,   *went about*
On my folye° I thoghte.   *folly*
Menen I gon my mourning
15   To hire that ber the Hevene King,
Of mercy hire besoghte:[12]
"Ledy, preye° thy sone for ous,°   *pray to / us*
That us dere bought,[13]
And shild° us from the lothe° hous   *shield / hateful*
20   That to the Fend is wroghte."°   *made*
Mine herte of dedes wes fordred,
Of sinne that I have my flesh fed
And folewed all my time:[14]
That I not° whider I shall be led   *know not*
25   When I lie on dethes bed,
In joy or into pyne.°   *pining, sorrow*
On o° ledy myn hope is,   *one*
Moder and virgine;
We shulen° into hevene° bliss   *shall [go] / heavenly*
30   Thurgh hire° medicine.   *through her*

Betere is hire medicine
Then any mead or any wyn.
Hire erbes smulleth swete;
From Catenas° into Dyvelyn°   *Caithness / Dublin*
35   Nis ther non leche so fyn
Oure serewes to bete.[15]
Mon that feleth eny sor,
Ant his folie wol lete,[16]
Without gold other° eny tresor°   *or / treasure*
40   He may be sound° and sete.°   *healthy / content*

---

[11] *Whoso wol ... abide* Whoever will forgo fleshly lust, and wait for the bliss of Heaven.

[12] *Menen ... besoghte* I began to make my mourning complaint to her that bore the King of Heaven, and sought her mercy.

[13] *That ... bought* Who redeemed us at great cost.

[14] *Mine herte ... my time* My heart was full of dread for my deeds of sin that I have fed my body (on) and followed all my life.

[15] *Nis ther ... bete* There is no doctor so able to make our troubles better.

[16] *Mon ... wol lete* Anyone who feels pain and will leave behind his own folly.

Of penaunce is his plaster° all,   *remedy*
And ever serven hire I shall,
Now and all my live;°   *life*
Now is free that ere wes thrall°   *slave*
45   Al thourh that levedy gent° and small   *noble lady*
Heried° be hir joyes five!   *praised*
Wher-so eny sek is,
Thider hie blyve;[1]
Thurh hire beoth ybroht° to bliss   *are brought*
50   Bo° maiden ant wive.   *both*

For he that dude° his body on tree,   *put*
Of° oure sinnes have piete°   *for / pity*
That weldes heovene boures![2]
Wimmon,° with thy jolyfte,°   *woman / merrymaking*
55   Thou thench on° Godes shoures!°   *think about / suffering*
Thagh thou be whyt and bryth on ble,°   *face*
Falewen shule thy floures.[3]
Jesu, haue mercy of vs,
That° all this world honoures.   *[you] whom*
—LATER 13TH CENTURY–EARLY 14TH CENTURY

Lenten is come with love to toune

L enten° is come with love to toune,°   *spring / town*
  With blosmen° and with briddes
      roune,[4]   *blossoms, flowers*
That all this blisse bringeth.
Dayeseyes° in this dales,°   *daisies / valleys*
5   Notes swete of nightegales,
Uch° fowl song singeth.   *each*
The threstelcok him threteth oo.[5]
Away is huere° winter wo   *their*
When woderofe° springeth.   *woodruff*
10   This fowles singeth ferly fele,[6]

And wliteth on huere wynne wele,[7]
That all the wode° ringeth.   *wood*

The rose raileth° hire rode,°   *adorns / face, complexion*
The leves on the lighte° wode   *bright*
15   Waxen all with wille.[8]
The mone mandeth hire ble,[9]
The lilye is lossom° to se,   *lovely*
The fennel and the fille.°   *thyme*
Wowes this[10] wilde drakes,
20   Miles murgeth huere makes,[11]
Ase strem that striketh stille.[12]
Mody meneth, so doth mo;[13]
Ichot° ich am on of tho[14]   *I know*
For love that likes ille.°   *goes badly*

25   The mone mandeth hire light,
So doth the semly° sonne bright,   *lovely, beautiful*
When briddes singeth breme.°   *loudly*
Deawes donketh the dounes,[15]
Deores° with huere derne rounes[16]   *animals*
30   Domes for to deme.[17]
Wormes woweth under cloude,°   *earth*
Wimmen waxeth wounder[18] proude,
So well it wol hem seme.[19]
Yef me shall wonte wille of on,[20]
35   This wunne wele I wole forgon,[21]
And wiht° in wode be fleme.°   *quickly / in exile*
—LATER 13TH CENTURY–EARLY 14TH CENTURY

---

[1] *Wher-so … hie blyve* Wherever there is anyone sick, (let him)
hasten to that place.

[2] *That weldes heovene boures* That rules the bowers of heaven.

[3] *Thagh thou … floures* Even if you are fair and bright of face, your
flowers shall fade.

[4] *briddes roune* Song of birds.

[5] *The threstelcok … oo* The song thrush always quarrels.

[6] *This fowles … fele* These many birds sing wonderfully.

[7] *And wliteth … wele* And warble about their abundance of joys.

[8] *Waxen … wille* Grow with joy.

[9] *The mone … ble* The moon sends her light.

[10] *Wowes this* Woo these.

[11] *Miles … makes* Animals are happy with their mates.

[12] *Ase … stille* Like a stream that flows softly.

[13] *Mody … mo* The passionate man mourns, so do others.

[14] *ich … tho* I am one of those.

[15] *Deawes … dounes* Dews wet the hills.

[16] *Derne rounes* Mysterious cries.

[17] *Domes … deme* In making their judgments.

[18] *waxeth wounder* Grow wondrously.

[19] *hem seme* Appear to them.

[20] *Yef me … of on* If I shall lack pleasure of one.

[21] *This wunne …forgon* I will give up this abundance of joys.

Stond well, moder, under Rode

"Stond well, moder,° under Rode.°   *mother / rood, cross*
Behold thy sone with glade mode°—   *mind, heart*
Blithe° moder might thou be."   *joyful*
"Sone, how shulde I blithe stonde?
5 I se thine fet,° I se thine honde,°   *feet / hands*
Nailed to the harde Tree."

"Moder, do wey° thy wepinge.   *away*
I thole° deth for monkinde—   *suffer*
For my gult° thole I non."   *sin*
10 "Sone, I fele the dedestounde:°   *hour of death*
The swerd is at mine herte grounde,
That me bihet Simeon."[1]

"Moder, thou rewe all of thy bern:[2]
Thou woshe° away the blody tern°—   *wash / tears*
15 It doth me worse then my ded."°   *death*
"Sone, how may I teres werne?[3]
I se the blody stremes erne°   *run*
From thine herte to my fet."

"Moder, now I may thee seye,°   *say*
20 Betere is that ich one deye[4]
Then all monkunde° to helle go."   *mankind*
"Sone, I se thy body beswungen,°   *hung*
Fet and honden thourhout stongen°—   *pierced*
No wonder thah me be wo."[5]

25 "Moder, now I shall thee telle,
Yef I ne deye thou gost to helle:[6]
I thole ded for thine sake."
"Sone, thou art so meke and minde,[7]

30 Ne wit me naht, it is my kinde[8]
That I for thee this sorewe make."

"Moder, mercy, let me deye!
For Adam out of helle beye,°   *to redeem*
And his kun that is forlore."[9]
"Sone, what shall me to rede?[10]
35 My peine pineth me to dede.[11]
Lat° me deye thee before."   *let*

"Moder, now thou might well leren°   *learn*
Whet sorewe haveth that children beren,[12]
Whet sorewe it is with childe gon."
40 "Sorewe, iwis,° I con thee telle!   *indeed, truly*
Bote it be the pine of helle,
More sorewe wot° I non."   *know*

"Moder, rew of moder care,[13]
For now thou wost of moder fare,[14]
45 Thou thou be clene maiden-mon."[15]
"Sone, help at alle nede
Alle tho that to me grede,°   *cry out*
Maiden, wif and fol wimmon."°   *prostitute*

"Moder, may I no lengore° dwelle.   *longer*
50 The time is come I shall to helle.
The thridde° day I rise upon."   *third*
"Sone, I will with thee founden.°   *go*
I deye, iwis, for° thine wounden,°   *of / wounds*
So soreweful ded nes never non."[16]

55 When he ros tho° fell hire sorewe,   *then*
Hire blisse sprong the thridde morewe:°   *morrow, morning*
Blithe moder were thou tho.

---

[1] *The swerd ... Simeon* The sword that Simeon promised me has pierced the bottom of my heart. See Luke 2.25–35.

[2] *rewe ... bern* Have pity on your child.

[3] *how ... werne* How may I deny my tears?

[4] *Betere ... deye* It is better that I alone die.

[5] *No wonder ... wo* No wonder though I grieve.

[6] *Yef ... helle* If I do not die you will go to hell.

[7] *meke and minde* Gentle and thoughtful.

[8] *Ne wit ... kinde* Do not blame me, it is my nature.

[9] *kun ... forlore* Kin that is lost.

[10] *what shall ... rede* What shall I do?

[11] *peine ... dede* Pain tortures me to death.

[12] *sorewe ... beren* Sorrow they have who bear children.

[13] *rew ... care* Pity a mother's care.

[14] *wost ... fare* Know of motherhood.

[15] *clene maiden-mon* Pure virgin.

[16] *So soreweful ... non* There was never such a sorrowful death.

Levedy, for that ilke blisse,[1]
Besech thy sone of sunnes lisse—[2]
60   Thou be oure sheld ayein oure fo.[3]

Blessed be thou, full of blisse,
Let us never Hevene misse,
Thourh thy swete sones might.
Louerd,° for that ilke blod   *Lord*
65   That thou sheddest on the Rod,
Thou bring us into Hevene light.
Amen.
—LATER 13TH CENTURY–EARLY 14TH CENTURY

Maiden in the mor lay

Maiden in the mor° lay,   *wilds*
In the mor lay;
Sevenight° fulle,   *seven nights, one week*
Sevenight fulle,
5   Maiden in the mor lay;
In the mor lay,
Sevenightes fulle and a day.

Welle° was hire mete.°   *good / food*
What was hire mete?
10   The primerole[4] and the—
The primerole and the—
Welle was hire mete.
What was hire mete?
The primerole and the violet.

15   Welle was hire dring.°   *drink*
What was hire dring?
The chelde° water of the—   *cold*
The chelde water of the—
Welle was hire dring.
20   What was hire dring?
The chelde water of the welle-spring.

---

[1] *Levedy ... blisse* Lady, for that same joy.

[2] *of sunnes lisse* Relief of sins.

[3] *ayein oure fo* Against our foe.

[4] *primerole* Early spring flowers (e.g., daisy and primrose).

Welle was hire bowr.°   *chamber*
What was hire bowr?
The rede rose and the—
25   The rede rose and the—
Welle was hire bowr.
What was hire bowr?
The rede rose and the lilye flour.
—EARLIER 14TH CENTURY

I lovede a child of this cuntree

Were it undo that is ido,
I wolde bewar.[5]

I lovede a child of this cuntree,°   *country*
And so I wende° he had do me;[6]   *thought*
Now myself the sothe° I see,   *truth*
That he is far.°   *far away, remote*

He seide to me he wolde be true,
And change me for non other new;
Now I sikke° and am pale of hue,   *sigh*
10   For he is far.

He said his sawes° he wolde fulfille: *promises*
Therfore I let him have all his wille;
Now I sikke and mourn stille,[7]
For he is far.
—C. 14TH CENTURY

Erthe tok of erthe erthe with woh

Erthe tok° of erthe erthe with woh;°   *took / evil, wrong*
Erthe other erthe to the erthe droh;°   *pulled, added*
Erthe leide erthe in erthene throh.°   *grave, coffin*
Tho hevede erthe of erthe erthe inoh.[8]
—C. 14TH CENTURY

---

[5] *Were it ... bewar* If whatever done could be undone, I would be careful (possibly a refrain to be repeated following each stanza).

[6] *I lovede ... do me* I loved a young man of this country, and so I believed he also loved me.

[7] *stille* Continually.

[8] *Tho hevede ... inoh* Then had earth of earth, earth enough.

When Adam delf

When Adam delf,°   *dug*
  And Eve span,°   *spun*
Spir, if thou will spede,[1]
Whare was than
5   The pride of man
That now merres° his mede?°   *restricts / reward*
Of erth and slame,°   *slime*
Als° was Adam,   *as*
Maked° to noyes° and nede,   *made / misfortune*
10 Ar we als he
Maked to be,
Whil we this lif shall lede.
With I and E,
Born ar we,
15 Als Salomon us hight,°   *promised, called*
To travel here,
Whils we ar fere,°   *alive*
Als fowls° to the flight.   *birds*

In worlde we ware°   *were*
20 Cast for to care,
To° we be broght to wende°   *until / go*
Till wele or wa—[2]
An of tha twa—[3]
To won° withouten ende.   *live, dwell*
25 Forthy,° whils thou   *therefore*
May helpe thee now,
Amend thee and haf minde
When thou shall ga°   *go*
He bese thy fa[4]
30 That ar° was here thy frende.   *before*
With E and I,
I rede,° forthy,   *advise*
Thou think upon these three,
What we are,
35 And what we ware,
And what we shall be.

War thou als wise,
Praised in price,°   *excellence, esteem*
Als was Salomon,
40 Fairer fode°   *child*
Of bone and blode
Then° was Absalon,   *than*
Strengthy and strang°   *strong*
To wreke° thy wrang   *avenge*
45 Als ever was Sampson,
Thou ne might a day,
Na mare then thay,
Dede° withstand allon.[5]   *death*
With I and E,
50 Dede to thee
Shall com, als I thee kenne.°   *know, teach*
Thou ne wate[6]
In what state,
How, ne whare, ne when.

55 Of erth aght°   *anything*
That thee was raght[7]
Thou shall not have, I hete,°   *promise*
Bot seven fote
Therin to rote,°   *rot*
60 And thy windingshete.°   *winding-sheet, shroud*
Forthy gif
Whils thou may lif,
Or all gase that thou gete—
Thy gast fra God,
65 Thy godes olod,
Thy flesh fouled under fete.[8]
With I and E,
Siker° thou be   *certain*
That thy secutours°   *executor*
70 Of thee ne will rek,°   *care*
Bot skelk and skek[9]
Full boldly in thy bowrs.°   *dwellings*

---

[1] *Spir … spede* Ask, for your success/advantage.

[2] *Till wele or wa* To happiness or woe.

[3] *An of tha twa* One of those two.

[4] *He bese … fa* He will be your foe/enemy.

[5] *Thou ne might … allon* No more than they were, would you be able to stand in the way of death even for a day.

[6] *Thou ne wate* You do not know.

[7] *That thee … raght* That was given to you.

[8] *Forthy gif … under fete* Therefore give (what is due to God), while you still live, or all you receive will go—your spirit from God, your goods scattered, and your flesh trampled in the grave.

[9] *Bot skelk and skek* But mock and attack.

Of welth and wit
This shall be hitt,°   *be fulfilled*
75 In world that thou here wroght.
Reckon thou mon
And yelde reson
Of thing that thou here thoght.[1]
May no falas°   *fallacy, sophism*
80 Help in this case,
Ne counsel getes thou noght;
Gift ne grace
Nane thare gase,
Bot brok als thou hase boght.[2]
85 With I and E,
The Boke biddes thee,
Man, beware of thy werkes:
Terme° of the yere   *time*
Hase thou nan here,[3]
90 Thy mede bese ther thy merkes.[4]

What may this be
That I here se,
The fairehede° of thy face?   *beauty*
Thy ble° so bright,   *complexion*
95 Thy main,° thy might,   *strength*
Thy mouth that miry mas?[5]
All mon als was
To powder passe,
To dede, when thou gase;[6]
100 A grisely geste°   *guest*
Bese than thy breste
In armes til° enbrase.   *to*
With I and E,
Siker thou be
105 Thare es nane, I thee hete,°   *promise*
Of all thy kith°   *kin*

---

[1] *Reckon thou ... here thoght*   Think on yourself and give reasons for what you thought here.

[2] *Gift ne ... boght*   No gift or favor works there; you will get what you have bought (i.e., you'll get what you deserve).

[3] *Terme of ... here*   The end of your days does not come here (on earth).

[4] *Thy mede ... merkes*   Your reward will be final (?).

[5] *miry mas*   Rejoices.

[6] *All mon ... gase*   All men who have lived turn to dust in death, when you die (i.e., as you will also).

Wald slepe thee with
A night under shete.
—14TH CENTURY?

The Lady Dame Fortune is both frende and foe

The Lady Dame Fortune is both frende and foe:
Of pore hee maketh riche and ryche of pore also;[7]
Hee turneth woe to wele° and wele also to woe.   *happiness*
Ne trist noght to hir word, the whele turneth so.[8]
—MID-14TH CENTURY

I have a gentil cock

I have a gentil° cock,   *noble*
Croweth° me day: *who crows*
He doth° me risen erly   *makes*
My matins° for to say.   *morning prayers*

5 I have a gentil cock,
Comen he is of gret:°   *great or noble family*
His comb° is of° red coral,   *crest / like*
His tail is of jet.

I have a gentil cock,
10 Comen he is of kinde:
His comb is of red coral,
His tail is of inde.°   *indigo*

His legges ben of asor,[9]
So gentle and so smale;
15 His spores° arn of silver whit   *spurs*
Into the wortewale.[10]

His eynen° arn of cristal,   *eyes*
Loken° all in aumber:°   *set / amber*

---

[7] *Of pore ... pore also*   She makes the poor rich, and also the rich poor.

[8] *Ne trist ... turneth so*   Do not trust her word, because the wheel (Fortune's wheel) turns so.

[9] *ben of asor*   Are like azure.

[10] *Into the wortewale*   Up to the root (of the cock's spur).

And every night he percheth him
20   In mine ladye's chaumber.
   —EARLIER 15TH CENTURY

I sing of a maiden

I sing of a maiden
   That is makeles:°   *matchless, unique*
King of alle kinges
To here sone she ches.[1]

5   He cam also° stille°   *as / quietly, gently*
Ther his moder was,
As dew in Aprille
That falleth on the grass.

He cam also stille
10   To his moderes bowr,°   *chamber*
As dew in Aprille
That falleth on the flowr.

He cam also stille
Ther his moder lay,
15   As dew in Aprille
That falleth on the spray.

Moder and maiden
Was never non but she:[2]
Well may swich° a lady   *such*
20   Godes moder be.
   —EARLIER 15TH CENTURY

Adam lay ibounden

Adam lay ibounden,°   *bound*
   Bounden in a bond:
Foure thousand winter
Thought he not too long.
5   And all was for an apple,

---

[1] *To here … ches* She chose for her son.

[2] *Moder … but she* Never was any but she both mother and
maiden.

And apple that he tok,
As clerkes° finden   *scholars*
Wreten in here° book.   *their*

Ne hadde the apple take ben,[3]
10   The apple taken ben,
Ne hadde never our Lady
A ben Hevene Quen.[4]
Blissed be the time
That apple take was!
15   Therfore we moun° singen,   *may*
   "Deo gracias!"[5]
   —EARLIER 15TH CENTURY

Farewell this world, I take my leve forever

Farewell this world, I take my leve forever,
   I am arrestid° to appere affore°   *at rest, waiting / before*
      Godis face.
O mercyfull God, Thow knowest that I had lever°   *rather*
Than all this worldis good to haue an owre° space   *hour*
5   For to make aseth° for my gret trespace. *amends*
My harte, alas, is brokyn for that sorow.
Som be this day that shall not be tomorow.

This world, I see, is but a chery fayre,[6]
All thyngis passith and so moste I algate.°   *inevitably*
10   This day I satt full royally in a chayre
Tyll sotyll° deth knokkid at my gate   *subtle*
And vnavised° he said to me, "Chekmate!"   *unexpected*
Loo,° how sodynly he maketh a devorce°   *look / separation*
And wormes to fede° here he hath layde my
      corse.°   *feed / corpse*
15   Speke softe, ye folkis,° for I am layde a° slepe. *folks / to*
I haue my dreme,° in triste is myche   *dream, vision*
      treason.[7]

---

[3] *Ne hadde … ben* Had the apple never been taken.

[4] *A ben … Quene* Been Queen of Heaven.

[5] *"Deo gracias!"* I.e., *Deo gratias.* Latin: Thanks be to God!

[6] *is but … fayre* Is only a cherry festival (i.e., is passing or transient,
like the time of cherry harvest).

[7] *in triste … treason* Proverbial: "in trust is much treason," i.e.,
confidence is often deceived.

From dethis° hold fayn° wold I make a lepe   *death's / glad*
But my wisdom ys torned into feble° reason: *weak*
I see this worldis joye lastith but a season.
20   Wold God I had remembrid this beforne!
I say no more but beware of an horne.°   *summons (?)*

This febyll world, so false and so vnstable,
Promoteth his lovers but for a lytill while,
But at last he geveth them a bable°   *bauble, toy*
25   Whan his payntid trowth° is torned into
         gile.°   *painted truth / deceit*
Experyence cawsith° me the trowth to
         compile,°   *causes / gather*
Thynkyng this: to° late, alas, that I began;   *too*
For foly and hope disseyveth° many a man.   *tricks, deceives*

Farewell my frendis, the tide° abidith°   *time / waits for*
         no man;
30   I moste departe hens° and so shall ye,   *hence*
But in this passage° the beste songe that I can   *journey*
Is Requiem Eternam.[1] I pray God grant it me.
Whan I haue endid all myn adversite°   *adversity*
Graunte me in paradise to haue a mancyon,°   *mansion*
35   That shede his blode for my redempcion.
Beati mortui qui in Domino moriuntur.
Humiliatus sum vermis.[2]

         —15TH CENTURY

To dy, to dy. What haue I

To dy°, to dy. What° haue I   *die / how*
Offendit,° that deth° is so
         hasty?   *offended, displeased / death*

O marcyfull God, maker of all mankynd,
What menyth° dethe in hys mynd   *intends, means*
5   And I so young of age?
Now deth is unkynd
For he seyth, "Man, stop thy wynde."°   *complaint*
Thus he doth rage.

         —LATE 15TH–EARLY 16TH CENTURY

---

[1] *Requiem Eternam*   Latin: Eternal rest (a requiem is a mass sung for
the dead).

[2] *Beati … vermis*   Latin: Blessed are the dead who die in the Lord.
I am humbled by (or with) worms.

Bring us in good ale

Bring us in good ale, and bring us in good ale,
Fore our blessed Lady sak,° bring us in   *sake*
   good ale.

Bring us in no browne bred, fore that is mad of brane;[3]
Nor bring us in no whit bred, fore therin is no game:
5   But bring us in good ale.

Bring us in no befe, for ther is many bones;
But bring us in good ale, for that goth downe at
   ones,°   *once*
And bring us in good ale.

Bring us in no bacon, for that is passing fat;
10   But bring us in good ale, and give us inought°   *enough*
   of that,
And bring us in good ale.

Bring us in no mutton, for that is ofte lene;[4]
Nor bring us in no tripes, for they be seldom clene:
But bring us in good ale.

15   Bring us in no egges, for ther ar many shelles;
But bring us in good ale, and give us nothing elles,°   *else*
And bring us in good ale.

Bring us in no butter, for therin ar many heres;°   *hairs*
Nor bring us in no pigges flesh, for that will mak
   us bores:°   *boars*
20   But bring us in good ale.

Bring us in no podinges, for therin is all gotes blod;[5]
Nor bring us in no venison, for that is not for our good:
But bring us in good ale.

Bring us in no capon's° flesh, for that is ofte
   der;°   *fowl's / dear, costly*

---

[3] *mad of brane*   Made of bran.

[4] *ofte lene*   Often lean.

[5] *gotes blod*   I.e., goat's blood puddings.

25 Nor bring us in no dokes° flesh for they slobber in
    the mer:°   *ducks' / pond*
But bring us in good ale.
  —LATER 15TH CENTURY

Of all creatures women be best

Of all creatures women be best,
Cuius contrarium verum est.[1]

In every place ye may well see
That women be trewe° as tirtill° on tree,   *true / turtledove*
5 Not liberal° in langage but ever in secree,[2]   *licentious*
And gret joye amonge them is for to be.

The stedfastnes of women will never be don,
So gentil,° so curtes,° they be everichon,[3] *noble / courteous*
Meke° as a lambe, still° as a stone,   *meek / quiet*
10 Croked° nor crabbed° find ye none. *perverse / twisted*

Men be more cumbers° a thousandfold, *troublesome*
And I mervail° how they dare be so bold *marvel*
Against women for to hold,
Seeing them so pascient,° softe and cold. *patient*

15 For tell a woman all your counsaile
And she can kepe it wonderly well:
She had lever° go quik° to hell *rather / alive*
Than to her neighbour she wold it tell.

Now say well by women or elles° be still, *else*
20 For they never displesed man by ther will:
To be angry or wroth they can no skill,[4]
For I dare say they think non° ill. *no*

Trow ye that women list to smater,[5]
Or against ther husbondes for to clater?° *make noise*

---

[1] *Cuius ... est* Latin: The opposite of this is true.

[2] *in secree* In secret, i.e., discreet.

[3] *they be everychon* Is each one.

[4] *can no skill* Are completely unable.

[5] *Trow ye ... smater* Do you believe that women enjoy chattering?

25 Nay! they had lever fast, bred and water,
Then for to dele° in suche a matter. *deal, act*

To the tavern they will not go,
Nor to the alehous never the mo,° *more*
For, God wot,° ther hartes wold be wo° *knows / sorry*
30 To spende ther husbondes money so.
  —LATER 15TH CENTURY

My lefe is faren in a lond[6]

My lefe is faren in a lond—
  Alas! why is she so?
And I am so sore bound
I may nat com her to.
5 She hath my hert in hold,° *imprisoned*
Where-ever she ride or go,
With trew love a thousandfold.
  —LATER 15TH CENTURY

A god and yet a man

A god and yet a man,
  A maide and yet a mother:
Wit° wonders what wit can *human knowledge, wit*
  Conceave this or the other.

5 A god and can he die?
  A dead man, can he live?
What wit can well reply?
  What reason reason give?

God, Truth itself, doth teach it.
10 Man's wit senkis° too far under *sinks*
By reason's power to reach it:
  Believe and leave to wonder.
  —16TH CENTURY

---

[6] *My lefe ... lond* My love has gone away (to another land). This lyric is referred to in Chaucer's *Nun's Priest's Tale* (1.112).

THE CRISES OF THE FOURTEENTH CENTURY

CONTEXTS

Britain in the fourteenth century suffered an unprecedented series of crises and catastrophes. The first of these was the great famine of 1315-18. Whereas we tend to think of famine as resulting from drought, the famine of the early fourteenth century was the result of too much water rather than too little. In Britain, as in the rest of Europe, a pattern of extraordinarily wet weather was repeated for several years; as the chronicle account below details, rot was followed by hunger, pestilence, and universal hardship.

The next great upheaval was the series of conflicts that eventually became known as the Hundred Years' War. Since the time of Henry II in the early thirteenth century, the English had held considerable territory in what is now France, and English kings continued to nurture ambitions of increasing their power on the other side of the English Channel. The French nobles' refusal to recognize Edward III's claim to the French throne acted as a spark to ignite conflict, and hostilities broke out in 1337 which would not truly end until 1453. With the help of the new technology of the longbow English forces at first enjoyed great success—most notably at the battles of Crécy (1346) and Poitiers (1356) under the leadership of Edward the Black Prince. Under the leadership of Henry V they inflicted a massive defeat upon the French armies at Agincourt (1415), but with the death of Henry V in 1422 and the extraordinary rise to military glory of the sixteen-year-old peasant Jeanne D'Arc (who is credited for leading the French to victory at Orléans in 1429) the tide of the conflict turned. By 1450 the English had abandoned almost all their possessions on the Continent, and the map of France had come to resemble closely its present-day shape. France had been left exhausted and impoverished by the struggle, but the events of the previous century helped to nurture a national myth that before long carried the French nation to new prosperity. The war gave rise to a national mythology in England too; the fact that the British had lost a vast expanse of territory was largely forgotten, while the famous victories of the Black Prince and of Henry V provided an ongoing source of nourishment for national pride.

The upheaval caused by the plague known as the Black Death that swept across Europe in the 1340s turned out to be just as long-lasting as that of the Hundred Years' War—and even more severe in its effects. The Black Death (so named for the color of the sores it brought with it) probably originated in China in 1320. Initially its spread was gradual, but once it reached the Crimean port of Calla in 1346 it began to spread much more rapidly; by the end of 1347 it was devastating much of continental Europe, and in the summer of 1348 it reached Britain. In many areas of Europe close to half the population succumbed; in some areas the figure exceeded seventy percent. The toll in Britain is believed to be in the range of a third of the people dead; not until a century later did the population begin to recover substantially. As the documents below indicate, the effects of such a vast and sudden demographic event were wide-ranging. One of the most significant was a persistent shortage of labor, which in turn contributed to scarcities and price increases. The almost universal response from the authorities was to attempt to impose wage and price controls, with mixed results; the aftershocks of the plague continued to ripple through the economic system, contributing significantly to the destabilizing and eventual disappearance of the feudal order.

Both the Hundred Years' War and the Black Death were underlying causes for another great fourteenth-century upheaval—the Uprising of 1381, sometimes called the Peasants' Revolt (though many non-peasants were involved). The shortage of labor caused by the Black Death—and the attempts of the authorities to suppress it, most notably Edward III's 1351 Statute of Laborers—had created a climate of restlessness among the peasantry. Thirty years on, when Parliament responded to the mounting costs of the wars with France by imposing a new tax on all adults (termed a "poll tax"), the action sparked the first widespread rebellion of commoners in English history. Though the revolt was suppressed, in its wake the peasantry were emboldened in dealing with their lords; feudal relationships of outright servitude began to die out, replaced by lease-hold arrangements under the terms of which peasants paid rent for the land they farmed.

⌘ ⌘ ⌘

The Great Famine

The chronicle excerpt below is of interest for its comments about such matters as price controls and relations between the Scots and the English as well as for its description of the effects of the famine itself.

from Anonymous (the "Monk of Malmesbury"), *Life of Edward the Second* (fourteenth century)

In this parliament [of February–March, 1315], because merchants going about the country selling victuals charged excessively, the earls and barons, looking to the welfare of the state, appointed a remedy for this malady; they ordained a fixed price for oxen, pigs and sheep, for fowls, chickens, and pigeons, and for other common foods. ... These matters were published throughout the land, and publicly proclaimed in shire courts and boroughs. ...

By certain portents the hand of God appears to be raised against us. For in the past year there was such plentiful rain that men could scarcely harvest the corn or bring it safely to the barn. In the present year worse has happened. For the floods of rain have rotted almost all the seed, so that the prophecy of Isaiah might seem now to be fulfilled; for he says that "ten acres of vineyard shall yield one little measure and thirty bushels of seed shall yield three bushels":[1] and in many places the hay lay so long under water that it could neither be mown nor gathered. Sheep generally died and other animals were killed in a sudden plague. It is greatly to be feared that if the Lord finds us incorrigible after these visitations, he will destroy at once both men and beasts; and I firmly believe that unless the English Church had

interceded for us, we should have perished long ago. ...

After the feast of Easter [in 1316] the dearth of corn[2] was much increased. Such a scarcity has not been seen in our time in England, nor heard of for a hundred years. For the measure of wheat sold in London and the neighboring places for forty pence, and in other less thickly populated parts of the country thirty pence was a common price. Indeed during this time of scarcity a great famine appeared, and after the famine came a severe pestilence, of which many thousands died in many places. I have even heard it said by some, that in Northumbria dogs and horses and other unclean things were eaten. For there, on account of the frequent raids of the Scots, work is more irksome, as the accursed Scots despoil the people daily of their food. Alas, poor England! You who once helped other lands from your abundance, now poor and needy are forced to beg. Fruitful land is turned into a salt-marsh; the inclemency of the weather destroys the fatness of the land; corn is sown and tares[3] are brought forth. All this comes from the wickedness of the inhabitants. Spare, O Lord, spare thy people! For we are a scorn and a derision to them who are around us. Yet those who are wise in astrology say that these storms in the heavens have happened naturally; for Saturn, cold and heedless, brings rough weather that is useless to the seed; in the ascendant now for three years he has completed his course, and mild Jupiter duly succeeds him. Under Jupiter these floods of rain will cease, the valleys will grow rich in corn, and the fields will be filled with abundance. For the Lord shall give that which is good and our land shall yield her increase. ...

---

[1] *ten acres ... bushels* Cf. Isaiah 5.10.

[2] *corn* Grain.

[3] *tares* Weeds.

[In 1318] the dearth that had so long plagued us ceased, and England became fruitful with a manifold abundance of good things. A measure of wheat, which the year before was sold for forty pence, was now freely offered to the buyer for sixpence. . . .

The Hundred Years' War

The *Chronicle* of Jean Froissart of Valenciennes is among the most valuable historical records we possess of the course of fourteenth-century history. Froissart (c. 1337–c. 1404) was in direct contact with many of the nobility on both sides of the conflict between France and England. His *Chronicle* appeared in four volumes between 1370 and 1400, and survives in over one hundred manuscript copies. The excerpt below describes the battle fought at Crécy in 1346, beginning with a French lord's unsuccessful attempt to give the French King, Philip VI, good tactical advice.

The second excerpt below may perhaps be regarded as an early equivalent of a newspaper; it is from a letter sent by Edward the Black Prince to the people of London, recounting the story of the English victory at Poitiers (1356).

from Jean Froissart, *Chronicle* (late fourteenth century)

The lord Moyne said [to the king of France], "Sir, I will speak, since it pleases you to order me, but with the assistance of my companions. We have advanced far enough to reconnoitre your enemies. Know, then, that they are drawn up in three battalions and are awaiting you. I would advise, for my part (submitting, however, to better counsel), that you halt your army here and quarter them for the night; for before the rear shall come up and the army be properly drawn out, it will be very late. Your men will be tired and in disorder, while they will find your enemies fresh and properly arrayed. On the morrow, you may draw up your army more at your ease and may reconnoitre at leisure on what part it will be most advantageous to begin the attack; for, be assured, they will wait for you."

The King commanded that it should be so done; and the two marshals rode, one towards the front, and the other to the rear, crying out, "Halt banners, in the name of God and St. Denis." Those that were in the front halted; but those behind said they would not halt until they were as far forward as the front. When the front perceived the rear pushing on, they pushed forward; and neither the king nor the marshals could stop them, but they marched on without any order until they came in sight of their enemies. As soon as the foremost rank saw them, they fell back at once in great disorder, which alarmed those in the rear, who thought they had been fighting. There was then space and room enough for them to have passed forward, had they been willing to do so. Some did so, but others remained behind.

All the roads between Abbeville and Crécy were covered with common people, who, when they had come within three leagues of their enemies, drew their swords, crying out, "Kill, kill"; and with them were many great lords who were eager to make show of their courage. There is no man, unless he had been present, who can imagine, or describe truly, the confusion of that day, especially the bad management and disorder of the French, whose troops were beyond number.

The English, who were drawn up in three divisions and seated on the ground, on seeing their enemies advance, arose boldly and fell into their ranks. That of the Prince was the first to do so, whose archers were formed in the manner of a portcullis, or harrow, and the men-at-arms in the rear.[1] The earls of Northampton and Arundel, who commanded the second division, had posted themselves in good order on his wing to assist and succor the Prince, if necessary.

You must know that these kings, dukes, earls, barons, and lords of France did not advance in any regular order, but one after the other, or in any way most pleasing to themselves. As soon as the King of France came in sight of the English his blood began to boil, and he cried out to his marshals, "Order the

---

[1] *archers were formed … in the rear* A portcullis (a kind of gate) and a harrow (a farming implement) both have prongs or teeth; in this formation, lines of bowmen would probably have advanced like the arms of a V ahead of the main troops. Lines of bowmen were roughly "vertical" in relation to the "horizontal" line of men-at-arms.

Genoese[1] forward, and begin the battle, in the name of God and St. Denis." There were about fifteen thousand Genoese cross-bowmen; but they were quite fatigued, having marched on foot that day six leagues, completely armed, and with their cross-bows. They told the constable that they were not in a fit condition to do any great things that day in battle. The Earl of Alençon, hearing this, said, "This is what one gets by employing such scoundrels, who fail when there is any need for them."

During this time a heavy rain fell, accompanied by thunder and a very terrible eclipse of the sun; and before this rain a great flight of crows hovered in the air over all those battalions, making a loud noise. Shortly afterwards it cleared up and the sun shone very brightly; but the Frenchmen had it in their faces, and the English at their backs.

When the Genoese were somewhat in order they approached the English and set up a loud shout in order to frighten them; but the latter remained quite still and did not seem to hear it. They then set up a second shout and advanced a little forward; but the English did not move. They hooted a third time, advancing with their cross-bows presented, and began to shoot. The English archers then advanced one step forward and shot their arrows with such force and quickness that it seemed as if it snowed.

When the Genoese felt these arrows, which pierced their arms, heads, and through their armor, some of them cut the strings of their cross-bows, others flung them on the ground, and all turned about and retreated, quite discomfited. The French had a large body of men-at-arms on horseback, richly dressed, to support the Genoese. The King of France, seeing them fall back, cried out, "Kill me those scoundrels; for they stop up our road, without any reason." You would then have seen the above-mentioned men-at-arms lay about them, killing all that they could of these runaways.

The English continued shooting as vigorously and quickly as before. Some of their arrows fell among the horsemen, who were sumptuously equipped, and, killing and wounding many, made them caper and fall among the Genoese, so that they were in such confusion they could never rally again. In the English army there were some Cornish- and Welshmen on foot who had armed themselves with large knives. These, advancing through the ranks of the men-at-arms and archers, who made way for them, came upon the French when they were in this danger and, falling upon earls, barons, knights and squires, slew many, at which the king of England was afterwards much exasperated.[2]

From a fifteenth-century manuscript of
Froissart's *Chronicles*, "The Battle of Crécy,"
from a fifteenth-century manuscript of Froissart's *Chronicles*,

"The Battle of Poitiers."

---

[1] *Genoese* The Genoese (from Genoa, in Italy) are here fighting for the French as mercenaries; hence the comment of the Earl of Alençon, below.

[2] *slew many ... much exasperated* It would have been typical at this time to capture aristocratic enemy fighters and return them for ransom, rather than killing them.

Late after vespers,[1] the King of France had not more about him than sixty men, every one included. Sir John of Hainault, who was of the number, had once remounted the king; for the latter's horse had been killed under him by an arrow. He said to the king, "Sir, retreat while you have an opportunity, and do not expose yourself so needlessly. If you have lost this battle, another time you will be the conqueror." After he had said this, he took the bridle of the king's horse and led him off by force; for he had before entreated him to retire.

The king rode on until he came to the castle of La Broyes, where he found the gates shut, for it was very dark. The king ordered the governor of it to be summoned. He came upon the battlements and asked who it was that called at such an hour. The king answered, "Open, open, governor; it is the fortune of France." The governor, hearing the king's voice, immediately descended, opened the gate, and let down the bridge. The king and his company entered the castle; but he had with him only five barons—Sir John Hainault, the lord Charles of Montmorency, the lord of Beaujeu, the lord of Aubigny, and the lord of Montfort. The king would not bury himself in such a place as that, but, having taken some refreshments, set out again with his attendants about midnight, and rode on, under the direction of guides who were well acquainted with the country, until, about daybreak, he came to Amiens, where he halted.

This Saturday the English never quitted their ranks in pursuit of anyone, but remained on the field, guarding their positions and defending themselves against all who attacked them. The battle was ended at the hour of vespers. When, on this Saturday night, the English heard no more hooting or shouting, nor any more crying out to particular lords, or their banners, they looked upon the field as their own and their enemies as beaten.

They made great fires and lighted torches because of the darkness of the night. King Edward [III] then came down from his post, who all that day had not put on his helmet, and, with his whole battalion, advanced to the prince of Wales [Edward the "Black Prince"], whom he embraced in his arms and kissed, and said, "Sweet son, God give you good preference. You are my son, for most loyally have you acquitted yourself this day. You are worthy to be a sovereign." The prince bowed down very low and humbled himself, giving all honor to the king his father.

The English, during the night, made frequent thanksgivings to the Lord for the happy outcome of the day, and without rioting; for the King had forbidden all riot or noise.

from Prince Edward, Letter to the People of London (1356)

Very dear and very much beloved: As concerning news in the parts where we are, know that since the time when we informed our most dread lord and father, the King [Edward III], that it was our purpose to ride forth against the enemies in the parts of France, we took our road through the country of Périgueux and of Limousin, and straight on towards Bourges in Vienne, where we expected to have found the [French] King's son, the count of Poitiers. ...[2]

And then our people pursued them as far as Chauvigny, full three leagues further; for which reason we were obliged that day to take up our quarters as near to that place as we could, that we might collect our men. And on the morrow we took our road straight towards the king, and sent out our scouts, who found him with his army; set himself[3] in battle array at one league from Poitiers, in the fields; and we went as near to him as we could take up our post, we ourselves on foot and in battle array, and ready to fight with him.

Where came the said Cardinal [Talleyrand], requesting very earnestly for a little respite, that so there might parley together certain persons of either side, and so attempt to bring about an understanding and good peace; the which he undertook that he would bring about to a good end. Whereupon we took counsel, and granted him his request; upon which there were ordered

---

[1] *vespers* The hour for evening service in monastic practice; probably around 6:00 in the evening. This is one of the "canonical hours" used for telling time in monasteries.

[2] *the King's son ... Poitiers* I.e., the French king, who at this time was Jean II, son of Philip VI; his son, the Dauphin, was later to become Charles V.

[3] set himself I.e., the French king.

certain persons of the one side and the other to treat upon this matter; which treating was of no effect. And then the said Cardinal wished to obtain a truce, by way of putting off the battle at his pleasure; to which truce we would not assent. And the French asked that certain knights on the one side and the other should take equal shares, so that the battle might not in any manner fail: and in such manner was that day delayed; and the battalions on the one side and the other remained all night, each one in its place, and until the morrow, about half prime;[1] and as to some troops that were between the said main armies, neither would give any advantage in commencing the attack upon the other. And for default of victuals, as well as for other reasons, it was agreed that we should take our way, flanking them, in such manner that if they wished for battle or to draw towards us, in a place that was not very much to our disadvantage, we should be the first; and so forthwith it was done. Whereupon battle was joined, on [September 19,] the eve of the day before St. Matthew; and, God be praised for it, the enemy was discomfited, and the King was taken, and his son; and a great number of other great people were both taken and slain; as our very dear bachelor Messire Neele Lorraine, our chamberlain, the bearer hereof, who has very full knowledge thereon, will know how to inform and show you more fully, as we are not able to write to you. To him you should give full faith and credence; and may our Lord have you in his keeping. Given under our privy seal, at Bordeaux, the 22nd day of October.

The Black Death

The letter excerpted below by Ralph of Shrewsbury, Bishop of Bath and a distinguished scholar as well as an administrator, was sent to several of his subordinates just after the plague had begun. The second excerpt, from the *Chronicle* of Henry Knighton, provides a much more wide-ranging sense of the devastation wrought by the Black Death.

from Ralph of Shrewsbury, Letter (17 August 1348)

… Since the disaster of such a pestilence has come from the eastern parts to a neighboring kingdom, it is greatly to be feared, and being greatly to be feared, it is to be prayed devoutly and without ceasing that such a pestilence not extend its poisonous growth to the inhabitants of this kingdom, and torment and consume them.

Therefore, to each and all of you we mandate, with firm enjoining, that in your churches you publicly announce this present mandate in the vulgar tongue[2] at opportune times, and that in the bowels of Jesus Christ you exhort your subordinates—regular, secular, parishioners, and others—or have them exhorted by others, to appear before the Face of the Lord in confession, with psalms and other works of charity.

Remember the destruction that was deservedly pronounced by prophetic utterance on those who, doing penance, were mercifully freed from the destruction threatened by the judgment of God. …

from Henry Knighton, *Chronicle* (1378–96)

In that year and the following year there was a universal mortality of men throughout the world. It began first in India, then in Tarsus, then it reached the Saracens and finally the Christians and Jews. …

On a single day 1,312 people died in Avignon, according to a calculation made in the pope's presence. On another day more than 400 died. 358 of the Dominicans in Provence died during Lent. At Montpellier only seven friars survived out of 140. At Magdalen seven survived out of 160, which is quite enough. From 140 Minorites [i.e., Franciscans] at Marseilles not one remained to carry the news to the rest. … At the same time the plague raged in England. It began in the autumn in various places and after racing across the country it ended at the same time in the following year.

… Then the most lamentable plague penetrated the coast through Southampton and came to Bristol, and virtually the whole town was wiped out. It was as if sudden death had marked them down beforehand, for few lay sick for more than two or three days, or even for

---

[1] *half prime* About 9:30 in the morning. Like vespers, prime is part of the monastic way of measuring time, the "canonical hours."

[2] *vulgar tongue* I.e., the vernacular (the language of the land) rather than Latin.

half a day. Cruel death took just two days to burst out all over a town. At Leicester, in the little parish of St. Leonard, more than 380 died; in the parish of Holy Cross more than 400; in the parish of St. Margaret 700; and a great multitude in every parish. The Bishop of Lincoln sent word through the whole diocese, giving general power to every priest (among the regular as well as the secular clergy) to hear confession and grant absolution with full and complete authority except only in cases of debt.[1] In such cases the penitent, if it lay within his power, ought to make satisfaction while he lived, but certainly others should do it from his goods after his death. Similarly the Pope granted plenary remission of all sins to those at the point of death, the absolution to be for one time only, and the right to each person to choose his confessor as he wished.[2] This concession was to last until the following Easter.

In the same year there was a great murrain[3] of sheep throughout the realm, so much so that in one place more than 5,000 sheep died in a single pasture, and their bodies were so corrupt that no animal or bird would touch them. And because of the fear of death everything fetched a low price. For there were very few people who cared for riches, or indeed for anything else. A man could have a horse previously valued at 40s. for half a mark, a good fat ox for 4s., a cow for 12d., a bullock for 6d., a fat sheep for 4d., a ewe for 3d., a lamb for 2d., a large pig for 5d., a stone of wool for 9d. And sheep and cattle roamed unchecked through the fields and through the standing corn, and there was no one to chase them and round them up. For want of watching animals died in uncountable numbers in the fields and in bye-ways and hedges throughout the whole country;

for there was so great a shortage of servants and laborers that there was no one who knew what needed to be done. There was no memory of so inexorable and fierce a mortality since the time of Vortigern, King of the Britons, in whose time, as Bede testifies in his *De gestis Anglorum*,[4] there were not enough living to bury the dead. In the following autumn it was not possible to hire a reaper for less than 8d. and his food, or a mower for 12d. with his food.[5] For which reason many crops rotted unharvested in the fields; but in the year of the pestilence, as mentioned above, there was so great an abundance of all types of grain that no one cared.

The Scots, hearing of the cruel plague of the English, declared that it had befallen them through the revenging hand of God, and they took to swearing "by the foul death of England"—or so the common report resounded in the ears of the English. And thus the Scots, believing that the English were overwhelmed by the terrible vengeance of God, gathered in the forest of Selkirk with the intention of invading the whole realm of England. The fierce mortality came upon them, and the sudden cruelty of a monstrous death winnowed the Scots. Within a short space of time around 5,000 died, and the rest, weak and strong alike, decided to retreat to their own country. But the English, following, surprised them and killed many of them. …

After the aforesaid pestilence many buildings of all sizes in every city fell into total ruin for want of inhabitants. Likewise, many villages and hamlets were deserted, with no house remaining in them, because everyone who had lived there was dead, and indeed many of these villages were never inhabited again. In the following winter there was such a lack of workers in all areas of activity that it was thought that there had hardly ever been such a shortage before; for a man's farm animals and other livestock wandered about without a shepherd and all his possessions were left unguarded. And as a result all essentials were so expensive that something which had previously cost 1d. was now worth 4d. or 5d.

---

[1] *among the regular … cases of debt* "Regular" clergy are those bound by a rule of communal life (i.e., most commonly, monks), who ordinarily would not have the "care of souls," that is, the duty of hearing confession or other interactions with lay people. That was the job of the "secular" clergy, the clergy who lived and worked in the outside world, such as parish priests or bishops.

[2] *the right … as he wished* Like the call for regular clergy to take on the care of souls, the concessions on remission (i.e., forgiveness) of sins and on the right to choose a confessor reflect the church's anxiety about the salvation of the faithful in a time of crisis. Ordinarily one would have been expected to confess to one's parish priest.

[3] *murrain* Infectious disease of livestock.

[4] *Bede … Anglorum De Gestis Anglorum (On the Deeds of the English)* by Venerable Bede (673–735), English scholar.

[5] *In the following autumn … with his food* Before the Black Death, laborers were typically hired for 2 or 3 pence per day, so these wages represent a roughly four-fold increase. (The abbreviation "d." is of the Latin *denarius*, or penny.)

Confronted by this shortage of workers and the scarcity of goods the great men of the realm, and the lesser landowners who had tenants, remitted part of the rent so that their tenants did not leave. Some remitted half the rent, some more and some less; some remitted it for two years, some for three and some for one—whatever they could agree with their tenants. Likewise those whose tenants held by the year, by the performance of labor services (as is customary in the case of serfs), found that they had to release and remit such works, and either pardon rents completely or levy them on easier terms, otherwise houses would be irretrievably ruined and land left uncultivated. And all victuals and other necessities were extremely dear.

Fourteenth-century manuscript: plague victims.

The Uprising of 1381

The following excerpts from a 1350 set of London wage and price regulations and from the Statute of Laborers imposed the following year by King Edward III provide some sense of the economic background for the Uprising of 1381 (or "The Peasants' Revolt"). As the Statute of 1363 demonstrates, regulations continued to tighten thereafter in an attempt to maintain traditional social distinctions between ranks, which were threatened by the economic upheaval that followed the plague. The passage by Froissart recounts a sermon by one of the leading figures of the rebellion, John Ball, while the extended passage

from the *Chronicle* of Henry Knighton, a canon of St. Mary's Abbey in the city of Leicester, provides a vivid account of the climax of the rebellion.

from Regulations, London (1350)

To amend and redress the damages and grievances which the good folks of the city, rich and poor, have suffered and received within the past year, by reason of masons, carpenters, plasterers, tilers, and all manner of laborers, who take immeasurably more than they have been wont to take, by assent of Walter Turk, mayor, the aldermen, and all the commonalty of the city, the points under-written are ordained, to be held and firmly observed for ever; that is to say:

In the first place, that the masons, between the Feasts of Easter and St. Michael,[1] shall take no more by the working-day than 6d., without victuals or drink; and from the Feast of St. Michael to Easter, for the working-day, 5d. And upon Feast Days, when they do not work, they shall take nothing. And for the making or mending of their implements they shall take nothing.

Also, that the carpenters shall take, for the same time, in the same manner.

Also, that the plasterers shall take the same as the masons and carpenters take.

Also, that the tilers shall take for the working-day, from the Feast of Easter to St. Michael 5 ½ d., and from the Feast of St. Michael 4 ½ d.

Also, that the laborers shall take in the first half year 3 ½ d., and in the other half 3d....

Also, that the tailors shall take for making a gown, garnished with fine cloth and silk, 18d.

Also, for a man's gown, garnished with linen thread and with buckram, 14d.

Also, for a coat and hood, 10d.

Also, for a long gown for a woman, garnished with fine cloth or with silk, 2s. 6d.

Also, for a pair of sleeves, to change, 4d.

Also, that the porters of the city shall not take more for their labor than they used to take in olden time, on pain of imprisonment.

---

[1] *St. Michael* The Feast of St. Michael the Archangel is held on September 29.

Also, that no vintner shall be so daring as to sell the gallon of wine of Vernaccia for more than 2s., and wine of Crete, wine of the River, Piement, and Clare, and Malveisin, at 16d. ...

Also, that a pair of spurs shall be sold for 6d., and a better pair for 8d., and the best at 10d. or 12d., at the very highest.

Also, that a pair of gloves of sheepskin shall be sold for one penny, and a better pair at 1 ½ d., and a pair at 2d., so going on to the very highest.

Also, that the shearmen shall not take more than they were wont to take; that is to say, for a short cloth 12d., and for a long cloth 2s.; and for a cloth of striped serge, for getting rid of the stripes, and shearing the same, 2s.

Also, that the farriers[1] shall not take more than they were wont to take before the time of the pestilence, on pain of imprisonment and heavy ransom; that is to say, for a horse-shoe of six nails 1½ 2d., and for a horse-shoe of eight nails 2d.; and for taking off a horse-shoe of six nails or of eight, one halfpenny; and for the shoe of a courser 2 ½ d., and the shoe of a charger 3d.; and for taking off the shoe of a courser or charger, one penny.

Also, if any workman or laborer will not work or labor as is above ordained, let him be taken and kept in prison until he shall have found good surety, and have been sworn to do that which is so ordained. And if anyone shall absent himself, or go out of the city, because he does not wish to work and labor, as is before mentioned, and afterwards by chance be found within the city, let him have imprisonment for a quarter of the year, and forfeit his chattels which he has in the city, and then let him find surety, and make oath, as is before stated. And if he will not do this, let him forswear the city for ever.

from Statute of Laborers (1351)

Because a great part of the people and especially of the workers and servants has now died in the pestilence, some, seeing the needs of the masters and the scarcity of servants, are not willing to serve unless they receive excessive wages, and others, rather than gain their living through labor, prefer to beg in idleness. We,

considering the grave inconveniences which might come from such a shortage, especially of ploughmen and such laborers, have held deliberation and discussion concerning this with the prelates and nobles and other learned men sitting by us, by whose consenting counsel we have seen fit to ordain that every man and woman of our kingdom of England, of whatever condition, whether serf or free, who is able bodied and below the age of 60 years, not living from trade or carrying on a definite craft, or having private means of living or private land to cultivate, and not serving another—if such a person is sought after to serve in a suitable service appropriate to that person's status, that person shall be bound to serve whomever has seen fit so to offer such employment, and shall take only the wages, liveries, reward or salary usually given in that place in the twentieth year of our reign in England, or the usual year of the five or six preceding ones. This is provided so that in thus retaining their service, lords are preferred before others by their serfs or land tenants, so that such lords nevertheless thus retain as many as shall be necessary, but not more. And if any man or woman, being thus sought after for service, will not do this, the fact being proven by two faithful men before the sheriffs or the bailiffs of our Lord the King, or the constables of the town where this happens to be done, immediately through them, or some one of them, that person shall be taken and sent to the next jail, and remain there in strict custody until offering security for serving in the aforesaid form. And if a reaper or mower, or other worker or servant, of whatever standing or condition, who is retained in the service of anyone, departs from the said service before the end of the agreed term without permission or reasonable cause, that person shall undergo the penalty of imprisonment, and let no one, under the same penalty, presume to receive or retain such a person for service. Let no one, moreover, pay or permit to be paid to anyone more wages, livery, reward or salary than was customary, as has been said.

... Likewise saddlers, skinners, tawyers,[2] cordwainers,[3] tailors, smiths, carpenters, masons, tilers, shipwrights, carters and all other artisans and laborers shall not take for their labor and handiwork more than

---

[1] *farriers* Shoe-smiths, shoers of horses.

[2] *tawyers* Producers of white leather.

[3] *cordwainers* Shoemakers.

what, in the places where they happen to labor, was customarily paid to such persons in the said twentieth year and in the other usual years preceding, as has been said. And anyone who takes more shall be committed to the nearest jail in the aforesaid manner.

Likewise, let butchers, fishmongers, innkeepers, brewers, bakers, those dealing in foodstuffs and all other vendors of any victuals, be bound to sell such victuals for a reasonable price, having regard for the price at which such victuals are sold in the adjoining places, so that such vendors may have moderate gains, and not excessive ones, according as the distance of the places from which such victuals are carried may seem reasonably to require. And if anyone sells such victuals in another manner, and is convicted of it in the aforesaid way, that person shall pay double what was received to the injured party, or in default of the injured party, to another who shall be willing to prosecute in this behalf. …

And because many sturdy beggars refuse to labor so long as they can live from begging alms, giving themselves up to idleness and sin and, at times, to robbery and other crimes, let no one, under the aforesaid pain of imprisonment, presume, under color of piety or alms, to give anything to those who can very well work, or to cherish them in their sloth, so that thus they may be compelled to work for the necessities of life.

from Statute (1363)

… Item. Regarding the outrageous and excessive apparel of diverse people, violating their estate and degree, to the great destruction and impoverishment of the whole land, it is ordained that grooms (both servants of lords and those employed in crafts) shall be served meat or fish once a day, and the remaining occasions shall be served milk, butter, and cheese, and other such food, according to their estate. They shall have clothes for their wear worth no more than two marks, and they shall wear no cloth of higher price which they have bought themselves or gotten in some other way. Nor shall they wear anything of silver, embroidered items, nor items of silk, nor anything pertaining to those things. Their wives, daughters, and children shall be of the same condition in their clothing and apparel, and

they shall wear no veils worth more than 12 pence a veil.

Item. Artisans and yeomen[1] shall not take or wear cloth for their clothing or stockings of a higher price than 40 shillings for the whole cloth, by way of purchase or by any other means. Nor may they take or wear silk, silver, or jeweled cloth, nor shall they take or wear silver or gold belts, knives, clasps, rings, garters, or brooches, ribbons, chains, or any manner of silk apparel which is embroidered or decorated. And their wives, daughters and children are to be of the same condition in their dress and apparel. And they are to wear no veils made of silk, but only of yarn made within the kingdom, nor are they to wear any manner of fur or of budge,[2] but only of lamb, rabbit, cat, or fox. …

Item. Knights who have land or rent valued up to 200 marks a year shall take and wear clothes of cloth valued at 6 marks for the whole cloth, and nothing of more expensive cloth. And they shall not wear cloth of gold or mantles or gowns furred with pure miniver[3] or ermine, or any apparel embroidered with jewels or anything else. Their wives, daughters, and children will be of the same condition. And they shall not wear ermine facings or lettice[4] or any jeweled apparel, except on their heads. All knights and ladies, however, who have land or rent of more than 400 marks a year, up to the sum of 1,000 marks, shall wear what they like, except ermine and lettice, and apparel with jewels and pearls, unless on their heads.

Item. Clergy who have any rank in a church, cathedral, college, or schools, or a cleric of the King who has an estate that requires fur, will wear and use it according to the constitution of the same. All other clergy who have 200 marks from land a year will wear and do as knights who receive the same rent. Other clergy with the same rent will wear what the esquires who have 100 pounds in rent wear. All of them, both clergy and knights, may wear fur in winter, and in the same manner will wear linure[5] in summer.

Item. Carters, ploughmen, ploughdrivers, cowherds,

---

1 *yeomen* Freeholders; those who farm their own land.

2 *budge* Lamb's wool fur.

3 *miniver* Ermine when taken in its white winter coat.

4 *lettice* White-grey fur.

5 *linure* Fine linen.

shepherds, swineherds, and all other keepers of animals, wheat threshers and all manner of people of the estate of a groom occupied in husbandry, and all other people who do not have 40 shillings' worth of goods or chattels will not take or wear any kind of cloth but blanket, and russet worth 12 pence, and shall wear belts of linen according to their estate. And domestic servants shall come to eat and drink in the manner pertaining to them, and not excessively. And it is ordained that if anyone wears or does contrary to the above, that person will forfeit to the King all the apparel thus worn against this ordinance.

Item. In order to maintain this ordinance and keep it in all points without exception, it is ordained that all makers of cloth within the realm, both men and women, shall confirm that they make their cloth according to the price set by this ordinance. And all the clothmakers shall buy and sell their varieties of cloth according to the same price, so that a great supply of such cloths will be made and put up for sale in every city, borough, and merchant town and elsewhere in the realm, so that no lack of supply of such cloths shall cause the violation of this ordinance. And to that end the said clothmakers will be constrained in any way that shall seem best to the King and his council. And this ordinance on new apparel shall take effect at the next Candlemas.[1]

from Jean Froissart, *Chronicle* (late fourteenth century), Account of a Sermon by John Ball

There was a foolish priest in the county of Kent called John Ball, who, for his foolish words, had been three times in the Archbishop of Canterbury's prison; for this priest used oftentimes, on the Sundays after Mass, when the people were going out of the minster,[2] to go into the cloister[3] and preach, and made the people to assemble about him, and would say thus, "Ah, ye good people, things are not going well in England, nor shall they do so till everything be common, and till there be no

villeins[4] nor gentlemen, but we be all united together, and the lords be no greater masters than we be. What have we deserved, or why should we be kept thus in serfdom? We be all come from one father and one mother, Adam and Eve; whereby can they say or show that they be greater lords than we be, except that they cause us to earn and labor for what they spend? They are clothed in velvet and camlet furred with gris,[5] and we be vestured with poor cloth; they have their wines, spices, and good bread, and we have the drawing out of the chaff and drink water; they dwell in fair houses and we have the pain and travail, rain and wind in the fields; and by what cometh of our labors they keep and maintain their estates: we be called their bondmen, and unless we readily do them service, we be beaten; and we have no sovereign to whom we may complain, nor that will hear us and do us right. Let us go to the King—he is young—and show him what serfage we be in, and show him how we will have it otherwise, or else we will provide us with some remedy, either by fairness or otherwise."[6] Thus John Ball said on Sundays, when the people issued out of the churches in the villages; wherefore many of the lowly people loved him, and such as intended to no goodness said how he said truth; and so they would murmur one with another in the fields and in the ways as they went together, affirming how John Ball spoke the truth.

from Henry Knighton, *Chronicle* (1378–96)

In the year 1381, the second of the reign of King Richard II, during the month of May ... that impious band began to assemble from Kent, from Surrey, and from many other surrounding places. Apprentices also, leaving their masters, rushed to join these. And so they gathered on Blackheath, where, forgetting themselves in their multitude, and neither contented with their former

---

[1]   *Candleman*   The Feast of the Purification of the Virgin Mary, celebrated on 2 February.

[2]   *minster*   Cathedral church.

[3]   *cloister*   Here, covered walkway connecting buildings of the Cathedral.

[4]   *villeins*   Peasants subject to lords or attached to manors.

[5]   *camlet furred with gris*   Fabric imported from the East and trimmed with gray fur.

[6]   *the King ... fairness or otherwise*   The young King mentioned here is Richard II, who had come to the throne at the age of only ten years old, after the death of his grandfather, Edward III, in 1377; for the first three years of his kingship the kingdom was actually ruled by a Council of nobles. This problematic royal transition contributed to the general uncertainties and tensions in England.

cause nor appeased by smaller crimes, they unmercifully planned greater and worse evils and determined not to desist from their wicked undertaking until they should have entirely extirpated the nobles and great men of the kingdom.

So at first they directed their course of iniquity to a certain town of the Archbishop of Canterbury called Maidstone, in which there was a jail of the said Archbishop, and in the said jail was a certain John Ball, a chaplain who was considered among the laity to be a very famous preacher; many times in the past he had foolishly spread abroad the word of God, by mixing tares with wheat, too pleasing to the laity and extremely dangerous to the liberty of ecclesiastical law and order, execrably introducing into the Church of Christ many errors among the clergy and laymen. For this reason he had been tried as a clerk and convicted in accordance with the law, being seized and assigned to this same jail for his permanent abiding place. On [June 12,] the Wednesday before the Feast of the Consecration, they came into Surrey to the jail of the King at Marshalsea, where they broke the jail without delay, forcing all imprisoned there to come with them to help them; and whomsoever they met, whether pilgrims or others of whatever condition, they forced to go with them.

On [June 14,] the Friday following the Feast of the Consecration, they came over the bridge to London; here no one resisted them, although, as was said, the citizens of London knew of their advance a long time before; and so they directed their way to the Tower where the King was surrounded by a great throng of knights, esquires, and others. It was said that there were in the Tower about one hundred and fifty knights together with one hundred and eighty others. ...

John Leg and a certain John, a Minorite, a man active in warlike deeds, skilled in natural sciences, an intimate friend of Lord John, duke of Lancaster, hastened with three others to the Tower for refuge, intending to hide themselves under the wings of the King. The people had determined to kill the Archbishop and the others above mentioned with him; for this reason they came to this place, and afterwards they fulfilled their vows. The King, however, desired to free the Archbishop and his friends from the jaws of the wolves, so he sent to the people a command to assemble

outside the city, at a place called Mile End, in order to speak with the King and to treat with him concerning their designs. The soldiers who were to go forward, consumed with folly, lost heart, and gave up, on the way, their boldness of purpose. Nor did they dare to advance but, unfortunately, struck as they were by fear, like women, kept themselves within the Tower.

But the King advanced to the assigned place, while many of the wicked mob kept following him. ... More, however, remained where they were. When the others had come to the King they complained that they had been seriously oppressed by many hardships and that their condition of servitude was unbearable, and that they neither could nor would endure it longer. The King, for the sake of peace, and on account of the violence of the times, yielding to their petition, granted to them a charter with the great seal, to the effect that all men in the kingdom of England should be free and of free condition, and should remain both for themselves and their heirs free from all kinds of servitude and villeinage forever. This charter was rejected and decided to be null and void by the King and the great men of the kingdom in the Parliament held at Westminster in the same year, after the Feast of St. Michael.

While these things were going on, behold those degenerate sons, who still remained, summoned their father the Archbishop with his above-mentioned friends without any force or attack, without sword or arrow, or any other form of compulsion, but only with force of threats and excited outcries, inviting those men to death. But they did not cry out against it for themselves, nor resist, but, as sheep before the shearers, going forth barefooted with uncovered heads, ungirt, they offered themselves freely to an undeserved death, just as if they had deserved this punishment for some murder or theft. And so, alas! before the King returned, seven were killed at Tower Hill, two of them lights of the kingdom, the worthy with the unworthy. John Leg and his three associates were the cause of this irreparable loss. Their heads were fastened on spears and sticks in order that they might be told from the rest. ...

Whatever representatives of the law they found or whatever men served the kingdom in a judicial capacity, these they slew without delay.

On the following day, which was Saturday, they

gathered in Smithfield, where there came to them in the morning the King, who although only a youth in years yet was in wisdom already well versed. Their leader, whose real name was Wat Tyler, approached him; already they were calling him by the other name of Jack Straw. He kept close to the King, addressing him for the rest. He carried in his hand an unsheathed weapon which they call a dagger, and, as if in childish play, kept tossing it from one hand to the other in order that he might seize the opportunity, if the King should refuse his requests, to strike the King suddenly (as was commonly believed); and from this thing the greatest fear arose among those about the King as to what might be the outcome.

They begged from the King that all the warrens, and as well waters as park and wood, should be common to all, so that a poor man as well as a rich should be able freely to hunt animals everywhere in the kingdom—in the streams, in the fish ponds, in the woods, and in the forest; and that he might be free to chase the hare in the fields, and that he might do these things and others like them without objection. When the King hesitated about granting this concession Jack Straw came nearer, and, speaking threatening words, seized with his hand the bridle of the horse of the King very daringly. When John de Walworth, a citizen of London, saw this, thinking that death threatened the King, he seized a sword and pierced Jack Straw in the neck. Seeing this, another soldier, by name Radulf Standyche, pierced his side with another sword. He sank back, slowly letting go with his hands and feet, and then died. A great cry and much mourning arose: "Our leader is slain." When this dead man had been meanly dragged along by the hands and feet into the church of St. Bartholomew, which was near by, many withdrew from the band, and, vanishing, betook themselves to flight, to the number it is believed of ten thousand....

After these things had happened and quiet had been restored, the time came when the king caused the offenders to be punished. So Lord Robert Tresillian, one of the judges, was sent by order of the king to inquire into the uprisings against the peace and to punish the guilty. Wherever he came he spared no one, but caused great slaughter....

For whoever was accused before him in this said cause, whether justly or as a matter of spite, he immediately passed upon him the sentence of death. He ordered some to be beheaded, others to be hanged, still others to be dragged through the city and hanged in four different parts thereof; others to be disemboweled, and the entrails to be burned before them while they were still alive, and afterwards to be decapitated, quartered, and hanged in four parts of the city according to the greatness of the crime and its desert. John Ball was captured at Coventry and led to St. Albans, where, by order of the King, he was drawn and hanged, then quartered, and his quarters sent to four different places.

From a fifteenth-century manuscript of Froissart's *Chronicle,* "The Death of Wat Tyler."

SIR ORFEO

c. 1325

The Breton *lai* is a poetic form that evolved in England and France during the twelfth century. Originally composed in Anglo-Norman, these relatively brief poems ostensibly originated in the oral legends of Brittany. The Breton *lais* generally retain the themes of longer chivalric poems—tales of adventure and noble love often colored by the supernatural—but their overall structure is much more concise and they are notable for the ways in which they often call attention to their own supposed origins in Breton stories. It is possible that the recitation of the tales was accompanied by music—the *lai* proper—and that (as in *Sir Orfeo*) the narrative originally served as something like a frame for a musical performance.

Eventually, English writers began to produce these works in their own language; *Sir Orfeo* is considered by many critics to be one of the best examples of the Breton *lai* in any language. As with many medieval English poems, the author of *Sir Orfeo* is unknown; the poem shows some signs of having been translated from a French original. The poem exists in three separate manuscripts, the earliest of which dates from the second quarter of the fourteenth century, the other two from the fifteenth century.

Sir Orfeo consists of a mixture of classical, romance, and Celtic elements. Its plot structure and main characters mirror those of the Greek myth of Orpheus and Eurydice, familiar to the Middle Ages particularly through versions in Ovid and Virgil. But the setting has been "domesticated" (the ancient city of Thrace is identified with Winchester) and many of the story's most distinctive plot elements have been altered to align it with romance rather than with classical myth. Whereas in the classical version Orpheus attempts to rescue Eurydice from Hades, the land of the dead, in this English version Sir Orfeo's task is to rescue Heurodis from the land of the fairies. The queen is not dead but merely "taken"; the king's descent into the wilderness precedes rather than follows his attempted rescue of the queen. Most strikingly, while the classical versions end in tragedy and loss—as he leads Eurydice from Hades, Orpheus glances back at her and thereby loses her forever—*Sir Orfeo* ends in reunion, recuperation and recovery. The couple are reunited, the king regains his kingdom, and all live happily ever after. We cannot say with any certainty whether the author knowingly replaced the tragic ending of the classical version with this happier one, or why he did so, or whether readers of the story would have recognized or appreciated such a striking reversal. But these puzzling uncertainties about sources and form do not detract from the skill of the storytelling, in which even the most familiar plot devices are presented with precision, grace, and admirable narrative economy.

The poem was influential not only in its time (Chaucer's *Franklin's Tale* and *Wife of Bath's Tale* drew on some of the story material of *Sir Orfeo*) but also in the twentieth century; J.R.R. Tolkien studied the poem extensively and may well have been influenced by it in writing some portions of *The Lord of the Rings*.

⌘⌘⌘

Sir Orfeo

W̶e redeth oft and findeth y-write,°   *written*   40
And this clerkes° wele it wite,°   *scholars / know*
Layes that ben in harping°   *are in song*
Ben y-founde of ferli thing:° *composed about marvelous things*
Sum bethe of wer° and sum of wo,°   *some are of war / grief*   5
And sum of joie° and mirthe also,°   *gaiety*
And sum of trecherie and of gile,°   *deceit (or, trickery)*
Of old aventours° that fel while;° *adventures / happened once*
And sum of bourdes° and ribaudy,°   *jokes / ribaldry*
And mani ther beth of fairy.[1]   10
Of al thinges that men seth,°   *relate*
Mest o° love, forsothe,° they beth.   *most of / in truth*
In Breteyne this° layes were wrought,° *Brittany these / made*
First y-founde° and forth y-brought,°   *composed / produced*
Of aventours that fel bi dayes,°   *happened in olden times*   15
Wherof Bretouns maked her° layes.   *their*
When kinges might our y-here°   *anywhere hear*
Of ani mervailes° that ther were,   *marvels*
Thai token° an harp in gle° and game   *took / minstrelsy*
And maked a lay and gaf° it name.   *gave*   20
Now of this aventours that weren y-falle   *have happened*
Y° can tel sum, ac° nought alle.   *I / but*
Ac herkneth,° lordinges that ben trewe,   *but listen*
Ichil° you telle of "Sir Orfewe."   *I will*
Orfeo mest° of ani thing   *most*   25
Lovede the gle° of harping.[2]   *glee or music*
Siker° was everi gode° harpour   *sure / good*
Of him to have miche° honour.   *much*
Himself he lerned forto° harp,   *he taught himself to*
And leyd° theron his wittes scharp;   *applied*   30
He lerned so ther nothing° was   *in no way*
A better harpour in no plas.°   *anywhere*
In al the warld was no man bore°   *born*
That ones° Orfeo sat before—   *once*
And° he might° of his harping here—   *if / could*   35
Bot he schuld thenche° that he were   *think*
In on° of the joies of Paradis,   *one*

Swiche melody in his harping is.
  Orfeo was a king,
In Inglond an heighe° lording,   *high*   40
A stalworth man and hardi bo;°   *brave as well*
Large° and curteys[3] he was also.   *generous*
His fader was comen° of King Pluto,   *descended from*
And his moder of King Juno,[4]
That sum time° were as godes°   45
  yhold   *who once / considered to be gods*
For aventours that thai dede° and told.   *did*
This king sojournd° in Traciens,   *dwelled*
That was a cité of noble defens—°   *fortifications*
For Winchester was cleped° tho°   *called / then*
Traciens,[5] withouten no.°   50   *denial*
  The king hadde a quen of priis°   *queen of excellence*
That was y-cleped° Dame Heurodis,   *called*
The fairest levedi, for the nones,°   *lady indeed*
That might gon on° bodi and bones,   *walk about in*
Ful of love and godenisse—°   55   *goodness*
Ac no man may telle hir fairnise.°   *beauty*

  Bifel° so in the comessing° of
  May   *it happened / beginning*
When miri° and hot is the day,   *merry (pleasant)*
And oway° beth winter schours,   *away*
And everi feld° is ful of flours,   60   *field*
And blosme breme° on everi bough   *blossoms bright*
Over al wexeth° miri anought,°   *everywhere grow / enough*
  This ich° quen, Dame Heurodis,   *same*
Tok to° maidens of priis,   *two*
And went in an undrentide°   65   *late morning*
To play° bi an orchardside,   *enjoy themselves*
To se the floures sprede and spring
And to here the foules° sing.   *birds*
Thai sett hem° doun al thre   *sat themselves*
Under a fair ympe-tre,°   70   *grafted tree*
And wel sone° this fair quene   *very quickly*

---

[1] *fairy* The word "fairy" here and elsewhere in the poem means "land of the fays" or the "fays" themselves. The word "fay" comes from Old French "fée" derived from the Latin "fata," "the Fates."

[2] *Orfeo … harping* Orfeo's name had a long tradition of being associated with music, art, and the power of eloquence; his name had been understood to mean "beautiful voice."

[3] *curteys* In medieval texts this word carries much greater weight than today's "courteous" or "polite"; it connotes courtly, elite, valuable, and cultured behavior as well as generosity.

[4] *King Pluto … King Juno* Pluto was, according to classical myth, god of the underworld. Juno was a goddess, the wife of Jupiter, not a king.

[5] *This king … Traciens* Because the poet has set the poem in England, classical and medieval places are conflated; hence, Winchester, the old capital, becomes Thrace.

Fel on slepe° opon the grene.   *asleep*
The maidens durst° hir nought awake,   *dared*
Bot lete hir ligge° and rest take.   *let her lie*
75 So sche slepe til after none,°   *noon*
That undertide° was al y-done.°[1]   *until midday / past*
Ac, as sone as sche gan° awake,   *began (to)*
Sche crid, and lothli bere gan make;°   *terrible outcry made*
Sche froted° hir honden° and hir fete,   *rubbed / hands*
80 And crached hir visage°—it bled
        wete—°   *scratched her face / profusely*
Hir riche robe hye al to-rett°   *she tore all to pieces*
And was reveyd° out of hir wit.   *driven*
The two maidens hir biside
No durst with hir no leng° abide,   *longer*
85 Bot ourn° to the palays ful right°   *ran / immediately*
And told bothe squier and knight
That her° quen awede wold,°   *their / was going mad*
And bad° hem go and hir at-hold.°   *bade / seize*
Knightes urn° and levedis also,   *ran*
90 Damisels sexti and mo.°   *numbering sixty and more*
In the orchard to the quen hye come,°   *they came*
And her up in her armes nome,°   *their arms took*
And brought hir to bed atte last,
And held hir there fine fast.°   *very securely*
95 Ac ever she held in o° cri   *persisted in one*
And wold° up and owy.°   *wished (to go) / away*
When Orfeo herd° that tiding   *heard*
Never him nas wers for
        nothing.°   *had he been as grieved by anything*
He come with knightes tene°   *ten*
100 To chaumber, right bifor the quene,
And bi-held,° and seyd with grete pité,° *beheld her / sorrow*
"O lef liif,° what is te,°   *dear life / with you*
That° ever yete° hast ben so stille°   *who / yet / calm*
And° now gredest wonder schille?°   *but / cries strangely shrilly*
105 Thy bodi, that was so white y-core,°   *exquisitely*
With thine nailes is all to-tore.°   *torn to pieces*
Allas! thy rode,° that was so red,   *face*
Is al wan, as° thou were ded;   *pale as (if)*
And also thine fingres smale°   *slender*
110 Beth al blodi and al pale.
Allas! thy lovesum eyyen to°   *lovely two eyes*
Loketh so° man doth on his fo!°   *as / foe*

A, dame, ich biseche,° merci!   *I beg you*
Lete ben° al this reweful° cri,   *let be / pitiful*
115 And tel me what the is,° and
        hou,°   *what's bothering you / how*
And what thing may the help now."
Tho° lay sche stille atte last   *then*
And gan to wepe swithe fast,°   *very hard*
And seyd thus the King to:
120 "Allas, mi lord, Sir Orfeo!
Sethen° we first togider were,   *since*
Ones wroth never we
        nere;°   *we were never once angry with each other*
Bot ever ich have yloved the
As mi liif and so thou me;
125 Ac now we mot delen ato;°   *must separate*
Do thi best, for y mot° go."   *I must*
"Allas!" quath he, "forlorn icham!°   *I am utterly lost*
Whider wiltow° go, and to wham?° *where will you / whom*
Whider thou gost, ichil° with the,   *I will go*
130 And whider y go, thou schalt with me."[2]
"Nay, nay, Sir, that nought nis!°   *cannot be*
Ichil the telle al hou° it is: *all how*
As ich lay this undertide
And slepe under our orchardside,
135 Ther come to me to fair knightes,
Wele y-armed al to rightes,°   *quite properly*
And bad me comen an heighing°   *in haste*
And speke with her lord the king.
And ich answerd at° wordes bold,   *with*
140 Y durst nought, no y nold.°   *dared not, nor did I want to*
Thai priked oyain as thai might drive;
Tho° com her king, also blive,°   *then / as quickly*
With an hundred knightes and mo,
And damisels an hundred also,
145 Al on snowe-white stedes;
As white as milke were her wedes.°[3]   *their garments*
Y no seighe° never yete bifore   *saw*

---

[1] *So sche slepe … al y-done* Midday, or noon, was considered a perilous time in both folktales and Christian literature.

[2] *Whider wiltow go … schalt with me* Cf. Ruth 1.16: "Wither ever thou gost I schal gon and where thou abidest I and thou together shall abide." Although Ruth speaks these words, not to her husband, but to her mother-in-law, Naomi, the lines were frequently associated with marriage.

[3] *Al … her wedes* The white horse and the white clothes worn by those who escort or meet the protagonists at the boundary of the Otherworld are common in romance and dream vision literature.

So fair creatours y-core.
The king hadde a croun on hed;
150 It nas of silver, no of gold red,
Ac it was of a precious ston—
As bright as the sonne it schon.
And as son as he to me cam,
Wold ich, nold ich, he me
    nam,°   *whether I wished or not he took me*
155 And made me with him ride
Opon a palfray° bi his side;   *horse*
And brought me to his palays,
Wele atird° in ich ways,°   *adorned / every way*
And schewed me castels and tours,°   *towers*
160 Rivers, forestes, frith with flours,°   *woods with flowers*
And his riche stedes ichon.°   *gorgeous steeds each one*
And sethen° me brought oyain hom°*afterwards / back home*
Into our owhen° orchard,   *own*
And said to me thus afterward,
165 "Loke, dame, tomorwe thatow° be   *that you*
Right here under this ympe-tre,
And than thou schalt with ous° go   *us*
And live with ous evermo.
And yif thou makest ous y-let,°   *a hindrance for us*
170 Whar° thou be, thou worst y-fet,° *wherever / will be fetched*
And totore° thine limes° al   *torn apart / limbs*
That nothing help the no schal;
And thei thou best so totorn,° *though (even if) you are so torn*
Yete thou worst with ous y-born."°   *will be carried with us*

175   When King Orfeo herd this cas,°   *matter*
"O we!"° quath he, "Allas, allas!   *woe*
Lever me were to lete° mi liif   *I'd rather lose*
Than thus to lese° the quen, mi wiif!"   *lose*
He asked conseyl at ich man,°   *advice from each person*
180 Ac no man him help no can.
Amorwe° the undertide is come   *the next day*
And Orfeo hath his armes y-nome,°   *taken*
And wele ten hundred knightes with him,
Ich y-armed, stout° and grim;°   *strong / fierce*
185 And with the quen wenten he
Right unto that ympe-tre.

Thai made scheltrom[1] in
    ich a side   *a rank of armed men*
And sayd thai wold there abide
And dye° ther everichon,°   *die / everyone*
190 Er° the quen schuld fram° hem gon.   *before / from*
Ac yete amiddes hem ful right° *yet amidst them straightaway*
The quen was oway y-twight,°   *snatched*
With fairi° forth y-nome.°   *enchantment / taken*
Men wist never° wher sche was bicome.° *never knew / gone*
195 Tho° was ther criing, wepe and wo!   *then*
The king into his chaumber is go,°   *went*
And oft swoned° opon the ston,° *swooned / stone (i.e., floor)*
And made swiche diol° and swiche mon° *such lament / moan*
That neighe° his liif was y-spent—° *almost / ended*
200 Ther was non amendement.°   *no remedy (for it)*
He cleped° togider his barouns,   *called*
Erls, lordes of renouns,
And when thai al y-comen were,
"Lordinges," he said, "bifor you here
205 Ich ordainy° min heighe steward[2]   *I ordain*
To wite° mi kingdom afterward;° *rule / henceforth*
In mi stede° ben he schal   *place*
To kepe mi londes overal.
For now ichave° mi quen y-lore,°   *I have / lost*
210 The fairest levedi that ever was bore,
Never eft y nil no woman
    se.°   *never again will I see another woman*
Into wildernes ichil te°   *I will go*
And live ther evermore
With wilde bestes in holtes hore;°   *woods grey*
215 And when ye understond that y be spent,° *dead*
Make you than a parlement,
And chese° you a newe king.   *choose*
Now doth° your best with al mi thing."°   *do / affairs*

    Tho was ther wepeing in the halle
220 And grete cri among hem alle;
Unnethe° might old or yong°   *hardly / young*
For wepeing speke a word with tong.
Thai kneled adoun al y-fere°   *together*

---

[1] *scheltrom* From the OE "scyld-truma," a tribal battle formation in which warriors used their shields to create a wall of defence.

[2] *steward* High court official from the nobility.

And praid° him, yif his wille were,   *prayed*
225 That he no schuld nought fram hem go.
"Do way!"° quath he, "It schal be so!"   *enough!*
Al his kingdom he forsoke;
Bot° a sclavin° on him he toke.[1]   *only / pilgrim's mantle*
He no hadde kirtel no hode,°   *had neither tunic nor hood*
230 Schert,° ne no nother gode,°   *shirt / goods*
Bot his harp he tok algate°   *at any rate*
And dede him barfot° out atte gate;   *passed barefoot*
No man most° with him go.   *might*
O way! What ther was wepe and wo,
235 When he that hadde ben king with croun
Went so poverlich out of
      toun!°   *in such poverty out of his town*
Thurth° wode and over heth°   *through / heath*
Into the wildernes he geth.°   *goes*
Nothing he fint° that him° is ays,°   *finds / for him / comfort*
240 Bot ever he liveth in gret malais.°   *distress*
He that hadde y-werd the fowe and
      griis,°   *worn the variegated and grey fur*
And on bed the purper biis,°   *purple linen*
Now on hard hethe he lith,°   *lies*
With leves and gresse he him writh.°   *covers himself*
245 He that hadde had castels and tours,
River, forest, frith with flours,
Now, thei it comenci° to snewe° and
      frese,°   *although it begins / snow / freeze*
This king mot° make his bed in mese.°   *must / moss*
He that had y-had knightes of priis
250 Bifor him kneland,° and levedis,   *kneeling*
Now seth he nothing that him liketh,
Bot wilde wormes° bi him striketh.°   *snakes / glide*
He that had y-had plenté
Of mete and drink, of ich deynté,°   *delicacy*
255 Now may he al day digge° and wrote°   *dig / grub*
Er he finde his fille of rote.°   *roots*
In somer he liveth bi wild frut,°   *fruit*
And berien bot gode lite;°   *berries of little worth*
In winter may he nothing finde
260 Bot rote, grases, and the rinde.°   *bark*

Al his bodi was oway dwine°   *away dwindled*
For missays,° and al to-chine.°   *hardship / chapped*
Lord! who may telle the sore°   *sorrow*
This king sufferd ten yere and more?
265 His here° of his berd,° blac and rowe,°   *hair / beard / rough*
To his girdel-stede° was growe.   *waist*
His harp, whereon was al his gle,°   *pleasure*
He hidde in an holwe° tre;   *hollow*
And when the weder° was clere and bright,   *weather*
270 He toke his harp to him wel right
And harped° at his owhen wille.°   *played / own desire*
Into alle the wode the soun gan
      schille,°   *sound began to resound*
That alle the wilde bestes that ther beth
For joie abouten him thai teth,°   *gathered*
275 And alle the foules° that ther were   *birds*
Come and sete° on ich a brere°   *sat / every briar*
To here his harping a-fine—
So miche° melody was therin;   *much*
And when he his harping lete wold,°   *would leave off*
280 No best° bi him abide nold.°[2]   *beast / would remain*
  He might se him bisides,°   *nearby*
Oft in hot undertides,
The king o fairy with his rout°   *company*
Com to hunt him al about
285 With dim cri and bloweing,°   *blowing (of horns)*
And houndes also with him berking;°   *barking*
Ac no best thai no nome,°   *but they took no beast (game)*
No never he nist whider they
      bicome°   *nor did he ever know where they went*
And other while° he might him se   *at other times*
290 As a gret ost° bi him te,°   *army / went*
Wele atourned,° ten hundred knightes,   *equipped*
Ich y-armed to his rightes,°   *all properly armed*
Of cuntenaunce° stout and fers,   *appearance*
With mani desplaid° baners,   *unfurled*
295 And ich his swerd y-drawe hold—
Ac never he nist whider° thai
      wold.°   *knew not whither / went*
And otherwile he seighe° other thing: *saw*
Knightes and levedis com daunceing

---

[1] *Al his kingdom … he toke*   Among scholars, considerable disagreement surrounds Orfeo's exile. It has been seen as an act of despair, atonement, or spiritual retreat, as part of a process of initiation for Orfeo, as an expression of the great love (or too great a love) Orfeo has for Heurodis.

[2] *He toke his harp … abide nold*   The tradition of harping as a way of "taming" the animals has roots in pre-Christian material as well as in the classical myth of Orpheus and in the Biblical story of David.

In queynt° atire, gisely,°   *elegant / skilfully*
300 Queynt pas° and softly;   *graceful steps*
Tabours and trunpes yede° hem
            bi,   *drums and trumpets went*
And al maner menstraci.°   *sorts of minstrelsy*

     And on a day° he seighe him biside   *on a certain day*
Sexti° levedis on hors ride,   *sixty*
305 Gentil and jolif as brid on ris;°   *lively as a bird on bough*
Nought o man amonges hem ther
            nis;°   *not a single man was with them*
And ich a faucoun on hond
            bere,°   *each a falcon on her hand bore*
And riden on haukin bi o° rivere.   *a-hawking by a*
Of game thai founde wel gode haunt—°   *great plenty*
310 Maulardes,° hayroun,° and
            cormeraunt;°   *mallards / heron / cormorant*
The foules of the water ariseth,
The faucouns hem wele deviseth;°   *marked*
Ich faucoun his pray slough—°   *prey killed*
That seigh Orfeo, and lough:°   *laughed*
315 "Parfay!"° quath he, "ther is fair game;   *by my faith*
Thider ichil,° bi Godes name;   *I'll go*
Ich was y-won swiche werk° to se!"   *I was wont such sport*
He aros, and thider gan te.°   *began to approach*
To a levedi he was y-come,
320 Biheld, and hath wele undernome,°   *perceived*
And seth bi al thing that it is
His owhen quen, Dam Heurodis.
Yern° he biheld hir, and sche him eke,°   *eagerly / also*
Ac noither° to other a word no speke;   *neither*
325 For messais° that sche on him seighe,   *sadness*
That° had ben so riche and so heighe,   *who*
The teres fel out of her eighe.°   *eye*
The other levedis this y-seighe
And maked hir oway to ride—
330 Sche most with him no lenger abide.
"Allas!" quath he, "now me is wo!"
Whi nil° deth now me slo?°   *will not / slay*
Allas, wreche, that y no might
Dye now after this sight!
335 Allas! to long last° mi liif,   *too long lasts*
When y no dar nought with mi wiif,
No hye° to me, o° word speke.   *nor she / one*
Allas! Whi nil min hert breke!

Parfay!" quath he, "tide wat bitide,°   *come what may*
340 Whiderso this° levedis ride,   *wherever these*
The selve° way ichil streche—°   *same / hasten*
Of liif no° deth me no reche."°   *nor / I do not care*
His sclavain he dede on also
            spac°   *pilgrim's gown he put on quickly*
And henge his harp opon his bac,
345 And had wel gode wil to gon—°   *great desire to go*
He no spard° noither stub° no ston.   *avoided / stump*
In at a roche° the levedis rideth,   *Into a rock*
And he after, and nought abideth.
When he was in the roche y-go,°   *gone*
350 Wele thre mile other mo,
He com into a fair cuntray°   *country*
As bright so sonne on somers° day,   *as sun on summer's*
Smothe and plain° and al grene—   *smooth and level*
Hille no dale nas ther non y-sene.°   *was not to be seen*
355 Amidde the lond a castel he sighe,
Riche and real° and wonder heighe.°   *royal / wondrously high*
Al the utmast wal°   *all of the outermost wall*
Was clere and schine° as cristal;   *bright*
An hundred tours ther were about,
360 Degiselich and batailld stout.[1]
The butras° com out of the diche°   *buttresses / moat*
Of rede gold y-arched riche.
The vousour° was avowed° al   *vaulting / adorned*
Of ich maner divers aumal.°   *with every kind of enamel*
365 Within ther wer wide wones,°   *spacious dwellings*
Al of precious stones;
The werst piler on to biholde
Was al of burnist° gold.   *burnished*
Al that lond was ever° light,   *always*
370 For when it schuld be therk° and night,   *dark*
The riche stones light gonne°   *stone's light shone*
As bright as doth at none° the sonne.   *noon*
No man may telle, no thenche° in thought,   *nor think*
The riche° werk that ther was wrought.°   *exquisite / made (done)*
375 Bi al thing him think° that it is   *it seems to him*
The proude court of Paradis.
In this castel the levedis alight;°   *dismounted*
He wold in after, yif° he might.   *wished to enter if*
     Orfeo knokketh atte gate;
380 The porter was redi therate
And asked what he wold hav y-do.°   *wanted (to do)*

---

[1] *Degiselich and batailld stout* Wonderful with strong battlements.

"Parfay!" quath he, "icham° a minstrel, lo!   *I am*
To solas° thi lord with mi gle,°   *entertain / minstrelsy*
Yif his swete wille be."
385 The porter undede° the gate anon   *undid*
And lete him into the castel gon.

Than he gan bihold about al,°   *look all around*
And seighe liggeand° within the wal   *remaining, living*
Of folk that were thider y-brought
390 And thought dede, and nare
    nought.°   *believed to be dead, but were not*
Sum stode° withouten hade,°   *stood / head*
And sum non armes nade,°   *had no arms*
And sum thurth° the bodi hadde wounde,   *through*
And sum lay wode,° y-bounde,   *mad*
395 And sum armed on hors sete,°   *sat*
And sum astrangled as thai ete;°   *they ate*
And sum were in water adreynt,°   *drowned*
And sum with fire al forschreynt.°   *shriveled*
Wives ther lay on childe bedde,
400 Sum ded and sum awedde,°   *driven mad*
And wonder fele° ther lay bisides   *wondrous many*
Right as° thai slepe her° undertides;   *just as / their*
Eche was thus in this warld y-nome,°   *taken*
With fairi thider y-come.°   *enchantment brought there*
405 Ther he seighe his owhen wiif,
Dame Heurodis, his lef liif,°   *dear life*
Slepe under an ympe-tre—
Bi her clothes he knewe that it was he.°   *she*
    And when he hadde bihold this mervails
    alle,°   *all these marvels*
410 He went into the kinges halle.
Than seighe he ther a semly° sight,   *fair*
A tabernacle blisseful° and bright,   *canopy beautiful*
Therin her maister king sete
And her quen, fair and swete.
415 Her crounes, her clothes schine so bright
That unnethe° bihold he him might.   *scarcely*
When he hadde biholden al that thing,
He kneled adoun bifor the king:
"O lord," he seyd, "yif it thi wille were,
420 Mi menstraci thou schust y-here."°   *should hear*
The king answered, "What man artow,°   *are you*
That art hider y-comen now?
Ich, no non° that is with me,   *neither I, nor no one*

No sent never after the.°   *you*
425 Sethen° that ich here regni° gan,   *since / reign*
Y no fond never so folehardi° man   *foolhardy*
That hider to ous durst wende°   *to us dared come*
Bot that ic him wald ofsende."[1]
"Lord," quath he, "trowe° ful wel,   *believe*
430 Y nam bot a pover menstrel;
And, sir, it is the maner of ous
To seche mani° a lordes hous—   *seek many*
Thei° we nought welcom no be,   *although (even if)*
Yete we mot proferi° forth our gle."   *must offer*

435 Bifor the king he sat adoun
And tok his harp so miri° of soun,°   *merry / sound*
And trempreth° his harp, as he wele
    can,°   *tunes / knows well how to do*
And blisseful notes he ther gan,°   *began*
That al that in the palays were
440 Com to him forto here,°   *to listen*
And liggeth° adoun to his fete—   *lie*
Hem thenketh° his melody so swete.   *they think*
The king herkneth° and sitt ful stille;°   *listens / sits quietly*
To here his° gle he° hath gode
    wille.   *his (Orfeo's) / he (the king)*
445 Gode bourde° he hadde of his gle;°   *great pleasure / songs*
The riche quen also hadde he.°   *she*
When he hadde stint° his harping,   *stopped*
Than seyd to him the king,
"Menstrel, me liketh° wel thi gle.   *pleases me*
450 Now aske of me what it be,°   *whatever you wish*
Largelich° ichil the pay;   *generously*
Now speke, and tow might asay."°   *if you wish to find out*
"Sir," he seyd, "ich biseche the°   *beseech you*
Thatow° woldest give me   *that you*
455 That ich° levedi, bright on ble,   *same / of complexion*
That slepeth under the ympe-tree."
"Nay!" quath the king, "that nought
    nere!°   *that could never be*
A sori° couple of you it were,   *ill-matched*
For thou art lene, rowe° and blac,   *lean, rough*
460 And sche is lovesum,° withouten lac;°   *beautiful / blemish*
A lothlich° thing it were, forthi,°   *loathly / therefore*
To sen° hir in thi compayni."   *see*
"O sir!" he seyd, "gentil king,

---
[1] *Bot that ... ofsende* Unless I wished him summoned.

Yete were it a wele fouler thing°   *much more disgraceful*

465 To here a lesing of° thi mouthe!   *hear a lie from*

So, sir, as ye seyd nouthe,°   *just now*

What ich wold aski,° have y

    schold,°   *wished to ask for / I should*

And nedes° thou most thi word hold."   *by necessity*

The king seyd, "Sethen it is so,

470 Take hir bi the hond and go;

Of° hir ichil thatow be

    blithe."°   *with / I wish that you be happy*

He kneled adoun and thonked him swithe.°   *quickly*

His wiif he tok bi the hond,°   *hand*

And dede° him swithe out of that lond,°   *went / land*

475 And went him out of that thede—°   *country*

Right as he come, the way he yede.°   *went*

So long he hath the way y-nome°   *taken*

To Winchester he is y-come,

That was his owhen cité;

480 Ac no man knewe that it was he.

No forther° than the tounes ende   *further*

For knoweleche no durst he wende,[1]

Bot with a begger, y-bilt ful

    narwe,°   *whose house was very small*

Ther he tok his herbarwe°   *lodging*

485 To him and to° his owhen wiif   *for himself and for*

As a minstrel of pover liif,

And asked tidinges of that lond,

And who the kingdom held in hond.

The pover begger in his cote°   *cottage*

490 Told him everich a grot:°   *every scrap*

Hou her quen was stole owy,°   *away*

Ten yer gon,° with fairy,°   *ago / by magic*

And hou her king en° exile yede,°   *into / went*

But no man nist° in wiche thede;°   *no one knew / country*

495 And how the steward the lond gan hold,

And other mani thinges him told.

    Amorwe, oyain nonetide,°   *the next day, towards noon*

He maked his wiif ther abide;°   *stay there*

The beggers clothes he borwed anon

500 And heng his harp his rigge° opon,   *back*

And went him into that cité

That men might him bihold and se.

Erls and barouns bold,

Buriays° and levedis him gun bihold.   *burgeses (citizens)*

505 "Lo!" thai seyd, "swiche a man!

Hou long the here° hongeth him opan!°   *hair / upon*

Lo! Hou his berd hongeth to his kne!

He is y-clongen also° a tre!"   *gnarled like*

And, as he yede in the strete,

510 With his steward he gan mete,

And loude he° sett on him° a

    crie: *he (Orfeo) / him (the steward)*

"Sir steward!" he seyd, "merci!

Icham° an harpour of hethenisse;°   *I am / from heathendom*

Help me now in this destresse!"

515 The steward seyd, "Com with me, come;

Of that ichave,° thou schalt have some.   *what I have*

Everich gode harpour is welcom me to

For mi lordes love, Sir Orfeo."

    In the castel the steward sat atte mete,°   *table*

520 And mani lording was bi him sete;

Ther were trompours° and tabourers,°   *trumpeters / drummers*

Harpours fele,° and crouders—[2]   *many*

Miche melody thai maked alle.

And Orfeo sat stille in the halle

525 And herkneth; when thai ben al stille,

He toke his harp and tempred schille;°   *tuned it loudly*

The blissefulest° notes he harped there   *most beautiful*

That ever ani man y-herd with ere—

Ich man liked wele his gle.

530 The steward biheld and gan y-se,°   *began to perceive*

And knewe the harp als blive.°   *at once*

"Menstrel!" he seyd, "so mot thou

    thrive,°   *if you wish to thrive*

Where hadestow° this harp, and hou?°   *did you get / how*

Y pray that thou me telle now."

535 "Lord," quath he, "in uncouthe° thede   *unknown*

Thurth a wildernes as y yede,

Ther y founde in a dale

With lyouns a man totorn smale,°   *torn in small pieces*

And wolves him frete° with teth so scharp.   *had devoured*

540 Bi him y fond this ich° harp;   *same*

---

[1] *For knoweleche ... wende*   He did not dare go lest he be recognized.

[2] *crouders* "Croud-players." The word probably derives from the Welsh "crwth," a Celtic string instrument which was played with a bow and plucked with the fingers. However, the *MED* refers to this line in *Sir Orfeo* and interprets the word as "one who plays the crowd."

Wele ten yere it is y-go."
"O!" quath the steward, "now me is wo!
That was mi lord, Sir Orfeo!
Allas, wreche, what schal y do,
545 That have swiche a lord y-lore?°   *lost*
A, way° that ich was y-bore!   *O, woe*
That him° was so hard grace   *to him / bitter fortune allotted*
   y-yarked,°
And so vile deth y-marked!"°   *(a) death was ordained*
Adoun he fel aswon° to grounde;   *in a faint*
550 His barouns him tok up in that stounde°   *moment*
And telleth him how it° geth—   *it (the world)*
"It is no bot of mannes
   deth!"   *there is no remedy for man's death!*
   King Orfeo knewe wele bi than
His steward was a trewe man
555 And loved him as he aught to do,
And stont up, and seyt thus, "Lo,
Steward, herkne now this thing:
Yif ich were Orfeo the king,
And hadde y-suffred ful yore°   *very long ago*
560 In wildernisse miche sore,
And hadde ywon mi quen o-wy
Out of the lond of fairy,
And hadde y-brought the levedi hende°   *gracious*
Right here to the tounes ende,
565 And with a begger her in y-nome,°   *had placed her*
And were mi-self hider y-come
Poverlich to the, thus stille,
For to asay° thi gode wille,   *test*
And ich founde the thus trewe,
570 Thou no schust it never rewe.°   *should never regret it*
Sikerlich,° for love or ay,°   *surely / fear*
Thou schust° be king after mi day;   *should*
And yif° thou of mi deth hadest ben
   blithe,°   *but if / happy*

Thou schust have voided, also
   swithe."°   *been banished immediately*
575 Tho all tho° that therin sete   *then all those*
That it was King Orfeo underyete,   *recognized that it was*
And the steward him wele knewe—
Over and over the bord he threwe,°   *overturned the table*
And fel adoun to his° fet;   *his (Sir Orfeo)*
580 So dede everich lord that ther sete,
And all thai seyd at o criing:°   *in one cry*
"Ye beth our lord, sir, and our king!"
Glad thai were of his live;°   *life*
To chaumber thai ladde him als belive° *led him immediately*
585 And bathed him and schaved his berd,
And tired° him as a king apert;°   *clothed / openly*
And sethen,° with gret processioun,   *afterwards*
Thai brought the quen into the toun
With al maner menstraci—
590 Lord! ther was grete melody!
For joie thai wepe with her eighe
That hem so sounde y-comen seighe.
Now King Orfeo newe coround° is,   *newly crowned*
And his quen, Dame Heurodis,
595 And lived long afterward,
And sethen° was king the steward.   *and after that*
Harpours in Bretaine after than
Herd hou this mervaile bigan,
And made herof° a lay of gode
   likeing,°   *made of it / great delight*
600 And nempned° it after the king.   *named*
That lay "Orfeo" is y-hote;°   *called*
Gode is the lay, swete is the note.
Thus com Sir Orfeo out of his care:°   *sorrow*
God graunt ous alle wele to fare! Amen!

Explicit.°   *the end*
—c. 1325

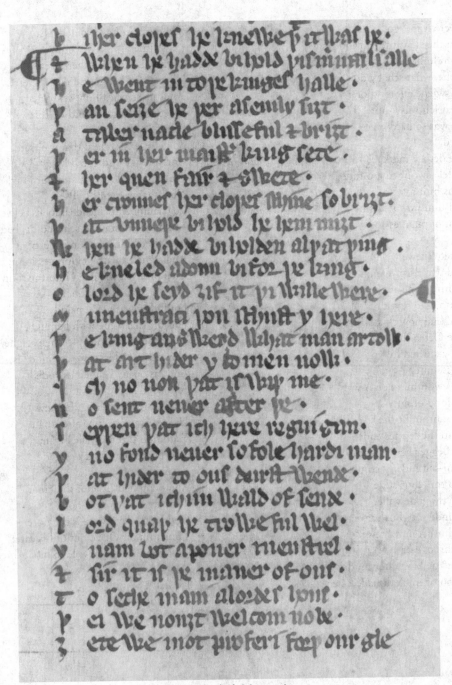

The Auchinleck Manuscript
(National Library of Scotland, Advocates' MS. 19.2.1),
fol. 302r, the last 26 lines of the first column (lines 417–34).

THE MABINOGI

The group of tales that are known as *The Mabinogi* form the core of the earliest known major collection of Welsh literature. They provide a unique window into the world of pre-literate Celtic culture that came to assume a vital role in the literature of England as well as that of Scotland, Ireland, and Wales. (Indeed, they connect in various ways with several of the major works of Middle English literature—from *Sir Gawain and the Green Knight* to Malory's Arthurian romances.) But *The Mabinogi* are also remarkable works in themselves—remarkable in the richness of the quasi-mythical world they evoke, in the intensely human conflicts and dilemmas they present, and in the sheer narrative interest of their story material.

The written form of these tales dates from the early fourteenth century; the manuscript referred to as the *White Book of Rhydderch*, which provides a near-complete manuscript of the four tales known as *The Mabinogi*, together with seven other early Welsh tales, dates from c. 1325. But it has generally been concluded (from both internal and external evidence) that the tales were in all likelihood shaped through several centuries of oral transmission before this. An early twelfth-century manuscript includes fragments of the tales, and some linguistic and cultural evidence suggests that they may well have existed in something resembling their present form in the eleventh and twelfth centuries.

By the period 1000–1250, the Celtic peoples, who in pre-Roman times had populated a good deal of what is now England, had been driven first by the Romans and later by the Anglo-Saxons into the further reaches of the British Isles: Wales, Scotland, and Ireland. Though the language and culture of the people developed various individual characteristics in each of these areas, they also retained a recognizably Celtic character. Free-spirited and tempestuous, colorful, as fond of storytelling as of feasting and of other physical pleasures, yet deeply imbued with a sense of the supernatural world—in such terms have the Celtic peoples often been characterized, by themselves as often as by outsiders, and the appeal of these tales has doubtless rested in no small part on the degree to which they convey that spirit in vivid and elemental fashion. Just as much, though, the appeal of the tales is rooted in a narrative strength that partakes of myth, folklore and history.

Many parallels to these stories exist in early Irish literature (as, for example, in the *Fled Bricrend* tale that was a key source for the Gawain poet): ritualized competitions between two noblemen to win the hand of a lady; ritualized missions or "errands," always involving some request; battles in which the combatants are pledged to return to the same place in exactly a year's time; elaborate tricks in which the participants make similar arrangements; repeated chains of events in which the supernatural figures prominently. As well, in the versions that have come down to us the Welsh tales seem to be touched by something of the chivalric spirit. The Welsh language did not import new words to denote such concepts as "knight" and "armor" (instead adapting exiting vocabulary to serve additional purposes or take on new connotations), and it is thus difficult to speak with any certainty of the extent to which the chivalric world permeates the world of *The Mabinogi*. In the other direction, however, we do know that Malory and other writers of Middle English romance borrowed here and there from the old Welsh tales; Malory, for example, borrows the names of Bedivere and Guinevere, and the Gawain poet evidently drew on the story of Pwyll being tempted by the availability of Arrawn's wife during the year in which he and Arrawn assumed each other's appearance.

"Pwyll Lord of Dyved" is the first of a group of four tales with which all manuscript versions of the early Welsh tales open; each of these four ends with a close variant of the expression "So ends this part [or "branch"] of the mabinogi [or "tale"]." Like other tales in the group, "Pwyll Lord of Dyved" includes several more or less self-contained narratives. The four are generally thought to display a sufficient degree of structural and thematic affinity so as to justify the supposition that one individual was involved in shaping the written form we now know. The other seven tales included in the early manuscripts are more diverse, and for the most part less clear in their narrative structure. (Charlotte Guest, who in the nineteenth century was instrumental in introducing the tales to the English-speaking world, applied a word she invented, "Mabinogion," to the entire collection of eleven tales, and since then they have continued to be referred to most frequently in that way.)

Even in a tale such as "Pwyll Lord of Dyved" there are numerous loose ends and inconsistencies—especially in the last of the three narratives that comprise the tale. Why and by whom is the baby abducted? Why is he abandoned with Teirnyon? What significance do the horses have? Why is the boy given away almost as soon as he has been returned to Pwyll and Rhiannon? None of this is made clear. It has been suggested that the presence of this sort of narrative inconsistency in even the most tightly structured of the tales is an indication of the degree to which they represent a long process of oral transmission in which elements of story material may be altered, combined and recombined many times over. Unquestionably the stories of *The Mabinogi* are often inconsistent, and often seem incomplete. Yet they continue to convey a mythic and narrative resonance; the tales continue to hold for readers a fascination that is at least as much literary as it is anthropological.

⌘ ⌘ ⌘

Pwyll,[1] Prince of Dyfed

Pwyll,[2] Prince of Dyfed, was lord of the seven cantrefs[3] of Dyfed. Once upon a time he was at Arberth, his chief court, and he was seized by the desire to go hunting. The part of his dominions in which he wished to hunt was Glyn Cuch, so he set forth from Arberth that night, and went as far as Llwyn Diarwyd. And that night he stayed there, and early the next day he rose and came to Glyn Cuch; there he let loose the dogs in the wood, and sounded the horn, and began the chase. And as he followed the dogs, he lost his companions, and while he listened to the hounds, he heard the cry of other hounds, a different cry, and coming from the opposite direction.

Pwyll beheld a glade in the wood forming a level plain, and as his dogs came to the edge of the glade he saw a stag in front of the other dogs. As it reached the middle of the glade, the dogs that had been following it overtook it and brought it down. Then he looked at the color of the dogs (not paying any attention to the stag); of all the hounds that he had seen in the world, he had never seen any like these. Their hair was of a brilliant shining white, and their ears were red, and as the whiteness of their bodies shone, so did the redness of their ears glisten. And he came towards the dogs, and drove away those that had brought down the stag, and set his own dogs upon the dying animal.

As he was urging on his dogs he saw a horseman coming towards him, upon a large light-gray steed, with a hunting horn around his neck, and clad in garments of gray woolen in the fashion of a hunter. The horseman drew near and spoke to him. "Chieftain," said he, "I know who you are, and I refuse to greet you."

"Perhaps," said Pwyll, "you are of such high position that you feel it would be inappropriate to do so."

"God knows," answered he, "it is not my dignity that prevents me."

"What is it then, chieftain?" asked Pwyll.

"By heaven, it is by reason of your own rudeness and want of courtesy."

"What discourtesy, chieftain, have you seen in me?"

"Greater discourtesy I have never seen," said he, "than to drive away the dogs that were killing the stag, and to set your dogs upon it. This was discourteous, and though I will not take revenge upon you, yet I declare to heaven that I will claim dishonor on you to the value of one hundred stags."

---

[1] *Pwyll, Prince of Dyfed* The present text, prepared for *The Broadview Anthology of British Literature*, is based very largely upon the English translation of Charlotte Guest. Certain passages referring to expressions of sexuality that were omitted from the Guest translation are here restored, and the text has been substantially modernized. Certain spellings have also been returned to their usual Welsh form.

[2] *Pwyll* Welsh: good sense, judgment.

[3] *cantrefs* Districts each containing a hundred townships.

"Chieftain," Pwyll replied, "if I have done wrong I will win your friendship."

"How will you do that?"

"According to your rank—but who are you?"

"A crowned king am I in the land from which I have come."

"Lord," said Pwyll, "may the day prosper with you. And from what land do you come?"

"From Annwn," he answered: "Arawn, King of Annwn, am I."

"Lord," said Pwyll, "how may I gain your friendship?"

"In this way," he said. "There is a man whose dominions border directly on mine, and who is always making war against me. His name is Hafgan, and he too is a king of Annwn. By ridding me of this oppression, which you can easily do, you shall gain my friendship."

"Gladly will I do this," said Pwyll. "Show me how I may."

"I will show you. I will make a firm friendship with you, and I will do the following. I will send you to Annwn in my place, and I will give you the fairest lady you ever beheld as your companion, and I will put my form and appearance upon you, so that not a page of the chamber, nor the steward, nor any other man that has followed me shall know that you are not I. This shall be for the space of a year from tomorrow, and then we will meet in this place."

"Yes," said Pwyll, "but when I have been there for a space of a year, how shall I recognize the man you are speaking of?"

"One year from this night," he answered, "it has already been arranged that he and I will meet at the ford; assume my appearance and take my place there, and with one stroke that you give him, he shall no longer live. And if he asks you to give him another, do not do so, no matter how much he may entreat you. For when I did so, he fought with me the next day as well as he had ever done before."

"Very well," said Pwyll, "but what shall I do concerning my kingdom if I must be away from it for a twelvemonth?"

Arawn said, "I will make sure that no one in your dominions, neither man nor woman, will know that I am not you; I will take on your appearance, and act in your place."

"Gladly then," said Pwyll, "I will set forward."

"Your path shall be clear, and nothing will detain you until you come into my dominions, and I myself will be your guide."

So Arawn conducted Pwyll until he came in sight of the court and its dwellings. "The court and the kingdom," he said, "are now in your power. Enter the court; there is no one there who will know you, and when you observe how things are done there, you will know the customs of the court."

So Pwyll went forward to the court, and when he came there he beheld sleeping rooms, and halls, and chambers—the most beautiful buildings ever seen. He went into the hall to change, and youths and pages came to dress him, and all as they entered saluted him. Two knights came and removed his hunting dress, and clothed him in a vesture of silk and gold. The hall was prepared, and behold he saw the household and the troops come in, the most refined and noble troops that he had ever seen. With them came the queen, who was the fairest woman he had ever yet beheld; she had on a yellow robe of silk and gold. They washed and went to the table and sat down, the queen upon one side of him, and one who seemed to be an earl on the other side.

Pwyll began to speak with the queen, and he thought from her speech that she was the most gracious, lively, and most noble lady he had ever spoken with. And they partook of food and drink, and there were songs and celebrations. Of all the courts upon the earth, this was the best supplied with food and drink, all served in vessels of gold, decorated with royal jewels.

When the time came for them to go to bed, Pwyll and the queen retired. As soon as they got into the bed, he turned away from her, and from then until the next day he did not speak a word to her. The next day they spoke affectionately to each other, but however tender they were to each other during the day, each night was like the first.

Pwyll spent the year before the night that had been fixed for the conflict in hunting, feasting, singing, dancing, and enjoying himself with his companions. When that night finally came, it was remembered even by those who lived in the most distant parts of his dominions. He went to the meeting, and the nobles of the kingdom went with him. When he came to the ford, a knight rode up to him and spoke. "Good men," he said, "listen well. It is between two kings that this meeting is, and between them only. Each has made a claim on the other's land and territory; all of you must stand aside and leave the fight to be between them."

Thereupon the two kings approached each other in the middle of the ford, and prepared to do battle. And from first thrust, the man who was taking the place of Arawn struck Hafgan on the centre of the boss of his shield, so that it was split in two, and his armor was broken, and Hafgan himself was thrown to the ground an arm's and a spear's length over the back of his horse, and he received a deadly blow. "Oh chieftain," said Hafgan, "what right have you to cause my death? I was doing you no harm, and I know not why you would slay me. But, for the love of heaven, since you have begun to slay me, finish the job."

"Ah, chieftain," he replied, "I may yet repent this, but, whoever else may slay you now, I will not do so."

"My trusted lords," said Hafgan, "take me away from here. My death has come. I shall not be able to uphold you any longer."

"My nobles," said the one who was in Arawn's place, "take counsel and know who ought to be my subjects."

"Lord," they said, "all should be your subjects, for there is no king ruling over the whole of Annwn but you."

"Agreed," he replied. "It is right that he who comes humbly should be received graciously—but he that does not come with obedience shall be compelled by the force of swords."

Thereupon he received the homage of the men, and he began to conquer the country, and the next day by noon the two kingdoms were in his power. And thereupon he went to keep his tryst, and came to Glyn Cuch. When he came there, the king of Annwn was there to meet him; the two rejoiced to see each other. "Truly," said Arawn, "may heaven reward you for your friendship towards me; I have heard what you have done."

"When you return to your own land," said Pwyll, "you will see what I have done for you."

"Whatever you have done for me," said Arawn, "may heaven repay you for it."

Then Arawn gave back to Pwyll Prince of Dyfed his proper form and semblance, and he himself resumed his own form and semblance, and Arawn set forth towards the court of Annwn. He rejoiced when he beheld his troops and his household, whom he had not seen for so long—but they had not known of his absence, and wondered no more at his coming than they would have on any other day. That day was spent on joy and merriment as Arawn sat and conversed with his wife and his nobles. And when it was time for them to go to bed rather than carouse, they retired.

Arawn's wife then came to him in bed, and he spoke to her and they joined each other in love and pleasure. It had been a year since she had been treated in this way, and for a long time she thought to herself, "How he differs now from what he had been!" Eventually he awoke and spoke to her—once, twice, three times—but she provided no answer. "Why do you not reply?" he asked her. To which she replied, "For one year now I have said nothing in this place."

"What can you mean?" asked her husband. "We always talk in bed."

"For the past year this bed has seen no words and no pleasure between us, or even you turning your face towards me, let alone anything else that might have happened." And Arawn thought for a moment and then said, "Oh God, how faithful is this one I have taken for a friend!" To his wife he said, "My lady, I am not to blame, for I have not been with you or slept beside you for the space of one full year." He then told her all that had happened, and she said, "To God I declare it: the bond between you and your friend must have been strong for him to resist temptation and remain loyal to you."

"My lady, such were my own thoughts when I was silent." "No wonder," she replied. Meanwhile, Pwyll Prince of Dyfed had come to his country and dominions, and had begun to ask the nobles of the land how his rule had been during the previous year, compared with what it had been before. "Lord," they said, "your wisdom was never so great, and you were never so kind or so free in bestowing gifts, and justice was never more seen than it has been in this past year."

"By heaven," said Pwyll, "for all the good you have enjoyed, you should thank the one who has been with you; thus has this matter been." Thereupon Pwyll related everything to them.

"Truly, lord," they said, "let us give thanks unto heaven that you have such a friendship. We ask you not to withhold from us a continuation of the sort of rule that we have enjoyed for the past year."

"I take heaven as my witness that I will not withhold it," answered Pwyll. And thenceforth Arawn and Pwyll made strong the friendship that was between them, and each sent unto the other horses, and greyhounds, and hawks, and such jewels as they thought would be pleasing to each other. And by reason of having lived a year in Annwn, and having ruled there so prosperously and united the two kingdoms in one day by his valor and prowess, Pwyll lost the name Pwyll Prince of Dyfed and was called Pwyll Head of Annwn from that time forward.

One day Pwyll was at Arberth, his chief court, where a feast had been prepared for him, and with him was a great host of men. And after the first part of the feast Pwyll arose to walk, and he went to the top of a mound that was above the court, and was called Gorsedd Arberth.

"My lord," said one of the court, "it is peculiar to the mound that whatever nobly born man sits upon it cannot leave without either receiving wounding blows, or else seeing a wonder."

"I fear not to receive wounding blows in the midst of such a host as this," said Pwyll, "but as to the wonder, gladly would I see it. I will therefore go and sit upon the mound."

And upon the mound he sat. And while he sat there, they all saw a lady on a great white horse, with a garment of shining gold around her, coming along the road that led past the mound. And the horse seemed to move at a slow and even pace, and to be coming up towards the mound. "Men," asked Pwyll, "is there any among you who knows that lady on horseback?"

"There is not, my lord," said they.

"One of you go and meet her," Pwyll commanded, "so that we may know who she is." One of the men arose, and as he came upon the road to meet her, she passed by. He followed as fast as he could on foot, but the more he increased his speed, the further she was from him. And when he saw that it was no use to follow her, he returned to Pwyll and said to him, "Lord, it is useless for anyone in the world to follow her on foot."

"In that case," said Pwyll, "go unto the court, and take the fleetest horse that you see, and go after her." The man to whom Pwyll had spoken took the horse

and went forward as he had been told. And he came to an open level plain, and put spurs to his horse; and the more he urged on his horse, the further was the mysterious lady in front of him. Yet she held the same pace as she had at first. His horse began to fail, and when his horse's feet failed him, he returned to the place where Pwyll was. "My lord," said he, "it will be useless for anyone to follow yonder lady. I know of no horse in these realms swifter than this one, and it was no help to me as I tried to pursue her."

"Of a truth," said Pwyll, "there must be some illusion here. Let us go towards the court." So to the court they went, and they spent that night there. And the next day they arose, and that day also they spent at court until it was time to go to meat.

And after the first part of the feast Pwyll began to speak. "Of a truth," said Pwyll, "we will go to the same place as yesterday, to the top of the mound. And you," he commanded one of his young men, "take the swiftest horse that you know in the field." And this the young man did. They went towards the mound, taking the horse with them. And as they were sitting down they beheld the lady on the same horse as she had ridden before, and in the same clothing, coming along the same road. "Behold," said Pwyll, "here is the lady of yesterday on horseback. Make ready, young man, to learn who she is."

"My lord," said he, "that I will gladly do." And thereupon the lady on horseback came alongside them. So the youth mounted his horse; and before he had settled himself in the saddle, she passed by, and there was a clear space between them. But her speed was no greater than it had been the day before. Then he put his horse into a trot, and thought that, despite the gentle pace at which his horse went, he would soon overtake her. But he was proved wrong, so he broke into a gallop. And still he came no nearer to her than if he had been on foot. The more he urged on his horse, the further she was from him. Yet she did not ride faster than before. When he saw that it was useless to follow her, he returned to where Pwyll was. "Lord," said he, "the horse can do no more than you have seen."

"I see indeed that it is useless for anyone to try and follow her," said Pwyll. "By heaven," he said, "she must have a message for someone on this plain if only she were willing to give it! Let us go back to the court." And to court they went, and they spent that night in songs and in feasting, as it pleased them.

And the next day they amused themselves until it was time to go to meat. When the feasting was ended Pwyll said, "Where are the troops that went with me yesterday and the day before to the top of the mound?"

"Lord, we are here," said they.

"Let us go," he said, "to the mound, to sit there. And you," said he to the page who tended his horse, "saddle my horse and hasten with him to the road, and bring my spurs with you." And the youth did this.

They went and sat upon the mound, and they had been there only a short time before they saw the lady on horseback coming by the same road, and in the same clothing, and at the same pace. "Young man," said Pwyll, "I see the lady on horseback coming; give me my horse!" No sooner had he mounted his horse than she passed. And he turned after her and followed her. And he let his horse go bounding energetically, and thought that at the second step or the third he would catch up with her. But he came no nearer to her than at first. Then he urged his horse to its utmost speed, and still he found that it brought him no closer. Then Pwyll said, "Oh maiden, for the sake of the one whom you love best, wait for me."

"I will do so gladly," said she. "It would have been better for your horse if you had asked this of me much earlier." So the maiden stopped, and she threw back that part of her headdress that covered her face, and fixed her eyes upon him, and began to talk with him.

"Lady," he asked, "where do you come from, and where do you journey to?"

"I travel on my own errand," said she, "and very glad I am to see you."

"And I am glad to see you," said he. Already he was beginning to think that the beauty of all the women and girls he had ever seen was as nothing compared to her beauty. "Lady," he said, "will you tell me anything concerning your purpose?"

"Between myself and God, I will," said she. "My chief quest was to seek you out."

"By heaven," said Pwyll, "that is to me the most pleasing quest on which you could have come. Will you tell me who you are?"

"I will tell you, lord," said she. "I am Rhiannon,[1] the daughter of Hefeydd Hên. They sought to give me to a husband against my will, but no husband would I have, and that because of my love for you. Nor will I yet have one now, unless you reject me. Hither have I come to hear your answer."

"By heaven," said Pwyll, "this is my answer: if I could choose from all the women and girls in the world, you are the one I would choose."

"Truly," said she, "if you mean what you say, make a pledge to meet me before I am given to another."

"The sooner I may do so, the more pleasing it will be to me," said Pwyll. "Wherever you wish, there will I meet you."

"Then meet me on this day a year from now at the court of Hefeydd Hên. I will cause a feast to be prepared, and it will be ready for your arrival."

"Gladly," said he, "will I keep this tryst."

"My lord," said she, "remain in health, and remember to keep your promise. Now I will go from here." So they parted, and he went back to his troops and the people of his household, and whenever they asked him questions about the damsel, he always turned the talk to other matters.

When a year had passed, he caused one hundred knights to equip themselves and to go with him to the court of Hefeydd Hên. And he came to the court, and there was great joy concerning him; there had been vast preparations for his coming, and the people milled about amongst great rejoicing. And the whole court was placed under his command.

The hall was decorated, and they sat down to dinner. Hefeydd Hên was on one side of Pwyll, and Rhiannon on the other, and all the rest according to their rank. And they ate and feasted and talked one with another, and at the beginning of the carousing after the meal there entered a tall auburn-haired youth of royal bearing, clothed in a garment of satin brocaded silk. When he came to the hall, he saluted Pwyll and his companions.

"The greeting of heaven be unto you," said Pwyll,

---

[1] *Rhiannon*   The character of Rhiannon appears in several of the early Welsh tales; like Arawn, she is always portrayed as a being who is to a greater or lesser degree otherworldly, and is possessed of magical powers. She is particularly associated with the horse-goddess Epona.

"come and sit down."

"No," said he, "I come with a request, and I will do my errand."

"Do so freely," said Pwyll.

"My lord," said the stranger, "my errand is with you; it is to make a request of you that I have come."

"Whatever favour you ask of me," said Pwyll, "so far as I am able to grant it, it shall be yours."

"Ah!" said Rhiannon, "why ever did you give that answer?"

"Has he not said this in the presence of all these nobles?" asked the young stranger.

"Sir," said Pwyll, "tell me what is the favor you request."

"The lady I love best is to sleep with you this night; I have come to ask you for her to be given to me with this wedding feast."

And Pwyll sat for a long time in silence because of the answer he had given. "You may well be silent," said Rhiannon. "Never did a man make worse use of his wits than you have just done."

"My lady," said Pwyll to her, "I did not know who he was, or what he would ask for."

"He is the man to whom they would have given me against my will," said she. "He is Gwawl the son of Clud, a man of great power and wealth. Now you have given him your word, and you are obliged to bestow me upon him, or shame will befall you."

"My lady," said he, "I do not understand your answer. Never can I do as you say."

"Bestow me upon him," said Rhiannon, "and I will make sure that I shall never be his."

"How can you make that happen?" asked Pwyll.

"In your hand I will place a small bag," she said. "See that you keep it well. He has asked you for this banquet, but the preparations for it are not in your power to give. For the knights and the rest of the household I prepared this feast—such will be your answer respecting this. And as for myself, I will agree to sleep with him on this night in a year's time. At the end of the year, return here," said she, "and bring this bag with you, and let your one hundred knights be in the orchard over there. And when he is in the midst of joy and feasting, come in by yourself, clad in ragged clothes, and holding your bag in your hand. Ask nothing but a bag full of food, and I will so arrange things that if all

the meat and drink in these seven cantrefs were put into the bag, it would be no fuller than before. And after a great deal has been put in the bag, he will ask you whether your bag will ever be full. Say then that it never will, until a man of noble birth and of great wealth shall arrive and shall press down on everything that is in the bag with both his feet, saying, 'Enough has now been put herein'; and I will cause him to go and press down on the food in the bag. When he does so, you must turn the bag so that he is in over his head, and then you must tie a knot with the thongs of the bag. Make sure you have a good horn around your neck, and as soon as you have bound him in the bag, put wind in your horn, and let that be a signal between you and your knights. When they hear the sound of the horn, let them come down upon the court."

The two had been talking quietly between themselves; now Gwawl spoke up, saying to Pwyll, "My lord, I must have an answer to my request."

"As much of what you have asked for as it is in my power to give, you shall have," replied Pwyll.

"My lord," added Rhiannon to Gwawl, "as for the feast and the banquet that are laid out here, I have bestowed them upon the men of Dyfed, and the household and the warriors that are with us. These things I cannot allow to be given to any others. But in a year from tonight a banquet shall be prepared for you in this court when you sleep with me."

So Gwawl went forth to his lands, and Pwyll went back to Dyfed. In their own lands they both spent that year, and at the end of the twelvemonth it was time for the feast at the court of Hefeydd Hên. Then Gwawl the son of Clud set out to the feast that had been prepared for him, and he came to the court, and he was received there with rejoicing. Pwyll head of Annwn came to the orchard with his one hundred knights, as Rhiannon had commanded him, and he had brought the bag with him. And Pwyll was clad in coarse and ragged clothes, and wore large clumsy old shoes upon his feet. When he knew that the carousing after the meal had begun, he went towards the hall, and when he came into the hall he saluted Gwawl the son of Clud, and his company, both men and women.

"Heaven prosper you," said Gwawl, "and the greeting of heaven be unto you."

"My lord," said Pwyll, "may heaven reward you! I

have an errand with you."

"Welcome to you and to your errand; if you ask of me something which is just, you shall be granted what you wish."

"That is only fair," answered Pwyll. "I ask only from need; the favor that I ask is to have this small bag that you see filled with meat and drink."

"This is a reasonable request," said Gwawl, "and gladly shall I grant it. Bring him food." A great number of attendants arose and began to fill the bag, but no matter how much they put into it, it was no fuller than at first. "Friend," said Gwawl, "will your bag ever be full?"

"It will not, I declare to heaven," said Pwyll, "unless one who is possessed of land and many valuables shall arise and tread down with both his feet the food that is within the bag and shall say, 'Enough has been put herein.'"

Then Rhiannon said to Gwawl the son of Clud, "rise up quickly."

"I will willingly arise," said Gwawl. So he rose up and put his two feet into the bag. And Pwyll turned up the sides of the bag, so that Gwawl was over his head in it. And Pwyll shut it up quickly and slipped a knot upon the thongs, and blew his horn. And behold, thereupon his household came down upon the court. And they seized all the host that had come with Gwawl, and took each one prisoner. And Pwyll threw off his rags, and his old shoes, and his tattered clothes; and as they came in, every one of Pwyll's knights struck a blow upon the bag, and asked, "What is here?"

"A badger," another would say. And in this manner they played, each of them striking the bag, either with his foot or with a staff. And thus they played with the bag. Everyone as he came in asked, "What game are you playing at?"

"The game of badger in the bag," he would be told. And then was the game of badger-in-the-bag first played.

"Lord," said the man in the bag, "if you would only listen to me! I do not deserve to be slain in a bag."

Then said Hefeydd Hên, "My lord, he speaks truth. It is fitting that you listen to him; he does not deserve this death."

"Truly," said Pwyll to Rhiannon and Hefeydd, "I will take your advice concerning him."

"My lord, this then is my counsel," said Rhiannon to Pwyll. "You are now in a position in which it behooves you to satisfy petitioners and minstrels; let Gwawl give unto them in your place, and take a pledge from him that he will never seek to avenge what has been done to him. This will be punishment enough."

"I will do this gladly," said Gwawl from within the bag.

"And gladly will I accept your assurance," said Pwyll, "if this is what Hefeydd Hên and Rhiannon counsel me to do."

"Such is our counsel," they answered.

"I accept it," said Pwyll. "But surely we should demand some bond to guarantee his good behavior."

"We will answer for him," said Hefeydd, "until his men are free to do so." And upon this Gwawl was let out of the bag and his liegemen were also freed. "Let us now demand of Gwawl his bond," said Hefeydd. "We know what should be taken from him." And Hefeydd listed the sureties. Said Gwawl, "You may draw up the agreement yourself."

"It will be enough that all shall be as Rhiannon said," answered Pwyll. So on those terms were the sureties pledged.

"Truly, my lord," said Gwawl, "I am greatly hurt, and I have many wounds. I am in need of healing; with your permission I will now go forth. I will leave nobles in my place to answer for me in everything that you require."

"Willingly," said Pwyll, "will we allow you to do this." So Gwawl went off towards his own lands.

The hall was then set in order for Pwyll and the men of his company, and also for the people of the court, and they went to the tables and sat down; as they had sat at the same time twelve months earlier, so they sat that night. And they ate, and feasted, and spent the night in mirth and tranquillity. And the time came that they should retire, and Pwyll and Rhiannon went to their chamber, and for them the night was a time of pleasure and delight.

Next morning at the break of day Rhiannon said, "My lord, arise and begin to give your gifts to the minstrels. Refuse no one today that may ask you to be generous."

"Gladly shall it be done," said Pwyll, "both today and every day while this feast shall last." So Pwyll arose, and he caused silence to be proclaimed, and he instructed all the petitioners and the minstrels to show and to point out what gifts they desired. This being done, the feast went on, and he denied no one while it lasted. And when the feast was ended, Pwyll said unto Hefeydd, "My lord, with your permission, I will set out for Dyfed tomorrow."

"Certainly," said Hefeydd. "May heaven help you to prosper. Fix also a time when Rhiannon may follow you."

"By heaven," said Pwyll, "we will leave here together."

"Is that your will, my lord?" said Hefeydd.

"Yes, by heaven," answered Pwyll.

The next day they set out for Dyfed, and journeyed to the court of Arberth, where a feast was made ready for them. And there came to them great numbers of the most important men and most noble ladies of the land, and of these there was none to whom Rhiannon did not give some rich gift, either a bracelet, a ring or a precious stone. And Pwyll and Rhiannon ruled the land prosperously both that year and the next.

In the third year the nobles of the land began to be sorrowful at seeing a man whom they loved so much, and who was their lord and their foster-brother, without an heir, and they came to him. The place where they met was Preseleu, in Dyfed. "Lord," said they, "we know that you are not so young as some of the men in this country, and we fear that you may not be provided with an heir by the wife you have taken. Take therefore another wife—one by whom you may have heirs. You cannot always remain with us, and though you desire things to stay as they are, we do not wish to stand idly by."

"Truly," said Pwyll, "Rhiannon and I have not long been joined together, and many things may yet happen. Grant me a year from this time; for the space of twelve months the two of us will remain together and after that I will abide by your wishes if nothing has changed." So they agreed. And before the end of a year a son was born unto Pwyll, and in Arberth was he born. On the night that he was born, women were brought to watch the mother and the boy. And the women slept, as did also Rhiannon and her son. And the number of the women that were brought into the chamber was six. They

watched for a good portion of the night, and then before midnight every one of them fell asleep. Towards break of day they awoke, and when they awoke they looked to where they had put the boy, and behold, he was not there. "Oh," said one of the women, "the boy is lost!"

"Yes," said another, "and we will be lucky if we are merely burnt to death for losing him!"

"Is there any counsel for us in the world in this matter?" asked another of the women.

"There is," answered another, "I offer you good counsel."

"What is that?" all the others asked.

"There is a deer-hound nearby, and she has a litter of puppies. Let us kill some one of them and rub the blood on the face and the hands of Rhiannon as she sleeps, and lay the bones before her, and say when she wakes that she herself has killed her son; she alone will not be able to go against the word of all six of us." According to this counsel it was settled.

Towards morning Rhiannon awoke, and she said, "Women, where is my son?"

"Lady," they said, "do not ask us about your son. We are still nursing the blows and the bruises we got while struggling with you; truly we never saw any woman so violent as you were. It was of no use to struggle with you. Did you not yourself destroy your own son? Do not therefore ask us for him."

"Oh wretched creatures!" said Rhiannon, "for the sake of the Lord God who knows all things, do not bring false charges against me. God, who knows all things, knows that this accusation is not true. If you are telling me this because you are afraid, I swear before heaven I will protect you."

"Truly," they said, "we would not bring evil on ourselves for anyone in the world."

"Oh wretched creatures," said Rhiannon, "you will receive no evil by telling the truth." But for all her words, whether kind or harsh, Rhiannon received the same answer from the women.

And Pwyll the head of Annwn arose, and so did his knights and those in his household. The death of the child could not be concealed, but the story went forth throughout the land, and all the nobles heard it. And the nobles came to Pwyll, and beseeched him to send his wife away for the great crime that she had done. Pwyll answered them, saying that they had put forward no reason to blame his wife other than her having had no children. "There was no reason given to put aside my wife except that she was childless. But a child she now has had, and therefore I will not send her away. If she has done any wrong, let her do penance for it."

So Rhiannon sent for the teachers and the wise men, and, since she preferred doing penance to contending with the women, she took upon herself a penance. The penance that was imposed upon her was this: that she should remain in that court of Arberth until the end of seven years, and that she should sit every day near a horse-block that was outside the gate. She had to relate the story to all who should come there whom she might suppose not to know it already, and she should make the offer to all guests and strangers, that if they would permit her to do so, she would carry them upon her back to the court. But it rarely happened that any would permit this. And thus did she spend the next part of the year.

Now at that time, Teyrnon Twryf Lliant was lord of Gwent-Ys-Coed, and he was the best man in the world. And unto his house belonged a mare more beautiful than any other horse in the kingdom. And on the night of the first of May[1] every year she foaled, and no one knew what became of the foals. And one night Teyrnon said to his wife, "Wife, we are fools that our mare should foal every year, and that we never have any of her colts."

"What can be done in the matter?" she asked.

"This is the night of the first of May," said he. "The vengeance of heaven be upon me if I am not able to learn what misfortune it is that takes away the colts." So he caused the mare to be brought into a house, and he armed himself, and that night he began to watch. And in the beginning of the night the mare gave birth to a large and beautiful colt, and it stood up in that place. And Teyrnon got up and looked at the size of the colt, and as he did so he heard a great commotion. And behold, after the commotion an arm ending in a claw came through the window into the house, and it seized the colt by the mane. Then Teyrnon drew his sword, and struck off the arm at the elbow, so that a portion of

the arm, together with the colt, remained in the house with him, and then did he hear a tumult and wailing, both at once. And he went out of the door in the direction of the noise, and he could not see the cause of the tumult because of the darkness of the night, but he rushed after it, following the noise. Then he remembered that he had left the door open and he returned. And behold, at the door there was an infant boy in swaddling clothes, wrapped in a mantle of brocaded silk. And Teyrnon took up the boy, and beheld that he was very strong for such a small baby.

Then he shut the door, and went into the chamber where his wife was. "My lady," he said, "are you sleeping?"

"No, my lord," said she. "I was asleep, but as you came in I did awake."

"Behold, here is a child for you if you will take him," said Teyrnon, "since you have never had one."

"My lord," said she, "what adventure has led to this?"

"It happened in this way," said Teyrnon, and he told her how it all had befallen.

"Truly, lord," said she, "what sort of garments are there upon the child?"

"A mantle of brocaded silk," said he.

"He is then a boy of noble birth," she replied. "My lord," she said, "if you will permit it, I should like to play a trick that will bring us great comfort and pleasure. I would like to get the support of my women, and say that I had been pregnant."

"I will readily let you do this," he answered. And so they did, and they caused the boy to be baptized with the ceremony that they used in that time, and the name which they gave to him was Gwri Wallt Euryn, because what hair was on his head was as yellow as gold.[2] And they had the boy raised in the court until he was a year old. Before the year was over he could walk stoutly, and he was stronger than a boy of three years old, even one of great growth and size. And the boy was raised the second year, and then he was as large as a child six years old. And before the end of his fourth year, he would bribe the grooms to allow him to take the horses to water.

"My lord," said his wife to Teyrnon, "where is the colt which you saved on the night that we got the boy?"

---

[1] The first day in May (or "May eve") in the Celtic calendar marked the beginning of summer. On the night before the first day of May, visits from the otherworld were often said to occur.

[2] *Wallt Euryn* Welsh: golden hair.

"I have commanded the grooms of the horses to take care of him," he said.

"Would it not be well, my lord," said she, "for you to cause him to be broken in, and given to the boy, seeing that on the same night that you found the boy the colt was foaled and you saved him?"

"I will not go against you in this matter," said Teyrnon. "I will allow you to give the colt to the boy."

"My lord," said she, "may heaven reward you; I will give it to him." So the horse was given to the boy. Then she went to the grooms and those who tended the horses and commanded them to be careful of the horse, so that it might be broken in by the time the boy could ride it.

And while these things were going forward, Teyrnon and his wife heard tidings of Rhiannon and her punishment. And Teyrnon Twryf Lliant, by reason of what he had heard, began to listen for news and inquired closely, until he had heard laments from many of those who had been to the court about Rhiannon's wretched fate and her penance. Then Teyrnon, often lamenting this sad history, pondered within himself, and looked steadfastly on the boy. As he looked upon him, it seemed that he had never beheld so great a likeness between father and son as the likeness he saw now between the boy and Pwyll the head of Annwn. The appearance of Pwyll was well known to Teyrnon, for he had long before been one of Pwyll's followers.

And immediately he began to regret the wrong that he had done, in keeping with him a boy whom he knew to be the son of another man. And the first time after that that he was alone with his wife, he asked her if it was right that they should keep the boy with them, and allow so excellent a lady as Rhiannon to be punished so greatly on his account; the boy was the son of Pwyll the head of Annwn. And Teyrnon's wife agreed with him that they should send the boy to Pwyll. "Three things, my lord," said she, "shall we gain by doing this: thanks and gratitude for releasing Rhiannon from her punishment; and thanks from Pwyll for raising his son and restoring him unto him; and thirdly, if the boy is of gentle nature he will be our foster-son, and he will do for us all the good that is in his power." So it was settled according to this counsel.

And no later than the next day Teyrnon equipped himself and set off with two other knights accompanying him. The boy was the fourth in their company, riding upon the horse that Teyrnon had given him. And they journeyed towards Arberth, and it was not long before they reached that place. And as they drew near to the court, they saw Rhiannon sitting beside a horse-block, and when they were opposite her she said, "Chieftain, do not go any further. I will carry every one of you who shall permit it to the court; this is my penance for slaying my own son and destroying him."

"Ah, fair lady," said Teyrnon, "I don't think a single one of us shall be carried upon your back."

"Let him go who wants to, but I will not," said the boy.

"Upon my soul, truly we will not have you carry us," said Teyrnon. So they went forward to the court, and there was great joy at their coming. At the court a feast had been prepared, because Pwyll had come back from the confines of Dyfed. And they went into the hall and washed, and Pwyll welcomed Teyrnon. And in this order they sat: Teyrnon between Pwyll and Rhiannon, and Teyrnon's two companions on the other side of Pwyll, with the boy between them. And after they had eaten their meat they began to carouse and to talk. And Teyrnon's talk was of the adventure of the mare and the boy, and how he and his wife had nursed and reared the child as their own. "And behold, here is your son, my lady," said Teyrnon to Rhiannon. "Whoever told that lie about you has done wrong. When I heard of your sorrow, I was troubled and grieved. And I believe that there is none of the company here who will not perceive that this boy is the son of Pwyll."

"There is none," said they all, "who is not certain of this."

"I declare to heaven," said Rhiannon, "that if this be true, there is indeed an end to my trouble."

"My lady," said Pendaran Dyfed,[1] "well have you named your son Pryderi,[2] and the name of Pryderi, son of Pwyll, head of Annwn, well becomes him."

"Look," said Rhiannon, "will not his own name be more suitable?"

"What name is that?" asked Pendaran Dyfed.

"Gwri Wallt Euryn is the name that we gave him."

"His name should be Pryderi," said Pendaran.

---

[1] *Pendaran Dyfed* Either a title ("Chieftain of Dyfed") or a proper name.

[2] *Pryderi* Welsh: worry, anxiety.

"It would be more appropriate," said Pwyll, "for the boy to take his name from the word his mother spoke when she received the joyful tidings of him." And thus it was arranged.

"Teyrnon," said Pwyll, "heaven reward you for bringing up the boy to his time; it would be fitting for him to repay you for it."

"My lord," said Teyrnon, "it was my wife who raised him, and there is no one in the world so saddened as she is at parting with him. It were well that he should bear in mind what I and my wife have done for him."

"I call heaven to witness," said Pwyll, "that while I live I will give support to you and your land. If it so pleases you, and pleases my nobles, I shall decree that, as you have raised the boy up to the present time, he may be brought up by Pendaran Dyfed from now on. And you shall be companions, and both be foster-parents unto him."

"This is good counsel," they all said. So the boy was given to Pendaran Dyfed, and the nobles of the land formed an alliance with him. Teyrnon Twryf Lliant and his companions then set out for his own country, with love and with gladness. And he went not without being offered the fairest jewels and the fairest horses, and the choicest dogs, but he would take none of them.

Thereafter they all remained in their own dominions, and Pryderi, the son of Pwyll the head of Annwn, was cared for well, so that he became the fairest youth and the most handsome, and the most skilled in games of any in the kingdom. And in this way years and years passed until the end of Pwyll the head of Annwn's life came, and he died.

And Pryderi ruled the seven cantrefs of Dyfed prosperously, and he was beloved by his people, and by all around him. And at length he added unto them the three cantrefs of Ystrad Twyi, and the four cantrefs of Ceredigion, and these seven cantrefs were called Seisyllwch. And when he added these lands to his territory, Pryderi the son of Pwyll the head of Annwn desired to take a wife, and the wife he chose was Cigfa the daughter of Gwynn Gohoyw, the son of Gloyw Lydan, the son of Casnar Wledic, one of the nobles of this island.

And thus ends this branch of the Mabinogi.

—? 12TH CENTURY

Sir Gawain and the Green Knight

Little is known about *Sir Gawain and the Green Knight* apart from what the poem itself tells us. Its author is anonymous. The work is preserved in a single manuscript copy that was originally bound up with three other poems, *Pearl, Cleannesse,* and *Patience,* which was generally regarded as having the same author. Like *Sir Gawain and the Green Knight* they are written in alliterative verse. The collection is known to have belonged to a private library in Yorkshire during the late sixteenth and early seventeenth centuries. It came to light in the nineteenth century, and *Sir Gawain and the Green Knight* was edited and printed for the first time in 1839. By the middle of the twentieth century the great interest and imaginative power of the poem had been generally acknowledged, and had attracted an increasing number of scholarly studies and commentaries.

The poem is written in a regional dialect characteristic of northwestern England at the time of its probable composition during the last quarter of the fourteenth century. That would mean that the *Gawain*-poet was a contemporary of Chaucer, who died in 1400; but even a brief comparison of their work shows how widely they were separated linguistically and culturally.

In the northern country reflected in the wintry landscapes of *Sir Gawain and the Green Knight,* an older literacy language seems to have persisted, relatively unmarked by French, a language which the poet associates with the elaborately courtly manners displayed by Gawain and his hostess. In Chaucer a reader may gain the impression that the English and French components of his language have formed a comfortable liaison, so much so that he uses both indifferently and without reserving either for particular tasks. *Sir Gawain and the Green Knight* creates a different impression: that the two elements have not yet reached an accommodation, and that the poet and his audience are sufficiently alive to the nuances of words still novel and alien to their regional culture that French words tend to be used for distinctive purposes.

The poem is composed in a unique stanza form, made up of a varying number of long alliterative lines followed by a "bob and wheel": five short lines rhyming *ababa,* of which the first consists of only two syllables. The number of stressed alliterative words in each long line also varies, the norm being three.

Evidently it suits the poet's purposes to present himself as a simple popular entertainer whose occasional comments to his audience—"I schal telle yow how thay wroght"—and explanatory remarks about incidents in the story—"Wyt ye wel, hit watz worth wele ful hoge"—create an impression of the close relationship that a storyteller must maintain with his listeners. In oral narration such remarks would arise spontaneously, but here they are contrived as part of a deliberate purpose. It is not difficult to understand why the poet should have adopted the manner of an oral tale in a written work. Alliterative poetry is addressed to the ear, not to the eye, and its effects are not fully realized unless what Chaucer called the "rum-ram-ruf" of its pounding consonants is heard. Until displaced by rhyming verse it was also the established form of English poetry, and it seems evident from *Sir Gawain and the Green Knight* that its author felt a strong attachment to native tradition and culture. That may explain why he adopted the persona of a popular storyteller in addressing his audience, when the tale itself—particularly the three episodes in Gawain's bedchamber—prove him unusually cultivated and well acquainted with the literature of courtly manners and ideals.

Sir Gawain and the Green Knight represents the close fusion of three separate stories which may have been individually familiar to the poet's audience, but which have not survived in any similar combination in England or any other country. The first is the legend of the beheading game, which provides the opening and closing episodes of the poet's story. The second is the "exchange of winnings" proposed by Gawain's host in the central episodes of his adventure, which overlaps with the third motif, the sexual testing of Gawain. Combining these three elements into a single romance was not in itself a remarkable feat. The poet's achievement lies in having amalgamated them in such a way that while they appear unrelated, the outcome of one is determined by Gawain's behavior in the quite separate circumstances of the other.

In *Sir Gawain and the Green Knight* the story takes substantially the same form as in *Fled Bricrend* (see *Contexts* below), but with many changes of detail. The giant is no longer terrifying and ugly but physically attractive, splendidly dressed, and mounted on a horse which like himself is emerald green. He makes his challenge on New Year's Day and requires his opponent to stand the return blow a year and a day later at the Green Chapel, which must be found without directions. Gawain is chosen as the court's representative, promises to meet the Green Knight as stipulated, and decapitates him. The victim picks up his head, leaps into his saddle, and after reminding Gawain of his undertaking gallops away. At the Green Chapel a year later Gawain stands three swings from the Green Knight's axe. The first two are checked just short of his neck, and the third gashes the flesh as punishment for Gawain's dishonesty in a matter which has no evident connection with the beheading game. In this and other respects *Sir Gawain and the Green Knight* is a much more elaborate and ingenious reworking of the legend, but its dependence upon that primitive story is obvious. There are reasons for supposing that the major changes in the *Gawain*-poet's version of the tale—the challenger's color, the midwinter setting, and the year's interval between blows, for instance—were of his own devising, for these are not inconsequential details but parts of the imaginative purpose that integrates the whole poem.

None of the analogues of the temptation theme used by the poet are very closely related to his story of Gawain's attempted seduction, and no source of the motif has been found in legend. In the Welsh *Mabinogi* Pwyll spends a year at the court of Arawn in his friend's likeness, sleeping beside the queen but respecting her chastity; but while his self-restraint is tested no attempt is made to seduce him. The story is one of many legends which require the hero or heroine to undergo a trial of patience, forbearance or self-denial, usually in preparation for some task that demands special powers. The French romance of *Le Chevalier à l'Épée* is distantly related to this theme, and one of several works which seem to have contributed to the *Gawain*-poet's version of the temptation story.

The James Winny translation of the poem which appears below has been widely praised for its sensitivity to nuances of meaning; given the facing-text presentation, the translator has not felt it necessary to imitate the alliterative qualities of the Middle English verse, and has thus been able to convey the sense of the original as clearly as possible for the modern reader.

⌘⌘⌘

Sir Gawayn and the Grene Knyght

FITT I

Sithen the sege and the assaut watz sesed at Troye,
The borgh brittened and brent to brondez and askez,
The tulk that the trammes of tresoun ther wroght
Watz tried for his tricherie, the trewest on erthe.

Sir Gawain and the Green Knight[1]

PART I

When the siege and the assault were ended at Troy,
The city laid waste and burnt into ashes,
The man who had plotted the treacherous scheme
Was tried for the wickedest trickery ever.

---

[1] *Sir Gawain and the Green Knight*   The translation is that of James Winny.

5 Hit watz Ennias the athel and his highe kynde[1]
   That sithen depreced provinces, and patrounes bicome
   Welneghe of al the wele in the west iles.
   Fro riche Romulus to Rome ricchis hym swythe,
   With gret bobbaunce that burghe he biges upon fyrst,
10 And nevenes hit his aune nome, as hit now hat;
   Tirius to Tuskan and teldes bigynnes,
   Langaberde in Lumbardie lyftes up homes,
   And fer over the French flod Felix Brutus
   On mony bonkkes ful brode Bretayn he settez
15   with wynne;
         Where werre and wrake and wonder
         Bi sythez hatz wont therinne,
         And oft both blysse and blunder
         Ful skete hatz skyfted synne.

20 Ande quen this Bretayn watz bigged bi this burn rych,
   Bolde bredden therinne, baret that lofden,
   In mony turned tyme tene that wroghten.
   Mo ferlyes on this folde han fallen here oft
   Then in any other that I wot, syn that ilk tyme.
25 Bot of alle that here bult, of Bretaygne kynges,
   Ay watz Arthur the hendest, as I haf herde telle.
   Forthi an aunter in erde I attle to schawe,
   That a selly in syght summe men hit holden,
   And an outtrage awenture of Arthurez wonderez.
30 If ye wyl lysten this laye bot on little quile
   I schal telle hit as-tit, as I in toun herde,[2]
         with tonge,[3]
         As hit is stad and stoken[4]
         In stori stif and stronge,
35   With lel letteres loken,
         In londe so hatz ben longe.

   This kyng lay at Camylot upon Krystmasse
   With mony luflych lorde, ledez of the best,
   Rekenly of the Rounde Table alle tho rich brether,
40 With rych revel oryght and rechles merthes.

It was princely Aeneas and his noble kin
Who then subdued kingdoms, and came to be lords
Of almost all the riches of the western isles.
Afterwards noble Romulus hastened to Rome,
45 With great pride he gave that city its beginnings,
And calls it by his own name, which it still has.
Tirius goes to Tuscany and sets up houses,
Langobard in Lombardy establishes homes,
And far over the French sea Felix Brutus
On many broad hillsides settles Britain
15   with delight;
         Where war and grief and wonder
         Have visited by turns,
         And often joy and turmoil
         Have alternated since.

20 And when Britain had been founded by this noble lord,
Valiant men bred there, who thrived on battle.
In many an age bygone they brought about trouble.
More wondrous events have occurred in this country
Than in any other I know of, since that same time.
25 But of all those whose dwelt there, of the British kings
Arthur was always judged noblest, as I have heard tell.
And so an actual adventure I mean to relate
Which some men consider a marvelous event,
And a prodigious happening among tales about Arthur.
30 If you will listen to this story just a little while
I will tell it at once, as I heard it told
         in court.
         As it is written down
         In story brave and strong,
35   Made fast in truthful words,
         That has endured long.

The king spent that Christmas at Camelot
With many gracious lords, men of great worth,
Noble brothers-in-arms worthy of the Round Table,
40 With rich revelry and carefree amusement, as was right.

---

[1] *Ennias the athel* Here *athel* is used as a title appropriate to a prince (Aeneas), but at 2065 the word is applied to Gawain's guide.

[2] *as I toun herde* It seems unlikely that the poet had either read or heard this particular tale recited. Although the beheading game figures in an Irish legend and the test of chastity has many analogues, no other surviving story combines them in a single narrative. But originality was not expected of medieval storytellers.

[3] *with tonge* Compare *wyth syght*, 197 and 226, and *meled with his muthe*, 447, for similar constructions.

[4] *stad and stoken* Set down and fixed.

Ther tournayed tulkes by tymez ful mony,
Justed ful jolilé thise gentyle knightes,
Sythen kayred to the court caroles to make.
For ther the fest watz ilyche ful fiften dayes,
45   With alle the mete and the mirthe that men couthe avyse;
Such glaume and gle glorious to here,
Dere dyn upon day, daunsyng on nyghtes,
Al watz hap upon heghe in hallez and chambrez
With lordez and ladies, as levest him thoght.
50   With all the wel of the worlde thay woned ther samen,
The most kyd knyghtez under Krystes selven,
And the lovelokkest ladies that ever lif haden,
And he the comlokest kyng that the court haldes;
For al watz this fayre folk in her first age,[1]
55   on sille,
        The hapnest under heven,
        Kyng hyghest mon of wylle;
        Hit were now gret nye to neven
        So hardy a here on hille.

60   Wyle Nwe Yer watz so yep that hit watz nwe cummen,
That day doubble on the dece watz the douth served.
Fro the kyng watz cummen with knyghtes into the halle,
The chauntré of the chapel cheved to an ende,
Loude crye watz ther kest of clerkez and other,
65   Nowel[2] nayted onewe, nevened ful ofte;
And sythen riche forth runnen to reche hondeselle,
Yeghed yeres-giftes on high, yelde hem bi hond,[3]
Debated busyly aboute tho giftes;
Ladies laghed ful loude, thogh thay lost haden,
70   And he that wan watz not wrothe, that may ye wel trawe.[4]
Alle this mirthe thay maden to the mete tyme;
When thay had waschen worthyly thay wenten to sete,
The best burne ay abof, as hit best semed,[5]
Whene Guenore, ful gay, graythed in the myddes,
75   Dressed on the dere des, dubbed al aboute,
Smal sendal bisides, a selure hir over
Of tryed tolouse, of tars tapites innoghe,

There knights fought in tournament again and again,
Jousting most gallantly, these valiant men,
Then rode to the court for dancing and song.
For there the festival lasted the whole fifteen days
45   With all the feasting and merry-making that could be devised:
Such sounds of revelry splendid to hear,
Days full of uproar, dancing at night.
Everywhere joy resounded in chambers and halls
Among lords and ladies, whatever pleased them most.
50   With all of life's best they spent that time together,
The most famous warriors in Christendom,
And the loveliest ladies who ever drew breath,
And he the finest king who rules the court.
For these fair people were then in the flower of youth
        in the hall.
55   Luckiest under heaven,
        King of loftiest mind
        Hard it would be
        Bolder men to find.

60   When New Year was so fresh that it had hardly begun,
Double helpings of food were served on the dais that day.
By the time the king with his knights entered the hall
When the service in the chapel came to an end,
Loud cries were uttered by the clergy and others,
65   "Nowel" repeated again, constantly spoken;
And then the nobles hurried to hand out New Year's gifts,
Cried their wares noisily, gave them by hand,
And argued excitedly over those gifts.
Ladies laughed out loud, even though they had lost,
70   And the winner was not angry, you may be sure.
All this merry-making went on until feasting time.
When they had washed as was fit they took their places,
The noblest knight in a higher seat, as seemed proper;
Queen Guenevere gaily dressed and placed in the middle,
75   Seated on the upper level, adorned all about;
Fine silk surrounding her, a canopy overhead
Of costly French fabric, silk carpets underfoot

---

[1] *in her first age* In their youth.

[2] *Nowel* I.e., Noël, a Christmas greeting.

[3] *And sythen ... head* Some have suggested that *hondeselle* are given to servants and *yeres-giftes* to equals. But Arthur is said figuratively to have received a *hanselle* at 491.

[4] *Ladies ... trawe* The lines refer to some kind of Christmas game, perhaps involving guesses and paying a forfeit of kisses when the guess is wrong.

[5] *The best burne ay abof* Members of the court are seated according to social degree, at the *hyghe table*, 107, or at *sidbordez*, 115. The reference to *lordes and ladis that longed to the Table*, 2515, suggests that the poet saw the Round Table as a social institution.

That were enbrawded and beten wyth the best gemmes
That myght be preved of prys wyth penyes to bye,[1]
80   in daye.[2]
     The comlokest to discrye
     Ther glent with yghen gray,[3]
     A semloker that ever he syghe
     Soth moght no mon say.

85   Bot Arthure wolde not ete til al were served,
     He watz so joly of his joyfnes, and sumquat childgered:
     His lif liked hym lyght, he lovied the lasse
     Auther to longe lye or to longe sitte,
     So bisied him his yonge blod and his brayn wylde.
90   And also an other maner meved him eke
     That he thurgh nobelay had nomen, he wolde never ete
     Upon such a dere day er hym devised were
     Of sum aventurus thyng an uncouthe tale,
     Of sum mayn mervayle, that he myght trawe,
95   Of alderes, of armes, of other aventurus,
     Other sum segg hym bisoght of sum siker knyght
     To joyne wyth hym in justyng, in jopardé to lay
     Lede, lif for lyf, leve uchon other,
     As fortune wolde fulsun hom, the fayrer to have.
100 This watz the kynges countenaunce where he in court were,
     At uch farande fest among his fre meny
               in halle.
     Therfore of face so fere
     He stightlez stif in stalle,
105 Ful yep in that Nw Yere
     Much mirthe he mas withalle.

     Thus ther stondes in stale the stif kyng hisselven,
     Talkkande bifore the hyghe table of trifles ful hende.
     There gode Gawan[4] watz graythed Gwenore bisyde,
110 And Agravain à la dure mayn on that other syde sittes,
     Bothe the kynges sistersunes and ful siker knightes;
     Bischop Bawdewyn abof biginez the table,
     And Ywan, Uryn son, ette with hymselven.
     Thise were dight on the des and derworthly served,
115 And sithen mony siker segge at the sidbordez.

That were embroidered and studded with the finest gems
That money could buy at the highest price
          anywhere.
     The loveliest to see
120 Glanced round with eyes blue-grey;
     That he had seen a fairer one
     Truly could no man say.

But Arthur would not eat until everyone was served,
He was so lively in his youth, and a little boyish.
125 He hankered after an active life, and cared very little
To spend time either lying or sitting,
His young blood and restless mind stirred him so much.
And another habit influenced him too,
Which he had made a point of honor: he would never eat
130 On such a special day until he had been told
A curious tale about some perilous thing,
Of some great wonder that he could believe,
Of princes, of battles, or other marvels;
Or some knight begged him for a trustworthy foe
135 To oppose him in jousting, in hazard to set
His life against his opponent's, each letting the other,
As luck would assist him, gain the upper hand.
This was the king's custom when he was in court,
At each splendid feast with his noble company
140   in hall.
     Therefore with proud face
     He stands there, masterful,
     Valiant in that New Year,
     Joking with them all.

145 So there the bold king himself keeps on his feet,
Chatting before the high table of charming trifles.
There good Gawain was seated beside Guenevere,
And Agravain à la Dure Main on the other side;
Both the king's nephews and outstanding knights.
150 Bishop Baldwin heads the table in the highest seat,
And Ywain, son of Urien, dined as his partner.
These knights were set on a dais and sumptuously served,
115 And after them many a true man at the side tables.

---

1   *preved of prys* Proved of value.

2   *in daye* Literally, ever.

3   *yghen gray* Virtually obligatory in medieval heroines.

4   *gode Gawan* So characterized throughout the story, even after his disgrace. The spelling of the hero's name varies considerably. He is *Gawan* consistently throughout Part 1. Later the poet or his scribe prefers the form *Gawayn* or *Gawayne*, which is used throughout Part 4. For alliterative purposes he is occasionally referred to as *Wawan*, *Wawen*, *Wowayn*, or *Wowen*. Less frequently he is *Gavan* or *Gavayn*.

Then the first cors come with crakkyng of trumpes,
Wyth mony baner ful bryght that therbi henged;
Nwe nakryn noyse with the noble pipes,
Wylde werbles and wyght wakned lote,
120   That mony hert ful highe hef at her towches.
Dayntés dryven therwyth of ful dere metes,
Foysoun of the fresche, and on so fele disches
That pine to fynde the place the peple biforne
For to sette the sylveren that sere sewes halden
125   on clothe.
        Iche lede as he loved hymselve
        Ther laght withouten lothe;
        Ay two had disches twelve,
        Good ber and bryght wyn bothe.

130   Now wyl I of hor servise say yow no more,
For uch wyghe may wel wit no wont that ther were.
An other noyse ful newe neghed bilive
That the lude myght haf leve liflode to cache;[1]
For unethe watz the noyce not a whyle sesed,
135   And the fyrst cource in the court kyndely served,
Ther hales in at the halle dor an aghlich mayster,
On the most on the molde on mesure hyghe;[2]
Fro the swyre to the swange so sware and so thik,
And his lyndes and his lymes so longe and so grete,
140   Half etayn in erde I hope that he were,
Bot mon most I algate mynn hym to bene,
And that the myriest in his muckel that myght ride;
For of his bak and his brest al were his bodi sturne,
Both his wombe and his wast were worthily smale,
145   And alle his fetures folyande, in forme that he hade,
        ful clene;
        For wonder of his hwe men hade,
        Set in his semblaunt sene;
        He ferde as freke were fade,
150   And overal enker-grene.

And al grathed in grene this gome and his wedes:
A strayte cote ful streght, that stek on his sides,
A meré mantile abof, mensked withinne
With pelure pured apert, the pane ful clene
155   With blythe blaunner ful bryght, and his hode bothe,
That watz laght fro his lokkez and layde on his schulderes;

Then the first course was brought in with trumpets blaring,
Many colorful banners hanging from them.
The novel sound of kettledrums with the splendid pipes
Waked echoes with shrill and tremulous notes,
120   That many hearts leapt at the outburst of music.
At the same time servings of such exquisite food,
Abundance of fresh meat, in so many dishes
That space could hardly be found in front of the guests
To set down the silverware holding various stews
125   on the board.
        Each man who loved himself
        Took ungrudged, pair by pair,
        From a dozen tasty dishes,
        And drank good wine or beer.

130   Now I will say nothing more about how they were served,
For everyone can guess that no shortage was there.
Another noise, quite different, quickly drew near,
So that the king might have leave to swallow some food.
For hardly had the music stopped for a moment,
135   And the first course been properly served to the court,
When there bursts in at the hall door a terrible figure,
In his stature the very tallest on earth.
From the waist to the neck so thick-set and square,
And his loins and his limbs so massive and long,
140   In truth half a giant I believe he was,
But anyway of all men I judge him the largest,
And the most attractive of his size who could sit on a horse.
For while in back and chest his body was forbidding,
Both his belly and waist were becomingly trim,
145   And every part of his body equally elegant
        in shape.
        His hue astounded them,
        Set in his looks so keen;
        For boldly he rode in,
150   Completely emerald green.

And all arrayed in green this man and his clothes:
A straight close-fitting coat that clung to his body,
A pleasant mantle over that, adorned within
With plain trimmed fur, the facing made bright
155   With gay shining ermine, and his hood of the same
Thrown back from his hair and laid over his shoulders.

---

[1] *haf leve liflode to cache* Arthur will not eat until he has *sen a selly* 475, which is about to arrive.

[2] *On the most* Not "one of the biggest" but "the very biggest."

Heme wel-haled hose of that same,
That spenet on his sparlyr, and clene spures under
Of bryght golde, upon silk bordes barred ful ryche,
160 And scholes under schankes[1] there the schalk rides;
And all his vesture verayly watz clene verdure,
Bothe the barres of his belt and other blythe stones,
That were richely rayled in his aray clene
Aboutte hymself and his sadel, upon silk werkez.
165 That were to tor for to telle of tryfles[2] the halve
That were enbrauded abof, wyth bryddes and flyghes,
With gay gaudi of grene, the gold ay inmyddes.
The pendauntes of his payttrure, the proude cropure,
His molaynes, and alle the metail anamayld was thenne,
170 The steropes that he stod on stayned of the same,
And his arsounz al after and his athel skyrtes,
That ever glemered and glent al of grene stones;
The fole that he ferkkes on fyn of that ilke,
　　　sertayn.
175 　A grene hors gret and thikke,
　A stede ful stif to strayne,
　In brawden brydel quik;
　To the gome he watz ful gayn.

Wel gay watz this gome gered in grene,
180 And the here of his hed of his hors swete.
Fayre fannand fax umbefoldes his schulderes;
A much berd as a busk over his brest henges,
That wyth his highlich here that of his hed reches
Watz evesed al umbetorne abof his elbowes,
185 That half his armes ther-under were halched in the wyse
Of a kyngez capados[3] that closes his swyre;
The mane of that mayn hors much to hit lyke,
Wel cresped and cemmed, wyth knottes ful mony
Folden in with a fildore aboute the fayre grene,
190 Ay a herle of the here, an other of golde;
The tayl and his toppyng twynnen of a sute,
And bounden bothe wyth a bande of a bryght grene,
Dubbed wyth ful dere stonez, as the dok lasted,
Sythen thrawen wyth a thwong a thwarle knot alofte,
195 Ther mony bellez ful bryght of brende golde rungen.
Such a fole upon folde, ne freke that hym rydes,

Neat tightly-drawn stockings colored to match
Clinging to his calf, and shining spurs below
Of bright gold, over embroidered and richly striped silk;
160 And without shoes on his feet there the man rides.
And truly all his clothing was brilliant green,
Both the bars on his belt and other gay gems
That were lavishly set in his shining array
Round himself and his saddle, on embroidered silk.
165 It would be hard to describe even half the fine work
That was embroidered upon it, the butterflies and birds,
With lovely beadwork of green, always centered upon gold.
The pendants on the breast-trappings, the splendid crupper,
The bosses on the bit, and all the metal enameled.
170 The stirrups he stood in were colored the same,
And his saddlebow behind him and his splendid skirts
That constantly glittered and shone, all of green gems;
The horse that he rides entirely of that color,
　　　in truth.
175 　A green horse huge and strong,
　A proud steed to restrain,
　Spirited under bridle,
　But obedient to the man.

Most attractive was this man attired in green,
180 With the hair of his head matching his horse.
Fine outspreading locks cover his shoulders;
A great beard hangs down over his chest like a bush,
That like the splendid hair that falls from his head
Was clipped all around above his elbows,
185 So that his upper arms were hidden, in the fashion
Of a royal capados that covers the neck.
That great horse's mane was treated much the same,
Well curled and combed, with numerous knots
Plaited with gold thread around the fine green,
190 Always a strand of his hair with another of gold.
His tail and his forelock were braided to match,
Both tied with a ribbon of brilliant green,
Studded with costly gems to the end of the tail,
Then tightly bound with a thong to an intricate knot
195 Where many bright bells of burnished gold rang.
No such horse upon earth, nor such a rider indeed,

---

[1] *scholes under schankes* Meaning that he was not wearing the steel shoes belonging to a suit of armor; see 574. The Green Knight's feet are covered by the *wel-haled hose* of 157.

[2] *tryfles* Decorative emblems, such as are embroidered on Gawain's silk uryson, 611–12, and on the old lady's headdress, 960.

[3] *capados* Hood.

Watz never sene in that sale wyth syght er that tyme,
    with yghe.
    He loked as layt so lyght,
200   So sayd al that hym syghe;
    Hit semed as no mon myght
    Under his dynttez dryghe.

Whether hade he no helme ne no hawbergh[1] nauther,
Ne no pysan ne no plate that pented to armes,
205 Ne no schafte ne no schelde to schwve ne to smyte,
Bot in his on honde he hade a holyn bobbe,
That is grattest in grene when grevez ar bare,
And an ax in his other, a hoge and unmete,
A spetos sparthe to expoun in spelle, quoso myght.
210 The lenkthe of an elnyerde the large hede hade,
The grayn al of grene stele and of golde hewen,
The bit burnyst bryght, with a brod egge
As wel schapen to schere as scharp rasores,
The stele of a stif staf the sturne hit bi grypte,
215 That watz wounden wyth yrn to the wandez ende,
And al bigraven with grene in gracios werkes;
A lace lapped aboute, that louked at the hede,
And so after the halme halched ful ofte,
Wyth tryed tasselez therto tacched innoghe
220 On botounz of the bryght grene brayden ful ryche.
This hathel heldez hym in and the halle entres,
Drivande to the heghe dece, dut he no wothe,
Haylsed he never one, bot heghe he over loked.
The fyrst word that he warp, "Where is," he sayd,
225 "The governour of this gyng? Gladly I wolde
Se that segg in syght, and with hymself speke
    raysoun."[2]
    To knyghtez he kest his yghe,
    And reled hym up and doun;
230   He stemmed, and con studie
    Quo walt ther most renoun.

Ther watz lokyng on lenthe the lude to beholde,
For uch mon had mervayle quat hit mene myght

Had any man in that hall before thought to see
    with his eyes.
    His glance was lightning swift,
200   All said who saw him there;
    It seemed that no one could
    His massive blows endure.

Yet he had no helmet nor hauberk either,
No neck-armour or plate belonging to arms,
205 No spear and no shield to push or to strike;
But in one hand he carried a holly-branch
That is brilliantly green when forests are bare,
And an axe in the other, monstrously huge;
A cruel battle-axe to tell of in words, if one could.
210 The great head was as broad as a measuring-rod,
The spike made entirely of green and gold steel,
Its blade brightly burnished, with a long cutting-edge
As well fashioned to shear as the keenest razor.
The grim man gripped the handle, a powerful staff,
215 That was wound with iron to the end of the haft
And all engraved in green with craftsmanly work.
It had a thong wrapped about it, fastened to the head,
And then looped round the handle several times,
With many splendid tassels attached to it
220 With buttons of bright green, richly embroidered.
This giant bursts in and rides through the hall,
Approaching the high dais, disdainful of peril,
Greeting none, but haughtily looking over their heads.
The first words he spoke, "Where is," he demanded,
225 "The governor of this crowd? Glad should I be
To clap eyes on the man, and exchange with him
    a few words."
    He looked down at the knights,
    As he rode up and down,
230   Then paused, waiting to see
    Who had the most renown.

For long there was only staring at the man,
For everyone marveled what it could mean

---

1 *hawbergh* I.e., hauberk, coat of chain mail.

2 *raysoun* Words, implicit in *speke* but evidently idiomatic.

That a hathel and a horse myght such a hwe lach
235 As growe gren as the gres and grener hit semed,
Then grene aumayl on golde glowande bryghter.
Al studied that ther stod, and stalked hym nerre
With al the wonder of the worlde what he worche schulde.
For fele sellyez had thay sen, bot such never are;
240 Forthi for fantoun and fayryye the folk there hit demed.
Therfore to answare watz arghe mony athel freke,
And al stouned at his steven and stonstil seten
In a swogh sylence thurgh the sale riche;
As al were slypped upon slepe so slaked hor lotez
245   in hyghe;
     I deme hit not al for doute,
     Bot sum for cortaysye,
     Bot let hym that al schulde loute
     Cast unto that wyghe.

250 Thenne Arthour bifore the high dece that aventure byholdez,
And rekenly hym reverenced, for rad was he never,
And sayde, "Wyghe, welcum iwys to this place,
The hede of this ostel Arthour I hat;
Lyght luflych adoun and lenge, I the praye,
255 And quat-so thy wylle is we schal wyt after."
"Nay, as help me," quoth the hathel, "he that on hygh syttes,
To wone any quyle in this won hit watz not myn ernde;
Bot for the los of the, lede, is lyft up so hyghe,
And thy burgh and thy burnes best ar holden,
260 Stifest under stel-gere on stedes to ryde,
The wyghtest and the worthyest of the worldes kynde,
Preve for to playe wyth in other pure laykez,
And here is kydde cortaysye, as I haf herd carp,
And that hatz wayned me hider, iwyis, at this tyme.
265 Ye may be seker bi this braunch that I bere here
That I passe as in pes, and no plyght seche;
For had I founded in fere in feghtyng wyse,
I have a hauberghe at home and a helme bothe,
A schelde and a scharp spere, schinande bryghte,
270 Ande other weppenes to welde, I wene wel, als;
Bot for I wolde no were, my wedez ar softer.
Bot if thou be so bold as alle burnez tellen,
Thou wyl grant me godly the gomen that I ask
          bi ryght."
275   Arthour con onsware,
       And sayd, "Sir cortays knyght,

That a knight and a horse might take such a color
235 And become green as grass, and greener it seemed
Than green enamel shining brightly on gold.
All those standing there gazed, and warily crept closer,
Bursting with wonder to see what he would do;
For many marvels they had known, but such a one never;
240 So the folk there judged it phantasm or magic.
For this reason many noble knights feared to answer:
And stunned by his words they sat there stock-still,
While dead silence spread throughout the rich hall
As though everyone fell asleep, so was their talk stilled
245   at a word.
     Not just for fear, I think,
     But some for courtesy;
     Letting him whom all revere
     To that man reply.

250 Then Arthur confronts that wonder before the high table,
And saluted him politely, for afraid was he never,
And said, "Sir, welcome indeed to this place;
I am master of this house, my name is Arthur.
Be pleased to dismount and spend some time here, I beg,
255 And what you have come for we shall learn later."
"No, by heaven," said the knight, "and him who sits there,
To spend time in this house was not the cause of my coming,
But because your name, sir, is so highly regarded,
And your city and your warriors reputed the best,
260 Dauntless in armor and on horseback afield,
The most valiant and excellent of all living men,
Courageous as players in other noble sports,
And here courtesy is displayed, as I have heard tell,
And that has brought me here, truly, on this day.
265 You may be assured by this branch that I carry
That I approach you in peace, seeking no battle.
For had I traveled in fighting dress, in warlike manner,
I have a hauberk at home and a helmet too,
A shield and a keen spear, shining bright,
270 And other weapons to brandish, I assure you, as well;
But since I look for no combat I am not dressed for battle.
But if you are as courageous as everyone says,
You will graciously grant me the game that I ask for
          by right."
275   In answer Arthur said,
       "If you seek, courteous knight,

If thou crave batayl bare,[1]
Here faylez thou not to fyght."

"Nay, frayst I no fyght, in fayth I the telle,
280 Hit arn aboute on this bench bot berdlez chylder.
If I were hasped in armes on a heghe stede,
Here is no mon me to mach, for myghtez so wayke.
Forthy I crave in this court a Crystemas gomen,[2]
For hit is Yol and Nwe Yer, and here ar yep mony.
285 If any so hardy in this hous holdez hymselven,
Be so bolde in his blod, brayn in hys hede,[3]
That dar stifly strike a strok for an other,
I schal gif hym of my gyft thys giserne ryche,
This ax, that is hevé innogh, to hondele as hym lykes,
290 And I schal bide the fyrst bur as bare as I sitte.[4]
If any freke be so felle to fonde that I telle,
Lepe lyghtly me to, and lach this weppen,
I quit-clayme hit for ever, kepe hit as his awen,
And I schal stonde hym a strok, stif on this flet,
295 Ellez thou wyl dight me the dom to dele hym an other
    barlay;[5]
    And yet gif hym respite
    A twelmonyth and a day;
    Now hyghe, and let se tite
300   Dar any herinne oght say."

If he hem stouned upon fyrst, stiller were thanne
Alle the heredmen in halle, the hyghe and the lowe.
The renk on his rouncé hym ruched in his sadel,
And runischly his red yghen he reled aboute,
305 Bende his bresed browez, blycande grene,
Wayved his berde for to wayte quo-so wolde ryse.
When non wolde kepe hym with carp he coghed ful hyghe,
Ande rimed hym ful richely, and ryght hym to speke:
"What, is this Arthures hous?" quoth the hathel thenne,
310 "That al the rous rennes of thurgh ryalmes so mony?
Where is now your sourquydrye and your conquestes,
Your gryndellayk and your greme, and your grete wordes?"

A combat without armor,
You will not lack a fight."

"No, I seek no battle, I assure you truly;
280 Those about me in this hall are but beardless children.
If I were locked in my armor on a great horse,
No one here could match me with their feeble powers.
Therefore I ask of the court a Christmas game,
For it is Yule and New Year, and here are brave men in plenty.
285 If anyone in this hall thinks himself bold enough,
So doughty in body and reckless in mind
As to strike a blow fearlessly and take one in return,
I shall give him this marvelous battle-axe as a gift,
This ponderous axe, to use as he pleases;
290 And I shall stand the first blow, unarmed as I am.
If anyone is fierce enough to take up my challenge,
Run to me quickly and seize this weapon,
I renounce all claim to it, let him keep it as his own,
And I shall stand his blow unflinching on this floor,
295 Provided you assign me the right to deal such a one
    in return;
    And yet grant him respite
    A twelvemonth and a day.
    Now hurry, and let's see
300   What any here dare say."

If he petrified them at first, even stiller were then
All the courtiers in that place, the great and the small.
The man on the horse turned himself in his saddle,
Ferociously rolling his red eyes about,
305 Bunched up his eyebrows, bristling with green,
Swung his beard this way and that to see whoever would rise.
When no one would answer he cried out aloud,
Drew himself up grandly and started to speak.
"What, is this Arthur's house?" said the man then,
310 "That everyone talks of in so many kingdoms?
Where are now your arrogance and your victories,
Your fierceness and wrath and your great speeches?

---

[1] *batayl bare* Either "without armor" (compare 290) or—as suggested by *thre bare mote*, 1141—"in single combat."

[2] *a Crystemas gomen* In earlier times the midwinter festival included many games and sports now forgotten. Many of them involved mock-violence, of which traces remained in Blind Man's Buff, played by striking a blindfolded victim and inviting him to guess who had struck him. Others exposed a victim to ridicule by playing a trick on him.

[3] *brayn* Crazy, reckless; usually *braynwod*, as at 1461.

[4] *as bare as I sitte* Without the protection of armor.

[5] *barlay* An obscure term, possibly meaning "by law," or here, "by agreement."

Now is the revel and the renoun of the Rounde Table
Overwalt wyth a worde of on wyghes speche,
315 For al dares for drede withoute dynt schewed!"
Wyth this he laghes so loude that the lorde greved;
The blod schot for scham into his schyre face
    and lere;
    He wex as wroth as wynde,
320   So did alle that ther were.
    The kyng as kene bi kynde
    Then stod that stif mon nere,

And sayde, "Hathel, by heven, thy askyng is nys,
And as thou foly hatz frayst, fynde the behoves.
325 I know no gome that is gast of thy grete wordes,
Gif me now thy geserne, upon Godez halve,
And I schal baythen thy bone that thou boden habbes."
Lyghtly lepez he him to, and laght at his honde,
Then feersly that other freke upon fote lyghtis.
330 Now hatz Arthure his axe, and the halme grypez,
And sturnely sturez hit aboute, that stryke wyth hit thoght.
The stif mon hym bifore stod upon hyght,
Herre then ani in the hous by the hede and more.
With sturne schere ther he stod he stroked his berde,
335 And wyth a countenaunce dryghe he drogh doun his cote,
No more mate ne dismayd for hys mayn dintez[1]
Then any burne upon bench hade broght hym to drynk
    of wyne.
    Gawan, that sate bi the quene,
340   To the kyng he can enclyne:
    "I beseche now with sayez sene
    This melly mot be myne."[2]

"Wolde ye, worthilych lorde," quoth Wawan to the kyng,
"Bid me boghe fro this benche, and stonde by yow there,
345 That I wythoute vylanye myght voyde this table,
And that my legge lady lyked not ille,[3]
I wolde com to your counseyl bifore your cort riche.
For me think hit not semly, as hit is soth knawen,
Ther such an askyng is hevened so hyghe in your sale,
350 Thagh ye yourself be talenttyf, to take hit to yourselven,
Whil mony so bolde yow aboute upon bench sytten
That under heven I hope non hagherer of wylle,
Ne better bodyes on bent ther baret is rered.

Now the revelry and repute of the Round Table
Are overthrown with a word from one man's mouth,
315 For you all cower in fear before a blow has been struck!"
Then he laughs so uproariously that the king took offence;
The blood rushed into his fair face and cheek
    for shame.
    Arthur grew red with rage,
320   As all the others did.
    The king, by nature bold,
    Approached that man and said,

"Sir, by heaven, what you demand is absurd,
And since you have asked for folly, that you deserve.
325 No man known to me fears your boastful words;
Hand over your battle-axe, in God's name,
And I shall grant the wish that you have requested."
He quickly goes to him and took the axe from his hand.
Then proudly the other dismounts and stands there.
330 Now Arthur has the axe, grips it by the shaft,
And grimly swings it about, as preparing to strike.
Towering before him stood the bold man,
Taller than anyone in the court by more than a head.
Standing there grim-faced he stroked his beard,
335 And with an unmoved expression then pulled down his coat,
No more daunted or dismayed by those powerful strokes
Than if any knight in the hall had brought him a measure
    of wine.
    Seated by Guenevere
340   Then bowed the good Gawain:
    "I beg you in plain words
    To let this task be mine."

Said Gawain to the king, "If you would, noble lord,
Bid me rise from my seat and stand at your side,
345 If without discourtesy I might leave the table,
And that my liege lady were not displeased,
I would offer you counsel before your royal court.
For it seems to me unfitting, if the truth be admitted,
When so arrogant a request is put forward in hall,
350 Even if you are desirous, to undertake it yourself
While so many brave men sit about you in their places
Who, I think, are unrivalled in temper of mind,
And without equal as warriors on field of battle.

---

[1] *for hys mayn dintez* Because of Arthur's great practice blows.

[2] *This melly mot be myne* Let this be my combat.

[3] *that my legge lady lyked not ille* That the Queen (beside whom Gawain is sitting) would not be offended if I left her side.

I am the wakkest, I wot, and of wyt feblest,
355 And lest lur of my lyf, quo laytes the sothe:
Bot for as much as ye are myn em I am only to prayse,
No bounté bot your blod I in my bodé knowe;
And sythen this note is so nys that noght hit yow falles,
And I have frayned hit at yow fyrst, foldez hit to me;
360 And if I carp not comlyly, let alle this cort rych
        bout blame.”
        Ryche togeder con roun,
        And sythen thay redden alle same,
        To ryd the kyng wyth croun
365   And gif Gawan the game.

Then comaunded the kyng the knyght for to ryse;
And he ful radly upros, and ruchched hym fayre,
Kneled doun bifore the kyng, and cachez that weppen;
And he luflyly hit hym laft, and lyfte up his honde
370 And gef hym Goddez blessyng, and gladly hym biddes
That his hert and his honde schulde hardi be bothe.
“Kepe the, cosyn,” quoth the kyng, “that thou on kyrf sette,
And if thou redez hym ryght, redly I trowe
That thou schal byden the bur that he schal bede after.”[1]
375 Gawan gotz to the gome with giserne in honde,
And he baldly hym bydez, he bayst never the helder.
Then carppez to Sir Gawan the knyght in the grene,
“Refourme we oure forwardes, er we fyrre passe.
Fyrst I ethe the, hathel, how that thou hattes
380 That thou me telle truly, as I tryst may.”
“In god fayth,” quoth the goode knyght, “Gawan I hatte,
That bede the this buffet, quat-so bifallez after,
And at this tyme twelmonyth take at the an other
Wyth what weppen so thou wylt, and wyth no wygh ellez
385   on lyve.”
        That other onswarez agayn,
        “Sir Gawan, so mot I thryve,
        As I am ferly fayn
        This dint that thou schal dryve.

390 “Bigog,” quoth the grene knyght, “Sir Gawan, me lykes
That I schal fange at thy fust that I haf frayst here.[2]
And thou hatz redily rehersed, bi resoun ful trwe,
Clanly al the covenaunt that I the kynge asked,
Saf that thou schal siker me, segge, bi thi trawthe,

I am the weakest of them, I know, and the dullest-minded,
355 So my death would be least loss, if truth should be told;
Only because you are my uncle am I to be praised,
No virtue I know in myself but your blood;
And since this affair is so foolish and unfitting for you,
And I have asked you for it first, it should fall to me.
360 And if my request is improper, let not this royal court
        bear the blame.”
        Nobles whispered together
        And agreed on their advice,
        That Arthur should withdraw
365   And Gawain take his place.

Then the king commanded Gawain to stand up,
And he did so promptly, and moved forward with grace,
Kneeled down before the king and laid hold of the weapon;
And Arthur gave it up graciously, and lifting his hand
370 Gave Gawain God’s blessing, and cheerfully bids
That he bring a strong heart and firm hand to the task.
“Take care, nephew,” said the king, “that you strike one blow,
And if you deal it aright, truly I believe
You will wait a long time for his stroke in return.”
375 Gawain approaches the man with battle-axe in hand,
And he waits for him boldly, with no sign of alarm.
Then the knight in the green addresses Gawain,
“Let us repeat our agreement before going further.
First I entreat you, sir, that what is your name
380 You shall tell me truly, that I may believe you.”
“In good faith,” said that virtuous knight, “I am called Gawain,
Who deals you this blow, whatever happens after,
On this day next year to accept another from you
With what weapon you choose, and from no other person
385   on earth.”
        The other man replied,
        “Sir Gawain, as I live,
        I am extremely glad
        This blow is yours to give.

390 By God,” said the Green Knight, “Sir Gawain, I am pleased
That I shall get from your hands what I have asked for here.
And you have fully repeated, in exact terms,
Without omission the whole covenant I put to the king;
Except that you shall assure me, sir, on your word,

---

[1] *thou schal byden the bur* You’ll be kept waiting for his blow.

[2] *“Bigog.” … here* The Green Knight does not explain why he is especially pleased that Gawain accepts the challenge.

395 That thou schal seche me thiself, where-so thou hopes
I may be funde upon folde, and foch the such wages
As thou deles me to-day bifore this douthe ryche."
"Where schulde I wale the?" quoth Gawan, "Where is thy
    place?
I wot never where thou wonyes, bi hym that me wroght,
400 Ne I know not the, knyght, thy cort ne thi name.
Bot teche me truly therto, and telle me how thou hattes,
And I schal ware alle my wyt to wynne me theder,
And that I swere the for sothe, and by my seker traweth."
"That is innogh in Nwe Yer, hit nedes no more,"[1]
405 Quoth the gome in the grene to Gawan the hende;
"Yif I the telle trwly quen I the tape have,
And thou me smothely hatz smyten, smartly I the teche
Of my hous and my home and myn owen nome,
Then may thou frayst my fare and forwardez holde;
410 And if I spende no speche, thenne spedez thou the better,
For thou may leng in thy londe and layt no fyrre—
      bot slokes!
    Ta now thy grymme tole to the,
    And lat se how thou cnokez."
415 "Gladly, sir, for sothe,"
    Quoth Gawan: his ax he strokes.

The grene knyght upon grounde graythely hym dresses,
A littel lut with the hed, the lere he discoverez,
His longe lovelych lokkez he layd over his croun,
420 Let the naked nec to the note schewe.
Gawan gripped to his ax and gederes hit on hyght,
The kay fot on the folde he before sette,
Let hit doun lyghtly lyght on the naked,
That the scharp of the schalk schyndered the bones,
425 And schrank thurgh the schyire grece, and schade hit in twynne,
That the bit of the broun stel bot on the grounde.[2]
The fayre hede fro the halce hit to the erthe,
That fele hit foyned wyth hir fete, there hit forth roled;
The blod brayed from the body, that blykked on the grene;
430 And nawther faltered ne fel the freke never the helder,
Bot stythly he start forth upon styf schonkes,
And runyschly he raght out, there as renkkez stoden,
Laght to his lufly hed, and lyft hit up sone;
And sythen bowez to his blonk, the brydel he cachchez,

395 That you will seek me yourself, wherever you think
I may be found upon earth, to accept such payment
As you deal me today before this noble gathering."
"Where shall I find you?" said Gawain, "Where is your
    dwelling?
I have no idea where you live, by him who made me;
400 Nor do I know you, sir, your court nor your name.
Just tell me truly these things, and what you are called,
And I shall use all my wits to get myself there,
And that I swear to you honestly, by my pledged word."
"That is enough for the moment, it needs nothing more,"
405 Said the man in green to the courteous Gawain,
"If I answer you truly after taking the blow,
And you have dextrously struck me, I will tell you at once
Of my house and my home and my proper name,
Then you can pay me a visit and keep your pledged word;
410 And if I say nothing, then you will fare better,
For you may stay in your country and seek no further—
      but enough!
    Take up your fearsome weapon
    And let's see how you smite."
415 Said Gawain, "Gladly, indeed,"
    Whetting the metal bit.

The Green Knight readily takes up his position,
Bowed his head a little, uncovering the flesh,
His long lovely hair he swept over his head,
420 In readiness letting the naked neck show.
Gawain grasped the axe and lifts it up high,
Setting his left foot before him on the ground,
Brought it down swiftly on the bare flesh
So that the bright blade slashed through the man's spine
425 And cut through the white flesh, severing it in two,
So that the shining steel blade bit into the floor.
The handsome head flew from the neck to the ground,
And many courtiers kicked at it as it rolled past.
Blood spurted from the trunk, gleamed on the green dress,
430 Yet the man neither staggered nor fell a whit for all that,
But sprang forward vigorously on powerful legs,
And fiercely reached out where knights were standing,
Grabbed at his fine head and snatched it up quickly,
And then strides to his horse, seizes the bridle,

---

[1] *innogh in Nwe Yer* Literally, "enough for this New Year's Day";
meaning that Gawain need say nothing more, as the Green Knight
goes on to say.

[2] *broun* Burnished.

435 Steppez into stelbawe and strydez alofte,
And his hede by the here in his honde haldez.
And as sadly the segge hym in his sadel sette
As non unhap had hym ayled, thagh hedlez he were
        in stedde.
440   He brayde his bulk aboute,
        That ugly bodi that bledde;
        Moni on of hym had doute
        Bi that his resounz were redde.

For the hede in his honde he haldez up even,
445 Toward the derrest on the dece he dressez the face,
And hit lyfte up the yghe-lyddez and loked ful brode,
And meled thus much with his muthe, as ye may now
        here:
"Loke, Gawan, thou be graythe to go as thou hettez,
And layte as lelly til thou me, lude, fynde,
450 As thou hatz hette in this halle, herande thise knyghtes;
To the grene chapel thou chose, I charge the, to fotte
Such a dunt as thou hatz dalt, disserved thou habbez
To be yederly yolden on Nw Yeres morn.
The knyght of the grene chapel men knowen me mony,
455 Forthi me for to fynde if thou fraystez, faylez thou never.
Therfore com, other recreaunt be calde thou behoves."
With a runisch rout the raynez he tornez,
Halled out at the hal dor, his hed in his hande,
That the fyr of the flynt flaghe fro fole hoves.
460 To quat kyth he becom knwe non there,
Never more then thay wyste from quethen he watz wonnen.
        What thenne?
        The kyng and Gawan thare
        At that grene thay laghe and grenne;
465   Yet breved watz hit ful bare
        A mervayl among tho menne.

Thagh Arther the hende kyng at hert hade wonder,
He let no semblaunt be sene, bot sayde ful hyghe
To the comlych quene wyth cortays speche,
470 "Dere dame, to-day demay yow never;
Wel bycommes such craft upon Cristmasse,[1]
Laykyng of enterludez, to laghe and to syng,
Among thise kynde caroles of knyghtez and ladyez.
Never the lece to my mete I may me wel dres,

435 Puts foot into stirrup and swings into his seat,
His other hand clutching his head by the hair;
And the man seated himself on horseback as firmly
As if he had suffered no injury, though headless he sat
        in his place.
440   He turned his body round,
        That gruesome trunk that bled;
        Many were struck by fear
        When all his words were said.

For he holds up the head in his hand, truly,
445 Turns its face towards the noblest on the dais,
And it lifted its eyelids and glared with wide eyes,
And the mouth uttered these words, which you shall now
        hear:
"See, Gawain, that you carry out your promise exactly,
And search for me truly, sir, until I am found,
450 As you have sworn in this hall in the hearing of these knights.
Make your way to the Green Chapel, I charge you, to get
Such a blow as you have dealt, rightfully given,
To be readily returned on New Year's Day.
As the Knight of the Green Chapel I am widely known,
455 So if you make search to find me you cannot possibly fail.
Therefore come, or merit the name of craven coward."
With a fierce jerk of the reins he turns his horse
And hurtled out of the hall door, his head in his hand,
So fast that flint-fire sparked from the hoofs.
460 What land he returned to no one there knew,
Any more than they guessed where he had come from.
        What then?
        Seeing that green man go,
        The king and Gawain grin;
465   Yet they both agreed
        They had a wonder seen.

Although inwardly Arthur was deeply astonished,
He let no sign of this appear, but loudly remarked
To the beautiful queen with courteous speech,
470 "Dear lady, let nothing distress you today.
Such strange goings-on are fitting at Christmas,
Putting on interludes, laughing and singing,
Mixed with courtly dances of ladies and knights.
None the less, I can certainly go to my food,

---

[1] *such craft* Display of skill. Arthur speaks as though the beheading
had been a conjuring trick.

475 For I haf sen a selly, I may not forsake."
He glent upon Sir Gawen, and gaynly he sayde,
"Now sir, heng up thyn ax, that hatz innogh hewen."[1]
And hit watz don abof the dece on doser to henge,
Ther alle men for mervayl myght on hit loke,
480 And bi trwe tytel therof to telle the wonder.
Thenne thay bowed to a borde thise burnes togeder,
The kyng and the gode knyght, and kene men hem served
Of alle dayntyez double, as derrest myght falle;
Wyth alle maner of mete and mynstralcie bothe,
485 Wyth wele walt thay that day, til worthed an ende
        in londe.
    Now thenk wel, Sir Gawan,
    For wothe that thou ne wonde
    This aventure for to frayn
490   That thou hatz tan on honde.

10 For I have witnessed a marvel, I cannot deny."
He glanced at Sir Gawain, and aptly he said,
"Now sir, hang your axe up, for it has severed enough."
And it was hung above the dais, on a piece of tapestry,
Where everyone might gaze on it as a wonder,
515 And the living proof of this marvelous tale.
Then these two men together walked to a table,
The king and the good knight, and were dutifully served
With delicious double helpings befitting their rank.
With every kind of food and minstrelsy
520 They spent that day joyfully, until daylight ended
        on earth.
    Now take good care, Gawain,
    Lest fear hold you back
    From leaving on the quest
525   You have sworn to undertake.

FITT 2

This hanselle hatz Arthur of aventurus on fyrst
In yonge yer, for he yerned yelpyng to here.
Thagh hym wordez were wane when thay to sete wenten,[2]
Now ar thay stoken of sturne werk, stafful her hond.
495 Gawan watz glad to begynne those gomnez in halle,
Bot thagh the ende be hevy haf ye no wonder;
For thagh men ben mery quen thay han mayn drynk,
A yere yernes ful yerne, and yeldez never lyke,
The forme to the fynisment foldez ful selden.
500 Forthi this Yol overyede, and the yere after,
And uche sesoun serlepes sued after other:
After Crystenmasse com the crabbed lentoun
That fraystez flesch wyth the fysche and fode more symple;
Bot thenne the weder of the worlde wyth wynter hit threpez,[3]
505 Colde clengez adoun, cloudez upliften,[4]
Schyre schedez the rayn in schowrez ful warme,
Fallez upon fayre flat, flowrez there schewen,
Bothe groundez and the grevez grene ar her wedez,
Bryddez busken to bylde, and bremlych syngen

PART 2

This wonder has Arthur as his first New Year's gift
When the year was newborn, for he loved hearing challenges.
Though words were wanting when they sat down at table,
Now a grim task confronts them, their hands are cram-full.
495 Gawain was glad enough to begin those games in the hall,
But if the outcome prove troublesome don't be surprised;
For though men are light-hearted when they have strong drink,
A year passes swiftly, never bringing the same;
Beginning and ending seldom take the same form.
500 And so that Yule went by, and the year ensuing,
Each season in turn following the other.
After Christmas came mean-spirited Lent,
That tries the body with fish and plainer nourishment;
But then the weather on earth battles with winter,
505 The cold shrinks downwards, clouds rise higher,
And shed sparkling rain in warming showers,
Falling on smiling plains where flowers unfold.
Both open fields and woodlands put on green dress;
Birds hasten to build, and rapturously sing

---

[1] *heng up thyn ax* Arthur *gaynly* or aptly quotes a proverbial saying, meaning "end your strife."

[2] *wordez were wane* Because the Green Knight had taken their breath away.

[3] *wyth wynter hit threpez* The seasons do not simply follow each other quietly but fight for succession: see 525, where autumn wind *wrastelez with the sunne.*

[4] *Colde clengez adoun* Winter is driven down into the earth, waiting to emerge again.

510 For solace of the softe somer that sues therafter
               bi bonk;
          And blossumez bolne to blowe
          Bi rawez rych and ronk,
          Then notez noble innoghe
515   Ar herde in wod so wlonk.

     After the sesoun of somer wyth the soft wyndez,
     Quen Zeferus[1] syflez hymself on sedez and erbez,
     Wela wynne is the wort that waxes theroute,
     When the donkande dewe dropez of the levez,
520 To bide a blysful blusch of the bryght sunne.
     Bot then hyghes hervest, and hardenes hym sone,
     Warnez hym for the wynter to wax ful rype.
     He dryves wyth droght the dust for to ryse
     Fro the face of the folde to flyghe ful hyghe;
525 Wrothe wynde of the welkyn wrastelez with the sunne,
     The levez lancen fro the lynde and lyghten on the grounde,
     And al grayes the gres that grene watz ere.
     Thenne al rypez and rotez that ros upon fyrst,
     And thus yirnez the yere in yisterdayez mony,
530 And wynter wyndez agayn, as the worlde askez,
               no fage;
          Til Meghelmas[2] mone
          Watz cumen wyth wynter wage;
          Then thenkkez Gawan ful sone
535   Of his anious vyage.

     Yet quyl Al-hal-day[3] with Arther he lenges;
     And he made a fare on that fest for the frekez sake,
     With much revel and ryche of the Rounde Table.
     Knyghtez ful cortays and comlych ladies
540 Al for luf of that lede in longynge thay were,
     Bot never the lece ne the later thay nevened bot merthe;
     Mony joylez for that jentyle japez ther maden.
     And aftter mete with mournyng he melez to his eme,
     And spekez of his passage, and pertly he sayde,
545 "Now, lege lorde of my lyf, leve I yow ask;
     Ye knowe the cost of this cace, kepe I no more
     To telle yow tenez therof, never bot trifel;
     Bot I am boun to the bur barely to-morne
     To sech the gome of the grene, as God wyl me wysse."
550 Then the best of the burgh bowed togeder,

---

[1] *Zeferus* God of the West Wind.

[2] *Meghelmas* I.e., Michaelmas, the feast of St. Michael, celebrated on 29 September.

510 For joy of gentle summer that follows next
               on the slopes.
          And flowers bud and blossom
          In hedgerows rich with growth,
          And many splendid songs
515   From woodlands echo forth.

     Then comes the summer season with gentle winds,
     When Zephirus blows softly on seeding grasses and plants,
     Beautiful is the growth that springs from the seed,
     When the moistening dew drips from the leaves
520 To await a joyful gleam of the bright sun.
     But then autumn comes quickly and urges it on,
     Warns it to ripen before winter's approach.
     Dry winds of autumn force the dust to fly
     From the face of the earth high into the air;
525 Fierce winds of heaven wrestle with the sun,
     Leaves are torn from the trees and fall to the ground,
     And all withered is the grass that was green before.
     Then all ripens and rots that had sprung up at first,
     And in so many yesterdays the year wears away,
530 And winter comes round again, as custom requires,
               in truth;
          Until the Michaelmas moon
          Brought hint of winter's frost,
          And into Gawain's mind
535   Come thoughts of his grim quest.

     Yet until All Saints' Day he lingers in court,
     And Arthur made a feast on that day to honor the knight,
     With much splendid revelry at the Round Table.
     The most courteous of knights and beautiful ladies
540 Grieved out of love for that noble man,
     But no less readily for that spoke as if unconcerned.
     Many troubled for that nobleman made joking remarks.
     And after the feast sorrowfully he addressed his uncle,
     Raised the matter of his quest, and openly said,
545 "Liege lord of my being, I must ask for your leave;
     You know the terms of this matter, and I have no wish
     To bother you with them, saving one small point;
     But tomorrow without fail I set out for the blow,
     To seek this man in green, as God will direct me."
550 Then the noblest in the court gathered together,

---

[3] *Al-hal-day* I.e., All Hallows' Day, or All Saints' Day, celebrated 1 November.

Aywan and Errik, and other ful mony,
Sir Doddinaval de Savage, the duc of Clarence,
Launcelot and Lyonel, and Lucan the gode,
Sir Boos and Sir Bydver, big men bothe,
555 And mony other menskful, with Mador de la Port.
Alle this compayny of court com the kyng nerre
For to counseyl the knyght, with care at her hert.
There watz much derve doel driven in the sale
That so worthé as Wawan schulde wende on that ernde,
560 To dryve a delful dynt, and dele no more
          wyth bronde.
      The knyght mad ay god chere,
      And sayde, "Quat schuld I wonde?
      Of destinés derf and dere
565   What may mon do bot fonde?"

He dowellez ther al that day, and dressez on the morn,
Askez erly hys armez, and alle were thay broght.
Fyrst a tulé tapit tyght over the flet,
And miche watz the gild gere that glent theralofte.
570 The stif mon steppez theron, and the stel hondelez,
Dubbed in a dublet of a dere tars,
And sythen a crafty capados, closed aloft,
That wyth a bryght blaunner was bounden withinne.
Thenne set thay the sabatounz upon the segge fotez,
575 His legez lapped in stel with luflych greves,
With polaynez piched therto, policed ful clene,
Aboute his knez knaged wyth knotez of golde;
Queme quyssewes then, that coyntlych closed
His thik thrawen thyghez, with thwonges to tachched;
580 And sythen the brawden bryné of bryght stel ryngez
Umbeweved that wygh upon wlonk stuffe,
And wel bornyst brace upon his bothe armes,
With gode cowters and gay, and glovez of plate,
And alle the godlych gere that hym gayn schulde
585   that tyde;
      Wyth ryche cote-armure
      His gold sporez spend with pryde,
      Gurde wyth a bront ful sure
      With silk sayn umbe his syde.

590 When he watz hasped in armes, his harnays watz ryche:
The lest lachet other loupe lemed of golde.
So harnayst as he watz he herknez his masse,
Offred and honoured at the heghe auter.
Sythen he come to the kyng and to his cort-ferez,

Ywain and Eric, and many others,
Sir Dodinal le Sauvage, the duke of Clarence,
Lancelot and Lionel, and Lucan the good,
Sir Bors and Sir Bedevere, both powerful men,
555 And several other worthy knights, including Mador de la Port.
This group of courtiers approached the king,
To give advice to Gawain with troubled hearts.
Much deep sorrowing was heard in the hall
That one as noble as Gawain should go on that quest,
560 To stand a terrible blow, and never more brandish
          his sword.
      Keeping an unchanged face,
      "What should I fear?" he said;
      "For whether kind or harsh
565   A man's fate must be tried."

He stays there all that day, and makes ready the next,
Calls early for his accouterment, and all was brought in.
First a crimson carpet was stretched over the floor,
A heap of gilded armor gleaming brightly piled there.
570 The brave knight steps on it and examines his armour,
Dressed in a costly doublet of silk
Under a well-made capados, fastened at the top
And trimmed with white ermine on the inside.
Then they fitted metal shoes upon the knight's feet,
575 Clasped his legs in steel with elegant greaves
With knee-pieces attached to them, highly polished
And fastened to his knees with knots of gold.
Next fine cuisses that neatly enclosed
His thick muscular thighs, with thongs attached,
580 And then the linked mail-shirt made of bright steel rings
Covered that man and his beautiful clothes:
Well burnished braces on both his arms,
With fine elbow-pieces and gloves of steel plate,
And all the splendid equipment that would benefit him
585   at that time;
      With costly coat-armor,
      His gold spurs worn with pride,
      Girt with a trusty sword,
      A silk belt round him tied.

590 All locked in his armor his gear looked noble:
The smallest fastening or loop was gleaming with gold.
In armor as he was, he went to hear mass
Offered and celebrated for him at the high altar.
Then he comes to the king and his fellows at court,

595 Lachez lufly his leve at lordez and ladyez;
And thay him kyst and conveyed, bikende hym to Kryst.
Bi that watz Gryngolet grayth, and gurde with a sadel
That glemed ful gayly with mony golde frenges,
Ayquere naylet ful nwe, for that note ryched;
600 The brydel barred aboute, with bryght golde bounden,
The apparayl of the payttrure and of the proude skyrtez,
The cropore and the covertor, acorded wyth the arsounez;
And al watz rayled on red ryche golde naylez,
That al glytered and glent as glem of the sunne.
605 Thenne hentes he the helme, and hastily hit kysses,
That watz stapled stifly, and stoffed wythinne.
Hit watz hyghe on his hede, hasped bihynde,
Wyth a lyghtly urysoun over the aventayle,
Enbrawden and bounden wyth the best gemmez
610 On brode sylkyn borde, and bryddez on semez,
As papjayez paynted pervyng bitwene,
Tortors and trulofez entayled so thyk
As many burde theraboute had ben seven wynter
in toune.
615   The cercle watz more o prys
       That umbeclypped hys croun,
       Of diamauntez a devys
       That bothe were bryght and broun.[1]

Then thay schewed hym the schelde, that was of schyr goulez,
620 Wyth the pentangel depaynt of pure gold hwez.
He braydez hit by the bauderyk, aboute the hals kestes,
That bisemed the segge semlyly fayre.
And quy the pentangel apendez to that prynce noble
I am in tent yow to telle, thof tary hyt me schulde:
625 Hit is a syngne that Salomon set sumquyle
In bytoknyng of trawthe, bi tytle that hit habbez,
For hit is a figure that haldez fyve poyntez,
And uche lyne umbelappez and loukez in other,
And ayquere hit is endelez; and Englych hit callen
630 Overal, as I here, the endeles knot.[2]
Forthy hit acordez to this knyght and to his cler armez,
For ay faythful in fyve and sere fyve sythez
Gawan watz for gode knawen, and as golde pured,
Voyded of uche vylany, wyth vertuez ennourned
635   in mote;

595 Graciously takes his leave of lords and ladies;
And they kissed and escorted him, commending him to Christ.
By then Gringolet was ready, fitted with a saddle
That splendidly shone with many gold fringes,
Newly studded all over for that special purpose;
600 The bridle striped all along, and trimmed with bright gold;
The adornment of the trapping and the fine saddle-skirts,
The crupper and the horse-cloth matched the saddle-bows,
All covered with gold studs on a background of red,
So that the whole glittered and shone like the sun.
605 Then Gawain seizes his helmet and kisses it quickly,
That was strongly stapled and padded inside.
It stood high on his head, fastened at the back
With a shining silk band over the mailed neck-guard,
Embroidered and studded with the finest gems
610 On a broad border of silk with birds covering the seams—
Popinjays depicted between periwinkles,
Turtledoves and true-love flowers embroidered so thick
As if many women had worked on it seven years
in town.
615   A circlet still more precious
       Was ringed about his head,
       Made with perfect diamonds
       Of every brilliant shade.

Then they brought out the shield of shining gules,
620 With the pentangle painted on it in pure gold.
He swings it over his baldric, throws it round his neck,
Where it suited the knight extremely well.
And why the pentangle should befit that noble prince
I intend to explain, even should that delay me.
625 It is a symbol that Solomon designed long ago
As an emblem of fidelity, and justly so;
For it is a figure consisting of five points,
Where each line overlaps and locks into another,
And the whole design is continuous, and in England is called
630 Everywhere, I am told, the endless knot.
Therefore it suits this knight and his shining arms,
For always faithful in five ways, and five times in each case,
Gawain was reputed as virtuous, like refined gold,
Devoid of all vice, and with all courtly virtues
635   adorned.

---

[1] *bryght and broun* Clear and colored.

[2] *the endeles knot* No other use of this phrase is known. Like the poet's claim to have heard the story recited, and his closing of refer- ence to its place in *the best boke of romaunce*, 2521, the remark should probably be regarded as poetic license. The line does not alliterate.

Forthy the pentangel nwe
He ber in schelde and cote,
As tulk of tale most trwe
And gentylest knyght of lote.

640 Fyrst he watz funden fautlez in his fyve wyttez,
And eft fayled never the freke in his fyve fyngres,
And alle his afyaunce upon folde watz in the fyve woundez
That Cryst caght on the croys, as the crede tellez;
And quere-so-ever thys mon in melly watz stad,
645 His thro thoght watz in that, thurgh alle other thyngez,
That alle his forsnes he feng at the fyve joyez
That the hende heven-quene had of hir chylde;
At this cause the knyght comlyche hade
In the inore half of his schelde hir image depaynted,
650 That quen he blusched therto his belde never payred.
The fyft fyve that I fynde that the frek used
Watz fraunchyse and felaghschyp forbe al thyng,
His clannes and his cortaysye croked were never,
And pité,[1] that passez alle poyntez: thyse pure fyve
655 Were harder happed on that hathel then on any other.
Now alle these fyve sythez, for sothe, were fetled on this
      knyght,
And uchone halched in other, that non ende hade,
And fyched upon fyve poyntez, that fayld never,
Ne samned never in no syde, ne sundred nouther,
660 Withouten ende at any noke I oquere fynde,
Whereever the gomen bygan, or glod to an ende.
Therfore on his schene schelde schapen watz the knot
Ryally wyth red golde upon rede gowlez,
That is the pure pentaungel wyth the peple called
665   with lore.
      Now graythed is Gawan gay,
      And laght his launce ryght thore,
      And gef them alle goud day,
      He wende for evermore.

670 He sperres the sted with the spurez and sprong on his way,
So stif that the ston-fyr stroke out therafter.
Al that sey that semly syked in hert,
And sayde sothly al same segges til other,[2]
Carande for that comly, "Bi Kryst, hit is scathe
675 That thou leude, schal be lost, that art of lyf noble!

So this new-painted sign
He bore on shield and coat,
As man most true of speech
And fairest-spoken knight.

640 First he was judged perfect in his five senses,
And next his five fingers never lost their dexterity;
And all his earthly faith was in the five wounds
That Christ suffered on the cross, as the creed declares.
And wherever this man found himself in battle
645 His fixed thought was that, above all other things,
All his fortitude should come from the five joys
That the mild Queen of Heaven found in her child.
For this reason the gracious knight had
Her image depicted on the inside of his shield,
650 So that when he glanced at it his heart never quailed.
The fifth group of five the man respected, I hear,
Was generosity and love of fellow-men above all;
His purity and courtesy were never lacking,
And surpassing the others, compassion: these noble five
655 Were more deeply implanted in that man than any other.
Now truly, all these five groups were embodied in that
      knight,
Each one linked to the others in an endless design,
Based upon five points that was never unfinished,
Not uniting in one line nor separating either;
660 Without ending anywhere at any point that I find,
No matter where the line began or ran to an end.
Therefore the knot was fashioned on his bright shield
Royally with red gold upon red gules,
That is called the true pentangle by learned people
665   who know.
      Now Gawain, lance in hand,
      Is ready to depart;
      He bade them all farewell,
      Not to return, he thought.

670 He set spurs to his horse and sprang on his way
So vigorously that sparks flew up from the stones.
All who watched that fair knight leave sighed from the heart,
And together whispered one to another,
Distressed for that handsome one, "What a pity indeed
675 That your life must be squandered, noble as you are!

---

[1] *pité* Cannot readily be translated in one word, as it means both pity and piety.

[2] *sothly* A dialect term meaning "quietly."

To fynde hys fere upon folde, in fayth, is not ethe.
Warloker to haf wrogt had more wyt bene,
And haf dygt yonder dere a duk to have worthed;
A lowande leder of ledez in londe hym wel semez,
680 And so had better haf ben then britned to nogt,
Hadet wyth an alvisch mon, for angardez pryde.
Who knew ever any kyng such counsel to take
As knygtez in cavelaciounz on Crystmasse gomnez!"
Wel much watz the warme water that waltered of yghen,
685 When that semly syre sogt fro tho wonez
      thad daye.
      He made non abode,
      Bot wygtly went hys way;
      Mony wylsum way he rode,
690   The bok as I herde say.

Now ridez this renk thurgh the ryalme of Logres,
Sir Gawan, on Godez halve, thagh hym no gomen thogt.
Oft leudlez and alone he lengez on nygtez
Ther he fonde nogt hym byfore the fare that he lyked.
695 Hade he no fere bot his fole by frythez and dounez,
Ne no gome bot God bi gate wyth to carp,
Til that he neghed ful neghe into the Northe Walez.
Alle the iles of Anglesay on lyft half he haldez,
And farez over the fordez by the forlondez,
700 Over at the Holy Hede, til he hade eft bonk
In the wyldrenesse of Wyrale; wonde ther bot lyte
That auther God other gome wyth goud hert lovied.
And ay he frayned as he ferde, at frekez that he met,
If thay hade herde any karp of a knygt grene,
705 In any grounde theraboute, of the grene chapel;
And al nykked hym wyth nay, that never in her lyve
Thay seye never no segge that watz of suche hwez
      of grene.
      The knygt tok gates straunge
710   In mony a bonk unbene,
      His cher ful oft con chaunge
      That chapel er he mygt sene.

Mony klyf he overclambe in contrayez straunge,
Fer floten fro his frendez fremedly he rydez.
715 At uche warthe other water ther the wyghe passed
He fonde a foo hym byfore, bot ferly hit were,
And that so foule and so felle that fegt hym byhode.

To find his equal on earth is not easy, in faith.
To have acted more cautiously would have been much wiser,
And have appointed that dear man to become a duke:
To be a brilliant leader of men, as he is well suited,
680 And would better have been so than battered to nothing,
Beheaded by an ogrish man out of excessive pride.
Whoever knew a king to take such foolish advice
As knights offer in arguments about Christmas games?"
A great deal of warm water trickled from eyes
685 When that elegant lord set out from the city
      that day.
      He did not linger there,
      But swiftly went his way;
      Taking perplexing roads
690   As I have heard books say.

Now rides this knight through the realm of England,
Sir Gawain, in God's name, though he found it no pleasure.
Often friendless and alone he passes his nights,
Finding before him no food that he liked.
695 He had no fellow but his horse by forest and hill,
And no one but God to talk to on the way,
Until he came very close to the north part of Wales.
All the islands of Anglesey he keeps on his left,
And crosses over the fords at the headlands,
700 There at the Holyhead, and came ashore again
In the wilderness of Wirral. There few people lived
Whom either God or good-hearted men could love.
And always as he rode he asked those whom he met
If they had heard anyone speak of a green knight
705 Or of a green chapel in any place round about;
And they all answered him no, that never in their lives
Had they ever seen a man who had such color
      of green.
      Strange roads the knight pursued
710   Through many a dreary space,
      Turning from side to side
      To find the meeting-place.

Many fells he climbed over in territory strange,
Far distant from his friends like an alien he rides.
715 At every ford or river where the knight crossed
He found an enemy facing him, unless he was in luck,
And so ugly and fierce that he was forced to give fight.

So mony mervayl bi mount ther the mon fyndez,
Hit were to tore for to telle of the tenthe dole.
720 Sumwhyle wyth wormez he werrez, and with wolves als,
Sumwhyle wyth wodwos that woned in the knarrez,
Bothe wyth bullez and berez, and borez otherquyle,
And etaynez that hym anelede of the heghe felle;
Nade he ben dughty and dryghe, and Dryghtyn had served,
725 Douteles he hade ben ded and dreped ful ofte.
For werre wrathed hym not so much that wynter nas wors,
When the colde cler water fro the cloudez schadde,
And fres er hit falle myght to the fale erthe.
Ner slayn wyth the slete he sleped in his yrnes
730 Mo nyghtez then innoghe in naked rokkez,
Ther as claterande fro the crest the colde borne rennez,
And henged heghe over his hede in hard iisse-ikkles.
Thus in peryl and payne and plytes ful harde
Bi contray caryez this knyght, tyl Krystmasse even,
735   al one;
        The knyght wel that tyde
        To Mary made his mone,
        That ho hym red to ryde
        And wysse hym to sum wone.

740 Bi a mounte on the morne meryly he rydes
Into a forest ful dep, that ferly watz wylde;
Highe hillez on uche a halve, and holtwodez under
Of hore okez ful hoge a hundreth togeder;
The hasel and the haghthorne were harled al samen,
745 With roghe raged mosse rayled aywhere,
With mony bryddez unblythe upon bare twyges,
That pitosly ther piped for pyne of the colde.
The gome upon Gryngolet glydez hem under,
Thurgh mony misy and myre, mon al hym one,
750 Carande for his costes, lest he ne kever schulde
To se the servyse of that syre, that on that self nyght
Of a burde watz borne, our baret to quelle;
And therfore sykyng he sayde, "I beseche the, lorde,
And Mary, that is myldest moder so dere,
755 Of sum herber ther heghly I myght here masse,
And thy matynez[1] to-morne, mekely I ask,
And therto prestly I pray my pater and ave
        and crede."[2]

So many wonders befell him in the hills,
It would be tedious to recount the least part of them.
720 Sometimes he fights dragons, and wolves as well,
Sometimes with wild men who dwelt among the crags;
Both with bulls and with bears, and at other times boars,
And ogres who chased him across the high fells.
Had he not been valiant and resolute, trusting in God,
725 He would surely have died or been killed many times.
For fighting troubled him less than the rigorous winter,
When cold clear water fell from the clouds
And froze before it could reach the faded earth.
Half dead with the cold Gawain slept in his armor
730 More nights than enough among the bare rocks,
Where splashing from the hilltops the freezing stream runs,
And hung over his head in hard icicles.
Thus in danger, hardship and continual pain
This knight rides across the land until Christmas Eve
735   alone.
        Earnestly Gawain then
        Prayed Mary that she send
        Him guidance to some place
        Where he might lodging find.

740 Over a hill in the morning in splendour he rides
Into a dense forest, wondrously wild;
High slopes on each side and woods at their base
Of massive grey oaks, hundreds growing together;
Hazel and hawthorn were densely entangled,
745 Thickly festooned with coarse shaggy moss,
Where many miserable birds on the bare branches
Wretchedly piped for torment of the cold.
The knight on Gringolet hurries under the trees,
Through many a morass and swamp, a solitary figure,
750 Troubled about his plight, lest he should be unable
To attend mass for that lord who on that same night
Was born of a maiden, our suffering to end;
And therefore sighing he prayed, "I beg of you, Lord,
And Mary, who is gentlest mother so dear,
755 For some lodging where I might devoutly hear mass
And your matins tomorrow, humbly I ask;
And to this end promptly repeat my Pater and Ave
        and Creed."

---

[1] *matynez* I.e., matins, Morning prayer, but here a church service specifically devoted to Mary as the mother of Jesus Christ ("matins of the blessed Virgin Mary").

[2] *Pater ... Crede Pater* Latin: father, i.e., "The Lord's Prayer" ("Our Father, who art in Heaven ..."); *Ave* Latin: hail, i.e., Ave Maria ("Hail Mary"); *Creed* Latin: I believe ("The Creed").

He rode in his prayere,
760　　And cryed for his mysdede,
He sayned hym in sythes sere,[1]
And sayde, "Cros Kryst me spede!"

Nade he sayned hymself, segge, bot thrye,
Er he watz war in the wod of a wone in a mote,
765　　Abof a launde, on a lawe, loken under boghez
Of mony borelych bole aboute bi the diches:
A castle the comlokest that ever knyght aghte,
Pyched on a prayere, a park al aboute,
With a pyked palays pyned ful thik,
770　　That umbeteye mony tre mo then two myle.
That holde on that on syde the hathel avysed
As hit schemered and schon[2] thurgh the schyre okez;
Thenne hatz he hendly of his helme, and heghly he thonkez
Jesus and sayn Gilyan,[3] that gentyle ar bothe,
775　　That cortaysly had hym kydde, and his cry herkened.
"Now bone hostel,"[4] cothe the burne, "I beseche yow yette!"
Thenne gerdez he to Gryngolet with the gilt helez,
And he ful chauncely hatz chosen to the chef gate,
That broght bremly the burne to the bryge ende
780　　　　in haste.
　　　　The bryge watz breme upbrayde,
　　　　The gatez were stoken faste,
　　　　The wallez were wel arayed
　　　　Hit dut no wyndez blaste.

785　　The burne bode on blonk, that on bonk hoved
Of the depe double dich that drof to the place;
The walle wod in the water wonderly depe,
And eft a ful huge heght hit haled upon lofte
Of harde hewen ston up to the tablez,
790　　Enbaned under the abataylment in the best lawe;
And sythen garytez ful gaye gered bitwene,
Wyth mony luflych loupe that louked ful clene:
A better barbican that burne blusched upon never.
And innermore he behelde that halle ful hyghe,
795　　Towres telded bytwene, trochet ful thik,
Fayre fylyolez that fyghed, and ferlyly long,

Bewailing his misdeeds,
760　　And praying as he rode,
He often crossed himself
Crying "Prosper me, Christ's cross!"

Hardly had he crossed himself, that man, three times,
Before he caught sight through the trees of a moated building
765　　Standing over a field, on a mound, surrounded by boughs
Of many a massive tree-trunk enclosing the moat:
The most splendid castle ever owned by a knight,
Set on a meadow, a park all around,
Closely guarded by a spiked palisade
770　　That encircled many trees for more than two miles.
That side of the castle Sir Gawain surveyed
As it shimmered and shone through the fine oaks;
Then graciously takes off his helmet, and devoutly thanks
Jesus and St. Julian, who kindly are both,
775　　Who had treated him courteously, and listened to his prayer.
"Now good lodging," said the man, "I beg you to grant!"
Then he urged Gringolet forward with his gilt spurs,
And by good chance happened upon the main path
That led the knight directly to the end of the drawbridge
780　　　　with speed.
　　　　The bridge was drawn up tight,
　　　　The gates were bolted fast.
　　　　The walls were strongly built,
　　　　They feared no tempest's blast.

785　　The knight sat on his horse, pausing on the slope
Of the deep double ditch that surrounded the place.
The wall stood in the water incredibly deep,
And then soared up above an astonishing height,
Made of squared stone up to the cornice,
790　　With coursings under battlements in the latest style.
At intervals splendid watch-towers were placed,
With many neat loop-holes that could be tightly shut:
Better outworks of a castle the knight had never seen.
Further inside he noticed a lofty hall
795　　With towers set at intervals, richly ornate,
Splendid pinnacles fitted into them, wonderfully tall,

---

[1] *in sythes sere*　Every time he prayed.

[2] *hit schemered and schon*　See also *that blenked ful quyte*, 799.

[3] *sayn Gilyan*　I.e., St. Julian, patron saint of hospitality.

[4] *bone hostel*　"Good lodging," a traditional invocation to St. Julian.

With corvon coprounez craftyly sleghe.[1]
Chalkwhyt chymnees ther ches he innoghe[2]
Upon bastel rovez, that blenked ful quyte;
800 So mony pynakle paynted watz poudred ayquere,
Among the castel carnelez clambred so thik
That pared out of papure purely hit semed.[3]
The fre freke on the fole hit fayre innoghe thoght,
If he myght kever to com the cloyster wythinne,
805 To herber in that hostel whyl halyday lested,
            avinant.
      He calde, and son ther com
      A porter pure plesaunt,
      On the wal his ernde he nome,
810   And haylsed the knyght erraunt.

"Gode sir," quoth Gawan, "woldez thou go myn ernde,
To the hegh lorde of this hous, herber to crave?"
"Ye, Peter,"[4] quoth the porter, "and purely I trowee
That ye be, wyghe, welcum to wone quyle yow lykez."
815 Then yede the wyghe yerne and com agayn swythe,
And folke frely hym wyth, to fonge the knyght.
Thay let doun the grete draght and derely out yeden,
And kneled doun on her knes upon the colde erthe
To welcum this ilk wygh as worthy hom thoght;
820 Thay yolden hym the brode gate, yarked up wyde,
And he hem raysed rekenly, and rod over the brygge.
Sere segges hym sesed by sadel, quel he lyght,
And sythen stabled his stede stif men innoghe.
Knyghtez and swyerez comen doun thenne
825 For to bryng this buurne wyth blys into halle;
Quen he hef up his helme, ther hyghed innoghe
For to hent it at his honde, the hende to serven;
His bronde and his blasoun both thay token.
Then haylsed he ful hendly tho hathelez uchone,
830 And mony proud mon ther presed that prynce to honour.
Alle hasped in his hegh wede to halle thay hym wonnen,

Topped by carved crocketing, skillfully worked.
Chalk-white chimneys he saw there without number
On the roofs of the towers, that brilliantly shone.
800 So many painted pinnacles were scattered everywhere,
Thickly clustered among the castle's embrasures,
That, truly, the building seemed cut out of paper.
To the noble on the horse it was an attractive thought
That he might gain entrance into the castle,
805 To lodge in that building during the festival days
            at his ease.
      A cheerful porter came
      In answer to his shout,
      Who stationed on the wall
810   Greeted the questing knight.

"Good sir," said Gawain, "will you carry my message
To the master of this house, to ask for lodging?"
"Yes, by St. Peter," said the porter, "and I truly believe
That you are welcome, sir, to stay as long as you please."
815 Then the man went speedily and quickly returned,
Bringing others with him, to welcome the knight.
They lowered the great drawbridge and graciously came out,
Kneeling down on their knees upon the cold ground
To welcome this knight in the way they thought fit.
820 They gave him passage through the broad gate, set open wide,
And he courteously bade them rise, and rode over the bridge.
Several men held his saddle while he dismounted,
And then strong men in plenty stabled his horse.
Knights and squires came down then
825 To escort this man joyfully into the hall.
When Gawain took off his helmet, several jumped forward
To receive it from his hand, serving that prince.
His sword and his shield they took from him both.
Then he greeted politely every one of these knights,
830 And many proud men pressed forward to honor that noble.
Still dressed in his armor they brought him into hall,

---

[1] *craftyly sleghe* The castle architecture abounds with crafts-manship. *Sleghe*, meaning skillful, intricate, subtle, is a term of some significance in the poem. Gawain's fellow-guests hope to see *sleghtez of thewez*, 916, skillful displays of good manners; and after creeping into his bedchamber the lady calls him *a sleper unslyghe*, 1209 or unwary, a related term. On being told that he cannot be killed *for slyght upon erthe*, 1854, while wearing the belt, Gawain tells himself that such a *sleght were noble*, 1858. Here the word shades off towards modern "sleight," with overtones of trickery or deceit appropriate to

the story. But many passages of the poem illustrate the poet's fondness for the elaborate craftsmanship or *wylyde werke* that is evident in his own writing, particularly in the *entrelacement* of Part 3.

[2] *ches he innoghe* He saw enough of them, meaning there were very many.

[3] *papure* Paper, a word newly introduced into English, perhaps by the poet.

[4] *Peter* I.e., St. Peter, one of Christ's twelve apostles and, tradi-tionally, the gate-keeper of Heaven.

Ther fayre fyre upon flet fersly brenned.
Thenne the lorde of the lede loutez fro his chambre
For to mete wyth menske the mon on the flor;
835 He sayde, "Ye ar welcum to welde as yow lykez
That here is: al is yowre awen, to have at yowre wylle
          and welde."
          "Graunt mercy," quoth Gawayn,
          "Ther Kryst hit yow foryelde."
840   As frekez that semed fayn
          Ayther other in armez con felde.

Gawan glynte on the gome that godly hym gret,
And thught hit a bolde burne that the burgh aghte;
A hoge hathel for the nonez, and of hyghe eldee;
845 Brode, bryght, watz his berde, and al bever-hwed,
Sturne, stif on the stryththe on stalworth schonkez,
Felle face as the fyre, and fre of hys speche,
And wel hym semed, for sothe, as the segge thught,
To lede a lortschyp in lee of leudez ful gode.
850 The lorde hym charred to a chambre, and chefly cumaundez
To delyver hym a leude, hym lowly to serve;
And there were boun at his bode burnez innoghe,
That broght hym to a bryght boure, ther beddyng was
          noble,
Of cortynes of clere sylk wyth cler golde hemmez,
855 And covertorez ful curious with comlych panez
Of bryght blaunner above, enbrawded bisydez,
Rudelez rennande on ropez, red golde ryngez,
Tapitez tyght to the wowe of tuly and tars,
And under fete, on the flet, of folyande sute.
860 Ther he watz dispoyled, wyth speches of myerthe,
The burne of his bruny and of his bryght wedez.
Ryche robes ful rad renkkez hym broghten,
For to charge and to chaunge, and chose of the best.
Sone as he on hent, and happed therinne,
865 That sete on hym semly wyth saylande skyrtez,
The ver by his visage verayly hit semed
Welnegh to uche hathel, alle on hwes
Lowande and lufly alle his lymmez under,
That a comloker knyght never Kryst made,
          hem thoght.
870   Whethen in worlde he were,
          Hit semed as he moght

Where a blazing fire was fiercely burning.
Then the lord of that company comes down from his chamber,
To show his respect by meeting Gawain there.
835 He said, "You are welcome to do as you please
With everything here: all is yours, to have and command
          as you wish."
          Said Gawain, "Thanks indeed,
          Christ repay your noblesse."
840   Like men overjoyed
          Each hugged the other close.

Gawain studied the man who greeted him courteously,
And thought him a bold one who governed the castle,
A great-sized knight indeed, in the prime of life;
845 Broad and glossy was his beard, all reddish-brown,
Stern-faced, standing firmly on powerful legs;
With a face fierce as fire, and noble in speech,
Who truly seemed capable, it appeared to Gawain,
Of being master of a castle with outstanding knights.
850 The lord led him to a chamber and quickly orders
A man to be assigned to him, humbly to serve;
And several attendants stood ready at his command
Who took him to a fine bedroom with marvelous
          bedding:
Curtains of pure silk with shining gold borders,
855 And elaborate coverlets with splendid facing
Of bright ermine on top, embroidered all around;
Curtains on golden rings, running on cords,
Walls covered with hangings from Tharsia and Toulouse
And underfoot on the floor of a matching kind.
860 There he was stripped, with joking remarks,
That knight, of his mail-shirt and his fine clothes.
Men hurried to bring him costly robes
To choose from the best of them, change and put on.
As soon as he took one and dressed himself in it,
865 Which suited him well with its flowing skirts,
Almost everyone truly supposed from his looks
That spring had arrived in all its colors;
His limbs so shining and attractive under his clothes
That a handsomer knight God never made,
          it seemed.
870   Wherever he came from,
          He must be, so they thought,

Be prynce withouten pere
In felde ther felle men foght.

875   A cheyer[1] byfore the chemné, ther charcole brenned,
      Watz grathed for Sir Gawan graythely with clothez,
      Whyssynes upon queldepoyntes that koynt wer bothe;
      And thenne a meré mantyle watz on that mon cast
      Of a broun bleeaunt, enbrauded ful ryche
880   And fayre furred wythinne with fellez of the best,
      Alle of ermyn in erde, his hode of the same;
      And he sette in that settel semlych ryche,
      And achaufed hym chefly, and thenne his cher mended.
      Sone watz telded up a tabil on trestez ful fayre,
885   Clad wyth a clene clothe that cler quyt schewed,
      Sanap, and salure, and sylverin sponez.
      The wyghe wesche at his wylle and went to his mete:
      Seggez hym served semly innoghe,
      Wyth sere sewes and sete, sesounde of the best,
890   Double-felde, as hit fallez, and fele kyn fischez,[2]
      Summe baken in bred, summe brad on the gledez,
      Summe sothen, summe in sewe savered with spyces,
      And ay sawes so sleghe that the segge lyked.
      The freke calde hit a fest ful frely and ofte
895   Ful hendely, quen alle the hatheles rehayted hym at onez,
            as hende,
         "This penaunce now ye take,
         And eft hit schal amende."
         That mon much merthe con make,
900   For wyn in his hed that wende.

      Thenne watz spyed and spured upon spare wyse
      Bi prevé poyntez of that prynce, put to hymselven,
      That he biknew cortaysly of the court that he were
      That athel Arthure the hende haldez hym one,
905   That is the ryche ryal kyng of the Rounde Table,
      And hit watz Wawen hymself that in that won syttez,
      Comen to that Krystmasse, as case hym then lymped.
      When the lorde hade lerned that he the leude hade,
      Loude laghed he therat, so lef hit hym thoght,

A prince unparalleled
In field where warriors fought.

875   A chair before the fireplace where charcoal glowed
      Was made ready with coverings for Gawain at once:
      Cushions set on quilted spreads, both skilfully made,
      And then a handsome robe was thrown over the man
      Made of rich brown material, with embroidery rich,
880   And well fur-lined inside with the very best pelts,
      All of ermine in fact, with a matching hood.
      Becomingly rich in attire he sat in that chair,
      Quickly warmed himself, and then his expression softened.
      Soon a table was deftly set up on trestles,
885   Spread with a fine tablecloth, brilliantly white,
      With overcloth and salt-cellar, and silver spoons.
      When he was ready Gawain washed and sat down to his meal.
      Men served him with every mark of respect,
      With many excellent dishes, wonderfully seasoned,
890   In double portions, as is fitting, and all kinds of fish:
      Some baked in pastry, some grilled over coals,
      Some boiled, some in stews flavored with spices,
      Always with subtle sauces that the knight found tasty.
      Many times he graciously called it a feast,
895   Courteously when the knights all urged him together,
            as polite,
         "Accept this penance now,
         Soon you'll be better fed."
         Gawain grew full of mirth
900   As wine went to his head.

      Then he was tactfully questioned and asked
      By discreet enquiry addressed to that prince,
      So that he must politely admit he belonged to the court
      Which noble Arthur, that gracious man, rules alone,
905   Who is the great and royal king of the Round Table;
      And that it was Gawain himself who was sitting there,
      Having arrived there at Christmas, as his fortune chanced.
      When the lord of the castle heard who was his guest,
      He laughed loudly at the news, so deeply was he pleased;

---

[1] *A cheyer* Chairs were relatively rare, and to be given one was a
mark of respect. The usual form of seat is indicated by the Green
Knight's reference to knights *aboute on this bench*, 280, and by
Gawain's request for permission to *boghe fro this benche*, 344.

[2] *fele kyn fischez* Many kinds of fish. Because Christmas Eve is a
fast-day, no red meat is served. The meal is jokingly referred to as
penance, 897, and Gawain is promised something better on the next
day, 898.

910 And alle the men in that mote maden much joye
To apere in his presense prestly that tyme,
That alle prys and prowes and pured thewes[1]
Apendes to hys persoun, and praysed is ever;
Byfore alle men upon molde his mensk is the most.
915 Uch segge ful softly sayde to his fere:
"Now schal we semlych se sleghtez of thewez
And the teccheles termes of talkyng noble,
Wich spede is in speche unspurd may we lerne,[2]
Syn we haf fonged that fyne fader of nurture.
920 God hatz geven us his grace godly for sothe,
That such a gest as Gawan grauntez us to have,
When burnez blythe of his burthe schal sitte
            and synge.
      In menyng of manerez mere
925   This burne now schal us bryng,
      I hope that may hym here
      Schal lerne of luf-talkyng."

Bi that the diner watz done and the dere up
Hit watz negh at the niyght neghed the tyme.
930 Chaplaynez to the chapeles chosen the gate,
Rungen ful rychely, ryght as thay schulden,
To the hersum evensong of the hyghe tyde.
The lorde loutes therto, and the lady als,
Into a cumly closet coyntly ho entrez.
935 Gawan glydez ful gay and gos theder sone;
The lorde laches hym by the lappe and ledez hym to sytte,
And couthly hym knowez and callez hym his nome,
And sayde he watz the welcomest wyghe of the worlde;
And he hym thonkked throly, and ayther halched other,
940 And seten soberly samen the servise quyle.
Thenne lyst the lady to loke on the knyght,
Thenne com ho of hir closet with mony cler burdez.
Ho watz the fayrest in felle,[3] of flesche and of lyre,
And of compas and colour and costes, of all other,
945 And wener then Wenore, as the wyght thoght.
Ho ches thurgh the chaunsel to cheryche that hende:
An other lady hir lad bi the lyft honde,
That watz alder then ho, an auncian hit semed,
And heghly honowred with hathelez aboute.

910 And all the men in the castle were overjoyed
To make the acquaintance quickly then
Of the man to whom all excellence and valor belongs,
Whose refined manners are everywhere praised,
And whose fame exceeds any other person's on earth.
915 Each knight whispered to his companion,
"Now we shall enjoy seeing displays of good manners,
And the irreproachable terms of noble speech;
The art of conversation we can learn unasked,
Since we have taken in the source of good breeding.
920 Truly, God has been gracious to us indeed,
In allowing us to receive such a guest as Gawain,
Whose birth men will happily sit down and celebrate
            in song.
      In knowledge of fine manners
925   This man has expertise;
      I think that those who hear him
      Will learn what love-talk is."

When dinner was finished and Gawain had risen,
The time had drawn on almost to night:
930 Chaplains made their way to the castle chapels,
Rang their bells loudly, just as they should,
For devout evensong on that holy occasion.
The lord makes his way there, and his lady too,
Who gracefully enters a finely carved pew.
935 Gawain hastens there, smartly dressed, and quickly arrives;
The lord takes him by the sleeve and leads him to a seat,
And greets him familiarly, calling him by his name,
And said he was the welcomest guest in the world.
Gawain thanked him heartily, and the two men embraced,
940 And sat gravely together while the service lasted.
Then the lady wished to set eyes on the knight
And left her pew with many fair women.
She was the loveliest on earth in complexion and features,
In figure, in coloring and behavior above all others,
945 And more beautiful than Guenevere, it seemed to the knight.
She came through the chancel to greet him courteously,
Another lady leading her by the left hand,
Who was older than she, an aged one it seemed,
And respectfully treated by the assembled knights.

---

[1] *alle prys and prowes and pured thewes* Great excellence, military valor, and refined manners.

[2] *Wich spede is in speche unspurd may we lerne* We may learn without asking what success in conversation consists of.

[3] *the fayrest in felle* Literally, the most beautiful in skin.

950	Bot unlyke on to loke tho ladyes were,
	For if the yonge watz yep, yolwe watz that other;
	Riche red on that on rayled ayquere,
	Rugh ronkled chekez that other on rolled;
	Kerchofes of that on, wyth mony cler perlez,
955	Hir brest and hir bryght throte bare displayed,
	Schon schyrer then snawe that schedez on hillez;
	That other wyth a gorger watz gered over the swyre,
	Chymbled over hir blake chyn with chalkquyte vayles,
	Hir frount folden in sylk, enfoubled ayquere,
960	Toreted and treleted with tryfles aboute,
	That noght watz bare of that burde bot the blake browes,
	The tweyne yghen and the nase, the naked lyppez,
	And those were soure to se and sellyly blered;
	A mensk lady on molde mon may hire calle,
965	for Gode!
	Hir body watz schort and thik,
	Hir buttokez balgh and brode,
	More lykkerwys on to lyk
	Watz that scho hade on lode.

970	When Gawayn glent on that gay, that graciously loked,
	Wyth leve laght of the lorde he lent hem agaynes;
	The alder he haylses, heldande ful lowe,
	The loveloker he lappez a lyttel in armez,
	He kysses hir comlyly, and knyghtly he melez.
975	Thay kallen hym of aquoyntaunce, and he hit quyk askez
	To be hir servaunt sothly, if hemself lyked.
	Thay tan hym bytwene hem, wyth talkyng hym leden
	To chambre, to chemné, and chefly thay asken
	Spycez,[1] that unsparely men speded hom to bryng,
980	And the wynnelych wyne therwith uche tyme.
	The lorde luflych aloft lepez ful ofte,
	Mynned merthe to be made upon mony sythez,
	Hent heghly of his hode, and on a spere henged,
	And wayned hom to wynne the worchip therof,
985	That most myrthe myght meve that Crystenmasse whyle:[2]
	"And I schal fonde, bi my fayth, to fylter wyth the best
	Er me wont the wede, with help of my frendez."
	Thus wyth laghande lotez the lorde hit tayt makez,
	For to glade Sir Gawayn with gomnez in halle
990	that nyght,

950	But very different in looks were those two ladies,
	For where the young one was fresh, the other was withered;
	Every part of that one was rosily aglow:
	On that other, rough wrinkled cheeks hung in folds.
	Many bright pearls adorned the kerchiefs of one,
955	Whose breast and white throat, uncovered and bare,
	Shone more dazzling than snow new-fallen on hills;
	The other wore a gorget over her neck,
	Her swarthy chin wrapped in chalkwhite veils,
	Her forehead enfolded in silk, muffled up everywhere,
960	With embroidered hems and lattice-work of tiny stitching,
	So that nothing was exposed of her but her black brows,
	Her two eyes and her nose, her naked lips,
	Which were repulsive to see and shockingly bleared.
	A noble lady indeed you might call her,
965	by God!
	With body squat and thick,
	And buttocks bulging broad,
	More delectable in looks
	Was the lady whom she led.

970	Gawain glanced at that beauty, who favored him with a look,
	And taking leave of the lord he walked towards them.
	The older one he salutes with a deep bow,
	And takes the lovelier one briefly into his arms,
	Kisses her respectfully and courteously speaks.
975	They ask to make his acquaintance, and he quickly begs
	Truly to be their servant, if that would please them.
	They place him between them and lead him, still chatting,
	To a private room, to the fireplace, and immediately call
	For spiced cakes, which men hurried to bring them unstinted,
980	Together with marvelous wine each time they asked.
	The lord jumps up politely on several occasions,
	Repeatedly urging his guests to make merry;
	Graciously pulled off his hood and hung it on a spear,
	And encouraged them to gain honor by winning it,
985	So that the Christmas season would abound with mirth.
	"And I shall try, on my word, to compete with the best,
	Before I lose my hood, with the help of my friends."
	Thus with laughing words the lord makes merry,
	To keep Sir Gawain amused with games in hall
990	that night,

---

1 *Spycez* Spiced cakes, still a Christmas tradition. Cloves, ginger, and cinnamon were available.

2 *Hent heghly … Crystenmasse whyle* Another Christmas game, evidently a jumping contest, typically boisterous in character.

Til that hit watz tyme
The lord comaundet lyght;
Sir Gawen his leve con nyme
And to his bed hym dight.

Until it was so late
That lights were ordered in;
Then taking courteous leave
To chamber went Gawain.

995 On the morne, as uch mon mynez that tyme
That Dryghtyn for oure destyné to deye watz borne,
Wele waxez in uche a won in world for his sake;
So did hit there on that day thurgh dayntés mony.
Bothe at mes and at mele messes ful quaynt[1]
1000 Derf men upon dece drest of the best.
The olde auncian wyf heghest ho syttez,
The lorde lufly her by lent, as I trowe;
Gawan and the gay burde togeder thay seten,
Even inmyddez, as the messe metely come,
1005 And sythen thurgh al the sale as hem best semed.
Bi uche grome at his degré graythely watz served,
Ther watz mete, ther watz myrthe, ther watz much joye,
That for to telle therof hit me tene were,
And to poynte hit yet I pyned me paraventure.
1010 Bot yet I wot that Wawen and the wale burde
Such comfort of her compaynye caghten togeder
Thurgh her dere dalyaunce of her derne wordez,
Wyth clene cortays carp closed fro fylthe,
That hor play watz passande uche prynce gomen,
1015   in vayres.
       Trumpes and nakerys,
       Much pypyng ther repayres;
       Uche mon tented hys,[2]
       And thay two tented thayres.

1020 Much dut watz ther dryven that day and that other,
And the thryd as thro thronge in therafter;
The joye of sayn Jonez day[3] watz gentyle to here,
And watz the last of the layk, leudez ther thoghten.
Ther wer gestes to go upon the gray morne,
1025 Forthy wonderly thay woke, and the wyn dronken,
Daunsed ful dreghly wyth dere carolez.
At the last, when hit watz late, thay lachen her leve,
Uchon to wende on his way that watz wyghe straunge.[4]

995 On the next day, when everyone remembers the time
When God who died for our salvation was born,
Joy spreads through every dwelling on earth for his sake.
So did it there on that day, through numerous pleasures;
Both light meals and great dishes cunningly prepared
1000 And of exquisite quality bold men served on the dais.
The ancient lady sits in the place of honor,
The lord politely taking his place by her, I believe.
Gawain and the lovely lady were seated together,
Right in the middle of the table, where food duly came,
1005 And was then served throughout the hall in proper sequence.
By the time each man had been served according to rank,
Such food and such merriment, so much enjoyment were there
That to tell you about it would give me much trouble,
Especially if I tried to describe it in detail.
1010 Yet I know that Gawain and his beautiful partner
Found such enjoyment in each other's company,
Through a playful exchange of private remarks,
And well-mannered small-talk, unsullied by sin,
That their pleasure surpassed every princely amusement,
1015   for sure.
       Trumpets, kettledrums
       And piping roused all ears.
       Each man fulfilled his wishes,
       And those two followed theirs.

1020 Great joy filled that day and the one following,
And a third as delightful came pressing after;
The revelry on St. John's Day was glorious to hear,
And was the end of the festivities, the people supposed.
The guests were to leave early next morning,
1025 And so they reveled all night, drinking the wine
And ceaselessly dancing and caroling songs.
At last, when it was late, they take their leave,
Each one who was a guest there to go on his way.

---

[1] *messes ful quaynt* Finely prepared meals, set out (*drest*) on the high table. Elsewhere *koynt*, 877 is a variant spelling, again indicating skillfully made things.

[2] *Uche mon tented hys* Each man attended to his own needs or pleasures.

---

[3] *sayn Jonez day* 27 December, but three days later it is New Year's Eve—a day too early. Some editors have suggested a line may be missing here.

[4] *wyghe straunge* Stranger or visitor to the castle.

Gawan gef hym god day, the godmon hym lachchez,
1030 Ledes hym to his awen chambre, the chemné bysyde,
And there he drawez hym on dryghe, and derely hym thonkkez
Of the wynne worschip that he hym wayved hade,
As to honour his hous on that hygh tyde,
And enbelyse his burgh with his bele chere.[1]
1035 "Iwysse, sir, quyl I leve, me worthez the better
That Gawayn hatz ben my gest at Goddez awen fest."
"Grant merci, sir," quoth Gawayn, "in god fayth hit is yowrez,
Al the honour is your awen—the heghe kyng yow yelde!
And I am wyghe at your wylle to worch youre hest,
1040 As I am halden therto, in hyghe and in lowe,
        bi right."
    The lorde fast can hym payne
    To holde lenger the knyght;
    To hym answarez Gawayn
1045 Bi non way that he myght.[2]

Then frayned the freke ful fayre at himselven
Quat derve dede had hym dryven at that dere tyme
So kenly fro the kyngez kourt to kayre al his one,
Er the halidayez holly were halet out of toun.[3]
1050 "For sothe, sir," quoth the segge, "ye sayn bot the trawthe,
A heghe ernde and a hasty me hade fro tho wonez,
For I am sumned myselfe to sech to a place,
I ne wot in the worlde whederwarde to wende hit to fynde.
I nolde bot if I hit negh myght on Nw Yeres morne
1055 For alle the londe inwyth Logres, so me oure lorde help!
Forthy, sir, this enquest I require yow here,
That ye telle me with trawthe if ever ye tale herde
Of the grene chapel, quere hit on grounde stondez,
And of the knyght that hit kepes, of colour of grene.
1060 Ther watz stabled bi statut a steven us bitwene
To mete that mon at that mere, yif I myght last;
And of that ilk Nw Yere bot neked now wontez,
And I wolde loke on that lede, if God me let wolde,
Gladloker, bi Goddez sun, then any god welde!
1065 Forthi, iwysse, bi yowre wylle, wende me bihoves,
Naf I now to busy bot bare thre dayez,
And me als fayn to falle feye as fayly of myyn ernde."
Thenne laghande quoth the lorde, "Now leng the byhoves,

Gawain bids goodbye to his host, who takes hold of him,
1030 Leads him to his own room, beside the fire,
And there he detains him, thanks him profusely
For the wonderful kindness that Gawain had shown
By honoring his house at that festive time,
And by gracing the castle with his charming presence.
1035 "Indeed, sir, as long as I live I shall be the better
Because Gawain was my guest at God's own feast."
"All my thanks, sir," said Gawain, "in truth it is yours,
All the honor falls to you, and may the high king repay you!
And I am at your commandment to act on your bidding,
1040 As I am duty bound to in everything, large or small,
        by right."
    The lord tried strenuously
    To lengthen Gawain's stay,
    But Gawain answered him
1045 That he could not delay.

Then the lord politely enquired of the knight
What pressing need had forced him at that festive time
So urgently from the royal court to travel all alone,
Before the holy days had completely passed.
1050 "Indeed, sir," said the knight, "you are right to wonder;
A task important and pressing drove me into the wild,
For I am summoned in person to seek out a place
With no idea whatever where it might be found.
I would not fail to reach it on New Year's morning
1055 For all the land in England, so help me our Lord!
Therefore, sir, this request I make of you now,
That you truthfully tell me if you ever heard talk
Of a Green Chapel, wherever it stands upon earth,
And of a knight who maintains it, who is colored green.
1060 A verbal agreement was settled between us
To meet that man at that place, should I be alive,
And before that New Year little time now remains;
And I would face that man, if God would allow me,
More gladly, by God's son, than come by great wealth!
1065 With your permission, therefore, I must indeed leave:
I have now for my business only three short days,
And would rather be struck dead than fail in my quest."
Then the lord said, laughing, "Now you must stay,

---

[1] *enbelyse ... bele chere* Bertilak (Gawain's host) makes an uncharacteristic sortie into courtly French terms.

[2] *Bi non way that he myght* He could not by any means.

[3] *Er the halidayez holly were halet* Before the holidays were completely over. A curious remark. Gawain reaches the castle, Hautdesert, after a long journey (*towen fro ferre*, 1093) as the festivities are reaching their height, having left Camelot long before the holiday season began.

For I schal teche yow to that terme bi the tymes ende,
1070 The grene chapayle upon grounde greve yow no more;
Bot ye schal be in yowre bed, burne, at thyn ese,
Quyle forth dayez, and ferk on the fyrst of the yere,
And cum to that merk at mydmorn, to make quat yow likez
          in spenne.
1075   Dowellez whyle New Yeres daye,
      And rys, and raykez thenne,
      Mon schal yow sette in waye,
      Hit is not two myle henne."

Thenne watz Gawan ful glad, and gomenly he laghed:
1080 "Now I thonk yow thryvandely thurgh alle other thynge,
Now acheved is my chaunce, I schal at your wylle
Dowelle, and ellez do quat ye demen."
Thenne sesed hym the syre and set hym bysyde,
Let the ladiez be fette to lyke hem the better.
1085 Ther watz seme solace by hemself stille;
The lorde let for luf lotez so myry
As wygh that wolde of his wyte, ne wyst quat he myght.
Thenne he carped to the knyght, criande loude,
"Ye han demed to do the dede that I bidde;
1090 Wyl ye halde this hes here at thys onez?"
"Ye, sir, for sothe," sayd the segge trwe,
"Whyl I byde in yowre borghe, be bayn to yowre hest."
"For ye haf travayled," quoth the tulk, "towen fro ferre,
And sythen waked me wyth, ye arn not wel waryst
1095 Nauther of sostnaunce ne of slepe, sothly I knowe;
Ye schal lenge in your lofte, and lyghe in your ese
To-morn quyle the messequyle, and to mete wende
When ye wyl, wyth my wyf, that wyth yow schal sitte
And comfort yow with compayny, til I to cort torne;
1100   ye lende,
    And I schal erly ryse,
    On huntyng wyl I wende."
    Gavayn grantez alle thyse,
    Hym heldande, as the hende.

1105 "Yet firre," quoth the freke, "a forwarde we make:
Quat-so-ever I wynne in the wod hit worthez to yourez,
And quat chek so ye acheve chaunge me therforne.[1]
Swete, swap we so, sware with trawthe,

For I shall direct you to your meeting at the year's end.
1070 Let the whereabouts of the Green Chapel worry you no more;
For you shall lie in your bed, sir, taking your ease
Until late in the day, and leave on the first of the year,
And reach that place at midday, to do whatever pleases you
          there.
1075   Stay till the year's end,
      And leave on New Year's Day;
      We'll put you on the path,
      It's not two miles away."

Then Gawain was overjoyed, and merrily laughed:
1080 "Now I thank you heartily for this, above everything else,
Now my quest is accomplished, I shall at your wish
Remain here, and do whatever else you think fit."
Then the host seized him, set Gawain by his side,
And bid the ladies be fetched to increase their delight.
1085 They had great pleasure by themselves in private;
In his excitement the lord uttered such merry words
Like a man out of his mind, not knowing what he did.
Then he said to the knight exuberantly,
"You have agreed to carry out whatever deed I ask;
1090 Will you keep this promise now, at this very instant?"
"Yes, sir, assuredly," said the true knight,
"While I am under your roof, I obey your bidding."
"You have wearied yourself," said the man, "traveling from far,
And then reveled all night with me: you have not recovered
1095 Either your lost sleep or your nourishment, I am sure.
You shall stay in your bed and lie at your ease
Tomorrow until mass-time, and then go to dine
When you like, with my wife, who will sit at your side
And be your charming companion until I come home.
1100   You stay;
    And I shall rise at dawn
    And hunting will I go."
    All this Gawain grants,
    With a well-mannered bow.

1105 "Yet further," said the man, "let us make an agreement:
Whatever I catch in the wood shall become yours,
And whatever mishap comes your way give me in exchange.
Dear sir, let us swap so, swear me that truly,

---

[1] *quat chek so ye acheve* Whatever fortune you win. The remark is equivocal. *Chek* also has the sense of misfortune—see 1857 and 2195.

Quether, leude, so lymp, lere other better."[1]
1110 "Bi God," quoth Gawayn the gode, "I grant thertylle,
And that yow lyst for to layke, lef hit me thynkes."
"Who bryngez uus this beverage, this bargayn is maked":
So sayde the lorde of that lede; thay laghed uchone,
Thay dronken and dalyeden and dalten untyghtel,
1115 Thise lordez and ladyez, quyle that hem lyked;
And sythen with Frenkysch fare and fele fayre lotez[2]
Thay stoden and stemed and stylly speken,
Kysten ful comlyly and kaghten her leve.
With mony leude ful lyght and lemande torches
1120 Uche burne to his bed watz broght at the laste,
          ful softe.
      To bed yet er thay yede,
      Recorded covenauntez ofte;
      The olde lorde of that leude
1125 Cowthe wel halde layk alofte.

FITT 3

Ful erly bifore the day the folk uprysen,
Gestes that go wolde hor gromez thay calden,
And thay busken up bilyve blonkkez to sadel,
Tyffen her takles, trussen her males,
1130 Richen hem the rychest, to ryde alle arayde,
Lepen up lightly, lachen her brydeles,
Uche wyghe on his way ther hym wel lyked.
The leve lorde of the londe watz not the last
Arayed for the rydyng, with renkkes ful mony;
1135 Ete a sop hastyly, when he hade herde masse,
With bugle to bent-felde he buskez bylyve.
By that any daylyght lemed upon erthe
He with his hatheles on hyghe horsses weren.
Thenne thise cacheres that couthe cowpled hor houndez,
1140 Unclosed the kenel dore and calde hem theroute,
Blwe bygly in buglez thre bare mote;[3]
Braches bayed therfore and breme noyse maked;
And thay chastysed and charred on chasyng that went,

Whatever falls to our lot, worthless or better."
1110 "By God," said the good Gawain, "I agree to that,
And your love of amusement pleases me much."
"If someone brings us drink, it will be an agreement,"
Said the lord of that company: everyone laughed.
They drank wine and joked and frivolously chatted
1115 For as long as it pleased them, these lords and ladies;
And then with exquisite manners and many gracious words
They stood at a pause, conversing quietly,
Kissed each other affectionately and then took their leave.
With many brisk servingmen and gleaming torches
1120 Each man was at last escorted to a bed
          downy soft.
      Yet first, and many times
      Again the terms were sworn;
      The master of those folk
1125 Knew how to foster fun.

PART 3

Early before daybreak the household arose;
Guests who were leaving called for their grooms,
And they hurried quickly to saddle horses,
Make equipment ready and pack their bags.
1130 The noblest prepare themselves to ride finely dressed,
Leap nimbly into saddle, seize their bridles,
Each man taking the path that attracted him most.
The well-loved lord of the region was not the last
Prepared for riding, with a great many knights;
1135 Snatched a hasty breakfast after hearing mass,
And makes ready for the hunting-field with bugles blowing.
By the time the first glimmers of daylight appeared
He and his knights were mounted on horse.
Then experienced huntsmen coupled the hounds,
1140 Unlocked the kennel door and ordered them out,
Loudly blowing three long notes on their horns.
Hounds bayed at the sound and made a fierce noise;
And those who went straying were whipped in and turned back,

---

[1] *Quether, leude, so lymp, lere other better* Whichever man wins
something worthless or better. The literal sense of *lymp* is "falls to
his lot."

[2] *Frenkysch fare* Refined manners, modeled on courtly French
behavior.

[3] *thre bare mote* Three single notes on the horn, ordering the
release of the hounds.

A hundreth of hunteres, as I haf herde telle,
1145   of the best.
To trystors vewters yod,[1]
Couples huntes of kest;
Ther ros for blastez gode
Gret rurd in that forest.

1150 At the fyrst quethe of the quest quaked the wylde;
Der drof in the dale, doted for drede,
Highed to the hyghe, bot heterly thay were
Restayed with the stablye, that stoutly ascryed.
Thay let the herttez haf the gate, with the hyghe hedes,
1155 The breme bukkez also with hor brode paumez;
For the fre lorde hade defende in fermysoun tyme
That ther schulde no mon meve to the male dere.
The hindez were halden in with hay! and war!
The does dryven with gret dyn to the depe sladez.
1160 Ther myght mon se, as thay slypte, slenting of arwes—
At uche wende under wande wapped a flone—
That bigly bote on the broun with ful brode hedez.
What! thay brayen and bleden, bi bonkkez thay deyen,
And ay rachches in a res radly hem folwes,
1165 Hunterez wyth hyghe horne hasted hem after
Wyth such a crakkande kry as klyffes haden brusten.
What wylde so atwaped wyghes that schotten
Watz al toraced and rent at the resayt,
Bi thay were tened at the hyghe and taysed to the wattres;
1170 The ledez were so lerned at the lowe trysteres,
And the grehoundez so grete, that geten hem bylyve
And hem tofylched, as fast as frekez myght loke,
        ther-ryght.
The lorde for blys abloy
1175 Ful ofte con launce and lyght,
And drof that day wyth joy
Thus to the derk nyght.

Thus laykez this lorde by lynde-wodez evez,
And Gawayn the god mon in gay bed lygez,
1180 Lurkkez[2] quyl the daylyght lemed on the wowes,
Under covertour ful clere, cortyned aboute;
And as in slomeryng he slode, sleghly he herde
A littel dyn at his dor, and dernly upon;
And he hevez up his hed out of the clothes,

By a hundred hunters, as I have been told,
1145   of the best.
With keepers at their posts
Huntsmen uncoupled hounds;
Great clamor in the woods
From mighty horn-blasts sounds.

1150 At the first sound of the hunt the wild creatures trembled;
Deer fled from the valley, frantic with fear,
And rushed to the high ground, but were fiercely turned back
By the line of beaters, who yelled at them savagely.
They let the stags with their tall antlers pass,
1155 And the wonderful bucks with their broad horns;
For the noble lord had forbidden in the close season
Anyone to interfere with the male deer.
The hinds were held back with shouts of hay! and war!
The does driven with great noise into the deep valleys.
1160 There you might see, as they ran, arrows flying—
At every turn in the wood a shaft whistled through the air—
Deeply piercing the hide with their wide heads.
What! they cry out and bleed, on the slopes they are slaughtered,
And always swiftly pursued by the rushing hounds;
1165 Hunters with screaming horns gallop behind
With such an ear-splitting noise as if cliffs had collapsed.
Those beasts that escaped the men shooting at them
Were all pulled down and killed at the receiving points,
As they were driven from the high ground down to the streams.
1170 The men at the lower stations were so skilful,
And the greyhounds so large, that they seized them quickly
And tore them down as fast as men could number,
        right there.
On horseback and on foot
1175 The lord, filled with delight,
Spent all that day in bliss
Until the fall of night.

Thus this nobleman sports along the edges of woods,
And the good man Gawain lies in his fine bed,
1180 Lying snug while the daylight gleamed on the walls,
Under a splendid coverlet, shut in by curtains.
And as he lazily dozed, he heard slily made
A little noise at his door and it stealthily open;
And he raised up his head from the bedclothes,

---

[1] *To trystors vewters yod* Keepers of hounds went to their hunting-stations.

[2] *Lurkkez* Lay snug; but the term has pejorative overtones that are heard again at 1195.

1185	A corner of the cortyn he caght up a lyttel,
	And waytez warly thiderwarde quat hit be myght.
	Hit watz the ladi, loflyest to beholde,
	That drow the dor after hir ful dernly and stylle,
	And bowed towarde the bed; and the burne schamed,[1]
1190	And layde hym doun lystyly and let as he slepte;
	And ho stepped stilly and stel to his bedde,
	Kest up the cortyn and creped withinne,
	And set hir ful softly on the bed-syde,
	And lenged there selly longe to loke quen he wakened.
1195	The lede lay lurked a ful longe quyle,
	Compast in his concience to quat that cace myght
	Meve other mount—to mervayle hym thoght,
	Bot yet he sayde in hymself, "More semly hit were
	To aspye wyth my spelle in space quat ho wolde."
1200	Then he wakenede, and wroth, and to hir warde torned,
	And unlouked his yghe-lyddez, and let as hym wondered,
	And sayned hym, as bi his saghe the saver to worthe,
	with hande.
	Wyth chynne and cheke ful swete,
1205	Both quit and red in blande,
	Ful lufly con ho lete
	Wyth lyppez smal laghande.
	"God moroun, Sir Gawayn," sayde that gay lady,
	"Ye ar a sleper unslyghe, that mon may slyde hider;
1210	Now ar ye tan as-tyt![2] Bot true uus may schape,
	I schal bynde yow in your bedde, that be ye trayst."
	Al laghande the lady lanced tho bourdez.
	"Goud moroun, gay," quoth Gawayn the blythe,
	"Me schal worthe at your wille, and that me wel lykez,[3]
1215	For I yelde me yederly, and yeghe after grace,
	And that is the best, be my dome, for me byhovez nede":
	And thus he bourded agayn with mony a blythe laghter.
	"Bot wolde ye, lady lovely, then leve me grante,
	And deprece your prysoun, and pray hym to ryse,
1220	I wolde bowe of this bed, and busk me better;
	I schulde kever the more comfort to karp yow wyth."
	"Nay, for sothe, beau sire," sayde that swete,

1185	Lifted a corner of the curtain a little,
	And takes a glimpse warily to see what it could be.
	It was the lady, looking her loveliest,
	Who shut the door after her carefully, not making a sound,
	And came towards the bed. The knight felt confused,
1190	And lay down again cautiously, pretending to sleep;
	And she approached silently, stealing to his bed,
	Lifted the bed-curtain and crept within,
	And seating herself softly on the bedside,
	Waited there strangely long to see when he would wake.
1195	The knight shammed sleep for a very long while,
	Wondering what the matter could be leading to
	Or portend. It seemed an astonishing thing,
	Yet he told himself, "It would be more fitting
	To discover straightway by talking just what she wants."
1200	Then he wakened and stretched and turned towards her,
	Opened his eyes and pretended surprise,
	And crossed himself as if protecting himself by prayer
	and this sign.
	With lovely chin and cheek
1205	Of blended color both,
	Charmingly she spoke
	From her small laughing mouth.
	"Good morning, Sir Gawain," said that fair lady,
	"You are an unwary sleeper, that one can steal in here:
1210	Now you are caught in a moment! Unless we agree on a truce,
	I shall imprison you in your bed, be certain of that!"
	Laughing merrily the lady uttered this jest.
	"Good morning, dear lady," said Gawain gaily,
	"You shall do with me as you wish, and that pleases me much,
1215	For I surrender at once, and beg for your mercy,
	And that is best, in my judgment, for I simply must."
	Thus he joked in return with a burst of laughter.
	"But if, lovely lady, you would grant me leave
	And release your captive, and ask him to rise,
1220	I would get out of this bed and put on proper dress,
	And then take more pleasure in talking with you."
	"No, indeed not, good sir," said that sweet one,

---

[1] *and the burne schamed* And the knight was embarrassed.

[2] *Now ar ye tan as-tyt!* Now are you captured in a moment! There may be a suggestion here of another traditional game, played by women on Hock Monday, the week after Easter. It consisted of seizing and binding men, who were released after paying a small sum of money.

[3] *that me wel lykez* That pleases me very much.

"Ye schal not rise of your bedde, I rych yow better.
I schal happe yow here that other half als,
1225 And sythen karp wyth my knyght that I kaght have;
For I wene wel, iwysse, Sir Wowen ye are,
That alle the worlde worchipez quere-so ye ride;
Your honour, your hendelayk is hendely praysed
With lordez, wyth ladyes, with alle that lyf bere.
1230 And now ye are here, iwysse, and we bot oure one;
My lorde and his ledez ar on lenthe faren,
Other burnez in her bedde, and my burdez als,
The dor drawen and dit with a derf haspe;
And sythen I have in this hous hym that al lykez,
1235 I schal ware my whyle wel, quyl hit lastez,
      with tale.
        Ye ar welcum to my cors,[1]
        Yowre awen won to wale,
        Me behovez of fyne force
1240   Your servaunt be, and schale."

"In god fayth," quoth Gawayn, "gayn hit me thynkkez,
Thagh I be not now he that ye of speken;
To reche to such reverence as ye reherce here
I am wyghe unworthy, I wot wel myselven.
1245 Bi God, I were glad, and yow god thoght,
At saghe other at servyce that I sette myght
To the plesaunce of your prys—hit were a pure joye."[2]
"In god fayth, Sir Gawayn," quoth the gay lady,
"The prys and the prowes that plesez al other,
1250 If I hit lakked other set at lyght, hit were little daynté;
Bot hit ar ladyes innoghe that lever were nowthe
Haf the, hende, in hor holde, as I the habbe here,
To daly with derely your daynté wordez,
Kever hem comfort and colen her carez,
1255 Then much of the garysoun other gold that thay haven.
Bot I louve that ilk lorde that the lyfte haldez
I have hit holly in my honde that al desyres,
        thurghe grace."
        Scho made hym so gret chere,
1260   That watz so fayr of face,
        The knyght with speches skere
        Answered to uche a case.

"You shall not leave your bed, I intend something better.
I shall tuck you in here on both sides of the bed,
1225 And then chat with my knight whom I have captured.
For I know well, in truth, that you are Sir Gawain,
Whom everyone reveres wherever you go;
Your good name and courtesy are honorably praised
By lords and by ladies and all folk alive.
1230 And now indeed you are here, and we two quite alone,
My husband and his men have gone far away,
Other servants are in bed, and my women too,
The door shut and locked with a powerful hasp;
And since I have under my roof the man everyone loves,
1235 I shall spend my time well, while it lasts,
      with talk.
        You are welcome to me indeed,
        Take whatever you want;
        Circumstances force me
1240   To be your true servant."

"Truly," replied Gawain, "I am greatly honored,
Though I am not in fact such a man as you speak of.
To deserve such respect as you have just described
I am completely unworthy, I know very well.
1245 I should be happy indeed, if you thought it proper,
That I might devote myself by words or by deed
To giving you pleasure: it would be a great joy."
"In all truth, Sir Gawain," replied the beautiful lady,
"If the excellence and gallantry everyone admires
1250 I were to slight or disparage, that would hardly be courteous;
But a great many ladies would much rather now
Hold you, sir, in their power as I have you here,
To spend time amusingly with your charming talk,
Delighting themselves and forgetting their cares,
1255 Than much of the treasure or wealth they possess.
But I praise that same lord who holds up the heavens,
I have completely in my grasp the man everyone longs for,
        through God's grace."
        Radiant with loveliness
1260   Great favor she conferred;
        The knight with virtuous speech
        Answered her every word.

---

[1] *Ye are welcum to my cors*   A suggestive ambiguity that cannot be translated. *My cors* may mean "me," just as "your honor" or "your worship" mean "you." But the literal sense of the phrase, "my body," is present.

[2] *To the plesaunce of your prys*   To pleasing you, or to carrying out your wishes, *your prys* meaning your noble self.

"Madame," quoth the myry mon, "Mary yow yelde,
For I haf founden, in god fayth, yowre fraunchis nobele,
1265 And other ful much of other folk fongen bi hor dedez,
Bot the daynté that thay delen, for my disert nys even,
Hit is the worchyp of yourself, that noght bot wel connez."
"Bi Mary," quod the menskful, "me thynk hit an other;
For were I worth al the wone of wymmen alyve,
1270 And al the wele of the worlde were in my honde,
And I schulde chepen and chose to cheve me a lorde,
For the costes that I haf knowen upon the, knyght, here,
Of bewté and debonerté and blythe semblaunt,
And that I haf er herkkened and halde hit here trwee,
1275 Ther schulde no freke upon folde bifore yow be chosen."
"Iwysse, worthy," quoth the wyghe, "ye haf waled wel
        better,[1]
Bot I am proude of the prys that ye put on me,
And soberly your servaunt, my soverayn I holde yow,
And yowre knyght I becom, and Kryst yow foryelde."
1280 Thus thay meled of muchquat til mydmorn paste,
And ay the lady let lyk as hym loved mych.
The freke ferde with defence, and feted ful fayre;
Thagh ho were burde bryghtest the burne in mynde hade,[2]
The lasse luf in his lode for lur that he soght
1285   bout hone—
        The dunte that schulde hym deve,
        And nedez hit most be done.
        The lady thenn spek of leve,
        He granted hir ful sone.

1290 Thenne ho gef hym god day, and wyth a glent laghed,
And as ho stod, ho stonyed hym wyth ful stor wordez:
"Now he that spedez uche spech this disport yelde yow!
Bot that ye be Gawan, hit gotz in mynde."
"Querfore?" quoth the freke, and freschly he askez,
1295 Ferde lest he hade fayled in fourme of his castes;
Bot the burde hym blessed, and "Bi this skyl" sayde:
"So god as Gawayn gaynly is halden,
And cortaysye is closed so clene in hymselven,
Couth not lightly haf lenged so long wyth a lady,
1300 Bot he had craved a cosse, bi his courtayse,

"Lady," said the man pleasantly, "may Mary repay you,
For I have truly made proof of your great generosity,
1265 And many other folk win credit for their deeds;
But the respect shown to me is not at all my deserving:
That honor is due to yourself, who know nothing but good."
"By Mary," said the noble lady, "to me it seems very different;
For if I were the worthiest of all women alive,
1270 And held all the riches of the earth in my hand,
And could bargain and pick a lord for myself,
For the virtues I have seen in you, sir knight, here,
Of good looks and courtesy and charming manner—
All that I have previously heard and now know to be true—
1275 No man on earth would be picked before you."
"Indeed, noble lady," said the man, "you have chosen
        much better,
But I am proud of the esteem that you hold me in,
And in all gravity your servant, my sovereign I consider you,
And declare myself your knight, and may Christ reward you."
1280 So they chatted of this and that until late morning,
And always the lady behaved as if loving him much.
The knight reacted cautiously, in the most courteous of ways,
Though she was the loveliest woman he could remember:
He felt small interest in love because of the ordeal he must face
1285   very soon—
        To stand a crushing blow,
        In helpless sufferance.
        Of leaving then she spoke,
        The knight agreed at once.

1290 Then she bade him goodbye, glanced at him and laughed,
And as she stood astonished him with a forceful rebuke:
"May he who prospers each speech repay you this pleasure!
But that you should be Gawain I very much doubt."
"But why?" said the knight, quick with his question,
1295 Fearing he had committed some breach of good manners;
But the lady said "Bless you" and replied, "For this cause:
So good a knight as Gawain is rightly reputed,
In whom courtesy is so completely embodied,
Could not easily have spent so much time with a lady
1300 Without begging a kiss, to comply with politeness,

---

[1] *ye haf waled wel better*   You have made a much better choice;
reminding the lady that she has a husband.

[2] *Thagh ho were burde bryghtest the burne in mynde hade*   The
frightening prospect facing Gawain (*the lur that he soght*, 1284) does

not allow him to become distracted by the lady's beauty, though her
loveliness surpasses anything he can remember. The manuscript
reading of this line, *Thagh I were burde bryghtest the burde in mynde
hade*, is usually amended as shown.

Bi sum towch of summe tryfle at sum talez ende."
Then quoth Wowen, "Iwysse, worthe as yow lykez;
I schal kysse at your comaundement, as a knyght fallez,
And fire, lest he displese yow, so plede hit no more."
1305 Ho comes nerre with that and cachez hym in armez,
Loutez luflych adoun and the leude kysses.
Thay comly bykennen to Kryst ayther other;
Ho dos hir forth at the dore withouten dyn more;
And he ryches hym to ryse and rapes hym sone,
1310 Clepes to his chamberlayn, choses his wede,
Bowez forth, quen he watz boun, blythely to masse;
And thenne he meved to his mete that menskly hym keped,
And made myry al day, til the mone rysed,
        with game.
1315   Watz never freke fayrer fonge
        Bitwene two so dyngne dame,
        The alder and the yonge;
        Much solace set thay same.

And ay the lorde of the londe is lent on his gamnez,
1320 To hunt in holtez and hethe at hyndez barayne;
Such a sowme he ther slowe bi that the sunne heldet,
Of dos and of other dere, to deme were wonder.
Thenne fersly thay flokked in folk at the laste,
And quykly of the quelled dere a querré thay maked.
1325 The best bowed therto with burnez innoghe,
Gedered the grattest of gres that ther were,
And didden hem derely undo as the dede askez;
Serched hem at the asay summe that ther were,
Two fyngeres thay fonde of the fowlest of alle.
1330 Sythen thay slyt the slot, sesed the erber,
Schaved wyth a scharp knyf, and the schyre knitten;
Sythen rytte thay the four lymmes, and rent of the hyde,
Then brek thay the balé, the bowelez out token
Lystily for laucyng the lere of the knot;
1335 Thay gryped to the gargulun, and graythely departed
The wesaunt fro the wynt-hole, and walt out the guttez;
Then scher thay out the schulderez with her scharp knyvez,
Haled hem by a lyttel hole to have hole sydes.
Sithen britned thay the brest and brayden hit in twynne,
1340 And eft at the gargulun bigynez on thenne,
Ryvez hit up radly ryght to the byght,
Voydez out the avanters, and verayly therafter
Alle the rymez by the rybbez radly thay lance;
So ryde thay of by resoun bi the rygge bonez,

By some hint or suggestion at the end of a remark."
Then Gawain said, "Indeed, let it be as you wish;
I will kiss at your bidding, as befits a knight,
And do more, rather than displease you, so urge it no further."
1305 With that she approaches him and takes him in her arms,
Stoops graciously over him and kisses the knight.
They politely commend each other to Christ's keeping:
She goes out of the room without one word more.
And he prepares to get up as quickly as he can,
1310 Calls for his chamberlain, selects his clothes,
Makes his way, when he was ready, contentedly to mass;
And then went to his meal that worthily awaited him,
And made merry all day until the moon rose
        with games.
1315   Never knight was entertained
        By such a worthy pair,
        One old, the other young;
        Much pleasure did they share.

And still the lord of that land is absorbed his sport,
1320 Chasing through woodland and heath after barren hinds.
What a number he killed by the time the day ended
Of does and other deer would be hard to imagine.
Then proudly the hunters flocked together at the end,
And quickly made a quarry of the slaughtered deer.
1325 The noblest pressed forward with many attendants,
Gathered together the fattest of the deer,
And neatly dismembered them as ritual requires.
Some of those who examined them at the assay
Found two inches of flesh in the leanest of them.
1330 Then they slit the base of the throat, took hold of the gullet,
Scraped it with a sharp knife and knotted it shut;
Next they cut off the four legs and ripped off the hide,
Then broke open the belly and took out the entrails
Carefully to avoid loosening the ligature of the knot.
1335 They took hold of the throat, and quickly separated
The gullet from the windpipe, and threw out the guts.
Then they cut round the shoulders with their keen knives,
Drawing them through an aperture to keep the sides whole.
Next they cut open the breast and split it in two,
1340 And then one of them turns again to the throat
And swiftly lays open the body right to the fork,
Throws out the neck-offal, and expertly then
Quickly severs all the membranes on the ribs.
So correctly they cut off all the offal on the spine

1345 Evenden to the haunche, that henged al samen,
And heven it up al hole, and hwen hit of there,
And that thay neme for the noumbles bi nome, as I trowe,
bi kynde;
Bi the byght al of the thyghes
1350 The lappez thay lance bihynde;
To hewe hit in two thay hyghes,
Bi the bakbon to unbynde.

Bothe the hede and the hals thay hwen of thenne,
And sythen sunder thay the sydez swyft fro the chyne,
1355 And the corbeles fee[1] thay kest in a greve;
Thenn thurled they ayther thik side thurgh bi the rybbe,
And henged thenne ayther bi hoghes of the fourchez,
Uche freke for his fee, as fallez for to have.
Upon a felle of the fayre best fede thay thayr houndes
1360 Wyth the lyver and the lyghtez, the lether of the paunchez,
And bred bathed in blod blende theramongez.
Baldely thay blw prys,[2] bayed thayr rachchez,
Sythen fonge thay her flesche, folden to home,
Strakande ful stoutly mony stif motez.
1365 Bi that the daylyght watz done the douthe watz al wonen
Into the comly castel, ther the knyght bidez
ful stille,
Wyth blys and bryght fyr bette.
The lorde is comen thertylle;
1370 When Gawayn wyth hym mette
Ther watz bot wele at wylle.

Thenne comaunded the lorde in that sale to samen alle the
meny,
Bothe the ladyes on lowe to lyght with her burdes
Bifore alle the folk on the flette, frekez he beddez
1375 Verayly his venysoun to fech hym byforne,
And al godly in gomen Gawayn he called,
Techez hym to the tayles[3] of ful tayt bestes,
Schewez hym the schyree grece schorne upon rybbes.
"How payez yow this play? Haf I prys wonnen?
1380 Have I thryvandely thonk thurgh my craft served?"
"Ye, iwysse," quoth that other wyghe, "here is wayth fayrest
That I sey this seven yere in sesoun of wynter."
"And al I gif yow, Gawayn," quoth the gome thenne,

1345 Right down to the haunches, in one unbroken piece,
And lifted it up whole, and cut it off there;
And to that they give the name of numbles, I believe,
as is right.
Then where the hind legs fork
1350 At the back they cut the skin,
Then hacked the carcass in two,
Swiftly along the spine.

Both the head and the neck they cut off next,
And then rapidly separate the sides from the chine;
1355 And the raven's fee in a thicket they threw.
Then they pierced both thick sides through the ribs,
Hanging each of them by the hocks of their legs,
For each man's payment, as his proper reward.
They put food for their hounds on a fine beast's skin—
1360 The liver and lights, the lining of the stomach,
And bread soaked in blood, mixed up together.
Noisily they blew capture, their hounds barking,
Then shouldering their venison they started for home,
Vigorously sounding many loud single notes.
1365 By the time daylight failed they had ridden back
To the splendid castle, where the knight waits
undisturbed,
With joy and bright fire warm.
Then into hall the lord
1370 Came, and the two men met
In joyfullest accord.

Then the lord commanded the household to assemble in
hall,
And both ladies to come downstairs with their maids.
In front of the gathering he orders his men
1375 To lay out his venison truly before him;
And with playful courtesy he called Gawain to him,
Reckons up the tally of well-grown beasts,
Points out the splendid flesh cut from the ribs.
"Does this game please you? Have I won your praise?
1380 Do I deserve hearty thanks for my hunting skill?"
"Yes indeed," said the other, "this is the finest venison
That I have seen for many years in the winter season."
"And I give it all to you, Gawain," said the man then,

---

[1] *the corbeles fee* A piece of gristle thrown to the birds as part of the ritual.

[2] *blw prys* A blast on the horn when the quarry is taken.

[3] *the tayles* Left on the carcasses to facilitate the tally, or count.

"For by acorde of covenaunt ye crave hit as your awen."
1385 "This is soth," quoth the segge, "I say yow that ilke:
That I haf worthyly wonnen this wonez wythinne,
Iwysse with as god wylle hit worthez to yourez."
He hasppez his fayre hals his armez wythinne,
And kysses hym as comlyly as he couthe awyse:
1390 "Tas yow there my chevicaunce, I cheved no more;
I wowche hit saf fynly, thagh feler hit were."
"Hit is god," quoth the godmon, "grant mercy therfore.
Hit may be such hit is the better, and ye me breve wolde
Where ye wan this ilk wele bi wytte of yorselven."
1395 "That watz not forward," quoth he, "frayst me no more.
For ye haf tan that yow tydez, trawe non other
        ye mowe."
        Thay laghed, and made hem blythe
        Wyth lotez that were to lowe;
1400   To soper thay yede as-swythe,
        Wyth dayntés nwe innowe.

And sythen by the chymné in chamber thay seten,
Wyghez the walle wyn weghed to hem oft,
And efte in her bourdyng thay baythen in the morn
1405 To fylle the same forwardez that thay byfore maden:
Wat chaunce so bytydez hor chevysaunce to chaunge,
What nwez so thay nome, at naght quen they metten.
Thay acorded of the covenauntez byfore the court alle;
The beverage watz broght forth in bourde at that tyme,
1410 Thenne thay lovelych leghten leve at the last,
Uche burne to his bedde busked bylyve.
Bi that the coke hade crowen and cakled bot thryse[1]
The lorde watz lopen of his bedde, the leudez uchone;
So that the mete and the masse watz metely delyvered,
1415 The douthe dressed to the wod er any day sprenged,
        to chace;
        Hegh with hunte and hornez
        Thurgh playnez thay passe in space,
        Uncoupled among tho thornez
1420   Rachez that ran on race.

Sone thay calle of a quest in a ker syde,
The hunt rehayted the houndez that hit fyrst mynged,
Wylde wordez hym warp wyth a wrast noyce;
The howndez that hit herde hastid thider swythe,

"For by the terms of our compact you may claim it as yours."
1385 "That is true," said the knight, "and I say the same to you:
What I have honorably won inside this castle,
With as much good will truly shall be yours."
He takes the other's strong neck in his arms,
And kisses him as pleasantly as he could devise.
1390 "Take here my winnings, I obtained nothing else;
I bestow it on you freely, and would do so were it more."
"It is excellent," said the lord, "many thanks indeed.
It could be even better if you would inform me
Where you won this same prize by your cleverness."
1395 "That was not in our agreement," said he, "ask nothing else;
For you have had what is due to you, expect to receive
        nothing more."
        They laughed and joked awhile
        In speech deserving praise;
1400   Then quickly went to sup
        On new delicacies.

Afterwards they sat by the fire in the lord's chamber,
And servants many times brought in marvelous wine;
And once again in their jesting they agreed the next day
1405 To observe the same covenant as they had made before:
Whatever fortune befell them, to exchange what they won,
Whatever new things they were, at night when they met.
They renewed the agreement before the whole court—
The pledge-drink was brought in with jokes at that time—
1410 Then they graciously took leave of each other at last,
Every man hastening quickly to bed.
By the time cock-crow had sounded three times
The lord had leapt out of bed and each of his men,
So that breakfast and mass were duly done,
1415 And long before daybreak they were all on their way
        to the chase.
        Through fields they canter soon,
        Loud with hunting-horns;
        Headlong the hounds run
1420   Uncoupled among the thorns.

Soon they give tongue at the edge of a marsh;
The huntsman urged on the hounds that found the scent first,
Shouting at them wildly in a loud voice.
The hounds who heard him raced there in haste

---

[1] *crowen ... bot thryse* Cocks supposedly crowed at midnight, 3
a.m., and 6 a.m.

1425	And fellen as fast to the fuyt, fourty at ones;
	Thenne such a glaver ande glam of gedered rachchez
	Ros that the rocherez rungen aboute;
	Hunterez hem hardened with horne and wyth muthe.
	Then al in a semblé sweyed togeder
1430	Bitwene a flosche in that fryth and a foo cragge;
	In a knot bi a clyffe, at the kerre syde,
	Ther as the rogh rocher unrydely was fallen,
	Thay ferden to the fyndyng, and frekez hem after;
	Thay umbekesten the knarre and the knot bothe,
1435	Wyghez, whyl thay wysten wel wythinne hem it were,
	The best that ther breved watz wyth the blodhoundez.
	Thenne thay beten on the buskez, and bede hym upryse,
	And he unsoundyly out soght seggez overthwert;
	On the sellokest swyn swenged out there,
1440	Long sythen fro the sounder that sighed for olde,
	For he watz borelych and brode, bor alther-grattest,
	Ful grymme quen he gronyed; thenne greved mony,
	For thre at the fyrst thrast he thryght to the erthe,
	And sparred forth good sped boute spyt more.
1445	Thise other halowed hyghe! ful hyghe, and hay! hay!
	cryed,
	Haden hornez to mouthe, heterly rechated;
	Mony watz the myry mouthe of men and of houndez
	That buskkez after this bor with bost and wyth noyse
	to quelle.
1450	Ful ofte he bydez the baye,
	And maymez the mute inn melle;
	He hurtez of the houndez, and thay
	Ful yomerly yaule and yelle.
	Schalkez to shote at hym schowen to thenne,
1455	Haled to hym of her arewez, hitten hym oft;
	Bot the poyntez payred at the pyth that pyght in his scheldez,
	And the barbez of his browe bite non wolde;
	Thagh the schaven schafte schyndered in pieces,
	The hede hypped agayn were-so-ever hit hitte.
1460	Bot quen the dyntez hym dered of her dryghe strokez,
	Then, braynwod for bate, on burnez he rasez,
	Hurtz hem ful heterly ther he forth hyghez,
	And mony arghed therat, and on lyte droghen.
	Bot the lorde on a lyght horce launces hym after,
1465	As burne bolde upon bent his bugle he blowez,
	He rechated, and rode thurgh ronez ful thyk,
	Suande this wylde swyn til the sunne schafted.

1425	And rushed towards the trail, forty of them together.
	Then such a deafening babel from gathered hounds rose
	That the rocky bank echoed from end to end.
	Huntsmen encouraged them with horn-blasts and shouts;
	And then all in a throng they rushed together
1430	Between a pool in that thicket and a towering crag.
	On a wooded knoll near a cliff at the edge of the marsh
	Where fallen rocks were untidily scattered,
	They ran to the dislodging, with men at their heels.
	The hunters surrounded both the crag and the knoll
1435	Until they were certain that inside their circle
	Was the beast which had made the bloodhounds give tongue.
	Then they beat on the bushes and called him to come out;
	And he broke cover ferociously through a line of men.
	An incredible wild boar charged out there,
1440	Which long since had left the herd through his age,
	For he was massive and broad, greatest of all boars,
	Terrible when he snorted. Then many were dismayed,
	For three men in one rush he threw on their backs,
	And made away fast without doing more harm.
1445	The others shouted "hi!" and "hay, hay!" at the tops of
	their voices,
	Put horns to mouth and loudly sounded recall.
	Many hunters and hounds joyfully gave tongue,
	Hurrying after this boar with outcry and clamor
	to kill.
1450	Often he stands at bay,
	And maims the circling pack,
	Wounding many hounds
	That piteously yelp and bark.
	Men press forward to shoot at him then,
1455	Loosed their arrows at him, hit him many times;
	But those that struck his shoulders were foiled by their toughness,
	And none of them could pierce through the bristles on his brow.
	Although the polished shaft shivered into pieces,
	The head rebounded away wherever it struck.
1460	But when the hits hurt him with their constant blows,
	Frenzied with fighting he turns headlong on the men,
	And injures them savagely when he charges out,
	So that many grew fearful and drew back further.
	But the lord on a lively horse races after him,
1465	Like a valiant hunter, blowing his horn.
	He urged the hounds on, and through dense thickets rode
	Following this wild boar until the sun went down.

This day wyth this ilk dede thay dryven on this wyse,
Whyle oure luflych lede lys in his bedde,
1470 Gawayn graythely at home, in gerez ful ryche
            of hewe.
        The lady noght forgate
        Com to hym to salue;
        Ful erly ho watz hym ate[1]
1475   His mode for to remwe.

Ho commes to the cortyn, and at the knyght totes.
Sir Wawen her welcumed worthy on fyrst,
And ho hym yeldez agayn ful yerne of hir wordez,
Settez hir softly by his syde, and swythely ho laghez,
1480 And wyth a luflych loke ho layde hym thyse wordez:
"Sir, yif ye be Wawen, wonder me thynkkez,
Wyghe that is so wel wrast alway to god,
And connez not of compaynye[2] the costez undertake;
And if mon kennes yow hom to knowe, ye kest hom of
            our mynde;
1485 Thou hatz foryeten yederly that yisterday I taght te
Bi alder-trest token of talk that I cowthe."
"What is that?" quoth the wyghe, "Iwysse I wot never;
If hit be sothe that ye breve, the blame is myn awen."
"Yet I kende yow of kyssyng," quoth the clere thenne,
1490 "Quere-so countenaunce is couthe quikly to clayme;[3]
That bicumes uche a knyght that cortaysye uses."
"Do way," quoth that derf mon, "my dere, that speche;
For that durst I not do, lest I devayed were.[4]
If I were werned, I were wrang, iwysse, yif I profered."
1495 "Ma fay,"[5] quoth the meré wyf, "ye may not be werned,
Ye ar stif innoghe to constrayne wyth strenkthe, yif yow lykez,
Yif any were so vilanous that yow devaye wolde."
"Ye, be God," quoth Gawayn, "good is your speche;
Bot threte is unthryvande in thede ther I lende,
1500 And uche gift that is geven not with goud wylle.
I am at your comaundement, to kysse quen yow lykez,
Ye may lach quen yow lyst, and leve quen yow thynkkez,
            in space."
        The lady loutez adoun
1505   And comlyly kysses his face;

So they spent the day in this manner, in this wild chase,
While our gracious knight lies in his bed:
1470 Gawain, happily at home amid bright-colored bedding
            so rich.
        Nor did the lady fail
        To wish her guest good day;
        Early she was there
1475   His mood to mollify.

She comes to the curtain and peeps in at the knight.
Sir Gawain welcomes her politely at once,
And she returns his greeting with eager speech,
Seats herself gently at his side and quickly laughs,
1480 And with a charming glance at him uttered these words:
"Sir, if you are Gawain, it astonishes me
That a man always so strongly inclined to good,
Cannot grasp the rules of polite behavior,
And if someone instructs him, lets them drop out of
            mind.
1485 You have quickly forgotten what I taught you yesterday,
By the very truest lesson I could put into words."
"What was that?" said the knight, "Indeed, I don't know at all.
If what you say is true, the blame is all mine."
"Yet I told you about kissing," the fair lady replied,
1490 "To act quickly wherever a glance of favor is seen;
That befits every knight who practises courtesy."
"Dear lady, enough of such talk," said that brave man,
"For I dare not do that, lest I were refused.
If repulsed, I should be at fault for having presumed."
1495 "Ma foi," said the gay lady, "you could not be refused;
You are strong enough to force your will if you wish,
If any woman were so ill-mannered as to reject you."
"Yes, indeed," said Gawain, "what you say is quite true;
But in my country force is considered ignoble,
1500 And so is each gift that is not freely given.
I am at your disposal, to kiss when it pleases you,
You may take one when you like, and stop as seems good,
            in a while."
        She bends down over him
1505   And gives the knight a kiss;

---

[1] *watz hym ate*   At him in one of two senses or both: in his bedchamber, and bothering him.

[2] *compaynye*   Critics have suggested that the term may have amorous connotations.

[3] *Quere-so countenaunce is couthe*   Wherever looks of favor are shown.

[4] *devayed*   Denied, refused: a neologism from Old French, repeated by the lady at 1497.

[5] *"Ma fay"*   I.e., *ma foi*, French: "by my faith," as asseveration.

Much speche thay ther expoun
Of druryes greme and grace.

"I woled wyt at yow, wyghe," that worthy then sayde,
"And yow wrathed not therwyth, what were the skylle
1510 That so yong and so yepe as ye at this tyme,
So cortayse, so knyghtly, as ye ar knowen oute—
And of alle chevalry to chose, the chef thyng alosed
Is the lel layk of luf, the lettrure of armes;
For to telle of this tevelyng of this trwe knyghtez,
1515 Hit is the tytelet token and tyxt of her werkkez;
How ledes for her lel lufe hor lyvez han auntered,
Endured for her drury dulful stoundez,
And after wenged with her walour and voyded her care,
And broght blysse into boure with bountees hor awen—[1]
1520 And ye ar knyght comlokest kyd of your elde,
Your worde and your worchip walkez ayquere,
And I haf seten by yourself here sere twyes,
Yet herde I never of your hed helde no wordez
That ever longed to luf, lasse ne more;
1525 And ye, that are so cortays and coynt of your hetes,[2]
Oghe to a yonke thynk yern to schewe
And teche sum tokenez of trweluf craftes.
Why, ar ye lewed, that alle the los weldez?
Other elles ye demen me to dille your dalyaunce to herken?
1530   For schame!
I com hider sengel, and sitte
To lerne at yow sum game;
Dos, techez me of your wytte
Whil my lorde is fro hame."

1535 "In goud faythe," quoth Gawayn, "God yow foryelde!
Gret is the gode gle, and gomen to me huge,
That so worthy as ye wolde wynne hidere,
And pyne yow with so pouer a man, as play wyth your
            knyght
With anyskynnez countenaunce, hit keverez me ese;
1540 Bot to take the torvayle to myself to trwluf expoun,
And towche the temez of tyxt and talez of armez
To yow that, I wot wel, weldez more slyght
Of that art, bi the half, or a hundreth of seche
As I am, other ever schal, in erde ther I leve,
1545 Hit were a folé felefolde, my fre, by my trawthe.

1480 For long they then discuss
Love's misery and bliss.

"I would learn from you, sir," said that gentle lady,
"If the question was not irksome, what the reason was
That someone as young and valiant as yourself,
1485 So courteous and chivalrous as you are known far and wide—
And of all the aspects of chivalry, the thing most praised
Is the true practice of love, knighthood's very lore;
For to speak of the endeavors of true knights,
The written heading and text of their deeds is that:
1490 How knights have ventured their lives for true love,
Suffered for their love-longings dismal times,
And later taken revenge on their misery through valor,
Bringing joy to their ladies through their personal merits.
1520 And you are the outstanding knight of your time,
Your fame and your honor are known everywhere,
And I have sat by you here on two separate occasions
Yet never heard from your mouth a solitary word
Referring to love, of any kind at all.
1525 And you, who make such courteous and elegant vows,
Should be eager to instruct a youthful creature,
And teach her some elements of skill in true love.
What, are you ignorant, who enjoy such great fame?
Or do you think me too silly to take in courtly chat?
1530   For shame!
I come here alone, and sit
To learn your special play;
Show me your expertise
While my husband is away."

1535 "In good faith," said Gawain, "may God reward you!
It gives me great gladness and pleases me hugely
That one as noble as yourself should make your way here,
And trouble yourself with a nobody, trifling with your
            knight
With any kind of favor: it gives me delight.
1540 But to take the task on myself of explaining true love,
And treat the matter of romance and chivalric tales
To you whom—I know well—have more expertise
In that subject by half than a hundred such men
As myself ever can, however long I may live,
1545 Would be absolute folly, noble lady, on my word.

---

[1] *into boure* Into the lady's bower.

[2] *coynt of your hetes* Gracious in your promises of knightly service.

I wolde yowre wylnyng worche at my myght,
As I am hyghly bihalden, and evermore wylle
Be servaunt to yourselven, so save me Dryghtyn!"
Thus hym frayned that fre, and fondet hym ofte,
1550 For to haf wonnen hym to woghe, what-so scho thoght ellez;[1]
Bot he defended hym so fayr that no faut semed,
Ne non evel on nawther halve, nawther thay wysten
        bot blysse.
        Thay laghed and layked long;
1555   At the last scho con hym kysse,
        Hir leve fayre con scho fonge,
        And went hir waye, iwysse.

Then ruthes hym the renk and ryses to the masse,
And sithen hor diner watz dyght and derely served.
1560 The lede with the ladyez layked alle day,
Bot the lorde over the londez launced ful ofte,
Swez his uncely swyn, that swyngez bi the bonkkez
And bote the best of his braches the bakkez in sunder
Ther he bode in his bay, tel bawemen hit breken,
1565 And madee hym mawgref his hed for to mwe utter,[2]
So felle flonez ther flete when the folk gedered.
Bot yet the styffest to start bi stoundez he made,
Til at the last he watz so mat he myght no more renne,
Bot in the hast that he myght he to a hole wynnez
1570 Of a rasse bi a rokk ther rennez the boerne.
He gete the bonk at his bak, bigynez to scrape,[3]
The frothe femed at his mouth unfayre bi the wykez,
Whettez his whyte tuschez; with hym then irked
Alle the burnez so bolde that hym by stoden
1575 To nye hym on-ferum, bot neghe hym non durst
        for wothe;
        He hade hurt so mony byforne
        That al thught thenne ful lothe
        Be more wyth his tusches torne
1580   That breme watz and braynwode bothe.

Til the knyght com hymself, kachande his blonk,
Sygh hym byde at the bay, his burnez bysyde;
He lyghtes luflych adoun, levez his corsour,
Braydez out a bryght bront and bigly forth strydez,
1585 Foundez fast thurgh the forth ther the felle bydez.

I will carry out your desires with all my power,
As I am in all duty bound, and always will be
The servant of your wishes, may God preserve me!"
Thus that lady made trial of him, tempting him many times
1550 To have led him into mischief, whatever her purpose;
But he defended himself so skillfully that no fault appeared,
Nor evil on either side, nor anything did they feel
        but delight.
        They laughed and bantered long;
1555   Then she kissed her guest;
        Charmingly took her leave,
        And went her way at last.

Then Gawain rouses himself and dresses for mass,
And afterwards dinner was cooked and splendidly served.
1560 The knight diverted himself with the ladies all day,
But the lord raced ceaselessly over the countryside,
After his menacing boar, that scurries over the hills,
And bit the backs of his bravest hounds asunder
Where he stood at bay, until archers broke it,
1565 And forced him unwillingly to move into the open;
So thickly the arrows flew when the hunters gathered.
But yet he made the bravest of them flinch at times,
Until at last he was so tired that he could run no more,
And as fast as he can he makes his way to a hole
1570 By a rocky ledge overlooking the stream.
He gets the river-bank at his back, begins to scrape—
The froth foamed hideously at the corners of his mouth—
And whets his white tusks. Then it grew irksome
For all the bold men who surrounded him trying
1575 To wound him from afar, but for the danger none dared
        to get close;
        So many had been hurt
        That no one wished to risk
        To be more savaged by
1580   A maddened boar's tusk.

Until the lord himself came, spurring his horse,
Saw the boar standing at bay, ringed by his men;
He nimbly dismounts, leaving his courser,
Unsheathes a bright sword and mightily strides,
1585 Hastens quickly through the stream towards the waiting boar.

---

[1] *to haf wonnen hym to woghe* It is uncertain whether *woghe* means "wrong" or "woo."

[2] *mawgref his hed* In spite of himself.

[3] *bigynez to scrape* Angrily scrapes (the earth with his feet).

The wylde watz war of the wyghe with weppen in honde,
Hef heghly the here, so hetterly he fnast
That fele ferde for the freke, lest felle hym the worre.
The swyn settez hym out on the segge even,
1590 That the burne and the bor were both upon hepez
In the wyghtest of the water: the worre hade that other,
For the mon merkkez hym wel, as thay mette fyrst,
Set sadly the scharp in the slot even,
Hit hym up to the hult, that the hert schyndered,
1595 And he yarrande hym yelde, and yedoun the water
         ful tyt.
         A hundreth houndez hym hent,
         That bremely con hym bite,
         Burnez him broght to bent,
1600   And doggez to dethe endite.

There watz blawyng of prys in mony breme horne,
Heghe halowing on highe with hathelez that myght;
Brachetes bayed that best, as bidden the maysterez
Of that chargeaunt chace that were chef huntes.
1605 Thenne a wyghe that watz wys upon wodcraftez
To unlace this bor lufly bigynnez.
Fyrst he hewes of his hed and on highe settez,
And sythen rendez him al roghe bi the rygge after,
Braydez out the boweles, brennez hom on glede,
1610 With bred blent therwith his braches rewardez.
Sythen he britnez out the brawen in bryght brode cheldez,
And hatz out the hastlettez, as hightly bisemez;
And yet hem halchez al hole the halvez togeder,
And sythen on a stif stange stoutly hem henges.
1615 Now with this ilk swyn thay swengen to home;
The bores hed watz borne bifore the burnes selven
That him forferde in the forthe thurgh forse of his honde
         so stronge.
         Til he seye Sir Gawayne
1620   In halle hym thoght ful longe;
         He calde, and he com gayn
         His feez ther for to fonge.

The lorde ful lowde with lote and laghter myry,
When he seye Sir Gawayn, with solace he spekez;
1625 The goude ladyez were geten, and gedered the
         meyny,
He schewez hem the scheldez, and schapes hem the tale
Of the largesse and the lenthe, the lithernez alse

The beast saw the man with his weapon in hand,
Raised his bristles erect, and so fiercely snorted
That many feared for the man, lest he got the worst of it.
The boar charged out, straight at the man,
1590 So that he and the beast were both in a heap
Where the water was swiftest. The other had the worse;
For the man takes aim carefully as the two met,
And thrust the sword firmly straight into his throat,
Drove it up to the hilt, so that the heart burst open,
1595 And squalling he gave up, and was swept through the water
         downstream.
         Seized by a hundred hounds
         Fierce and sharp of tooth,
         Men dragged him to the bank,
1600   And dogs do him to death.

There was sounding of capture from many brave horns,
Proud shouting by knights as loud as they could,
Hounds bayed at that beast, as bidden by the masters
Who were the chief huntsmen of that wearisome chase.
1605 Then a man who was expert in hunting practice
Skilfully begins to dismember this boar.
First he cuts off the head and sets it on high,
And then roughly opens him along the spine,
Throws out the entrails, grills them over embers,
1610 And rewards his hounds with them, mixed with bread.
Next he cuts out the boar's-meat in broad glistening slabs,
And takes out the haslets, as properly follows;
Yet he fastens the two sides together unbroken,
And then proudly hangs them on a strong pole.
1615 Now with this very boar they gallop towards home;
Carrying the boar's head before the same man
Who had killed it in the stream by force of his own
         strong hand.
         Until he saw Gawain
1620   It seemed a tedious time,
         He gladly came when called,
         His due reward to claim.

The lord, noisy with speech and merry laughter,
Joyfully exclaims at the sight of Sir Gawain.
1625 The good ladies were brought down and the household
         assembled;
He shows them the sides of meat, and gives an account
Of the boar's huge size and the ferocity

Of the were of the wylde swyn in wod ther he fled.

That other knyght ful comly comended his dedez,

1630 And praysed hit as a gret prys that he proved hade,

For suche a brawne of a best, the bolde burne sayde,

Ne such sydes of a swyn segh he never are.

Thenne hondeled thay the hoge hed, the hende mon hit praysed,

And let lodly therat the lorde for to here.

1635 "Now, Gawayn," quoth the godmon, "this gomen is your awen

By fyn forwarde and faste, faythely ye knowe."

"Hit is sothe," quoth the segge, "and as siker trwe

Alle my get I schal yow gif agayn, bi my trawthe."

He hent the hathel aboute the halse, and hendely hym kysses,

1640 And eftersones of the same he served hym there.

"Now ar we even," quoth the hathel, "in this eventide,

Of alle the covenauntes that we knyt, sythen I com hider, bi lawe."

The lorde sayde, "Bi saynt Gile,

1645 Ye ar the best that I knowe!

Ye ben ryche in a whyle,

Such chaffer and ye drowe."[1]

Thenne thay teldet tablez trestes alofte,

Kesten clothez upon; clere lyght thenne

1650 Wakned by wowes, waxen torches;

Segges sette and served in sale al aboute;

Much glam and gle glent up therinne

Aboute the fyre upon flet, and on fele wyse

At the soper and after, mony athel songez,

1655 As coundutes of Krystmasse and carolez newe,

With al the manerly merthe that mon may of telle.

And ever oure luflych knyght the lady bisyde,

Such semblaunt to that segge semly ho made

Wyth stille stollen countenaunce, that stalworth to plese,

1660 That al forwondered watz the wyghe, and wroth with hymselven,

Bot he nolde not for his nurture nurne hir agaynez,

Bot dalt with hir al in daynté, how-se-ever the dede turned towrast.

Quen thay hade played in halle

1665 As longe as hor wylle hom last,

Of the fight with the beast in the wood where he fled.

The other knight warmly commended his deeds,

1630 And praised his action as proof of his excellence,

For such boar's-meat, the brave knight declared,

And such sides of wild boar he had never seen before.

Then they picked up the huge head, the polite man praised it

And pretended to feel horror, to honor the lord.

1635 "Now, Gawain," said his host, "this quarry is all yours,

By fully ratified covenant, as you well know."

"That is so," said the knight, "and just as truly indeed

I shall give you all I gained in return, by my pledged word."

He grasped the lord round the neck and graciously kisses him,

1640 And then a second time treated him in the same way.

"Now we are quit," said Gawain, "at the end of the day,

Of all the agreements we have made since I came here, in due form."

The lord said, "By St. Giles,

1645 You're the best man I know!

You'll be a rich one soon

If you keep on trading so."

Then tables were set up on top of trestles,

And tablecloths spread on them: bright light then

1650 Glittered on the walls from waxen torches.

Attendants laid table and served throughout hall.

A great noise of merry-making and joking arose

Round the fire in the center; and of many kinds,

At supper and afterwards, noble songs were sung,

1655 Such as Christmas carols and the newest dances,

With all the fitting amusement that could be thought;

Our courteous knight sitting with the lady throughout.

Such a loving demeanor she displayed to that man,

Through furtive looks of affection to give him delight,

1660 That he was utterly astonished and angry inside;

But he could not in courtesy rebuff her advances,

But treated her politely, even though his actions might be misconstrued.

When the revelry in hall

1665 Had lasted long enough,

---

[1] *Such chaffer and ye drowe* If you carry on such a trade (since on the second day Gawain has doubled his takings). Bertilak makes another joking allusion to marketing at the third exchange: see 1938–9.

To chambre he con hym calle,
And to the chemné thay past.

Ande ther thay dronken, and dalten, and demed eft nwe
To norne on the same note on Nwe Yerez even;
1670 Bot the knyght craved leve to kayre on the morn,
For hit watz neghe at the terme that he to schulde.
The lorde hym letted of that, to lenge hym resteyed,
And sayde, "As I am trwe segge, I siker my trawthe
Thou schal cheve to the grene chapel thy charres to make,
1675 Leude, on Nw Yeres lyght, longe bifore pryme.[1]
Forthy thow lye in thy loft and lach thyn ese,
And I schal hunt in this holt, and halde the towchez,[2]
Chaunge wyth the chevisaunce, bi that I charre hider;
For I haf fraysted the twys, and faythful I fynde the.
1680 Now 'thrid tyme throwe best' thenk on the morne,
Make we mery quyl we may and mynne upon joye,
For the lur may lach when-so mon lykez."
This watz graythely graunted, and Gawayn is lenged,
Blithe broght watz hym drynk, and thay to bedde yeden
1685   with light.
     Sir Gawayn lis and slepes
     Ful stille and softe al night;
     The lorde that his craftez kepes,[3]
     Ful erly he watz dight.

1690 After messe a morsel he and his men token;
Miry watz the mornyng, his mounture he askes.
Alle the hatheles that on horse schulde helden hym after
Were boun busked on hor blonkkez bifore the halle gatez.
Ferly fayre watz the folde, for the forst clenged;
1695 In red rudede upon rak rises the sunne,
And ful clere castez the clowdes of the welkyn.
Hunteres unhardeled bi a holt syde,
Rocheres roungen bi rys for rurde of her hornes;
Summe fel in the fute ther the fox bade,
1700 Traylez ofte a traveres bi traunt of her wyles;[4]
A kenet kryes therof, a hunt on hym calles;
His felawes fallen hym to, that fnasted ful thike,
Runnen forth in a rabel in his ryght fare,

To the fireside in his room
The lord took Gawain off.

And there they drank and chatted, and spoke once again
To repeat the arrangement on New Year's Eve;
1670 But the knight begged leave to depart the next day,
For it was near time for the appointment that he had to keep.
The lord held him back, begging him to remain,
And said, "As I am an honest man, I give you my word
That you shall reach the Green Chapel to settle your affairs,
1675 Dear sir, on New Year's Day, well before nine.
Therefore lie in your bed enjoying your ease,
And I shall hunt in the woods, and keep the compact,
Exchange winnings with you when I return here;
For I have tested you twice, and find you trustworthy.
1680 Now tomorrow remember, 'Best throw third time';
Let us make merry while we can and think only of joy,
For misery can be found whenever a man wants it."
This was readily agreed, and Gawain is stayed;
Drink was gladly brought to him, and with torches they went
1685   to their beds.
     Sir Gawain lies and sleeps
     All night taking his rest;
     While eager for his sport
     By dawn the lord was dressed.

1690 After mass he and his men snatched a mouthful of food:
The morning was cheerful, he calls for his horse.
All the knights who would ride after him on horses
Were ready arrayed in the saddle outside the hall doors.
The countryside looked splendid, gripped by the frost;
1695 The sun rises fiery through drifting clouds,
And then dazzling bright drives the rack from the sky.
At the edge of a wood hunters unleashed the hounds;
Among the trees rocks resounded with the noise of their horns.
Some picked up the scent where a fox was lurking,
1700 Search back and forwards in their cunning practice.
A small hound gives tongue, the huntsman calls to him,
His fellows rally around, panting loudly,
And dash forward in a rabble right on the fox's track.

---

[1] *Thou schal cheve … bifore pryme* Prime begins either at 6 a.m. or at sunrise. At 1073 Bertilak promises that Gawain will *cum to that merk at mydmorn*, meaning at 9 a.m. In fact the sun rises when he is on the way to the Green Chapel, 2085–86. In northwest England midwinter sunrise would not occur before 8 a.m. Two hours earlier it would be completely dark.

[2] *halde the towchez* Keep the terms of the agreement.

[3] *that his craftez kepes* Who attends to his pursuits.

[4] *Traylez ofte a traveres* Track the scent by working back and forth across the line.

And he fyskez hem byfore; thay founden hym sone,
1705 And quen thay seghe hym with syght thay sued hym fast,
Wreghande hym ful weterly with a wroth noyse;
And he trantes and tornayeez thurgh mony tene greve,
Havilounez, and herkenez bi hegges ful ofte.
At the last bi a littel dich he lepez over a spenne,
1710 Stelez out ful stilly bi a strothe rande,
Went half wylt of the wode with wylez fro the houndes;[1]
Thenne watz he went, er he wyst, to a wale tryster,
Ther thre thro at a thrich thrat hym at ones,
        al graye.
1715   He blenched agayn bilyve,
        And stifly start on-stray,[2]
        With alle the wo on lyve
        To the wod he went away.

Thenne watz hit list upon lif to lythen the houndez,
1720 When alle the mute hade hym met, menged togeder:
Such a sorwe at that syght thay sette on his hede
As alle the clamberande clyffes hade clatered on hepes;
Here he watz halawed, when hathelez hym metten,
Loude he watz yayned with yarande speche;
1725 Ther he watz threted and ofte thef called,
And ay the titleres at his tayl, that tary he ne myght.
Ofte he watz runnen at, when he out rayked,
And ofte reled in agayn, so Reniarde watz wylé.
And ye, he lad hem bi lagmon,[3] the lorde and his meyny,
1730 On this maner bi the mountes quyle myd-over-under,[4]
Whyle the hende knyght at hom holsumly slepes
Withinne the comly cortynes, on the colde morne.
Bot the lady for luf let not to slepe,
Ne the purpose to payre that pyght in hir hert,
1735 Bot ros hir up radly, rayked hir theder,
In a mery mantyle, mete to the erthe,
That watz furred ful fyne with fellez wel pured;
No hwez[5] goud on hir hede bot the hagher stones
Trased aboute hir tressour by twenty in clusteres;
1740 Hir thryven face and hir throte throwen al naked,

He scampers ahead of them, they soon found his trail,
1705 And when they caught sight of him followed fast,
Abusing him furiously with an angry noise.
He twists and dodges through many a dense copse,
Often doubling back and listening at the hedges.
At last he jumps over a fence by a little ditch,
1710 Creeps stealthily by the edge of a bush-covered marsh,
Thinking to escape from the wood and the hounds by his wiles.
Then he came, before he knew it, to a well-placed station,
Where three fierce greyhounds flew at him at once
        in a rush.
1715   Undaunted changing course
        He quickly swerved away,
        Pursued into the woods
        With hideous outcry.

Then it was joy upon earth to hear the hounds giving tongue
1720 When all the pack had come upon him, mingled together:
Such a cursing at that sight they called down on his head
As if all the clustering cliffs had crashed down in a mass.
Here he was yelled at when hunters happened upon him,
Loudly he was greeted with chiding speech;
1725 There he was reviled and often called thief,
And always the hounds at his tail, that he could not pause.
Many times he was run at when he made for the open,
And many times doubled back, so cunning was Reynard.
And yes! strung out he led them, the lord and his followers,
1730 Across the hills in this manner until mid-afternoon,
While the knight in the castle takes his health-giving sleep
Behind splendid bed-curtains on the cold morn.
But out of love the lady did not let herself sleep,
Nor the purpose to weaken that was fixed in her heart;
1735 But rose from her bed quickly and hastened there
In a charming mantle reaching to the ground,
That was richly lined with well-trimmed furs:
No modest coif on her head, but skillfully cut gems
Arranged about her hair-fret in clusters of twenty;
1740 Her lovely face and throat displayed uncovered,

---

[1] *Went haf wylt of the wode*   Thought to have escaped out of the wood.

[2] *on-stray*   In a different direction.

[3] *he lad hem bi lagmon*   The critic Norman Davis explains *lagmon* as "the last man in a line of reapers," who would advance diagonally across a field; hence "strung out."

[4] *quyle myd-over-under*   Variously explained as mid-morning, midday, or afternoon. When the fox is killed it is *niegh nyght* (1922).

[5] *hwez*   So the manuscript; some critics prefer *hwef*. The sense of the passage is that the lady is not wearing the headdress of a married woman.

Hir brest bare bifore, and bihinde eke.
Ho comez withinne the chambre dore, and closes hit hir after,
Wayvez up a wyndow, and on the wyghe callez,
And radly thus rehayted hym with hir riche wordes,
1745   with chere:
      "A, mon, how may thou slepe,
      This morning is so clere?"
      He watz in drowping depe,
      Bot thenne he con hir here.

1750 In dregh droupyng of dreme draveled that noble,[1]
As mon that watz in mornyng of mony thro thoghtes,
How that destiné schulde that day dele hym his wyrde
At the grene chapel, when he the gome metes,
And bihoves his buffet abide withoute debate more;
1755 Bot quen that comly com he kevered his wyttes,
Swenges out of the swevenes, and swarez with hast.
The lady luflych com laghande swete,
Felle over his fayre face, and fetly hym kyssed;
He welcumez hir worthily with a wale chere.
1760 He sey hir so glorious and gayly atyred,
So fautles of hir fetures and of so fyne hewes,
Wight wallande joye warmed his hert.
With smothe smylyng and smolt thay smeten into merthe,
That al watz blis and bonchef that breke hem bitwene,
1765   and wynne.
      Thay lanced wordes gode,
      Much wele then watz therinne;
      Gret perile bitwene hem stod,
      Nif Maré of hir knyght mynne.

1770 Fo that prynces of pris depressed hym so thikke,
Nurned hym so neghe the thred, that nede hym bihoved
Other lach ther hir luf other lodly refuse.
He cared for his cortaysye, lest crathayn he were,
And more for his meschef yif he schulde make synne,
1775 And be traytor to that tolke that that telde aght.
"God schylde," quoth the schalk, "that schal not befalle!"
With luf-laghyng a lyt he layd hym bysyde
Alle the spechez of specialté that sprange of her mouthe.
Quoth that burde to the burne, "Blame ye disserve
1780 Yif ye luf not that lyf that ye lye nexte,

Her breast was exposed, and her shoulders bare.
She enters the chamber and shuts the door after her,
Throws open a window and calls to the knight,
Rebuking him at once with merry words
1745   in play:
      "Ah, sir, how can you sleep?
      The morning is so clear!"
      Deep in his drowsiness
      Her voice broke in his ear.

1750 In the stupor of a dream that nobleman muttered,
Like a man overburdened with troublesome thoughts;
How destiny would deal him his fate on the day
When he meets the man at the Green Chapel,
And must stand the return blow without any more talk:
1755 But when that lovely one spoke he recovered his wits,
Broke out of his dreaming and hastily replied.
The gracious lady approached him, laughing sweetly,
Bent over his handsome face and daintily kissed him.
He welcomes her politely with charming demeanor;
1760 Seeing her so radiant and attractively dressed,
Every part of her so perfect, and in color so fine,
Hot passionate feeling welled up in his heart.
Smiling gently and courteously they made playful speech,
So that all that passed between them was happiness, joy
1765   and delight.
      Gracious words they spoke,
      And pleasure reached its height.
      Great peril threatened, should
      Mary not mind her knight.

1770 For that noble lady so constantly pressed,
Pushed him so close to the verge, that either he must
Take her love there and then or churlishly reject it.
He felt concerned for good manners, lest he behaved like a boor,
And still more lest he shame himself by an act of sin,
1775 And treacherously betray the lord of the castle.
"God forbid!" said the knight, "That shall not come about!"
With affectionate laughter he put to one side
All the loving inducements that fell from her mouth.
Said that lady to the knight, "You deserve rebuke
1780 If you feel no love for the person you are lying beside,

---

[1] *In dregh droupyng of dreme draveled that noble*   A literal translation —"In a heavy troubled sleep that nobleman muttered"—misses the grinding effect of the alliterated words.

Bifore alle the wyghez in the worlde wounded in hert,
Bot if ye haf a lemman, a lever, that yow lykez better,
And folden fayth to that fre, festned so harde
That yow lausen ne lyst—and that I leve nouthe;
1785 And that ye telle me that now trwly I pray yow,
For alle the lufez upon lyve layne not the sothe
      for gile."
    The knyght sayde, "Be sayn Jon,"
    And smethely con he smyle,
1790   "In fayth I welde right non,
    Ne non wil welde the quile."

"That is a worde," quoth that wyght, "that worst is of alle,
Bot I am swared for sothe, that sore me thinkkez.
Kysse me now comly, and I schal cach hethen,
1795 I may bot mourne upon molde, as may that much lovyes."
Sykande ho sweghe doun and semly hym kyssed,
And sithen ho severes hym fro, and says as ho stondes,
"Now, dere, at this departyng do me this ese,
Gif me sumquat of thy gifte, thi glove if hit were,
1800 That I may mynne on the, mon, my mournyng to lassen."
"Now iwysse," quoth that wyghe, "I wolde I hade here
The levest thing for thy luf that I in londe welde,
For ye haf deserved, for sothe, sellyly ofte
More rewarde bi resoun then I reche myght;
1805 Bot to dele yow for drurye that dawed bot neked,
Hit is not your honour to haf at this tyme
A glove for a garysoun of Gawaynez giftez;
And I am here an erande in erdez uncouthe,
And have no men wyth no males with menskful thingez;
1810 That mislykez me, ladé, for luf at this tyme,
Iche tolke mon do as he is tan, tas to non ille
      ne pine."
    "Nay, hende of hyghe honours,"
    Quoth that lufsum under lyne,
1815   "Thagh I hade noght of yourez,
    Yet schulde ye have of myne."

Ho raght hym a riche rynk of red golde werkez,
With a starande ston stondande alofte
That bere blusshande bemez as the bryght sunne—
1820 Wyt ye wel, hit watz worth wele ful hoge.
Bot the renk hit renayed, and redyly he sayde,
"I wil no giftez, for God, my gay, at this tyme;
I haf none yow to norne, ne noght wyl I take."

More than anyone on earth wounded in her heart;
Unless you have a mistress, someone you prefer,
And have plighted troth with that lady, so strongly tied
That you wish not to break it—which now I believe;
1785 And I beg you now to confess that honestly:
For all the loves in the world hide not the truth
      in guile."
    The knight said, "By St. John,"
    And gave a pleasant smile,
1790   "In truth I have no one,
    Nor seek one for this while."

"That remark," said the lady, "is the worst you could make,
But I am answered indeed, and painfully, I feel.
Kiss me now lovingly, and I will hasten from here,
1795 I must spend my life grieving, as a woman deeply in love."
Sighing she stooped down and kissed him sweetly,
And then moves away from him and says, standing there,
"Now, dear sir, do me this kindness at parting,
Give me something as a present, for instance your glove,
1800 That I may remember you by, to lessen my sorrow."
"Now truly," said that man, "I wish I had here
The dearest thing in the world I possess for your love,
For you have truly deserved, wonderfully often,
More recompense by right than I could repay.
1805 But to give you as love-token something worth little
Would do you no honor, or to have at this time
A glove for a keepsake, as Gawain's gift.
I am here on a mission in unknown country,
And have no servants with bags full of precious things;
1810 That grieves me, lady, for your sake at this time,
But each man must do as conditions allow; take no offense
      or pain."
    "No, most honored sir,"
    Then said that lady free,
1815   "Though I get no gift from you,
    You shall have one from me."

She held out a precious ring of finely worked gold
With a sparkling jewel standing up high,
Its facets flashing as bright as the sun:
1820 Take my word, it was worth an enormous sum.
But the knight would not accept it, and straightaway said,
"I want no gifts, I swear, dear lady, at this time;
I have nothing to offer you, and nothing will I take."

Ho bede hit hym ful bysily, and he hir bode wernes,
1825 And swere swyfte by his sothe that he hit sese nolde,
And ho soré that he forsoke, and sayde therafter,
"If ye renay my rynk, to ryche for hit semez,
Ye wolde not so hyghly halden be to me,
I schal gif yow my girdel, that gaynes yow lasse."
1830 Ho lacht a lace lyghtly that leke umbe hir sydez,
Knit upon hir kyrtel under the clere mantyle;
Gered hit watz with grene sylke and with golde schaped,
Noght bot arounde brayden, beten with fyngrez;[1]
And that ho bede to the burne, and blythely bisoght,
1835 Thagh hit unworthi were, that he hit take wolde.
And he nay that he nolde neghe in no wyse
Nauther golde ne garysoun, er God hym grace sende
To acheve to the chaunce that he hade chosen there.
"And therfore, I pray yow, displese yow noght,
1840 And lettez be your bisinesse, for I baythe hit yow never
          to graunte.
     I am derely to yow biholde
     Bicause of your sembelaunt,
     And ever in hot and colde
1845   To be your trwe servaunt."

"Now forsake ye this silke," sayde the burde thenne,
"For hit is symple in hitself? and so wel hit semez.
Lo, so hit is littel, and lasse hit is worthy;
But who-so knew the costes that knit ar therinne,
1850 He wolde hit prayse at more prys, paraventure.
For quat gome so is gorde with this grene lace,
While he hit hade hemely halched aboute,
Ther is no hathel under heven tohewe hym that myght,
For he myght not be slayn for slyght upon erthe."
1855 Then kest the knyght, and hit come to his hert
Hit were a juel for the jopardé that hym jugged were:
When he acheved to the chapel his chek for to fech,
Myght he haf slypped to be unslayn, the sleght were noble.
Thenne he thulged with hir threpe and tholed hir to speke,
1860 And ho bere on hym the belt and bede hit hym swythe—
And he granted and hym gafe with a goud wylle—
And bisoght hym, for hir sake, discever hit never,
Bot to lelly layne fro hir lorde; the leude hym acordez
That never wyghe schulde hit wyt, iwysse, bot thay twayne
1865   for noghte.

She pressed him insistently, and he declines her request,
1825 Swearing quickly on his word that he would never touch it,
And she was grieved that he refused it, and said to him then,
"If you reject my ring because you think it too precious,
And wish not to be so deeply indebted to me,
I shall give you my girdle, that profits you less."
1830 Quickly she unbuckled a belt clipped round her waist,
Fastened over her kirtle beneath the fine mantle;
It was woven of green silk and trimmed with gold,
Embroidered at the edges and decorated by hand;
And this she offered to the knight, and sweetly implored him
1835 That despite its slight value he would accept it.
And he declared absolutely that he would never agree
To take either gold or keepsake before God gave him grace
To finish the task he had undertaken.
"And therefore I beg you, do not be displeased,
1840 And cease your insisting, for I shall never be brought
          to consent.
     I am deeply in your debt
     Because of your kind favor,
     And will through thick and thin
1845   Remain your servant ever."

"Now, do you refuse this belt," the lady said then,
"Because it is worth little? and so truly it appears.
See, it is indeed a trifle, and its worth even less;
But anyone who knew the power woven into it
1850 Would put a much higher price on it, perhaps.
For whoever is buckled into this green belt,
As long as it is tightly fastened about him
There is no man on earth who can strike him down,
For he cannot be killed by any trick in the world."
1855 Then the knight reflected, and it flashed into his mind
This would be a godsend for the hazard he must face
When he reached the chapel to receive his deserts;
Could he escape being killed, the trick would be splendid.
Then he suffered her pleading and allowed her to speak,
1860 And she pressed the belt on him, offering it at once—
And he consented and gave way with good grace—
And she begged him for her sake never to reveal it,
But loyally hide it from her husband. Gawain gives his word
That no one should ever know of it, not for anything,
1865   but themselves.

----

[1] *Noght bot arounde brayden*   No part of which was not embroidered at the edges.

He thonkked hir oft ful swythe,
Ful thro with hert and thoght.
Bi that on thrynne sythe
Ho hatz kyst the knyght so toght.

He gave her heartfelt thanks
With earnest mind and sense;
By then she has three times
Kissed that valiant prince.

1870 Thenne lachchez ho hir leve, and levez hym there,
For more myrthe of that mon moght ho not gete,
When ho watz gon, Sir Gawayn gerez hym sone,
Rises and riches him in araye noble,
Lays up the luf-lace the lady hym raghte,
1875 Hid hit ful holdely, ther he hit eft fonde.
Sythen chevely to the chapel choses he the waye,
Prevély aproched to a prest, and prayed hym there
That he wolde lyste his lyf [1] and lern hym better
How his sawle schulde be saved when he schuld seye hethen.
1880 There he schrof hym schyrly and schewed his mysdedez,
Of the more and the mynne, and merci besechez,
And of absolucioun he on the segge calles;
And he asoyled hym surely and sette hym so clene
As domezday schulde haf ben dight on the morn.
1885 And sythen he mace hym as mery among the fre ladyes,
With comelych caroles and alle kynnes joye,
As never he did bot that daye, to the derk nyght,
    with blys.
    Uche mon hade daynté thare
1890   Of hym, and sayde, "Iwysse,
    Thus mery he watz never are,
    Syn he com hider, er this."

1870 Then she takes her departure, leaving him there,
For more pleasure from that man was not to be had.
When she had gone, Gawain quickly makes himself ready,
Gets up and dresses himself in splendid array,
Puts away the love-token the lady gave him,
1875 Hid it carefully where he could find it again.
Then quickly to the chapel he makes his way,
Approached a priest privately, and besought him there
To hear his confession and instruct him more clearly
How his soul could be saved when he leaves this world.
1880 There he confessed himself honestly and admitted his sins,
Both the great and the small, and forgiveness begs,
And calls on the priest for absolution.
And the priest absolved him completely, and made him as clean
As if the Judgment were appointed for the next day.
1885 And then Gawain makes merry with the noble ladies,
With charming dance-songs and gaiety of all kinds,
As he never did before that day, until darkness fell,
    with joy.
    Each man had courtesy
1890   From him, and said, "Sure,
    So merry since he came
    He never was before."

Now hym lenge in that lee, ther luf hym bityde!
Yet is the lorde on the launde ledande his gomnes.
1895 He hatz forfaren this fox that he folwed longe;
As he sprent over a spenne to spye the schrewe,
Ther as he herd the howndes that hasted hym swythe,
Renaud com richchande thurgh a roghe greve,
And alle the rabel in a res ryght at his helez.
1900 The wyghe watz war of the wylde, and warly abides,
And braydez out the bryght bronde, and at the best castez.
And he schunt for the scharp, and schulde haf
    arered;

Let him stay in that shelter, and love come his way!
But still the lord is afield, enjoying his sport.
1895 He has headed off the fox that he pursued so long;
As he leapt over a hedge to look for the villain,
Where he heard the hounds barking as they chased him fast,
Reynard came running through a rough thicket
With the pack howling behind him, right at his heels.
1900 The man caught sight of the fox, and warily waits,
Unsheathes his bright sword and slashes at the beast;
And he swerved away from the blade and would have
    turned back.

---

[1] *lyste his lyf* Hear his confession. Much ink has been spilt over the passage. If Gawain tells the priest about his love-token he would be obliged to return it; if he does not reveal the liaison he cannot be *schrof schyrly* or given absolution.

A rach rapes hym to, ryght er he myght,
And ryght bifore the hors fete thay fel on hym alle,
1905 And woried me this wyly wyth a wroth noyse.[1]
The lorde lyghtez bilyve, and lachez hym sone,
Rased hym ful radly out of the rach mouthes,
Haldez heghe over his hede, halowez faste,
And ther bayen aboute hym mony brath houndez.
1910 Huntes hyghed hem theder with hornez ful mony,
Ay rechatande aryght til thay the renk seyen.
Bi that watz comen his compeyny noble
Alle that ever ber bugle blowed at ones,
And alle thise other halowed that had no hornes;
1915 Hit watz the myriest mute that ever men herde,
The rich rurd that ther watz raysed for Renaude saule
                with lote.
        Hor houndez thay ther rewarde,
        Her hedez thay fawne and frote,
1920   And sythen thay tan Reynarde
        And tyrven of his cote.

And thenne thay helden to home, for hit watz niegh nyght,
Strakande ful stoutly in hor store hornez.
The lorde is lyght at last at hys lef home,
1925 Fyndez fire upon flet, the freke ther-byside,
Sir Gawayn the gode, that glad watz withalle,
Among the ladies for luf he ladde much joye.
He were a bleaunt of blwe that bradde to the erthe,
His surkot semed hym wel that softe watz forred,
1930 And his hode of that ilke henged on his schulder,
Blande al of blaunner were bothe al aboute.
He metez me this godmon inmyddez the flore,
And al with gomen he hym gret, and goudly he sayde,
"I schal fylle upon fyrst oure forwardez nouthe,
1935 That we spedly han spoken, ther spared watz no drynk."
Then acoles he the knyght and kysses hym thryes,
As saverly and sadly as he hem sette couthe.
"Bi Kryst," quoth that other knyght, "ye cach much sele
In chevisaunce of this chaffer, yif ye hade goud chepez."[2]

A hound rushed at him before he could turn,
And right at the horse's feet the pack fell on him all,
1905 Tearing at the wily one with an enraged noise.
The lord swiftly dismounts, grabs the fox at once,
Lifted it quickly out of the hounds' mouths,
Holds it high over his head, halloos loudly,
And many fierce hounds surround him there, baying.
1910 Hunters hurried towards him with many horns blowing,
Sounding rally in proper fashion until they saw the lord.
When his noble company was all assembled,
Everyone carrying a bugle blew it at once,
And the others, without horns, raised a great shout.
1915 It was the most glorious baying that man ever heard,
The noble clamor set up there for Reynard's soul
                with din.
        Hunters reward their hounds,
        Heads they rub and pat;
1920   And then they took Reynard
        And stripped him of his coat.

And then they set off for home, for it was nearly night,
Stridently sounding their mighty horns.
At last the lord dismounts at his well-loved home,
1925 Finds a fire burning in hall, the knight waiting beside,
Sir Gawain the good, completely content,
Taking great pleasure from the ladies' affection.
He wore a blue mantle of rich stuff reaching the ground;
His softly furred surcoat suited him well,
1930 And his hood of the same stuff hung on his shoulder,
Both trimmed with ermine along the edges.
He meets his host in the middle of the hall,
Laughingly greeted him, and courteously said,
"Now I shall first carry out the terms of our covenant,
1935 Which we readily agreed on when wine was not spared."
Then he embraces the lord and gives him three kisses,
With as much relish and gravity as he could contrive.
"By God," said that other knight, "you had much luck
In winning this merchandise, if the price was right."

---

[1] *woried me this wyly* Tore at the fox. The ethic dative *me* is
colloquial. Other examples occur at 2014 and 2144.

[2] *yif ye hade goud chepez* If you struck a good bargain.

1940 "Ye, of the chepe no charg," quoth chefly that other,
"As is pertly payed the porchaz that I aghte."
"Mary," quoth that other man, "myn is bihynde,
For I haf hunted al this day, and noght haf I geten
Bot this foule fox felle—the fende haf the godez!
1945 And that is ful pore for to pay for suche prys thinges
As ye haf thryght me here thro, suche thre cosses
so gode."
"Inogh," quoth Sir Gawayn,
"I thonk yow, bi the rode";[1]
1950 And how the fox watz slayn
He tolde hym as thay stode.

With merthe and mynstralsye, wyth metez at hor wylle,
Thay maden as mery as any men moghten
With laghyng of ladies, with lotez of bordez.
1955 Gawayn and the godemon so glad were thay bothe
Bot if the douthe had doted, other dronken ben other.[2]
Both the mon and the meyny maden mony japez
Til the sesoun watz seghen that thay sever moste;
Burnez to hor bedde behoved at the laste.
1960 Thenne lowly his leve at the lorde fyrst
Fochchez this fre mon, and fayre he hym thonkkez:
"Of such a selly sojorne as I haf hade here,
Your honour at this hyghe fest, the hyghe kyng yow yelde!
I gef yow me for on of yourez, if yowreself lykez,
1965 For I mot nedes, as ye wot, meve to-morne,
And ye me take sum tolke to teche, as ye hyght,
The gate to the grene chapel,[3] as God wyl me suffer
To dele on Nw Yerez day the dome of my wyrdes."[4]
"In god faythe," quoth the godmon, "wyth a goud wylle
1970 Al that ever I yow hyght halde schal I redé."
Ther asyngnes he a servaunt to sette hym in the waye,
And coundue hym by the downez, that he no drechch had,
For to ferk thurgh the fryth[5] and fare at the gaynest
bi greve.

1940 "Oh, never mind the price," replied the other quickly,
"So long as the goods I got have been honestly paid."
"Marry," said the other man, "mine don't compare,
For I have hunted all day, and yet have caught nothing
But this stinking fox pelt—the devil take the goods!
1945 And that is a meager return for such precious things
As you have warmly pressed on me, three such kisses
so good."
"Enough," said Gawain,
"I thank you, by the Rood";
1950 And how the fox was killed
He heard as there they stood.

With mirth and minstrelsy, and all the food they would wish,
They made as much merriment as any men could
With laughter of ladies and jesting remarks.
1955 Both Gawain and the lord were ravished with joy
As if the company had gone crazy or taken much drink.
Both the lord and his retainers played many tricks
Until the time came round when they must separate:
Folk to their beds must betake them at last.
1960 Then humbly this noble knight first takes leave
Of the lord, and graciously gives him thanks:
"For such a wonderful stay as I have had here,
Honored by you at this holy feast, may God repay you!
I offer myself as your servant, if you agree,
1965 For I am compelled, as you know, to leave tomorrow,
If you will assign someone to show me, as you promised,
The road to the Green Chapel, as God will allow me,
To get what fate ordains for me on New Year's Day."
"In good faith," said the lord, "very willingly,
1970 Everything I ever promised you I shall readily give."
There he appoints a servant to put Gawain on the road
And guide him over the fells, so that he would not be delayed,
To ride through the woods and take the shortest path
in the trees.

---

[1] bi the rode   I.e., by the Cross (on which Christ was crucified).

[2] Gawayn … other   The syntax of these two lines seems erratic. Instead of following so glad with a comparison "as if" the poet continues Bot if, meaning unless. The intended sense of the passage seems to be, "They could only have been more deliriously happy if the whole company had gone crazy or got drunk."

[3] I gef yow … grene chapel   Gawain politely offers to become Bertilak's servant (on of yourez) if he will give him a man (take sum tolke) to guide him to the Green Chapel.

[4] the dome of my wyrdes   The judgment of my fate.

[5] to ferk thurgh the fryth   To ride through the wood, as Gawain does at 2084. Bi greve refers to it again.

1975	The lorde Gawayn con thonk,
	Such worchip he wolde hym weve.
	Then at tho ladyez wlonk
	The knyght hatz tan his leve.
	With care and wyth kyssyng he carppez hem tille,
1980	And fele thryvande thonkkez he thrat hom to have,
	And thay yelden hym agayn yeply that ilk.
	Thay bikende hym to Kryst with ful colde sykyngez.
	Sythen fro the meyny he menskly departes;
	Uche mon that he mette, he made hem a thonke
1985	For his servyse and his solace and his sere pyne,
	That thay wyth busynes had ben aboute hym to serve;
	And uche segge as soré to sever with hym there
	As thay hade wonde worthyly with that wlonk ever.
	Then with ledes and lyght he watz ladde to his chambre,
1990	And blythely broght to his bedde to be at his rest.
	Yif he ne slepe soundyly say ne dar I,
	For he hade muche on the morn to mynne, yif he wolde,
	in thoght.
	Let hym lyghe there stille,
1995	He hatz nere that he soght;
	And ye wyl a whyle be stylle[1]
	I schal telle yow how thay wroght.

FITT 4

	Now neghez the Nw Yere, and the nyght passez,
	The day dryvez to the derk, as Dryghtyn biddez;
2000	Bot wylde wederez of the worlde wakned theroute,
	Clowdes kesten kenly the colde to the erthe,
	Wyth nyghe innoghe of the northe the naked to tene.
	The snawe snitered ful snart, that snayped the wylde;
	The werbelande wynde wapped fro the hyghe,
2005	And drof uche dale ful of dryftes ful grete.
	The leude lystened ful wel that ley in his bedde,
	Thagh he lowkez his liddez, ful lyttel he slepes;
	Bi uch kok that crue he knwe wel the steven.
	Deliverly he dressed up, er the day sprenged,
2010	For there watz lyght of a laumpe that lemed in his chambre;
	He called to his chamberlayn, that cofly hym swared,

1975	Gawain thanked the lord,
	Paying him great respect;
	Then from those noble ladies
	Took leave, as was correct.
	With tears and with kisses he addresses them both,
1980	And begged them to accept many profuse thanks,
	And they immediately returned the same words to him.
	They commended him to Christ with many deep sighs.
	Then from the household he takes courteous leave;
	To each man whom he met he expressed his thanks
1985	For his service and kindness and the personal pains
	They had taken in busying themselves for his sake;
	And each man was as sorry to part from him there
	As if they had honorably lived with that nobleman ever.
	Then with attendants and torches he was led to his room,
1990	And cheerfully brought to his bed and his rest.
	Whether or not he slept soundly I dare not say,
	For he had much about the next day to turn over, if he wished,
	in his mind.
	Let him lie there undisturbed,
1995	He is close to what he sought;
	Be quiet a short while,
	And I'll tell how things turned out.

PART 4

	Now the New Year approaches and the night wears away,
	The dawn presses against the darkness, as the Creator bids,
2000	But rough weather blows up in the country outside,
	Clouds empty their bitter cold contents on the earth,
	With enough malice from the north to torment the ill-clad.
	Snow pelted down spitefully, stinging the wild creatures;
	The wind shrilly whistled down from the fells,
2005	Choking the valleys with enormous drifts.
	The knight lay in bed listening intently,
	Although his eyelids are shut very little he sleeps;
	Each cock-crow reminded him of his undertaking.
	He got up quickly before the day dawned,
2010	For there was light from a lamp burning in his room;
	He called to his chamberlain, who answered him promptly,

---

[1] *stille ... stylle* Literary convention of the time allowed homonyms to be used as rhyme-words different in sense; here "without moving," 1994, and "without noise," 1996.

And bede hym bryng hym his bruny and his blonk sadel;
That other ferkez hym up and fechez hym his wedez,
And graythez me Sir Gawayn upon a grett wyse.
2015 Fyrst he clad hym in his clothez the colde for to were,
And sythen his other harnays, that holdely watz keped,
Bothe his paunce and his platez, piked ful clene,
The ryngez rokked of the roust of his riche bruny;
And al watz fresch as upon fyrst, and he watz fayn thenne
2020   to thonk.
        He hade upon uche pece,
        Wypped ful wel and wlonk;
        The gayest unto Grece
        The burne bede bryng his blonk.

2025 Whyle the wlonkest wedes he warp on hymselven—
His cote wyth the conysaunce of the clere werkez
Ennurned upon velvet, vertuus stonez
Aboute beten and bounden, enbrauded semez,
And fayre furred withinne wyth fayre pelures—
2030 Yet laft he not the lace, the ladiez gifte,
That forgat not Gawayn for gode of hymselven.
Bi he hade belted the bronde upon his balghe haunchez,
Thenn dressed he his drurye double hym aboute,
Swythe swethled umbe his swange swetely that knyght
2035 The gordel of the grene silk, that gay wel bisemed,
Upon that ryol red clothe that ryche watz to schewe.
Bot wered not this ilk wyghe for wele this gordel,
For pryde of the pendauntez, thagh polyst thay were,
And thagh the glyterande golde glent upon endez,
2040 Bot for to saven hymself, when suffer hym byhoved,
To byde bale withoute dabate of bronde hym to were
        other knyffe.
        Bi that the bolde mon boun
        Wynnez theroute bilyve,
2045   Alle the meyny of renoun
        He thonkkez ofte ful ryve.

Thenne watz Gryngolet graythe, that gret watz and huge,
And hade ben sojourned saverly and in a siker wyse,
Hym lyst prik for poynt, that proude hors thenne.
2050 The wyghe wynnez hym to and wytez on his lyre,
And sayde soberly hymself and by his soth swerez:
"Here is a meyny in this mote that on menske thenkkez,
The mon hem maynteines, joy mot thay have;
The leve lady on lyve luf hir bityde;

Bade him bring his mail-shirt and saddle his horse.
The man leaps out of bed and fetches him his clothes,
And gets Gawain ready in splendid attire.
2015 First he puts clothing on him to keep out the cold,
And then the rest of his gear, that had been well looked after,
His body-armor and his plate, all polished clean,
The rings of his fine mail-shirt rocked free of rust;
Everything unstained as at first, for which he gladly
2020   gave thanks.
        Wearing each metal piece
        Rubbed clean of stain and spot,
        The best-dressed man on earth
        Ordered his horse be brought.

2025 While he dressed himself in his noblest clothes—
His coat with its finely embroidered badge
Set upon velvet, with stones of magical power
Inlaid and clasped round it, with embroidered seams,
And richly lined on the inside with beautiful furs—
2030 He did not leave out the belt, the lady's present:
For his own good Gawain did not forget that.
When he had buckled his sword on his curving hips,
That noble knight bound his love-token twice
Closely wrapped round his middle, with delight;
2035 The girdle of green silk, whose color went well
Against that splendid red surcoat that showed so fine.
But the knight did not wear the belt for its costliness,
Or for pride in its pendants, however they shone,
Or because its edges gleamed with glittering gold,
2040 But to safeguard himself when he had to submit,
To await death without sword to defend himself
        or blade.
        When he was fully dressed
        The knight hurries outside,
2045   And pays that noble household
        His debt of gratitude.

Then Gringolet was ready, that great horse and huge,
Who had been stabled securely, keeping him safe;
In such fine condition that he was eager to gallop.
2050 The knight walks up to him and examines his coat,
And said gravely to himself, swearing by his true word,
"There is a company in the castle that keeps courtesy in mind;
And a lord who supports them, may he have joy,
And may the dear lady be loved all her life!

2055	Yif thay for charyté cherysen a gest,
	And halden honour in her honde, the hathel hem yelde
	That haldez the heven upon hyghe, and also yow alle!
	And yif I myght lyf upon londe lede any quyle,
	I schuld rech yow sum rewarde redyly, if I myght."
2060	Thenn steppez he into stirop and strydez alofte;
	His schalk schewed hym his schelde, on schulder he hit laght,
	Gordez to Gryngolet with his gilt helez,
	And he startez on the ston, stod he no lenger
	to praunce.
2065	His hathel on hors watz thenne,
	That bere his spere and launce.
	"This kastel to Kryst I kenne":
	He gef hit ay god chaunce.[1]
	The brygge watz brayed doun, and the brode gatez
2070	Unbarred and born open upon bothe halve.
	The burne blessed hym bilyve, and the brede passed—
	Prayses the porter bifore the prynce kneled,
	Gef hym God and goud day, that Gawayn he save—
	And went on his way with his wyghe one,
2075	That schulde teche hym to tourne to that tene place
	Ther the ruful race he schulde resayve.
	Thay bowen bi bonkkez ther boghez ar bare,
	Thay clomben bi clyffez ther clengez the colde.
	The heven watz uphalt, bot ugly ther-under;
2080	Mist muged on the mor, malt on the mountez,
	Uche hille hade a hatte, a myst-hakel huge.
	Brokez byled and breke bi bonkkez about,
	Schyre schaterande on schorez ther thay doun showved.
	Wela wylle watz the way ther thay bi wod schulden,
2085	Til hit watz sone sesoun that the sunne ryses
	that tyde.
	Thay were on a hille ful hyghe,
	The quyte snaw lay bisyde;
	The burne that rod hym by
2090	Bede his mayster abide.
	"For I haf wonnen yow hider, wyghe, at this tyme,
	And now nar ye not fer fro that note place
	That ye han spied and spuryed so specially after;
	Bot I schal say yow for sothe, sythen I yow knowe,

2055	If out of kindliness they cherish a guest
	And dispense hospitality, may the noble lord
	Who holds up heaven repay them, and reward you all!
	And were I to live any long time on earth
	I would gladly recompense you, if I could."
2060	Then he sets foot in stirrup and vaults on to his horse;
	His servant gave him his shield, he slung it on his shoulder,
	Strikes spurs into Gringolet with his gilt heels,
	And he leaps forward on the paving, he waited no longer
	to prance.
2065	His man was mounted then,
	Carrying his spear and lance.
	"I commend this house to God,
	May it never meet mischance."
	The drawbridge was lowered, and the broad gates
2070	Unbarred and pushed open upon both sides.
	The knight blessed himself quickly and rode over the planks,
	Praises the porter who knelt before him
	Commending Gawain to God, that he should the knight save,
	And went on his way with his single guide,
2075	Who would show him the way to that perilous place
	Where he must submit to a fearful stroke.
	They struggled up hillsides where branches are bare,
	They climbed up past rock-faces gripped by the cold.
	The clouds were high up, but murky beneath them,
2080	Mist shrouded the moors, melted on the hills.
	Each summit wore a hat, a huge cloak of mist.
	Streams foamed and splashed down the slopes around them,
	Breaking white against the banks as they rushed downhill.
	Very wandering was the way they must take to the wood,
2085	Until soon it was time for sunrise at that point
	of the year.
	They were high up in the hills,
	By snow surrounded then;
	The servant at his side
2090	Bade Gawain draw rein.
	"For I have guided you here, sir, on this day,
	And now you are not far from that notorious place
	That you have searched and enquired for so specially.
	But I shall tell you truly—since I know who you are,

---

[1] *He gef hit ay god chaunce* Either Gawain wishes the castle lasting good fortune or, continuing his prayer in the previous line, hopes that Christ will do so, *He gef* then meaning "May he give."

2095	And ye are a lede upon lyve that I wel lovy,
	Wolde ye worch bi my wytte, ye worthed the better.
	The place that ye prece to ful perelous is halden;
	Ther wonez a wyghe in that waste, the worst upon erthe,
	For he is stiffe and sturne, and to strike lovies,
2100	And more he is then any mon upon myddelerde,
	And his body bigger then the best fowre
	That ar in Arthurez hous, Hestor, other other.
	He chevez that chaunce at the chapel grene,
	Ther passes non bi that place so proude in his armes
2105	That he ne dyngez hym to dethe with dynt of his honde;
	For he is a mon methles, and mercy non uses,
	For be hit chorle other chaplayn that bi the chapel rydes,
	Monk other masseprest, other any mon elles,
	Hym thynk as queme hym to quelle as quyk go hymselven.
2110	Forthy I say the, as sothe as ye in sadel sitte,
	Com ye there, ye be kylled, I may the knyght rede;[1]
	Trawe ye me that trwely, thagh ye had twenty lyves
	to spende.
	He hatz wonyd here ful yore,
2115	On bent much baret bende,
	Agayn his dyntez sore
	Ye may not yow defende.

"Forthy, goude Sir Gawayn, let the gome one,
And gotz away sum other gate, upon Goddez halve!

2120	Cayrez bi sum other kyth, ther Kryst mot yow spede,
	And I schal hygh me hom agayn, and hete yow fyrre
	That I schal swere bi God and alle his gode halwez,
	As help me God and the halydam, and othez innoghe,
	That I schal lelly yow layne,[2] and lance never tale
2125	That ever ye fondet to fle for freke that I wyst."
	"Grant merci," quoth Gawayn, and gruchyng he sayde,
	"Wel worth the, wyghe, that woldez my gode,
	And that lelly me layne I leve wel thou woldez.
	Bot helde thou hit never so holde, and I here passed,
2130	Founded for ferde for to fle, in fourme that thou tellez,
	I were a knyght kowarde, I myght not be excused.
	Bot I wyl to the chapel, for chaunce that may falle,
	And talk wyth that ilk tulk the tale that me lyste,

2095	And you are a man whom I love dearly—
	If you would follow my advice, it would be better for you.
	The place you are going to is extremely dangerous;
	There lives a man in that wilderness, the worst in the world,
	For he is powerful and grim, and loves dealing blows,
2100	And is bigger than any other man upon earth:
	His body is mightier than the four strongest men
	In Arthur's household, Hector or any other.
	He so brings it about at the Green Chapel
	That no one passes that place, however valiant in arms,
2105	Who is not battered to death by force of his hand;
	For he is a pitiless man who never shows mercy.
	For whether peasant or churchman passes his chapel,
	Monk or mass-priest, or whatever man else,
	To him killing seems as pleasant as enjoying his own life.
2110	Therefore I tell you, as sure as you sit in your saddle,
	If you go there you'll be killed, I warn you, sir knight,
	Believe that for certain, though you had twenty lives
	to lose.
	He has dwelt there long,
2115	And brought about much strife;
	Against his brutal blows
	Nothing can save your life.

"Therefore, good Sir Gawain, let the man be,
And for God's sake get away from here by some other road!

2120	Ride through some other country, where Christ be your help,
	And I will make my way home again, and further I vow
	That I shall swear by God and all his virtuous saints—
	As help me God and the holy thing, and many more oaths—
	That I shall keep your secret truly, and never reveal
2125	That ever you took flight from a man that I knew."
	"Many thanks," replied Gawain, and grudgingly he spoke,
	"Good luck to you, man, who wishes my good,
	And that you would loyally keep my secret I truly believe.
	But however closely you kept it, if I avoided this place,
2130	Took to my heels in fright, in the way you propose,
	I should be a cowardly knight, and could not be excused.
	But I will go to the chapel, whatever may chance,
	And discuss with that man whatever matter I please,

---

[1] *I may the knyght rede*   I can tell you, knight. The original text does not include the first personal pronoun.

[2] *I schal lelly yow layne*   The guide repeats Gawain's promise to the lady at 1863.

Worthe hit wele other wo, as the wyrde lykez
     hit hafe.
    Thaghe he be a sturn knape
    To stightel, and stad with stave,
    Ful wel con Dryghtyn schape
    His servauntez for to save."

2140 "Mary!" quoth that other man, "now thou so much spellez
That thou wylt thyn awen nye nyme to thyselven,
And the lyste lese thy lyf, the lette I ne kepe.
Haf here thi helme on thy hede, thi spere in thi honde,
And ryde me doun this ilke rake bi yon rokke syde,
2145 Til thou be broght to the bothem of the brem valay;
Thenne loke a littel on the launde, on thy lyfte honde,
And thou schal se in that slade the self chapel,
And the borelych burne on bent that hit kepez.
Now farez wel, on Godez half, Gawayn the noble!
2150 For alle the golde upon grounde I nolde go wyth the,
Ne bere the felaghschip thurgh this fryth on fote fyrre."
Bi that the wyghe in the wod wendez his brydel,
Hit the hors with the helez as harde as he myght,
Lepez hym over the launde, and levez the knyght there
2155   al one.
    "Bi Goddez self," quoth Gawayn,
    "I wyl nauther grete ne grone;
    To Goddez wylle I am ful bayn,
    And to hym I haf me tone."

2160 Thenne gyrdez he to Gryngolet, and gederez the rake,
Schowvez in bi a schore at a schawe syde,
Ridez thurgh the roghe bonk ryght to the dale;
And thenne he wayted hym aboute, and wylde hit hym thoght,
And seye no syngne of resette bisydez nowhere,
2165 Bot hyghe bonkkez and brent upon bothe halve,
And rughe knokled knarrez with knorned stonez;
The skwez of the scowtes skayned hym thoght.
Thenne he hoved, and wythhylde his hors at that tyde,
And ofte chaunged his cher the chapel to seche:
2170 He seye non suche in no syde, and selly hym
    thoght,
Save, a lyttle on a launde, a lawe as hit were;
A balgh berw bi a bonke the brymme bysyde,
Bi a forgh of a flode that ferked thare;
The borne blubred therinne as hit boyled hade.
2175 The knyght kachez his caple and com to the lawe,

Whether good or ill come of it, as destiny
     decides.
    Though an opponent grim
    To deal with, club in hand,
    His faithful servants God
    Knows well how to defend."

2140 "Mary!" said the other man, "since your words make it clear
That you will deliberately bring harm on yourself,
And lose your life by your own wish, I won't hinder you.
Put your helmet on your head, take your spear in your hand,
And ride down this track beside the rock over there
2145 Until it brings you to the bottom of the wild valley;
Then look to your left, some way off in the glade,
And you will see in that dale the chapel itself,
And the giant of a man who inhabits the place.
Now in God's name, noble Gawain, farewell!
2150 For all the wealth in the world I would not go with you,
Nor keep you company through this wood one further step."
With that the man at his side tugs at his bridle,
Struck his horse with his heels as hard as he could,
Gallops over the hillside and leaves the knight there
2155   alone.
    Said Gawain, "By God himself,
    I shall not moan or cry;
    My life is in his hands,
    His will I shall obey."

2160 Then he sets spurs to Gringolet and picks up the path,
Makes his way down a slope at the edge of a wood,
Rides down the rugged hillside right to the valley,
And then looked about him, and it seemed a wild place,
And saw no sign of a building anywhere near,
2165 But high and steep hillsides upon both sides,
And rough rocky crags of jagged stones:
The clouds grazing the jutting rocks, as it seemed.
Then he halted, and checked his horse for a while,
Often turning his face to look for the chapel.
2170 He saw nothing of the kind anywhere, which he thought
    strange,
Except a way off in a glade, something like a mound;
A rounded hillock on the bank of a stream,
Near the bed of a torrent that tumbled there;
The water foamed in its course as though it had boiled.
2175 The knight urges his horse and comes to the mound,

Lightez doun luflyly, and at a lynde tachez
The rayne and his riche with a roghe braunche.
Thenne he bowez to the berwe, aboute hit he walkez,
Debatande with hymself quat hit be myght.
2180 Hit hade a hole on the ende and on ayther syde,
And overgrowen with gresse in glodes aywhere,
And al watz holw inwith, nobot an olde cave,[1]
Or a crevisse of an olde cragge, he couthe hit noght deme
          with spelle.
2185   "We, lorde!" quoth the gentyle knyght,
          "Whether this be the grene chapelle?
          Here myght aboute mydnyght
          The dele his matynnes telle!

     "Now iwysse," quoth Wowayn, "wysty is here;
2190 This oritore is ugly, with erbez overgrowen;
Wel bisemez the wyghe wruxled in grene
Dele here his devocioun on the develez wyse.
Now I fele hit is the fende, in my fyve wyttez,
That hatz stoken me this steven to strye me here.
2195 This is a chapel of meschaunce, that chekke hit bytyde!
Hit is the corsedest kyrk that ever I com inne!"
With hegh helme on his hede, his launce in his honde,
He romez up to the roffe of the rogh wonez.
Thene herde he of that hyghe hil, in a harde roche
2200 Biyonde the broke, in a bonk, a wonder breme noyse:
Quat! hit clatered in the clyff, as hit cleve schulde,
As one upon a gryndelston hade grounden a sythe.
What! hit wharred and whette, as water at a mulne;
What! hit rusched and ronge, rawthe to here.
2205 Thenne "Bi Godde," quoth Gawayn, "that gere, as I trowe,
Is ryched at the reverence me, renk, to mete
          bi rote.[2]
          Let God worche! 'We loo'
          Hit helppez me not a mote.
2210   My lif thagh I forgoo,
          Drede dotz me no lote."

Thenne the knyght con calle ful hyghe,
"Who stightlez in this sted me steven to holde?

Alights nimbly, and makes fast to a tree
The reins and his noble steed with a rough branch.
Then he goes to the mound and walks around it,
Wondering to himself what it could be.
2180 It had a hole at the end and on either side,
And was covered all over with patches of grass,
And was all hollow inside; nothing but an old cave,
Or a fissure in an old rock: what to call it he hardly
          could tell.
2185   "Good lord!" said the noble knight,
          "Can the Green Chapel be this place?
          Here probably at midnight
          The devil his matins says!

     "Now truly," said Gawain, "this is a desolate place;
2190 This chapel looks evil, with grass overgrown;
Here fittingly might the man dressed in green
Perform his devotions, in devilish ways.
Now all my senses tell me that the devil himself
Has forced this agreement on me, to destroy me here!
2195 This is a chapel of disaster, may ill-luck befall it!
It is the most damnable church I was ever inside."
With tall helmet on head, his lance in his hand,
He climbs to the top of that primitive dwelling.
Then he heard up the hillside, from behind a great rock,
2200 On the slope across the stream, a deafening noise:
What! it echoed in the cliffs, as though they would split,
As if someone with a grindstone were sharpening a scythe.
What! it whirred and sang, like water at a mill;
What! it rasped and it rang, terrible to hear.
2205 Then said Gawain, "By God, these doings, I suppose,
Are a welcoming ceremony, arranged in my honor
          as a knight.
          God's will be done: 'Alas'
          Helps me no whit here.
2210   Although my life be lost,
          Noise cannot make me fear."

Then the knight shouted at the top of his voice,
"Who is master of this place, to keep tryst with me?

---

1   *nobot an olde cave*   An unlikely guess. The hollow mound half-covered with grass, with *a hole on the ende and on ayther syde*, has the characteristic form of a prehistoric burial chamber.

2   *Is ryched … bi rote*   Is intended in honor of me, in order to meet a knight with due ceremony; or, if *renk* means a field of combat or a dueling-place, the noise is intended to mark (*mete*) it out ceremoniously.

For now is gode Gawayn goande ryght here.[1]
2215 If any wyghe oght wyl, wynne hider fast,
Other now other never, his nedez to spede."
"Abyde," quoth on on the bonke aboven his hede,
"And thou schal haf al in hast that I the hyght ones."
Yet he rusched on that rurde rapely a throwe,
2220 And wyth quettyng awharf, er he wolde lyght;
And sythen he keverez bi a cragge, and comez of a hole,
Whyrlande out of a wro wyth a felle weppen,
A denez ax nwe dyght, the dynt with to yelde,
With a borelych bytte bende bi the halme,
2225 Fyled in a fylor, fowre foot large—
Hit watz no lasse bi the lace that lemed ful bryght—[2]
And the gome in the grene gered as fyrst,
Bothe the lyre and the leggez, lokkez and berde,
Save that fayre on his fote he foundez on erthe,
2230 Sette the stele to the stone, and stalked bysyde.
When he wan to the watter, ther he wade nolde,
He hypped over on hys ax, and orpedly strydez,
Bremly brothe on a bent that brode watz aboute,
    on snawe.
2235   Sir Gawayn the knyght con mete,
    He ne lutte hym nothyng lowe;
    That other sayde, "Now, sir swete,
    Of steven mon may the trowe.

"Gawayn," quoth that grene gome, "God the mot loke!
2240 Iwysse thou art welcom, wyghe, to my place,
And thou hatz tymed thi travayl as truee mon schulde,
And thou knowez the covenauntez kest uus bytwene:
At this tyme twelmonyth thou toke that the falled,
And I schulde at this Nwe Yere yeply the quyte.
2245 And we ar in this valay verayly oure one;
Here are no renkes us to rydde, rele as uus lykez.
Haf thy helme of thy hede, and haf here thy pay.
Busk no more debate then I the bede thenne
When thou wypped of my hede at a wap one."
2250 "Nay, bi God," quoth Gawayn, "that me gost lante,

For now is good Gawain waiting right here.
2215 If anyone wants something, let him hurry here fast,
Either now or never, to settle his affairs."
"Wait," said someone on the hillside above,
"And you shall quickly have all that I promised you once."
Yet he kept making that whirring noise for a while,
2220 And turned back to his whetting before he would come down;
And then makes his way among the rocks, bursting out of a hole,
Whirling out of a nook with a fearsome weapon—
A Danish axe newly made—for dealing the blow,
With a massive blade curving back on the shaft,
2225 Honed with a whetstone, four feet across—
No less than that, despite the gleaming green girdle—
And the man in the green, dressed as at first,
Both his flesh and his legs, hair and beard,
Except that grandly on foot he stalked on the earth,
2230 Set the handle to the ground and walked beside it.
When he came to the stream he refused to wade:
He hopped over on his axe and forcefully strides,
Fiercely grim on a clearing that stretched wide about,
    under snow.
2235   Sir Gawain met the knight,
    Made him a frosty bow;
    The other said, "Good sir,
    A man may trust your vow.

"Gawain," said that green man, "may God protect you!
2240 You are indeed welcome, sir, to my place;
You have timed your journey as a true man should,
And you know the agreement settled between us:
A twelvemonth ago you took what fell to your lot,
And I was to repay you promptly at this New Year.
2245 And we are in this valley truly by ourselves,
With no knights to separate us, so we can fight as we please.
Take your helmet off your head, and here get your pay.
Make no more argument than I offered you then,
When you slashed off my head with a single stroke."
2250 "No, by God," said Gawain, "who gave me a soul,

---

[1] *goande ryght here* Walking right here, with a suggestion of being ready to leave immediately if no one answers.

[2] *Hit watz no lasse bi that lace that lemed ful bryght* Commentators disagree about which lace the poet is referring to. The axe used by Gawain has *a lace lapped aboute, that louked at the hede*, 217 as part of its decoration. But the axe which the Green Knight has just finished sharpening is a different weapon, newly made and not apparently decorated. The other lace is the green girdle or *luf-lace*;

see 1830, *a lace ... that leke umbe hir sydez*, and 2030, *the lace, the ladiez gifte*. The belt is so designated at least eight times between 1830 and 2505, while lace in the first sense is not clearly mentioned again after 217. The more likely reading of the line is that the axe seemed enormous to Gawain, despite the assurance of the green belt, whose *glyterande golde* decoration explains *lemed ful bryght*.

I schal gruch the no grwe for grem that fallez.
Bot styghtel the upon on strok, and I schal stonde stylle
And warp the no wernyng to worch as the lykez,
         nowhare."[1]
2255   He lened with the nek, and lutte,
         And schewed that schyre al bare,
         And lette as he noght dutte;
         For drede he wolde not dare.

Then the gome in the grene graythed hym swythe,
2260   Gederez up hys grymme tole Gawayn to smyte;
With alle the bur in his body he ber hit on lofte,
Munt as maghtyly as marre hym he wolde;
Hade hym dryven adoun as dregh as he atled,
Ther hade ben ded of his dynt that doghty watz ever.[2]
2265   Bot Gawayn on that giserne glyfte hym bysyde,
As hit com glydande adoun on glode hym to schende,
And schranke a lytel with the schulderes for the scharp yrne.
That other schalk wyth a schunt the schene wythhaldez,
And thenne repreved he the prynce with many prowde wordez:
2270   "Thou art not Gawayn," quoth the gome, "that is so goud
         halden,
That never arghed for no here by hylle ne be vale,
And now thou fles for ferde er thou fele harmez!
Such cowardise of that knyght cowthe I never here.
Nawther fyked I ne flaghe, freke, quen thou myntest,
2275   Ne kest no cavelacioun in kyngez hous Arthor.
My hede flagh to my fote, and yet flagh I never;
And thou, er any harme hent, arghez in hert.
Wherfore the better burne me burde be called
         therfore."
2280   Quoth Gawayn, "I schunt onez,
         And so wyl I no more;
         Bot thagh my hede falle on the stonez,
         I con not hit restore.

"But busk, burne, bi thi fayth, and bryng me to the poynt.
2285   Dele to me my destiné, and do hit out of honde,[3]
For I schal stonde the a strok, and start no more
Til thy ax have me hitte: haf here my trawthe."
"Haf at the thenne!" quoth that other, and hevez hit alofte,
And waytez as wrothely as he wode were.

I shall bear you no grudge at all, whatever hurt comes about.
Just limit yourself to one blow, and I will stand still
And not resist whatever it pleases you to do
         at all."
2255   He bent his neck and bowed,
         Showing the flesh all bare,
         And seeming unafraid;
         He would not shrink in fear.

Then the man dressed in green quickly got ready,
2260   Raised his terrible axe to give Gawain the blow;
With all the strength in his body he heaved it in the air,
Swung it as fiercely as if meaning to mangle him.
Had he brought the axe down as forcibly as he acted,
That courageous knight would have been killed by the blow;
2265   But Gawain glanced sideways at that battle-axe
As it came sweeping down to destroy him there,
And hunched his shoulders a little to resist the sharp blade.
The other man checked the bright steel with a jerk,
And then rebuked the prince with arrogant words:
2270   "You're not Gawain," said the man, "who is reputed so
         good,
Who never quailed from an army, on valley or on hill,
And now flinches for fear before he feels any hurt!
I never heard of such cowardice shown by that knight.
I neither flinched nor fled, sir, when you aimed one at me,
2275   Nor raised any objections in King Arthur's house.
My head fell to the floor, yet I gave no ground;
But you, though not wounded, are trembling at heart,
So I deserve to be reckoned the better man
         for that."
2280   Gawain said, "I flinched once,
         But won't twice hunch my neck,
         Though if my head should fall
         I cannot put it back.

"But hurry up, man, by your faith, and come to the point.
2285   Deal out my fate to me, and do it out of hand,
For I shall let you strike a blow, and not move again
Until your axe has hit me, take my true word."
"Have at you then!" said the other, and raises it up,
Contorting his face as though he were enraged.

----

[1] *nowhare*   Anywhere you like. Gawain is only concerned that the
Green Knight shall restrict himself to one stroke (2253).

[2] *that doghty watz ever*   The man who was always brave.

----

[3] *out of honde*   I.e., out of hand: at once. The first recorded use of
the phrase.

2290 He myntez at hym maghtyly, bot not the mon rynez,
Withhelde heterly his honde er hit hurt myght.
Gawayn graythely hit bydez, and glent with no membre,
Bot stode stylle as the ston, other a stubbe auther
That ratheled is in roché grounde with rotez a hundreth.
2295 Then muryly efte con he mele, the mon in the grene,
"So, now thou hatz thi hert holle, hitte me bihovs.
Halde the now the hyghe hode that Arthur the raght,
And kepe thy kanel at this kest, yif hit kever may."
Gawayn ful gryndelly with greme thenne sayde:
2300 "Wy! thresch on, thou thro mon, thou thretez to longe;
I hope that thi hert arghe wyth thyn awen selven."
"For sothe," quoth that other freke, "so felly thou spekez,
I wyl no lenger on lyte lette thin ernde[1]
          right nowe."
2305   Thenne tas he hym strythe to stryke,
          And frounsez bothe lyppe and browe,
          No mervayle thagh hym myslyke
          That hoped of no rescowe.

He lyftes lyghtly his lome, and let hit doun fayre
2310 With the barbe of the bitte bi the bare nek;
Thagh he homered heterly, hurt hym no more
Bot snyrt hym on that on syde, that severed the hyde.
The scharp schrank to the flesche thurgh the schyre grece,
That the schene blod over his schulderes schot to the erthe;
2315 And quen the burne sey the blode blenk on the snawe,
He sprit forth a spenne-fote[2] more then a spere lenthe,
Hent heterly his helme, and his hed cast,
Schot with his schulderes his fayre schelde under,
Braydez out a bryght sworde, and bremly he spekez—
2320 Never syn that he watz burne borne of his moder
Watz he never in this worlde wyghe half so blythe—
"Blynne, burne, of thy bur, bede me no mo!
I haf a stroke in this sted withoute stryf hent,
And if thow rechez me any mo, I redyly schal quyte,
2325 And yelde yederly agayn—and therto ye tryst—
          and foo.
          Bot on stroke here me fallez—
          The covenaunt ryght schop so,
          Fermed in Arthurez hallez—
2330   And therfore, hende, now hoo!"

He swings the axe at him savagely, without harming the man,
Checked his blow suddenly before it could inflict hurt.
Gawain awaits it submissively, not moving a limb,
But stood as still as a stone, or the stump of a tree
Anchored in rocky ground by hundreds of roots.
Then the man in green spoke mockingly again,
"So, now you have found courage it is time for the blow.
Now may the order of knighthood given you by Arthur
Preserve you and your neck this time, if it has power!"
Then Gawain replied angrily, mortified deeply,
"Why, strike away, you fierce man, you waste time in threats;
I think you have frightened yourself with your words."
"Indeed," said that other man, "you speak so aggressively
That I will no longer delay or hinder your business
          at all."
He takes his stance to strike,
Puckering mouth and brow;
No wonder if Gawain feels
No hope of rescue now.

He swiftly raises his weapon, and brings it down straight
With the cutting edge of the blade over Gawain's bare neck;
Although he struck fiercely, he hurt him no more
Than to slash the back of his neck, laying open the skin.
The blade cut into the body through the fair flesh
So that bright blood shot over his shoulders to the ground.
And when the knight saw his blood spatter the snow
He leapt forward with both feet more than a spear's length,
Snatched up his helmet and crammed it on his head,
Jerked his shoulders to bring his splendid shield down,
Drew out a gleaming sword and fiercely he speaks—
Never since that man was born of his mother
Had he ever in the world felt half so relieved—
"Hold your attack, sir, don't try it again!
I have passively taken a blow in this place,
And if you offer me another I shall repay it promptly
And return it at once—be certain of that—
          with force.
          One single blow is due;
          The contract is my proof,
          Witnessed in Arthur's hall;
          And therefore, sir, enough!"

---

[1] *I wyl no lenger on lyte lette thin ernde*   Literally: I will no longer in delay hinder your mission.

[2] *spenne-fote*   With feet together.

The hathel heldet hym fro, and on his ax rested,
Sette the schaft upon schore, and to the scharp lened,
And loked to the leude that on the launde yede,
How that doghty, dredles, dervely ther stondez
2335 Armed, ful aghles: in hert hit hym lykez.
Thenn he melez muryly wyth a much steven,
And with a rynkande rurde he to the renk sayde:
"Bolde burne, on this bent be not so gryndel.
No mon here unmanerly the mysboden habbez,
2340 Ne kyd bot as covenaunde at kyngez kort schaped.
I hyght the a strok and thou hit hatz, halde the wel payed;
I relece the of the remnaunt of ryghtes alle other.
Iif I deliver had bene, a boffet paraunter
I couthe wrotheloker haf waret, to the haf wroght anger.
2345 Fyrst I mansed the muryly with a mynt one,
And rove the wyth no rofe-sore, with ryght I the profered
For the forwarde that we fest in the fyrst nyght,[1]
And thou trystyly the trawthe and trwly me haldez,
Al the gayne thow me gef, as god mon schulde.
2350 That other munt for the morne, mon, I the profered,
Thou kyssedes my clere wyf—the cosses me raghtez.
For bothe two here I the bede bot two bare myntes
        boute scathe.[2]
    Trwe mon trwe restore,
2355 Thenne thar mon drede no wathe.
    At the thrid thou fayled thore,
    And therfore that tappe ta the.

"For hit is my wede that thou werez, that ilke woven girdel,
Myn owen wyf hit the weved, I wot wel for sothe.
2360 Now know I wel thy cosses, and thy costes als,
And the wowyng of my wyf: I wroght it myselven.
I sende hir to asay the, and sothly me thynkkez
On the fautlest freke that ever on fote yede;
As perle bi the quite pese is of prys more,
2365 So is Gawayn, in god fayth, bi other gay knyghtez.
Bot here yow lakked a lyttel, sir, and lewté yow wonted;
Bot that watz for no wylyde werke,[3] ne wowyng nauther,
Bot for ye lufed your lyf; the lasse I yow blame."
That other stif mon in study[4] stod a gret whyle,
2370 So agreved for greme he gryed withinne;
Alle the blod of his brest blende in his face,

The knight kept his distance, and rested on his axe,
Set the shaft on the ground and leaned on the blade,
Contemplating the man before him in the glade;
Seeing how valiant, fearlessly bold he stood there
2335 Armed and undaunted, he admired him much.
Then he spoke to him pleasantly in a loud voice,
And said to the knight in a resounding tone,
"Brave sir, don't act so wrathfully in this place.
No one has discourteously mistreated you here,
2340 Or acted contrary to the covenant sworn at the king's court.
I promised you a blow and you have it; think yourself well paid;
I free you from the rest of all other obligations.
Had I been more dextrous, maybe I could
Have dealt you a more spiteful blow, to have roused your anger.
2345 First I threatened you playfully with a pretence,
And avoided giving you a gash, doing so rightly
Because of the agreement we made on the first night,
When you faithfully and truly kept your pledged word,
Gave me all your winnings, as an honest man should.
2350 That other feint, sir, I gave you for the next day,
When you kissed my lovely wife and gave me those kisses.
For both occasions I aimed at you two mere mock blows
        without harm.
    True man must pay back truly,
2355 Then he need nothing fear;
    You failed me the third time
    And took that blow therefore.

"For it is my belt you are wearing, that same woven girdle,
My own wife gave it to you, I know well in truth.
2360 I know all about your kisses, and your courteous manners,
And my wife's wooing of you: I arranged it myself.
I sent her to test you, and to me truly you seem
One of the most perfect men who ever walked on the earth.
As pearls are more valuable than the white peas,
2365 So is Gawain, in all truth, before other fair knights.
Only here you fell short a little, sir, and lacked fidelity,
But that was not for fine craftsmanship, nor wooing either,
But because you wanted to live: so I blame you the less."
That other brave man stood speechless a long while,
2370 So mortified and crushed that he inwardly squirmed;
All the blood in his body burned in his face,

---

[1] *fyrst nyght* The night before the first hunt.

[2] *boute scathe* Without injury, unscathed.

[3] *wylyde werke* Intricate workmanship (of the belt).

[4] *in study* Lost in thought, speechless.

That al he schranke for schome that the schalk talked.
The forme worde upon folde that the freke meled:
"Corsed worth cowarddyse and covetyse bothe!
2375 In yow is vylany and vyse that vertue disstryez."
Thenne he kaght to the knot, and the kest lawsez,
Brayde brothely the belt to the burne selven:
"Lo, ther the falssyng, foule mot hit falle!
For care of thy knokke cowardyse me taght
2380 To acorde me with covetyse, my kynde to forsake,
That is larges and lewté that longez to knyghtez.
Now am I fawty and falce, and ferde haf ben ever
Of trecherye and untrawthe: bothe bityde sorwe
          and care!
2385   I biknowe yow, knyght, here stylle,
          Al fawty is my fare;
          Letez me overtake your wylle
          And efte I schal be ware."

The loghe that other leude and luflyly sayde,
2390 "I halde hit hardily hole, the harme that I hade.[1]
Thou art confessed so clene, beknowen of thy mysses,
And hatz the penaunce apert of the poynt of myn egge,
I halde the polysed of that plyght, and pured as clene
As thou hadez never forfeted sythen thou watz fyrst borne;
2395 And I gif the, sir, the gurdel that is golde-hemmed;
For hit is grene as my goune, Sir Gawayn, ye maye
Thenk upon this ilke threpe, ther thou forth thryngez
Among prynces of prys, and this a pure token
Of the chaunce of the grene chapel at chevalrous
          knyghtez.
2400 And ye schal in this Nwe Yer agayn to my wonez,
And we schyn revel the remnaunt of this ryche fest
          ful bene."
          Ther lathed hym fast the lorde
          And sayde, "Wyth my wyf, I wene,
2405   We schal yow wel acorde,
          That watz your enmy kene."

"Nay, for sothe," quoth the segge, and sesed hys helme,
And hatz hit of hendely, and the hathel thonkkez,
"I haf sojorned sadly; sele yow bytyde
2410 And he yelde hit yow yare that yarkkez al menskes!
And comaundez me to that cortays, your comlych fere,
Bothe that on and that other, myn honoured ladyez,

So that he winced with shame at what the man said.
The first words that the knight uttered there
Were, "A curse upon cowardice and coveteousness!
2375 You breed boorishness and vice that ruin virtue."
Then he took hold of the knot and looses the buckle,
Flung the belt violently towards that man:
"There it is, the false thing, may the devil take it!
For fear of your blow taught me cowardice,
2380 To give way to covetousness, be false to my nature,
The generosity and fidelity expected of knights.
Now I am false and unworthy, and have always dreaded
Treachery and deceit: may misfortune and grief
          befall both!
2385   Sir, humbly I confess
          My good name is marred.
          Let me regain your trust,
          Next time I'll be on guard."

Then the other man laughed, and graciously said,
2390 "The wrong you did me I consider wiped out.
You have so cleanly confessed yourself, admitted your fault,
And done honest penance on the edge of my blade.
I declare you absolved of that offence, and washed as clean
As if you had never transgressed since the day you were born.
2395 And I make you a gift, sir, of my gold-bordered belt;
Since it is green like my gown, Sir Gawain, you may
Remember this meeting in the world where you mingle
With princes of rank: it will be a true token
Of the exploit of the Green Chapel among chivalrous
          knights.
2400 And you shall come back to my castle at this New Year,
And we will see out the revelry of this high feast
          with joy."
          He pressed him earnestly
          And said, "We shall, I know,
2405   Reconcile you with my wife,
          Who was your cunning foe."

"No, indeed," said the knight, and seizing his helmet
Takes it off politely and gives the lord thanks;
"I have stayed long enough: good fortune attend you,
2410 And may he who gives all honors soon send you reward!
And commend me to that gracious one, your lovely wife,
Both the one and the other of those honorable ladies

---

[1] *the harme that I hade*   I.e., being cheated of his winnings.

That thus hor knyght wyth hor kest han koyntly bigyled.
Bot hit is no ferly thagh a fole madde,
2415 And thurgh wyles of wymmen be wonen to sorwe,
For so watz Adam in erde with one bygyled,
And Salamon with fele sere, and Samson eftsonez—
Dalyda dalt hym hys wyrde—and Davyth therafter
Watz blended with Barsabe, that much bale tholed.[1]
2420 Now these were wrathed wyth her wyles, hit were a wynne huge
To luf hom wel and leve hem not, a leude that couthe.
For thes wer forne the freest, that folwed alle the sele
Exellently of alle thyse other, under hevenryche
         that mused;
2425   And alle thay were biwyled
      With wymmen that thay used.
      Thagh I be now bigyled
      Me think me burde be excused.

"Bot your gordel," quoth Gawayn, "God yow foryelde!
2430 That wyl I welde wyth goud wylle, not for the wynne golde,
Ne the saynt, ne the sylk, ne for syde pendaundes,
For wele ne for worchyp, ne for the wlonk werkkez,
Bot in syngne of my surfet I schal se hit ofte,
When I ride in renoun, remorde to myselven
2435 The faut and the fayntyse of the flesche crabbed,
How tender hit is to entyse teches of fylthe;
And thus, quen pryde schal me pryk for prowes of armes,
The loke to this luf-lace schal lethe my hert.
Bot on I wolde yow pray, displeses yow never:
2440 Syn ye be lorde of the yonder londe her I haf lent inne
Wyth yow wyth worschyp—the wyghe hit yow yelde
That uphaldez the heven and on hygh sittez—
How norne ye yowre ryght nome, and thenne no more?"
"That schal I telle the trwly," quoth that other thenne,
2445 "Bertilak de Hautdesert I hat in this londe.
Thurgh myght of Morgne la Faye, that in my hous lenges,
And koyntyse of clergye, bi craftes wel lerned,
The maystrés of Merlyn mony hatz taken—
For ho hatz dalt drwry ful dere sumtyme
2450 With that conable klerk, that knowes alle your knyghtez
         at hame.
      Morgne the goddes
      Therfore hit is hir name:
      Weldez non so hyghe hawtesse
2455   That ho ne con make ful tame—

Who have so cleverly deluded their knight with their game.
But it is no wonder if a fool acts insanely
2415 And is brought to grief through womanly wiles;
For so was Adam beguiled by one, here on earth,
Solomon by several women, and Samson was another—
Delilah was cause of his fate—and afterwards David
Was deluded by Bathsheba, and suffered much grief.
2420 Since these were ruined by their wiles, it would be a great gain
To love women and not trust them, if a man knew how.
For these were the noblest of old, whom fortune favored
Above all others on earth, or who dwelt
         under heaven.
2425   Beguiled were they all
      By women they thought kind.
      Since I too have been tricked
      Then I should pardon find.

"But for your belt," said Gawain, "God repay you for that!
2430 I accept it gratefully, not for its wonderful gold,
Nor for the girdle itself nor its silk, nor its long pendants,
Nor its value nor the honor it confers, nor its fine workmanship,
But I shall look at it often as a sign of my failing,
And when I ride in triumph, recall with remorse
2435 The corruption and frailty of the perverse flesh,
How quick it is to pick up blotches of sin.
And so, when pride in my knightly valor stirs me,
A glance at this girdle will humble my heart.
Just one thing I would ask, if it would not offend you,
2440 Since you are the lord of the country that I have dwelt in,
Honorably treated in your house—may he reward you
Who holds up the heavens and sits upon high!—
What do you call yourself rightly, and then no more demands?"
"I will tell you that truthfully," replied that other man,
2445 "Bertilak of Hautdesert I am called in this land.
Through the power of Morgan le Fay, who lives under my roof,
And her skill in learning, well taught in magic arts,
She has acquired many of Merlin's occult powers—
For she had love-dealings at an earlier time
2450 With that accomplished scholar, as all your knights know
         at home.
      Morgan the goddess
      Therefore is her name;
      No one, however haughty
2455   Or proud she cannot tame.

---

1 *For so watz Adam ... tholed* Famous stories of female betrayal
from the Old Testament.

"Ho wayned me upon this wyse to your wynne halle
For to assay the surquidré, yif hit soth were
That rennes of the grete renoun of the Rounde Table.
Ho wayned me this wonder your wyttez to reve,
2460 For to have greved Gaynour and gart hir to dyghe
With glopnyng of that ilke gome that gostlych speked
With his hede in his honde bifore the hyghe table.
That is ho that is at home, the auncian lady;
Ho is even thyn aunt, Arthurez half-suster,
2465 The duches doghter of Tyntagelle, that dere Uter after
Hade Arthur upon, that athel is nowthe.
Therfore I ethe the, hathel, to com to thyn aunt,
Make myry in my hous; my meny the lovies,
And I wol the as wel, wyghe, bi my faythe,
2470 As any gome under God for thy grete trauthe."
And he nikked hym naye, he nolde bi no wayes.
Thay acolen and kyssen and kennen ayther other
To the prynce of paradise, and parten ryght there
        on coolde;
2475   Gawayn on blonk ful bene
        To the kyngez burgh buskez bolde,
        And the knyght in the enker-grene
        Whiderwarde-so-ever he wolde.

Wylde wayez in the worlde Wowen now rydez
2480 On Gryngolet, that the grace hade geten of his lyve;
Ofte he herbered in house and ofte al theroute,
And mony aventure in vale, and venquyst ofte,
That I ne tyght at this tyme in tale to remene.
The hurt watz hole that he hade hent in his nek,
2485 And the blykkande belt he bere theraboute
Abelef as a bauderyk bounden by his syde,
Loken under his lyfte arme, the lace, with a knot,
In tokenyng he watz tane in tech of a faute.
And thus he commes to the court, knyght al in sounde.
2490 Ther wakned wele in that wone when wyst the grete
That gode Gawayn watz commen; gayn hit hym thoght.
The kyng kysses the knyght, and the whene alce,
And sythen mony syker knyght that soght hym to haylce,
Of his fare that hym frayned; and ferlyly he telles,
2495 Biknowez alle the costes of care that he hade,
The chaunce of the chapel, the chere of the knyght,
The luf of the ladi, the lace at the last.
The nirt in the neck he naked hem schewed

"She sent me in this shape to your splendid hall
To make trial of your pride, and to judge the truth
Of the great reputation attached to the Round Table.
She sent me to drive you demented with this marvel,
2460 To have terrified Guenevere and caused her to die
With horror at that figure who spoke like a specter
With his head in his hand before the high table.
That is she who is in my castle, the very old lady,
Who is actually your aunt, Arthur's half-sister,
2465 The duchess of Tintagel's daughter, whom noble Uther
Afterwards begot Arthur upon, who now is king.
So I entreat you, good sir, to visit your aunt
And make merry in my house: my servants all love you,
And so will I too, sir, on my honor,
2470 As much as any man on earth for your great truth."
But Gawain told him no, not for any persuasion.
They embrace and kiss, and commend each other
To the prince of paradise, and separate there
        in the cold;
2475   On his great horse Gawain
        To the king's court quickly goes,
        And the knight in emerald green
        Went wheresoever he chose.

Over wild country Gawain now makes his way
2480 On Gringolet, after his life had been mercifully spared.
Sometimes he lodged in a house and often out of doors,
And was vanquisher often in many encounters
Which at this time I do not intend to relate.
The injury he had received in his neck was healed,
2485 And over it he wore the gleaming belt
Across his body like a baldric, fastened at his side,
And this girdle tied under his left arm with a knot,
To signify he had been dishonored by a slip.
And so safe and sound he arrives at the court.
2490 Joy spread through the castle when the nobles learnt
That good Gawain had returned: they thought it a wonder.
The king kisses the knight, and the queen too,
And then many true knights who came to embrace him,
Asking how he had fared; he tells a marvelous story,
2495 Describes all the hardships he had endured,
What happened at the chapel, the Green Knight's behavior,
The lady's wooing, and finally the belt.
He showed them the scar on his bare neck

That he laght for his unleuté at the leudes hondes
2500   for blame.
  He tened quen he schulde telle,
  He groned for gref and grame;
  The blod in his face con melle,
  When he hit schulde schewe, for schame.

2505 "Lo, lorde," quoth the leude, and the lace hondeled,
"This is the bende of this blame I bere in my nek,
This is the lathe and the losse that I laght have
Of cowardise and covetyse that I haf caght thare,
This is the token of untrawthe that I am tane inne,
2510 And I mot nedez hit were wyle I may last;
For mon may hyden his harme, bot unhap ne may hit,
For ther hit onez is tachched twynne wil hit never."
The kyng comfortez the knyght, and alle the court als
Laghen loude therat, and luflyly acorden
2515 That lordes and ladis that longed to the Table,
Uche burne of the brotherhede, a bauderyk schulde have,
A bende abelef hym aboute of a bryght grene,
And that, for sake of that segge, in swete to were.
For that watz acorded the renoun of the Rounde Table,
2520 And he honoured that hit hade evermore after,
As hit is breved in the best boke of romaunce.
Thus in Arthurus day this aunter bitidde,
The Brutus bokez therof beres wyttenesse;
Sythen Brutus, the bolde burne, bowed hider fyrst,
2525 After the segge and the asaute watz sesed at Troye,[1]
  iwysse,
  Mony aunterez here-biforne
  Haf fallen suche er this.
  Now that bere the croun of thorne
2530   He bryng uus to his blysse! AMEN.

HONY SOYT QUI MAL PENCE.[2]

That he received for his dishonesty at the lord's hands
2500   in rebuke.
  Tormented by his tale
  He groaned for grief and hurt;
  The blood burned in his face
  When he showed the shameful cut.

2505 "See, my lord," said the man, and held up the girdle,
"This belt caused the scar that I bear on my neck;
This is the injury and damage that I have suffered
For the cowardice and covetousness that seized me there;
This is the token of the dishonesty I was caught committing,
2510 And now I must wear it as long as I live.
For a man may hide his misdeed, but never erase it,
For where once it takes root the stain can never be lifted."
The king consoles the knight, and the whole court
Laughs loudly about it, and courteously agrees
2515 That lords and ladies who belong to the Table,
Each member of the brotherhood, should wear such a belt,
A baldric of bright green crosswise on the body,
Similar to Sir Gawain's and worn for his sake:
And that became part of the renown of the Round Table,
2520 And whoever afterwards wore it was always honored,
As is set down in the most reputable books of romance.
So in the time of Arthur this adventure happened,
And the chronicles of Britain bear witness to it;
After the brave hero Brutus first arrived here,
2525 When the siege and the assault were ended at Troy,
  indeed.
  Many exploits before now
  Have happened much like this.
  Now may the thorn-crowned God
2530   Bring us to his bliss! AMEN.

HONI SOIT QUI MAL Y PENSE.

---

[1] *After the segge and the asaute watz sesed at Troye* The last long line of the poem repeats the first one, as though bringing the story full circle after its hundred and one stanzas.

[2] *Hony Soyt Qui Mal Pence* I.e., Latin: evil be to him who evil thinks, the motto embroidered on the blue velvet garter worn by Knights of the Garter, the highest order of English knighthood bestowed by the sovereign. According to Froissart, the order was instituted about 1344. The poet's use of the motto has not been accounted for.

IN CONTEXT

Fled Bricrend

The earliest known example of the beheading-game legend appears in the Irish story *Fled Bricrend*, written down about the year 1100 but probably a good deal older. It tells how a terrifying ogre enters the hall where several heroes are gathered, carrying a huge club in one hand and an enormous axe in the other. He explains that he is searching for a man who will deal with him fairly, and that the reputation of the Ulaid has brought him there in the hope of finding one. The terms of fair play that he proposes are that he will cut off the head of one of the heroes, who on the following night will decapitate him. This arrangement is not accepted, and the ogre agrees to reverse the conditions by standing a blow forthwith and returning on the next day to give one in return. One of the heroes accepts the challenge and cuts off the ogre's head, filling the hall with blood; but the ogre rises, picks up his head and the axe, and leaves the hall, still bleeding profusely. When he returns on the following night his opponent shirks his undertaking to stand the return blow. Two further heroes take up the challenge with the same result, but when the ogre returns on the fourth night contemptuous of the false and cowardly Ulaid, Cú Chulaind (Cuchulainn) is present. He too decapitates the ogre and smashes the head for good measure. On the next night Cú Chulaind places his neck on the block to receive the return blow, and is mocked by the ogre because his neck does not cover the enormous block. Cú Chulaind rebukes the ogre for tormenting him, and insists on being despatched at once. The ogre raises the huge axe and brings it down on Cú Chulaind's neck with the blade uppermost. After praising Cú Chulaind's courage and fidelity the ogre vanishes. In a shorter version of the story he swings the axe at Cú Chulaind three times, each time with the blade reversed.

from *Fled Bricrend/Bricriu's Feast*

Once, when the Ulaid were at Emuin Machae, tired after the fair and the games, Conchubur and Fergus and the other Ulaid chieftains returned from the playing field to sit in Conchubur's Cráebrúad. Lóegure and Conall and Cú Chulaind were not there that evening, but the best of the other warriors of Ulaid were. As night drew on, they saw a huge, ugly churl coming towards them in the house, and it seemed to them that there was not in all Ulaid a warrior half as tall. His appearance was frightful and terrifying: a hide against his skin, and a dun cloak round him, and a great bushy tree overhead where a winter shed for thirty calves could fit. Each of his two yellow eyes was the size of an ox-cauldron; each finger was as thick as a normal man's wrist. The tree trunk in his left hand would have been a burden for twenty yoked oxen; the axe in his right hand, whence had gone three fifties of glowing metal pieces, had a handle that would have been a burden for a team of oxen, yet it was sharp enough to cut hairs against the wind.

He came in this guise and stood beneath the forked beam at one end of the fire. "Do you find the house so narrow," said Dubthach Dóeltenga, "that there is no place to stand but under the forked beam? You may wish to contest the position of house candlebearer, but you are more likely to burn the house than to illuminate the company inside." "Although that is my gift," the churl replied, "perhaps you will grant that, despite my height, the entire household may be lit without the house's being burnt. But that is not my primary gift, and I have others. That which I have come to seek I have not found in Ériu or the Alps or Europe or Africa or Asia or Greece or Scythia or Inis Orc or the Pillars of Hercules or Tor mBregoind or Inis Gaid. Nowhere have I found a man to keep my bargain. Since you Ulaid surpass the hosts of every land in anger and prowess and weaponry, in rank and pride and dignity, in honor and generosity and excellence, let one of you keep faith with me in the matter over which I have come."

"It is not right," said Fergus, "to dishonor a province because of one man's failure to keep his word—perhaps death is no nearer to him than it is to you." "It is not I who shirk death," replied the churl. "Then let us hear your proposal," said Fergus. "Only if I am allowed fair play," said the churl. "It is right to allow him that," said Senchae son of Ailill, "for it would be no fair play if a great host broke faith with a completely unknown individual. Besides, it would seem to us that if you are to find the man you seek, you will find him here." "I exempt Conchubur, for he is the king, and I exempt Fergus, for he is of equal rank," said the churl. "Whoever else may dare, let him come that I may cut off his head tonight, he mine tomorrow."

"After those two," said Dubthach, "there is certainly no warrior here worthy of that." "Indeed, there is," said Muinremur son of Gerrgend, and he sprang into the center of the house. Now, Muinremur had the strength of one hundred warriors, and each arm had the strength of one hundred. "Bend down, churl," he said, "that I may cut off your head tonight—you may cut off mine tomorrow night." "I could make that bargain anywhere," said the churl. "Let us rather make the bargain I proposed: I will cut off your head tonight, and you will avenge that by cutting off my head tomorrow night." "I swear by what my people swear by," said Dubthach Dóeltenga, "such a death would not be pleasant if the man you killed tonight clung to you tomorrow. But you alone have the power to be killed one night and to avenge it the next." "Then whatever conditions you propose I will fulfil, surprising as you may find that," said the churl, whereupon he made Muinremur pledge to keep his part of the bargain the following night.

With that, Muinremur took the churl's axe, whose two edges were seven feet apart. The churl stretched his neck out on the block, and Muinremur so swung the axe that it stuck in the block underneath; the head rolled to the foot of the forked beam, and the house was filled with blood. At once, the churl rose, gathered his head and his block and his axe and clutched them to his chest, and left the house, blood streaming from the neck and filling the Cráebrúad on every side. The household were horrorstruck by the wondrousness of the event they had witnessed. "I swear by what my people swear by," said Dubthach Dóeltenga, "if that churl returns tomorrow after having been killed tonight, not a man in Ulaid will be left alive."

The following night, the churl returned, but Muinremur avoided him. The churl complained, saying "Indeed, it is not fair of Muinremur to break his part of the bargain." Lóegure Búadach, however, was present that night, and when the churl continued, "Who of the warriors who contest the champion's portion of Ulaid will fulfil this bargain with me tonight? Where is Lóegure Búadach?", Lóegure said, "Here I am!" The churl pledged Lóegure as he had pledged Muinremur, but Lóegure, like Muinremur, failed to appear the following night. The churl then pledged Conall Cernach, and he too failed to appear and keep his pledge.

When he arrived on the fourth night, the churl was seething with rage. All the women of Ulaid had gathered there that night to see the marvel that had come to the Cráebrúad, and Cú Chulaind had come as well. The churl began to reproach them, then, saying, "Men of Ulaid, your skill and courage are no more. Your warriors covet the champion's portion, yet they are unable to contest it. Where is that pitiful stripling you call Cú Chulaind? Would his word be better than that of his companions?" "I want no bargain with you," said Cú Chulaind. "No doubt you fear death, wretched fly," said the churl. At that, Cú Chulaind sprang towards the churl and dealt him such a blow with the axe that his head was sent to the rafters of the Cráebrúad, and the entire house shook. Cú

Chulaind then struck the head with the axe once more, so that he shattered it into fragments. The churl rose nonetheless.

The following day, the Ulaid watched Cú Chulaind to see if he would avoid the churl the way his companions had done; they saw that he was waiting for the churl, and they grew very dejected. It seemed to them proper to begin his death dirge, for they feared greatly that he would live only until the churl appeared. Cú Chulaind, ashamed, said to Conchubur, "By my shield and by my sword, I will not go until I have fulfilled my pledge to the churl—since I am to die, I will die with honor."

Towards the end of the day, they saw the churl approaching them. "Where is Cú Chulaind?" he asked. "Indeed, I am here," said Cú Chulaind. "You speak low, tonight, wretch, for you fear death greatly," said the churl. "Yet for all that, you have not avoided me." Cú Chulaind rose and stretched his neck out on the block, but its size was such that his neck reached only halfway across. "Stretch out your neck, you wretch," said the churl. "You torment me," said Cú Chulaind. "Kill me quickly. I did not torment you last night. Indeed, I swear, if you torment me now, I will make myself as long as a heron above you." "I cannot dispatch you, not with the length of the block and the shortness of your neck," said the churl.

Cú Chulaind stretched himself, then, until a warrior's foot would fit between each rib, and he stretched his neck until it reached the other side of the block. The churl raised his axe so that it reached the rafters of the house. What with the creaking of the old hide that he wore and the swish of his axe as he raised it with the strength of his two arms, the sound he made was like that of a rustling forest on a windy night. The churl brought the axe down, then, upon Cú Chulaind's neck—with the blade turned up. All the chieftains of Ulaid saw this.

"Rise, Cú Chulaind!" the churl then said. "Of all the warriors in Ulaid and Ériu, whatever their merit, none is your equal for courage and skill and honor. You are the supreme warrior of Ériu, and the champion's portion is yours, without contest; moreover, your wife will henceforth enter the drinking house before all the other women of Ulaid. Whoever might dispute this judgment, I swear by what my people swear by, his life will not be long." After that, the churl vanished. It was Cú Rui son of Dáre, who in that guise had come to fulfil the promise he had made to Cú Chulaind.

Illustrations from the Original Manuscript

In the manuscript in which *Sir Gawain and the Green Knight* appears the text is accompanied by four illustrations. Two of these are reproduced below. The first, which appears before the text in the original manuscript, brings together two scenes from the poem in a single illustration. Gawain is shown both taking the axe from King Arthur (who appears with the Queen on his left), and holding the axe (having just decapitated the Green Knight); the Green Knight is shown on horseback, holding his head.

In the second illustration reproduced here, the lady of the castle is shown visiting Gawain. (The two lines appearing above the illustration were written in a hand other than that of the manuscript scribe, and are not connected to the poem.)

The two illustrations not reproduced here are somewhat indistinct in the manuscript; they portray Gawain at the Green Chapel with the Green Knight above, axe in hand, and Gawain kneeling in front of Arthur and Guenevere.

The Thorn and the Yogh

The "original" text of *Sir Gawain and the Green Knight* as provided above substitutes modern English letters for two letters in Middle English that have now died out. One of these, the letter þ ("thorn"), was sounded very much as we sound the letters "th" today. The other, 3 ("yogh"), various represented sounds that we represent with "gh," "y," and "z." Following is the first part of the poem with Middle English letters.

> Siþþen þe sege and þe assaut watz sesed at Troye,
> Þe bor3 brittened and brent to bronde3 and askez,
> Þe tulk þat þe trammes of tresoun þer wro3t
> Watz tried for his tricherie, þe trewest on erþe:
> Hit watz Ennias þe athel, and his highe kynde,
> Þat siþþen depreced prouinces, and patrounes bicome
> Welne3e of al þe wele in þe west iles.
> Fro riche Romulus to Rome ricchis hym swyþe,
> With gret bobbaunce þat bur3e he biges vpon fyrst,
> And neuenes hit his aune nome, as hit now hat;
> Tirius to Tuskan and teldes bigynnes,
> Langaberde in Lumbardie lyftes vp homes,
> And fer ouer þe French flod Felix Brutus
> On mony bonkkes ful brode Bretayn he settez wyth wynne,
> Where werre and wrake and wonder
> Bi syþez hatz wont þerinne,
> And oft boþe blysse and blunder
> Ful skete hatz skyfted synne.

LOVE AND MARRIAGE IN MEDIEVAL BRITAIN
CONTEXTS

Most Old English literature focuses on the bonds between men, whether heroic retainers and their lords or pious saints and their God, and there seems to have been little interest in depicting domestic relationships and values. Even the elegiac lyric known as "The Wife's Lament" uses the language of heroic loyalty and service to express the female speaker's longing for her absent lover. Domestic life certainly existed, of course, and we may assume that men and women had various types of close and meaningful relationships; these did not, however, generally attract the interest of the authors of surviving literary works, at any rate not to the extent that they would fascinate later centuries. Apart from a few isolated passages, and the domestic scenes depicted from the peculiar perspective of the Exeter Book *Riddles*, the realm of private or personal feelings in the Anglo-Saxon period is closed to us. Several sets of laws from the early medieval period, however, give some sense of the social customs and attitudes surrounding marriage in the Anglo-Saxon world.

The literary traditions of courtly love that appeared in the south of France in the twelfth century spread rapidly throughout Europe, and had enormous impact both on literature and on the culture of European courts. It seems likely, however, that the ideology of romantic love was not shared by most members of society during this period; the early Middle English *Owl and the Nightingale* recounts, tongue in cheek, a debate on the moral implications of courtly love, and texts such as *Piers Plowman* convey some of the realities of love and marriage for the English in the later medieval period.

From its earliest days the Church had an interest in regularizing private behavior, but in general, marriage and divorce in the early medieval world appear to have been as much a matter of secular custom as of law or religion. With the Fourth Lateran Council of 1215 marriage procedures began much more widely to be brought under ecclesiastical control, but the status of marriage as one of the seven sacraments in the Roman Catholic Church was not firmly established until the late medieval period (at the Councils of Florence and of Trent in 1439 and 1547 respectively). Arranged marriages, often at a very young age, were common among the upper classes in the later medieval period, and the letter below concerning Elizabeth Paston's situation in the mid fifteenth century speaks to the seriousness of the consequences if the arrangements were resisted. Arranged marriages of this sort were almost certainly much less common among the peasantry, who constituted the vast majority of the population.

Evidence concerning same-sex love in the Middle Ages is for the most part scant and inconclusive. Specific accounts of sexual activity (such as that attributed to Robert Grosseteste) are rare—indeed, in the case of female same-sex sexual activity, entirely unknown. The term "sodomy" begins to be widely used by Christian theologians beginning in the eleventh and twelfth centuries, but it is often unclear precisely what sorts of activity are being condemned; the term often comes to be applied to all sexual practices that by their nature cannot lead to procreation (including masturbation), and even to heterosexual intercourse in an unconventional position. As the excerpts below from the letters of Anselm attest, expressions of same-sex love could be highly eroticized even when no explicitly sexual element was acknowledged.

The reputation the English acquired in later centuries as being less romantically inclined than, for example, the French or the Italians, may well have had no basis in fact in any age; the views on this matter expressed by an Italian traveler in the late fifteenth century may nevertheless be of interest.

⌘ ⌘ ⌘

Anglo-Saxon Laws

from the Laws of Æthelberht (c. 600 CE)

At the height of his power Æthelberht of Kent (560–616) controlled almost all of Britain south of the Humber River. With his permission Augustine of Canterbury began his missionary work during this period, and Æthelberht himself converted to Christianity, no doubt motivated in part by familiarity with the new faith: his wife Bertha was a Frankish Christian. His exposure to Christianity and the Latin culture that accompanied it was presumably the inspiration for the recording of his laws in writing, but Æthelberht's code of law contains few explicit references to Christianity. Æthelberht's laws were probably recorded some time around 600, though they survive only in a twelfth-century copy; they are the oldest extant vernacular laws in a Germanic language, and the earliest legal text from Britain. The laws set out an elaborate system of compensation for injury, varying according to the status of the injured person and the seriousness of the injury. Such monetary payments, called *wergild*, were meant to prevent the escalation of acts of revenge.

The translation is adapted from that of Dorothy Whitelock. See also Lisi Oliver, "The Laws of Æthelberht: A Student Edition," *Old English Newsletter* 38.1 (2004), 58–72, for a newly-edited text and very useful commentary.

16.   If anyone lies with a maiden belonging to the king, he is to pay 50 shillings compensation. If she is a grinding slave,[1] he is to pay 25 shillings compensation; [if a

slave of] the third [class], 12 shillings.

17.   The king's *fedesl*[2] is to be paid for with 20 shillings.

18.   If anyone kills a man on a nobleman's estate, he is to pay 12 shillings compensation.

19.   If anyone lies with a nobleman's serving-woman, he is to pay 12 shillings compensation.[3]

20.   A free peasant's protection is six shillings.

21.   If anyone lies with a free peasant's serving-woman, he is to pay six shillings compensation; [if] with a slave-woman of the second [class], 50 *sceattas*; [if with one of] the third [class], 30 *sceattas*.[4] …

31.   If a freeman lies with the wife of another freeman, he is to atone with his wergild,[5] and to obtain another wife with his own money, and bring her to the other's home. …

72.   If a freewoman with control of a household[6]

---

[2]   *fedesl*   The meaning of *fedesl* is not known; it may mean a boarder in the king's household, under royal protection. It may also refer to the duty of subjects to provide food and drink for the king; if one defaults on this obligation, he owes twenty shillings.

[3]   *If anyone … compensation*   I.e., to the nobleman, not the woman.

[4]   *sceattas*   In Kent at this period a *shilling* was a gold piece containing 20 sceattas; a *sceatta* was a smaller gold piece equal in weight to a grain of barley.

[5]   *his wergild*   Or "her wergild"; the Old English is ambiguous. *Wergild* is the monetary valuation placed on the worth of an individual in order to assign compensation in the event of wrongdoing.

[6]   The Old English words *friwif locbore* are not clearly understood. It has often been interpreted as referring to an unmarried young woman who did not need to bind up her hair; more recently it has been suggested that it refers to a woman "in charge of the locks," i.e.,

---

[1]   *grinding slave*   A "grinding slave" was presumably one whose job it was to prepare meal from grain; she had a higher status than a simple house slave, but a lower status than the king's own slaves.

commits any misconduct, she is to pay 30 shillings compensation.

73.   The compensation for [injury to] a maiden is to be as for a freeman.

74.   [Breach of] guardianship over a noble-born widow of the highest class is to be compensated for with 50 shillings; over one of the second class, with 20 shillings; over one of the third class, with 12 shillings; over one of the fourth, with six shillings.

75.   If a man takes a widow who does not belong to him, the [penalty for breach of the] guardianship is to be doubled.

76.   If anyone buys a maiden with a payment, if there is no fraud, then let the transaction stand. If, however, there is any fraud, she is to be taken back home, and he is to be given back his money. If she bears a living child, she is to inherit half the goods if her husband dies first. If she wishes to remain with the children,[1] she is to inherit half the goods. If she wishes to take [another] husband, [she is to inherit the same share] as a child. If she does not bear a child, [her] paternal kinsmen are to have [her] goods and the morning-gift.[2]

77.   If anyone carries off a maiden by force, [he is to pay] to the owner[3] 50 shillings, and afterwards buy from the owner his consent [to the marriage]. If she is betrothed to another man at a [bride] price, he is to pay 20 shillings compensation. If a return [of the woman] takes place, [he is to pay] 35 shillings, and 15 shillings to the king.

---

the provisions.

[1] *If she wishes to remain with the children*   I.e., after her husband's death. This phrase has sometimes been translated "if she wishes to go away with the children," but there is no real evidence for Anglo-Saxon divorce laws, and the sequence of ideas suggests that the translation offered here (which is that of Carole Hough in *Anglo-Saxon England* 23 [1994], 19–34, and Lisi Oliver) is more likely.

[2] *If she wishes to take … the morning-gift*   This apparently means that the dowry originally paid by her paternal kin is returned, and they also keep the "morning gift" given to her by her husband when the marriage has been consummated.

[3] *owner*   Or possibly "protector."

78.   If anyone lies with the woman of a poor freeman while her husband is alive, he is to pay a two-fold compensation.

from the Laws of Cnut (c. 1021)

Cnut (r. 1016–35) was a Danish prince who defeated Æthelred in 1016 to become king of England; he was also king of Denmark from 1018 until his death in 1035. He secured the goodwill of the English and minimized opposition to his reign through strong policy, generous patronage, and a marriage to Emma, the widow of Æthelred. His law code was drafted in part by the homilist and archbishop Wulfstan. Though there is a much stronger Christian presence in these laws than in those of Æthelberht from some four centuries earlier, there are many points of similarity; the increasing strictness in the laws concerning the sexual conduct of women, however, suggests that the state was taking a greater interest in regulating the moral lives of its subjects.

51.   If anyone commit adultery, let him make amends for it as the deed may be. It is a wicked adultery when a married man commits fornication with a single woman, and much worse with another's wife, or with a consecrated nun.

52.   If anyone commit incest, let him make amends for it according to the degree of kinship [between them] with wergild or punishment or [by the forfeiture] of all his possessions. The cases are by no means alike whether a man lie with a sister, or with a distant relative.

53.   If anyone rapes a widow, let him make amends for it with his wergild. If anyone rapes a maiden, let him make amends for it with his wergild.

54.   If a woman commits adultery with another man while her husband is alive, and it becomes public, she shall be disgraced, and let her lawful husband have all that she possesses; and let her then lose both her nose

and her ears: and if it be a prosecution,[1] and the attempt to refute it fails, let the bishop use his power, and judge severely.

55. If a married man commits adultery with his own slave, let him lose her, and make amends for himself to God and to men: and he who has a lawful wife, and also a concubine,[2] let no priest administer to him any of those rites which ought to be administered to a Christian man before he desist, and make amends as seriously as the bishop may instruct him; and let him ever afterwards desist from such things.

56. If foreigners will not correct their fornications,[3] let them be driven from the land with their possessions, departing in sin. ...

74. And let every widow continue husbandless for twelve months: afterwards let her choose what she wishes. And if she choooses a husband within the space of a year, then let her forfeit her morning-gift and all the possessions which she inherited through her first husband; and let the nearest kinsmen take the land and the possessions that she had before. And let the husband be liable for his wergild to the king, or to whomever has jurisdiction over him. And even if she is taken forcibly, let her forfeit the possessions, unless she be willing to go home again from the man, and never again be his. And let not a widow take the veil too hastily. And let every widow pay her heriot[4] without penalty within twelve months, unless it be convenient to her earlier.

75. And let no one compel either a woman or maiden to marry someone whom she herself dislikes, nor exchange her for money, unless he is willing to give anything voluntarily.[5]

"King Canute and Queen Aelfgyfu give the cross," from the *Liber Vitae* of New Minster (London, British Library, MS Stowe 944, Fol. 6r).

from the Canons of the Fourth Lateran Council (1215)

As discussed more fully elsewhere in this volume, the Fourth Lateran Council did much to regularize Christian law and practice. On the subject of marriage the Council devoted considerable space to

---

[1] *If a woman commit adultery ... prosecution* Presumably, if there is some doubt, as opposed to getting caught *in flagrante*.

[2] *lawful wife, and also a concubine* In the early Middle Ages a married man could legally have a concubine as a servant. Surprisingly, the church accepted such practices for many centuries, though it did not endorse them.

[3] *If foreigners will not correct their fornications* I.e., regularize their state as married couples.

[4] *heriot* A death-tax consisting of the return of the weapons with which a lord had outfitted his man. The heriot of a lesser-class thane in Wessex was a horse, its trappings, and a set of personal weapons (spear, shield, helmet, and coat of mail); in some parts of England this could be commuted into a cash payment.

[5] *And let no one compel ... unless he is willing to give anything voluntarily* I.e., unless a man is willing to offer money to the bride's family of his own accord.

the issue of consanguinity: to what degree should marriages between those related by blood be permitted? As the following articles detail, the Council was also at pains to extend and formalize the general authority of the church over marriage, and to combat the fairly widespread practice of priests having "wives" or concubines, a situation that, as the canon notes, was treated differently in different regions.

14. In order that the morals and general conduct of clerics may improve, let them all, particularly those in sacred orders, strive to live chastely and virtuously. Let them guard against every vice of desire, especially that on account of which the anger of God came from heaven upon the children of unbelief,[1] so that they may perform their duties in the sight of Almighty God with a pure heart and a chaste body. But lest the ease of obtaining pardon should become an incentive to do wrong, we decree that whoever may be found to indulge in the vice of incontinence shall, in proportion to the gravity of his sin, be punished in accordance with the canonical statutes. We command that these statutes be strictly and rigorously observed, so that if the fear of God does not restrain a man from evil, he may at least be held back from sin by an earthly punishment. If, therefore, anyone suspended for this reason should presume to celebrate the divine mysteries [i.e., perform mass], let him not only be deprived of his ecclesiastical benefices but for this twofold offense let him be forever deposed [from the priesthood]. Prelates who dare support such men in their iniquities, especially with an eye to money or other temporal advantages, shall be subject to a similar punishment. But those who, in accordance with the practice of their region, have not renounced the marriage bond should be punished more severely if they fall into the vice of impurity, since they can lawfully be married.

51. Since the prohibition against marriage in the three remotest degrees has been revoked, we wish it to be strictly observed in the other degrees. Following in the footsteps of our predecessors, we altogether forbid clandestine marriages and we forbid any priest to presume to be present at such a marriage. Extending the special custom of certain regions to other regions generally, we decree that when marriages are to be contracted they shall be publicly announced in the churches by priests, with a suitable time being fixed beforehand within which whoever wishes and is able to may adduce a lawful impediment. The priests themselves shall also investigate whether there is any impediment. When there appears a credible reason why the marriage should not be contracted, the contract shall be expressly forbidden until there has been established from clear documents what ought to be done in the matter. If any persons presume to enter into clandestine marriages of this kind, or forbidden marriages within a prohibited degree, even if done in ignorance, the offspring of the union shall be deemed illegitimate and shall have no help from their parents' ignorance, since the parents in contracting the marriage could be considered as not devoid of knowledge, or even as affecters of ignorance. Likewise the offspring shall be deemed illegitimate if both parents know of a legitimate impediment and yet dare to contract a marriage in the presence of the church, contrary to every prohibition. Moreover the parish priest who refuses to forbid such unions, or even any member of the regular clergy who dares to attend them, shall be suspended from office for three years and shall be punished even more severely if the nature of the fault requires it. Those who presume to be united in this way, even if it is within a permitted degree, are to be given a suitable penance. Anybody who maliciously proposes an impediment in order to prevent a legitimate marriage will not escape the church's vengeance.

---

[1] *children of unbelief* The inhabitants of Sodom and Gomorrah, whose destruction is told in Genesis 19.

Lancelot and Guinevere in bed, from
Le Livre de Lancelot del Lac (c. 1316, f. 312v).

from Andreas Capellanus, *The Art of Courtly Love* (c. 1180)

The Art of Courtly Love (in Latin, *De Amore*) was one of the most wide-ranging and influential treatises on the subject, although it should not be taken at face value as a depiction of social practices at the time. Andreas addressed the work to a young man named Walter, promising to make known to him "the way in which a state of love between two lovers may be kept unharmed, and likewise how those who do not love may get rid of the darts of Venus that are in their hearts." Little is known of Andreas himself, though he is believed to have been a chaplain with some connection to the court of Marie de Champagne. The work is divided into three books, the first of which offers a wide range of definitions and descriptions as well as a series of entertaining dialogues between men trying to seduce women and the women who cleverly fend them off, the second advice on how to behave in a love affair, and the third (under the heading "The Rejection of Love") reasons why one should in fact never conduct love affairs of the sort described in the second book.

from BOOK 1

Chapter 1. What Love Is

Love is a certain inborn suffering derived from the sight of and excessive meditation upon the beauty of the opposite sex, which causes each one to wish above all things the embraces of the other and by common desire to carry out all of love's precepts in the other's embrace.

Chapter 3. Where Love Gets Its Name

Love gets its name *(amor)* from the word for hook *(amus),* which means "to capture" or "to be captured," for he who is in love is captured in the chains of desire and wishes to capture someone else with his hook. Just as a skillful fisherman tries to attract fishes by his bait and to capture them on his crooked hook, so the man who is a captive of love tries to attract another person by his allurements and exerts all his efforts to unite two different hearts with an intangible bond, or if they are already united he tries to keep them so forever.

Chapter 4. What the Effect of Love Is

Now it is the effect of love that a true lover cannot be degraded with any avarice. Love causes a rough and uncouth man to be distinguished for his handsomeness; it can endow a man even of the humblest birth with nobility of character; it blesses the proud with humility; and the man in love becomes accustomed to performing many services gracefully for everyone. O what a wonderful thing is love, which makes a man shine with so many virtues and teaches everyone, no matter who he is, so many good traits of character! There is another thing about love that we should not praise in few words: it adorns a man, so to speak, with the virtue of chastity, because he who shines with the light of one love can hardly think of embracing another woman, even a beautiful one. For when he thinks deeply of his beloved the sight of any other woman seems to his mind rough and rude.

Chapter 8. The Love of Nuns

You may be interested enough to ask what we have to say regarding the love of nuns. What we say is that their solaces must be absolutely avoided just as though they were a pestilence of the soul, because from them comes the great wrath of our heavenly Father and the civil authorities are greatly stirred up and threaten the most severe punishments, and by all of this we become infamous among men and our good reputation is destroyed. Even Love's commandment warns us not to choose for our love any woman whom we may not properly seek to marry.[1] ...

Chapter 9. Love Got with Money

Now let us see whether real love can be got with money or any other gift. Real love comes only from the affection of the heart and is granted out of pure grace and genuine liberality, and this most precious gift of love cannot be paid for at any set price or be cheapened by a matter of money. If any woman is so possessed with a feeling of avarice as to give herself to a lover for the sake of pay, let no one consider her a lover, but rather a counterfeiter of love, who ought to join those shameful women in the brothel. Indeed the wantonness of such women is more polluted than the passion of harlots who ply their trade openly, for they do what one expects them to, and they deceive no one since their intentions are perfectly obvious. But those others who pretend to be fine ladies of the very best breeding force men to languish for love of them, and under the false veil of affection they gleefully rob of all their wealth those who have been smitten by Cupid's arrow. Men are deceived by their fallacious looks, outwitted by their crafty beckonings, and impelled by their clever and deceitful demands; they are kept busy giving them as many good things as they can, and they get more pleasure out of what they give away than from what they keep for their own use. These women have all sorts of ways of asking for things, and so long as they see that a man can respond to their greedy desire for gifts, they say that he is their adored lover, and they never cease to drain away his property or ruin him by their constant demands. But when his substance is gone and his patrimony is exhausted they despise and hate him and cast him aside like an unproductive bee, and then they begin to appear in their real colors. Any man who would seek for the love of women like these ought to be classed with shameless dogs and deserves no help from anybody. ...

Chapter 11. The Love of Peasants

But lest you should consider that what we have already said about the love of the middle class applies also to farmers, we will add a little about their love. We say that it rarely happens that we find farmers serving in Love's court, but naturally, like a horse or a mule, they give themselves up to the work of Venus, as nature's urging teaches them to do. For a farmer hard labor and the uninterrupted solaces of plough and mattock are sufficient. And even if it should happen at times, though rarely, that contrary to their nature they are stirred up by Cupid's arrows, it is not expedient that they should be instructed in the theory of love, lest while they are devoting themselves to conduct which is not natural to them the kindly farms which are usually made fruitful by their efforts may through lack of cultivation prove useless to us. And if you should, by some chance, fall in love with some of their women, be careful to puff them up with lots of praise and then, when you find a convenient place, do not hesitate to take what you seek and to embrace them by force. For you can hardly soften their outward inflexibility so far that they will grant you their embraces quietly or permit you to have the solaces you desire unless first you use a little compulsion as a convenient cure for their shyness. We do not say these things, however, because we want to persuade you to love such women, but only so that, if through lack of caution you should be driven to love them, you may know, in brief compass, what to do.

from BOOK 2: THE RULES OF LOVE

1. Marriage is no real excuse for not loving.
2. He who is not jealous cannot love.
3. No one can be bound by a double love.
4. It is well known that love is always increasing or decreasing.
5. That which a lover takes against the will of his beloved has no relish.
6. Boys do not love until they arrive at the age of maturity.

---

[1] *Even Love's commandment ... properly seek to marry* As will become clear below, Andreas does not here include women who are already married; instead, he means those whom, for reasons of class, religious status, or moral shortcomings, a man would avoid marrying on principle.

7.   When one lover dies, a widowhood of two years is required of the survivor.

8.   No one should be deprived of love without the very best of reasons.

9.   No one can love unless he is impelled by the persuasion of love.

10.   Love is always a stranger in the home of avarice.

11.   It is not proper to love any woman whom one should be ashamed to seek to marry.

12.   A true lover does not desire to embrace in love anyone except his beloved.

13.   When made public love rarely endures.

14.   The easy attainment of love makes it of little value; difficulty of attainment makes it prized.

15.   Every lover regularly turns pale in the presence of his beloved.

16.   When a lover suddenly catches sight of his beloved his heart palpitates.

17.   A new love puts to flight an old one.

18.   Good character alone makes any man worthy of love.

19.   If love diminishes, it quickly fails and rarely revives.

20.   A man in love is always apprehensive.

21.   Real jealousy always increases the feeling of love.

22.   Jealousy, and therefore love, are increased when one suspects his beloved.

23.   He whom the thought of love vexes, eats and sleeps very little.

24.   Every act of a lover ends with in the thought of his beloved.

25.   A true lover considers nothing good except what he thinks will please his beloved.

26.   Love can deny nothing to love.

27.   A lover can never have enough of the solaces of his beloved.

28.   A slight presumption causes a lover to suspect his beloved.

29.   A man who is vexed by too much passion usually does not love.

30.   A true lover is constantly and without intermission possessed by the thought of his beloved.

31.   Nothing forbids one woman being loved by two men or one man by two women.

Anonymous, Images of Troubadours: illustrations for a song by Bernart de Ventadorn (13th century). The figure here is believed to be Bernart.

from *The Owl and the Nightingale* (late 12th century)

The Owl and the Nightingale is a long poem touching on three topics: questions of religion, questions of fortune (with particular reference to astrological portents), and questions of love and marriage. In the debate between the two on this third topic the Owl represents herself as the defender of traditional marriage and attempts to characterize the Nightingale as a source of the sort of romantic love through which young maidens are ruined. In the discussion it becomes clear, however, that the distinctions between the two points of view are not always clear-cut.

The Owl was now angry, ready for battle, and after this speech she rolled her eyes. "You say that you guard the dwellings of men where there are leaves and beautiful flowers, and where two lovers lie in bed, well protected in each other's arms. Once you sang—I know well where—near to a dwelling. You told the lady of unlawful love and, with song high and low, taught her to abandon herself to a shameful and evil passion. Her lord, soon seeing how things were, set bird-lime and snares and many other things in order to capture you. You soon came to the window, and you were caught in a trap.[1] Your legs paid the price: the doom decreed was none other than that you should be torn asunder by wild horses. Try again, then, if you can, to seduce either wife or maiden; your singing, indeed, may prove so successful that you shall flutter helplessly in a snare!" …

[The Nightingale says:] "… You vile creature, you hide and reproach me viciously for singing near the dwellings of men and teaching wives to break their vows. You lie for certain, you loathsome creature! I have never harmed marriage. Yet I sing and declaim where there are ladies and fair maidens, and it is also true that I sing of love. For a virtuous wife can, in her married state, love her own husband far better than any philanderer, and a maiden can take a lover without loss of honor, loving with true affection the man to whom she grants her favor. Such love as this I teach and commend; this is the sense of all my utterances. But if a woman is weak of will—for women are soft-hearted by nature—so that through the wiles of a fool, who eagerly entreats her with many a sad sigh, she happens to go astray and do wrong on occasion, should I in that case be held to blame? If women love in foolish ways, am I to be scolded for their misdeeds? Even if a woman is bent on a secret love, I cannot nevertheless refrain from singing. A woman may frolic as she will, either honestly or viciously, and as a result of my song, she may do as she will, either well or badly. For there is nothing in the wide world so good that it may not do evil if turned to wrong uses. Gold and silver, for instance, are always valuable, yet one can use them to pay for adultery and

other such crimes. Weapons, again, are useful in keeping the peace, yet men are unlawfully killed with them in lands where they are used by thieves. And so it is with my singing: though it be chaste, it can still be abused and connected with foolish and evil deeds. But must you, wretched creature, speak evil of love? All love between man and woman, of whatever kind it may be, is pure unless it be stolen; in that case it is impure and also corrupt. May the wrath of the Holy Cross descend upon those who thus transgress the laws of nature! It is strange that they do not go mad—yet indeed they do, for they are mad who go to brood without a nest. Women's flesh is weak, and since carnal lust is hard to crush, it is no wonder that it persists. But even if fleshly lusts make women stray, not all those who trip at the stumbling-block of the flesh are completely lost. For many a woman who has gone wrong rises again out of the mire.

"Nor are all sins quite the same; they are, indeed, of two different kinds. One is the fruit of carnal lust: the other, of the spiritual nature. For whereas the flesh leads men to drunkenness, to sloth and also to wantonness, the spirit goes wrong through malice and anger, and through the joy felt at another's shame. It also longs for more and more, having little regard for mercy and grace: and, ascending on high through haughtiness, it proudly disdains what is below. Tell me truly, if you can, which is worse, the flesh or the spirit? You may answer, if you like, that the flesh is the less evil, for many a man is pure of body, who in his heart is of a devilish nature. No man should therefore loudly condemn a woman, rebuking her for the lusts of the flesh; he may blame her for wantonness while he indulges in the greater sin of pride.

"Yet if through my singing I cause a wife or maiden to fall in love, I would take the side of the maiden—if you can grasp my meaning correctly. Listen now and I'll tell you why, the whole reason from beginning to end. If a maiden loves secretly, she stumbles and falls according to nature, for though she may frolic for a time, she has not gone very far astray. She can escape lawfully from her sin through the rites of the church, and afterwards have her lover as husband, free from all blame, and in the full light of day go to the man whom before she had received under cover of darkness. A young maiden knows nothing about such things; her

---

[1]   *You soon came … caught in a trap*   This story is told in a slightly different form in Marie de France's "Laüstic," below, as well as in other medieval texts.

young blood leads her astray, and some foolish fellow entices her to evil with all the tricks at his command. He comes and goes, he commands and entreats, he pays her attention, then neglects her, and sighs after her often and persistently. How can the girl help but go wrong? She never knew what things were, and so she thought she would experiment, and learn for certain of the sport that tames high spirits. And when I see the drawn expression which love gives to the young maid, I cannot refrain, out of sheer pity, from singing to her some song of cheer. Thus do I teach them by my singing, that love of this kind does not last long. For my song is short-lived, and love merely alights upon such girls; it soon passes, and the hot passion quickly subsides. I sing with them for a while; I begin high and end low, and after a time I cease completely. The maiden knows, when I have finished, that love is just like my singing, for it is but a brief excitement that soon comes and soon goes. The girl understands things through me, and her naivety is turned to wisdom. She sees clearly from my song that unbridled love does not last long.

"But I want you to know that I find hateful the lapses of wives. And if a married woman will take note of me, she will see that I do not sing in the breeding season. Though marriage bonds may seem harsh, a wife should ignore the teaching of fools. And to me it appears most astounding, how a man could find it in his heart to wrong another's wife. For it means one of two alternatives; there can be no other possibility. Either, on the one hand, the husband is worthy; or else he is feeble and of no account. If he is honored and courageous, no man who is wise will wish to shame him, especially through his wife, for he will fear the good man's anger and the loss of his thing that dangles down there. And even if he is not afraid of that, yet it is wicked and extremely stupid to injure a worthy in this way and lure his partner away from him. If, on the other hand, the husband is a failure, feeble in bed and at the table, how could there be any love when such a churl's body lies on top of her? How can there be any sort of love, when such a man is pawing her thigh? From this you can to see clearly that in one case there is sorrow, in the other, disgrace, as a result of stealing another man's wife. For if her husband is a brave man, you can look out for trouble when lying by her side, and if the husband be

good for nothing, what pleasure can be derived from the deed? If you remember who lies with her, you will pay for her favors with loathing. I do not know how any man with self-respect can make advances to her after that. If he thinks about whom he's lying beside, all his love will immediately vanish."

The Owl was glad to hear these words, for she thought that the Nightingale, though she had argued well to begin with, had in the end come to grief. And so she exclaimed, "Now I can see that maidens are your special interest; you take their side, defending them and praising them beyond all reason. The married women turn to me: to me they make their complaints. For it very often happens that a husband and wife are at odds, and so the man goes astray and takes delight in loose living, spending all the money he has on another woman, making love to one without claim on him, and leaving his lawful wife at home with bare walls and an empty house, leaving her, too, thinly clad and poorly fed, without food and without clothing. And when he comes home to his wife again, she dare not utter a single word: he storms and shouts like a madman—and this is all the kindness he brings. All that she does merely annoys him, all that she says is utterly wrong, and often when she does nothing amiss, her reward is his fist in her teeth. There is no man living who cannot send his wife astray by such treatment. Such a one may be so often maltreated that on occasion she may consult her own pleasure. God knows she cannot help it even if she makes a cuckold of him. For it happens, time and again that the wife is tender and gentle, fair of face and of good figure, and this only makes it the more unjust that he should shower his love on one who is not worth a hair of her head. And there are plenty of men who do not know how to treat their wives properly. No man can speak to her, for he thinks that she is at any moment about to betray him if she so much as looks at a man or speaks sweetly to him. And so he puts her under lock and key, with the result that marriage ties are often broken, for if she is brought to such a pass, she does what before she never thought of. A curse on anyone who talks too much, if such wives proceed to avenge themselves.

"Wives complain to me concerning this matter, and they grieve me sadly. My heart, indeed, almost breaks when I see their great distress. I weep bitter tears with them, and pray that Christ shall have mercy on them, so that he may quickly help the wife, and send her a better husband. And moreover I can tell you this, that you shall find no answer to what I have said , even to save your skin; all your talking shall now be futile. Many a merchant and many a knight loves and cherishes his wife properly, and so does many a peasant. And then the good wife behaves accordingly, rendering him service at bed and at table, with gentle deeds and kindly words, anxiously striving how to please him." …

Royal Couples

For the first century and a half after the Norman conquest most English monarchs were buried in their French territories, not their English ones. The first illustration below shows the tombs at the abbey of Fontevrault of Henry II (on the right), Eleanor of Aquitaine (in the center), and their son Richard I the Lion-Hearted (on the left). Eleanor and Henry's son John, who also became king of England, was buried at Worcester Cathedral, but the tomb of his wife, Isabella of Angoulême, is at Fontevrault.

The second illustration is of two of the Lewes chess pieces, found on the island of Lewes in Scotland's Outer Hebrides in the early nineteenth century. Carvings in the same style have also been found in Scandinavia and East Anglia; it is not known whether the carvings were made in Scandinavia or in Britain.

The tombs of the Plantagenets at Fotrevault.

Lewes Chess Pieces: King and Queen (12th century).

from *The Paston Letters*

A large body of the fifteenth-century correspondence of the Paston family of Norfolk has survived; it is a rich source of information about many aspects of English life in this period.

The first of the two letters below concerns twenty-year old Elizabeth Paston (referred to by the letter-writer, Elizabeth Clere, as "my cousin your sister"), whose family wished her to marry fifty-year old Stephen Scrope. (In the end the marriage did not occur, though at one point Elizabeth indicated a willingness to accede to the family's demands.)

The second letter concerns the clandestine marriage a generation later of Margery Paston to Richard Calle, the family steward. Such marriages were deeply disapproved of, particularly when, as in this case, there was a considerable difference in social standing between the two participants. The church did consider such unions to be valid, however, unless it could be shown after the fact that some "impediment" existed, such as the two being too closely related or one being already married.

from Letter from Agnes Paston to her son John Paston I (not later than 1449)

Son, I greet you well with God's blessing and mine and to let you know that my cousin [Elizabeth] Clere wrote to me that she has spoken with [Stephen] Scrope after he had been with me at Norwich, and told her what hospitality I had given him, and he said to her he very much liked the reception I gave him.

He told my cousin Clere that unless you gave him a warm reception and comforting words at London, he would speak no more of the matter.

My cousin Clere thinks that it would be folly to forsake him unless you knew of another as good or better; and I have consulted your sister and I've never found her so willing toward anyone as she is to him, if it be the case that his land stands clear.[1] ...

Soon, I grete ȝow wel wyth Goddys blyssyng and myn; and I latte ȝow wette þat my cosyn Clere wrytted to me þat sche spake wyth Schrowpe aftyre þat he had byen wyth me at Norwyche, and tolde here what chere þat I had made hym; and he seyde to here he lyked wel by þe chere þat I made hym. He had swyche wordys to my cosyn Clere þat lesse þan ȝe made hym good chere and ȝaf hym wordys of conforth at London he wolde no more speke of þe matyre. My cosyn Clere thynkyth þat it were a foly to forsake hym lesse þan ȝe knew of on owdyre as good ore bettere, and I haue assayde ȝowre sustere and I fonde here neuer so wylly to noon as sche is to hym, ȝyf it be so þat his londe stande cleere. I sent ȝow a letter by Brawnton fore sylke and fore þis matyre be-fore my cosyn Clere wrote to me, þe qwyche was wrytten on þe Wednysday nexȝt aftyre Mydsomere Day. Ser Herry Ynglows is ryȝth besy a-bowt Schrowpe fore on of his doȝthteres. I prey ȝow fore-ȝette noȝth to brynge me my mony fro Horwelbery as ȝe com fro London, edyre all ore a grete parte. þe dew dette was at Crystemesse last paste, no thynge a-lowyd, vij li. xiiij s. viij d., and at þis Mydsomere it is v li. more; and thow I a-low hym all his askyng it is but xxvj s. vj d. lesse, but I am noȝth so avysyth ȝytt. As fore þe frere, he hath byen at Sent Benettys and at Norwyche, and made grete bowste of þe sewte þat he hath a-ȝens me, and bowȝthe

many boxes, to what jntent I wett neuer. It is well doen to be ware at London in drede ȝyf he bryng ony syse at Sent Margaretys tyme. I kan no more, but Almȝty God be owre good lorde, who have ȝow euer in kepyng. Wryten at Oxnede in grete hast on þe Satyr-[day] next aftyre Mydsomere. By ȝowre modyre A. P.

from Letter from Richard Calle to Margery Paston (1469)

My own lady and mistress, and before God my very true wife, with a heart full of sorrow I recommend me to you, as one that cannot be merry, nor shall be until it be otherwise with us than it now is. For this life that we now lead is neither pleasing to God nor to the world, considering the great bond of matrimony that is between us, and also the great love that has been, and I trust is still between us, and on my part has never been greater. On this account I beseech almighty God to comfort us as soon as it pleases him, for we who ought by right to be together are torn apart; it seems to me that it is a thousand years since I spoke with you. I would rather be with you than have all the goods in the world. Alas, alas, good lady, consider little them and what they do to keep us apart. Four times in the year they who obstruct matrimony are cursed. It causes many men to reflect inwardly who have a great conscience in matters other than matrimony. But, lady, suffer as you must and make merry as you can, for certainly, lady, in the long run God will from his righteousness help his servants who mean well and wish to live according to his laws, etc.

I understand, lady, that you have had as much sorrow for me as any gentlewoman has had in the world. I wish to God that all the sorrow that you have had rested upon me, so that you would be free of it. For certainly, lady, it is like death for me to hear that you are being treated otherwise than you ought to be. This is a painful life that we lead. I cannot live thus without it being a great displeasure to God.

Also, I would like you to know that I had sent you a letter from London by my lad, and he told me he was not allowed to speak with you, and was made to wait there for you a long time. He told me that John Thresh-

---

[1] *land stands clear* I.e., is not pledged as collateral on a debt.

er came to him in your name and said that you sent him to my lad for a letter or a token which I should have sent you. But he didn't trust him and he would not deliver anything to him. After that he brought him a ring, saying that you sent it to him, commanding him that he should deliver the letter or token to him, which I have affirmed by my lad was not sent by you, but was sent by my mistress and on Sir James Gloys' advice. Alas, what do they intend? I suppose that they consider us not to be pledged together. And if they think that, I am amazed, for then they are not well advised, remembering the plainness with which I broke the matter to my mistress at the very beginning, and I suppose by you as well, if you did as you ought to have done by right. And if you have done the contrary, as I have been informed you have done, you did it neither from conscience nor to God's pleasure, unless you did it from fear and to please for the time those who were around you. And if you did so for this reason it was a reasonable cause, considering the great and unbearable demands you had, and the many untrue tales being told you about me, which God knows I was never guilty of.

My lad told me that my mistress your mother asked him if he had brought any letter to you, and she insinuated many other things to him. Among all the others she said to him, that I would not tell her about it at the beginning but she supposed I would at the end. And as to that, God knows she knew of it first from me and no other. I do not know what her ladyship means, for upon my word there is no gentlewoman alive whom my heart cherishes more than her, nor is more loathe to displease, except only your person, which by right I ought to cherish and love best, for I am bound to you by the law of God, and so I will do while I am alive, whatsoever results from it. I suppose if you told them plainly the truth they would not damn their souls for us. Although I tell them the truth, they will not believe me as well as they will you. And therefore, good lady, at the reverence of God be plain to them and tell the truth. And if they will by no means agree to it, it will be between God, the devil, and them, and the peril that we should be in, I beg God that it may lie on them and not upon us. I am grieving and sorry to remember their disposition. God send them grace to guide all things

well, as well as I wish they did. God be their guide, and send them peace and rest, etc.

I marvel greatly that they should take this matter so hard, as I understand they do, remembering that it is a situation that cannot be remedied. My desire on behalf of everyone is for it to be thought there is no obstacle against it and also that their honor is not in your marriage; it is in their own marriage, which I pray God send them such as may be to their honor and pleasing to God, and to ease their hearts, for otherwise it would be a great pity. Mistress, I am afraid to write to you, for I understand you have shown my letters that I have sent you previously, but I ask you to let no one see this letter. As soon as you have read it, let it be burned for I wish that no man should see it in any way. You have had no letters from me for these two years, nor will I send you any more. Therefore I send this whole matter to your wisdom. Almighty Jesus preserve, keep, and give you your heart's desire, which I know well to be God's pleasure, etc.

This letter was written with as great pain as was anything I ever wrote, I think, in my whole life, for in good faith I have been sick and am not yet very well recovered, God amend it, etc.

from William Langland, *The Vision of Piers the Plowman* (late 14th century)

Langland's fiercely satirical poem speaks out against many abuses, including the corruption of many members of the clergy, and also comments on many aspects of the social world of his time, from professions to education to church practice. The following excerpt discusses and offers advice concerning love and marriage, and shows an approval of and interest in ordinary married people ("true wedded living folk") that is in line with much of the poem's view of the laity as potential models of Christian behavior, although, typically for Langland, it also has much to say about lay failings.

In this world is Do-well true wedded living folk,
For they mote° work and win and the world   *must*
sustain.

For of hir° kind they come that confessors   *this*
    been nempned°,   *called*
Kings and knights, kaysers° and clerks,°   *rulers / clerics*
5   Maidens and martyrs—out of one man come.
The wife was made the wye° for to help work,   *man*
And thus was wedlock wrought with a mene°   *intermediary*
    person—
First by the father's will and the friends' counsel,
And sithenes° by assent of himself, as they two   *then*
    might accord,°   *agree*
10   And thus was wedlock wrought, and God himself
    it made;°   *made it*
In earth the heaven is—himself was the witness.
    Ac° false folk faithless, thieves and liars,   *but*
Wasters and wretches out of wedlock, I trowe,°   *believe*
Conceived been in evil time, as Cain was on Eve.
15   Of switch° sinful shrews° the   *such / wretches*
    Sauter° maketh mind: *psalter*
Concepit dolorem et peperit iniquitatem[1]
And all that come of that Cain[2] come to evil end.
    For God sent to Seth and said by° an angel,   *through*
'Thine issue in thine issue, I will that they be wedded,
20   And not thy kind with Cain's coupled ne° spoused.'   *nor*
Yet some, against the sonde° of our   *commandment*
    saviour of heaven,
Cain's kind and his° kind coupled together—   *their*
Till God wrathed° with hir° works, and   *grew angry / their*
    such a word said,
'That I maked man, now it me forthinketh.'[3]
25   *Penitet me fecisse hominem.*'[4]
    And came to Noah anon° and bade him   *at once*
    nought let:[5]
'Swith° go shape a ship of shides° and   *quickly / planks*
    of boards.
Thyself and thy sons three and sithen your wifes,
Busketh° you to that boat and bideth° therein   *hurry / stay*
30   Till forty days be fulfilled, that flood have washed

Clean away the cursed blood° that Cain   *lineage*
    hath maked.
    'Beasts that now been shall ban° the time   *curse*
That ever that cursed Cain come on this earth.
All shall die for his deeds by dales and hills,
35   And the fowls that fly forth with other beasts,
Except oonliche° of each kind a couple   *only*
That in thy shingled ship shall be saved.'
    Here abought° the bairns the belsires'   *paid for*
    guilts,°   *ancestors' sins*
And all for hir forefathers they fared the worst.
40   The gospel is hereagainst in o degree,[6] I find:
Filius non portabit iniquitatem patris et pater non portabit
    iniquitatem filii.[7]
Ac I find, if the father be false and a shrew,°   *wretch*
That somdel° the son shall have the sire's   *somewhat*
    tacches.°   *qualities*
Impe° on an alder, and if thine apple be sweet   *graft*
45   Muchel° marvel me thinketh; and more of a shrew   *much*
That bringeth forth any bairn, but if he be the same
And have a savour after the sire —selde seestow other:[8]
Numquam colligunt de spinis uvas nec de tribulis ficus.[9]
    And thus through cursed Cain came care°   *trouble*
    upon earth,
50   And all for° they wrought wedlock against   *because*
    God's will.
Forthi have they maugre of their marriages, that marry
    so their children.[10]
For some, as I see now, sooth° for to tell   *truth*
For coveting of cattle unkindly been wedded.[11]
As careful° conception cometh of swich   *sorrowful*
    marriages

---

[1] *Concepit dolorem et peperit iniquitatem* Latin: He has conceived sorrow, and brought forth iniquity.

[2] *all that come of that Cain* All of Cain's descendants.

[3] *it me forthinketh* I regret it.

[4] *Penitet me fecisse hominem* Latin: I regret that I created humankind.

[5] *bade him nought let* Told him not to delay.

[6] *hereagainst in o degree* Against this in one way.

[7] *Filius non portabit iniquitatem patris et pater non portabit iniquitatem filii* The son shall not bear the father's iniquity, and the father shall not carry the son's iniquity.

[8] *have a savour ... other* Taste like (i.e., have qualities like) his parent—you seldom see [it happen] otherwise.

[9] *Numquam colligunt de spinis uvas nec de tribulis ficus* Latin: Men never gather grapes from thorn bushes, or figs from thistles.

[10] *Forthi ... their children* Thus those who allow their children to be married in this way will be blamed for their marriages.

[11] *For coveting of cattle unkindly been wedded* Out of a desire for wealth have married unnaturally.

55 As befell other folk that I before of told.[1]
   For good should wed good, though° they no   *even if*
       goods have;
   'I am *via et veritas*,'[2] saith Christ. 'I may advance all.'
       It is an uncomely couple, by Christ! as me
           thinketh–
   To yeven° a young wench to an old feeble°   *give / weak man*
60 Or wed any widow for wealth of her goods
   That never shall bairn bear but if it be in arms![3]
   In jealousy joyless and jangling° on bed,   *quarreling*
   Many a pair sithen° the pestilence have   *since*
       plight° them together.   *joined*
   The fruits that they bring forth are many foul words;
65 Have they no children but cheeste° and   *fighting*
       chops° them between …   *blows*
       Forthi° I counsel all Christians covet not [to] be   *therefore*
           wedded
   For coveting of cattle ne of kindred rich;
   Ac maidens and maydens,° match you   *bachelors*
       together;
   Widowers and widows, work the same;
70 For no lands, but for love, look ye be wedded,
   And then get ye the grace of God, and goods enough to
       live with.
       And every manner secular° that may not   *layperson*
           continue [chaste],
   Wisely go wed, and ware° him[4] from sin;   *guard*
   For lechery in liking is limeyard of hell.[5]
75 Whiles thou art young, and thy weapon keen,°   *sharp*
   Wreak° thee with wiving, if thou   *give vent to [your lust]*
       will be excused;[6]
   Dum sis vir fortis, ne des tua robora scortis.

Scribitur in portis, meretrix est ianua mortis.[7]
   "When you have wived, be wary, and work in
       time[8] —
80 Not as Adam and Eve when Cain was engendered.
   For in un-time, truly, between man and woman
   Ne should no bed-board be: but if they both were clean
   Of life and in soul, and in law also,
   That ilk derne° deed do no man ne should.   *private, secret*
85 Ac if they lead thus their life, it liketh° God   *pleases*
       almighty,
   For he made wedlock first and himself it said:
   *Bonum est ut unusquisque uxorem suam habeat propter
       fornicacionem.*[9]
       "That othergates been gotten, for gedelings are
           holden,[10]
   And false folk, fondlings,° faitours° and   *bastards / deceivers*
       liars,
90 Ungracious° to get good or love of the   *unsuccessful (at)*
       people;
   Wander and waste what they catch mowe.°   *can acquire*
   Against Do-well they do evil and the devil serve,
   And after hir death-day shall dwell with the same
   But° God give them grace here themselves to   *unless*
       amend."

from Robert Grosseteste (attr.), *Speculum Confessionis* (early 13ᵗʰ century)

The work on confession in which the following passages appear is attributed to Robert Grosseteste, Bishop of Lincoln from 1235 to 1253. One of the most important thinkers and church leaders of his day, he left important writings in both science and theology and demanded a high level of learning

---

[1] *As befell other folk that I before of told* As happened to the people that I told of before (i.e., those that were destroyed in the Flood).

[2] *via et veritas* Latin: the way and the truth.

[3] *never shall bairn bear but if it be in arms* Never shall bear a child except by carrying it in her arms.

[4] *ware him* Guard himself from.

[5] *For lechery … of hell* For taking pleasure in lechery is the snare of hell.

[6] *if thou will be excused* If you want an excuse [for your lustful behavior].

---

[7] *Dum sis vir fortis, ne des tua robora scortis. Scribitur in portis, meretrix est ianua mortis* Latin: While you are a strong man, do not give your strength to harlots. For as it is written on the gates, a harlot is the entrance to death.

[8] *work in time* Have sex at the proper time.

[9] *Bonum est ut unusquisque uxorem suam habeat propter fornicacionem* Latin: It is good that every man have his own wife in order to avoid fornication.

[10] *That othergates … holden* Those who are otherwise begotten (i.e., are born out of wedlock) are considered vagabonds.

from the clergy under his direction. The *Speculum* reflects the self-scrutiny that confession required of the penitent.

Often I stroked forbidden members, shameful members, both on me and on others ... often I returned my hand to my lap, caressing the flesh and weakening it and rendering it more prone to titillation and excitement from touches of this kind. [...] I also oftentimes provoked others to evil, either by a light touch or more brashly and irreverently, because I exposed myself to him, showing him my erection, or by a gesture of my body, or by some other means which is too disgusting to mention, whence those who were previously innocent afterwards, at my provocation, were violently tempted or perhaps cast down, and this because of me.

from Eadmer, *The Life of Saint Anselm* (early 12th century)

Anselm of Bec, who was born in Italy, later became abbot at a monastery in Normandy, Archbishop of Canterbury, and one of the most respected theologians of the age. Anselm was a defender of the then-common practice of oblation, in which families placed children in the care of religious houses as oblates or "offerings"—a move that was generally binding on the child for life. He was also, however, a voice of moderation on the issue of how the boys should be treated.

The language that Anselm and other monks sometimes employed with one another may strike modern readers as homoerotic, but would probably not have been read in the same fashion in the eleventh or early twelfth centuries. Anselm sometimes used a similarly fervid devotional style both in addressing female correspondents and in speaking of the Virgin Mary—and numerous others followed his lead. The wording of the Benedictine Rule, however, is perhaps an indication that the possibility of overtly sexual behavior between males was tacitly acknowledged.

1.4 *How he left his native land because of his father's great hostility to him*

From that time, with health of body, youth, and worldly well-being smiling upon him, he began little by little to cool in the fervor of his desire for a religious life—so much so that he began to desire to go the way of the world rather than to leave the world for a monastic life. He gradually turned from study, which had formerly been his chief occupation, and began to give himself up to youthful amusements. His love and reverence for his mother held him back to some extent from these paths, but she died and then the ship of his heart had as it were lost its anchor and drifted almost entirely among the waves of the world. But almighty God, foreseeing what he was going to make of him, stirred up for him a hateful and domestic strife, lest in enjoying a transitory peace he should lose his soul. That is to say, he stirred up in his father's mind so keen a hatred against him that he persecuted him as much, or even more, for the things he did well as for those which he did ill. Nor could he soften his father by any degree of humility, but the more humble he showed himself towards his father, the sharper did he feel his father's anger towards him. When he saw that this was becoming more than he could bear, he feared that worse might come of it, and he chose rather to renounce both his patrimony and his country than to bring some disgrace upon either himself or his father by continuing to live with him. He gathered together those things that were necessary for the journey, and left his country, with a clerk as his companion and servant. As they were crossing Mount Cenis, he grew weary and his strength failed him, being unequal to the toil. He tried to revive himself by eating snow, for there was nothing else at hand that he could eat. His servant was grieved to see this and began to make a careful search in the bag that was carried on the ass's back to see if by chance there was anything to eat. Soon, against all expectation, he found some bread of exceptional whiteness and, having eaten and been refreshed, Anselm set out once more on the road with renewed strength....

1.11 *The reason for his giving more attention to the training of young men than of others*

Nevertheless his chief care was for the youths and young men, and when men asked him why this was, he replied by way of a simile. He compared the time of youth to a piece of wax of the right consistency for the impress of a seal. "For if the wax," he said, "is too hard or too soft it will not, when stamped with the seal, receive a perfect image. But if it preserves a mean between these extremes of hardness and softness, when it is stamped with the seal, it will receive the image clear and whole. So it is with the ages of men. Take a man who has been sunk in the vanity of this world from infancy to extreme old age, knowing only earthly things, and altogether set in these ways. Converse with such a man about spiritual things, talk to him about the fine points of divine contemplation, show him how to explore heavenly mysteries, and you will find he cannot see the things you wish him to. And no wonder. He is the hardened wax; his life has not moved in these paths; he has learnt to follow other ways. Now consider a boy of tender years and little knowledge, unable to distinguish between good and evil, or even to understand you when you talk about such things. Here indeed the wax is soft, almost liquid, and incapable of taking an image of the seal. Between these extremes is the youth and young man, aptly tempered between the extremes of softness and hardness. If you teach him, you can shape him as you wish. Realizing this, I watch over the young men with greater solicitude, taking care to nip all their faults in the bud, so that being afterwards properly instructed in the practice of holy exercises they may form themselves in the image of a spiritual man." ...

1.22 *Concerning the discretion that he taught a certain abbot to practice toward boys who were being educated in his school*

On one occasion then, a certain abbot, who was considered to be a sufficiently religious man, was talking with him about matters of monastic discipline, and among other things he said something about the boys brought up in the cloister, adding: "What, I ask you, is to be done with them? They are incorrigible ruffians.

We never give over beating them day and night, and they only get worse and worse." Anselm replied with astonishment: "You never give over beating them? And what are they like when they grow up?" "Stupid brutes," he said. To which Anselm retorted, "You have spent your energies in rearing them to good purpose: from men you have reared beasts." "But what can we do about it?" he said. "We use every means to force them to get better, but without success." "You force them? Now tell me, my lord abbot, if you plant a tree-shoot in your garden, and straightway shut it in on every side so that it has no space to put out its branches, what kind of tree will you have in after years when you let it out of its confinement?" "A useless one, certainly, with its branches all twisted and knotted." "And whose fault would this be, except your own for shutting it in so unnaturally? Without doubt, this is what you do with your boys. At their oblation they are planted in the garden of the church, to grow and bring forth fruit for God. But you terrify them and hem them in on all sides with threats and blows so that they are utterly deprived of their liberty. And being thus injudiciously oppressed, they harbor and welcome and nurse within themselves evil and crooked thoughts like thorns, and cherish these thoughts so passionately that they doggedly reject everything which could minister to their correction. Hence, feeling no love or pity, good-will or tenderness in your attitude towards them, they have in future no faith in your goodness but believe that all your actions proceed from hatred and malice against them. The deplorable result is that as they grow in body so their hatred increases, together with their apprehension of evil, and they are forward in all crookedness and vice. They have been brought up in no true charity towards anyone, so they regard everyone with suspicion and jealousy." ...

from Letters of Anselm to fellow monks (late 11th century)

Brother Anselm to Dom Gilbert, brother, friend, beloved lover [*dilecto dilectori*] ... sweet to me, sweetest friend, are the gifts of sweetness, but they cannot begin to console my desolate heart for want of your love. Even if you sent every scent of perfume, every glitter of metal, every precious gem, every texture of clothes, still it would not make up to my soul for this separation unless it returned the separated half. The anguish of my heart just thinking about this bears witness, as do the tears dimming my eyes and wetting my face and the fingers writing this. You recognized, as I do know, my love for you, but I did not. Our separation from one another has shown me how much I love you; a man does not in fact have knowledge of good and evil unless he has experienced both. Not having experienced your absences, I did not realize how sweet it was to be with you and how bitter it was to be without you. But you have gained from our separation the company of someone else, whom you love no less—or even more—than [you love] me; while I have lost you, and there is no one to take your place. You are thus enjoying your consolation, while nothing is left to me but heartbreak.

[Anselm] To Gondulph— I put no other or longer salutations at the head of my letter, because I can say nothing more to him whom I love. All who know Gondulph and Anselm know well what this means, and how much love is understood in these two names. ... How could I forget thee? Can a man forget one who is placed like a seal upon his heart? In thy silence I know that thou lovest me; and thou also, when I say nothing, thou knowest that I love thee. Not only have I no doubt of thee, but I answer for thee that thou art sure of me. What can my letter tell thee that thou knowest not already, thou who art my second soul? Go into the secret place of thy heart, look there at thy love for me, and thou shalt see mine for thee.... Thou knewest how much I love thee, but I knew it not. He who has separated us has alone instructed me how dear to me thou wert. No, I knew not before the experience of thy absence how sweet it was to have thee, how bitter to have thee not. Thou hast another friend whom thou hast loved as much or more than me to console thee, but I have no longer thee, thou understandest? and nothing to replace thee. Those who rejoice in the possession of thee may perhaps be offended by what I say. Ah, I let them content themselves with their joy, and permit me to weep for him whom I ever love.

from *Rule of Saint Benedict*, Chapter 22 How the Brothers [or Sisters] Are to Sleep

Let each one sleep in a separate bed. Let them receive bedding suitable to their manner of life, according to the abbot's directions. If possible let all sleep in one place; but if the number does not allow this, let them take their rest by tens or twenties with the seniors who have charge of them.

A candle shall be kept burning in the room until morning.

Let them sleep clothed and girded with belts or cords—but not with their knives at their sides, lest they cut themselves in their sleep—and thus be always ready to rise without delay when the signal is given and hasten to be before one another at the Work of God, yet with all gravity and decorum. The younger shall not have beds next to one another, but among those of the older ones. When they rise for the Work of God let them gently encourage one another, that the drowsy may have no excuse.

from Anonymous, *A Relation, or Rather a True Account, of the Island of England, with Sundry Particulars of the Customs of these People, and of the Royal Revenues under King Henry the Seventh* (late 15th century)

The report from which the following extract is taken was written by an official from Venice who visited England in 1496–97.

[The English] have an antipathy to foreigners, and imagine that they never come into their island, but to make themselves masters of it, and to usurp their goods; neither have they any sincere and solid friendships amongst themselves, insomuch that they do not trust each other to discuss either public or private affairs together, in the confidential manner we do in Italy. And although their dispositions are somewhat licentious, I never have noticed anyone, either at court or amongst the lower orders, to be in love; whence one must necessarily conclude, either that the English are the most discreet lovers in the world, or that they are incapable of love. I say this of the men, for I understand it is quite the contrary with the women, who are very violent in their passions. Howbeit the English keep a very jealous guard over their wives, though anything may be compensated in the end, by the power of money.

The want of affection in the English is strongly manifested towards their children; for after having kept them at home till they arrive at the age of 7 or 9 years at the utmost, they put them out, both males and females, to hard service in the houses of other people, binding them generally for another 7 or 9 years. And these are called apprentices, and during that time they perform all the most menial offices; and few are born who are exempted from this fate, for everyone, however rich he may be, sends away his children into the houses of others, whilst he, in return, receives those of strangers into his own. And on inquiring their reason for this severity, they answered that they did it in order that their children might learn better manners. But I, for my part, believe that they do it because they like to enjoy all their comforts themselves, and that they are better served by strangers than they would be by their own children. Besides which the English being great epicures, and very avaricious by nature, indulge in the most delicate fare themselves and give their household the coarsest bread, and beer, and cold meat baked on Sunday for the week, which, however, they allow them in great abundance. If they had their own children at home, they would be obliged to give them the same food they made use of for themselves. ...

GEOFFREY CHAUCER
1343 – 1400

Little is known about the private life of the greatest English author of the Middle Ages, but because Geoffrey Chaucer spent most years of his adult life in service to the Crown and the government, medieval records tell us much about his working life. These records, in which Chaucer's name is mentioned some 500 times, document decades of work for various royal households—as a page, a controller of customs, and a justice of the peace, among other positions. What they fail to provide are any details about Chaucer's education, literary life, or personal life.

As the author of the exquisite *Troilus and Criseyde* and of a variety of shorter poems and prose works, Chaucer would be regarded among the most important medieval English writers. But it is *The Canterbury Tales* that has secured his place as one of the greatest English authors of any era. From the time of its first appearance in the late fourteenth century, this linked series of stories has remained one of the most popular works of literature of the Middle Ages. The *Tales* were, in fact, among the first works ever printed in England, after William Caxton introduced the printing press to the country in 1474, some two decades after Gutenberg's invention of moveable type. In his Preface to *Fables Ancient and Modern* (1700), John Dryden called Chaucer the "father of English poetry," not only for his great influence upon future generations, but also for the fact that he was one of the first poets to compose his works in English, rather than French, Latin, or Anglo-Norman. Indeed, like Dante before him, Chaucer used the everyday language of the common people and proved its poetic capacity.

Chaucer was born at a time that saw the beginnings of a breakdown in strict divisions between the aristocracy, the Church, and the commoners. Although he was not born into the noble class, he was able to transcend the restrictions of the old social order and to procure a variety of high positions. Chaucer was born to Agnes Copton and John Chaucer just a few years before the beginning of the Hundred Years' War between France and England; his childhood also saw the outbreak of bubonic plague in England (which eventually killed between thirty and forty per cent of the population). Both of his parents held court positions at various times, but his father was primarily a prosperous wine merchant in London. With his knowledge of Latin, French, and Italian, the young Chaucer was likely educated in a good London grammar school; later he may have attended university. Court documents show that in his early teens he held a position as page in the household of the Countess of Ulster and Prince Lionel, son of the ruling monarch, Edward III.

In 1359 Chaucer took part in the war in France and was captured and ransomed to the king, who procured his release in 1360. Speculation has it that during this period on the continent Chaucer began his literary career, translating from the French the popular and influential allegorical poem *Le Roman de la Rose* (*The Romance of the Rose*), written by Guillaume de Lorris and Jean de Meun. In 1366 Chaucer married Philippa Roet, a lady-in-waiting to the queen. The couple had at least two children; Chaucer addressed *A Treatise on Astrolabe* (1391) to "little Lewis," and another son, Thomas, was eventually knighted.

The first page of *Chaucer's Tale of Melibee*, from the Ellesmere manuscript of *The Canterbury Tales*. The figure on horseback is generally taken to be a representation of Chaucer. The actual size of pages in the Ellesmere manuscript is approximately 15¾ x 11⅛". (This item is reproduced by permission of *Huntington Library*, San Marino, California. EL26C9F72r.)

Over the course of the next twenty years, Chaucer continued his work for the royal household, serving in the army in France under John of Gaunt and in 1372 traveling on a diplomatic mission to Italy, where he probably acquired his knowledge of the works of Dante, Petrarch, and Boccaccio. *The Book of the Duchess* (1368), written when he was twenty-five, is already an accomplished work. After his trip to Italy, however, Chaucer's writing began to show a new level of maturity and innovative technique, as well as a vast knowledge of both classical and contemporary literature and the various languages associated with these writings. *The House of Fame* (c. 1377) owes a debt to Dante, *The Parliament of Fowls* (1380) to Boccaccio and Cicero, and *Troilus and Criseyde* (c. 1385) again to Boccaccio; it is a reworking of Boccaccio's *Il Filostrato*.

Troilus, a long romantic poem recounting the fateful love of the Trojan Prince Troilus for Criseyde, has often been considered the most perfectly realized of all Chaucer's works. Although it exhibits less range than *The Canterbury Tales*, its elegant and supple verse, sustained narrative accomplishment, and depth of characterization are unsurpassed in medieval poetry in English.

In his next (and unfinished) work, *The Legend of Good Women*, written as a series of tales, Chaucer parodies his own authorial persona, taking himself to task for the writing of Criseyde's betrayal of Troilus by telling the stories of famous women who were themselves deceived by men.

Although the beginning of the 1380s were difficult times for Chaucer and for the country (he was accused of abduction or rape by a young woman named Cecilia Chaumpaigne, and 1381 saw the uprising against the poll tax), he seemed to regain inspiration in the latter part of the decade, at the same time as he held some important positions in the court. He became Controller of Customs and Justice of the Peace, and in 1386 was elected Member of Parliament for Kent; in 1389 Chaucer was appointed Clerk of the King's Works, a vital and challenging position in which he oversaw repairs and maintenance of government buildings. During these years he began work on *The Canterbury Tales*, generally considered his masterpiece. Rather than adapting old legends or reworking ancient stories of heroes, as was the norm, Chaucer told the stories of a gallery of English characters, from knight to clerk, parson to cook, nobility and commoners alike. Frequently hilarious, sometimes bawdy, and often revealing, *The Canterbury Tales* is composed of a series of stories told by a group of pilgrims on their way from London to Canterbury to visit the shrine of the martyr St. Thomas à Becket. Similar framing devices had been used by other writers of the Middle Ages, but Chaucer's inclusion of various classes and types of people, some of whom had never before been represented in literature, as well as his tonal range and his melding of diverse styles, were without precedent in English.

Although the work as it stands includes 24 tales and runs to over 17,000 lines, *The Canterbury Tales* was far from complete at the end of Chaucer's life. *The General Prologue*, in which the narrator introduces some thirty pilgrims, suggests that Chaucer intended to write more than 100 tales, with each narrator telling two tales on the journey to Canterbury and two on the way back. Chaucer must have known that such a plan was entirely unrealistic, however. Perhaps he allowed it to stand in the *General Prologue*, which he probably revised on several occasions, to indicate that *The Canterbury Tales* was a work that could never be finished. The narratives we do have are fleshed out by linking passages recounting exchanges among the pilgrims. Although these characters are fictional, the text provides a wealth of insight into the customs and practices of the time. Many of the pilgrims are medieval "types," but by providing and by varying narrative styles with each speaker, Chaucer breathes imaginative life into the characters as individuals and into their world as a whole.

Chaucer's moral stance in *The Canterbury Tales* has been the subject of much discussion. The *Retraction* that follows *The Parson's Tale* disavows on moral grounds not only the *Tales*, but virtually all his more secular writings. Is this "Geoffrey Chaucer" merely another imaginary personage, or did the aging author truly repent of all "worldly vanitees"? At so great a remove as we are from medieval sensibilities, it is impossible to be sure. It can be said, however, that through most of *The Canterbury Tales* the author refrains from moralizing or casting judgment. The whole notion of a religious pilgrimage is frequently undermined by the actions of the characters, many of whom show themselves to be more interested in carnal than spiritual quests. Other characters, such as the Pardoner, may seem at first to be of high moral character, but deliberately or unwittingly expose their own compromised morality as they tell their stories. More broadly, there is an ongoing and unresolved tension in the tales between the spiritual and the worldly. This tension operates not only within many of the individual tales but also in the work as a whole, with the elevated tone of *The Knight's Tale,* for example, standing in marked contrast to the bawdiness of *The Miller's Tale*, the irreverence of the Wife of Bath's fantasy, or the elaborate pretense of artlessness in the fable recounted by the Nun's Priest. There is tension as well between the social classes represented among the pilgrims, between different religious views, between the sexes, and over the extent to which the traditions and conventions of the past should still be respected and adhered to. *The Canterbury Tales* is of all the classics of English literature one of the most entertaining and also one of the most open: open-minded in its underlying sensibilities, and open to an extraordinary range of interpretation.

The final year of Chaucer's life saw great upheaval in England's monarchy. In 1399, Richard II, who had supported Chaucer, was overthrown by Henry Bolingbroke (Henry IV), the oldest son of Richard's uncle, John of Gaunt, Duke of Lancaster, who had also been one of Chaucer's patrons. It may have been due to his gifts as a poet that Chaucer managed to retain the favor of the new regime, which was anxious for respectability. Chaucer wrote his final poem, "Complaint to His Purse," as a plea to King Henry to pay income owing from Richard II's reign; while the king did promise payment, Chaucer never collected the money. He died in October of 1400 and was buried in the south transept of Westminster Abbey. A century and a half later a monument to Chaucer was erected on the spot; thus began the tradition of the abbey's "Poets' Corner."

⌘⌘⌘

The Canterbury Tales

It is some indication of its popularity that *The Canterbury Tales* survives in so many manuscripts: fifty-five complete or nearly complete collections and a further twenty-eight manuscripts that contain one or more tales. Of these manuscripts, two of the earliest, the Hengwrt, now in the National Library in Wales, and the Ellesmere, now in the Huntington Library in Pasadena, California, have provided the basis for most editions. The two manuscripts were copied by the same scribe, Adam Pynkhurst, in the first few years after Chaucer's death in 1400, or just possibly in the last year or two of Chaucer's life. The differences between the two manuscripts raise one of the great puzzles in Chaucerian scholarship: how close Chaucer came to finishing *The Canterbury Tales*. Ellesmere, generally agreed to be slightly later, presents the tales in an order that many modern readers have found to make strong artistic sense; Ellesmere also contains material—most notably the *Canon's Yeoman's Tale*, an account of a fraudulent alchemical workshop—that is missing from Hengwrt. On the other hand, many individual lines in Ellesmere contain small errors or are missing words. Why Pynkhurst, having managed to get an accurate (although incomplete) text from which to copy when he was writing the Hengwrt manuscript, should then have failed to do so when writing Ellesmere remains unclear. This edition reproduces the text of the Ellesmere manuscript, preserving its spellings and modifying only its word division and punctuation. Where the text of the Ellesmere is clearly deficient or does not make sense, the editors have drawn on Hengwrt. In each case, these alterations are noted.

The Ellesmere manuscript includes a considerable number of marginal notes, or glosses. In the tales included in this anthology, these glosses are particularly numerous in *The Wife of Bath's Tale* and in *The Franklin's Tale*. Who first composed these glosses is still an open question, although there are strong grounds for believing that Chaucer himself composed quite a few of them. In these pages the texts of a number of the more interesting marginal glosses have been included in the notes at the bottom of the page.

The Ellesmere manuscript is large, its pages measuring roughly 15 by 11 inches, and elegantly decorated. It is the kind of luxury volume that might have been commissioned by an aristocrat, a prosperous London merchant, or a senior civil servant of the early fifteenth century. Various personal inscriptions in the manuscript indicate that it once belonged to John de Vere, who became the twelfth earl of Oxford in 1417, and whose guardians (possibly the book's first owners) were Thomas Beaufort, Duke of Exeter (one of the sons of John of Gaunt) and Henry IV's third son, John, Duke of Bedford, a great book collector.

The General Prologue

Chaucer's account of meeting a group of twenty-nine pilgrims at the Tabard Inn in Southwark, on the south bank of the Thames, has such an air of verisimilitude that it was once read as an account of an actual pilgrimage, with much attention devoted to determining just when it took place (1387 being the most favored date), how many days it took the pilgrims to get to Canterbury, and who the pilgrims were in real life. In fact, *The Canterbury Tales* draws on a tradition of medieval estates satire, poems that describe members of the three estates (those who pray, i.e., monks and nuns; those who fight, i.e., knights; and those who work, i.e., peasants) in terms of their characteristic vices. Many of Chaucer's most memorable and vivid characters, including his Friar and the Wife of Bath, are drawn from satirical figures found in such works as *Le Roman de la Rose* (*The Romance of the Rose*), in which a lover's quest for his lady (the rose) serves as an occasion for broad social commentary.

Chaucer knew the work well, having translated it from French, and also knew the major example of English estates satire, William Langland's *Piers Plowman*, which Langland composed and then repeatedly reworked in the 1370s and 1380s.

Chaucer includes a Knight and a Plowman among his pilgrims, but for the most part they are drawn from the middle ranks of society, including prosperous members of the clergy, or first estate, such as the Friar, the Monk, and the Prioress, and those of the third estate who no longer fitted among the peasantry, such as the five prosperous Guildsmen, the Wife of Bath, the Merchant, the Physician, the Sergeant of Law, and the Manciple. Energetic and often clever, or at least sophisticated, the pilgrims are all professionally successful and—with a few exceptions—they thrive in the vibrant money economy of the later fourteenth century. To describe these people, Chaucer employs an affable and naively enthusiastic narrator, who mingles easily with them, admiring and even echoing their speeches, all apparently uncritically. As George Lyman Kittredge has observed, however, Chaucer was a professional tax collector and "a naïf collector of Customs would be a paradoxical monster." The poet and his narrator must not be confused.

The framing device of the pilgrimage allows Chaucer to explore the social tensions and moral debates of his day more freely than would otherwise be possible, transposing all conflict into an apparently innocent tale-telling competition. The question of who will tell the tale that offers the "best sentence and moost solaas" (line 798), i.e., the best moral meaning and the most enjoyment, is a standing invitation to probe beneath the surface and ask what the meaning of each tale really is. The pilgrimage frame also allows Chaucer to experiment with almost every major literary genre of his day and to assemble an encyclopedic compilation of ancient wisdom, history, and moral lessons. The learned aspect of this compilation is reinforced in the Ellesmere manuscript by the large number of marginal glosses, which identify the source for quotations and draw attention to particularly sententious passages.

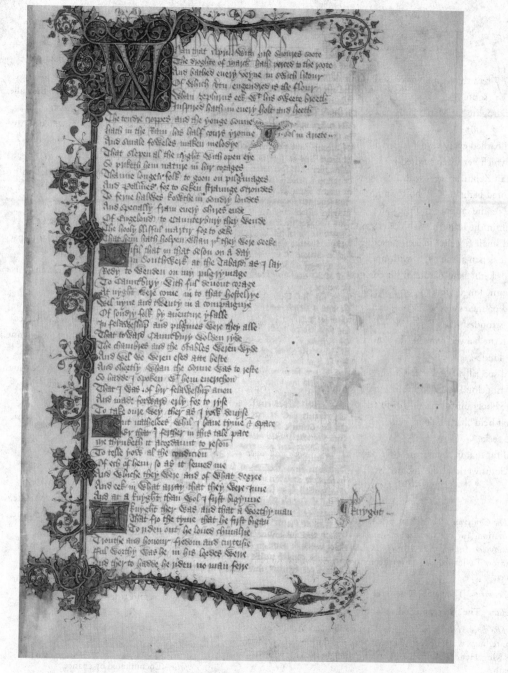

Opening page of *The General Prologue*, Ellesmere manuscript.
(This item is reproduced by permission of the *Huntington Library*, San Marino, California. EL26C9F72r.)

The Canterbury Tales[1]

THE GENERAL PROLOGUE

Whan that Aprill with hise shoures°   showers
    soote°   sweet
The droghte° of March hath perced° to the
    roote   drought / pierced
And bathed every veyne° in swich° licour°   vein / such / liquid
Of which vertu° engendred is the flour,°   power / flower
5   Whan Zephirus[2] eek° with his sweete breeth   also
Inspired hath in every holt° and heeth°   wood / heath
The tendre croppes and the yonge sonne
Hath in the Ram[3] his half cours yronne°   run
And smale foweles° maken melodye   birds
10 That slepen al the nyght with open eye,
So priketh° hem nature in hir corages,°   excites / their hearts
Thanne longen folk to goon° on pilgrimages   go
And palmeres° for to seken° straunge
    strondes°   pilgrims / seek / shores
To ferne halwes° kowthe° in sondry
    londes.   far-off shrines / known
15 And specially, fram° every shires° ende   from / shire's
Of Engelond to Caunterbury they wende,°   travel
The hooly blisful martir[4] for to seke
That hem° hath holpen° whan that they were
    seeke.°   them / helped / sick
Bifil° that in that seson° on a day   it happened / season
20 In Southwerk[5] at the Tabard[6] as I lay

Redy to wenden° on my pilgrymage   travel
To Caunterbury with ful devout corage,°   heart
At nyght were come into that hostelrye°   inn
Wel nyne° and twenty in a compaignye   nine
25 Of sondry° folk by aventure yfalle[7]   various
In felaweshipe, and pilgrimes were they alle
That toward Caunterbury wolden° ryde.   would
The chambres° and the stables weren wyde,°   bedrooms / wide
And wel we weren esed° atte beste.   fed
30 And shortly, whan the sonne was to reste,
So hadde I spoken with hem° everichon°   them / everyone
That I was of hir° felaweshipe anon°   their / soon
And made forward° erly° for to ryse   a pact / early
To take oure wey ther as I yow devyse.°   as I will tell you
35 But nathelees,° whil I have tyme and space   nevertheless
Er that I ferther° in this tale pace,°   further / go
Me thynketh it° acordaunt° to resoun   it seems to me / according
To telle yow al the condicioun°   i.e., character and estate
Of ech of hem,° so as it semed me,   each of them
40 And whiche they were and of what degree°   rank
And eek° in what array° that they were inne,   also / clothing
And at a knyght than wol I first bigynne.
A Knyght ther was and that a worthy man,
That fro the tyme that he first bigan
45 To riden out, he loved chivalrie,
Trouthe and honour, fredom and curteisie.[8]
Ful worthy was he in his lordes werre°   war
And therto hadde he riden no man ferre°   further
As wel in Cristendom as in hethenesse°   pagan lands
50 And evere honoured for his worthynesse.
At Alisaundre he was whan it was wonne.
Ful ofte tyme he hadde the bord bigonne[9]
Aboven alle nacions in Pruce.
In Lettow hadde he reysed° and in Ruce,   raided
55 No Cristen man so ofte of his degree.
In Gernade at the seege eek° hadde he be   also
Of Algezir, and riden in Belmarye.

---

[1] *The Canterbury Tales*   The present text of introductions to, and quotations for *the Canterbury Tales* have been prepared for *The Broadview Anthology of British Literature* by Robert Boenig and Andrew Taylor from their forthcoming Broadview edition of the *Tales*.

[2] *Zephirus*   The name given to the personified west wind.

[3] *Ram*   The sign of the Zodiac for the early spring.

[4] *The hooly blisful martir*   St. Thomas Becket, Archbishop of Canterbury, was killed on 29 December 1170 during a dispute with his King, Henry II, by four knights who thought the king wished his death.

[5] *Southwerk*   Southwark is the region, now officially part of London but not so during Chaucer's time, on the southern bank of the Thames, directly across from the old city of London.

[6] *Tabard*   This is the name of Harry Bailly's inn. A "tabard" was a type of tunic often worn over chain-mail armor.

[7] *yfalle*   Encountered by chance.

[8] *Trouthe ... curteisie*   Keeping one's word, preserving one's reputation or honor, generosity, and courtesy or courtly manners are central values in the code of chivalry.

[9] *hadde the bord bigonne*   Sat at the first table—an honor in victory banquets.

At Lyeys was he and at Satalye
Whan they were wonne and in the Grete See.
60 At many a noble armee° hadde he be.   *army*
At mortal batailles hadde he been fiftene
And foughten for oure feith° at Tramyssene   *faith*
In lystes° thries—and ay slayn his foo.   *jousting arenas*
This ilke° worthy knyght hadde been also   *same*
65 Somtyme with the lord of Palatye
Agayn another hethen° in Turkye,[1]   *heathen*
And everemoore he hadde a sovereyn° prys.°   *sovereign / reputation*
And though that he were worthy,° he was wys,°   *brave / prudent*
And of his port° as meeke as is a mayde.   *behavior*
70 He nevere yet no vileynye ne sayde
In al his lyf unto no maner wight.[2]
He was a verray,° parfit,° gentil° knyght.   *true / perfect / noble*
But for to tellen yow of his array,°   *appearance*
His hors° weren goode, but he was nat gay.°   *horses / gaudy*
75 Of fustian° he wered a gypon°   *rough cloth / tunic*
Al bismotered° with his habergeon,°   *soiled / mail coat*
For he was late ycome° from his viage°   *arrived / voyage*
And wente for to doon° his pilgrymage.   *do*
　　With hym ther was his sone, a yong Squier,[3]
80 A lovyere° and a lusty° bacheler   *lover / vigorous*
With lokkes crulle° as they were leyd in presse.   *curled locks*
Of twenty yeer of age he was, I gesse.°   *guess*
Of his stature he was of evene lengthe°   *moderate height*

And wonderly delyvere° and of greet strengthe.   *quick*
85 And he hadde been somtyme in chyvachie°   *calvary expedition*
In Flaundres, in Artoys, and Pycardie[4]
And born hym weel as of so litel space°   *in so short a time*
In hope to stonden° in his lady grace.°   *stand / lady's favor*
Embrouded° was he as it were a meede,°   *embroidered / meadow*
90 Al ful of fresshe floures whyte and reede.°   *white and red*
Syngynge he was or floytynge° al the day.   *playing the flute*
He was as fressh as is the monthe of May.
Short was his gowne with sleves longe and wyde.
Wel koude he sitte on hors and faire ryde.
95 He koude songes make and wel endite,°   *compose verse*
Juste and eek daunce and weel putreye° and write.   *draw*
So hoote° he lovede, that by nyghtertale°   *hotly / nighttime*
He slepte namoore° than dooth a nyghtyngale.   *no more*
Curteis he was, lowely,° and servysable°   *humble / helpful*
100 And carf° biforn his fader at the table.   *carved (meat)*
　　A Yeman[5] hadde he and servantz namo°   *no more*
At that tyme for hym liste° ride so,   *desired*
And he was clad in cote° and hood of grene.   *coat*
A sheef of pecok arwes° bright and kene°   *peacock arrows / sharp*
105 Under his belt he bar ful thriftily.°   *very carefully*
Wel koude he dresse his takel° yemanly.   *equipment*
His arwes drouped° noght with fetheres° lowe, *drooped / feathers*
And in his hand he baar° a myghty bowe.   *bore*
A not heed° hadde he, with a broun visage.°   *curly head / face*
110 Of wodecraft wel koude° he al the usage.°   *knew / customs*
Upon his arm he baar° a gay bracer,°   *bore / leather bracelet*
And by his syde a swerd° and a bokeler°   *sword / small shield*
And on that oother syde a gay° daggere   *bright*
Harneised wel° and sharpe as point of spere;   *well-sheathed*
115 A cristophere° on his brest of silver
　　sheene.°   *St. Christopher medal / bright*
An horn he bar;° the bawdryk° was of grene. *bore / shoulder-belt*
A forster° was he, soothly° as I gesse.°   *forester / truly / guess*

---

[1] *Alisaundre … Turkye*   The locations of the Knight's battles are as follows: Alexandria in Egypt (1365), Prussia, Lithuania, Russia (the scenes of much fighting against hold-out pagans in the last decades of the fourteenth century), Grenada (in Spain) whose city Algezir was captured in 1344, Banu Merin (in North Africa), Ayash (Lyeys in Syria, captured in 1367), Antalya (Satalye, in modern Turkey, captured in 1361), Tlemcen (in modern Algeria), Balat (Palatye, in modern Turkey, involved in campaigning in both the 1340s and 1365), and Turkey. The places not identified with a specific date of battle saw protracted hostilities between Christians and non-Christians during the period in question. The "great sea" is the Mediterranean. It would, of course, have been impossible for a knight to have taken part in all these campaigns.

[2] *In … wight*   He was never rude to anyone. Middle English often uses double or even triple negatives to intensify each other rather than to cancel each other out.

[3] *yong Squier*   A squire would serve a knight, especially by helping to arm him, and would fight with him in battle. In some cases, as here, squires were young men training to be knights, but squires could also be older men, such as Chaucer.

[4] *In … Pycardie*   These places in Flanders saw military action in 1383, as the English troops fought for Pope Urban VI against his rival, Anti-Pope Clement VII. The campaign, led by the war-loving Bishop of Norwich, was a great disaster for the English.

[5] *A Yeman*   Yeoman, a small landholder or tenant farmer, often prosperous enough to serve as an infantryman or archer in a knight's retinue.

Ther was also a Nonne,° a Prioresse,[1]   *nun*
That of hir smylyng was ful° symple and coy.°   *very | modest*
120 Hire gretteste ooth was but "By Seint Loy!"[2]
And she was cleped° Madame Eglentyne.[3]   *called*
Ful weel she soong° the service dyvyne,[4]   *sung*
Entuned°in hir nose ful semely.°   *intoned | seemly*
And Frenssh she spak ful faire and fetisly°   *elegantly*
125 After the scole° of Stratford atte Bowe:[5]   *school*
For Frenssh of Parys was to hire unknowe.°   *unknown*
At mete° wel ytaught° was she withalle.   *dinner | taught*
She leet° no morsel from hir lippes falle,   *let*
Ne wette hir fyngres in hir sauce depe.
130 Wel koude she carie a morsel and wel kepe,°   *take care*
That no drope ne fille upon hire brist.°   *breast*
In curteisie° was set ful muchel° hir list.°   *courtesy | much | pleasure*
Hir over-lippe° wyped° she so clene,°   *upper lip | wiped | clean*
That in hir coppe° ther was no ferthyng°
sene   *cup | coin-sized spot*
135 Of grece° whan she dronken hadde hir draughte.°   *grease | draft*
Ful semely after hir mete° she raughte.°   *food | reached*
And sikerly° she was of greet desport°   *surely | geniality*
And ful plesaunt and amyable° of port°   *amiable | disposition*
And peyned° hire to counterfete cheere°   *took pains | manners*
140 Of court and to been estatlich° of manere   *stately*

And to ben holden° digne° of reverence.   *held | worthy*
But for to speken° of hire conscience,°   *speak | conscience*
She was so charitable and so pitous,°   *compassionate*
She wolde wepe° if that she saugh° a mous°   *weep | saw | mouse*
145 Kaught in a trappe if it were deed° or bledde.°   *dead | bleeding*
Of smale houndes hadde she that she fedde
With rosted flessh or milk and wastel breed.[6]
But soore wepte she if any of hem were deed°   *dead*
Or if men smoot it with a yerde° smerte.°   *yardstick | smartly*
150 And al was conscience and tendre herte.°   *tender heart*
Ful semyly hir wympul[7] pynched was;
Hir nose tretys,° hir eyen° greye as glas,   *shapely | eyes*
Hir mouth ful smal, and therto softe and reed.°   *red*
But sikerly, she hadde a fair forheed.
155 It was almoost a spanne brood,° I
trowe,°   *a hand's span across | believe*
For hardily° she was nat undergrowe.°   *certainly | not undergrown*
Full fetys° was hir cloke, as I was war.°   *elegant | aware*
Of smal coral aboute hire arm she bar
A peire° of bedes, gauded° al with grene,[8]   *pair | divided*
160 And theron heng a brooch of gold ful sheene,°   *very shiny*
On which ther was first write° a crowned "A"   *written*
And after, "Amor vincit omnia."[9]
Another Nonne with hire hadde she
That was hir chapeleyne,° and Preestes° thre.   *chaplain | priests*
165 A Monk ther was, a fair for the maistrie,°   *i.e., better than all*
An outridere[10] that lovede venerie,°   *hunting*
A manly man, to been an abbot able.
Ful many a deyntee° hors hadde he in stable.   *fine*
And whan he rood, men myghte his brydel heere°   *hear*
170 Gynglen° in a whistlynge wynd als cleere°   *jingling | as clear*

---

[1] *Prioresse* A prioress is either the second-in-command of an abbey, a large convent governed by an abbess, or is in charge of a priory, a smaller convent.

[2] *Seint Loy* St. Eligius, a seventh-century Bishop of Noyon in France. He is patron saint of both goldsmiths and blacksmiths.

[3] *Eglentyne* Eglantine, also known as sweet briar, is an early species of rose. It is known for its sweet, apple-like smell (which even the leaves emit if crushed) and five-petaled coral flowers, which appear once a year, in spring. Eglantine was not a common name in the Middle Ages.

[4] *service dyvyne* Divine service; the phrase refers to the Office (or Canonical Hours)—the round of services dominated by psalm-singing that monks and nuns perform on a daily basis. The names of the individual services are Matins, Lauds, Prime, Terce, Sext, None, Vespers, and Compline.

[5] *Stratford atte Bowe* Stratford-at-Bow is in Middlesex, just to the west of London. Chaucer's point, elaborated in the next line, is that the Prioress does not speak French properly but with a provincial accent. The Benedictine Priory of St. Leonard's was at Stratford-at-Bow and in Chaucer's day it had nine nuns, one of them named Argentine. The similarity of the names is suggestive, but Argentine was not the prioress there.

[6] *wastel breed* White bread (which, in the Middle Ages, was a delicacy reserved for the nobility).

[7] *wympul* Cloth folded cover the neck sides of the head, leaving only the face exposed. It was worn by both nuns and lay women.

[8] *A ... grene* She carries a set of coral rosary beads, a chain of prayer-beads. These are divided at intervals by green beads. The green beads indicated the end of the "decade," one set of prayers, and the beginning of the next.

[9] *Amor vincit omnia* Latin: love conquers all.

[10] *An outridere* An outrider was a monk whose job was to leave the cloister (which, as Chaucer makes clear below, was not the ideal thing for a monk to do) to take care of his monastery's business in the world at large. One of the common accusations made against monks was that they loved the secular world more than the cloister.

And eek as loude as dooth the chapel belle

Theras° this lord was kepere of the celle.[1] *since*

The Reule° of Seint Maure or of Seint Beneit,[2] *rule*

Bycause that it was old and somdel streit,° *somewhat restrictive*

175 This ilke monk leet olde thynges pace° *pass*

And heeld after the newe world the space.° *course*

He yaf nat° of that text a pulled° hen *gave not / plucked*

That seith that hunters beth nat hooly° men, *not holy*

Ne that° a monk whan he is recchelees° *nor when / reckless*

180 Is likned til° a fissh that is waterlees. *likened to*

This is to seyn,° a monk out of his cloystre.° *say / cloister*

But thilke° text heeld he nat worth an oystre. *that same*

And I seyde his opinioun was good.

What° sholde he studie and make hymselven
        wood° *why / crazy*

185 Upon a book in cloystre° alwey to poure° *cloister / poor*

Or swynken° with his handes and laboure° *work / labor*

As Austyn[3] bit?° How shal the world be served? *commanded*

Lat Austyn have his owene swynk° to hym reserved! *work*

Therfore he was a prikasour aright.° *hard rider*

190 Grehoundes he hadde as swift as fowel° in flight. *bird*

Of prikyng° and of huntyng for the hare *riding*

Was al his lust.° For no cost wolde he spare. *pleasure*

I seigh his sleves° ypurfiled° at the hond° *sleeves / lined / hand*

With grys°—and that the fyneste° of a
        lond.° *expensive gray fur / finest / the land*

195 And for to festne° his hood under his chyn° *fasten / chin*

He hadde of gold ywroght° a ful° curious pyn:° *made / very / pin*

A love knotte in the gretter° ende ther was. *bigger*

His heed was balled,[4] that shoon as any glas,

And eek his face as it hadde been enoynt.° *anointed*

200 He was a lord ful fat and in good poynt,[5]

Hise eyen° stepe° and rollynge in his heed, *eyes / bright*

That stemed as a forneys° of a leed, *furnace*

His bootes souple,° his hors in greet estaat.° *supple / in best shape*

Now certeinly he was a fair prelaat.° *prelate*

205 He nas nat° pale as a forpyned goost.° *was not / distressed ghost*

A fat swan loved he best of any roost.° *roast*

His palfrey[6] was as broun as is a berye.° *berry*

A Frere° ther was, a wantowne° and a
        merye,° *friar / pleasure-seeking / merry*

A lymytour,[7] a ful solempne° man. *distinguished*

210 In alle the ordres foure[8] is noon° that kan° *no one / knows*

So muchel° of daliaunce° and fair langage. *much / flirtation*

He hadde maad° ful many a mariage *made*

Of yonge wommen at his owene cost.

Unto his ordre he was a noble post!° *pillar*

215 And wel biloved and famulier was he

With frankeleyns° ever al in his contree *franklins (gentry)*

And with worthy wommen of the toun,

For he hadde power of confessioun,

As seyde hymself, moore than a curat,° *curate (local priest)*

220 For of his ordre he was licenciat.° *licensed*

Ful swetely° herde he confessioun, *sweetly*

And plesaunt was his absolucioun.

He was an esy° man to yeve° penaunce, *easy / give*

Theras° he wiste° to have a good
        pitaunce.° *where / thought / donation*

225 For unto a povre° ordre for to yive° *poor / give*

Is signe that a man is wel yshryve.° *confessed*

For if he yaf,° he dorste° make avaunt,° *gave / dared / assert*

---

[1] *celle* Priory or outlying house governed by the central monastery.

[2] *Seint Maure … Seint Beneit* Monks. St. Benedict, a sixth-century Italian monk and abbot, compiled the famous Rule that goes by his name. It became normative for most of Western monasticism. St. Maurus, by legend one of his monks, was credited with bringing his Rule to France.

[3] *Austyn* "Austin" is the typical Middle English abbreviation for Augustine, the great Doctor of the Church and Bishop of Hippo in Northern Africa (354–430 CE). He was famous for his theological writings, particularly *The City of God* and *The Confessions*, the latter his spiritual autobiography. He is also credited with writing the Rule (followed by Augustinian canons and monks) to which this passage alludes.

[4] *His heed was balled* Monks shaved the crowns of their heads in a haircut known as a tonsure.

[5] *in good poynt* Idiomatic: in good condition.

[6] *palfrey* Everyday horse, as opposed to a destrier (war-horse) or a plowhorse.

[7] *lymytour* Friar licensed to preach, minister, and hear confessions in a specified, limited area.

[8] *In … foure* There were four main orders of friars in the later Middle Ages—the Franciscans, the Dominicans, the Carmelites, and the Augustinians. Like monks, the friars took vows of poverty, chastity, and obedience, but they were supposed to go out in the world and preach to the laity, whereas monks were supposed to live apart from the world and devote themselves to prayer.

He wiste that a man was repentaunt.[1]
For many a man so hard is of his herte,
230 He may nat wepe° althogh hym soore
   smerte.°   *weep / sorely hurts*
Therfore instede of wepynge° and preyeres,°   *weeping / prayers*
Men moote yeve° silver to the povre freres!   *should give*
His typet[2] was ay farsed° ful of knyves   *stuffed*
And pynnes° for to yeven yonge
   wyves.°   *pins / give to young women*
235 And, certeinly, he hadde a murye note;°   *merry melody*
Wel koude he synge and pleyen on a rote.°   *play on a lyre*
Of yeddynges° he baar outrely° the
   pris.°   *songs / completely / prize*
His nekke° whit° was as the flour-de-lys.°   *neck / white / lily*
Therto he strong was as a champion.
240 He knew the tavernes wel° in al the toun   *well*
And everich hostiler and
   tappestere°   *each innkeeper and barmaid*
Bet° than a lazar° or a beggestere.°   *better / leper / female beggar*
For unto swich° a worthy man as he   *such*
Acorded nat as by his facultee[3]
245 To have with sike lazars aqueyntaunce.°   *sick lepers acquaintance*
It is nat honeste,° It may nat avaunce,°   *respectable / advance (one)*
For to deelen° with no swich poraille°   *deal / poor folk*
But al with riche° and selleres of vitaille.°   *rich / sellers of food*
And overal theras profit sholde arise,
250 Curteis he was and lowely° of servyse.   *humble*
Ther nas no° man nowher so vertuous;   *was not*
He was the beste beggere in his hous.°[4]   *convent*
For thogh a wydwe° hadde noght a sho,°   *widow / not a shoe*
So plesaunt was his "In principio,"[5]

255 Yet wolde he have a ferthyng° er he wente.   *farthing (coin)*
His purchas° was wel bettre than his rente,°   *income / expenses*
And rage° he koude as it were right a whelp.°   *cavort / dog*
In love-dayes ther koude he muchel° help,   *could he (offer) much*
For ther he was nat lyk a cloystrer°   *monk*
260 With a thredbare cope° as is a povre scoler,°   *cloak / poor student*
But he was lyk a maister or a pope.
Of double worstede° was his semycope°   *thick cloth / short-cloak*
That rounded as a belle out of the presse.°   *mold*
Somwhat he lipsed° for his wantownesse°   *lisped / affectation*
265 To make his Englissh sweete upon his tonge.
And in his harpyng, whan that he hadde songe,
Hise eyen° twynkled in his heed aryght°   *eyes / aright*
As doon° the sterres° in the frosty nyght.   *do / stars*
This worthy lymytour° was cleped Huberd.   *limiter*
270   A Marchant was ther with a forked berd;°   *beard*
In motlee° and hye° on horse he sat,   *multi-colored cloth / high*
Upon his heed a Flaundryssh° bevere° hat,   *Flemish / beaver*
His bootes clasped faire and fetisly.
Hise resons° he spak ful solempnely,   *opinions*
275 Sownynge° alwey th'encrees° of his
   wynnyng.°   *concerning / increase / profit*
He wolde° the see° were kept for anythyng   *wished / sea*
Bitwixe° Middelburgh and Orewelle.[6]   *between*
Wel koude he in eschaunge° sheeldes selle.[7]   *exchange*
This worthy man ful wel his wit bisette;°   *employed*
280 Ther wiste no wight that he was in dette,[8]
So estatly° was he of his governaunce,°   *dignified / management*
With his bargaynes and with his
   chevyssaunce.°   *commerce for interest*
Forsothe,° he was a worthy man withalle.°   *truly / for all that*
But sooth to seyn, I noot how men hym calle.[9]

---

[1] *For ... repentaunt* For if a man gave money then he (the Friar) knew that man was repentant. The Friar is imposing a light penance in exchange for a donation to his order.

[2] *typet* Long ornamental piece of cloth worn either as kind of scarf or as part of a hood or as sleeves. It provided a convenient place to put small objects.

[3] *For ... facultee* It was not appropriate according to his profession.

[4] The Hengwrt manuscript at this point includes the following two lines, usually numbered 252b and 252c: "And yaf a certeyn ferme for the graunt / Noon of his bretheren cam ther in his haunt" (And he paid a certain annual amount for the rights [to beg] / so that none of his brother friars came into his territory).

[5] *In principio* Latin: "in the beginning was the Word," the opening line of the Gospel of John.

---

[6] *Middelburgh and Orewelle* These two ports were in the Netherlands and in England respectively. There was much trade in the late Middle Ages between the two countries, particularly in textiles.

[7] *sheeldes selle* A shield, or *écu*, was a French coin. This kind of trade between national currencies was regarded with suspicion. It was often illegal and could be used as a way of surreptitiously charging interest on a loan (which the Church condemned as usury).

[8] *Ther ... dette* The syntax is ambiguous. Either "No one knew that he was in debt" (implying he was) or "No one knew him to be in debt" (implying he was not) or, since merchants were normally in debt, "No one knew how much he was in debt."

[9] *sooth ... calle* To tell the truth, I don't know what he was called.

285　A Clerk ther was of Oxenford° also[1]　*Oxford*
　　That unto logyk hadde longe ygo,°　*who had [committed himself] to*
　　And leene° was his hors as is a rake.　*lean*
　　And he nas nat right° fat, I undertake,°　*was not very / declare*
　　But looked holwe° and therto sobrely.°　*hollow / soberly*
290　Ful thredbare was his overeste courtepy,°　*overcoat*
　　For he hadde geten hym yet no benefice[2]
　　Ne was so worldly for to have office.
　　For hym was levere° have at his beddes
　　　heed°　*would rather / bed's head*
　　Twenty bookes clad° in blak or reed°　*bound / red*
295　Of Aristotle and his philosophie
　　Than robes riche or fithele° or gay sautrie.°　*fiddle / psaltery*
　　But al be that he was a philosophre,
　　Yet hadde he but litel gold in cofre.°[3]　*little gold in a chest*
　　But al that he myghte of his freendes° hente,°　*friends / obtain*
300　On bookes and on lernynge° he it spente　*learning*
　　And bisily° gan for the soules preye°　*busily / prayed*
　　Of hem° that yaf° hym wherwith to
　　　scoleye.°　*them / gave / the means to study*
　　Of studie took he moost cure° and moost heede.　*care*
　　Noght o° word spak he moore than was neede,　*one*
305　And that was seyd in forme° and reverence　*formally*
　　And short and quyk and ful of hy sentence.°　*meaning*
　　Sownynge in° moral vertu was his speche,　*tending towards*
　　And gladly wolde he lerne and gladly teche.

　　A Sergeant of the Lawe[4] war° and wys°　*shrewd / wise*
310　That often hadde been at the Parvys[5]
　　Ther was also, ful riche of excellence.
　　Discreet he was and of greet reverence.
　　He semed swich, his wordes weren so wise.
　　Justice° he was ful often in assise°　*judge / court*
315　By patente and by pleyn commissioun,[6]
　　For his science° and for his heigh renoun.°　*knowledge / renown*
　　Of fees and robes hadde he many oon;°　*many a one*
　　So greet a purchasour[7] was nowher noon.°　*nowhere at all*
　　Al was fee symple[8] to hym in effect.
320　His purchasyng myghte nat been infect.°　*invalidated*
　　Nowher so bisy° a man as he ther nas,°　*busy / was not*
　　And yet he semed bisier° than he was.　*seemed busier*
　　In termes° hadde he caas° and doomes
　　　alle°　*files / cases / judgments*
　　That from the tyme° of Kyng William[9] were
　　　yfalle.°　*time / given*
325　Therto he koude endite° and make a thyng.°　*write / brief*
　　Ther koude no wight° pynchen° at his
　　　writyng.　*nobody / quibble*
　　And every statut koude he pleyn by rote.°　*recite by heart*
　　He rood but hoomly° in a medlee° cote,　*simply / multi-colored*
　　Girt with a ceint° of silk with barres° smale.　*belt / ornaments*
330　Of his arraye tell I no lenger tale.

---

[1] *Clerk*　The term clerk can mean student or professor, priest or priest's assistant, or learned man or philosopher, depending on the context. University students were supposed to be preparing for the priesthood. Some became priests, which required a vow of celibacy, and could then win promotion in the ranks of the Church. Others only took minor orders (which meant they could marry), and either remained at university or, in many cases, became members of the growing royal, baronial, and civic administration. Chaucer's Clerk, who is studying advanced logic, is roughly the equivalent of a graduate student or junior professor.

[2] *benefice*　Position as a priest or clergyman. In the Middle Ages there had developed a much-criticized custom of granting the income from some benefices to people who would apportion a small amount of the income to a poorer clergyman to do the work and then live off the rest. This practice made some bishops with multiple benefices very wealthy, and it became a means of supporting a well-connected scholar at one of the universities.

[3] *But … cofre*　Chaucer is punning on the word philosopher, which can also mean alchemist. The search for the Philosopher's Stone, thought to be the key to turning metal to gold, was a particular study of alchemists.

[4] *Sergeant of the Lawe*　In late fourteenth-century England, a Sergeant of Law was not simply a lawyer; he was one of about twenty or so lawyers who functioned as legal advisors to the king and served as judges.

[5] *Parvys*　Shortened form of "Paradise," a name given to the porch in front of large churches. Here the reference is to the porch of Saint Paul's Cathedral in London, where lawyers would meet with their clients, the lawyer's office being unknown to late-fourteenth-century England.

[6] *By … commissioun*　Letters patent were royal letters of appointment that were open, i.e., public, documents that anyone was allowed to read. The full commission gives the Sergeant the right to hear all legal cases in the Court of Assizes, circuit courts that would move from county to county.

[7] *purchasour*　I.e., purchaser, someone who acquired feudal property by money rather than feudal service.

[8] *fee symple*　Ownership without feudal obligations.

[9] *Kyng William*　William the Conqueror, who ruled England from 1066 to 1087. His reign marked a turning point in English governance.

A Frankeleyn[1] was in his compaignye.
Whit° was his heed° as is a dayesye.°   *white | head | daisy*
Of his complexioun he was sangwyn;[2]
Wel loved he by the morwe a sope in wyn.[3]

335   To lyven° in delit° was evere his wone,°   *live | delight | custom*
For he was Epicurus[4] owene sone°   *son*
That heeld opinioun that pleyn delit°   *full delight*
Was verray° felicitee parfit.°   *true | perfect happiness*
An housholdere and that a greet was he;

340   Seint Julian[5] was he in his contree.
His breed,° his ale was alweys after oon;[6]   *bread*
A bettre envyned man° was nevere noon.   *man stocked with wine*
Withoute bake mete° was nevere his hous   *baked food*
Of fissh and flessh, and that so plentevous°   *plentiful*

345   It snewed° in his hous of mete and drynke,   *snowed*
Of alle deyntees° that men koude thynke.   *delicacies*
After the sondry° sesons° of the yeer   *various | seasons*
So chaunged he his mete° and his soper.°   *food | meals*
Ful° many a fat partrich° hadde he in
muwe°   *very | partridge | coop*

350   And many a breem° and many a luce° in
stuwe.°   *bream | pike | pond*
Wo° was his cook but if° his sauce were   *woe | unless*
Poynaunt° and sharpe° and redy al his
geere.°   *pungent | spicy | utensils*

His table dormant[7] in his halle alway
Stood redy covered al the longe day.
355   At sessiouns° ther was he lord and sire;   *court sessions*
Ful ofte tyme he was Knyght of the Shire.[8]
An anlaas° and a gipser° al of silk   *dagger | pouch*
Heeng° at his girdel whit° as morne°
milk.   *hung | white | morning*
A shirreve° hadde he been and countour.°   *sheriff | tax-collector*
360   Was nowher swich a worthy vavasour.°   *feudal land holder*

An Haberdasshere[9] and a Carpenter,
A Webbe,° a Dyere, and a Tapycer,°   *weaver | tapestry-maker*
And they were clothed alle in o° lyveree[10]   *one*
Of a solempne and a greet fraternitee.[11]
365   Ful fressh and newe hir geere° apiked° was.   *equipment | polished*
Hir knyves were chaped° noght° with bras   *mounted | not | brass*
But al with silver, wroght ful clene° and weel   *made very elegantly*
Hire girdles° and hir pouches everydeel.°   *belts | every bit*
Wel semed° ech of hem a fair burgeys°   *seemed | citizen*
370   To sitten in a yeldehalle° on a deys.°   *guildhall | raised platform*
Everich° for the wisdom that he kan°   *everyone | knew*

---

[1] *Frankeleyn*   From the word franc or free, a wealthy independent landowner and a member of the minor gentry.

[2] *Of … sangwyn*   The Franklin's physiological makeup is dominated by blood, one of the four humors, which makes him red-faced and cheerful.

[3] *Wel … wyn*   He greatly loved in the morning bread soaked in wine. Such was the preferred breakfast for those wealthy enough to afford wine, which had to be imported from Gascony, the sole remaining territory England retained in what we now call France.

[4] *Epicurus*   The Greek philosopher Epicurus (341–270 BCE) maintained that the pursuit of pleasure was the natural state of humankind.

[5] *Seint Julian*   St. Julian, the patron saint of hospitality in the Middle Ages. Julian set up a way-station for travelers in penance for unwittingly killing his parents, who had unknowingly lodged in his house while journeying.

[6] *after oon*   Consistent, i.e., consistently good.

---

[7] *His table dormant*   Always standing. Most medieval tables on which meals were set were trestle tables, i.e., a long board placed on top of what we would call saw-horses. After the meal was over, the table would normally be taken down. Not so the Franklin's.

[8] *Knyght of the Shire*   Official designation for people chosen to represent their region in Parliament. Chaucer himself, while he was never knighted and only held the rank of squire, served as Knight of the Shire for Kent in 1386, the year before the fictitious pilgrimage to Canterbury takes place. The Franklin has also presided at the sessions of the Justices of the Peace (line 355) and served as Sheriff, the chief royal officer in a county who was responsible for collecting its taxes, and as the county auditor, who assisted the Sheriff.

[9] *Haberdasshere*   Seller of ribbons, buttons, hats, gloves, and small articles of clothing.

[10] *lyveree*   Uniform. Members of craft or religious guilds, as well as retainers of various lords, wore liveries. At this time the wearing of liveries encouraged factionalism and attendant violence, and there were some legal attempts to curb abuses.

[11] *fraternitee*   Trade guilds or religious guilds. The trade guilds regulated who was allowed to follow a given trade in a given town, and the religious guilds functioned as mutual aid societies, burying their dead and helping members who were sick or had fallen into poverty. These guildsmen, though identified by their trades, are members of a religious guild, since trade guilds admitted only members of a single trade.

Was shaply° for to been an alderman.[1]   *suitable*

For catel° hadde they ynogh° and rente,°*belongings / enough / rent*

And eek hir wyves° wolde it wel assente°   *wives / agree*

375 And elles° certeyn were they to blame.   *otherwise*

It is ful fair to been ycleped° "Madame"   *called*

And goon to vigilies[2] al bifore

And have a mantel roialliche ybore.°   *cloak royally carried*

A Cook° they hadde with hem° for the
nones°   *cook / them / occasion*

380 To boille° the chiknes° with the
marybones°   *boil / chickens / marrowbones*

And poudre-marchant tart and galyngale.[3]

Wel koude he knowe a draughte of Londoun ale.

He koude rooste and sethe° and boille° and frye, *simmer / boil*

Maken mortreux° and wel bake a pye.   *stews*

385 But greet harm° was it as it thoughte me°   *pity / seemed to me*

That on his shyne° a mormal° hadde he.   *shin / ulcer*

For blankmanger[4] that made he with the beste.

A Shipman was ther wonynge° fer by
weste.°   *living / far in the west*

For aught I woot,° he was of Dertemouthe.[5]   *all I know*

390 He rood° upon a rouncy° as he kouthe°   *rode / nag / could*

In a gowne of faldyng° to the knee.   *woollen cloth*

A daggere hangynge on a laas° hadde he   *lace*

About his nekke under his arm adoun.°   *downwards*

The hoote° somer hadde maad° his hewe°   *hot / made / color*
al broun,

395 And certeinly he was a good felawe.

Ful many a draughte° of wyn° had he
drawe°   *draft / wine / drawn*

Fro Burdeuxward whil that the chapman° sleepe.[6]   *merchant*

Of nyce° conscience took he no keepe.°   *scrupulous / notice*

If that he faught° and hadde the hyer
hond,°   *if he fought / upper hand*

400 By water he sente hem hoom° to every lond.[7]   *home*

But of his craft° to rekene° wel his tydes,° *ability / reckon / tides*

His stremes° and his daungers° hym
bisides,°   *currents / dangers / all around him*

His herberwe° and his moone,° his
lodemenage,°   *harborage / moon / piloting*

Ther nas noon swich° from Hull to
Cartage.[8]   *was not such a one*

405 Hardy he was and wys to undertake;°   *wise in his endeavors*

With many a tempest hadde his berd° been
shake.°   *beard / shaken*

He knew alle the havenes° as they were   *havens*

Fro Gootlond to the Cape of Fynystere[9]

And every cryke° in Britaigne° and in
Spayne.°   *inlet / Brittany / Spain*

410 His barge ycleped was the Maudelayne.

With us ther was a Doctour of Physik.[10]

In al this world ne was ther noon hym
lik°   *there was no one like him*

To speke of phisik° and of surgerye,   *medicine*

For he was grounded in astronomye.[11]

415 He kepte° his pacient a ful greet deel   *watched over*

---

[1] *alderman* In late medieval England, as in some cities today, the board of aldermen governs under the mayor. The five guildsmen have prospered, rising from artisans to masters. They are successful businessmen who run their own shop or shops, participate in civic government, and aspire, with their wives, to the status of the lesser gentry.

[2] *vigilies* Church services held the night before an important holy day. The aldermen and their wives would lead the procession, with their cloaks carried by a servant.

[3] *And ... galyngale* And tart ground spice and aromatic roots (such as ginger).

[4] *blankmanger* Stew of milk, rice, almonds, and chicken or fish.

[5] *Dertemouthe* I.e., Dartmouth, a port on the English Channel in the southwest of England, near Plymouth.

[6] *Ful ... sleepe* Sailing home from Bordeaux with a cargo of wine, the Shipman would secretly steal some while the wine merchant (chapman) was asleep.

[7] *By ... lond* I.e., he threw his defeated opponents overboard.

[8] *Hull to Cartage* Hull is a port in northern England; Cartage is either Carthage on the Mediterranean coast of North Africa or Cartagena in Spain.

[9] *Fro ... Fynystere* Gotland is an island in the Baltic Sea off the coast of southern Sweden; Cape Finisterre is the point of land that juts out into the Atlantic Ocean in northwest Spain.

[10] *Doctour of Physik* Physician. The term "doctor" means "teacher," as everyone in the Middle Ages knew, so the type of doctor who taught medicine and sometimes practiced it needed to be distinguished from other types of doctors, who taught academic subjects in the universities.

[11] *For ... astronomye* In the Middle Ages, physicians often based their schedules of treatment on astrological tables.

In houres by his magyk natureel.[1]

Wel koude he fortunen the ascendent° — *calculate a planet's position*

Of hise ymages[2] for his pacient.

He knew the cause of everich° maladye, — *every*

420 Were it of hoot or coold or moyste or drye,[3]

And where they engendred and of what humour.

He was a verray, parfit praktisour:° — *practitioner*

The cause yknowe° and of his harm the roote,° — *known / root*

Anon he yaf° the sike man his boote.° — *gave / remedy*

425 Ful redy hadde he hise apothecaries° — *pharmacists*

To sende hym drogges° and his letuaries,° — *drugs / syrups*

For ech° of hem° made oother for to wynne.° — *each / them / profit*

Hir° frendshipe nas nat newe° to bigynne.° — *their / recently / begun*

Wel knew he the olde Esculapius[4]

430 And Deyscorides and eek Rufus,

Olde Ypocras, Haly, and Galyen,

Serapion, Razis, and Avycen,

Averrois, Damascien, and Constantyn,

Bernard and Gatesden and Gilbertyn.

435 Of his diete° mesurable° was he, — *diet / moderate*

For it was of no superfluitee° — *excess*

But of greet norissyng° and digestible. — *nourishment*

His studie was but litel on the Bible.[5]

In sangwyn° and in pers° he clad was al, — *red / blue*

440 Lyned with taffata and with sendal.[6]

And yet he was but esy of dispence.° — *moderate in spending*

He kepte that he wan° in pestilence.[7] — *what he earned / plague*

For gold in phisik° is a cordial.° — *medicine / heart-medicine*

Therfore he lovede gold in special.° — *especially*

445 A good Wif was ther of biside Bathe,[8]

But she was somdel deef,° and that was scathe.° — *somewhat deaf / a shame*

Of clooth makyng she hadde swich an haunt,° — *skill*

She passed hem of Ypres and of Gaunt.[9]

In al the parisshe° wif ne was ther noon — *parish*

450 That to the offrynge[10] bifore hire sholde goon. — *offering*

And if ther dide, certeyn so wrooth° was she, — *angry*

That she was out of alle charitee.

Hir coverchiefs° ful fyne were of ground—° — *kerchiefs / texture*

I dorste swere° they weyeden° ten pound— — *dare swear / weighed*

455 That on a Sonday weren upon hir heed.

Hir hosen weren of fyn° scarlet reed,° — *fine / red*

Ful streite yteyd° and shoes ful moyste° and newe. — *tightly laced / supple*

---

[1] *In … natureel* Hours are the times in the day when the various planetary influences were pronounced, when the Physician watched over (kepte) his patient. Natural magic is opposed to black magic, which involves contact with malicious spirits.

[2] *Of hise ymages* The practice of astrologically-based medicine involved the use of images of the planets as talismans.

[3] *He … drye* Medieval medicine was also based on a theory, traceable back to Greek physicians such as the ones Chaucer mentions below, of the balance of the four bodily humors (blood, phlegm, black bile, and yellow bile) and their qualities of hot, cold, moist, and dry mentioned in this line.

[4] *Wel … Esculapius* Aesculapius was a mythological demi-god, son to Apollo. Dioscorides, Rufus of Ephesus, Hippocrates (associated with the Hippocratic Oath physicians still swear), and Galen were famous Greek physicians. Galen (129–199) was particularly influential, since he set out the theory of four humors which was the basis of medieval medicine. "Haly" is probably the Persian physician Ali Ben el-Abbas (d. 994). Rhazes (d. c. 930) was an Arab astronomer and physician. Avicenna, or Ibn Sina (980–1037), and Averroes (1126–98) were Islamic philosophers and physicians. John of Damascus was a Syrian physician of the ninth century. Constantine the African came from Carthage, converted to Christianity, became a Benedictine monk, and taught at Salerno in Italy in the eleventh century. His work on aphrodisiacs earns him the title the "cursed monk" in *The Merchant's Tale*, line 1810. Islamic science was widely influential in the Middle Ages; it first brought Greek thought to the Latin West. The last three authorities are British. Bernard Gordon was a Scottish physician who taught at Montpellier in the fourteenth century. John Gaddesden (d. c. 1349) taught at Oxford and served as court doctor to Edward II. Gilbert was an English physician in the thirteenth century and the author of a major medical treatise.

[5] *His … Bible* In the Middle Ages physicians were often thought to be religious skeptics, partly because of their knowledge of classical astronomy.

[6] *Lyned … sendal* Taffeta and sendal are types of silk cloth; silk, imported from Asia, was a mark of status and wealth.

[7] *He … pestilence* Possibly a reference to the Black Death, which killed at least a third of the population of England between 1348 and 1349, although there were later outbreaks of plague in 1362, 1369, and 1376.

[8] *Bathe* I.e., Bath, a town in southwest England near Bristol. It is famous for its hot springs (hence its name) and Roman ruins. The parish of St Michael's, just north of Bath, was famous for its weavers.

[9] *Ypres … Gaunt* Cities in Flanders (now north-western Belgium) known for cloth trading. There were also skilled weavers from these cities working in England.

[10] *offrynge* In eucharistic services, gifts are brought to the altar during the Offering, or Offertory.

Boold° was hir face and fair and reed of hewe.°   *bold / color*

She was a worthy womman al hir lyve.

460 Housbondes at chirche dore° she hadde fyve,°[1] *church door / five*

Withouten° oother compaignye in youthe.   *apart from*

But therof nedeth nat to speke as nowthe.°   *for now*

And thries° hadde she been at Jerusalem.[2]   *three times*

She hadde passed many a straunge strem.°   *foreign water*

465 At Rome she hadde been and at Boloigne,

In Galice at Seint Jame and at Coloigne.

She koude muchel of wandrynge by the weye.[3]

Gat-tothed was she, soothly for to seye.[4]

Upon an amblere° esily° she sat,   *saddle-horse / easily*

470 Ywympled[5] wel, and on hir heed° an hat   *head*

As brood° as is a bokeler or a targe,°   *broad / shields*

A foot mantel° aboute hir hipes large   *outer skirt*

And on hir feet a paire of spores° sharpe.   *spurs*

In felaweshipe wel koude she laughe and carpe.°   *joke*

475 Of remedies of love she knew perchaunce,°   *as it happened*

For she koude° of that art the olde daunce.   *knew*

  A good man was ther of religioun

And was a povre Persoun° of a toun,   *poor parson*

But riche he was of hooly thoght° and werk.°*holy thought / work*

480 He was also a lerned man, a clerk,

That Cristes° gospel trewely wolde preche.°   *Christ's / preach*

Hise parisshens° devoutly wolde he teche.   *parishioners*

Benygne° he was and wonder diligent   *benign*

And in adversitee ful pacient,

485 And swich° he was preved° ofte sithes.°   *such / proven / many times*

Ful looth° were hym to cursen° for hise tithes,[6]   *reluctant / excommunicate*

But rather wolde he yeven° out of doute°   *give / without doubt*

Unto his povre parisshens aboute

Of his offryng and eek of his substaunce.

490 He koude in litel thyng have suffisaunce.[7]

Wyd° was his parisshe and houses fer asonder,°   *wide / far apart*

But he ne lefte° nat for reyn° ne thonder   *did not neglect / rain*

In siknesse nor in meschief° to visite   *trouble*

The ferreste° in his parisshe muche and lite,°   *farthest / of greater or lesser (rank)*

495 Upon his feet and in his hand a staf.°   *staff*

This noble ensample° to his sheepe he yaf,   *example*

That firste he wroghte° and afterward that he taughte.   *acted*

Out of the gospel he tho° wordes caughte,°   *those / took*

And this figure° he added eek therto,°   *figure of speech / to it*

500 "That if gold ruste, what shal iren° do?"   *iron*

For if a preest be foul on whom we truste,

No wonder is a lewed man° to ruste,   *layman*

And shame it is if a preest take keepe—°   *heed*

A shiten° shepherde and a clene sheepe.   *soiled with excrement / clean*

505 Wel oghte° a preest ensample for to yeve   *ought*

By his clennesse how that his sheepe sholde lyve.

He sette nat° his benefice to hyre   *did not offer*

And leet° his sheepe encombred° in the myre°   *left / stuck / mud*

And ran to Londoun unto Seint Poules[8]

510 To seken hym a chauntrie° for soules   *seek for himself / chantry*

Or with a bretherhed° to been withholde,°[9]   *guild / hired*

But dwelleth at hoom and kepeth wel his folde°   *sheepfold (i.e., flock)*

---

[1] *Housbondes … fyve* Marriage vows were exchanged on the church steps and were followed by a Mass inside the church.

[2] *And … Jerusalem* Jerusalem was the greatest of all pilgrimages. From England, a trip there and back could take a couple of years. The other pilgrimages mentioned below are Rome, where the Apostles Peter and Paul were buried; Boulogne-sur-mer in France, famous for its miraculous image of the Blessed Virgin; Compostella in Galicia, where the relics of St. James were venerated; and Cologne, where the relics of the Three Kings (or Three Magi) were kept.

[3] *She … weye* She knew much about wandering along the road.

[4] *Gat-tothed … seye* According to medieval physiognomy, a gap between the teeth was a sign that a woman was bold, lecherous, faithless, and suspicious.

[5] *Ywympled* Wearing a wimple.

[6] *tithes* Periodic assessments made to determine one tenth of a person's goods, harvest, and animals, which would then be claimed by the Church. Parish priests could excommunicate parishioners who would not pay them.

[7] *He … suffisaunce* He was able to have enough in little things.

[8] *Seint Poules* St. Paul's Cathedral in London. The custom Chaucer refers to is related to the issue of benefices. A chantry is an endowed position, usually at large churches and cathedrals, in which a priest sings masses for the soul of the person who left money for the endowment. It involved very little work, unlike the Parson's toil described in his section of the General Prologue.

[9] *Or … withholde* The brotherhood here is a guild. Guilds hired priests to serve as their chaplains.

So that the wolf ne made° it nat
    myscarie.°   *would not make / come to grief*
He was a shepherde and noght° a mercenarie,° *not / mercenary*
515 And though he hooly were and vertuous,
He was nat to synful men despitous,°   *scornful*
Ne of his speche daungerous° ne digne,°   *proud / haughty*
But in his techyng discreet and benygne,°   *kind*
To drawen folk to hevene by fairnesse,
520 By good ensample. This was his bisynesse.
But it were any persone obstinat,[1]
Whatso° he were of heigh or lough estat,° *whether / low class*
Hym wolde he snybben° sharply for the
    nonys.°   *rebuke / occasion*
A bettre preest I trowe° that nowher noon ys. *believe*
525 He waiteth after° no pompe and reverence, *expected*
Ne maked° hym a spiced° conscience. *affected / overly fastidious*
But Cristes loore° and hise apostles twelve *teaching*
He taughte, but first he folwed it hymselve.
    With hym ther was a Plowman, was° his brother, *(who) was*
530 That hadde ylad° of dong ful many a fother.° *hauled / cartload*
A trewe swynkere° and a good was he,   *true worker*
Lyvynge in pees and parfit charitee.
God loved he best with al his hoole herte
At alle tymes, thogh he gamed or smerte,[2]
535 And thanne° his neighebore right° as hymselve. *then / just*
He wolde thresshe° and therto dyke° and
    delve°   *thresh / dig / shovel*
For Cristes sake for every povre wight°   *poor person*
Withouten hire° if it lay in his myght.   *pay*
Hise tithes payde he ful faire and wel,
540 Bothe of his propre swynk° and his catel.° *own work / possessions*
In a tabard° he rood upon a mere.°   *over-shirt / mare*
    Ther was also a Reve° and a Millere,   *reeve*
A Somnour°[3] and a Pardoner[4] also,   *summoner*

A Maunciple°[5] and myself. Ther were namo.° *manciple / no more*
545 The Millere was a stout carl° for the nones.   *sturdy fellow*
Ful byg he was of brawn and eek of bones.
That proved wel,° for overal ther° he
    cam°   *was clear / everywhere / came*
At wrastlynge° he wolde have alwey the ram.[6] *wrestling*
He was short-sholdred,° brood,° a thikke
    knarre.°   *stocky / broad / thick fellow*
550 Ther was no dore that he ne wolde heve of harre[7]
Or breke it at a rennyng° with his heed. *by running at it*
His berd as any sowe° or fox was reed,   *sow*
And therto brood as though it were a spade.
Upon the cope° right of his nose he hade   *ridge*
555 A werte° and theron stood a toft of herys,° *wart / tuft of hairs*
Reed as the brustles° of a sowes erys.° *bristles / sow's ears*
Hise nosethirles° blake were and wyde.°   *nostrils / wide*
A swerd and a bokeler bar° he by his syde.   *bore*
His mouth as greet was as a greet forneys.° *furnace*
560 He was a janglere° and a goliardeys,[8]   *joker*
And that was moost of synne° and harlotries.° *sin / obscenities*
Wel koude he stelen° corn° and tollen
    thries,[9]   *steal / grain / take his toll (percentage) thrice*
And yet he hadde a thombe° of gold,
    pardee.°   *thumb / by God*
A whit cote° and a blew° hood wered° he. *white coat / blue / wore*
565 A baggepipe wel koude he blowe and sowne,° *sound*
And therwithal he broghte us out of towne.
    A gentil° Maunciple was ther of a temple   *gracious*
Of which achatours° myghte take exemple   *buyers*
For to be wise in byynge° of vitaille.° *buying / food*
570 For wheither that he payde or took by taille,°   *credit*
Algate he wayted so in his achaat
That he was ay biforn and in good staat.[9]

---

[1] *But ... obstinat* But if anyone were obstinate.

[2] *At ... smerte* At all times, whether he gamed (i.e., did pleasant things) or hurt.

[3] *A Somnour* Deliverer of legal summonses to either secular or ecclesiastical courts, although more often the latter. The ecclesiastical courts were run by the Church and had jurisdiction over all clerics but also over any lay person charged with a moral offense such as adultery or fornication.

[4] *Pardoner* Seller of indulgences, which were writs authorized by the Church to raise money for charitable causes. Indulgences usually promised reduction of time in penance and, after death, in Purgatory.

[5] *Maunciple* Servant at one of the Inns of Court, the legal brotherhoods in London. The Inns of Court were also called temples.

[6] *ram* Typical prize for victors at trade fairs.

[7] *Ther ... harre* There was not a door that he would not heave off its hinges.

[8] *goliardeys* The reference is to Goliards, wandering scholars in the eleventh and twelfth centuries who were known for their rowdy life.

[9] *Algate ... staat* He was always so watchful in his purchasing (achaat) / That he always came out ahead (biforn) and did well.

Now is nat that of God a ful faire grace

That swich a lewed° mannes wit shal pace°   *unlearned | surpass*

575 The wisdom of an heepe° of lerned men?   *heap*

Of maistres hadde he mo° than thries ten°   *more | three times ten*

That weren° of lawe° expert and curious,°   *were | law | skilled*

Of whiche ther weren a duszeyne° in that hous   *dozen*

Worthy to been stywardes° of rente and lond   *stewards*

580 Of any lord that is in Engelond,

To maken hym lyve by his propre good°   *own means*

In honour detteleees°—but if he were wood—   *without debt*

Or lyve as scarsly° as hym list desire,°   *frugally | as he wanted*

And able for to helpen al a shire°   *an entire county*

585 In any caas° that myghte falle or happe,°   *situation | happen*

And yet this Manciple sette hir aller cappe.°   *cheated them all*

The Reve was a sclendre,° colerik° man.[1]   *slender | angry*

His berd was shave° as ny° as ever he kan,   *shaven | closely*

His heer° was by his erys° ful round yshorn.°   *hair | ears | cut*

590 His tope was dokked° lyk a preest biforn.[2]   *clipped*

Ful longe were his legges and ful lene°—   *lean*

Ylyk° a staf° ther was no calf ysene.°   *like | staff | seen*

Wel koude he kepe a gerner° and a bynne;°   *granary | bin*

Ther was noon auditour koude of hym

wynne.°   *get the better of*

595 Wel wiste° he by the droghte° and by the

reyn°   *knew | drought | rain*

The yeldynge° of his seed and of his greyn.°   *yield | grain*

His lordes sheepe, his neet,° his dayerye,°   *cattle | dairy cows*

His swyn,° his hors, his stoor,° and his

pultrye°   *swine | livestock | poultry*

Was hoolly° in this Reves governyng,   *wholly*

600 And by his covenant° yaf the rekenyng°   *contract | reckoning*

Syn° that his lord was twenty yeer of age.   *since*

Ther koude no man brynge hym in arrerage.°   *arrears*

Ther nas baillif ne hierde nor oother hyne,

That he ne knew his sleighte and his covyne.[3]

605 They were adrad° of hym as of the deeth.°[4]   *afraid | death*

His wonyng° was ful faire upon an heeth;°   *dwelling | heath*

With grene trees shadwed was his place.

He koude bettre than his lord purchace.°   *buy land*

Full riche he was, astored pryvely.°   *privately stocked*

610 His lord wel koude he plesen subtilly,°   *please subtly*

To yeve and lene° hym of his owene good   °   *loan | goods*

And have a thank and yet a gowne and hood.[5]

In youthe he hadde lerned° a good myster:°   *learned | craft*

He was a wel good wrighte,° a carpenter.   *craftsman*

615 This Reve sat upon a ful good stot°   *farm horse*

That was al pomely° grey and highte° Scot.   *dappled | named*

A long surcote° of pers upon he hade,   *overcoat*

And by his syde he baar a rusty blade.

Of Northfolk° was this Reve of which I telle,   *Norfolk*

620 Biside a toun men clepen Baldeswelle.[6]

Tukked° he was as is a frere° aboute,[7]   *belted | friar*

And ever he rood the hyndreste° of oure route.°   *last | company*

A Somonour was ther with us in that place

That hadde a fyr reed,° cherubynnes° face,[8]   *fire red | cherub-like*

625 For saucefleem° he was with eyen narwe.°   *blotchy | narrow eyes*

As hoot he was and lecherous as a sparwe,°[9]   *sparrow*

With scaled browes blake and piled berd.[10]

Of his visage° children were aferd.°   *face | afraid*

---

[3] *Ther nas … covyne* There was not a bailiff (foreman), herdsman, or other worker whose tricks and deception he did not know.

[4] *adrad … deeth* Death in general, or possibly the plague.

[5] *His lord … hood* This reeve cheats his lord by storing away the lord's goods as his own and then using them to provide loans to the lord, receiving payment and thanks. Payment in the Middle Ages was most often in tangible goods, like the clothing mentioned here, rather than in money.

[6] *Baldeswelle* I.e., Bawdeswell, a town in the northern part of Norfolk, the northernmost county in East Anglia on the east coast of England.

[7] *Tukked … aboute* Franciscan friars wore habits tied about the waist with ropes.

[8] *That … face* Cherubim, the second highest order of angels, were bright red. See Ezekiel 1.13.

[9] *sparwe* Since sparrows travel in flocks, they had a reputation in the Middle Ages for being lecherous, similar to the more modern reputation of rabbits.

[10] *With … berd* The Summoner's eyebrows have a disease called the scall, and his beard has been losing tufts of hair.

---

[1] *The … man* A reeve was someone, often originally a peasant, who served as a supervisor on a lord's estate. Among other things, reeves collected the portion of the harvest due to the lords and made sure peasants performed their customary labor for the lords. They were much resented. Chaucer's Reeve is dominated by choler, or yellow bile, which makes him suspicious and irritable.

[2] *His … biforn* The top of his head was cut short in the front like a priest's haircut. This would have been an unfashionable cut for a layman, and suitable to a man who was poor, or miserly, or austere.

Ther nas quyksilver, lytarge, ne brymstoon,
630 Boras, cerice, ne oille of Tartre noon,[1]
Ne oynement° that wolde clense° and   *ointment | cleanse | bite*
     byte°
That hym myghte helpen of the whelkes° white   *blemishes*
Nor of the knobbes sittynge° on his chekes.°   *sitting | cheeks*
Wel loved he garleek, oynons, and eek lekes°   *leeks*
635 And for to drynken strong wyn reed as blood.
Thanne wolde he speke and crie° as he were wood.   *yell*
And whan that he wel dronken hadde the wyn,
Thanne wolde he speke no word but Latyn.
A fewe termes hadde he, two or thre,
640 That he had lerned out of som decree.°   *legal document*
No wonder is, he herde it al the day,
And eek ye knowen wel how that a jay°   *chattering bird*
Kan clepen "Watte"° as wel as kan the Pope.   *Walter*
But whoso koude in oother thyng him grope,°   *examine*
645 Thanne hadde he spent al his philosophie.
Ay° "Questio quid iuris!"[2] wold he crie.   *always*
He was a gentil harlot and a kynde;°   *noble and kindly scoundrel*
A bettre felawe° sholde men noght° fynde.   *fellow | not*
He wolde suffre for a quart of wyn
650 A good felawe to have his concubyn°   *mistress*
A twelf monthe° and excuse hym atte fulle.°   *a year | fully*
Ful prively° a fynch° eek koude he pulle.[3]   *secretly | finch*
And if he foond° owher° a good felawe,   *found | anywhere*
He wolde techen° hym to have noon awe°   *teach | no respect*
655 In swich caas of the Ercedekenes curs—[4]
But if° a mannes° soule were in his purs.°   *unless | man's | purse*
For in his purs he sholde ypunysshed be:°   *be punished*
Purs is the Ercedekenes Helle, seyde he.
But wel I woot° he lyed° right in dede.°   *know | lied | indeed*
660 Of cursyng° oghte ech gilty man him drede;   *excommunication*
For curs wol slee° right as° assoillyng°   *kill | just as | absolution*

savith.
And also war° him of a "Significavit"![5]   *beware*
In daunger° hadde he at his owene gise°   *power | pleasure*
The yonge girles[6] of the diocise°   *diocese*
665 And knew hir conseil° and was al hir reed.[7]   *their secrets*
A gerland° hadde he set upon his heed   *garland*
As greet as it were for an ale stake.[8]
A bokeleer hadde he, maad° hym of a cake.°   *made | loaf of bread*
   With hym ther was a gentil° Pardoner   *noble*
670 Of Rouncivale,[9] his freend and his compeer,°   *companion*
That streight° was comen fro the court of Rome.   *straight*
Ful loude he soong "Com Hider, Love, to Me;"[10]
This Somonour bar to hym a stif burdoun.[11]
Was nevere trompe° of half so greet a soun!   *trumpet*
675 This Pardoner hadde heer as yelow as wex,°   *wax*
But smothe it heeng as dooth a strike° of flex.°   *bunch | flax*
By ounces° henge hise lokkes that he hadde,   *strands*
And therwith he hise shuldres°
     overspradde,°   *shoulders | spread over*
But thynne° it lay by colpons° oon° and oon. *thin | strands | one*
680 But hood for jolitee° wered° he noon,   *fun | wore*
For it was trussed° up in his walet.°   *packed | bag*
Hym thoughte° he rood al of the newe
     jet.°   *it seemed to him | fashion*

---

[5] *Significavit* Latin: it signified. It is the first word in a writ authorizing the civil court to imprison someone who had been excommunicated.

[6] *yonge girles* In Middle English, girls can mean young people of both sexes, but here it may just mean young women.

[7] *was al hir reed* Was all their advice. Idiomatic: the Summoner was in their confidence.

[8] *ale stake* Ale-sign; a long pole that stuck out into the street and showed that ale was being sold on the premises.

[9] *Of Rouncivale* The Pardoner belongs to the Hospital of the Blessed Mary of Roncesvalles in London, a dependent house of the larger one at Roncesvalles, the mountain pass between Spain and France which many pilgrims used when they traveled to St. James of Compostela. Hospitals in the Middle Ages were not purely medical facilities; they also served as inns and poor houses.

[10] *Com Hider, Love, to Me* This song, "Come Here, Love, to Me," does not survive.

[11] *This ... burdoun* The Summoner accompanied him with a strong bass. In medieval carols, each sung verse was separated by a burden, a kind of refrain. Carols originally had many subjects, not just the joys of Christmas.

---

[1] *Ther ... noon* The unsuccessful remedies are mercury (sometimes known as quicksilver), lead monoxide (lytarge), sulfur (sometimes known as brimstone), borax, white lead (cerice), and cream of tartar.

[2] *Questio quid iuris* Latin: Question: what point of the law? The expression was often used in the ecclesiastical courts.

[3] *Ful ... pulle* Obscene expression that meant, literally, "to pluck a bird."

[4] *In ... curs* In such a case of the excommunication (curse) of the archdeacon. An archdeacon was the ecclesiastical official in charge of the ecclesiastical court of a diocese.

Dischevelee° save° his cappe° he rood° al
bare.   *with his hair loose | except | cap | rode*
Swiche glarynge° eyen hadde he as an hare.[1]   *bulging*
685 A vernycle[2] hadde he sowed° upon his cappe;   *sewn*
His walet° biforn° hym in his lappe,°   *wallet | before | lap*
Bretful° of pardoun, comen from Rome al hoot.   *brimful*
A voys° he hadde as smal° as hath a
goot.°   *voice | high-pitched | goat*
No berd hadde he, ne never sholde° have: *would*
690 As smothe° it was as° it were late yshave.°   *smooth | as if | shaven*
I trowe° he were a geldyng° or a mare.[3]   *believe | gelding*
But of his craft fro° Berwyk into Ware[4]   *from*
Ne was ther swich° another pardoner.   *there was not such*
For in his male° he hadde a pilwe beer,°   *bag | pillow-case*
695 Which that he seyde was oure Lady veyl;°[5]   *Virgin Mary's veil*
He seyde he hadde a gobet° of the seyl°   *piece | sail*
That Seint Peter hadde when that he wente
Upon the see til Jhesu Crist hym hente.°[6]   *grabbed him*
He hadde a croys° of latoun° ful of stones,   *cross | brass*
700 And in a glas° he hadde pigges bones.   *glass*
But with thise relikes whan that he fond
A povre person dwellynge upon lond,
Upon a day he gat hym° moore moneye   *got himself*
Than that the person gat in monthes tweye.
705 And thus with feyned° flaterye and japes°   *pretended | jokes*
He made the person and the peple his apes.°   *dupes*
But trewely, to tellen atte laste,
He was in chirche a noble ecclesiaste.°   *churchman*

Wel koude he rede a lessoun° or a
storie,°   *lesson | story (from the Bible)*
710 But alderbest° he song° an offertorie,[7]   *best of all | sang*
For wel he wiste whan that song was songe
He moste preche° and wel affile° his
tonge°   *must preach | sharpen | tongue*
To wynne° silver as he ful wel koude.   *acquire*
Therfore he song the murierly° and loude.   *more merrily*
715 Now have I toold yow shortly° in a clause   *briefly*
Th'estaat,° th'array,° the nombre, and eek the
cause   *social position | appearance*
Why that assembled was this compaignye
In Southwerk at this gentil hostelye
That highte the Tabard, faste by the Belle.[8]
720 But now is tyme to yow° for to telle   *you*
How that we baren° us that ilke nyght   *behaved*
Whan we were in that hostelrie alyght,°   *arrived*
And after wol I tell of oure viage
And al the remenaunt of oure pilgrimage.
725 But first I pray yow of youre curteisye
That ye n'arette it nat my vileynye,[9]
Thogh that I pleynly° speke in this mateere   *plainly*
To telle yow hir wordes and hir cheere,°   *comportment*
Ne thogh I speke hir wordes proprely.°   *exactly*
730 For this ye knowen also wel as I:
Whoso° shal telle a tale after a man,   *whoever*
He moot° reherce as ny° as ever he kan   *should | closely*
Everich a word° if it be in his charge,   *every word*
Al° speke he never so rudeliche° or
large,°   *although | crudely | freely*
735 Or ellis° he moot° telle his tale untrewe,   *else | must*
Or feyne thyng,° or fynde wordes newe.   *falsify something*
He may nat spare althogh he were his brother;
He moot as wel seye o word as another.

---

[1] *hare* According to medieval lore, hares were hermaphroditic, becoming both male and female in order to reproduce. Bulging eyes were thought to be a sign of lust and folly.

[2] *vernycle* Badge depicting St. Veronica's veil, a relic at Rome. St. Veronica wiped Jesus's face with her veil as he carried the cross, and by miracle his image was imprinted upon it. Pilgrims collected such badges.

[3] *I ... mare* I believe he was either a gelding (a castrated horse) or a mare.

[4] *Berwyk into Ware* Berwick is in the extreme north of England near the border with Scotland; Ware is near London.

[5] *For ... veyl* Chaucer's point is that the Pardoner sells fraudulent relics (sacred objects associated with Jesus or the saints).

[6] *That ... hente* The reference is to Peter's unsuccessful attempt to imitate Christ by walking on the water. Christ had to rescue him. See Matthew 14.22–33.

[7] *offertorie* The Offertory was chanted when the congregation was bringing gifts to the altar.

[8] *Belle* Previous editors have capitalized this word, guessing that it was the name of another inn—there were several called the Bell in that area — or perhaps a house of prostitution. Perhaps the word should not be capitalized, as it may imply a notable bell in the neighborhood.

[9] *That ... vileynye* That you not attribute it to my lack of manners. Vileynye does not mean villainy in the modern sense. A villein was originally an inhabitant of a rural village; thus the word signifies the state of being rustic rather than civilized.

Crist spak hymself ful brode° in Hooly
    Writ,°   *freely | Holy Scripture*
740 And wel ye woot no vileynye is it.
Eek Plato seith, whoso kan hym rede,
The wordes moote be cosyn° to the dede.°[1]   *cousin | deed*
Also I prey yow to foryeve° it me   *forgive*
Al° have I nat set folk in hir degree°   *although| according to rank*
745 Heere in this tale as that they sholde stonde.
My wit° is short, ye may wel understonde.   *intelligence*
  Greet chiere° made oure Hoost us everichon,°   *cheer | everyone*
And to the soper sette he us anon.
He served us with vitaille at the beste;
750 Strong was the wyn, and wel to drynke us leste.°   *it pleased us*
A semely° man oure Hoost was withalle   *suitable*
For to been a marchal° in an halle.[2]   *marshal*
A large man he was, with eyen stepe.°   *bright*
A fairer burgeys° was ther noon in Chepe,[3]   *citizen*
755 Boold of his speche and wys and wel ytaught,°   *learned*
And of manhod hym lakked° right naught.°   *lacked | nothing*
Eek therto° he was right a myrie man,   *in addition*
And after soper pleyen° he bigan°   *play | began*
And spak of myrthe amonges othere thynges
760 Whan that we hadde maad oure rekenynges[4]
And seyde thus, "Now lordynges, trewely,
Ye been° to me right welcome hertely.°   *are | heartily*
For by my trouthe, if that I shal nat lye,
I saugh nat this yeer so myrie a compaignye
765 Atones° in this herberwe° as is now.   *at once | inn*
Fayn° wolde I doon yow myrthe, wiste I°
    how.   *gladly | if I knew*
And of a myrthe I am right now bythoght°   *in mind*
To doon yow ese,° and it shal coste noght.°   *do you ease | nothing*
  Ye goon to Caunterbury: God yow
    speede!°   *God bring you success!*
770 The blissful martir quite° yow youre meede!°   *pay | reward*

And wel I woot as ye goon by the weye,
Ye shapen yow° to talen° and to pleye.°   *intend | tell tales | play*
For trewely,° confort ne myrthe is noon   *truly | comfort*
To ride by the weye doumb as the stoon.[5]
775 And therfore wol I maken yow disport,°   *entertainment*
As I seyde erst,° and doon yow som
    confort.°   *first | bring you some comfort*
And if yow liketh° alle by oon assent°   *pleases you | unanimously*
For to stonden at° my juggement°   *abide by | judgment*
And for to werken° as I shal yow seye,   *proceed*
780 Tomorwe, whan ye riden by the weye,
Now by my fader soule° that is deed,°   *father's soul | dead*
But if ye be myrie, I wol yeve yow myn heed!
Hoold up youre hondes withouten moore speche."
  Oure conseil° was nat longe for to seche.°   *counsel | not | seek*
785 Us thoughte° it was noght worth to make it wys,[6]   *we thought*
And graunted hym withouten moore avys°   *more debate*
And bad° hym seye his voirdit° as hym
    leste.°   *asked | verdict | as he wanted*
"Lordynges," quod he, "now herkneth for the beste,
But taak it nought, I prey° yow, in desdeyn.°   *beg | disdain*
790 This is the poynt, to speken short and pleyn,
That ech of yow to shorte° with oure weye   *shorten*
In this viage shal telle tales tweye°   *two*
To Caunterburyward,° I mene° it so,   *towards Canterbury | mean*
And homward he shal tellen othere two
795 Of aventures that whilom° han bifalle.°   *once | have happened*
And which of yow that bereth hym° best of
    alle,   *conducts himself*
That is to seyn, that telleth in this caas°   *occasion*
Tales of best sentence° and moost solaas,°   *meaning | enjoyment*
Shal have a soper at oure aller cost°   *at all our cost*
800 Heere in this place, sittynge by this post,
Whan that we come agayn fro Caunterbury.
As for to make yow the moore mury,°   *merry*
I wol myself goodly° with yow ryde,   *gladly*
Right at myn owene cost, and be youre gyde.
805 And whoso wole my juggement withseye°   *resist*
Shal paye al that we spenden by the weye.°   *along the way*
And if ye vouchesauf° that it be so,   *grant*
Tel me anon withouten wordes mo,

---

[1] *Eek ... dede* The reference is to Plato's *Timaeus*, the only one of his dialogues available in translation to the Latin West in the Middle Ages. The quotation is found in section 29. The passage is also discussed by Boethius in his *Consolation of Philosophy* (3, prose 12), a work that Chaucer had translated and drew upon frequently.

[2] *For ... halle* A marshal is a steward or chief butler; a hall is a manor house or town house of a lord.

[3] *Chepe* Cheapside was the merchants' district in London.

[4] *Whan ... rekenynges* When we had paid our bills.

---

[5] *For ... stoon* For truly there is neither comfort nor mirth in riding along as silent as a stone.

[6] *to make it wys* Idiomatic: to make a big deal of it.

And I wol erly° shape me° therfore."°   *early | get ready | for it*

810   This thyng was graunted and oure othes° swore°   *oaths | sworn*
With ful glad herte, and preyden° hym also   *asked*
That he wolde vouchesauf for to do so
And that he wolde been oure governour
And of oure tales juge° and reportour°   *judge | referee*
815   And sette a soper at a certeyn pris°   *price*
And we wol reuled been at his devys°   *wish*
In heigh and lough.° And thus by oon° assent   *all matters | one*
We been acorded° to his juggement,   *agreed*
And therupon the wyn was fet° anon.°   *fetched | immediately*
820   We dronken and to reste wente echon°   *each one*
Withouten any lenger taryynge.°   *longer delaying*
Amorwe,° whan that day gan° for to
sprynge,°   *the next day | began | dawn*
Up roos° oure Hoost and was oure aller cok°   *rose | rooster for us all*
And gadrede° us togidre° all in a flok.°   *gathered | together | flock*
825   And forth we ridden,° a litel moore than
paas,°   *rode | a horse's walking pace*
Unto the Wateryng of Seint Thomas.[1]
And there oure Hoost bigan his hors areste°   *rein in*
And seyde, "Lordynges, herkneth if yow leste!°   *please*
Ye woot youre foreward° and it yow recorde;°   *contract | recall*
830   If evensong° and morwesong° accorde,[2]   *Evensong | Matins*
Lat se° now who shal telle the firste tale.   *let us see*
As evere mote° I drynke wyn or ale,   *might*
Whoso be rebel to my juggement
Shal paye for al that by the wey is spent.

835   Now draweth cut er that we ferrer twynne;[3]
He which that hath the shorteste shal bigynne.
Sire Knyght," quod he, "my mayster and my lord,
Now draweth cut,° for that is myn accord.°   *a straw | decision*
Cometh neer," quod he, "my lady Prioresse,
840   And ye, sire Clerk, lat be youre shamefastnesse,°   *shyness*
Ne studieth noght.° Ley° hond° to every
man."   *stop studying | lay | hand*
Anon to drawen every wight° bigan,   *person*
And shortly for to tellen as it was,
Were it by aventure or sort or cas,[4]
845   The sothe° is this: the cut° fil° to the knyght,   *truth | straw | fell*
Of which ful blithe° and glad was every wyght.   *very happy*
And telle he moste his tale as was resoun,°   *reasonable*
By foreward° and by composicioun,°   *agreement | arrangement*
As ye han herd. What nedeth wordes mo?
850   And whan this goode man saugh° that it was so,   *saw*
As he that wys was and obedient
To kepe his foreward by his free assent,
He seyde, "Syn° I shal bigynne the game,   *since*
What, welcome be the cut, a Goddes° name!   *in God's*
855   Now lat us ryde and herkneth what I seye."
And with that word we ryden forth oure weye.
And he bigan with right a myrie cheere°   *cheerful expression*
His tale anon, and seyde in this manere.[5]

---

[1] *Wateryng of Seint Thomas*   The Watering of St. Thomas was the name given to a brook just outside London on the way to Canterbury.

[2] *If ... accorde*   I.e., if you still say in the morning what you said last evening.

[3] *Now ... twynne*   "Now draw a straw before we depart further."

[4] *Were ... cas*   Adventure, sort, and case mean roughly the same thing: chance.

[5] *His ... manere*   Hengwrt and some other manuscripts read "and seyde as ye may heere," not "and seyde in this manere," a suggestion that *The Canterbury Tales* were to be read aloud as well as silently.

The Knight's Tale

The Knight has the highest social status of the pilgrims and it is appropriate that he should initiate the tale-telling and do so with a work that reflects the interests of his class, a philosophical romance. As befits the teller, the poem is stately in tone and pace and filled with lengthy descriptions of aristocratic rituals, including the great final tournament and the funeral of one of the two lovers. It offers a fantasy of idealized aristocratic love, set in a world of violence to which the love sometimes contributes. In so doing it also raises questions of free will and astrological determinism, inviting us to ask whether a providential order can be reconciled with the violence and disorder of earthly life.

Chaucer originally composed *The Knight's Tale* as a separate work, probably during the 1380s. His source was Boccaccio's story of Theseus, the *Teseida* (written c. 1340), a work of nearly 10,000 lines, in twelve books, and written in Italian to provide a vernacular rival to Virgil's Latin epic, the *Aeneid*. The 2350 lines of *The Knight's Tale* make it Chaucer's longest single poem after *Troilus and Criseyde*, although it is only a quarter of the length of Boccaccio's *Teseida*.

The Knight's central subject is the love of two young nobles, Palamon and Arcite, for the beautiful Emelye, which follows the conventions of *amour courtois* or courtly love, a refined love that is inspired by the sight of the beloved and is violent in its intensity, demanding absolute devotion and years of painful service. Palamon and Arcite fall in love with Emelye while gazing from their prison window and without exchanging a word with her, their passion remains as intense as ever seven years later. The literature of courtly love often takes a legalistic turn, inviting readers or listeners to join in a debate on a formal question, known as a *demande d'amour*; in this case, the question is whether the lover who can see his lady but do nothing to win her is in a worse position than the lover who can struggle to win her but can never see her.

Chaucer, or his Knight, complicates the basic love story by repeated references to cosmic forces. The three earthly lovers are in the character of pagan gods of love, war, and chastity, whose conflict is ultimately resolved by Saturn, the oldest of the gods and a source of destruction. Chaucer takes the sub-plot of the pagan gods from Boccaccio, but he greatly expands the descriptions of the grim effects of Mars and Saturn on human life, evoking the wars, rebellions, plagues, and devastation of his own day. One might describe this world as a thoroughfare of woe, as Theseus's father Egeus does (line 1987). Alternatively, one could look beyond it to a higher order, as Theseus does, in an evocation of cosmic harmony that draws on one of Chaucer's most important sources, the *Consolation of Philosophy* of the late Roman philosopher Boethius. For Theseus, the principle that maintains this order is either Jupiter, chief of the pagan gods, or the First Mover of Aristotelian philosophy (l. 2127), but Chaucer's readers would have understood this principle in Christian terms. In many respects, Theseus speaks for the Knight's values, but whether the tale always confirms them is more questionable.

Detail, opening page of *The Knight's Tale*, Ellesmere manuscript.
(This item is reproduced by permission of the *Huntington Library*, San Marino, California. EL26C9F72r.)

Opening page of *The Knight's Tale*, Ellesmere manuscript.
(This item is reproduced by permission of the *Huntington Library*, San Marino, California. EL26C9F72r.)

THE KNIGHT'S TALE

Iamque domos patrias, Scithice post aspera gentis
Prelia, laurigero[1]

HEERE BIGYNNETH THE KNYGHTES TALE

Whilom,° as olde stories tellen us,   *once*
    Ther was a duc° that highte° Theseus.   *duke / was named*
Of Atthenes° he was lord and governour,   *Athens*
And in his tyme swich° a conquerour   *such*
5 That gretter° was ther noon° under the sonne.   *greater / none*
Ful many a riche contree hadde he wonne,°   *won*
What with his wysdom and his chivalrie.°   *knightly prowess*
He conquered al the regne of Femenye[2]
That whilom was ycleped° Scithia[3]   *called*
10 And wedded the queene Ypolita°   *Hippolita*
And broghte hire hoom° with hym in° his contree   *home / to*
With muchel° glorie and greet
    solempnytee,°   *much / great ceremony*
And eek° hir faire suster° Emelye.°   *also / sister / Emily*
And thus with victorie and with melodye
15 Lete° I this noble duc to Atthenes ryde   *let*
And al his hoost° in armes hym bisyde.°   *host / beside him*
    And certes,° if it nere to long to
    heere,°   *certainly / were not too long to hear*
I wolde° yow have toold fully the manere°   *would / manner*
How wonnen° was the regne of Femenye   *won*
20 By Theseus and by his chivalrye°   *knights*
And of the grete bataille° for the
    nones°   *great battle / on that occasion*
Bitwixen° Atthenes and Amazones   *between*
And how asseged° was Ypolita,   *besieged*

The faire, hardy queene of Scithia,
25 And of the feste° that was at hir weddynge   *feast*
And of the tempest at hir hoomcomynge.°   *homecoming*
But al that thyng I moot° as now
    forbere.°   *must / for the moment resist (telling)*
I have, God woot,° a large feeld to ere,°   *God knows / plow*
And wayke° been° the oxen in my plough.   *weak / are*
30 The remenant of the tale is long ynough:°   *enough*
I wol nat letten° eek noon° of this route.°   *hinder / none / company*
Lat° every felawe° telle his tale aboute!°   *let / fellow / in turn*
And lat se° now, who shal the soper wynne?   *let us see*
And ther° I lefte I wol ayeyn° bigynne.   *where / again*
35   This duc of whom I make mencioun,
Whan he was come almoost unto the toun
In al his wele° and in his mooste pride,°   *prosperity / great pride*
He was war° as he caste his eye aside   *aware*
Where that ther° kneled° in the weye°   *there / kneeled / road*
40 A compaignye of ladyes tweye and tweye,°   *two by two*
Ech after oother clad in clothes blake.
But swich a cry and swich a wo° they make,   *woe*
That in this world nys° creature lyvynge   *is no*
That herde° swich another waymentynge.°   *heard / sorrowing*
45 And of this cry they nolde° nevere stenten°   *would not / cease*
Til they the reynes of his brydel henten.°   *grasped*
    "What folk been° ye, that at myn homcomynge   *are*
Perturben° so my feste with criynge?"   *disturb*
Quod° Theseus. "Have ye so greet envye°   *said / envy*
50 Of myn honour that thus compleyne and crye?
Or who hath yow mysboden° or offended?   *harmed*
And telleth me if it may been amended
And why that ye been clothed thus in blak."
    The eldeste lady of hem alle spak,
55 Whan she hadde swowned° with a deedly°
    cheere°   *fainted / deathly / face*
That it was routhe° for to seen and heere,   *pity*
And seyde, "Lord to whom fortune hath yeven°   *given*
Victorie and as a conquerour to lyven,°   *live*
Nat greveth us° youre glorie and youre
    honour,   *we are not grieved by*
60 But we biseken° mercy and socour!°   *ask / help*
Have mercy on oure wo° and oure distresse!   *woe*
Som drope of pitee thurgh° thy gentillesse°   *through / nobility*
Upon us wrecched wommen lat thou falle.
For certes,° lord, ther is noon of us alle   *certainly*
65 That she ne hath been a duchesse or a queene.
Now be we caytyves,° as it is wel seene,   *miserable people*

---

[1] *Iamque … laurigero* Latin: "And now Theseus, [drawing near] his native land in a chariot covered with laurels, after fierce battle with the Scythians [is heralded by glad applause and the shouts of the people to the heavens and the merry trumpet celebrating the end of the war]." This passage occurs at the end of Latin poet Statius's epic poem about the Theban War, *The Thebaid*, which was one of Chaucer's sources for *The Knight's Tale*. This passage describes the triumphant return of Theseus at the very end of the poem.

[2] *Femenye* Land of the Amazons, a race of female warriors.

[3] *Scithia* Scythia was an ancient country of nomads who inhabited the Caucasus region and was believed to be the homeland of the Amazons.

Thanked be Fortune and hire false wheel,[1]

That noon estaat assureth to be weel!° · *assures no estate prospers*

And certes, lord, to abyden° youre presence, · *await*

70 Heere in the temple of the goddesse

Clemence° · *clemency (mercy)*

We han° been waitynge al this

fourtenyght.° · *have / two-week period*

Now help us, lord, sith° it is in thy myght! · *since*

"I, wrecche° which that wepe° and crie thus, · *wretched one / weep*

Was whilom wyf to Kyng Cappaneus[2]

75 That starf° at Thebes, cursed be that day! · *died*

And alle we that been in this array° · *condition*

And maken al this lamentacioun,

We losten alle oure housbondes at that toun

Whil° that the seege° theraboute lay. · *while / siege*

80 And yet now the olde Creon,[3] weylaway,° · *alas*

That lord is now of Thebes the citee,

Fulfild of ire° and of iniquitee,° · *filled with anger / wickedness*

He for despit° and for his tirannye · *spite*

To do the dede bodyes vileynye° · *disgrace*

85 Of alle oure lordes whiche that been slawe,° · *killed*

He hath alle the bodyes on an heepe°

ydrawe° · *heap / gathered together*

And wol nat suffren hem by noon

assent° · *permit them on any terms*

Neither to been yburyed° nor ybrent,° · *buried / burned*

But maketh houndes° ete° hem in despit!"° · *dogs / eat / spite*

90   And with that word, withouten° moore respit, · *delay*

They fillen gruf° and criden° pitously, · *fell groveling / cried*

"Have on us wrecched wommen som mercy,

And lat oure sorwe synken° in thyn herte!" · *sink*

This gentil° duc doun from his courser°

sterte° · *noble / horse / jumped*

95 With herte pitous° whan he herde hem speke. · *pitying*

Hym thoughte that his herte wolde breke

Whan he saugh° hem so pitous and so maat,° · *saw / downcast*

That whilom weren of so greet estaat.

And in his armes he hem alle up hente° · *took*

100 And hem conforteth in ful good entente° · *with good will*

And swoor his ooth as he was trewe knyght

He wolde doon so ferfortly° his myght · *completely*

Upon the tiraunt° Creon, hem to wreke,° · *tyrant / avenge*

That al the peple of Grece sholde speke

105 How Creon was of Theseus yserved° · *dealt with*

As he that hadde his deeth ful wel deserved.

And right anoon° withouten moore abood,° · *immediately / delay*

His baner° he desplayeth and forth rood° · *banner / rode*

To Thebesward° and al his hoost° biside. · *towards Thebes / army*

110 No neer° Atthenes wolde he go ne° ride · *nearer / Athens / nor*

Ne take his ese° fully half a day, · *rest*

But onward on his wey that nyght he lay

And sente anon Ypolita the queene

And Emelye hir yonge suster sheene° · *bright*

115 Unto the toun of Atthenes to dwelle.

And forth he rit;° ther is namoore to telle. · *rode*

The rede° statue of Mars with spere° and

targe° · *red / spear / shield*

So shyneth in his white baner large

That alle the feeldes glyteren° up and doun, · *glitter*

120 And by his baner born° is his penoun° · *carried / pennant*

Of gold ful riche, in which ther was ybete° · *embroidered*

The Mynotaur[4] which that he slough° in Crete. · *killed*

Thus rit this duc. Thus rit this conquerour,

And in his hoost of chivalrie the flour,° · *flower*

125 Til that he cam to Thebes and alighte° · *dismounted*

Faire in a feeld theras° he thoughte fighte. · *where*

But shortly for to speken of this thyng,

With Creon, which° that was of Thebes kyng, · *who*

He faught and slough hym manly as a knyght

130 In pleyn bataille,° and putte the folk to flyght. · *open battle*

And by assaut° he wan° the citee after · *assault / captured*

And rente adoun° bothe wall and sparre° and

rafter. · *pulled down / beam*

And to the ladyes he restored agayn

The bones of hir housbondes that weren slayn

---

[1] *Fortune ... wheel* The Wheel of Fortune appears in Boethius's *Consolation of Philosophy*, a work Chaucer translated into English. The goddess Fortune turns her Wheel, and those on the top, in prosperity, fall to the bottom, and misery.

[2] *Kyng Cappaneus* King Cappaneus was one of seven leaders who attacked and besieged Thebes.

[3] *Creon* Creon was the king of Thebes and brother of Jocasta, mother of Oedipus.

---

[4] *The Mynotaur* An earlier deed of Theseus's is his killing of the Minotaur, a half-bull, half-human monster, who was kept in the labyrinth on the island of Crete and there given Athenian youths to devour for food. The Cretan King Minos's daughter, Ariadne, helped Theseus in this feat by giving him a ball of thread to roll out behind him so he could find his way out of the labyrinth once his deed was done.

135 To doon obsequies° as was tho the
      gyse.°   *funeral rites / then the custom*
    But it were al to longe for to devyse°   *narrate*
    The grete clamour and the waymentynge°   *lamentation*
    That the ladyes made at the brennynge°   *cremation*
    Of the bodies and the grete° honour   *great*
140 That Theseus the noble conquerour
    Dooth to the ladyes whan they from hym wente;
    But shortly for to telle is myn entente.
       Whan that this worthy duc, this Theseus
    Hath Creon slayn and wonne Thebes thus,
145 Stille° in that feeld he took al nyght his reste   *quietly*
    And dide with al the contree as hym leste.°   *desired*
       To ransake in the taas° of the bodyes dede   *pile*
    Hem for to strepe° of harneys° and of
      wede°   *strip / armor / clothes*
    The pilours° diden bisynesse and cure[1]   *scavengers*
150 After the bataille and disconfiture.°   *defeat*
    And so bifel that in the taas they founde,
    Thrugh girt° with many a grevous, blody wounde,   *pierced*
    Two yonge knyghtes liggynge° by and by,°   *lying / side by side*
    Bothe in oon armes wroght ful richely,[2]
155 Of whiche two, Arcita highte° that oon   *was named*
    And that oother knyght highte Palamon.
    Nat fully quyke° ne fully dede they were,   *alive*
    But by hir cote-armures° and by hir gere°   *coat of arms / equipment*
    The heraudes° knewe hem best in special°   *heralds / particularly*
160 As they that weren of the blood roial°   *were / royal*
    Of Thebes, and of sustren° two yborn.°   *sisters / born*
    Out of the taas the pilours han hem torn°   *had pulled them*
    And han hem caried softe° unto the tente   *softly*
    Of Theseus. And ful soone he hem sente
165 To Atthenes to dwellen in prisoun
    Perpetuelly. He nolde° no raunsoun.[3]   *would take*
    And whan this worthy duc hath thus ydon,
    He took his hoost and hoom he rood anon

With laurer° crowned as a conquerour.   *laurel*
170 And ther he lyveth in joye and in honour
    Terme of lyve.° What nedeth wordes
      mo?°   *for the rest of his life / more*
    And in a tour° in angwissh° and in wo   *tower / anguish*
    This Palamon and his felawe° Arcite   *companion*
    For everemoore; ther° may no gold hem
      quite.°   *where / buy them back*
175   This passeth yeer by yeer and day by day,
    Til it fil° ones° in a morwe° of May   *happened / once / morning*
    That Emelye, that fairer was to sene°   *see*
    Than is the lylie° upon his stalke grene   *lily*
    And fressher than the May with floures newe—
180 For with the rose colour stroof° hire hewe; *competed*
    I noot° which was the fyner° of hem two!—   *know not / finer*
    Er it were day, as was hir wone° to do,   *custom*
    She was arisen and al redy dight,°   *dressed*
    For May wol have no slogardrie° anyght!°   *laziness / at night*
185 The sesoun° priketh° every gentil herte°   *season / incites / heart*
    And maketh hym out of his slep to sterte
    And seith, "Arys and do thyn observaunce!"° *pay your respects*
    This maked Emelye have remembraunce
    To doon honour to May and for to ryse.
190 Yclothed was she fressh for to devyse.
    Hir yelow heer° was broyded° in a tresse° *hair / braided / plait*
    Bihynde hir bak, a yerde° long, I gesse.   *yard*
    And in the gardyn at the sonne upriste°   *sunrise*
    She walketh up and doun, and as hire liste
195 She gadereth° floures, party° white and rede,   *gathers / mingled*
    To make a subtil° gerland for hire hede.   *intricate*
    And as an aungel hevenysshly° she soong.   *heavenly*
    The grete tour that was so thikke and stroong
    Which of the castel was the chief dongeoun,[4]
200 Theras° the knyghtes weren in prisoun,   *where*
    Of whiche I tolde yow and tellen shal,
    Was evene joynaunt° to the gardyn wal   *next to*
    Theras this Emelye hadde hir pleyynge.°   *enjoyment*
    Bright was the sonne and cleer that morwenynge.
205 And this Palamoun, this woful prisoner,
    As was his wone° by leve° of his gayler°   *custom / leave / jailor*
    Was risen and romed° in a chambre an heigh° *roamed / on high*

---

[1] *diden ... cure* Worked hard.

[2] *Bothe ... richely* Both in one coat of arms fashioned very richly. As members of the same family, Palamon and Arcite have the same heraldic markings on a light cloth jacket worn over their armor.

[3] *He ... raunsoun* In the fourteenth century, the custom was to try to capture enemy soldiers in battle rather than kill them, for ransoming was profitable. Although the tale is ostensibly set in classical antiquity, the descriptions of warfare and the social customs are based on those of Chaucer's own day.

[4] *dongeoun* In the Middle Ages, a tower, often part of a castle. Dungeons were sometimes indeed used as prisons, as is the case here, but they had other functions as well, both domestic and military. The word here does not imply a miserable place of imprisonment.

In which he al the noble citee seigh°   *saw*
And eek the gardyn ful of braunches grene
210 Theras this fresshe Emelye the shene°   *bright*
Was in hir walk and romed up and doun.
This sorweful prisoner, this Palamoun
Goth in the chambre romynge° to and fro,   *roaming*
And to hymself compleynynge of his wo
215 That he was born. Ful ofte he seyde, "Allas!"
And so bifel by aventure° or cas°   *chance / accident*
That thurgh a wyndow thikke of many a
    barre°   *thickly set with bars*
Of iren° greet° and square as any sparre,°   *iron / great / beam*
He caste his eye upon Emelya.
220 And therwithal° he bleynte° and cride, "A!"   *with that / went pale*
As though he stongen° were unto the herte.   *stung*
And with that cry Arcite anon up sterte
And seyde, "Cosyn° myn, what eyleth° thee   *cousin / ails*
That art so pale and deedly° on to see?   *deathly*
225 Why cridestow?° Who hath thee doon offence?   *did you cry*
For Goddes love, taak° al° in pacience   *take / all*
Oure prisoun, for it may noon oother be!°   *may not be otherwise*
Fortune hath yeven° us this adversitee.   *given*
Som wikke° aspect or disposicioun   *wicked*
230 Of Saturne by som constellacioun
Hath yeven us this, although we hadde it sworn.
So stood the hevene whan that we were born.[1]
We moste endure! This is the short and playn!"°   *simple (truth)*
   This Palamon answerde and seyde agayn,
235 "Cosyn, forsothe° of this opinioun   *in truth*
Thow hast a veyn° ymaginacioun!°   *foolish / misconception*
This prison caused me nat for to crye.
But I was hurt right now thurghout myn eye
Into myn herte, that wol my bane° be!   *death-blow*
240 The fairnesse of that lady that I see
Yond° in the gardyn romen to and fro   *yonder*
Is cause of al my crying and my wo.
I noot where° she be woman or goddesse,   *whether*
But Venus[2] is it, soothly° as I gesse!"   *truly*
245 And therwithal on knees doun° he fil   *down*

And seyde, "Venus, if it be thy wil,
Yow in this gardyn thus to transfigure°   *change shape*
Bifore me, sorweful wrecche° creature,   *wretched*
Out of this prisoun helpe that we may scapen!°   *escape*
250 And if so be my destynee be shapen°   *predetermined*
By eterne° word to dyen in prisoun,   *eternal*
Of oure lynage° have som compassioun   *lineage*
That is so lowe ybroght by tirannye!"
And with that word Arcite gan espye°   *to see*
255 Wheras° this lady romed to and fro,   *where*
And with that sighte hir beautee hurte hym so
That if that Palamon was wounded soore,
Arcite is hurt as muche as he or moore.
And with a sigh he seyde pitously,
260 "The fresshe beautee sleeth me sodeynly
Of hire that rometh in the yonder place,
And but° I have hir mercy and hir grace,   *unless*
That I may seen hire atte leeste° weye,   *at least*
I nam° but deed! Ther is namoore° to seye."   *am not / no more*
265   This Palamon, whan he tho° wordes herde,   *those*
Dispitously° he looked and answerde,   *angrily*
"Wheither seistow° this in ernest or in pley?"°   *do you say / jest*
   "Nay," quod Arcite, "in ernest, by my fey!°   *faith*
God helpe me so, me list ful yvele pleye!"[3]
270   This Palamon gan knytte° his browes tweye.   *knit*
"It nere,"° quod he, "to thee no greet honour   *were not*
For to be fals ne for to be traitour
To me that am thy cosyn and thy brother,
Ysworn° ful depe, and ech of° us til oother,   *sworn / each to*
275 That nevere, for to dyen in the peyne,[4]
Til that deeth departe shal us tweyne,
Neither of us in love to hyndre° oother   *hinder*
Ne in noon oother cas, my leeve° brother,   *beloved*
But that thou sholdest trewely forthren° me   *help*
280 In every cas as I shal forthren thee.
This was thyn ooth and myn also, certeyn,
I woot° right wel, thou darst it nat withseyn.°   *know / deny*
Thus artow° of my conseil° out of
    doute,°   *are you / counsel / doubtless*
And now thow woldest falsly been aboute°   *set about*
285 To love my lady, whom I love and serve
And evere shal, til that myn herte sterve.°   *dies*

---

[1] *So ... born* Some evil aspect or alignment of Saturn with some other constellation has given us this fate, which we must endure although we had sworn to do otherwise. The stars were arranged that way when we were born. (Saturn was the Roman god of time and old age.)

[2] *Venus* Roman goddess of love, reproduction, and peace.

[3] *me ... pleye* I desire to play very little.

[4] *That ... peyne* Even if we were to die by torture.

Nay, certes, false Arcite, thow shalt nat so.

I loved hire first, and tolde thee my wo

As to my conseil° and to my brother sworn　　*my counsellor*

290　To forthre° me, as I have toold biforn,°　　*help / before*

For which thou art ybounden° as a knyght　　*obligated*

To helpen me if it lay in thy might,

Or elles artow fals, I dar wel seyn."

　This Arcite ful proudly spak ageyn.

295　"Thow shalt," quod he, "be rather fals than I.

And thou art fals, I telle thee outrely,°　　*completely*

For paramour° I loved hire first er thow.°　　*as a lover / you*

What wiltow seyn? Thou wistest nat yet
　　now°　　*did not yet know just now*

Wheither she be a womman or goddesse!

300　Thyn is affeccioun° of hoolynesse,°　　*feeling / religious devotion*

And myn is love, as to a creature,°　　*human being*

For which I tolde thee myn aventure

As to my cosyn and my brother sworn.

I pose° that thow lovedest hire biforn:　　*suppose*

305　Wostow nat wel the olde clerkes sawe[1]

That 'Who shal yeve° a lovere any lawe?'　　*give*

Love is a gretter° lawe, by my pan,°　　*greater / skull*

Than may be yeve° of any erthely man.　　*given*

And therfore positif lawe[2] and swich decree

310　Is broken alday,° for love in ech degree.°　　*daily / social rank*

A man moot nedes love, maugree his heed.°　　*despite his intentions*

He may nat flee it thogh he sholde be deed,°　　*dead*

Al be she° mayde° or wydwe° or elles°
　　wyf.　　*even if she is / maiden / widow / else*

And eek, it is nat likly al thy lyf

315　To stonden in hir grace;° namoore° shal I.　　*favor / no more*

For wel thou woost° thyselven° verraily°　　*know / yourself / truly*

That thou and I be dampned° to prisoun　　*condemned*

Perpetuelly. Us gayneth no raunsoun.°　　*no ransom will free us*

We stryven° as dide the houndes for the boon;°　　*quarrel / bone*

320　They foughte al day, and yet hir° part was noon:　　*their*

Ther cam a kyte° whil they weren so wrothe°　　*buzzard / angry*

And baar awey° the boon bitwixe hem bothe.　　*carried away*

And therfore at the kynges court, my brother,

Ech man for hymself! Ther is noon oother!

325　Love if thee list, for I love and ay° shal.　　*always*

And soothly,° leeve brother, this is al.　　*truly*

Heere in this prisoun moote we endure°　　*must we remain*

And everich° of us take his aventure!"　　*each*

　Greet was the strif and long bitwix hem tweye,

330　If that I hadde leyser° for to seye.　　*leisure*

But to th'effect:° It happed on a day,　　*result*

To telle it yow as shortly as I may,

A worthy duc that highte Perotheus,

That felawe° was to Duc Theseus　　*companion*

335　Syn° thilke° day that they were children lite,　　*since / the same / little*

Was come to Atthenes his felawe to visite

And for to pley, as he was won° to do.　　*accustomed*

For in this world he loved no man so,

And he loved hym als° tendrely agayn.　　*as*

340　So wel they lovede, as olde bookes sayn,

That whan that oon was deed, soothly to telle,

His felawe wente and soughte hym doun in Helle![3]

But of that storie, list me nat° to write.　　*I do not desire*

Duc Perotheus loved wel Arcite

345　And hadde hym knowe at Thebes yeer by yere.

And finally at requeste and preyere

Of Perotheus, withouten any raunsoun,

Duc Thesuus hym leet out of prisoun

Frely° to goon wher that hym liste overal　　*freely*

350　In swich a gyse° as I you tellen shal.　　*such a manner*

　This was the forward,° pleynly for
　　t'endite,°　　*agreement / to write it plainly*

Bitwixen Theseus and hym Arcite:

That if so were that Arcite were yfounde°　　*found*

Evere in his lif by day or nyght or stounde°　　*hour*

355　In any contree of this Theseus

And he were caught, it was acorded° thus:　　*agreed*

That with a swerd he sholde lese° his heed.°　　*lose / head*

Ther nas noon oother remedie ne reed,°　　*counsel*

But taketh his leve° and homward he him spedde.　　*leave*

360　Lat hym bewar! His nekke lith to wedde!°　　*lies as a pledge*

　How greet a sorwe suffreth now Arcite!

---

[1]　*Wostow … sawe*　Do you not know well the old scholar's saying.

[2]　*Positif lawe*　Positive law is that written into the statute books, as opposed to natural law, which is self-evident from God's creation.

[3]　*His … Helle*　The classical legend is that Theseus accompanied Pirithous (Chaucer's Perotheus) to the Underworld in his unsuccessful attempt to rescue Proserpina, who had been abducted by Pluto, king of that region. Both men eventually returned alive, although Theseus was imprisoned and rescued by Hercules. The suggestion that Theseus went down to rescue Pirithous because he had died probably comes from the long thirteenth-century medieval allegory *The Romance of the Rose*, which Chaucer translated from French.

The deeth he feeleth thurgh his herte smyte!°   *strike*
He wepeth, wayleth, crieth pitously.
To sleen hymself he waiteth prively.°   *secretly*
365 He seyde, "Allas that day" that he "was born!¹
Now is my prisoun worse than biforn!
Now is me shape° eternally to dwelle   *ordained*
Nat in my Purgatorie but in Helle!
Allas, that evere knew I Perotheus,
370 For elles hadde I dwelled with Theseus
Yfetered° in his prisoun everemo!   *chained*
Thanne hadde I been in blisse and nat in wo!
Oonly the sighte of hire whom that I serve,
Though that I nevere hir grace may deserve,
375 Wolde han suffised right ynough for me!
O deere cosyn Palamon," quod he,
"Thyn is the victorie of this aventure.
Ful blissfully in prisoun maistow dure.°   *may you remain*
In prisoun? certes nay,° but in Paradys!   *no*
380 Wel hath Fortune yturned thee the dys°   *dice*
That hast the sighte of hire, and I th'absence.
For possible is, syn° thou hast hire presence   *since*
And art a knyght, a worthy and an able,
That som cas,° syn Fortune is chaungeable,   *(by) some event*
385 Thow maist to thy desir somtyme atteyne.°   *attain*
But I that am exiled and bareyne°   *lacking*
Of alle grace and in so greet dispeir
That ther nys° erthe, water, fir, ne eir,°   *is not / nor air*
Ne creature that of hem maked is
390 That may me heele° or doon confort° in
    this,   *heal / bring comfort*
Wel oughte I sterve in wanhope° and distresse!   *despair*
Farwel my lif,° my lust,° and my gladnesse!   *life / desire*
   "Allas, why pleynen° folk so in commune°   *complain / commonly*
On° purveiaunce° of God or of Fortune   *against / foresight*
395 That yeveth hem° ful ofte in many a gyse°   *gives them / way*
Wel bettre than they kan hemself devyse?
Som man desireth for to han richesse
That cause is of his moerdre° or greet siknesse,   *murder*
And som man wolde out of his prisoun fayn°   *gladly (get)*
400 That in his hous is of his meynee° slayn.   *his retinue*

---

¹ *Allas … born* Many editions prefer the reading, found in several other manuscripts, "Allas the day that I was born." The Ellesmere variant (which we have preserved, although it may indeed be an error) would originally have been less awkward, since the quotation marks are a modern addition.

Infinite harmes been in this mateere.°   *matter*
We witen nat° what we preyen heere;°   *know not / pray for*
We faren° as he that dronke is as a mous.°   *behave / mouse*
A dronke man woot wel that he hath an hous,
405 But he noot° which the righte wey is
    thider,°   *does not know / there*
And to a dronke man the wey is slider.°   *slippery*
And certes in this world so faren° we: *fare*
We seken faste° after felicitee,°   *determinedly / happiness*
But we goon wrong ful often, trewely.
410 Thus may we seyn° alle and namely° I,   *see / especially*
That wende° and hadde a greet opinioun   *expected*
That if I myghte escapen from prisoun,
Thanne hadde I been in joye and parfit heele°   *well-being*
That now I am exiled fro my wele,°   *happiness*
415 Syn° that I may nat seen you, Emelye!   *since*
I nam° but deed! Ther nys no remedye!"   *am not*
   Upon that oother syde° Palamon,   *side*
Whan that he wiste Arcite was agon,°   *gone*
Swich sorwe° he maketh that the grete tour   *sorrow*
420 Resouned° of his youlyng° and clamour.   *resounded / yowling*
The pure fettres° on his shynes°
    grete°   *very chains / shins / swollen*
Weren of his bittre salte teeres wete.°   *wet*
"Allas," quod he, "Arcita, cosyn myn!
Of al oure strif,° God woot, the fruyt° is thyn!   *strife / fruit*
425 Thow walkest now in Thebes at thy large,°   *freely*
And of my wo thow yevest° litel° charge!   *give / little*
Thou mayst, syn° thou hast wisdom and
    manhede,°   *since / manhood*
Assemblen alle the folk of oure kynrede°   *kindred*
And make a werre so sharpe on this citee
430 That by som aventure or som tretee°   *treaty*
Thow mayst have hire° to lady and to wyf   *her*
For whom that I moste nedes lese° my lyf.   *lose*
For as by wey of possibilitee,
Sith thou art at thy large of prisoun free
435 And art a lord, greet is thyn avauntage
Moore than is myn that sterve here in a cage.
For I moot° wepe and wayle whil I lyve   *must*
With al the wo that prison may me yeve°   *give*
And eek with peyne that love me yeveth also
440 That doubleth al my torment and my wo!"
Therwith the fyr° of jalousie up sterte   *fire*
Withinne his brest and hente° him by the herte   *grabbed*
So woodly° that he lyk was to biholde   *madly*

The boxtree[1] or the asshen° dede and colde.   *ashes*

445   Thanne seyde he, "O crueel goddes that governe
This world with byndyng° of youre word eterne   *binding*
And writen in the table of atthamaunt°   *adamant (diamond)*
Youre parlement and youre eterne graunt,°   *eternal decree*
What is mankynde moore unto you holde°   *indebted*

450   Than is the sheepe that ronketh° in the folde?   *huddles*
For slayn is man right as another beest
And dwelleth eek in prison and arreest°   *arrest*
And hath siknesse and greet adversitee
And ofte tymes giltlees,° pardee!°   *guiltless | by God*

455   What governance is in this prescience
That giltlees tormenteth innocence?[2]
And yet encresseth° this al my penaunce,   *increases*
That man is bounden to his observaunce
For Goddes sake to letten of° his wille,   *restrain*

460   Theras° a beest may al his lust fulfille.   *whereas*
And whan a beest is deed, he hath no peyne,
But after his deeth man moot wepe and pleyne,
Though in this world he have care and wo;
Withouten doute it may stonden so!

465   The answere of this lete° I to dyvynys,°   *leave | religious scholars*
But wel I woot that in this world greet pyne ys.
Allas, I se° a serpent or a theef°   *see | thief*
That many a trewe man hath doon mescheef
Goon at his large° and where hym list may turne.   *go freely*

470   But I moot been in prisoun thurgh Saturne
And eek thurgh Juno,[3] jalous° and eek wood,°   *jealous | crazy*
That hath destroyed wel ny° al the blood   *very nearly*
Of Thebes with hise° waste° walles wyde,   *its | wasted*
And Venus sleeth me on that oother syde

475   For jalousie and fere° of hym Arcite."   *fear*
    Now wol I stynte° of Palamon a lite°   *stop (speaking) | little*
And lete hym in his prisoun stille° dwelle   *quietly*
And of Arcita forth I wol yow telle.

    The sonne passeth, and the nyghtes longe

480   Encressen doublewise° the peynes stronge   *double*
Bothe of the lovere and the prisoner.
I noot° which hath the wofuller°
    mester.°   *do not know | sadder | profession*
For shortly for to seyn,° this Palamoun   *say*
Perpetuelly is dampned° to prisoun   *condemned*

485   In cheynes and in fettres to been deed,°   *to die*
And Arcite is exiled upon his heed°   *upon pain of losing his head*
Forever mo as out of that contree,
Ne nevere mo he shal his lady see.

    Yow loveres, axe° I now this questioun: *ask*

490   Who hath the worse, Arcite or Palamoun?
That oon may seen his lady day by day,
But in prison he moot dwelle alway.
That oother wher hym list may ride or go,
But seen his lady shal he nevere mo.[4]

495   Now demeth° as you list, ye that kan,   *judge*
For I wol telle forth as I bigan.

EXPLICIT PRIMA PARS

SEQUITUR PARS SECUNDA[5]

    Whan that Arcite to Thebes comen was,
Ful ofte a day he swelte° and seyde, "Allas,"   *fainted*
For seen his lady shal he nevere mo.

500   And shortly to concluden° al his wo,   *summarize*
So muche sorwe hadde nevere creature
That is or shal° whil° that the world may
    dure.°   *shall be | while | endure*
His slepe, his mete,° his drynke is hym biraft°   *food | taken away*
That lene° he wexeth° and drye as is a shaft.°   *lean | grows | arrow*

505   Hise eyen holwe° and grisly° to biholde,   *hollow | grim*
His hewe° falow° and pale as asshen colde,   *complexion | yellow*
And solitarie he was and evere allone
And waillynge al the nyght, makynge his mone.°   *moan*
And if he herde song or instrument,

510   Thanne wolde he wepe. He myghte nat be stent.°   *stopped*
So feble eek were hise spiritz and so lowe
And chaunged so that no man koude knowe

---

[1] *The boxtree*   The box tree is known for its light yellow wood. Palamon is as pale as ashes.

[2] *What ... innocence*   What governing principle is in this foresight that torments innocent people who are guiltless?

[3] *Juno*   In Roman mythology, Juno, wife of Jupiter (king of the gods), was the goddess of the hearth and of domesticity, and was frequently jealous of Jupiter's love affairs. Juno hated Thebes because of Jupiter's love affairs with the Theban women Semele, mother of Bacchus, and Alcmena, mother of Hercules.

[4] *But ... mo*   This is a typical *demande d'amour* (French: question of love) that sets forth a problem in the aristocratic code of love for courtiers to debate.

[5] *Explicit ... Secunda*   Latin: Here ends the first part. The second part follows.

His speche nor his voys,° though men it herde,   voice
And in his geere° for al the world he ferde°   manner / fared
515 Nat oonly lik the loveris maladye
Of hereos[1] but rather lyk manye°   mania
Engendred of humour malencolik[2]
Biforn his owene celle fantastik.[3]
And shortly, turned was al up so doun°   upside-down
520 Bothe habit and eek disposicioun
Of hym this woful lovere daun Arcite.°   Sir Arcite
    What sholde I al day of his wo endite?°   write
Whan he endured hadde a yeer or two
This crueel torment and this peyne and wo
525 At Thebes in his countree, as I seyde,
Upon a nyght in sleepe as he hym leyde,°   lay
Hym thoughte° how that the wynged god Mercurie[4]   it seemed
Biforn hym stood and bad° hym to be murie.°   commanded / merry
His slepy yerde° in hond he bar°
    uprighte;   sleep-producing staff / bore
530 An hat he werede° upon hise heris° brighte.   wore / hairs
Arrayed was this god, as I took keepe,°   noticed
As he was whan that Argus[5] took his sleepe,
And seyde hym thus: "To Atthenes shaltou
    wende.°   shall you go
Ther is thee shapen° of thy wo an ende."   for you ordained
535 And with that word Arcite wook° and sterte.°   woke / got up
"Now trewely, hou° soore° that me
    smerte,"°   however / sore / it may injure
Quod he, "to Atthenes right now wol I fare.°   travel
Ne for the drede of deeth shal I nat spare°   avoid
To se my lady that I love and serve.
540 In hire presence I recche nat° to sterve!"   care not
    And with that word he caughte° a greet mirour°   seized / mirror

And saugh° that chaunged was al his colour   saw
And saugh his visage° al in another kynde.°   face / nature
And right anon it ran hym in his mynde
545 That sith his face was so disfigured
Of maladye, the which he hadde endured,
He myghte wel, if that he bar hym lowe,°   acted humbly
Lyve in Atthenes everemoore unknowe
And seen his lady wel ny day by day.°   nearly every day
550 And right anon he chaunged his array°   dress
And cladde hym as a povre° laborer.   poor
And al allone save only a squier
That knew his privetee° and al his cas,°   secret / case
Which was disguised povrely as he was,
555 To Atthenes is he goon the nexte way,°   shortest way
And to the court he wente upon a day,
And at the gate he profreth° his servyse   offered
To drugge° and drawe° what so men wol
    devyse.°   drudge / draw (water) / demand
And shortly of this matere for to seyn,
560 He fil in office° with a chamberleyn°   was employed / chamberlain
The which that dwellynge was with Emelye,
For he was wys° and koude soone espye°   wise / see
Of every servaunt which that serveth here.°   her
Wel koude he hewen° wode and water bere,°   cut / carry
565 For he was yong and myghty for the nones.°   occasion
And therto he was long° and big of bones   tall
To doon that° any wight° kan hym devyse.   whatever / person
A yeer or two he was in this servyse,
Page° of the chambre° of Emelye the
    brighte,   young servant / chamber
570 And Philostrate[6] he seyde that he highte.°   was named
But half so wel biloved a man as he
Ne was ther nevere in court of his degree.
He was so gentil° of condicioun   noble
That thurghout al the court was his renoun.°   renown
575 They seyden that it were a charitee°   would be an act of charity
That Theseus wolde enhauncen his degree°   promote him
And putten hym in worshipful servyse°   honorable service
Theras° he myghte his vertu excercise.°   where / demonstrate
And thus withinne a while his name is spronge°   spread about
580 Bothe of hise dedes and his goode tonge,°   elegant speech
That Theseus hath taken hym so neer°   close (to himself)

---

[1] *hereos* Hereos or amor hereos was the name given for the "disease" of love.

[2] *humour malencolik* Melancholic humor is one of the four humors of the body according to classical and medieval medicinal theory. The other humors are the choleric, phlegmatic, and sanguine. Melancholic humor, of course, makes one sad—hence our word "melancholy."

[3] *celle fantastik* The portion of the brain where the imagination resided. The other two cells were those of memory and reason.

[4] *Mercurie* Roman messenger of the gods.

[5] *Argus* In Roman mythology, Argus had a hundred eyes and bore watch over Io, whom Jupiter loved. Mercury put him to sleep with his staff and then killed him.

[6] *Philostrate* Greek: one knocked down by love.

That of his chambre[1] he made hym a squier
And gaf° hym gold to mayntene° his
    degree.°   *gave / maintain / rank*
And eek men broghte hym out of his contree
585 From yeer to yeer ful pryvely° his rente.[2]   *privately*
But honestly and slyly° he it spente,   *discreetly*
That no man wondred how that he it hadde.
And thre yeer° in this wise° his lif he ladde°   *years / way / led*
And bar hym so, in pees° and eek in
    werre,°   *conducted himself / peace / war*
590 Ther was no man that Theseus hath derre.°   *held more dear*
And in this blisse lete I now Arcite
And speke I wole of Palamon a lite.°   *little*
    In derknesse and horrible and strong prisoun
Thise seven yeer hath seten Palamoun
595 Forpyned,° what for wo and for distresse.   *tormented*
Who feeleth double soor° and hevynesse° *soreness / heaviness*
But Palamon that love destreyneth° so,   *afflicts*
That wood° out of his wit he goth° for wo?   *crazy / goes*
And eek therto he is a prisoner
600 Perpetuelly, noght oonly for a yer.
    Who koude ryme° in Englyssh proprely   *rhyme*
His martirdom? Forsothe, it am nat I!
Therfore I passe as lightly° as I may.   *quickly*
    It fel that in the seventhe yer in May,
605 The thridde° nyght, as olde bookes seyn   *third*
That al this storie tellen moore pleyn,°   *plainly*
Were it° by aventure or destynee,   *whether it were*
As whan a thyng is shapen° it shal be,   *ordained*
That soone after the mydnyght Palamoun
610 By helpyng of a freend° brak° his prisoun *friend / escaped*
And fleeth° the citee faste as he may go.   *flees*
For he hadde yeve° his gayler° drynke so, *given / jailor*
Of a clarree° maad° of a certeyn wyn *spiced drink / made*
Of nercotikes° and opie° of Thebes fyn° *narcotics / opium / fine*
615 That al that nyght thogh that men wolde him shake,

This gayler sleepe; he myghte nat awake!
And thus he fleeth as faste as evere he may.
The nyght was short and faste by the day° *it was almost day*
That nedes cost° he moot° hymselven hyde, *necessarily / must*
620 And til° a grove faste therbisyde°   *to / nearby*
With dredeful° foot thanne stalketh°
    Palamon.   *fearful / walks quietly*
For shortly, this was his opinion
That in that grove he wolde hym hyde al day,
And in the nyght thanne wolde he take his way
625 To Thebesward,° his freendes for to preye° *towards Thebes / ask*
On Theseus to helpe hym to werreye.°   *make war*
And shortly outher° he wolde lese° his lif *either / lose*
Or wynnen° Emelye unto his wyf.   *win*
This is th'effect and his entente pleyn.° *plain intent*
630 Now wol I turne to Arcite ageyn,°   *again*
That litel wiste how ny° that was his care,   *near*
Til that Fortune had broght him in the snare.
    The bisy larke, messager of day,
Salueth° in hir song the morwe gray,   *salutes*
635 And firy Phebus[3] riseth up so brighte
That al the orient° laugheth of the lighte   *east*
And with hise stremes° dryeth° in the
    greves°   *beams / dries / branches*
The silver dropes hangynge on the leves.°   *leaves*
And Arcita that is in the court roial
640 With Theseus, his squier principal,
Is risen and looketh on the myrie° day.   *merry*
And for to doon his observaunce to May,[4]
Remembrynge on the poynt° of his desir,   *point*
He on a courser° startlynge° as the fir° *war-horse / prancing / fire*
645 Is riden into the feeldes° hym to pleye.   *fields*
Out of the court were it a myle° or tweye,   *mile*
And to the grove of which that I yow tolde
By aventure his wey he gan to holde
To maken hym a gerland of the greves,°   *branches*
650 Were it of wodebynde° or hawethorn
    leves.°   *woodbine / hawthorn leaves*
And loude he song ayeyn the sonne shene,° *in the bright sunshine*
"May, with alle thy floures and thy grene,°   *green*
Welcome be thou, faire, fresshe May,

---

[1] *That of his chambre* Medieval English kings relied heavily on knights of their chamber for administrative duties of government. Originally servants who performed various domestic functions, these people had honorific titles implying these duties but took on the duties of governmental administration instead.

[2] *From … rente* The rent here referred to is not something Arcite must pay but what is owed to him. Medieval lords possessed land and were owed various rents and services from those whom they allowed use it. A high lord like Arcite would have had much income from such sources.

---

[3] *Phebus* Name for Apollo, god of the sun.

[4] *And … May* The custom was for courtly people to rise early in mornings in May and roam about in the countryside to enjoy the good weather that had recently returned.

In hope that I som grene° gete may." — *something green*

655 And from his courser° with a lusty
  herte° — *war-horse / spirited heart*

Into a grove ful hastily he sterte,

And in a path he rometh° up and doun — *roams*

Theras° by aventure this Palamoun — *where*

Was in a bussh that no man myghte hym se,° — *see*

660 For soore aferd of his deeth thanne was he.

Nothyng ne knew he° that it was Arcite. — *he did not know*

God woot, he wolde have trowed° it ful lite!° — *believed / very little*

But sooth is seyd, so sithen° many yeres,° — *after / years*

That "Feeld hath eyen and the wode° hath eres."° — *wood / ears*

665 It is ful fair a man to bere hym evene,

For al day meeteth men at unset stevene.[1]

Ful litel woot Arcite of his felawe

That was so ny to herknen° al his sawe,° — *listen to / speech*

For in the bussh he sitteth now ful stille.

670   Whan that Arcite hadde romed all his fille

And songen al the roundel[2] lustily,

Into a studie° he fil° al sodeynly, — *meditative mood / fell*

As doon thise loveres in hir queynte° geres.° — *curious / customs*

Now in the crope,° now doun in the breres,° — *tree-top / briars*

675 Now up, now doun as boket° in a welle. — *bucket*

Right as the Friday, soothly°for to telle, — *truly*

Now it shyneth, now it reyneth° faste: — *rains*

Right so kan geery° Venus overcaste — *fickle*

The hertes of hir folk. Right as hir day[3]

680 Is gereful,° right so chaungeth she array. — *fickle*

Selde° is the Friday al the wowke
  ylike.° — *seldom / like the rest of the week*

  Whan that Arcite had songe,° he gan to sike° — *sung / sigh*

And sette hym doun withouten any moore.

"Allas," quod he, "that day that I was bore!

685 How longe, Juno, thurgh thy crueltee

Woltow werreyen° Thebes the citee? — *make war on*

Allas, ybroght° is to confusioun — *brought*

The blood roial of Cadme and Amphioun[4]—

Of Cadmus which that was the firste man

690 That Thebes bulte,° or first the toun bigan, — *built*

And of the citee first was crouned kyng.

Of his lynage am I and his ofspryng

By verray ligne° as of the stok° roial, — *true lineage / stock*

And now I am so caytyf° and so thral,° — *captive / enslaved*

695 That he that is my mortal enemy

I serve hym as his squier povrely.° — *poorly*

And yet dooth Juno me wel moore° shame, — *much more*

For I dar noght biknowe° myn owene name! — *reveal*

But theras I was wont to highte Arcite,

700 Now highte I Philostrate, noght worth a myte!° — *small coin*

Allas, thou felle° Mars,[5] allas, Juno! — *cruel*

Thus hath youre ire° oure kynrede° al
  fordo,° — *anger / kindred / destroyed*

Save oonly me and wrecched Palamoun

That Theseus martireth° in prisoun. — *martyrs*

705 And over al this to sleen me outrely,° — *completely*

Love hath his firy dart so brennyngly° — *burningly*

Ystiked° thurgh my trewe,° careful° herte, — *stuck / true / sorrowful*

That shapen° was my deeth° erst than my
  sherte.°[6] — *ordained / death / shirt*

Ye sleen me with youre eyen, Emelye!

710 Ye been the cause wherfore that I dye!

Of al the remenant of myn oother care,

Ne sette I nat° the montance° of a tare,° — *I do not set / value / weed*

So that I koude doon aught to youre plesaunce."

And with that word he fil doun in a traunce

715 A longe tyme, and after he up sterte.

  This Palamoun that thoughte that thurgh his herte

He felte a coold swerd sodeynliche° glyde, — *suddenly*

For ire° he quook.° No lenger wolde he
  byde.° — *anger / shook / wait*

And whan that he had herd Arcites tale,

720 As he were wood,° with face deed° and pale, — *crazy / dead*

He stirte hym up out of the buskes° thikke° — *bushes / thick*

And seide, "Arcite, false traytour wikke,° — *wicked*

Now artow° hent° that lovest my lady so, — *are you / caught*

---

[1] *It ... stevene* It is very desirable for a man to behave with restraint, for every day people meet at an unexpected time.

[2] *roundel* Type of popular song in both France and England in the fourteenth century. It was characterized by repeated phrases of both music and words.

[3] *Right as hir day* The days of the week were originally devoted to the various gods and goddesses, as our names for them still attest (Saturn's day—Saturday; Thor's day—Thursday). Venus's day was Friday (*Veneris dies*) in the Romance languages; the Germanic goddess most resembling Venus was named Freya.

[4] *Cadme and Amphioun* Earlier kings of Thebes.

[5] *Mars* Roman god of war.

[6] *That ... sherte* The reference here is probably to the *first* shirt made for Arcite when he was a baby.

For whom that I have al this peyne and wo!
725 And art my blood° and to my conseil°
        sworn,   *of my blood | counsel*
As I ful ofte have seyd thee heer biforn,
And hast byjaped° heere Duc Theseus   *tricked*
And falsly chaunged hast thy name thus—
I wol be deed or elles thou shalt dye!
730 Thou shalt nat love my lady Emelye!
But I wol love hire oonly and namo,°   *no more*
For I am Palamon, thy mortal foo!°   *foe*
And though that I no wepene have in this place,
But out of prison am astert° by grace,   *escaped*
735 I drede noght° that outher° thow shalt dye   *fear not | either*
Or thow ne shalt nat loven Emelye.
Chees° which thou wolt,° or thou shalt nat
        asterte!"   *choose | wish*
    This Arcite, with ful despitous° herte,   *scornful*
Whan he hym knew° and hadde his tale herd,   *recognized*
740 As fiers as leoun pulled out his swerd
And seyd thus: "By God that sit above,
Nere it° that thou art sik° and wood for love, *were it not | sick*
And eek that thow no wepne° hast in this place,   *weapon*
Thou sholdest nevere out of this grove pace°   *escape*
745 That thou ne sholdest dyen of° myn hond!   *by*
For I defye° the seurete° and the bond   *defy | promise*
Which that thou seist that I have maad° to thee.   *made*
What, verray fool, thynk wel that love is free,
And I wol love hire maugree° al thy myght!   *despite*
750 But for as muche thou art a worthy knyght
And wilnest to darreyne hire by bataille,[1]
Have heer° my trouthe:° tomorwe I wol nat faille,   *here | vow*
Withoute wityng° of any oother wight,°   *the knowledge | person*
That heere I wol be founden as a knyght,
755 And bryngen harneys° right ynough° for thee, *armor | enough*
And chese the best and leve the worste for me.
And mete° and drynke this nyght wol I brynge   *food*
Ynough for thee and clothes for thy beddynge.
And if so be that thou my lady wynne°   *win*
760 And sle° me in this wode ther I am inne,°   *kill | in*
Thow mayst wel have thy lady as for me!"
    This Palamon answerde, "I graunte it thee!"
And thus they been departed til amorwe,°   *the next day*

Whan ech of hem had leyd his feith° to
        borwe.°   *word | as a pledge*
765 O Cupide,[2] out of all charitee!
O regne,° that wolt no felawe° have with thee!   *reign | equal*
Ful sooth is seyd that love ne lordshipe
Wol noght, hir thankes, have no felaweshipe.[3]
Wel fynden that Arcite and Palamoun!
770 Arcite is riden anon unto the toun,
And on the morwe er it were dayes light
Ful prively two harneys° hath he dight,°   *suits of armor | prepared*
Bothe suffisaunt° and mete° to
        darreyne°   *sufficient | fitting | decide*
The bataille in the feeld bitwix hem tweyne.
775 And on his hors allone as he was born
He carieth al the harneys hym biforn.
And in the grove at tyme and place yset,°   *appointed*
This Arcite and this Palamon ben° met.   *are*
To chaungen gan the colour in hir° face,   *their*
780 Right as the hunters in the regne of
        Trace°   *(Greek) kingdom of Thrace*
That stondeth at the gappe° with a spere,°   *gap | spear*
Whan hunted is the leoun and the bere°   *bear*
And hereth hym come russhyng in the greves°   *brush*
And breketh bothe bowes and the leves
785 And thynketh, "Heere cometh my mortal enemy!
Withoute faille, he moot be deed or I!
For outher I moot sleen hym at the gappe
Or he moot sleen me if that me myshappe"°—   *I am unlucky*
So ferden° they in chaungyng of hir hewe   *fared*
790 As fer as everich of hem oother knewe.°   *knew the other*
    Ther nas no° good day ne no saluyng,° *was neither | saluting*
But streight° withouten word or
        rehersyng°   *immediately | conversation*
Everich of hem heelpe for to armen oother°   *to arm the other*
As freely° as he were his owene brother.   *friendly*
795 And after that with sharpe speres stronge
They foynen° ech at oother wonder° longe. *thrust | wonderfully*
Thou myghtest wene° that this Palamoun   *expect*
In his fightyng were a wood leoun,
And as a crueel tigre was Arcite.
800 As wilde bores gonne° they to smyte,   *began*

[1] *And ... bataille* And wish to vindicate your right to her by battle.

[2] *Cupide* Cupid, son of Venus, is the Roman god of love.

[3] *Ful ... felaweshipe* Truly it is said that neither love nor lordship will willingly have company.

That frothen whit as foom for ire wood.[1]
Up to the anclee° foghte they in hir blood,   *ankle*
And in this wise I lete hem fightyng dwelle°   *still fighting*
And forth I wole of Theseus yow telle.
805   The destinee, ministre° general   *agent*
That executeth in the world over al
The purveiaunce° that God hath seyn° biforn,   *foresight | seen*
So strong it is that though the world had sworn
The contrarie of a thyng by ye or nay,
810   Yet somtyme it shal fallen° on a day   *happen*
That falleth nat eft° withinne a thousand yeere.   *not again*
For certeinly oure appetites heere,
Be it of werre or pees° or hate or love,   *war or peace*
Al is this reuled° by the sighte above.   *ruled*
815   This mene° I now by myghty Theseus,   *mean*
That for to hunten is so desirus,°   *eager*
And namely at the grete hert° in May,   *deer*
That in his bed ther daweth° hym no day   *dawns*
That he nys clad° and redy° for to ryde   *is not clothed | ready*
820   With hunte and horn and houndes hym bisyde,
For in his huntyng hath he swich delit
That it is al his joye and appetit°   *desire*
To been hymself the grete hertes bane.°   *slayer*
For after Mars he serveth now Dyane.[2]
825   Cleer was the day, as I have toold er this,
And Theseus with alle joye and blis
With his Ypolita the faire queene
And Emelye clothed al in grene
On huntyng° be they riden° roially.   *a-hunting | are they riding*
830   And to the grove that stood ful faste by°   *very nearby*
In which ther was an hert, as men hym tolde,
Duc Theseus the streighte wey° hath holde.°   *road | has held*
And to the launde° he rideth hym ful right,°   *clearing | directly*
For thider° was the hert wont° have his flight, *there | accustomed*
835   And over a brook and so forth in his weye,
This duc wol han a cours° at hym or tweye   *chase*
With houndes swiche as hym list comaunde.°   *to command*
And whan this duc was come unto the launde
Under the sonne he looketh. And anon
840   He was war° of Arcite and Palamon,   *aware*
That foughten breme° as it were bores° two.   *boldly | boars*

The brighte swerdes wenten to and fro
So hidously that with the leeste strook°   *stroke*
It semed as it wolde fille° an ook!°   *fell | oak*
845   But what they were, nothyng he ne woot.[3]
This duc his courser with his spores° smoot,°   *spurs | struck*
And at a stert° he was bitwix hem two   *in an instant*
And pulled out a swerd and cride, "Hoo!°   *whoa!*
Namoore, upon peyne of lesynge° of youre heed!   *losing*
850   By myghty Mars, he shal anon be deed
That smyteth any strook° that I may seen.   *stroke*
But telleth me what mystiers men ye been[4]
That been so hardy° for to fighten here   *bold*
Withouten juge° or oother officere   *judge (referee)*
855   As it were in a lystes° roially."   *jousting ground*
This Palamon answerde hastily
And seyde, "Sire, what nedeth wordes mo?
We have the deeth disserved bothe two.[5]
Two woful wrecches been we, two caytyves°   *wretches*
860   That been encombred of° oure owene lyves.   *burdened by*
And as thou art a rightful lord and juge,
Ne yeve° us neither mercy ne refuge.   *do not give*
But sle° me first, for Seinte Charitee,[6]   *slay*
But sle my felawe eek as wel as me.
865   Or sle hym first! For though thow knowest it lite,°   *little*
This is thy mortal foo.° This is Arcite   *foe*
That fro thy lond is banysshed on his heed,[7]
For which he hath deserved to be deed.
For this is he that cam unto thy gate
870   And seyde that he highte Philostrate.
Thus hath he japed° thee ful many a yer,   *fooled*
And thou hast maked hym thy chief squire,
And this is he that loveth Emelye.

---

[1] *That ... wood* That froth (at the mouth), white as foam, with raging anger.

[2] *Dyane* Roman goddess of the hunt.

[3] *But ... woot* He did not know anything about who they were.

[4] *But ... been* But tell me what occupation you follow, i.e., what kind of men you are. Mystiers is cognate with mystery, which in the Middle Ages meant a trade or occupation and gave the name to the religious plays the trade guilds put on in various cities—mystery plays.

[5] *We ... two* They deserve death because of the terms of their conditional sentence: Palamon must stay in prison or die, while Arcite must remain in exile or die.

[6] *Seinte Charitee* Holy Charity. Charity is the old word for God's love.

[7] *banysshed on his heed* Banished with the consequence of losing his head should he return without pardon.

For sith the day is come that I shal dye,
875 I make pleynly° my confessioun   *fully*
That I am thilke° woful Palamoun   *the same*
That hath thy prisoun broken° wikkedly.   *escaped*
I am thy mortal foo, and it am I
That loveth so hoote° Emelye the brighte,   *hotly*
880 That I wol dye,° present in hir sighte.   *die*
Wherfore I axe° deeth and my juwise.°   *ask | sentence*
But sle my felawe in the same wise,
For bothe han we deserved to be slayn!"
    This worthy duc answerde anon agayn
885 And seyde, "This is a short conclusioun!°   *quick decision*
Youre owene mouth by youre confessioun
Hath dampned° yow, and I wol it recorde.   *damned*
It nedeth noght to pyne yow with the corde:[1]
Ye shal be deed, by myghty Mars the rede!"°   *red*
890   The queene anon for verray wommanhede°   *womanhood*
Gan for to wepe and so dide Emelye
And alle the ladyes in the compaignye.
Greet pitee was it as it thoughte hem alle,°   *it seemed to them*
That evere swich a chaunce° sholde falle.°   *event | happen*
895 For gentil men they were, of greet estaat,
And no thyng but for love was this debaat,°   *quarrel*
And saugh hir blody woundes wyde and soore
And alle crieden° bothe lasse and
    moore,°   *cried | the lesser and the greater*
"Have mercy, lord, upon us wommen alle!"
900 And on hir bare knees adoun they falle
And wolde have kist° his feet theras° he stood,   *kissed | where*
Til at the laste aslaked° was his mood.   *calmed*
For pitee renneth° soone in gentil herte.   *runs*
And though he first for ire quook° and sterte,   *shook*
905 He hath considered shortly° in a clause   *briefly*
The trespas° of hem bothe and eek the cause.   *crime*
And although that his ire hir gilt° accused,   *their guilt*
Yet in his resoun° he hem bothe excused   *reason*
As thus: he thoghte wel that every man
910 Wol° helpe hymself in love if that he kan°   *will*
And eek delivere hymself out of prisoun.
And eek his herte hadde compassioun
Of wommen, for they wepen evere in oon.°   *in unity*
And in his gentil herte he thoughte anon
915 And softe unto hymself he seyde, "Fy°   *shame*

Upon a lord that wol have no mercy
But been a leoun bothe in word and dede
To hem that been in repentaunce and drede,
As wel as to a proud, despitous° man   *scornful*
920 That wol mayntene that he first bigan.
That lord hath litel of discrecioun
That in swich cas kan° no divisioun   *knows*
But weyeth° pride and humblesse after oon."°   *weighs | equally*
And shortly, whan his ire is thus agoon,°   *gone*
925 He gan to looken up with eyen lighte
And spak thise same wordes al on highte:°   *aloud*
"The god of love, a, *benedicite*,°[2]   *bless you*
How myghty and how greet a lord is he!
Ayeyns° his myght ther gayneth° none
    obstacles!   *against | prevails*
930 He may be cleped° a god for hise myracles.   *called*
For he kan maken at his owene gyse°   *in his own way*
Of everich herte as that hym list divyse.°   *as he wishes to arrange*
Lo heere this Arcite and this Palamon,
That quitly° weren out of my prisoun   *freely*
935 And myghte han lyved in Thebes roially,
And witen° I am hir mortal enemy   *know*
And that hir deth lith° in my myght also,   *lies*
And yet hath love maugree hir° eyen two[3]   *despite their*
Broght hem hyder° bothe for to dye.   *here*
940 Now looketh: is nat that an heigh° folye?   *great*
Who may been a fool but if he love?°   *unless he who loves*
Bihoold, for Goddes sake that sit above:
Se how they blede! Be they noght wel arrayed?°   *decorated*
Thus hath hir lord, the god of love, ypayed°   *paid*
945 Hir wages and hir fees for hir servyse!
And yet they wenen for to been ful
    wyse°   *consider (themselves) very wise*
That serven love, for aught that may
    bifalle.°   *anything that may happen*
But this is yet the beste gam° of alle,   *game*
That she for whom they han° this jolitee°   *have | amusement*
950 Kan° hem therfore as muche thank as me.   *owes*
She woot namoore° of al this hoote°
    fare,°   *knows no more | rash | business*

---

[1] *It ... corde* There is no need to torture you with a rope (i.e., with a rope twisted about the prisoner's head).

[2] *benedicite* Latin: bless you.

[3] *maugree ... two* Despite anything they could do.

By God, than woot a cokkow° of an hare.[1]   *cuckoo*
But al moot been assayed,° hoot and coold!   *tried*
A man moot been a fool or yong or oold.[2]
955 I woot it by myself ful yore agon,°   *very long ago*
For in my tyme a servant[3] was I oon,
And therfore syn° I knowe of loves peyne   *since*
And woot hou soore° it kan a man
    distreyne,°   *how painfully / afflict*
As he that hath been caught ofte in his laas,°   *trap*
960 I yow° foryeve° al hoolly° this trespass   *you / forgive / completely*
At requeste of the queene that kneleth heere
And eek of Emelye, my suster deere.°   *dear sister(-in-law)*
And ye shul bothe anon unto me swere
That nevere mo ye shal my contree° dere,°   *country / harm*
965 Ne make werre° upon me nyght ne day   *war*
But been my freendes in al that ye may.
I yow foryeve this trespas every deel."°   *completely*
And they hym sworen his axyng° faire and weel   *asking*
And hym of lordshipe° and of mercy
    preyde,   *his protection as lord*
970 And he hem graunteth grace,° and thus he seyde: *his favor*
    "To speke of roial lynage and richesse,
Though that she were a queene or a princesse,
Ech of you bothe is worthy, doutelees,
To wedden whan tyme is, but nathelees—
975 I speke as for my suster Emelye,
For whom ye have this strif° and jalousye.   *strife*
Ye woot yourself she may nat wedden two
Atones,° though ye fighten everemo.   *at once*
That oon of you, al be hym looth or lief,°   *whether he likes it or not*
980 He moot pipen in an yvy leef.°[4]   *pipe in an ivy leaf*
This is to seyn, she may nat now han bothe,
Al be° ye never so jalouse ne so wrothe.   *although*
And forthy° I yow putte in this degree,°   *therefore / situation*
That ech of yow shal have his destynee
985 As hym is shape,° and herkneth in what wyse;°   *ordained / way*
Lo heere° youre ende of that I shal devyse.   *here is*

"My wyl° is this for plat° conclusioun,   *will / plain*
Withouten any repplicacioun:°   *reply*
If that you liketh, take it for the beste,
990 That everich° of you shal goon where hym leste   *each*
Frely° withouten raunson or daunger,   *freely*
And this day fifty wykes fer ne ner[5]
Everich of you shal brynge an hundred knyghtes
Armed for lystes° up at alle rightes,°[6]   *arena / points*
995 Al redy° to darreyne° hire by bataille.   *ready / decide*
And this bihote° I yow withouten faille°   *promise / fail*
Upon my trouthe and as I am a knyght:
That wheither of yow bothe that hath myght,
This is to seyn, that wheither he or thow
1000 May with his hundred as I spak° of now   *spoke*
Sleen his contrarie° or out of lystes dryve,   *opponent*
Thanne shal I yeve° Emelya to wyve   *give*
To whom that Fortune yeveth so fair a grace.
The lystes shal I maken in this place,
1005 And God so wisly° on my soule rewe,°   *wisely / have mercy*
As I shal evene° juge been and trewe.   *fair*
Ye shul noon oother ende° with me maken,   *resolution*
That oon of yow ne shal be deed or taken.°   *captured*
And if yow thynketh this is weel ysayd,°   *well said*
1010 Seyeth youre avys° and holdeth you apayd.°   *opinion / satisfied*
This is youre ende and youre conclusioun."
    Who looketh lightly now but Palamoun?
Who spryngeth up for joye but Arcite?
Who kouthe° telle or who kouthe endite°   *could / write*
1015 The joye that is maked in the place
Whan Theseus hath doon so fair a grace?°   *behaved so graciously*
But doun on knees wente every maner wight°   *manner of person*
And thonken hym with al hir herte and myght,
And namely the Thebans often sithe.°   *many times*
1020 And thus with good hope and with herte blithe°   *happy*
They taken hir leve and homward gonne° they ride   *began*
To Thebes with hise° olde walles wyde.   *its*

EXPLICIT SECUNDA PARS

---

[1] *of an hare* Many editors prefer the reading "or a hare," which is found in many manuscripts, but "less than a cuckoo knows about a hare" also makes sense.

[2] *A ... oold* A man must be a fool, either when he is young or when he is old.

[3] *For ... servant* I.e., a servant of Cupid.

[4] *pipen in an yvy leef* I.e., make an attempt at an impossible task.

---

[5] *fifty ... ner* Fifty weeks from this day, neither more nor less.

[6] *Armed ... rightes* Lists were the spaces fenced off for a medieval tournament, in which knights fought in two groups, and for individual jousts. The description of the lists set up by Theseus in the lines below, however, is based on accounts of Roman arenas, like the Coliseum in Rome.

SEQUITUR PARS TERTIA[1]

I trowe° men wolde deme° it necligence   *believe / judge*
If I foryete° to tellen the dispence°   *forget / expense*
1025 Of Theseus that gooth so bisily
To maken up the lystes° roially   *arena*
That swich a noble theatre° as it was,   *ampitheater*
I dar wel seyn in this world ther nas.°   *was not*
The circuit a myle was aboute,
1030 Walled of stoon° and dyched° al withoute.   *stone / ditched*
Round was the shape, in manere of compas,
Ful of degrees, the heighte of sixty pas,°   *spaces*
That whan a man was set on o° degree,   *one*
He lette nat° his felawe for to see.   *hindered not*
1035 Estward ther stood a gate of marbul whit,°   *white marble*
Westward right swich another in the opposit.
And shortly to concluden, swich a place
Was noon in erthe° as in so litel space,   *earth*
For in the lond ther was no crafty° man   *skillful*
1040 That geometrie or ars metrik° kan,°   *arithmetic / knew*
Ne portreitour,° ne kervere° of
    ymages°   *portrait-painter / carver / statues*
That Theseus ne yaf° mete° and wages   *did not give / food*
The theatre for to maken and devyse.
And for to doon his ryte° and sacrifise   *ceremonies*
1045 He estward hath upon the gate above
In worshipe of Venus, goddesse of love,
Doon make° an auter° and an oratorie,°   *had made / altar / chapel*
And on the westward in memorie
Of Mars, he maked hath right swich° another,   *just such*
1050 That coste largely of gold a fother.[2]
And northward in a touret° on the wal   *turret*
Of alabastre° whit and reed° coral   *alabaster / red*
An oratorie riche for to see
In worshipe of Dyane of chastitee
1055 Hath Theseus doon wrought in noble wyse.°   *manner*
    But yet hadde I foryeten° to devyse°   *forgotten / describe*
The noble kervyng° and the portraitures,°   *carving / portraits*
The shape, the contenaunce, and the figures
That weren in thise oratories thre.
1060   First, in the temple of Venus maystow se°   *you may see*

Wroght on the wal ful pitous° to biholde   *pitiful*
The broken slepes° and the sikes° colde,   *sleeps / sighs*
The sacred teeris° and the waymentynge,°   *tears / lamentation*
The firy strokes and the desirynge
1065 That loves servantz° in this lyf enduren,   *love's servants*
The othes° that hir covenantz assuren,°   *oaths / assure*
Plesaunce° and Hope, Desir, Foolhardynesse,   *pleasure*
Beautee and Youthe, Bauderie,° Richesse,   *bawdiness*
Charmes and Force, Lesynges,° Flaterye,   *lies*
1070 Despense,° Bisyness,° and Jalousye,   *spending / anxiety*
That wered° of yelewe° gooldes° a
    gerland   *wore / yellow / marigolds*
And a cokkow° sittynge on hir hand.   *cuckoo*
Festes,° instrumentz, caroles,[3] daunces,   *feasts*
Lust,° and array,° and all the circumstaunces   *pleasure / dress*
1075 Of love, whiche that I rekned° have and rekne shal,   *reckoned*
By ordre weren peynted on the wal,
And mo than I kan make of mencioun.°   *make mention*
For soothly, al the Mount of Citheroun[4]
Ther° Venus hath hir principal dwellynge,   *where*
1080 Was shewed on the wal in portreyynge°   *painting*
With al the gardyn and the lustynesse.
Nat was forgyeten the porter Ydelnesse
Ne Narcisus[5] the faire of yore agon,°   *days of old*
And yet the folye of Kyng Salomon,[6]
1085 And eek the grete strengthe of Ercules,°   *Hercules*
Th'enchauntementz of Medea and Circes,[7]
Ne of Turnus[8] with the hardy fiers corage,
The riche Cresus,[9] kaytyf° in servage.°   *captive / servitude*

---

[1] *Explicit … Tertia*   Latin: Here ends the second part. The third part follows.

[2] *That … fother*   That cost many a cart-load of gold.

[3] *caroles*   Dances performed to the accompaniment of singing.

[4] *Mount of Citheroun*   In Roman mythology, Venus rose from the sea fully-formed at the island of Cythera. In a number of medieval texts, including *The Knight's Tale,* Mount Cithaeron is confused with this island.

[5] *Narcisus*   Narcissus fell in love with his own image when he saw it in a pool. See Ovid's *Metamorphoses.*

[6] *folye of Kyng Salomon*   King Solomon, famously the wisest of men, fell into folly under the influence of the many wives and concubines in his harem.

[7] *Medea and Circes*   In Greek mythology, Medea and Circe were sorceresses. They were in love with Jason and Odysseus respectively.

[8] *Turnus*   In the later books of Virgil's *Aeneid,* Turnus is Aeneas's main antagonist and his rival for the hand of Lavinia in marriage.

[9] *The riche Cresus*   In Roman mythology, Croesus, King of Lydia, was fabulously rich but died a wretched death, captured by Cyrus.

Thus may ye seen that wysdom ne richesse,

1090 Beautee ne sleighte,° strengthe, hardynesse   *trickery*

Ne may° with Venus holde
    champartie.°   *may not / equal partnership*

For as hir list,° the world than° may she
    gye.°   *she desires / then / rule*

Lo, alle thise folk so caught were in hir las,°   *snare*

Til they for wo ful ofte seyde, "Allas!"

1095 Suffiseth° heere ensamples° oon or two,   *it is enough / examples*

And though I koude rekene a thousand mo.

    The statue of Venus glorious for to se

Was naked, fletynge° in the large see,°   *floating / sea*

And fro° the navele doun al covered was   *from*

1100 With wawes° grene and brighte as any glas.   *waves*

A citole[1] in hir right hand hadde she,

And on hir heed, ful semely° for to se,   *very beautiful*

A rose gerland fressh and wel smellynge;°   *sweet smelling*

Above hir heed hir dowves° flikerynge.°   *doves / fluttering*

1105 Biforn hire stood hir sone Cupido.

Upon his shuldres wynges hadde he two,

And blynd° he was as it was often seene.   *blind*

A bowe he bar° and arwes° brighte and
    kene.°   *carried / arrows / sharp*

    Why sholde I noght° as wel eek telle yow al   *not*

1110 The portreiture that was upon the wal

Withinne the temple of myghty Mars the rede?

Al peynted was the wal in lengthe and brede°   *breadth*

Lyk to the estres° of the grisly place   *interior*

That highte° the grete temple of Mars in
    Trace°   *was called / Thrace*

1115 In thilke° colde, frosty regioun   *the same*

Theras° Mars hath his sovereyn° mansioun.[2]   *where / chief*

    First on the wal was peynted a forest

In which ther dwelleth neither man ne best,

With knotty, knarry,° bareyne° trees olde,   *gnarled / barren*

1120 Of stubbes° sharpe and hidouse° to biholde,   *stumps / hideous*

In which ther ran a rumbel° and a
    swough°   *rumble / rush of wind*

As though a storm sholde bresten° every bough.   *break*

---

[1] *A citole* Musical instrument that had a fingerboard and was plucked with a plectrum. It was a distant descendant of the classical lyre.

[2] *mansioun* A "mansion" of a god/planet was, in astrological terms, its appropriate region in the sky, but here the reference is to Mars's greatest temple, in Thracia in northern Greece.

And dounward from an hille under a bente,°   *slope*

Ther stood the temple of Mars Armypotente,°   *powerful in arms*

1125 Wroght al of burned° steel of which the
    entree°   *polished / entrance*

Was long and streit° and gastly for to see.   *narrow*

And therout cam a rage° and swich a veze,°   *roar of wind / blast*

That it made al the gate for to rese.°   *shake*

The northren lyght in at the dores° shoon,   *doors*

1130 For wyndowe on the wal ne was ther noon

Thurgh which men myghten any light discerne.

The dore was al of adamant eterne,°   *eternal*

Yclenched° overthwart° and
    endelong°   *supported / crosswise / lengthwise*

With iren tough, and for to make it strong

1135 Every pyler° the temple to sustene   *pillar*

Was tonne-greet° of iren° bright and shene.   *big as a barrel / iron*

    Ther saugh I first the dirke ymaginyng°   *dark plotting*

Of Felonye° and the compassyng,°   *crime / scheming*

The crueel Ire, reed° as any gleede,°   *red / ember*

1140 The pykepurs° and the pale Drede,°   *pick-pocket / dread*

The smylere° with the knyf° under the
    cloke,°   *smiler / knife / cloak*

The shepne° brennynge° with the blake smoke,   *stable / burning*

The tresoun of the mordrynge° in the bedde,°   *murdering / bed*

The open werre° with woundes al bibledde,°   *war / bleeding*

1145 Contek° with blody knyf and sharpe manace;°   *conflict / menace*

Al ful of chirkyng° was that sory° place.[3]   *groaning / sorry*

The sleere of hymself° yet saugh° I ther: *suicide / saw*

His herte blood hath bathed al his heer,°   *hair*

The nayl° ydryven° in the shode°
    anyght,°   *nail / driven / temple / at night*

1150 The colde deeth with mouth gapyng upright.

Amyddes° of the temple sat
    Meschaunce°   *in the middle / misfortune*

With disconfort° and sory contenaunce.   *distress*

Yet saugh I Woodnesse° laughynge in his rage,   *madness*

Armed Compleint,° Outhees,° and fiers
    Outrage,°   *grievance / outcry / violence*

1155 The careyne° in the busk° with throte
    ycorne,°   *corpse / forest / cut throat*

A thousand slayn and nat oon of qualm
    ystorve,°   *killed by plague*

---

[3] *The tresoun … place* The images and statues on the walls of the temple of Mars show the planet's influence, which causes not only war but other sorts of violence and catastrophe.

The tiraunt° with the pray° by force yraft,°   *t yrant / prey / seized*
The toun° destroyed: ther was nothyng laft!   *town*
Yet saugh I brent° the shippes
    hoppesteres,°   *burned / dancing ships*
1160 The hunte° strangled with° the wilde
    beres,°   *hunter / killed by / bears*
The sowe° freten° the child right in the cradel,   *sow / eat*
The cook yscalded° for al his longe ladel.°   *scalded / ladle*
Noght was foryeten° by the infortune° of
    Marte:°   *forgotten / adverse influence / Mars*
The cartere,° overryden° with his carte.   *carter / run over by*
1165 Under the wheel ful lowe° he lay adoun.   *very low*
Ther were also of Martes divisioun°   *company*
The laborer and the bocher° and the smyth   *butcher*
That forgeth sharpe swerdes° on his styth.°[1]   *swords / anvil*
And al above depeynted° in a tour°   *painted / tower*
1170 Saugh I Conquest sittynge in greet honour
With the sharpe swerd over his heed
Hangynge by a soutil twynes threed.°   *thin twine's thread*
Depeynted° was the slaughtre° of Julius,   *painted / assassination*
Of grete Nero and of Antonius.[2]
1175 Al° be that thilke tyme they were
    unborn,°   *although / not yet born*
Yet was hir deth° depeynted ther biforn°   *death / painted before*
By manasynge° of Mars, right by figure.°   *menacing / by horoscope*
So was it shewed in that protreiture
As is depeynted in the certres[3] above
1180 Who shal be slayn or elles deed for love.
Suffiseth° oon ensample in stories olde;   *suffices*
I may nat rekene° hem alle, though I wolde.°   *count / wanted to*
    The statue of Mars upun a carte° stood   *upon a chariot*
Armed, and looked grym° as he were wood.°   *looking grim / crazy*
1185 And over his heed ther shynen° two figures   *shone*
Of sterres° that been cleped in
    scriptures,°   *stars / called in writings*
That oon Puella, that oother Rubeus.[4]
This god of armes was arrayed thus:

A wolf ther stood biforn° hym at his feet   *before*
1190 With eyen rede,° and of a man he eet.°   *red / ate*
With soutil pencel° was depeynted this storie   *brush*
In redoutynge° of Mars and of his glorie.°   *honor / glory*
    Now to the temple of Dyane the chaste
As shortly as I kan I wol me haste
1195 To telle yow al the descripsioun.
Depeynted been the walles up and doun
Of huntyng and of shamefast° chastitee.   *modest*
Ther saugh I how woful Calistopee,[5]
Whan that Diane agreved° was with here,°   *angry / her*
1200 Was turned from a womman til° a bere,°   *into / bear*
And after was she maad° the loode sterre.°   *made / pole-star*
Thus was it peynted. I kan° sey you no ferre.°   *can / further*
Hir sone[6] is eek a sterre, as men may see.
Ther saugh I Dane[7] yturned° til a tree—   *turned*
1205 I mene° nat the goddesse Diane,   *mean*
But Penneus doghter° which that highte°
    Dane.   *Penneus's daughter / named*
Ther saugh I Attheon[8] an hert° ymaked°   *deer / made*
For vengeaunce that he saugh Diane al naked.
I saugh how that hise houndes have hym caught
1210 And freeten° hym for that they knewe hym
    naught.°   *ate / did not know him*
Yet peynted a litel forthermoor°   *further away*
How Atthalante[9] hunted the wilde boor°   *boar*

---

[1] *The laborer ... styth* These trades, which all use sharp tools, are under the protection of Mars.

[2] *Depeynted ... Antonius* Julius Caesar, the Emperor Nero, and Marc Antony all met violent deaths.

[3] *As ... certres* Depicted in the astrological certainties.

[4] *Puella ... Rubeus* Patterned figures used in the method of predicting the future known as geomancy—a method of arranging dots into columns according to chance.

[5] *Calistopee* Callisto was a favorite companion of Diana. In order to sleep with Callisto, Jupiter disguised himself as Diana. Diana discovered the trick and forced Callisto from her company. Shortly after she left Diana, she found she was pregnant. She gave birth to a boy, Arcas. Juno, Jupiter's wife, jealously changed Callisto into a bear. When her son Arcas was about to kill her mistakenly in a hunt, Jupiter changed her into the constellation Ursa Major, the Great Bear.

[6] *Hir sone* Callisto's son is Arcas, whom Jupiter transformed into the constellation Ursa Minor, the Little Bear.

[7] *Dane* I.e., Daphne, who was chased by the god Apollo. At her request, the gods turned her into a laurel tree to protect her from him. See Ovid's *Metamorphoses*.

[8] *Attheon* I.e., Actaeon, who saw the naked Diana taking a bath. She changed him into a deer to punish him and he was killed by his own hunting dogs.

[9] *Atthalante* I.e., Atalanta, a maiden, a hunter who acquitted herself well in the Calydonian Boar Hunt.

And Meleagree[1] and many another mo,

For which Dyane wroghte hym° care and wo.   *fashioned for him*

1215 Ther saugh I many another wonder° storie,   *wonderful*

The whiche me list nat drawen to memorie.[2]

This goddesse on an hert ful wel hye seet,°   *sat very high*

With smale houndes al aboute hir feet,

And undernethe hir feet she hadde a moone.°   *moon*

1220 Wexynge° it was and sholde wanye° soone.   *waxing / wane*

In gaude grene° hir statue clothed was,   *yellow-green*

With bowe in honde and arwes in a cas.°   *quiver*

Hir eyen caste she ful lowe adoun

Ther° Pluto[3] hath his derke regioun.   *where*

1225 A womman travaillynge° was hire biforn,   *in labor*

But for° hir child so longe was unborn   *because*

Ful pitously, "Lucyna!"[4] gan she calle

And seyde, "Helpe! For thow mayst best° of

alle!"   *may best (help)*

Wel koude he peynten lifly° that it wroghte;°   *life-like / made*

1230 With many a floryn° he the hewes°

boghte.°   *gold coin / colors / bought*

Now been the lystes maad° and Theseus   *made*

That at his grete cost arrayed° thus   *arranged*

The temples and the theatre every deel,°   *part*

Whan it was doon, hym lyked wonder

weel.°   *it pleased him very well*

1235 But stynte° I wole of Theseus a lite   *stop speaking*

And speke of Palamon and of Arcite.

The day approcheth of hir retournynge

That everich sholde an hundred knyghtes brynge

The bataille to darreyne° as I yow tolde.   *decide*

1240 And til Atthenes,° hir covenantz° for to

holde,   *to Athens / agreement*

Hath everich of hem broght an hundred knyghtes

Wel armed for the werre at alle rightes.°   *in all aspects*

And sikerly,° ther trowed° many a man   *surely / believed*

That nevere sithen° that the world bigan,   *never since*

1245 As for to speke of knyghthod° of hir hond,   *deeds of knighthood*

As fer as God hath maked see or lond

Nas° of so fewe so noble a compaignye.   *there was not*

For every wight° that lovede chivalrye   *person*

And wolde his thankes° han a passant° name   *gladly / surpassing*

1250 Hath preyd° that he myghte been of°   *prayed / (part) of*

that game.

And wel was hym that therto chosen was,

For if ther fille° tomorwe swich a cas,   *befell*

Ye knowen wel that every lusty knyght

That loveth paramours° and hath his myght,   *as a lover*

1255 Were it in Engelond or elleswhere,

They wolde hir thankes° wilnen° to be there   *gladly / wish*

To fighte for a lady, benedicitee.

It were a lusty° sighte for to see!   *pleasant*

And right so ferden° they with Palamon.   *did*

1260 With hym ther wenten knyghtes many on.°   *one*

Som wol ben° armed in an haubergeon°   *one would be / mail-coat*

And in bristplate° and in light gypon,°   *breast-plate / over-garment*

And somme woln have a paire plates,[5]

And somme woln have a Pruce-sheeld° or a   *Prussian shield*

targe.

1265 Somme woln ben armed on hir legges° weel°   *legs / well*

And have an ax, and somme a mace[6] of steel.

There is no newe gyse° that it nas° old.   *fashion / was not*

Armed were they as I have yow told,

Everych after his opinioun.

1270 Ther maistow seen comynge° with Palamoun   *see coming*

Lygurge[7] hymself, the grete kyng of Trace.

Blak was his berd, and manly was his face.

The cercles of hise eyen in his heed,

They gloweden bitwixen yelow and reed,

1275 And lik a grifphon[8] looked he aboute,

With kempe heeris° on hise browes stoute,°   *combed hairs / large*

Hise lymes° grete, his brawnes° harde and

stronge,   *limbs / muscles*

His shuldres brode,° hise armes rounde and

longe.   *shoulders broad*

And as the gyse° was in his contree,   *fashion*

1280 Ful hye upon a chaar° of gold stood he   *chariot*

---

[1] *Meleagree*   Meleager was awarded Atalanta after the hunt for the Calydonian boar, occasioning jealousy between him and his family.

[2] *The … memorie*   Which I do not wish to call to memory.

[3] *Pluto*   God of the Underworld, the realm of the dead.

[4] *Lucyna*   Lucina is another name for Diana. One of Diana's attributes was the goddess of childbirth.

[5] *paire plates*   Plate armor, as opposed to chain-mail armor.

[6] *mace*   Here, a spiked metal club.

[7] *Lygurge*   King of Sparta, in Greece, known for his austere militarism.

[8] *grifphon*   Mythological beast with a lion's hindquarters and an eagle's torso and head.

With foure white boles° in the trays.°   *bulls | harness*
Instede of cote armure° over° his
    harnays,°   *coat of arms | on | armor*
With nayles° yelewe and brighte as any gold,   *nails*
He hadde a beres skyn, col blak for old.°   *coal-black with age*

1285 His longe heer was kembd° bihynde his bak;   *combed*
As any ravenes fethere° it shoon° for blak.   *raven's feather | shone*
A wrethe° of gold, arm-greet,° of huge
    wighte°   *wreath | arm-thick | weight*
Upon his heed, set ful of stones° brighte,   *jewels*
Of fyne rubyes° and of dyamauntz.°   *rubies | diamonds*

1290 Aboute his chaar ther wenten white alauntz,°   *wolfhounds*
Twenty and mo, as grete as any steer
To hunten at the leoun or the deer,
And folwed hym with mosel° faste ybounde,   *muzzle*
Colered° of gold and tourettes° fyled°
    rounde.   *collared | leash-rings | filed*

1295 An hundred lordes hadde he in his route,
Armed ful wel with hertes stierne° and stoute.   *stern*
    With Arcite in stories as men fynde
The grete Emetreus,[1] the kyng of Inde,°   *India*
Upon a steede bay,° trapped in steel,   *bay horse*

1300 Covered in clooth of gold dyapred[2] weel,
Cam ridynge lyk the god of armes, Mars.
His cotearmure° was of clooth of Tars,°   *cloth tunic | Tartary*
Couched° with perles white and rounde and grete.   *decorated*
His sadel° was of brend° gold newe ybete,[3]   *saddle | burnished*

1305 A mantel° upon his shulder hangynge   *tunic*
Bratful° of rubyes rede as fyr sparklynge;   *full to the brim*
His crispe heer° lyk rynges was yronne,°   *curly hair | curled*
And that was yelow and glytered as the sonne.
His nose was heigh, hise eyen bright citryn,°   *lemon-colored*

1310 Hise lippes rounde, his colour was sangwyn;°   *red*
A fewe frakenes° in his face yspreynd,°   *freckles | sprinkled*
Bitwixen yelow and somdel blak°
    ymeynd;°   *somewhat black | mixed*

And as a leoun he his lookyng caste;°   *he looked about*
Of fyve and twenty yeer his age I caste.°   *guess*
1315 His berd was wel bigonne for to sprynge.°   *grow*
His voys was as a trompe thondrynge. °   *thundering trumpet*
Upon his heed he wered° of laurer° grene   *wore | laurel-leaves*
A gerland fressh and lusty° for to sene.   *pleasant*
Upon his hand he bar° for his deduyt°   *carried | pleasure*
1320 An egle° tame as any lilye whyt.   *eagle*
An hundred lordes hadde he with hym there,
Al armed save hir heddes° in al hir gere,°   *except their heads | armor*
Ful richely in alle maner thynges.
For trusteth wel that dukes, erles, kynges
1325 Were gadered° in this noble compaignye   *gathered*
For love and for encrees° of chivalrye.   *increase*
Aboute this kyng ther ran on every part
Ful many a tame leoun and leopard,
And in this wise thise lordes alle and some
1330 Been on the Sonday to the citee come
Aboute pryme, and in the toun alight.°   *arrived*
    This Theseus, this duc, this worthy knyght,
Whan he had broght hem into his citee
And inned hem° everich in his
    degree,°   *lodged them | according to his rank*
1335 He festeth° hem and dooth so greet labour   *feasted*
To esen° hem and doon hem al honour, °   *refresh | every honor*
That yet man weneth° that no maner wit   *imagines*
Of noon estaat ne koude amenden it. °   *make it better*
    The mynstralcye,° the service at the feeste,   *musical performances*
1340 The grete yiftes° to the meeste and
    leeste,°   *gifts | most and least (important)*
The riche array° of Theseus paleys,   *decoration*
Ne who sat first ne last upon the deys,°   *dais (high table)*
What ladyes fairest been or best daunsynge,
Or which of hem kan dauncen best and synge,
1345 Ne who moost felyngly speketh of love,
What haukes° sitten on the perche above,   *hawks*
What houndes liggen° in the floor adoun,   *lie*
Of al this make I now no mencioun,
But al th'effect° that thynketh me° the
    beste.[4]   *only the general effect | seems to me*
1350 Now cometh the point, and herkneth° if yow
    leste.°   *listen | wish*

---

[1] *The grete Emetreus* King Emetreus is not attested in classical mythology nor is he to be found in Chaucer's sources.

[2] *dyapred* "Diapered" is a technical term drawn from the world of medieval manuscript illumination that indicates the diamond-shaped patterns used as the background for many paintings in medieval books. King Emetreus's horse wears a decorative cloth covered with this type of pattern.

[3] *newe ybete* I.e., newly beaten. A goldsmith works goldplate jewelry into pleasing patterns by beating it with a small hammer.

---

[4] *But ... beste* Here Chaucer offers an example of *occupatio*, the rhetorical figure in which one lists at great length the things one is not going to describe, thus describing them.

The Sonday nyght er day bigan to sprynge,
Whan Palamon the larke herde synge,
Although it nere nat day by houres two,
Yet song the larke and Palamon also.
1355 With hooly herte and with an heigh corage°   high spirit
He roos° to wenden° on his pilgrymage   rose / go
Unto the blisful Citherea° benigne.°   Venus / kind
I mene Venus, honurable and digne.°   worthy
And in hir houre he walketh forth a pas°   slowly
1360 Unto the lystes ther hire temple was,
And doun he kneleth with ful humble cheere°   expression
And herte soor, and seyde in this manere:
     "Faireste of faire, O lady myn, Venus,
Doughter to Jove and spouse of Vulcanus,
1365 Thow gladere° of the mount of Citheron,   one who delights
For thilke° love thow haddest to° Adoon,[1]   the same / for
Have pitee of my bittre teeris smerte°   bitter, painful tears
And taak myn humble preyere at° thyn herte.   to
Allas, I ne have no langage° to telle   words
1370 Th'effectes ne° the tormentz of myn helle!°   nor / my hell
Myn herte may myne harmes° nat biwreye.°   wrongs / reveal
I am so confus, that I kan noght seye
But 'Mercy!' Lady bright, that knowest weele
My thought and seest what harmes that I feele,
1375 Considere al this and rewe° upon my soore,°   have mercy / pain
As wisly° as I shal for everemore,   surely
Emforth° my myght, thy trewe servant be,   according to
And holden werre° alwey with chastitee,   be at war
That make I myn avow,° so° ye me helpe.   promise / if
1380 I kepe noght° of armes for to yelpe,°   do not care / boast
Ne I ne axe° nat tomorwe to have victorie   nor do I ask
Ne renoun in this cas,° ne veyneglorie°   event / pride
Of pris° of armes blowen up and
     doun.°   reputation / made widely known
But I wolde have fully possessioun
1385 Of Emelye, and dye in thy servyse.
Fynd thow the manere hou° and in what
     wyse.°   means how / way
I recche nat but° it may bettre be   do not care whether
To have victorie of hem or they of me,
So that I have my lady in myne armes!
1390 For though so be that Mars is god of armes,
Youre vertu° is so greet in hevene above,   power

That if yow list, I shal wel have my love.
Thy temple wol I worshipe everemo,
And on thyn auter, where° I ride or go,   wherever
1395 I wol doon sacrifice and fires beete.°   kindle fires (of sacrifice)
And if ye wol nat so,° my lady sweete,   you will not (do) so
Thanne preye I thee tomorwe with a spere
That Arcita me thurgh the herte bere!°   pierce
Thanne rekke° I noght whan I have lost my lyf,   care
1400 Though that Arcita wynne hire to° his wyf.   as
This is th'effect and ende of my preyere.°   prayer
Yif° me my love, thow blisful lady deere."   give
     Whan the orison was doon° of Palamon,   done
His sacrifice he dide and that anon
1405 Ful pitously with alle circumstaunce,°   ritual
Al° telle I noght as now° his observaunce.   although / for now
But atte laste the statue of Venus shook
And made a signe wherby that he took
That his preyere accepted was that day.
1410 For thogh the signe shewed a delay,
Yet wiste he wel that graunted was his boone.°   request
And with glad herte he wente hym hoom ful soone.
     The thridde houre inequal[2] that Palamon
Bigan to Venus temple for to gon,°   go
1415 Up roos the sonne, and up roos Emelye,
And to the temple of Dyane gan hye.°   went
Hir maydens,° that she thider with hire
     ladde,°   ladies-in-waiting / led
Ful redily with hem the fyr° they
     hadde,.°   fire (for sacrifice) / carried
Th'encens,° the clothes, and the remenant al   the incense
1420 That to the sacrifice longen shal,°   belongs
The hornes° fulle of meeth,° as was the
     gyse;°   drinking horns / mead / custom
Ther lakked noght to doon hir sacrifise.
Smokynge° the temple ful of clothes
     faire,°   incensing / beautiful cloth hangings

---

[1] *Adoon* Adonis was a youth whom Venus loved. He was killed by a boar, and Venus transformed his blood into a flower.

---

[2] *houre inequal* In Chaucer's day there were two ways of dividing up time into hours. "Artificial" hours are those we use today, where both day and night are divided into twelve hours equal in amount. "Unequal" hours, the older system used in an age that did not have the clocks that made the artificial hours possible, was the division of the daylight time into twelve hours and the time of dark into twelve. The length of these hours would change according to the seasons. They were the same as the artificial hours only at the spring and autumn equinoxes. Each hour of the day was devoted to one of the gods/planets.

This Emelye, with herte debonaire,°   *gentle*
1425 Hir body wessh° with water of a welle.   *washed*
But hou° she dide hir ryte,° I dar nat telle,   *how / rite*
But° it be anythyng in general.   *unless*
And yet it were a game° to heeren al.   *joy*
To hym that meneth wel, it were no charge,°   *burden*
1430 But it is good a man been at his large.°   *free (to speak)*
Hir brighte heer was kembd, untressed° al;   *unbraided*
A coroune° of a grene ook° cerial¹   *crown / oak*
Upon hir heed was set ful fair and meete.°   *fitting*
Two fyres on the auter gan she beete°   *kindled*
1435 And dide hir thynges° as men may biholde   *performed her duties*
In Stace° of Thebes and thise bookes olde.   *Statius*
Whan kyndled was the fyr, with pitous cheere
Unto Dyane she spak as ye may heere:
"O chaste goddesse of the wodes grene,
1440 To whom bothe hevene and erthe and see° is sene,°   *sea / seen*
Queene of the regne of Pluto derk° and lowe,   *dark*
Goddesse of maydens° that myn herte hast
     knowe°   *maidens / known*
Ful many a yeer, and woost° what I desire,   *knows*
As keepe me fro thy vengeaunce and thyn ire,
1445 That Attheon aboughte° cruelly.   *paid for*
Chaste goddesse, wel wostow° that I   *you know*
Desire to ben a mayden al my lyf.
Ne nevere wol I be no love ne wyf!
I am, thow woost, yet of thy compaignye,
1450 A mayde, and love huntynge° and venerye°   *hunting / the chase*
And for to walken in the wodes wilde
And noght to ben a wyf and be with childe.
Noght° wol I knowe the compaignye of man.   *by no means*
Now helpe me, lady, sith ye may and kan,
1455 For tho° thre formes² that thou hast in thee,   *those*
And Palamon that hath swich love to me
And eek Arcite that loveth me so soore,
This grace I preye thee withoute
     moore:°   *without any more (words)*
And sende love and pees° bitwixe hem two,   *peace*
1460 And fro me turne awey hir hertes so
That al hire hoote love and hir desir
And al hir bisy° torment and hir fir°   *intense / fire*

Be queynt° or turned in another place.   *quenched*
And if so be thou wolt do° me no grace,°   *grant / favor*
1465 And if my destynee be shapen so
That I shal nedes° have oon of hem two,   *necessarily*
As sende me hym that moost° desireth me.   *most*
Bihoold, goddesse of clene° chastitee,   *pure*
The bittre teeris that on my chekes falle!
1470 Syn° thou art mayde and kepere° of us alle,   *since / keeper*
My maydenhede° thou kepe and wel
     conserve,°   *virginity / preserve*
And whil I lyve, a mayde I wol thee serve."
    The fires brenne upon the auter cleere°   *bright*
Whil Emelye was thus in hir preyere,
1475 But sodeynly she saugh a sighte queynte.°   *curious*
For right anon oon of the fyres queynte°   *went out*
And quyked agayn,° and after that anon   *kindled again*
That oother fyr was queynt° and al
     agon.°   *quenched / completely gone*
And as it queynte, it made a whistlynge,
1480 As doon thise wete° brondes° in hir brennynge,   *wet / sticks*
And at the brondes ende out ran anon
As it were blody dropes° many oon,°   *bloody drops / many a one*
For which so soore° agast° was Emelye,   *sorely / appalled*
That she was wel ny mad° and gan to crye,   *almost crazy*
1485 For she ne wiste° what it signyfied,   *did not know*
But oonly for the feere° thus hath she cried   *fear*
And weepe, that it was pitee for to heere.
And therwithal° Dyane gan appeere   *with all of this*
With bowe° in honde, right as an hunteresse,   *bow*
1490 And seyde, "Doghter, stynt° thyn hevynesse!°   *stop / laments*
Among the goddes hye,° it is affermed°   *high / affirmed*
And by eterne word writen and confermed:
Thou shalt ben wedded unto oon of tho°   *those*
That han for thee so muchel care and wo,
1495 But unto which of hem, I may nat telle.
Farwel, for I ne may no lenger dwelle.
The fires whiche that on myn auter brenne
Shulle° thee declaren, er that thou go henne,°   *shall / away*
Thyn aventure° of love as in this cas."   *fortune*
1500 And with that word, the arwes in the caas°   *quiver*
Of the goddesse clateren° faste and rynge,°   *clatter / ring*
And forth she wente and made a vanysshynge,°   *vanished*
For which this Emelye astoned° was   *astonished*
And seyde, "What amounteth this,° allas?   *what does this mean*
1505 I putte me in thy proteccioun,
Dyane, and in thy disposicioun."°   *care*

---

¹ *cerial* Distinct species of oak, *quercus cerris.*

² *thre formes* I.e., three attributes of Diana, goddess of the hunt, of the underworld, and of chastity.

And hoom she goth anon the nexte weye.
This is th'effect. Ther is namoore to seye.
   The nexte houre of Mars folwynge this,
1510 Arcite unto the temple walked is
Of fierse Mars to doon his sacrifise
With alle the rytes of his payen wyse.°   *rites / pagan customs*
With pitous herte and heigh devocioun
Right thus to Mars he seyde his orisoun:
1515   "O stronge god that in the regnes° colde   *kingdoms*
Of Trace honoured art and lord yholde,°   *considered lord*
And hast in every regne and every lond
Of armes al the brydel in thyn hond,[1]
And hem fortunest° as thee lyst
   devyse,°   *give fortune to them / wish to arrange*
1520 Accepte of me my pitous° sacrifise.   *pious*
If so be that my youthe may deserve
And that my myght° be worthy for to serve   *strength*
Thy godhede,° that I may been oon of thyne,   *divinity*
Thanne preye I thee to rewe° upon my pyne.   *have pity*
1525 For thilke peyne and thilke hoote fir°   *the same hot fire*
In which thow whilom° brendest for desir   *once*
Whan that thow usedest° the beautee   *used*
Of faire, yonge, fresshe Venus fre°   *noble*
And haddest hire in armes at thy wille
1530 (Although thee ones° on a tyme mysfille°   *once / had a misfortune*
Whan Vulcanus hadde caught thee in his las°   *trap*
And foond thee liggynge° by his wyf, allas!)[2]—   *lying*
For thilke sorwe° that was in thyn herte,   *sorrow*
Have routhe as wel upon my peynes smerte!°   *smart*
1535 I am yong and unkonnynge,° as thow
   woost,°   *unknowing / know*
And, as I trowe,° with love offended° moost   *believe / injured*
That evere was any lyves° creature.   *living*
For she that dooth° me al this wo endure°   *does / enduring woe*
Ne reccheth° nevere wher° I synke° or
   fleete!°   *does not care / whether / sink / float*
1540 And wel I woot er° she me mercy heete,°   *before / promise*
I moot with strengthe wynne hire in the place.

And wel I woot withouten helpe or grace
Of thee ne may° my strengthe noght availle.°   *may not / succeed*
Thanne helpe me, lord, tomorwe in my bataille
1545 For thilke fyr that whilom brente° thee   *once burned*
As wel as° thilke fyr now brenneth me,   *just as*
And do° that I tomorwe have victorie.   *cause it*
Myn be the travaille° and thyn be the glorie!   *trouble*
Thy sovereyn temple wol I moost honouren
1550 Of any place, and alwey moost labouren
In thy plesaunce° and in thy craftes[3] stronge,   *pleasure*
And in thy temple I wol my baner honge.°   *hang*
And alle the armes of my compaignye,
And evere mo unto that day I dye
1555 Eterne fir I wol biforn thee fynde,°   *provide*
And eek to this avow° I wol me bynde: *promise*
My beerd, myn heer that hongeth° long adoun   *hangs*
That nevere yet ne felte offensioun°   *felt offense (was cut)*
Of rasour° nor of shere° I wol thee yeve°   *razor / scissors / give*
1560 And ben° thy trewe servant whil I lyve.   *be*
Now, lord, have routhe upon my sorwes soore.
Yif° me the victorie. I aske thee namoore."°   *give / no more*
   The preyere stynt° of Arcita the stronge.   *ends*
The rynges on the temple dore that honge,°   *hung*
1565 And eek the dores, claterede° ful faste,   *clattered*
Of which Arcita somwhat hym agaste.°   *was somewhat afraid*
The fyres brenden upon the auter brighte,
That it gan al the temple for to lighte,
And sweete smel the ground anon up yaf.°   *immediately gave*
1570 And Arcita anon his hand up haf°   *raised*
And moore encens° into the fyr he caste°   *incense / threw*
With othere rytes° mo. And atte laste   *rites*
The statue of Mars bigan his hauberk° rynge,   *mail-coat*
And with that soun° he herde a
   murmurynge°   *sound / murmuring*
1575 Full lowe and dym,° and seyde thus: "Victorie,"   *low and dim*
For which he yaf° to Mars honour and glorie.   *gave*
And thus with joye and hope wel° to fare,   *well*
Arcite anon unto his in° is fare°   *inn / has gone*
As fayn° as fowel° is of the brighte sonne.   *happy / bird*
1580   And right anon swich strif° ther is bigonne   *strife*
For thilke grauntyng° in the hevene
   above   *this granting (of answers to prayers)*
Bitwixe Venus the goddesse of love

---

[1] *Of armes … hond* Mars has complete control (has the bridle, or as might be said now, the reins) of all matters relating to arms.

[2] *Although … allas* Arcite refers here to the story of Vulcan's jealousy over the affair his wife, Venus, had with Mars. As the greatest of smiths, he fashioned an invisible net, which fell upon Mars and Venus when they were in bed together, trapping them for all the gods to see their shame.

---

[3] *craftes* I.e., those that belong to war—wielding the sword and lance and horsemanship foremost among them.

And Mars the stierne° god armypotente,°   *stern / strong in arms*
That Juppiter was bisy it to stente,°   *stop*
1585 Til that the pale Saturnus the colde
That knew so manye of aventures olde
Foond° in his olde experience and art   *found*
That he ful soone hath plesed every part.°   *each side*
As sooth° is seyd, elde° hath greet avantage;   *truly / age*
1590 In elde is bothe wysdom and usage.°   *experience*
Men may the olde atrenne° and noght
    atrede.°   *outrun / not out-wit*
Saturne anon, to stynten strif and drede,°   *stop strife and fear*
Albeit that it is agayn° his kynde,°   *against / nature*
Of al this strif he gan remedie fynde.°   *found a remedy*
1595   "My deere doghter, Venus," quod Saturne,
"My cours° that hath so wyde° for to
    turne   *course (across the sky) / wide*
Hath moore power than woot any man.[1]
Myn is the drenchyng° in the see° so wan.°   *drowning / sea / pale*
Myn is the prison° in the derke cote.°   *imprisonment / dark cell*
1600 Myn is the stranglyng and hangyng by the throte,°   *throat*
The murmure° and the cherles
    rebellyng,°   *murmur / peasants' rebellion*
The groynynge° and the pryvee
    empoysonyng.°   *groaning / secret poisoning*
I do vengeance and pleyn correccioun°   *full punishment*
Whil I dwelle in signe of the leoun.[2]
1605 Myn is the ruyne° of the hye° halles,   *ruin / high*
The fallynge of the toures° and of the walles   *towers*
Upon the mynour° or the carpenter.[3]   *miner*
I slow° Sampsoun shakynge the piler.[4]   *killed*

---

[1] *My ... man*   Saturn, in the Middle Ages the farthest known planet
from the sun, was believed to have a cold and harmful influence. The
following speech of Saturn enumerates disasters that he as god and
planet (i.e., as an astrological influence) typically causes.

[2] *signe of the leoun*   Saturn is most harmful when he is in the
astrological house of Leo.

[3] *mynour or the carpenter*   Here, military men who helped dig
tunnels under besieged walls of towns and castles. The walls would
be shored up with timber, and then, at the right time for an attack
to start, the timbers would be set on fire, thus insuring the collapse
of the walls. The disaster envisioned here is that which would occur
if the miners and carpenters did not leave the tunnel in time before
the walls collapsed.

[4] *I slow ... piler*   Samson, blinded and enslaved by his enemies,
pulled down the pillars supporting their temple, killing them and
himself as well. See Judges 13–16.

And myne be the maladyes colde,[5]
1610 The derke tresons° and the castes° olde.   *treasons / plots*
My lookyng is the fader° of pestilence.   *father*
Now weepe namoore. I shal doon diligence°   *take care*
That Palamon, that is thyn owene knyght,
Shal have his lady as thou hast hym hight.°   *promised*
1615 Though Mars shal helpe his knyght, yet nathelees
Bitwixe yow ther moot be somtyme pees,°   *peace*
Al° be ye noght of o compleccioun,°   *although / one temperament*
That causeth al day swich divisioun.
I am thyn aiel,° redy at thy wille.   *your grandfather*
1620 Weepe now namoore. I wol thy lust fulfille."°   *satisfy your desire*
    Now wol I stynten° of the goddes above,   *stop speaking*
Of Mars and of Venus, goddesse of love,
And telle yow as pleynly as I kan
The grete effect° for which that I bygan.   *result*

EXPLICIT TERCIA PARS
SEQUITUR PARS QUARTA[6]

1625   Greet was the feeste in Atthenes that day,
And eek the lusty seson° of that May   *pleasant season*
Made every wight to been in swich plesaunce°   *enjoyment*
That al that Monday justen° they and daunce   *joust*
And spenten it in Venus heigh servyse.
1630 And by the cause° that they sholde ryse°   *because / had to rise*
Eerly for to seen the grete fight,
Unto hir reste wenten they at nyght,
And on the morwe whan that day gan sprynge,
Of hors° and harneys,° noyse and claterynge   *horse / equipment*
1635 Ther was in hostelryes° al aboute,   *inns*
And to the paleys° rood° ther many a route°*palace / rode / crowd*
Of lordes upon steedes and palfreys.
Ther maystow seen divisynge of harneys°   *preparation of gear*
So unkouth° and so riche and wroght so weel   *unusual*
1640 Of goldsmythrye,° of browdynge,° and of
    steel,   *goldsmithery / embroidering*
The sheeldes brighte, testeres,° and
    trappures,°   *horses' headpieces / horse-armor*
Gold-hewen helmes, hauberkes,° cote-armures,   *mail-coats*
Lordes in paremen tz° on hir courseres,   *robes*

---

[5] *And ... colde*   Diseases caused by a preponderance of the cold
humor.

[6] *Explicit ... Quarta*   Latin: here ends the third part. The fourth
part follows.

Knyghtes of retenue and eek squieres

1645 Nailynge the speres° and helmes

bokelynge,°   *nailing spears | buckling helmets*

Giggynge of sheeldes° with layneres

lacynge°   *setting straps | lacing straps*

(Thereas° nede° is, they weren nothyng

ydel°),   *where | need | idle*

The fomy° steedes on the golden brydel°   *foamy | bridle*

Gnawynge,° and faste° the armurers°

also   *gnawing | quickly | armorers*

1650 With fyle° and hamer prikynge° to and fro,   *file | galloping*

Yemen° on foote and communes° many oon   *yeomen | commoners*

With shorte staves thikke° as they may goon,   *densely*

Pypes, trompes,° nakerers,° clariounes,°   *trumpets | drums | bugles*

That in the bataille blowen° blody sounes,°   *blow | bloody sounds*

1655 The paleys ful of peples up and doun,

Heere thre, ther ten, holdynge° hir questioun, *debating*

Dyvynynge of° thise Thebane knyghtes two.   *guessing about*

Somme seyden thus; somme seyde it shal be so;

Somme helden with° hym with the blake berd;   *sided with*

1660 Somme with the balled,° somme with the thikke

herd;°   *bald | thick-haired*

Somme seyde he looked grymme° and he wolde

fighte;°   *fierce | wanted to fight*

"He hath a sparth° of twenty pound of wighte!"° *axe | weight*

Thus was the halle ful of divynynge

Longe after that the sonne gan to sprynge.

1665   The grete Theseus that of his sleepe awaked

With mynstralcie° and noyse that was maked   *music*

Heeld yet the chambre of his paleys riche

Til that the Thebane knyghtes, bothe yliche°   *equally*

Honured, were into the paleys fet.°   *fetched*

1670 Duc Theseus was at a wyndow set,

Arrayed right as he were a god in trone.°   *on (his) throne*

The peple preesseth thiderward° ful soone   *towards there*

Hym for to seen and doon heigh reverence

And eek to herkne his heste° and his

sentence.°   *command | decision*

1675 An heraud° on a scaffold made an "Oo!"°   *herald | whoa!*

Til al the noyse of peple was ydo.°   *stopped*

And whan he saugh the noyse of peple al stille,

Tho° shewed he the myghty dukes wille.   *then*

"The lord hath of his heigh discrecioun

1680 Considered that it were destruccioun

To gentil° blood to fighten in the gyse°   *noble | manner*

Of mortal bataille now in this emprise.°   *enterprise*

Wherfore to shapen° that they shal nat dye,°   *ensure | die*

He wolde his firste purpos modifye.

1685 No man therfore up° peyne of los of lyf   *upon*

No maner shot,° polax,° ne short knyf   *arrow | battle-axe*

Into the lystes sende ne thider brynge,°   *bring there*

Ne short swerd for to stoke° with poynt

bitynge°   *stab | biting point*

Ne man ne drawe ne bere° by his syde.   *carry*

1690 Ne no man shal unto his felawe° ryde   *against his opponent*

But o° cours° with a sharpe ygrounde

spere;°   *one | turn | sharpened spear*

Foyne, if hym list, on foote hymself to were.[1]

And he that is at meschief° shal be take°   *in trouble | taken*

And noght slayn,° but be broght unto the stake *not killed*

1695 That shal ben ordeyned° on either syde,   *set up*

But thider he shal° by force and there abyde.   *shall (go)*

And if so be the chieftayn° be take°   *leader | taken*

On outher syde or elles sleen° his make,°   *killed | opponent leader*

No lenger shal the turneiynge° laste.   *tourneying*

1700 God spede you! Gooth forth and ley° on faste! *lay*

With long swerd and with maces fighteth youre fille!

Gooth now youre wey! This is the lordes wille!"

The voys° of peple touched the hevene,°   *voice | sky*

So loude cride they with murie stevene,°   *merry voice*

1705 "God save swich a lord that is so good!

He wilneth° no destruccion of blood!"   *wills*

Up goon the trompes and the melodye,

And to the lystes rit° the compaignye,   *rides*

By ordinance° thurghout the citee large,   *decree*

1710 Hanged with clooth of gold and nat° with

sarge.°   *not | serge (plain cloth)*

Ful lik a lord this noble duc gan ryde,

Thise two Thebans upon either syde.

And after rood the queene and Emelye,

And after that another compaignye

1715 Of oon and oother after hir degree.

And thus they passen thurghout the citee

And to the lystes come they by tyme.°   *in time*

---

[1] *Foyne … were* Let him parry, if he wishes, to protect himself when he is on foot. Knights who had been dismounted in a tournament would often continue to fight on foot. Although set in an arena and conducted under the eyes of the Roman gods, the tournament will follow the customs of Chaucer's own day.

It nas nat° of the day yet fully pryme[1]   *was not*
Whan set was Theseus ful riche and hye,

1720 Ypolita the queene, and Emelye,
And othere ladys in degrees aboute.
Unto the seetes° preesseth al the route.   *seats*
And westward thurgh the gates under Marte°   *Mars*
Arcite, and eek the hondred of his parte,°   *party*

1725 With baner reed is entred right anon.
And in that selve° moment Palamon   *same*
Is under Venus estward° in the place   *eastward*
With baner whyt and hardy chiere and face.
In al the world to seken° up and doun   *seek*

1730 So evene, withouten variacioun,
Ther nere° swiche compaignyes tweye!   *were not*
For ther was noon so wys that koude seye
That any hadde of oother° avauntage   *(the) other*
Of worthynesse ne of estaat ne age,

1735 So evene were chosen for to gesse.°   *guess*
And in two renges° faire they hem
  dresse°   *ranks / arrange themselves*
Whan that hir names rad° were everichon,   *read*
That in hir nombre° gyle° were ther noon.   *number / trickery*
Tho° were the gates shet° and cried was loude: *then / shut*

1740 "Do now youre devoir,° yonge° knyghtes proude!" *duty / young*
  The heraudes lefte hir prikyng° up and doun.   *riding*
Now ryngen trompes loude and clarioun.°   *bugle*
Ther is namoore to seyn, but west and est
In goon the speres ful sadly° in arrest;°   *firmly / holder*

1745 In gooth the sharpe spore° into the syde.   *spur*
Ther seen men who kan° juste° and who kan
  ryde.   *know how (to) / joust*
Ther shyveren° shaftes upon sheeldes thikke;   *shiver*
He feeleth thurgh the herte-spoon° the prikke.°   *breast / point*
Up spryngen speres twenty foot on highte,

1750 Out gooth the swerdes as the silver brighte;
The helmes they tohewen° and toshrede.°   *cut up / shred up*
Out brest° the blood with stierne stremes rede;   *bursts*
With myghty maces the bones they tobreste.°   *break up*
He thurgh the thikkeste of the throng° gan
  threste.°   *crowd / thrust*

1755 Ther semblen° steedes stronge, and doun gooth al! *stumble*
He rolleth under foot as dooth a bal.°   *ball*
He foyneth° on his feet with his tronchon,°   *parries / spear-shaft*

And he hym hurtleth° with his hors adoun.   *strikes*
He thurgh the body is hurt and sithen
  ytake,°   *afterwards captured*

1760 Maugree his heed,° and broght unto the
  stake;   *despite all he could do*
As forward° was, right there he moste abyde.   *the agreement*
Another lad° is on that oother syde.   *led*
And somtyme dooth hem° Theseus to reste,   *causes them*
Hem to fresshen° and drynken if hem
  leste.°   *take refreshment / they wanted*

1765 Ful ofte° a day han thise Thebanes two   *very often*
Togydre ymet and wroght° his felawe wo.   *caused*
Unhorsed hath ech oother° of hem tweye.   *each other*
Ther nas no tygre in the vale of Galgopheye[2]
Whan that hir whelpe° is stole° whan it is lite   *cub / stolen*

1770 So crueel on the hunte as is Arcite
For jelous herte° upon this Palamoun,   *heart*
Ne in Belmarye[3] ther nys so fel leoun°   *is not so fierce a lion*
That hunted is or for his hunger wood
Ne of his praye° desireth so the blood   *prey*

1775 As Palamoun to sleen his foo Arcite.
The jelous strokes on hir helmes byte;°   *bite*
Out renneth blood on bothe hir sydes rede.
  Somtyme an ende ther is of every dede,°   *deed*
For er the sonne unto the reste wente,

1780 The stronge Kyng Emetreus gan hente°   *captured*
This Palamon as he faught with Arcite
And made his swerd depe in his flessh to byte.
And by the force of twenty is he take°   *taken*
Unyolden° and ydrawe° unto the stake.   *not yielding / drawn*

1785 And in the rescus° of this Palamon   *rescue*
The stronge Kyng Lygurge is born adoun,°   *knocked down*
And Kyng Emetreus for al his strengthe
Is born° out of his sadel a swerdes lengthe,   *carried*
So hitte hym Palamoun er he were take.°   *taken*

1790 But al for noght.° He was broght to the stake;   *nothing*
His hardy herte myghte hym helpe naught.°   *by no means*
He moste abyde° whan that he was caught   *had to stay*
By force and eek by composicioun.°   *agreement*
  Who sorweth now but woful Palamoun,
1795 That moot namoore goon agayn° to fighte?   *go again*

---

[1] *pryme* Roughly three hours after sunrise; i.e., some time towards 9 a.m.

[2] *Galgopheye* I.e., Galgophia, a valley in Greece.

[3] *Belmarye* I.e., Benmarin, a region of Morocco. In the General Prologue, we find that the Knight has fought there.

And whan that Theseus hadde seyn° this sighte,   *seen*
Unto the folk that foghten° thus echon,°   *fought / each one*
He cryde, "Hoo!° Namoore! For it is doon!   *stop!*
I wol be trewe juge and no partie.°   *partisan*
1800 Arcite of Thebes shal have Emelie,
That by his fortune hath hire faire ywonne!"°   *won fairly*
Anon ther is a noyse of peple bigonne
For joye of this so loude and heighe withalle
It semed that the lystes sholde falle.
1805   What kan now faire Venus doon° above?   *do*
What seith she now? What dooth this queene of love
But wepeth so for wantynge° of hir wille   *lack*
Til that hir teeres in the lystes fille?
She seyde, "I am ashamed doutelees!"°   *doubtless*
1810 Saturnus seyde, "Doghter, hoold thy pees!
Mars hath his wille. His knyght hath al his bone.°   *request*
And by my heed, thow shalt been esed° soone!"   *be eased*
    The trompes with the loude mystralcie,°   *music*
The heraudes that ful loude yolle° and crie   *yell*
1815 Been° in hire wele° for joye of Daun° Arcite.   *be / prosperity / sir*
But herkneth me,° and stynteth° now a
    lite   *listen to me / keep quiet*
Which a myracle ther bifel anon.
    This fierse Arcite hath of his helm ydon,°   *removed*
And on a courser for to shewe his face
1820 He priketh endelong° the large place,   *from end to end of*
Lokynge upward upon Emelye.
And she agayn° hym caste a freendlich° eye¹   *towards / friendly*
And was al his chiere as in his herte.
    Out of the ground a furie infernal sterte,°   *infernal fury arose*
1825 From Pluto sent at requeste of Saturne,
For which his hors for fere° gan to turne   *fear*
And leepe° aside and foundred° as he
    leepe.°   *leap / stumbled / leapt*
And er that Arcite may taken keepe,°   *care*
He pighte hym° on the pomel° of his
    heed,   *knocked himself / crown*
1830 That in the place he lay as he were deed.

His brest tobrosten° with his sadel bowe,   *broken up*
As blak he lay as any cole° or crowe,   *coal*
So was the blood yronnen° in his face.   *run*
Anon he was yborn° out of the place   *carried*
1835 With herte soor° to Theseus paleys.   *sore*
Tho° was he korven° out of his harneys°   *then / cut / armor*
And in a bed ybrought° ful faire and blyve,°   *brought / quickly*
For he was yet in memorie° and alyve°   *conscious / alive*
And alwey criynge° after Emelye.   *crying*
1840   Duc Theseus with al his compaignye
Is comen hoom to Atthenes his citee
With alle blisse and greet solempnitee.°   *ceremony*
Albeit° that this aventure° was
    falle,°   *although / mishap / had happened*
He nolde noght° disconforten° hem alle.   *would not / distress*
1845 Men seyde eek that Arcite shal nat dye.°   *not die*
He shal been heeled° of his maladye!   *be healed*
And of another thyng they weren as fayn,°   *glad*
That of hem alle was ther noon yslayn.°   *killed*
Al° were they soore yhurt and namely
    oon°   *although / especially one*
1850 That with a spere was thirled° his brest
    boon.°   *pierced / breast-bone*
To othere woundes and to broken armes
Somme hadden salves, and somme hadden charmes.²
Fermacies° of herbes and eek save°   *medicines / sage*
They dronken, for they wolde hir lymes
    have.°   *to save their limbs*
1855 For which this noble duc, as he wel kan,
Conforteth and honoureth every man
And made revel al the longe nyght
Unto the straunge° lordes, as was right,   *foreign*
Ne ther was holden no disconfitynge
1860 But as a justes or a tourneiynge.³
For soothly, ther was no disconfiture.°   *dishonor*
For fallyng nys nat° but an aventure,   *is nothing*
Ne to be lad by force unto the stake
Unyolden° and with twenty knyghtes take,   *unyielded*
1865 O° persone allone withouten mo,   *one*
And haryed° forth by arm, foot and too,°   *dragged / toe*

---

¹ *And ... eye* The following lines occur in most editions of *The Canterbury Tales* after this one: "For wommen, as to speken in comune, / Thei folwen alle the favour of Fortune." Ellesmere and Hengwrt both omit these lines. They are found in Oxford, Corpus Christi College MS 198. Dated c. 1410–20, this manuscript, like Ellesmere and Hengwrt, is a very early witness to the text of *The Canterbury Tales*.

² *Somme ... charmes* Some had salves and some had charms. Herbal medicine and medicinal magic were widely practiced in the Middle Ages.

³ *Ne ... tourneiynge* Nor was it considered a defeat for anyone except of the kind appropriate to a joust or tournament.

And eek his steede dryven forth with staves,°   *spears*
With footmen, bothe yemen° and eek knaves,°   *yeomen / boys*
It nas arretted hym no vileynye.[1]
1870 Ther may no man clepen° it cowardye.°   *call / cowardice*
For which anon Duc Theseus leet crye°   *proclaimed*
To stynten alle rancour and envye,
The gree° as wel of o° syde as of oother,   *victory / one*
And eyther syde ylik° as ootheres brother,   *either side like*
1875 And yaf hem yiftes° after hir degree   *gave them gifts*
And fully heeld° a feeste dayes three   *held*
And convoyed° the kynges worthily   *accompanied*
Out of his toun a journee° largely.   *day's ride*
And hoom went every man the righte way.
1880 Ther was namoore but "Farewel! Have good day!"
Of this bataille I wol namoore endite
But speke of Palamoun and of Arcite.
  Swelleth° the brest of Arcite, and the soore°   *swells / sore*
Encreesseth at his herte moore and moore.
1885 The clothered° blood for any lechecraft°   *clotted / skill in medicine*
Corrupteth° and is in his bouk° ylaft,°   *corrupts / chest / left*
That neither veyne-blood ne ventusynge[2]
Ne drynke of herbes may ben° his helpynge.°   *be / helping*
The vertu expulsif[3] or animal
1890 Fro thilke vertu° cleped° natural[4]   *power / called*
Ne may the venym° voyden° ne expelle.   *poison / purge*
The pipes of his longes° gonne° to swelle,   *lungs / began*
And every lacerte° in his brest adoun°   *muscle / down*
Is shent° with venym° and corrupcioun.   *destroyed / poison*
1895 Hym gayneth° neither, for to gete° his lif,   *it helps him / preserve*
Vomyt° upward ne dounward laxatif.°   *vomit / laxative*
Al is tobrosten thilke regioun;
Nature hath now no dominacioun.
And certeinly ther° nature wol nat wirche,°   *where / work*
1900 Farewel phisik!° Go ber° the man to
    chirche!°   *medicine / carry / church*
This al and som:° that Arcita moot dye,   *this briefly (means)*

For which he sendeth after Emelye
And Palamon, that was his cosyn deere.°   *dear cousin*
Thanne° seyde he thus, as ye shal after heere: *then*
1905 "Naught° may the woful spirit in myn herte   *by no means*
Declare o° point of alle my sorwes smerte°   *one / painful sorrows*
To yow, my lady that I love moost,
But I biquethe the servyce of my goost°   *spirit*
To yow aboven every creature,
1910 Syn that my lyf may no lenger dure.°   *last*
Allas the wo! Allas the peynes stronge
That I for yow have suffred and so longe!
Allas the deeth! Allas, myn Emelye!
Allas, departynge of oure compaignye!
1915 Allas, myn hertes queene! Allas my wyf,[5]
Myn hertes lady, endere of my lyf!°   *one who ends my life*
What is this world? What asketh men to have?
Now with his love, now in his colde grave,
Allone, withouten any compaignye.
1920 Farewel, my sweete foo, myn Emelye!
And softe, taak° me in youre armes tweye   *take*
For love of God, and herkneth what I seye:
  I have heer with my cosyn Palamon
Had strif and rancour many a day agon°   *past*
1925 For love of yow and for my jalousye.
And Juppiter so wys° my soule gye°   *wise / guide*
To speken of a servaunt° proprely   *a servant (of love)*
With alle circumstances trewely—
That is to seyn, trouthe, honour, knyghthede,°   *knighthood*
1930 Wysdom, humblesse,° estaat, and heigh
    kynrede,°   *humility / high kindred*
Fredom, and al that longeth° to that art—   *pertains*
So Juppiter have of my soule part
As in this world right now ne knowe I non°   *I know none*
So worthy to ben loved as Palamon,
1935 That serveth yow and wol doon° al his lyf.   *will do*
And if that evere ye shul ben a wyf,
Foryet nat° Palamon, the gentil man."   *forget not*
And with that word his speche faille gan,°   *speech began to fail*
And from his herte up to his brest was come
1940 The coold of deeth, that hadde hym overcome.
And yet moreover,° for in hise armes two   *and that is not all*

---

[1] *It ... vileynye* It was not attributed to him as any dishonor.

[2] *veyne-blood ne ventusynge* *Vein-blood* Blood-letting; *ventusing* Cupping. Two medieval medical procedures.

[3] *expulsif* The power of the body to expel unhealthy humors, medieval medicine's version of modern immune theory. "Animal" was a term applied to this power, which was supposed to reside in one's brain.

[4] *Fro ... natural* Natural power in medieval medicine was supposed to reside in the liver, and it too helped combat illness.

[5] *Allas ... wyf* Arcite may simply be thinking of Emily as the woman who is destined to be his wife, but in Boccaccio's *Teseida*, Chaucer's immediate source, Arcite actually marries Emily on his death-bed.

The vital strenghe° is lost and al ago.°   *power of life / gone*
Oonly the intellect withouten moore
That dwelled in his herte syk and soore,
1945 Gan faillen whan the herte felte deeth.[1]
Dusked° hise eyen two, and failled breeth.   *darkened*
But on his lady yet caste he his eye.
His laste word was "Mercy, Emelye!"
His spirit chaunged hous° and wente ther°   *its dwelling / where*
1950 As I can nevere;° I kan nat tellen wher.   *can never know*
Therfore I stynte. I nam no divinistre.°   *theologian*
Of soules fynde I nat in this registre,°   *list*
Ne me ne list° thilke opinions to telle   *I do not wish*
Of hem° though that they writen wher they
dwelle.   *them (other writers)*
1955 Arcite is coold. Ther Mars his soule gye!°   *guide*
Now wol I speken forth of Emelye.
Shrighte° Emelye, and howleth Palamon,   *shrieks*
And Theseus his suster took anon,
Swownynge,° and baar° hire fro the corps
away.   *fainting / carried*
1960 What helpeth it to tarien forth° the day   *while away*
To tellen how she weepe bothe eve and morwe?°   *morning*
For in swich cas wommen have swich sorwe,
Whan that hir housbond is from hem ago,°   *gone*
That for the moore part they sorwen° so   *sorrow*
1965 Or ellis fallen in swich maladye
That at the laste certeinly they dye.
Infinite been the sorwes and the teeres
Of olde folk and eek of tendre yeeres°   *(those of) tender years*
In al the toun for deeth of this Theban.
1970 For hym ther wepeth bothe child and man.
So greet a wepyng was ther noon, certayn,
Whan Ector[2] was ybroght al fressh yslayn°   *freshly killed*
To Troye. Allas, the pitee that was ther,
Cracchynge° of chekes, rentynge° eek of
heer!°   *scratching / tearing / hair*
1975 "Why woldestow° be deed," thise wommen crye,   *would you*
"And haddest gold ynough and Emelye?"
No man myghte gladen° Theseus   *make glad*
Savynge° his olde fader° Egeus,   *except for / father*
That knew this worldes transmutacioun,°   *changing*

As he hadde seyn° it up and doun—   *seen*
Joye after wo and wo after gladnesse—
And shewed hem ensamples° and liknesse.°   *examples / analogies*
"Right as ther dyed° nevere man," quod he,   *died*
"That he ne lyvede° in erthe° in som degree,   *did not live / earth*
1985 Right so ther lyvede never man," he seyde,
"In al this world that somtyme he ne deyde.°   *did not die*
This world nys° but a thurghfare°   *is nothing / thoroughfare*
ful of wo,
And we been pilgrymes passynge to and fro.
Deeth is an ende of every worldes soore."°   *sorrow*
1990 And over al this yet seyde he muchel more
To this effect, ful wisely to enhorte°   *exhort*
The peple that they sholde hem reconforte.°   *comfort themselves*
Duc Theseus with al his bisy cure°   *anxious care*
Cast° now wher that the sepulture°   *considered / grave*
1995 Of goode Arcite may best ymaked be
And eek moost honurable in his degree.°   *according to his rank*
And at the laste he took conclusioun
That theras° first Arcite and Palamoun   *where*
Hadden for love the bataille hem bitwene,°   *between them*
2000 That in that selve° grove swoote° and grene   *same / sweet*
Theras° he hadde hise amorouse desires,   *where*
His compleynte,° and for love hise hoote° fires,   *lament / hot*
He wolde make a fyr in which the office°   *ceremony*
Funeral he myghte al accomplice,°   *accomplish*
2005 And leet comande° anon to hakke and hewe°   *ordered / cut*
The okes° olde and leye hem on a rewe°   *oaks / row*
In colpons° wel arrayed° forto brenne.   *piles / arranged*
Hise officers with swifte feet they renne°   *run*
And ryden anon at his comandement.°   *commandment*
2010 And after this Theseus hath ysent°   *has sent*
After a beere,° and it al overspradde   *bier*
With clooth of gold, the richeste that he hadde,
And of the same suyte° he cladde° Arcite.   *material / clothed*
Upon his hondes hadde he gloves white,
2015 Eek on his heed a coroune° of laurer° grene,   *crown / laurel*
And in his hond a swerd ful bright and kene.°   *sharp*
He leyde hym, bare the visage,° on the beere,   *bare-faced*
Therwith° he weepe that pitee was to heere.   *thus*
And for the peple sholde seen hym alle,
2020 Whan it was day, he broghte hym to the halle,
That roreth° of the criyng and the soun.°   *roars / sound*
Tho° cam° this woful Theban Palamoun   *then / came*

---

1 *Oonly ... deeth* Only when the heart felt death did the intellect
begin to fail.

2 *Ector* I.e., Hector, the greatest of Trojan warriors, killed by the
Greek Achilles. See Homer's *Iliad*.

With flotery° berd° and rugged, asshy heeres,[1]   *fluttering / beard*
In clothes blake,° ydropped° al with teeres,   *black / wet*
2025   And passynge° othere of wepynge,° Emelye,   *surpassing / weeping*
The rewefulleste° of al the compaignye.   *most pitiful*
Inasmuche as the servyce sholde be
The moore noble and riche in his degree,
Duc Theseus leet forth thre steedes brynge,[2]
2030   That trapped° were in steel al gliterynge°   *equipped / glittering*
And covered with the armes° of Daun Arcite.   *coat of arms*
Upon thise steedes grete and white
Ther sitten folk of whiche oon baar° his sheeld,   *carried*
Another his spere in his hondes heeld,
2035   The thridde baar with hym his bowe Turkeys°   *Turkish bow*
(Of brend gold was the caas° and eek the harneys),   *quiver*
And riden forth a paas° with sorweful cheere   *slowly*
Toward the grove, as ye shul after heere.
The nobleste of the Grekes that ther were
2040   Upon hir shuldres caryeden the beere
With slak° paas and eyen rede and wete   *slow*
Thurghout the citee by the maister strete,°   *main street*
That sprad°was al with blak, and wonder
    hye°   *spread / wonderfully high*
Right of the same is the strete ywrye.[3]
2045   Upon the right hond wente olde Egeus,
And on that oother syde Duc Theseus
With vessel° in hir hand of gold ful fyn,°   *jar / fine*
Al ful of hony,° milk, and blood, and wyn,°   *honey / wine*
Eek Palamon with ful greet compaignye.
2050   And after that cam woful Emelye
With fyr in honde as was that tyme the gyse°   *custom*
To do the office of funeral servyse.
    Heigh labour and ful greet apparaillynge°   *preparation*
Was at the service and the fyr makynge,°   *making of the fire*
2055   That with his grene tope° the hevene raughte°[4]   *top / reached*

And twenty fadme° of brede° the armes
    straughte°—   *fathoms / breadth / stretched*
This is to seyn, the bowes° weren so brode.°   *boughs / broad*
Of stree° first ther was leyd° ful many a lode.°   *straw / laid / load*
But how the fyr was maked upon highte°   *high*
2060   Ne eek the names that the trees highte°—   *were called*
As ook, firre, birch, aspe, alder, holm, popeler,
Wylugh, elm, plane, assh, box, chasteyn, lynde, laurer,
Mapul, thorn, bech, hasel, ew, whippeltree—[5]
How they weren fild° shal nat be toold for me,   *cut down*
2065   Ne hou° the goddes ronnen up and doun,   *nor how*
Disherited° of hire habitacioun°   *disinherited / dwelling*
In whiche they woneden° in reste and pees—   *lived*
Nymphus,° fawnes, and amadrides°—[6]   *nymphs / hamadryads*
Ne hou the beestes and the briddes° alle   *birds*
2070   Fledden° for fere whan the wode° was
    falle,°   *fled / wood / cut down*
Ne how the ground agast was° of the light   *was frightened*
That was nat wont° to seen the sonne bright,   *accustomed*
Ne how the fyr was couched° first with stree°   *made / straw*
And thanne with drye stokkes cloven athre°   *sticks cut in three*
2075   And thanne with grene wode and spicerye°   *spices*
And thanne with clooth of gold° and with
    perrye°   *golden cloth / jewels*
And gerlandes hangynge with ful many a flour,
The mirre,° th'encens, withal so greet odour,   *myrrh / incense*
Ne how Arcite lay among al this,
2080   Ne what richesse aboute his body is,
Ne how that Emelye, as was the gyse,
Putte in the fyr of funeral servyse,
Ne how she swowned whan men made fyr,
Ne what she spak, ne what was hir desir,
2085   Ne what jeweles men in the fyre caste
Whan that the fyr was greet and brente faste,

---

1   *With … heeres* To throw ashes on one's hair is an ancient form of mourning.

2   *Duc Theseus … brynge* Duke Theseus commanded that three horses be brought out.

3   *ywrye* Draped. The walls of the houses along the main street have been draped high with black cloth, a standard practice in the late Middle Ages for the funerals of great nobles.

4   *That … raughte* The huge pile of trees, with its branches still green, reaches to the sky and is 120 feet (twenty fathoms) wide. Chaucer draws his description of the funeral from Boccaccio's *Teseida* (Book 11) and also probably from the Statius's *Thebaid*

(6.98–106), which in turn draws on Virgil's *Aeneid*. Unlike the warfare, courtship, and tournament in the *Knight's Tale*, the funeral rituals are those of classical antiquity and not of Chaucer's own day.

5   *Ne … whippeltree* Catalogues of trees are a feature of several epic poems from ancient times. The trees here listed are oak, fir, birch, aspen, alder, holm-oak, poplar, willow, elm, plane, ash, boxtree, chestnut, linden, laurel, maple, thorn, beech, hazel, yew, and dogwood.

6   *Disherited … amadrides* In Roman mythology, lesser gods and goddesses like those listed here lived in the woods and fields. Since the grove is cut down for the funeral, the gods and goddesses normally inhabiting it no longer have a home.

Ne how somme caste hir sheeld° and   *some threw in their shields*
    somme hir spere
And of hire vestimentz° whiche that they
    were°   *clothing | were wearing*
And coppes° fulle of wyn and milk and blood   *cups*
2090 Into the fyr that brente as it were wood,
Ne how the Grekes with an huge route
Thries° riden al the place about   *thrice*
Upon the left hand° with a loud shoutynge   *counter-clockwise*
And thries with hir speres claterynge,
2095 And thries how the ladyes gonne crye
And how that lad was homward Emelye,
Ne how Arcite is brent to asshen colde,
Ne how that lych-wake° was yholde°   *funeral wake | held*
Al thilke nyght, ne how the Grekes pleye
2100 The wake-pleyes,° ne kepe° I nat to seye   *funeral games | care*
What° wrastleth° best naked with oille
    enoynt,°   *who | wrestles | anointed*
Ne who that baar hym best in no disjoynt.°   *difficulty*
I wol nat tellen eek how that they goon
Hoom til Atthenes° whan the ple° is   *to Athens | funeral game(s)*
    doon,
2105 But shortly to the point thanne wol I wende°   *turn*
And maken of my longe tale an ende.
    By processe° and by lengthe of certeyn yeres,   *in due course*
Al stynted is the moornynge° and the teres   *mourning*
Of Grekes by oon general assent.
2110 Thanne semed me° ther was a
    parlement°   *it seemed to me | parliament*
At Atthenes upon certein pointz° and caas,°   *points | cases*
Among the whiche pointz yspoken° was   *spoken*
To have with certein contrees° alliaunce°   *countries | alliance*
And have fully of Thebans obeisaunce,°   *obedience*
2115 For which this noble Theseus anon
Leet senden° after gentil Palamon,   *had sent*
Unwist of hym° what was the cause and why,   *unknown by him*
But in hise blake clothes sorwefully
He cam at his comandement in hye.°   *in haste*
2120 Tho° sente Theseus for Emelye   *then*
Whan they were set and hust° was al the place.   *quieted*
And Theseus abiden° hadde a space   *waited*
Er° any word cam fram his wise brest.   *before*
Hise eyen sette he theras was his lest,°   *where he wished*
2125 And with a sad visage he siked stille,°   *sighed quietly*
And after that right thus he seyde his wille:

"The Firste Moevere[1] of the cause above,
Whan he first made the faire cheyne° of love,   *chain*
Greet was th'effect and heigh was his entente.
2130 Wel wiste he why and what therof he ment.
For with that faire cheyne of love he bond°   *bound*
The fyr, the eyr, the water, and the lond[2]
In certeyn boundes, that they may nat flee.
That same prince and that same Moevere," quod he,
2135 Hath stablissed° in this wrecched° world
    adoun°   *established | wretched | below*
Certeyne dayes and duracioun°   *duration*
To al that is engendred° in this place,   *born*
Over the which day they may nat pace,°   *not go beyond*
Al mowe° they yet tho° dayes wel
    abregge.°   *although | those | shorten*
2140 Ther nedeth noght noon auctoritee allegge,[3]
For it is preeved° by experience.   *proven*
But that me list declaren° my sentence.°   *I wish to give | judgment*
Thanne may men by this ordre° wel discerne   *order*
That thilke Moevere stable is and eterne.
2145 Wel may men knowe, but it be° a fool,   *unless (the man) is*
That every part dirryveth° from his hool.°   *derives | its wholeness*
For Nature hath taken his bigynnyng°   *its beginning*
Of no partie° or of cantel° of a thyng,   *part | portion*
But of a thyng that parfit° is and stable,   *perfect*
2150 Descendynge° so til it be corrumpable.°   *descending | corruptible*
And therfore of his wise purveiaunce°   *foresight*
He hath so wel biset° his ordinaunce°   *well established | laws*
That speces° of thynges and
    progressiouns°   *species | natural processes*
Shullen enduren° by successiouns,°   *last | one after another*
2155 And nat eterne,° withouten any lye.°   *not (be) eternal | lie*
This maystow understonde and seen at eye.°   *see with your eye*
    "Loo, the ook° that hath so long a norisshynge°   *oak | growing*
From tyme that it first bigynneth sprynge°   *begins to grow*
And hath so long a lif, as we may see,

---

[1]   *The Firste Moevere* I.e., God. According to Aristotle, the First Mover is the principle that sets all other things into motion. The idea that love unites all the elements, each of which is linked to the others in a hierarchical order (the Great Chain of Being), goes back to Plato and is described in Boethius's *Consolation of Philosophy* (Book 2, meter 8), on which this passage is based.

[2]   *The ... lond* Four elements from which everything was thought to be made.

[3]   *Ther ... allegge* There is no need to cite authority.

2160 Yet at the laste wasted is the tree.
      "Considereth eek how that the harde stoon
      Under oure feet, on which we trede° and goon,°   *tread / go*
      Yet wasteth it° as it lyth by the weye.°   *it wastes / lies along the road*
      The brode ryver° somtyme wexeth dreye,°   *broad river / grows dry*
2165 The grete toures° se° we wane and
           wende;.°   *towers / see / diminishing and changing*
      Thanne may ye se that al this thyng hath ende.
      "Of man and womman seen we wel also
      That nedeth in oon of thise termes two,
      This is to seyn, in youthe or elles age,
2170 He moot be deed—the kyng as shal a page:
      Som in his bed, som in the depe see,
      Som in the large feeld, as men may see.
      Ther helpeth noght.° Al goth that ilke weye.   *nothing can help*
      Thanne may I seyn al this thyng moot deye.
2175   What maketh this° but Juppiter the kyng,[1]   *who does this*
      That is prince and cause of alle thyng,
      Convertynge al unto his propre welle,°   *own source*
      From which it is dirryved,° sooth° to telle?   *derived / truth*
      And heer agayns no creature on lyve
2180 Of no degree availleth for to stryve.[2]
          "Thanne° is it wysdom, as it thynketh me°   *then / seems to me*
      To maken vertu of necessitee
      And take it weel that we may nat eschue,°   *avoid*
      And namely that to us alle is due.
2185 And whoso gruccheth° ought, he dooth
           folye,°   *whoever / complains at all / folly*
      And rebel is to hym that al may gye.°   *who may guide all (Jupiter)*
      And certeinly a man hath moost honour
      To dyen° in his excellence and flour°   *die / flower*
      Whan he is siker° of his goode name: *sure*
2190 Thanne hath he doon° his freend ne hym° no
           shame.   *done / nor himself*
      And gladder oghte° his freend been of his deeth   *ought*
      Whan with honour up yolden° is his breeth   *yielded up*
      Than whan his name apalled° is for age,   *faded*
      For al forgeten is his vassellage.°   *service in arms*
2195 Thanne is it best as for a worthy fame
      To dyen whan that he is best of name.
          "The contrarie of al this is wilfulnesse.

_____

[1] *What ... kyng* Theseus here identifies Jupiter, as the King of the
classical gods, with the First Mover.

[2] *And ... stryve* And against this it is of no use for any living
creature, of whatever rank, to struggle.

Why grucchen° we? Why have we hevynesse°   *complain / sadness*
      That goode Arcite, of chivalrie flour,
2200 Departed is with duetee° and honour   *duty*
      Out of this foule prisoun of this lyf?
      Why grucchen heere his cosyn and his wyf
      Of his welfare, that loved hem so weel?
      Kan he hem thank? Nay, God woot, never a deel,°   *not a bit*
2205 That bothe his soule and eek hemself offende,°   *harm*
      And yet they mowe° hir lustes nat amend.   *can*
      What may I concluden of this longe serye,°   *series of arguments*
      But after wo I rede° us to be merye°   *advise / merry*
      And thanken Juppiter of al his grace?
2210 And er that we departen from this place,
      I rede we make of sorwes two
      O° parfit joye, lastynge everemo.   *one*
      And looketh now, wher° moost sorwe is
           herinne,°   *where / in this matter*
      Ther wol we first amenden° and bigynne.   *amend*
2215 "Suster," quod he, "this is my fulle assent,°   *desire*
      With al th'avys° heere° of my parlement,   *advice / here*
      That gentil Palamon, thyn owene° knyght,   *your own*
      That serveth yow with wille,° herte, and myght   *(all his) will*
      And evere hath doon syn that ye first hym knewe,
2220 That ye shul of youre grace upon hym rewe°   *have pity upon him*
      And taken hym for housbonde and for lord.
      Lene° me youre hond, for this is oure accord.   *give*
      Lat se° now of youre wommanly pitee.   *let (us) see*
      He is a kynges brother sone, pardee,°   *by God*
2225 And though he were a povre bacheler,°   *poor young knight*
      Syn he hath served yow so many a yeer
      And had for yow so greet adversitee,
      It moste been° considered, leeveth me.°   *must be / believe me*
      For gentil mercy oghte to passen right."°   *prevail over justice*
2230   Thanne seyde he thus to Palamon ful right,°   *forthrightly*
      "I trowe ther nedeth litel sermonyng°   *few words*
      To make yow assente to this thyng.
      Com neer, and taak youre lady by the hond!"
      Bitwixen hem was maad° anon the bond   *made*
2235 That highte matrimoigne° or mariage,   *matrimony*
      By al the conseil° and the baronage,°   *council / company of barons*
      And thus with alle blisse and melodye
      Hath Palamon ywedded Emelye.
      And God that al this wyde world hath wroght°   *made*
2240 Sende hym his love that it deere aboght.°   *who purchased it dearly*
      For now is Palamon in alle wele,°   *good fortune*
      Lyvynge in blisse, in richesse, and in heele,°   *health*

And Emelye hym loveth so tendrely,
And he hire serveth so gentilly,°   *nobly*
2245 That nevere was ther no word hem bitwene
Of jalousie or any oother teene.°   *discord*

Thus endeth Palamon and Emelye.
And God save al this faire compaignye! Amen.

HEERE IS ENDED THE KNYGHTES TALE

The Miller's Prologue and Tale

When the Knight has finished his tale, much applauded by the "gentles," the Host turns to the pilgrim who, after the Prioress, ranks next in the social hierarchy: the Monk, a senior brother from a wealthy monastery. But the Miller, who has already placed himself at the head of the pilgrims to lead them out of town with his discordant bagpipes, has no respect for social hierarchy. He insists that he will "quyte" the Knight, that is, repay him or match him, and his tale does just that. With the insertion of *The Miller's Tale*, Chaucer breaks decisively from less dynamic frame narratives such as Boccaccio's *Decameron*, in which the stories are told by a homogeneous and harmonious group of aristocrats, and launches a social comedy in which the various tellers will contest each other's authority and values.

The Miller's Tale belongs to the medieval genre of the *fabliau*, a short tale of trickery often set among lower-class or bourgeois characters. These tales may have circulated orally, but they were also written down, and the written versions were enjoyed by aristocratic, not peasant, readers. Chaucer draws on two well-established *fabliau* plots. In the first, a young scholar cuckolds an old husband by making him believe that a second flood is coming; in the second, a young lover humiliates a rival by tricking him into a misdirected kiss. Chaucer may have drawn on a source that had already combined these two plots or may have combined them himself. Early critics, embarrassed by the tale's vulgarity, tended to regard it as a regrettable lapse and take Chaucer at his word when he apologizes in *The General Prologue* for his boorish lower-class characters, whom he designates as "churls" who insist on telling churlish stories. But Chaucer devoted all his powers of comic timing, sensual description, and social satire to expanding the basic story line into a comic masterpiece, in which the two plots come together when Nicholas calls for water.

The Miller tells his tale, a "legend or a life" (which would normally mean a saint's life) of the cuckolding of an old carpenter, in part to attack the Reeve, who is also a carpenter—and a professional rival, since reeves were expected to catch dishonest millers. The Miller's rivalry with the Knight, however, and his claim that he will "quyte" him, invite readers to observe how extensively his tale parallels that of the Knight. These parallels all serve to subvert the values of *The Knight's Tale*, calling into question its lengthy tribute to cosmic order, its chivalric dignity, and its depiction of refined love from afar. Whereas Palamon and Arcite are almost interchangeable, Nicholas, who is "hende" or handy in so many ways, is completely unlike the squeamish Absolon; and Alison, in complete contrast to the passive Emelye, is an energetic schemer, who participates gleefully in Absolon's humiliation.

Set in Oxford, *The Miller's Tale* gives a vivid sense of medieval student life and reveals the tensions between the more prosperous members of the peasantry and cunning clerics. Most unusually, the butt of the story, the old cuckolded husband, becomes a complex and often sympathetic character. John the carpenter is allowed to expand upon his philosophy of life, warning against prying into God's secrets, just as the Miller warns the Reeve not to pry into his wife's secrets. With the fast pace of burlesque or a modern situation comedy, *The Miller's Tale* is filled with vivid details of domestic life; it could not be more different from the Knight's, and its insistence that cleverness or proximity will triumph over high ideals is one of its many possible morals. The tale offers solace and *sentens*, but exactly what this *sentens* is remains the source of continual debate.

Opening page to *The Miller's Tale*, Ellesmere manuscript.
(This item is reproduced by permission of the *Huntington Library*, San Marino, California. EL26C9F72r.)

THE MILLER'S PROLOGUE

HERE FOLWEN THE WORDES BITWENE THE HOOST AND THE MILLERE

Whan that the Knyght hath thus his tale ytoold,° *told*
In al the route° ne was ther° yong ne° oold *company / there was not / nor*
That he ne seyde° it was a noble storie *did not say*
And worthy for to drawen to memorie,° *learn by heart*
5 And namely° the gentils° everichon.° *especially / gentlefolk / every one*
Oure Hoost lough° and swoor,° "So moot I gon,[1] *laughed / swore*
This gooth aright!° Unbokeled° is the male.° *goes well / unbuckled / purse*
Lat se,° now, who shal telle another tale? *let's see*
For trewely, the game is wel bigonne.
10 Now telleth on, Sire Monk, if that ye konne,° *if you can*
Somwhat to quite with° the knyghtes tale." *match*
The Millere, that for dronken° was al pale *being drunk*
So that unnethe° upon his hors he sat, *scarcely*
He nolde° avalen° neither hood ne hat *would not / take off*
15 Ne abyde° no man for his curteisie,° *put up with / courtesy*
But in Pilates[2] voys° he gan° to crie *voice / began*
And swoor, "By armes and by blood and bones,[3]
I kan° a noble tale for the nones° *know / occasion*
With which I wol now quite° the Knyghtes tale!" *match*
20 Oure Hoost saugh° that he was dronke of ale *saw*
And seyde, "Abyd,° Robyn, my leeve° brother, *wait / dear*
Som bettre man shal telle us first another.
Abyde, and lat° us werken° thriftily."° *let / work / respectably*
    "By Goddes soule," quod° he, "that wol° nat I. *said / will*
25 For I wol speke or elles° go my wey."° *else / way*
Oure Hoost answerde, "Tel on a devele wey!° *in the devil's name*
Thou art a fool! Thy wit is overcome!"
    "Now herkneth,"° quod the Millere, "alle and some.° *listen / one and all*

30 But first I make a protestacioun° *protest*
That I am dronke; I knowe it by my soun.° *sound*
And therfore if that I mysspeke or seye,° *say something wrong*
Wyte it° the ale of Southwerk, I preye.° *blame it on / pray*
For I wol tell a legende and a lyf[4]
Bothe of a carpenter and of his wyf,
35 How that a clerk° hath set the wrightes cappe."[5] *student*
    The Reve answerde and seyde, "Stynt thy clappe!° *shut your mouth*
Lat be thy lewed,° dronken° harlotrye!° *ignorant / drunken / bawdiness*
It is a synne° and eek° a greet° folye° *sin / also / great / folly*
To apeyren° any man or hym° defame° *harm / him / slander*
40 And eek to bryngen wyves in swich° fame.° *such / dishonor*
Thou mayst ynogh° of othere thynges seyn."° *enough / speak*
    This dronke° Millere spak° ful° soone agayn° *drunken / spoke / very / again*
And seyde, "Leve brother Osewold,
Who hath no wyf, he is no cokewold.[6]
45 But I sey nat therfore that thou art oon.° *one*
Ther been ful goode wyves many oon,° *a one*
And evere a thousand goode ayeyns° oon badde.° *against / bad*
That knowestow wel° thyself, but if° thou madde.° *you know well / unless / are mad*
Why artow° angry with my tale now? *are you*
50 I have a wyf, perdee,° as wel as thow, *by God*
Yet nolde° I for the oxen in my plogh° *would not / plow*
Take upon me moore than ynogh,° *enough*
As demen° of myself that I were oon.° *judge / one (i.e., a cuckold)*
I wol bileve° wel that I am noon.° *believe / none*
55 An housbonde shal nat been inquisityf° *inquisitive*
Of Goddes pryvetee° nor of his wyf. *secrets*
So he may fynde° Goddes foyson° there, *find / abundance*
Of the remenant nedeth nat enquere!"° *he need not inquire*
    What sholde I moore seyn, but this Millere,
60 He nolde° his wordes for no man forbere,° *would not / bear patiently*
But tolde his cherles° tale in his manere.° *boor's / manner*
M'athynketh° that I shal reherce° it heere, *I regret / repeat*

---

[1] *So ... goon* I.e., as I hope to live.

[2] *But in Pilates* I.e., Pontius Pilate, the Roman governor who condemned Jesus to be crucified. In medieval religious plays he was depicted as a loud, rampaging villain.

[3] *By ... bones* Swearing during the Middle Ages and Renaissance often involved taking oaths on various parts of God's body—here God's arms, blood, and bones.

[4] *legende and a lyf* Normally a "saint's life," or biography of a Christian saint.

[5] *set the wrightes cappe* Made a fool of the carpenter.

[6] *cokewold* I.e., cuckold: a husband whose wife has sex with another man.

And therfore every gentil° wight° I preye,° *noble / person / pray*
For Goddes love demeth° nat° that I seye° *judge / not / speak*
65 Of yvel entente,° but that I moot reherce° *evil intent / repeat*
Hir° tales, all be they° bettre or werse, *their / although they be*
Or elles° falsen° som of my mateere.° *else / falsify / matter*
And therfore,° whoso° list° it nat
yheere,° *whoever / wishes / not to hear*
Turne over the leef,° and chese° another tale. *page / choose*
70 For he shal fynde° ynowe,° grete° and
smale,° *find / enough / great / small*
Of storial° thyng that toucheth gentillesse° *historical / nobility*
And eek moralitee° and hoolynesse.° *morality / holiness*
Blameth nat me if that ye chese amys.° *choose wrongly*
The millere is a cherl.° Ye knowe wel this. *boor*
75 So was the Reve, and othere manye mo,° *more*
And harlotrie° they tolden bothe two. *bawdiness*
Avyseth yow;° putteth me out of blame, *be advised*
And eek men shal nat maken ernest° of game.° *seriousness / joke*

THE MILLER'S TALE

HEERE BIGYNNETH THE MILLERE HIS TALE

Whilom° ther was dwellynge° at
Oxenford° *once / living / Oxford*
80 A riche gnof° that gestes° heeld to bord,[1] *fellow / guests*
And of his craft° he was a carpenter. *profession*
With hym ther was dwellynge a povre° scoler° *poor / student*
Hadde lerned° art, but al his fantasye° *learned / interest*
Was turned for to lerne astrologye,
85 And koude a certeyn of conclusiouns[2]
To demen° by interrogaciouns° *judge / questions*
If that men asked hym in certein houres[3]
Whan that men sholde have droghte° or elles
shoures,° *drought / rain*
Or if men asked hym what sholde bifalle° *happen*
90 Of every thyng—I may nat rekene° hem° all. *count up / them*
This clerk was cleped° hende° Nicholas. *named / handy*

---

[1] *heeld to bord* Rented out rooms.
[2] *koude a certeyn of conclusiouns* Knew some (astrological) calculations.
[3] *houres* I.e., astrological hours—times when certain planets exerted a certain influence.

Of deerne° love he koude° and of solas,° *secret / knew / pleasure*
And therto he was sleigh° and ful privee° *sly / very secretive*
And lyk° a mayden meke° for to see. *like / meek*
95 A chambre° hadde he in that hostelrye,° *room / lodging*
Allone° withouten any compaignye. *alone*
Ful fetisly° ydight° with herbes[4]
swoote,° *fashionably / decorated / sweet*
And he hymself as swete as is the roote° *root*
Of lycorys° or any cetewale.[5] *licorice*
100 His *Almageste*[6] and bookes grete and smale,
His astrelabie[7] longynge for° his art, *pertaining to*
Hise augrym stones[8] layen° faire apart° *lay / somewhat away*
On shelves couched° at his beddes heed,° *arranged / bed's head*
His presse° ycovered° with a faldyng°
reed,° *cupboard / covered / cloth / red*
105 And al above ther lay a gay sautrie[9]
On which he made a nyghtes° melodie° *nightly / melody*
So swetely that al the chambre rong.° *rang*
And *Angelus ad virginem*[10] he song,
And after that he song *The Kynges Noote*;[11]
110 Full often blessed was his myrie° throte!° *merry / throat*
And thus this sweete clerk his tyme spente
After his freendes fyndyng[12] and his rente.° *income*

---

[4] *ydight with herbes* Spread with dried and sweet smelling herbs.

[5] *cetewale* The spice zedoary, similar to ginger.

[6] *Almageste* I.e., *Almagest*, the basic textbook for medieval astronomy. It was the work of Claudius Ptolemy (2nd century CE), who gives his name to the Ptolemaic system, in which the sun revolves around the earth. According to Ptolemy, the heavens comprised nine concentric crystal spheres that revolved and on which the planets and stars were affixed.

[7] *astrelabie* I.e., astrolabe, a scientific instrument used to measure angles of heavenly bodies. Chaucer wrote *The Treatise on the Astrolabe*, a prose work that is one of the first pieces of technical writing in the English language.

[8] *augrym stones* I.e., Augrim stones; they were marked with numbers and were used for making mathematical calculations.

[9] *sautrie* I.e., psaltery, a stringed musical instrument.

[10] *Angelus ad virginem* Latin: The Angel to the Virgin. The song, an antiphon used in liturgical service, depicts the conversation between the angel Gabriel and the Virgin Mary about the coming birth of Jesus.

[11] *The Kynges Noote* This song has not survived.

[12] *After his freendes fyndyng* According to what his friends found to give him.

This carpenter hadde wedded newe° a wyf   *newly married*
Which that he lovede moore than his lyf.
115   Of eighteteene yeer she was of age.
Jalous° he was and heeld hire narwe° in cage,[1]   *jealous / closely*
For she was yong and wylde and he was old,
And demed° hymself been° lik° a
      cokewold.°   *guessed / to be / likely / cuckold*
He knew nat Catoun,[2] for his wit° was
      rude,°   *intelligence / unformed*
120   That bad° man sholde wedde his
      simylitude.°   *who advised / equal*
Men sholde wedden after hire° estaat,°   *their / condition*
For youthe and elde° is often at debaat.°   *age / in dispute*
But sith° that he was fallen in the snare,°   *since / trap*
He moste endure as oother folk his care.°   *sorrow*
125   Fair was this yonge wyf and therwithal
As any wezele° hir body gent° and smal.   *weasel / delicate*
A ceynt° she werede° ybarred° al of silk,   *girdle / wore / striped*
A barmclooth° as whit° as morne° milk   *apron / white / morning*
Upon hir lendes,° ful of many a goore.°   *hips / pleat*
130   Whit° was hir smok° and broyden° al
      bifoore°   *white / undergarment / embroidered / in front*
And eek bihynde on hir coler° aboute   *collar*
Of col-blak° silk withinne and eek withoute.   *coal-black*
The tapes° of hir white voluper°   *ribbons / cap*
Were of the same suyte° of hir coler,   *pattern*
135   Hir filet° brood° of silk and set ful hye,°   *headband / broad / high*
And sikerly° she hadde a likerous° eye.   *certainly / flirtatious*
Ful smale ypulled° were hire browes° two,   *plucked / eyebrows*
And tho° were bent and blake° as any
      sloo.°   *they / black / sloeberry*
She was ful moore blisful° on to see   *much more pleasant*
140   Than is the newe perejonette tree,°   *pear tree*
And softer than the wolle° is of a wether.°   *wool / male sheep*
And by hir girdel° heeng a purs of
      lether°   *belt / hung a purse of leather*
Tasseled with grene° and perled° with
      latoun.°   *green / decorated / brass*
In al this world to seken° up and doun   *seek*

145   Ther nas° no man so wys° that koude
      thenche°   *was not / wise / imagine*
So gay a popelote° or swich a wenche.°   *doll / peasant girl*
Full brighter was the shynyng° of hir hewe°   *shining / complexion*
Than in the Tour° the noble° yforged°
      newe![3]   *tower / gold coin / forged*
But of hir song, it was as loude and yerne°   *eager*
150   As any swalwe° sittynge on a berne.°   *swallow / barn*
Therto she koude skippe° and make game°   *dance / play*
As any kyde° or calf folwynge his dame.°   *kid (young goat) / mother*
Hir mouth was sweete as bragot° or the
      meeth°   *ale / mead (fermented honey)*
Or hoord° of apples leyd° in hey° or
      heeth.°   *hoard / stored / hay / heather*
155   Wynsynge° she was as is a joly° colt,   *skittish / pretty*
Long as a mast and uprighte° as a bolt.°   *straight / arrow*
A brooch° she baar° upon hir loue
      coler°   *broach / wore / low collar*
As brood° as is the boos[4] of a bokeler.°   *broad / shield*
Hir shoes were laced on hir legges hye.°   *high*
160   She was a prymerole,° a piggesnye°   *primrose / pig's eye (flower)*
For any lord to leggen° in his bedde   *lay*
Or yet for any good yeman° to wedde.   *yeoman*
      Now sire° and eft° sire, so bifel° the cas°   *sir / again / befell / event*
That on a day this hende° Nicholas   *handy*
165   Fil° with this yonge wyf to rage° and pleye   *fell / romp*
Whil that hir housbonde was at Oseneye,[5]
As clerkes been ful subtile° and ful queynte,°   *subtle / clever*
And prively° he caughte hire by the queynte[6]   *secretly / genitals*
And seyde, "Ywis,° but if° ich° have my wille,   *indeed / unless / I*
170   For deerne° love of thee, lemman,° I
      spille,"°   *secret / sweetheart / die*
And heeld hire harde by the haunche bones°   *thighs*

---

[1]   *in cage*   In a cage; i.e., he guarded her carefully.
[2]   *Catoun*   I.e., Cato. The *Distichs*, a widely circulating collection of proverbs and wise sayings in verse couplets, often used for teaching Latin in schools, were ascribed in the Middle Ages to the Roman writer Dionysius Cato.

[3]   *Than ... newe*   Gold coins were forged in the Tower of London.
[4]   *boos*   I.e., boss, the center bulge of a shield, occasionally used to injure an enemy.
[5]   *Oseneye*   I.e., Oseney, a small town just to the west of Oxford (now part of the modern city) where there was an abbey.
[6]   *queynte*   A rhyme on two homonyms (such as *blue / blew* or *guest / guessed*), near homonyms (such as *seke / seke*, i.e., *seek* and *sick* in the General Prologue, lines 18–19) or on two different meanings of the same word, as here with *queynte*, was known as "rime riche" and was much valued by the French court poets of Chaucer's day. The modern term "rich rhyme" has a slightly narrower meaning and is confined to rhymes on homonyms.

And seyde, "Lemman,° love me al at
   ones°   *sweetheart | immediately*

Or I wol dyen,° also° God me save!"   *die | as*

And she sproong° as a colt dooth° in the
   trave,°   *sprang | does | stall*

175 And with hir heed she wryed° faste awey.   *twisted*

She seyde, "I wol nat kisse thee, by my fey!°   *faith*

Why, lat be, quod ich,°¹ lat be Nicholas,   *I say*

Or I wol crie 'Out, harrow, and allas!'²

Do wey° youre handes, for youre curteisye!"   *let go*

180   This Nicholas gan mercy for to crye

And spak so faire and profred° hire so faste   *urged*

That she hir love hym graunted atte last°   *at last*

And swoor hir ooth,° "By Seint Thomas of
   Kent,"°   *oath | St. Thomas à Becket*

That she wol° been at his comandement   *would*

185 Whan that she may hir leyser° wel espie.°   *leisure | see*

"Myn housbonde is so ful of jalousie

That but° ye wayte° wel and been privee,° *unless | wait | secretive*

I woot° right wel I nam° but deed," quod she. *know | am not*

"Ye moste been ful deerne° as in this cas."° *secretive | business*

190   "Nay, therof care thee noght,"° quod Nicholas, *have no care*

"A clerk hadde lutherly biset his whyle³

But if° he koude a carpenter bigyle."°   *unless | trick*

And thus they been accorded° and ysworn° *agreed | sworn*

To wayte a tyme° as I have told biforn.° *wait (for a time) | before*

195   Whan Nicholas had doon° thus everideel° *done | every bit*

And thakked° hire aboute the lendes° weel,° *patted | loins | well*

He kiste hire sweete and taketh his sawtrie° *psaltery*

And pleyeth° faste and maketh melodie.   *plays*

Thanne fil it° thus that to the paryssh chirche *it happened*

200 Cristes owene werkes° for to wirche,°   *works | perform*

This goode wyf wente on an haliday.⁴

Hir forheed° shoon° as bright as any day, *forehead | shone*

So was it wasshen° whan she leet° hir werk.° *washed | left | work*

Now was ther of that chirche° a parissh clerk⁵ *church*

205 The which that was ycleped° Absolon.⁶   *called*

Crul° was his heer, and as the gold it shoon, *curled*

And strouted° as a fanne° large and
   brode;°   *stretched out | fan | broad*

Ful streight and evene lay his joly shode.° *parting of his hair*

His rode° was reed,° hise eyen greye as
   goos,°   *complexion | red | goose*

210 With Poules wyndow⁷ corven° on his shoos.° *carved | shoes*

In hoses° rede° he wente fetisly.° *stockings | red | elegantly*

Yclad° he was ful smal° and proprely *clothed | very tightly*

Al in a kirtel° of a lyght waget.°   *tunic | blue*

Ful faire and thikke° been the poyntes° set, *thick | laces*

215 And therupon he hadde a gay surplys° *surplice (liturgical garment)*

As whit as is the blosme upon the rys.°   *twig*

A myrie° child° he was, so God me save. *merry | young man*

Wel koude he laten blood° and clippe and shave⁸ *let blood*

And maken a chartre° of lond° or
   acquitaunce.°   *contract | land | quit-claim*

220 In twenty manere koude he trippe and daunce

After the scole° of Oxenford tho,°   *school | then*

And with his legges casten to and fro

And pleyen songes on a smal
   rubible.°   *rebec (bowed stringed instrument)*

Therto he song somtyme a loud quynyble,° *falsetto*

225 And as wel koude he pleye on his
   giterne.°   *gittern (plucked stringed instrument)*

In al the toun° nas° brewhous ne taverne *town | was not*

That he ne visited° with his solas° *did not visit | comfort*

Ther any gaylard tappestere° was. *merry bar-maid*

But sooth to seyn, he was somdeel
   squaymous°   *somewhat squeamish*

---

¹ *quod ich* Both Ellesmere and Hengwrt read "ich" here, yet modern editors emend to "she," under the assumption that Chaucer is here slipping in and out of direct discourse. The manuscript readings can be defended on the basis of her uttering these words: "Let me be, I said, let me be, Nicholas…!"

² *Out, harrow, and allas* Common cries of alarm to summon assistance.

³ *lutherly biset his whyle* Wasted his time.

⁴ *haliday* I.e., holy day; a saint's day or the day of a major religious celebration.

⁵ *a parissh clerk* Absolon is an assistant to the parish priest. He is a member of the clergy and probably in minor orders and might, in due course, be ordained as a priest himself.

⁶ *Absolon* The Biblical Absalom, son of King David, was famous for his beauty. Cf. 2 Samuel 14.25–26.

⁷ *Poules wyndow* Fancy shoes were sometimes cut to produce a lattice pattern, which Chaucer compares to the stained glass rose window at St. Paul's Cathedral, London, which burned down in the disastrous fire in 1666.

⁸ *clippe and shave* Medieval barbers not only worked on one's hair but also did minor surgery like letting blood. This procedure, which involved opening a vein and allowing blood to flow out, was considered important in keeping the body's four humors (one of which was blood) in balance, thus insuring good health.

230　Of fartyng, and of speche daungerous.° — *fastidious*
　　This Absolon that jolif° was and gay — *jolly*
　　Gooth° with a sencer° on the haliday,[1] — *goes / incense censer*
　　Sensynge° the wyves° of the parisshe
　　　faste.° — *incensing / wives / diligently*
　　And many a lovely look on hem° he caste, — *them*
235　And namely° on this carpenteris wyf. — *especially*
　　To looke on hire hym thoughte a myrie lyf.
　　She was so propre and sweete and likerous,
　　I dar wel seyn if she hadde been a mous° — *mouse*
　　And he a cat, he wolde hire° hente° anon. — *her / grab*
240　This parissh clerk, this joly Absolon,
　　Hath in his herte swich a love longynge
　　That of no wyf took he noon offrynge.° — *no offering*
　　For curteisie, he seyde, he wolde noon.° — *wanted none*
　　　The moone, whan it was nyght, ful brighte shoon,
245　And Absolon his gyterne° hath ytake;° — *gittern / taken*
　　For paramours° he thoghte for to wake.° — *love's sake / stay awake*
　　And forth he gooth, jolif° and amorous, — *jolly*
　　Til he cam to the carpenteres hous
　　A litel after cokkes° hadde ycrowe° — *roosters / crowed*
250　And dressed° hym up by a
　　　shot-wyndowe° — *approached / hinged window*
　　That was upon the carpenteris wal.° — *wall*
　　He syngeth in his voys° gentil° and
　　　smal,° — *voice / refined / high-pitched*
　　"Now deere lady, if thy wille be,
　　I pray yow that ye wole thynke on me,"
255　Ful wel acordaunt° to his
　　　gyternynge.° — *in accord / playing of the gittern*
　　This carpenter awook and herde synge
　　And spak unto his wyf and seyde anon,
　　"What, Alison, herestow nat° Absolon — *don't you hear*
　　That chaunteth° thus under oure boures°
　　　wal?" — *who sings / bedroom's*
260　And she answerde hir housbonde therwithal,
　　"Yis, God woot,° John! I heere it every deel."°*God knows / every bit*
　　　This passeth forth. What wol ye bet than
　　　weel?° — *what more do you want?*
　　Fro day to day this joly Absolon
　　So woweth° hire that hym is wobigon.° — *woos / filled with woe*
265　He waketh al the nyght and al the day.

He kembeth° hise lokkes° brode and made hym
　gay. — *combs / hair*
He woweth hire by meenes° and brocage° — *go-betweens / agents*
And swoor he wolde been hir owene page.° — *young servant*
He syngeth brokkynge° as a nyghtyngale. — *twittering*
270　He sent hire pyment,° meeth,° and spiced ale *spiced wine / mead*
And wafres° pipyng hoot° out of the
　gleede,° — *wafer cakes / hot / fire*
And for° she was of towne, he profreth meede.° — *because / money*
For som folk wol ben wonnen° for richesse, — *won*
And somme for strokes,° and somme for
　gentillesse.° — *force / nobility*
275　Somtyme to shewe his lightnesse° and maistrye° — *agility / ability*
He playeth Herodes[2] upon a scaffold° hye.° — *stage / high*
But what availleth hym as in this cas?
She loveth so this hende Nicholas
That Absolon may blowe the bukkes° horn.[3] — *buck's*
280　He ne hadde° for his labour but a scorn. — *did not have*
And thus she maketh Absolon hire ape,
And al his ernest° turneth til a jape.° — *seriousness / joke*
Ful sooth° is this proverbe, it is no lye,° — *true / lie*
Men seyn right thus: "Alwey the nye slye° — *near sly one*
285　Maketh the ferre° leeve° to be looth."° — *far / loved one / hated*
For though that Absolon be wood° or wrooth,° — *crazy / angry*
Bycause that he fer° was from hire sighte, — *far*
This nye Nicholas stood in his lighte.
　　Now bere° thee wel, thou hende Nicholas, — *bear*
290　For Absolon may waille° and synge "Allas!" — *complain*
And so bifel it° on a Saterday — *it happened*
This carpenter was goon° til Osenay,° — *gone / to Oseney*
And hende Nicholas and Alisoun
Acorded° been to this conclusioun — *agreed*
295　That Nicholas shal shapen° hym a wyle° — *fabricate / scheme*
This sely,° jalous housbonde to bigyle,° — *simple / trick*
And if so be the game wente aright,
She sholde slepen° in his arm al nyght, — *sleep*
For this was his desir and hire° also. — *hers*
300　And right anon, withouten wordes mo,
This Nicholas no lenger wolde tarie,° — *delay*
But dooth ful softe° unto his chambre carie° — *quietly / carry*

1　*Gooth ... holiday* It was and is the custom in liturgical churches to burn incense in a censer, a metal container which hung from a chain and was swung about by a cleric called a thurifer.

2　*Herodes* I.e., King Herod. Told of the birth of the Messiah, Herod ordered the slaughter of all male children born in Bethlehem, an event depicted in some religious plays.

3　*blowe the bukkes horn* The expression "blow the buck's horn" more or less means "go whistle."

Bothe mete° and drynke for a day or tweye°   *food | two*
And to hire housbonde bad hire for to seye,°   *asked her to say*
305   If that he axed° after Nicholas,   *asked*
She sholde seye she nyste° where he was;   *did not know*
Of al that day she saugh° hym nat° with eye.   *saw | not*
She trowed° that he was in maladye,°   *believed | sickness*
For° for° no cry hir mayde koude hym calle.   *because | with*
310   He nolde° answere for thyng° that myghte
          falle.°   *would not | anything | happen*
    This passeth forth al thilke° Saterday,   *that same*
That Nicholas stille° in his chambre lay   *quietly*
And eet° and sleepe° or dide what hym
          leste,°   *ate | slept | what he wanted*
Til Sonday that the sonne gooth to reste.
315   This sely carpenter hath greet merveyle°   *wondered greatly*
Of Nicholas or what thyng myghte hym eyle°   *ail (trouble)*
And seyde, "I am adrad,° by Seint Thomas,   *afraid*
It stondeth nat aright with Nicholas.
God shilde° that he deyde° sodeynly!   *forbid | died*
320   This world is now ful tikel,° sikerly.°   *uncertain | certainly*
I saugh today a cors° yborn° to chirche   *body | carried*
That now on Monday last I saugh hym wirche!°   *work*
    Go up," quod he unto his knave°
          anoon,°   *serving boy | immediately*
"Clepe° at his dore or knokke with a stoon.   *call*
325   Looke how it is and tel me boldely."
    This knave gooth hym up ful sturdily
And at the chambre dore whil that he stood,
He cride and knokked as that he were wood,
"What how! What do ye, maister Nicholay?
330   How may ye slepen al the longe day?"
    But al for noght. He herde nat a word.
An hole he foond ful lowe upon a bord°   *board*
Theras° the cat was wont° in for to
          crepe,°   *where | accustomed | creep*
And at that hole he looked in ful depe
335   Til at the laste he hadde of hym a sighte.
This Nicholas sat capyng evere uprighte°   *gaping upwards*
As he had kiked° on the newe moone.   *looked*
Adoun° he gooth and tolde his maister soone   *down*
In what array° he saugh that ilke° man.   *condition | same*
340   This carpenter to blessen[1] hym bigan°   *began*

And seyde, "Help us, Seinte Frydeswyde![2]
A man woot litel what hym shal bityde!°   *shall happen to him*
This man is falle° with his astromye°   *fallen | astronomy*
In som woodnesse° or in som agonye.°   *madness | fit*
345   I thoghte ay° wel how that it sholde be.   *I always thought*
Men sholde nat knowe of Goddes pryvetee.°   *secrets*
Yblessed° be alwey a lewed° man   *blessed | uneducated*
That noght but oonly° his Bileve[3] kan.°   *nothing other than | knows*
So ferde° another clerk with astromye:°   *it happened | astronomy*
350   He walked in the feeldes° for to prye°   *fields | pry (study foolishly)*
Upon the sterres,° what ther sholde bifalle,   *stars*
Til he was in a marleput[4] yfalle.°   *fallen*
He saugh nat that! But yet by Seint Thomas,
Me reweth° soore of hende Nicholas.   *I have pity*
355   He shal be rated of° his studiyng   *scolded for*
If that I may, by Jhesus hevene° kyng!   *Heaven's*
Get me a staf° that I may underspore,°   *staff | pry*
Whil that thou, Robyn, hevest of the dore.°   *heave off the door*
He shal out of his studiyng, as I gesse."°   *guess*
360   And to the chambre dore° he gan hym dresse.°   *door | approached*
His knave° was a strong carl° for the
          nones,°   *servant | fellow | occasion*
And by the haspe° he haaf it of°
          atones;°   *hinge | heaved it off | at once*
Into° the floor the dore° fil° anon.   *onto | door | fell*
This Nicholas sat ay° as stille as stoon°   *ever | stone*
365   And evere caped° upward into the eir.°   *gaped | air*
This carpenter wende° he were in despeir,   *believed*
And hente° hym by the sholdres° myghtily   *grabbed | shoulders*
And shook hym harde and cride spitously,°   *loudly*
"What Nicholay! What, how! What! Looke adoun!
370   Awake and thenk° on Cristes Passioun!   *think*
I crouche° thee from elves and fro
          wightes."°   *sign with the cross | evil creatures*
Therwith the nyght spel[5] seyde he anonrightes°   *right away*

---

[2]   *Seinte Frydeswyde*   The Anglo-Saxon St. Frideswide, a young noblewoman who was persecuted for her desire to be a nun, is the patron saint of the town of Oxford. She was abbess of a monastery that was on the site of the present Christ Church, Oxford.

[3]   *Bileve*   Carpenter John's "Believe" is his Creed—the Apostle's Creed, which, along with the Lord's Prayer, was to be memorized by every Christian.

[4]   *marleput*   I.e., marl-pit, a ditch on a farm for keeping marl, a type of soil rich in clay and used for fertilizing fields.

[5]   *nyght spel*   Spell or charm said at night to ward off evil spirits.

---

[1]   *blessen*   I.e., to bless oneself, to make the sign of the cross.

On foure halves° of the hous aboute   *four corners*
And on the thresshfold° of the dore withoute.   *threshold*
375 "Jhesu Crist and Seint Benedight[1]
Blesse this hous from every wikked wight
For nyghtes nerye° the white Pater Noster:°   *save | Lord's Prayer*
Where wentestow,° Seint Petres soster?"[2]
    And atte laste this hende Nicholas
380 Gan for to sike° soore and seyde, "Allas!   *sigh*
Shal al this world be lost eftsoones° now?"   *immediately*
    This carpenter answerde, "What seystow?°   *do you say*
What! Thynk on God as we doon, men that swynke."[3]
    This Nicholas answerde, "Fecche° me drynke,   *get*
385 And after wol I speke in pryvetee
Of certeyn thyng that toucheth me and thee.
I wol telle it noon oother° man certeyn."   *(to) no other*
    This carpenter goth doun and comth ageyn°   *comes again*
And broghte of myghty ale a large quart.
390 And whan that ech of hem had dronke his part,
This Nicholas his dore faste shette°   *shut*
And doun the carpenter by hym he sette.
    He seyde, "John, myn hoost, lief° and deere,   *beloved*
Thou shalt upon thy trouthe swere me here
395 That to no wight thou shalt this conseil° wreye,°   *counsel | betray*
For it is Cristes conseil that I seye!
And if thou telle man, thou art forlore,°   *lost*
For this vengeaunce thou shalt han therfore:°   *for it*
That if thou wreye° me, thou shalt be wood."   *betray*
400 "Nay, Crist forbede it for his hooly blood!"
Quod tho this sely man, "I nam no labbe.°   *am no blabber*
Ne, though I seye, I am nat lief to gabbe.°   *accustomed to gab*
Sey what thou wolt, I shal it nevere telle
To child ne wyf, by hym that harwed helle!"[4]

---

405 "Now John," quod Nicholas, "I wol nat lye.
I have yfounde° in myn astrologye   *found*
As I have looked in the moone bright
That now a Monday next° at quarter nyght[5]   *next Monday*
Shal falle a reyn,° and that so wilde and wood   *rain*
410 That half so greet° was nevere Noees° Flood.   *great | Noah's*
This world," he seyde, "in lasse than an hour   *less*
Shal al be dreynt,° so hidous is the shour.°   *drowned | downpour*
Thus shal mankynde drenche° and lese hir lyf."   *drown*
    This carpenter answerde, "Allas, my wyf!
415 And shal she drenche? Allas, my Alisoun!"
For sorwe° of this he fil° almoost adoun   *sorrow | fell*
And seyde, "Is ther no remedie in this cas?"
    "Why, yis, for Gode," quod hende Nicholas.
"If thou wolt werken° after loore° and reed.° *act | teaching | advice*
420 Thou mayst nat werken after thyn owene
    heed,°   *head (intelligence)*
For thus seith Salomon,[6] that was ful trewe:
'Werk° al by conseil and thou shalt nat rewe!'°   *do | regret*
And if thou werken wolt by good conseil,
I undertake withouten mast and seyl°   *sail*
425 Yet shal I saven hire° and thee and me.   *save her*
Hastou nat herd how saved was Noe°   *Noah*
Whan that oure Lord hadde warned hym biforn°   *before*
That al the world with water sholde be lorn?"°   *lost*
    "Yis," quod this carpenter, "ful yoore ago."°   *very long ago*
430 "Hastou nat herd," quod Nicholas, "also,
The sorwe of Noe with his felaweshipe
Er that he myghte brynge his wyf to shipe?[7]
Hym hadde be levere,° I dar° wel
    undertake,°   *he had rather | dare | affirm*
At thilke tyme° than alle hise wetheres
    blake°   *at that time | black sheep*
435 That she hadde had a shipe hirself° allone.   *to herself*
And therfore woostou° what is best to doone?   *do you know*

---

[1] *Seint Benedight* St. Benedict of Nursia was an early sixth-century abbot who wrote the famous Rule for monasteries.

[2] *For nyghtes ... soster* These lines have never been satisfactorily explained and probably represent John's mangling of popular charms or invocations; *Where wentestow* Where did you go; *soster* Sister.

[3] *men that swynke* Men who labor. John is making the old distinction between the three estates here. The first estate comprises those who pray (the profession for which Nicholas is studying), the second, those who fight (the nobility), and the third, those who work and thus provide the food for all three estates.

[4] *harwed helle* The Harrowing of Hell (another subject of medieval religious drama) was the victorious entry Christ made into Hell between his death and resurrection to save the righteous souls held in limbo.

[5] *quarter nyght* One-fourth of the way through the night.

[6] *Salomon* Solomon, the ancient King of Israel, was known for his wisdom and was thought to be the author of several books of the Hebrew Bible. The reference here is to Ecclesiasticus 32.24. John makes a mistake here: Ecclesiasticus, part of the Greek Old Testament considered apocryphal by Protestants or deuterocanonical by Catholics, was written by Jesus ben Sirach, not Solomon, as Saint Augustine (among others) noted.

[7] *to shipe* On board. The difficulty Noah has in getting his wife aboard the Ark is depicted in medieval drama.

This asketh° haste, and of an hastif thyng° *requires / urgent business*

Men may nat preche or maken tariyng.° *delay*

 "Anon, go gete us faste into this in° *house*

440 A knedyng trogh° or ellis a kymelyn° *kneading pot / tub*

For ech° of us—but looke that they be large— *each*

In whiche we mowe swymme° as in a barge, *may float*

And han therinne vitaille suffissant° *enough food*

But for a day. Fy on° the remenant! *disregard*

445 The water shal aslake° and goon away *ebb*

Aboute pryme° upon the nexte day. *prime (an early hour of prayer)*

But Robyn may nat wite° of this, thy knave,° *know / servant*

Ne eek thy mayde Gille I may nat save.

Axe nat° why, for though thou aske me, *ask not*

450 I wol nat tellen Goddes pryvetee.° *secrets*

Suffiseth thee, but if thy wittes madde,

To han as greet a grace as Noe hadde.[1]

Thy wyf shal I wel saven, out of doute.° *doubtless*

Go now thy wey, and speed thee heer aboute.

455 "But whan thou hast for hire and thee and me

Ygeten° us thise knedyng tubbes thre, *gotten*

Thanne shaltow hange hem° in the roof ful hye, *hang them*

That° no man of oure purveiaunce° spye. *so that / preparations*

And whan thou thus hast doon as I have seyd

460 And hast oure vitaille faire in hem yleyd,° *laid*

And eek an ax to smyte the corde° atwo° *rope / in two*

Whan that the water comth, that we may go,

And breke an hole anheigh° up on the gable *on high*

Unto the gardynward° over the stable, *towards the garden*

465 That we may frely passen forth oure way

Whan that the grete shour is goon away.

Thanne shal I swymme as myrie,° I undertake, *merrily / expect*

As dooth the white doke° after hire drake.° *duck / male duck*

Thanne wol I clepe,° 'How, Alison! How, John! *call*

470 Be myrie, for the flood wol passe anon!'

And thou wolt seyn, 'Hayl,° maister Nicholay, *hail*

Good morwe! I se thee wel, for it is day.'

And thanne shul° we be lordes al oure lyf *shall*

Of al the world, as Noe and his wyf.

475 "But of o° thyng I warne thee ful right:° *one / directly*

Be wel avysed on that ilke nyght° *that same night*

That we ben entred° into shippes bord *entered*

That noon of us ne speke nat a word,

Ne clepe,° ne crie, but been in his preyere, *call*

480 For it is Goddes owene heeste° deere. *commandment*

 "Thy wyf and thou moote hange fer° atwynne,° *far / apart*

For that bitwixe yow shal be no synne,° *sin*

Namoore in lookyng than ther shal in deede.

This ordinance° is seyd. Go, God thee speede! *commandment*

485 Tomorwe at nyght, whan folk ben alle aslepe,

Into oure knedyng tubbes wol we crepe,

And sitten there abidyng Goddes grace.

Go now thy wey. I have no lenger space° *no more time*

To make of this no lenger sermonyng.° *speech*

490 Men seyn thus: 'Sende the wise and sey nothing.'

Thou art so wys, it nedeth thee nat to preche.° *preach*

Go save oure lyf, and that I bise che."° *implore*

 This sely carpenter goth forth his wey.

Ful ofte he seith "Allas!" and "Weylawey!"

495 And to his wyf he tolde his pryvetee.° *secret*

And she was war° and knew it bet° than he *aware / better*

What al this queynte cast° was for to seye. *unusual scheme*

But nathelees she ferde as° she wolde deye, *acted as if*

And seyde, "Allas! Go forth thy wey anon.

500 Help us to scape° or we been lost echon!° *escape / everyone*

I am thy trewe, verray° wedded wyf. *faithful*

Go, deere spouse, and help to save oure lyf!"

 Lo, which a greet° thyng is affeccioun! *what a great*

Men may dyen° of ymaginacioun,° *die / imagination*

505 So depe° may impressioun be take.° *deep / taken*

This sely carpenter bigynneth quake.° *to shake*

Hym thynketh verraily° that he may see *it truly appears to him*

Noees° Flood come walwynge° as the see *Noah's / surging*

To drenchen° Alisoun, his hony deere. *drown*

510 He wepeth, weyleth, maketh sory cheere.° *a sorry face*

He siketh with ful many a sory swogh.° *groan*

He gooth and geteth hym a knedyng trogh,

And after that a tubbe and a kymelyn,

And pryvely he sente hem to his in° *house*

515 And heng hem in the roof in pryvetee.

His owene hand made laddres thre

To clymben by the ronges and the stalkes° *shafts*

Into the tubbes hangynge in the balkes,° *beams*

And hem vitailleth,° bothe trogh and tubbe, *provides food for*

520 With breed and chese and good ale in a jubbe,° *jug*

Suffisynge right ynogh as for a day.

But er that he hadde maad al this array° *these preparations*

He sente his knave and eek his wenche also

Upon his nede° to London for to go. *need*

---

[1] *Suffiseth … hadde* It is enough for you (i.e., you should be grateful), unless you are insane, to have as much favor as Noah had (by being warned of the Flood).

525	And on the Monday whan it drow to nyght,° *approached night*
He shette° his dore withoute candel lyght *shut*
And dresseth° alle thyng as it shal be. *arranged*
And shortly, up they clomben alle thre.
They sitten stille, wel a furlong way.[1]
530	Now, "Pater Noster, clom!"° seyde Nicholay. *be quiet*
And "Clom," quod John. And "Clom," seyde Alisoun.
This carpenter seyde his devocioun,° *prayers*
And stille he sit and biddeth his preyere,° *offers his prayers*
Awaitynge on the reyn, if he it heere.
535	The dede° sleepe, for wery° bisynesse, *dead / weary*
Fil° on this carpenter, right as I gesse,° *fell / guess*
About corfew° tyme[2] or litel moore. *curfew*
For travaille° of his goost° he groneth soore *labor / spirit*
And eft° he routeth,° for his heed°
myslay.° *also / snores / head / lay wrong*
540	Doun of the laddre stalketh Nicholay,
And Alisoun ful softe adoun she spedde.° *hastens*
Withouten wordes mo they goon to bedde
Theras° the carpenter is wont to lye. *where*
Ther was the revel° and the melodye, *fun*
545	And thus Alison and Nicholas
In bisynesse of myrthe and of solas
Til that the belle of laudes[3] gan to rynge
And freres° in the chauncel[4] gonne synge.° *friars / began to sing*
This parissh clerk, this amorous Absolon
550	That is for love alwey so wobigon,° *sorrowful*
Upon the Monday was at Oseneye
With a compaignye hym to disporte and
pleye,° *play and have fun*
And axed upon cas° a cloistrer° *asked by chance / monk*
Ful prively° after John the carpenter. *very secretly*
555	And he drough hym apart° out of the chirche *drew him aside*
And seyde, "I noot.° I saugh hym heere nat wirche *don't know*
Syn° Saterday.[5] I trowe° that he be went° *since / believe / is gone*

For tymber ther° oure abbot hath hym sent, *timber where*
For he is wont° for tymber for to go *accustomed*
560	And dwellen° at the grange° a day or two.[6] *stay / farm-house*
Or elles he is at his hous, certeyn.
Where that he be, I kan nat soothly seyn."° *truly say*
This Absolon ful joly was and light
And thoghte, "Now is tyme wake° al nyght, *to stay awake*
565	For sikirly,° I saugh hym nat stirynge° *certainly / not stirring*
Aboute his dore syn day bigan to sprynge.° *dawn*
"So moot I thryve,° I shall at cokkes crowe *thrive*
Ful pryvely knokke at his wyndowe
That stant ful lowe upon his boures wal.° *bedroom's wall*
570	To Alison now wol I tellen al
My love-longynge, for yet I shal nat mysse
That at the leeste wey° I shal hire kisse; *very least*
Som maner° confort shal I have, parfay.° *kind of / in faith*
My mouth hath icched° al this longe day: *itched*
575	That is a signe of kissyng atte leeste!
Al nyght me mette° eek I was at a feeste.° *I dreamed / feast*
Therfore I wol goon slepe an houre or tweye
And al the nyght thanne° wol I wake and pleye." *then*
Whan that the firste cok° hath crowe anon, *rooster*
580	Up rist° this joly lovere Absolon *rose*
And hym arraieth° gay at poynt devys.[7] *dresses*
But first he cheweth greyn° of lycorys° *a grain / licorice*
To smellen sweete er he hadde kembd his heer.
Under his tonge° a trewe-love[8] he beer,° *tongue / carried*
585	For therby wende° he to ben gracious.° *expected / attractive*
He rometh° to the carpenteres hous, *roams*
And stille he stant° under the *stands / hinged window*
shot-wyndowe—°
Unto his brist° it raughte,° it was so lowe— *breast / reached*
And softe he knokketh with a semy soun.° *quiet sound*
590	"What do ye, honycomb, sweete Alisoun,
My faire bryd,° my sweete cynamone?° *bird / cinnamon*
Awaketh, lemman myn,° and speketh to me. *my sweetheart*
Wel litel° thynken ye upon my wo, *very little*
That for youre love I swete° ther° I go. *sweat / where*
595	No wonder is thogh° that I swelte° and *is it though / swelter*
swete;

---

[1] *They … way* For the time it takes to walk a furlong (about an eighth of a mile).

[2] *corfew tyme* Curfew, from the French for "cover your fire," announced the time when all fires had to be covered and houses were shut up for the night.

[3] *laudes* I.e., Lauds, the monastic hour of prayer that occurs very early in the morning, before dawn.

[4] *chauncel* Chancel, the area of a church or chapel near the altar.

[5] *I … Saterday* I do not know. I have not seen him work here since Saterday.

[6] *And … two* Abbeys usually had outlying estates, such as this one where John the carpenter is working.

[7] *at poynt devys* I.e., at point devise: perfectly.

[8] *a trewe-love* Four-leaved clover.

I moorne° as dooth° a lamb after the tete.°   *yearn / does / teat*
Ywis,° lemman,° I have swich love longynge   *indeed / sweetheart*
That lik a turtel° trewe is my moornynge.°   *turtle-dove / mourning*
I may nat ete namoore° than a mayde."   *anymore*
600   "Go fro the wyndow, Jakke fool,"° she sayde.   *Jack-fool*
"As help me God, it wol nat be 'com pa me.'°   *come kiss me*
I love another, and elles° I were to blame,   *else*
Wel bet° than thee, by Jhesu, Absolon.   *better*
Go forth thy wey, or I wol caste a ston,°   *throw a stone*
605   And lat me slepe, a twenty devel wey!"[1]
    "Allas," quod Absolon, "and weylawey,
That trewe love was evere so yvel biset!°   *ill bestowed*
Thanne kys me, syn° it may be no bet,°   *since / better*
For Jhesus love and for the love of me."
610   "Wiltow thanne go thy wey?" quod she.
    "Ye, certes, lemman," quod this Absolon.
    "Thanne make thee redy," quod she. "I come anon."
And unto Nicholas she seyde stille,°   *quietly*
"Now hust,° and thou shalt laughen al thy fille."   *shush*
615   This Absolon doun sette hym on his knees
And seyde, "I am lord at alle degrees,°   *in every way*
For after this I hope ther cometh moore.
Lemman, thy grace, and sweete bryd,° thyn oore!"°   *bird / favor*
    The wyndow she undoth° and that in haste.   *unlatched*
620   "Have do," quod she. "Com of and speed the faste,[2]
Lest that oure neighebores thee espie."°   *see you*
    This Absolon gan wype his mouth ful drie.
Dirk° was the nyght as pich° or as the cole,°   *dark / pitch / coal*
And at the wyndow out she pitte° hir hole.   *put*
625   And Absolon hym fil° no bet° ne wers,°   *fell / better / worse*
But with his mouth he kiste° hir naked ers°   *kissed / ass*
Ful savourly° er he was war° of this.   *with relish / aware*
Abak° he stirte° and thoughte it was
    amys,°   *backwards / jumped / wrong*
For wel he wiste a womman hath no berd.°   *beard*
630   He felte a thyng al rough and longe yherd°   *long-haired*
And seyde, "Fy! Allas! What have I do?"°   *done*
    "Tehee!" quod she, and clapte° the wyndow to,   *slammed*
And Absolon gooth forth a sory° pas.°   *sorry / step*
    "A berd,° a berd!" quod hende Nicholas.   *beard, trick*
635   "By Goddes corpus,° this goth° faire and weel!"   *body / goes*
    This sely° Absolon herde every deel°   *foolish / part*

And on his lippe° he gan for anger byte,°   *lip / began to bite*
And to hymself he seyde, "I shall thee quyte!"°   *repay*
    Who rubbeth now, who froteth° now his lippes   *wipes*
640   With dust, with sond, with straw, with clooth, with
    chippes°   *chips (of wood)*
But Absolon, that seith ful ofte, "Allas!
My soule bitake° I unto Sathanas°   *commit / Satan*
But me were levere° than al this toun," quod he,   *rather*
"Of this despit° awroken° for to be.   *insult / avenged*
645   Allas," quod he, "Allas, I ne hadde
    ybleynt!"°   *had not restrained (myself)*
His hoote love was coold and al yqueynt.°   *quenched*
For fro that tyme that he hadde kist hir ers,
Of paramours° he sette nat a kers,[3]   *lovemaking*
For he was heeled of his maladie.
650   Ful ofte paramours he gan deffie,°   *defied*
And weepe as dooth a child that is ybete.°   *beaten*
A softe paas° he wente over the strete°   *quiet step / street*
Until° a smyth° men cleped daun°
    Gerveys,   *unto / blacksmith / master*
That in his forge smythed plough° harneys.   *plow*
655   He sharpeth shaar° and kultour° bisily.   *plowshare / plow-blade*
This Absolon knokketh al esily°   *quietly*
And seyde, "Undo,° Gerveys, and that anon."   *open up*
    "What! Who artow?" "I am heere Absolon."   *are you*
"What! Absolon, for Cristes sweete tree,°   *cross*
660   Why rise ye so rathe?° Ey,° benedicitee!   *early / ah*
What eyleth° yow? Som gay gerl,° God it
    woot,°   *ails / girl / knows*
Hath broght yow thus upon the viritoot.[4]
By Seinte Note,[5] ye woot wel what I mene."
    This Absolon ne roghte nat a bene°   *did not care a bean*
665   Of al his pley. No word agayn he yaf.°   *gave*
He hadde moore tow° on his distaf[6]   *flax*
Than Gerveys knew, and seyde, "Freend so deere,°   *kind*
That hoote° kultour° in the chymenee heere,   *hot / plow-blade*
As lene° it me. I have therwith to doone,°   *lend / do*
670   And I wol brynge it thee agayn ful soone."

---

[1]   *a twenty devel wey*   For the sake of twenty devils.

[2]   *Com … faste*   "Hurry up," she said, "make haste and be quick."

[3]   *sette nat a kers*   Cared nothing. (A *kers* is a watercress.)

[4]   *upon the viritoot*   Up and about.

[5]   *Seinte Note*   I.e., St. Neot, a ninth-century monk from Glastonbury who became a hermit.

[6]   *distaf*   I.e., distaff, a tool used in making thread to be spun into cloth.

Gerveys answerde, "Certes, were it gold
Or in a poke° nobles° alle untold,°   *bag / gold coins / unnumbered*
Thou sholdest have,° as I am trewe smyth.   *have (it)*
Ey, Cristes foo,° what wol ye do therwith?"   *foe*
675   "Therof," quod Absolon, "be as be may.
I shal wel telle it thee tomorwe day,"
And caughte the kultour by the colde stele.
Ful softe out at the dore he gan to stele°   *began to steal*
And wente unto the carpenteris wal.
680 He cogheth° first and knokketh therwithal   *coughs*
Upon the wyndowe right° as he dide er.   *just*
   This Alison answerde, "Who is ther
That knokketh so? I warante it a theef."
   "Why, nay," quod he, "God woot, my sweete leef,°   *loved one*
685 I am thyn Absolon, my deerelyng.°   *darling*
Of gold," quod he, "I have thee broght a ryng.
My mooder yaf° it me, so God me save.   *gave*
Ful fyn° it is and therto wel ygrave.°   *fine / engraved*
This wol I yeve° thee if thou me kisse."   *give*
690   This Nicholas was risen for to pisse
And thoughte he wolde amenden° al the jape: *make better*
He sholde kisse his ers er that he scape.°   *escape*
And up the wyndowe dide he hastily,
And out his ers he putteth pryvely
695 Over the buttok to the haunche bon.°   *thigh*
And therwith spak this clerk, this Absolon:
"Spek, sweete bryd,° I noot nat° where thou
   art."   *bird / do not know*
   This Nicholas anon leet fle° a fart   *let fly*
As greet as it had been a thonder dent,°   *thunder-clap*
700 That with the strook he was almoost yblent.°   *blinded*
And he was redy with his iren hoot,°   *hot iron*
And Nicholas amydde the ers° he
   smoot.°   *in the middle of the ass / struck*
Of gooth° the skyn° an hande brede°
   about,   *off goes / skin / a hand-breadth*
The hoote kultour brende° so his toute,°   *burned / rear*
705 And for the smert° he wende° for to dye.°   *pain / expected / die*
As he were wood for wo, he gan to crye,
"Help, water, water, help, for Goddes herte!"
   This carpenter out of his slomber sterte°   *jumped*
And herde oon crien,° "Water!" as he were wood,   *heard one cry*
710 And thoughte, "Allas, now comth Nowelis Flood!"
He sit hym up withouten wordes mo,
And with his ax he smoot the corde atwo,

And doun gooth al! He foond neither to selle,
Ne breed ne ale, til he cam to the celle[1]
715 Upon the floor, and there aswowne° he lay.   *in a faint*
   Up stirte hire Alison and Nicholay,
And criden, "Out!" and "Harrow!" in the strete.
The neighebores, bothe smale and grete,°   *big*
In ronnen° for to gauren on° this man   *ran in / gape at*
720 That yet aswowne he lay, bothe pale and wan,
For with the fal° he brosten hadde° his arm.   *fall / had broken*
But stonde he moste unto his owene harm.[2]
For whan he spak, he was anon bore doun°   *shouted down*
With° hende Nicholas and Alisoun.   *by*
725 They tolden every man that he was wood,
He was agast° so of Nowelis Flood   *afraid*
Thurgh fantasie° that of his vanytee°   *fantasy / folly*
He hadde yboght° hym knedyng tubbes thre   *bought*
And hadde hem hanged in the rove° above,   *roof*
730 And that he preyde° hem for Goddes love   *asked*
To sitten in the roof par compaignye.°   *for company*
   The folk gan laughen at his fantasye.
Into the roof they kiken° and they cape°   *stare / gape*
And turned al his harm unto a jape.°   *joke*
735 For what° so that this carpenter answerde,   *whatever*
It was for noght.° No man his reson° herde.   *nothing / explanation*
With othes° grete he was so sworn adoun°   *oaths / shouted down*
That he was holde° wood in al the toun,   *considered*
For every clerk° anonright heeld° with oother;   *scholar / agreed*
740 They seyde, "The man was wood, my leeve° brother."   *dear*
And every wight gan laughen of this stryf.°   *strife*
Thus swyved° was this carpenteris wyf   *made love to*
For al his kepyng° and his jalousye,   *guarding*
And Absolon hath kist hir nether° eye,   *lower*
745 And Nicholas is scalded in the towte.°   *rear*
This tale is doon, and God save al the rowte!°   *company*

HEERE ENDETH THE MILLERE HIS TALE

---

[1] *Ne ... celle* He did not find bread or ale to sell until he came to the bottom; i.e., he did not stop on his way down.

[2] *moste ... harm* This idiomatic expression has been interpreted differently. John the Carpenter must endure (or put up with, or take responsibility for) his own injury, or he must stand up for himself even though it turned out badly.

The Wife of Bath's
Prologue and Tale

With the opening words of her extremely long prologue, the Wife of Bath introduces one of her central themes, the conflict between the experience of life, which for the Wife means sexual experience foremost, and "auctoritee," the written commentary of learned men on religious, moral, and philosophical issues. These men, who included both the patristic writers (such as Saints Ambrose and Jerome) and classical philosophers, have little good to say about women, whom they repeatedly depict as deceitful, quarrelsome, and lecherous. Escape from this tradition, as the Wife herself indicates in her account of the debate between the man and the lion, is not easy. Just as all paintings of lions will always be painted by men, so in classical and medieval society almost all writing, especially writing that had official authority, was done by men. The Wife herself, in one of the tale's many layers of ventriloquism, places traditional criticisms of women in the mouths of her first three husbands, whom she accuses of abusing her with these repeated insults. The criticisms can also be found in her fifth husband's book, a compilation of misogynistic texts from Jerome and others, all counseling against marriage.

The great irony is that the Wife herself is drawn from this tradition. Her character is based in part on the Old Woman in *The Romance of the Rose*, a sexually experienced cynic who teaches young people the tricks of love, and both the Wife's history and the literary shape of her prologue and tale conform to many of the traditional misogynistic stereotypes found in her husband's book. The subtle layering of the text makes its final moral elusive. Readers continue to argue whether the Wife should be taken as a moral warning against unbridled carnality or admired for her independence, courage, and vitality. The glosses in the Ellesmere manuscript tend to support the first view, but the Wife herself has some telling comments to offer on men who write glosses.

The tale that the Wife finally tells is an Arthurian romance. It follows a well-established folk-tale plot in which a knight is given a year to answer a question or die and can only get the answer from an old and ugly woman who will not give it to him unless he promises either to marry her or, as in Chaucer's version, to give her whatever she wants, which later turns out to be marriage. In several versions, including *The Tale of Florent* in John Gower's *Confessio Amantis*, the question the knight must answer is what women most desire. Chaucer modifies the familiar story in a number of ways, so that the tale contributes to the argument the Wife has been making in her prologue. The knight in the Wife's version is not innocent—he is a rapist—and he objects to the marriage not just because the woman is old and ugly, but also because she is of low birth, an objection she counters in a long disquisition on the nature of true gentility. Even the knight's final choice, which in the other versions takes the form of "foul by day and fair by night" or the reverse, is subtly altered in keeping with the Wife's interests.

Detail, opening page of the Prologue to *The Wife of Bath's Tale*, Ellesmere manuscript;
see color insert for full page.
(This item is reproduced by permission of the *Huntington Library*, San Marino, California. EL26C9F72r.)

THE WIFE OF BATH'S PROLOGUE

THE PROLOGUE OF THE WYVVES TALE OF BATHE

"Experience, though noon auctoritee
Were in this world, were right ynogh to me[1]
To speke° of wo° that is in mariage.   *speak | woe*
For lordynges,° sith° I twelve yeer was of age,   *lords | since*
5   Ythonked° be God that is eterne on lyve,°   *thanked | eternally alive*
Housbondes at chirche dore° I have had fyve,°   *church door | five*
For I so ofte have ywedded° bee,°[2]   *wedded | been*
And alle were worthy men in hir° degree.   *their*
But me was toold certeyn° nat longe
    agoon° is,   *certain | not long ago*
10 That sith that Crist ne wente° nevere but onis°   *did not go | once*
To weddyng in the Cane° of Galilee,[3]   *Cana*
By the same ensample° thoughte me°   *example | it seemed to me*
That I ne sholde° wedded be but ones.°   *should not | once*
Herkne eek° which a sharpe word for the
    nones°   *listen also | for the occasion*
15 Biside° a welle Jhesus, God and man,   *beside*
Spak° in repreeve° of the Samaritan;[4]   *spoke | rebuke*
'Thou hast yhad° fyve housbondes,' quod° he,   *have had | said*
'And that man the which that hath now thee°   *who now has you*
Is noght thyn housbonde.' Thus seyde he certeyn.
20 What that he mente therby,° I kan nat
    seyn.°   *meant by this | cannot say*
But that I axe,° why that the fifthe man   *ask*
Was noon housbonde to the Samaritan?
How manye myghte she have in mariage?
Yet herde I nevere tellen° in myn age   *never heard told*
25 Upon this nombre° diffinicioun.°   *number | definition*
Men may devyne° and glosen°[5] up and doun,° *guess | gloss | down*
But wel I woot° expres° withoute lye,°   *well I know | clearly | lie*

God bad° us forto wexe° and multiplye.   *commanded | to increase*
That gentil° text kan° I understonde!   *noble | can*
30 Eek wel I woot, he seyde myn housbonde
Sholde lete fader and mooder° and take
    me.[6]   *should leave father and mother*
But of no nombre° mencioun made
    he°   *number | did he make mention*
Of bigamye° or of octogamye.°   *bigamy | marriage to eight spouses*
Why sholde men speke° of it vileynye?°   *speak | as villainy*
35 "Lo heere° the wise kyng daun° Salamon: *consider | master*
I trowe° he hadde wyves mo° than oon.°[7]   *believe | more | one*
As wolde God, it were leveful unto me[8]
To be refresshed° half so ofte° as he!   *refreshed | often*
Which yifte° of God hadde he for alle hise wyvys;°   *gift | wives*
40 No man hath swich° that in this world alyve° is.   *such | alive*
God woot,° this noble kyng, as to my
    wit,°   *knows | as far as I know*
The first nyght° had many a myrie° fit   *night | merry*
With ech° of hem,° so wel was hym° on
    lyve.   *each | them | he was so lucky*
Yblessed be God that I have wedded five![9]
45 Welcome the sixte, whanevere he shal.°   *whenever he shall arrive*
Forsothe,° I wol nat kepe me chaast in al° *in truth | entirely chaste*
Whan myn housbonde is fro° the world ygon.°   *from | gone*
Som° Cristen° man shal wedde me
    anon,°   *some | Christian | immediately*
For thanne° th'apostle seith[10] I am free   *then | the apostle says*
50 To wedde, a Goddes half, where it liketh me.[11]

---

[1] *Experience ... me* Experience, even if there were no written
authority in the world, would be quite enough for me. Authority, in
this sense, refers to the writings of learned men, especially the
patristic writers and ancient philosophers.

[2] *For ... bee* Many manuscripts have "If I so ofte myghte have
ywedded be," i.e., if these multiple marriages were indeed lawful.

[3] *Cane of Galilee* See John 2.1–11.

[4] *Samaritan* See John 4.1–42.

[5] *glosen* Crucial points in the Bible, and other religious, philosophical, or legal texts were explained in glosses (comments written in the
margins or between the lines).

[6] *myn housbonde ... me* See Genesis 2.24.

[7] *I ... oon* According to the Bible, King Solomon had seven
hundred wives and three hundred concubines. See 1 Kings 11.33.

[8] *As wolde ... me* If only God would permit that it should be lawful
for me.

[9] *Yblessed ... five* Some manuscripts contain the following six-line
passage:

> "Of whiche I have pyked out the beste
> Bothe of here nether purs and of here cheste.
> Diverse scoles maken parfyt clerkes,
> And diverse practyk in many sondry werkes,
> Maken the workman parfit, sekirly;
> Of five husbandes scoleiyng am I."

John Manly and Edith Rickert suggest that these lines are "a late
Chaucerian insertion," i.e., part of a late rough draft of the poem.

[10] *th'apostle seith* I.e., St. Paul. See 1 Corinthians 7.25–38.

[11] *To wedde ... me* To wed, by God's permission, wherever I wish.

He seith to be wedded is no synne:°   *sin*
"Bet° is to be wedded than to brynne."°¹   *better | burn*
What rekketh me,° thogh folk seye°
   vileynye°   *what do I care | say | villainy*
Of shrewed° Lameth² and of bigamye?°   *cursed | bigamy*
55 I woot wel° Abraham³ was an hooly° man   *know well | holy*
And Jacob eek, as ferforth as I kan,°   *as far as I know*
And ech of hem° hadde wyves mo than two   *them*
And many another man also.
Whanne° saugh° ye evere in manere° age   *when | saw | any*
60 That hye° God defended° mariage   *high | forbade*
By expres° word? I pray yow, telleth me.   *specific*
Or where comanded he virginitee?°   *virginity*
I woot as wel as ye,° it is no drede,⁴   *know as well as you*
Whan th'apostel° speketh of maydenhede°   *virginity*
65 He seyde that precept° therof hadde° he
   noon.°⁵   *commandment | about | none*
Men may conseille° a womman to been oon,°   *counsel | single*
But conseillyng is nat comandement.
He putte it in oure owene juggement.°   *left it to our own judgment*
For hadde° God comanded maydenhede,   *had*
70 Thanne° hadde he dampned° weddyng with the
   dede.°   *then | condemned | in the act*
And certein,° if ther were no seed ysowe°   *certainly | sown*
Virginitee, wherof thanne° sholde° it growe?   *how then | should*
Poul° ne dorste nat° comanden atte
   leeste°   *St. Paul | dared not | command at least*
A thyng of which his maister° yaf° noon
   heeste.°   *master | gave | no command*
75 The dart⁶ is set up of virginitee:
Cacche whoso may. Who renneth best, lat see!⁷

"But this word is nat taken of every
   wight,°   *does not apply to everyone*
But theras God lust gyve it of his myght.⁸
I woot wel the apostel was a mayde.°   *virgin*
80 But nathelees,° thogh° that he wroot° and
   sayde   *nevertheless | though | wrote*
He wolde° that every wight° were swich° as
   he,   *wished | person | such*
Al nys but conseil° to virginitee.   *is not but advice*
And for to been° a wyf he yaf° me leve°   *be | gave | leave*
Of indulgence,° so it is no repreve°   *by permission | reproach*
85 To wedde me if my make° dye,°   *mate | should die*
Withouten excepcioun° of bigamye.°   *objection | bigamy*
Al° were it good no womman for to touche,   *although*
He mente° as in his bed or in his couche.°   *meant | couch*
For peril is bothe fyr and tow t'assemble.⁹
90 Ye knowe what this ensample° may resemble.   *example*
This is al and som,° that virginitee   *the whole matter*
Moore profiteth than weddyng in freletee;¹⁰
Freletee° clepe I° but if° that he and she   *weakness | I call it | unless*
Wolde lede° al hir lyf° in chastitee.   *would lead | their life*
95 "I graunte° it wel; I have noon envie,°   *grant | no envy*
Thogh maydenhede preferre bigamye.¹¹
Hem liketh° to be clene,° body and
   goost.°   *they prefer | pure | spirit*
Of myn estaat° I nyl nat° make no
   boost.°   *my condition | will not | boast*
For wel ye knowe, a lord in his houshold,
100 He nath nat° every vessel al of gold.   *does not have*
Somme been of tree° and doon° hir° lord
   servyse.   *wood | do | their*
God clepeth° folk to hym in sondry wyse.°   *calls | in different ways*
And everich hath° of God a propre
   yifte°—   *everyone has | particular gift*
Som this, som that, as hym liketh shifte.°   *as he pleases to give*
105 "Virginitee is greet perfeccioun
And continence eek with devocioun.°   *religious devotion*

---

¹ *Bet … brynne* See 1 Corinthians 7.9.

² *Lameth* Lamech is the first to marry two wives. See Genesis 4.19.

³ *Abraham* The patriarch Abraham, as recounted in the book of Genesis, was favored by God, yet he had more than one wife, as did his grandson Jacob.

⁴ *it is no drede* Do not doubt it.

⁵ *He … noon* Paul admits that he could find no justification for his view in the Old Testament. See 1 Corinthians 7.25.

⁶ *dart* A spear was sometimes given as a prize for a race in England in the Middle Ages. Many editors prefer the reading "for virginity" (found in many other manuscripts), which makes virginity the competitor rather than the prize.

⁷ *Cacche … see* Let whoever can catch it. Let us see who runs best.

---

⁸ *But … myght* Except where God wishes, through his might, to impose this principle (of virginity).

⁹ *fyr … t'assemble* To assemble fire and flax (flammable material of which wicks are made).

¹⁰ *Moore … freletee* Remaining a virgin is better than marrying through weakness.

¹¹ *Thogh … bigamye* Though virginity be preferred to bigamy.

But Crist that of perfeccioun° is welle°   *perfection | well (source)*
Bad° nat every wight sholde go selle   *commanded*
Al that he hadde and gyve° it to the poore   *give*
110   And in swich wise folwe hym[1] and his foore.°   *steps*
He spak to hem that wolde lyve parfitly.°   *wished to live perfectly*
And, lordynges, by youre leve,° that am nat I!   *leave*
I wol bistowe° the flour° of myn age   *will bestow | flower*
In the actes and in fruyt° of mariage.   *fruit*
115   "Telle me also, to what conclusioun
Were membres ymaad° of generacioun?[2]   *made*
And for what profit° was a wight ywroght?°   *purpose | person made*
Trusteth° right wel, they were nat maad° for
    noght.°   *believe me | not made | nothing*
Glose whoso wole and seye bothe up and doun,[3]
120   That they were maad for purgacioun°   *releasing*
Of uryne° and oure bothe thynges
    smale,°   *urine | our two small things (sexual organs)*
And eek to knowe° a femele from a male,   *distinguish*
And for noon oother cause: sey° ye no?   *say*
The experience woot wel° it is   *experience (in general) knows well*
    noght so.
125   So that the clerkes° be nat with me wrothe,°   *theologians | angry*
I sey yis,° that they beth maked° for
    bothe!   *say yes | are made*
That is to seye, for office and for ese°   *pleasure*
Of engendrure,[4] ther we nat God
    displese.°   *where we do not displease God*
Why sholde men elles° in hir bookes sette°   *otherwise | set down*
130   That a man shal yelde to his wyf hire dette?[5]
Now, wherwith° sholde he make his
    paiement°   *with what | payment*
If he ne used° his sely° instrument?   *did not use | innocent*
Thanne were they maad upon a creature
To purge uryne° and for engendrure.°   *release urine | conception*
135   "But I seye noght° that every wight is holde°   *not | obligated*

That hath swich harneys,° as I of tolde,   *such equipment*
To goon° and usen hem° in engendrure.   *go | them*
They shul° nat take of chastitee no cure.°   *shall | attention*
Crist was a mayde° and shapen° as a man,   *virgin | formed*
140   And many a seint sith° the world bigan,   *since*
Yet lyved they evere in parfit° chastitee.   *perfect*
I nyl nat envye° no virginitee.   *will not envy*
Lat hem° be breed° of pured whete°
    seed,   *let them | bread | pure wheat*
And lat us wyves hoten° barly breed.   *be called*
145   And yet with barly breed, Mark[6] telle kan,
Oure Lord refresshed° many a man.   *gave food to*
In swich estaat° as God hath cleped us°   *condition | has called us*
I wol persevere.° I nam nat precius.°   *remain | fastidious*
In wyfhode I wol use myn instrument°   *sexual organ*
150   As frely° as my makere hath it sent.   *freely*
If I be daungerous,° God yeve° me sorwe.   *stand-offish | give*
Myn housbonde shal it have bothe eve and morwe
Whan that hym list com forth and paye his dette.[7]
An housbonde I wol have, I nyl nat lette,°   *will not stop*
155   Which shal° be bothe my dettour° and my
    thral°   *who shall | debtor | slave*
And have his tribulacioun° withal°   *tribulation | also*
Upon his flessh whil I am his wyf.
I have the power durynge° al my lyf   *during*
Upon his propre° body, and noght he.   *own*
160   Right thus the apostel[8] tolde it unto me
And bad° oure housbondes for to love us
    weel.°   *commanded | well*
Al this sentence me liketh every deel."[9]
    Up stirte° the Pardoner and that anon.°   *jumped | immediately*
"Now, Dame," quod he, "by God and by Seint John,
165   Ye been° a noble prechour° in this cas!°   *are | preacher | matter*
I was aboute to wedde a wyf, allas!
What sholde I bye it on my flessh so deere?[10]

---

[1] *swich wise* Such a manner; *folwe hym* Follow him.

[2] *membres ... of generacioun* Sexual organs.

[3] *Glose ... doun* Let whoever wishes to do so offer an interpretation and say both up and down.

[4] *Of engendrure* Of conception. The phrase "office and ease of engendrure" means for a purpose (that is, conceiving children) and for the pleasure of procreation.

[5] *yelde ... dette* Having sex. I.e., both partners owed each other a certain sexual fulfillment, lest sexual frustration drive one of them to adultery. The line is a quotation from 1 Corinthians 7.3.

[6] *And ... man* The reference here is to John 6.9 and the miracle of the loaves and fishes, not to a passage in the Gospel of Mark.

[7] *Whan ... dette* When he wishes to come forth and pay his debt.

[8] *the apostel* I.e., St. Paul, whose insights on marriage the Wife of Bath has been mentioning since she began to speak. In addition to the passage referred to above in note 5, Paul's other major pronouncement on marriage is in Ephesians 5.21–33.

[9] *Al ... deel* All this lesson (of Scripture) pleases me, every part (of it).

[10] *What ... deere* Why should I pay so dearly for it with my flesh.

Yet hadde I levere° wedde no wyf to yeere!"°   *rather / this year*

  "Abyde,"° quod she, "my tale is nat bigonne!   *wait*

170 Nay, thou shalt drynken° of another

    tonne°   *drink / cask (of wine)*

Er that I go, shal savoure wors° than ale!   *that shall taste worse*

And whan that I have toold forth my tale

Of tribulacioun that is in mariage,

Of which I am expert in al myn age°—   *throughout my life*

175 This to seyn,° myself have been the whippe°—   *say / whip*

Than maystow chese wheither° thou wolt

    sippe°   *choose whether / will sip*

Of that tonne that I shal abroche.°   *open*

Bewar of it er thou to ny° approche,°   *too near / approach*

For I shal telle ensamples° mo° than ten.   *examples / more*

180 Whoso that wol nat bewar by othere men,[1]

By hym shul othere men corrected be.

The same wordes writeth Protholomee.°   *Ptolemy*

Rede° it in his *Almageste* and take it there!"[2]   *read*

  "Dame, I wolde praye° if youre wyl° it were,"   *ask / will*

185 Seyde this Pardoner, "as ye bigan

Telle forth youre tale. Spareth° for no man,   *spare*

And teche us yonge men of youre praktike!"°   *practice*

  "Gladly, sires,° sith it may yow like.°   *sirs / it may please you*

But yet I praye to al this compaignye,

190 If that I speke after my fantasye,°   *fancy*

As taketh it nat agrief° that° I seye,   *take it not wrong / what*

For myn entente is but for to pleye.

  "Now sire, now wol I telle forth my tale.

As evere moote° I drynken wyn or ale,   *might*

195 I shal seye sooth° of tho housbondes that I hadde,   *say the truth*

As thre of hem were goode and two were badde.

The thre men were goode and riche and olde.

Unnethe° myghte they the statut° holde   *scarcely / regulation*

In which that they were bounden° unto me.[3]   *bound*

200 Ye woot wel what I meene° of this, pardee.°   *mean / by God*

As help me God, I laughe whan I thynke

How pitously anyght° I made hem swynke!°   *at night / work*

And by my fey,° I tolde of it no stoor.°   *faith / set no store by it*

They had me yeven° hir° gold and hir

    tresoor.°   *given / their / treasure*

205 Me neded nat do lenger diligence[4]

To wynne hir love or doon hem reverence.°   *honor them*

They loved me so wel, by God above,

That I ne tolde no deyntee of hir love.[5]

A wys° womman wol sette hire evere in

    oon°   *wise / will always determine*

210 To gete hire° love theras° she hath

    noon.°   *get herself / where / has none*

But sith I hadde hem° hoolly° in myn hond,   *them / wholly*

And sith they hadde me yeven° al hir lond,°   *given / all their land*

What sholde I taken heede° hem for to plese,°   *bother / please*

But if° it were for my profit and myn ese?°   *unless / pleasure*

215 I sette hem so a werk,° by my fey,°   *to work / faith*

That many a nyght they songen° 'Weilawey!'°   *sang / alas*

The bacon was nat fet° for hem, I trowe,°   *fetched / believe*

That som° men han° in Essex at Dunmowe.[6]   *some / have*

I governed hem so wel after my lawe,

220 That ech°of hem was ful blisful° and fawe°   *each / very happy / eager*

To brynge me gaye thynges° fro the fayre.°   *pretty things / fair*

They were ful glad whan I spak to hem faire,°   *nicely*

For, God it woot, I chidde hem spitously!°   *scolded them spitefully*

  "Now herkneth hou° I baar me° properly,   *how / bore myself*

225 Ye wise wyves that kan understonde.

Thus shul ye speke and beren hem on honde.[7]

For half so boldely kan ther no man

Swere° and lye° as kan a womman.   *swear / lie*

I sey nat this by° wyves that been wyse,   *about*

230 But if° it be whan they hem

    mysavyse.°   *unless / give themselves bad advice*

A wys wyf, if that she kan hir good,°   *knows what is good for her*

Shal bere hym on hond the cow is wood[8]

And take witnesse of hir owene mayde°   *own maid*

---

[1] *Whoso ... men* The one who will not be warned (by examples offered) by others.

[2] *Rede ... there* The aphorism is not found in the *Almagest*, the great astrological treatise of Claudius Ptolemy (second century CE), but in the preface to one of the translations of his work.

[3] *In ... me* I.e., the three old husbands could barely fulfill their obligation to pay the marriage debt.

[4] *Me ... diligence* I did not need to make any more effort.

[5] *ne tolde ... love* Did not put any value on their love.

[6] *The bacon ... Dunmowe* In the village of Dunmow, it was the custom to award a side of bacon to a married couple if they did not quarrel for a year.

[7] *beren hem on honde* Either to deceive them or to accuse them falsely. The Wife does both to her husbands.

[8] *A wys ... wood* A wise woman can convince her husband that a tale-telling cowbird (a kind of jackdaw) who tells him she has been unfaithful is mad and use her own maid as a witness.

Of hir° assent, but herkneth° how I
    sayde:°   *her | listen to | how I spoke*

235 "'Sire olde kaynard,° is this thyn array?°*fool | your way of behaving*
Why is my neighebores wyf so gay?°   *well dressed*
She is honoured over al ther she gooth.°   *wherever she goes*
I sitte at hoom. I have no thrifty clooth.°   *appropriate clothing*
What dostow° at my neighebores hous?   *are you doing*

240 Is she so fair? Artow° so amorous?   *are you*
What rowne° ye with oure mayde,° benedicite?   *whisper | maid*
Sire olde lecchour,° lat thy japes be!   *sir old lecher | tricks*
And if I have a gossib° or a freend,°   *confidant | friend*
Withouten gilt,° thou chidest° as a feend!° *guilt | complain | fiend*

245 If that I walke or pleye unto his hous,
Thou comest hoom as dronken as a mous[1]
And prechest° on thy bench, with yvel
    preef!°   *preach | bad luck to you*
"'Thou seist° to me it is a greet
    meschief°   *you say | great misfortune*
To wedde a povre° womman for costage.°   *poor | expense*

250 And if she be riche and of heigh parage,°   *lineage*
Thanne seistow° it is a tormentrie°   *you say | torment*
To suffren° hire pride and hire malencolie.   *endure*
And if she be fair, thou verray knave,[2]
Thou seyst that every holour° wol hire have: *lecher*

255 She may no while in chastitee abyde°   *remain*
That is assailled upon ech a syde.°   *every side*
    Thou seyst that som folk desiren us for richesse,
Somme for oure shape, somme for oure fairnesse
And som for she kan synge and daunce

260 And som for gentillesse° and som for
    daliaunce,°   *nobility | flirtation*
Som for hir handes and hir armes smale.°   *slender*
Thus goth al to the devel,° by thy tale!   *devil*
Thou seyst men may nat kepe° a castel wal,° *not hold | wall*
It may so longe assailled been overal!°   *everywhere*

265 "'And if that she be foul,° thou seist that she   *ugly*
Coveiteth every man that she may se.°   *see*
For as a spaynel° she wol on hym lepe,°   *spaniel | leap*
Til that she fynde som man hire to chepe.°   *to buy her*
Ne noon so grey goos gooth in the lake

270 As, seistow, wol been withoute make.[3]
And seyst it is an hard thyng for to welde,°   *control*
A thyng that no man wole his thankes helde.° *willingly hold*
"'Thus seistow, lorel,° whan thow goost to bedde,   *fool*
And that no wys man nedeth° for to wedde,   *needs*

275 Ne° no man that entendeth unto
    hevene.°   *nor | intends to go to heaven*
With wilde thonder dynt° and firy
    levene°   *thunder claps | fiery lightening*
Moote° thy welked nekke° be
    tobroke!°   *may | withered neck | broken*
"'Thow seyst that droppyng° houses and eek smoke *dripping*
And chidyng° wyves maken men to flee   *nagging*

280 Out of hir owene houses. A, benedicitee,
What eyleth° swich an old man for to chide?   *ails*
"'Thow seyst that we wyves wol oure vices hide
Til we be fast,° and thanne we wol hem shewe.° *secure | show*
Wel may that be a proverbe of a shrewe!°   *villain*

285 "'Thou seist that oxen, asses, hors,° and houndes,   *horses*
They been assayd° at diverse stoundes;° *tried | different times*
Bacyns,° lavours° er that men hem bye,° *basins | bowls | buy them*
Spoones and stooles and al swich
    housbondrye,°   *household equipment*
And so been pottes,° clothes, and array.° *pots | ornaments*

290 But folk of wyves maken noon assay° *do not try them out*
Til they be wedded. Olde dotard° shrewe!   *foolish*
Thanne seistow we wol oure vices shewe.
    "'Thou seist also that it displeseth me
But if° that thou wolt preyse° my beautee   *unless | will praise*

295 And but° thou poure° alwey upon my face   *unless | gaze*
And clepe° me "faire dame!" in every place,   *call*
And but thou make a feeste° on thilke° day *feast | the same*
That I was born, and make me fressh and gay,
And but thou do to my norice[4] honour

300 And to my chambrere° withinne my
    bour.°   *chambermaid | bedroom*
And to my fadres° folk° and his allyes: *father's | relatives*
Thus seistow, olde barel° ful of lyes!°   *barrel | lies*
    "'And yet of oure apprentice Janekyn,

---

[1] *dronken as a mous*   It is not clear why mice are thought to be drunk, but the expression was common in medieval England.

[2] *thou verray knave*   You true villain.

[3] *Ne noon ... make*   Proverbial: There is no goose in the lake, no matter how grey, who does not have a mate.

[4] *norice*   Nurse. Wealthy medieval people were attended to in their childhood by wet nurses, who often became, for a time, surrogate mothers.

For his crispe heer° shynynge° as gold so
    fyn,°   *curly hair | shining | fine*

305 And for he squiereth° me bothe up and doun,   *escorts*

Yet hastow° caught a fals suspecioun.   *you have*

I wol° hym noght,° though thou were deed
    tomorwe!   *want | not*

    "'But tel me, why hydestow° with sorwe°   *do you hide | sorrow*

The keyes of my cheste° awey fro me?   *chest (safety box)*

310 It is my good° as wel as thyn, pardee!°   *possession | by God*

What, wenestow to make an ydiot of oure dame?[1]

Now by that lord that called is Seint Jame,°   *Saint James*

Thou shalt nat bothe, thogh° thou were wood,°   *though | crazy*

Be maister° of my body and of my good!°   *master | possessions*

315 That oon thou shalt forgo, maugree thyne eyen![2]

What nedeth thee of me to enquere° or spyen?°   *inquire | spy*

I trowe thou woldest loke me in thy chiste![3]

Thou sholdest seye, "Wyf, go wher thee liste.[4]

Taak youre disport!° I wol leve° no
    talys.°   *enjoyment | believe | tales*

320 I knowe yow for a trewe wyf, Dame Alys!"

We love no man that taketh kepe or charge°   *takes heed or cares*

Wher that we goon. We wol ben at oure large.°   *free*

    "'Of alle men, blessed moot° he be,   *may*

The wise astrologien° Daun
    Protholome°   *astronomer/ Master Ptolemy*

325 That seith this proverbe in his *Almageste*,

"Of alle men his wysdom is the hyeste°   *highest*

That rekketh nevere who hath the world in honde."[5]

By this proverbe thou shalt understonde:

Have thou ynogh, what thar thee recche or care[6]

330 How myrily° that othere folkes fare?°   *merrily | behave*

For certeyn, olde dotard,° by youre leve,°   *fool | leave*

Ye shul have queynte[7] right ynogh° at eve!°   *enough | at night*

He is to greet° a nygard° that wolde
    werne°   *too great | skinflint | refuse*

A man to lighte his candle at his lanterne.

335 He shal have never the lasse° light, pardee!   *less*

Have thou ynogh, thee thar nat pleyne thee.[8]

    "'Thou seyst also that if we make us gay

With clothyng and with precious array,°   *expensive adornment*

That it is peril of° oure chastitee.   *a danger to*

340 And yet with sorwe thou most° enforce
    thee°   *must | support yourself*

And seye thise wordes in the apostles name:[9]

"In habit° maad° with chastitee and shame   *clothing | made*

Ye wommen shul apparaille yow,"° quod he   *dress yourselves*

"And noght° in tressed heer° and gay
    perree,°   *not | braided hair | jewels*

345 As perles,° ne with gold ne clothes riche."   *pearls*

After thy text° ne after thy rubriche°   *quotation | rubric*

I wol nat wirche° as muchel as a gnat![10]   *work*

    "'Thou seydest this, that I was lyk° a cat.   *like*

For whoso wolde senge° a cattes skyn,   *singe*

350 Thanne wolde the cat wel dwellen in his in.°   *lodgings*

And if the cattes skyn be slyk° and gay,   *sleek*

She wol nat dwelle in house half a day,

But forth she wole° er any day be dawed°   *will go | dawned*

To shewe hir skyn and goon a caterwawed.[11]

355 This is to seye, if I be gay, sire shrewe,°   *sir villain*

I wol renne out my borel° for to shewe!   *cheap clothing*

    "'Sire olde fool, what eyleth° thee to spyen?°   *ails | spy*

---

[1] *What ... dame* What, do you expect to make an idiot of our lady? I.e., the Wife herself.

[2] *That ... eyen* You must give up one of them, despite your eyes! (I.e., despite anything you can do.)

[3] *I trowe ... chiste* I believe you would lock me in your chest. Medieval merchants used large locked chests to lock up their coins and their valuables.

[4] *Thou ... liste* You should say, "Wife, go wherever you want."

[5] *That ... honde* Who does not care who possesses the world.

[6] *Have ... care* If you have enough, why do you need to bother yourself or care.

[7] *queynte* Literally meaning elegant, clever, or pleasing thing, queynte is also a medieval euphemism for the female sexual organs.

[8] *Have ... thee* If you have enough, you do not need to complain for yourself.

[9] *the apostles name* St. Paul. The following quotation is from 1 Timothy 2.9.

[10] *After thy ... gnat* I will not follow (work after) your quotation or your text in the smallest way, or, any more than a gnat would. In medieval service books and books of devotion, rubrics (whose name comes from the red ink in which they were written) were directions about how to use the texts to which they referred either in communal worship or private devotion.

[11] *caterwawed* Caterwauling, the loud noise cats make while they are mating.

Thogh thou preye Argus[1] with hise hundred eyen
To be my wardecors,° as he kan° best.   *bodyguard | knows how*
360 In feith, he shal nat kepe me but me lest!° *unless I want to be kept*
Yet koude I make his berd,° so moot I thee![2]   *fool him*
    "'Thou seydest eek that ther been thynges thre,° *three things*
The whiche thynges troublen° al this erthe   *trouble*
And that no wight may endure the ferthe.°   *fourth*
365 O leeve° sire shrewe! Jhesu° shorte° thy lyf! *dear | Jesus | shorten*
Yet prechestow° and seyst an hateful wyf   *still you preach*
Yrekned is for° oon of thise
    meschances.°   *is counted as | misfortunes*
Been ther none othere resemblances
That ye may likne° youre parables to,   *liken*
370 But if a sely° wyf be oon of tho?°   *innocent | those*
    "'Thou liknest° wommenes love to helle,   *liken*
To bareyne° lond° ther° water may nat
    dwelle.   *barren | land | where*
Thou liknest it also to wilde fyr:
The moore° it brenneth,° the moore it hath
    desir°   *more | burns | desires*
375 To consumen° everythyng that brent wole be.   *consume*
Thou seyst, right as wormes° shendeth° a tree,   *grubs | harm*
Right so a wyf destroyeth hire housbond;
This knowe they that been to wyves bonde.'°   *bound*
    "Lordynges, right thus as ye have understonde
380 Baar I stifly myne olde housbondes on honde,
That thus they seyden in hir dronkenesse![3]
And al was fals, but that I took witnesse
On Janekyn and on my nece° also.   *niece*
O Lord, the pyne° I dide hem° and the wo,   *pain | to them*
385 Ful giltlees,° by Goddes sweete pyne!°   *guiltless | pain*
For as an hors I koude byte and whyne.°   *whinny*
I koude pleyne° thogh° I were in the
    gilt,°   *complain | though | guilty*
Or elles oftentyme hadde I been spilt.°   *destroyed*
Whoso comth° first to mille,° first
    grynt.°   *whoever comes | mill | grinds*
390 I pleyned first, so was oure werre° ystynt.°   *war | concluded*
They were ful glad to excuse hem° blyve°   *them | quickly*

Of thyng of which they nevere agilte hir lyve.[4]
Of wenches° wolde I beren hym on honde,°   *girls | accuse him*
Whan that for syk° unnethes° myghte he
    stonde.   *sickness | scarcely*
395 "Yet tikled° it his herte,° for that° he   *tickled | heart | because*
Wende° that I hadde of hym° so greet
    chiertee.°   *thought | for him | love*
I swoor° that al my walkynge° out by
    nyghte°   *swore | walking | night*
Was for t'espye° wenches that he dighte.°   *spy | had sex with*
Under that colour° hadde I many a myrthe,°   *pretense | mirth*
400 For al swich thyng was yeven° us in oure byrthe.°   *given | birth*
Deceite, wepyng, spynnyng° God hath yeve°   *spinning | given*
To wommen kyndely° whil that they may lyve.   *naturally*
And thus of o° thyng I avaunte° me: *one | boast*
Atte ende, I hadde the bettre° in ech
    degree°   *at the | better | instance*
405 By sleighte,° or force, or by som maner
    thyng,°   *deceit | manner of thing*
As by continueel murmure° or
    grucchyng.°   *continual murmur | complaining*
Namely° abedde° hadden they
    meschaunce;°   *especially | in bed | misfortune*
Ther wolde I chide° and do hem no plesaunce.°   *nag | pleasure*
I wolde no lenger° in the bed abyde°   *longer | remain*
410 If that I felte his arm over my syde°   *side*
Til he had maad his raunsoun° unto me.   *paid his ransom*
Thanne wolde I suffre hym do his nycetee.°   *foolishness*
And therfore every man this tale I telle:
Wynne° whoso may, for al is for to selle.°   *win | for sale*
415 With empty hand men may none° haukes° lure;   *no | hawks*
For wynnyng° wolde I al his lust endure   *profit*
And make me a feyned° appetit.   *pretended*
And yet in bacon[5] hadde I nevere delit.°   *delight*
That made me that evere I wolde hem chide,
420 For thogh the Pope hadde seten hem biside,°   *sat beside them*
I wolde nat spare hem at hir owene bord.°   *table*
For by my trouthe, I quitte hem,° word for word,   *requited them*
As° helpe me verray° God omnipotent!   *so | true*
Though I right now sholde make my testament,
425 I ne owe hem nat a word that it nys quit.°   *was not paid back*

1   *Argus*   Hundred-eyed creature of Greek mythology hired by Hera to guard her husband Zeus's mistress Io. He was killed by Hermes.

2   *so moot I thee*   I.e., indeed, or by my word.

3   *Baar … dronkenesse*   I bore witness firmly to my old husbands that they said this when they were drunk.

4   *Of … lyve*   Of a thing that they had never been guilty of in their lives.

5   *bacon*   Old meat preserved by salting; in other words, old men.

I broghte° it so aboute, by my wit,   *brought*
That they moste yeve it up° as for the beste   *had to give it up*
Or elles hadde we nevere been in reste.°   *at rest*
For thogh° he looked as a wood leoun,°   *although / crazy lion*
430 Yet sholde he faille of his conclusion.°   *intent*
        "Thanne wolde I seye, 'Goodlief, taak keepe
How mekely looketh Wilkyn oure sheepe! [1]
Com neer, my spouse. Lat me ba° thy cheke.   *kiss*
Ye sholde been al pacient and meke°   *meek*
435 And han° a sweete, spiced conscience,°   *have / delicate conscience*
Sith ye so preche° of Jobes pacience.°[2]   *preach / Job's patience*
Suffreth alwey,° syn ye so wel kan preche,   *endure always*
And but° ye do, certein we shal yow teche°   *unless / teach you*
That it is fair to have a wyf in pees.°   *peace*
440 Oon of us two moste bowen,° doutelees,°   *must bow / doubtless*
And sith a man is moore resonable
Than womman is, ye moste been suffrable.°   *you must be patient*
What eyleth yow,° to grucche° thus and
        grone?°   *ails you / complain / groan*
Is it for ye wolde have my queynte°
        allone?°   *female sexual organs / alone*
445 Wy,° taak it al! Lo, have it everydeel!°   *why / every bit*
Peter, I shrewe yow but ye love it weel! [3]
For if I wolde selle my bele chose,[4]
I koude walke as fressh as is a rose. [5]
But I wol kepe it for youre owene tooth.°   *own taste (pleasure)*
450 Ye be to blame, by God, I sey yow sooth!°   *tell you the truth*
        "Swiche manere wordes hadde we on honde.[6]
Now wol I speken of my fourthe housbonde.
        "My fourthe housbonde was a revelour°—   *party-goer*
This is to seyn, he hadde a paramour°—   *lover*
455 And I was yong and ful of ragerye,°   *high spirits*
Stibourne° and strong and joly° as a
        pye.°   *stubborn / pretty / magpie*

Wel koude I daunce to an harpe smale°   *small harp*
And synge,° ywis,° as any nyghtyngale   *sing / indeed*
Whan I had dronke a draughte of sweete wyn.°   *wine*
460 Metellius,[7] the foule cherl, the swyn,°   *swine*
That with a staf° birafte° his wyf hir lyf   *club / stole from*
For° she drank wyn, thogh I hadde been his wyf,   *because*
He sholde nat han daunted me fro drynke![8]
And after wyn, on Venus[9] moste° I thynke.   *must*
465 For also siker° as cold engendreth hayl,°   *as sure / causes hail*
A likerous° mouth moste han° a likerous
        tayl.°   *lecherous / must have / tail*
In wommen vinolent is no defence.[10]
This knowen lecchours° by experience.   *lechers*
        "But, Lord Crist, whan that it remembreth
        me°   *when I remember*
470 Upon my yowthe° and on my jolitee,°   *youth / gaiety*
It tikleth° me aboute myn herte roote.°   *tickles / heart's root*
Unto this day it dooth myn herte boote°   *does my heart good*
That I have had my world as in my tyme.°   *time*
But age, allas, that al wole envenyme,°   *will poison all*
475 Hath me biraft° my beautee and my pith.° *stolen from me / strength*
Lat go! Farewel! The devel go therwith!°   *with it*
The flour is goon,° ther is namoore° to telle;   *gone / no more*
The bren° as I best kan now moste° I selle.   *bran / must*
But yet to be right myrie° wol I fonde.°   *merry / try*
480 Now wol I tellen of my fourthe housbonde.
        "I seye I hadde in herte° greet despit°   *heart / great anger*
That he of any oother° had delit.°   *any other (woman) / delight*
But he was quit,° by God and by Seint Joce![11]   *punished*
I made hym of the same wode° a croce.°   *wood / cross*
485 Nat of my body in no foul manere,°   *manner*
But certein I made folk swich cheere,°   *hospitality*
That in his owene grece° I made hym frye°   *own grease / fry*
For angre and for verray jalousie.°   *true jealousy*
By God, in erthe I was his purgatorie,°   *purgatory*

---

[1] *Thanne ... sheepe* Then would I say, "Sweetheart, note well, how meekly Willie, our sheep (i.e., her husband) looks."

[2] *Jobes pacience* God allowed Satan to attempt to shake Job's faith through a series of terrible misfortunes. See the Biblical Book of Job.

[3] *Peter ... weel* By St. Peter!, I curse you unless you love it well, i.e., do you ever love it well.

[4] *bele chose* French: beautiful thing, i.e. sexual organs.

[5] *I ... rose* In other words, if I sold myself sexually, I could dress myself beautifully with the proceeds.

[6] *Swiche ... honde* We were occupied by this kind of conversation.

---

[7] *Metellius* See *Facta et dicta memorabilia* (*Memorable Facts and Deeds*), a collection of short stories for orators, written by Valerius Maximus (1st century CE).

[8] *He ... drynke* He should not have prevented me from drink.

[9] *Venus* Goddess of love.

[10] *In ... defence* There is no defense in drunken women, i.e., they are defenseless.

[11] *Seint Joce* St. Judoc or St. Joyce was a seventh-century prince in Brittany who gave up his succession to the throne to become a priest. He was also famous for going on a pilgrimage to Rome.

490   For which I hope his soule be in glorie.
       For God it woot,° he sat ful ofte and song°   *knows it / sang*
       Whan that his shoo° ful bitterly hym
          wrong.°   *shoe / hurt him very bitterly*
       Ther was no wight save God and he that wiste°   *who knew*
       In many wise° how soore° I hym twiste.°   *ways / sorely / tormented*
495   He deyde° whan I cam fro°
          Jerusalem   *died / came from (a pilgrimage to)*
       And lith ygrave° under the roode beem,[1]   *lies buried*
       Al° is his tombe° noght so curyus°   *although / tomb / elaborate*
       As was the sepulcre of hym Daryus,°   *Darius*
       Which that Appeles wroghte° subtilly.°[2]   *made / subtly*
500   It nys° but wast to burye hym preciously.°   *is not / expensively*
       Lat hym° fare wel! God yeve° his soule reste.   *may he / give*
       He is now in his grave and in his cheste.°   *coffin*
          "Now of my fifthe housbonde wol I telle.
       God lete his soule nevere come in Helle!
505   And yet was he to me the mooste shrewe.
       That feele I on my ribbes° al by rewe,°   *ribs / in a row*
       And evere shal unto myn endyng day.
       But in oure bed he was ful fressh and gay.
       And therwithal so wel koude he me glose,°   *flatter*
510   Whan that he wolde han my bele chose,
       That thogh he hadde me bet° on every bon,°   *beaten / bone*
       He koude wynne agayn my love anon.
       I trowe° I loved hym best for that he   *believe*
       Was of his love daungerous° to me.   *standoffish*
515   We wommen han, if that I shal nat lye,
       In this matere a queynte fantasye:°   *odd whim*
       Wayte,° what° thyng we may nat lightly   *know (that) / whatever*
          have,
       Therafter° wol we crie al day and crave!   *after it*
       Forbede° us thyng,° and that desiren we;   *forbid / something*
520   Preesse on us faste, and thanne wol we fle.°   *flee*
       With daunger oute we al oure chaffare;[3]

       Greet prees° at market maketh deere
          ware,°   *crowd / expensive goods*
       And to greet cheepe° is holde at litel
          prys.°   *too much merchandise / little price*
       This knoweth every womman that is wys.
525   My fifthe housbonde, God his soule blesse,
       Which that I took for love and no richesse,
       He somtyme° was a clerk° of Oxenford°   *once / student / Oxford*
       And hadde left scole° and wente at hom° to
          bord°   *school / home / rent a room*
       With my gossib,° dwellynge in oure toun.   *confidant*
530   God have hir soule! Hir name was Alisoun.
       She knew myn herte and eek my privetee°   *secrets*
       Bet° than oure parisshe preest, as moot I
          thee!°   *better / may I thrive*
       To hire biwreyed° I my conseil° al.   *revealed / counsel*
       For hadde myn housbonde pissed on a wal°   *wall*
535   Or doon a thyng that sholde han cost his lyf,
       To hire and to another worthy wyf
       And to my nece,° which that I loved weel,   *niece*
       I wolde han toold his conseil everydeel.°   *every bit*
       And so I dide ful often, God it woot!°   *God knows it*
540   That made his face ful often reed and hoot°   *hot*
       For verray° shame, and blamed hymself, for he   *true*
       Had toold to me so greet a pryvetee.
          "And so bifel° that ones° in a Lente[4]—   *it happened / once*
       So oftentymes I to my gossyb° wente,   *confidant*
545   For evere yet I loved to be gay
       And for to walke in March, Averill, and May
       Fro hous to hous to heere sondry talys°—   *various tales*
       That Jankyn clerk and my gossyb Dame Alys
       And I myself into the feeldes° wente.   *fields*
550   Myn housbonde was at Londoun al the Lente;
       I hadde the bettre leyser° for to pleye   *better opportunity*
       And for to se° and eek for to be seye°   *see / seen*
       Of lusty folk. What wiste I wher my grace
       Was shapen for to be or in what place?[5]
555   Therfore I made my visitaciouns°   *visits*

---

[1] *And ... beem* Her fourth husband was buried inside the local parish church under the cross-beam of the cross near the high altar, a place reserved for only the most influential members of a parish.

[2] *As was ... subtilly* The legendary tomb of Darius the Mede, fashioned by the Jewish sculptor Appeles, was famous for its beauty.

[3] *With ... chaffare* Either (where we are greeted) with scorn, we (put) out all our goods (i.e., are anxious to sell), or we (put) out all our goods with (a show of) scorn (i.e., as if we did not care if anyone buys them).

[4] *Lente* Period in the late winter and early spring when Christians prepare for Easter by fasting and doing penance.

[5] *What wiste ... place* How could I know where or in what place my good luck was destined to be? or possibly (to avoid the redundancy) how could I know whether I was destined to have good luck, or where?

To vigilies and to processiouns,[1]

To prechyng° eek and to thise pilgrimages,   *preaching*

To pleyes° of myracles and to mariages,   *plays*

And wered upon° my gaye scarlet gytes.°   *wore / robes*

560   Thise wormes, ne thise motthes,° ne thise mytes°   *moths / mites*

Upon my peril frete° hem never a deel,°   *eat / never a bit*

And wostow° why? For they were used weel.   *do you know*

   "Now wol I tellen forth what happed me.°   *happened to me*

I seye that in the feeldes walked we

565   Til trewely we hadde swich daliance,°   *flirtation*

This clerk and I, that of my purveiance°   *foresight*

I spak to hym and seyde° hym how that he,   *said to*

If I were wydwe,° sholde wedde me.   *widowed*

For certeinly I sey for no bobance,°   *pride*

570   Yet was I nevere withouten purveiance

Of mariage n'of° othere thynges eek.   *nor of*

I holde a mouses herte° nat worth a leek   *mouse's heart*

That hath but oon hole forto sterte° to,   *escape*

And if that faille,° thanne is al ydo.°[2]   *should fail / completely done for*

575   "I bar hym on honde° he hadde enchanted me;   *accused him*

My dame° taughte me that soutiltee.°   *mother / trick*

And eek I seyde I mette° of hym al nyght: *dreamed*

He wolde han slayn° me as I lay upright,°   *killed / on my back*

And al my bed was ful of verray blood.

580   But yet I hope that he shal do me good,

For blood bitokeneth° gold, as me was taught.[3]   *signifies*

And al was fals! I dremed of it right naught.°   *not at all*

But I folwed ay° my dammes

loore,°   *followed ever / mother's teaching*

As wel of this as othere thynges° moore.°   *matters / more*

585   "But now sire, lat me se° what I shal seyn.   *see*

Aha! By God, I have my tale ageyn!°   *again*

"Whan that my fourthe housbonde was on beere,°[4]   *bier*

I weepe algate° and made sory cheere,°   *continuously / face*

As wyves mooten,° for it is usage,°   *must / custom*

590   And with my coverchief° covered my visage.°   *kerchief / face*

But for that° I was purveyed of° a

make,°   *because / provided with / mate*

I wepte but smal,° and that I undertake.°   *little / attest*

   "To chirche° was myn housbonde born

amorwe,°   *church / in the morning*

With neighebores that for hym maden sorwe,°   *sorrow*

595   And Jankyn oure clerk was oon of tho.°   *one of those*

As help me God, whan that I saugh° hym go   *saw*

After the beere, me thoughte he hadde a paire

Of legges and of feet so clene° and faire,°   *neat / attractive*

That al myn herte I yaf° unto his hoold.°   *gave / possession*

600   He was, I trowe,° a twenty wynter oold,   *believe*

And I was fourty, if I shal seye sooth.°   *say the truth*

And yet I hadde alwey a coltes° tooth.   *colt's*

Gat-tothed I was, and that bicam me weel;[5]

I hadde the prente° of Seint Venus seel.[6]   *print*

605   As help me God, I was a lusty oon,

And faire and riche and yong and wel bigon.°   *established*

And trewely, as myne housbondes tolde me,

I hadde the beste 'quonyam'° myghte be.   *sexual organ*

For certes, I am al venerien[7]

610   In feelynge,° and myn herte is marcien.[8]   *feeling*

Venus me yaf° my lust, my likerousnesse,°   *gave / lecherousness*

And Mars yaf me my sturdy hardynesse.°   *courage*

Myn ascendent was Taur, and Mars therinne.[9]

Allas! Allas! That evere love was synne!°   *sin*

615   I folwed° ay° myn inclinacioun°   *followed / ever / inclination*

By vertu° of my constellacioun,°   *influence / constellation*

---

[1] *To … processiouns* To vigils and to processions. Vigils were church services held on the evening before the feast day of a saint. Ceremonial processions formed part of the service on the day itself.

[2] *I holde … y do* The mouse who has only one hole to which it can escape appears in various proverbs as well as in the *Romance of the Rose* (line 13554), whose character La Vieille, the old woman who knows all about love, is one of the models for the Wife of Bath. Not worth a leek means worth nothing at all.

[3] *blood … taught* Blood could serve as a token or symbol of gold, which was often described as red.

[4] *beere* Bier, i.e., in his coffin.

[5] *Gat-tothed … weel* I was gap-toothed, and that suited me well. Women with gaps between their teeth were said to have lustful and licentious natures.

[6] *I hadde … seel* I had the imprint of Venus's seal; in other words, Venus has given the Wife of Bath a birthmark, another supposed indication of a lascivious nature.

[7] *venerien* In astrology, one who is influenced by the planet Venus—i.e., prone to love.

[8] *marcien* In astrology, one who is influenced by the planet Mars—i.e., war-like.

[9] *Myn … therinne* At the moment when the Wife was born the constellation of stars known as Taurus (the Bull) was coming over the horizon (ascendant) along with the planet Mars. It was believed that if a woman is born with Venus and Mars ascending together she will be unchaste.

That made me I koude noght withdrawe° *withhold*
My chambre° of Venus from a good felawe.° *organ / fellow*
Yet have I Martes° mark[1] upon my face— *Mars's*
620 And also in another privee place.
For God so wys° be my savacioun,° *wise / salvation*
I ne loved nevere° by no discrecioun *never loved*
But evere folwed myn appetit,° *appetite*
Al° were he short or long° or blak° or
whit.° *whether / tall / dark / fair*
625 I took no kepe,° so that he liked° me, *did not care / pleased*
How poore he was ne eek of what degree.
    "What sholde I seye, but at the monthes ende,
This joly° clerk Jankyn that was so hende° *pretty / handy*
Hath wedded me with greet solempnytee.° *ceremony*
630 And to hym yaf° I al the lond and fee° *gave / property*
That evere was me yeven° therbifoore.° *given / before this*
But afterward repented me ful soore!° *I regretted it sorely*
He nolde suffre nothyng of my list.[2]
By God, he smoot° me ones° on the lyst,° *hit / once / ear*
635 For that° I rente° out of his book a leef,° *because / tore / page*
That of the strook° myn ere° wax° al
deef.° *blow / ear / grew / completely deaf*
Stibourne° I was as is a leonesse° *stubborn / lioness*
And of my tonge° a verray°
jangleresse.° *tongue / true / ceaseless talker*
And walke I wolde as I had doon biforn° *before*
640 From hous to hous, although he had it sworn.° *forbidden*
For which he often tymes wolde preche° *preach*
And me of olde Romayn geestes[3] teche° *teach*
How he Symplicius Gallus lefte his wyf
And hire forsook for terme° of al his lyf, *the rest*
645 Noght but for open heveded,[4] he hir say,
Lookynge out at his dore° upon a day. *door*
    "Another Romayn tolde he me by name,
That, for° his wyf was at a someres game° *because / entertainment*
Withouten his wityng,° he forsook hire eke. *knowledge*
650 And thanne wolde he upon his Bible seke° *seek*

That ilke° proverbe of Ecclesiaste[5] *same*
Where he comandeth and forbedeth faste° *firmly*
Man shal nat suffre° his wyf go roule° aboute. *allow / wander*
Thanne wolde he seye right thus, withouten doute:
655 'Whoso that buyldeth his hous al of salwes[6]
And priketh° his blynde hors° over the
falwes° *spurs / blind horse / fields*
And suffreth his wyf to go seken halwes° *shrines*
Is worthy to been° hanged on the galwes.'°[7] *be / gallows*
But al for noght! I sette noght an hawe° *hawthorn berry*
660 Of his proverbes n'of° his olde lawe, *nor of*
Ne I wolde nat of hym° corrected be. *by him*
I hate hym that my vices telleth me° *tells me about*
And so doo mo,° God woot,° of us than I. *do more / knows*
This made hym with me wood° al outrely:° *crazy / entirely*
665 I nolde noght° forbere° hym in no cas.° *would not / endure / case*
    "Now wol I seye° yow° sooth,° by Seint
Thomas,[8] *tell / you / the truth*
Why that I rente out of his book a leef,
For which he smoot me so that I was deef.
    "He hadde a book that gladly, nyght and day,
670 For his desport° he wolde rede° alway. *fun / read*
He cleped° it *Valerie and Theofraste*,[9] *called*
At which book he lough° alwey ful faste.° *laughed / very much*
And eek ther was somtyme° a clerk° at Rome, *once / theologian*
A cardinal that highte° Seint Jerome,[10] *was named*

---

1 *Martes mark* Red birthmark.

2 *He … list* He would not allow anything I desired.

3 *Romayn geestes* Roman stories. Like the reference to Metellius above in line 460, the following are old misogynistic or antimatrimonial stories dating back to ancient Rome.

4 *Noght … heveded* Just because he saw her bare-headed.

5 *That … Ecclesiaste* See Ecclesiasticus 25.34.

6 *Whoso … salwes* Whoever builds his house of all willow branches

7 *Whoso … galwes* Proverb.

8 *Seint Thomas* There are three possible candidates for this St. Thomas: Thomas the apostle, mentioned in the Gospels; St. Thomas Aquinas, the thirteenth-century theologian (though his second name was more often used than not); and St. Thomas Becket, whose shrine the Canterbury pilgrims are journeying to visit. Thomas the apostle was often referred to as "Thomas of India." Becket is the likely reference.

9 *Valerie and Theofraste* The Wife of Bath is actually referring to two separate works, often bound together into one volume in the Middle Ages—the *Dissuasio Valerii ad Rufinum* by the English scholar and courtier Walter Map (c. 1140–c. 1208) and the *Golden Book of Marriages* by Theophrastus, a supposed disciple of Aristotle. Both books were full of stories attacking women and discouraging men from marrying.

10 *Seint Jerome* Late fourth and early fifth centuries and was a theologian who wrote many influential works, including a translation of the Bible into Latin. *Against Jovinian*, which extolls virginity,

675 That made a book, *Agayn° Jovinian,*   against
In which book eek ther was Tertulan,[1]
Crisippus,[2] Trotula,[3] and Helowys[4]
That was abbesse nat fer° fro Parys,   not far
And eek the *Parables of Salomon,*[5]
680 Ovides° *Art,*[6] and bookes many on.°   Ovid's / many (other) books
And alle thise were bounden in o° volume.   one
And every nyght and day was his custume,
Whan he hadde leyser° and vacacioun°   leisure / opportunity
From oother worldly occupacioun
685 To reden on this *Book of Wikked Wyves.*[7]
He knew of hem mo legendes and lyves°   biographies
Than been° of goode wyves in the Bible.   there are
For, trusteth wel, it is an inpossible°   impossibility
That any clerk wol speke good of wyves
690 But if° it be of hooly seintes lyves,   unless
Ne of noon other womman never the mo.
Who peynted the leoun,[8] tel me who?
By God, if wommen hadde writen stories
As clerkes han° withinne hire° oratories,°   have / their / chapels
695 They wolde han writen of men moore wikkednesse
Than al the mark of Adam° may redresse.   male sex (i.e., men)
The children of Mercurie and Venus[9]

Been in hir wirkyng ful contrarius.[10]
Mercurie loveth wysdam° and science,°   wisdom / knowledge
700 And Venus loveth ryot° and dispence.°   parties / squandering money
And for hire diverse disposicioun,°   natures
Ech falleth in otheres exaltacioun,°   exaltation
And thus, God woot, Mercurie is desolat
In Pisces, wher Venus is exaltat,°   exalted
705 And Venus falleth ther° Mercurie is reysed.   where
Therfore no womman of no clerk is preysed.
The clerk, whan he is oold and may noght° do   cannot
Of Venus werkes[11] worth his olde sho,°   shoe
Thanne sit he doun and writ in his dotage[12]
710 That wommen kan nat kepe hir mariage.
    "But now to purpos° why I tolde thee   the reason
That I was beten° for a book, pardee.°   beaten / by God
Upon a nyght Jankyn, that was oure sire,°   master
Redde on his book as he sat by the fire
715 Of Eva° first, that for hir wikkednesse   Eve
Was al mankynde broght to wrecchednesse,
For which Crist hymself was slayn,
That boghte° us with his herte blood agayn.   who bought
Lo, heere,° expres° of womman may ye fynde   here, specifically
720 That womman was the los° of al mankynde.   destruction
    "Tho° redde he me how Sampson[13] loste hise
    heres:°   then / hairs
Slepynge, his lemman° kitte° it with hir
    sheres,°   lover / cut / scissors
Thurgh° which tresoun° loste he bothe hise
    eyen.°   through / betrayal
    "Tho redde he me, if that I shal nat lyen,°   lie
725 Of Hercules and of his Dianyre,[14]
That caused hym to sette hymself afyre.°   on fire
Nothyng° forgat he the sorwe and wo   not at all

---

is one of Chaucer's major sources for the "Wife of Bath's Prologue."

[1] *Tertulan* Early third-century theologian who wrote several treatises about the value of virginity.

[2] *Crisippus* Mentioned in Jerome's treatise, referred to in line 671, but none of his works survive.

[3] *Trotula* Female doctor who taught medicine at the University of Salerno in the eleventh century and wrote a treatise about gynecology.

[4] *Helowys* Tried to persuade her lover Abelard not to marry her, giving typical anti-matrimonial reasons. She eventually became the abbess of the Paraclete, a convent of nuns near Paris.

[5] *Parables of Solomon* Biblical Book of Proverbs.

[6] *Ovides Art* Ovid's *Art of Love* concludes with a long argument about why it is prudent to avoid love.

[7] *Book of Wikked Wyves* Title of the whole compendium volume mentioned above.

[8] *Who ... leoun* In medieval versions of the fable of Aesop, a man and a lion were having a dispute about who was the stronger. For proof, the man showed the lion a picture of a man killing a lion, and the lion then asked the man who painted the lion—implying the painting is biased. Then the lion ate the man.

[9] *The children ... Venus* I.e., scholars and lovers.

---

[10] *Been ... contrarius* In addition to influencing the body's humors (Cf. *General Prologue*, lines 413 ff.), the planets were thought to govern various parts of the body and various trades. Mercury was the planet of scholars and merchants, who, in their ways of doing things, are completely at odds with lovers.

[11] *Venus werkes* I.e., sex.

[12] *Thanne ... dotage* Then he sits down and writes in his old age.

[13] *Tho ... Sampson* See Judges 16.15–22.

[14] *Hercules ... Dianyre* Deianira was the wife of Hercules and inadvertently caused his death by giving him a shirt that she thought would keep him faithful. It was in fact poisoned and he had himself burned alive to escape the pain.

That Socrates hadde with hise wyves two,
How Xantippa[1] caste° pisse° upon his heed.°   *threw / urine / head*
730   This sely° man sat stille° as he were
          deed.°   *innocent / quietly / dead*
He wiped his heed. Namoore dorste° he seyn   *dared*
But, 'Er° that thonder stynte,° comth a
          reyn.°'   *before / stops / rain*
          "Of Phasipha, that was the queene of Crete,
For shrewednesse° hym thoughte the tale
          swete.°   *nastiness / sweet*
735   Fy! Spek namoore! It is a grisly thyng,
Of hire horrible lust and hir likyng!²
          "Of Clitermystra,³ for hire lecherye,
That falsly made hire housbonde for to dye,°   *die*
He redde it with ful good devocioun.
740   "He tolde me eek for what occasioun
Amphiorax at Thebes loste his lyf:⁴
Myn housbonde hadde a legende° of his wyf,   *story*
Eriphilem, that for an ouche° of gold   *brooch*
Hath prively° unto the Grekes told   *secretly*
745   Wher that hir housbonde hidde hym in a place,
For which he hadde at Thebes sory° grace.   *sorry*
          "Of Lyvia tolde he me and of Lucye.⁵
They bothe made° hir° housbondes for to dye—   *caused / their*
That oon for love, that oother was for hate.
750   Lyvia hir housbonde upon an even° late   *evening*
Empoysoned° hath, for that she was his fo;°   *poisoned / foe*
Lucia likerous° loved hire housbonde so,   *lustfully*

That, for he sholde alwey upon hire thynke,
She yaf° hym swich a manere° love drynke°   *gave / type of / potion*
755   That he was deed° er it were by the morwe.°   *dead / morning*
And thus algates° housbondes han sorwe.°   *always / have sorrow*
          "Thanne tolde he me how that oon Latumyus⁶
Compleyned unto his felawe° Arrius   *friend*
That in his gardyn growed swich a tree
760   On which he seyde how that hise wyves thre
Hanged hemself° for herte° despitus.°   *themselves / heart / cruel*
'O leeve° brother,' quod this Arrius,   *dear*
'Yif° me a plante° of thilke° blissed tree,   *give / seedling / that*
And in my gardyn planted it shal bee.'
765   "Of latter date of wyves hath he red,
That somme han slayn hir housbondes in hir bed
And lete hir lecchour dighte hire al the nyght⁷
Whan that the corps lay in the floor upright,
And somme han dryve° nayles° in hir brayn⁸   *driven / nails*
770   Whil that they slepte, and thus they han hem slayn;
Somme han hem yeve poysoun in hire drynke.⁹
He spak moore harm than herte may bithynke.°   *imagine*
And therwithal° he knew of mo proverbes   *with all this*
Than in this world ther growen gras or herbes.
775   'Bet° is,' quod he, 'thyn habitacioun°   *better / dwelling place*
Be with a leoun or a foul dragoun
Than with a womman usynge° for to chyde.   *accustomed*
Bet is,' quod he, 'hye° in the roof abyde   *high*
Than with an angry wyf doun in the hous,
780   They been° so wikked and contrarious;   *are*
They haten that hir housbondes loveth ay.'¹⁰
He seyde, 'A womman cast° hir shame away   *throws*
Whan she cast of° hir smok.° And forthermo,   *off / undergarment*
A fair womman, but° she be chaast° also,   *unless / chaste*
785   Is lyk a gold ryng in a sowes° nose.'   *pig's*
Who wolde leeve or who wolde suppose°   *believe*
The wo that in myn herte was and pyne?°   *pain*
          "And whan I saugh he wolde nevere fyne°   *finish*
To reden on this cursed book al nyght,

---

¹ *Xantippa* I.e., Xanthippe (late fifth c. BCE) famously shrewish wife of the philosopher Socrates (469–399 BCE).

² *Phasipha … likyng* In Greek mythology, Queen Pasiphae of Crete had sex with a bull and gave birth to the monster Minotaur; *likyng* Desire.

³ *Clitermystra* I.e., Clytemnestra, who with her lover Aegisthus murdered her husband Agamemnon when he returned from the Trojan war.

⁴ *Amphiorax … lyf* Amphiaraus hid so he would not have to fight in war, but his hiding place was betrayed by his wife Eriphyle, and he was killed in battle.

⁵ *Of … Lucye* Livia was either Augustus's wife, who poisoned several prominent Romans (including her own husband) for political gain, or Livilla, Livia's granddaughter, who poisoned her husband at the instigation of her lover Sejanus. Lucilla poisoned her husband, the Roman philosopher Lucretius (c. 99–c. 55 BCE), author of *On the Nature of Things*, with a love-potion intended to increase his desire for her.

---

⁶ *Thanne … Latumyus* The incident related below is another misogynistic story from ancient Rome, for which Chaucer's source is probably Walter Map's *Dissuasio Valerii*.

⁷ *And … nyght* And let her lover have sex with her all night.

⁸ *And … brayn* See Judges 4.17–22.

⁹ *Somme … drynke* Some have given them poison in their drink.

¹⁰ *They … ay* They always hate what their husbands love.

790 Al sodeynly thre leves have I plyght° — *plucked*
Out of his book, right as he radde. And eke
I with my fest° so took° hym on the cheke, — *fist / hit*
That in oure fyr he fil° bakward adoun. — *fell*
And he up stirte° as dooth a wood leoun, — *jumps*
795 And with his fest he smoot me on the heed,
That in° the floor I lay as I were deed. — *on*
And whan he saugh how stille that I lay,
He was agast° and wolde han fled his way.° — *afraid / away*
Til atte laste out of my swogh° I breyde.° — *faint / awoke*
800 'O hastow° slayn me, false theef?' I seyde. — *have you*
'And for my land thus hastow mordred me!
Er° I be deed, yet wol I kisse thee.' — *before*
        "And neer he cam and kneled faire° adoun — *pleasantly*
And seyde, 'Deere suster° Alisoun, — *sister*
805 As help me God, I shal thee nevere smyte!
That I have doon, it is thyself to wyte.° — *blame*
Foryeve it me, and that I thee biseke!'° — *beg*
And yet eftsoones° I hitte hym on the cheke — *once more*
And seyde, 'Theef, thus muchel am I wreke.° — *avenged*
810 Now wol I dye. I may no lenger speke.'
But atte laste, with muchel care and wo,
We fille acorded° by usselven° two. — *came to an agreement / ourselves*
He yaf me al° the bridel° in myn hond — *completely / bridle*
To han the governance of hous and lond,
815 And of his tonge and his hond also,
And made hym brenne his book anon right tho.° — *there*
And whan that I hadde geten° unto me — *gotten*
By maistrie° al the soveraynetee, — *mastery*
And that he seyde, 'Myn owene trewe wyf,
820 Do as thee lust to terme of al thy lyf:[1]
Keepe thyn honour and keepe eek myn estaat.'—
After that day we hadden never debaat.° — *disagreement*
God helpe me so, I was to hym as kynde
As any wyf from Denmark unto Ynde° — *India*
825 And also trewe, and so was he to me.
I prey to God that sit in magestee,
So blesse his soule for his mercy deere.
Now wol I seye° my tale, if ye wol heere." — *tell*

BIHOLDE THE WORDES BITWENE THE SOMONOUR AND THE FRERE

The Frere° lough° whan he hadde herd al this. — *friar / laughed*
830 "Now dame," quod he, "so have I joye or blis,
This is a long preamble of a tale!"
And whan the Somonour herde the Frere gale,° — *speak up*
"Lo," quod the Somonour, "Goddes armes two![2]
A frere wol entremette hym evere mo![3]
835 Lo, goode men, a flye and eek a frere
Wol falle in every dyssh and mateere![4]
What spekestow° of preambulacioun?° — *what do you say / preambling*
What! Amble or trotte° or pees° or go sit doun! — *trot / pace*
Thou lettest° oure disport° in this manere." — *spoil / fun*
840   "Ye, woltow so,° sire Somonour?" quod the
        Frere. — *will you say so*
"Now by my feith, I shal er that I go
Telle of a somonour swich a tale or two,
That alle the folk shal laughen in this place!"
        "Now elles,° Frere, I bishrewe° thy face!" — *otherwise / curse*
845 Quod this Somonour, "and I bishrewe me
But if° I telle tales two or thre — *unless*
Of freres er I come to Sidyngborne![5]
That I shal make thyn herte for to morne,° — *mourn*
For wel I woot thy pacience is gon."
850   Oure Hoost cride, "Pees,° and that anon!" — *peace*
And seyde, "Lat the womman telle hire tale.
Ye fare° as folk that dronken were of ale! — *behave*
Do, dame, telle forth youre tale, and that is best."
        "Alredy,° sire," quod she, "right as yow lest,° — *ready / wish*
855 If I have licence of this worthy Frere."
        "Yis, dame," quod he, "tel forth, and I wol heere."

HEERE ENDETH THE WYF OF BATHE HIR PROLOGE AND BIGYNNETH HIR TALE

---

1 *Do ... lyf* Do as you wish as long as you live.

2 *Goddes armes two* God's two arms. This is an oath like those uniformly condemned by the Church.

3 *A ... mo* A friar will always put himself in the middle of things.

4 *Wol ... mateere* Will fall into every dish and matter.

5 *Sidyngborne* I.e., Sittingbourne, a small town about forty miles from London on the road to Canterbury.

THE WIFE OF BATH'S TALE

In th'olde dayes of Kyng Arthour,[1]
Of which that Britons speken greet honour,
Al was this land fulfild of° fairye.[2]   *filled up with*
860 The Elf Queene with hir joly compaignye
Daunced ful ofte in many a grene mede.°   *meadow*
This was the olde opinion, as I rede°—   *read*
I speke of manye hundred yeres ago.
But now kan no man se none elves mo,°   *no more elves*
865 For now the grete charitee and prayeres
Of lymytours[3] and othere hooly° freres   *holy*
That serchen every lond and every streem,
As thikke as motes° in the sonne beem,   *dust particles*
Blessynge halles, chambres, kichenes, boures,°   *bedrooms*
870 Citees, burghes,° castels, hye toures,°   *fortified towns / towers*
Thropes,° bernes,° shipnes,°
dayeryes°—   *villages / barns / stables / dairies*
This maketh° that ther been° no fairyes.   *causes it / are*
For theras° wont° to walken was an elf,   *where / accustomed*
Ther walketh now the lymytour° hymself   *friar*
875 In undermeles° and in morwenynges,   *early afternoons / mornings*
And seyth his matyns° and his hooly
thynges°   *morning service / prayers*
As he gooth in his lymytacioun.°   *limited area*
Wommen may go saufly° up and doun: *safely*
In every bussh or under every tree
880 Ther is noon oother incubus[4] but he,
And he ne wol doon hem but dishonour.[5]
And so bifel° that this Kyng Arthour   *it happened*
Hadde in hous a lusty bachelor°   *young knight*
That on a day cam ridynge fro ryver,°   *from a river*
885 And happed that, allone° as he was born,   *alone*
He saugh a mayde° walkynge hym biforn,°   *maid / in front of him*
Of° which mayde anon, maugree° hir heed,°   *from / despite / will*
By verray° force birafte° hire maydenhed,   *true / stole*

---

[1] *Kyng Arthour … honour* Legendary British king of roughly the
fifth or sixth century CE, the subject of many medieval tales and
romances.

[2] *fairye* Supernatural beings known as elves or fairies.

[3] *lymytours* Friars who were licensed to preach in a limited area in
a parish or county.

[4] *incubus* Devilish spirit who would appear to women in dreams
and thereby impregnate them.

[5] *ne … dishonour* Will do them nothing but dishonor.

For which oppressioun was swich clamour°   *outcry*
890 And swich pursute° unto the Kyng Arthour,   *appeal*
That dampned° was this knyght for to be
deed°   *condemned / dead*
By cours of lawe, and sholde han lost his heed—
Paraventure° swich was the statut tho°—   *by chance / then*
But that the queene and othere ladyes mo
895 So longe preyden° the kyng of grace,°   *requested / mercy*
Til he his lyf hym graunted in the place
And yaf hym to the queene al at hir wille
To chese° wheither she wolde hym save or spille.°   *choose / kill*
The queene thanketh the kyng with al hir myght
900 And after this thus spak she to the knyght
Whan that she saugh hir tyme upon a day:
"Thou standest yet," quod she, "in swich array°   *condition*
That of thy lyf yet hastow° no suretee.°   *have you / certainty*
I grante thee lyf if thou kanst tellen me
905 What thyng is it that wommen moost desiren.
Bewar and keepe thy nekke boon° from iren!°   *bone / iron*
And if thou kanst nat tellen it anon,
Yet shal I yeve thee leve for to gon°   *go*
A twelf month and a day to seche° and leere°   *seek / learn*
910 An answere suffisant° in this mateere.   *sufficient*
And suretee° wol I han er that thou pace°—   *guarantee / leave*
Thy body for to yelden° in this place."   *return*
Wo° was this knyght, and sorwefully he siketh,°   *sad / sighs*
But he may nat do al as hym liketh.°   *as he wishes*
915 And at the laste he chees° hym for to wende,°   *chooses / go*
And come agayn right at the yeres° ende   *year's*
With swich answere as God wolde hym purveye,°   *provide*
And taketh his leve and wendeth forth his weye.
He seketh every hous and every place
920 Whereas° he hopeth for to fynde grace   *where*
To lerne what thyng wommen loven moost,
But he ne koude arryven in no coost°   *region*
Wheras he myghte fynde in this mateere
Two creatures accordynge° in feere.°   *agreeing / together*
925 Somme seyde wommen loven best richesse;
Somme seyde honour, somme seyde jolynesse,°   *jollity*
Somme riche array.° Somme seyden lust
abedde°   *clothing / in bed*
And oftetyme to be wydwe° and wedde.°   *widowed / married*
Somme seyde that oure hertes been moost esed°   *refreshed*
930 Whan that we been° yflatered and yplesed.   *are*

He gooth ful ny the sothe, I wol nat lye!¹
A man shal wynne us best with flaterye
And with attendance° and with bisynesse°   *attention / diligence*
Been we° ylymed² bothe moore and lesse.   *we are*
935 And somme seyn that we loven best
For to be free and so do right° as us lest°   *just / wish*
And that no man repreve us° of oure vice   *complain to us*
But seye that we be wise and nothyng° nyce.°   *not / foolish*
For trewely, ther is noon° of us alle,   *none*
940 If any wight° wol clawe° us on the galle,°   *person / claw / a sore*
That we nel kike,° for he seith us sooth.   *will not kick*
Assay° and he shal fynde it that so dooth.   *try*
For be we never so vicious° withinne,°   *wicked / within*
We wol been holden° wise and clene   *wish to be considered*
        of synne.
945 And somme seyn that greet delit han we
For to been holden stable and eek secree,°   *discreet*
And in o° purpos stedefastly to dwelle,   *one*
And nat biwreye° thyng° that men us telle.   *betray / something*
But that tale is nat worth a rake-stele!°   *handle of a rake*
950 Pardee, we wommen konne nothyng hele.³
Witnesse on Myda.⁴ Wol ye heere the tale?
Ovyde, amonges othere thyngs smale,
Seyde Myda hadde under his longe heres°   *hairs*
Growynge upon his heed two asses eres,
955 The which vice he hydde as he best myghte
Ful subtilly° from every mannes sighte,   *carefully*
That save his wyf, ther wiste of it namo.°   *no one else*
He loved hire moost and triste° hire also.   *trusted*
He preyde° hire that to no creature   *asked*
960 She sholde tellen of his disfigure.°   *disfigurement*
She swoor hym nay: for al this world to wynne°   *gain*
She nolde° do that vileynye or synne   *would not*
To make hir housbonde han so foul a name.
She nolde nat telle it for hir owene shame.
965 But nathelees, hir thoughte that she dyde,°   *would die*
That° she so longe sholde a conseil° hyde.   *if / secret*

Hir thoughte it swal so soore aboute hir herte⁵
That nedely som word hire moste asterte.⁶
And sith she dorste° telle it to no man,   *dared*
970 Doun to a mareys° faste by° she ran;   *marsh / close by*
Til she cam there hir herte was afyre.°   *on fire*
And as a bitore⁷ bombleth° in the myre,°   *calls out / mud*
She leyde hir mouth unto the water doun.
"Biwreye me nat, thou water, with thy soun,"°   *sound*
975 Quod she. "To thee I telle it and namo:
Myn housbonde hath longe asses erys two!
Now is myn herte al hool.° Now is it oute!   *whole*
I myghte no lenger kepe it, out of doute."°   *without doubt*
Heere may ye se,° thogh we a tyme° abyde,   *see / for a time*
980 Yet out it moot!° We kan no conseil hyde.   *must (go)*
The remenant of the tale if ye wol heere,
Redeth Ovyde, and ther ye may it leere.°   *learn*
This knyght of which my tale is specially,
Whan that he saugh he myghte nat come therby,
985 This is to sey, what wommen love moost,
Withinne his brest ful sorweful was the goost.°   *spirit*
But hoom he gooth. He myghte nat sojourne.°   *delay*
The day was come that homward moste he tourne.
And in his wey it happed hym to ryde
990 In al this care under a forest syde
Wheras he saugh upon a daunce⁸ go
Of ladyes foure and twenty and yet mo,
Toward the which daunce he drow ful yerne°   *drew very eagerly*
In hope that som wysdom sholde he lerne.
995 But certeinly, er he cam fully there,
Vanysshed was this daunce he nyste° where.   *knew not*
No creature saugh he that bar lyf,°   *bore life*
Save on the grene° he saugh sittynge a wyf—   *meadow*
A fouler° wight ther may no man devyse.°   *uglier / imagine*
1000 Agayn° the knyght this olde wyf gan ryse°   *towards / rose up*
And seyde, "Sire Knyght, heer forth ne lith° no
        wey.°   *lies / road*
Tel me what that ye seken by youre fey.°   *faith*

---

¹ *He ... lye* He gets very near the truth, I will not lie.

² *ylymed* Limed. Lime was used to catch birds.

³ *Pardee ... hele* By God, we women know nothing about how to keep a secret.

⁴ *Myda* I.e., Midas. See Ovid's *Metamorphoses*, Book 11 (although in Ovid's version it is the king's barber, not his wife, who whispers the secret).

⁵ *Hir ... herte* It seemed to her that it became so sorely swollen around her heart.

⁶ *That ... asterte* That by necessity some word had to burst out from her.

⁷ *bitore* I.e., bittern, a small heron.

⁸ *Wheras ... daunce* One way in which mortals were said to encounter elves was at night in the woods, where the elves performed a ritual dance.

Paraventure it may the bettre be;

Thise olde folk kan° muchel° thyng," quod she.   *know / many*

1005 "My leeve° mooder,"° quod this knyght certeyn,   *dear / mother*

"I nam but° deed but if° that I kan seyn   *am as good as / unless*

What thyng it is that wommen moost desire.

Koude ye me wisse, I wolde wel quite youre hire."[1]

"Plight° me thy trouthe° heere in myn hand,"   *pledge / word*

    quod she,

1010 "The nexte thyng that I requere° thee,   *ask of*

Thou shalt it do if it lye in thy myght,

And I wol telle it yow° er it be nyght."   *to you*

"Have heer my trouthe," quod the knyght. "I grante."

"Thanne," quod she, "I dar° me wel avante.°   *dare / boast*

1015 Thy lyf is sauf,° for I wol stonde therby.   *safe*

Upon my lyf, the queene wol seye as I.

Lat se° which is the proudeste of hem alle   *let's see*

That wereth on a coverchief° or a calle°   *kerchief / hairnet*

That dar seye nay of that I shal thee teche.°   *teach*

1020 Lat us go forth withouten lenger speche."

Tho° rowned° she a pistel° in his ere   *then / whispered / lesson*

And bad hym to be glad and have no fere.

Whan they be comen to the court, this knyght

Seyde he had holde° his day as he hadde hight°   *kept / promised*

1025 And redy was his answere, as he sayde.

Full many a noble wyf and many a mayde

And many a wydwe,° for that they been° wise,   *widow / are*

The queene hirself sittynge as justise,°   *sitting as a judge*

Assembled been° his answere for to heere,   *are*

1030 And afterward this knyght was bode°

    appeere.°   *commanded / to appear*

To every wight comanded was silence

And that the knyght sholde telle in audience°   *in their hearing*

What thyng that worldly wommen loven best.

This knyght ne stood nat° stille as doth a

    best,°   *did not stand / beast*

1035 But to his questioun anon answerde

With manly voys,° that al the court it herde.   *voice*

"My lige° lady, generally," quod he,   *liege*

"Wommen desiren to have sovereynetee   *to have sovereignty*

As wel over hir housbond as hir love

1040 And for to been in maistrie hym above.

This is youre mooste° desir, thogh ye me kille.   *greatest*

Dooth as yow list. I am at youre wille."

In al the court ne was ther° wyf ne mayde   *there was neither*

Ne wydwe that contraried that he sayde,

1045 But seyden he was worthy han° his lyf.   *to have*

And with that word up stirte° the olde wyf   *jumped*

Which that the knyght saugh sittynge in the grene.

"Mercy," quod she, "my sovereyn lady queene!

Er that youre court departe, do me right.

1050 I taughte this answere unto the knyght,

For which he plighte° me his trouthe° there,   *promised / word*

The firste thyng I wolde hym requere,

He wolde it do if it lay in his myght.

Bifore the court thanne preye° I thee, sire knyght,"   *ask*

1055 Quod she, "that thou me take unto thy wyf.

For wel thou woost° that I have kept thy lyf.   *know*

If I seye fals, sey nay, upon thy fey!"°   *faith*

This knyght answerde, "Allas and weylawey!°   *woe is me*

I woot° right wel that swich° was my

    biheste.°   *know / such / promise*

1060 For Goddes love, as chees° a newe requeste!   *choose*

Taak° al my good,° and lat° my body go!"   *take / possessions / let*

"Nay thanne,"° quod she, "I shrewe° us bothe two,   *then / curse*

For thogh that I be foul, oold, and poore,

I nolde° for al the metal ne for oore°   *would not / ore*

1065 That under erthe° is grave° or lith° above   *earth / buried / lies*

But if thy wyf I were and eek thy love."

"My love!" quod he. "Nay, my dampnacioun!°   *damnation*

Allas, that any of my nacioun°   *family*

Sholde evere so foule disparaged° be!"   *badly shamed*

1070 But al for noght! Th'end is this: that he

Constreyned° was. He nedes moste hire wedde,   *compelled*

And taketh his olde wyf and gooth to bedde.

Now wolden som men seye paraventure°   *perhaps*

That for my necligence I do no cure°   *care*

1075 To tellen yow the joye and al th'array°   *the arrangements*

That at the feeste was that ilke° day   *same*

To which thyng shortly answere I shal.

I seye ther nas° no joye ne feeste at al.   *was no*

Ther nas° but hevynesse and muche sorwe.   *was nothing*

1080 For prively he wedded hire on a morwe,°   *morning*

And al day after hidde hym as an owle,

So wo was hym, his wyf looked so foule.

Greet was the wo the knyght hadde in his thoght

Whan he was with his wyf abedde ybroght.[2]

---

[1] *Koude … hire* If you could inform me, I would pay you back well.

[2] *Whan … ybroght* It was a custom for wedding guests to escort the bride and groom to their bedroom.

1085 He walweth,° and he turneth to and fro.   *writhes about*
His olde wyf lay smylynge° evere mo   *smiling*
And seyde, "O deere housbonde, benedicitee,°   *bless you*
Fareth° every knyght thus with his wyf as ye?   *behaves*
Is this the lawe of Kyng Arthures hous?
1090 Is every knyght of his so dangerous?°   *standoffish*
I am youre owene love and youre wyf;
I am she which that saved hath youre lyf.
And certes, yet ne dide° I yow nevere unright:°   *did not / injustice*
Why fare ye thus with me this firste nyght?
1095 Ye faren lyk a man had lost his wit.
What is my gilt?° For Goddes love, tel it,   *guilt*
And it shal been amended if I may."
"Amended!" quod this knyght. "Allas, nay! Nay!
It wol nat been amended nevere mo.°   *forever more*
1100 Thou art so loothly° and so oold° also,   *ugly / old*
And therto comen of so lough° a kynde,°   *low / lineage*
That litel wonder is thogh° I walwe° and
wynde.°   *though / writhe / twist about*
So wolde God myn herte wolde breste!"°   *burst*
"Is this," quod she, "the cause of youre unreste?"
1105 "Ye, certeinly," quod he, "no wonder is!"
"Now sire," quod she, "I koude amende al this
If that me liste° er it were dayes thre,°   *I wished / three days*
So wel ye myghte bere yow unto me.¹
But for° ye speken of swich gentillesse   *because*
1110 As is descended out of old richesse,
That therfore sholden ye be gentilmen,
Swich arrogance is nat worth an hen!
Looke who that is moost vertuous alway,
Pryvee and apert and moost entendeth ay
1115 To do the gentil dedes that he kan:²
Taak hym for the grettest gentilman.
Crist wole° we clayme° of hym oure
gentillesse,   *desires that / claim*
Nat of oure eldres° for hire old richesse.   *ancestors*
For thogh they yeve us al hir heritage,
1120 For which we clayme to been of heigh parage,°   *lineage*
Yet may they nat biquethe° for nothyng   *bequeath*
To noon° of us hir vertuous lyvyng°   *none / living*
That made hem° gentilmen ycalled be,   *them*

And bad us folwen hem in swich degree.
1125 Wel kan the wise poete of Florence
That highte Dant° speken in this
sentence.°   *is named Dante / matter*
Lo, in swich maner rym° is Dantes tale: *such a kind of rhyme*
'Ful selde up riseth by his branches smale
Prowesse of man.³ For God of his goodnesse
1130 Wole° that of hym we clayme oure gentillesse.'   *wishes*
For of oure eldres may we nothyng clayme
But temporel thyng° that man may hurte and
mayme.°   *temporal things / maim*
Eek every wight woot this as wel as I.
If gentillesse were planted natureelly°   *implanted by nature*
1135 Unto a certeyn lynage doun the lyne,°   *line (of generations)*
Pryvee nor apert thanne wolde they nevere fyne
To doon of gentillesse the faire office.⁴
They myghte do no vileynye or vice.
Taak fyr° and ber° it in the derkeste hous   *fire / carry*
1140 Bitwix this and the mount of Kaukasous°   *Caucasus*
And lat men shette the dores and go thenne:°   *go away*
Yet wole the fyr as faire lye° and brenne°   *blaze / burn*
As twenty thousand men myghte it biholde.
His° office natureel ay° wol it holde,   *its / ever*
1145 Up peril of my lyf, til that it dye.⁵
Heere may ye se wel how that genterye
Is nat annexed° to possessioun,   *linked*
Sith folk ne doon hir operacioun°   *do not behave*
Alwey as dooth the fyr, lo, in his kynde.°   *according to its nature*
1150 For God it woot, men may wel often fynde
A lordes sone do shame and vileynye,
And he that wole han° pris of° his gentrye,   *will have / esteem for*
For he was born of a gentil hous
And hadde hise eldres noble and vertuous,
1155 And nel hymselven° do no gentil dedis°   *will not himself / deeds*
Ne folwen his gentil, auncestre that deed° is.   *dead*
He nys nat° gentil be he duc° or erl,°   *is not / duke / earl*
For vileyns synful dedes make a cherl.°   *churl*
For gentillesse nys but° renomee°   *is not / renown*

---

¹ *So ... me* Provided that you might behave yourself well towards me.

² *Looke ... kan* Look for whoever is always most virtuous in private and in public and always strives to do the most noble deeds.

---

³ *Ful ... man* The excellence of a man seldom extends to the further branches (of his family tree); i.e., the sons are seldom worthy of the father. Cf. Dante's *Convivio* 4 and *Purgatorio* 7.121.

⁴ *Pryvee ... office* Then they would never stop doing the fair office of gentle deeds either in private or in public.

⁵ *His ... dye* Upon my life, it will always perform its natural function (i.e., burn) until it dies.

1160 Of thyne auncestres for hire heigh bountee,° *their high goodness*
Which is a strange° thyng to thy persone. *separate*
Thy gentillesse cometh fro God allone.
Thanne comth oure verray gentillesse of grace;
It was nothyng biquethe us° with oure
place.° *bequeathed to us / social position*
1165 Thenketh how noble, as seith Valerius,
Was thilke° Tullius Hostillius,[1] *that*
That out of poverte roos° to heigh noblesse. *rose*
Reed Senek and redeth eek Boece:[2]
Ther shul ye seen expres° that no drede° is *specifically / doubt*
1170 That he is gentil that dooth gentil dedis.
And therfore, leeve housbonde, I thus conclude,
Al° were it that myne auncestres weren
rude,° *although / of low birth*
Yet may the hye° God—and so hope I— *high*
Grante me grace to lyven° vertuously. *live*
1175 Thanne am I gentil whan that I bigynne° *begin*
To lyven vertuously and weyve synne.° *avoid sin*
And theras° ye of poverte me repreeve,° *since / reproach*
The hye God on whom that we bileeve
In wilful° poverte chees° to lyve his lyf. *voluntary / chose*
1180 And certes, every man, mayden, or wyf
May understonde that Jesus Hevene kyng° *King of Heaven*
Ne wolde nat chesen° vicious lyvyng. *choose*
Glad° poverte is an honeste thyng, certeyn. *joyful*
This wole Senec and othere clerkes° seyn.° *writers / say*
1185 Whoso that halt hym payd of° his poverte, *satisfied with*
I holde° hym riche, al° hadde he nat a sherte. *consider / although*
He that coveiteth° is a povere wight, *covets*
For he wolde han that° is nat in his myght. *what*
But he that noght hath ne coveiteth have° *and does not covet*
1190 Is riche, although ye holde hym but a knave.
Verray poverte, it syngeth properly.
Juvenal[3] seith of poverte myrily,° *merrily*
'The povre man, whan he goth by the weye,° *along the road*
Bifore the theves he may synge and pleye.'
1195 Poverte is hateful good and, as I gesse,

A ful greet bryngere° out of bisynesse,° *very great bringer / busyness*
A greet amendere° eek of sapience° *improver / wisdom*
To hym that taketh it in pacience.° *patience*
Poverte is this, although it seme alenge:° *wretched*
1200 Possessioun that no wight wol chalenge.° *claim*
Poverte ful ofte, whan a man is lowe,
Maketh° his God and eek hymself to knowe. *causes*
Poverte a spectacle is, as thynketh me,
Thurgh° which he may hise verray° freendes see. *through / true*
1205 And therfore sire, syn that I noght yow greve,° *do not grieve you*
Of my poverte namoore° ye me repreve. *no more*
Now sire, of elde° ye repreve me, *old age*
And certes, sire, thogh noon auctoritee
Were in no book, ye gentils° of honour *nobles*
1210 Seyn that men sholde an oold wight doon favour° *do honor*
And clepe° hym fader for youre gentillesse. *call*
And auctours° shal I fynden, as I gesse. *authorities*
Now ther° ye seye that I am foul and old: *where*
Than drede° you noght to been a cokewold.[4] *fear*
1215 For filthe and eelde, also moot I thee,° *might I thrive*
Been grete wardeyns upon° chastitee. *guardians of*
But nathelees, syn I knowe youre delit,° *delight*
I shal fulfille youre worldly appetit.
Chese now," quod she, "oon of thise thynges tweye:° *two*
1220 To han me foul and old til that I deye
And be to yow a trewe, humble wyf
And nevere yow displese° in al my lyf, *displease you*
Or elles° ye wol han me yong and fair *else*
And take youre aventure of the repair
1225 That shal be to youre hous bycause of me,
Or in som oother place, may wel be.[5]
Now chese yourselven wheither that yow
liketh."° *whichever pleases you*
This knyght avyseth° hym and sore siketh,° *considers / sorely sighs*
But atte laste he seyde in this manere:
1230 "My lady and my love and wyf so deere,
I put me in youre wise governance.
Cheseth youreself which may be moost plesance° *most pleasant*
And moost honour to yow and me also.
I do no fors° the wheither of the two, *I do not care*
1235 For as yow liketh, it suffiseth me."

---

[1] *Valerius … Hostillius* Tullius Hostillius started life as a peasant and rose to become king. The story is told by the Roman writer Valerius Maximus.

[2] *Senek* I.e., Seneca, Stoic philosopher (c. 5 BCE–65 CE); *Boece* I.e., Boethius. See his *Consolation of Philosophy*, book 3, prose 6 and metre 3.

[3] *Juvenal* Roman poet and satirist (55–127 CE).

[4] *cokewold* I.e., cuckold, a man whose wife has been unfaithful to him.

[5] *And … be* And take your chances of the visiting (i.e., by lovers) at your house, or perhaps in some other places, in order to see me.

"Thanne have I gete° of yow maistrie,"° quod she, — *gotten / mastery*

"Syn I may chese and governe as me lest?"° — *as I wish*

"Ye certes, wyf," quod he, "I holde it best."

"Kys me," quod she, "we be no lenger wrothe.° — *angry*

1240 For by my trouthe,° I wol be to yow bothe. — *truth*

This is to seyn, ye, bothe° fair and good. — *indeed both*

I prey to God that I moote sterven wood° — *die crazy*

But° I to yow be also good and trewe — *unless*

As evere was wyf, syn that the world was newe.

1245 And but° I be tomorn° as fair to seene — *unless / tomorrow*

As any lady, emperice,° or queene — *empress*

That is bitwixe the est and eke the west,

Dooth° with my lyf and deth right° as yow lest.° — *do / just / wish*

Cast up the curtyn. Looke how that it is."

1250 And whan the knyght saugh verraily al this,

That she so fair was and so yong therto,

For joye he hente° hire in hise armes two. — *held*

His herte° bathed in a bath of blisse. — *heart*

A thousand tyme arewe° he gan hire kisse. — *in a row*

1255 And she obeyed hym in everythyng

That myghte doon hym plesance or likyng.° — *enjoyment*

And thus they lyve unto hir lyves ende

In parfit° joye. And Jesu Crist us sende — *perfect*

Housbondes meeke, yonge, and fressh abedde° — *in bed*

1260 And grace to t'overbyde° hem that we, wedde. — *control*

And eek I pray Jhesu shorte hir lyves° — *shorten their lives*

That nat wol be governed by hir wyves.

And olde and angry nygardes° of dispence,° — *skinflints / spending*

God sende hem soone verray pestilence!

HEERE ENDETH THE WYVES TALE OF BATHE

The Merchant's Prologue and Tale

The Clerk's tale of an impossibly patient wife, Griselda, provokes the Merchant, who has been married for two months. Although he says that he will say no more about his own sorrow, his tale of January, the wealthy old knight cuckolded by his young wife and his squire, seems to represent his own disillusioning experience. The Merchant's voice is bitter and cynical, describing a world of lust and self-delusion concealing itself behind respectability.

Like that of the Miller, *The Merchant's Tale* is a *fabliau*, and turns on the efforts of a blind man to guard his young wife and her ability to trick him into doubting his own eyes. However, it is a *fabliau* that repeatedly breaks the conventions of the genre. The business of the *fabliau* plot, centering around the lover in the pear tree, is largely confined to the last hundred lines and the bulk of the tale is given over to the discussion of marriage in theory and the description of marriage in practice. The tale makes its characters members of the knightly class, but their world is anything but chivalric. Most unattractive is January's calculation that, having spent his life in lechery, he can now save his soul and spend the rest of his days in comfort and sexual pleasure by marrying a young wife since, as he claims, a man cannot sin with his own wife any more than he can cut himself with his own knife (line 628). This view, one that a medieval theologian would regard as utterly mistaken, is enthusiastically supported by the toadying courtier Placebo.

The tale is set in January's castle, where Placebo triumphs over the wise Justinus, and in the enclosed garden, a symbolically charged location with ironic echoes of the garden of Paradise or the garden of love in works such as *The Romance of the Rose*. Like *The Knight's Tale*, *The Merchant's Tale* introduces a second level where the struggle of the earthly characters is echoed by the debate between the pagan gods. The debate between Pluto and Proserpina echoes the discussion of experience and authority in *The Wife of Bath's Prologue*, but the appearance of the gods in this *fabliau* world, even though they are the gods of the underworld, is disconcerting. More disconcerting still is the role of the three human lovers, especially January. His appeal to May to enter the garden, couched in language borrowed from *The Song of Songs* (l. 927–33) or his claim that he did not choose her for covetousness but for love (lines 954–56) make him a far more complex, if not necessarily sympathetic, character than the standard figure of the old cuckold in the *fabliau*.

Opening page of *The Merchant's Tale*, Ellesmere manuscript.
(This item is reproduced by permission of the *Huntington Library*, San Marino, California. EL26C9F72r.)

THE MERCHANT'S PROLOGUE

THE PROLOGE OF THE MARCHANTES TALE

"Wepyng° and waylyng,° care and oother
    sorwe°   *weeping / wailing / other sorrow*
I knowe ynogh° on even° and
    amorwe,"°   *enough / evening / morning*
Quod° the Marchant, "and so doon° othere
    mo°   *said / do / many others*
That wedded been.° I trowe° that it be so,   *are married / believe*
5 For wel° I woot° it fareth° so with me!   *well / know / fares*
I have a wyf,° the worste that may be,   *wife*
For thogh the feend° to hire° ycoupled°   *devil / her / married*
    were,
She wolde hym overmacche,° I dar wel swere!°   *overcome / swear*
What° sholde I yow° reherce° in
    special°   *why / to you / describe / specially*
10 Hir hye° malice? She is a shrewe° at
    al.°   *her extreme / nag / completely*
Ther is a long and large difference
Bitwix Grisildis[1] grete pacience°   *great patience*
And of my wyf the passyng° crueltee.   *surpassing*
Were I unbounden,° also moot I thee,°   *released / might I thrive*
15 I wolde nevere eft° comen° in the snare   *would never again / come*
We wedded men lyve in—sorwe and care.
Assaye° whoso wole,° and he shal fynde   *try / who will*
I seye sooth,° by Seint Thomas of Ynde![2]   *say truth*
As for the moore part,° I sey nat alle.°   *greater part / say not all*
20 God shilde° that it sholde so bifalle!°   *prevent / happen*
   "A,° good sire Hoost, I have ywedded bee°   *ah / been*
Thise monthes two and moore nat,° pardee,°   *not more / by God*
And yet I trowe he that al his lyve°   *life*
Wyflees° hath been, though that men wolde him
    ryve°   *wifeless / stab*
25 Unto the herte,° ne koude° in no
    manere°   *heart / could not / manner*
Tellen so muchel° sorwe as I now heere°   *much / here*
Koude tellen of my wyves cursednesse!"
   "Now," quod oure Hoost, "Marchaunt, so God yow blesse,
Syn° ye so muchel knowen of that art,   *since*

30 Ful hertely° I pray yow, telle us part."   *heartily*
   "Gladly," quod he, "but of myn owene soore,
For soory herte I telle may namoore."[3]

THE MERCHANT'S TALE

HEERE BIGYNNETH THE MARCHANTES TALE

Whilom° ther was dwellynge° in
    Lumbardye°   *once / living / Lombardy*
A worthy knyght that born was of Pavye,°   *Pavia*
35 In which he lyved in greet prosperitee.
And sixty yeer a wyflees man was hee
And folwed ay° his bodily delyt°   *always followed / delight*
On wommen, theras° was his appetyt,°   *where / appetite*
As doon thise fooles that been seculeer.°   *worldly*
40 And whan that he wes passed sixty yeer,
Were it° for hoolynesse° or for
    dotage°   *whether it was / holiness / senility*
I kan nat seye, but swich a greet corage°   *desire*
Hadde this knyght to been a wedded man,
That day and nyght he dooth al that he kan
45 T'espien° where he myghte wedded be,   *to find out*
Preyinge° oure Lord to graunten° him that he   *praying to / grant*
Mighte ones° knowe of thilke blisful lyf°   *once / that happy life*
That is bitwixe° an housbonde and his wyf,   *between*
And for to lyve under that hooly boond,°   *bond*
50 With which that first God man and womman bond.°   *bound*
"Noon oother lyf," seyde he, "is worth a bene,°   *bean*
For wedlok is so esy° and so clene,°   *comforting / pure*
That in this world it is a Paradys."
Thus seyde this olde knyght, that was so wys.°   *wise*
55   And certeinly, as sooth° as God is kyng,   *true*
To take a wyf, it is a glorious thyng!
And namely° whan a man is oold° and
    hoor.°   *especially / old / gray*
Thanne° is a wyf the fruyt° of his
    tresor.°   *then / best part / treasure*
Thanne sholde he take a yong wyf and a feir,°   *fair*
60 On which he myghte engendren hym° an heir   *beget himself*
And lede° his lyf in joye and in solas,°   *lead / comfort*

---

[1] *Grisildis* Griselda, the subject of the previous tale by the Clerk, was a wife extolled for her patience and fidelity.

[2] *Seint Thomas of Ynde* St. Thomas of India is the Apostle Thomas of the Gospels. His legend made him the Evangelist of India.

[3] *but of … namoore* But I can tell no more of my own sorrow because of my sorrowful heart.

Whereas° thise bacheleris° synge° *while | these young knights | sing*
   allas,

Whan that they fynden° any adversitee°   *find | adversity*

In love, which nys° but childyssh vanytee.°   *is nothing | foolishness*

65   And trewely,° it sit wel° to be so   *truly | is fitting*

That bacheleris have often peyne° and wo.°   *pain | woe*

On brotel ground they buylde, and brotelnesse

They fynde whan they wene sikernesse.°[1]   *expect security*

They lyve but as a bryd° or as a beest—   *bird*

70   In libertee and under noon arreest,°   *no hindrance*

Theras° a wedded man in his estaat°   *whereas | condition*

Lyveth a lyf blisful and ordinaat,°   *ordered*

Under this yok° of mariage ybounde.   *yoke*

Wel may his herte in joye and blisse habounde,°   *abound*

75   For who kan be so buxom° as a wyf?   *obedient*

Who is so trewe and eek so ententyf°   *attentive*

To kepe hym syk and hool as is his make?[2]

For wele° or wo, she wole hym nat forsake.   *wellness*

She nys nat° wery° hym to love and serve,   *is not | wearied*

80   Thogh° that he lye bedrede° til he sterve.°   *though | bedridden | die*

And yet somme clerkes° seyn it nys nat so,   *scholars*

Of whiche he, Theofraste,[3] is oon° of tho.°   *one | those*

What force° though Theofraste liste lye?°   *who cares | wants to lie*

"Ne take no wyf," quod he, "for housbondrye,°   *economy*

85   As for to spare in houshold thy dispence.°   *expenses*

A trewe servant dooth moore diligence°   *takes more care*

Thy good° to kepe° than thyn owene wyf,   *possessions | preserve*

For she wol clayme° half part al hir lyf.   *claim*

And if thou be syk,° so God me save,   *sick*

90   Thy verray freendes° or a trewe knave°   *own friends | true servant*

Wol kepe thee bet° than she that waiteth ay°   *better | ever*

After thy good° and hath doon many a day.   *possessions*

And if thou take a wyf unto thyn hoold,°   *under your protection*

Ful lightly° maystow been° a cokewold."[4]   *easily | may you be*

95   This sentence and an hundred thynges° worse   *things*

Writeth this man, ther God his bones corse!°   *curse*

But take no kepe° of al swich vanytee.   *heed*

Deffie° Theofraste and herke° me.   *defy | listen to*

   A wyf is Goddes yifte,° verraily.°   *gift | truly*

100   Alle otherere maner yiftes,° hardily,°   *kinds of gifts | certainly*

As londes,° rentes, pasture, or   *lands | rights to common land*
   commune,°

Or moebles,° alle been yiftes of Fortune   *movable property*

That passen as a shadwe° upon a wal.   *shadow*

But dredelees,° if pleynly° speke I shal,   *doubtless | plainly*

105   A wyf wol laste and in thyn hous endure°   *remain*

Wel lenger than thee list,° paraventure.°   *you wish | perhaps*

   Mariage is a ful greet° sacrement.[5]   *very great*

He which that hath no wyf, I holde hym
   shent!°   *consider him ruined*

He lyveth helplees and al desolat.

110   I speke of folk in seculer estaat.[6]

And herke° why. I sey nat° this for noght:°   *listen to | not | nothing*

That womman is for mannes helpe ywroght.°   *created*

The hye° God, whan he hadde Adam maked   *high*

And saugh hym al allone, bely-naked,°   *completely naked*

115   God of his grete goodnesse seyde than,°   *then*

"Lat us now make an helpe° unto this man   *helper*

Lyk to hymself."[7] And thanne he made him Eve.

Heere may ye se° and heerby may ye preve°   *see | prove*

That wyf is mannes helpe and his confort,

120   His Paradys terrestre° and his disport.°   *earthly | enjoyment*

So buxom° and so vertuous is she,   *obedient*

They moste nedes° lyve in unitee.   *necessarily must*

O° flessh they been, and o flessh as I gesse,   *one*

Hath but oon herte in wele° and in distresse.   *prosperity*

125   A wyf—a,° Seinte Marie, benedicite°—   *ah | bless you*

How myghte a man han° any adversitee   *have*

That hath a wyf? Certes, I can nat seye.

The blisse which that is bitwixe hem tweye,°   *them two*

Ther may no tonge° telle or herte° thynke.   *tongue | heart*

130   If he be povre,° she helpeth hym to swynke.°   *poor | work*

She kepeth his good and wasteth never a deel.°   *a bit*

---

[1]   *On brotel ... sikernesse*   They build on brittle (i.e., promiscuous) ground and they find brittleness when they expect security (i.e., fidelity).

[2]   *Who ... make*   Who is as true and attentive as his mate to take care of him when he is sick or healthy?

[3]   *Theofraste*   Theophrastus wrote *The Golden Book on Marriage*, a work that attacked marriage.

[4]   *cokewold*   Cuckold, a man whose wife has committed adultery.

[5]   *Mariage ... sacrement*   This is a quotation from Paul's Letter to the Ephesians, 5.32, "sacramentum hoc magnum est," often translated from the Latin to "This is a great mystery." By the thirteenth century marriage had come to be regarded as a sacrament by most Christian theologians.

[6]   *in seculer estaat*   As opposed to priests, who were forbidden to marry but, by implication, were not destroyed by celibacy.

[7]   *Lat ... hymself*   See Genesis 2.18.

Al that hire housbonde lust,° hire liketh
    weel;°   *desires / pleases her well*

She seith nat ones° nay whan he seith ye.   *once*

"Do this," seith he. "Al redy, sire," seith she.

135   O, blisful order of wedlok precious,

Thou art so murye° and eek° so vertuous   *merry / also*

And so commended and approved° eek,   *approved*

That every man that halt hym worth a leek[1]

Upon his bare knees oughte al his lyf

140 Thanken his God that hym hath sent a wyf

Or elles preye to God hym for to sende

A wyf to laste unto his lyves ende.

For thanne his lyf is set in sikernesse.°   *security*

He may nat be deceyved, as I gesse,

145 So° that he werke after° his wyves reede.° *provided / follow / advice*

Thanne may he boldely kepen up his heed,°   *head*

They been so trewe and therwith al so wyse.

For which, if thow wolt werken° as the wyse, *will do / wise (man)*

Do alwey so as wommen wol thee rede.°   *advise*

150 Lo how that Jacob, as thise clerkes rede,° *these scholars recount*

By good conseil of his mooder° Rebekke,   *mother*

Boond the kydes skyn° aboute his nekke,   *kid's skin*

Thurgh which his fadres benysoun he wan.[2]

  Lo Judith, as the storie eek telle kan,

155 By wys conseil she Goddes peple kepte°   *saved*

And slow° hym, Olofernus, whil he slepte.[3]   *killed*

  Lo Abigayl, by good conseil how she

Saved hir housbonde Nabal whan that he

Sholde han be slayn.[4] And looke, Ester also

160 By good conseil delyvered out of wo

The peple of God and made hym, Mardochee,°   *Mordecai*

Of Assuere° enhaunced° for to be.[5] *Ahasuerus (Xerxes) / promoted*

  Ther nys nothyng in gree superlatyf,°   *highest degree*

As seith Senek, above an humble wyf.[6]

165 Suffre thy wyves tonge, as Catoun bit:[7]

She shal comande, and thou shalt suffren it.

And yet she wole obeye of curteisye.

A wyf is kepere of thyn housbondrye.°   *household*

Wel may the sike° man biwaille° and wepe,   *sick / complain*

170 Theras° ther nys no wyf the hous to kepe.   *where*

I warne thee if wisely thou wolt wirche,°   *work*

Love wel thy wyf, as Crist loved his Chirche.

If thou lovest thyself, thou lovest thy wyf;

No man hateth his flessh, but in his lyf

175 He fostreth° it.[8] And therfore bidde° I thee *nurtures / command*

Cherisse thy wyf, or thou shalt nevere thee.°   *thrive*

Housbonde and wyf, whatso men jape° or

    pleye,°   *whatever people say in joke / play*

Of worldly folk holden the siker weye.°   *sure way*

They been so knyt,° ther may noon harm

    bityde°—   *joined together / befall*

180 And namely upon the wyves syde.

For which° this Januarie, of whom I

    tolde,°   *these reasons / told you*

Considered hath, inwith hise dayes olde,°   *in his old age*

The lusty° lyf, the vertuous quyete°   *vigorous / quiet*

That is in mariage hony-sweete.°   *honey-sweet*

185 And for hise freendes on a day he sente

---

[1] *halt … leek* Holds himself worth a leek (i.e., worth anything at all).

[2] *Thurgh … wan* Through which he won his father's blessing. See Genesis 27.5–29. It also appears, along with the following examples of Judith, Esther, and Abigail, the saying misattributed to Seneca, the saying of Cato, and the passages from Paul's Letter to the Ephesians, in Albertano da Brescia's *Book of Consolation and Counsel*.

[3] *Lo Judith … slepte* The Book of Judith, in the apocryphal portion of the Bible, recounts the story of the widow Judith, who captivates Nebuchadnezzar's general Holofernes with her beauty and then, taking advantage of his drunkenness, beheads him, thus liberating the Jews of Bethulia.

[4] *Lo Abigayl … slayn* David sought vengeance upon Nabal, who had refused to help him in his time of need. Nabal's wife, Abigail, saved her husband's life by secretly meeting David and giving him provisions. See 1 Samuel 25.

[5] *And looke … be* When one of Xerxes's ministers secures a royal decree authorizing the slaughter of all the Jews, Esther, his second wife, reveals herself as a Jew and begs her husband to save her people. Xerxes overturns the decree and replaces the offending minister with Esther's own cousin and adopted father, Mordecai. See the Book of Esther.

[6] *Senek* Seneca, the Stoic philosopher (c. 5 BCE–65 CE); *Ther nys … wyf* The quotation actually comes from the *Mythologies* of Fabius Planciades Fulgentius, a late fifth-century Christian writer known for his elaborate allegorical interpretation of classical writers such as Ovid and Virgil.

[7] *Suffre … bit* Endure your wife's tongue, as Cato commanded. Cf. Cato's *Distichs* 3.23. The Roman moralist Dionysius Cato was reputed in the Middle Ages to be the author of a widely circulating collection of proverbs and wise sayings, often used for teaching Latin in schools.

[8] *Love wel … it* From Paul's Letter to the Ephesians 5.25 and 5.28–29, 33.

To tellen hem th'effect° of his entente.°   *the substance / intent*
  With face sad,° his tale he hath hem toold.   *serious*
He seyde, "Freendes, I am hoor and oold
And almoost, God woot,° on my pittes
    brynke;°   *knows / grave's brink*
190 Upon the soule somwhat moste° I thynke.   *must*
I have my body folily despended.°   *foolishly spent*
Blessed be God that it shal been amended!
For I wol be, certeyn, a wedded man—
And that anoon,° in al the haste I kan,   *at once*
195 Unto som mayde° fair and tendre of age.   *maid*
I prey° yow, shapeth° for my mariage   *ask / arrange*
Al sodeynly,° for I wol nat abyde.°   *quickly / wait*
And I wol fonde t'espien° on my syde   *attempt to find out*
To whom I may be wedded hastily.
200 But forasmuche as ye been mo° than I,   *be more*
Ye shullen° rather swich a thyng espyen   *shall*
Than I, and where me best were to
    allyen.°   *ally myself (through marriage)*
  But o thyng warne I yow, my freendes deere:
I wol noon oold wyf han in no manere.°   *no way*
205 She shal nat passe° twenty yeer, certain.   *exceed*
Oold fissh° and yong flessh wolde I have fayn.°   *fish / gladly*
Bet° is," quod he, "a pyk° than a
    pykerel,°   *better / pike / young pike*
And bet than olde boef° is the tendre veel.°   *beef / veal*
I wol° no womman thritty° yeer of age—   *want / thirty*
210 It is but benestraw and greet forage.[1]
And eek thise olde wydwes,° God it woot,   *widows*
They konne so muchel craft on Wades boot,
So muchel broken harm whan that hem lest,[2]
That with hem sholde I nevere lyve in reste,
215 For sondry scoles maken sotile clerkis.[3]
Womman of manye scoles° half a clerk° is.   *schools / scholar*
But certeynly, a yong thyng may men gye°   *guide*
Right as men may warm wex° with handes
    plye.°   *wax / manipulate*

Wherfore I sey yow pleynly° in a clause,   *plainly*
220 I wol noon oold wyf han, for this cause:
For if so were that I hadde swich myschaunce,°   *misfortune*
That I in hire ne koude han no plesaunce,°   *pleasure*
Thanne sholde I lede° my lyf in avoutrye°—   *spend / adultery*
And streight unto the devel whan I dye!°   *die*
225 Ne children sholde I none upon hire geten.°   *beget*
Yet were me levere° that houndes° had me
    eten°   *I would rather / dogs / eaten*
Than that myn heritage[4] sholde falle
In straunge hand. And this I telle yow alle:
I dote nat.° I woot° the cause why   *am not senile / know*
230 Men sholde wedde. And forthermore, woot I
Ther speketh many a man of mariage
That woot namoore of it than woot my page°   *boy servant*
For whiche causes man sholde take a wyf:
Siththe° he may nat lyven° chaast his
    lyf,°   *since / live / chaste (all) his life*
235 Take hym° a wyf with greet devocioun   *let him take*
Bycause of leveful procreacioun°   *lawful procreation*
Of children to th'onour° of God above,   *the honor*
And nat oonly for paramour° or love;   *sex*
And for° they sholde leccherye° eschue°   *because / lechery / avoid*
240 And yelde hir dettes whan that they ben due;[5]
Or for that ech of hem sholde helpen oother
In meschief,° as a suster° shal the brother,   *misfortune / sister*
And lyve in chastitee ful holily.°   *very devoutly*
But sires,° by youre leve,° that am nat
    I.°   *sirs / leave / I am not like that*
245 For God be thanked, I dar make avaunt:°   *boast*
I feele my lymes° stark° and suffisaunt°   *limbs / strong / capable*
To do al that a man bilongeth to.°   *is appropriate for a man*
I woot myselven best what I may do.
Though I be hoor, I fare as dooth a tree
250 That blosmeth er that fruyt° ywoxen° bee,   *fruit / ripened*
And blosmy° tree nys neither drye ne deed.   *blossom-filled*
I feele me nowhere hoor but on myn heed.
Myn herte and alle my lymes been as grene
As laurer° thurgh° the yeer is for to
    sene.°   *laurel / throughout / be seen*
255 And syn° that ye han herd al myn entente,   *since*

---

[1] *It … forage* It is (nothing) but bean-straw and great fodder. In other words, marrying an older woman is a waste.

[2] *They konne … lest* They have so much skill in Wade's boat (they know), so much about how to cause harm when they wish. Wade was once a famous hero, but only passing references to him survive (including one in Chaucer's *Troilus and Criseyde*, 3.164). The significance of his boat remains obscure.

[3] *For … clerkis* For a variety of schools makes subtle scholars.

[4] *heritage* I.e., lands and property.

[5] *And … due* And yield their debts when they are due. The reference here is to the marriage debt, of having sex with one's spouse. Cf. *Wife of Bath's Prologue*, line 130.

I prey yow to my wyl° ye wole assente."   *will*
    Diverse men diversely hym tolde
Of mariage manye ensamples° olde.   *examples*
Somme blamed it. Somme preysed° it,
    certeyn.°   *praised / certainly*
260 But atte laste, shortly for to seyn,[1]
As al day falleth altercacioun°   *disagreement*
Bitwixen freendes in disputisoun,°   *debate*
Ther fil° a stryf° bitwixe hise bretheren°
    two,   *fell / strife / his brothers*
Of whiche that oon was cleped° Placebo;   *named*
265 Justinus[2] soothly° called was that oother.   *truly*
    Placebo seyde, "O Januarie brother,
Ful litel nede° hadde ye, my lord so deere,   *little need*
Conseil to axe° of any that is heere,   *ask*
But that ye been so ful of sapience°   *wisdom*
270 That yow ne liketh° for youre heighe
    prudence°   *it does not please you / wisdom*
To weyven fro° the word of Salomon.°   *depart from / Solomon*
This word seyde he unto us everychon:°   *every one*
'Wirk° alle thyng by conseil,' thus seyde he,   *work (do)*
'And thanne shaltow° nat repente° thee.'[3]   *shall you / regret*
275 But though that Salomon spak swich a word,
Myn owene deere brother and my lord,
So wysly God my soule brynge at reste,°   *bring to rest*
I holde youre owene conseil is the beste.
For brother myn, of me taak this motyf:°   *thought*
280 I have now been a court-man° al my lyf,   *courtier*
And God it woot, though I unworthy be,
I have stonden° in ful greet° degree   *stood / very high*
Abouten lordes of ful heigh estaat.
Yet hadde I nevere with noon of hem debaat;
285 I nevere hem contraried,° trewely.   *disagreed with them*
I woot wel that my lord kan moore than I.
What that° he seith I holde it ferme° and
    stable;°   *whatever / firm / certain*
I seye the same or elles thyng semblable.°   *a similar thing*
A ful greet fool is any conseillour
290 That serveth any lord of heigh honour
That dar presume or elles thenken° it,   *think*
That his conseil sholde passe° his lordes wit.   *surpass*

Nay, lordes been no fooles, by my fay!°   *faith*
Ye han youreselven seyd heer today
295 So heigh sentence,° so holily° and weel,° *judgment / devoutly / well*
That I consente and conferme everydeel°   *every part*
Youre wordes alle and youre opinioun.
By God, ther nys no man in al this toun
Nyn Ytaille° that koude bet han sayd.   *nor in Italy*
300 Crist halt hym of this conseil ful wel apayd.[4]
And trewely, it is an heigh corage°   *act of high courage*
Of any man that stapen is in age°   *is stooped by age*
To take a yong wyf, by my fader kyn.°   *father's kin*
Youre herte hangeth on a joly pyn.°   *peg*
305 Dooth° now in the matiere right° as yow leste,° *do / just / wish*
For finally, I holde it for the beste."
    Justinus, that ay° stille° sat and herde   *ever / quiet*
Right in this wise,° he to Placebo answerde,   *way*
"Now, brother myn, be pacient, I preye,
310 Syn ye han seyd,° and herkneth what I seye.   *have spoken*
Senek among his othere wordes wyse
Seith that a man oghte hym right wel avyse°   *be advised*
To whom he yeveth° his lond or his catel.° *gives / possessions*
And syn I oghte avyse me right wel
315 To whom I yeve my good° awey fro me,   *possessions*
Wel muchel moore° I oghte avysed be   *all the more*
To whom I yeve my body for alwey.°   *always*
I warne yow wel, it is no childes pley
To take a wyf withouten avysement.°   *advice*
320 Men moste enquere—this is myn assent°—   *my counsel*
Wher° she be wys or sobre or dronkelewe°   *whether / drunken*
Or proud or elles ootherweys a shrewe,
A chidestere° or wastour° of thy good   *nag / waster*
Or riche or poore or elles mannyssh wood.[5]
325 Albeit so that no man fynden shal
Noon in this world that trotteth hool in al,[6]
Ne man ne beest which as men koude devyse;°   *imagine*
But nathelees, it oghte ynough suffise°   *to be enough*
With any wyf, if so were that she hadde
330 Mo° goode thewes° than hire vices badde.   *more / customs*
And al this axeth leyser° for t'enquere.   *requires time*

---

[1] *shortly … seyn* To say it shortly (i.e., to make a long story short).

[2] *Placebo* Latin: I will please; *Justinus* Implies truth, justice.

[3] *Wirk … thee* See Ecclesiasticus 32.24.

[4] *apayd* Christ considers himself very well paid by this counsel; i.e., it is pious.

[5] *mannysshe wood* Man-mad; i.e., either as fiercely crazy as a man or, possibly, crazy for men.

[6] *Noon … al* There is no one in this world who trots perfectly in all respects. The metaphor is drawn from buying horses.

For God it woot, I have wept many a teere°   *tear*
Ful pryvely° syn I have had a wyf.   *privately*
Preyse° whoso wole° a wedded mannes
    lyf,   *praise / whoever wishes to*
335 Certein, I fynde in it but cost and care
And observances° of alle blisses bare.°   *duties / lacking all happiness*
And yet, God woot, my neighebores aboute,
And namely of wommen many a route,°   *crowd*
Seyn that I have the mooste stedefast wyf
340 And eek the mekeste oon° that bereth lyf.°   *meekest one / bears life*
But I woot best where wryngeth° me my sho.°   *pinches / shoe*
Ye mowe for me right as yow liketh do.[1]
Avyseth yow—ye been a man of age—
How that ye entren° into mariage,   *enter*
345 And namely with a yong wyf and a fair.
By hym that made water, erthe, and air,
The yongeste man that is in al this route
Is bisy° ynough to bryngen it aboute   *hard pressed*
To han his wyf allone,[2] trusteth me.
350 Ye shul nat plesen hire fully yeres thre°—   *for three years*
This is to seyn, to doon hire ful plesaunce.°   *do her great pleasure*
A wyf axeth° ful many an observaunce.°   *asks / attention*
I prey yow that ye be nat yvele apayd."°   *displeased*
    "Wel," quod this Januarie, "and hastow
    ysayd?°   *have you finished speaking*
355 Straw for thy Senek and for thy proverbes!
I counte nat a panyer° ful of herbes   *basket*
Of° scole termes.[3] Wyser men than thow,°   *for / you*
As thou has herd, assenteden° right now   *agree*
To my purpos. Placebo, what sey ye?"
360   "I seye it is a cursed man," quod he,
"That letteth° matrimoigne,° sikerly."°   *hinders / matrimony / surely*
And with that word they rysen sodeynly
And been assented fully° that he sholde   *completely agreed*
Be wedded whanne hym liste and where he wolde.
365   Heigh fantasye and curious bisynesse°   *elaborate concern*
Fro day to day gan in the soule impresse
Of Januarie aboute his mariage.
Many fair shape and many a fair visage°   *face*

Ther passeth thurgh his herte nyght by nyght,
370 As whoso° took a mirour° polisshed bryght   *as if someone / mirror*
And sette it in a commune° market place,   *common*
Thanne sholde he se ful many a figure pace°   *pass*
By his mirour,° and in the same wyse°   *in his mirror / way*
Gan Januarie inwith° his thoght devyse°   *within / imagine*
375 Of maydens whiche that dwellen hym bisyde.°   *lived near him*
He wiste nat wher that he myghte abyde,°   *settle*
For if that oon have beaute in hir face,
Another stant° so in the peples grace°   *stands / favor*
For hire sadnesse° and hire benyngnytee°   *constancy / kindness*
380 That of the peple grettest voys° hath she.   *fame*
And somme were riche and hadden badde name.
But nathelees, bitwixe ernest° and game,°   *seriousness / jest*
He atte laste apoynted hym on oon°   *decided himself upon one*
And leet alle othere from his herte goon
385 And chees° hire of his owene auctoritee.°   *chose / authority*
For love is blynd° alday° and may nat see.   *blind / all day (always)*
And whan that he was in his bed ybroght,
He purtreyed° in his herte and in his thoght   *imagined*
Hir fresshe beautee and hir age tendre,
390 Hir myddel smal,° hire armes longe and
    sklendre,°   *small waist / slender*
Hir wise governaunce,° hir gentillesse,°   *behavior / nobility*
Hir wommanly berynge and hire sadnesse.
And whan that he on hire was condescended,°   *decided*
Hym thoughte his choys° myghte nat ben
    amended.°   *choice / improved upon*
395 For whan that he hymself concluded hadde,°   *had decided*
Hym thoughte ech oother mannes wit° so badde,   *intelligence*
That inpossible it were to repplye°   *object*
Agayn his choys. This was his fantasye.°   *delusion*
Hise freendes sente he to° at his instaunce°   *for / insistence*
400 And preyed hem° to doon hym that
    plesaunce°   *asked them / pleasure*
That hastily they wolden to hym come.
He wolde abregge° hir labour alle and
    some:°   *shorten / one and all*
Nedeth namoore for hym° to go ne ryde.°   *them / walk nor ride*
He was apoynted° ther he wolde
    abyde.°   *had decided / abide (by his decision)*
405 Placebo cam and eek hise freendes soone,
And alderfirst° he bad° hem alle a boone,°   *first of all / asked / favor*
That noon of hem none argumentz make
Agayn the purpos which that he hath take,
Which purpos was "plesant to God," seyde he,

---

[1] *Ye ... do* You may, as far as I am concerned, do as you wish to
do.

[2] *allone* I.e., to himself.

[3] *scole termes* School terms, the type of debates engaged in at the
universities, and the language used in such debates.

410 And verray ground° of his prosperitee.°   *true basis | prosperity*

He seyde ther was a mayden in the toun

Which that of beautee hadde greet renoun;

Al° were it so she were of smal degree,°   *although | low-born family*

Suffiseth hym° hir yowthe and hir beautee.   *sufficed for him*

415 Which° mayde, he seyde, he wolde han to his wyf,   *this*

To lede in ese and hoolynesse his lyf,

And thanked God that he myghte han hire al,°   *might have her all*

That no wight° his blisse parten° shal,   *person | share*

And preyde hem° to laboure in this nede°   *asked them | need*

420 And shapen° that he faille nat to
spede.°   *arrange | not fail to succeed*

For thanne, he seyde, his spirit was at ese.°   *ease*

"Thanne is," quod he, "nothyng may me displese,

Save o thyng priketh° in my conscience,   *sticks*

The which I wol reherce° in youre presence.

425 "I have," quod he, "herd seyd ful yoore ago,°   *very long ago*

Ther may no man han parfite blisses two.°   *two perfect happinesses*

This is to seye, in erthe and eek in Hevene.

For though he kepe hym from the synnes
sevene°   *seven (deadly) sins*

And eek from every branche of thilke tree,[1]

430 Yet is ther so parfit felicitee°   *happiness*

And so greet ese° and lust° in mariage,   *comfort | pleasure*

That evere I am agast° now in myn age   *afraid*

That I shal lede now so myrie° a lyf,   *merry*

So delicat,° withouten wo and stryf,   *delightful*

435 That I shal have myn Hevene in earthe here.

For sith that verray Hevene is boght so deere°   *dearly*

With tribulacioun and greet penance,

How sholde I thane, that lyve in swich plesaunce

As alle wedded men doon with hire wyvys,

440 Come to the blisse ther° Crist eterne° on lyve
ys?°   *where | eternal | is alive*

This is my drede, and ye, my bretheren tweye,

Assoilleth° me this questioun, I preye."   *resolve*

Justinus, which that hated his folye,°   *folly*

Answerde anon right° in his japerye,°   *right away | mockery*

445 And for he wolde his longe tale abregge,°   *shorten*

He wolde noon auctoritee allegge°   *quote*

But seyde, "Sire, so ther be noon obstacle

Oother than this, God of his hygh myracle

And of his hygh mercy may so for yow wirche°   *work*

450 That er ye have youre right of Hooly Chirche,[2]

Ye may repente of wedded mannes lyf

In which ye seyn ther is no wo ne stryf.

And elles, God forbede° but° he sente   *forbid | unless*

A wedded man hym grace to repente

455 Wel ofte, rather° than a sengle° man.   *sooner | single*

And therfore, sire—the beste reed° I kan°—   *advice | I know*

Dispeire° yow noght, but have in youre
memorie,°   *despair | keep in mind*

Paraunter° she may be youre Purgatorie.   *perhaps*

She may be Goddes meene° and Goddes
whippe.°   *means | whip*

460 Thanne shal youre soule up to Hevene skippe°   *skip*

Swifter than dooth an arwe° out of the bowe.   *arrow*

I hope to God herafter° shul ye knowe   *after this*

That ther nys no so greet felicitee

In mariage ne nevere mo shal bee,

465 That yow shal lette of youre
savacioun,°   *shall hinder your salvation*

So that ye use, as skil° is and resoun,°   *reasonable | sensible*

The lustes° of youre wyf attemprely°   *desires | temperately*

And that ye plese hire° nat to° amorously   *please her | not too*

And that ye kepe yow eek from oother synne.

470 My tale is doon, for my wit is thynne.°   *thin*

Beth nat agast herof,° my brother deere,   *be not afraid of this*

But lat us waden° out of this mateere!   *wade*

The Wyf of Bathe, if ye han understonde,

Of mariage, which ye have on honde,°   *hand*

475 Declared hath ful wel in litel space.

Fareth now wel! God have yow in his grace!"

And with this word this Justyn and his brother

Han take hir leve and ech of hem of oother.

For whan they saugh° that it moste be,   *saw*

480 They wroghten so° by sly and wys
tretee°   *made it happen | negotiations*

That she this mayden, which that Mayus°
highte,°   *May | was named*

As hastily as evere that she myghte

Shal wedded be unto this Januarie.

I trowe° it were to longe° yow to tarie   *believe | too long | delay*

485 If I yow tolde of every scrit° and bond°   *contract | agreement*

---

[1] *thilke tree* The seven deadly sins were often described by preachers as the branches of a tree.

[2] *er ... Chirche* Before you receive your last rites from the Holy Church.

By which that she was feffed¹ in his lond
Or for to herknen of° hir riche array.   *hear about*
But finally ycomen is the day
That to the chirche bothe be they went°   *have they gone*
490 For to receyve the hooly sacrement.°   *holy sacrament (of marriage)*
Forth comth the preest with stole° aboute his nekke   *vestment*
And bad hire be lyk to Sarra and Rebekke²
In wysdom and in trouthe° of mariage   *constancy*
And seyde hir orisons° as is usage°   *prayers / customary*
495 And croucheth hem and bad God sholde hem blesse³
And made al siker ynogh° with hoolynesse.   *certain enough*
     Thus been they wedded with solempnitee,°   *ceremony*
And at the feeste sitteth he and she
With othere worthy folk upon the deys.°   *dais (high table)*
500 Al ful of joye and blisse is the paleys,°   *palace*
And ful of instrumentz° and of
     vitaille,°   *musical instruments / food*
The mooste deyntevous° of al Ytaille.°   *choice / Italy*
Biforn hem stooden instrumentz of swich soun°   *sound*
That Orpheus ne of Thebes Amphioun⁴
505 Ne maden° nevere swich a melodye.   *made*
At every cours° thanne cam loud mynstralcye,°   *course / music*
That nevere tromped° Joab⁵ for to heere   *trumpeted*
Nor he Theodomas yet half so cleere
At Thebes whan the citee was in doute.⁶
510 Bacus⁷ the wyn hem skynketh° al aboute   *pours*
And Venus⁸ laugheth upon every wight°—   *person*
For Januarie was bicome hire knyght

And wolde° bothe assayen° his corage°   *wanted / try / vigor*
In libertee and eek in mariage—
515 And with hire fyr brond° in hire hand aboute   *her fiery torch*
Daunceth biforn the bryde and al the route.°   *company*
And certeinly, I dar right wel seyn this:
Ymeneus⁹ that god of weddyng is,
Saugh nevere his lyf so myrie a wedded man.
520 Hoold thou thy pees,° thou poete Marcian,¹⁰   *peace*
That writest us that ilke° weddyng murie°   *same / merry*
Of hire, Philologie, and hym, Mercurie
And of the songes that the Muses song!¹¹
To smal is bothe thy penne and eek thy tonge
525 For to discryven° of this mariage.   *describe*
Whan tendre youthe hath wedded stoupyng° age   *stooping*
Ther is swich myrthe° that it may nat be writen.   *mirth*
Assayeth it yourself. Thanne may ye witen°   *know*
If that I lye or noon° in this matiere.   *not*
530 Mayus, that sit with so benyngne° a chiere,°   *kind / face*
Hire to biholde, it semed fairye.°   *magical*
Queene Ester looked nevere with swich an eye
On Assuer, so meke° a look hath she.¹²   *meek*
I may yow nat devyse al hir beautee.
535 But thus muche of hire beautee telle I may,
That she was lyk the brighte morwe° of May,   *morning*
Fulfild of alle beautee and plesaunce.
     This Januarie is ravysshed in a traunce
At every tyme he looked on hir face.
540 But in his herte he gan hire to manace,°   *menace*
That he that nyght in armes wolde hire streyne°   *embrace*
Harder than evere Parys dide Eleyne.¹³
But nathelees, yet hadde he greet pitee
That thilke nyght offenden° hire moste he   *harm*
545 And thoughte, "Allas, o tendre creature!
Now wolde God ye myghte wel endure
Al my corage,° it is so sharpe and keene!   *sexual prowess*

---

¹ *feffed* Enfeoffed; i.e., she was given possession of some of his land.

² *Sarra and Rebekke* I.e. Sarah and Rebecca, two good wives in the Book of Genesis. The actual ceremony of marriage is performed on the church steps and is followed by a nuptial mass inside.

³ *And croucheth … blesse* And blesses them with the sign of the cross and asked that God should bless them.

⁴ *That … Amphioun* In Greek mythology, Orpheus could charm beasts, rocks, and trees and was almost able to rescue his wife Eurydice from Hades by playing his lyre. King Amphion was a famous harper who helped build Thebes by using the magical power of his harp to assemble the stones.

⁵ *Joab* King David's trumpeter. See 2 Samuel 2.28.

⁶ *Nor he … doute* In Greek legend, Theodomas was a Theban prophet whose pronouncements were heralded by a trumpet.

⁷ *Bacus* I.e., Bacchus, Greek god of wine.

⁸ *Venus* Greek goddess of love.

⁹ *Ymeneus* I.e., Hymen, god of marriage.

¹⁰ *thou poete Marcian* The North African poet Martianus Capella (c. 5th century CE) wrote an allegorical account of the seven liberal arts, *The Marriage of Philology and Mercury*, i.e., the union of the science of language with eloquence, represented by the god Mercury.

¹¹ *Muses song* In classical mythology, the Muses were the goddesses of the arts and sciences.

¹² *Queene … she* See Esther 2.

¹³ *Harder … Eleyne* Paris's seduction of Helen and their subsequent flight to Troy occasioned the Trojan war.

I am agast° ye shul it nat susteene.°   *afraid / sustain*
But God forbede that I dide al my myght!¹
550   Now wolde God that it were woxen° nyght   *turned to*
And that the nyght wolde lasten everemo!
I wolde that al this peple were ago!"°   *gone*
And finally he dooth al his labour
As he best myghte, savyng his honour,
555   To haste hem fro the mete° in subtil wyse.°   *food / subtle way*
     The tyme cam that resoun° was to ryse,   *reasonable*
And after that men daunce and drynken faste,
And spices al aboute the hous they caste.²
And ful of joye and blisse is every man—
560   Al but a squyer° highte Damyan,   *squire*
Which carf° biforn the knyght ful many a day.³   *carved*
He was so ravysshed on° his lady May,   *in love with*
That for the verray peyne° he was ny
     wood.°   *true pain / nearly crazy*
Almoost he swelte° and swowned° ther he stood,   *died / fainted*
565   So soore hath Venus hurt hym with hire brond,°   *torch*
As that she bar° it daunsynge° in hire hond,   *carried / dancing*
And to his bed he wente hym hastily.
Namoore of hym at this tyme speke I,
But there I lete hym wepe ynogh and pleyne,⁴
570   Til fresshe May wol rewen° on his peyne.   *have pity*
     O perilous fyr, that in the bedstraw⁵ bredeth,°   *breeds*
O famulier foo,° that his servyce bedeth,°   *foe / offers*
O servant traytour, false, hoomly hewe,°   *domestic color*
Lyk to the naddre° in bosom, sly, untrewe!   *snake*
575   God shilde° us alle from youre aqueyntaunce!   *shield*
O Januarie, dronken in plesance,
In mariage se how thy Damyan,
Thyn owene squier and thy born man,⁶

---

¹ *But ... myght* But God forbid that I should perform as powerfully as I can (i.e., because that would be too much for May).

² *And ... caste* An old marriage custom was to throw spices on the
floor during a wedding feast. This symbolized the beginning of the
marriage, because medieval floors were often bare dirt strewn with
straw and herbs. The old material would be removed before the new
was strewn about.

³ *Which ... day* One of the duties of a squire was to carve the meat
and serve his lord at dinner.

⁴ *But ... pleyne* But there I leave him weeping enough and
complaining.

⁵ *bedstraw* Straw used for stuffing mattresses.

⁶ *Thyn ... man* Your own man, born into your service.

Entendeth for to do thee vileynye.
580   God graunte thee thyn hoomly fo° t'espye.°   *foe at home / to see*
For in this world nys° worse pestilence   *there is no*
Than hoomly foo alday in thy presence.
     Parfourned° hath the sonne° his ark diurne,⁷   *performed / sun*
No lenger may the body of hym sojurne°   *its body travel*
585   On th'orisonte° as in that latitude.   *horizon*
Night with his mantel that is derk° and rude°   *dark / rough*
Gan oversprede° the hemysperie°
     aboute,   *to spread over / hemisphere*
For which departed is this lusty route°   *energetic crowd*
Fro Januarie with thank on every syde.
590   Hoom to hir hous° lustily they ryde,   *their houses*
Whereas they doon hir thynges as hem leste,⁸
And whan they sye° hir tyme° goon to reste.   *see / their time*
Soone after that this hastif° Januarie   *impatient*
Wolde go to bedde. He wolde no lenger tarye.
595   He drynketh ypocras, clarree, and vernage⁹
Of spices hoote° t'encreessen his corage.°   *hot spices / potency*
And many a letuarie° hath he ful fyn,   *potion*
Swiche as the monk Daun Constantyn
Hath writen in his book, *De Coitu*.¹⁰
600   To eten hem alle he nas nothyng eschu,°   *by no means avoided*
And to hise privee° freendes thus seyde he,   *close*
"For Goddes love, as soone as it may be,
Lat voyden° al this hous in curteys
     wyse!"°   *empty / a courteous manner*
And they han doon right° as he wol devyse.°   *just / would have it*
605   Men drynken and the travers° drawe anon.   *curtains*
The bryde was broght abedde° as stille° as
     stoon.°   *to bed / quiet / stone*
And whan the bed was with° the preest yblessed,   *by*
Out of the chambre hath every wight hym dressed.¹¹
And Januarie hath faste° in armes take°   *firmly / taken*
610   His fresshe May, his Paradys, his make.°   *mate*

---

⁷ *ark diurne* I.e., diurnal arc: the sun has set.

⁸ *Whereas ... leste* Where they go about their affairs as they wish.

⁹ *ypocras ... vernage* I.e., hypocras, clary, and vernaccia, types of
spiced wine, thought to heat the blood, i.e., increase desire.

¹⁰ *Swiche as ... Coitu* Constantine the African, who came from
Carthage and converted to Christianity, wrote a medical treatise
entitled *About Intercourse* (*De Coitu*) which, among other things,
recommends various remedies for impotence similar to those here
consumed by January.

¹¹ *Out ... dressed* Out of the room everyone has gone.

He lulleth° hire, he kisseth hire ful ofte,   *speaks softly to*
With thilke brustles° of his berd°
    unsofte°   *those bristles | beard | rough*
Lyk to the skyn of houndfyssh° sharpe as brere.°   *dogfish | briar*
For he was shave° al newe in his manere.   *shaven*
615   He rubbeth hire aboute hir tendre face
And seyde thus: "Allas, I moot trespace°   *do wrong*
To yow, my spouse, and yow greetly offende
Er tyme come that I wil doun° descende.   *down*
But nathelees, considereth this," quod he,
620   "Ther nys no werkman what so evere he be
That may bothe werke wel and hastily.
This wol be doon at leyser,° parfitly.°   *leisure | perfectly*
It is no fors° how longe that we pleye:°   *it does not matter | play*
In trewe wedlok wedded be we tweye,
625   And blessed be the yok° that we been inne!   *yoke*
For in actes we mowe° do no synne.°   *can | sin*
A man may do no synne with his wyf
Ne hurte hymselven with his owene knyf.°   *own knife*
For we han leve to pleye us by the lawe."[1]
630   Thus laboureth he til that the day gan dawe.°   *began to dawn*
And thanne he taketh a sope in fyn clarree,[2]
And upright in his bed thanne sitteth he.
And after that he sang ful loude and cleere
And kiste his wyf and made wantowne
    cheere.°   *behaved flirtatiously*
635   He was al coltissh,° ful of ragerye°   *like a colt | lechery*
And ful of jargon° as a flekked pye.°   *chatter | spotted magpie*
The slakke skyn aboute his nekke shaketh
Whil that he sang, so chaunteth° he and craketh.° *sings | croaks*
But God wot° what that May thoughte in hir herte   *knows*
640   Whan she hym saugh up sittynge° in his
    sherte,°   *sitting up | nightshirt*
In his nyght cappe, and with his nekke lene.°   *skinny*
She preyseth nat his pleyyng° worth a bene.° *love-making | bean*
Thanne seide he thus: "My reste wol I take
Now day is come; I may no lenger wake."
645   And doun he leyde his heed and sleepe til pryme.[3]

And afterward, whan that he saugh his tyme,
Up ryseth Januarie. But fresshe May
Heeld hire chambre° unto the fourthe day,   *kept in her room*
As usage° is of wyves for the beste.   *custom*
650   For every labour somtyme moot han reste,
Or elles longe may he nat endure.
This is to seyn, no lyves creature,°   *living creature*
Be it of fyssh or bryd or beest or man.
    Now wol I speke of woful Damyan,
655   That langwissheth° for love, as ye shul here.   *languishes*
Therfore I speke to° hym in this manere: *about*
I seye, "O sely° Damyan, allas!   *foolish*
Andswere to my demaunde,° as in this
    cas:°   *question | situation*
How shaltow to thy lady, fresshe May,
660   Telle thy wo? She wole alwey seye nay.
Eek° if thou speke, she wol thy wo biwreye.° *and | betray*
God be thyn helpe; I kan no bettre seye."
    This sike° Damyan in Venus fyr°   *sick | fire*
So brenneth,° that he dyeth for desyr,   *burns*
665   For which he putte his lyf in aventure.°   *danger*
No lenger myghte he in this wise° endure,   *way*
But prively a penner° gan he borwe,[4]   *pen case*
And in a lettre wroot he al his sorwe
In manere of a compleynt or a lay[5]
670   Unto his faire, fresshe lady May.
And in a purs of sylk heng° on his sherte   *that hung*
He hath it put and leyde° it at his herte.   *laid*
    The moone, that at noon was thilke day
That Januarie hath wedded fresshe May
675   In two of Tawr,[6] was into Cancre° glyden,°   *Cancer | glided*
So longe hath Mayus in hir chambre byden°   *stayed*
As custume is unto thise noble alle.°   *for all these nobles*
A bryde shal nat eten in the halle
Til dayes foure or thre dayes atte leeste
680   Ypassed been. Thanne lat hire go to feeste.
The fourthe day compleet, fro noon to noon,
Whan that the heighe masse was ydoon

---

[1] *For ... lawe* The law permits us to enjoy ourselves. Church law, known as canon law, governed matters of sexual morality. It actually placed many restrictions on sexual activity within marriage.

[2] *And ... clarree* And then he takes a piece of bread (soaked) in fine wine.

[3] *And ... pryme* And he put his head down and slept until prime (the first of the canonical hours, around 7 a.m.).

---

[4] *But ... borwe* But secretly he borrowed a pen case (or box with writing materials). Pen cases normally belonged to scholars or clerics. Damyan is literate but does not write very often.

[5] *compleynt ... lay* Complaints and lais were types of short poems, often expressing a lover's sorrow.

[6] *two of Tawr* The second (degree) of Taurus (a sign of the zodiac).

In halle sit this Januarie and May,
As fressh as is the brighte someres day.
685 And so bifel how that this goode man
Remembred hym upon this Damyan
And seyde, "Seynte Marie, how may this be
That Damyan entendeth nat° to me?   *does not attend*
Is he ay syk? Or how may this bityde?"°   *happen*
690 His squieres, whiche that stooden ther bisyde,
Excused hym bycause of his siknesse,
Which letted hym° to doon his
     bisynesse.°   *prevented him / duty*
Noon oother cause myghte make hym tarye.
"That me forthynketh,"° quod this Januarie.   *grieves*
695 "He is a gentil° squier, by my trouthe!   *noble*
If that he deyde, it were harm and routhe.°   *pity*
He is as wys, discreet, and as secree°   *private*
As any man I woot of his degree,
And therto manly and eek servysable°   *eager to serve*
700 And for to been a thrifty° man
     right able.°   *successful / very qualified*
But after mete° as soone as evere I may   *food*
I wol myself visite hym and eek May,
To doon hym al the confort that I kan."
And for that word hym blessed every
     man,°   *every man blessed him*
705 That of his bountee° and his gentillesse°   *generosity / nobility*
He wolde so conforten in siknesse
His squier, for it was a gentil dede.
"Dame," quod this Januarie, "taak good hede.°   *heed*
At afternoon ye with youre wommen alle,
710 Whan ye han been in chambre out of this halle,
That alle ye go se this Damyan.
Dooth hym disport.° He is a gentil man.   *cheer him up*
And telleth hym that I wol hym visite
Have I nothyng but° rested me a lite.   *when I have only*
715 And spede° yow faste, for I wole abyde°   *speed / wait*
Til that ye slepe faste by my syde."
And with that word he gan to hym to calle
A squier that was marchal° of his
     halle   *marshall (master of ceremonies)*
And tolde hym certeyn thynges what he wolde.°   *wanted*
720 This fresshe May hath streight hir wey
     yholde°   *immediately taken her way*
With alle hir wommen unto Damyan.
Doun by his beddes syde sit she than,
Confortynge hym as goodly as she may.

This Damyan, whan that his tyme he
     say,°   *he saw his opportunity*
725 In secree wise° his purs and eek his bille,°   *secret way / letter*
In which that he ywriten hadde his wille,°   *desire*
Hath put into hire hand withouten moore,
Save that he siketh° wonder° depe and soore,   *sighs / wondrously*
And softely to hire right thus seyde he:
730 "Mercy, and that ye nat discovere° me,   *betray*
For I am deed if that this thyng be kyd!"°   *known*
This purs hath she inwith° hir bosom hyd°   *inside / hidden*
And wente hire wey. Ye gete namoore of me.
But unto Januarie ycomen is she,
735 That on his beddes syde sit ful softe,°   *quietly*
And taketh hire and kisseth hire ful ofte,
And leyde hym° doun to slepe, and that anon.   *lay himself*
She feyned° hire as that she moste gon°   *pretended / had to go*
Theras° ye woot that every wight moot neede,   *where*
740 And whan she of this bille hath taken heede,°   *paid attention*
She rente° it al to cloutes° atte laste,°   *tore / pieces / at the last*
And in the pryvee° softely it caste.   *privy*
     Who studieth° now but faire, fresshe May?   *considers*
Adoun by olde Januarie she lay,
745 That sleepe° til that the coughe hath hym awaked. *who sleeps*
Anon he preyde hire strepen° hire al naked: *strip*
He wolde of hire, he seyde, han som plesaunce;
He seyde hir clothes dide hym encombraunce.°   *got in his way*
And she obeyeth, be hire lief or looth.°   *whether she wished to or not*
750 But lest ye precious° folk be with me wrooth,°   *prudish / angry*
How that he wroghte,° I dar nat to yow telle,   *acted*
Or wheither that hire thoughte it Paradys or Helle.
But heere I lete hem° werken° in hir wyse   *leave them / acting*
Til evensong° rong and that they moste aryse.   *evening service*
755 Were it° by destynee or by aventure,°   *whether it were / chance*
Were it by influence° or by
     nature°   *(astrological) influence / natural cause*
Or constellacioun, that in swich estaat°   *condition*
The hevene stood that tyme fortunaat[1]
Was for to putte a bille of Venus werkes°—   *Venus's works*
760 For alle thyng hath tyme, as seyn thise clerkes°— *scholars*
To any womman for to gete hire love,
I kan nat seye. But grete God above,
That knoweth that noon act is causelees,°   *without cause*
He deme° of al, for I wole holde my pees.   *may he judge*

---

[1] *The … fortunaat*   The heavens stood in such an arrangement that
the time was fortunate, i.e., the planetary influences were favorable.

765   But sooth is this, how that this fresshe May
      Hath take° swich impressioun that day   *has taken*
      For pitee of this sike Damyan
      That from hire herte she ne dryve kan°   *cannot drive*
      The remembrance for to doon hym
          ese.°   *memory (thought) of comforting him*
770   "Certeyn," thoghte she, "whom that this thyng displese,
      I rekke noght,° for heere I hym assure   *care not*
      To love hym best of any creature,
      Though he namoore° hadde than his
          sherte."   *no more possessions*
      Lo, pitee renneth soone in gentil herte!
775   Heere may ye se how excellent franchise°   *generosity*
      In wommen is whan they hem narwe
          avyse.°   *consider things carefully*
      Som tyrant° is, as ther be many
          oon,°   *cruel woman / many a one*
      That hath an herte as hard as any stoon,
      Which wolde han lat hym storven° in the place   *die*
780   Wel° rather than han graunted hym hire
          grace,°   *much / favor*
      And hem rejoysen in hire crueel pryde[1]
      And rekke° nat to been an homycide.°   *care / murderer*
         This gentil May, fulfilled° of pitee,   *full*
      Right of hire hand a lettre made she
785   In which she graunteth hym hire verray grace.°   *true favor*
      Ther lakketh noght° oonly but day and place   *nothing*
      Wher that she myghte unto his lust
          suffise,°   *satisfy his desire*
      For it shal be right° as he wole devyse.°   *just / determine*
      And whan she saugh hir tyme,° upon a day   *opportunity*
790   To visite this Damyan gooth May,
      And sotilly° this lettre doun she threste°   *subtly / thrust*
      Under his pilwe,° rede° it if hym
          leste.°   *pillow / to read / wishes*
      She taketh hym by the hand and harde hym
          twiste°   *squeezes*
      So secrely that no wight of it wiste°   *knew*
795   And bad hym been al hool.° And forth he°
          wente   *whole / she*
      To Januarie whan that he for hym° sente.   *her*
         Up riseth Damyan the nexte morwe:
      Al passed was his siknesse and his sorwe.

      He kembeth hym.° He preyneth° hym and
          pyketh.°   *combs himself / preens / cleans*
800   He dooth al that his lady lust° and lyketh.°   *desires / likes*
      And eek to Januarie he gooth as lowe°   *meekly*
      As evere dide a dogge for the bowe.°   *bow (for hunting)*
      He is so plesant unto every man—
      For craft is al, whoso that do it kan—[2]
805   That every wight is fayn° to speke hym good,°   *glad / well of him*
      And fully in his lady grace° he stood.   *lady's favor*
      Thus lete° I Damyan aboute his nede,   *leave*
      And in my tale forth I wol procede.
         Somme clerkes° holden that felicitee   *scholars*
810   Stant° in delit, and therfore certeyn he,   *stands*
      This noble Januarie, with al his myght,
      In honeste wyse as longeth to a knyght,
      Shoope hym° to lyve ful deliciously.°   *determined / delightfully*
      His housynge,° his array as honestly°   *housing / honorably*
815   To his degree was maked as a kynges.
      Amonges othere of hise honeste thynges,
      He made a gardyn walled al with stoon.
      So fair a gardyn woot I nowher noon.[3]
      For out of doute,° I verraily suppose   *without doubt*
820   That he that wroot *The Romance of the Rose*[4]
      Ne koude of it the beautee wel devyse!
      Ne Priapus[5] ne myghte nat suffise,
      Though he be god of gardyns, for to telle
      The beautee of the gardyn and the welle°   *well*
825   That stood under a laurer° alwey grene.   *laurel tree*
      Ful ofte tyme he Pluto and his queene
      Proserpina, and al hire fairye,[6]

---

1   *And ... pryde*   And rejoice themselves in their cruel pride.

---

2   *For ... kan*   For cunning is all that matters, as whoever can practice it knows.

3   *So ... noon*   I do not know of so fair a garden anywhere.

4   *The Romance of the Rose*   Thirteenth-century French poem begun by Guillaume de Lorris and completed by Jean de Meun. In it is depicted the Garden of Love, where Cupid holds his court. Chaucer translated part of this very influential poem into English.

5   *Priapus*   Greek and Roman god of gardens. Priapus was also associated with male sexuality and fertility.

6   *Pluto ... fairye*   In Greek mythology, Pluto was the god of the underworld who abducted Proserpina and forcibly made her his queen. As a result, Proserpina's mother, Ceres, the goddess of the earth, caused the world to suffer perpetual winter until Pluto agreed to return her daughter. Since Proserpina had eaten some seeds from a pomegranate while in the underworld, however, she was forced to reside there for half the year. Her mother mourns when she is there,

Disporten hem and maken melodye
Aboute that welle, and daunced as men tolde.
830   This noble knyght, this Januarie the olde
Swich deyntee° hath in it to walke and pleye   *delight*
That he wol no wight suffren bere the keye°   *to have the key*
Save he hymself. For of the smale wyket
He baar alwey of silver of a clyket,[1]
835   With which whan that hym leste he it unshette.°   *unlocked*
And whan he wolde paye his wyf hir dette°   *marriage-debt*
In somer sesoun thider° wolde he go   *thither*
And May his wyf, and no wight but they two.
And thynges whiche that were nat doon abedde
840   He in the gardyn parfourned° hem and
       spedde°   *performed / succeeded*
And in this wyse many a murye° day   *merry*
Lyved this Januarie and fresshe May.
But worldly joye may nat alwey dure°   *endure*
To Januarie ne to no creature.
845   O sodeyn hape!° O thou Fortune instable,°   *chance / unstable*
Lyk to the scorpion so deceyvable°   *deceptive*
That flaterest with thyn heed° whan thou wolt
       stynge!°   *head / sting*
Thy tayl is deeth thurgh° thyn
       envenymynge.°   *through / poisoning*
O brotil° joye, o sweete venym queynte,°   *brittle / strange*
850   O monstre that so subtilly kanst peynte°   *paint*
Thy yiftes° under hewe of stidefastnesse   *gifts*
That thou deceyvest bothe moore and lesse!
Why hastow Januarie thus deceyved,
That haddest hym for thy ful° freend receyved?   *close*
855   And now thou hast biraft° hym bothe hise
       eyen,°   *taken from / eyes*
For sorwe of which desireth he to dyen.
       Allas, this noble Januarie free
Amydde his lust and his prosperitee
Is woxen° blynd, and that al sodeynly!   *grown*
860   He wepeth and he wayleth pitously
And therwithal the fyr of jalousie,
Lest that his wyf sholde falle in swich folye,°   *folly (i.e., adultery)*
So brente° his herte that he wolde fayn   *burned*
That som man bothe hym and hire had slayn.

865   For neither after his deeth nor in his lyf
Ne wolde he° that she were love° ne wyf   *he did not want / lover*
But evere lyve as wydwe° in clothes blake,   *widow*
Soul° as the turtle° that lost hath hire make.   *single / turtledove*
But atte laste, after a monthe or tweye,
870   His sorwe gan aswage, sooth to seye.
For whan he wiste° it may noon oother be,   *knew*
He paciently took his adversitee,°   *adversity (i.e., blindness)*
Save° out of doute° he may nat
       forgoon°   *except / without a doubt / stop*
That he nas jalous everemoore in oon,[2]
875   Which jalousye it was so outrageous
That neither in halle n'yn noon oother° hous   *nor in any other*
N'yn noon other place never the mo
He nolde suffre° hire for to ryde or go   *would not allow*
But if° that he had hond° on hire alway.   *unless / hand*
880   For which ful ofte wepeth fresshe May,
That loveth Damyan so benyngnely°   *kindly*
That she moot outher dyen° sodeynly   *either die*
Or elles she moot han hym as hir leste.°   *she wished*
She wayteth whan° hir herte wolde breste.   *expects that*
885   Upon that oother syde, Damyan
Bicomen is the sorwefulleste man
That evere was, for neither nyght ne day
Ne myghte he speke a word to fresshe May
As to his purpos of no swich mateere
890   But° if that Januarie moste it heere,   *except*
That hadde an hand upon hire everemo.
But nathelees by writyng to and fro
And privee signes° wiste° he what she mente,   *secret signs / knew*
And she knew eek the fyn° of his entente.   *aim*
895   O Januarie, what myghte it thee
       availle°   *what good would it do you*
Thogh thou myghtest se as fer° as shippes saille?   *far*
For as good is blynd deceyved be°   *to be deceived*
As to be deceyved whan a man may se.
Lo Argus,[3] which that hadde an hondred eyen,
900   For al that evere he koude poure° or pryen,°   *investigate / pry*
Yet was he blent.° And God woot, so been mo   *blinded*

---

dooming the earth to winter.

[1] *For of … clyket* For he always carried the silver key to the small wicket gate.

[2] *That … oon* Being jealous forever in one (matter).

[3] *Argus* In Greek mythology, Juno asked Argus, a shepherd with one hundred eyes, to guard her husband's mistress, Io, to prevent him from seeing her. Argus was killed by Mercury at Jove's request.

That wenen wisly that it be nat so.[1]
Passe over is an ese.[2] I sey namoore.

    This fresshe May that I spak of so yoore°   *long ago*
905 In warm wex° hath emprented the clyket°   *wax / key*
That Januarie bar° of the smale wyket,   *carried*
By which into his gardyn ofte he wente.
And Damyan, that knew al hire entente,
The cliket countrefeted pryvely.
910 Ther nys namoore° to saye but hastily   *is no more*
Som wonder by this clyket shal bityde,°   *happen*
Which ye shul heeren if ye wole abyde.

    O noble Ovyde, ful sooth° seystou,° God woot,   *truth / you say*
"What sleighte° is it, thogh it be long and hoot,°   *trick / hot*
915 That he nyl fynde it out in som manere?"
By Piramus and Tesbee may men leere,°   *learn*
Thogh they were kept ful longe streit
    overal,°   *long guarded most carefully*
They been accorded rownynge° thurgh a wal   *whispering*
Ther no wight koude han founde out swich a sleighte.°[3] *trick*
920   But now to purpose. Er that dayes eighte
Were passed er the monthe of Juyl bifille,°   *July arrived*
That Januarie hath caught so greet a wille,°   *desire*
Thurgh eggyng° of his wyf, hym for to pleye   *incitement*
In his gardyn, and no wight but they tweye,
925 That in a morwe° unto this May seith he,[4]   *on one morning*
"Rys up, my wyf, my love, my lady free!
The turtle voys° is herd, my dowve sweete;   *turtledove's voice*
The wynter is goon with his reynes weete.°   *wet rains*
Com forth now with thyne eyen columbyn;°   *dove-like*
930 How fairer been thy brestes than is wyn!
The gardyn is enclosed al aboute.
Com forth, my white spouse; out of doute
Thou hast me wounded in myn herte, o wyf!
No spot of thee ne knew I° al my lyf.   *did I know*

935 Com forth, and lat us taken som disport;
I chees° thee for my wyf and my confort."   *choose*
    Swiche olde, lewed wordes used he.
On° Damyan a signe made she   *to*
That he sholde go biforn with his cliket.
940 This Damyan thanne hath opened the wyket,
And in he stirte,° and that in swich manere   *jumps*
That no wight myghte it se neither yheere,°   *see nor hear*
And stille° he sit under a bussh anon.   *quietly*
    This Januarie, as blynd as is a stoon,
945 With Mayus° in his hand and no wight mo°   *May / no one else*
Into his fresshe gardyn is ago°   *gone*
And clapte to° the wyket sodeynly.   *slammed*
    "Now wyf," quod he, "heere nys but thou and I,
That art the creature that I best love.
950 For by that Lord that sit in Hevene above,
Levere ich hadde° to dyen on a knyf   *rather I had*
Than thee offende, trewe, deere wyf!
For Goddes sake, thenk° how I thee chees,°   *think / chose*
Noght° for no coveitise,° doutelees,   *not / greed*
955 But oonly for the love I had to thee.
And though that I be oold and may nat see
Beth° to me trewe, and I shal telle yow why: *be*
Thre thynges, certes, shal ye wynne therby.
First, love of Crist, and to youreself honour,
960 And al myn heritage,° toun° and tour.°   *property / town / tower*
I yeve it yow. Maketh chartres° as yow
    leste.°   *charters (legal documents) / desire*
This shal be doon tomorwe er sonne reste,°   *before sunset*
So wisly° God my soule brynge in° blisse.   *surely / into*
I prey yow first, in covenat° ye me kisse,   *(to seal the) covenant*
965 And though that I be jalous, wyte° me noght;   *blame*
Ye been so depe enprented° in my thoght,   *deeply imprinted*
That whan I considere youre beautee
And therwithal the unlikly elde° of me,   *unsuitable old age*
I may nat, certes, though I sholde dye
970 Forbere° to been out of youre compaignye,   *bear*
For verray° love this is withouten doute.   *true*
Now kys me, wyf, and lat us rome° aboute."   *roam*
    This fresshe May, whan she thise wordes herde,
Benyngnely° to Januarie answerde,   *kindly*
975 But first and forward she bigan to wepe.
"I have," quod she, "a soule for to kepe°   *guard*
As wel as ye, and also myn honour,
And of my wyfhod thilke tendre flour°   *that tender flower*

---

[1] *And God … so* And, God knows, so are many others who believe firmly that it is not so (i.e., that they are not being deceived).

[2] *Passe … ese* To pass over something is a comfort or is the best course (i.e., what you don't know won't hurt you).

[3] *Ovyde … sleighte* The quotation is from Roman poet Ovid's *Metamorphoses*, book 4.68, in which he tells the story of the star-crossed lovers Pyramus and Thisbe. Their families forbade them to see one another, but they could whisper through a crack in the wall between their houses.

[4] *seith he* The following speech quotes from various passages from the Song of Songs in the Bible.

Which that I have assured in youre
    hond° *given over to your control*
980 Whan that the preest to yow my body bond.° *bound*
Wherfore° I wole answere in this manere: *therefore*
By the leve° of yow, my lord so deere, *leave*
I prey to God that nevere dawe° the day *dawn*
That I ne sterve,° as foule° as womman may, *do not die / foully*
985 If evere I do unto my kyn° that shame *my relatives*
Or elles I empeyre° so my name *damage*
That I be fals. And if I do that lakke,° *offence*
Do strepe° me and put me in a sakke,° *strip / sack*
And in the nexte ryver do me drenche.° *drown*
990 I am a gentil womman and no wenche.° *peasant girl or mistress*
Why speke ye thus? But men been evere untrewe,
And wommen have repreve° of yow ay
    newe.° *reproach / continually*
Ye han noon oother contenance,° I leeve,° *behavior / believe*
But speke to us of untrust° and repreeve!" *mistrust*
995   And with that word she saugh wher Damyan
Sat in the bussh. And coughen she bigan,
And with hir fynger signes made she
That Damyan sholde clymbe upon a tree
That charged° was with fruyt. And up he wente. *laden*
000 For verraily, he knew al hire entente
And every signe that she koude make,
Wel bet° than Januarie, hir owene make,° *much better / mate*
For in a lettre she had toold hym al
Of this matere, how he werchen shal.° *what he should do*
005 And thus I lete hym sitte upon the pyrie° *pear tree*
And Januarie and May romynge myrie.° *merrily*
    Bright was the day and blew° the firmament.° *blue / sky*
Phebus[1] hath of gold hise stremes° doun ysent *beams*
To gladen every flour with his warmnesse.
010 He was that tyme in Geminis, as I gesse,° *guess*
But litel fro his declynacioun
Of Cancer, Jovis exaltacioun.[2]
And so bifel that brighte morwetyde° *morning*

That in that gardyn in the ferther syde
1015 Pluto, that is kyng of Fairye,[3]
And many a lady in his compaignye,
Folwynge his wyf, the queene Proserpyne,
Ech after oother, right as a lyne,° *line*
Whil that she gadered° floures in the mede.° *gathered / meadow*
1020 In Claudyan[4] ye may the stories rede.
And in his grisly carte° he hire sette,° *gruesome chariot / placed*
This kyng of Fairye, thanne adoun hym sette
Upon a bench of turves fressh and grene.[5]
And right anon thus seyde he to his queene:
1025   "My wyf," quod he, "ther may no wight seye nay.° *deny*
Th'experience so preveth° every day *proves*
The tresons whiche that wommen doon to man.
Ten hondred thousand tellen I kan
Notable of youre untrouthe and brotilnesse.° *unreliability*
1030 O Salomon wys and richest of richesse,
Fulfild of sapience° and of worldly glorie, *full of wisdom*
Ful worthy been thy wordes to memorie° *to be remembered*
To every wight that wit and reson kan.° *who has wit and reason*
Thus preiseth he yet the bountee° of man: *goodness*
1035 'Amonges° a thousand men yet foond I oon, *amongst*
But of wommen alle foond I noon.'
    "Thus seith the kyng that knoweth youre wikkednesse.
And Jesus *filius* Syrak,[6] as I gesse,
Ne speketh of yow but seelde° reverence. *seldom*
1040 A wyldefyr[7] and corrupt pestilence° *plague*
So falle upon youre bodyes yet tonyght!
Ne se ye nat° this honurable knyght, *do you not see*
Bycause, allas, that he is blynd and old,
His owene man shal make hym cokewold?
1045 Lo, heere he sit, the lechour, in the tree!
Now wol I graunten° of my magestee *grant*
Unto this olde, blynde, worthy knyght
That he shal have ayeyn hise eyen syght° *eyesight*

---

[1] *Phebus* I.e., Phoebus, another name for Apollo, god of the sun in classical mythology.

[2] *He was ... exaltacioun* The sun (Phoebus) is in the sign of Gemini (often represented in the Middle Ages by a couple embracing). The sun has almost entered its maximum northern declination and will reach it a few days later when it moves into the astrological sign of Cancer. Cancer is the "exaltation" of Jupiter, i.e., the astrological sign in which he was considered to be most powerful.

[3] *Pluto ... Fairye* Pluto, also known as Hades, the god of the underworld in Greek mythology, is here made the king of the Celtic otherworld.

[4] *Claudyan* I.e., Roman author Claudian (c. 400 CE). His *Rape of Proserpina* recounts the story of Pluto and his queen.

[5] *Upon ... grene* Medieval gardens often contained turf benches made by piling up earth and then growing grass on it.

[6] *Jesus filius Syrak* Jesus, son of Sirach (not Jesus Christ) is the author of the apocryphal or deuterocanonical Book of Ecclesiasticus.

[7] *wyldefyr* I.e., wildfire, or erysipelas, a painful skin disease.

Whan that his wyf wold doon hym vileynye.
1050 Thanne shal he knowen al hire harlotrye,
Bothe in repreve of hire and othere mo."
    "Ye shal?" quod Proserpyne, "wol° ye so?   will
Now by my moodres sires soule[1] I swere
That I shal yeven° hire suffisant answere   give
1055 And alle wommen after for hir sake,
That though they be in any gilt ytake,°   taken
With face boold they shulle hemself excuse
And bere hem doun° that wolden hem accuse!   bear them down
For lakke of answere noon of hem shal dyen,°   die
1060 Al hadde man seyn a thyng with bothe hise eyen![2]
Yit shul° we wommen visage it hardily° yet shall / outface it boldly
And wepe and swere and chide° it subtilly,   accuse
So that ye men shul been as lewed° as gees.°   ignorant / geese
    What rekketh me° of youre auctoritees?   what do I care
1065 I woot wel that this Jew, this Salomon,
Foond of us wommen fooles many oon.[3]
But though that he ne foond no good womman,
Yet that ther founde many another man
Wommen ful trewe, ful goode and vertuous.
1070 Witnesse on hem that dwelle in Cristes hous:[4]
With martirdom they preved° hire
    constance.°   proved / their constancy
The Romayn geestes° eek maken
    remembrance°   Roman stories / also record
Of many a verray, trewe wyf also.
But sire, ne be nat wrooth° albeit so,   angry
1075 Though that he seyde he foond no good womman:
I prey yow, take the sentence° of the man.   meaning
He mente thus: that in sovereyn bontee°   supreme goodness
Nis noon but God, that sit in Trinitee.
    Ey,° for verray God, that nys but oon.   ah
1080 What make ye so muche of Salomon?
What though he made a temple, Goddes hous?
What though he were riche and glorious?
So made he eek a temple of false goddis.
How myghte he do a thyng that moore

forbode° is?   more forbidden
1085 Pardee,° as faire as ye his name emplastre,[5]   by God
He was a lecchour and an ydolastre!°   idolater
And in his elde° he verray God forsook.   old age
And if God ne hadde, as seith the book,
Yspared hym for his fadres sake, he sholde
1090 Have lost his regne rather than he wolde.[6]
I sette right noght° of al the vileynye,   consider nothing
That ye of wommen write, a boterflye!°   not a butterfly
I am a womman. Nedes moot I° speke   I must needs
Or elles swelle til myn herte breke.
1095 For sithen he seyde that we been jangleresses,° chatterboxes
As evere hool I moote brouke my tresses,[7]
I shal nat spare for no curteisye
To speke hym harm that wolde us vileynye!"°   do harm to us
    "Dame," quod this Pluto, "be no lenger wrooth!
1100 I yeve° it up. But sith I swoor myn ooth,   give
That I wolde graunten hym his sighte ageyn,
My word shal stonde.° I warne yow certeyn   stand
I am a kyng. It sit me noght° to lye!"   would not be fitting for me
    "And I," quod she, "a queene of Fairye.
1105 Hir answere shal she have, I undertake.
Lat us namoore wordes heerof make.
For sothe, I wol no lenger yow contrarie."°   disagree with you
    Now lat us turne agayn to Januarie,
That in the gardyn with his faire May
1110 Syngeth ful murier° than the papejay,° much more merrily / parrot
"Yow love I best and shal and oother noon."°   none other
So longe aboute the aleyes° is he goon,°   paths / he walked
Til he was come agayns° thilke pyrie,° upon / that same pear tree
Whereas this Damyan sitteth ful myrie
1115 An heigh° among the fresshe leves grene.   on high
    This fresshe May that is so bright and sheene°   shining
Gan for to syke° and seyde, "Allas my syde!°   sigh / side
Now sire," quod she, "for aught that may bityde,
I moste han of the peres° that I see,   pears
1120 Or I moot dye, so soore longeth me°   I long
To eten of the smale peres grene!

---

[1] *moodres sires soule* Mother's father's soul. Proserpina was the daughter of Ceres, whose father Saturn was known for his wisdom but also for his destructive power.

[2] *Al ... eyen* Although a man had seen a thing with both of his eyes.

[3] *Foond ... oon* Found many a one of us women to be fools.

[4] *hem that ... hous* I.e., martyrs in Heaven.

[5] *emplastre* Apply a medicinal plaster over a wound, hence to plaster over or gloss over.

[6] *if God ... wolde* If God had not spared him for his father's sake, as the Bible says, he would have lost his kingdom sooner than he wished. See 1 Kings 11.12–13.

[7] *As ... tresses* As ever I enjoy my braids, i.e., as long as I am a woman.

Help for hir love that is of Hevene queene![1]
I telle yow wel, a womman in my plit[2]
May han to fruyt° so greet an appetit   *have for fruit*
1125 That she may dyen but° she of it have!"   *unless*
    "Allas," quod he, "that I ne had° heer a
    knave°   *if only I had / servant*
That koude clymbe! Allas! Allas," quod he,
"That I am blynd!" "Ye sire, no fors,"° quod   *it does not matter*
    she.
"But wolde ye vouchesauf° for Goddes sake   *grant (or deign)*
1130 The pyrie inwith youre armes for to take[3]—
For wel I woot that ye mystruste me—
Thanne sholde I clymbe wel ynogh," quod she,
"So° I my foot myghte sette upon youre bak."   *if*
    "Certes," quod he, "theron shal be no lak,
1135 Mighte I yow helpen with myn herte blood."
He stoupeth doun, and on his bak she stood
And caughte hire° by a twiste,° and up she
    gooth—   *raised herself / branch*
    Ladyes, I prey yow that ye be nat wroth:
I kan nat glose,° I am a rude° man—   *speak delicately / rough*
1140 And sodeynly anon this Damyan
Gan pullen up the smok,° and in he
    throng.°   *undergarment / thrust*
    And whan that Pluto saugh this grete wrong,
To Januarie he gaf agayn° his sighte   *gave back*
And made hym se as wel as evere he myghte.
1145 And whan that he hadde caught° his sighte agayn,   *gained*
Ne was ther nevere man of thyng so fayn,°   *eager*
But on his wyf his thoght was everemo.
Up to the tree he caste hise eyen two
And saugh that Damyan his wyf had dressed°   *treated*
1150 In swich manere it may nat been expressed
But if I wolde speke uncurteisly.
And up he yaf a roryng and a cry
As dooth the mooder whan the child shal dye.
"Out! Helpe! Allas! Harrow!"[4] he gan to crye.
1155 O stronge lady stoore,° what dostow?"°   *bold / what are you doing*

And she answerde, "Sire, what eyleth° yow?   *ails*
Have pacience and resoun in youre mynde.
I have yow holpe on° bothe youre eyen blynde.   *helped you with*
Up° peril of my soule, I shal nat lyen:°   *on peril / lie*
1160 As me was taught,° to heele with youre
    eyen°   *was taught to me / heal your eyes*
Was nothyng bet° to make yow to see   *better*
Than strugle° with a man upon a tree.   *struggle*
God woot, I dide it in ful good entente!"
    "Strugle?" quod he. "Ye, algate in it wente![5]
1165 God yeve yow bothe on shames deth° to dyen!   *a shameful death*
He swyved thee!° I saugh it with myne eyen!   *had sex with you*
And elles be I hanged by the hals!"°   *neck*
    "Thanne is," quod she, "my medicyne fals.°   *false*
For certeinly, if that ye myghte se,
1170 Ye wolde nat seyn thise wordes unto me.
Ye han som glymsyng° and no parfit° sighte."   *glimpsing / perfect*
    "I se," quod he, "as wel as evere I myghte,
Thonked be God, with bothe myne eyen two.
And by my trouthe me thoughte he dide thee so!"
1175   "Ye maze,° maze, goode sire," quod she.   *you are dazed*
"This thank° have I, for I have maad yow see.   *this is all the thanks*
Allas," quod she, "that evere I was so kynde!"
    "Now dame," quod he, "lat al passe out of mynde.
Com doun, my lief,° and if I have myssayd,°   *dear / said wrong*
1180 God helpe me so as I am yvele apayd.°   *evilly paid back*
But by my fader soule, I wende° han seyn   *thought to*
How that this Damyan hadde by thee leyn°   *lain*
And that thy smok hadde leyn upon his brest."
    "Ye sire," quod she, "ye may wene as yow
    lest.°   *think as you wish*
1185 But, sire, as man that waketh out of his sleepe,
He may nat sodeynly wel taken keepe
Upon a thyng ne seen° it parfitly   *see*
Til that he be adawed verraily,°   *truly awakened*
Right so a man that longe hath blynd ybe°   *been*
1190 Ne may nat sodeynly so wel yse°   *see*
First whan his sighte is newe come ageyn
As he that hath a day or two yseyn.
Til that youre sighte ysatled be awhile°   *is settled for awhile*
Ther may ful many a sighte yow bigile.°   *trick*
1195 Beth war,° I prey yow for by Hevene kyng   *beware*
Ful many a man weneth° to seen a thyng,   *thinks*
And it is al another° than it semeth.   *different*

---

[1] *for ... queene* For the love of Her that is Heaven's Queen (i.e., the Virgin Mary).

[2] *plit* Plight. May obliquely refers to her pregnancy.

[3] *The ... take* To encircle the pear tree with your arms.

[4] *Out! Helpe! Allas! Harrow!* Cries to raise help when one is in trouble.

---

[5] *Ye ... wente* Yes, it went all the way in!

He that mysconceyveth,° he mysdemeth."°*misperceives / misjudges*

And with that word she leepe° doun fro the tree.   *leapt*

1200   This Januarie, who is glad but he?

He kisseth hire and clippeth° hire ful ofte,   *hugs*

And on hire wombe° he stroketh hire ful softe,   *belly*

And to his palays° hoom° he hath hire   lad.°   *palace / home / has led her*

Now goode men, I pray yow be glad;

1205 Thus endeth heere my tale of Januarie.

God blesse us and his mooder, Seinte Marie!

Heere is ended the Marchantes Tale of Januarie

━━━━━━━

The Franklin's Prologue and Tale

In the full *Canterbury Tales*, this tale is preceded by *The Squire's Tale*, which the Squire never manages to finish. The Franklin, a wealthy landowner with a reputation for generous hospitality, interrupts the Squire when he has reached line 672 of a tale that promises to go on for several thousand lines more, complimenting him on his eloquence (although in a rather back-handed way) and saying that he wishes his own son might learn "gentilesse" from the Squire. This prologue introduces what is clearly, for the Franklin, the main theme of his own tale. For him, the point of the tale lies in the final question: who was "most fre," that is, most liberal or magnanimous, these being qualities of a gentleman. Many readers, however, have found the behavior of all three men, the squire, the knight, and the magician, far from ideal, and that of Dorigen, who invokes at length noble women who have committed suicide rather than face dishonor and who postpones her own death indefinitely, far from heroic.

While the nature of gentilesse is the central concern of the Franklin, his tale also contributes to another major theme in *The Canterbury Tales*, the value of marriage and the nature and status of women. Earlier critics tended to see the balanced marriage of Dorigen and the knight Arveragus as the ideal resolution of a debate that pitted the Wife of Bath and her spirited defense of women's sovereignty against the views of the Merchant and the Clerk, but the resolution is not entirely assured. Dorigen's questioning of divine Providence suggests she may have had too much freedom by medieval standards' while her ultimate dependence on her husband to solve her dilemma suggests that by the end of the tale she has lost it.

The Franklin says that his tale is a Breton *lai*, a short romance of the kind told by Celtic storytellers or minstrels from Wales or Brittany. In fact, the tale comes from Boccaccio, who told it twice, once in his *Decameron* and once in the *Filocolo*. Chaucer does not always acknowledge his sources (and the modern notion of plagiarism was not part of a medieval textual culture in which works were adapted and translated freely), but in this case the misrepresentation may be significant. Casting the tale in a distant Celtic past is an important part of Chaucer's artistic strategy. Like many folktales, *The Franklin's Tale* revolves around a rash promise, in this case Dorigen's promise to sleep with the squire Aurelius if he can remove the black rocks along the coast. Arveragus decides that Dorigen must keep her promise, her truth, because it is "the highest thing that man may keep" (l. 807), and the conflict between truth and illusion is one of the tale's central concerns.

Opening page of the *Franklin's Tale*, Ellesmere manuscript.
(This item is reproduced by permission of the *Huntington Library*, San Marino, California. EL26C9F72r.)

THE FRANKLIN'S PROLOGUE

HEERE FOLWEN THE WORDES OF THE FRANKELEYN TO THE SQUIER AND THE WORDES OF THE HOOST TO THE FRANKELEYN

"In feith, Squier, thow hast thee wel yquit°   *done well*
    And gentilly.° I preise° wel thy wit,"   *nobly / praise*
Quod° the Frankeleyn, "considerynge° thy
    yowthe.°   *said / considering / youth*
So feelyngly° thou spekest,° sire, I allowe
    the,°   *sensitively / speak / grant you*
5   As to my doom,° ther is noon° that is heere   *judgment / no one*
Of eloquence that shal be thy peere°   *be your equal*
If that thou lyve.° God yeve° thee good chaunce   *live / give*
And in vertu° sende thee continuaunce!°   *virtue / continuing*
For of thy speche I have greet deyntee.°   *delight*
10 I have a sone,° and by the Trinitee,°   *son / Trinity*
I hadde levere° than twenty pound worth lond,[1]   *rather*
Though it right now were fallen in my hond,°   *into my hand*
He were a man of swich discrecioun°   *such discretion*
As that ye been.° Fy° on possessioun,°   *are / fie / possession*
15 But if° a man be vertuous withal!°   *unless / as well*
I have my sone snybbed,° and yet shal,   *scolded*
For he to vertu listeth nat entende,[2]
But for to pleye° at dees° and to despende°   *play / dice / spend*
And lese° al° that he hath is his usage.°   *lose / all / custom*
20 And he hath levere° talken with a page   *would rather / boy servant*
Than to comune° with any gentil wight,°   *talk / noble person*
Where he myghte lerne gentillesse[3] aright."°   *properly*
    "Straw for youre gentillesse!" quod oure Hoost.
    "What, Frankeleyn, pardee° sire, wel thou
    woost°   *by God / well you know*
25 That ech° of yow° moot° tellen atte
    leste°   *each / you / must / at least*
A tale or two or breken his biheste."°   *break his promise*

"That knowe I wel, sire," quod the Frankeleyn.
"I prey yow, haveth me nat in desdeyn°   *do not disdain me*
Though to this man I speke a word or two."
30 "Telle on thy tale withouten wordes
    mo."°   *without more words*
"Gladly, sire Hoost," quod he. "I wole obeye°   *obey*
Unto youre wyl.° Now herkneth° what I seye.   *will / listen to*
I wol yow nat contrarien in no wyse,[4]
As fer° as that my wittes° wol suffyse.°   *far / wits / suffice*
35 I prey to God that it may plesen yow;°   *please you*
Thanne woot° I wel that it is good ynow."°   *know / enough*

EXPLICIT[5]

THE PROLOGUE OF THE FRANKELEYNS TALE

Thise olde, gentil Britouns[6] in hir dayes°   *their days*
    Of diverse° aventures maden layes,°   *various / made songs*
Rymeyed° in hir firste° Briton tonge,°   *rhymed / original / language*
40 Whiche layes with hir° instrumentz they songe   *their*
Or elles redden hem° for hir plesaunce.   *read them*
And oon of hem° have I in
    remembraunce,°   *one of them / memory*
Which I shal seyn° with good wyl° as I kan.   *say / will*
    But sires, bycause I am a burel° man,   *uneducated*
45 At my bigynnyng first I yow biseche,
Have me excused of my rude° speche.   *rough*
I lerned nevere rethorik,° certeyn.°   *rhetoric / certainly*
Thyng that I speke,° it moot° be bare and
    pleyn.°   *what I speak / must / plain*
I sleepe nevere on the Mount of Pernaso,[7]
50 Ne lerned° Marcus Tullius Scithero.[8]   *nor did I learn*

---

1   *twenty ... lond* Twenty pounds worth of land is that which provides an annual income of twenty pounds—a considerable sum in the late fourteenth century, equal to half a year's income for a well-off knight.

2   *For ... entende* Because he does not want (listeth nat) to pay attention to virtue.

3   *gentillesse* The quality that makes someone a gentleman or woman. In the Middle Ages it normally implied distinguished birth as well as refined manners and moral virtue.

4   *I ... wyse* I will not contradict you in any way.

5   *Explicit* Latin: here it ends.

6   *Britouns* Bretons, who came from Brittany, the northwest corner of modern-day France. They were a Celtic people, many of whom had, almost a thousand years before Chaucer's time, fled from Britain to escape the Anglo-Saxon invaders and joined the earlier Celtic inhabitants.

7   *Mount of Pernaso* Mount Parnassus, the home of the Muses (the goddesses of learning and the arts).

8   *Marcus Tullius Scithero* Cicero (106–43 BCE), the famous Roman orator who wrote about rhetoric, among other subjects.

Colours[1] ne° knowe I none, withouten
    drede,°   *nor | without doubt*
But swiche° colours as growen in the mede,°   *such | meadow*
Or elles° swiche as men dye or peynte.°   *else | paint*
Colours of rethoryk been to queynte!°   *are too unusual*
55 My spirit feeleth noght° of swich
    mateere.°   *understands nothing | matter*
But if yow list,° my tale shul ye heere.°   *desire | hear*

THE FRANKLIN'S TALE

HEERE BIGYNNETH THE FRANKELEYNS TALE

In Armorik,° that called is Britayne,°   *Armorica | Brittany*
Ther was a knyght that loved and dide his
    payne°   *took pains*
To serve a lady in his beste wise,°   *manner*
60 And many a labour, many a greet emprise°   *undertaking*
He for his lady wroghte° er° she were wonne.°   *did | before | won*
For she was oon° the faireste under sonne°   *one of | sun*
And eek° therto comen of so heigh kynrede°   *also | high lineage*
That wel unnethes° dorste° this knyght for
    drede°   *scarcely | dared | fear*
65 Telle hire° his wo,° his peyne,° and his distresse.   *her | woe | pain*
But atte laste, she for his worthynesse°   *worth*
And namely° for his meke obeysaunce°   *especially | meek obedience*
Hath swich a pitee° caught of his penaunce°   *pity | penance*
That pryvely° she fil of his
    accord°   *secretly | fell in agreement with him*
70 To take hym for hir housbonde and hir lord—
Of swich lordshipe as men han° over hir
    wyves.°   *have | their wives*
And for to lede° the moore in blisse hir lyves,   *lead*
Of his free wyl he swoor hire° as a knyght   *swore to her*
That nevere in al his lyf he, day ne nyght,
75 Ne sholde° upon hym take no maistrie°   *he would not | control*
Agayn hir wyl° ne kithe hire° jalousie   *against her will | show her*
But hire obeye and folwe° hir wyl in al   *follow*

As any lovere to his lady shal,
Save° that the name of soveraynetee,   *except*
80 That wolde he have for shame of his
    degree.°   *lest it shame his rank*
She thanked hym and with ful greet
    humblesse°   *great humility*
She seyde, "Sire, sith° of youre gentillesse   *since*
Ye profre° me to have so large a reyne,°   *offer | rein*
Ne wolde nevere God bitwixe us tweyne,
85 As in my gilt, were outher werre or stryf.[2]
Sire, I wol be youre humble, trewe wyf:
Have heer my trouthe° til that myn herte breste."°   *pledge | burst*
Thus been° they bothe in quiete and in reste.   *are*
For o thyng,° sires, saufly° dar I seye,   *one thing | safely*
90 That freendes everych oother° moot obeye   *each other*
If they wol longe holden compaignye.°   *remain in company*
Love wol nat been constreyned by maistrye.°   *control*
Whan maistrie comth, the god of love anon°   *immediately*
Beteth hise wynges,° and, farewel, he is gon!   *beats his wings*
95 Love is a thing—as any spirit—free.
Wommen of kynde° desiren libertee   *by nature*
And nat to been constreyned as a thral.°   *slave*
And so doon° men, if I sooth° seyen shal.   *do | truth*
Looke, who that is moost pacient° in love,   *patient*
100 He is at his avantage° al above.   *advantage*
Pacience is an heigh° vertu, certeyn,   *great*
For it venquysseth,° as thise clerkes°   *vanquishes | learned men*
    seyn,
Thynges that rigour° sholde° nevere
    atteyne.°   *harshnes | could | achieve*
For every word men may nat chide° or pleyne.°   *nag | complain*
105 Lerneth to suffre° or elles,° so moot I goon,[3]   *endure | else*
Ye shul it lerne wherso° ye wole or noon!°   *whether | not*
For in this world, certein, ther no wight° is   *person*
That he ne dooth or seith° som tyme°
    amys;   *neither does or says | sometimes*
Ire, siknesse,° or constellacioun,[4]   *sickness*

---

[1] *Colours* The colors of rhetoric were the stylistic devices and figures of speech recommended by rhetoricians for use in effective public speaking and writing. Despite the Franklin's protestation that he knows no rhetoric, his tale has several ornate passages that make heavy use of these rhetorical colors.

[2] *Ne … stryf* May God never wish that there were (i.e., may there never be) any quarrel or strife between us two through any fault of mine.

[3] *So moot I gon* As I might go, an idiomatic expression meaning roughly "By my word" or "I assure you."

[4] *constellacioun* By the influence of the stars and planets.

110 Wyn,° wo, or chaungynge° of complexioun[1]   *wine / changing*
Causeth ful ofte to doon amys or speken.°   *do or speak wrong*
On every wrong a man may nat be wreken.°   *avenged*
After the tyme moste be temperaunce[2]
To every wight that kan on governaunce.°   *knows about governing*

115 And therfore hath this wise, worthy knyght,
To lyve in ese,° suffrance hire
    bihight,°   *ease / promised her (his) patience*
And she to hym ful wisly gan to swere°   *swore*
That nevere sholde ther be defaute° in here.°   *fault / her*
    Heere may men seen° an humble, wys accord.   *see*

120 Thus hath she take° hir servant and hir lord—   *has she taken*
Servant in love and lord in mariage.
Thanne° was he bothe in lordshipe and servage.°   *then / service*
Servage? Nay, but in lordshipe above,
Sith he hath bothe his lady and his love—

125 His lady, certes, and his wyf also,
The which that lawe of love acordeth to.°   *agrees to*
And whan he was in this prosperitee,°   *prosperity*
Hoom° with his wyf he gooth° to his
    contree,°   *home / goes / country*
Nat fer fro° Pedmark,[3] ther° his dwellyng
    was,   *not far from / where*

130 Whereas° he lyveth in blisse and in solas.°   *where / comfort*
    Who koude telle, but he hadde wedded
    be,°   *he who had married*
The joye, the ese,° and the prosperitee   *ease*
That is bitwixe° an housbonde and his wyf?   *between*
A yeer and moore lasted this blisful lyf,

135 Til that the knyght of which I speke of thus,
That of Kayrrud[4] was cleped° Arveragus,   *called*
Shoope hym° to goon and dwelle a yeer or
    tweyne°   *prepared / two*
In Engelond, that cleped° was eek° Briteyne,   *called / also*
To seke in armes worshipe° and honour.   *knightly reputation*

140 For al his lust° he sette in swich labour—   *pleasure*
And dwelled there two yeer. The book seith thus.

Now wol I stynten° of the Arveragus,   *cease speaking*
And speken I wole of Dorigene his wyf,
That loveth hire housbonde as hire hertes lyf.

145 For his absence wepeth she and siketh,°   *sighs*
As doon° thise noble wyves whan hem
    liketh.°   *do / when they like*
She moorneth, waketh, wayleth, fasteth, pleyneth![5]
Desir of his presence hire so destreyneth,°   *afflicts*
That al this wyde world she sette at noght.°   *set at nothing*

150 Hire freendes,° whiche that knewe hir hevy
    thoght,°   *friends / sad thoughts*
Conforten hire in al that ever they may.
They prechen hire.° They telle hire nyght and day   *preach to her*
That causelees° she sleeth° hirself, allas!   *without cause / kills*
And every confort possible in this cas°   *case*

155 They doon to hire° with al hire bisynesse,°   *her / their efforts*
Al for to make hire leve° hire hevynesse.°   *leave / sadness*
    By proces,° as ye knowen everichoon,°   *gradually / everyone*
Men may so longe graven° in a stoon°   *engrave / stone*
Til som figure° therinne emprented° be.   *image / engraved*

160 So longe han° they conforted hire, til she   *have*
Receyved hath by hope and by resoun°   *reason*
The emprentyng° of hire consolacioun,   *imprinting*
Thurgh which hir grete sorwe gan aswage.°   *began to lessen*
She may nat alwey duren° in swich rage.°   *endure / passion*

165   And eek Arveragus in al this care
Hath sent hire lettres hoom of his welfare,
And that he wol come hastily agayn,
Or elles hadde this sorwe hir herte slayn.
    Hire freendes sawe hir sorwe gan to slake°   *lessen*

170 And preyde° hire on knees, for Goddes sake   *asked*
To come and romen hire° in compaignye   *roam about*
Awey to dryve hire derke fantasye.°   *dark imaginings*
And finally she graunted that requeste,
For wel she saugh° that it was for the beste.   *saw*

175   Now stood hire castel° faste° by the see,°   *castle / close / sea*
And often with hire freendes walketh shee
Hire to disporte° upon the bank an
    heigh,°   *to enjoy herself / on high*
Whereas° she many a shipe and barge seigh°   *where / sees*
Seillynge hir cours, whereas hem liste go.[6]

180 But thanne was that a parcel° of hire wo,°   *part / her woe*

---

[1] *complexioun* Temperament. Medieval medical theory maintained that what we now call "personality" was a function of the balance in the body of the four bodily fluids known as humors.

[2] *After … temperaunce* Moderation must be suited to the time or occasion.

[3] *Pedmark* Penmarch, a town in Brittany.

[4] *Kayrrud* In modern Brittany there are several towns called Kerru (from the Celtic name for red fort), but none is near Penmarch.

[5] *She … pleyneth* She mourns, lies sleepless, wails, fasts, complains.

[6] *Seillynge … go* Sailing their course, where they wished to go.

For to hirself ful ofte "Allas!" seith she.
"Is ther no shipe of so manye as I se
Wol bryngen hom° my lord? Thanne were myn herte   *bring home*
Al warisshed° of hise bittre peynes smerte!"°   *cured / the hurt of its bitter pains*

185   Another tyme ther wolde she sitte and thynke
And caste hir eyen dounward fro the brynke.°   *from the brink*
But whan she saugh the grisly rokkes blake,°   *horrible black rocks*
For verray feere° so wolde hir herte quake   *true fear*
That on hire feet she myghte hire noght° sustene.°   *not / keep*
190 Thanne wolde she sitte adoun° upon the grene°   *sit down / green*
And pitously into the see° biholde°   *sea / gaze*
And seyn right thus with sorweful sikes colde,[1]
   "Eterne° God, that thurgh° thy purveiaunce°   *eternal / through / foresight*
Ledest° the world by certein governaunce,   *lead*
195 In ydel,° as men seyn, ye nothyng make.   *vain*
But, Lord, thise grisly, feendly° rokkes blake   *fiendish*
That semen° rather a foul confusioun   *seem*
Of werk than any fair creacioun
Of swich a parfit,° wys° God and a stable,°   *perfect / wise / unchanging*
200 Why han ye wroght° this werk unresonable?°   *made / irrational work*
For by this werk south, north, ne° west, ne eest,   *nor*
Ther nys yfostred° man ne bryd ne beest.   *is not helped*
It dooth no good, to my wit,° but anoyeth.°   *understanding / harms*
Se ye nat, Lord, how mankynde it destroyeth?
205 An hundred thousand bodyes° of mankynde   *bodies*
Han rokkes slayn, al° be they nat in mynde,°   *although / remembered*
Which mankynde is so fair part of thy werk,
That thou it madest lyk to thyn owene merk.°   *image*
Thanne semed it ye hadde a greet chiertee°   *love*
210 Toward mankynde. But how thanne may it bee
That ye swiche meenes° make it to destroyen—   *means*
Whiche meenes do no good but evere anoyen?°   *harm*
I woot wel clerkes wol seyn as hem leste[2]
By argumentz that al is for the beste,
215 Though I kan the causes nat yknowe.
But thilke God that made wynd to blowe,

As kepe my lord! This my conclusioun.[3]
To clerkes° lete° I al this disputisoun.°   *theologians / leave / debate*
But wolde God that alle thise rokkes blake
220 Were sonken into Helle for his[4] sake!
Thise rokkes sleen° myn herte for the feere!"°   *kill / fear*
Thus wolde she seyn with many a pitous teere.°   *pitiful tear*
   Hire freendes sawe that it was no disport°   *comfort*
To romen by the see, but disconfort,°   *distress*
225 And shopen° for to pleyen° somwher elles.   *arranged / play*
They leden hire by ryveres° and by welles°   *rivers / springs*
And eek in othere places delitables.°   *delightful*
They dauncen, and they pleyen at ches° and tables.°   *chess / backgammon*
So on a day, right in the morwetyde,°   *morning*
230 Unto a gardyn that was ther bisyde,°   *nearby*
In which that they hadde maad hir ordinaunce°   *their arrangements*
Of vitaille° and of oother purveiaunce,°   *food / other provisions*
They goon° and pleye hem° al the longe day.   *go / enjoy themselves*
And this was in the sixte morwe° of May—   *sixth morning*
235 Which May hadde peynted with his softe shoures°   *showers*
This gardyn ful of leves° and of floures,   *leaves*
And craft of mannes hand so curiously°   *cleverly*
Arrayed° hadde this gardyn trewely,°   *adorned / truly*
That nevere was ther gardyn of swich prys°   *value*
240 But if it were the verray Paradys.°   *Paradise itself*
The odour of floures and the fresshe sighte
Wolde han maked° any herte lighte   *have made*
That evere was born, but if to greet siknesse°   *too great sickness*
Or to greet sorwe° helde it in distresse,   *too great sorrow*
245 So ful it was of beautee with plesaunce.°   *pleasure*
At after dyner° gonne° they to daunce   *dinner / began*
And synge also—save° Dorigen allone,   *except*
Which° made alwey hir compleint °and hir moone.°   *who / lament / moan*
For she ne saugh° hym on the daunce go   *saw*
250 That was hir housbonde and hir love also.
But nathelees, she moste a tyme abyde°   *wait for a time*

---

[1] *And ... colde* And say just like this with sorrowful, cold sighs.

[2] *I ... leste* I know well that theologians will say as they wish.

[3] *But ... conclusioun* (May) that same God that caused the wind to blow take care of my lord. That is my conclusion. (Dorigen closes her discussion of the theological question of God's foreknowledge with the word "conclusion," the formal term for the end of a scholastic argument.)

[4] *his* Refers here to her husband, Arveragus, rather than to God.

And with good hope lete hir sorwe slyde.° — *go away*
   Upon this daunce, amonges othere men,
Daunced a squier biforn° Dorigen — *before*
255 That fressher was and jolyer of array,° — *more finely dressed*
As to° my doom,° than is the monthe of — *according to / judgment*
   May.
He syngeth, daunceth passynge° any man — *surpassing*
That is or was sith that the world bigan.
Therwith° he was, if men sholde hym
   discryve,° — *moreover / describe*
260 Oon of the beste faryinge° man onlyve°— — *behaving / alive*
Yong, strong, right vertuous and riche and wys,
And wel biloved and holden° in greet prys.° — *held / value*
And shortly, if the sothe° I tellen shal, — *truth*
Unwityng° of this Dorigen at al — *not knowing*
265 This lusty° squier, servant to Venus,[1] — *vigorous*
Which that ycleped was° Aurelius, — *was called*
Hadde loved hire best of any creature,
Two yeer and moore, as was his aventure.° — *chance*
But nevere dorste° he tellen hire his grevaunce.° — *dared / grief*
270 Withouten coppe he drank al his penaunce.[2]
He was despeyred.° Nothyng dorste he seye, — *in despair*
Save in his songes somwhat wolde he wreye° — *reveal*
His wo, as in a general compleynyng.° — *lamenting*
He seyde he lovede and was biloved
   nothyng.° — *by no means beloved*
275 Of swich matere made he manye layes,
Songes, compleintes, roundels, virelayes,[3]
How that he dorste nat° his sorwe telle — *dared not*
But langwisseth° as a Furye[4] dooth° in Helle. — *languishes / does*
And dye he moste, he seyde, as dide Ekko
280 For Narcisus, that dorste nat telle hir wo.[5]

In oother manere than ye heere me seye
Ne dorste he nat to hire his wo biwreye,
Save that paraventure° somtyme at daunces — *perhaps*
Ther° yong folk kepen hir
   observaunces,° — *where / keep their rituals*
285 It may wel be he looked on hir face
In swich a wise as man that asketh grace.° — *for favor*
But nothyng wiste she of his entente.° — *intent*
Nathelees, it happed er they thennes wente,[6]
Bycause that he was hire neighebour
290 And was a man of worshipe and honour
And hadde yknowen hym of tyme yore,[7]
They fille in speche,[8] and forth moore and moore
Unto° this purpos drough° Aurelius, — *towards / drew*
And whan he saugh his tyme, he seyde thus:
295   "Madame," quod he, "by God that this world made,
So that° I wiste it myghte youre herte glade,° — *provided / gladden*
I wolde that day that youre Arveragus
Wente over the see that I, Aurelius,
Hadde went ther. Nevere I sholde have come agayn,
300 For wel I woot, my servyce is in vayn.° — *vain*
My gerdoun° is but brestyng° of myn herte. — *reward / breaking*
Madame, reweth° upon my peynes
   smerte,° — *have pity / sharp pains*
For with a word ye may me sleen° or save. — *kill*
Heere at youre feet God wolde that I were grave!° — *buried*
305 I ne have as now no leyser° moore to seye. — *leisure*
Have mercy, sweete, or ye wol do me deye!"° — *cause my death*
   She gan to looke upon Aurelius.
"Is this youre wyl?"° quod she. "And sey ye thus? — *will*
Nevere erst,"° quod she, "ne wiste I what ye
   mente!° — *before / meant*
310 But now, Aurelie, I knowe youre entente.
By thilke° God that yaf° me soule and lyf, — *that same / gave*
Ne shal I nevere been untrewe wyf,
In word ne° werk,° as fer° as I have wit. — *nor / deed / far*
I wol been his to whom that I am knyt.° — *knit*
315 Taak this for fynal answere as of me."

---

[1] *servant to Venus* Aurelius, like Chaucer's Squire or Palamon in *The Knight's Tale*, is devoted to courtly love (Venus was the goddess of love), which was conceived of as a form of service, demanding total loyalty and subservience to one's lady.

[2] *Withouten ... penaunce* He drank his penance without a cup. The expression may suggest he suffered intensely or even eagerly (without bothering with a cup), but its exact meaning is unclear.

[3] *Songes ... virelayes* Genres of songs popular in fourteenth-century France and England.

[4] *Furye* Winged goddess.

[5] *Ekko ... wo* In Greek mythology, Narcissus looked into a well, saw his image, and fell in love with himself. Echo, who could only repeat the last words of others, loved him but died because he did

not return her love, fading away until only her voice was left. This story is told by the Roman poet Ovid (43 BCE–18 CE) in his *Metamorphoses* 3.353–407.

[6] *Nathelees ... wente* But nevertheless, it happened before they went from there.

[7] *And ... yore* And (she) had known him for a long time.

[8] *fille in speche* Fell into speech (i.e., began to talk together).

But after that in pley thus seyde she:
"Aurelie," quod she, "by heighe God above,
Yet wolde I graunte° yow to been youre love,   *grant you to be*
Syn° I yow see so pitously complayne.   *since*
320 Looke what day¹ that endelong° Britayne   *all along the edge of*
Ye remoeve° alle the rokkes, stoon by stoon,   *remove*
That they ne lette° shipe ne boot° to goon,   *hinder | boat*
I seye whan ye han maad the coost so clene°   *clear*
Of rokkes, that ther nys no stoon ysene,°   *is no stone seen*
325 Thanne wol I love yow best of any man.
Have heer my trouthe in al that evere I kan."²
    "Is ther noon oother grace° in yow?" quod he.   *no other mercy*
    "No, by that Lord," quod she, "that maked° me!   *made*
For wel I woot that it shal never bityde!°   *happen*
330 Lat swiche folies out of youre herte slyde!³
What deyntee° sholde a man han° in his lyf   *delight | have*
For to go love another mannes wyf,
That hath hir body whan so that hym
    liketh?"°   *whenever he wishes*
    Aurelius ful ofte soore siketh.°⁴   *sighs sorely*
335 Wo was Aurelie whan that he this herde,
And with a sorweful herte he thus answerde:
    "Madame," quod he, "this were an
    inpossible!°   *impossible (thing)*
Thanne moot° I dye of sodeyn° deth horrible!"   *must | sudden*
And with that word he turned hym
    anon.°   *turned away immediately*
340 Tho° coome hir° othere freendes, many
    oon,°   *then | her | a one*
And in the aleyes° romeden° up and doun,   *alleys | roamed*
And nothyng wiste of this conclusioun°   *matter*
But sodeynly bigonne° revel newe,°   *began | new revelry*
Til that the brighte sonne loste his hewe.°   *color*
345 For th'orisonte° hath reft° the sonne his   *horizon | taken from*
    light—
This is as muche to seye as it was nyght.

And hoom they goon in joye and in solas,
Save° oonly wrecche° Aurelius, allas!   *except | wretched*
He to his hous is goon with sorweful herte.
350 He seeth he may nat fro his deeth asterte.°   *escape*
Hym semed that he felte his herte colde.⁵
Up to the Hevene hise handes he gan holde,°   *raised*
And on hise knowes bare° he sette hym doun,   *bare knees*
And in his ravyng° seyde his orisoun.°   *raving | prayer*
355 For verray wo° out of his wit° he breyde.°   *true woe | mind | went*
He nyste° what he spak. But thus he seyde   *did not know*
With pitous herte. His pleynt hath he bigonne
Unto the goddes and first unto the sonne:
    He seyde, "Appollo,⁶ god and governour
360 Of every plannte, herbe, tree, and flour
That yevest° after° thy declinacioun⁷   *gives | according to*
To ech of hem his tyme and his sesoun,
As thyn herberwe⁸ chaungeth lowe or heighe,
Lord Phebus, cast thy merciable eighe°   *merciful eye*
365 On wrecche Aurelie, which am but lorn.°   *lost*
Lo, Lord, my lady hath my deeth
    ysworn°—   *sentenced me to death*
Withoute gilt° but° thy benignytee,°   *guilt | unless | kindness*
Upon my dedly° herte have som pitee.   *deathly*
For wel I woot, Lord Phebus, if yow lest,°   *wish*
370 Ye may me helpen, save° my lady, best.   *except for*
Now vouchethsauf° that I may yow devyse°   *grant | describe*
How that I may been holpen° and in what
    wyse.°   *be helped | way*
    Youre blisful suster° Lucina⁹ the sheene,°   *sister | bright*
That of the see is chief goddesse and queene—
375 Though Neptunus¹⁰ have deitee° in the see,   *divine rule*
Yet emperisse° aboven hym is she—   *empress*
Ye knowen wel, Lord, that right° as hir desir   *just*

---

¹ *Looke what day* On whatever day.

² *Have … kan* Have here my word, as far as I am able.

³ *Lat … slide* Let such follies slide out of your heart.

⁴ *Aurelius … siketh* The awkward position of this line, which seems an interruption, may be an error, but it is found in many manuscripts, including both Ellesmere and Hengwrt. Three manuscripts whose readings are on the whole considered less reliable have lines 327 and 328 following after 334, which removes the problem.

⁵ *Hym … colde* It seemed to him that he felt his heart grow cold.

⁶ *Appollo* Phoebus Apollo is the god of the sun.

⁷ *declinacioun* Angle of a planet from the celestial equator. As Walter Skeat notes in his edition, "The change of season depends on the sun's change of position (called *herbrewe* or 'harbor' in line 1035) to be high or low in the sky."

⁸ *herberwe* Harbor (i.e., position in the sky).

⁹ *Lucina* Another name for Diana, goddess of the moon. A gloss above the name Lucina provides the more familiar "Luna."

¹⁰ *Neptunus* Neptune, god of the sea.

Is to be quyked° and lightned of°   *animated / illuminated by*
   youre fir,
For which she folweth yow ful bisily,°   *eagerly*
380 Right° so the see desireth naturelly   *just*
To folwen hire as she that is goddesse,
Bothe in the see and ryveres moore° and lesse.°   *greater / lesser*
Wherfore,° Lord Phebus, this is my requeste: *therefore*
Do this miracle or do myn herte breste°—   *make burst*
385 That now next at this opposicioun,°   *opposition (of planets)*
Which in the signe shal be of the leoun,[1]
As preieth° hire so greet a flood to brynge   *ask*
That fyve fadme° at the leeste it
   oversprynge°   *five fathoms / overwhelm*
The hyeste rokke in Armorik Briteyne,°   *Armorican Brittany*
390 And lat this flood endure yeres tweyne.°   *two years*
Thanne, certes, to my lady may I seye,
'Holdeth° youre heste.° The rokkes been°   *keep / promise / are*
   aweye!'
    Lord Phebus, dooth this miracle for me!
Preye° hire she go no faster cours° than ye.   *ask / orbit*
395 I seye, preyeth youre suster that she go
No faster cours than ye thise yeres two.
Thanne shal she been evene atte fulle alway,[2]
And spryng° flood laste bothe nyght and day.   *spring*
And but she vouchesauf in swich manere
400 To graunte me my sovereyn lady deere,
Prey hire to synken° every rok adoun°   *sink / down*
Into hir owene dirke° regioun   *dark*
Under the ground, ther° Pluto dwelleth inne,[3]   *where*
Or neveremo shal I my lady wynne.
405 Thy temple in Delphos[4] wol I barefoot seke.°   *seek*
Lord Phebus, se° the teeris° on my cheke,   *see / tears*
And of my peyne have som compassioun."

And with that word in swowne° he fil adoun,   *faint*
And longe tyme he lay forth in a traunce.
410   His brother, which that° knew of his penaunce,°   *who / grief*
Up caughte hym, and to bedde he hath hym
   broght°   *raised him up*
Dispeyred° in this torment and this thoght   *despairing*
Lete° I this woful creature lye.   *leave*
Chese he for me wheither he wol lyve or dye![5]
415 Arveragus, with heele° and greet honour,   *health*
As he that was of chivalrie the flour,°   *flower*
Is comen hoom and othere worthy men.
O blisful artow° now, thou Dorigen,   *are you*
That hast thy lusty° housbonde in thyne armes!   *vigorous*
420 The fresshe° knyght, the worthy man of armes   *lively*
That loveth thee as his owene hertes lyf,
Nothyng list hym to been ymaginatyf[6]
If any wight hadde spoke whil he was oute°   *abroad*
To hire of love. He hadde of it no doute.°   *fear*
425 He noght entendeth° to no swich mateere   *pays no attention*
But daunceth, justeth,° maketh hire good cheere.   *jousts*
And thus in joye and blisse I lete hem° dwelle,   *them*
And of the sike° Aurelius I wol yow telle.   *sick*
    In langour and in torment furyus°   *extreme*
430 Two yeer and moore lay wrecche° Aurelyus   *wretched*
Er any foot° he myghte on erthe gon.°   *step / walk*
Ne confort in this tyme hadde he noon,
Save of his brother, which that was a clerk.°   *scholar*
He knew of al this wo and al this werk,°   *effort*
435 For to noon oother creature, certeyn,
Of this matere he dorste no word seyn.°   *say*
Under his brest he baar° it moore secree°   *carried / more secretly*
Than evere dide Pamphilus for Galathee.[7]
His brest was hool° withoute° for to
   sene,°   *healthy / outside / to be seen*
440 But in his herte ay° was the arwe° kene,°   *ever / arrow / sharp*
As wel ye knowe that of a sursanure[8]
In surgerye is perilous the cure,

---

[1] *signe ... leoun* Constellation Leo (the lion), part of the zodiac. The sun's influence is strongest in this sign, which is his house or mansion. When the sun and the moon are in opposition, i.e., 180° apart, their effect on the earth is strongest and the tides highest.

[2] *evene ... always* Completely even with you. Aurelius wishes the sun and moon to align in the sky for two years, thus causing abnormally high tides.

[3] *Under ... inne* Pluto was the god of the underworld and husband of Persephone (Roman Proserpina), who was sometimes associated with the moon goddess, Luna.

[4] *Thy ... Delphos* Apollo's oracle at the temple at Delphi provided clues from the gods to help solve difficult problems.

---

[5] *Chese ... dye* Let him choose, for all I care, whether he live or die.

[6] *Nothyng ... ymaginatyf* He by no means wishes to be inquisitive.

[7] *Pamphilus ... Galathee* Main characters in the thirteenth-century Latin romance, *Pamphilus de amore* (*Pamphilus on Love*).

[8] *sursanure* Wound healed only on outside.

But men myghte touche the arwe or come therby.[1]

His brother weepe and wayled pryvely,° · *privately*

445 Til atte laste hym fil in remembraunce° · *he remembered*

That whiles he was at Orliens° in Fraunce[2] · *Orléans*

As yonge clerkes that been lykerous° · *eager*

To reden artz° that been curious,° · *sciences / exotic*

Seken in every halke° and every herne° · *nook / corner*

450 Particuler° sciences° for to lerne, · *specialized / types of knowledge*

He hym remembred that upon a day

At Orliens in studie° a book he say° · *(a hall of) study / saw*

Of magyk natureel,[3] which his felawe° · *friend*

That was that tyme a bacheler of lawe,° · *student of law*

455 Al° were he ther to lerne another craft,° · *although / subject*

Hadde prively upon his desk ylaft,° · *left*

Which book spak° muchel° of the

operaciouns° · *spoke / much / operations*

Touchynge° the eighte and twenty mansiouns[4] · *pertaining to*

That longen° to the moone and swich folye,° · *belong / such folly*

460 As in oure dayes is nat worth a flye.° · *fly*

For Hooly Chirches feith in oure bileve

Ne suffreth noon illusioun us to greve.[5]

And whan this book was in his remembraunce,

Anon for joye his herte gan to daunce,

465 And to hymself he seyde pryvely,

"My brother shal be warisshed° hastily, · *healed*

For I am siker° that ther be sciences · *certain*

By whiche men make diverse apparences,° · *different illusions*

Swiche as thise subtile° tregetours° pleye.[6] · *clever / magicians*

470 For ofte at feestes, have I wel herd seye,° · *said*

That tregetours withinne an halle large

Have maad come in a water and a barge

And in the halle rowen up and doun.

Somtyme hath semed come a grym leoun,[7]

475 And somtyme floures sprynge° as in a mede; · *spring up*

Somtyme a vyne° and grapes white and rede, · *vine*

Somtyme a castel al of lym° and stoon, · *lime*

And whan hym lyked° voyded it° · *they wished / it disappeared*

anon.

Thus semed it to every mannes° sighte. · *man's*

480 Now thanne, conclude I thus: that if I myghte

At Orliens som oold felawe° yfynde° · *old friend / find*

That hadde this moones° mansions in mynde · *moon's*

Or oother magyk natureel above,

He sholde wel make my brother han° his love. · *have*

485 For with an apparence a clerk may make

To mannes sighte that alle the rokkes blake

Of Britaigne weren yvoyded° everichon° · *removed / every one*

And shippes by the brynke° comen and gon · *shore*

And in swich forme enduren a wowke° or two. · *week*

490 Thanne were my brother warisshed of his wo.

Thanne moste she nedes° holden hire biheste, · *necessarily*

Or elles he shal shame hire atte leeste."° · *at the least*

What sholde° I make a lenger tale of this? · *why should*

Unto his brotheres bed he comen is,

495 And swich confort he yaf hym for to gon° · *go*

To Orliens, that he up stirte° anon, · *started*

And on his wey forthward° thanne is he fare° · *forward / gone*

In hope for to been lissed° of his care. · *relieved*

Whan they were come almoost to that citee,

500 But if it were a two furlong[8] or thre,

A yong clerk romynge° by hymself they mette, · *roaming*

Which that in Latyn° thriftily° hem

grette.° · *Latin / appropriately / greeted*

And after that he seyde a wonder° thyng. · *wonderful*

"I knowe," quod he, "the cause of youre comyng."

505 And er they ferther any foote wente,

He tolde hem al that was in hire entente.° · *their intent*

This Briton clerk hym asked of° felawes, · *about*

The whiche that he had knowe in olde dawes,° · *days*

And he answerde hym that they dede were,

510 For which he weep ful ofte many a teere.

---

[1] *In … therby* Is hard to cure in medicine, unless one can find the arrow head.

[2] *Orliens in Fraunce* The university at Orléans, south of Paris, was famous for the study of law and had a more dubious reputation as a center for the study of magic.

[3] *magyk natureel* Natural magic, such as that of Chaucer's Physician (see *General Prologue*, line 416), is based on a knowledge of the powers of the planets and the physical world, as opposed to black magic, which makes use of spirits or devils.

[4] *eighte … mansiouns* The twenty-eight houses of astrology.

[5] *For … greve* Because the faith in Holy Church (set out) in our creed does not allow any illusion to grieve us. The passage reminds us that the story ostensibly takes place in pagan times, even though the social customs are more or less those of Chaucer's day.

[6] *Swiche … pleye* Tregetours produced special effects and illusions, often for banquets.

[7] *Sometyme … leoun* Sometimes a fierce lion seems to come.

[8] *furlong* Measurement equal to 220 yards.

Doun of his hors° Aurelius lighte° anon,　　　*horse / alighted*
And with this magicien forth is he gon
Hoom to his hous, and maden hem° wel at ese;°　　*them / ease*
Hem lakked no vitaille that myghte hem plese.[1]
515　So wel arrayed hous as ther was oon
Aurelius in his lyf saugh nevere noon.[2]

He shewed hym er he wente to sopeer°　　　*supper*
Forestes, parkes ful of wilde deer.
Ther saugh he hertes° with hir hornes
hye,°　　　　　　　　　　　　*harts (deer) / high horns*
520　The gretteste that evere were seyn with eye.
He saugh of hem an hondred slayn with houndes°　*by dogs*
And somme with arwes blede of bittre woundes.
He saugh, whan voyded° were thise wilde deer,　　*gone*
Thise fauconers° upon a fair ryver,　　　*these falconers*
525　That with hir haukes° han the heroun slayn.　　*their hawks*

Tho saugh he knyghtes justyng° in a playn.°　*jousting / plain*
And after this he dide° hym swich plesaunce°　*gave / pleasure*
That he hym shewed his lady on a daunce,°　　*at a dance*
On° which hymself he° daunced, as hym　　*at / he himself*
thoughte.°　　　　　　　　　　*as it seemed to him*
530　And whan this maister° that this magyk
wroughte°　　　　　　*master (of Arts) / performed*
Saugh it was tyme, he clapte° hise handes two,　　*clapped*
And, farewel, al oure revel° was ago!°　　*revelry / gone*
And yet remoeved° they nevere out of the hous　　*moved*
Whil they saugh al this sighte merveillous,°　*marvelous sight*
535　But in his studie thereas° hise bookes be　　*where*
They seten stille and no wight but they thre.°　　*three*

To hym this maister called his squier[3]
And seyde hym thus: "Is redy oure soper?°　　*supper*
Almoost an houre it is, I undertake,°　　*I suppose*
540　Sith I yow bad° oure soper for to make,　　*commanded*
Whan that thise worthy men wenten with me
Into my studie, theras my bookes be."

"Sire," quod this squier, "whan it liketh° yow,　　*pleases*
It is al redy, though ye wol° right now."　　*wish*
545　"Go we thanne soupe,"° quod he, "as for the beste.　*to eat*

This amorous folk somtyme moote han hir reste!"
At after soper° fille° they in tretee°　*after supper / fell / negotiations*
What somme° sholde this maistres gerdoun° be　*sum / payment*
To remoeven alle the rokkes of Britayne
550　And eek from Gerounde° to the mouth of
Sayne.°　　　　　　　　　　*Gironde / Seine*
He made it straunge° and swoor, so God　*made difficulties*
hym save,
Lasse than a thousand pound he wolde nat have,
Ne gladly for that somme he wolde nat goon.[4]
Aurelius with blisful herte anoon°　　　*immediately*
555　Answerde thus: "Fy° on a thousand pound!　　*fie*
This wyde world which that men seye is round,[5]
I wolde it yeve° if I were lord of it.　　*give*
This bargayn is ful dryve,° for we been knyt.°　*fully made / agreed*
Ye shal be payed trewely, by my trouthe.°　　*pledge*
560　But looketh now, for no necligence° or
slouthe°　　　　　　　　*negligence / laziness*
Ye tarie° us heere no lenger than tomorwe."　　*keep*
"Nay," quod this clerk, "have heer my feith° to
borwe!"°　　　　　　　*faith / as a pledge*
To bedde is goon Aurelius whan hym leste,°　　*he wished*
And wel ny° al that nyght he hadde his reste.　*very nearly*
565　What for his labour and his hope of blisse,
His woful herte of penaunce° hadde a lisse.°　*grief / relief*
Upon the morwe whan that it was day
To Britaigne tooke they the righte° way,　　*direct*
Aurelius and this magicien bisyde,°　　*as well*
570　And been descended° ther° they wolde abyde.　*are arrived / where*
And this was, as thise° bookes me remembre,°　*these / remind me*
The colde, frosty sesoun of Decembre.
Phebus° wax° old and hewed lyk
latoun,°　　　　　*the sun / grew / colored like brass*
That in his hoote declynacioun°　　*hot declination*
575　Shoon as the burned° gold with stremes°　*polished / streams*
brighte.
But now in Capricorn adoun he lighte,°[6]　　*alights*

---

[1] *Hem ... plese* They lacked no food that might please them.

[2] *So ... noon* Aurelius, in his life, never saw any house so well arranged (or supplied) as the one that was there.

[3] *squier* The squire is not a knight in training but a personal servant. The title nevertheless suggests that his master is a man of consequence.

[4] *Ne ... goon* Nor, at that price, would he not gladly refuse the job, i.e., it was the minimum he would accept.

[5] *This ... round* Contrary to popular modern belief, educated people in the Middle Ages knew the world was round.

[6] *That ... lighte* The declination is the distance above or below the equator. The hot declination is the sign of Cancer, which the sun enters in June. When it was in Cancer the sun shone hot, but now in December it enters Capricorn, where it is at its lowest altitude and

Whereas° he shoon ful pale, I dar wel seyn. — *where*
The bittre frostes with the sleet and reyn° — *rain*
Destroyed hath the grene in every yerd.° — *yard*
580 Janus[1] sit by the fyr with double berd° — *beard*
And drynketh of his bugle horn° the wyn.° — *drinking horn / wine*
Biforn hym stant° brawen° of the tosked swyn,[2] — *stands / meat*
And "Nowel!"° crieth every lusty man. — *Noël*
      Aurelius in al that evere he kan
585 Dooth to his maister chiere and reverence[3]
And preyeth hym to doon his diligence° — *do his best*
To bryngen hym out of his peynes smerte,
Or with a swerd° that he wolde slitte° his herte. — *sword / pierce*
      This subtil° clerk swich routhe° had of this man — *clever / pity*
590 That nyght and day he spedde hym that he
      kan° — *tried as best he could*
To wayten° a tyme of his conclusioun. — *watch for*
This is to seye, to maken illusioun
By swich a apparence° of jogelrye°— — *an appearance / trickery*
I ne kan no termes of astrologye°— — *know no astrological jargon*
595 That she and every wight sholde wene° and seye — *think*
That of Britaigne the rokkes were aweye
Or ellis they were sonken under grounde.
So atte laste he hath his tyme yfounde° — *found*
To maken hise japes° and his — *tricks*
      wrecchednesse° — *wretchedness*
600 Of swich a supersticious cursednesse.
Hise tables Tolletanes[4] forth he brought,

Ful wel corrected, ne° ther lakked° nought,° — *nor / lacked / nothing*
Neither his collect° ne hise expans
      yeeris° — *collect (years) / expanse-years*
Ne hise rootes° ne hise othere geeris,° — *roots (dates) / equipment*
605 As been his centris° and his argumentz — *centric tables*
And hise proporcioneles convenientz° — *fitting proportionals*
For hise equacions° in everythyng. — *equations*
And by his eighte speere in his wirkyng[5]
He knew ful wel how fer Alnath[6] was shone° — *had shone*
610 Fro the heed° of thilke fixe° Aries[7] above, — *head / that fixed*
That in the ninthe speere° considered is. — *sphere*
Ful subtilly° he hadde kalkuled° al this. — *cleverly / calculated*
      Whan he hadde founde his firste
      mansioun,° — *position (of the moon)*
He knew the remenaunt° by proporcioun° — *the rest / proportion*
615 And knew the arisyng of his moone weel
And in whos face and terme[8] and everydeel° — *every part*
And knew ful weel the moones mansioun
Acordaunt to his operacioun° — *calculation*
And knew also hise othere observaunces,° — *ceremonies*
620 For swich illusiouns and swiche meschaunces° — *evil practices*
As hethen° folk useden° in thilke° dayes, — *heathen / used / those*
For which no lenger maked° he delayes, — *made*
But thurgh his magik for a wyke or tweye,
It semed that alle the rokkes were aweye.
625   Aurelius, which that yet despeired is° — *is still in despair*
Wher° he shal han his love or fare amys,° — *whether / lose out*
Awaiteth nyght and day on this myracle.
And whan he knew that ther was noon obstacle,
That voyded° were thise rokkes everychon, — *gone*
630 Doun to hise maistres feet he fil anon
And seyde, "I, woful wrecche Aurelius,
Thanke yow, lord, and lady myn Venus,

shines most faintly.

[1] *Janus* In Roman mythology, Janus is the double-faced god who represents the exit of the old year and the entrance of the new. The month of January is named after him.

[2] *tosked swyn* Boar. The roasted boar's head was a favorite meal during the twelve days of Christmas.

[3] *Dooth ... reverence* Treats the magician in a friendly and respectful manner.

[4] *tables Tolletanes* I.e., Toledan tables. astrological tables drawn up for the latitude of Toledo, Spain, in the thirteenth century by King Alfonso the Wise. The tables allow the astronomer or astrologer to predict the motions of the planets relative to the earth. Lines 1273–80 are full of the language of astrology, which Chaucer explains in his *Treatise on the Astrolabe*, the instrument used for measuring the angles of various planets. The complete calculation required adding together figures for the planet's motion during the collect years (periods of twenty to 300 years), expanse years (periods of one to twenty years), and fractions of years. Roots are quantities, such as dates or the longitude of a planet, which are used when

consulting the tables. "Centres" are probably not parts of the astrolabe but rather centric tables of planetary distances, while "arguments," are angles or arcs from which the planets' motions can be measured. Fitting proportionals are figures used when taking into account the passage of fractions of a year.

[5] *And ... wirkyng* And by the eighth sphere in his calculation. According to medieval cosmology, the universe was made up of nine concentric crystalline spheres on which the planets and stars were affixed and which moved them across the sky.

[6] *Alnath* Name of a star.

[7] *Aries* Constellation and a sign in the zodiac.

[8] *face and terme* Subdivisions of a sign of the zodiac.

That me han holpen° fro my cares° colde!"   *helped / sorrows*
And to the temple his wey forth hath he holde,°   *gone*
635   Whereas he knew he sholde his lady see.[1]
And whan he saugh his tyme, anon right hee
With dredful° herte and with ful humble
    cheere°   *fearful / manner*
Salewed° hath his sovereyn lady deere.   *greeted*
    "My righte lady," quod this woful man,
640   "Whom I moost° drede and love as I best kan   *most*
And lothest° were of al this world displese,   *most unwilling*
Nere it° that I for yow have swich disese°   *were it not / misery*
That I moste dyen heere at youre foot anon,
Noght° wolde I telle how me is
    wobigon,°   *by no means / afflicted by woe*
645   But certes, outher° moste I dye or pleyne.   *either*
Ye sle° me giltlees° for verray peyne!   *kill / guiltless*
But of my deeth, thogh that ye have no routhe,°   *pity*
Avyseth° yow er that ye breke youre trouthe.°   *consider / promise*
Repenteth yow, for thilke God above,
650   Er ye me sleen bycause that I yow love.
For, madame, wel ye woot what ye han hight°—   *promised*
Nat that I chalange° anythyng of right   *claim*
Of yow, my sovereyn lady, but youre grace°—   *favor*
But in a gardyn yond,° at swich a place,   *yonder*
655   Ye woot right wel what ye bihighten me
And in myn hand youre trouthe plighten
    ye°   *you gave your promise*
To love me best. God woot, ye seyde so,
Al° be that I unworthy am therto.   *although*
Madame, I speke it for the honor of yow
660   Moore than to save myn hertes lyf right now.
I have do° so as ye comanded me,   *done*
And if ye vouchesauf, ye may go see.
Dooth as yow list.° Have youre biheste in mynde.   *wish*
For quyk° or deed,° right there ye shal me fynde.   *living / dead*
665   In yow lith al to do me lyve or deye.[2]
But wel I woot the rokkes been aweye."
    He taketh his leve, and she astoned° stood.   *stunned*

In al hir face nas° a drope of blood.   *was not*
She wende nevere han come in swich a trappe.[3]
670   "Allas," quod she, "that evere this sholde happe!
For wende° I nevere by possibilitee°   *expected / it possible*
That swich a monstre° or merveille° myghte
    bee.   *monstrosity / marvel*
It is agayns the proces of nature!"
And hoom she goth, a sorweful creature.
675   For verray feere° unnethe° may she go.   *fear / scarcely*
She wepeth, wailleth al a day or two
And swowneth that it routhe was to see.
But why it was to no wight tolde shee,
For out of towne was goon Arveragus.
680   But to hirself she spake and seyde thus,
With face pale and with ful sorweful cheere,
In hire compleynt, as ye shal after heere:
    "Allas," quod she, "on thee, Fortune, I pleyne,
That unwar wrapped hast me in thy cheyne![4]
685   For which t'escape woot I no socour,°   *help*
Save oonly deeth or dishonour.
Oon of thise two bihoveth me° to chese.   *I am compelled*
But nathelees, yet have I levere° to lese   *rather*
My lif than of my body have a shame,
690   Or knowe myselven fals or lese my name.
And with my deth I may be quyt,° ywis.°   *freed / indeed*
Hath ther nat° many a noble wyf er this   *has not*
And many a mayde yslayn hirself, allas,
Rather than with hir body doon trespas?°   *do a wrong*
695   "Yis, certes; lo, thise stories beren witnesse:
Whan thritty tirauntz° ful of
    cursednesse°   *thirty tyrants / wickedness*
Hadde slayn Phidoun in Atthenes[5] at feste,°   *a feast*
They comanded hise doghtres for t'areste°   *to be arrested*
And bryngen hem biforn hem in despit°   *scorn*
700   Al naked to fulfille hir foul delit,
And in hir fadres blood they made hem daunce
Upon the pavement. God yeve hem
    myschaunce!°   *give them misfortune*
For which thise woful maydens ful of drede
Rather than they wolde lese hir maydenhede,°   *chastity*

---

[1] *And to ... see* In the Middle Ages lovers often used church services as an opportunity to meet. Chaucer here gives the social customs of his day a pagan coloring by having Dorigen go to the temple. Chaucer frequently alternates between the simple past (Aurelius *knew*) and present or perfect forms (Aurelius *has gone* rather than *had gone*).

[2] *In ... deye* In you lies everything to make me live or die.

---

[3] *She ... trappe* She never expected to come into such a trap.

[4] *That ... cheyne* That have tangled me unawares in your chain.

[5] *Whan ... Atthenes* Thirty oligarchs ruled Athens briefly in 403 BCE before being overthrown by the naval commander Thrasybulus.

705	They prively been stirt° into a welle	*jumped*
	And dreynte° hemselven, as the bookes telle.	*drowned*
	They of Mecene° leet enquere° and	*Messene / make an inquiry*
	seke	
	Of Lacedomye° fifty maydens eke,	*Sparta*
	On whiche they wolden doon° hir lecherye.	*exercise*
710	But was ther noon of al that compaignye	
	That she nas slayn and with a good entente	
	Chees° rather for to dye than assente	*choose*
	To been oppressed° of hir maydenhede.	*robbed*
	Why sholde I thanne to dye been in drede?	
715	Lo eek, the tiraunt Aristoclides,	
	That loved a mayden heet° Stymphalides,[1]	*named*
	Whan that hir fader slayn was on a nyght,	
	Unto Dianes temple goth she right°	*right away*
	And hente° the ymage° in hir handes two,	*grasped / statue*
720	Fro which ymage wolde she nevere go.°	*let go*
	No wight ne myghte hir handes of it arace°	*pull away*
	Til she was slayn right in the selve° place.	*same*
	Now sith that maydens hadden swich despit	
	To been defouled with mannes° foul delit,	*men's*
725	Wel oghte° a wyf rather hirselven slee	*ought*
	Than be defouled, as it thynketh me!°	*seems to me*
	What shal I seyn of Hasdrubales wyf,	
	That at Cartage° birafte hirself hir lyf?[2]	*Carthage*
	For whan she saugh that Romayns wan° the toun,	*conquered*
730	She took hir children alle and skipte adoun°	*jumped down*
	Into the fyr and chees rather to dye	
	Than any Romayn dide° hire vileynye.	*should do*
	Hath nat Lucresse yslayn hirself, allas,	
	At Rome whan she oppressed was	
735	Of° Tarquyn?[3] For hire thoughte it was a shame	*by*
	To lyven whan she had lost hir name.°	*(good) name*
	The sevene° maydens of Melesie° also	*seven / Miletus*
	Han slayn hemself for drede and wo	

	Rather than folk of Gawle hem sholde oppresse.[4]	
740	Mo than a thousand stories, as I gesse,	
	Koude I now telle as touchynge this mateere.	
	Whan Habradate was slayn, his wyf so deere	
	Hirselven slow° and leet hir blood to glyde°	*killed / flow*
	In Habradates woundes depe and wyde	
745	And seyde, 'My body at the leeste way	
	Ther shal no wight defoulen, if I may.'[5]	
	"What sholde I mo ensamples heerof sayn,	
	Sith that so manye han hemselven slayn,	
	Wel rather than they wolde defouled be?	
750	I wol conclude that it is bet° for me	*better*
	To sleen myself than been defouled thus.	
	I wol be trewe unto Arveragus	
	Or rather sleen myself in som manere	
	As dide Demociones doghter deere,	
755	Bycause that she wolde nat defouled be.[6]	
	O Cedasus, it is ful greet pitee	
	To reden how thy doghtren deyde, allas,	
	That slowe hemself for swich manere cas![7]	
	As greet a pitee was it or wel° moore	*even*
760	The Theban mayden that for Nichanore	
	Hirselven slow,° right for swich manere wo.[8]	*slew*
	Another Theban mayden dide right so,°	*the same*
	For oon° of Macidonye hadde hire oppressed.	*someone*
	She with hire deeth hir maydenhede redressed.[9]	
765	What shal I seye of Nicerates wyf,	

---

[1] *Lo eek … Stymphalides* Aristoclides was a tyrant of Orchomenos who fell in love with a virgin called Stymphalides.

[2] *What … lyf* Hasdrubal, king of Carthage, the North African empire that threatened Rome, committed suicide when the Romans took the city in 146 BCE, although only after his wife had rebuked him for his cowardice.

[3] *Hath … Tarquyn* Lucretia ("Lucresse") committed suicide after being raped by Tarquinus Sextus, prince of Rome. The people then rebelled and drove the Tarquins out. The story is told by Ovid in his *Fasti* 2.685–852 and by Chaucer in his *Legend of Good Women*.

[4] *The sevene … oppresse* Miletus, in Asia Minor (now Turkey) was conquered by the Galatians in 276 BCE.

[5] *Whan Habradate … may* King Abradates of Susi was killed fighting the Egyptians, and his wife, Panthea, killed herself on his body.

[6] *As dide … be* When she heard that her husband, the general Leosthenes, had been killed in battle, the daughter of Demotion committed suicide rather than re-marry.

[7] *O Cedasus … cas* The daughters of Scedasus offered hospitality to two youths who then got drunk and raped them. Afterwards, the daughters stabbed each other to death; *swich manere cas* Such a situation.

[8] *The Theban … wo* Nicanor, one of Alexander the Great's officers, fell in love with one of the captured Thebans after taking the city in 336 BCE. She killed herself rather than submit to him.

[9] *She … redressed* She made up for (the loss of) her chastity with her death.

That for swich cas birafte hirself hir lyf?[1]
How trewe eek was to Alcebiades
His love, rather for to dyen chees
Than for to sufre° his body unburyed be.[2]   *allow*
770 Lo, which° a wyf was Alceste!" quod she.   *what*
"What seith Omer of goode Penalopee?
Al Grece knoweth of hire chastitee.[3]
Pardee, °of Lacedomya is writen thus: *by God*
That whan at Troie was slayn Protheselaus,
775 No lenger wolde she lyve after his day.[4]
The same of noble Porcia telle I may.
Withoute Brutus koude she nat lyve,
To whom she hadde al hool° hir herte yeve.[5]   *completely*
The parfit wyfhod of Arthemesie
780 Honored is thurgh al the Barbarie.[6]
O Teuta Queene, thy wyfly chastitee
To alle wyves may a mirour bee![7]
The same thyng I seye of Bilyea,
Of Rodogone and eek of Valeria."[8]

---

[1] *What … lyf* The wife of Nicerates killed herself to escape the lust of the thirty oligarchs (the same ones that commanded Phidoun's daughters to dance before them) (*Against Jovinian* 1.44).

[2] *How … be* Alcibiades, the friend of Socrates, was beheaded at the command of the Spartan general Lysander. His mistress risked her life to bury him.

[3] *Lo which … chastitee* The story of Penelope, wife of Ulysses, and how she kept her unwanted suitors at bay is told by Homer in *The Odyssey*. It was known in the Middle Ages in various translations.

[4] *Pardee … day* Protesilaus, the husband of Lacedomia (or Laodamia) was the first of the Greeks to be killed at the siege of Troy. At her entreaty he was brought briefly back to life and when he died a second time she died with him. Ovid tells the story in *Heroides* 13.

[5] *The same … yeve* Brutus joined the conspiracy against Julius Caesar and committed suicide when defeated by Marc Antony. Portia, Brutus's wife, committed suicide by swallowing hot coals after she learned of her husband's death.

[6] *The parfit … Barbarie* Arthemesia built the famous mausoleum at Halicarnasus for her husband Mausolus, king of Caria, in what is now northern Greece. It was with this sepulcher that the term "mausoleum" was coined.

[7] *O Teuta … bee* Teuta assumed the throne of Illyria, on the Dalmatian coast, on the death of her husband in 231 BCE.

[8] *The same … Valeria* Bilyea's martyrdom consisted in enduring her husband's bad breath. When he reproached her for not having told him about it, she replied that she thought all men's breath was that foul. Rhodogune, daughter of Darius, king of Persia, killed her nurse for suggesting she remarry. The Roman Valeria also refused to

---

785 Thus pleyned Dorigene a day or tweye,
Purposynge° evere that she wolde deye.   *intending*
But nathelees, upon the thridde nyght
Hoom cam Arveragus, this worthy knyght,
And asked hire why that she weepe so soore.
790 And she gan wepen ever lenger the moore.
"Allas," quod she, "that evere I was born!
Thus have I seyd," quod she. "Thus have I sworn!"
And toold hym al as ye han herd bifore.
It nedeth nat reherce° it yow namoore.   *repeat*
795 This housbonde with glad chiere° in freendly wyse   *expression*
Answerde and seyde as I shal yow devyse.°   *describe*
"Is ther oght elles, Dorigen, but this?"
     "Nay, nay," quod she, "God helpe me so, as wys°   *certainly*
This is to muche, and° it were Goddes wille!"   *even if*
800 "Ye, wyf," quod he, "lat slepen that° is stille.°   *what / quiet*
It may be wel paraventure yet today.
Ye shul youre trouthe holden, by my fay!°   *faith*
For God so wisly have mercy upon me,
I hadde wel levere ystiked° for to be   *stabbed*
805 For verray° love which that I to yow have,   *true*
But if ye sholde youre trouthe kepe and save!
Trouthe is the hyeste thyng that man may kepe."
But with that word he brast° anon to wepe   *burst out*
And seyde, "I yow forbede up° peyne deeth,   *on*
810 That nevere whil° thee lasteth lyf ne breeth   *while*
To no wight telle thou of this aventure.°   *misfortune*
As I may best, I wol my wo endure.
Ne make no contenance of hevynesse°   *sadness*
That folk of yow may demen harm or gesse."[9]
815   And forth he cleped° a squier and a mayde.   *called*
"Gooth forth anon with Dorigen," he sayde,
"And bryngeth hire to swich a place anon!"
They take hir leve, and on hir wey they gon.
But they ne wiste why she thider° wente.   *there*
820 He nolde no wight tellen his entente.
     Paraventure an heepe° of yow, ywis,°   *many / indeed*
Wol holden hym a lewed° man in this,   *foolish*
That he wol putte his wyf in jupartie.°   *jeopardy*
Herkneth° the tale er ye upon hire
     crie:°   *listen to / cry out against her*

---

remarry.

[9] *That … gesse* That people may think or guess that there is anything wrong with you.

825 She may have bettre fortune than yow semeth,°   *it seems to you*
And whan that ye han herd the tale, demeth.°   *judge*
   This squier which that highte Aurelius
On Dorigen that was so amorus,
Of aventure° happed hire to meete   *by chance*
830 Amydde the toun, right in the quykkest° strete,   *busiest*
As she was bown° to goon the wey forthright   *prepared*
Toward the gardyn theras° she had hight.°   *where / promised*
And he was to the gardynward also,
For wel he spyed whan she wolde go
835 Out of hir hous to any maner place.
But thus they mette, of° aventure° or grace,°*by / chance / fortune*
And he saleweth° hire with glad entente   *greets*
And asked of hire whiderward° she wente.   *where*
And she answerde half as she were mad,
840 "Unto the gardyn, as myn housbonde bad,°   *commanded*
My trouthe for to holde, allas! Allas!"
   Aurelius gan wondren on this cas°   *situation*
And in his herte hadde greet compassioun
Of hire and of hire lamentacioun
845 And of Arveragus, the worthy knyght,
That bad hire holden al that she had hight,
So looth hym was his wyf sholde breke hir trouthe.
And in his herte he caughte° of this greet routhe,   *had*
Considerynge the beste on every syde,
850 That fro his lust yet were° hym levere
     abyde°   *would / rather abstain*
Than doon so heigh° a cherlyssh wrecchednesse   *great*
Agayns franchise° and alle gentillesse.   *generosity*
For which in fewe wordes seyde he thus:
   "Madame, seyeth to youre lord Arveragus
855 That sith I se his grete gentillesse
To yow, and eek I se wel youre distresse,
That him were levere han shame—and that were°
     routhe°—   *would be / a pity*
Than ye to me sholde breke thus youre trouthe,
I have wel levere evere to suffre wo
860 Than I departe° the love bitwix yow two.   *separate*
I yow relesse, madame, into youre hond
Quyt every serement and every bond
That ye han maad to me as heer biforn[1]

Sith thilke tyme which that ye were born.
865 My trouthe I plighte:° I shal yow never repreve° *pledge / reproach*
Of no biheste. And heere I take my leve
As of the treweste and the beste wyf
That evere yet I knew in al my lyf.
But every wyf bewar of hire biheeste!
870 On Dorigene remembreth, atte leeste.
Thus kan a squier doon a gentil dede
As wel as kan a knyght, withouten drede."[2]
   She thonketh hym upon hir knees al bare,
And hoom unto hir housbonde is she fare°   *gone*
875 And tolde hym al as ye han herd me sayd.
And be ye siker,° he was so weel apayd,°   *certain / paid back*
That it were inpossible me to wryte.[3]
What° sholde I lenger of this cas endyte?°   *why / relate*
   Arveragus and Dorigene his wyf
880 In sovereyn° blisse leden forth hir lyf.   *highest*
Nevere eft° ne was ther angre hem bitwene.   *again*
He cherisseth hire as though she were a queene,
And she was to hym trewe for everemoore.
Of thise folk ye gete of me namoore.
885   Aurelius, that his cost° hath al forlorn,°   *money / lost*
Curseth the tyme that evere he was born.
"Allas," quod he, "allas that I bihighte
Of pured° gold a thousand pound of wighte°   *pure / weight*
Unto this philosophre!° How shal I do?   *wise man*
890 I se namoore but that I am fordo.°   *ruined*
Myn heritage° moot I nedes selle   *inheritance*
And been a beggere. Heere may I nat dwelle
And shamen° al my kynrede° in this place,   *shame / kindred*
But° I of hym may gete bettre grace.   *unless*
895 But nathelees, I wole of hym assaye
At certeyn dayes yeer by yeer to paye[4]
And thanke hym of his grete curteisye.
My trouthe wol I kepe; I wol nat lye."

---

[1] *I yow … biforn* I release you, my lady, into your power (hand), discharged of every oath (*serement*, from Latin *sacramentum*) and pledge that you have made to me before. Aurelius is using the language of a formal legal contract.

[2] *But every … drede* Most editors attribute lines 1541–44 to Aurelius and place the quotation marks accordingly. The lines could also be attributed to the Franklin. The medieval manuscripts leave the matter open, since they contain almost no punctuation; *drede* Doubt.

[3] *wryte* An apparent slip, since the Franklin is telling, not writing, the story.

[4] *But … paye* But, nonetheless, I will try to get from him (an agreement) to pay back the money in fixed installments over the years.

With herte soor he gooth unto his cofre°   *money chest*
900   And broghte gold unto this philosophre,
The value of fyve hundred pound, I gesse,
And hym bisecheth of his gentillesse
To graunte hym dayes of the remenaunt°   *for the rest*
And seyde, "Maister, I dar wel make avaunt°   *boast*
905   I failled nevere of my trouthe as yit.
For sikerly,° my dette shal be quyt°   *surely / repaid*
Towardes yow, howevere that I fare
To goon a begged° in my kirtel° bare.   *begging / shirt*
But wolde ye vouchesauf upon seuretee[1]
910   Two yeer or thre for to respiten me,°   *give me respite*
Thanne were I wel, for elles° moot I selle   *otherwise*
Myn heritage. Ther is namoore to telle."
This philosophre sobrely answerde
And seyde thus whan he thise wordes herde:
915   "Have I nat holden covenant° unto thee?"   *kept (my) promise*
"Yes, certes, wel and trewely," quod he.
"Hastow nat had thy lady as thee liketh?"
"No, no!" quod he, and sorwefully he siketh.°   *sighs*
"What was the cause? Tel me, if thou kan."
920   Aurelius his tale anon bigan
And tolde hym al as ye han herd bifoore.
It nedeth nat to yow reherce it moore.
He seide, "Arveragus of gentillesse
Hadde levere dye in sorwe and in distresse
925   Than that his wyf were of hir trouthe fals."
The sorwe of Dorigen he tolde hym als,
How looth hire was to been a wikked wyf

And that she levere had lost that day hir lyf
And that hir trouthe she swoor thurgh innocence.
930   She nevere erst hadde herd speke of apparence.[2]
"That made me han of hire so greet pitee.
And right as frely as he sente hire me,
As frely sente I hire to hym ageyn!
This al and som.[3] Ther is namoore to seyn."
935   This philosophre answerde, "Leeve brother,
Everich° of yow dide° gentilly til° oother.   *each / acted / to*
Thou art a squier, and he is a knyght;
But God forbede for his blisful myght
But if° a clerk koude doon a gentil dede   *unless*
940   As wel as any of yow, it is no drede!°   *doubt*
Sire, I releese thee° thy thousand pound,   *you from*
As thou right now were cropen° out of the ground,   *had crept*
Ne nevere er now ne haddest knowen me.
For sire, I wol nat taken a peny of thee
945   For al my craft ne noght for my travaille.°   *trouble*
Thou hast ypayed wel for my vitaille;°   *food*
It is ynogh, and farewell. Have good day!"
And took his hors and forth he goth his way.
Lordynges, this questioun thanne wolde I aske now:
950   Which was the mooste fre,° as thynketh yow?   *generous*
Now teleth me er that ye ferther wende.°   *go further*
I kan° namoore. My tale is at an ende.   *know*

HEERE IS ENDED THE FRANKELYNS TALE

---

[1]   *seuretee*   In effect, Aurelius is here offering to mortgage his land in return for time to pay back the full thousand pounds of gold.

[2]   *She ... apparence*   Never before had she heard (someone) speak of illusion.

[3]   *This ... som*   This is the whole.

The Pardoner's Prologue and Tale

The Pardoner calls himself "a full vicious man," yet, paradoxically, his tale is one of the few that has a completely straightforward moral: covetousness is the root of all evil. The tale is actually a popular sermon of the kind that the Pardoner has given so often that he knows it by rote. A story of three men who go in search of death, *The Pardoner's Tale* has at its core an *exemplum*, a short and gripping story with a clear moral message. To this exemplum a preacher might add, as the Pardoner does, dramatic denunciations of the Seven Deadly Sins, supported by Biblical quotations, and calls for repentance. Medieval popular preachers were often excellent storytellers, but the level of detail in *The Pardoner's Tale* goes beyond the needs of any sermon. Like the Miller, the Pardoner is a churl, and their two tales share an interest in the concrete and seamy aspects of daily life, down to such matters as how people rented rooms or poisoned rats. Although the time period is not specified the Pardoner's story captures the brutal joys of the tavern and the grim atmosphere of England in a time of plague, with the death cart making the rounds to retrieve the bodies, as it would have done during the Black Death of 1348–49. The enigmatic old man who cannot die but knows where death is to be found further enriches the basic *exemplum*.

The Pardoner's greatest modification of a popular sermon, however, is to offer a full commentary on his own art, describing his motivation (simple covetousness) and the various tricks, including blackmail, which he uses to persuade his listeners to buy his spurious relics and pardons. By holding out false promises of salvation, the Pardoner is endangering the souls of others and his own. His character has fascinated readers, perhaps because it is so enigmatic. There has been much discussion of what drives the Pardoner to such extensive self-revelation and why, having just explained his methods to the pilgrims, he is so rash as to make a final sales pitch for his relics. In one much-discussed line in *The General Prologue*, "I trowe [I believe] he were a gelding [a castrated stallion] or a mare," the narrator indicates that he does not precisely know what to make of the Pardoner, while defining him as other than "masculine." Based on this line and other features of his depiction, some have seen the Pardoner as a tormented outsider, anxious to win group approval, others as a figure of spiritual sterility, corrupted by his own covetousness and in turn corrupting those who listen to him.

Opening page of *The Pardoner's Tale*,
Ellesmere manuscript (detail).
(This item is reproduced by permission of the *Huntington Library*, San Marino, California. EL26C9F72r.)

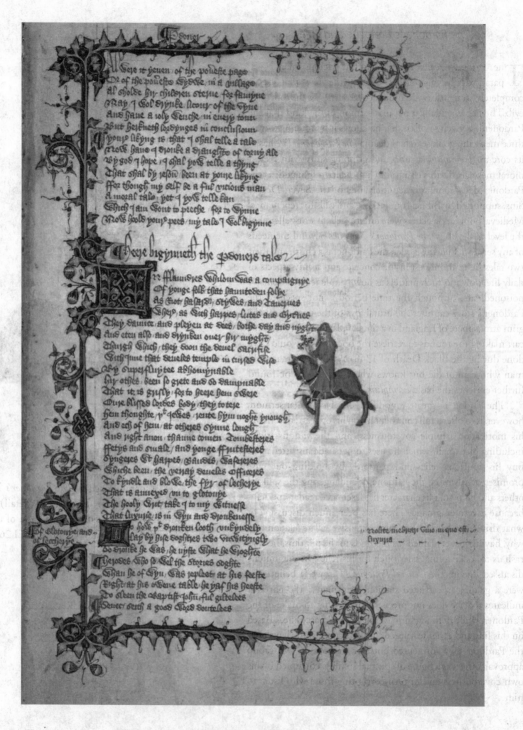

Opening page of *The Pardoner's Tale*, Ellesmere manuscript.
(This item is reproduced by permission of the *Huntington Library*, San Marino, California. EL26C9F72r.)

THE INTRODUCTION TO THE PARDONER'S TALE

THE WORDES OF THE HOOST
TO THE PHISICIEN AND THE PARDONER

O ure Hoost gan to swere° as° he were
    wood.°   *began to swear | as if | crazy*
"Harrow!" quod he. "By nayles and by blood!¹
This was a fals° cherl° and a fals justice.° *false | churl | judge*
As shameful deeth° as herte° may devyse° *death | heart | imagine*
5 Come to thise° false juges° and hire
    advocatz!°   *these | judges | their lawyers*
Algate° this sely° mayde° is slayn,°
    allas!²   *but | innocent | maid | killed*
Allas, to deere° boughte she beautee! *too dearly*
Wherfore° I seye° al day as men may see, *therefore | say*
That yiftes° of Fortune and of nature   *gifts*
10 Been° cause of deeth to many a creature.   *are*
Of bothe yiftes that I speke of now
Men han ful ofte° moore for harm than
    prow.°   *have very often | profit*
But trewely,° myn owene maister° deere,° *truly | master | dear*
This is a pitous° tale for to here.°   *pitiful | hear*
15 But nathelees,° passe over.° Is no
    fors.° *nevertheless | let it pass | matter*
I pray to God so save thy gentil cors°   *noble body*
And eek thyne urynals and thy jurdones,³
Thyn ypocras° and eek thy galiones° *hypocras | galians (medicines)*
And every boyste° ful of thy letuarie.°   *box | medicine*
20 God blesse hem° and oure Lady, Seint Marie!   *them*
So moot° I theen,° thou art a propre° man *might | thrive | fine*
And lyk° a prelat,° by Seint Ronyan!⁴ *like | prelate (high clergyman)*

Seyde I nat wel? I kan nat speke in terme,° *in the right jargon*
But wel I woot,° thou doost myn herte to
    erme,°   *know | make my heart grieve*
25 That I almoost have caught a cardynacle.⁵
By corpus bones,° but° I have triacle⁶ *by God's bones | unless*
Or elles a draughte° of moyste° and corny°
    ale,   *drink | moist | malty (strong)*
Or but I heere anon° a myrie° tale, *immediately | merry*
Myn herte is lost for pitee of this mayde.
30 Thou beel amy,° thou Pardoner," he sayde, *good friend*
"Telle us som myrthe or japes° right anon."   *jokes*
  "It shal be doon!" quod he, "by Seint Ronyon!
But first," quod he, "heere at this ale-stake⁷
I wol bothe drynke and eten° of a cake."°   *eat | bread*
35 And right anon the gentils° gonne° to crye, *gentle folk | began*
"Nay, lat hym telle us of no ribaudye!°   *ribald story*
Telle us som moral thyng that we may leere°   *learn*
Som wit,° and thanne wol we gladly here." *piece of wisdom*
  "I graunte, ywis,"° quod he. "But I moot
    thynke°   *indeed | must think*
40 Upon som honeste thyng° whil that I drynke."*respectable subject*

THE PARDONER'S PROLOGUE

HEERE FOLWETH THE PROLOGE OF THE PARDONERS TALE

Radix malorum est Cupiditas. Ad Thimotheum 6.10⁸

"L ordynges,"° quod he, "in chirches° whan I
   preche,°   *lords | churches | preach*

---

¹ *Harrow ... blood Harrow* Help; *Nails and blood* By Christ's nails and by Christ's blood, i.e., alas. Medieval swearing often referred to parts of Christ's body.

² *Harow ... alas* The tale told previously, by the Physician, involved an innocent young girl who agrees to let her father kill her in order to save her from the lewd desires of a corrupt judge.

³ *urynals* Vessels to hold urine; *jurdones* Jars. These were both part of the equipment medieval doctors used.

⁴ *Seint Ronyan* There were several medieval saints called St. Ronan—a seventh-century Scottish hermit, a Breton bishop who died in Cornwall, a Scottish bishop who helped settle a dispute about the date of Easter, and an early bishop of Caesarea, whose arm was kept as a relic at Canterbury Cathedral. Most editors state that it was the Scottish hermit to whom the Host refers here, but the last

Saint Ronan, given his association with Canterbury, seems the most likely reference, for the pilgrims are traveling to the place where his relic was kept. There may also be a pun on runnions (male sexual organs).

⁵ *cardynacle* The Host means heart attack, though he blunders for the proper word, which is cardiacle.

⁶ *triacle* Medicine or cordial, usually made primarily from molasses.

⁷ *ale-stake* Post set up outside a house when the people who lived there had brewed up some ale and were ready to sell it to those passing by.

⁸ *Radix ... Cupiditas* Latin: the root of evils is cupidity. From 1 Timothy 6.10. Cupidity is often translated as avarice, or love of money, but, like the word covetousness, it can also refer to any excessive or sinful love of earthly things.

I peyne me to han° an hauteyn
    speche°   *take pains to have | dignified speech*
And rynge° it out as round° as gooth a
    belle,°   *ring | roundly | rings a bell*
For I kan° al by rote° that I telle.°   *know | by memory | say*
45 My theme[1] is alwey oon° and evere was: *always one*
Radix malorum est cupiditas.

    First I pronounce° whennes° that I come,   *say | whence*
And thanne my bulles[2] shewe I alle and some.°   *one and all*
Oure lige lordes seel° on my
    patente,°   *liege lord's (i.e., the bishop's) seal | license*
50 That shewe I first, my body to warente,°   *protect*
That no man be so boold,° ne preest ne clerk,[3]   *bold*
Me to destourbe° of Cristes hooly werk.   *disturb*
And after that thanne° telle I forth my tales.   *then*
Bulles of popes and of cardynales,°   *cardinals*
55 Of patriarkes° and bisshopes° I shewe,   *patriarchs | bishops*
And in Latyn° I speke a wordes fewe   *Latin*
To saffron with[4] my predicacioun°   *preaching*
And for to stire hem° to devocioun.   *stir them*
Thanne shewe I forth my longe cristal stones,°   *glass cases*
60 Ycrammed° ful of cloutes° and of bones.   *crammed | rags*
Relikes been they, as wenen they echoon.°   *as everyone believes*
Thanne have I in latoun° a sholder boon°
bone   *brass | shoulder*
Which that was of an hooly Jewes sheepe.°   *holy Jew's sheep*
65 "Goode men," I seye, "taak of my wordes keepe.°   *heed*
If that this boon be wasshe° in any welle,   *washed*
If cow or calf or sheepe or oxe swelle°   *swell*
That any worm° hath ete° or worm
    ystonge,°   *snake | has eaten | stung*
Taak water of that welle and wassh his tonge,
And it is hool° anon. And forthermoor,   *healthy*

70 Of pokkes° and of scabbe° and every soor°   *pocks | scab | sore*
Shal every sheepe be hool that of this welle
Drynketh a draughte. Taak kepe° eek° what I
    telle!   *take heed | also*
If that the goode man that the beestes° oweth°   *beasts | owns*
Wol every wyke° er° that the cok° hym
    croweth°   *week | before | rooster | crows*
75 Fastynge° drynke of this welle a draughte,   *while fasting*
As thilke° hooly Jew oure eldres° taughte,   *that | ancestors*
Hise beestes and his stoor° shal multiplie.   *possessions*
    And sire, also it heeleth° jalousie.   *heals*
For though a man be falle° in jalous rage,   *fallen*
80 Lat maken with this water his potage,°   *stew*
And nevere shal he moore his wyf mystriste,°   *mistrust*
Though he the soothe° of hir defaute°
    wiste,°   *truth | default | knew*
Al had she taken preestes two or thre.[5]
    Heere is a miteyn° eek that ye may se.   *mitten*
85 He that his hand wol putte in this mitayn,
He shal have multipliyng of his grayn°   *grain*
Whan he hath sowen, be it whete° or otes,°   *wheat | oats*
So that he offre pens or elles grotes.[6]
    Goode men and wommen, o° thyng warne I yow: *one*
90 If any wight° be in this chirche now   *person*
That hath doon° synne° horrible, that he   *committed | sin*
Dar nat for shame of it yshryven° be,   *confessed*
Or any womman, be she yong or old,
That hath ymaked° hir housbonde cokewold,[7]   *made*
95 Swich folk shal have no power ne no grace
To offren° to my relikes in this place.   *make an offering*
And whoso fyndeth hym out° of swich
    fame,°   *is not subject to | (ill-) repute*
They wol come up and offre on° Goddes name,   *in*
And I assoille hem° by the auctoritee°   *absolve them | authority*
100 Which that by bulle ygraunted was to me.
    By this gaude° have I wonne° yeer° by yeer   *trick | gained | year*
An hundred mark sith I was pardoner.[8]

---

[1] *theme* "Text." Medieval sermons were usually organized around a short passage from the Bible.

[2] *bulles* I.e., papal bulls (written documents which put official policy into effect). Pardoners had licenses from the Pope to raise money for charitable causes by selling indulgences (certificates that reduce the number of years the buyer must serve in Purgatory after death).

[3] *ne preest ne clerk* The term clerk can refer to students, scholars, or assistants to priests (as in *The Miller's Tale*), so neither priest nor clerk means not a member of the clergy. The parish clergy often regarded wandering preachers as interlopers.

[4] *To saffron with* To season with saffron, a very expensive yellow spice imported from the East.

[5] *Al ... thre* Even if she had taken two or three priests as lovers.

[6] *So ... grotes* Provided that he offers pennies or else groats (a coin worth fourpence).

[7] *cokewold* I.e., cuckold, a man whose wife has committed adultery.

[8] *An ... pardoner* A hundred marks equaled over £66, making the Pardoner a wealthy man. In comparison, in 1367 Chaucer was granted an annual pension of 20 marks.

I stonde lyk a clerk° in my pulpet,   *theologian*
And whan the lewed peple[1] is doun yset,°   *settled down*
105 I preche so as ye han herd bifoore°   *have heard before*
And telle an hundred false japes° moore.   *tricks*
Thanne peyne I me° to strecche° forth the
      nekke   *I take pains / stretch*
And est° and west upon the peple° I bekke°   *east / people / nod*
As dooth a dowve° sittynge on a berne.°   *sitting / barn*
110 Myne handes and my tonge goon so yerne°   *eagerly*
That it is joye to se° my bisynesse.°   *see / busyness*
Of avarice and of swich cursednesse°   *cursedness*
Ys° al my prechyng, for to make hem free°   *is / generous*
To yeven hir pens°—and namely unto me.   *give their pence*
115 For myn entente° is nat but for to wynne°   *intent / profit*
And nothyng° for correccioun° of synne.   *by no means / correction*
I rekke° nevere whan they been beryed,°   *care / buried*
Though that hir soules goon a blakeberyed![2]
For certes, many a predicacioun°   *sermon*
120 Comth ofte tyme of yvel entencioun°—   *evil intent*
Som for plesance° of folk and flaterye   *pleasure*
To been avaunced by ypocrisye°   *hypocrisy*
And som for veyneglorie° and som for hate.   *pride*
For whan I dar noon oother weyes° debate,   *in no other way*
125 Thanne wol I stynge° hym[3] with my tonge
      smerte°   *sting / sharp*
In prechyng, so that he shal nat asterte°   *escape*
To been defamed falsly if that he
Hath trespased° to my bretheren or to me.   *has done harm*
For though I telle noght° his propre° name,   *not / own*
130 Men shal wel knowe that it is the same
By signes and by othere circumstances.
Thus quyte° I folk that doon us displesances.° *pay back / offenses*
Thus spitte I out my venym under hewe°   *guise*
Of hoolynesse, to semen° hooly and trewe.   *seem*
135   But shortly, myn entente I wol devyse:°   *describe*
I preche of nothyng but for coveityse.°   *covetousness*
Therfore my theme is yet and evere was

Radix malorum est cupiditas.
Thus kan I preche agayn° that same vice   *against*
140 Which that I use, and that is avarice.
But though myself be gilty in that synne,
Yet kan I maken oother folk to twynne°   *turn away*
From avarice and soore° to repente.   *sorely*
But that is nat my principal entente;°   *intent*
145 I preche nothyng but for coveitise.°   *covetousness*
Of this mateere it oghte ynogh suffise.°   *should be sufficient*
  Thanne telle I hem ensamples° many
      oon°   *examples / many a one*
Of olde stories longe tyme agoon,°   *ago*
For lewed peple° loven tales olde;   *laypeople*
150 Swiche thynges kan they wel reporte and holde.°   *remember*
What? Trowe ye,° the whiles I may preche   *do you believe*
And wynne° gold and silver for I teche,°   *gain / because I teach*
That I wol lyve in poverte wilfully?°   *willingly*
Nay, nay! I thoghte it nevere, trewely.
155 For I wol preche and begge in sondry landes;° *different countries*
I wol nat do no labour with myne handes
Ne make baskettes and lyve therby,
Bycause I wol nat beggen ydelly.°   *beg in vain*
I wol noon of the apostles countrefete![4]
160 I wol have moneie,° wolle,° chese, and
      whete,°   *money / wool / wheat*
Al° were it yeven°of the povereste page° *even if / given / poorest boy*
Or of the povereste wydwe° in a village,   *widow*
Al sholde hir children sterve° for famyne.   *die*
Nay, I wol drynke licour of the vyne
165 And have a joly wenche° in every toun.   *pretty girl*
But herkneth,° lordynges, in conclusioun: *listen*
Youre likyng° is that I shal telle a tale.   *pleasure*
Now have I dronke a draughte of corny ale,
By God, I hope I shal yow telle a thyng
170 That shal by resoun° been at youre liking.   *with reason*
For though myself be a ful° vicious man,   *very*
A moral tale yet I yow telle kan,
Which I am wont° to preche for to wynne.   *accustomed*
Now hoold youre pees!° My tale I wol bigynne.   *peace*

---

[1] *lewed peple* Uneducated, illiterate (in the medieval sense—i.e., unable to read Latin), or simple, but it can also refer to lay people in general. It does not have the modern meaning of sexual offensiveness.

[2] *a blakeberyed* Go picking blackberries (i.e., wandering).

[3] *hym* I.e., any opponent. Pardoners were much criticized by the parish clergy and by reformers.

[4] *noon ... countrefete* In the Gospels and the Book of Acts the apostles were enjoined to live in poverty so as to give surplus goods to the poor.

THE PARDONER'S TALE

HEERE BIGYNNETH THE PARDONERS TALE

175 In Flaundres° whilom° was a
    compaignye°   *Flanders / once / company*
Of yonge folk that haunteden folye
As riot, hasard, stywes, and tavernes,[1]
Whereas° with harpes, lutes, and gyternes[2]   *where*
They daunce and pleyen° at dees° bothe day and   *play / dice*
    nyght
180 And eten also and drynken over hir myght,°   *capacity*
Thurgh which they doon the devel sacrifise°   *sacrifice to the devil*
Withinne that develes temple[3] in cursed wise°   *manner*
By superfluytee° abhomynable.   *excess*
Hir othes° been so grete and so dampnable°   *oaths / damnable*
185 That it is grisly° for to heere hem swere.   *horrible*
Oure blissed° Lordes body they to-tere°—   *blessed / tear apart*
Hem thoughte that Jewes rente hym noght ynough![4]
And ech of hem at otheres synne° lough.°   *sin / laughed*
And right anon thanne comen tombesteres°   *female acrobats*
190 Fetys° and smale° and yonge
    frutesteres,°   *elegant / slender / fruit-sellers*
Syngeres with harpes, baudes,° wafereres,°   *pimps / pastry-sellers*
Whiche been° the verray devels officeres   *who are*
To kyndle and blowe the fyr of lecherye
That is annexed unto° glotonye.°   *allied with / gluttony*
195 The Hooly Writ° take I to my witnesse   *Bible*
That luxurie° is in wyn° and dronkenesse.   *lust / wine*
  Lo how that dronken Looth[5] unkyndely°   *unnaturally*
Lay by hise doghtres° two unwityngly!°   *daughters / unknowingly*
So dronke he was, he nyste° what he
    wroghte.°   *did not know / did*

200 Herodes,[6] whoso wel the stories soghte,[7]
Whan he of wyn was replest° at his feeste,°   *most filled / feast*
Right at his owene table he yaf° his heeste°   *gave / command*
To sleen° the Baptist John ful giltelees.[8]   *kill*
Senec[9] seith a good word, doutelees.°   *doubtless*
205 He seith he kan no difference fynde
Bitwix° a man that is out of his mynde   *between*
And a man which that is dronkelewe,°   *often drunk*
But that woodnesse,° fallen° in a
    shrewe,°   *madness / occurring / villain*
Persevereth° lenger than dooth dronkenesse.   *lasts*
210 O glotonye, ful of cursednesse,
O cause first of oure confusioun,
O original of oure dampnacioun,[10]
Til Crist hadde boght° us with his blood agayn!   *redeemed*
Lo how deere,° shortly for to seyn,°   *expensively / say*
215 Aboght° was thilke° cursed vileynye!   *purchased / that*
Corrupt was al this world for glotonye.
  Adam oure fader and his wyf also
Fro° Paradys to labour and to wo°   *from / woe*
Were dryven° for that vice, it is no drede.°   *driven / doubt*
220 For whil that Adam fasted, as I rede,°   *read*
He was in Paradys, and whan that he
Eet° of the fruyt deffended° on the tree,   *ate / prohibited*
Anon he was outcast to wo and peyne.
O glotonye, on thee wel oghte us pleyne!°   *complain*
225 O, wiste a man how manye maladyes°   *diseases*
Folwen of excesse and of glotonyes,
He wolde been the moore mesurable°   *temperate*
Of his diete, sittynge at his table.
Allas, the shorte throte,° the tendre mouth   *throat*
230 Maketh that° est and west and north and south,   *causes*
In erthe, in eir, in water man to swynke°   *labor*
To gete a glotoun° deyntee° mete° and
    drynke.   *glutton / delicious / meat*

---

[1] *Of yonge … tavernes* Of young folk that gave themselves to
foolish living, such as loud parties, gambling, brothels, and taverns.

[2] *gyternes* Like the harp and the lute, the medieval gittern was a
plucked stringed instrument.

[3] *develes temple* I.e., a tavern.

[4] *Hem … ynough* They thought that Jews did not tear him apart
enough. The oaths figuratively tore God's body apart, according to
the moralists. In the Middle Ages, Jews were usually blamed for
Christ's crucifixion.

[5] *Looth* I.e., Lot. The story of how Lot, while drunk, made his
daughters pregnant is recounted in Genesis 19.30–38.

---

[6] *Herodes* I.e., Herod, King of the Jewish people (74–3 BCE).

[7] *whoso … soghte* As whoever consulted the stories carefully can
confirm.

[8] *ful giltelees* Entirely guiltless. See Matthew 14.1–12.

[9] *Senec* I.e., Seneca, Roman playwright, orator, and philosopher (4
BCE–65 CE).

[10] *O cause … dampnacioun* A reference to the role of gluttony in
causing Adam and Eve to eat the forbidden fruit of the Tree of
Knowledge in the Garden of Eden. See Genesis 2–3.

Of this matiere, O Paul,[1] wel kanstow trete:°   *can you write*

"Mete unto wombe° and wombe eek unto mete: *stomach*

235 Shal God destroyen bothe," as Paulus seith.[2]

Allas, a foul thyng is it, by my feith,

To seye this word, and fouler is the dede

Whan man so drynketh of the white and

rede,°   *white and red wine*

That of his throte he maketh his pryvee,°   *latrine*

240 Thurgh thilke cursed superfluitee.°   *excess*

The apostel[3] wepyng seith ful pitously,°   *pitifully*

"Ther walken manye of whiche yow toold have I.°   *I have told you*

I seye it now wepyng with pitous voys:°   *pitiful voice*

Ther been° enemys of Cristes croys°   *are / cross*

245 Of whiche the ende is deeth.° Wombe is hir god."[4]   *death*

O wombe, o bely, o stynkyng cod,°   *stinking bag (stomach)*

Fulfilled of donge° and of corrupcioun,   *filled with dung*

At either ende of thee foul is the soun!°   *sound*

How greet labour and cost is thee to fynde.°   *provide for*

250 Thise cookes, how they stampe° and streyne° and

grynde   *pound / strain*

And turnen substaunce into accident[5]

To fulfillen al thy likerous° talent!°   *lecherous / inclination*

Out of the harde bones knokke they

The mary,° for they caste° noght awey   *marrow / throw*

255 That may go thurgh the golet° softe and swoote.°   *throat / sweet*

Of spicerie° of leef and bark and roote   *spices*

Shal been his sauce ymaked,° by delit°   *made / through delight*

To make° hym yet a newer appetit.   *give*

But certes, he that haunteth° swiche delices°   *follows / delights*

260 Is deed whil that he lyveth in tho° vices.[6]   *those*

A lecherous thyng is wyn, and dronkenesse

Is ful of stryvyng° and of wrecchednesse.   *quarreling*

O dronke man, disfigured is thy face!

Sour is thy breeth! Foul artow° to embrace!   *are you*

265 And thurgh thy dronke nose semeth the

soun°   *the sound seems to come*

As though thou seydest ay° "Sampsoun, Sampsoun!"   *ever*

And yet, God woot,° Sampsoun drank nevere no

wyn![7]   *God knows*

Thou fallest as it were a styked swyn.°   *stuck (i.e., speared) pig*

Thy tonge is lost and al thyn honeste cure.°   *care*

270 For dronkenesse is verray sepulture°   *tomb*

Of mannes wit and his discrecioun.

In whom that drynke hath dominacioun,

He kan no conseil° kepe, it is no drede.°   *counsel / doubt*

Now kepe yow fro the white and fro the rede

275 And namely fro the white wyn of Lepe[8]

That is to selle° in Fyssh Strete or in Chepe.[9]   *for sale*

This wyn of Spaigne° crepeth subtilly   *Spain*

In othere wynes growynge faste° by,[10]   *near*

Of which ther ryseth swich fumositee°   *such vapors*

280 That whan a man hath dronken draughtes thre°   *three*

And weneth° that he be at hoom° in Chepe,   *thinks / home*

He is in Spaigne, right at the toune of Lepe—

Nat at the Rochele ne at Burdeux toun—[11]

And thanne wol he seye, "Sampsoun, Sampsoun!"

285 But herkneth, lordes, o° word, I yow preye,   *one*

That alle the sovereyn actes, dar I seye,

Of victories in the Olde Testament

Thurgh verray° God that is omnipotent   *true*

Were doon in abstinence and in preyere.

290 Looketh the Bible, and ther ye may it leere.°   *learn*

Looke, Attilla[12] the grete conquerour

---

[1] *Paul* I.e., St. Paul.

[2] *Shal … seith* See 1 Corinthians 6.13.

[3] *apostel* I.e., apostle, here St. Paul.

[4] *Ther walken … god* See Philippians 3.18–19.

[5] *And … accident* This distinction between the basic food and the flavors the cooks give to it draws on Aristotle's distinction between substance (essential inner reality) and its superficial qualities (accidents). This line could be read as an allusion to contemporary philosophical debates between Nominalists and Realists or to contemporary theological controversies concerning the process through which the bread and wine of the Eucharist are transformed into the body and blood of Christ.

[6] *he that … vices* Cf. 1 Timothy 5.6: "But she that lives in pleasure is dead while she lives."

[7] *And yet … wyn* As recounted in Judges 13, in which it is written that Samson's mother did not drink wine during her pregnancy.

[8] *Lepe* Town in Spain.

[9] *Fyssh … Chepe* I.e., Fish Street and Cheapside, two market districts in London.

[10] *This wyn … by* Expensive French wines, shipped through Bordeaux and La Rochelle, were often surreptitiously mixed with cheaper, but stronger, Spanish wines.

[11] *the Rochele … Burdeaux toun* I.e., La Rochelle and Bordeaux.

[12] *Attilla* I.e., Attila the Hun, a fifth-century nomadic chieftain who ravaged vast stretches of central Europe. According to medieval histories, such as those of Jordanes and Paul the Deacon, he died from drink on the night that he took a new bride.

Deyde° in his sleepe with shame and dishonour,   *died*
Bledynge° ay at his nose in dronkenesse.   *bleeding*
A capitayn° sholde lyve in sobrenesse.   *leader*
295 And over al this° avyseth yow° right wel   *above all | consider*
What was comaunded unto Lamwel.[1]
Nat Samuel[2] but Lamwel, seye I.
Redeth the Bible, and fynde it expresly°   *specifically*
Of wyn yevyng° to hem that han
    justise.°   *giving wine | have legal power*
300 Namoore of this, for it may wel suffise.
    And now I have spoken of glotonye,
Now wol I yow deffenden° hasardrye.°   *prohibit | gambling*
Hasard is verray mooder° of lesynges°   *mother | lying*
And of deceite and cursed forswerynges,°   *perjury*
305 Blasphemyng of Crist, manslaughtre, and
    wast° also   *wasteful spending*
Of catel° and of tyme. And forthermo,   *goods*
It is repreeve° and contrarie of° honour   *reproach | to*
For to ben holde° a commune hasardour.°   *be considered | gambler*
And ever the hyer° he is of estaat°   *higher | condition*
310 The moore is he holden° desolaat.°   *regarded as | vile*
If that a prynce° useth hasardrye,°   *prince | frequently gambles*
In alle governaunce and policye
He is as by commune opinioun
Yholde° the lasse° in reputacioun.   *held | less*
315 Stilboun,[3] that was a wys embassadour,
Was sent to Cornythe° in ful greet honour   *Corinth*
Fro Lacidomye° to maken hire alliaunce,   *Sparta*
And whan he cam, hym happed par chaunce[4]
That alle the gretteste that were of that lond
320 Pleyynge atte hasard he hem fond,
For which, as soone as it myghte be,
He stal hym° hoom agayn to his contree   *stole away*
And seyde, "Ther wol I nat lese° my name!   *lose*
Ne I wol nat take on me so greet defame°   *dishonor*
325 Yow for to allie° unto none hasardours.   *ally*
Sendeth otherewise° embassadours.   *other*

For by my trouthe, me were levere dye°   *rather die*
Than I yow sholde to hasardours allye.
For ye that been so glorious in honours
330 Shul nat allyen yow with hasardours,
As by my wyl,° ne as by my tretee."°   *will | treaty*
This wise philosophre thus seyde hee.
    Looke eek that to the kyng Demetrius,
The kyng of Parthes,° as the book seith° us,[5]   *Parthia | tells*
335 Sente him a paire of dees° of gold in scorn,   *dice*
For he hadde used hasard ther-biforn,°   *often gambled before this*
For which he heeld his glorie or his renoun
At no value or reputacioun.
Lordes may fynden oother maner pley°   *kinds of amusement*
340 Honeste ynough to dryve the day awey.
    Now wol I speke of othes° false and grete   *oaths*
A word or two, as olde bookes trete.
Greet sweryng° is a thyng abhominable,   *swearing*
And fals sweryng° is yet moore reprevable.°   *perjury | disgraceful*
345 The heighe God forbad sweryng at al,[6]
Witnesse on Mathew, but in special°   *specially*
Of sweryng seith the hooly Jeremye,°   *Jeremiah*
"Thou shalt seye sooth thyne othes° and nat lye *truly your oaths*
And swere in doom° and eek in rightwisnesse."[7]   *judgment*
350 But ydel sweryng is a cursednesse.
Bihoold and se that in the firste table°   *tablet (of Moses)*
Of heighe Goddes heestes° honorable   *commandments*
Hou that the seconde heeste of hym° is this   *them*
"Take nat my name in ydel or amys."[8]
355 Lo, rather° he forbedeth swich   *earlier (in the commandments)*
    sweryng
Than homycide or any cursed thyng.
I seye that as by ordre thus it stondeth.°   *stands*

---

[1] *Lamwel* I.e., Lemuel, King of Massa, whose mother warns him not to drink wine. See Proverbs 31.4–5.

[2] *Samuel* I.e., the prophet Samuel. See 1 Samuel.

[3] *Stilboun* I.e., Chilon, an ambassador who is mentioned in John of Salisbury's *Polycraticus*, 1.5.

[4] *And ... chaunce* And when he came, it happened to him by chance.

---

[5] *The kyng ... us* King Demetrius of Parthia has not been securely identified, but John of Salisbury tells his story in the *Policraticus* immediately after that of Chilon.

[6] *The heighe ... al* See Matthew 5.34.

[7] *Thou ... rightwisnesse* See Jeremiah 4.2; *rightwisnesse* Righteousness.

[8] *Take ... amys* See Deuteronomy 5.7–21. In the Middle Ages the first two commandments were normally grouped as one, making what is now considered the third commandment the second, as it is here. The tenth commandment was then broken into two to make up the difference; *amys* In vain.

This knowen that hise heestes understondeth,[1]
How that the seconde heeste° of God is
    that.   *second commandment*
360 And forther over,° I wol thee telle al plat°   *furthermore / plainly*
That vengeance shal nat parten° from his hous   *depart*
That of his othes° is to° outrageous.   *oaths / too*
"By Goddes precious herte!" and "By his nayles"°   *nails*
And "By the blood of Crist that is in Hayles,[2]
365 Sevene is my chaunce and thyn is cynk° and treye!"°[3]   *five / three*
By Goddes armes, if thou falsly pleye,
This daggere shal thurghout thyn herte go!"°   *pierce*
This fruyt° cometh of the bicched bones two—[4]   *fruit*
Forsweryng,° ire,° falsnesse, homycide.   *perjury / anger*
370 Now for the love of Crist that for us dyde,
Lete° youre othes, bothe grete and smale.   *leave*
But sires, now wol I telle forth my tale.

    Thise riotours° thre of whiche I telle   *party-goers*
Longe erst er° prime° rong° of any belle   *before / early morning / rang*
375 Were set hem in a taverne to drynke.
And as they sat, they herde a belle clynke°   *ring*
Biforn° a cors° was° caried to his
    grave.   *before / corpse / that was being*
That oon of hem gan callen to his knave,°   *servant*
"Go bet,"° quod he, "and axe° redily°   *quickly / ask / eagerly*
380 What cors is this that passeth heer forby,
And looke that thou reporte his name weel."
    "Sire," quod this boy, "it nedeth never a deel.°   *it is not necessary*
It was me toold er ye cam heer two houres.[5]
He was, pardee,° an old felawe° of youres,   *by God / friend*
385 And sodeynly he was yslayn tonyght.
For dronke as he sat on his bench upright
Ther cam a privee theef° men clepeth° Deeth,   *secret thief / call*
That in this contree al the peple sleeth,
And with his spere he smoot° his herte atwo°   *cut / in two*

390 And wente his wey withouten wordes mo.
He hath a thousand slayn this pestilence.°[6]   *during this epidemic*
And maister, er ye come in his presence,
Me thynketh that it were necessarie
For to bewar of swich an adversarie.
395 Beth° redy for to meete hym everemoore.°   *be / always*
Thus taughte me my dame.° I sey namoore."   *mother*
"By seinte Marie," seyde this taverner,°   *tavern-keeper*
"The child seith sooth, for he hath slayn this yeer
Henne° over a mile withinne a greet° village   *from here / large*
400 Bothe man and womman, child and hyne° and
    page.   *hired hand*
I trowe° his habitacioun° be there.   *believe / dwelling*
To been avysed° greet wysdom it were,   *warned*
Er° that he dide° a man a dishonour."°   *lest / cause / harm*
    "Ye, Goddes armes," quod this riotour,
405 "Is it swich peril with hym for to meete?°   *encounter*
I shal hym seke by wey° and eek by strete,°   *road / street*
I make avow° to Goddes digne° bones.   *a vow / worthy*
Herkneth, felawes, we thre been al ones.°   *are three together*
Lat ech of us holde up his hand til oother,°   *to the other*
410 And ech of us bicomen° otheres brother,   *become*
And we wol sleen this false traytour, Deeth!
He shal be slayn, which that so manye sleeth,
By Goddes dignitee er it be nyght!"
    Togidres° han thise thre hir trouthes plight°   *together / promised*
415 To lyve and dyen ech of hem for oother
As though he were his owene yborn° brother.   *born*
And up they stirte° al dronken in this rage.   *jumped*
And forth they goon towardes that village
Of which the taverner hadde spoke biforn.
420 And many a grisly° ooth thanne han they sworn,   *horrible*
And Cristes blessed body they torente.°   *tear apart (with their oaths)*
Deeth shal be deed, if that they may hym hente!°   *catch him*
    Whan they han goon[7] nat fully half a mile

---

[1] *This … understondeth* Those who understand his commandments know this.

[2] *Hayles* I.e., Hales Abbey in Gloucestershire, a monastery that
claimed to have some of Christ's blood as a relic.

[3] *Sevene … treye* The modern game of craps is a version of
medieval hazard, in which the player rolling the dice must call out
the numbers he hopes to get.

[4] *bicched bones two* Two cursed bones; i.e., the dice, which were
made of bone in the Middle Ages.

[5] *It … houres* It was told to me two hours ago, before you came
here.

---

[6] *Ther cam … pestilence* The reference here is doubtless to plague,
the Black Death that spread from Italy across Europe, hit England
in 1348, and in the space of a year killed at least a third of the
population. There were further outbreaks in 1361–62, 1369, and
1375–76.

[7] *han goon* Have gone. Chaucer frequently alternates between the
simple past (the rioters jumped up, the old man met with them) and
the present or the perfect forms (the rioters have gone rather than
had gone or went, which we would expect in modern English).

Right° as they wolde han troden over a stile,[1]   *just*
425   An oold man and a povre° with hem   *poor / encountered them*
        mette.°
        This olde man ful mekely° hem grette°   *meekly / greeted*
        And seyde thus: "Now, lordes, God yow see!"°   *watch over*
           The proudeste of thise riotours three
        Answerde agayn, "What, carl,° with sory   *peasant / bad luck to you*
           grace!°
430   Why artow al forwrapped,° save thy face?   *wrapped up*
        Why lyvestow° so longe in so greet age?"   *live you*
           This olde man gan looke in his visage°   *face*
        And seyde thus: "For° I ne kan nat fynde   *because*
        A man, though that I walked into Ynde,°   *India*
435   Neither in citee nor in no village,
        That wolde chaunge his youthe for myn age.
        And therfore moot I han myn age stille,
        As longe tyme as it is Goddes wille.
        Ne deeth, allas, ne wol nat han my lyf.
440   Thus walke I lyk a restelees° kaityf,°   *restless / wretch*
        And on the ground which is my moodres° gate   *mother's*
        I knokke with my staf° bothe erly and late   *walking stick*
        And seye, 'Leeve° Mooder, leet me in!   *dear*
        Lo how I vanysshe°—flessh and blood and skyn!   *waste away*
445   Allas, whan shul my bones been at reste?
        Mooder, with yow wolde I chaunge my cheste°   *money box*
        That in my chambre° longe tyme hath be,°   *room / been*
        Ye, for an heyre clowt° to wrappe me.'[2]   *hair-shirt*
        But yet to me she wol nat do that grace,°   *favor*
450   For which ful pale and welked° is my face.   *withered*
           "But sires, to° yow it is no curteisye   *in*
        To speken to an old man vileynye,°   *insults*
        But° he trespasse° in word or elles in dede.   *unless / offend*
        In Hooly Writ ye may yourself wel rede
455   'Agayns° an oold man hoor° upon his   *in the presence of / gray*
           heed
        Ye sholde arise.'[3] Wherfore° I yeve° yow   *therefore / give*
           reed:°   *advice*
        Ne dooth unto an oold man noon harm now,

Namoore than that ye wolde° men did to yow[4]   *desire*
In age—if that ye so longe abyde.°   *live long enough*
460   And God be with yow, where° ye go° or ryde.   *wherever / walk*
        I moot go thider as° I have to go."   *thither where*
           "Nay, olde cherl, by God thou shalt nat so!"
        Seyde this oother hasardour° anon.   *gambler*
        "Thou partest nat° so lightly, by Seint John!   *do not get away*
465   Thou spak right now of thilke traytour Deeth,
        That in this contree° alle oure freendes sleeth.   *country*
        Have heer my trouthe:° as thou art his espye,°   *on my word / spy*
        Telle where he is, or thou shalt it abye,°   *pay for it*
        By God and by the hooly sacrement!°   *holy sacrament (the Eucharist)*
470   For soothly, thou art oon of his assent°   *plot*
        To sleen us yonge folk, thou false theef!"
           "Now sires," quod he, "if that ye be so leef,°   *desirous*
        To fynde Deeth, turne up this croked wey.°   *crooked way*
        For in that grove I lafte hym, by my fey,°   *faith*
475   Under a tree, and there he wole abyde.°   *wait*
        Noght for youre boost he wole him nothyng hyde.[5]
        Se ye that ook?° Right there ye shal hym fynde.   *oak*
        God save yow that boghte agayn° mankynde[6]   *redeemed*
        And yow amende!"° Thus seyde this olde man.   *make you better*
480   And everich° of thise riotours ran   *each*
        Til he cam to that tree, and ther they founde
        Of floryns° fyne of gold ycoyned° rounde   *florins (coins) / coined*
        Wel ny° an eighte busshels, as hem   *very nearly / it seemed to them*
           thoughte.°
        No lenger thanne° after Deeth they soughte,   *then*
485   But ech of hem so glad was of that sighte,
        For that the floryns been so faire and brighte,
        That doun° they sette hem° by this precious   *down / themselves / hoard*
           hoord.°
        The worste of hem, he spak the firste word.
           "Bretheren," quod he, "taak kepe° what I seye.   *pay attention to*
490   My wit is greet, though that I bourde° and pleye.   *joke*
        This tresor hath Fortune unto us yeven°   *given*
        In myrthe and joliftee° oure lyf to lyven.   *jollity*
        And lightly° as it comth, so wol we spende.   *easily*
        Ey, Goddes precious dignitee! Who wende°   *expected*

---

[1] *stile* Steps to get over a wall or fence.

[2] *Mooder ... me* People in the Middle Ages sometimes wore shirts made of hair, which irritated the body, expecting the pain to gain them spiritual benefit. Here the old man wishes be buried in such a shirt, exchanging it for the chest that holds his money.

[3] *Agayns ... arise* See Leviticus 19.3.

---

[4] *Namoore ... yow* Cf. the Golden Rule from Matthew 7:12: "So whatever you wish that men would do to you, do so to them."

[5] *Noght ... hyde* He will not hide himself in any way because of your boasting.

[6] *God ... mankynde* May God, who redeemed mankind (by sending his Son Jesus Christ to die on the Cross), save you.

495 Today that we sholde han so fair a grace?
But myghte this gold be caried fro this place
Hoom to myn hous, or elles unto yours—
For wel ye woot that al this gold is oures—
Thanne were we in heigh felicitee.°   *great happiness*
500 But trewely, by daye it may nat bee.°   *not be*
Men wolde seyn that we were theves stronge°   *downright thieves*
And for oure owene tresor doon us honge.° *cause us to be hanged*
This tresor moste ycaried be by nyghte
As wisely and as slyly as it myghte.
505 Wherfore I rede° that cut° among us alle,   *advise / lots*
Be drawe° and lat se wher the cut wol falle,   *drawn*
And he that hath the cut with herte blithe°   *happy*
Shal renne to towne, and that ful swithe,°   *quickly*
And brynge us breed and wyn ful prively.°   *secretly*
510 And two of us shul kepen subtilly°   *cleverly*
This tresor wel. And if he wol nat tarie,°   *delay*
Whan it is nyght we wol this tresor carie
By oon assent° whereas us thynketh best."   *in agreement*
That oon of hem the cut° broghte in his fest°   *lots / fist*
515 And bad hem drawe and looke where it wol falle.
And it fil on the yongeste of hem alle,
And forth toward the toun he wente anon.
And also soone as that he was gon,
That oon spak thus unto that oother:
520 "Thow knowest wel thou art my sworn brother;
Thy profit° wol I telle thee anon.   *your advantage*
Thou woost wel that oure felawe is agon,
And heere is gold, and that ful greet plentee,°   *a great deal of it*
That shal departed° been among us thre.   *divided*
525 But nathelees, if I kan shape it so,
That it departed were among us two,
Hadde I nat doon a freendes torn° to thee?"   *friend's turn*
    That oother answerde, "I noot hou° that   *do not know how*
      may be.
He woot how that the gold is with us tweye.°   *two*
530 What shal we doon? What shal we to hym seye?"
    "Shal it be conseil?"° seyde the firste shrewe.°   *our plan / villain*
"And I shal tellen in a wordes fewe
What we shal doon and bryngen it wel aboute."
    "I graunte," quod that oother, "out of doute,°   *without doubt*
535 That by my trouthe I shal thee nat biwreye."°   *betray*
    "Now," quod the firste, "thou woost wel we be tweye,
And two of us shul strenger be than oon.

Looke whan that he is set, that right anoon
Arys° as though thou woldest with hym pleye,   *arise*
540 And I shal ryve° hym thurgh the sydes tweye°   *stab / two sides*
Whil that thou strogelest° with hym as in game,°   *struggle / jest*
And with thy daggere, looke thou do the same.
And thanne shal al this gold departed be,
My deere freend, bitwixen me and thee.
545 Thanne may we bothe oure lustes° all fulfille   *pleasures*
And pleye at dees° right at oure owene wille."   *dice*
And thus acorded been° thise shrewes tweye   *are agreed*
To sleen° the thridde, as ye han herd me seye.   *kill*
    This yongeste, which that wente unto the toun,
550 Ful ofte in herte he rolleth up and doun
The beautee of thise floryns newe and brighte.
"O Lord," quod he, "if so were that I myghte
Have al this tresor to myself allone,
Ther is no man that lyveth under the trone°   *throne*
555 Of God that sholde lyve so murye° as I!"   *merry*
And atte laste the feend° oure enemy   *devil*
Putte in his thought that he sholde poyson beye°   *buy*
With which he myghte sleen hise felawes tweye,   *kill*
For why the feend foond hym in swich lyvynge
560 That he hadde leve hym to sorwe brynge.[1]
For this was outrely° his fulle entente,   *utterly*
To sleen hem bothe and nevere to repent.
And forth he gooth—no lenger wolde he tarie—
Into the toun unto a pothecarie°   *apothecary*
565 And preyde hym that he hym wolde selle
Som poysoun that he myghte hise rattes° quelle.°   *rats / kill*
And eek ther was a polcat in his hawe,
That, as he seyde, hise capouns hadde yslawe.[2]
And fayn° he wolde wreke hym,° if he   *gladly / avenge himself*
    myghte,
570 On vermyn that destroyed° hym by nyghte.   *harmed*
    The pothecarie answerde, "And thou shalt have
A thyng that, also° God my soule save,   *as*
In al this world ther is no creature
That eten or dronken hath of this confiture°   *concoction*

---

[1] *For why … brynge* Because the devil found him living in such a way (i.e., so sinfully) that he had permission (from God) to bring him to sorrow (i.e., damnation).

[2] *And eek … yslawe* And also there was a polecat (a type of weasel) in his yard that, as he said, had killed his poultry.

575 Noght° but the montance° of a corn° of
        whete,   *nothing | size | grain*
    That he ne shal his lif anon° forlete.°   *immediately | lose*
    Ye, sterve° he shal, and that in lasse while°   *die | less time*
    Than thou wolt goon a paas° nat but a mile,   *at a walking pace*
    The poysoun is so strong and violent."
580 This cursed man hath in his hond yhent°   *taken*
    This poysoun in a box, and sith° he ran   *afterwards*
    Into the nexte strete° unto a man   *street*
    And borwed hym° large botels thre.   *borrowed from him*
    And in the two his poyson poured he.
585 The thridde he kepte clene for his owene drynke.
    For al the nyght he shoope° hym for to swynke°   *intended | labor*
    In cariynge of the gold out of that place.
    And whan this riotour with sory grace°   *wretched misfortune*
    Hadde filled with wyn hise grete botels thre,
590 To hise felawes agayn repaireth he.
        What nedeth it to sermone° of it moore?   *talk*
    For right so° as they hadde cast° his deeth
        bifoore,   *just as | determined*
    Right so they han hym slayn, and that anon.
    And whan that this was doon, thus spak that oon:° *the first*
595 "Now lat us sitte and drynke and make us merie,
    And afterward we wol his body berie."°   *bury*
    And with that word it happed hym par cas°   *by chance*
    To take the botel ther the poysoun was,
    And drank and yaf his felawe drynke also,
600 For which anon they storven° bothe two.   *died*
        But certes, I suppose that Avycen[1]
    Wroot° nevere in no *Canoun* ne in no fen°   *wrote | chapter*
    Mo wonder° signes° of
        empoisonyng°   *more terrible | symptoms | poisoning*
    Than hadde thise wrecches two er hir endyng.°   *before their death*
605 Thus ended been thise homycides° two   *murderers*
    And eek the false empoysonere° also.   *poisoner*
        O cursed synne of alle cursednesse,
    O traytours° homycide, o wikkednesse,   *traitorous*
    O glotonye, luxurie,° and hasardrye,   *lust*

610 Thou blasphemour of Crist with vileynye
    And othes grete° of usage° and of pride!   *great oaths | habit*
    Allas, mankynde, how may it bitide°   *happen*
    That to thy creatour, which that the wroghte°   *who made you*
    And with his precious herte blood thee boghte,°   *redeemed*
615 Thou art so fals and so unkynde,° allas?   *unnatural*
        Now goode men, God foryeve yow youre trespas
    And ware° yow fro the synne of avarice!   *guard*
    Myn hooly pardoun may yow all warice,°   *save*
    So° that ye offre nobles or sterlynges[2]   *provided*
620 Or elles silver broches, spoones, rynges.
    Boweth youre heed under this hooly bulle.°   *license*
    Com up, ye wyves, offreth of youre wolle;°   *wool*
    Youre names I entre heer in my rolle° anon.   *list*
    Into the blisse of Hevene shul ye gon.
625 I yow assoille° by myn heigh power,   *pardon*
    As ye were born. And lo, sires, thus I preche.
    And Jesu Crist that is oure soules leche°   *soul's physician*
    So graunte yow his pardoun to receyve.
    For that is best; I wol yow nat deceyve.
630   "But sires, o° word forgat I in my tale.   *one*
    I have relikes and pardoun in my male°   *pouch*
    As faire as any man in Engelond,
    Whiche were me yeven° by the Popes hond.°   *given | hand*
    If any of yow wole of devocioun°   *in devotion*
635 Offren and han myn absolucioun,
    Com forth anon, and kneleth heere adoun,
    And mekely° receyveth my pardoun.   *meekly*
    Or elles taketh pardoun as ye wende,°   *go*
    Al newe and fressh at every miles ende,
640 So that ye offren alwey newe° and newe   *anew*
    Nobles or pens,° whiche that be goode and trewe.[3] *pence*
    It is an honour to everich° that is heer   *everyone*
    That ye mowe° have a suffisant° pardoneer   *may | capable*
    T'assoille yow in contree° as ye ryde   *the country*
645 For aventures° whiche that may bityde.°   *accidents | befall*
    Paraventure° ther may fallen oon or two   *perhaps*
    Doun of his hors and breke his nekke atwo.°   *in two*

---

[1] *Avycen*   I.e., Avicenna or Ibn Sina (980–1037 CE), a Persian
philosopher who wrote, among other things, a treatise about
medicine entitled *Liber Canonis Medicinae* (*The Book of the Canon
of Medicine*). The word *Canon* in the next line refers to this book. It
was divided into chapters called "fens," from the Arabic word for a
part of a science.

[2] *nobles or sterlynges*   Gold and silver coins respectively.

[3] *Nobles ... trewe*   Forgery and also the clipping of coins (i.e.,
shaving off some of the silver or gold from the edges) were major
concerns in Chaucer's day.

Looke which a seuretee° is it to yow alle   *guarantee*
That I am in youre felaweshipe yfalle,°   *fallen into your company*
650 That may assoille yow bothe moore and
        lasse°   *greater and lesser (of rank)*
Whan that the soule shal fro the body passe.
I rede° that oure Hoost heere shal bigynne,°   *advise / begin*
For he is moost envoluped in synne.
Com forth, sire Hoost, and offre first anon,
655 And thou shalt kisse my relikes everychon.
Ye, for a grote unbokele anon thy purs."[1]
        "Nay, nay," quod he, "thanne have I Cristes curs!°   *curse*
Lat be,"° quod he. "It shal nat be so, thee'ch!   *leave it be*
Thou woldest make me kisse thyn olde breech°   *pants*
660 And swere it were a relyk of a seint—
Though it were with thy fundement° depeint!°   *anus / stained*
But by the croys which that Seint Eleyne[2] fond,
I wolde I hadde thy coillons° in myn hond   *testicles*
Instide of relikes or of seintuarie!°   *reliquaries*
665 Lat kutte hem of!° I wol with thee hem
        carie.°   *let them be cut off / carry*

They shul be shryned° in an hogges
        toord!"°   *enshrined / hog's turd*
    This Pardoner answerde nat a word.
So wrooth° he was, no word ne wolde he seye.   *angry*
    "Now," quod oure Hoost, "I wol no lenger pleye°   *joke*
670 With thee ne with noon oother angry man!"
But right anon the worthy knyght bigan°   *began*
Whan that he saugh that al the peple lough,°   *laughed*
"Namoore of this! For it is right ynough!°   *quite enough*
Sire Pardoner, be glad and myrie of cheere.°   *merry of face*
675 And ye, sire Hoost, that been to me so deere,
I prey yow that ye kisse the Pardoner.
And Pardoner, I prey thee, drawe thee neer,
And as we diden,° lat us laughe and pleye!"   *did*
Anon they kiste and ryden forth hir weye.°   *their way*

HEERE IS ENDED THE PARDONERS TALE

---

[1] *Ye ... purs* Yes, unbuckle your purse immediately for a groat
(fourpenny coin).

[2] *Seint Eleyne* I.e., St. Helena, the mother of the fourth-century
Roman emperor Constantine. Legend had it that she went to the
Holy Land and found there the cross on which Christ was crucified.

The Prioress's Prologue and Tale

*T*he Prioress's Tale belongs to the genre of the miracles of the Virgin, collections of stories recounting the Virgin Mary's dramatic interventions to save people who had shown her particular devotion. These melodramatic stories were enormously popular, In these miracle stories, Jews often figure as villains, and there are several in which they are depicted murdering or trying to murder a Christian child, whom the Virgin rescues or takes to Heaven. One such legend concerned the boy-saint Hugh of Lincoln. The Prioress describes his death as happening "but a little while ago" (line 686), but all Jews had been expelled from England in 1290 and Hugh was in fact killed in 1255.

Chaucer's presentation of this anti-Semitic story, a version of the so-called "blood libel," which accuses Jews of killing Christian children, has troubled modern readers, who have often debated whether Chaucer's own attitudes are to any degree distanced from those of the Prioress. The contrast between the sentimentality she is shown to display in *The General Prologue* (as a character who weeps if a man beats one of her lap dogs) and the extreme virulence of her hatred of the Jews—who are punished more savagely at the end of her tale than in other versions of the story—might suggest a narrative distancing. On the other hand, *The Prioress's Tale* was popular in the fifteenth century, and was copied separately in several manuscripts, with no reference to *The General Prologue*; the opening Hymn to the Virgin, the *Alma redemptoris*, is set above any possible parody; the Man of Law is no less hostile to Islam; and there are anti-Semitic lines in *The Parson's Tale* as well. In short, it is difficult not to think it likely that Chaucer shared substantially in the anti-Semitism that was so prevalent in fourteenth-century England.

Also of interest is the style of *The Prioress's Tale*. Written in rhyme-royal stanzas, and drawing on the language of the liturgy, it has moments of stately elegance, as the Prioress employs a high rhetorical style in formal praise of the Virgin. But it also contains lurid details of the murder and the disposal of the body in a privy which seem at odds with the Prioress's courtly manners.

The relation between the teller and the tale has attracted much critical attention. The Prioress clearly identifies with the innocent little *clergeon*, who is absolute in his devotion to the Virgin, even to the point of neglecting his education. His faith, like hers, is child-like in its innocence, or so she would have us believe. The tale can perhaps be explained as Chaucer's exploration of a particular kind of devotional story, the emotionally charged saint's life or miracle of the Virgin, which was immensely popular in his day.

Detail of the opening page of *The Prioress's Tale*, Ellesmere manuscript.
(This item is reproduced by permission of the *Huntington Library*, San Marino, California. EL26C9F72r.)

Opening page of *The Prioress's Tale*, Ellesmere manuscript.
(This item is reproduced by permission of the *Huntington Library*, San Marino, California. EL26C9F72r.)

THE PRIORESS'S PROLOGUE

BIHOOLD THE MURIE WORDES OF THE HOOST TO THE SHIPMAN AND TO THE LADY PRIORESSE

"Wel seyd,° by *corpus dominus*,"[1] quod° oure
   Hoost.°   *well said / said / host*
"Now longe moote° thou saille° by the cost,° *may / sail / coast*
Sire gentil° maister,° gentil maryneer!° *noble / master / mariner*
God yeve° this monk a thousand last quade
   yeer!°   *give / cart-loads of bad years*
5 Aha, felawes,° beth war° of swich° a
   jape!°   *fellows / beware / such / joke*
The monk putte in the mannes hood an ape,[2]
And in his wyves° eek,° by Seint
   Austyn!°   *wife's / also / St. Augustine*
Draweth° no monkes moore unto youre
   in.°   *take / into your house*
  "But now passe over,° and lat° us seke° aboute *on / let / seek*
10 Who shal now telle first of al° this route° *all / company*
Another tale." And with that word he sayde
As curteisly° as it had been a mayde,° *courteously / maid (speaking)*
"My Lady Prioresse, by youre leve,°   *leave*
So that I wiste° I sholde yow nat
   greve,°   *knew / would not distress you*
15 I wolde demen° that ye tellen sholde° *would judge / should tell*
A tale next, if so were that ye wolde.
Now wol° ye vouchesauf,° my lady deere?"° *will / agree / dear*
  "Gladly," quod she, and seyde° as ye shal heere.° *said / hear*

EXPLICIT[3]

THE PROLOGUE OF THE PRIORESS'S TALE

Domine Dominus noster[4]

20 "O Lord, oure Lord, thy name how merveillous° *marvelous*
   Is in this large world ysprad,"° quod she. *spread about*
"For noght oonly° thy laude° precious   *not only / praise*
Parfourned° is by men of dignitee,   *proclaimed*
But by the mouth of children thy bountee°   *goodness*
Parfourned is, for on the brest° soukynge° *breast / sucking*
25 Somtyme° shewen° they thyn heriynge.° *sometimes / show / praise*

Wherfore° in laude, as I best kan° or may, *therefore / know how*
Of thee and of the lylye flour°   *lily flower*
Which that° thee bar° and is a mayde°
   alway,[5]   *who / bore you / virgin*
To telle a storie I wol do my labour--
30 Nat that I may encreessen° hir honour,   *increase*
For she hirself is honour and the roote°   *root*
Of bountee, next hir sone, and soules boote.[6]

O mooder° mayde,° o mayde mooder
   free,°   *mother / maid / noble*
O bussh unbrent, brennynge in Moyses sighte,[7]
35 That ravysedest° doun° fro° *allured, entranced / down / from*
   the Deitee,
Thurgh thyn humblesse, the goost that in th'alighte,[8]
Of whos vertu whan he thyn herte lighte[9]

---

[1] *corpus dominus* Incorrect Latin: "The Lord's body"; a reference to the sacrament of the Eucharist, in which the communion bread was transubstantiated into Christ's body.

[2] *The ... ape* Literally, "The monk put an ape in the man's hood." I.e., he made a fool of him (to "put an ape" was an expression meaning "to fool").

[3] *Explicit* Latin: Here it ends.

---

[4] *Domine Dominus noster* Latin: "O Lord, our Lord." These are the first words of Psalm 8, which the Prioress paraphrases in the first stanza of her Prologue.

[5] *lylye ... alway* In medieval iconography, the Virgin Mary is presented with a lily, a symbol of her purity, by the angel Gabriel during the Annunciation of the birth of Christ.

[6] *Of ... boote* Of goodness, next to her son, and the soul's help.

[7] *O ... sighte* O unburned bush, burning in Moses's sight. The reference is to the encounter Moses has in Exodus 3 with God in the form of a burning bush that is unconsumed by the fire. This became a popular image for Mary, who preserved her virginity despite being a mother.

[8] *Thurgh ... alighte* Through your humility, the spirit that alighted in you.

[9] *Of ... lighte* Of whose power when he illumined your heart.

Conceyved° was the Fadres sapience,[1]   *conceived*
40 Helpe me to telle it in thy reverence.°   *for your honor*

Lady, thy bountee,° thy magnificence,°   *goodness | majesty*
Thy vertu,° and thy grete humylitee°   *power | great humility*
Ther may no tonge expresse in no
   science.°   *whatever its knowledge*
For somtyme,° Lady, er° men praye to thee,   *sometimes | before*
Thou goost biforn° of thy benyngnytee°   *anticipate | goodness*
45 And getest us thurgh lyght° of thy preyere°   *light | prayer*
To gyden° us unto thy Sone° so deere.   *guide | Son*

My konnyng° is so wayk,° o blisful°
   queene,   *knowledge | weak | blessed*
For to declare thy grete worthynesse,
That I ne may the weighte° nat susteene,°   *the weight | not sustain*
50 But as a child of twelf monthe oold or lesse
That kan unnethe° any word expresse,°   *can scarcely | pronounce*
Right° so fare I. And therfore I yow preye,°   *just | pray you*
Gydeth my song that I shal of yow seye."°   *tell of you*

EXPLICIT

THE PRIORESS'S TALE

HEERE BIGYNNETH THE PRIORESSES TALE

Ther was in Asye[2] in a greet cite°   *great city*
55 Amonges Cristene° folk a Jewerye°   *Christian | Jewish quarter*
Sustened° by a lord of that contree°   *sustained | country*

For foul usure° and lucre° of vileynye,[3]   *interest (rates) | profit*
Hateful to Crist and to his
   compaignye.°   *company (i.e., Christians)*
And thurgh this strete° men myghte ride or wende,°   *street | go*
60 For it was free and open at eyther ende.

A litel scole° of Cristen folk ther stood   *little school*
Doun at the ferther ende, in which ther were
Children an heepe° ycomen° of Cristen   *many children | come*
   blood,
That lerned in that scole yeer by yere
65 Swich manere doctrine° as men used there.   *such kind of teaching*
This is to seyn, to syngen° and to rede,°   *sing | read*
As smale children doon in hire childhede.°   *their childhood*

Among thise° children was a wydwes sone,°   *these | widow's son*
A litel clergeoun[4] seven yeer of age,
70 That day by day to° scole was his wone.°   *to [go to] | custom*
And eek also whereas° he saugh°
   th'ymage°   *where | saw | the image*
Of Cristes mooder, he hadde in usage,°   *he had the habit*
As hym was taught, to knele adoun and seye
His *Ave Marie*[5] as he goth by the weye.°   *goes along the road*

75 Thus hath this wydwe hir litel sone ytaught°   *taught*
Oure blisful lady, Cristes mooder deere,
To worshipe ay.° And he forgat it naught,°   *always | not*
For sely° child wol alwey soone leere.°   *innocent | learn*
But ay° whan I remembre on this mateere,   *ever*
80 Seint Nicholas[6] stant° evere in my presence,   *stands*
For he so yong to Crist dide° reverence.   *did*

---

[1] *Fadres sapience* Father's wisdom (i.e., Christ). Although each member of the Christian Trinity is equal, they are often associated with particular qualities. Christ, the word or logos, is associated with wisdom; the Father with power, and the Holy Spirit with love.

[2] *Ayse* Asia. In the Middle Ages, the geographical term "Asia" meant Asia Minor, which today is the country of Turkey and part of northern Greece. All Jews were expelled from England in 1290. In Chaucer's day there were some Jews living in France (from which they were expelled first in 1306 and again in 1394), some in central and eastern Europe, the Balkans and Asia Minor. There were also significant Jewish communities in Spain, Italy, North Africa, and the Middle East.

[3] *For ... vileynye* In the Middle Ages, the Church prohibited Christians from lending money at interest rates. Such commerce, increasingly necessary for the economy of the time, was engaged in by the few non-Christian peoples of Europe, especially the Jews. See the section on "Religion and Spiritual Life" elsewhere in this volume for a further discussion of this issue.

[4] *clergeoun* Term meaning pupil but also choir boy. Young boys often served in choirs in exchange for education.

[5] *Ave Marie* Latin: "Hail Mary," the words of the angel Gabriel to the Virgin at the Annunciation. His speech was set to music and frequently sung in church services in the Middle Ages.

[6] *Seint Nicholas* Fourth-century bishop of Myra in Asia Minor who became the patron saint of children. His legend maintained that as an infant he fasted on Wednesdays and Fridays by refusing his mother's breast-milk.

This litel child, his litel book lernynge,° *learning*
As he sat in the scole at his prymer,° *primer (school book)*
He *Alma redemptoris*[1] herde synge° *heard being sung*
85   As children lerned hire° antiphoner.[2] *their*
And as he dorste,° he drough hym° *dared | drew himself |*
     ner° and ner *nearer*
And herkned ay° the wordes and the *ever listened (to) |*
     noote° *melody*
Til he the firste vers koude° al by rote.° *knew | by heart*

Noght wiste he° what this Latyn was to *he did not know |*
     seye,° *meant*
90   For he so yong and tendre was of age.
But on a day his felawe° gan he preye° *his friend | he began to ask*
T'expounden hym° this song in his langage, *to explain to him*
Or telle hym why this song was in usage;
This preyde he hym to construe° and declare *translate*
95   Ful often tyme° upon hise knowes° bare. *very often | knees*

His felawe, which that elder was than he,
Answerde hym thus: "This song, I have herd seye,° *heard said*
Was maked of° oure blisful lady free,° *made for | noble*
Hir to salue° and eek hire for to preye *honor*
100 To been° oure helpe and socour° whan we deye.° *be | aid | die*
I kan namoore expounde in this mateere.
I lerne song; I kan° but smal° grammeere." *know | little*

"And is this song maked° in reverence° *made | honor*
Of Cristes mooder?" seyde this innocent.
105 "Now, certes,° I wol do my diligence° *certainly | will work hard*
To konne° it al er Cristemasse is went,° *learn | has passed*
Though that I for my prymer shal be shent[3]
And shal be beten° thries° in an houre. *beaten | three times*
I wol it konne,° oure Lady for to honoure." *will learn it*

110 His felawe taughte hym homward prively[4]
Fro day to day, til he koude it by rote.
And thanne he song° it wel and boldely *sang*
Fro word to word, acordynge with the
     note.° *according to the melody*
Twies° a day it passed thurgh his throte, *twice*
115 To scoleward° and homward whan he wente; *towards school*
On Cristes mooder set was his entente.

As I have seyd, thurghout° the Juerie *throughout*
This litel child, as he cam to and fro,
Ful murily° wolde he synge and crie *merrily*
120 *O Alma redemptoris* everemo.
The swetnesse his herte perced° so *pierced*
Of Cristes mooder, that to hire° to preye *her*
He kan nat stynte° of syngyng° by the weye. *cannot stop | singing*

Oure firste foo,° the serpent Sathanas,° *foe | Satan*
125 That hath in Jues herte° his waspes° nest *Jewish hearts | wasp's*
Up swal° and seide, "O Hebrayk *swelled up | Hebrew people*
     peple,° allas!
Is this to yow° a thyng that is honest,° *you | respectable*
That swich a boy shal walken as hym lest° *wishes*
In youre despit,° and synge of swich *scorn of you | subject*
     sentence°
130 Which is agayn° oure lawes reverence?" *against*

Fro thennes° forth the Jues han° conspired *thence | have*
This innocent out of this world to chace.° *chase*
An homycide° therto han they hyred *murderer*
That in an aleye° hadde a privee° place, *alley | secret*
135 And as the child gan forby for to pace,° *to pass by*
This cursed Jew hym hente° and heeld hym faste *grabbed*
And kitte° his throte and in a pit hym caste.° *cut | threw*

I seye° that in a wardrobe° they hym threwe, *say | latrine*
Whereas° thise Jewes purgen° hire
     entraille.° *where | empty | bowels*
140 O cursed folk of Herodes[5] al newe,
What may youre yvel° entente° yow availle? *evil | intent*
Mordre wol out! Certeyn, it wol nat faille,

---

[1] *Alma redemptoris* I.e., "Alma redemptoris mater" (Latin: Gracious mother of the redeemer), an antiphon used in church services in the Middle Ages during Advent.

[2] *antiphoner* Book containing the words and music of antiphons like *Alma Redemptoris*.

[3] *Though ... shent* Although I shall be punished for [neglecting] my school book. Corporal punishment was the norm in medieval schools for students who were slow at learning their lessons.

[4] *His ... prively* On the way home, his friend taught him privately.

[5] *O ... Herodes* In Matthew 2.1–18, Herod causes all the children of the region to be murdered in his effort to kill the baby Jesus.

And namely, ther th'onour of God shal sprede.[1]
The blood out crieth° on youre cursed dede!　　　　　*cries out*

145　O martir° sowded° to virginitee,　　　　　*martyr / united*
Now maystow° syngen, folwynge evere in
　　　oon°　　　　　*may you / following ever in unity*
The white Lamb celestial,[2] quod she,[3]
Of which the grete evaungelist Seint John
In Pathmos wroot,[4] which seith that they that goon°　　　　　*go*
150　Biforn this Lamb and synge a song al newe
That nevere flesshly° wommen they ne knewe.[5]　　　　　*carnally*

　　This povre wydwe awaiteth° al that nyght　　　　　*waits*
After hir litel child. But he cam noght.°　　　　　*did not come*
For which, as soone as it was dayes lyght,
155　With face pale of drede° and bisy thoght° *for fear / hectic thoughts*
She hath at scole and elleswhere hym soght,
Til finally she gan so fer espie,°　　　　　*found out this much*
That he last seyn was in the Juerie.

With moodres pitee° in hir brest enclosed,　　　　　*mother's pity*
160　She gooth as she were half out of hir mynde
To every place where she hath supposed
By liklihede° hir litel child to fynde.　　　　　*it likely*
And evere on Cristes mooder meeke and kynde
She cride. And atte laste thus she wroghte:°　　　　　*did thus*
165　Among the cursed Jues she hym soghte.

She frayneth,° and she preyeth pitously°　　　　　*asks / begs pitifully*
To every Jew that dwelte in thilke place
To telle hire if hir child wente oght forby.°　　　　　*by at all*
They seyde nay, but Jesu of his grace

170　Yaf in hir thoght inwith a litel space,[6]
That in that place after hir sone she cryde,
Where he was casten in a pit bisyde.°　　　　　*nearby*

O grete God, that parfournest° thy laude°　　　　　*proclaims / praise*
By mouth of innocentz, lo heere° thy myght!　　　　　*behold here*
175　This gemme° of chastite, this emeraude,°　　　　　*gem / emerald*
And eek of martirdom° the ruby bright,　　　　　*martyrdom*
Ther° he with throte ykorven° lay
　　upright,°　　　　　*where / cut / on his back*
He *Alma redemptoris* gan to synge
So loude that al the place gan to rynge!

180　The Cristene folk that thurgh° the strete wente　　　　　*through*
In coomen° for to wondre upon this thyng,　　　　　*came*
And hastily they for the provost[7] sente.
He cam anon withouten tariyng°　　　　　*delay*
And herieth° Crist that is of Hevene kyng　　　　　*praises*
185　And eek his mooder, honour of mankynde,
And after that the Jewes leet he°
　　bynde.°　　　　　*he commanded / to be bound*

This child with pitous lamentacioun
Up taken° was, syngynge his song alway,　　　　　*lifted up*
And with honour of greet processioun
190　They carien hym unto the nexte abbay.°　　　　　*nearest monastery*
His mooder swownynge° by his beere° lay.　　　　　*fainting / bier*
Unnethe° myghte the peple that was theere　　　　　*scarcely*
This newe Rachel[8] brynge fro his beere.

With torment° and with shameful deeth°
　　echon,°　　　　　*torture / death / each one*
195　This provost dooth° the Jewes for to sterve,°　　　　　*causes / die*
That of this mordre wiste,° and that anon.°　　　　　*knew / immediately*
He nolde° no swich cursednesse°
　　observe.°　　　　　*would not / villainy / tolerate*
Yvele° shal he have that yvele wol deserve!　　　　　*evil*

---

[1] *Mordre ... sprede* Murder will come to light. Certainly, it will not fail, and especially wherever the honor of God shall spread.

[2] *Lamb celestial* Heavenly lamb. The reference is to Revelation 14.1–5, in which Christ appears as the Lamb of God.

[3] *she* I.e., the Prioress. This line-filler reinforces momentarily the fiction that the Prioress is telling this tale on the road to Canterbury.

[4] *of which ... wroot* The writer of Revelation identifies himself as John, who was exiled for his faith on the island of Patmos off the coast of Turkey, where he had the visions that form the basis of the book of Revelation.

[5] *That ... knewe* Reference to the virginity of those who praise the Lamb.

[6] *Yaf ... space* Brought to her mind within a little while.

[7] *provost* Medieval judge who oversaw legal matters within a town.

[8] *This newe Rachel* Reference to Matthew 2.18, which quotes Jeremiah 31.15: "Rachel weeping for her children, and would not be comforted, because they are not." Rachel, according to Matthew, is a metaphor for the Jewish mothers whose children were slaughtered by Herod.

Therfore with wilde hors° he dide hem
    drawe,°   *horses | had them drawn*
200 And after that he heng° hem by° the lawe. *hanged | according to*

Upon this beere ay lith° this innocent   *ever lies*
Biforn° the chief auter° whil the masse° laste, *before | altar | mass*
And after that the abbot with his covent°   *group of monks*
Han sped° hem for to burien° hym ful faste. *have hurried | bury*
205 And whan they hooly water on hym caste,
Yet spak° this child whan spreynd° was   *spoke | sprinkled*
    hooly water
And song° *O alma redemptoris mater.*   *sang*

This abbot, which that was an hooly man,
As monkes been° or elles oghte be,   *are*
210 This yonge child to conjure he bigan°   *began to call upon*
And seyde, "O deere child, I halse° thee   *ask*
In vertu of the Hooly Trinitee,
Tel me what is thy cause for to synge,
Sith that thy throte is kut, to my semynge."° *as it seems to me*

215 "My throte is kut unto my nekke boon,"°   *neck-bone*
Seyde this child, "and as by wey° of kynde° *way | nature*
I sholde have dyed, ye,° longe tyme agon.° *yes | ago*
But Jesu Crist, as ye in bookes fynde,
Wil° that his glorie laste and be in mynde,° *wishes | remembered*
220 And for the worship of his mooder deere,
Yet may I synge *O alma* loude and cleere.

"This welle° of mercy, Cristes mooder sweete, *well (source)*
I loved alwey, as after my konnynge.° *according to my knowledge*
And whan that I my lyf sholde forlete,°   *have lost*
225 To me she cam and bad° me for to synge *commanded*
This anthephen° verraily° in my
    deyynge,°   *antiphon | truly | dying*
As ye han herd. And whan that I hadde songe,
Me thoughte she leyde a greyn° upon my tonge.° *grain*

"Wherfore I synge, and synge I moot, certeyn,
230 In honour of that blisful mayden free,
Til fro my tonge of taken° is the greyn.   *taken off*
And afterward thus seyde she to me:

'My litel child, now wol I fecche° thee   *fetch*
Whan that the greyn is fro thy tonge ytake.° *taken*
235 Be nat agast.° I wol thee nat forsake!'"   *not afraid*

This hooly monk, this abbot, hym meene I,° *I mean him*
His tonge out caughte° and took awey the greyn, *pulled out*
And he yaf° up the goost ful softely.° *gave | very quietly*
And whan this abbot hadde this wonder seyn,° *seen*
240 Hise salte teeris° trikled doun as reyn,° *salty tears | rain*
And gruf° he fil° al plat° upon the grounde, *on his face | fell | flat*
And stille he lay as he had leyn ybounde.° *lain bound*

The covent eek lay on the pavement,
Wepynge and herying Cristes mooder deere.
245 And after that they ryse and forth been went° *are gone away*
And tooken awey this martir from his beere,
And in a temple of marbul stones cleere
Enclosen they his litel body sweete.
Ther he is now, God leve° us alle for to meete! *allow*

250 O yonge° Hugh of Lyncoln,[1] slayn also   *young*
With° cursed Jewes, as it is notable,° *by | well known*
For it is but a litel while ago,
Preye eek for us, we synful folk unstable,° *unsteadfast*
That of his mercy God so merciable°   *merciful*
255 On us his grete mercy multiplie
For reverence of his mooder Marie. Amen.

HEERE IS ENDED THE PRIORESSES TALE

---

[1] *Hugh of Lyncoln* Child supposedly murdered by Jews in 1255. He was one of the two principal saints associated with Lincoln, a town midway up England's east coast. In 1386 Henry, Earl of Derby (John of Gaunt's son by his first wife and the future Henry IV), became a member of the fraternity of Lincoln Cathedral, to which Edward III and John of Gaunt already belonged. Chaucer's wife Philippa, who was a member of the household of John of Gaunt's wife, Constance or Constanza of Castille, also became a member of the fraternity at the same ceremony. Chaucer may have had a special interest in Hugh of Lincoln because of this connection to the Cathedral's fraternity, although he was not a member himself.

The Nun's Priest's Prologue and Tale

In the full *Canterbury Tales* this tale is preceded by *The Monk's Tale*, in which the Monk recites a long list of tragedies, which for him are simply stories of those who have fallen suddenly from great rank. This wearies the Knight, who interrupts him. When the Monk refuses to tell stories of hunting instead, the Host calls peremptorily upon the Nun's Priest. The Nun's Priest, who is not even described in the *General Prologue*, is at first almost a nonentity. By the end of his tale, however, he will have won whole-hearted admiration, at least from the rather undiscerning Host, whose response (also included here) is contained in a passage that does not appear in the Ellesmere Manuscript.

The tale offered by the Nun's Priest is a beast fable of the kind told by Aesop. It revolves around animals who are all too human in their follies, and it teaches a clear moral lesson: beware of flatterers. The Nun's Priest expands on this simple structure, beginning with a rich rhetorical evocation of the rooster Chauntecleer's crowing, which he contrasts to the austere life of the poor widow who owns him. The tale then moves into an elaborate debate on dream lore, in which the hen Pertelote speaks for the materialist for whom dreams are the result of indigestion, and Chauntecleer for those who see them as veiled prophecies. This debate alone takes up nearly half the lines in the tale. Throughout, the tale fluctuates between a world in which Chauntecleer and Pertelote are aristocratic lovers and a world in which they are just barnyard fowl. Much of the comedy lies in the elaborate rhetorical language, which is both celebrated and mocked. The Nun's Priest is clearly a master of this art, and it is typical of the tale's comic approach to the eloquence it proudly displays that he should invoke Geoffrey of Vinsauf and his basic textbook on rhetoric. This is a work that, while it is several steps up on Pertelote's only written authority, an elementary grammar drawn from the moral writings of Cato, is scarcely sophisticated. For all its comedy, the tale contains one of Chaucer's grimmest and most pointed historical references, to the rebels in 1381 who hunted down and murdered Flemish weavers.

The Nun's Priest ends by suggesting that the tale exists only for its moral, the fruit, and that we should discard the story, the chaff. All that is written, he tells us, is written for our doctrine, a line Chaucer repeats in his *Retraction*. But the Nun's Priest also tells us that his story is as true as that of Lancelot de Lake (line 445), that he speaks only in game (line 495), and that when he criticizes women his words are those of Chauntecleer (line 498). Filled with references to books and sayings, such as Chauntecleer's comment that "Mulier est hominis confusio" (Latin: Woman is man's confusion, line 397), that are misrepresented or otherwise untrustworthy, the tale does not allow such an easy distinction between literary art and moral content.

Opening page of *The Nun's Priest's Tale*, Ellesmere manuscript (detail).
(This item is reproduced by permission of the *Huntington Library*, San Marino, California. EL26C9F72r.)

Opening page of *The Nun's Priest's Tale*, Ellesmere manuscript.
(This item is reproduced by permission of the *Huntington Library*, San Marino, California. EL26C9F72r.)

THE NUN'S PRIEST'S PROLOGUE

HEERE STYNTETH THE KNYGHT THE MONK OF HIS TALE[1]

THE PROLOGE OF THE NONNES PREESTES TALE

"Hoo,"° quod° the Knyght, "good sire, namoore° of
   this!   *whoa / said / no more*
That ye han seyd is right ynough, ywis,[2]
And muchel moore,° for litel
   hevynesse°   *much more / a little heaviness*
Is right ynough° to muche folk,° I gesse. *enough / many people*
5 I seye° for me it is a greet disese,°   *say / great discomfort*
Whereas° men han been in greet welthe° and
   ese,°   *where / wealth / ease*
To heeren° of hire° sodeyn fal,° allas! *hear / their / sudden fall*
And the contrarie° is joye and greet solas,° *contrary / comfort*
As whan a man hath been in povre° estaat,° *poor / condition*
10 And clymbeth° up, and wexeth° fortunate, *climbs / grows*
And there abideth° in prosperitee.   *remains*
Swich° thyng is gladsom,° as it
   thynketh° me,   *such a / pleasant / seems to*
And of swich thyng were goodly for to telle."
  "Ye,"° quod oure Hoost, "by Seint Poules belle,[3] *yes*
15 Ye seye right sooth.° This Monk, he clappeth
   lowed.°   *truth / chatters loudly*
He spak how Fortune covered with a clowde° *cloud*
I noot° nevere what, and also of a tragedie *know not*
Right now ye harde,° and, pardee,° no
   remedie°   *heard / by God / remedy*
It is for to biwaille° ne° compleyne° *bewail / nor / lament*
20 That that° is doon,° and als° it is a
   peyne,°   *which / done / also / pain*
As ye han seyd, to heere of hevynesse.°   *sadness*
  "Sire Monk, namoore of this, so God yow blesse!
Youre tale anoyeth al this compaignye.
Swich talkyng is nat worth a boterflye!°   *butterfly*
25 For therinne is ther no desport° ne game. *sport*

Wherfore,° sire Monk, daun° Piers by youre
   name,   *therefore / sir*
I pray yow hertely° telle us somwhat elles.° *heartily / something else*
For sikerly,° nere° clynkyng° of youre
   belles   *surely / were not / clinking*
That on youre bridel° hange on every syde, *bridle*
30 By Hevene Kyng° that° for us alle
   dyde,°   *the King of Heaven / who / died*
I sholde er° this han° fallen doun for sleepe, *before / have*
Althogh the slough° had never been so deepe. *mud*
Thanne hadde youre tale al be° toold in veyn.° *been / vain*
For certeinly, as that thise clerkes seyn,° *these scholars say*
35 Whereas° a man may have noon° audience, *where / no*
Noght helpeth it° to tellen his sentence.° *it is of no use / meaning*
And wel I woot, the substance is in me
If anythyng shal wel reported be.[4]
Sire, sey° somwhat of huntyng, I yow preye." *tell us*
40 "Nay," quod this Monk, "I have no lust° to
   pleye.°   *desire / play*
Now lat° another telle as I have toold."   *let*
  Thanne spak oure Hoost with rude speche° and
   boold°   *rough speech / bold*
And seyde unto the Nonnes Preest°
   anon,°   *Nun's Priest / immediately*
"Com neer, thou Preest. Com hyder,° thou sire John![5] *here*
45 Telle us swich thyng as may oure hertes glade.° *gladden*
Be blithe,° though thou ryde upon a jade.° *happy / bad horse*
What thogh° thyn hors be bothe foul and lene?° *though / lean*
If he wol serve thee, rekke nat a bene!° *do not care a bean*
Looke that thyn herte be murie° everemo." *merry*
50 "Yis sire," quod he, "yis, Hoost, so moot I go.° *as I may go*
But° I be myrie, ywis,° I wol be blamed." *unless / indeed*
And right anon his tale he hath attamed,° *has begun*
And thus he seyde unto us everichon,° *everyone*
This sweete preest, this goodly man, sire John.

EXPLICIT[6]

THE NUN'S PRIEST'S TALE

HEERE BIGYNNETH THE NONNES PREESTES TALE OF THE COK AND HEN, CHAUNTECLEER AND PERTELOTE

55 A povre° wydwe° somdeel° stape° in
   age *poor / widow / somewhat / advanced*
  Was whilom° dwellyng° in a narwe° cottage *once / living / small*
  Biside° a grene[1] stondynge° in a dale. *beside / standing*
  This wydwe of which I telle yow my tale,
  Syn° thilke° day that she was last a wyf *since / that*
60 In pacience ladde° a ful° symple lyf, *led / very*
  For litel° was hir catel° and hir rente.° *little / possessions / income*
  By housbondrie° of swich° as God
   hire° sente *frugal use / such / her*
  She foond° hirself and eek° hir
   doghtren° two. *provided for / also / daughters*
  Thre° large sowes hadde she and namo,° *three / no more*
65 Thre keen,° and eek a sheepe that highte° *cows / was called*
   Malle.
  Ful sooty° was hir bour° and eek hir
   halle° *dirty / bedroom / dining hall*
  In which she eet° ful many a sklendre meel.° *ate / meager meal*
  Of poynaunt° sauce hir neded never a deel;° *spicy / portion*
  No deyntee° morsel passed thurgh hir throte.° *dainty / throat*
70 Hir diete was accordant to hir cote.° *in accord with her cottage*
  Repleccioun° ne made hire nevere sik.° *gluttony / sick*
  Attempree° diete was al hir phisik,° *temperate / medical remedy*
  And excercise and hertes suffisaunce.° *heart's content*
  The goute lette hire nothyng for to daunce,[2]
75 N'apoplexie° shente° nat hir heed.° *nor stroke / harmed / head*
  No wyn ne drank she, neither whit ne reed.
  Hir bord° was served moost with whit and blak— *table*
  Milk and broun breed, in which she foond no lak,[3]
  Seynd bacoun° and somtyme an ey° or
   tweye.° *smoked bacon / egg / two*

80 For she was, as it were, a maner° deye.° *kind of / dairy farmer*
  A yeerd° she hadde enclosed al aboute *yard*
  With stikkes° and a drye dych[4] withoute, *sticks*
  In which she hadde a cok° heet° Chauntecleer.[5] *rooster / named*
  In al the land of crowyng° nas° his peer. *crowing / there was not*
85 His voys° was murier° than the murie
   orgon° *voice / merrier / organ*
  On messedayes that in the chirche gon.[6]
  Wel sikerer° was his crowing in his logge° *reliable / lodging*
  Than is a clokke or an abbey orlogge.° *monastery clock*
  By nature he crew° ech ascencioun° *crowed / each ascension*
  Of the equynoxial[7] in thilke° toun. *that*
90 For whan degrees fiftene weren ascended,
  Thanne crew he that it myghte nat been
   amended.° *could not be improved*
  His coomb° was redder than the fyn° coral *coxcomb / fine*
  And batailled° as it were a castel wal.[8] *crenellated*
  His byle° was blak, and as the jeet° it
   shoon.° *bill / jet (gemstone) / shone*
95 Lyk asure° were his legges and his toon,° *azure / toes*
  Hise nayles° whitter than the lylye flour,° *nails / lily flower*
  And lyk the burned° gold was his colour. *polished*
  This gentil° cok hadde in his governaunce° *noble / control*
  Sevene hennes for to doon° al his plesaunce,° *do / pleasure*
100 Whiche were hise sustres° and his paramours° *his sisters / lovers*
  And wonder lyk° to hym as of colours, *marvelously similar*
  Of whiche the faireste hewed° on hir throte° *colored / her throat*
  Was cleped° faire damoysele° Pertelote. *called / damsel*
  Curteys° she was, discreet, and debonaire° *courteous / gracious*
105 And compaignable,° and bar° hyrself so
   faire° *friendly / behaved / well*

---

1 *grene* I.e., green, a common area in a village used for pasturage or other agricultural pursuits that did not demand the plowing of the green into a field.

2 *The goute … daunce* The gout (a disease affecting the feet and brought on by over-eating or drinking) by no means hindered her from dancing.

3 *in … lak* Either defect or lack, so either: In which she found no fault, or of which she had no shortage.

4 *drye dych* Contrasts with the moat of a castle.

5 *Chauntecleer* From the French, "clear singer." Chauntecleer is the name of the rooster in *The Romance of Renard*, which tells the adventures of a wily fox and contains one of the best known medieval versions of the story told by the Nun's Priest.

6 *On … gon* That go (i.e., are played—the organ, an instrument of many pipes, was spoken of as plural) in Church on feast days.

7 *By nature … equynoxial* The sense of this passage is that Chauntecleer crows when each hourly point of the celestial equator rises past the horizon.

8 *And … wal* The crenelation on a castle's walls is the alternation of high, squared masonry with blank spaces. This would provide cover for the archers defending the castle against the arrows of the attackers.

Syn thilke day that she was seven nyght oold,°   *nights old*
That trewely, she hath the herte in hoold°   *holds the heart*
Of Chauntecleer, loken° in every lith.°   *locked / limb*
He loved hire so, that wel was hym therwith.
110 And swich a joye was it to here hem° synge,   *them*
Whan that the brighte sonne bigan to sprynge,°   *rise*
In sweete accord,° "My Lief Is Faren in Londe."[1]   *harmony*
For thilke tyme,° as I have understonde,   *at that time*
Beestes and briddes° koude speke and synge.   *birds*
115   And so bifel° that in the dawenynge,°   *it happened / at dawn*
As Chauntecleer among hise wyves alle
Sat on his perche° that was in the halle,   *perch*
And next hym sat this faire Pertelote,
This Chauntecleer gan gronen° in his throte   *began to groan*
120 As man that in his dreem is drecched soore.°   *sorely disturbed*
And whan that Pertelote thus herde hym roore,°   *roar*
She was agast° and seyde, "O herte deere,   *afraid*
What eyleth° yow to grone in this manere?   *ails*
Ye been° a verray° slepere. Fy!° For shame!"   *are / good / fie*
125   And he answerde and seyde thus: "Madame,
I pray yow that ye take it nat agrief.°   *amiss*
By God, me thoughte I was in swich meschief°   *such trouble*
Right now, that yet myn herte is soore afright.
Now God," quod he, "my swevene recche aright,[2]
130 And kepe my body out of foul prisoun!
Me mette° how that I romed up and doun   *I dreamed*
Withinne oure yeerd, wheereas° I saugh a beest   *where*
Was lyk an hound, and wolde han maad areest°   *grabbed hold*
Upon my body and han had me deed!°   *have had me dead*
135 His colour was bitwixe yelow and reed,°   *red*
And tipped was his tayl° and bothe hise eeris°   *tail / his ears*
With blak, unlyk° the remenant of hise heeris;°   *unlike / hairs*
His snowte° smal with glowynge eyen tweye.°   *nose / two*
Yet° of his look for feere° almoost I deye.   *still / fear*
140 This caused me my gronyng, doutelees."°   *doubtless*
    "Avoy!"° quod she. "Fy on yow, hertelees!°   *shame / coward*
Allas," quod she, "for by that God above,
Now han ye lost myn herte and al my love.
I kan nat love a coward, by my faith!
145 For certes,° whatso° any womman seith,   *certain / whatever*

We alle desiren, if it myghte bee,
To han housbondes hardy,° wise, and free,°   *brave / generous*
And secree° and no nygard° ne no fool,   *discreet / cheapskate*
Ne hym that is agast° of every tool,°   *afraid / weapon*
150 Ne noon avauntour,° by that God above.   *nor any braggart*
How dorste° ye seyn, for shame, unto youre love   *dare*
That anythyng myghte make yow aferd?°   *afraid*
Have ye no mannes herte,° and han a berd?°   *man's heart / beard*
Allas, and konne ye been agast of swevenys?°   *be afraid of dreams*
155 Nothyng, God woot,° but vanitee° in swevene
is!   *knows / foolishness*
Swevenes engendren of° replecciouns°   *are caused by / overeating*
And ofte of fume° and of complecciouns[3]   *stomach- gas*
Whan humours been° to habundant° in a
wight.°   *are / too abundant / person*
Certes, this dreem which ye han met° tonyght   *have dreamed*
160 Cometh of greet superfluytee°   *excess*
Of youre rede colera, pardee,[4]
Which causeth folk to dreden° in hir dremes   *fear*
Of arwes° and of fyr° with rede lemes,°   *arrows / fire / red flames*
Of grete beestes that they wol hem byte,°   *will bite them*
165 Of contek° and of whelpes° grete and lyte,°   *conflict / dogs / small*
Right° as the humour of malencolie[5]   *just*
Causeth ful many a man in sleepe to crie
For feere of blake beres° or boles° blake   *black bears / bulls*
Or elles blake develes wole hem take.
170 Of othere humours koude I telle also
That werken° many a man in sleepe ful wo,°   *cause / much woe*
But I wol passe° as lightly as I kan.   *pass over*
"Lo Catoun,[6] which that was so wys° a man,   *wise*
Seyde he nat thus: 'Ne do no fors of dremes'?[7]

---

[1] *My ... Londe* My dear one has traveled into (a foreign) land. This is the title of a popular song, one version of which, from c. 1500, has survived in a manuscript at Trinity College, Cambridge.

[2] *Now ... aright* "Now God," he said, "interpret my dream correctly."

---

[3] *compleicciouns* I.e., complexions, or temperaments. Medieval medical theory maintained that what we now call personality was a function of the balance in the body of the four bodily fluids known as humors. If these fluids were unbalanced, disease would result.

[4] *Of ... pardee* Of your red choler, by God. Choler was one of the four bodily temperaments. It was formed by the combination of yellow bile (which was hot and dry) with blood (which was hot and moist).

[5] *malencolie* I.e., melancholy, another of the four temperaments.

[6] *Catoun* I.e., Dionysius Cato, a Roman politician who was believed in the Middle Ages to be the author of a widely-circulating collection of proverbs which was often used to teach basic Latin grammar.

[7] *Seyde ... dremes* Said he not this: "Do not pay attention to dreams"?

175 "Now sire," quod she, "whan ye flee° fro the
            bemes,°   *fly down / beams*
    For Goddes love, as taak som laxatyf!°   *take some laxative*
    Up° peril of my soule and of my lyf,   *upon*
    I conseille° yow the beste—I wol nat lye°—   *counsel / lie*
    That bothe of colere° and of malencolye   *choler*
180 Ye purge yow,° and for ye shal nat
            tarie,°   *yourself / so you do not delay*
    Though in this toun is noon apothecarie,°   *no pharmacist*
    I shal myself to herbes° techen yow,   *about herbs*
    That shul been for youre heele° and for youre
            prow,°   *health / profit*
    And in oure yeerd° tho° herbes shal I fynde,   *yard / those*
185 The whiche han of hire propretee° by
            kynde°   *their property / nature*
    To purge yow bynethe and eek above.
    Foryet nat this, for Goddes owene love!
    Ye been ful coleryk of compleccioun.
    Ware the sonne in his ascencioun
190 Ne fynde yow nat repleet of humours hoote.[1]
    And if it do, I dar wel leye° a grote[2]   *bet*
    That ye shul° have a fevere terciane[3]   *shall*
    Or an agu° that may be youre bane.°   *ague (fever) / cause of death*
    A day or two ye shul have digestyves°   *stomach medicines*
195 Of wormes, er ye take youre laxatyves[4]
    Of lawriol,° centaure,° and fumetere,°   *laurel / centaury / fumaria*
    Or elles of ellebor,° that groweth there;   *hellebore*
    Of katapuce° or of gaitrys beryis,°   *euphorbia / rhamus berries*
    Of herbe yve,° growyng in oure yeerd ther mery
            is.°   *herb-ivy / where it is merry*
200 Pekke hem up right as they growe, and ete hem
            yn.°   *eat them up*
    Be myrie, housbonde, for youre fader kyn!°   *merry / father's kin*
    Dredeth no dreem. I kan sey yow namoore."

    "Madame," quod he, "*graunt mercy*[5] of youre loore!°   *advice*
    But nathelees, as touchyng° daun
            Catoun,°   *pertaining to / Master Cato*
205 That hath of° wysdom swich a greet renoun,°   *for / fame*
    Though that he bad° no dremes for to drede,   *commanded*
    By God, men may in olde bookes rede
    Of many a man moore of auctorite
    Than evere Caton was, so moot I thee,°   *so might I thrive*
210 That al° the revers° seyn of this sentence,   *completely / opposite*
    That han wel founden° by experience   *have found out well*
    That dremes been significacïouns°   *are signs*
    As wel of joye as of tribulacïouns°   *troubles*
    That folk enduren in this lif present.
215 Ther nedeth make of this noon argument.
    The verray preeve° sheweth it in dede.   *true proof / deed*
    "Oon of the gretteste auctour[6] that men rede
    Seith thus: that whilom° two felawes wente   *once*
    On pilgrimage in a ful good entente,
220 And happed so° they coomen in a toun,   *it so happened*
    Wheras ther was swich congregacïoun°   *a gathering*
    Of peple, and eek so streit of
            herbergage,°   *such a shortage of lodging*
    That they ne founde as muche as o° cotage   *one*
    In which they bothe myghte logged bee,
225 Wherfore they mosten of necessitee
    As for that nyght departen compaignye.°   *part company*
    And ech of hem gooth to his hostelrye°   *lodging place*
    And took his loggyng as it wolde falle.°   *would happen*
    That oon of hem was logged in a stalle°   *stall*
230 Fer° in a yeerd, with oxen of the plough.   *far*
    That oother man was logged wel ynough,
    As was his aventure° or his fortune,   *chance*
    That us governeth alle as in commune.°   *in common*
    "And so bifel that, longe er it were day,
235 This man mette in his bed, theras° he lay,   *where*
    How that his felawe gan upon hym calle°   *to call*
    And seyde, 'Allas, for in an oxes stalle
    This nyght I shal be mordred ther I lye!
    Now helpe me, deere brother, or I dye.

---

[1] *Ware … hoote* Beware that the sun when it is climbing does not find you when you are (already) full of hot humors. The movements of the planets were thought to affect a patient's balance of humors.

[2] *grote* Coin equal to four pence.

[3] *fevere terciane* I.e., tertian fever. Medieval people classified the types of fevers they would contract by how frequently they recurred. This one would return every third day—meaning every other day, in which the first day is counted, as is the non-fever day and the recurring-fever day. The disease is possibly malaria.

[4] *laxatyves* The laxatives listed by the hen are all types of bitter herbs.

[5] *graunt mercy* From the French "grand merci" or "much thanks." Chauntecleer, as an aristocrat, employs French phrases.

[6] *Oon … auctour* The Roman orator and writer (auctour) Cicero (106–43 BCE) tells the story in *On Divination*, and it is also found in the *Memorable Deeds and Sayings of Valerius Maximus* (see *The Wife of Bath's Prologue*, line 168).

240 In alle haste com to me,' he sayde.
This man out of his sleepe for feere abrayde,° *woke up*
But whan that he was wakened of his sleepe,
He turned hym° and took of it no keepe.° *turned over / notice*
Hym thoughte his dreem nas but a vanitee.° *folly*
245 Thus twies in his slepyng dremed hee,
And atte thridde tyme yet his felawe
Cam as hym thoughte and seide, 'I am now slawe.° *slain*
Bihoold my bloody woundes depe and wyde.
Arys° up erly in the morwe tyde,° *arise / morning-time*
250 And at the west gate of the toun,' quod he,
'A carte ful of donge° ther shaltow° se° *dung / shall you / see*
In which my body is hid ful prively.° *secretly*
Do thilke carte arresten boldely.[1]
My gold caused my mordre, sooth to sayn,'° *true to say*
255 And tolde hym every point how he was slayn
With a ful pitous face, pale of hewe.° *color*
And truste wel, his dreem he foond ful trewe.
For on the morwe, as soone as it was day,
To his felawes in° he took the way, *friend's inn*
260 And whan that he cam to this oxes stalle,
After his felawe he bigan to calle.
    "The hostiler° answerde hym anon *innkeeper*
And seyde, 'Sire, youre felawe is agon.° *gone*
As soone as day he wente out of the toun.'
265   "This man gan fallen in suspicioun,° *to be suspicious*
Remembrynge on hise dremes that he mette.° *dreamed*
And forth he gooth—no lenger wolde he lette°— *delay*
Unto the west gate of the toun and fond° *found*
A dong-carte, as it were to donge lond° *to manure a field*
270 That was arrayed in that same wise° *way*
As ye han herd the dede man devyse.° *describe*
And with an hardy herte he gan to crye,
'Vengeance and justice of this felonye!
My felawe mordred is this same nyght,
275 And in this carte heere he lith,° gapyng
upright.° *lies / facing upright*
I crye out on the ministres,'° quod he, *magistrates*
'That sholden kepe° and reulen° this citee! *care for / rule*
Harrow!° Allas! Heere lith my felawe slayn!' *help*
What sholde I moore unto this tale sayn?
280 The peple out sterte° and caste the cart to grounde, *jumped up*
And in the myddel of the dong they founde

The dede man that mordred was al newe.° *recently*
"O blisful° God that art so just and trewe, *blessed*
Lo how that thou biwreyest° mordre alway! *reveal*
285 Mordre wol out.° That se we day by day. *will be found out*
Mordre is so wlatsom° and abhomynable° *repulsive / abominable*
To God, that is so just and resonable,
That he ne wol nat suffre it heled° be, *concealed*
Though it abyde a yeer or two or thre.
290 Mordre wol out! This my conclusioun.
And right anon, ministres of that toun
Han hent° the cartere, and so soore° hym
pyned,° *arrested / sorely / tortured*
And eek the hostiler so soore engyned,° *tortured on a rack*
That they biknewe° hire wikkednesse anon *confessed*
295 And were anhanged° by the nekke bon.° *hanged / neck-bone*
    "Heere may men seen that dremes been to
drede.° *are to be feared*
And certes, in the same book I rede,
Right in the nexte chapitre after this—
I gabbe° nat, so have I joye or blis— *babble*
300 Two men that wolde han° passed over see° *would have / the sea*
For certeyn cause into a fer contree,° *distant country*
If that the wynd° ne hadde been contrarie, *wind*
That made hem in a citee for to tarie° *delay*
That stood ful myrie° upon an haven-syde.° *merrily / harbor-side*
305 But on a day agayn the eventyde,° *towards evening*
The wynd gan chaunge and blew right as hem
leste.° *they wanted*
Jolif° and glad, they wente unto hir reste *jolly*
And casten° hem ful erly for to saille. *decided*
But herkneth: to that o man fil a greet mervaille.[2]
310 That oon of hem, in slepyng as he lay,
Hym mette° a wonder dreem agayn the
day.° *dreamed / toward daybreak*
Hym thoughte a man stood by his beddes syde
And hym comanded that he sholde abyde° *wait*
And seyde hym thus: 'If thou tomorwe wende,° *go*
315 Thow shalt be dreynt.° My tale is at an ende.' *drowned*
He wook and tolde his felawe what he mette
And preyde hym his viage° to lette;° *voyage / delay*
As for that day he preyde hym to byde.° *wait*
His felawe, that lay by his beddes syde,
320 Gan for to laughe, and scorned hym ful faste.° *very much*

---

[1] *Do ... boldely* Cause that cart to be seized boldly.

[2] *But ... mervaille* But listen! To one man there happened a great marvel.

'No dreem,' quod he, 'may so myn herte agaste°   *frighten*
That I wol lette for to do my thynges.°   *business*
I sette nat a straw by thy dremynges!°   *dreams*
For swevenes been but vanytees° and japes.°   *nonsense / tricks*
325   Men dreme al day of owles or of apes,
And of many a maze° therwithal.°   *delusion / with it all*
Men dreme of thyng that nevere was ne shal.°   *nor shall be*
But sith I see that thou wolt heere abyde,
And thus forslewthen° wilfully thy tyde,°   *waste / time*
330   God woot, it reweth me!° And have good day!'   *I regret it*
And thus he took his leve° and wente his way.   *leave*
But er that he hadde half his cours yseyled,°   *sailed*
Noot I nat° why, ne what myschaunce° it
     eyled,   *I know not / went wrong*
But casuelly° the shippes botme° rente,°   *by chance / bottom / split*
335   And shipe and man under the water wente
In sighte of othere shippes it bisyde°   *beside it*
That with hem seyled at the same tyde.°   *tide*
And therfore, faire Pertelote, so deere,
By swiche ensamples olde yet maistow leere°   *may you learn*
340   That no man sholde been to recchelees°   *too careless*
Of dremes. For I seye thee doutelees
That many a dreem ful soore is for to drede!
     Lo in the *Lyf of Seint Kenelm*[1] I rede,
That was Kenulphus sone,° the noble kyng   *Cenwulf's son*
345   Of Mertenrike,° how Kenelm mette° a thyng   *Mercia / dreamed*
A lite er° he was mordred on a day.   *little before*
His mordre in his avysioun° he say.°   *vision / saw*
His norice° hym expowned° every deel°   *nurse / explained / part*
His swevene, and bad hym for to kepe hym
     weel°   *protect himself*
350   For traisoun.° But he nas but° sevene yeer
     oold,   *from treason / was only*
And therfore litel tale hath he toold°   *paid little attention*
Of any dreem, so hooly° is his herte.   *holy*
By God, I hadde levere than my sherte
That ye hadde rad his Legende as have I,[2]
355   Dame Pertelote! I sey yow trewely,
Macrobeus, that writ the avisioun

In Affrike of the worthy Cipioun,[3]
Affermeth° dremes and seith that they   *affirms (the validity of)*
     been
Warnynge of thynges that men after seen.°   *see afterwards*
360   And forthermoore, I pray yow, looketh wel
In the Olde Testament of Daniel,
If he heeld° dremes any vanitee.°   *considered / folly*
Reed eek of Joseph,[4] and ther shul ye see
Wher dremes be somtyme—I sey nat alle°—   *not always*
365   Warnynge of thynges that shul after falle.°   *happen*
Looke of Egipte° the kyng daun Pharao,°   *Egypt / Lord Pharoah*
His bakere and his butiller° also,   *butler*
Wher° they ne felte noon° effect in
     dremes.   *whether / did not feel any*
Whoso wol seken actes of sondry remes°   *various realms*
370   May rede of dremes many a wonder thyng.
Lo Cresus,[5] which that was of Lyde kyng,
Mette he nat° that he sat upon a tree,   *did he not dream*
Which signified he sholde anhanged° bee?   *hanged*
Lo heere Adromacha,° Ectores° wyf,   *Andromache / Hector's*
375   That day that Ector sholde lese his lyf
She dremed on the same nyght biforn
How that the lyf of Ector sholde be lorn°   *lost*
If thilke day he wente into bataille.
She warned hym, but it myghte nat availle.°   *could not help*
380   He wente for to fighte natheles,°   *nevertheless*

---

1   *Lyf ... Kenelm* This is a saint's life, or hagiography, of Kenelm (Cenhelm), a seven-year-old Anglo-Saxon king of Mercia who was murdered at the command of his aunt.

2   *I hadde ... I* I would rather that you had read this saint's life than that I had my shirt, or, as we might say, I'd give my shirt to have you read it.

3   *In ... Cipioun* The Roman writer Macrobius (c. 400 CE) wrote a commentary on the part of Cicero's *Republic* called "The Dream of Scipio." This book tells how Scipio Africanus Minor, a Roman consul, dreamed of meeting his famous ancestor, Scipio Africanus Major (so-called because he defeated Hannibal, the great general of Carthage, in North Africa) and urged him to pursue virtue for the sake of reward in a future life. Chauntecleer misinterprets his name, assuming the dream happened in Africa.

4   *Daniel ... Joseph* Both Daniel and Joseph were famous for their ability to interpret dreams. Daniel interpreted the dream of King Nebuchadnezzar to predict that the king would be banished for seven years (see Daniel 4). Joseph interpreted his own dream to predict that he would be lord over his brothers, interpreted the dreams of Pharaoh's butler and his baker to predict that the former would be restored to office but the latter hanged, and interpreted Pharaoh's dream to predict that Egypt would have seven years of good harvest followed by seven years of famine (see Genesis 37.5–11; 40.1–23; 41.1–32).

5   *Cresus* The Monk had mentioned the dream of Croesus, the fabulously rich king of Lydia who was conquered by King Cyrus of Persia, in the previous tale.

But he was slayn anon of Achilles.[1]
But thilke is al to° longe for to telle,   too
And eek it is ny° day. I may nat dwelle.°   near / not delay
Shortly I seye, as for conclusioun,
385 That I shal han of this avisioun
Adversitee. And I seye forthermoor
That I ne telle of laxatyves no stoor!°   set no store in laxatives
For they been venymes,° I woot° it weel.   venomous / know
I hem diffye,° I love hem never a deel!°   reject them / not at all
390   "Now lat us speke of myrthe° and
        stynte° al this.   mirth / be silent about
Madame Pertelote, so have I blis,°   happiness
Of o° thyng God hath sent me large grace,°   one / great favor
For whan I se the beautee of youre face—
Ye been so scarlet reed° aboute youre eyen—   red
395 It maketh al my drede for to dyen.
For also siker° as In principio,[2]   as certain
Mulier est hominis confusio.[3]
Madame, the sentence° of this Latyn is,   meaning
'Womman is mannes joye and al his blis.'
400 For whan I feele anyght° youre softe side—   at night
Albeit that I may nat on yow ryde,°   ride
For that oure perche is maad° so narwe,° allas!   made / narrow
I am so ful of joye and of solas
That I diffye° bothe swevene and dreem!"[4]   defy
405 And with that word he fly° doun fro the beem,°   flew / beam
For it was day, and eek hise hennes alle,°   did also all his hens
And with a "chuk" he gan hem for to calle,
For he hadde founde a corn lay° in the yerd.   kernel that lay
Real° he was. He was namoore aferd,   regal
410 And fethered Pertelote twenty tyme

And trad as ofte er it was pryme.[5]
He looketh as it were° a grym leoun,°   as if he were / fierce lion
And on hise toos° he rometh° up and doun.   his toes / roams
Hym deigned nat to sette his foot to grounde.
415 He chukketh° whan he hath a corn yfounde,   clucks
And to hym rennen thanne° hise wyves alle.   run then
Thus roial° as a prince is in an halle   regal
Leve° I this Chauntecleer in his pasture,   leave
And after wol I telle his aventure.
420   Whan that the monthe in which the world bigan,
That highte March, whan God first maked man,[6]
Was compleet, and passed were also,
Syn March bigan, thritty dayes and two,[7]
Bifel° that Chauntecleer in al his pryde,   it happened
425 Hise sevene wyves walkynge by his syde,
Caste up hise eyen to the brighte sonne,
That in the signe of Taurus hadde yronne
Twenty degrees and oon° and somwhat   twenty-one degrees
        moore,
And knew by kynde° and by noon oother
        loore°   nature / teaching
430 That it was pryme,° and crew with blisful
        stevene.°   early morning / voice
"The sonne," he seyde, "is clomben upon hevene
Fourty degrees and oon and moore, ywis.
Madame Pertelote, my worldes blis,
Herkneth thise blisful briddes,° how they synge,   birds
435 And se the fresshe floures, how they sprynge.°   bloom
Ful is myn herte of revel° and solas."   amusement
But sodeynly hym fil° a sorweful cas,°   befell / event
For evere the latter ende of joye is wo.
God woot that worldly joye is soone ago!°   gone
440 And if a rethor° koude faire endite,°   rhetorician / write well

---

[1] Lo heere ... Achilles The narrative of the Trojan war recounted by Dares Phrygius (one of the standard versions of the story in the Middle Ages) includes the story of the dream of Hector's wife. Homer's *Iliad*, which was not well known in western Europe at the time, does not include the episode.

[2] In principio Latin: in the beginning; i.e., as certain as the Bible. These words begin both the book of Genesis and the Gospel of John.

[3] Mulier ... confusio Latin: woman is the confusion of man.

[4] That ... dreem Chauntecleer appears to distinguish between two kinds of dreams here, but it is not clear what the difference is. Medieval dream theory distinguished between prophetic dreams and those that had no special significance, but the terms swevene and dreme (and also mete) cover both.

---

[5] And fethered ... pryme He covered Pertelote with his feathers twenty times and copulated with her as often before it was the hour of prime (early morning).

[6] That ... man According to various medieval authorities, including Saint Basil and the English monastic writer Bede, God created the world at the spring equinox.

[7] Was compleet ... two The phrasing is ambiguous but the events seem to take place on May 3, when all of March and a further thirty-two days had passed. This date is in keeping with the position of the sun in the sky and the other astrological information. May 3 was considered an unlucky day and is also the day on which Palamon escapes from prison in *The Knight's Tale* (line 1462).

He in a cronycle saufly° myghte it write   *safely*
As for a sovereyn notabilitee.°   *very notable thing*
Now every wys man, lat hym herkne me.°   *listen to me*
This storie is also trewe, I undertake,°   *swear*
445 As is *The Book of Launcelot de Lake*,[1]
That wommen holde in ful greet reverence.
Now wol I come agayn to my sentence.°   *purpose*
   "A colfox° ful of sly iniquitee,°   *coal-black fox / malice*
That in the grove hadde woned° yeeres three,   *lived*
450 By heigh ymaginacioun forncast,[2]
The same nyght thurghout° the hegges°
     brast°   *through / hedge / burst*
Into the yerd ther° Chauntecleer the faire   *where*
Was wont, and eek hise wyves, to repaire,°   *retire*
And in a bed of wortes° stille° he lay   *herbs / quietly*
455 Til it was passed undren° of the day,   *dawn*
Waitynge his tyme° on Chauntecleer to falle,   *opportunity*
As gladly doon thise homycides alle°   *all these murderers*
That in await liggen° to mordre men.   *lie in wait*
O false mordrour, lurkynge in thy den!
460 O newe Scariot,° newe Genylon!°   *(Judas) Iscariot / Ganelon*
False dissymulour,° o Greek Synon,   *liar*
That broghtest Troye al outrely° to sorwe![3]   *utterly*
O Chauntecleer, acursed be that morwe
That thou into that yerd flaugh° fro the bemes!   *flew*
465 Thou were ful wel ywarned by thy dremes
That thilke day was perilous to thee,
But what that God forwoot° moot nedes
     bee,°   *foreknows / necessarily be*
After° the opinioun of certein clerkis.°   *according to / scholars*

Witnesse on hym that any parfit clerk is,[4]
470 That in scole° is greet altercacioun°   *the universities / debate*
In this mateere, and greet disputisoun,
And hath been of an hundred thousand men.[5]
But I ne kan nat bulte it to the bren[6]
As kan the hooly doctour Augustyn,°   *holy scholar Augustine*
475 Or Boece, or the Bisshope Bradwardyn—[7]
Wheither that Goddes worthy forwityng°   *foreknowledge*
Streyneth° me nedely° to doon a thyng—   *constrains / necessarily*
"Nedely" clepe° I symple necessitee—   *call*
Or elles, if free choys be graunted me
480 To do that same thyng or do it noght,
Though God forwoot it er that it was wroght,°   *done*
Or if his wityng° streyneth° never a
     deel°   *knowing / constrains / not at all*
But by necessitee condicioneel.[8]

---

[1] *The Book ... Lake* This is the title of any one of a number of Arthurian romances that recount the adventures of Sir Lancelot, including his love affair with Guinevere, wife of King Arthur.

[2] *By ... forncast* Foreseen by exalted imagination. What this means is disputed. Many editors take it to refer to the mind or conception (ymaginacioun) of God, which foresees all events. Others take "ymaginacioun" as a reference, expressed in deliberately and ridiculously grandiose language, to Chauntecleer's dream, or as a reference to the plotting of the fox. In each case, the word "forncast" introduces the theme of predestination discussed in lines 467–830.

[3] *O newe ... sorwe* In the Gospel, Judas Iscariot betrayed Christ by identifying him to the Roman soldiers who came to arrest him; in *The Song of Roland*, Ganelon betrayed Roland with a plot that led to his death in the pass at Roncesvalles; and in *The Iliad*, Sinon betrayed Troy by suggesting the Greeks conceal themselves in a wooden horse to gain access to the city.

---

[4] *Witnesse ... is* As any fully qualified scholar can testify.

[5] *But what ... men* The question of how God's foreknowledge could be reconciled with human free will was always important in medieval theology, but the debate flared up in Chaucer's day. The radical theologian John Wycliffe (d. 1394), best known for initiating the translation of the Bible into English, argued that God's omniscience gave him absolute knowledge of who would be saved or damned. This meant for Wycliffe that there was no justification for the institutions of the earthly church or for penitential practices such as confession or pilgrimage.

[6] *But ... bren* But I cannot separate (the kernels) from the bran. That is, the Nun's Priest cannot sort out the issues in the debate about God's foreknowledge.

[7] *As kan ... Bradwardyn* The great patristic writer St. Augustine (d. 430 CE), the late Roman scholar Boethius (d. 524 CE), and Thomas Bradwardine, chancellor of Oxford and very briefly Archbishop of Canterbury (who died of the Black Death in 1349), all wrote about the concept of predestination. Although stressing God's omniscience, all three were thoroughly orthodox in their insistence that humans have free will.

[8] *necessitee condicioneel* Boethius distinguishes between simple necessity and conditional necessity in his *Consolation of Philosophy* 5, prose 6, and then draws on God's status outside time to resolve the theological dilemma. To use Boethius's example, that a man must die is a matter of simple necessity. But if you know someone is walking, while he must then necessarily be walking, the necessity is only conditional; i.e., it depends on the condition of the man having decided to take a walk. From your perspective, he could have chosen not to do so. The issue here is whether God, in knowing in advance all future events and choices, necessarily removes free choice (for how can God be wrong?). The solution, proposed by Boethius, is this idea of conditional necessity: to know about an event is not

I wol nat han to do of° swich mateere.　　*have to do with*
485　My tale is of a cok, as ye may heere,
That took his conseil of his wyf with sorwe
To walken in the yerd upon that morwe
That he hadde met that dreem that I of tolde.
Wommennes conseils been ful ofte colde.°　　*bad*
490　Wommannes conseil broghte us first to wo
And made Adam out of Paradys to go,
Theras° he was ful myrie° and wel at ese.　　*where / merry*
But for I noot° to whom it myght displese,　　*since I do not know*
If I conseil of wommen wolde blame,
495　Passe over, for I seye it in my game.°　　*in jest*
Rede auctours° where they trete of swich mateere,　　*authors*
And what they seyn of wommen ye may heere.
Thise been the cokkes wordes and nat myne!
I kan noon harm of no womman divyne!°　　*imagine*
500　　Faire in the soond° to bathe hire myrily　　*sand*
Lith° Pertelote, and alle hire sustres by°　　*lies / nearby*
Agayn the sonne.° And Chauntecleer so free　　*in the sunshine*
Soong murier° than the mermayde in the　　*sang more merrily*
　　see—
For Phisiologus[1] seith sikerly°　　*surely*
505　How that they syngen wel and myrily—
And so bifel that as he caste his eye
Among the wortes° on a boterflye,　　*herbs*
He was war° of this fox that lay ful lowe.　　*aware*
Nothyng ne liste hym thanne for to crowe,[2]
510　But cride anon, "Cok! Cok!" and up he sterte
As man that was affrayed in his herte.
For natureely a beest desireth flee
Fro his contrarie° if he may it see,　　*enemy*
Though he never erst hadde seyn it with his eye.
515　　This Chauntecleer, whan he gan hym espye,°　　*spotted him*
He wolde han fled, but that the fox anon
Seyde, "Gentil sire, allas, wher wol ye gon?

Be ye affrayed of me, that am youre freend?
Now certes, I were worse than a feend°　　*fiend*
520　If I to yow wolde° harm or vileynye!　　*intended*
I am nat come youre conseil for t'espye.°　　*to spy on your council*
But trewely, the cause of my comynge
Was oonly for to herkne° how that ye synge.　　*listen*
For trewely, ye have as myrie° a stevene°　　*merry / voice*
525　As any aungel that is in Hevene.
Therwith ye han in musyk moore feelynge
Than hadde Boece[3] or any that kan synge.
My lord, youre fader, God his soule blesse,
And eek youre mooder of hire gentillesse
530　Han in myn hous ybeen to my greet ese.
And certes, sire, ful fayn° wolde I yow plese.　　*very gladly*
But for men speke of syngyng, I wol yow seye—
So moote I brouke wel myne eyen tweye—[4]
Save yow,° herde I nevere man yet synge　　*apart from yourself*
535　As dide youre fader in the morwenynge.
Certes, it was of herte° al that he song!　　*from the heart*
And for to make his voys the moore strong,
He wolde so peyne hym° that with bothe hise eyen　　*take pains*
He moste wynke°—so loude he wolde cryen—　　*had to wink*
540　And stonden on his tip-toon° therwithal,°　　*tip-toes / in doing so*
And strecche forth his nekke long and smal.°　　*slender*
And eek he was of swich discrecioun°　　*discernment*
That ther nas no man in no regioun
That hym in song or wisedom myghte passe.°　　*surpass*
545　I have wel rad° in *Daun Burnel the Asse*,[5]　　*read*
Among hise vers,° how that ther was a cok,　　*verses*
For that° a preestes sone yaf° hym a knok　　*because / gave*
Upon his leg whil he was yong and nyce,°　　*silly*
He made hym for to lese his benefice.
550　But certeyn, ther nys no° comparisoun　　*is no*

---

necessarily to cause it. As he says, "God sees those future events which happen of free will as present events; so that these things when considered with reference to God's sight of them do happen necessarily as a result of the condition of divine knowledge; but when considered in themselves they do not lose the absolute freedom of their nature."

[1] *Phisiologus* The supposed author of a bestiary, a book explaining the allegorical significances of various animals. According to this work, mermaids use their sweet singing to lure sailors to their deaths.

[2] *Nothyng … crowe* He did by no means want then to crow.

---

[3] *Boece* Boethius not only wrote *The Consolation of Philosophy*, which Chaucer translated, but also wrote the basic university textbook on music used in the Middle Ages.

[4] *So … tweye* So may I enjoy the use of my eyes, a common expression meaning little more than "indeed," but it is ill suited to express musical appreciation.

[5] *Daun … Asse* Title of a twelfth-century Latin satire by Nigel Wireker about a foolish donkey, Master Brunellus, who becomes a wandering scholar. The episode described below concerns a young man who was about to be ordained and to receive a benefice. The cock, whom he had injured in his youth, took its revenge by not crowing, causing the man to oversleep and miss his opportunity for a benefice.

Bitwixe the wisedom and discrecioun
Of youre fader and of his subtiltee.°   cleverness
Now syngeth, sire, for Seinte Charitee!°   Holy Charity
Lat se, konne ye youre fader countrefete?"°   imitate
555   This Chauntecleer hise wynges gan to bete°   beat
As man that koude his traysoun° nat espie,°   betrayal / perceive
So was he ravysshed with his flaterie.
Allas, ye lordes, many a fals flatour°   false flatterer
Is in youre courtes,° and many a losengeour°   courts / spy
560 That plesen yow wel moore, by my feith,
Than he that soothfastnesse° unto yow seith.   truth
Redeth Ecclesiaste[1] of° flaterye.   on
Beth war,° ye lordes, of hir trecherye!   beware
    This Chauntecleer stood hye upon his toos,
565 Strecchynge his nekke, and heeld his eyen cloos°   closed
And gan to crowe loude for the nones.°   occasion
And Daun Russell the fox stirte up atones°   jumped up at once
And by the gargat° hente° Chauntecleer   throat / grabbed
And on his bak toward the wode hym beer,
570 For yet° ne was ther no man that hym sewed.°   as yet / pursued
    O Destinee, that mayst nat been eschewed!°   avoided
Allas, that Chauntecleer fleigh fro the bemes!
Allas, his wyf ne roghte nat° of dremes!   paid no attention
And on a Friday fil al this meschaunce!
575   O Venus, that art goddesse of plesaunce,[2]
Syn that thy servant was this Chauntecleer,
And in thy servyce dide al his poweer°   all he could
Moore for delit than world to
        multiplye,°   to increase the world (procreate)
Why woldestow suffre° hym on thy day to
        dye?[3]   would you allow
580   O Gaufred,[4] deere maister soverayn,°   sovereign teacher

That whan thy worthy kyng Richard was slayn
With shot,° compleynedest° his deeth so soore,   arrow / lamented
Why ne hadde I now thy sentence° and thy
        loore°   meaning / learning
The Friday for to chide as diden ye?
585 For on a Friday soothly° slayn was he.   truly
Thanne wolde I shewe yow how that I koude pleyne
For Chauntecleres drede and for his peyne!
Certes swich cry ne lamentacioun
Was nevere of ladyes maad° whan Ylioun°   made / Ilion (Troy)
590 Was wonne,° and Pirrus° with his streite
        swerd,°   conquered / Pyrrhus / drawn sword
Whan he hadde hent° Kyng Priam by the berd°   seized / beard
And slayn hym, as seith us Eneydos,°   Aeneid
As maden alle the hennes in the clos°   yard
Whan they had seyn of Chauntecleer the sighte.
595 But sodeynly Dame Pertelote shrighte°   shrieked
Ful louder than dide Hasdrubales wyf
Whan that hir housbonde hadde lost his lyf
And that the Romayns hadde brend° Cartage.[5]   burned
She was so ful of torment and of rage
600 That wilfully into the fyr she sterte
And brende hirselven with a stedefast herte.
    O woful hennes, right so criden ye
As, whan that Nero[6] brende the citee
Of Rome, cryden senatours wyves,
605 For that hir housbondes losten alle hir lyves.
Withouten gilt this Nero hath hem slayn.
Now turne I wole to my tale agayn.
    This sely° wydwe and eek hir doghtres two   innocent
Herden thise hennes crie and maken wo,
610 And out at dores stirten they anon
And syen the fox toward the grove gon
And bar upon his bak the cok away,
And cryden, "Out! Harrow!" and "Weylaway!"°   alas
Ha! Ha! The fox!" And after hym they ran,

---

[1] *Ecclesiaste* Ecclesiasticus 12.16 warns against deceptive enemies but does not specifically mention flattery. The reference might be a mistake for Ecclesiastes or for Proverbs, other books of the Bible that were, like Ecclesiasticus, attributed to King Solomon.

[2] *O ... plesaunce* In classical mythology, Venus is the goddess of love.

[3] *Why ... dye* According to medieval astrology, each of the planets had special influence on a given day of the week. Venus, who gives her name to Friday (*Veneris dies*) in Romance languages, controlled that day.

[4] *Gaufred* I.e., Geoffrey of Vinsauf, whose treatise *Poetria Nova*, a basic manual on how to write rhetorically elaborate poetry, is alluded to by Chaucer in the following lines. King Richard is Richard I, the

---

Lion-hearted, who in 1199 was wounded on a Friday while besieging a castle and later died of his wound.

[5] *Hasdrubales ... Cartage* I.e., Hasdrubal (245–207 BCE), Carthaginian general, who died in battle at the Metaurus River in central Italy when he met the army of Caius Claudius Nero. Carthage was destroyed by Scipio Africanus in 146 BCE.

[6] *Nero* Nero (54–68 CE), Emperor of Rome, who had his city burned while he stood by, according to Suetonius, playing the bagpipes. In the previous tale the Monk narrates his tragedy.

615 And eek with staves° many another man;   clubs
    Ran Colle oure dogge, and Talbot and Gerland,[1]
    And Malkyn with a dystaf° in hir hand.   spinning staff
    Ran cow and calf and the verray hogges,
    So fered° for berkyng of the dogges   afraid
620 And shoutyng of the men and wommen eek.
    They ronne so hem thoughte hir herte breek;[2]
    They yolleden° as feendes° doon in Helle.   yelled / fiends
    The dokes° cryden as men wolde hem quelle,°   ducks / kill them
    The gees° for feere flowen° over the trees,   geese / flew
625 Out of the hyve° cam the swarm of bees.   hive
    So hydous° was the noyse,° a,
        benedicitee,°   hideous / noise / ah, bless us
    Certes he Jakke Straw and his meynee°   gang
    Ne made nevere shoutes half so shrille,
    Whan that they wolden any Flemyng kille,[3]
630 As thilke day was maad upon the fox.
    Of bras they broghten bemes and of box,
    Of horn, of boon, in whiche they blewe and powped,[4]
    And therwithal° they skriked° and they
        howped.°   with this / shrieked / whooped
    It semed as that Hevene sholde falle.
635   Now, goode men, I prey yow, herkneth alle.
    Lo how Fortune turneth sodeynly
    The hope and pryde of hir enemy.
    This cok that lay upon the foxes bak,
    In al his drede unto the fox he spak
640 And seyde, "Sire, if that I were as ye,
    Yet wolde I seyn, as wys° God helpe me,   wise
    'Turneth agayn, ye proude cherles° alle!   churls
    A verray pestilence upon yow falle!°   fall upon you
    Now I am come unto the wodes syde.°   border
645 Maugree youre heed,° the cok shal heere
        abyde.   despite your efforts

    I wol hym ete,° in feith, and that anon!'"   eat
        The fox answerde, "In feith, it shal be don!"
    And as he spak that word al sodeynly,
    This cok brak° from his mouth delyverly°   broke / quickly
650 And heighe upon a tree he fleigh anon.
    And whan the fox saugh that he was gon,
        "Allas!" quod he. "O Chauntecleer, allas!
    I have to yow," quod he, "ydoon trespas,°   done an insult
    In as muche as I maked yow aferd
655 Whan I yow hente° and broghte into this yerd.[5]   seized
    But sire, I dide it of no wikke° entente.   wicked
    Com doun, and I shal telle yow what I mente.
    I shal seye sooth° to yow, God help me so!"   tell the truth
        "Nay, thanne," quod he, "I shrewe° us bothe two!   curse
660 And first I shrewe myself, bothe blood and bones,
    If thou bigyle° me any ofter° than ones!°   trick / more often / once
    Thou shalt namoore thurgh thy flaterye
    Do me to synge and wynke with myn eye!
    For he that wynketh whan he sholde see
665 Al wilfully,° God lat hym nevere thee!"°   voluntarily / thrive
        "Nay," quod the fox, "but God yeve° hym
        meschaunce°   give / misfortune
    That is so undiscreet° of governaunce°   indiscreet / behavior
    That jangleth° whan he sholde holde his pees!"°   chatters / peace
        Lo, swich it is for to be recchelees°   reckless
670 And necligent° and truste on flaterye!   negligent
        But ye that holden° this tale a folye°   consider / folly
    As of a fox or of a cok and hen,
    Taketh the moralite,° goode men.   moral
    For Seint Paul seith that al that writen is,
675 To oure doctrine° it is ywrite, ywis.[6]   for our teaching
    Taketh the fruyt,° and lat the chaf be
        stille.°   fruit / let the chaff alone
    Now, goode God, if that it be thy wille,

---

[1] *Colle … Talbot and Gerland* Names for dogs.

[2] *They … breek* They ran so (fast) that they thought their hearts would burst.

[3] *Certes … kille* Jack Straw was the name of one of the leaders of the Uprising of 1381; about thirty or forty Flemish merchants and weavers were murdered in London during this period of violence and rioting. This is one of the few contemporary events Chaucer mentions directly in his writings.

[4] *Of bras … powped* They brought trumpets (bemes) made of brass and boxwood and of horn and of bone, on which they blew and puffed.

---

[5] *into this yerd* This seems an obvious slip that should instead read "out of this yerd," as this line does in some manuscripts. Derek Pearsall, however, in the Variorum edition, defends "into" by suggesting that the fox is still trying to deceive Chauntecleer and so refers to the place they have come to as "this yerd" as if it were the kind of safe enclosure the rooster were used to.

[6] *For Seint … ywis* Cf. Romans 15.4. Chaucer cites the same line in his "Retraction" and it is also paraphrased at the beginning of the medieval translation and allegorical interpretation of Ovid's *Metamorphoses*, the *Ovide Moralisé*.

As seith my lord,[1] so make us alle goode men,
And brynge us to his heighe blisse. Amen!

HEERE IS ENDED THE NONNES PREESTES TALE

THE NUN'S PRIEST'S EPILOGUE[2]

680   "Sire Nonnes Preest," oure Hoost seide anoon,
     "Iblissed° be thy breche° and every
            stoon!°   *blessed / buttocks / testicles*
     This was a murie tale of Chauntecleer.
     But by my trouthe, if thou were seculer°   *a lay man*
     Thow woldest be a tredefoul[3] aright.

685   For if thou have corage° as thou hast myght,°   *spirit / power*
     The were nede° of hennes, as I
            wene,°   *you would have need of / think*
     Ya, moo° than sevene tymes seventeen!   *more*
     Se which braunes° hath this gentil° preest,   *what muscle / fine*
     So gret a nekke and swich a large breest.°   *chest*
690   He loketh as a sperhauke° with hise eyen.   *sparrowhawk*
     Him nedeth nat his colour° for to dyghen°   *complexion / dye*
     With brasile ne with greyn of Portingale.[4]
     Now sire, faire falle yow° for your tale."   *may good befall you*
     And after that he with ful murie chere
     Seide unto another as ye shuln here.

Introduction to Chaucer's *Retraction*

The *Retraction* is found in all complete manuscripts of *The Canterbury Tales*, including the Ellesmere. In it Chaucer revokes most of his poems, including his early elegy *The Book of the Duchess*; his dream vision *The House of Fame*, which deals with worldly reputation; his great love poem *Troilus and Criseyde*; *The Legend of Good Women*, in which Chaucer compensates for telling the story of Criseyde's betrayal by telling of numerous good women; and those of *The Canterbury Tales* "that sownen into synne" (that tend to promote sin). Chaucer takes credit only for his translation of Boethius and for works of obvious moral or devotional content. Many critics, troubled by Chaucer's disavowal of so many of his poems as "worldly vanitees," have seen ironies in the *Retraction*. It effectively provides a list of his life's work, it does not name which of *The Canterbury Tales* it is revoking,

and it is found in manuscripts that contain all the tales, including the ones that would seem to "sownen into synne." As a confession of Chaucer's sins, however, the *Retraction* follows logically from *The Parson's Tale*, which is not a tale at all but a penitential treatise, calling for full confession and repentance. As a penitent should, Chaucer lists all his works that may be sinful, even those he cannot remember writing. The connection to *The Parson's Tale* may also explain the opening line, with its reference to those who read or hear this "lityl treatise," a description that can only rather awkwardly fit the entire *Canterbury Tales*. By this point, the tale-telling pilgrims have faded from the scene. If we accept the retraction as a sincere act of personal atonement, however, the crucial question becomes how far this act should affect our understanding of *The Canterbury Tales* as a whole.

---

[1]   *my lord*   The Nun's Priest might be referring to the Archbishop of Canterbury, Christ, or, since he is attached to the nunnery at Stratford-at-Bow near London, his immediate ecclesiastical superior, the Bishop of London.

[2]   *The ... Epilogue*   This epilogue is found in nine manuscripts but not in either Ellesmere or Hengwrt. It seems most likely that the epilogue is part of an earlier draft that Chaucer later abandoned, incorporating some of the lines into the Host's words to the Monk.

[3]   *tredefoul*   Copulator with chickens, a rooster.

[4]   *brasile ... Portingale*   Imported red dyes.

CHAUCER'S RETRACTION

HEERE TAKETH THE MAKERE OF THIS BOOK HIS LEVE

Now preye° I to hem alle° that herkne° this litel tretys° or rede,° that if ther be anythyng in it that liketh hem,° that therof° they thanken oure Lord Jhesu Crist, of whom procedeth al wit and al goodnesse. And if ther be anythyng that displese hem,° I preye° hem also that they arrette° it to the defaute° of myn unkonnynge° and nat to my wyl,° that wolde° ful fayn° have seyd bettre, if I hadde had konnynge.° For oure book seith, "Al that is writen is writen for oure doctrine."[1] And that is myn entente.° Wherfore I biseke° yow mekely° for the mercy of God that ye preye for me, that Crist have mercy on me and foryeve° me my giltes,° and namely° of my translacions and enditynges° of worldly vanitees,° the whiche I revoke in my retracciouns—as is *The Book of Troilus*, *The Book* also *of Fame*, *The Book of the Five and Twenty Ladies*, *The Book of the Duchesse*, *The Book of Seint Valentynes Day of the Parlement of Briddes*,° *The Tales of Caunterbury* (thilke° that sownen into synne°), *The Book of the Leoun*,[2] and many another book (if they were in my remembrance) and many a song and many a leccherous° lay—that Crist for his grete° mercy foryeve me the synne.

But of the translacioun of Boece, *De Consolacioun*[3] and othere bookes of legendes° of seintes and omelies° and moralitee and devocioun, that thanke I oure Lord Jhesu Crist and his blisful mooder° and alle the seintes of Hevene, bisekynge hem° that they from hennes° forth unto my lyves° ende sende me grace to biwayle° my giltes and to studie° to the salvacioun of my soule and graunte me grace of verray° penitence, confessioun, and satisfaccioun to doon° in this present lyf thurgh the benigne grace of hym that is Kyng of kynges and Preest over alle preestes, that boghte° us with the precious blood of his herte,° so that I may been oon° of hem at the Day of Doome° that shulle° be saved. *Qui cum patre, etc.*[4]

HEERE IS ENDED THE BOOK OF THE TALES OF CAUNTERBURY COMPILED BY GEFFREY CHAUCER, OF WHOS SOULE JHESU CRIST HAVE MERCY, AMEN.

pray / them all / listen to / treatise/ read [it]
pleases them / for it

them / ask / ascribe / default
my ignorance / will / would / very gladly
knowledge
my intent / ask / meekly
forgive / sins
especially / writings / acts of folly

Parliament of Fowles / those
tend towards sin
lecherous
great

moral stories / homilies
mother
asking them / hence / life's / lament
take thought
true / do

redeemed / heart / one
Judgment Day / shall

---

[1] *Al ... doctrine* From 2 Timothy 3.16; *doctrine* Instruction.

[2] *The ... Leoun* This text, probably a translation of the *Dit de Leon* by the French court poet Guillaume de Machaut (c. 1300 –77), one of Chaucer's major early influences, does not survive.

[3] *De Consolacioun* This is *The Consolation of Philosophy*, the famous treatise of the late Roman scholar and statesman Boethius.

[4] *Qui ... etc.* The full liturgical phrase is *Qui cum Patre et spiritu sancto vivit et regnat Deus per omnia secula, Amen*. Latin: Who with the Father and the Holy Spirit lives and reigns, God forever and ever, Amen.

To His Scribe Adam

Adam scriveyn,° if ever it thee bifalle   copyist
Boece or Troylus for to wryten newe,[1]
Under thy long lokkes thou most have the scalle,
But° after my makyng thow wryte more trewe;[2]   unless
5   So ofte adaye I mot° thy werk renewe,°   must / redo
It to correcte and eke° to rubbe and scrape,   also
And al is thorugh thy negligence and rape.°   haste
—1561 (WRITTEN C. 1380)

Complaint of Chaucer to His Purse[3]
A Supplication to King Henry

To yow, my purs, and to non other wight°   person
Complaine I, for ye ben my lady dere!
I am so sory, now that ye been light;°   empty
For certes, but if° ye make me hevy chere,   unless
5   Me were as lief be[4] laid upon my bier;
For which unto your mercy thus I crye,
Beth hevy ayeyn, or elles mot° I dye!   must

Now voucheth sauf° this day, or° hyt be   grant / ere
nyght,
That I of you the blissful soun° may hear,   sound
10 Or see your colour lyk the sonne bright,
That of yelownesse had never peer.
Ye be my lyf, ye be myne hertes stere,[5]
Quene of comfort and of good companye;
Beeth hevy again, or elles mot I dye!

15 Ye purs, that ben to me my lyves° light   life's
And saviour, as doun in this worlde here,
Out of this towne helpe me thurgh your might,
Syn° that ye wylle nat ben my tresorere;   since
For I am shave as nye as any frere.[6]
20 But yet I pray unto youre curtesye,
Beeth hevy ayeyn, or elles mot I dye!
—1477 (WRITTEN C. 1399)

Lenvoy de Chaucer[7]

O conquerour of Brutes Albyoun,[8]
Which that by line and free eleccioun
Been[9] verray° kyng, this song to you I sende;   true
And ye, that mowen° alle our harmes amende,   may
5   Have mynde upon my supplicacioun.
—1399

from *Troilus and Criseyde*

Troilus's Song[10]

If no love is, O God, what feele I so?
And if love is, what thing and which is he?
If love be good, from whennes commeth my wo?
If it be wikke, a wonder thinketh me,[11]
5   Whan every torment and adversitee
That cometh of him may to me savory°   pleasant
thinke,°   seem

---

[1] *if ever ... newe* If you ever have occasion to copy out Boethius (Chaucer's translation of Boethius's *Consolation of Philosophy*) or Troilus (Chaucer's *Troilus and Criseyde*). At the end of *Troilus* Chaucer also expresses concern about errors creeping in during the copying process, noting the "diversitee in English, and in writing of our tonge" and fearing that as a result someone may "miswrite" his book.

[2] *thou most ... trewe* May you have a scaly (or mangy) scalp if you do not follow more truly in your writing what I have made.

[3] The tradition in which this poem is written is that of courtly love; "complaints" to a lady concerning unrequited love were a staple of love poetry on French models.

[4] *Me were as lief be* I would be just as happy to be.

[5] *myne hertes stere* Rudder of my heart.

[6] *shave ... any frere* As close-cropped as any friar (i.e., with nothing left).

[7] *Lenvoy de Chaucer* The "envoy" or message at the close of a poem is addressed directly to the poem's recipient. Chaucer was requesting that the new king, Henry IV, renew the annual payments that the former monarch, Richard II, had authorized.

[8] *Brutes Albyoun* Geoffrey of Monmouth's claim that Britain ("Albion") had been founded by Brutus, the grandson of Aeneas, the founder of Rome, had long been accepted as true.

[9] *Which that ... Been* Who by your lineage and by choice are.

[10] *Troilus's Song* In Chaucer's long poem, Troilus composes a song on the theme of his feelings of love for Criseyde. Chaucer translated a sonnet of Petrarch's ("S'amor non è") for the purpose.

[11] *If it ... me* It if is wicked, I would be very surprised.

For ay° thurste I, the more that ich° drinke.   *always / I*

And if that at myn owene lust I breene,
From whennes cometh my wailing and my plainte?
10   If harm agree me, wherto plaine° I thenne?   *complain*
I noot, ne why unwary that I fainte.[1]
O quikke° deeth, O sweete harm so   *living*
    quainte,°   *strange*
How may of thee in me swich quantitee[2]
But° if that I consente that it be?   *except*

15   And if that I consente, I wrongfully
Complaine; ywis,° thus possed° to and fro   *truly / tossed*
All stereless° within a boot° am I   *rudderless / boat*
Amiddde the see, bitwixen windes two,
That in contrarye stonden everemo.
20   Allas, what is this wonder maladye?
For hoot° of colde, for cold of hoot I die.   *hot*
—1483 (WRITEN C. 1388)

---

[1] *I noot ... fainte* I do not know, any more than I know why I faint when I am not weary.

[2] *How may ... quantitee* How can there be such a great quantity of you in me.

The Travels of Sir John Mandeville
c. 1360

The Travels of Sir John Mandeville was among the most popular books of its time: more than 275 manuscripts survive, in 10 different languages. Despite the work's popularity and influence, however, the identity of its author remains unclear, and the veracity of the entire text has been the subject of considerable debate.

The book recounts the travels of Sir John Mandeville, whom the text identifies as an English knight from St. Albans (a town on the northern outskirts of London). Mandeville claims to have left England for a great journey in 1322, traveling first to Egypt and Palestine, and then further east to India and China. The book begins with a prologue that introduces the author and invites the reader to undertake a pilgrimage to the Holy Land; the first half of the book serves as a kind of guide for potential pilgrims on the way to Jerusalem, outlining travel routes and identifying highlights along the journey. It also contains a detailed and, for its time, fairly sympathetic description of Islamic history, customs, and beliefs.

The second half of the book contains what to us seems a fantastical account of the lands of South and East Asia—a world of hybrid creatures, half-human, half animal; cannibal nations who raise children for food; waterless seas of gravel and sand which nevertheless contain fish. Such travelogues fed the medieval hunger for information about the unknown world; Mandeville's *Travels* was in fact more widely read and accepted than what we now know is the more accurate account in Marco Polo's *Description of the World* (1298). Christopher Columbus, for example, is said to have taken a copy of Mandeville's *Travels* with him on his voyages; the popularity of Mandeville's book did not begin to wane until the later sixteenth century, when reports of the newly discovered lands to the west captured European imaginations.

Mandeville's identity went largely unexamined for 500 years. In the late nineteenth century scholars began to read the work more critically, and discovered that Mandeville's account was in fact a patchwork of allusions and borrowings from other sources. These include a pilgrimage narrative by a German Dominican monk, William of Boldensele (1336), a memoir of travels in India and China dictated by a Franciscan missionary, Orderic of Pordenone, an account of the first Crusade led by Albert of Aix in the mid-twelfth century, and the anonymous *Letter of Prester John* (c. 1165). In addition to these lengthier narratives, the work was sprinkled with excerpts gleaned from other travel books, encyclopedic works, and even from Julius Caesar's description of the Britons. Study of the surviving manuscripts also made it apparent that the original work was written in France. In light of these revelations it was widely suggested that "Sir John Mandeville" had never traveled—in fact, had never existed, except as the pen name of a resident of Liege.

In the mid-twentieth century, interest in Mandeville's *Travels* has resulted in the assertion by a number of scholars that John Mandeville, author/compiler of a work of fiction rather than a travel book, actually existed. Others have pointed out that most travelers would have embellished their adventures, and like many travelers to unknown lands (Columbus himself, for instance) the author of the *Travels* might well have seen in the East what his reading had led him to expect to see. Most modern readers accept that the matter may never be resolved with any certainty, and are content to read the *Travels* as a work of literature by an unknown author.

⌘ ⌘ ⌘

from *The Travels of Sir John Mandeville*

PROLOGUE

Forasmuch as the land beyond the sea, that is to say the Holy Land, that men call the Land of Promission[1] or of Behest,[2] passing all other lands, is the most worthy land, most excellent, and lady and sovereign of all other lands, and is blessed and hallowed of the precious body and blood of our Lord Jesu Christ; in the which land it liked him to take flesh and blood of the Virgin Mary, to environ that holy land with his blessed feet; and there he would of his blessedness enumber[3] him in the said blessed and glorious Virgin Mary, and become man, and work many miracles, and preach and teach the faith and the law of Christian men unto his children; and there it liked him to suffer many reprovings and scorns for us; and he that was king of heaven, of air, of earth, of sea and of all things that be contained in them would all only be clept[4] king of that land, when he said, *Rex sum Judeorum*, that is to say, "I am King of Jews"; and that land he chose before all other lands as the best and most worthy land, and the most virtuous land of all the world: for it is the heart and the midst of all the world, witnessing the philosopher, that saith thus, *Virtus rerum in medio consistit*, that is to say, "The virtue of things is in the midst";[5] and in that land he would lead his life, and suffer passion and death of Jews, for us, to buy and to deliver us from pains of hell, and from death without end; the which was ordained for us, for the sin of our forme[6]-father Adam, and for our own sins also; for as for himself, he had no evil deserved: for he thought never evil nor did evil: and he that was king of glory and of joy, might best in that place suffer death; because he chose in that land, rather than in any other, there to suffer his passion and his death. For he that will publish anything to make it openly known, he will make it to be cried and pronounced in the middle place of a town; so that the thing that is proclaimed and pronounced may evenly stretch to all parts: right so, he that was former of all the world would suffer for us at Jerusalem, that is the midst of the world; to that end and intent, that his passion and his death, that was published there, might be known evenly to all parts of the world.

See now, how dear he bought man, that he made after his own image, and how dear he again—bought us[7] for the great love that he had to us, and we never deserved it to him. For more precious chattel[8] nor greater ransom might he put for us, than his blessed body, his precious blood, and his holy life that he thralled for us;[9] and all he offered for us that never did sin.

Ah dear God! What love had he to us his subjects, when he that never trespassed, would for trespassers suffer death! Right well ought us for to love and worship, to dread and serve such a Lord; and to worship and praise such an holy land, that brought forth such fruit, through the which every man is saved, but it be his own default. Well may that land be called delectable and a fructuous[10] land, that was be-bled[11] and moistened

---

[1] *Promission* Promise.

[2] *Behest* Promise.

[3] *enumber* Enshroud himself in.

[4] *clept* Called.

[5] Cf. Psalms 74.12: "For God is my king of old, working salvation in the midst of the earth."

[6] *forme* Earliest in time or order.

[7] *again—bought us* Redeemed us. Jesus's blood is supposed to seal God's second covenant with humanity, the first one being made with Abraham. Cf. Genesis 17, Luke 1.73, Romans 4.13, 15.18.

[8] *chattel* Property, goods.

[9] *thralled for us* Enslaved for our good.

[10] *Fructuous* Fertile.

[11] *be-bled* Bled upon.

with the precious blood of our Lord Jesu Christ; the which is the same land that our Lord behight[1] us in heritage. And in that land he would die, as seised,[2] to leave it to us, his children.

Wherefore every good Christian man, that is of power, and hath whereof, should pain him with all his strength for to conquer our right heritage,[3] and chase out all the misbelieving men. For we be clept Christian men, after Christ our Father. And if we be right children of Christ, we ought for to challenge the heritage that our Father left us, and do it out of heathen men's hands. But now pride, covetise,[4] and envy have so inflamed the hearts of lords of the world that they are more busy for to dis-herit their neighbours, more than for to challenge or to conquer their right heritage before-said. And the common people, that would put their bodies and their chattels to conquer our heritage, they may not do it without the lords. For a sembly[5] of people without a chieftain, or a chief lord, is as a flock of sheep without a shepherd; the which departeth and disperpleth[6] and wit[7] never whither to go. But would God, that the temporal lords and all worldly lords were at good accord, and with the common people would take this holy voyage over the sea! Then I trow[8] well that within a little time, our right heritage before-said should be reconciled and put in the hands of the right heirs of Jesu Christ.

And forasmuch as it is long time passed that there was no general passage nor voyage over the sea, and many men desire for to hear speak of the Holy Land, and have thereof great solace and comfort, I, John Mandeville, Knight, albeit I be not worthy, that was born in England, in the town of St. Albans, and passed the sea in the year of our Lord Jesu Christ, 1322, in the day of St. Michael;[9] and hitherto been long time over the sea, and have seen and gone through many diverse lands, and many provinces and kingdoms and isles and have passed throughout Turkey, Armenia the little and the great; through Tartary, Persia, Syria, Arabia, Egypt the high and the low; through Libya, Chaldea, and a great part of Ethiopia; through Amazonia, Ind[10] the less and the more, a great part; and throughout many other Isles, that be about Ind; where dwell many diverse folk, and of diverse manners and laws, and of diverse shapes of men. Of which lands and isles I shall speak more plainly hereafter; and I shall devise you of some part of things that there be, when time shall be, after it may best come to my mind; and specially for them, that will and are in purpose for to visit the Holy City of Jerusalem and the holy places that are thereabout. And I shall tell the way that they shall hold thither. For I have often times passed and ridden that way, with good company of many lords. God be thanked!

And ye shall understand that I have[11] put this book out of Latin into French, and translated it again out of French into English, that every man of my nation may understand it. But lords and knights and other noble and worthy men that con[12] Latin but little, and have been beyond the sea, know and understand if I say truth or no, and if I err in devising, for forgetting or else, that they may redress it and amend it. For things passed out of long time from a man's mind or from his sight turn soon into forgetting, because that mind of man may not comprehend or withholden,[13] for the frailty of mankind.

---

[1] *behight* Promised.

[2] *seised* In legal possession (of it).

[3] *for to conquer our right heritage* This passage refers generally to the Crusades.

[4] *covetise* Covetousness.

[5] *sembly* I.e., assembly.

[6] *disperpleth* Scatters.

[7] *wit* Knows.

[8] *trow* Believe.

[9] *the day of St. Michael* The feast day of St. Michael the Archangel, 29 September.

[10] *Tartary* In Central Asia, anywhere from modern Armenia to Mongolia; *Persia* Modern Iran; *Chaldea* Modern Iraq; *Amazonia* Mythical land somewhere in Central Asia; *Ind* India.

[11] *I have* The English translator here inserted himself into the work's transmission. This sentence implies that one person translated the text from Latin to French and then from French to English. The French original reads at this point, "I should have written this in Latin in order to be briefer, but as I understand French better, I wrote it in French."

[12] *con* Know.

[13] *withholden* Retain.

CHAPTER 7

Of the country of Egypt; of the bird Phoenix of Arabia;
of the city of Cairo; of the cunning to know balm and
to prove it; and of the garners of Joseph

Egypt is a long country, but it is straight, that is to say narrow, for they may not enlarge it toward the desert for default of water. And the country is set along upon the river of Nile, by as much as that river may serve by floods or otherwise, that when it floweth it may spread abroad through the country; so is the country large of length. For there it raineth not but little in that country, and for that cause they have no water, but if it be of that flood of that river. And forasmuch as it raineth not in that country, but the air is alway pure and clear, therefore in that country be the good astronomers, for they find there no clouds to letten[1] them. Also the city of Cairo is right great and more huge than that of Babylon the less, and it sitteth above toward the desert of Syria, a little above the river above-said.

In Egypt there be two parts: the height, that is toward Ethiopia, and the lower, that is toward Arabia. In Egypt is the land of Rameses and the land of Goshen. Egypt is a strong country, for it hath many shrewd havens because of the great rocks that be strong and dangerous to pass by. And at Egypt, toward the east, is the Red Sea, that dureth unto the city of Coston;[2] and toward the west is the country of Libya, that is a full dry land and little of fruit, for it is overmuch plenty of heat, and that land is clept Fusthe. And toward the part meridional[3] is Ethiopia. And toward the north is the desert, that dureth unto Syria, and so is the country strong on all sides. And it is well a fifteen journeys[4] of length, and more than two so much of desert, and it is but two journeys in largeness. And between Egypt and Nubia it hath well a twelve journeys of desert. And men of Nubia be Christian, but they be black as the Moors[5] for great heat of the sun.

In Egypt there be five provinces: that one is Sahythe; that other Demeseer; another Resith, that is an isle in the Nile; another Alexandria; and another the land of Damietta. That city was wont to be right strong, but it was twice won of[6] the Christian men, and therefore after that the Saracens[7] beat down the walls; and with the walls of the tower thereof, the Saracens made another city more far from the sea, and clept it the new Damietta; so that now no man dwelleth at the rather town of Damietta. At that city of Damietta is one of the havens of Egypt; and at Alexandria is that other. That is a full strong city, but there is no water to drink but if[8] it come by conduit from Nile, that entereth into their cisterns; and whoso stopped that water from them, they might not endure there. In Egypt there be but few forcelets[9] or castles, because that the country is so strong of himself.

At the deserts of Egypt was a worthy man that was an holy hermit,[10] and there met with him a monster (that is to say, a monster is a thing deformed against kind both of man or of beast or of anything else, and that is clept a monster). And this monster that met with this holy hermit was as it had been a man, that had two horns trenchant on his forehead; and he had a body like a man unto the navel, and beneath he had the body like a goat. And the hermit asked him what he was. And the monster answered him, and said he was a deadly[11] creature, such as God had formed, and dwelt in those deserts in purchasing his sustenance, and besought the hermit that he would pray God for him, the which that came from heaven for to save all mankind, and was born of a maiden and suffered passion and death (as we well know) and by whom we live and be. And yet is the head with the two horns of that monster at Alexandria for a marvel.

In Egypt is the city of Heliopolis, that is to say, the city of the Sun. In that city there is a temple, made round after the shape of the Temple of Jerusalem. The priests of that temple have all their writings, under the

---

[1] *letten* Hinder.

[2] *city of Coston* Probably referring to Kus, a city just south of Luxor.

[3] *meridional* Of or relating to the south.

[4] *journey* Day's travel.

[5] *Moors* In Mandeville's time, natives of North Africa.

[6] *of* By.

[7] *Saracens* Medieval term used to denote Muslim Arabs.

[8] *but if* Unless.

[9] *forcelets* Small forts or castles.

[10] *an holy hermit* St. Anthony.

[11] *deadly* Mortal.

Woodcut illustrations to Chapter 7, from
Anton Sorg's second Augsburg edition (1481).

date of the fowl[1] that is clept phoenix; and there is none but one in all the world. And he cometh to burn himself upon the altar of that temple at the end of five hundred year; for so long he liveth. And at the five hundred years' end, the priests array their altar honestly,[2] and put thereupon spices and sulphur vif and other things that will burn lightly; and then the bird phoenix cometh and burneth himself to ashes. And the first day next after, men find in the ashes a worm; and the second day next after, men find a bird quick[3] and perfect; and the third day next after, he flieth his way. And so there is no more birds of that kind in all the world, but it alone, and truly that is a great miracle of God. And men may well liken that bird unto God, because that there is no God but one; and also, that our Lord arose from death to life the third day. This bird men see often-time fly in those countries; and he is not mickle[4] more than an eagle. And he hath a crest of feathers upon his head more great than the peacock hath; and his neck is yellow after colour of an oriel[5] that is a stone well shining, and his beak is coloured blue as ind;[6] and his wings be of purple colour, and his tail is barred overthwart[7] with green and yellow and red. And he is a full fair bird to look upon, against the sun, for he shineth full gloriously and nobly.

Also in Egypt be gardens that have trees and herbs, the which bear fruits seven times in the year. And in that land men find many fair emeralds and enough; and therefore they be greater cheap.[8] Also when it raineth once in the summer in the land of Egypt, then is all the country full of great mires. Also at Cairo, that I spake of before, sell men commonly both men and women of other laws[9] as we do here beasts in the market. And there is a common house in that city that is all full of small furnaces, and thither bring women of the town

their eyren[10] of hens, of geese, and or ducks for to be put into those furnaces. And they that keep that house cover them with heat of horse dung, without hen, goose or duck or any other fowl. And at the end of three weeks or of a month they come again and take their chickens and flourish them and bring them forth, so that all the country is full of them. And so men do there both winter and summer.

Also in that country and in others also, men find long apples to sell, in their season, and men clepe them apples of Paradise;[11] and they be right sweet and of good savour. And though ye cut them in never so many gobbets[12] or parts, overthwart or endlong, evermore ye shall find in the midst the figure of the Holy Cross of our Lord Jesu. But they will rot within eight days, and for that cause men may not carry of those apples to no far countries; of them men find the mountance[13] of a hundred in a basket, and they have great leaves of a foot and a half of length, and they be convenably large. And men find there also the apple tree of Adam, that have a bite at one of the sides; and there be also fig trees that bear no leaves, but figs upon the small branches; and men clepe them figs of Pharaoh.

Also beside Cairo, without that city, is the field where balm groweth;[14] and it cometh out on small trees, that be none higher than to a man's breeks' girdle,[15] and they seem as wood that is of the wild vine. And in that field be seven wells that our Lord Jesu Christ made with one of his feet, when he went to play with other children. That field is not so well closed, but that men may enter at their own list; but in that season that the balm is growing, men put thereto good keeping, that no man dare be hardy to enter.

This balm groweth in no place, but only there. And though that men bring of the plants for to plant in other countries, they grow well and fair; but they bring forth no

---

[1] *date of the fowl* I.e., the priests organize their writings by the period of the incarnation of the phoenix.

[2] *honestly* Appropriately.

[3] *quick* Alive.

[4] *mickle* Much. I.e., the bird is not much larger than an eagle.

[5] *oriel* Precious stone, unidentifiable.

[6] *ind* Indigo: a blue dye.

[7] *overthwart* Across.

[8] *greater cheap* A better bargain.

[9] *laws* I.e., religions.

---

[10] *eyren* Eggs.

[11] *long apples … apples of Paradise* Many fruits were called apples in this period; it has been suggested that Mandeville is referring to plantains, a type of banana.

[12] *gobbets* Portions.

[13] *mountance* Amount.

[14] *field where balm groweth* Probably the garden of El-Matariyeh, near Cairo.

[15] *breeks' girdle* Breeches' belt.

fructuous thing, and the leaves of balm fall not. And men cut the branches with a sharp flintstone, or with a sharp bone, when men will go to cut them; for whoso cut them with iron, it would destroy his virtue and his nature.

And the Saracens clepe the wood *Enonch-Balse*, and the fruit, the which is as cubebs,[1] they clepe *Abebissam*, and the liquor that droppeth from the branches they clepe *Guybalse*.[2] And men make always that balm to be tilled of the Christian men, or else it would not fructify; as the Saracens say themselves, for it hath been oftentime proved. Men say also that the balm groweth in Ind the more, in that desert where Alexander spake to the trees of the sun and of the moon, but I have not seen it; for I have not been so far above upward, because that there be too many perilous passages.

And wit ye well, that a man ought to take good keep for to buy balm[3] but if he can know it right well, for he may right lightly be deceived. For men sell a gum, that men clepe turpentine, instead of balm, and they put thereto a little balm for to give good odour. And some put wax in oil[4] of the wood of the fruit of balm, and say that it is balm. And some distil cloves of gilofre[5] and of spikenard[6] of Spain and of other spices, that be well smelling; and the liquor that goeth out thereof they clepe it balm, and they think that they have balm, and they have none. For the Saracens counterfeit it by subtlety of craft for to deceive the Christian men, as I have seen full many a time; and after them the merchants and the apothecaries counterfeit it eft sones,[7] and then it is less worth, and a great deal worse.

But if it like you, I shall shew how ye shall know and prove, to the end that ye shall not be deceived. First ye shall well know that the natural balm is full clear, and of citron colour and strongly smelling; and if it be thick, or red or black, it is sophisticate, that is to say,

counterfeited and made like it for deceit. And understand, that if ye will put a little balm in the palm of your hand against the sun, if it be fine and good, ye shall not suffer your hand against the heat of the sun. Also take a little balm with the point of a knife, and touch it to the fire, and if it burn it is a good sign. After take also a drop of balm, and put it into a dish, or in a cup with milk of a goat, and if it be natural balm anon it will take and beclippe[8] the milk. Or put a drop of balm in clear water in a cup of silver or in a clear basin, stir it well with the clear water; and if the balm be fine and of his own kind, the water shall never trouble; and if the balm be sophisticate, that is to say counterfeited, the water shall become anon[9] trouble; and also if the balm be fine it shall fall to the bottom of the vessel, as though it were quicksilver,[10] for the fine balm is more heavy twice than is the balm that is sophisticate and counterfeited. Now I have spoken of balm.

And now also I shall speak of another thing that is beyond Babylon, above the flood of the Nile, toward the desert between Africa and Egypt; that is to say, of the garners[11] of Joseph, that he let make for to keep the grains for the peril of the dear[12] years. And they be made of stone, full well made of masons' craft; of the which two be marvellously great and high, and the tother be not so great. And every garner hath a gate for to enter within, a little high from the earth; for the land is wasted and fallen since the garners were made. And within they be all full of serpents. And above the garners without be many scriptures of diverse languages. And some men say that they be sepultures[13] of great lords, that were sometime, but that is not true, for all the common rumour and speech is of all the people there, both far and near, that they be the garners of Joseph; and so find they in their scriptures, and in their chronicles. On the other part, if they were sepultures, they should not be void within, they should have no

---

[1] *cubebs* Peppercorns.

[2] *Enoch-Balse … Abebissam … Guybalse* Unidentified.

[3] *take good keep … balm* Be careful about buying balm.

[4] *put wax in oil …* Mistranslation from the French original where *cire*, wax, replaced *cuire*, boil. The sentence should have read: "And some boil the oil of the wood of the fruit of the balm."

[5] *gilofre* Gillyflower.

[6] *spikenard* Aromatic substance used in the creation of expensive oils, distilled from a relative of lavender.

[7] *eftsones* Often.

[8] *beclippe* Mix with; in this case, curdle.

[9] *anon* At once (or, immediately).

[10] *quicksilver* Mercury.

[11] *garners* Granaries. See Genesis 41.49. The pyramids at Giza and in other parts of Egypt were thought to have been granaries built by Joseph.

[12] *dear* Lean (i.e., "dear years" = famine).

[13] *sepultures* Crypts.

gates for to enter within; for ye may well know, that tombs and sepultures be not made of such greatness, nor of such highness; wherefore it is not to believe, that they be tombs or sepultures.

In Egypt also there be diverse languages and diverse letters, and of other manner and condition than there be in other parts. As I shall devise you, such as they be, and the names how they clepe them, to such intent, that ye may know the difference of them and of others,—Athoimis, Bimchi, Chinok, Duram, Eni, Fin, Gomor, Heket, Janny, Karacta, Luzanin, Miche, Naryn, Oldach, Pilon, Qyn, Yron, Sichen, Thola, Urmron, Yph and Zarm, Thoit.[1]...

CHAPTER 15

Of the customs of Saracens, and of their law. And how the Soldan[2] reasoned me, author of this book; and of the beginning of Mohammet.[3]

Now, because that I have spoken of Saracens and of their country—now, if ye will know a part of their law and of their belief, I shall tell you after what their book that is clept *Alkaron*[4] telleth. And some men clepe that book *Meshaf*. And some men clepe it *Harme*, after the diverse languages of the country. The which book Mohammet took them. In the which book, among other things, is written, as I have often-time seen and read, that the good shall go to paradise, and the evil to hell; and that believe all Saracens. And if a man ask them what paradise they mean, they say, to paradise that is a place of delights where men shall find all manner of fruits in all seasons, and rivers running of milk and honey, and of wine and of sweet water; and that they shall have fair houses and noble, every man after his desert, made of precious stones and of gold and of silver; and that every man shall have four score wives all

maidens, and he shall have ado every day with them, and yet he shall find them always maidens.

Also they believe and speak gladly of the Virgin Mary and of the Incarnation. And they say that Mary was taught of the angel; and that Gabriel said to her, that she was for-chosen from the beginning of the world and that he shewed to her the Incarnation of Jesu Christ and that she conceived and bare child maiden; and that witnesseth their book.

And they say also that Jesu Christ spake as soon as he was born; and that he was an holy prophet and a true in word and deed, and meek and piteous and rightful and without any vice.

And they say also that when the angel shewed the Incarnation of Christ unto Mary, she was young and had great dread. For there was then an enchanter in the country that dealt with witchcraft, that men clept Taknia, that by his enchantments could make him in likeness of an angel, and went often-times and lay with maidens. And therefore Mary dreaded lest it had been Taknia, that came for to deceive the maidens. And therefore she conjured the angel, that he should tell her if it were he or no. And the angel answered and said that she should have no dread of him, for he was very[5] messenger of Jesu Christ. Also their book saith that when that she had childed under a palm tree she had great shame that she had a child; and she greet[6] and said that she would that she had been dead. And anon the child spake to her and comforted her, and said, "Mother, dismay thee nought, for God hath hid in thee his privities for the salvation of the world." And in other many places saith their *Alkaron* that Jesu Christ spake as soon as he was born. And that book saith also that Jesu was sent from God Almighty for to be mirror and example and token to all men.

And the *Alkaron* saith also of the day of doom[7] how God shall come to doom all manner of folk. And the good he shall draw on his side and put them into bliss, and the wicked he shall condemn to the pains of hell. And among all prophets Jesu was the most excellent and the most worthy next God, and that he made the

---

[1] *Athomis, Bimchi … Thoit* Most manuscript copies of *Mandeville's Travels* include five alphabets: Greek, Egyptian, Hebrew, Saracen and Persian. None of these alphabets genuinely correspond to the languages they purport to represent. Here, the so-called Egyptian alphabet is corrupted past all recognition.

[2] *Soldan* Sultan.

[3] *Mohammet* Mohammed, revered in Islam as the final prophet of God.

[4] *Alkoran* The Koran (al-Quran), the Holy Book of Islam.

[5] *very* True.

[6] *greet* Cried.

[7] *doom* Judgment.

Woodcut illustrations to Chapter 15, from Anton Sorg's second Augsburg edition (1481).

gospels in the which is good doctrine and healthful, full of clarity and soothfastness[1] and true preaching to them that believe in God. And that he was a very prophet and more than a prophet, and lived without sin, and gave sight to the blind, and healed the lepers, and raised dead men, and styed[2] to heaven.

And when they may hold the Book of the Gospels of our Lord written, and namely *Missus est angelus Gabriel*,[3] that gospel they say, those that be lettered, oftentimes in their orisons, and they kiss it and worship it with great devotion.

They fast an whole month in the year and eat nought but by night. And they keep them from their wives all that month. But the sick men be not constrained to that fast.

Also this book speaketh of Jews and saith that they be cursed; for they would not believe that Jesu Christ was come of God. And that they lied falsely on Mary and on her son Jesu Christ, saying that they had crucified Jesu the son of Mary; for he was never crucified, as they say, but that God made him to sty up to him without death and without annoy. But he transfigured his likeness into Judas Iscariot, and him crucified the Jews, and weened[4] that it had been Jesus. But Jesus styed to heavens all quick. And therefore they say, that the Christian men err and have no good knowledge of this, and that they believe folily[5] and falsely that Jesu Christ was crucified.[6] And they say yet, that and he had been crucified, that God had done against his righteousness for to suffer Jesu Christ, that was innocent, to be put upon the cross without guilt. And in this article they say that we fail and that the great righteousness of God might not suffer so great a wrong: and in this faileth their faith. For they knowledge well, that the works of Jesu Christ be good, and his words and

his deeds and his doctrine by his gospels were true, and his miracles also true; and the blessed Virgin Mary is good, and holy maiden before and after the birth of Jesu Christ; and that all those that believe perfectly in God shall be saved. And because that they go so nigh our faith, they be lightly[7] converted to Christian law when men preach them and shew them distinctly the law of Jesu Christ, and when they tell them of the prophecies.

And also they say, that they know well by the prophecies that the law of Mahomet shall fail, as the law of the Jews did; and that the law of Christian people shall last to the day of doom. And if any man ask them what is their belief, they answer thus, and in this form: "We believe God, former of heaven and of earth, and of all other things that he made. And without him is nothing made. And we believe of the day of doom, and that every man shall have his merit, after[8] he hath deserved. And, we believe it for sooth, all that God hath said by the mouths of his prophets."

Also Mahomet commanded in his *Alkaron* that every man should have two wives, or three or four; but now they take unto nine, and of lemans[9] as many as he may sustain.[10] And if any of their wives misbear[11] them against their husband, he may cast her out of his house, and depart from her and take another; but he shall depart with her his goods.

Also, when men speak to them of the Father and of the Son and of the Holy Ghost, they say, that they be three persons, but not one God; for their *Alkaron* speaketh not of the Trinity. But they say well, that God hath speech, and else were he dumb. And God hath also a spirit they know well, for else[12] they say, he were not alive. And when men speak to them of the Incarnation, how that by the word of the angel God sent his wisdom in to earth and enumbred[13] him in the Virgin Mary, and by the word of God shall the dead be raised at the day of doom, they say, that it is sooth and that the word of

---

1   *soothfastness* Truthfulness.

2   *styed* Ascended, rose.

3   *Missus est angelus Gabriel* Latin: the Angel Gabriel was sent. See Luke 1.26: "And in the sixth month the angel Gabriel was sent from God unto a city of Galilee, named Nazareth."

4   *weened* Believed.

5   *folily* Foolishly, madly.

6   *Christian men err … crucified* This is what Christians call the heresy of Docetism, the belief that Christ only appeared or seemed to be a man, rather than being both God and human at once.

7   *lightly* Easily.

8   *after* According to what.

9   *lemans* Lovers or mistresses.

10   *sustain* Support.

11   *misbear* Misbehave.

12   *else* Otherwise.

13   *enumbred* Concealed. Cf. Luke 1035.

God hath great strength. And they say that whoso knew not the word of God he should not know God. And they say also that Jesu Christ is the word of God; and so saith their *Alkaron*, where it saith that the angel spake to Mary and said: "Mary, God shall preach thee the gospel by the word of his mouth and his name shall be clept[1] Jesu Christ."

And they say also that Abraham was friend to God, and that Moses was familiar speaker with God, and Jesu Christ was the word and the spirit of God, and that Mohammet was right messenger of God. And they say that of these four, Jesu was the most worthy and the most excellent and the most great. So that they have many good articles of our faith, albeit that they have no perfect law and faith as Christian men have; and therefore be they lightly converted, and namely those that understand the scriptures and the prophecies. For they have the gospels and the prophecies and the Bible written in their language; wherefore they ken[2] much of holy writ, but they understand it not but after the letter. And so do the Jews, for they understand not the letter ghostly,[3] but bodily; and therefore be they reproved of the wise, that ghostly understand it. And therefore saith Saint Paul: *Litera occidit; Spiritus autem vivificat*.[4] Also the Saracens say that the Jews be cursed, for they have befouled the law that God sent them by Moses; and the Christian be cursed also, as they say, for they keep not the commandments and the precepts of the gospel that Jesu Christ taught them.

And therefore I shall tell you what the Soldan told me upon a day in his chamber. He let void out[5] of his chamber all manner of men, lords and others, for he would speak with me in counsel.[6] And there he asked me how the Christian men governed them in our country. And I said him, "Right well, thanked be God!"

And he said me, "Truly nay! For ye Christian men reck right nought,[7] how untruly to serve God! Ye should give ensample[8] to the lewd[9] people for to do well, and ye give them ensample to do evil. For the commons, upon festival days, when they should go to church to serve God, then go they to taverns, and be there in gluttony all the day and all night, and eat and drink as beasts that have no reason, and wit[10] not when they have enough. And also the Christian men enforce themselves[11] in all manners that they may, for to fight and for to deceive that one that other. And therewithal[12] they be so proud that they know not how to be clothed; now long, now short, now strait, now large, now sworded, now daggered, and in all manner guises.[13] They should be simple, meek and true, and full of alms-deeds, as Jesu was, in whom they trow;[14] but they be all the contrary, and ever inclined to the evil, and to do evil. And they be so covetous, that, for a little silver, they sell their daughters, their sisters, and their own wives to put them to lechery. And one withdraweth the wife of another, and none of them holdeth faith to another; but they befoul their law that Jesu Christ betook[15] them to keep for their salvation. And thus, for their sins, have they lost all this land that we hold. For their sins, their God hath taken them into our hands, not only by strength of ourself, but for their sins. For we know well, in very sooth,[16] that when ye serve God, God will help you; and when he is with you, no man may be against you. And that know we well by our prophecies, that Christian men shall win again this land out of our hands, when they serve God more devoutly; but as long as they be of foul and of unclean living (as they be now) we have no dread of them in no kind, for their God will not help

---

[1] *clept* Called.

[2] *ken* Know.

[3] *ghostly* Spiritually.

[4] *Litera occidit ... vivificat* Latin: the letter kills, but the spirit gives life. See 2 Corinthians 3.6.

[5] *let void out* Sent away.

[6] *in counsel* Privately.

[7] *reck right nought* Do not care at all.

[8] *ensample* Example.

[9] *lewd* Unlearned, common.

[10] *wit* Know.

[11] *enforce themselves* Strive.

[12] *therewithal* Moreover.

[13] *all manner guises* All kinds of ways.

[14] *trow* Believe.

[15] *betook* Gave.

[16] *sooth* Truth.

them in no wise."[1]

And then I asked him, how he knew the state of Christian men. And he answered me, that he knew all the state of all courts of Christian kings and princes and the state of the commons also by his messengers that he sent to all lands, in manner as[2] they were merchants of precious stones, of cloths of gold and of other things, for to know the manner of every country amongst Christian men. And then he let clepe in[3] all the lords that he made void first out of his chamber, and there he shewed me four that were great lords in the country, that told me of my country and of many other Christian countries, as well as they had been of the same country; and they spake French right well, and the Soldan also; whereof I had great marvel.

Alas! that it is great slander to our faith and to our law, when folk that be without law shall reprove us and undernim[4] us of our sins, and they that should be converted to Christ and to the law of Jesu by our good ensamples and by our acceptable life to God, and so converted to the law of Jesu Christ, be, through our wickedness and evil living, far from us and strangers from the holy and very belief, shall thus appeal[5] us and hold us for wicked livers and cursed. And truly they say sooth, for the Saracens be good and faithful; for they keep entirely the commandment of the holy book *Alkaron* that God sent them by his messenger Mahomet, to the which, as they say, Saint Gabriel the angel oftentime told the will of God.

And ye shall understand that Mahomet was born in Arabia, that was first a poor knave that kept camels, that went with merchants for merchandise. And so befell that he went with the merchants into Egypt; and they were then Christian in those parts. And at the deserts of Arabia, he went into a chapel where a hermit dwelt. And when he entered into the chapel that was but a little and a low thing and had but a little door and a low, then the entry began to wax[6] so great, and so large and so high, as

though it had been of a great minster[7] or the gate of a palace. And this was the first miracle, the Saracens say, that Mahomet did in his youth.

After began he for to wax wise and rich. And he was a great astronomer. And after, he was governor and prince of the land of Corodane;[8] and he governed it full wisely, in such manner that when the prince was dead, he took the lady to wife that hight Gadrige.[9] And Mahomet fell often in the great sickness that men call the falling evil;[10] wherefore the lady was full sorry that ever she took him to husband. But Mahomet made her to believe that all times when he fell so, Gabriel the angel came for to speak with him, and for the great light and brightness of the angel he might not sustain him from falling; and therefore the Saracens say that Gabriel came often to speak with him.

This Mahomet reigned in Arabia, the year of our Lord Jesu Christ 610, and was of the generation of Ishmael that was Abraham's son, that he gat upon[11] Hagar his chamberer. And therefore there be Saracens that be clept Ishmaelites; and some Hagarenes, of Hagar. And the other properly be clept Saracens, of Sarah. And some be clept Moabites and some Ammonites, for the two sons of Lot, Moab and Ammon,[12] that he begat on his daughters that were afterward great earthly princes.

And also Mahomet loved well a good hermit that dwelled in the deserts a mile from Mount Sinai, in the way that men go from Arabia toward Chaldea and toward Ind, one day's journey from the sea, where the merchants of Venice come often for merchandise. And so often went Mahomet to this hermit that all his men were wroth; for he would gladly hear this hermit preach and make his men wake all night. And therefore his men thought to put the hermit to death. And so it befell upon a night, that Mahomet was drunken of good wine,

---

[1] *wise* Way.

[2] *in manner as* Disguised as though.

[3] *let clepe in* Called back in.

[4] *undernim* Reprove.

[5] *appeal* Accuse.

[6] *wax* Grow.

[7] *minster* Large church or cathedral.

[8] *governor and prince … Corodane* Mistranslation from the French original, "governour de la terre al prince de Corodane": governor of the land of the prince of Corodane. This land is called Khorsan in Crusade chronicles.

[9] *hight Gadrige* Was named Khadidjah.

[10] *falling evil* Possibly epilepsy.

[11] *gat upon* Fathered by.

[12] *Hagar … Moat and Ammon* See Genesis 16 and 19.37–38.

and he fell on sleep. And his men took Mahomet's sword out of his sheath, whiles he slept, and therewith they slew this hermit, and put his sword all bloody in his sheath again. And at morrow, when he found the hermit dead, he was full sorry and wroth,[1] and would have done his men to death. But they all, with one accord, said that he himself had slain him, when he was drunken, and shewed him his sword all bloody. And he trowed that they had said sooth. And then he cursed the wine and all those that drink it. And therefore Saracens that be devout drink never no wine. But some drink it privily; for if they drunk it openly, they should be reproved. But they drink good beverage and sweet and nourishing that is made of gallamelle[2] and that is that men make sugar of, that is of right good savour, and it is good for the breast.

Also it befalleth sometimes that Christian men become Saracens, either for poverty or for simpleness,[3] or else for their own wickedness. And therefore the archflamen or the flamen,[4] as our archbishop or bishop, when he receiveth them saith thus: *La ellec olla Sila, Machomete rores Alla*; that is to say, "There is no God but one, and Mahomet his messenger."

Now I have told you a part of their law and of their customs, I shall say you of their letters that they have, with their names and the manner of their figures what they be: Almoy, Bethath, Cathi, Ephoti, Delphoi, Fothi, Garothi, Hechum, Iotty, Kaythi, Lothum, Malach, Nabaloth, Orthi, Chesiri, Zoch, Ruth, Holath, Routhi, Salathi, Thatimus, Yrthom, Azazoth, Arrocchi, Zotipyn, Ichetus. And these be the names of their a. b. c. Now shall ye know the figures.[5] … And four letters they have more than other for diversity of their language and speech, forasmuch as[6] they speak in their throats; and we in England have in our language and speech two letters more than they have in their a. b. c.; and that is þ and ȝ, which be clept thorn and yogh.

---

[1]   *sorry and wroth*   Upset and angry.

[2]   *gallamelle*   Sugar cane.

[3]   *simpleness*   Foolishness or lack of intelligence.

[4]   *flamen*   Priest of any non-Christian religion.

[5]   *figures*   Numerals.

[6]   *forasmuch as*   Because.

CHAPTER 20

Of the evil customs used in the isle of Lamary.[7] And how the earth and the sea be of round form and shape, by proof of the star that is clept Antarctic, that is fixed in the south

From that country[8] go men by the sea ocean, and by many divers isles and by many countries that were too long for to tell of. And a fifty-two journeys[9] from this land that I have spoken of, there is another land, that is full great, that men clepe Lamary. In that land is full great heat. And the custom there is such that men and women go all naked. And they scorn when they see any strange folk going clothed. And they say that God made Adam and Eve all naked, and that no man should shame him to shew him such as God made him, for nothing is foul that is of kindly nature.[10] And they say that they that be clothed be folk of another world, or they be folk that trow not in God. And they say that they believe in God that formed the world, and that made Adam and Eve and all other things. And they wed there no wives, for all the women there be common and they forsake[11] no man. And they say they sin if they refuse any man; and so God commanded to Adam and Eve and to all that come of him, when he said, *Crescite Et Multiplicamini Et Replete Terram*.[12] And therefore may no man in that country say, This is my wife; and no woman may say, This my husband. And when they have children, they may give them to what man they will[13] that hath companied[14] with them. And also all the land is common; for all that a man holdeth one year, another man hath it another year; and every man taketh what part that him liketh. And also all the goods of the land

---

[7]   *Lamary*   One of the kingdoms of the isle of Sumatra, near Aceh.

[8]   *that country*   The text refers to a previous chapter, on India and Southeast Asia.

[9]   *journeys*   Days' travel.

[10]   *of kindly nature*   Natural.

[11]   *forsake*   Reject.

[12]   *Crescite et multiplicamini … terram*   Latin. Cf. Genesis 9.7. "And you, be ye fruitful, and multiply; bring forth abundantly in the earth, and multiply therein."

[13]   *what man they will*   Whatever man they like.

[14]   *companied*   Had intercourse.

Woodcut illustrations to Chapter 20, from Anton Sorg's
second Augsburg edition (1481).

be common, corns[1] and all other things: for nothing there is kept in close, and nothing there is under lock, and every man there taketh what he will without any contradiction, and as rich is one man there as is another.

But in that country there is a cursed custom, for they eat more gladly man's flesh than any other flesh; and yet is that country abundant of flesh, of fish, of corns, of gold and silver, and of all other goods. Thither go merchants and bring with them children to sell to them of the country, and they buy them. And if they be fat they eat them anon. And if they be lean they feed them till they be fat, and then they eat them. And they say that it is the best flesh and the sweetest of all the world.

In that land, nor in many other beyond that, no man may see the Star Transmontane, that is clept the Star of the Sea, that is unmovable and that is toward the north, that we clepe the Lode-star.[2] But men see another star, the contrary to him, that is toward the south, that is clept Antarctic.[3] And right as the ship-men take their advice[4] here and govern them by the Lode-star, right so do ship-men beyond those parts by the star of the south, the which star appeareth not to us. And this star that is toward the north, that we clepe the Lode-star, appeareth not to them. For which cause men may well perceive, that the land and the sea be of round shape and form; for the part of the firmament sheweth in one country that sheweth not in another country. And men may well prove by experience and subtle compassment[5] of wit, that if a man found passages by ships that would go to search the world, men might go by ship all about the world and above and beneath.

The which thing I prove thus after that I have seen.[6] For I have been toward the parts of Brabant, and beholden the Astrolabe[7] that the star that is clept the Transmontane is fifty-three degrees high;[8] and more further in Almayne and Bohemia it hath fifty-eight degrees; and more further toward the parts septentrional[9] it is sixty-two degrees of height and certain minutes; for I myself have measured it by the Astrolabe. Now shall ye know, that against the Transmontane is the t'other star that is clept Antarctic, as I have said before. And those two stars move never, and by them turneth all the firmament right as doth a wheel that turneth by his axle-tree. So that those stars bear the firmament in two equal parts, so that it hath as much above as it hath beneath. After this, I have gone toward the parts meridional, that is, toward the south, and I have found that in Libya men see first the star Antarctic. And so far I have gone more further in those countries, that I have found that star more high; so that toward the High Libya it is eighteen degrees of height and certain minutes (of the which sixty minutes make a degree). After going by sea and by land toward this country of that I have spoken, and to other isles and lands beyond that country, I have found the Star Antarctic of thirty-three degrees of height and more minutes. And if I had had company and shipping for to go more beyond, I trow well, in certain, that we should have seen all the roundness of the firmament all about. For, as I have said to you before, the half of the firmament is between those two stars, the which halvendel[10] I have seen. And of the tother halvendel I have seen, toward the north under the Transmontane, sixty-two degrees and ten minutes, and toward the part meridional I have seen under the Antarctic, thirty-three degrees and sixteen minutes. And then, the halvendel of the firmament in all holdeth not but nine score degrees. And of those nine score, I have seen sixty-two on that one part and thirty-three on that other part; that be, ninety-five degrees and nigh the halvendel of a degree. And so there ne faileth but that I have seen all the

---

[1] *corns* Grains.

[2] *Lode-star* Polaris, the North Star.

[3] *Antarctic* The star, obviously, does not exist, but acts as evidence for the assertion that the Earth is a sphere.

[4] *advice* Bearings.

[5] *compassment* Contrivance.

[6] *The which thing … seen* This (i.e., that the world is round) I prove from my own experience.

[7] *Astrolabe* Instrument used for practical astronomical purposes such as navigation.

[8] *degrees high* The part of the dome of the sky immediately above the observer's head is ninety degrees, descending to zero as you approach the horizon. A star like Polaris, which does not appear to move much in the night sky, can be used to determine the latitude at which a person is standing. In this passage, Brabant (the Netherlands) is at 53° North Latitude, and so on.

[9] *septentrional* Northern.

[10] *halvendel* A half part.

firmament, save four score and four degrees and the halvendel of a degree, and that is not the fourth part of the firmament; for the fourth part of the roundness of the firmament holds four score and ten degrees, so there faileth but five degrees and an half of the fourth part. And also I have seen the three parts of all the roundness of the firmament and more yet five degrees and a half. By the which I say you certainly that men may environ[1] all the earth of all the world, as well under as above, and turn again to his country, that had company and shipping and conduct. And always he should find men, lands and isles, as well as in this country. For ye wit well, that they that be toward the Antarctic, they be straight, feet against feet, of them that dwell under the Transmontane; also well as we and they that dwell under us be feet against feet. For all the parts of sea and of land have their opposites, habitable trepassable,[2] and they of this half and beyond half.

And wit well, that, after that that I may perceive and comprehend, the lands of Prester John,[3] Emperor of Ind, be under us. For in going from Scotland or from England toward Jerusalem men go upward always. For our land is in the low part of the earth toward the west, and the land of Prester John is in the low part of the earth toward the east. And they have there the day when we have the night; and also, high[4] to the contrary, they have the night when we have the day. For the earth and the sea be of round form and shape, as I have said before; and that that men go upward to one coast, men go downward to another coast.

Also ye have heard me say that Jerusalem is in the midst of the world. And that may men prove, and shew there by a spear, that is pight[5] into the earth, upon the hour of midday, when it is equinox, that sheweth no shadow on no side. And that it should be in the midst of the world, David witnesseth it in the Psalter,[6] where he saith, *Deus operatus est salutem in medio terrae.*[7] Then they that part from those parts of the west for to go toward Jerusalem, as many journeys as they go upward for to go thither, in as many journeys may they go from Jerusalem unto other confines of the superficiality of the earth beyond. And when men go beyond those journeys toward Ind and to the foreign isles, all is environing the roundness of the earth and of the sea under our countries on this half.

And therefore hath it befallen many times of one thing that I have heard counted[8] when I was young, how a worthy man departed some-time from our countries for to go search the world. And so he passed Ind and the isles beyond Ind, where be more than 5000 isles. And so long he went by sea and land, and so environed the world by many seasons, that he found an isle where he heard speak his own language, calling on oxen in the plough such words as men speak to beasts in his own country, whereof he had great marvel, for he knew not how it might be. But I say that he had gone so long by land and by sea, that he had environed all the earth; that he was come again environing, that is to say, going about, unto his own marches,[9] and if he would have passed further, till he had found his country and his own knowledge. But he turned again from thence, from whence he was come from. And so he lost much painful labour, as himself said a great while after that he was come home. For it befell after, that he went into Norway. And there tempest of the sea took him, and he arrived in an isle. And, when he was in that isle, he knew well that it was the isle where he had heard speak his own language before and the calling of oxen at the plough; and that was possible thing.

But how it seemeth to simple men unlearned, that men may not go under the earth, and also that men should fall toward the heaven from under. But that may not be, upon less than we may fall toward heaven from the earth where we be. For from what part of the earth that men dwell, either above or beneath, it seemeth always to them that dwell that they go more right than any other folk. And right as it seemeth to us that they be

---

[1] *environ* Circle around, circumnavigate.

[2] *trepassable* That may be passed through.

[3] *Prester John* Legendary priest-king from the East who headed a mighty army.

[4] *high* Exactly.

[5] *pight* Stuck.

[6] *Psalter* (Book of) Psalms.

[7] *Deus operatus ... Terrae* Latin: God has worked salvation in the midst of the earth. Cf. Psalms 73.12 (Vulgate).

[8] *counted* Told, recounted.

[9] *marches* Borders.

under us, right so it seemeth to them that we be under them. For if a man might fall from the earth unto the firmament, by greater reason the earth and the sea that be so great and so heavy should fall to the firmament; but that may not be, and therefore saith our Lord God, *Non timeas me, qui suspendi terram ex nihilo?*[1]

And albeit that it be possible thing that men may so environ all the world, natheles,[2] of a thousand persons, one might not happen to return into his country. For, for the greatness of the earth and of the sea, men may go by a thousand and a thousand other ways, that[3] no man could ready him perfectly toward the parts that he came from, but if it were by adventure and hap,[4] or by the grace of God. For the earth is full large and full great, and holds in roundness and about environ, by above and by beneath, 20,425 miles,[5] after the opinion of old wise astronomers; and their sayings I reprove nought. But after my little wit[6] it seemeth me, saving their reverence, that it is more.

And for to have better understanding I say thus. Be there[7] imagined a figure that hath a great compass. And, about the point of the great compass that is clept the centre, be made another little compass. Then after, be the great compass devised by lines in many parts, and that all the lines meet at the centre. So that in as many parts as the great compass shall be departed, in as many shall be departed the little, that is about the centre, albeit that the spaces be less. Now then, be the great compass represented for the firmament, and the little compass represented for the earth. Now then, the firmament is devised by astronomers in twelve signs, and every sign is devised in thirty degrees; that is, 360 degrees that the firmament hath above. Also, be the earth devised in as many parts as the firmament, and let every part answer to a degree of the firmament. And wit

it well that, after[8] the authors of astronomy, 700 furlongs of earth answer to a degree of the firmament, and those be eighty-seven miles and four furlongs. Now be that here multiplied by 360 sithes,[9] and then they be 31,500 miles every of eight furlongs, after miles of our country. So much hath the earth in roundness and of height environ, after mine opinion and mine understanding.

And ye shall understand that after the opinion of old wise philosophers and astronomers, our country nor Ireland nor Wales nor Scotland nor Norway nor the other isles coasting to them be not in the superficiality counted above the earth, as it sheweth by all the books of astronomy. For the superficiality of the earth is parted in seven parts for the seven planets, and those parts be clept climates. And our parts be not of the seven climates, for they be descending toward the west drawing towards the roundness of the world. And also these isles of Ind which be even against us be not reckoned in the climates. For they be against us that be in the low country. And the seven climates stretch them environing the world.

CHAPTER 29

Of the countries and isles that be beyond the land of Cathay;[10] *and of the fruits there; and of twenty-two kings enclosed within the mountains*

Now shall I say you, suingly,[11] of countries and isles that be beyond the countries that I have spoken of.

Wherefore I say you, in passing by the land of Cathay toward the high Ind and toward Bacharia,[12] men pass by a kingdom that men clepe Caldilhe,[13] that is a full fair country.

And there groweth a manner of fruit, as though it were gourds. And when they be ripe, men cut them a-two, and men find within a little beast, in flesh, in bone,

---

[1] *Non timeas me ..., nihilo* Latin: Do not fear me—who have suspended the earth from the void (cf. Psalms 104.5).

[2] *natheles* Nonetheless.

[3] *that* So that.

[4] *adventure and hap* Chance and fortune.

[5] *20,425 miles* In actuality, the earth is approximately 24,900 miles (40,000 km) in circumference.

[6] *after my little wit* According to my limited knowledge.

[7] *Be there* Let there be.

[8] *after* According to.

[9] *sithes* Times.

[10] *Cathay* I.e., China.

[11] *suingly* In due order.

[12] *Bacharia* Bactria, between the Hindu Kush and the Oxus.

[13] *Caldilhe* Thought to be a Tartar kingdom on the Volga.

and blood, as though it were a little lamb without wool. And men eat both the fruit and the beast. And that is a great marvel. Of that fruit I have eaten, although it were wonderful, but that I know well that God is marvellous in his works. And natheles I told them of as great a marvel to them, that is amongst us, and that was of the Bernakes.[1] For I told them that in our country were trees that bear a fruit that become birds flying, and those that fell in the water live, and they that fall on the earth die anon, and they be right good to man's meat. And hereof had they as great marvel, that some of them trowed it were an impossible thing to be.

In that country be long apples of good savour, whereof be more than an hundred in a cluster, and as many in another; and they have great long leaves and large, of two foot long[2] or more. And in that country, and in other countries thereabout, grow many trees that bear clove-gylofres and nutmegs, and great nuts of Ind, and of Canell[3] and of many other spices. And there be vines that bear so great grapes that a strong man should have enough to do for to bear one cluster with all the grapes.

In that same region be the mountains of Caspian that men clepe Uber[4] in the country. Between those mountains the Jews of ten lineages be enclosed, that men clepe Goth and Magoth,[5] and they may not go out on no side. There were enclosed twenty-two kings with their people, that dwelled between the mountains of Scythia. There King Alexander chased them between those mountains, and there he thought for to enclose them through work of his men. But when he saw that he might not do it, nor bring it to an end, he prayed to God of nature that he would perform that that he had begun. And all were it so, that he was a paynim[6] and not worthy to be heard, yet God of his grace closed the mountains together, so that they dwell there all fast

locked and enclosed with high mountains all about, save only on one side, and on that side is the sea of Caspian.[7]

Now may some men ask, since that the sea is on that one side, wherefore go they not out on the sea side, for to go where that them liketh?[8]

But to this question, I shall answer: that sea of Caspian goeth out by land under the mountains, and runneth by the desert at one side of the country, and after it stretcheth unto the ends of Persia, and although it be clept a sea, it is no sea, it toucheth to none other sea, but it is a lake, the greatest of the world; and though they would put them into that sea, they wist[9] never where that they should arrive; and also they can no language but only their own, that no man knoweth but they; and therefore may they not go out.

And also ye shall understand, that the Jews have no proper land of their own for to dwell in, in all the world, but only that land between the mountains. And yet they yield tribute for that land to the Queen of Amazonia, the which that maketh them to be kept in close full diligently, that they shall not go out on no side but by the coast of their land; for their land marcheth to[10] those mountains.

And often it hath befallen that some of the Jews have gone up the mountains and avaled[11] down to the valleys. But great number of folk may not do so, for the mountains be so high and so straight up that they must abide there, maugre[12] their might. For they may not go out, but by a little issue that was made by strength of men, and it lasteth well a four great mile.

And after is there yet a land all desert, where men may find no water, neither for digging nor for none other thing. Wherefore men may not dwell in that place, so is it full of dragons, of serpents and of other venomous beasts, that no man dare not pass, but if it be strong winter. And that strait[13] passage men clepe in that country Clyron. And that is the passage that the Queen

---

[1] *Bernakes* Bartlathes or Bernacae were mythical sea birds, supposedly related to barnacles, who began their life growing on the wool of sheep.

[2] *long* Mistranslation from the French original. The word should be "wide."

[3] *Canell* Cinnamon.

[4] *Uber* From Latin: *ubera aquilonis*, the breasts of the north wind.

[5] *Goth and Magoth* After devils Gog and Magog.

[6] *all were ... paynim* Although it was the case that he was a pagan.

[7] *Caspian* An inland sea of Central Asia.

[8] *where that them liketh* Where they please.

[9] *wist* Know.

[10] *marcheth to* Borders on.

[11] *avaled* Descended.

[12] *maugre* In spite of.

[13] *strait* Narrow.

of Amazonia maketh to be kept. And though it happen some of them by fortune to go out, they can no manner of language but Hebrew, so that they cannot speak to the people.

And yet, natheles, men say they shall go out in the time of anti-Christ, and that they shall make great slaughter of Christian men. And therefore all the Jews that dwell in all lands learn always to speak Hebrew, in hope that when the other Jews shall go out, that they may understand their speech, and to lead them into Christendom for to destroy the Christian people. For the Jews say that they know well by their prophecies that they of Caspia shall go out, and spread throughout all the world, and that the Christian men shall be under their subjection, as long as they have been in subjection of them.

And if that you will wit how that they shall find their way, after that I have heard say I shall tell you.

In the time of anti-Christ a fox shall make there his train,[1] and mine[2] an hole where King Alexander let make the gates;[3] and so long he shall mine and pierce the earth, till that he shall pass through towards that folk. And when they see the fox, they shall have great marvel of him, because that they saw never such a beast. For of all other beasts they have enclosed amongst them, save only[4] the fox. And then they shall chase him and pursue him so strait, till that he come to the same place that he came from. And then they shall dig and mine so strongly till that they find the gates that King Alexander let make of great stones, and passing huge, well cemented and made strong for the mastery. And those gates they shall break, and so go out by finding of that issue.

From that land go men toward the land of Bacharia, where be full evil folk and full cruel. In that land be trees that bear wool,[5] as though it were of sheep, whereof men make clothes and all things that may be made of wool.

In that country be many hippotaynes[6] that dwell sometime in the water and sometime on the land. And they be half man and half horse, as I have said before. And they eat men when they may take them.

And there be rivers of waters that be full bitter, three sithes[7] more than is the water of the sea.

In that country be many griffins, more plenty than in any other country. Some men say that they have the body upward as an eagle and beneath as a lion; and truly they say sooth, that they be of that shape. But one griffin hath the body more great and is more strong than eight lions, of such lions as be on this half, and more great and stronger than an hundred eagles such as we have amongst us. For one griffin there will bear, flying to his nest, a great horse, if he may find him at the point, or two oxen yoked together as they go at the plough. For he hath his talons so long and so large and great upon his feet, as though they were horns of great oxen or of bugles or of kine,[8] so that men make cups of them to drink of. And of their ribs and of the pens[9] of their wings, men make bows, full strong, to shoot with arrows and quarrels.[10]

From thence go men by many journeys through the land of Prester John, the great Emperor of Ind. And men clepe his realm the isle of Pentexoire.[11]

---

[1] *train*   Burrow (?).

[2] *mine*   Dig.

[3] *let make the gates*   Had the gates built.

[4] *save only*   Except.

[5] *trees that bear wool*   Cotton trees.

[6] *hippotaynes*   Hippopotami, possibly here confused with the hippocentaur.

[7] *sithes*   Times.

[8] *kine*   Cattle.

[9] *pens*   Feathers.

[10] *quarrels*   Crossbow bolts.

[11] *Pentexoire*   This name has never been satisfactorily explained.

JULIAN OF NORWICH

c. 1342 – c. 1416

We know very little of Julian of Norwich, one of the great medieval English mystics. It is possible that she was trained as Benedictine nun, and some have speculated that she may have received some form of education at Carrow Priory, the school attached to the Cathedral in Norwich. Her lineage, name, and even the date of her death are unknown. Given what we do know of her, though, it seems likely that she would want her readers to focus on her meditations—her "shewings" and what they revealed about the nature of God—rather than her own life.

Our knowledge of Julian of Norwich's life and mystical experiences is derived from the records she allowed others to keep. At the age of 30 years, on 8 May 1373, Julian of Norwich lay critically ill, her mother at her side. Her curate, called to administer the last rites, held a crucifix aloft at the foot of her bed. With her sight beginning to fail, she felt a creeping numbness spread from her toes to her waist. As her field of vision narrowed and she fixed her eyes on the crucifix near her bed, Julian reports that she suddenly saw the figure of Jesus begin to bleed from his forehead in drops that reminded her of rain falling from the eaves of a house. For several hours, while those around her presumed she was near death, Julian continued to experience what she termed a "bodely sight"—a total of sixteen visions. Soon after her recovery, Julian wrote a short narrative of her visions (the Short Text), and 20 years later, a longer and more theologically complex version (the

JULIAN OF NORWICH

Long Text) that incorporated the fruits of her years of intense and studied meditation on her sixteen original showings.

At some point after her miraculous recovery, Julian became an anchoress at St. Julian's church in Norwich, a bustling and thriving town in the north of England. Being an anchoress required taking a vow of seclusion, which would have meant that she lived the majority of her years in a small room within the sides of the church. This would probably have afforded her a certain autonomy; anchorites and anchoresses did not answer to any ecclesiastical authority other than the bishop. The ritual for enclosure included a Mass with prayers for the dead; as an anchoress Julian was, in effect, choosing to "die" to the world so that she could devote herself to prayer and meditation. Most anchoritic strongholds were small, perhaps no more than 12 or 15 feet square, with three windows. Through hers, Julian could view the altar and the Sacrament and hear Mass. She would have spoken to her confessor or counseled those, like Margery Kempe, who came to talk to her through this window. Another small window would have allowed access to those who saw to her physical needs, and a third, quite possibly facing the street but covered with a translucent cloth, would have allowed in light.

Although there is evidence that Julian, in her role as an anchoress, served her community for many years as a spiritual director and may have enjoyed at least a modicum of public attention, her written works did not garner much interest outside of ecclesiastical circles for over two centuries; in fact, the first time her writings are mentioned at length after her death is in the 1650s, during the Puritan Revolution. The anti-Catholic and anti-mystical temper of the political times led those who were sympathetic to her theological views to transfer their copies of her *Revelations* to several monastic houses in France, where, for all intents and purposes, her writings remained buried until the 1800s.

Early in the twentieth century the scholar Evelyn Underhill revived interest in Julian's writings, which began to be read again by lay, clerical, and academic readers. Over the last few decades, partly as the result of a growing interest in works by women, Julian's writings have become the focus of considerable critical attention. Along with her contemporaries Richard Rolle, Walter Hilton, and the anonymous author of the *Cloud of Unknowing*, Julian is now regarded as one of the great fourteenth-century English mystics.

Her writing is known for its innovative and sometimes startling theology: perhaps most strikingly, she says God is Mother as well as Father. Her meditations on her visions over the years persuaded her that God is not a vindictive God, prone to punish or rebuke, although she emphasized that she adhered to Church doctrine about sin and damnation, as about all other matters; for a woman writing in her time, it was essential to avoid the charge of heresy. Julian found herself unable to embrace the idea of eternal damnation, however, and perceived a God who saw His people through the eyes of love and through grace brought by Christ's death and resurrection. The strength of her unique vision, together with her ability to tap the deep potential for image and metaphor afforded by the Middle English of her time, make her texts a fascinating study of the intersection between affective piety and the flowering of the English language.

⌘⌘⌘

from *A Revelation of Love*[1]

CHAPTER 1—A PARTICULAR OF THE CHAPTERS

The First chapter—of the number of the revelations particularly.

This is a revelation of love that Jesus Christ, our endless bliss, made in sixteen showings or revelations particular; of the which the first is of His precious crowning with thorns; and therein was contained and specified the Trinity with the incarnation and unity betwixt God and man's soul, with many fair showings of endless wisdom and teaching of love, in which all the showings that follow be grounded and joined.

The second is the discolouring of His fair face in tokening of his dear-worthy[2] passion.

The third is that our Lord God almighty, all wisdom and all love, right as verily[3] as He hath made every thing that is, also verily He doth and worketh all thing that is done.

The fourth is the scourging[4] of His tender body with plenteous shedding of His blood.

The fifth is that the fiend[5] is overcome by the precious passion of Christ.

The sixth is the worshipful thanking of our Lord God in which He rewardeth his blessed servants in heaven.

The seventh is often times feeling of wele[6] and woe—the feeling of wele is gracious touching and lightening, with true sikerness[7] of endless joy; the feeling of woe is temptation by heaviness and irkehede[8] of our fleshly living—with ghostly understanding that we are kept also sekirly[9] in love, in woe as in wele, by the goodness of God.

The eighth is the last pains of Christ and His cruel dying.

The ninth is of the liking which is in the blissful Trinity of the hard passion of Christ after his rueful dying; in which joy and liking he will that we be solaced

---

[1] *A Revelation of Love* For the present text the edition of Marion Glasscoe has been used as a copy text. Spelling and punctuation have been substantially modernized for this anthology.

[2] *tokening* Signifying; *dear-worthy* Precious.

[3] *right as verily* Just as truly.

[4] *scourging* Whipping, beating.

[5] *the fiend* Satan.

[6] *wele* Well being.

[7] *sikerness* Certainty.

[8] *irkehede* Distastefulness.

[9] *sekirly* Certainly.

and mirth with him till when we come to the fullness in[1] heaven.

The tenth is our Lord Jesus showeth in love his blissful heart even cloven in two enjoined.

The eleventh is a high ghostly showing of his dearworthy mother.

The twelfth is that our Lord is the most worthy being.

The thirteenth is that our Lord God will we[2] have great regard to all the deeds that he hath done in the great nobility of all things making, and of the excellence of man making, which is above all his works, and of the precious amends that he hath made for man's sin, turning all our blame into endless worship; where also our Lord saith: Behold and see; for by the same mighty wisdom and goodness I shall make wele all that is not wele and thou[3] shalt see it. And in this he will we keep us in the faith and truth of Holy Church, not willing to wit his privities[4] now, but as it longeth to us in this life.

The fourteenth is that our Lord is ground of our beseeching.[5] Herein were seen two fair properties: that one is rightful prayer, that other is sekir trust, which he will both be alike large; and thus our prayers liketh him and he of his goodness fullfilleth it.

The fifteenth, that we shall suddenly be taken from all our pain and from all our woe and of his goodness we shall come up above where we shall have our Lord Jesus to our mede[6] and be fulfilled of joy and bliss in Heaven.

The sixteenth is that the blissful Trinity our Maker, in Christ Jesus our Saviour, endlessly dwells in our soul, worshipfully ruling and giving all things, us mightily and wisely saving and keeping for love, and we shall not be overcome of[7] our enemy.

CHAPTER 2

The Second chapter—of the time of these revelations, and how she asked three petitions.

These revelations were showed to a simple creature that could no letter,[8] the year of our Lord 1373, the 8th day of May; which creature desired afore three gifts of God: the first was mind[9] of the passion, the second was bodily sickness in youth at thirty years of age, the third was to have of God's gift three wounds. As in the first, methought I had some feeling in the passion of Christ but yet I desired more by the grace of God. Methought I would have been that time with Mary Magdalene and with other that were Christ's lovers,[10] and therefore I desired a bodily sight wherein I might have more knowledge of the bodily pains of our Saviour, and of the compassion of Our Lady and of all his true lovers that seen that time his pains, for I would be one of them and suffer with Him.[11] Other sight nor showing of God desired I never none[12] till the soul was departed from the body. The cause of this petition was that after the showing I should have the more true mind in the passion of Christ. The second came to my mind with contrition, freely desiring that sickness so hard as to death that I might, in that sickness, undertaken all my rites[13] of Holy Church, myself wening[14] that I should die, and that all creatures might suppose the same that saw me; for I would have no manner comfort of earthly life. In this sickness I desired to have all manner pains bodily and ghostly that I should have if I should die, with all the dreads and tempests of the fiend, except the outpassing of the soul. And this I meant for I would be purged by the mercy of God and after live more to the worship of God because of that sickness; and that for the more speed in my death, for I desired to be soon with my God. These two desires of the passion and the

---

[1] *in* Of.

[2] *will we* Wishes that we.

[3] *thou* In the Middle Ages, "thou" was the term of familiar address, and "you" was the term of formal address.

[4] *wit* Know; *privities* Private secrets.

[5] *beseeching* Prayers.

[6] *mede* Reward.

[7] *of* By.

[8] *could no letter* Could not read.

[9] *mind* Remembrance, recollection.

[10] *Christ's lovers* Those who loved Christ.

[11] *one of them* See John 19.25.

[12] *desired I never none* I never desired any. Middle English often uses a double negative.

[13] *rites* The Last Rites given to the dying.

[14] *wening* Thinking.

sickness I desired with a condition, saying thus: Lord, thou woteth[1] what I would—if it be Thy will that I have it; and if it be not Thy will, good Lord, be not displeased, for I will nought but as Thou wilt. For the third, by the grace of God and teaching of Holy Church, I conceived a mighty desire to receive three wounds in my life: that is to say the wound of very[2] contrition, the wound of kind compassion and the wound of wilful longing to God. And all this last petition I asked without any condition. These two desires foresaid passed from my mind, and the third dwelled with me continually.

CHAPTER 3

Of the sickness she obtained of God by petition—Third chapter.

And when I was thirty years old and half God sent me a bodily sickness in which I lay three days and three nights; and on the fourth night I took all my rites of Holy Church and wened not to have lived till day. And after this I lay for two days and two nights. And on the third night I wened oftentimes to have passed, and so wened they that were with me. And yet, I thought great sweeme[3] to die; but for nothing that was in earth that me liked to live for, for no pain that I was afraid of, for I trusted in God of his mercy; but it was to have lived that I might have loved God better and longer time, that I might have the more knowing and loving of God in bliss of heaven. For methought all the time that I had lived here, so little and so short in reward of that endless bliss, I thought nothing. Wherefore I thought: Good Lord, may my living no longer be to Thy worship! And I understood by my reason and by my feeling of my pains that I should die. And I assented fully with all, with all the will of my heart, to be at God's will.

Thus I dured[4] till day, and by then my body was dead from the middle downwards as to my feeling.

Then was I stered[5] to be set upright, underset[6] with help, for to have more freedom of my heart to be at God's will, and thinking on God while my life would last. My curate[7] was sent for to be at my ending, and before he came I had set my eyen[8] and might not speak. He set the cross before my face and said: I have brought thee the image of thy Maker and Saviour. Look thereupon and comfort thee therewith. Methought I was well, for my eyen were set uprightward into heaven where I trusted to come by the mercy of God. But nevertheless I assented to set my eyen in the face of the crucifix if I might, and so I did, for methought I might longer endure to look even forth[9] than right up. After this my sight began to fail and it was all dark about me in the chamber as it had be night, save in the image of the cross wherein I beheld a common light, and I wist[10] not how. All that was beside the cross was ugly to me as if it had been much occupied with the fiends.

After this the other part of my body[11] began to die so far forth that scarcely I had any feeling, with shortness of wind.[12] And then I went soothly to have passed.[13] And, in this, suddenly all my pain was taken from me and I was as whole, and namely in the other part of my body, as ever I was before. I marvelled at this sudden change for methought it was a privy working of God and not of kind.[14] And yet by the feeling of this ease I trusted never the more to live; nor the feeling of this ease was no full ease to me, for methought I had lever[15] to be delivered of this world.

Then came suddenly to my mind that I should desire the second wound, of Our Lord's gracious gift, that my body might be fulfilled with mind and feeling of his blessed passion; for I would that his pains were my

---

[1] *woteth* Know.

[2] *very* True.

[3] *sweeme* Regret, grief.

[4] *dured* Endured.

[5] *stered* Moved.

[6] *underset* Supported.

[7] *curate* Priest.

[8] *set my eyen* Fixed my eyes.

[9] *even forth* Parallel to the ground.

[10] *wist* Know.

[11] *other part … body* The upper part of her body.

[12] *wind* Breath.

[13] *went … passed* Truly believed I would die.

[14] *kind* Nature.

[15] *lever* Rather.

pains with compassion, and afterward longing to God. But in this I desired never bodily sight nor showing of God, but compassion, as a kind soul might have with our Lord Jesus, that for love would become a deadly[1] man; and therefore I desired to suffer with Him. …

CHAPTER 5

How God is to us everything that is good, tenderly wrapping us; and all thing that is made, in regard to Almighty God, it is nothing; and how man hath no rest till he knoweth himself and all thing for the love of God—the Fifth chapter.

In this same time Our Lord showed to me a ghostly sight of his homely[2] loving. I saw that he is to us everything that is good and comfortable for us. He is our clothing that for love wrappeth us, halseth[3] us and all becloseth us for tender love, that he may never leave us, being to us all things that are good, as to mine understanding. Also in this he showed a little thing, the quantity of a hazelnut in the palm of my hand; and it was as round as a ball. I looked thereupon with eye of my understanding and thought: What may this be? And it was generally answered thus: It is all that is made. I marvelled how it might last, for methought it might suddenly have fallen to nought for little. And I was answered in my understanding: It lasteth and ever shall, for God loveth it; and so all things hath their being by the love of God.

In this little thing I saw three properties: the first is that God made it, the second is that God loveth it, the third, that God keepeth it. But what is to me soothly the maker, the keeper, and the lover I cannot tell; for, till I am substantially united to him, I may never have full rest nor very bliss; that is to say, that I be so fastened to him that there be right nought that is made betwixt my God and me.

It needeth us[4] to have knowing of the littleness of creatures and to nought[5] all thing that is made for to love and have God that is unmade. For this is the cause why we be not all in ease of heart and soul: for we seek here rest in these things that is so little, wherein is no rest, and know not Our God that is almighty, all wise, all good; for he is the very rest. God will be known, and Him liketh that we rest in Him; for all that is beneath Him sufficeth not us; and this is the cause why that no soul is rested till it is noughted[6] of all things that is made. When he is wilfully noughted, for love to have Him that is all, then is he able to receive ghostly rest.

Also our Lord God showed that it is full great pleasure to Him that a silly[7] soul come to Him nakedly and plainly and homely. For this is the kind[8] yearning of the soul by the touching of the Holy Ghost, as by the understanding that I have in this showing: God, of Thy goodness, give me Thyself; for Thou art enough to me and I may nothing ask that is less that may be full worship to Thee. And if I ask anything that is less, ever me wanteth, but only in Thee I have all.

And these words are full lovesome to the soul and full near touch the will of God and His goodness; for His goodness comprehendeth all his creatures and all His blessed works, and overpasseth without end, for He is the endlessness. And He hath made us only to Himself and restored us by His blessed passion and keepeth us in His blessed love. And all this is of His goodness. …

CHAPTER 7

How Our Lady, beholding the greatness of her Maker, thought herself least, and of the great drops of blood running from under the garland, and how the most joy to man is that God most high and mighty is holiest and most courteous[9]—Seventh chapter.

And to learn[10] us this, as to mine understanding, our Lord God showed Our Lady Saint Mary in the same time; that is to mean the high wisdom and truth she had

---

[1] *deadly* Mortal.

[2] *homely* Familiar.

[3] *halseth* Embraces.

[4] *It needeth us* It is necessary for us, we must.

[5] *nought* Despise.

[6] *noughted* Freed.

[7] *silly* Simple.

[8] *kind* Natural.

[9] *most courteous* The word "courtesy" had more connotations in the medieval period than it does today: it was suggestive of chivalry, goodness, moral virtue, and divine grace.

[10] *learn* Teach.

in beholding of her Maker so great, so high, so mighty and so good. This greatness and this nobility of the beholding of God fulfilled her of reverend dread, and with this she saw herself so little and so low, so simple and so poor, in reward of[1] her Lord God, that this reverend dread fulfilled her of meekness. And thus, by this ground, she was fulfilled of grace and of all manner of virtues and overpasseth all creatures.

In all the time that he showed this that I have said now in ghostly sight, I saw the bodily sight lasting of the plenteous bleeding of the head. The great drops of blood fell down from under the garland like pellets seeming as it had come out of the veins; and in the coming out it were brown red, for the blood was full thick; and in the spreading abroad it were bright red; and when it come to the brows, then it vanished; notwithstanding the bleeding continued till many things were seen and understood. The fairness and the liveliness is like nothing but the same.

The plenteousness is like to the drops of water that fall on the eaves after a great shower of rain that fall so thick that no man may number them with bodily wit. And for the roundness, it were like to the scale of herring in the spreading on the forehead.[2]

These three come to my mind in the time: pellets, for roundness, in the coming out of the blood; the scale of herring, in the spreading in the forehead, for roundness; the drops of eaves, for the plenteousness innumerable. This showing was quick and lively, and hideous and dreadful, sweet and lovely. And of all the sight it was most comfort to me that our God and Lord, that is so reverent and dreadful, is so homely and courteous. And this most fulfilled me with liking and sikerness of soul.

And to the understanding of this he showed this open example: it is the most worship that a solemn king or a great lord may do a poor servant if he will be homely with him, and namely if he shows it himself, of a full true meaning and with a glad cheer, both privately and openly. Then thinketh this poor creature thus: Ah! What might this noble lord do more worship and joy to show me, that am so simple, this marvellous homeliness? Soothly it is more joy and liking to me than he gave me

great gifts and were himself strange[3] in manner. This bodily example was showed so high that man's heart might be ravished and almost forget himself for joy of this great homeliness.

Thus it fares by our Lord Jesus and by us; for soothly it is the most joy that may be, as to my sight, that He that is highest and mightiest, noblest and worthiest, is lowest and meekest, homeliest and most courteous. And truly and soothly this marvellous joy shall be shown us all when we see Him; and this will our Lord, that we believe and trust, joy and like, comfort us and solace us, as we may, with His grace and with His help, into the time that we see it verily;[4] for the most fullness of joy that we shall have, as to my sight, is the marvellous courtesy and homeliness of our Father that is our Maker, in our Lord Jesus Christ that is our brother and our Saviour. But this marvellous homeliness may no man wit in this time of life, but[5] he have it of special showing of our Lord, or of great plenty of grace inwardly given of the Holy Ghost. But faith and belief with[6] charity deserves the mede, and so it is had by grace; for in faith with hope and charity our life is grounded. The showing, made to whom that God will, plainly teaches the same, opened and declared with many privy points longing to our faith which be worshipful to known. And when the showing, which is given in a time, is passed and hid, then the faith keeps it by grace of the Holy Ghost unto our life's end. And thus by the showing it is not other than the faith, not less nor more, as it may be seen by Our Lord's meaning in the same matter by then[7] it come to the end....

CHAPTER II

The third revelation etc., how God doth all things except sin, never changing his purpose without end, for he hath made all things in fullness of goodness—Eleventh chapter.

And after this I saw God in a point, that is to say, in mine understanding, by which sight I saw that He is in

---

[1] *in reward of* By comparison to.

[2] *in the spreading... forehead* As they spread over the forehead.

[3] *strange* Distant.

[4] *verily* Truly.

[5] *but* Unless.

[6] *with* In.

[7] *by then* By the time.

all things. I beheld with advisement,[1] seeing and knowing in sight with a soft dread, and thought: What is sin? for I saw truly that God doth all things be it never so little. And I saw truly that nothing is done by hap[2] nor by adventure, but all things be the foreseeing wisdom of God. If it be hap or adventure in the sight of man, our blindness and our unforesight[3] is the cause, for the things that are in the foreseeing wisdom of God been from without beginning, which rightfully and worshipfully and continually He leads to the best end as they come about, falling to us suddenly, ourselves unwitting;[4] and thus, by our blindness and our unforesight, we say these been haps and adventures; but to Our Lord God they be not so.

Wherefore me behooveth needs to grant[5] that all things that are done, are well done, for our Lord God doth all; for in this time the working of creatures was not showed, but of Our Lord God in the creature; for He is in the mid point of all things and all He doth, and I was sekir He does no sin. And here I saw soothly that sin is no deed,[6] for in all this was not sin showed. And I would no longer marvel in this, but beheld Our Lord, what He would show. And thus, as it might be for the time, the rightfulness of God's working was showed to the soul. Rightfulness has two fair properties: it is right and it is full. And so are all the works of Our Lord God; and thereto needs neither the working of mercy nor grace, for it been all rightful, wherein fails not. And in another time He showed for the beholding of sin nakedly, as I shall say, where He uses working of mercy and grace.

And this vision was showed to mine understanding, for Our Lord will have the soul turned truly into the beholding of Him, and generally of all His works; for they are full good and all His doings be easy and sweet, and to great ease[7] bringing the soul that is turned from the beholding of the blind deeming[8] of man onto the faire sweet deeming of our Lord God; for a man beholds some deeds well done and some deeds evil, but Our Lord beholds them not so; for as all that has been in kind is of God's making, so are all things that are done in property of God's doing; for it is easy to understand that the best deed is well done; and so well as the best deed is done and the highest, so well is the least deed done; and all in property and in the order that Our Lord hath it ordained to from without beginning, for there is no doer but He.

I saw full sekirly that He changes never His purpose in no manner thing, nor never shall, without end; for there was nothing unknown to Him in His rightful ordinance from without beginning, and therefore all things was set in order, or[9] anything was made, as it should stand without end; and no manner thing shall fail of that point; for He made all things in fullness of goodness; and therefore the Blessed Trinity is ever full pleased in all His works. And all this showed he full blissfully, meaning thus: See I am God. See I am in all things. See I do all things. See I left never mine hands of mine works, nor never shall, without end. See I lead all things to the end I ordained it to from without beginning by the same might, wisdom and love that I made it. How should anything be amiss? Thus mightily, wisely and lovingly was the soul examined in this vision. Than saw I soothly that me behooved needs to assent[10] with great reverence, enjoying in God. ...

Chapter 27—The Thirteenth Revelation

The thirteenth revelation is that Our Lord God will that we have great regard to all His deeds that He have[11] done in the great nobleness of all of all things making and of etc., how sin is not known by the pain—Twenty-Seventh chapter.

After this the Lord brought to my mind the longing that I had to Him before; and I saw that nothing letted[12] me but

---

[1] *beheld with advisement* Viewed the vision contemplatively.

[2] *hap* Chance.

[3] *unforesight* Lack of foresight.

[4] *unwitting* Unknowing.

[5] *wherefore me behooveth ... grant* Thus I was compelled to admit.

[6] *no deed* Nothing.

[7] *ease* Rest.

[8] *deeming* Judgment.

[9] *or* Before.

[10] *me behooved ... assent* I was compelled to agree.

[11] *have* Has. Medieval verb forms have been maintained wherever the sense seems clear.

[12] *letted* Hindered.

sin, and so I beheld generally in us all. And methought if sin had not been, we should all have been clean and like to our Lord as He made us; and thus, in my folly, before this time often I wondered why by the great foreseeing wisdom of God the beginning of sin[1] was not letted; for then, thought I, should have been well.

This stering[2] was mikel[3] to be forsaken, and nevertheless mourning and sorrow I made therefore without reason and discretion. But Jesus, that in this vision informed me of all that me needeth, answered by this word and said: Sin is behovely,[4] but all shall be well, and all shall be well, and all manner of thing shall be well. In this naked word sin our Lord brought to my mind generally all that is not good, and the shameful despite and the utter noughting[5] that He bare for us in this life, and His dying, and all His pains, and passions of all His creatures, ghostly and bodily—for we be all in part noughted,[6] and we shall be noughted following our master Jesus till we be full purged: that is to say, till we be fully purged of our deadly flesh and of all our inward affections which are not very good[7]—and the beholding of this, with all the pains that ever were or ever shall be. And with all these I understood the passion of Christ for most pain and over passing. And all this was showed in a touch and readily passed over into comfort. For our good Lord would not that the soul were afeared of this ugly sight.

But I saw not sin; for I believe it hath no manner of substance nor party of[8] being, nor it might not be known but by the pain that it is cause of; and thus pain, it is something, as to my sight,[9] for a time, for it purgeth and maketh us to know ourselves and ask mercy; for the passion of Our Lord is comfort to us against all this, and so is His blessed will. And for the tender love that our good Lord hath to all that shall be saved He comforteth

readily and sweetly, meaning thus: It is sooth that sin is cause of all this pain, but all shall be well, and all shall be well, and all manner thing shall be well.

These words were showed full tenderly, showing no manner of blame to me,[10] nor to none that shall be safe. Than were it a great unkindness to blame or wonder on God for my sin, sith[11] He blameth not me for sin.

And in these same words I saw a marvellous high privity[12] hid in God, which privity He shall openly make known to us in heaven; in which knowing we shall verily see the cause why He suffered sin to come; in which sight we shall endlessly joy in our Lord God.

CHAPTER 28

How the children of salvation shall be shaken in sorrows, but Christ enjoyeth with compassion; and a remedy against tribulation—Twenty-Eighth chapter.

Thus I saw how Christ hath compassion on us for the cause of sin. And right as I was before in the passion of Christ fulfilled with pain and compassion, so in this I was fulfilled a party with compassion of all my even[13] Christians; for that well, well beloved people that shall be saved: that is to say, God's servants, Holy Church, shall be shaken in sorrows and anguish and tribulation in this world as men shake a cloth in the wind. And as to this Our Lord answered in this manner: A great thing shall I make hereof in heaven, of endless worships and everlasting joy. Yea, so far forth I saw that Our Lord enjoyeth of the tribulations of His servants with pity and compassion; to each person that He loveth to His bliss for to bring, He leaveth upon Him something that is no lack in His sight, whereby they are lowed[14] and despised in this world, scorned, and so outcast. And this He doth for to let[15] the harm that they should take of the pomp and the vainglory of this wretched life, and make their way ready to come to heaven in His bliss

---

[1] *beginning of sin*   See Romans 5.13.

[2] *stering*   Impulse.

[3] *mikel*   Much.

[4] *behovely*   Necessary. See Matthew 18.7.

[5] *noughting*   Belittling, disparagement.

[6] *noughted*   Freed.

[7] *not very good*   See Romans 6.12.

[8] *party of*   Share in.

[9] *as to my sight*   As far as I can see.

[10] *blame to me*   See John 8.10–11.

[11] *sith*   Since.

[12] *privity*   Mystery.

[13] *even*   Fellow. See I Peter 3.8.

[14] *lowed*   Humbled.

[15] *let*   Prevent.

without end lasting; for He saith: I shall all[1] to—break you for your vain affections and your vicious pride; and after that I shall together gather you and make you mild and meek, clean and holy, by joining to me.[2]

And then I saw that each kind compassion that man hath on[3] His even Christian with charity, it is Christ in him. That same noughting that was showed in His passion, it was showed again here in this compassion wherein were two manner of understandings in Our Lord's meaning:[4] the one was the bliss that we are bought to, wherein He wills that we enjoy. That other is for comfort in our pain; for He will that we wit[5] that it shall all be turned to worship and profit by virtue of His passion, and that we wit that we suffer not alone but with Him, and see Him our ground, and that we see His pains and His noughting pass so for all that we may suffer, that it may not be full thought. And the beholding of this will save us from grouching and despair in the feeling of our pains; and if we see soothly that our sin deserveth it, yet His love excuseth us, and of His great courtesy He does away all our blame, and He holdeth us with ruth[6] and pity, as children innocent and unlothful.[7] ...

CHAPTER 50

How the chosen soul was never dead in the sight of God, and of a marvel upon the same; and three things bolded her to ask of God the understanding of it— Fiftieth chapter.

And in this deadly life mercy and forgiveness is our way and evermore leadeth us to grace.[8] And by the tempest and the sorrow that we fall in on our part, we be often dead as to man's doom in earth, but in the sight of God the soul that shall be saved was never dead nor never shall. But yet here I wondered and marvelled with all the diligence of my soul, meaning[9] thus: Good Lord, I see Thee that Thou art very truth, and I know soothly that we sin grievously all day and be much blameworthy;[10] and I may neither leave the knowing of this sooth, nor I see not the showing to us no manner of blame. How may this be? For I knew by the common teaching of Holy Church and by mine own feeling that the blame of our sin continually hangeth upon us, from the first man[11] into the time that we come up into heaven. Then was this my marvel, that I saw our Lord God showing to us no more blame than if we were as clean as and holy as angels be in heaven.[12] And atwix[13] these two contraries my reason was greatly travailed[14] by my blindness, and could have no rest for dread that His blessed presence should pass from my sight and I to be left in unknowing how He beholdeth us in our sin. For either me behooved[15] to see in God that sin were all done away, or else me behooved to see in God how He seeth it, whereby I might truly know how it longeth to me to see sin and the manner of our blame.

My longing endured, Him continually beholding, and yet I could have no patience for great awe and perplexity, thinking: If I take it thus, that we be not sinners nor not blameworthy, it seemeth as I should err and fail of knowing of this sooth. And if it be so that we be sinners and blameworthy, good Lord, how may it then be that I cannot see this soothness in Thee, which art my God, my Maker, in whom I desire to see all truths?

For three points make me hardy to ask it: the first is for it[16] is so low a thing, for if it were a high I should be adread;[17] the second is that it is so common, for if it were special and privy, also I should be adread; the third

---

[1] *I shall all* I shall do all.

[2] *I shall together ... me* See Matthew 23.37, 11.28–29, Ephesians 5.25–26.

[3] *on* For.

[4] *nothing that was ... meaning* Christ's love of humanity made Him see all the pains of the Passion as nothing, and such stoicism is achieved through two means.

[5] *wit* Know.

[6] *ruth* Compassion.

[7] *unlothful* Innocent.

[8] See Psalm 118.132–33.

[9] *meaning* Saying.

[10] See Proverbs 24.16.

[11] *the first man* Adam.

[12] See Luke 20.35–36.

[13] *atwix* Between.

[14] *travailed* Tormented.

[15] *me behooved* It was incumbent upon me.

[16] *it* This question.

[17] *adread* Afraid.

is that it needeth me to wit it, as me thinketh, if I shall live here, for knowing of good and evil, whereby I may by reason and grace the more depart them asunder, and love goodness and hate evil as Holy Church teacheth. I cried inwardly with all my might, seeking unto God for help, meaning thus: Ah! Lord Jesus, King of bliss, how shall I be eased? Who that shall teach me and tell me that[1] me needeth to wit, if I may not at this time see it in Thee?

CHAPTER 51

The answer to the doubt afore by a marvellous example of a lord and a servant; and God will abide, for it was near twenty years after ere she fully understood this example; and how it is understood that Christ sitteth on the right hand of the Father—Fifty-First chapter.

And then our courteous Lord answered in showing full mystily[2] a wonderful example of a lord that hath a servant, and gave me sight to my understanding of both; which sight was showed double in the Lord, and the sight was showed double in the servant: than one party was showed ghostly in bodily likeness, and the other party was showed more ghostly without bodily likeness.[3] For the first thus: I saw two persons in bodily likeness, that is to say, a lord and a servant; and therewith God gave me ghostly understanding. The lord sitteth solemnly in rest and in peace, the servant standeth by, before his lord reverently, ready to do his lord's will. The lord looketh upon his servant full lovely and sweetly, and meekly he sendeth him to a certain place to do his will.[4] The servant, not only he goeth, but suddenly he starteth and runneth in great haste for love to don his lord's will. And anon he falleth in a slade[5] and taketh full great sore. And than he groaneth and moaneth and waileth and writheth, but he ne may risen[6] nor

help himself by no manner way. And of all this the most mischief that I saw him in was failing of comfort; for he could not turn his face to look upon his loving lord, which was to him full near, in whom is full comfort;[7] but as a man that was feeble and unwise for the time, he intended to his feeling, and endured in woe, in which woe he suffered seven great pains. The first was the sore bruising he took in his falling, which was to him much pain. The second was the heaviness of his body. The third was feebleness following of these two. The fourth, that he was blinded in his reason and stonied[8] in his mind so far forth that almost he had forgotten his own love. The fifth was that he might not rise. The sixth was most marvellous to me, and that was that he lay alone. I looked all about and beheld, and far nor near, high nor low, I saw to him no help. The seventh was that the place which he lay on was a long, hard and grievous.

I marvelled how this servant might meekly suffer there all this woe. And I beheld with avisement to wit if I could perceive in him any default, or if the Lord should assign in him any blame, and soothly there was none seen; for only his good will and his great desire was cause of his falling; and he was as unlothful[9] and as good inwardly as when he stood afore his lord ready to do his will.

And right thus continually his loving lord full tenderly beholdeth him; and now with a double cheer:[10] one outward, full meekly and mildly with great ruth and pity, and this was of the first; another inward, more ghostly, and this was showed with a leading of my understanding into the lord, which I saw him highly enjoy, for the worshipful resting and nobleth[11] that he will and shall bring his servant to by his plenteous grace. And this was of that other showing. And now my understanding led again into the first, both keeping in mind.

Then saith this courteous lord in his meaning: Lo, lo, my loved servant. What harm and disease[12] he hath

---

[1] *that* That which.

[2] *mystily* Mistily, darkly.

[3] *ghostly in bodily ... ghostly without bodily* This refers to the spiritual sight versus bodily sight distinction that Julian sets up in the First Revelation.

[4] *do his will* See John 17.18.

[5] *slade* Valley, dell.

[6] *ne may risen* Cannot rise.

[7] *full comfort* See 2 Corinthians 1.3.

[8] *stonied* Astonished, stunned.

[9] *unlothful* Innocent.

[10] *cheer* Countenance.

[11] *nobleth* Eminence, high standing.

[12] *disease* Distress.

taken in my service for my love, yea, and for his good will! Is it not reason that I award him[1] his fright and his dread, his hurt and his maim and all his woe? And not only this, but falleth it not to me to given a gift that be better to him and more worshipful than his own whole should have been? And else methinketh I did him no grace.

And in this an inward ghostly showing of the Lord's meaning descended[2] into my soul, in which I saw that it behoveth needs to be, standing His great and His own worship, that His dear-worthy servant which he loved so much should be verily and blissfully rewarded without end above that he should have been if he had not fallen; yea, and so far forth that his falling and his woe that he hath taken thereby shall be turned into high and over-passing worship and endless bliss.

And at this point the showing of the example vanished, and our good Lord led forth mine understanding in sight and in showing of the revelation to the end. But notwithstanding all this forth-leading, the marvelling[3] of the example came never from me; for methought it was given me for an answer to my desire. And yet could I not taken therein full understanding to mine ease at that time. For in the servant that was showed for Adam, as I shall say, I saw many diverse properties that might by no manner or way be directed to single Adam.[4] And thus in that time I stood mikel in unknowing. For the full understanding of this marvel-lous example was not given me in that time; in which misty example three privities of the revelation be yet mikel hid, and notwithstanding this I saw and under-stood that every showing is full of privities. And there-fore me behoveth now to tell three properties in which I am sumdele[5] eased.

The first is the beginning of teaching that I under-stood therein in the same time; the second is the inward learning that I have understood therein sithen;[6] the third all the whole revelation from the beginning to the end, that is to say, of this book, which our Lord God of his goodness bringeth oftentimes freely to the sight of mine understanding. And these three are so joined, as to my understanding, that I cannot, nor may, depart them. And by these three as one I have teaching whereby I owe to believe and trust in our Lord God, that of the same goodness that he showed it, and for the same end, right so of the same goodness and for the same end he shall declare it to us when it is His will.

For twenty years after the time of the showing, save three months, I had teaching inwardly, as I shall say: It longeth to thee to taken heed to all the properties and condition that were showed in the example though thou think that they been misty and indifferent to thy sight. I assented wilfully with great desire, seeing inwardly with avisement all the points and properties that were showed in the same time, as far forth as my wit and understanding would serve; beginning mine beholding at the lord and at the servant, and the manner of sitting of the lord, and the place that he sat on, and the colour of his clothing and the manner of shape, and his cheer without, and his nobleth and his goodness within; at the manner of standing of the servant and the place where and how, at his manner of clothing, the colour and the shape, at his outward having and at his inward goodness and his unlothfulness. The lord that sat solemnly in rest and in peace, I understand that he is God. The servant that stood before the lord, I understood that it was showed for Adam, that is to say, one man was showed that time, and his falling to make that thereby under-stand how God beholdeth a man and his falling; for in the sight of God all man is one man and one man is all man. This man was hurt in his might and made full feeble; and he was stonied in his understanding, for he turned from the beholding of his Lord. But his will was kept whole in God's sight; for his will I saw Our Lord commend and approve, but himself was letted and blinded of the knowing of this will. And this is to him great sorrow and grievous disease, for neither he sees clearly his loving lord, which is to him full meek and mild, nor he sees truly what himself is in the sight of his loving lord. And well I wot, when these two are wisely and truly seen, we shall getten rest and peace here in part, and the fullness of the bliss of heaven, by His

---

[1] *award him*   Remind him for.

[2] *descended*   This is the only place where Julian speaks of a revelation as coming from above.

[3] *marvelling*   Wonder.

[4] *to single Adam*   I.e., to Adam alone.

[5] *sumdele*   Somewhat.

[6] *sithen*   Since.

plenteous grace.

And this was a beginning of teaching which I saw in the same time whereby I might come to knowing in what manner he beholdeth us in our sin. And then I saw that only pains blameth and punisheth, and our courteous Lord comforteth and sorroweth; ever He is to the soul in glad cheer, loving and longing to bring us to His bliss.

The place that our Lord sat on was simple, on the earth barren and desert, alone in wilderness. His clothing was wide and syde,[1] and full seemly as falleth to a lord; the colour of his cloth was blue as azure, most sad[2] and fair. His cheer was merciful, the colour of his face was fair brown with fulsomely[3] features; his eyes were black, most fair and seemly, showing full of lovely pity; and within him an high ward,[4] long and broad, all full of endless heavens. And the lovely looking that he looked upon his servant continually, and namely in his falling, methought it might melt our hearts for love and brest[5] them in two for joy. The fair looking showed of a seemly medlur[6] which was marvellous to beholden: that one was ruth and pity, that other was joy and bliss. The joy and bliss passeth as far ruth and pity as heaven is above earth. The pity was earthly and the bliss was heavenly.

The ruth in the pity of the Father was of the falling of Adam, which is his most loved creature. The joy and the bliss was of his dear-worthy Son, which is even[7] with the Father. The merciful beholding of his lovely cheer fulfilled all earth and descended down with Adam into hell,[8] with which continuant pity Adam was kept from endless death. And this mercy and pity dwelleth with mankind until the time we come up into heaven. But man is blinded in this life, and therefore we may not see our Father, God, as He is. And what time that He of His goodness will show Him to man, He showeth Him homely[9] as man. Notwithstanding that, I saw verily we ought to know and believe that the Father is not man. But his sitting on the earth barren and desert is this to mean: he made man's soul to be his own city and his dwelling place, which is most pleasing to him of all his works; and what time that man was fallen into sorrow and pain he was not all seemly to serven of that noble office; and therefore our kind Father would dight[10] him no other place but to sit upon the earth abiding mankind, which is meddled[11] with earth, till what time by His grace His dear-worthy Son had brought again His city into the noble fairness with His hard travail.[12]

The blueness of the clothing betokeneth his steadfastness. The brownness of his fair face with the seemly blackness of the eyen was most according to show his holy soberness. The largeness of his clothing, which were fair, flamand[13] about, betokeneth that he hath beclosed in him all heavens and all joy and bliss. And this was showed in a touch where I say mine understanding was led into the lord, in which I saw him highly enjoy for the worshipful restoring that he will and shall bring his servant to be his plenteous grace. And yet I marvelled, beholding the lord and the servant before said.

I saw the lord sit solemnly, and the servant standing reverently before his lord, in which servant is double understanding: one without, another within. Outward, he was clad simply as a labourer which were disposed to travail, and he stood full near the lord, not even for against[14] him, but in part aside, that on the left. His clothing was a white kirtle,[15] single, old and all defaced, dyed with sweat of his body, strait[16] fitting to him and short, as it were an handful beneath the knee, bare,[17] seeming as it should soon be worn up, ready to be

---

[1] *syde* Ample.

[2] *sad* Deep or dark (blue).

[3] *fulsomely* Gracious.

[4] *high ward* Secure citadel, place of refuge. See 2 Kings 22.3, Psalm 58.17.

[5] *brest* Break.

[6] *medlur* Mixture.

[7] *even* Equal.

[8] *into hell* See Psalm 138.8–10.

[9] *homely* Familiarly.

[10] *dight* Prepare.

[11] *meddled* Mixed. See Genesis 2.7.

[12] *travail* Labor.

[13] *flamand* Flaming.

[14] *for against* In front of.

[15] *kirtle* Tunic.

[16] *strait* Close.

[17] *bare* Threadbare.

ragged and rent. And in this I marvelled greatly, think-ing: This is now an unseemly clothing for the servant that is so highly loved to stand afore so worshipful a lord. And inward, in him was showed a ground of love, which love he had to the lord was even like to the love that the lord had to him. The wisdom of the servant saw inwardly that there was one thing to do which should be to the worship of the lord. And the servant for love, having no reward to[1] himself nor to nothing that might fall of[2] him, hastily he started and ran at the sending of his lord to do that thing which was his will and his worship. For it seemed be his outward clothing as he had been a continuant labourer of long time. And by the inward sight that I had, both in the lord and in the servant, it seemed that he was anew, that is to say, new beginning for to travail, which servant was never sent out before.

There was a treasure in the earth[3] which the lord loved. I marvelled and thought what it might be. And I was answered in mine understanding: It is a meat[4] which is lovesome and pleasant to the lord. For I saw the lord sit as a man, and I saw neither meat nor drink wherewith to serve him; this was one marvel. Another marvel was that this solemn lord had no servant but one, and him he sent out. I beheld, thinking what manner labour it might be that the servant should do. And then I understood that he should do the greatest labour and hardest travail, that is, he should be a gardener; delving and diking,[5] swinking[6] and sweating, and turn the earth upside down, and seek the deepness, and water the plants in time. And in this he should continue his travail and make sweet floods to run, and noble and plenteous fruits to spring, which he should bring before the lord and serve him therewith to his liking. And he should never turn again till he had dight this meat,[7] all ready as he knew that it liked the lord, and then he should take this meat with the drink, and bear it full worshipfully

---

[1] *reward to* Regard for.

[2] *fall of* Happen to.

[3] *treasure in the earth* See Matthew 13.44.

[4] *meat* Food.

[5] *diking* Digging ditches.

[6] *swinking* Toiling.

[7] *dight this meat* Prepared this food.

before the lord. And all this time the lord should sit on the same place abiding his servant whom he sent out.

And yet I marvelled from whence the servant came; for I saw in the lord that he hath within himself endless life and all manner of goodness, save that treasure that was in the earth and that was grounded in the lord in marvellous deepness of endless love—but it was not all to the worship till this servant had dight thus nobly it, and brought it before him, in himself present. And without the lord was nothing but wilderness. And I understood not all what this example meant, and therefore I marvelled whence the servant came.

In the servant is comprehended the second person in the Trinity; and in the servant is comprehended Adam, that is to say, all men. And therefore when I say the Son, it meaneth the Godhead which is even with the Father, and when I say the servant, it meaneth Christ's man-hood which is rightful Adam. By the nearness of the servant is understood the Son, and by the standing on the left side is understood Adam. The lord is the Father, God. The servant is the Son, Christ Jesus. The Holy Ghost is even love which is in them both. When Adam fell, God's Son fell; for the ruthful joining which was made in heaven, God's Son might not be separated from Adam, for by Adam I understand all man. Adam fell from life to death into the slade of this wretched world and after that into hell. God's Son fell with Adam into the slade of the maiden's womb, which was the fairest daughter of Adam, and therefore to excuse Adam from blame in heaven and in earth; and mightily he fetched him out of hell.[8] By the wisdom and goodness that was in the servant is understood God's Son. By the poor clothing as a labourer standing near the left side is understood the manhood and Adam, with all the mischief[9] and feebleness that followeth; for in all this our good lord showed his own Son and Adam but one man. The virtue and the goodness that we have is of Jesus Christ, the feebleness and the blindness that we have is of Adam; which two were showed in the servant.

And thus hath our good Lord Jesus taken upon Him all our blame; and therefore our Father may, nor will, no more blame assign to us than to his own dear-worthy Son, Christ. Thus was He the servant before His com-

---

[8] Here the text alludes to the Harrowing of Hell.

[9] *mischief* Misfortune.

ing into the earth, standing ready before the Father in purpose till what time He would send him to do that worshipful deed by which mankind was brought again into heaven; that is to say, notwithstanding that He is God, even with the Father as against[1] the Godhead, but in His foreseeing purpose that He would be man to save man in fulfilling of his Father's will, so He stood afore his Father as a servant, wilfully taking upon Him all our charge. And then He start full readily at the Father's will, and anon he fell full low in the maiden's womb, having no reward to Himself nor to His hard pains.

The white kirtle is the flesh; the singleness is that there was right naught atwix[2] the Godhood and manhood; the straitness is poverty; the eld[3] is of Adam's wearing; the defacing of sweat, of Adam's travail; the shortness showeth the servant's labour.

And thus I saw the Son standing, saying in His meaning: Lo, my dear Father, I stand before Thee in Adam's kirtle all ready to start and to run. I would be in the earth to do Thy worship when it is Thy will to send me. How long shall I desire? Full soothfastly wist the Son when it was the Father's will and how long He shall desire; that is to say, against the Godhead, for He is the wisdom of the Father. Wherefore this meaning was showed in understanding of the manhood of Christ; for all mankind that shall be saved by the sweet incarnation and blissful passion of Christ, all is the manhood of Christ; for he is the head and we be his members;[4] to which members the day and the time is unknown when every passing woe and sorrow shall have an end, and the everlasting joy and bliss shall be fulfilled; which day and time for to see all the company of heaven longeth. And all that shall be under heaven that shall come thither, their way is by longing and desire; which desire and longing was showed in the servant standing afore the Lord, or else thus, in the Son's standing before the Father in Adam's kirtle; for the languor and desire of all mankind that shall be saved appeared in Jesus; for Jesus is all that shall be saved and all that shall be saved is Jesus; and all of the charity of God, with obedience,

meekness and patience, and virtues that longen[5] to us. Also in this marvellous example I have teaching with me, as it were the beginning of an ABC, whereby I may have some understanding of our Lord's meaning; for the privities of the revelation be hid therein, notwithstanding that all the showings are full of privities.

The sitting of the Father betokeneth His Godhead, that is to say, for showing of rest and peace; for in the Godhead may be no travail. And that he showed himself as lord betokeneth to our manhood. The standing of the servant betokeneth travail; on side and on the left betokeneth that he was not all worthy to stand even right before[6] the lord. His starting was the Godhead, and the running was the manhood; for the Godhead start from the Father into the maiden's womb, falling into the taking of our kind; and in this falling he took great sore; the sore that he took was our flesh in which he had feeling of deadly pains. By that he stood dreadfully before the lord, and not even right, betokeneth that his clothing was not honest to stand in even right before the Lord; nor that might not, nor should not, be his office while he was a labourer; nor also he might not sit in rest and peace with the Lord till he had won his peace rightfully with his hard travail; and by the left side, that the Father left His own Son wilfully in the manhood to suffer all man's pains without sparing of Him. By that his kirtle was in point to be ragged and rent is understood the rods and the scourges, the thorns and the nails, the drawing and the dragging, his tender flesh rending; as I saw in some part. The flesh was rent from the head-pan,[7] falling in pieces until the time the bleeding failed; and then it began to dry again, clinging to the bone. And by the wallowing and writhing, groaning and moaning is understood that he might never rise all mightily from the time that he was fallen into the maiden's womb till his body was slain and dead, he yielding the soul in the Father's hands with all mankind for whom he was sent.

And at this point He began first to show his might; for He went into hell, and when He was there He raised up the great right out of the deep deepness which rightfully was knit to Him in high heaven. The body

---

[1] *against* Regards.

[2] *right naught atwix* Nothing at all between.

[3] *eld* Age.

[4] Cf. Corinthians 12.12.

[5] *longen* Belong.

[6] *even right before* Directly in front of.

[7] *head-pan* Forehead.

was in the grave till Easter morrow, and from that time he lay never more. For then was rightfully ended the wallowing and the writhing, the groaning and the moaning; and our foul deadly flesh that God's Son took on him, which was Adam's old kirtle, strait, bare and short, then by Our Saviour was made fair now, white and bright and of endless cleanness, wide and syde, fairer and richer than was than the clothing which I saw on the Father; for that clothing was blue, and Christ's clothing is now of a fair, seemly medlur[1] which is so marvellous that I can it not discrien;[2] for it is all of very worships.

Now sitteth not the Lord on earth in wilderness, but He sitteth in his noblest seat which He made in heaven most to His liking. Now standeth not the Son before the Father as a servant dreadfully, unornly[3] clad, in part naked, but He standeth before the Father even right, richly clad in blissful largess, with a crown upon his head of precious riches; for it was showed that we be his crown, which crown is the Father's joy, the Son's worship, the Holy Ghost's liking, and endless marvellous bliss to all that be in heaven.

Now standeth not the Son before the Father on the left side as a labourer, but He sitteth on his Father's right hand in endless rest and peace. But it is not meant that the Son sitteth on the right hand, side by side, as one man sitteth by another in this life; for there is no such sitting, as to my sight, in the Trinity; but he sitteth on his Father's right hand, that is to say, in the highest nobleth of the Father's joys. Now is the spouse, God's Son, in peace with his loved wife, which is the fair maiden of endless joy. Now sitteth the Son, very God and man, in his city in rest and peace, which his Father hath adyte to[4] him of his endless purpose; and the Father in the Son, and the Holy Ghost in the Father and in the Son....

CHAPTER 58

God was never displeased with His chosen wife; and of three properties in the Trinity; Fatherhead, Motherhead and Lordhead; and how our substance is in every person, but our sensuality is in Christ alone— Fifty-Eighth chapter.

God, the blessed Trinity which is everlasting being, right as He is endless from without beginning, right so it was in His purpose endless to make mankind; which fair kind first was dight to His own Son, the second person. And when He would, by full accord of all the Trinity, He made us all at once; and in our making He knit us and joined us to himself; by which joining we are kept as clean and as noble as we were made. By the virtue of that ilke[5] precious joining we love our Maker and liken him, praise Him and thank Him and endlessly enjoy in him. And this is the work which is wrought continually in every soul that shall be saved; which is the godly will beforesaid.

And thus in our making God almighty is our kindly Father; and God all wisdom is our kindly Mother, with the love and the goodness of the Holy Ghost; which is all one God, one Lord. And in the knitting and in the joining He is our very true spouse, and we His loved wife and His fair maiden, with which wife He is never displeased; for He saith: I love thee and thou lovest me, and our love shall never be departed on two.

I beheld the working of all the blessed Trinity, in which beholding I saw and understood these three properties: the property of the Fatherhead, the property of the Motherhead and the property of the Lordship in one God. In our Father almighty we have our keeping and our bliss as our kindly substance, which is to us by our making without beginning; and in the second person, in wit and wisdom, we have our keeping as our sensuality, our restoring and our saving; for He is our Mother, Brother and Saviour. And in our good Lord the Holy Ghost we have our rewarding and our yielding for our living and our travail;[6] and endless overpassing all that we desire, in His marvellous courtesy, of His high plenteous grace. For all our life is in three. In the first we have our being and in the second we have our increasing and in the third we have our fulfilling. The first is kind;[7] the second is mercy; the third is grace.

---

[1] *medlur* Mixture.

[2] *descrien* Describe.

[3] *unornly* Wretchedly.

[4] *adyte to* Prepared for.

[5] *ilke* Same.

[6] *travail* Work.

[7] *kind* Nature.

For the first: I saw and understood that the high might of the Trinity is our Father, and the deep wisdom of the Trinity is our Mother, and the great love of the Trinity is our Lord; and all this have we in kind and in our substantial making. And furthermore, I saw that the second person, which is our Mother substantial, that same dear-worthy person is become our Mother sensual; for we are double of Gods making: that is to say, substantial and sensual. Our substance is the higher part, which we have in our Father, God Almighty; and the second person of the Trinity is our Mother in kind in our substantial making, in whom we are grounded and rooted, and He is our Mother in mercy in our sensuality taking. And thus our Mother is to us diverse manner working, in whom our parties are kept undeparted; for in our Mother, Christ, we profit and increase, and in mercy He reformeth us and restoreth, and, by the virtue of His passion and His death and uprising, joineth us to our substance. Thus worketh our Mother in mercy to all His children which are to Him buxom and obedient. And grace worketh with mercy, and namely in two properties as it was showed; which working longeth to the third person, the Holy Ghost. He worketh rewarding and giving; rewarding is a large giving of truth that the Lord doth to Him that hath travailed, and giving is a courtesy working which He doth freely of grace fulfil, and overpassing all that is deserved of creatures.

Thus in our Father, God Almighty, we have our being; and in our Mother of mercy we have our reforming and restoring, in whom our parties are joined and all made perfect man; and by yielding and giving in grace of the Holy Ghost we are fulfilled. And our substance is our Father, God Almighty, and our substance is our Mother, God all wisdom, and our substance is in our Lord the Holy Ghost, God all goodness; for our substance is whole in each person of the Trinity, which is one God. And our sensuality is only in the second person, Christ Jesus, in whom is the Father and the Holy Ghost; and in Him and by Him we are mightily taken out of hell and out of the wretchedness in earth, and worshipfully brought up into heaven and blissfully joined to our substance, increased in riches and nobleth, by all the virtue of Christ and by the grace and working of the Holy Ghost. . . .

CHAPTER 60

How we be bought again[1] and forth-spread by mercy and grace of our sweet, kind and ever loving Mother Jesus, and of the properties of Motherhead; but Jesus is our very Mother, not feeding us with milk but with Himself, opening His side unto us and challenging all our love—Sixtieth chapter.

But now behoveth to say a little more of this forth-spreading, as I understand in the meaning of our Lord, how that we be bought again by the Motherhead of mercy and grace into our kindly stead[2] where that we were made by the Motherhead of kind love; which kind love it never leaveth us.

Our kind Mother, our gracious Mother, for He would all wholly become our Mother in all things, He took the ground of His work full low and full mildly in the maiden's womb. And that He showed in the first, where He brought that meek maid before the eye of mine understanding in the simple stature as she was when she conceived; that is to say, our high God is sovereign wisdom of all, in this low place He raised him and dight him full ready in our poor flesh, himself to do the service and the office of Motherhead in all things. The Mother's service is nearest, readiest and surest, for it is most of kind.[3] This office nor might, nor could, nor never none do to the full[4] but He alone. We wit that all our Mother's bearing is us to pain and to dying; and what is that but our very Mother Jesus? He, all love, beareth us to joy and to endless living; blessed may He be! Thus He sustaineth us within himself in love, and travailed into the full time that He would suffer the sharpest thorns and the grievous pains that ever were or ever shall be, and died at the last. And when He had done, and so born us to bliss, yet might not all this make a seeth[5] to His marvellous love; and that showed He in these high over passing words of love: If I might suffer more, I would suffer more. He might no more die, but

---

[1] *bought again* Redeemed.

[2] *kindly stead* Natural place.

[3] *kind* Nature.

[4] *nor might ... full* None ever might, nor could, nor did fully.

[5] *make a seeth* Give satisfaction.

He would not stint[1] of working.

Wherefore Him behooveth to feed us, for the dear-worthy love of Motherhead hath made Him debtor to us. The mother may give her child suck her milk, but our precious Mother Jesus, He may feed us with him-self; and doth full courteously and full tenderly with the blessed sacrament that is precious food of very life. And with all the sweet Sacraments He sustaineth us full mercifully and graciously. And so meant He in this blessed word where that He said, I it am that Holy Church preacheth thee and teacheth thee. That is to say: All the health and life of sacraments, all the virtue and grace of my word, all the goodness that is ordained in Holy Church for thee, I it am.

The mother may lay the child tenderly to her breast, but our tender Mother Jesus, He may homely lead us into His blessed breast by His sweet open side,[2] and show therein part of the Godhead and the joys of heaven, with ghostly sekirnes[3] of endless bliss; and that showed in the giving the same understanding in this sweet word where He saith: Lo how I love thee, behold-ing into His side, enjoying.

This fair lovely word Mother, it is so sweet and so kind of the self that it may not verily be said of none but of Him, and to her that is very Mother of Him and of all. To the property of Motherhead longeth[4] kind love, wisdom and knowing, and it is good; for though it be so that our bodily forth-bringing be but little, low and simple in regard of our ghostly forth-bringing yet it is He that doth it in the creatures by whom that it is done. The kind, loving mother that wot and knoweth the need of her child, she keepeth it full tenderly as the kind and condition of motherhead will. And as it waxeth in age she changeth her working but not her love. And when it is waxen of more age, she suffered that it be chastised in breaking down of vices to make the child to receive virtues and graces. This working, with all that be fair and good, our Lord doth it in Him by whom it is done. Thus He is our Mother in kind by the working of grace in the lower part, for love of the higher part. And

He will that we know it; for He will have all our love fastened to Him. And in this I saw that all our debt that we owe, by God's bidding, by Fatherhead and Mother-head, for God's Fatherhead and Motherhead is fulfilled in true loving of God; which blessed love Christ work-eth in us. And this was showed in all, and namely in the high plenteous words where He saith: I it am that thou lovest. …

CHAPTER 86

The good Lord showed this book should be otherwise performed than at the first writing; and for His working [we] will thus pray, Him thanking, trusting, and in Him enjoy-ing; and how He made this showing because He will have it known, in which knowing He will give us grace to love him; for fifteen years after it was answered that the cause of all this showing was love, which Jesus grant us. Amen—Eighty-Sixth chapter.

This book is begun by God's gift and His grace, but it is not yet performed, as to my sight. For charity pray we all to God, with God's working, thanking, trusting, enjoying; for thus will our good Lord be prayed, as by the understanding that I took in all His own meaning, and in the sweet words where He saith full merrily: I am ground of thy beseeching. For truly I saw and under-stood in our Lord's meaning that He showed it for He will have it known more than it is, in which knowing He will give us grace to love Him and cleave to him; for He beheld His heavenly treasure with so great love on earth that He will give us more light and solace in heavenly joy in drawing of our hearts, for sorrow and darkness which we are in.

And from that time that it was showed I desired oftentimes to wit what was our Lord's meaning. And fifteen years after and more I was answered in ghostly understanding, saying thus: Wouldst thou wit thy Lord's meaning in this thing? Wit it well: love was His meaning. Who showed it thee? Love. What showed He thee? Love. Wherefore showed it he? For love. Hold thee therein and thou shalt wit and know more in the same; but thou shalt never know nor wit therein other thing without end.

Thus was I learned that love was our Lord's mean-ing. And I saw full sekirly in this and in all, that ere God

---

[1] stint Stop.

[2] open side Referring to the wound that Jesus received from a soldier's spear when he hung on the Cross. See John 19.34.

[3] sekirnes Certainly.

[4] longeth Belongeth, i.e., belongs.

made us He loved us; which love was never slaked, nor never shall. And in this love He hath done all His work; and in this love He hath made all things profitable to us; and in this love our life is everlasting. In our making we had beginning, but the love wherein He made us was in Him from without beginning; in which love we have our beginning. And all this shall be seen in God without end; which Jesus may grant us. Amen.

Thus endeth the revelation of love of the blessed Trinity showed by our Saviour Christ Jesus for our endless comfort and solace, and also to enjoy in Him in this passing journey of this life. Amen, Jesus, Amen.

I pray Almighty God that this book come not but to the hands of them that will be His faithful lovers, and to those that will submit them to the faith of Holy Church and obey the wholesome understanding and teaching of the men that be of virtuous life, sad[1] age and profound learning; for this revelation is high divinity and high wisdom, wherefore it may not dwell with him that is thrall to sin and to the devil. And beware thou take not one thing after thy affection and liking and leave another, for that is the condition of a heretic. But take everything with other and truly understand all is according to Holy Scripture and grounded in the same, and that Jesus, our very love, light and truth, shall show to all clean souls that with meekness ask perseverantly[2] this wisdom of Him. And thou, to whom this book shall come, thank highly and heartily our Saviour Christ Jesus that He made these showings and revelations for thee, and to thee, of His endless love, mercy and goodness, for thine and our safe guide and conduct to everlasting bliss; the which Jesus may grant us. Amen.

—LATE 14TH CENTURY

---

[1] *sad* Mature.

[2] *perseverantly* With perseverance.

Margery Kempe

c. 1373 – 1439

Widely varying descriptions of Margery Kempe have been proposed in the past century—mystic, eccentric, feminist, lunatic, saint, fanatic, heretic, visionary—but for literary purposes, one point about her is central: hers is often considered the first extant autobiography written in English. Dictated to two different scribes, *The Book of Margery Kempe* describes the spiritual awakening and religious fervor of a medieval woman who could neither read nor write, but who had a wide and heartfelt knowledge of theology from listening to sermons and lectures. Modeling herself after various female saints (Bridget of Sweden and Katherine of Alexandria, for example), Kempe was herself on a self-described quest for sainthood; in her autobiography she describes the many obstacles that stood in her spiritual path, as well as her shrewd approaches to dealing with the impediments. Her willingness to challenge powerful men—including the Archbishop of York—and her determination to follow her calling at any cost make her story as fascinating as it is remarkable.

Margery Brunham Kempe's early life was typical of a prosperous woman of the fifteenth century. Her father was an important man in the affluent port town of Bishop's Lynn (now called King's Lynn) in Norfolk, England. John Brunham was five times mayor of the town, two times Member of Parliament, and he held various other estimable positions. At the age of 20 Margery married John Kempe, also of Bishop's Lynn; the couple had 14 children over the following 20 years. Kempe's autobiography begins with her marriage, although she mentions having committed some sin, possibly of a sexual nature, before the age of 20 and having felt deeply remorseful about it ever since; she seemed to feel that no amount of penance or atonement would redeem her. Following the difficult birth of her first child, Kempe, believing she was near death, called for a priest and attempted to confess her "crime." The priest's response was so unsympathetic and threatening that Kempe was not able to continue her confession, nor would she ever again mention her misdeed to anyone. She subsequently suffered what most modern readers would describe as a mental breakdown and experienced visions of the Devil and of Christ; she would endure many more travails before experiencing salvation.

At the age of 60, Kempe dictated an account of these travails and of the happiness she eventually found in God. Narrated in a colloquial and often non-chronological manner, her book describes her progress from a strong-willed wife who ran her own businesses to a strong-willed ascetic who renounced her family and her conjugal bed and set out on a series of pilgrimages. Kempe candidly describes the various ways in which she alienated both priests and laypeople wherever she went. Weeping and sobbing were not unusual occurrences in the medieval church, but Kempe's unrestrained crying and her obsessive discourse on religious topics annoyed many townsfolk and travelers and led some to believe that she was insane. More than once she was taken into custody as a heretic, only to use her wiles and her knowledge of Scripture to assuage (if not always win over) her accusers.

Although she had not lived with her husband for some years, when he suffered a bad accident Kempe rushed to his side and nursed him for several years until his death in 1431. While settled in

Bishop's Lynn, she claimed to have performed a miracle that prevented the town from burning down, and her claim was widely believed. The last known mention of Kempe is in the town records of 1439, so she is presumed to have died around that time. These days Kempe is often studied alongside anchoress Julian of Norwich (in fact the two had once met when Kempe went to Julian to seek spiritual guidance), who also described mystical visions in her *Revelations of Divine Love*; Kempe's autobiography, however, affords greater insights into the lives of secular women and the lay spirituality of medieval England.

⌘⌘⌘

from *The Book of Margery Kempe*

THE PROEM

Here begins a short treatise, and a comforting one for sinful wretches, from which they can take great solace and comfort and understand the exalted and ineffable mercy of our sovereign Saviour Jesus Christ, whose name should be worshipped and exalted without end, who now in our time deigns to exercise His nobility and goodness upon us unworthy ones. All the works of our Savior serve as an example and instruction for us, and whatever grace He works in any creature is for our benefit, provided that a lack of charity does not hinder us.

And therefore, by leave of our merciful Lord Jesus Christ, for the exaltation of His Holy Name, Jesus, this little treatise will treat a small part of his wonderful works: how mercifully, how kindly, and how charitably He moved and stirred a sinful wretch[1] to love Him, a sinful wretch who for many years wished and intended, through the incitement of the Holy Spirit, to follow our Savior, and made great promises of fasting and many other acts of penance. And she was continually turned back from this in time of temptation, like a reed that bends with every wind and is never stable unless no wind blows, until the time when our merciful Lord Jesus Christ, taking pity and compassion on His handiwork and His creature, turned health into sickness, prosperity into adversity, honor into reproach, and love into hatred. With all these things turning upside down in this way, this creature, who for many years had gone astray and had always been unstable, was perfectly drawn and stirred to enter the way of noble righteousness, the righteous way that Christ our Savior exemplified in His own person. He trod it steadfastly and diligently prepared it.

Then this creature, whose way of life this treatise, through the mercy of Jesus, will partly show, was touched by the hand of our Lord with great bodily sickness, from which she lost her reason and her wits for a long time until our Lord restored her again by grace, as will be more clearly showed hereafter. Her worldly goods, which were plenteous and abundant at that time, shortly afterward became quite worthless and meager. Then pomp and pride were cast down and laid aside. Those who had honored her before reproached her most sharply; her kin and those who had been her friends were now her greatest enemies. Then she, considering this astonishing change, seeking help under the wings of her spiritual mother, Holy Church, went and submitted herself to her spiritual father, accusing herself of her misdeeds, and then did great bodily penance.

And in a short time our merciful Lord endowed this creature with plenteous tears of contrition, day by day, to such an extent that some men said she could weep at will, and slandered the work of God. She was so accustomed to being slandered and reproached, to being chided and rebuked by the world on account of the grace and virtue with which she was endowed through the strength of the Holy Spirit, that it was a kind of solace and comfort to her when she suffered any unhappiness for the love of God and for the grace that God worked in her. For the more slander and reproach that she suffered, the more she increased in grace and in devotion to holy meditation and deep contemplation and in the wonderful speech and conversation that our

---

[1] *a sinful wretch* Kempe refers to herself in the third person throughout her text.

Lord spoke and provided in her soul, teaching her how she would be despised for love of Him, how she should have patience, putting all her trust, all her love, and all her affection in Him alone. She knew and understood many secret and hidden things that were going to happen afterward, by inspiration of the Holy Spirit. And often, while she was engaged in such holy speech and conversation, she would weep and sob so much that many people were greatly astonished, for they little knew how much at home our Lord was in her soul. Nor could she herself ever tell the grace that she felt, it was so heavenly, so high above her reason and her bodily wits, and her body was so weak when grace was present in her that she could never express it in words as she felt it in her soul.

Then this creature was very much afraid of illusions and deceptions by her spiritual enemies. She went, at the bidding of the Holy Spirit, to many estimable learned men, both archbishops and bishops, teachers of divinity and scholars as well. She also spoke with many anchoresses[1] and showed them her way of life and the grace that the Holy Spirit, in His goodness, worked in her mind and in her soul, as well as her wits allowed her to express it. And all those to whom she showed her secrets said that she should greatly love our Lord for the grace that He showed her, and they counseled her to follow her movings and stirrings and trustingly believe they were from the Holy Spirit and not from an evil spirit.

Some of these worthy and estimable clerks accepted, on the peril of their souls and as they would answer to God for it, that this creature was inspired by the Holy Spirit, and asked her to have written and made for them a book of her experiences and her revelations. Some offered to write down her experiences with their own hands, and she would not by any means consent, for she was commanded in her soul not to write so soon. And so it was twenty years and more from the time when this creature had her first experiences and revelations before she had any of them written down. Afterward, when it pleased our Lord, He commanded and charged her that she should have her experiences and revelations and way of life written down so that His goodness might be known to all the world.

The creature had no writer who would fulfil her desire or give credence to her experiences until the time when a man living in Germany, who was an Englishman by birth and later was married in Germany and had both a wife and child there, having good knowledge of this creature and of her desire, moved, I trust, by the Holy Spirit, came to England with his wife and his belongings and lived with the aforementioned creature until he had written as much as she would tell him during the time they were together. And then he died. Then there was a priest for whom this creature had great affection, and so she conversed with him about this matter and brought him the book to read. The book was so badly written that he could do little with it, for it was neither good English nor German, and the letters were not shaped or formed as other letters are. Therefore the priest fully believed that no one would ever be able to read it, unless it were by special grace. Nevertheless, he promised her that if he could read it he would with good will copy it out and write it better.

Then there was such ill spoken of this creature and of her weeping that the priest, out of cowardice, did not dare speak with her often, and would not write as he had promised the aforementioned creature. And so he avoided and deferred the writing of this book well into the fourth year or more, despite the fact that the creature often asked him for it. At last he said to her that he could not read it, and so he would not do it. He would not, he said, put himself in danger from it. Then he advised her to go to a good man who had been well acquainted with the man who first wrote the book, on the supposition that he would be best able to read the book, for he had sometimes read letters in the other man's writing that were sent from overseas while he was in Germany. And so she went to that man, asking him to write this book down and never to let it be known as long as she lived, and granting him a large portion of goods for his labor. And this good man wrote about a page, and yet it was not much help, for he could not do much with it, the book was so badly presented and so poorly written.

Then the priest was troubled in his conscience, for he had promised her to write this book, if he could manage to read it, and had not done his part as well as he could have, and he asked this creature to get the book

---

[1] *anchoresses* Female religious ascetics who secluded themselves and devoted their lives to God.

back if she were able. Then she got the book back and brought it to the priest with a glad face, asking him to do his best, and she would pray to God for him and get him grace to read and also to write it. The priest, trusting in her prayers, began to read this book, and it was much easier, it seemed to him, than it had been before. And so he read it over in this creature's presence, every word, with her sometimes helping him when there was any difficulty.

This book is not written in order, each thing after another as it was done, but just as the material came to the creature's mind when it was being written down, for it was so long before it was written that she had forgotten the time and the order in which things happened. And therefore she had nothing written down unless she knew for certain it was really true. When the priest first began to write this book, his eyes failed him so that he could not see to form his letters, nor could he see to mend his pen. Everything else he could see well enough. He set a pair of spectacles on his nose, and then it was even worse than it had been before. He complained to the creature of his trouble. She said his enemy resented his good deed and would prevent him if he could, and she told him to do as well as God would give him grace to do, and not to stop. When he went back to his book, he could see as well, it seemed to him, as he had ever done before, by both daylight and candlelight. And for this reason, when he had written a quire,[1] he added a leaf to it, and then wrote this prologue to be clearer than the next one is, which was written before this one. *Anno domini*[2] 1436.

THE PREFACE

A short treatise of a creature living in great pomp and worldly pride, who then was drawn to our Lord by great poverty, sickness, shame, and great reproaches in many diverse countries and places, some of which tribulations will be depicted below, not in order as they happened but as the creature was able to recall them when it was written, for it was twenty years and more from the time when this creature had forsaken the world and eagerly devoted herself to our Lord before this book was writ-

ten, even though this creature was greatly advised to have her tribulations and experiences written down, and a Carmelite friar[3] offered to write them willingly, if she would agree. And she was warned in her spirit that she should not write so soon. And many years afterward she was bidden in her spirit to write. And yet then it was first written by a man who wrote neither good English nor German, so it was unreadable except by special grace, for there was so much malicious talk and slander of this creature that few people would believe her. And so at last a priest was greatly moved to write this treatise, and he could not easily read it for four whole years. And then at the request of this creature and the urging of his own conscience he tried again to read it, and it was much easier than it had been previously. And so he began to write in the year of our Lord 1436, on the day after Mary Magdalene's day,[4] according to the information of this creature.

BOOK 1

CHAPTER 1

When this creature was twenty years old or a little more, she was married to a respected townsman and was pregnant within a short time, as nature would have it. And after she had conceived, she was afflicted with great fever until the child was born, and then, because of the labor she had in giving birth and the sickness that had gone before, she despaired of her life, believing she might not survive. And then she sent for her spiritual father, for she had something on her conscience that she had never told before that time, in all her life. For she was always prevented by her enemy, the devil, continually saying to her while she was in good health that she did not need confession but should do penance alone, by herself, and all would be forgiven, for God is merciful enough. And therefore this creature often did great penance by fasting on bread and water, and other charitable deeds with devout prayers, but she

---

[1] *quire* Four large sheets of paper folded to create eight sheets.

[2] *Anno domini* Latin: In the year of our Lord.

[3] *Carmelite friar* Monk of the religious order of Our Lady of Mount Carmel, founded in the twelfth century; Kempe refers here to Alan of Lynn.

[4] *Mary Magdalene's day* July 23rd.

would not tell it in confession. And whenever she was sick or unwell, the devil said in her mind that she would be damned, for she was not absolved of that sin. Therefore, after the child was born, she, not trusting she would live, sent for her spiritual father, as was said before, with the full intention of being absolved for her entire life, as near as she could. And when she came to the point of saying the thing that she had concealed for so long, her confessor was a little too hasty, and began sharply to rebuke her before she had said everything she meant to, and so she would say no more for anything he could do.

And then, on account of the fear she had of damnation, on the one hand, and his sharp reproofs on the other hand, this creature went out of her mind and was terribly troubled and harassed by spirits for half a year, eight weeks and some days. And in this time she saw, as it seemed to her, devils opening their mouths, all aflame with burning flames of fire as though they would swallow her in, sometimes raging at her, sometimes threatening her, sometimes pulling her and dragging her, night and day, during this time. And also the devils cried out at her with great threats and told her to forsake her Christianity, her faith, and deny her God, His mother, and all the saints in heaven, her good works and all good virtues, her father, her mother, and all her friends. And so she did. She slandered her husband, her friends and her own self; she spoke many reproving words and many harsh words; she knew no virtue or goodness; she desired all wickedness; just as the spirits tempted her to say and do, so she said and did. She would have destroyed herself many times at their instigation, and been damned with them in hell. And in demonstration of this, she bit her own hand so violently that it could be seen for the rest of her life afterward. And she tore the skin of her body above her heart with her nails pitilessly, for she had no other instrument, and she would have done worse except that she was bound and strongly restrained both day and night, so that she could not do what she wished.

And when she had been oppressed for a long time by these and many other temptations, so that no one thought she would escape or live, then at one point, as she lay alone and her keepers were away, our merciful Lord Jesus Christ, who is ever to be trusted, worshiped

be His name, never forsaking His servant in time of need, appeared to His creature, who had forsaken Him, in the likeness of the loveliest, most beauteous, most pleasing man who could ever be seen with human eye, wearing a mantle of purple silk, sitting on her bedside, looking upon her with such a blessed face that she was strengthened in all her spirits, and He said to her these words: "Daughter, why have you forsaken me, and I never forsook you?"

And at once, as He said these words, she saw truly how the air opened, as bright as any light, and He rose up into the air, not hastily or quickly, but gently and easily so that she could see Him well in the air until it closed again.

And at once the creature was confirmed in her wits and her reason as well as she had ever been before, and asked her husband, as soon as he came to her, to give her the keys of the cellar so that she could get her food and drink as she had done before. Her maids and her keepers advised him not to give her any keys, for they said she would just give away whatever goods there were, for they believed she did not know what she was saying. Nevertheless, her husband, still having tenderness and compassion for her, commanded them to give her the keys. And she ate and drank as well as her bodily strength would allow her, and recognized her friends and her household and everyone else who came to her to see how our Lord Jesus Christ had worked His grace in her, so blessed may He be who is always near in tribulation. When people think He is far from them, He is very near, by His grace. Then this creature did all the other tasks that fell to her wisely and soberly enough, but she did not truly know the ecstasy of our Lord.

CHAPTER 2

And when this creature had in this way, by grace, come to herself again, she thought she was indebted to God and that she would be His servant. Still, she would not leave the pride and pompous display that she had been accustomed to beforehand, either at her husband's or at anyone else's advice. And yet she knew full well that men said many bad things of her, for she wore ornaments of gold wire on her head and her hoods were fringed with tassels. Her cloaks were fringed as well and decorated with many colors between the fringes, so that they would be more striking to men's eyes and she herself would be more admired. And when her husband would tell her to leave her pride, she answered harshly and sharply and said that she came from such a worthy family that he could never have expected to marry her, for her father had once been mayor of the town N. and then was alderman of the noble Guild of the Trinity[1] in N., and therefore she would defend the honor of her kin whatever anyone said.

She was very envious of her neighbours if they were dressed as well as she was. All her desire was to be admired by people. She would not be warned by any chastisement nor be content with the goods God had given her, as her husband was, but always wanted more and more. And then, for pure greed and to support her pride, she began to be a brewer, and was one of the main brewers in the town of N. for three or four years until she lost a great deal of money, for she had no experience at it. For no matter how good her servants were, nor how knowledgeable about brewing, it would never ferment with them. For when the air was standing as nicely under the froth as anyone could see, suddenly the froth would fall down so that all the ale was lost, one brewing after another, so that her servants were ashamed and would not stay with her.

Then this creature thought of how God had punished her previously and she would not take the warning, and now again by the loss of her goods, and then she left it and did no more brewing. And then she asked her husband's pardon for not following his advice before, and she said that her pride and sin were the cause of all her punishment and that she would make good what she had done wrong, with good will. And yet she did not entirely leave the world, for now she thought of a new business. She had a horse-mill. She got two good horses and a man to grind people's corn and in this way she thought she would make her living. This plan did not last long, for a short while after, on the eve of Corpus Christi,[2] this marvel took place. The man was in good bodily health, and his two horses, which were

strong and healthy, had pulled well in the mill before, but now he took one of these horses and put it in the mill as he had done before, and the horse would not pull at all in the mill, for anything the man might do. The man was upset and tried with all his wits to think how he could get the horse to pull. Now he led him by the head, now he beat him, now he coaxed him, and all to no avail, for he would rather go backward than forward. Then the man set a sharp pair of spurs on his heels and rode on the horse's back to make him pull, and still it was no better. When the man saw that it was not going to work, he put the horse back in the stable and gave him food, and he ate well and heartily. And then he took the other horse and put him in the mill, and just as his companion had done, so he did, for he would not pull for anything the man might do. And then the man gave up his position and would no longer stay with the aforesaid creature.

As soon as it was reported around the town of N. that no man or beast would work for the said creature, some said she was cursed; some said God took open vengeance on her; some said one thing and some said another. And some wise men, whose minds were more grounded in a love of our Lord, said it was the divine mercy of our Lord Jesus Christ that called and cried to her from the pride and vanity of the wretched world. And then this creature, seeing all the adversity coming on every side, thought it was the scourges of our Lord that were chastising her for her sin. Then she asked God's mercy and forsook her pride, her greed, and her desire for worldly honor, and did great bodily penance, and began to enter the way of everlasting life, as will be told hereafter.

CHAPTER 3

One night, as this creature lay in bed with her husband, she heard the sound of a melody as sweet and delectable, it seemed to her, as if she had been in Paradise. And at that she jumped out of bed and said, "Alas that ever I did sin; it is full merry in heaven."

This melody was so sweet that it surpassed, beyond comparison, all the melody that could ever be heard in this world, and caused this creature, when she heard any mirth or melody after that, to experience most plenteous

---

[1] *alderman ... Guild of the Trinity* Leader of an organization dedicated to the Holy Trinity that served as a social aid group; Kempe was inducted into the Guild in the 1440s.

[2] *Corpus Christi* Feast of the Blessed Sacrament, in early summer.

and abundant tears of sincere devotion, and great sobbing and sighing after the bliss of heaven, without dreading the shame and spite of the wretched world. And after this spiritual ecstasy she always had in her mind the mirth and melody that were in heaven, so much so that she could not easily restrain herself from speaking of it. For, whenever she was in company, she would often say, "It is full merry in heaven."

And those who knew her previous behavior and now heard her speak so much of the bliss of heaven said to her, "Why do you talk in this way of the mirth that is in heaven? You do not know it, and you have not been there any more than we have," and they were angry with her because she would not hear any talk of worldly things as they did and as she had done before.

And after this time she never wished to have intercourse with her husband, for the debt of matrimony was so abominable to her that it seemed to her she would rather eat or drink slime, or the muck in the gutter, than to consent to any bodily intercourse, except out of obedience. And so she said to her husband, "I cannot deny you my body, but the love of my heart and my affection is drawn away from all earthly creatures and set only on God."

He would have his will, and she obeyed with great weeping and lamenting because she could not live chastely. And often this creature lived chastely, advised her husband to live chastely, and said that she knew well that they had often displeased God by their excessive love and the great enjoyment that they both had in sleeping together, and now it was right that they should, by the will and consent of both of them, both punish and chastise themselves deliberately by abstaining from their bodily lust. Her husband said it would be good to do so, but that he could not yet, and he would when God wished him to. And so he slept with her as he had done before, he would not restrain himself. And she continually prayed to God that she might live chastely, and three or four years later, when it pleased our Lord, her husband made a vow of chastity, as will be written hereafter by leave of Jesus.

And also, after this creature heard this heavenly melody, she did great bodily penance. She was confessed sometimes twice or three times in a day, and especially of that sin that she had so long concealed and hidden, as is written in the beginning of the book. She gave herself to great fasting and keeping vigils. She got up at two or three o'clock and went to church, and stayed there in her prayers until noontime and also all afternoon. And then she was slandered and reproached by many people because she lived so strict a life. Then she got a rough haircloth[1] from a kiln, of the kind that men use to dry malt on, and put it under her gown as craftily and secretly as she could, so that her husband would not notice it, and he did not, even though she lay by him every night in bed and wore the haircloth every day, and bore children during this time.

Then she spent three years being greatly troubled by temptations, which she bore as meekly as she could, thanking our Lord for all His gifts, and was as happy when she was reproached, scorned, or jeered at for love of our Lord, as she had been before at worldly honor—indeed, much happier. For she knew full well that she had sinned greatly against God and was worthy of more shame and sorrow than any man could do to her, and that being despised by the world was the right path to heaven, since Christ Himself chose that path. All His apostles, martyrs, confessors and virgins, and all who ever came to Heaven, passed along the path of tribulation, and she desired nothing so much as Heaven. Then she was glad in her conscience when she believed that she was entering the path that would lead her to the place that she most desired. And this creature had contrition and great remorse, with plenteous tears and many loud sobs for her sins and for her unkindness to her maker. She contemplated her unkindness since her childhood, which our Lord would many times bring to her mind. And then she, beholding her own wickedness, could only lament and weep and keep praying for mercy and forgiveness. Her weeping was so plenteous and so continual that many people thought that she could weep and stop weeping at will, and therefore many people said she was a false hypocrite and wept for show, for support and worldly good. And then a great many forsook her who had loved her before, when she was in the world, and would not acknowledge her, and she continually thanked God for everything, desiring nothing but mercy and forgiveness of sin.

---

[1] *haircloth* Coarse shirt made from animal hair and worn by penitents.

CHAPTER 4

The first two years when this creature was drawn to our Lord in this way, she had great rest in spirit with regard to temptations. She could easily endure fasting, it did not cause her suffering. She hated the joys of the world. She felt no rebellion in her flesh. She was so strong, it seemed to her, that she feared no devil in hell, for she did such great bodily penance. She thought that she loved God more than He loved her. She was struck with the deadly wound of vainglory and did not feel it, for she desired many times that the crucifix should free His hands from the Cross and embrace her as a sign of love. Our merciful Lord Jesus Christ, seeing this creature's presumption, sent her, as is written above, three years of great temptations, of which I propose to write about one of the hardest, as an example to those who come after that they should not trust in themselves or have joy in themselves as this creature had, for assuredly our spiritual enemy does not sleep, but very busily searches our characters and our dispositions, and wherever he finds us weakest, there, by our Lord's permission, he lays his snare, which no one can escape by his own power. And so he laid before this creature the snare of lechery, when she thought that all fleshly lust had been wholly quenched in her. And for a long time she was tempted with the sin of lechery, in spite of anything she could do. And yet she often went to confession, she wore the haircloth and did great bodily penance and wept many a bitter tear, and very often prayed to our Lord that he should preserve her and keep her so that she should not fall into temptation, for she thought she would rather be dead than consent to that. And all this time she had no desire to have intercourse with her husband, but found it very painful and horrible.

In the second year of her temptations it so happened that a man she loved well said to her on the eve of St. Margaret's Day, before evensong,[1] that come what may he would lie by her and have his bodily pleasure, and she would not withstand him, for if he could not have his will this time, he said, he would have it another time, she had no choice. And he did it to test what she would do, but she thought he meant it entirely in earnest at that time, and said little in reply. So then they parted from one another and both went to hear evensong, for she attended St. Margaret's Church. This woman was so intent on the man's words that she could not hear evensong, or say her Lord's Prayer, or think any other good thought, but was more troubled than she had ever been before. The devil put it into her mind that God had forsaken her, and otherwise she would not have been so tempted. She believed the devil's persuasion and began to consent because she could not think any good thought. Therefore she believed that God had forsaken her. And when evensong was over, she went to the man and said that he should have his desire, as she thought he had wished, but he dissimulated[2] so that she did not know what he meant, and so they parted from one another for the night.

This creature was so troubled and vexed all that night that she had no idea what to do. She lay beside her husband, and having intercourse with him was so loathsome to her that she could not endure it, although it was lawful for her and at a lawful time[3] if she had wished. But she was continually thinking about the other man and about sinning with him, since he had spoken to her about it. At last she was overcome by the pressure of temptation and a lack of control, and consented in her mind, and went to the man to see if he would consent to her. And he said he would not do it for all the wealth in the world; he would rather be chopped up as small as meat for the cooking pot. She went away all ashamed and confused, seeing his stability and her own weakness. Then she thought of the grace God had given her before, how she had had two years of great rest in her soul, repentance for her sins with many bitter tears of compunction,[4] and a perfect will never to return to her sins, but to be dead rather than do so, it seemed to her. And now she saw how she had consented to do sin in her will. Then she fell half into despair. She thought she was in hell, she had such sorrow. She thought she was not worthy of any mercy because her consent was so willingly given, and not worthy to do

---

1. *St. Margaret's Day* June 20th, feast of St. Margaret of Antioch, patron saint of pregnant women; *evensong* Vespers, or evening prayer.

2. *dissimulated* Pretended not to understand her.

3. *at a lawful time* I.e., not during one of the many times when sex was prohibited—feast days, etc.

4. *compunction* Remorse.

him service because she was so false to him. Nevertheless she was absolved[1] many times and often, and did whatever penance her confessor would order her to do, and was guided by the rules of the Church. God gave this creature that grace, blessed may He be, but He did not withdraw her temptation, but instead increased it, it seemed to her. And therefore she believed He had forsaken her and dared not trust in His mercy, but was oppressed by horrible temptations of lechery and despair for almost the whole rest of the year, except that our Lord, in His mercy, as she said herself, gave her almost every day two hours of compunction for her sins, with many bitter tears. And then she was troubled by the temptation to despair, as she had been before, and was as far from feeling grace as those who never felt it at all. And that she could not bear, and therefore she continually despaired. Except when she felt grace, her troubles were so overwhelming that she could hardly manage them, but continually mourned and lamented as though God had forsaken her. …

CHAPTER 11

It happened one Friday, on Midsummer Eve in very hot weather, as this creature was coming from the direction of York, carrying a bottle of beer in her hand, and her husband with a cake tucked in his coat, that he asked his wife this question: "Margery, if a man came along with a sword and was going to cut off my head unless I had natural intercourse with you as I have done before, tell me the truth of your conscience—for you say you will not lie: would you allow my head to be cut off, or would you allow me to sleep with you again as I once did?"

"Alas, sir," she said, "why do you raise this matter, we having been chaste these eight weeks?"

"Because I want to know the truth of your heart."

And then she said with great sorrow, "Truly I would rather see you be killed than that we should go back to our uncleanness."

And he said to her, "You are no good wife."

And then she asked her husband why he had not slept with her for eight weeks before, since she lay beside him every night in his bed. And he said he was so afraid

when he went to touch her that he dared do no more.

"Now, good sir, amend yourself and ask God's mercy, for I told you nearly three years ago that you[2] would be killed, and here it is the third year, and still I hope I shall have my wish.[3] Good sir, I beg that you grant me what I ask, and I will pray that you may be saved through the mercy of our Lord Jesus Christ, and you will have greater reward in heaven than if you wore a hairshirt or a coat of mail. I beg you, allow me to make a vow of chastity by the hand of whatever bishop God wills."

"No," he said, "that I will not grant you, for now I can sleep with you without deadly sin, and then I could not do so."

Then she said again, "If it is the will of the Holy Spirit to fulfil what I have said, I pray God that you may consent to it; and if it is not the will of the Holy Ghost, I pray God you never consent."

Then they went on toward Bridlington in very hot weather, the aforesaid creature in a state of great sorrow and great fear for her chastity. And as they passed by a Cross, her husband sat himself down under the Cross, calling his wife to him and saying these words to her: "Margery, grant me my desire, and I shall grant you yours. My first desire is that we should continue to lie together in one bed as we have done before; the second that you shall pay my debts before you go to Jerusalem; and the third that you should eat and drink with me on a Friday as you used to do."

"Nay, sir," she said, "to break the Friday I will never grant you while I live."

"Well," he said, "then I shall sleep with you again."

She asked him to give her leave to make her prayers, and he granted it willingly. Then she kneeled down beside a Cross in the field and prayed in this manner, with a great abundance of tears: "Lord God, You know all things; You know what sorrow I have had to be chaste in my body for You these three years, and now I could have my will and I dare not for love of You. For if I were to break that custom of fasting that You commanded me to keep on Fridays, without meat or drink, I would now have my desire. But, blessed Lord, you know I will not go against Your will, and now my

---

[1] *she was absolved*   I.e., absolved of her sins through the sacrament of Confession.

[2] *you*   I.e., your sexual desire.

[3] *my wish*   To live chastely.

sorrow is great unless I find comfort in You. Now, blessed Jesus, make Your will known to me unworthy, that I may follow it and fulfil it with all my might."

And then our Lord Jesus Christ with great sweetness spoke to this creature, commanding her to go back to her husband and ask him to grant what she desired. "And he shall have what he desires. For, my most worthy daughter, this was the reason that I told you to fast, so that you should sooner obtain and get your desire, and it is granted you. I do not wish you to fast any longer, therefore I bid you in the name of Jesus, eat and drink as your husband does."

Then this creature thanked our Lord Jesus Christ for His grace and His goodness, and then rose up and went to her husband, saying to him, "Sir, if it please you, you shall grant me my desire, and you shall have your desire. Grant me that you shall not come into my bed, and I grant you to pay your debts before I go to Jerusalem. And put my body at God's disposal so that you never make any claims on me to ask me for any marriage debt after this day as long as you live, and I will eat and drink on Fridays at your bidding."

Then her husband said in reply, "May your body be as much at God's disposal as it has been at mine." This creature greatly thanked God, rejoicing that she had her desire, and asking her husband that they might say three Our Fathers in honor of the Trinity for the great grace that He had given them. And so they did, kneeling under a Cross, and then they ate and drank together in great gladness of spirit. This was on a Friday, on Midsummer Eve. Then they went on toward Bridlington and also to many other regions and spoke with God's servants, both hermits and recluses and many other lovers of our Lord, as well as many worthy clerks, doctors of divinity, and also scholars in many various places. And this creature showed to various of them her experiences and her contemplations, as she was commanded to do, to know if there were any deception in her experiences....

CHAPTER 50

When she got to York, she went to an anchoress who had loved her well before she went to Jerusalem to find out about her spiritual progress, and also wishing, for more spiritual conversation, to eat with the anchoress that day nothing but bread and water, for it was Our Lady's Eve.[1] And the anchoress would not receive her, for she had heard so much evil spoken of her. So she went off to other strangers and they made her very welcome for the love of our Lord.

One day, as she sat in a church in York, our Lord Jesus Christ said in her soul, "Daughter, there is much tribulation coming to you."

She was somewhat dejected and upset at that, and therefore, sitting still, she did not answer. Then our blessed Lord said again, "What, daughter, are you unwilling to suffer more tribulation for love of Me? If you do not wish to suffer any more, I will take it away from you."

And then she said in reply, "Nay, good Lord, let me be at Your will and make me mighty and strong to suffer all that You will ever wish me to suffer, and grant me meekness and patience as well."

And so, from that time forward, knowing it was our Lord's will that she suffer more tribulation, she received it willingly when our Lord wished to send it, and thanked Him greatly for it, being truly glad and merry on any day when she suffered any misfortune. And over the course of time, she was not as merry nor as glad on a day when she suffered no tribulation as on a day when she did suffer tribulation.

Then, when she was in the aforementioned Minster[2] at York, a clerk came to her, saying, "Damsel, how long will you stay here?"

"Sir," she said, "I plan to stay for the next fourteen days."

And so she did. And in that time many good men and women asked to meet her and made her warmly welcome and were very glad to hear her conversation, marvelling greatly at the fruitfulness of her speech. And she also had many enemies who slandered, scorned and despised her, of whom one, a priest, came to her while she was in the said minster and, taking her by the collar of her gown, said, "You wolf, what is this cloth that you

---

[1]   *Our Lady's Eve*   The eve of the Feast of St. Mary, i.e., 1 September.

[2]   *Minster*   Large church.

have on?"[1]

She stood still and would say nothing on her own behalf. Young men from the monastery who were going by said to the priest, "Sir, it is wool."

The priest was annoyed because she would not answer, and began to swear many great oaths. Then she spoke on God's behalf; she was not afraid. She said, "Sir, you should keep God's commandments and not swear so carelessly as you do."

The priest asked her who kept the commandments. She said, "Sir, those who keep them."

Then he said, "Do you keep them?"

She said in reply, "Sir, it is my will to keep them, for I am bound to do so, and so are you and every man who will be saved at last."

When he had grumbled at her for some time, he went away secretly before she was aware of it, so that she did not know what became of him.

CHAPTER 51

Another time a great clerk came to her asking how these words should be understood: "Be fruitful and multiply."[2]

She, answering, said, "Sir, these words should be understood to mean not only the bodily procreation of children, but also the attainment of virtue, which is spiritual fruit, such as by hearing the words of God, by setting a good example, by meekness and patience, charity and chastity, and other such things, for patience is worth more than miracle-working." And by the grace of God she answered that clerk in such a way that he was well pleased. And our Lord in His mercy always made some men love and support her.

And so in this city of York there was a doctor of divinity, Master John Aclom, also a canon of the Minster, Sir John Kendale, and another priest who sang by the Bishop's grace; these were her good friends among the clergy. So she remained in that city for fourteen days, as she had said before, and a little more, and on the Sundays she was absolved in the Minster

with great weeping, loud sobbing, and loud crying so that many people greatly wondered what was wrong with her. So afterward a priest came, who seemed like an honorable clerk, and said to her, "Damsel, you said when you first came here that you would stay here only fourteen days."

"Yes, sir, by your leave, I said that I would stay here fourteen days, but I did not say that I would stay here neither more nor less. But now, sir, I tell you truly that I am not going yet."

Then he set a day when he commanded her to appear before him in the chapterhouse. And she said that she would obey his order with a good will. Then she went to Master John Aclom, the aforesaid doctor, asking him to be there on her side, and so he was, and gained great favor among all of them. Another master of divinity had also promised her that he would be there with her, but he held back until he knew how things would go, whether for or against her. There were many people that day in the chapterhouse of the Minster to hear and see what would be said and done to the aforesaid creature.

When the day came, she was all ready in the Minster to answer for herself. Then her friends came to her and told her to be in good spirits. She, thanking them, said that she would. And soon a priest came very kindly and took her by the arm to help her through the crowd of people and brought her before a distinguished doctor, the one who had summoned her before to appear before him in the chapterhouse that day in York Minster. And with this doctor sat many other reverend and distinguished clerks, some of whom loved the said creature well. Then the eminent doctor said to her, "Woman, what are you doing here in this area?"

"Sir, I came on pilgrimage to make an offering here at St. William."[3]

Then he said again, "Do you have a husband?" She said, "Yes." "Do you have any letter of record?"[4]

"Sir," she said, "my husband gave me leave with his own mouth. Why do you behave like this with me more than with other pilgrims who are here, who do not have a letter any more than I have? Sir, you let them go in

---

[1] "*You wolf ... have on.*" See Matthew 7.15: "Beware of false prophets, which come to you in sheep's clothing, but inwardly they are ravening wolves."

[2] *Be fruitful and multiply.* From Genesis 1.22.

[3] *St. William* Shrine of William Fitzherbert, Archbishop of York (at the Cathedral of York).

[4] *letter of record* I.e., letter of consent to go on a pilgrimage.

peace and quiet and in rest, and I can get no rest among you. And sir, if there is any clerk among you all who can prove that I have said any word otherwise than I ought to do, I am ready to amend it with a good will. I will neither maintain error nor heresy, for it is my full will to believe as Holy Church believes and fully to please God."

Then the clerks examined her in the articles of the faith and in many other questions as they pleased, to which she answered well and truly so that they could find no excuse in her words to make trouble for her, thanks be to God.

And then the doctor who sat there as a judge ordered her to appear before the Archbishop of York and told her what day, at a town called Cawood, commanding that she be kept in prison until the day of her appearance. Then the secular people spoke for her and said that she should not go to prison, for they themselves would take responsibility for her and go to the Archbishop with her. And so the clerks said no more to her at that time, for they got up and went where they liked and let her go where she liked, praise be to Jesus. And soon afterward a clerk came to her, one of the same who had sat in judgment against her, and said, "Damsel, I beg that you not be displeased with me, though I sat with the doctor against you; he insisted so much that I did not dare do otherwise."

And she said, "Sir, I am not displeased with you for it."

Then he said, "I ask you then, pray for me."

"Sir," she said, "I will, gladly."

CHAPTER 52

There was a monk who was going to preach in York, who had heard much slander and much evil talk about the said creature. And when he was going to preach there was a great multitude of people there to hear him, and she was present with them. And so, when he was giving his sermon, he discussed many matters so openly that the people easily gathered that it was because of her, for which reason her friends who loved her well were very distressed and upset about it, and she was much happier, for she had something to test her patience and her charity, by which she hoped to please our Lord Jesus Christ. When the sermon was done, a doctor of divinity

who loved her well, along with many others, also came to her and said, "Margery, how are things with you today?"

"Sir," she said, "very well, blessed be God. I have reason to be truly merry and glad in my soul if I can suffer anything for His love, for He suffered much more for me."

Soon after there came a man who loved her well with a good will, along with his wife and others, and led her seven miles from there to the Archbishop of York, and brought her into a handsome room, and a good clerk came in, saying to the good man who had brought her there, "Sir, why have you and your wife brought this woman here? She will sneak away from you, and cause you to be disgraced."

The good man said, "I dare well say that she will remain, and be here to answer for herself with a good will."

The next day she was brought into the Archbishop's chapel, and many of the Archbishop's household came in, scorning her, calling her "Lollard"[1] and "heretic," and they swore many a horrible oath that she would be burned. And she, through the strength of Jesus, said in reply to them, "Sirs, I fear you will be burned endlessly in hell unless you improve yourselves with regard to your swearing, for you do not keep God's commandments. I would not swear as you do for all the goods of this world."

Then they went away as if they were ashamed. She then, making a silent prayer, asked grace to behave herself that day in the way that would be most pleasing to God and profit to her own soul and a good example to her fellow Christians. Our Lord, answering her, said it would be just so. At last the said Archbishop came into the chapel with his clerks, and said sharply to her, "Why do you wear white? Are you a maiden?"[2]

She, kneeling on her knees before him, said, "No, sir, I am no maiden; I am a wife."

He commanded his people to fetch a pair of shackles and said she would be shackled, for she was a false

---

[1] *Lollard* Follower of theologian John Wycliffe (1330–84), considered by some to be a heretic because of his severe criticisms of corruption in the institutional church and the failings of the clergy, as well as his views on certain church doctrines.

[2] *maiden* Virgin.

heretic. And then she said, "I am no heretic, nor shall you prove me to be one."

The Archbishop went away and let her stand there alone. Then she prayed for a long while to our Lord God Almighty to help her and support her against all her enemies, spiritual and bodily, and her flesh trembled and shuddered terribly so that she wanted to put her hands under her clothing in order that it would not be seen.

Then the Archbishop came back into the chapel with many worthy clerks, among whom was the same doctor who had examined her before and the monk who had preached against her a little while before in York. Some of the people asked whether she was a Christian woman or a Jew; some said she was a good woman and some said not. Then the Archbishop took his seat, and her clerks also, each of them according to his rank, there being many people present. And in the time while the people were gathering together and the Archbishop taking his seat, the said creature stood to the back, making her prayers with deep devotion for help and succor against her enemies, for such a long time that she melted all into tears. And at last she cried out loudly as well, so that the Archbishop and his clerks and many people were astonished at her, for they had not heard such crying out before.

When her crying had passed she came before the Archbishop and fell on her knees, the Archbishop saying rudely to her, "Why do you weep like that, woman?"

She, answering, said, "Sir, you will wish some day that you had wept as hard as I."

And shortly, after the Archbishop had put to her the articles of our faith, which God gave her grace to answer well and truly and readily without any great thought so that he could not find fault with her, then he said to the clerks, "She knows her faith well enough. What shall I do with her?"

The clerks said, "We know well that she knows the articles of the faith, but we will not allow her to remain among us, for the people have great faith in her conversation, and perhaps she might lead some of them astray."

Then the Archbishop said to her, "I hear bad reports of you; I hear tell that you are a very wicked woman."

And she said back to him, "Sir, so I hear tell that you are a wicked man. And if you are as wicked as men say, you shall never get to heaven unless you mend your ways while you are here."

Then he said very rudely, "Why, you, what do people say about me?"

She answered, "Other people, sir, can tell you well enough."

Then a great clerk with a furred hood said, "Peace! You speak of yourself and let him be."

Then the Archbishop said to her, "Lay your hand on the book here in front of me and swear that you will leave my diocese as soon as you can."

"Nay, sir," she said, "I beg you, give me leave to go back to York to take leave of my friends."

Then he gave her leave for a day or two. She thought it was too short a time, so she said again, "Sir, I cannot leave this diocese so hastily, for I must stay and speak with good men before I go, and I must, sir, by your leave, go to Bridlington and speak with my confessor, who was the confessor of the good prior who is now canonized."

Then the Archbishop said to her, "You shall swear that you will not teach or scold the people in my diocese."

"Nay, sir, I will not swear," she said, "for I shall speak of God and rebuke those who swear great oaths wherever I go, until the time that the Pope and Holy Church have ordained that no one shall be so bold as to speak of God, for God Almighty does not forbid, sir, that we shall speak of Him. And moreover the Gospel mentions that when the woman had heard our Lord preach, she came before Him with a loud voice and said, 'Blessed be the womb that bore you and the breasts that gave you suck.' Then our Lord said in reply to her, 'Truly, so are they blessed who hear the word of God and keep it.'[1] And therefore, sir, it seems to me that the Gospel gives me leave to speak of God."

"Ah, sir," said the clerks, "here we truly think that she has a devil in her, for she speaks of the Gospel."[2]

---

1   *Blessed be the womb ... and keep it*   From Luke 11.27–28.

2   *she has a devil ... Gospel*   Reading the Scriptures in English was one of the major points of debate in the Lollard conflict. The Catholic Church did not wish the Bible to be made available in the vernacular or for anyone other than the clergy to engage in Biblical interpretation. The Lollards took issue with the established Church on both counts.

At once a great clerk brought forth a book and for his part quoted St. Paul against her, that no woman should preach.[1] She, in response to this, said, "I do not preach, sir; I go into no pulpit. I use only conversation and good words, and that I will do as long as I live."

Then a doctor who had examined her previously said, "Sir, she told me the worst stories about priests that I ever heard."

The Bishop commanded her to tell that story.

"Sir, with all due respect, I spoke only of one priest by way of example, whom, as I have been told, God allowed to go astray in a wood, for the profit of his soul, until night came upon him. He, lacking in shelter, found a pleasant garden in which he rested that night, which had a lovely pear tree in the middle, all covered and adorned with flowers and blooms delightful to see, to which there came a big, rough bear, huge to behold, shaking the pear tree and knocking down the flowers. This dreadful beast greedily ate and devoured those fair flowers. And when he had eaten them, turning his tail end toward the priest, he excreted them out again from his hind parts.

"The priest, greatly disgusted at this loathsome sight, and struck with great doubt about its meaning, went on his way the next day melancholy and pensive, when it happened that it met with a handsome, aged man who looked like a palmer[2] or pilgrim, who asked the priest the cause of his melancholy. The priest, telling him what is written above, said he was struck by great fear and melancholy when he saw that loathsome beast defoul and devour such fair flowers and blooms and afterward excrete them from his backside so horribly in front of him, and that he did not understand what this could mean.

"Then the palmer, showing himself to be the messenger of God, explained it to him in this way: 'Priest, you yourself are the pear tree, partly flourishing and flowering by saying your service and administering the sacraments, though you do so undevoutly, for you pay little attention to how you say your matins[3] and your service, so long as you babble your way through it. Then you go to your Mass without devotion, and you have little contrition for your sin. You receive there the fruit of everlasting life, the Sacrament of the altar, in a most inappropriate state of mind. Then the whole day afterward you spend your time badly, devoting yourself to buying and selling, chopping and changing, as if you were a worldly man. You sit at your ale, giving yourself over to gluttony and excess, to bodily pleasure, through lechery and uncleanness. You break God's commandments by swearing, lying, slander, and backbiting and practicing other such sins. Thus through your misconduct you, like the loathsome bear, devour and destroy the flowers and blooms of virtuous living, to your endless damnation and the detriment of many people, unless you get the grace of repentance and amendment.'"

Then the Archbishop liked the story well and commended it, saying it was a good story. And the clerk who had examined her before in the absence of the Archbishop said, "Sir, this story strikes me to the heart."

The aforesaid creature said to the clerk, "Ah, honorable sir doctor, in the place where I mostly live there is a worthy clerk, a good preacher, who boldly speaks against the misconduct of the people and will flatter no one. He says many times in the pulpit, 'If any man dislikes my preaching, let him take note, for he is guilty.' And just so, sir," she said to the clerk, "is your experience with me, God forgive you."

The clerk did not know what to say to her. Afterward the same clerk came to her and asked her forgiveness for having been so much against her. He also asked her especially to pray for him.

And then soon after the Archbishop said, "Where can I find a man who will take this woman away from me?"

At once many young men jumped up, and every one of them said, "My lord, I will go with her."

The Archbishop answered, "You are too young; I will not have you." Then a good solid man of the Archbishop's household asked his lord what he would give him if he would take her. The Archbishop offered him five shillings and the man asked for a noble.[4] The Archbishop, answering, said, "I will not spend so much on her body." "Yes, good sir," said the aforesaid creature, "our Lord shall reward you well in return." Then the Archbishop said to the man, "See, here is five

---

[1]   *St. Paul … preach*   See 1 Timothy 2.11–12.

[2]   *palmer*   Pilgrim to the Holy Land.

[3]   *matins*   Morning services.

[4]   *noble*   English gold coin worth six shillings eightpence.

shillings, and take her quickly out of this region." She, kneeling down on her knees, asked his blessing. He, asking her to pray for him, blessed her and let her go. When she then went back to York she was welcomed by many people and worthy clerks, who rejoiced that our Lord had given her, who was unlearned, wit and wisdom to answer so many learned men without disgrace or blame, thanks be to God.

CHAPTER 53

Then the good man who was escorting her brought her out of town and then they went on to Bridlinton to her confessor, who was called Sleytham, and spoke with him and with many other good men who had entertained her previously and done much for her. Then she did not wish to stay but took her leave, to proceed on her journey. And then her confessor asked if she did not dare stay on account of the Archbishop of York, and she said, "No, indeed."

Then the good man gave her money, beseeching her to pray for him. And so she went on toward Hull. And there at one time, as they went in procession, a woman of high rank treated her with great contempt, and she said not a word. Many other people said she should be put in prison, and made great threats. And despite all their malice, a good man came and asked her to eat with him and made her very welcome. Then the malicious people who had scorned her before came to this man and told him not to be kind to her, for they believed that she was not a good woman. The next day in the morning her host led her out to the edge of town, for he did not dare entertain her any longer. And so she went to Hessle and wanted to cross the water at Humber.[1] Then she happened to find there two Dominican friars and two yeomen[2] of the Duke of Bedford. The friars told the yeomen who she was, and the yeomen arrested her as she was about to take her boat, and also arrested a man who was with her.

"For our lord the Duke of Bedford," they said, "has sent for you. And you are considered the greatest Lollard in this whole area and around London as well. And we have looked for you in many places, and we will have a hundred pounds for bringing you before our lord."

She said to them, "Sirs, I will willingly go with you where you want to take me."

Then they took her back to Hessle, and there people called her a Lollard, and women came running out of their houses with their distaffs,[3] crying out to the people, "Burn this false heretic."

And as she went on toward Beverley with the aforesaid yeomen and friars, they repeatedly met with people of that area who said, "Damsel, give up this life you are living, and go spin and card as other women do, and do not suffer so much shame and sorrow. We would not suffer so much for anything on earth."

Then she said to them, "I do not suffer as much sorrow as I wish to for our Lord's love, for I suffer only harsh words, and our merciful Lord Jesus Christ, worshipped be His name, suffered hard blows, bitter scourging, and at last shameful death for me and for all mankind, blessed may He be. And therefore what I suffer is truly nothing compared to what He suffered."

And so, as she went along with the aforesaid men, she said good things to them, until one of the Duke's men who had arrested her said, "I regret that I came upon you, for it seems to me that you say right good words."

Then she said to him, "Sir, do not regret or repent having come upon me. Do your lord's will, and I trust that all will be for the best, for I am very well pleased that you came upon me."

He said in reply, "Damsel, if ever you are a saint in heaven, pray for me."

She answered, saying to him in reply, "Sir, I hope you will be a saint yourself, and everyone that shall come to heaven."

So they went on until they came into Beverley, where the wife of one of the men who had arrested her lived. And they took her there and took her purse and her ring away from her. They prepared a pleasant room for her and a clean bed in it with the necessities, locking the door with the key and taking the key away with them. Then they took the man whom they had arrested with her, who was the Archbishop of York's man, and put him in prison. And soon after, that same day, word came that the Archbishop had come into the town where his man was in prison. The Archbishop was told

---

[1] *Humber* I.e., the River Humber.

[2] *yeomen* Attendants; men of high rank who serve a lord.

[3] *distaffs* Rods used for spinning wool.

of his man's imprisonment, and at once had them let him out. Then the man went angrily to the aforesaid creature, saying, "Alas that ever I knew you. I have been put in prison on your account."

She, comforting him, said, "Be meek and patient, and you will get a great reward in heaven for it."

So he went away from her. Then she stood looking out a window, saying many good words to those who wished to hear her, so that women wept hard and said with great sorrow in their hearts, "Alas, woman, why must you be burned?"

Then she asked the good woman of the house to give her something to drink, for she was ill with thirst. And the woman said her husband had taken the key away, and so she could not get to her nor give her anything to drink. And then the women got a ladder and put it up to the window and gave her a pint of wine in a pot and gave her some bread, beseeching her to put the pot and bread away secretly so that when the man of the house came he would not see it.

Chapter 54

The aforesaid creature, lying in her bed on the following night, heard with her bodily ears a loud voice calling, "Margery." At that voice she awoke, very frightened, and lying still in silence she made her prayers as devoutly as she could at the time. And soon our merciful Lord, who is present everywhere, comforting his unworthy servant, said to her, "Daughter, it is more pleasing to Me that you endure contempt and scorn, shame and reproof, wrongs and misfortunes than if your head were struck off three times a day, every day for seven years. And therefore, daughter, do not fear what any man may say to you; rather you have great reason to rejoice in My goodness and in the sorrows you have suffered for it, for when you come home to heaven, then every sorrow will turn to joy for you."

The next day she was brought into the chapterhouse of Beverley, and the Archbishop of York was there and many great clerks with him, priests, canons, and secular men. Then the Archbishop said to the aforesaid creature, "What, woman, have you come back? I would willingly be rid of you."

And then a priest brought her before him, and the Archbishop said, in the hearing of everyone present, "Sirs, I had this woman before me at Cawood, and there I and my clerks examined her in the faith and found no error in her. Furthermore, sirs, I have since that time spoken with good men who consider her a righteous woman and a good woman. Nevertheless, I gave one of my men five shillings to lead her out of this area to keep the people quiet. And as they were going on their journey, they were taken and arrested, my man put in prison on her account, and her gold and silver taken away from her, as well as her prayer beads and her ring, and she is brought before me again. Is there anyone here who can say anything against her?"

Then other men said, "Here is a friar who knows many things against her."

The friar came forth and said that she led everyone astray from Holy Church, and uttered many bad things about her at that time. He also said that she would have been burnt at Lynn if his order, that is, the Dominicans, had not been there. "And sir, she says that she can weep and feel contrition when she wishes."

Then the two men who had arrested her came, saying like the friar that she was Cobham's[1] daughter and was sent to carry letters around the country. And they said she had not been to Jerusalem nor in the Holy Land nor on other pilgrimages,[2] when in truth she had been. They denied all truth and insisted on what was wrong, as many others had done before. When they had said enough for a great while and a long time, they held their peace.

Then the Archbishop said to her, "Woman, what do you say to this?"

She said, "My lord, with all due respect, every word they say is a lie."

Then the Archbishop said to the friar, "Friar, these are not heretical words; they are slanderous and erroneous words."

"My lord," said the friar, "she knows her faith well enough. Nevertheless, my lord of Bedford is angry with her, and he wishes to see her."

---

[1]   *Cobham*   Sir John Oldcastle, Lord Cobham, one of the leaders of the Lollards in the early fifteenth century; he was executed as a heretic in 1417.

[2]   *pilgrimages*   Lollards did not condone pilgrimages.

"Well, friar," said the Archbishop, "then you shall take her to him."

"Nay, sir," said the friar, "it is not for a friar to lead a woman around."

"And I do not wish," said the Archbishop, "for the Duke of Bedford to be angry with me on her account."

Then the Archbishop said to his men, "Keep watch on the friar until I wish to see him again," and commanded another man to keep the aforesaid creature as well, until he wished to see her again another time at his pleasure. Then the aforesaid creature asked him by his lordship not to have her put among men, for she was a man's wife. And the Archbishop said, "No, you will not be harmed."

Then he who was entrusted with her took her by the hand and led her home to his house and asked her to sit with him at meat and drink, making her welcome. Soon afterwards many priests and other people came there to see her and speak with her, and many people felt great compassion that she was treated so badly.

Shortly afterward the Archbishop sent for her, and she came into his hall. His retinue was dining, and she was taken into his room and up to his bedside. Then she, obeying, thanked him for his gracious lordship that he had shown to her before.

"Yes, yes," said the Archbishop; "I am told worse of you than I ever was before."

She said, "My lord, if you would like to question me, I will tell the truth, and if I am found guilty, I will submit to your correction."

Then a Dominican who was a diocesan bishop[1] came forward and the Archbishop said to him, "Now, sir, say while she is present what you said to me when she was not present."

"Shall I really?" said the bishop.

"Yes," said the Archbishop.

Then the bishop said to the aforesaid creature, "Damsel, you were with Lady Westmoreland."

"When, sir?" she said.

"At Easter," said the suffragan.

She, not answering, said, "Well, sir?"

Then he said, "My lady herself was very pleased with you and liked your words, but you counselled Lady Greystoke to leave her husband, and she is a baron's wife and the daughter of Lady Westmoreland, and now you have said enough to be burnt for it." And so he spoke many harsh words in front of the Archbishop; it is not useful to repeat them.

At last she said to the Archbishop, "My lord, by your leave, I have not seen Lady Westmoreland for the past two years and more. Sir, she sent for me before I went to Jerusalem and, if you like, I will go to her again so she can attest that I never brought up any such matter."

"Nay," said those who stood about, "have her put in prison, and we will send a letter to the noble lady, and if what she says is true, let her go without any objection."[2]

And she said she was quite happy for it to be so. Then a great clerk who stood just beside the Archbishop, "Put her in prison for forty days and she will love God better all her life."

The Archbishop asked her what tale it was she had told Lady Westmoreland when she spoke with her.

She said, "I told her a good tale of a lady who was damned because she would not love her enemies and of a bailiff who was saved because he loved his enemies and forgave their trespasses against him, and yet he was considered a bad man."

The Archbishop said it was a good tale. Then his steward and many others said, crying out with a loud voice to the Archbishop, "Lord, we pray you, let her go away at this time, and if she should ever come back, we will burn her ourselves."

The Archbishop said, "I believe there was never a woman in England who was so much feared as she is and has been."

Then he said to the aforesaid creature, "I do not know what to do with you."

She said, "My lord, I pray you, let me have your letter and your seal to witness that I have defended myself against my enemies and nothing has been alleged against me, neither error nor heresy, that can be proved against me, thanked be our Lord, and have John, your man, take me back across the water."

And the Archbishop very kindly granted her all her desire, may our Lord reward him, and gave back her purse with her ring and prayer beads that the Duke of

---

[1] *diocesan bishop* Bishop suffragan: a bishop under the Archbishop's jurisdiction.

[2] *objection* I.e., resistance.

Bedford's men had taken from her before. The Archbishop was surprised that she had the means to travel around the country, and she said good men gave it to her asking her to pray for them.

Then she, kneeling down, received his blessing and took her leave in very good spirits, going out of his room. And the Archbishop's people asked her to pray for them, but the steward was angry because she laughed and was cheerful, and said to her, "Holy folk should not laugh."

She said, "Sir, I have great reason to laugh, for the more shame and contempt I suffer, the merrier I am in our Lord Jesus Christ."

Then she went down into the hall and there stood the Dominican friar who had caused her all that trouble. And so she left the town with one of the Archbishop's men, carrying the letter that the Archbishop had granted her as a witness, and the man brought her to the River Humber, and there he took his leave of her, returning to his lord and taking the letter back with him, and so she was left alone without anyone she knew. All this misfortune came to her on a Friday,[1] thanked be God of all.

CHAPTER 55

When she had crossed the River Humber she was immediately arrested as a Lollard and taken toward prison. There happened to be a person who had seen her stand before the Archbishop of York, and he obtained permission for her to go where she wished and defended her against the bailiff and vouched for her that she was no Lollard. And so she escaped in the name of Jesus. Then she met a man from London and his wife. And she went along with them until she got to Lincoln, and there she suffered much scorn and many injurious words, answering back in God's cause at once so wisely and prudently that many people marveled at her cleverness.

There were lawyers who said to her, "We have gone to school for many years, and we are still not capable of answering as you do. Where do you get such cleverness?"

And she said, "From the Holy Spirit."

Then they asked, "Do you have the Holy Spirit?"

"Yea, sirs," she said, "no one can say a good word

without the gift of the Holy Spirit, for our Lord Jesus Christ said to his disciples, 'Do not worry about what you will say, for it will not be your spirit that speaks in you, but the spirit of the Holy Ghost.'"[2] And thus our Lord gave her the grace to answer them, worshiped may He be.

Another time a great lord's men came to her and swore many great oaths, saying, "We have been told that you can tell us whether we shall be saved or damned."

She said, "Yes, indeed I can, for as long as you swear such horrible oaths and knowingly break the commandment of God as you do and will not give up your sin, I dare well say you will be damned. And if you will be contrite and confess your sin, willingly do penance and give it up while you can, with no intention of returning to it, I dare well say you will be saved."

"What, can you tell us nothing else but this?"

"Sirs," she said, "this is very good, it seems to me."

And then they went away from her.

After this she went on toward home again until she got to West Lynn. Once she was there, she sent to Bishop's Lynn for her husband, for Master Robert, her confessor, and for Master Alan, a doctor of divinity, and told them in part of her difficulties. And then she told them that she could not come home to Bishop's Lynn until she had gone to the Archbishop of Canterbury to get his letter and his seal. "For when I was called before the Archbishop of York," she said, "he would not believe what I said because I did not have a letter and seal from my lord of Canterbury. And so I promised him that I would not go to Bishop's Lynn until I had my lord's letter and the seal of Canterbury."

And then she took her leave of the aforesaid clerks, asking for their blessing, and went on with her husband to London. When she got there, she was provided with her letter at once by the Archbishop of Canterbury. And so she stayed in the city of London for a long time and was made very welcome by many worthy people.

Then she went toward Ely in order to get home to Lynn, and when she was three miles from Ely a man came riding after them at great speed and arrested her husband and her as well, intending to take them to prison. He cruelly rebuked and thoroughly insulted them, saying many chiding words. And at last she asked

---

[1] *on a Friday* The day of Christ's Passion.

[2] *Do not worry ... Holy Ghost* From Matthew 10.19–20.

her husband to show him my lord of Canterbury's letter. When the man had read the letter, he spoke politely and kindly to them, saying, "Why didn't you show me your letter before?"

And so they left him and went on to Ely and from there home to Lynn, where she suffered much contempt, much reproach, many a slander, many a harsh word, and many a curse. And one time a reckless man, thinking little of his own shame, wilfully and on purpose threw a bowlful of water on her head as she came down the street. She, not at all bothered by it, said, "May God make you a good man," greatly thanking God for that, as she did for many other occasions....

CHAPTER 86

One time our Lord spoke to this creature when it pleased him, saying to her spiritual understanding, "Daughter, as many times as you have received the blessed Sacrament of the altar[1] with many more holy thoughts than you can speak of, just so many times will you be rewarded in heaven with new joys and new comforts. And daughter, in heaven you will know how many days you have had of devout contemplation on earth, by My gift. And though all these are gifts and graces that I have given you, still you will have the same grace and reward in heaven as if they came from your own merits, for I have given them to you freely. But I thank you earnestly, daughter, for allowing Me to work My will in you and letting Me be so familiar with you. For there is nothing that you could do on earth, daughter, that would please Me better than allowing Me to speak to you in your soul, for then you understand My will and I understand your will.

"And also, daughter, you call My mother to come into your soul and take Me in her arms and put Me to her breast and give Me suck. Also, daughter, I know your holy thoughts and the good desires you have when you receive Me[2] and the true charity that you have for Me when you receive My precious body in your soul, and also how you call Mary Magdalene into your soul to welcome Me, for daughter, I know your thoughts well enough. You think that she is worthiest in your soul,

and you have the greatest trust in her prayers next to My mother's, and well you may, daughter, for she is a very great intercessor for you with Me in the bliss of heaven. And sometimes, daughter, you find your soul so large and wide that you call all the court of heaven into your soul to welcome Me. I know well, daughter, what you say: 'Come, all twelve apostles, who were so well beloved of God on earth, and receive your Lord in my soul.'

"You also ask Katherine, Margaret, and all holy virgins to welcome Me in your soul. And then you ask My blessed mother, and Mary Magdalene, all the apostles, martyrs, and confessors,[3] Katherine, Margaret, and all holy virgins that they should adorn the chamber of your soul with many beautiful flowers and with many sweet spices so that I might rest there.

"Furthermore you imagine sometimes, daughter, that you have a cushion of gold, another of red velvet, and the third of white silk in your soul. And you imagine that My Father sits on the cushion of gold, for to Him belong power and might. And you imagine that I, the second Person,[4] your love and your joy, sit on the cushion of red velvet, for all your thoughts are for Me because I redeemed you at such cost, and you think that you can never repay Me for the love that I have shown you, even if you were slain a thousand times a day, if that were possible, for love of Me. Thus you think in your soul, daughter, that I deserve to sit on a red cushion in remembrance of the red blood that I shed for you. Moreover you imagine that the Holy Spirit sits on a white cushion, for you consider that He is full of love and purity, and therefore it becomes Him to sit on a white cushion, for He is the giver of all holy thoughts and chastity.

"And yet I know well enough, daughter, that you think you cannot worship the Father unless you worship the Son, and you cannot worship the Son unless you worship the Holy Spirit. And you also think sometimes, daughter, that the Father is all-powerful and all-knowing and all grace and goodness, and you think the same of the Son, that He is all-powerful and all-knowing and all grace and goodness. And you think that the Holy Spirit has the same properties equally with the Father

---

[1] *blessed Sacrament of the altar*   The Eucharist; Communion.

[2] *you receive Me*   In Communion.

[3] *confessors*   Those who bore witness to the faith, often referring to saints who were not martyred.

[4] *second Person*   Of the Trinity.

and the Son, proceeding from them both. Also you think that each of the three Persons in the Trinity has what the other has in His Godhead, and so you believe truly in your soul, daughter, that there are three diverse Persons and one God in substance, and that each knows what the others know, and each can do what the others can, and each wills what the others will. And daughter, this is a true faith and a right faith, and this faith you have only by My gift. And therefore, daughter, if you will consider it carefully, you have great reason to love Me well and to give Me your whole heart so that I may fully rest in it as I myself wish to, for if you allow Me, daughter, to rest in your soul on earth, believe well that you shall rest eternally with Me in heaven.

"And therefore, daughter, do not be surprised that you weep hard when you take Communion and receive My blessed body in the form of bread, for you pray to me before you receive the Sacrament, saying to me in your mind, 'As surely, Lord, as you love me, make me clean from all sin and give me grace to receive your precious body worthily, with every kind of worship and reverence.'

"And daughter, know well that I hear your prayer, for you cannot say a better word to please Me than 'as surely as I love you,' for then I fulfil my grace in you and give you many a holy thought—it is impossible to tell them all. And for the great intimacy that I show you you are all the bolder to ask Me for grace for yourself, for your husband, and for your children, and you make every Christian man and woman your child in your soul for that time, and wish to have as much grace for them as for your own children. You also ask mercy for your husband, and you think you are greatly obliged to me for having given you such a man, who would allow you to live chaste while he is still alive and in good bodily health. Truly, daughter, you think rightly, and therefore you have great cause to love me well. Daughter, if you knew how many wives there are in this world that would love Me and serve Me well and diligently, if they could be as free of their husbands as you are of yours, you would say that you were very greatly obliged to Me. And yet they are prevented from having their will and suffer great pain, and therefore they will have great reward in Heaven, for I take every good will as a deed.

"Sometimes, daughter, I cause you to feel great sorrow for your spiritual father's sins, and especially that he should have as full forgiveness of his sins as you would hope to have of yours. And sometimes when you receive the precious Sacrament, I cause you to pray for your spiritual father in this way: that as many men and women might be inspired by his preaching as you hope may be inspired by the tears of your eyes, and that My holy words might sink as deep in their hearts as you wish them to sink in your heart. And you also ask the same grace for all good men who preach My word on earth, that they might benefit all rational creatures.

"And often, on the day when you receive my precious body, you ask grace and mercy for all your friends, and for all your enemies that ever shamed you or reproached you or scorned you or mocked you for the grace that I work in you, and for all this world both young and old, with many tears of heavy weeping and sobbing. You have suffered much shame and reproach, and therefore you will have great bliss in heaven.

"Daughter, do not be ashamed to receive My grace when I will give it to you, for I will not be ashamed of you when you are received into the bliss of heaven, where for every good thought, for every good word, and for every good deed, for every day of contemplation, and for all the good desires that you have had here in this world, you will be rewarded there with Me eternally as My beloved darling, as My blessed spouse, and as My holy wife.

"And therefore fear not, daughter, though the people wonder why you weep so hard when you receive Me, for if they knew what grace I put in you at that time, they would wonder instead why your heart did not burst asunder. And so it would if I did not measure that grace myself, but you see well yourself, daughter, that when you have received Me into your soul you are in peace and at rest, and sob no longer. And the people wonder at that, but it should be no wonder to you, for you know well that I act like a husband who is going to marry a wife. Once he has married her, it seems to him that he is sure enough of her and that no man will part them asunder, for then, daughter, they can go to bed together without any shame or dread of the people and sleep in rest and peace if they wish to. And so it goes, daughter, between you and Me, for you have every week, especially on Sunday, great fear and dread in your soul about how you can be sure of My love, and how, with great reverence and holy dread, you may best receive Me for the salvation of your soul with every kind of meekness, humility, and charity, as any lady in this world is eager to receive her husband when he comes home and has been away from her a long time.

"My beloved daughter, I thank you highly for all the sick people that you have taken care of in My name, and for all the goodness and service that you have done to them in any degree, for you shall have the same reward with Me in heaven as if you had protected Me Myself when I was here on earth. Also, daughter, I think you for all the times you have bathed Me in your soul at home in your room, as if I had been present there in My humanity, for I know well, daughter, all the holy thoughts that you have shown Me in your mind. And also, daughter, I thank you for all the times you have sheltered Me and My blessed mother in your bed. For these and for all other good thoughts and good deeds that you have thought in My name and done for love of Me you shall have, with Me and with My mother, with My holy angels, with My apostles, with My martyrs, confessors, and virgins, and with all My holy saints, all manner of joy and bliss everlasting."

BOOK TWO

...

CHAPTER 10

From London she went to Sheen[1] three days before Lammas Day[2] to get a pardon[3] through the mercy of our Lord. And when she was in the church at Sheen, she experienced great devotion and high contemplation. She had abundant tears of compunction and of compassion at the remembrance of the bitter pains and suffering that our merciful Lord Jesus Christ suffered in His blessed humanity. Those who saw her weep and heard her sob so loudly were greatly astonished and wondered what was the concern of her soul.

A young man who saw her appearance and her countenance, moved by the Holy Spirit, went to her when he was able to do so alone, with a fervent desire to understand what might be the cause of her weeping, and said to her, "Mother, if it please you, I ask that you show me the reason for your weeping, for I have not seen a person with such abundance of tears as you have, and I have, especially, never before heard anyone sob so hard as you do. And mother, though I am young, my desire is to please my Lord Jesus Christ and to follow Him as I can and may. And I intend by the grace of God to take the habit[4] of this holy religion, and therefore I beg you not to be distant with me. Show me your thoughts in a good and motherly way, as I trust in you."

She, kindly and meekly, with gladness of spirit, as it seemed right to her, commended him for his intention and told him in part that the cause of her weeping and sobbing was her great unkindness toward her Maker, by which she had many times offended His goodness, and the great disgust she felt at her sins caused her to sob and weep. Also the great and excellent charity of her Redeemer, who by virtue of suffering the Passion and shedding His precious Blood redeemed her from everlasting pain and through whom she hoped to be the inheritor of joy and bliss, moved her to sob and weep, and it was no wonder. She told him many good words of spiritual comfort, by which he was incited to great virtue, and afterward he ate and drank with her while she was there and was very glad to be in her company.

Lammas Day was the principal day of pardon,[5] and as the aforesaid creature went into the church of Sheen, she caught sight of the hermit who had led her out of Lynn when she went toward the sea with her daughter-in-law, as is written above. At once, with great joy of spirit, she presented herself to him, welcoming him with all the powers of her soul, saying to him, "Ah, Reynald, you are welcome. I trust our Lord sent you here, for now I hope that just as you led me out of Lynn, so you will bring me home again to Lynn."

The hermit had a cross face and a discouraging expression, neither wishing nor intending to bring her home to Lynn as she desired. Answering curtly, he said,

---

[1] *Sheen* Carthusian monastery founded by Henry V.

[2] *Lammas Day* Harvest festival on August 1.

[3] *pardon* Official grant by the Church for the remission of a sin after the sacrament of Penance and specified devotional duties are performed.

[4] *take the habit* Become a monk.

[5] *Lammas Day ... pardon* Pardons were often associated with major feast days.

"I think you should know that your confessor has forsaken you, for you went overseas and did not tell him a word about it. You got leave to take your daughter down to the shore; you did not ask leave any further. You had no friend who knew of your plan; therefore I imagine you will find little friendship when you get back there. I pray you, get your company where you can, for I was blamed for your absence after I last escorted you; I will not do it again." She spoke to him pleasantly and asked him for the love of God not to be displeased, for those who loved her for God's sake before she went away would love her for God's sake when she came home. She offered to pay his costs along the way home. So at last he, consenting, took her back to London and then home to Lynn, to the great worship of God and the merit of both their souls. When she got home to Lynn, she submitted herself to her confessor. He spoke sharply to her, for she was under obedience to him and had taken such a journey upon herself without his knowing. Therefore he was displeased with her, but our Lord helped her so that she had as good love from him and from other friends afterward as she had before, worshipped be God. Amen.

This creature, who is spoken of above, for many years used to begin her prayers in this way. First, when she got to church, kneeling before the sacrament in worship of the blessed Trinity (Father, Son, and Holy Spirit, one God and three Persons), of the glorious Virgin, Queen of Mercy, our Lady Saint Mary, and of the twelve apostles, she said the holy hymn "*Veni creator spiritus*"[1] with all the verses belonging to it, so that God would illuminate her soul, as He did with His apostles on Pentecost Day, and endow her with the gifts of the Holy Spirit so that she might have grace to understand His will and perform it in her works, and so that she might have grace to withstand the temptations of her spiritual enemies and avoid every kind of sin and wickedness.

When she had said "*Veni creator spiritus*" with its verses, she said as follows: "I call the Holy Spirit to witness, and our Lady Saint Mary, the mother of God, all the holy court of heaven, and all my spiritual fathers here on earth, that even if it were possible for me to

have all knowledge and understanding of the secrets of God by hearing them from a devil of hell, I would not do it. And as surely as I would not know, hear, see, feel, nor understand in my soul in this life more than it is God's will for me to know, may God just as surely help me in all my works, in all my thoughts, and in all my speech, eating and drinking, sleeping and waking. As surely as it is not my will nor my intention to worship any false devil as my God, nor any false faith, nor to have false belief, just so surely do I reject the devil and all his false counsel and everything that I have ever done, said, or thought on the devil's advice when I believed it to be the counsel of God and the inspiration of the Holy Spirit. If it has not been so, God, who sees into and knows the secrets of all men's hearts, have mercy on me for it and grant me in this life a well of abundantly flowing tears with which I can wash away my sins through Your mercy and goodness.

"And Lord, by Your exalted mercy, bring upon me, here on earth, all the tears that can increase my love for you and build up my merit in heaven, and help and profit the souls, lives, or deaths of my fellow Christians. Good Lord, do not spare the eyes in my head any more than You spared the Blood in Your body, which You shed abundantly for sinful mankind's soul, and grant me so much pain and sorrow in this world that I am not held back from Your bliss and the sight of Your glorious face when I pass from here.

"As for my crying, my sobbing and weeping, Lord God Almighty, as surely as You know what scorns, what shames, what contempt and blame I have had for it, as surely as it is not in my power to weep either loudly or quietly for any devotion or sweetness, but only by the gift of the Holy Spirit, just so surely, Lord, acquit me so that all this world may know and believe that it is Your work and Your gift to magnify Your name and increase other people's love for You, Jesus. And I beg You, Sovereign Lord Jesus Christ, that as many men may be inspired by my crying and my weeping as have scorned me or shall scorn me for it to the end of the world, and many more if it be Your will.

"And regarding the love of any earthly man, as surely as I would have no beloved but God to love above all things, and would love all things and all other creatures for God and in God, just so surely quench all fleshly lust

---

[1]   *Veni creator spiritus*   Latin: Come, Creator Spirit.

in me and in all those in whom I have beheld Your blissful body. And give us Your holy dread in our hearts for Your painful wounds. Lord, make my spiritual fathers fear You in me and love You in me, and make all the world have greater sorrow for their own sins for the sorrow that You have given me for other people's sins. Good Jesus, make my will Your will and Your will my will, so that I may have no will but Yours alone.

"Now, good Lord Jesus Christ, I ask Your mercy for all the ranks in Holy Church, for the Pope and all his cardinals, for all archbishops and bishops, and for the whole order of the priesthood, for all monks and nuns, especially those who are active in preserving and defending the faith of Holy Church. Lord, bless them of Your mercy and grant them victory over all their enemies and help them in all they do for Your worship; may God send all who are in grace at this time perseverance to the end of their lives. And make me worthy to share in their prayers, and they in mine, and each of us in others'.

"I ask Your mercy, blissful Lord, for the King of England and for all Christian kings and for all lords and ladies who are in this world. God, give them the governance by which they can most please You and be lords and ladies in heaven without end. I ask Your mercy, Lord, for the rich men of this world who have Your goods at their disposal; give them grace to spend these as it pleases You. I ask Your mercy, Lord, for Jews and Saracens,[1] and all heathen people. Good Lord, be mindful that there is many a saint in heaven who was once a heathen on earth. And as You have spread Your mercy to those on earth.[2] Lord, You say Yourself that no one shall come to You without Your help nor anyone be drawn to You without Your drawing him. And therefore, Lord, if there is any man undrawn, I pray that You draw him toward You. You have drawn me, Lord, and I never deserved to be drawn, but You have drawn me according to Your great mercy. If all this world knew all my wickedness as you do, they would marvel and wonder at the great goodness that You have shown me. I wish that all this world were worthy to thank You on my account, and as You have made unworthy creatures worthy, so make all this world worthy to thank and praise You.

"I ask Your mercy, Lord, for all false heretics and for all misbelievers, for all false tithers,[3] thieves, adulterers, and all prostitutes, and for all who live wickedly. Lord, of Your mercy have mercy on them if it is Your will, and bring them out of their wickedness the sooner for my prayers.

"I ask Your mercy, Lord, for all those who are tempted and troubled by their spiritual enemies, and that You of Your mercy give them grace to withstand their temptations and deliver them from these when it is most pleasing to You. I ask Your mercy, Lord, for all my spiritual fathers, that You deign to spread as much grace in their souls as I would wish You to do in mine.

"I ask Your mercy, Lord, for all my children, spiritual and bodily, and for all the people in this world, and ask that You give me contrition for their sins as if they were my own sins, and forgive them as I would wish You to forgive me.

"I ask Your mercy, Lord, for all my friends and for all my enemies, especially for all who are sick, for all lepers, for all bedridden men and women, for all who are in prison, and for all creatures in the world who have spoken either good or ill of me and ever shall do to the end of the world. Have mercy on them and be as gracious to their souls as I would wish You to be to mine. And those who have said any evil of me, forgive them for it of Your divine mercy; and those who have said well, Lord, I pray You reward them, for it is through their charity and not through my merits, for even if You allowed all this world to avenge You on me and to hate me for displeasing You, You would do me no wrong.

"I ask Your mercy, Lord, for all the souls that are in the pains of purgatory awaiting Your mercy and the prayers of Holy Church[4] as surely, Lord, as they are Your own chosen souls. Be as gracious to them as I would wish You to be to me if I were in the same pain that they are in.

"Lord Jesus Christ, I thank You for all health and wealth, for all riches and all poverty, for sickness and

---

[1] *Saracens* I.e., Muslims.

[2] The manuscript seems to have some text missing at this point, leaving an incomplete idea.

[3] *tithers* Those who tithe, or donate one-tenth of their incomes to the Church.

[4] *pains of purgatory … Holy Church* It was believed that prayer could help shorten a soul's time in purgatory.

scorns, for all the contempt and all the wrongs, and for all the various tribulations that have befallen or shall befall me as long as I live. I thank You earnestly for allowing me to suffer in this world in remission of my sins and to the increase of my merit in Heaven, as I surely have great reason to thank You.

"Hear my prayers, for even if I had as many hearts and souls enclosed in my soul as those that God without beginning knew would dwell in Heaven without end, and as there are drops of water, fresh and salt, chips of gravel, large and small stones, grasses growing in all the earth, kernels of corn, fish, birds, animals, and leaves on trees when they are most plentiful, feathers of birds or hair of animals, seed that grows into plant or weed or flower, on land or on water when they grow the most, and as many creatures as there have been on earth and ever shall be and can be by Your power, and as there are stars and angels in Your sight or other kinds of good that grow on the earth, and each were a soul as holy as our Lady Saint Mary was, who bore our Savior Jesus, and if it were possible that each could think and speak as much reverence and worship as our Lady Saint Mary ever did here in earth and now does in heaven and shall do without end, I may well think in my heart and say with my mouth at this time, to the honor of the Trinity and of all the court of Heaven and to the great shame and disgrace of Satan who fell from God's presence, and of all his wicked spirits, that all these hearts and souls could never thank God nor fully praise Him, fully bless Him nor fully worship Him, fully love Him nor fully give Him the glory, praise, and reverence that He deserves to have for the great mercy that He has shown me in earth; that I cannot and may not do.

"I ask my Lady, who alone is the Mother of God, the well of grace, the flower and fairest of all women that God ever made on earth, the worthiest in His sight, the most beloved, dear, and precious to Him, most worthy to be heard by God and the one who most truly deserved it in this life, kind Lady, meek Lady, charitable Lady, with all the reverence that is in heaven and with all Your holy saints, I ask you, Lady, to offer thanks and praise to the blissful Trinity for love of me, asking mercy and grace for me and for all my spiritual fathers and perseverance for the rest of our lives in the way of life that is most pleasing to God. I bless my God in my soul and all of you who are in heaven. Blessed may God be in you all and all of you in God.

"Blessed be You, Lord, for all the mercies that You have shown to all those in heaven and earth. And I especially bless You, Lord, for Mary Magdalene, for Mary the Egyptian, for Saint Paul, and for Saint Augustine. And as You have shown Your mercy to them, show Your mercy to me and to all who earnestly ask You for mercy. The peace and rest that You have bequeathed to Your disciples and those who love You, bequeath that same peace and rest to me on earth and in heaven without end. Be mindful, Lord, of the woman who was taken in adultery and brought before You, and as You drove away all her enemies from her and she stood alone beside You, so indeed may you drive away all my enemies from me, both bodily and spiritual, so that I may stand alone beside You and make my soul dead to all the joys of this world and alive and eager for devout contemplation in God.

"Be mindful, Lord, of Lazarus who lay dead in his grave for four days, and as I have been in that holy place where Your body was living and dead and crucified for mankind's sin and where Lazarus was raised from death to life, as surely, Lord, if any man or woman die in this hour by deadly sin, if any prayer can help them, hear my prayers for them and give them life without end. Many thanks, Lord, for all the sins You have kept me from and that I have not done, and many thanks, Lord, for all the sorrow You have given me for those I have done, for these graces and for all the other graces that are necessary to me and to all creatures on earth. And for all those who have faith and trust in my prayers, or will have faith and trust in them until the world's end, I pray You, Lord, grant them of the multitude of Your mercy such grace as they desire, spiritual or bodily, to the profit of their souls. Amen."

—1436–38

Religious and Spiritual Life

CONTEXTS

Religion was so central to life in the Middle Ages that it is impossible in a section of this sort to do more than touch on a few important developments and themes.

Celtic culture forms a strong thread through the Christian culture of the early Middle Ages; several striking visual examples are included here. Among the most important developments in the transition from the Christianity of the Early to that of the High Middle Ages was a dramatic change in religious architecture; again, illustrations are provided below.

The prayers that Christians were expected to be able to recite and two excerpts from works of advice and instruction may give some sense of the reality of religious life for the laity. The Canons of the Fourth Lateran Council in 1215 were of enormous importance in regularizing Church practice throughout Western Europe; several of these are reproduced below.

Monks and friars both played vital roles in medieval Christianity generally; both are touched on here. Beginning in the eleventh century the recovery of Aristotelian and other classical texts facilitated the development of new planes of theological argument among the Scholastics; represented here is the most influential argument of the leading theologian in Britain in the Middle Ages, St. Anselm. Scholasticism of the sort practised by St. Anselm, however, existed only in pockets; much more representative of the popular cast of mind are the accounts of miracles connected to saints' lives—those associated with Thomas Becket being a leading example.

Corruption within the Church was a recurring complaint—and a recurring reality—throughout the medieval period. During the fourteenth and early fifteenth centuries it was particularly pressing concern both for reformist clerics such as John Wycliffe and the Lollards and for lay writers such as William Langland; in both cases relevant excerpts are included below.

The regularizing of Christian practice in the later Middle Ages was accompanied by the growth of exclusionist attitudes towards those who did not follow the designated path; as several of the readings at the end of this section illustrate, attitudes towards both heretics and Jews hardened significantly.

⌘ ⌘ ⌘

Celtic Christianity

Celtic art is characterized by formal intricacy and an extraordinarily high level of decorative skill. Its most famous expressions in a Christian context are in Gospels such as the Book of Kells and the Lindisfarne Gospels, but for centuries Celtic designs also featured prominently in a variety of forms of stone and metalwork.

Decorative page from the Book of Durrow (c. 670).   Carpet page from the Lindisfarne Gospels (8th century).

First text page, Gospel of Saint Luke, from the
Lindisfarne Gospels (8th century).

St. John from The Book of Kells (9th century).

Ardagh chalice (c. 700).
This extraordinarily elaborate chalice was discovered in a hoard in a ring-fort in Limerick County in Ireland.

St. John, from The Macdurnan Gospels (9th century).

Pictish memorial stone (7th century?).
This stone stands at Glamis in Scotland; accompanying the "Celtic cross" are a variety of pictograms, the meaning of which is unknown.

Church and Cathedral

Greensted Church at Ongar, Essex (c. 850).
Thought to be the oldest wooden church in the world,
the walls of Greensted Church are formed of tree trunks
split in two, erected curved-side outward.

The Norman Crypt, Canterbury Cathedral (12th c.).
Round arches and heavy stone work are characteristic of
Romanesque church architecture of the Norman Period.

Interior, Durham Cathedral (1093–1133).
Durham is the most spare and imposing of the Norman
cathedrals in England.

Roger Fenton, "Salisbury Cathedral" (1858).
Salisbury Cathedral was built in the thirteenth century,
with work beginning in 1220. The spire, which was
completed near the end of the century, remains the
tallest in England at 404 feet. Until the latter part of the
nineteenth century it was one of the world's tallest
structures. (From the late medieval period until the
1890s all but one of the world's tallest buildings were
churches—the exception being the Pyramid of Cheops
at Giza.)

Roger Fenton, *Cloisters, Westminster Abbey* (c. 1858). The cloisters date from the 13th and 14th centuries. Like Salisbury and York Minster, Westminster Abbey is built in the Gothic style, with pointed rather than rounded arches and extensive vaulting giving a stronger sense of verticality than in Romanesque architecture.

Roger Fenton, *York Minster, from the South East* (c. 1856).
Built in the late thirteenth and fourteenth centuries, York Minster remains one of Britain's leading cathedrals.

Religion for All: The Apostles' Creed, the Pater Noster, and the Hail Mary

In the Middle Ages the Apostles' Creed was believed to have been jointly composed by the apostles, with each contributing one verse. Its origins are in fact unknown, though in its earliest forms the Creed almost certainly dates back to at least the fourth century. The following Latin text and English translation show the Creed divided into twelve constituent articles.

By the later medieval period all Christians were required to be able to recite the Apostles' Creed, the Pater Noster (or Lord's Prayer), and the Hail Mary in Latin rather than in the vernacular. The Pater Noster derives from two passages in the Gospels that were believed to contain Jesus's very words, Matthew 6.9–13 and Luke 11.2–4. The Pater Noster was ubiquitous throughout society, but few understood precisely what they were saying (the word "patter" derives from the sounds people made as they recited the Pater Noster quickly and without understanding); even among the clergy a working knowledge of Latin was far from universal.

The Hail Mary had come into wide use by the eleventh century, but it was not until the twelfth century that it became common for lay people to be required to be able to recite it.

The Apostle's Creed

Credo in Deum Patrem omnipotentem, Creatorem cæli et terræ.
Et in Jesum Christum, Fílium eius unicum, Dominum nostrum,
qui conceptus est de Spiritu Sancto, natus ex Maria Virgine,
passus sub Pontio Pilato, crucifixus, mortuus, et sepultus,
descendit ad infernos, tertia die resurrexit a mortuis, ascendit ad cælos, sedet ad dexteram Dei Patris omnipotentis,
inde venturus est iudicare vivos et mortuos.
Credo in Spiritum Sanctum,
sanctam Ecclesiam catholicam, sanctorum communionem,

remissionem peccatorum,
carnis resurrectionem,
vitam æternam. Amen.

I believe in God the Father Almighty,
    creator of heaven and earth,
    and in Jesus Christ, His only Son, our Lord;
    who was conceived by the Holy Spirit,
    born of the Virgin Mary,
    suffered under Pontius Pilate, was crucified, died,
        and was buried.
    He descended into hell; on the third day He arose
        again from the dead;
    He ascended into heaven and sits at the right hand
        of God the Father Almighty.
    From thence He shall come to judge the living and
        the dead.
I believe in the Holy Spirit,
    the Holy Catholic Church,
    the Communion of Saints,
    the forgiveness of sins,
    the resurrection of the body,
    and life everlasting. Amen.

The Pater Noster

Pater noster, qui es in caelis, sanctificetur nomen tuum. Adveniat regnum tuum. Fiat voluntas tua, sicut in caelo et in terra. Panem nostrum quotidianum da nobis hodie, et dimitte nobis debita nostra, sicut et nos dimittimus debitoribus nostris. Et ne nos inducas in tentationem: sed libera nos a malo. Amen.

Our Father, who art in heaven, hallowed be Thy name. Thy kingdom come. Thy will be done, on earth as it is in heaven. Give us this day our daily bread. And forgive us our trespasses, as we forgive those who trespass against us. And lead us not into temptation, but deliver us from evil. Amen.

[The following verse, which has never been part of the Roman Catholic Pater Noster, began to be added by various Protestant groups in the sixteenth century.]

For thine is the kingdom, the power and the glory, for ever and ever. Amen.

Illuminated page, Genesis-Job volume, Lambeth Bible (c. 1150).

This page illustrates the centrality of the Virgin Mary to medieval Christianity. During the Middle Ages the Latin words *virga* (stem) and *virgo* (virgin) were often assumed to be related. Here the illustration shows the stem of genealogy passing from Jesse through the Virgin Mary to Christ, with the four prophets (lower roundels), the four virtues of Mercy, Truth, Righteousness and Peace (middle roundels), and Moses with representatives of the Church Triumphant (upper roundels) looking on. In the corners are the four apostles.

The Hail Mary

Ave Maria, gratia plena, Dominus tecum, benedicta tu in mulieribus et benedictus fructus ventris tui.

Hail Mary, full of grace, the Lord is with thee, blessed

art thou among women and blessed is the fruit of thy
womb.

[The following verse began to be added during the fifteeth
and sixteenth centuries.]

Sante Maria, Mater Dei, ora pro nobis peccatoribus,
nunc et in hora mortis nostrae.

Holy Mary, Mother of God, pray for us sinners now
and at the hour of our death.

from Robert Manning of Brunne, *Handlyng Synne* (early 14th century)

Robert Manning (c. 1264–c. 1340) was a Gilbertine
monk at an abbey near Brunne (now Bourne) in
Lincolnshire. Manning's poem *Handlying Synne*,
written in English but very largely a translation of
a similar work in French by William of Wadding-
ton, is an educational text designed to set out in
everyday terms what is entailed in following the Ten
Commandments, avoiding the Seven Deadly Sins,
and so forth. Whereas most religious writing of the
time was in Latin, Manning wrote in the vernacular
for "lewd" men "that tales and rhyme will blithely
hear" rather than for the educated minority who
were literate in Latin. The extracts below set out
specific examples of forbidden or morally questionable activities. Interestingly, miracle plays performed
outside the church are included here on the list of
proscribed activities—though depicting the birth
and resurrection of Jesus within the church is
"without danger."

… Of tournaments that are forbade
in holy church, as men do read,
of tournaments I shall prove therein,
seven points of deadly sin:
5   first is pride, as thou well know'st,
vanity, pomp, and many a boast;
of rich attire there is great flaunting,
spurring her horse with much vaunting.
Know you well this is envy
10 when one sees another do mastery,

some in words, some in deeds;
envy most of all him leads.
Ire and wrath cannot be late;
oft are tournaments made for hate.
15 If all knights loved each other well,
tournaments would never be held;
And of course they fall into slothfulness,
they love it more than God or Mass;
And truly, there can be no doubt,
20 they spend more gold thereabout—
that is, they give it all to folly—
than on any deed of mercy.
And yet be very careful lest
you forget Dame Covetousness,
25 for she shall be foolish, in all ways,
to win a horse and some harness.
And a man shall also do robbery,
or beguile his host where he shall stay.
Gluttony also is them among,
30 delicious meats do make him strong;
and gladly he drinks wine untold,
with gluttony to make him bold.
Also is there Dame Lechery;
from here comes all her mastery.
35 Many times, for women's sake,
knights these tournaments do make;
and when he goes to the tournament
she sends him some secret present,
and bids him do, if he loves her best,
40 all that he can at her behest,
for which he gets so much the worst,
that he may not sit upon his horse,
and that peradventure, in all his life,
shall he never after thrive.
45 Consider whether such tournaments
should more truly be called torments? …

It is forbidden him, in the decree,
miracle plays for to make or see,
for, miracles if thou begin,
50 it is a gathering, a site of sin.
He may in the church, through this reason,
portray the resurrection—
that is to say, how God rose,
God and man in strength and loss—

55 to make men hold to belief good,
that he rose with flesh and blood;
and he may play, without danger,
how God was born in the manger,
to make men to believe steadfastly
60 that he came to us through the Virgin Mary. ...

A parson is slothful in holy church
who on his sheep will not work
how they should heed his own word
and please the church and their Lord.
65 The high Shepherd shall him blame,
for how he lets them go to shame.
If he should see in anything
that they have a lack of chastising,
unless he teach them and chastise so
70 that they from henceforth better do,
for them he shall, at God's assize,
be punished before the high Justice.
Also it behooves him to pray
that God, of grace, show him the way. ...

75 Man or woman that has a child
that with bad manners grows too wild,
that will both mis-say and –do,
chastisement behooves them too;
But chastise them with all your might,
80 Otherwise you'll be in their plight.
Better were the child unborn
than lack chastising, and thus be forlorn.
Thus says the wise king Solomon
to men and women every one,
85 "If you want your children to be good,
give them the smart end of the rod;"
and teach them good manners each one;
but take care that you break no bone. ...

Everywhere I see this custom:
90 that rich men have shrews for sons—
shrews in speech and in act—
Why? They hold no one in respect.
In his youth shall he mis-say
and scorn others by the way;
95 then says the father, "This child's story
doesn't hang together—sorry!"

And if he learns guilefulness,
false words and deceitful looks,
his father shouldn't acquit him then;
100 his sly wit will be his only friend.
If he injures foes in rages,
then says his father, "He shall be courageous,
he shall be hardy, and no man dread,
he begins early to be doughty in deed."
105 But right so shall it him befall
as it did with Eli's bad sons all. ...

from William of Pagula, *Priest's Eye* (c. 1320)

William of Pagula was an English curate who wrote a work entitled *Oculis Sacerdotis* (*Priest's Eye*) between 1320 and 1323, intended for use as a handbook of instruction for parish priests–many of whom remained poorly educated. Both the full book and excerpts taken from it circulated widely; the following constituted a selection of twenty-one instructions taken from the larger work and issued independently in 1385.

1. A parish priest should recommend as many things to his parishioners on Sundays as seem useful to him for their instruction, and he should repeat them often so they will not slip from memory. First he should teach them the formula for baptizing infants in the absence of a priest if it becomes necessary. This is the vernacular version: *I crysten thee in the name of the fadyr and the sone and the holy ghost.* While saying this, sprinkle water over the child or immerse it in water three times or at the very least once. Anyone, whether cleric or lay person, may baptize a child in an emergency. Even the father of the child or its mother may do so without putting restrictions on their conjugal relations unless there is someone else present who knows how and wishes to do it. And if someone must baptize a child in an emergency using the above formula, he should speak the words distinctly and clearly only once, in no manner repeating the words of the rite or anything like them over the child. And if an infant baptized in this manner recovers, it should be taken to the church, and those who bring it should tell the priest that the child was baptized at home so that the priest will not baptize it

again. But, excluding the immersion in water, he should perform the exorcism, the anointing, and the other customary actions that accompany baptism but were omitted. Let the priest teach his parishioners that they should baptize using only water, no other liquids. Likewise let him warn men and women who are appointed the godparents of children at baptism that, except in an emergency they should not delay having their godchildren confirmed by a bishop. They should teach them or have them be taught the Lord's Prayer and the Creed, and admonish them when they reach adulthood or are capable of learning that they should guard their chastity, love justice, and practice charity.

The baptism of children born within eight days of Easter or Pentecost should be postponed for a week if it is convenient and they may be held back without danger, and then they should be baptized.

2. He should also warn them that anyone who has children who are not confirmed should make arrangements to have them confirmed by the time they are five years old if it is possible.

3. Also he should warn them that they should never put their children in bed with them in case through negligence they should roll over and smother them, which would be reckoned a case of homicide according to canon law. Nor should they thoughtlessly bind them in swaddling clothes or leave them alone by day or by night without someone watching them because of various dangers.

4. Also the priest should teach his parishioners that a spiritual kinship is established among godparents, godchildren, and the parents of the godchildren. The same is true for sponsors at confirmation. Because of this kinship, marriage between any of these parties is prohibited. A spiritual kinship is established among ten people in baptism and the same number in confirmation.

5. He should also teach them that if a man and a woman shall have given their legitimate consent to contract a marriage by an exchange of words in the present tense, even though there has been no betrothal but only an oath, and even though, as is the custom, no carnal relations have occurred, still they have contracted a true marriage—so much so that if afterwards one of them should contract a second marriage and even have carnal relations with the new partner, they should be separated and that person should return to the first marriage. Also he should teach them that marriages should not be contracted except in the presence of a priest and legitimate witnesses. Prior to the marriage ceremony banns should be solemnly published to the people in the church on three consecutive feast days. And any cleric or priest or other person who is present at a clandestine marriage shall be suspended from his office for three years.

6. Also he should warn them that boys and girls older than seven years should not lie together in the same bed because of the danger of fornication, nor should a brother share a bed with his sister because of the danger of incest.

7. Also he should publicly announce that any member of the faithful who has reached the age of discretion [i.e, fourteen] ought to confess all his sins to his own parish priest at least once a year and he should fulfill the penance imposed on him for his vices. During Eastertide he should receive the Body of Christ unless, with the counsel of his priest, for some reason he should abstain; otherwise while he is alive he should be barred from entering a church, and when he dies he should be without Christian burial. But if anyone does not wish to confess to his parish priest for a specific and well-founded reason, he should seek and obtain permission from his own priest to confess to another suitable priest.

8. Also he should teach them that pregnant women should be confessed beforehand so that they are prepared to receive the Eucharist if life-threatening danger should arise during their delivery, since it would seem improper for the priest to stay with them [hearing confession] during the course of their labor.

9. Also he should teach his parishioners that when the Host is elevated during the consecration of the Mass, they should genuflect if they can comfortably do so,

and, adoring the Host, they should say in a low voice: "Hail salvation of the world, Word of the Father, true sacrifice, living flesh, fully God, truly man" or "Glory to you Lord who is born" or the Lord's Prayer or some other devout words. And they should also do this when they see the Body of Christ, preceded by lights and a ringing bell, carried to the sick.

10. Also he should warn his parishioners that they should faithfully pay their tithes on goods legitimately acquired. For faithfully paying tithes brings a fourfold reward: the first is an abundance of crops; the second is bodily health, according to Augustine; the third is the remission of sins; the fourth is reward in the kingdom of heaven. But those who tithe badly are punished in four ways: first because they transgress a divine commandment. Second because once they had an abundance of all things when they tithed well, but now since they tithe badly they will be forced to tithe. Third, when tithes are poorly paid, God does not ward off locusts or other harmful things, nor does he dispel plagues or bring rain, except short-lived ones. Fourth, because of a lack of tithes, men justly collect taxes and tolls from the people since what Christ does not take, taxes will. Besides, those who do not pay their tithes are cursed by God. And merchants and artisans as much as carpenters, blacksmiths, weavers, alewives and other such people, and all other hired laborers and boon laborers all ought to be admonished to pay tithes from their earnings or else reach a settlement with the rector of their church.

11. And the priest ought to announce to his people which days are feast days and which are days of fast.

12. Also he should instruct his parishioners that they should not practice the magical arts, incantations, or sorcery, since these things have no power to cure either man or beast and besides are utterly worthless and unlawful. Moreover clerics who do these things shall be degraded and lay people shall be excommunicated.

13. Also he should warn everyone not to lend money, grain, wine, oil or any other thing whatsoever by usury; namely by entering into a contract or having the intention to receive back more in repayment than he lent out.

And if a cleric shall do this he shall be suspended from office; and a lay person shall be excommunicated until he makes restitution. To be sure, usury is forbidden in both the Old and the New Testaments.

14. He should also warn his parishioners that they should not wait in order to sell their goods at a higher price, for they are obliged to repay what they have gained by this type of withholding. Likewise they should not sell their goods to travelers, pilgrims, and other wayfarers for a higher price than they charge to their neighbors or than they can receive at market.

15. Let him also warn them that if anyone shall receive land or a dwelling as a pledge for a loan of money, after deducting his expenses, he should return the pledge; and if he receives more than that, it is to be reckoned as usury.

16. Also he shall publicly announce three times yearly that all those men who wish to enjoy the privileges of the clergy shall be duly tonsured, displaying the crown of their head suitably shaved especially in the presence of their ordinaries and in churches and in congregations of the clergy.

17. Also one day during Lent he should publicly preach the Creed, that is to say, the articles of faith.

18. And he should admonish his parishioners that they should enter church humbly and devoutly and should behave reverently, peacefully, and devoutly while in it. And when they hear named the Name of Jesus they should genuflect at the very least in their hearts, or by bowing their head, or beating their breast.

19. He should admonish them that no one should cause a disturbance, or a disagreement, or hold discussions, or useless and profane conversations in a church or its graveyard; nor should they provoke disputes or fights or anything else which could interrupt the divine services or dishonor the holiness of the place. Likewise business should not be conducted in the church or its graveyard and especially not fairs or markets, nor should courts, pleas, or secular judgments be held there. And

dishonorable dances should not take place there, nor should improper songs be sung during the vigils of saints days or at other times, nor should there take place anything else by which the church or the graveyard could be dishonored.

20. Also he should instruct them that neither a husband nor a wife should make an oath swearing to practice chastity, to fast, or to go on pilgrimage (except for a vow to go to the Holy Land) without the consent of the other. For a man and a wife are to be judged as equals in this regard.

21. He should also warn his parishioners that no one should harbor or defend in his home anyone who he knows has committed a known robbery.

from the Canons of the Fourth Lateran Council (1215)

> The following selections touch on the behavior of clerics, on confession, and on regulating the display and sale of the relics of saints. The final selection, Canon 68, is an illustration of the manner in which, as the canons of the Council acted to unify and strengthen the practices of Christians, equally they strengthened Christian hostility towards non-Christians.

Canon 14. That the morals and general conduct of clerics may be better reformed, let all strive to live chastely and virtuously, particularly those in sacred orders, guarding against every vice of desire, especially that on account of which the anger of God came from heaven upon the children of unbelief so that in the sight of Almighty God they may perform their duties with a pure heart and chaste body. But lest the facility to obtain pardon be an incentive to do wrong, we decree that whoever shall be found to indulge in the vice of incontinence, shall, in proportion to the gravity of his sin, be punished in accordance with the canonical statutes, which we command to be strictly and rigorously observed, so that he whom divine fear does not restrain from evil, may at least be withheld from sin by

a temporal penalty. If therefore anyone suspended for this reason shall presume to celebrate the divine mysteries, let him not only be deprived of his ecclesiastical benefices but for this twofold offense let him be forever deposed. Prelates who dare support such in their iniquities, especially in view of money or other temporal advantages, shall be subject to a like punishment. But if those, who according to the practice of their country [i.e., the Latin East] have not renounced the conjugal bond, fall by the vice of impurity, they are to be punished more severely, since they can use matrimony lawfully.

Canon 15. All clerics shall carefully abstain from drunkenness. Wherefore, let them accommodate the wine to themselves, and themselves to the wine. Nor shall anyone be encouraged to drink, for drunkenness banishes reason and incites to lust. We decree, therefore, that that abuse be absolutely abolished by which in some localities the drinkers bind themselves in their manner to an equal portion of drink and he in their judgment is the hero of the day who outdrinks the others. Should anyone be culpable in this matter, unless he heeds the warning of the superior and makes suitable satisfaction, let him be suspended from his benefice or office.

We forbid hunting and fowling to all clerics: wherefore, let them not presume to keep dogs and birds for these purposes.

Canon 21. All the faithful of both sexes shall after they have reached the age of discretion [then accepted to be fourteen] faithfully confess all their sins at least once a year to their own [parish] priest and perform to the best of their ability the Penance imposed, receiving reverently at least at Easter the sacrament of the Eucharist, unless perchance at the advice of their own priest they may for a good reason abstain for a time from its reception; otherwise they shall be [barred from entering] the church during life and deprived of Christian burial in death. Wherefore, let this salutary decree be published frequently in the churches, that no one may find in the plea of ignorance a shadow of excuse. But if anyone for good reason should wish to confess his sins to another priest, let him first seek and obtain permission from his own priest, since otherwise the other priest cannot absolve or bind him.

Let the priest be discreet and cautious, ... carefully inquiring into the circumstances of the sinner and the sin, from the nature of which he may understand what kind of advice to give and what kind of remedy to apply, making use of different means to heal the sick one. But let him exercise the greatest precaution that he does not in any degree by word, sign, or any other manner make known the sinner, but should he need more prudent counsel, let him seek it cautiously without any mention of the person. He who dares to reveal a sin confided to him in the tribunal of penance, we decree that he be not only deposed from the priestly office but also relegated to a monastery of strict observance to do penance for the remainder of his life ...

Canon 62.   From the fact that some expose for sale and exhibit promiscuously the relics of the saints, great injury is sustained by the Christian religion. That this may not occur hereafter, we ordain in the present decree that in the future old relics may not be exhibited outside of a vessel or exposed for sale. And let no one presume to venerate publicly new ones unless they have been approved by the Roman pontiff. In the future prelates shall not permit those who come to their churches [for the sake of venerating relics] to be deceived by worthless fabrications or false documents as has been done in many places for the sake of gain. We forbid also that seekers of alms, some of whom, misrepresenting themselves, preach certain abuses, be admitted, unless they exhibit genuine letters either of the Apostolic See or of the diocesan bishop, in which case they may not preach anything to the people but what is contained in those letters. We give herewith a form which the Apostolic See commonly uses in granting such letters, that the diocesan bishops may model their own upon it....

Canon 68.   In some provinces a difference of dress distinguishes the Jews and Saracens from the Christians, but in others confusion has developed to such a degree that no difference is discernible. Whence it happens sometimes through error that Christians mingle with the women of Jews and Saracens, and, on the other hand, Jews and Saracens mingle with those of the Christians. Therefore, that such religious commingling

through error of this kind may not serve as a refuge for further excuse for excesses, we decree that such people of both sexes (that is, Jews and Saracens) in every Christian province and at all times be distinguished in public from other people by a difference in dress, since this was also enjoined on them by Moses. On the days of the Lamentations and on Passion Sunday they may not appear in public, because some of them, as we understand, on those days are not ashamed to show themselves more ornately attired and do not fear to amuse themselves at the expense of Christians, who in memory of the sacred passion go about attired in robes of mourning. That we most strictly forbid, lest they should presume in some measure to burst forth in contempt of the Redeemer. And, since we ought not be ashamed of him who blotted out our offenses, we command that the secular princes restrain presumptuous persons of this kind by condign punishment, lest they presume to blaspheme in some degree the one crucified for us.

Monks, Anchoresses, and Friars

from The Rule of St. Columba (6th century)

The monastic movement in Ireland in the sixth century exerted enormous influence on the spread of both Christianity and Celtic culture. Irish monks led by St. Columba (521–97) converted large areas of northern England, as well as much of Scotland, to Christianity.

Be alone in a separate place near a chief city, if thy conscience is not prepared to be in common with the crowd.

Be always naked in imitation of Christ and the Evangelists.

Whatsoever little or much thou possessest of anything, whether clothing, or food, or drink, let it be at the command of the senior and at his disposal, for it is not befitting a religious to have any distinction of property with his own free brother.

Let a fast place, with one door, enclose thee.

A few religious men to converse with thee of God and his Testament; to visit thee on days of solemnity; to strengthen thee in the Testaments of God, and the narratives of the Scriptures.

A person too who would talk with thee in idle words, or of the world; or who murmurs at what he cannot remedy or prevent, but who would distress thee more should he be a tattler between friends and foes, thou shalt not admit him to thee, but at once give him thy benediction should he deserve it.

Let thy servant be a discreet, religious, not tale-telling man, who is to attend continually on thee, with moderate labour of course, but always ready.

Yield submission to every rule that is of devotion.

A mind prepared for red martyrdom.

A mind fortified and steadfast for white martyrdom.

Forgiveness from the heart of every one.

Constant prayers for those who trouble thee.

Fervour in singing the office for the dead, as if every faithful dead was a particular friend of thine.

Hymns for souls to be sung standing.

Let thy vigils be constant from eve to eve, under the direction of another person.

Three labours in the day, viz., prayers, work, and reading.

The work to be divided into three parts, viz., thine own work, and the work of thy place, as regards its real wants; secondly, thy share of the brethen's [work]; lastly, to help the neighbours, viz. by instruction or writing, or sewing garments, or whatever labour they may be in want of, *ut Dominus ait, "Non apparebis ante Me vacuus"* [as the Lord says, "You shall not appear before me empty"].

Everything in its proper order; *Nemo enim coronabitur nisi qui legitime certaverit* [For no one is crowned except he who has striven lawfully].

Follow alms-giving before all things.

Take not of food till thou art hungry.

Sleep not till thou feelest desire.

Speak not except on business.

Every increase which comes to thee in lawful meals, or in wearing apparel, give it for pity to the brethren that want it, or to the poor in like manner.

The love of God with all thy heart and all thy strength;

The love of thy neighbour as thyself.

Abide in the Testament of God throughout all times.

Thy measure of prayer shall be until thy tears come;

Or thy measure of work of labour till thy tears come;

Or thy measure of thy work of labour, or of thy genuflexions, until thy perspiration often comes, if thy tears are not free.

from The Rule of St. Benedict (6ᵗʰ century)

By the end of the eighth century most monasteries both in Britain and on the continent were Benedictine; even many that had originally been Columban had adopted the full and precise set of rules that had been composed in the first half of the sixth century by St. Benedict.

Prologue. .... We are about to found, therefore, a school for the Lord's service; in the organization of which we trust that we shall ordain nothing severe and nothing burdensome. But even if, the demands of justice dictating it, something a little irksome shall be the result, for the purpose of amending vices or preserving charity;—thou shalt not therefore, struck by fear, flee the way of salvation, which can not be entered upon except through a narrow entrance. But as one's way of life and one's faith progresses, the heart becomes broadened, and, with the unutterable sweetness of love, the way of the mandates of the Lord is traversed. Thus, never departing from His guidance, continuing in the monastery in His teaching until death, through patience we are made partakers in Christ's passion, in order that we may merit to be companions in His kingdom.

Concerning the kinds of monks and their manner of living. It is manifest that there are four kinds of monks. The cenobites are the first kind; that is, those living in a monastery, serving under a rule or an abbot. Then the second kind is that of the anchorites; that is, the hermits—those who, not by the new fervour of a conversion but by the long probation of life in a monastery, have learned to fight against the devil, having already been taught by the solace of many. They, having been well prepared in the army of brothers for the solitary fight of the hermit, being secure now without the consolation of another, are able, God helping them, to fight with their own hand or arm against the vices of the flesh or of their thoughts.

But a third very bad kind of monks are the sarabaites, approved by no rule, experience being their teacher, as with the gold which is tried in the furnace. But, softened after the manner of lead, keeping faith with the world by their works, they are known through their tonsure to lie to God. These being shut up by twos or threes, or, indeed, alone, without a shepherd, not in the Lord's but in their own sheep-folds— their law is the satisfaction of their desires. For whatever they think good or choice, this they call holy; and what they do not wish, this they consider unlawful. But the fourth kind of monks is the kind which are called gyrovagues. During their whole life they are guests, for three or four days at a time, in the cells of the different monasteries, throughout the various provinces; always wandering and never stationary, given over to the service of their own pleasures and the joys of the palate, and in every way worse than the sarabaites. Concerning the most wretched way of living of all such monks it is better to be silent than to speak. These things therefore being omitted, let us proceed, with the aid of God, to treat of the best kind, the cenobites. …

Concerning humility. … The sixth grade of humility is, that a monk be contented with all lowliness or extremity, and consider himself, with regard to everything which is enjoined on him, as a poor and unworthy workman; saying to himself with the prophet: "I was reduced to nothing and was ignorant; I was made as the cattle before thee, and I am always with thee." The seventh grade of humility is, not only that he, with his tongue, pronounce himself viler and more worthless than all; but that he also believe it in the innermost workings of his heart; humbling himself and saying with the prophet, etc. … The eighth degree of humility is that a monk do nothing except what the common rule of the monastery, or the example of his elders, urges him to do. The ninth degree of humility is that a monk restrain his tongue from speaking; and, keeping silence, do not speak until he is spoken to. The tenth grade of humility is that he be not ready, and easily inclined, to laugh. … The eleventh grade of humility is that a monk, when he speaks, speak slowly and without laughter, humbly with gravity, using few and reasonable words; and that he be not loud of voice. … The twelfth

grade of humility is that a monk shall, not only with his heart but also with his body, always show humility to all who see him: that is, when at work, in the oratory in the monastery, in the garden, on the road, in the fields. And everywhere, sitting or walking or standing, let him always be with head inclined, his looks fixed upon the ground; remembering every hour that he is guilty of his sins. Let him think that he is already being presented before the tremendous judgment of God, saying always to himself in his heart what the publican of the gospel, fixing his eyes on the earth, said: "Lord I am not worthy, I a sinner, so much as to lift mine eyes unto Heaven."

Concerning the divine offices at night. In the winter time, that is from the Calends of November until Easter, according to what is reasonable, they must rise at the eighth hour of the night [i.e., around 2 a.m.), so that they rest a little more than half the night, and rise when they have already digested. But let the time that remains after vigils be kept for meditation by those brothers who are in any way behind hand with the psalter or lessons. From Easter, moreover, until the aforesaid Calends of November, let the hour of keeeeping vigils be so arranged that, a short interval being observed in which the brethren may go out for the necessities of nature, the matins, which are always to take place with the dawning light, may straightway follow.

How many psalms are to be said at night. In the winter first of all the verse shall be said: "O God, come to my assistance; O Lord, make haste to help me." Then, secondly, there shall be said three times: "Oh Lord open my lips, and my mouth shall proclaim Thy praise." To which is to be subjoined the third psalm and the Gloria. After this the ninety-fourth psalm is to be sung antiphonally or in unison. The Ambrosian chant shall then follow: then six psalms antiphonally. These having been said, the abbot shall, with the verse mentioned, give the blessing. And all being seated upon the benches, there shall be read in turn from the Scriptures—following out the analogy— three lessons; between which also three responses shall be sung. Two responses shall be said without the *Gloria* [i.e., The doxology "Glory to the father, the Son, and the Holy Spirit, as it was in the beginning, is now, and ever shall be"]; but, after the third lesson, he who chants shall say the *Gloria.* And, when the cantor begins to say this, all shall straightway rise from their seats out of honour and reverence for the Holy Trinity. Books, moreover, of the old as well as the New Testament of Divine authority shall be read at the Vigils; but also expositions of them which have been made by the most celebrated orthodox teachers and catholic Fathers. Moreover, after these three lessons with their responses, shall follow other six psalms to be sung with the Alleluia. After this a lesson of the Apostle shall follow, to be recited by heart; and verses and the supplication of the Litany, that is the *Kyrie eleison*: and thus shall end the nocturnal vigils. ...

How Divine Service shall be held through the day. As the prophet says: "Seven times in the day so I praise Thee." Which sacred number of seven will thus be fulfilled by us if, at matins, at the first, third, sixth, ninth hours [i.e., roughly 6 a.m., 9 a.m., noon, and 3 p.m.], at vesper time and at *completorium* we perform the duties of our service; for it is of these hours of the day that he said: "Seven times in the day do I praise Thee." For, concerning nocturnal vigils, the same prophet says: "At midnight I arose to confess unto thee." Therefore, at these times, let us give thanks to our Creator concerning the judgments of his righteousness; that is, at matins, etc. ... and at night we will rise and confess to Him ...

How the monks shall sleep. They shall sleep separately in separate beds. They shall receive positions for their beds, after the manner of their characters, according to the dispensation of their abbot. If it can be done, they shall all sleep in one place. If, however, their number do not permit it, they shall rest by tens or twenties, with elders who will concern themselves about them. A candle shall always be burning in that same cell until early in the morning. They shall sleep clothed, and girt with belts or with ropes; and they shall not have their knives at their sides while they sleep, lest perchance in a dream they should wound the sleepers. And let the monks be always on the alert; and, when the signal is given, rising without delay, let them hasten to mutually prepare themselves for the service of God—with all gravity and modesty, however. The younger brothers shall not have beds by themselves, but interspersed among those of the elder ones. And when they rise for

the service of God, they shall exhort each other mutually with moderation on account of the excuses that those who are sleepy are inclined to make. ...

Concerning the amount of food. ... We believe, moreover, that, for the daily refection of the sixth as well as of the ninth hour, two cooked dishes, on account of the infirmities of the different ones, are enough for all tables: so that whoever, perchance, can not eat of one may partake of the other. Therefore let two cooked dishes suffice for all the brothers: and, if it is possible to obtain apples or growing vegetables, a third may be added. One full pound of bread shall suffice for a day, whether there be one refection, or a breakfast and a supper. But if they are going to have supper, the third part of that same pound shall be reserved by the cellarer, to be given back to those who are about to sup. But if, perchance, some greater labour shall have been performed, it shall be in the will and power of the abbot, if it is expedient, to increase anything; surfeiting above all things being guarded against, so that indigestion may never seize a monk: for nothing is so contrary to every Christian as surfeiting, as our Lord says: "Take heed to yourselves, lest your hearts be overcharged with surfeiting." But to younger boys the same quantity shall not be served, but less than that to the older ones; moderation being observed in all things. But the eating of the flesh of quadrupeds shall be abstained from altogether by every one, excepting alone the weak and the sick. ...

Concerning the amount of drink. Each one has his own gift from God, the one in this way, the other in that. Therefore it is with some hesitation that the amount of daily sustenance for others is fixed by us. Nevertheless, in view of the weakness of the infirm we believe that a hemina[1] of wine a day is enough for each one. Those moreover to whom God gives the ability of bearing abstinence shall know that they will have their own reward. But the prior shall judge if either the needs of the place, or labour or the heat of summer, requires more; considering in all things lest satiety or drunkenness creep in. Indeed we read that wine is not suitable for monks at all. But because, in our day, it is

---

[1] *hemina* About half a pint.

not possible to persuade the monks of this, let us agree at least as to the fact that we should not drink till we are sated, but sparingly. For wine can make even the wise to go astray. Where, moreover, the necessities of the place are such that the amount written above can not be found—but much less or nothing at all—those who live there shall bless God and shall not murmur. And we admonish them to this above all: that they be without murmuring. …

Concerning the daily manual labour. Idleness is the enemy of the soul. And therefore, at fixed times, the brothers ought to be occupied in manual labour; and again, at fixed times, in sacred reading. Therefore we believe that, according to this disposition, both seasons ought to be arranged; so that, from Easter until the Calends of October, going out early, from the first until the fourth hour [i.e., roughly 6–10 a.m.] they shall do what labour may be necessary. Moreover, from the fourth hour until about the sixth, they shall be free for reading. After the meal of the sixth hour, moreover, rising from table, they shall rest in their beds with all silence; or, perchance, he that wishes to read may so read to himself that he do not disturb another. And the *nona* (the second meal) shall be gone through with more moderately about the middle of the eighth hour; and again they shall work at what is to be done until Vespers. But, if the exigency or poverty of the place demands that they be occupied by themselves in picking fruits, they shall not be dismayed: for then they are truly monks if they live by the labours of their hands; as did also our fathers and the apostles. Let all things be done with moderation, however, on account of the faint-hearted. From the Calends of October, moreover, until the beginning of Lent they shall be free for reading until the second full hour. At the second hour the *tertia* (morning service) shall be held, and all shall labour at the task which is enjoined upon them until the ninth. The first signal, moreover, of the ninth hour having been given, they shall each one leave off his work; and be ready when the second signal strikes. Moreover after the refection they shall be free for their reading or for psalms. But in the days of Lent, from dawn until the third full hour, they shall be free for their readings; and, until the tenth full hour, they shall do the labour that is enjoined on them. In which days of Lent they shall all

receive separate books from the library; which they shall read entirely through in order. These books are to be given out on the first day of Lent. Above all there shall certainly be appointed one or two elders, who shall go round the monastery at the hours in which the brothers are engaged in reading, and see to it that no troublesome brother chance to be found who is open to idleness and trifling, and is not intent on his reading; being not only of no use to himself, but also stirring up others.

from *The Ancrene Wisse*

As St. Benedict expressed it, anchorites and anchoresses lived "the solitary life of the hermit." Unlike hermits of the very early days of Christianity, however, they lived in groups rather than in absolute isolation. *The Ancrene Wisse*, a set of rules for a group of English anchoresses, dates from the early thirteenth century.

[Temptations] … An anchoress thinks that she shall be most strongly tempted in the first twelve months after she shall have begun her monastic life, and in the next twelve thereafter; and when, after many years, she feels them so strong, she is greatly amazed, and is afraid lest God may have quite forgotten her, and cast her off. Nay! it is not so. In the first years, it is nothing but ball-play; but now, observe well, by a comparison, how it fares. When a man has brought a new wife home, he, with great gentleness, observes her manners. Though he sees in her some thing that he does not approve, yet he takes no notice of it, and puts on a cheerful countenance toward her, and carefully uses every means to make her love him, affectionately in her heart; and when he is well assured that her love is truly fixed upon him, he may then, with safety, openly correct her faults, which he previously bore with as if he knew them not: he becomes right stern, and assumes a severe countenance, in order still to test whether her love toward him might give way. At last when he perceives that she is completely instructed—that for nothing that he does to her does she love him less, but more and more, if possible, from day to day, then he shows her that he loves her sweetly, and does whatsoever she desires, as to one whom he loves and knows—then is all that sorrow become joy. If Jesu Christ, your Spouse, does thus to you, my dear sisters, let it not seem strange to you. For in the beginning it is only courtship, to draw you into love; but as soon as he perceives that he is on a footing of affectionate familiarity with you, he will now have less forbearance with you; but after the trial—in the end—then is the great joy....

Of sight, and of speech, and of the other senses enough was said. Now this last part, as I promised you at the commencement, is divided and separated into seven small sections.

Men esteem a thing as less dainty when they have it often, and therefore you should be, as lay brethren are, partakers of the holy communion only fifteen times a year: at midwinter [December 25]; Candlemas [February 2]; Twelfth-day [January 6]; on Sunday halfway between that and Easter, or our Lady's Day [March 25], if it is near the Sunday, because of its being a holiday; Easter Day; the third Sunday thereafter; Holy Thursday [that is, Ascension Day, forty days after Easter]; Whitsunday [that is, Pentecost, six weeks after Easter]; and Midsummer Day [June 24]; St. Mary Magdalen's Day [July 22]; the Assumption [August 15]; the Nativity [of the Virgin Mary, September 8]; St. Michael's Day [September 29]; All Saints' Day [November 1]; St. Andrew's Day [November 30]. And before all these days, see that you make a full confession and undergo discipline; but never from any man, only from yourselves. And forego your pittance for one day. And if any thing happens out of the usual order, so that you may not have received the sacrament at these set times, you may make up for it the Sunday next following, or if the other set time is near, you may wait till then.

You shall eat twice every day from Easter until the later Holyrood Day [September 14], which is in harvest, except on Fridays, and Ember Days [that is, days of fasting and prayer in each season of the year], and procession days and vigils. In those days, and in the Advent, you shall not eat any thing white, except when necessity requires it. The other half year you shall fast always, except only on Sundays.

You shall eat no flesh nor lard except in great sickness; or whosoever is infirm may eat potage without scruple; and accustom yourselves to little drink.

Nevertheless, dear sisters, your meat and your drink have seemed to me less than I would have it. Fast no day upon bread and water, unless you have permission. There are anchoresses who make their meals with their friends outside the convent. That is too much friendship, because, of all orders, this is most ungenial, and most contrary to the order of an anchoress, who is quite dead to the world. We have often heard it said that dead men speak with living men; but that they eat with living men, I have never yet found. Make no banquetings, nor encourage any strange vagabond fellows to come to the gate; though no other evil come of it but their immoderate talking, it might sometimes prevent heavenly thoughts.

It is not fit that an anchoress should be liberal with other men's alms. Would we not laugh loud to scorn a beggar who should invite men to a feast? Mary and Martha were two sisters, but their lives were different. You anchorites have taken to yourselves Mary's part, whom our Lord himself commended. "Mary hath chosen the best part. Martha, Martha," said he, "thou art much cumbered. Mary hath chosen better, and nothing shall take her part from her." Housewifery is Martha's part, and Mary's part is quietness and rest from all the world's din, that nothing may hinder her from hearing the voice of God. And observe what God saith, "that nothing shall take away this part from you." Martha has her office; let her alone, and sit with Mary stone-still at God's feet, and listen to Him alone. Martha's office is to feed and clothe poor men, as the mistress of a house. Mary ought not to intermeddle in it, and if anyone blame her, God Himself supreme defends her for it, as Holy Writ bears witness. On the other hand, an anchoress ought to take sparingly only that which is necessary for her. Whereof, then, may she make herself liberal? She must live upon alms, as frugally as ever she can, and not gather that she may give it away afterwards. She is not a housewife, but a church anchoress. If she can spare any fragments for the poor, let her send them quite privately out of her dwelling. Sin is oft concealed under the semblance of goodness. And how shall those rich anchoresses that are tillers of the ground, or have fixed rents, do their alms privately to poor neighbors? Desire not to have the reputation of bountiful anchoresses, nor, in order to give much, be too eager to possess more. Greediness is the root of bitterness: all the boughs that spring from it are bitter. To beg in order to give away is not the part of an anchoress. From the courtesy of an anchoress, and from her liberality, sin and shame have often come in the end.

Make women and children who have labored for you to eat whatever food you can spare from your own meals; but let no man eat in your presence, except he be in great need; nor invite him to drink anything. Nor do I desire that you should be told that you are courteous anchoresses. From a good friend take whatever you have need of when she offers it to you; but for no invitation take anything without need, lest you get the name of gathering anchoresses. Of a man whom you distrust, receive neither less nor more—not so much as a race of ginger. It must be great need that shall drive you to ask any thing; yet humbly show your distress to your dearest friend.

You shall not possess any beast, my dear sisters, except only a cat. An anchoress that hath cattle appears as Martha was, a better housewife than anchoress; nor can she in any wise be Mary, with peacefulness of heart. For then she must think of the cow's fodder, and of the herdsman's hire, flatter the hayward, defend herself when her cattle is shut up in the pinfold, and moreover pay the damage. Christ knows, it is an odious thing when people in the town complain of anchoresses' cattle. If, however, anyone must needs have a cow, let her take care that she neither annoy nor harm anyone, and that her own thoughts be not fixed thereon. An anchoress ought not to have anything that draws her heart outward. Carry on no business. An anchoress that is a buyer and seller sells her soul to the chapman of hell. Do not take charge of other men's property in your house, nor of their cattle, nor their clothes, neither receive under your care the church vestments, nor the chalice, unless force compel you, or great fear, for oftentimes much harm has come from such care-taking. Let no man sleep within your walls. If, however, great necessity should cause your house to be used, see that, as long as it is used, you have therein with you a woman of unspotted life day and night.

Because no man sees you, nor do you see any man, you may be well content with your clothes, be they white, be they black; only see that they be plain, and

warm, and well made—skins well tawed; and have as many as you need, for bed and also for back.

Next to your flesh you shall wear no flaxen cloth, except it be of hard and coarse canvas … You shall sleep in a garment and belted. Wear no iron, nor haircloth, nor hedgehog-skins; and do not beat yourselves therewith, nor with a scourge of leather thongs, nor leaded; and do not with holly nor with briars cause yourselves to bleed without leave of your confessor; and do not, at one time, use too many flagellations. Let your shoes be thick and warm. In summer you are at liberty to go and to sit barefoot, and to wear hose without vamps, and whoever likes may sleep in them … She who wishes to be seen, it is no great wonder that she adorn herself; but, in the eyes of God, she is more lovely who is unadorned outwardly for his sake. Have neither ring, nor brooch, nor ornamented girdle, nor gloves, nor any such thing that is not proper for you to have.

I am always the more gratified, the coarser the works are that you do. Make no purses, to gain friends therewith …; but shape, and sew, and mend church vestments, and poor people's clothes. You shall give nothing away without leave from your father confessor. Assist with your own labor, as far as you are able, to clothe yourselves and your domestics, as St. Jerome teaches. Be never idle; for the fiend immediately offers his work to her who is not diligent in God's work, and he begins directly to talk to her. … An anchoress must not become a schoolmistress, nor turn her anchoress-house into a school for children. Her maiden may, however, teach any little girl concerning whom it might be doubtful whether she should learn among boys, but an anchoress ought to give her thoughts to God only.

You shall not send, nor receive, nor write letters without leave. You shall have your hair cut four times a year to unburden your head; and be bled as oft, and oftener if it is necessary; but if anyone can dispense with this, I may well suffer it. When you are bled, you ought to do nothing that may be irksome to you for three days; but talk with your maidens, and divert yourselves together with instructive tales. You may often do so when you feel dispirited, or are grieved about some worldly matter, or sick. Thus wisely take care of yourselves when you are bled, and keep yourselves in such rest that long thereafter you may labor the more vigorously in God's service, and also when you feel any sickness, for it is great folly, for the sake of one day, to lose ten or twelve. Wash yourselves wheresoever it is necessary, as often as you please.

When an anchoress does not have her food at hand, let two women be employed, one who stays always at home, another who goes out when necessary; and let her be very plain, or of sufficient age. ... Let neither of the women either carry to her mistress or bring from her any idle tales, or new tidings, nor sing to one another, nor speak any worldly speeches, nor laugh, nor play, so that any man who saw it might turn it to evil. ... No servant of an anchoress ought, properly, to ask stated wages, except food and clothing, with which, and with God's mercy, she may do well enough. ... Whoever has any hope of so high a reward will gladly serve, and easily endure all grief and all pain. With ease and abundance men do not arrive at heaven.

Franciscan Friars

Whereas the early monastic movements embodied a Christian striving for purity and simplicity, by the twelfth century monasteries were widely regarded as sites of wealth and corruption. The friars represented in later medieval Christianity many of the same ideals that the monks professed in earlier centuries. But rather than seeking a better life by removing themselves from the world, friars aimed to travel and preach and combat heresy and heal, all the while maintaining strict vows of poverty and chastity. St. Francis (c. 1182–1226) founded the largest order of friars; excerpts from his Rule appear below.

1. In the name of the Lord, the life of the lesser brothers begins.

The rule and life of the lesser brothers is this: To observe the Holy Gospel of our Lord Jesus Christ, living in obedience without anything of our own, and in chastity. Brother Francis promises obedience and reverence to the Lord Pope Honorius and his canonically elected successors, and to the Roman Church; and the rest of the brothers are obliged to obey Francis and his successors.

A Friar, preaching. Nineteenth-century copy of an illustration from British Library MS Royal XIVE (early 14th century). The friar stands barefoot, outdoors, on a portable pulpit.

2. Concerning those who wish to adopt this life.

... Let those who have promised obedience take one tunic with a hood, and let those who wish it have another without a hood. And those who must may wear shoes. All the brothers are to wear inexpensive clothing, and they can use sackcloth and other material to mend it with God's blessing.

3. Concerning the divine office and fasting; and how the brothers ought to travel through the world.

Clerics are to perform the divine office according to the rite of the Roman Church, except for the Psalter, and they can have breviaries for that purpose. Laymen are to say twenty-four "Our Fathers" at matins; five at lauds; seven each at prime, terce, sext and none; twelve at vespers; and seven at compline. They should also pray for the dead.

They should fast from the feast of all saints until Christmas. Those who voluntarily fast at Quadragessima, those forty days after Epiphany which the Lord consecrated with his own holy fasting, will themselves be blessed by the Lord; yet they are not required to do so if they do not want to. They must fast during Lent, but they are not required to do so at other times except on Fridays. In case of obvious necessity, however, they are excused from bodily fasting.

I counsel, admonish and beg my brothers that, when they travel about the world, they should not be quarrelsome, dispute with words, or criticize others, but rather should be gentle, peaceful and unassuming, courteous and humble, speaking respectfully to all as is fitting. They must not ride on horseback unless forced to so by obvious necessity or illness. Whatever house they enter, they are first to say, "Peace to this house" (Luke 10.5). According to the Holy Gospel they can eat whatever food is set before them.

4. That the brothers should not accept money.

I strictly forbid the brothers to receive money in any form either directly or through an intermediary. Nevertheless, the ministers and custodians can work through spiritual friends to care for the sick and clothe the brothers, according to place, season and climate, as necessity may seem to demand. This must be done, however, in such a way that they do not receive money.

5. On their manner of working.

Those brothers whom the Lord favors with the gift of working should do so faithfully and devotedly, so that idleness, the enemy of the soul, is excluded yet the spirit of holy prayer and devotion, which all other temporal things should serve, is not extinguished. As payment for their labor let them receive that which is necessary for themselves and their brothers, but not money. Let them receive it humbly as befits those who serve God and seek after the holiest poverty.

6. That the brothers should appropriate nothing for themselves; and on how alms should be begged; and concerning sick brothers.

The brothers should appropriate neither house, nor place, nor anything for themselves; and they should go confidently after alms, serving God in poverty and humility, as pilgrims and strangers in this world. Nor should they feel ashamed, for God made Himself poor in this world for us. This is that peak of the highest poverty which has made you, my dearest brothers, heirs and kings of the kingdom of heaven, poor in things but rich in virtues. Let this be your portion. It leads into the land of the living and, adhering totally to it, for the sake of our Lord Jesus Christ wish never to have anything else in this world, beloved brothers.

And wherever brothers meet one another, let them act like members of a common family. And let them securely make their needs known to one another, for if a mother loves and cares for her carnal son, how much more should one love and care for his spiritual son? And if one of them should become ill, let the other brothers serve him as they themselves would like to be served....

9. On preachers.

The friars must not preach in the diocese of any bishop if they have been forbidden to do so by him. And no brother should dare preach to the people unless he has been examined and approved by the minister general of his brotherhood and the office of preaching has been conceded to him. I also admonish and exhort the brothers that in their preaching their words be studied and chaste, useful and edifying to the people, telling them about vices and virtues, punishment and glory; and they ought to be brief, because the Lord kept His words brief when He was on earth.

10. On the admonition and correction of brothers.

Brothers who are ministers and servants of other brothers must visit and admonish their brothers, and they should correct them humbly and lovingly, prescribing nothing against their soul or our rule. Brothers who are subject to authority must remember that they have surrendered their own wills for the sake of God. ...

I admonish and exhort the brothers in the Lord Jesus Christ to beware of all pride, vainglory, envy, avarice, worldly care and concern, criticism and complaint. And I admonish the illiterate not to worry about studying but to realize instead that above all they should wish to have the spirit of the Lord working within them, and that they should pray to him constantly with a pure heart, be humble, be patient in persecution and infirmity, and love those who persecute, blame or accuse us....

11. That the brothers should not enter the convents of nuns.

I strictly order all the brothers to avoid suspicious meetings or conversations with women and to stay out of the convents of nuns except in cases where special permission has been granted by the Holy See. Nor should they be godfathers of men or women, lest it lead to scandal among or concerning the brothers.

12. Concerning those who go among the Saracens and other infidels.

Whoever should, by divine inspiration, wish to go among the Saracens and other infidels must ask permission from their provincial ministers. The ministers should grant permission only to those whom they consider qualified to be sent.

I enjoin the ministers by obedience to ask the Lord Pope for a cardinal of the Holy Roman Church to serve as governor, protector and corrector of their brotherhood so that we servants and subjects at the feet of Holy Church, firm in faith, will always observe the poverty, humility and Holy Gospel of our Lord Jesus Christ which we firmly promised.

Scholasticism

In the wake of the rediscovery of Aristotelian and other classical works of philosophy, theological discourse in the late eleventh and twelfth centuries began to become far more abstract and densely reasoned than had previously been the case; theologians were now keen to demonstrate that faith was in complete harmony with the dictates of reason. One of the most important of these university-influenced "scholastics" was St. Anselm, Archbishop of Canterbury from 1093 to 1109. Anselm's great contribution to theology was the argument that has come to be known as the "ontological proof" for the existence of God.

from St. Anselm, *Proslogion* (c. 1080)

I acknowledge, Lord, and I give thanks that you have created in me this Your image, so that I can remember You, think about You and love You. But it is so worn away by sins, so smudged over by the smoke of sins, that it cannot do what it was created to do unless You renew and reform it. I do not even try, Lord, to rise up to Your heights, because my intellect does not measure up to that task; but I do want to understand in some small measure Your truth, which my heart believes in and loves. Nor do I seek to understand so that I can believe, but rather I believe so that I can understand. For I believe this too, that "unless I believe I shall not understand."[1]

2. That God Really Exists

Therefore, Lord, You who give knowledge of the faith, give me as much knowledge as You know to be fitting for me, because you are as we believe and that which we believe. And indeed we believe You are something greater than which cannot be thought. Or is there no such kind of thing, for "the fool said in his heart, there is no God"?[2] But certainly that same fool, having heard what I just said, "something greater than which cannot be thought," understands what he heard, and what he understands is in his thought, even if he does not think it exists. For it is one thing for something to exist in a person's thought and quite another for the person to think that thing exists. For when a painter thinks ahead to what he will paint, he has that picture in his thought, but he does not yet think it exists, because he has not done it yet. Once he has painted it he has it in his thought and thinks it exists because he has done it. Thus even the fool is compelled to grant that something greater than which cannot be thought exists in thought, because he understands what he hears, and whatever is

---

[1] *unless I believe I shall not understand* See Isaiah 7.9.

[2] *the fool said ... no God* See Psalms 13.1, 52.1.

understood exists in thought. And certainly that greater than which cannot be understood cannot exist only in thought, for if it exists only in thought it could also be thought of as existing in reality as well, which is greater. If, therefore, that than which greater cannot be thought exists in thought alone, then that than which greater cannot be thought turns out to be that than which something greater actually can be thought, but that is obviously impossible. Therefore something than which greater cannot be thought undoubtedly exists both in thought and in reality.

3. That God Cannot Be Thought Not to Exist

In fact, it so undoubtedly exists that it cannot be thought of as not existing. For one can think there exists something that cannot be thought of as not existing, and that would be greater than something which can be thought of as not existing. For if that greater than which cannot be thought can be thought of as not existing, then that greater than which cannot be thought is not that greater than which cannot be thought, which does not make sense. Thus that than which nothing can be thought so undoubtedly exists that it cannot even be thought of as not existing.

And you, Lord God, are this being. You exist so undoubtedly, my Lord God, that you cannot even be thought of as not existing.

Truly there is a God, although the fool hath said in his heart, There is no God.

And so, Lord, do thou, who dost give understanding to faith, give me, so far as thou knowest it to be profitable, to understand that thou art as we believe; and that thou art that which we believe. And, indeed, we believe that thou art a being than which nothing greater can be conceived. Or is there no such nature, since the fool hath said in his heart, there is no God? But, at any rate, this very fool, when he hears of this being of which I speak—a being than which nothing greater can be conceived—understands what he hears, and what he understands is in his understanding; although he does not understand it to exist.

For, it is one thing for an object to be in the understanding, and another to understand that the object exists. When a painter first conceives of what he will afterwards perform, he has it in his understanding, but he does not yet understand it to be, because he has not yet performed it. But after he has made the painting, he both has it in his understanding, and he understands that it exists, because he has made it.

Hence, even the fool is convinced that something exists in the understanding, at least, than which nothing greater can be conceived. For, when he hears of this, he understands it. And whatever is understood, exists in the understanding. And assuredly that, than which nothing greater can be conceived, cannot exist in the understanding alone. For, suppose it exists in the understanding alone: then it can be conceived to exist in reality; which is greater.

Therefore, if that, than which nothing greater can be conceived, exists in the understanding alone, the very being, than which nothing greater can be conceived, is one, than which a greater can be conceived. But obviously this is impossible. Hence, there is no doubt that there exists a being, than which nothing greater can be conceived, and it exists both in the understanding and in reality. …

… For no one who understands what fire and water are can conceive fire to be water, in accordance with the nature of the facts themselves, although this is possible according to the words. So, then, no one who understands what God is can conceive that God does not exist; although he says these words in his heart, either without any, or with some foreign, signification. For, God is that than which greater cannot be conceived. And he who thoroughly understands this, assuredly understands that this being so truly exists, that not even in concept can it be non-existent. Therefore, he who understands that God so exists, cannot conceive that he does not exists. …

The Miraculous and the Strange

from *The Miracles of Thomas of Becket*

In the medieval period records of miracles associated with saints were often kept at saints' shrines. These miracles were alleged to be either a result of contact with a relic of a saint, or of the saint's direct involvement. The largest collection of such records is that associated with Thomas Becket, the Archbishop of Canterbury who was murdered (allegedly on the orders of King Henry II) in 1170.

[Miracles of 1171] Book 2, Chapter 7. Edilda, a woman from Canterbury, was left at the shrine, carried with the help of three women. It had now been about a year and half since she could stand on her foot. During that whole time she had lived as if on the brink of death, confined to bed. The disease was especially severe in her left knee, which through the contraction of the muscles prevented her from walking. Her knee reeled with pain if the woman happened to touch it even lightly with her hand. She was carried to the martyr by three women, as we said, and propped on a staff; she returned home with her pain relieved. In witness of her recovered health, before us all with her upraised fist she struck her knee a hard blow, which since the second year of her illness she could not touch because of the pain. The people saw her walking about and praising the Lord; they were filled with wonder and amazed over what had happened to her. But we refrain from discussing why she remained lame and did not regain complete health, considering it more prudent to keep totally silent about God's secret judgments than to draw rash conclusions from them.

Chapter 8. But we know that He who strengthened that woman's weak knee was capable of making her feet and soles completely firm so that she could have walked normally, just as we have no doubt that He did grant this to Wlviva, a woman from Canterbury. Satan had bound her for three years already, and she was bent over, unable to walk anywhere without a crutch. She fell down before the saint for a short prayer and, with the pain gone from her loins, she rose standing straight up without her crutch, wanting no longer to carry the thing that had once supported her. …

Chapter 12. Robert, a blacksmith from the Isle of Thanet, also found the grace of healing, but the vision that preceded the gift of his cure is no less wonderful. He had been blind for at least two years; the loss of his livelihood troubled him more than his lost sight. But then, after our venerable father had been called home from exile, around the time when he was called to heaven from the exile of this world [i.e., Dec. 29], this man heard this oracle in a dream: "Go, Robert, to Christ Church Canterbury; a monk will put milk in your eyes and you will recover your sight." But at first he thought he was deluded: he neither believed the promise nor obeyed the command. Yet later, when he heard that God's saint practically glittered with miracles, he recalled what he had heard and, equating this sweetest lamb's innocent blood to milk's sweetness, he began to hope for a cure. With the guidance of his wife and daughter (for we understand they accompanied him), he arrived where he had been ordered to go. After daubing his eyes with the longed-for blood of the martyr, he prostrated himself in prayer. While face-down, he felt his head racked by what seemed like a loud thunderclap and he regained his sight. Getting up, he publicly preached God's grace.

Chapter 13. But what is easier: to restore health to the body or the mind? He who restored sight to physical eyes restored sanity to the young man, Henry of Fordwich. He had been insane for some days and had accidentally wounded his friends due to his pain. With his hands bound behind him, he was dragged to the saint. He was presented to the saint even though he was struggling and shouting. He remained there insane for the whole day, but as the light of the sun waned, he started gradually to recover the light of reason. He spent the night in the church and went back home in the morning completely recovered.

Chapter 14. We received a woman from the vicinity of the same town who not only could not hear but was also troubled by an unbearable pain in the head. That universal medicine of the sick—water mixed with the blood—was poured into her stopped ears; she was also given some to drink, and then threw herself into prayer. While she prayed she suffered more bitterly than before and she thought [she heard] many twigs being snapped in pieces inside her head. She asked those standing around whether they heard the noise in her head. But while she was being racked this way, she cried out to the

Lord and he heard her. For as she shouted, a great deal of matter flowed out of her ears, as if some inner abscess had ruptured. The matter was followed by blood, and the blood by the gift [of the return] of her lost hearing.

Chapter 15. Eilward, a man from Tenham, for some years had lost the pleasures of the sense of smell and could smell absolutely nothing. He entered that place where rests that good odor of the anointed one, that sweet victim, that scented tree, whose aroma the whole world now senses; but before he had reached that fragrant flower of England, there came to him the sweetest perfume filling his nostrils, and he rejoiced to recover his smell.

Chapter 16. We think that it should not be forgotten that, while many people obtained a longed-for healing, one person was denied outright. For the holy father [Becket] came to a crippled boy who had gone seeking a favor from the martyr and had fallen asleep with his head resting on top of the tomb. "Why are you lying on me?" he asked, "You certainly will not be healed. Go away. I'll do nothing for you." These words woke him up, and he told us and his mother what he had heard with great sadness of heart. Convinced by the adamancy of the [saint's] words, he had himself taken elsewhere. Still, we urged him to press on with his prayers, and he agreed; but time passed and he did not regain his health....

Book 3, Chapter 2. There was a man of the common folk, Eilward by name, in the king's town of Weston in the county of Bedford. One of his neighbors, Fulk, owed him two pennies of rent for a portion of plowland; he had paid part but put off paying the rest until the following year with the excuse that he did not have the money. One day after the Feast of the Passion of the Blessed Martyr [Thomas] when they were both by chance going to the alehouse together (for it is the English custom to indulge in feasting and drinking on feast days, which makes them seem to be enemies and scorners of their holy days), Eilward asked for his money and Fulk swore that he did not owe him. Eilward asked him to pay half, as he was going to have some beer, and

keep the other half for himself, likewise for beer. When Fulk completely denied that he was in debt to him, the other said that he would get even with him.

After both of them got drunk at the tavern, getting up on some pretext, Eilward left before Fulk and turned aside to Fulk's cottage, tore away the bar to the door, and broke into the house, turned burglar as much through rashness as through drunkenness. Going through the house looking for what he could take, he stumbled upon a large grindstone and some gloves which country people are wont to wear on their hands to protect them from the sharp points of thorns. The poor robber stole these, both of them together scarcely worth a penny. The boys playing together in the yard of the house cried out, and running to the tavern, called out to their father to come get his property back. Striking him, Fulk wrenched the grindstone from him and, brandishing it over the robber's head, he as much broke the grindstone with Eilward's head as he smashed his head with the grindstone. Baring a sharp-pointed knife he carried, he stabbed him in the arm. Overcoming him, he bound the miserable man and led him as a thief and robber back to the house he had broken into. He summoned Fulk[1] the town beadle to find out what he should do with the prisoner. "The charge for which he has been seized," he said, "is not serious enough and insufficient. But if you make the robbery more serious by producing him loaded with other things that appear stolen, you can prosecute him to be punished for the crime." Fulk agreed and fastened around his prisoner's neck an awl, a two-edged axe, a net, and some clothes together with the grindstone and the gloves, and on the following day brought him thus before the king's officers.

Having been thus taken to Bedford, he was kept in prison there for a month. He sent for a priest, the reverend Paganus, so that, faced with the ultimate danger, he could prepare himself for death—or rather for life; and going over all the secrets of his conscience, whatever he found contrary to his salvation, he poured into the safely-sealed ears of the priest. Putting his trust in divine mercy for the deliverance of his body, he said, "Dearest sir, if I escape this moment of danger, I will go on foot to the land that the Son of God, our Lord Jesus made holy by his life on earth and death. And so I beg to have

---

[1] *Fulk* I.e., another man of the same name.

the sign of the cross branded on my right shoulder with a hot iron so that no one has the power to strip it from me even though my clothes are stripped away." The priest branded him accordingly, but also suggested that he should devoutly seek the protection of the saints, and especially of the glorious martyr St. Thomas whom the Lord magnified by such glorious signs. Moreover, he measured the length and breadth of his body with a thread with which to make a candle to be offered to the martyr for his release. He also gave him a scourge made of branches, saying, "Take these branches and five times a day before you take a little food, become your own torturer, and do not cease day and night to kneel to the martyr and call upon him except when, overcome by the annoyance of sleep, you are compelled to succumb to the weakness of human nature." Thus carefully instructing him, he left him, saying that the judges had forbidden any priest to have further access to him. However, he sent for him many times and he secretly announced himself at the window either to rouse him from negligence [in his devotions] or to further kindle his zeal. Also, Galfrid, the prior of the canons of Bedford (whose witness we have for this admirable miracle) often supplied him with needed food, visited him in prison, and—for him to have at least an hour of fresh air—took him from the jail and had him walk around under the open sky.

When four weeks had passed and the fifth begun, this poor man was led from jail and taken before the court for trial. His accuser charged him with the crime of theft; he consistently denied the charge, further objecting that he had taken none of the things hanging around his neck except for the grindstone and the gloves which he admitted taking, but only as a pledge for Fulk's debt, which had motivated the theft and the crime. The judgment was put off so he was again remanded into custody.

Brought out again in the fifth week and taken before the court, he was now charged by his accuser only with the theft of the grindstone and the gloves. For his accuser feared to undergo the trial by combat demanded by the accused, and his silence condemned all his previous charges; but—having the viscount and the judges on his side—he managed to free himself from the

obligation to fight, and to arrange that the accused should be tried by the ordeal of water.

Now it was the Sabbath, and the examination was put off until the third day of the following week, he himself being kept again in prison. The cruelty of his keeper forbade him to keep vigil in the church—a right conceded by the compassion of religion to all who are to purge themselves by ordeal from criminal charge. In prison, however, he devoutly kept the watch that he was not allowed to keep in the church.

When brought out to the water [for the ordeal], he was met by the priest Paganus, mentioned earlier, who exhorted him to bear everything patiently in remission of his sins, to hold no hatred and anger in his heart, to forgive sincerely all his enemies for all they had done to him, and not to despair of God's mercy. And he replied, "May the will of God and of the martyr Thomas be done in me."

After being plunged into the water, he was found guilty. The beadle Fulk now seized him, saying, "Follow me, rascal, follow me!" "Thanks be to God," he replied, "and to the holy martyr Thomas." Dragged to the place of punishment, he was deprived of his eyes and his genitals were lopped off. As for his left eye, they at once extracted that whole; but his right eye, after being sliced and cut in pieces, was at last with difficulty gouged out. The members which they had chopped off him they hid under the sod; and—like what is read about the man who "fell in with robbers"—"after both stripping him and beating him" (as described above) "they went their way, leaving him half-dead" [Luke 10.30].

His accuser Fulk and the official of the same name (by whose suggestion and advice this man is believed to have been brought into this misery) and also two other executioners with them mutilated him. When, however, they asked pardon for the love of God and St. Thomas the martyr, he willingly forgave them, crying aloud with a wonderful faith that he would go to the martyr's memorial, blind though he was, and he would not despair of the martyr's holiness and power, knowing that it was more glorious for the martyr to restore eyes that had been taken away than to preserve them when not taken.

He was escorted only by his twelve-year-old daughter, who had also begged food for him while he was incarcerated. For all his goods were confiscated, all his friends spurned him, and there was not one of all those dear to him to console him. Such a great amount of blood gushed from his wounds that, in fear of his death, those who were present sent for a priest to whom he confessed. By degrees, however, when the flow of blood was assuaged, led by the little girl, he returned to Bedford, where he threw himself down against the wall of a house; and all that day, until evening, no man showed him kindness. But at nightfall, one Eilbrict took compassion on him, especially since the weather was inclement and he was lying there vexed by a downpour of rain. He welcomed him rejoicing into his house.

He lay there in darkness for ten days, offering prayers and vigils. But at the first watch of the tenth night, after mourning, groaning, and sighing, as he relaxed in sleep he whom he had invoked appeared to him, clothed in snow-white garments. With his pastoral staff he painted the sign of the cross on his forehead and eyeless sockets and appeared to depart in silence. Waking up and disregarding the vision, he flung himself down again and went back to sleep. A second time before dawn he, who washed his garments in the blood of the Lamb, returned dressed in white. He said to the man, "Good man, are you sleeping?" When he acknowledged that he was awake, the man in white said, "Do not sleep, do not sleep, but watch and press on with your prayers. Do not despair but put your hope in God, the Blessed Virgin Mary, and St. Thomas who comes to visit you. If, tomorrow night, you keep watch with a waxen light before the Virgin's altar in the church of the Blessed Mary close by, and devote yourself in faith to praying, and have no doubts, you shall rejoice in the restoration of your eyes." Rousing from sleep, the man silently thought about what such a vision could mean—or rather whether once the hidden meaning was uncovered, the saint's promise would be fulfilled. Mulling over such a mysterious thing, taking it as news of a good omen, the maid-servant said, "Tonight, Eilward, I dreamed that you recovered sight in both your eyes." And he said, "So it may be when it shall please God and His blessed martyr Thomas."

When it was getting on toward evening, and daylight was declining, the eyelids of his left eye started itching. In order to scratch them, he removed a wax poultice which had been applied either to draw out the purulent matter in the empty orbs, or to close the eyelids themselves. Opening his eyelids, by the marvelous power of God it appeared to him as if a bright lantern were shining on the opposite wall of the house—it was the red sunlight, since the sun was by this time verging on setting. But he, ignorant of the truth and distrusting himself about the matter, called the master of the house and pointed out to him what he thought he saw. "You are mad, Eilward, you are mad," replied his host, "Be quiet. You don't know what you are saying." "I am not the least bit mad, sir," he said, "but I do seem to see what I say with my left eye." Shaken in his mind and anxious to ascertain the truth, his host spread out his hand before his eyes and said to him, "Do you see what I'm doing?" He answered, "I think your hand is waving before my eyes, moving back and forth." Then, starting with the beginning of the first vision, he told Eilbrict step by step what he had seen and what he had been ordered and promised.

Word about this spread among the neighborhood, and this novelty of novelties attracted not a small multitude of people. The deacon Osbern, lord—or rather, minister—of the church mentioned earlier comes running. When he hears about the vision from the man, he takes him to the church, brings him before the altar of the Blessed Virgin, and instructs and strengthens his faith. Putting a light in his hand, he declares that he distinctly sees the altar cloth, then the image of the Blessed Virgin Mary, and then any other objects of smaller size.

People's amazement grows over how this man was favored with sight. Thus, when the strength of the vision in his new eyes (or rather empty sockets without pupils) proceeds to be put to the test, they detect two small pupils concealed deeply in his head, scarcely equal in size to the pupils of a small bird, which, still constantly growing, prolonged by their gradual increase in size the ineffable and incredible wonder of those beholding them.

The shouts of the people rise up to heaven; due praises are paid to God; church bells are rung; crowds flock in who were just about to go to bed, and sleepless they await the sunlight with the man restored to light.

In the morning a crowd of the whole town massed together. Closely examining him in the bright light, they noticed that one eye was parti-colored, the other quite black, though from birth both his eyes had been particolored. Now among others the priest from the church of St. John, who had heard his confession after the mutilation, ran up. Seeing this miracle of God's power he said, "Why are we waiting for papal instructions? No more delaying for me! This very moment I will begin and conduct to the end a solemn service in the name of Thomas, the glorious friend of God, indeed, the martyr beyond price. Who can hesitate to give the name martyr to one who does such mighty and such merciful deeds?" So he ran to the church, set the bells ringing, and was as good as his word.

This man, however, now no longer bereft of light but bedecked with it, as he had been dragged in disgrace through the middle of the town to be punished, so now through the self-same street, amid the praise and applause of the people, he is led back to the church of St. Paul where he also passed the eve of the Lord's Day in vigil. Departing from there he hastened on the way toward St. Thomas, the author of his healing. Wherever he passed, a great multitude of people followed him, for his fame flying along in front of him excited anyone on his way. Whatever gifts they gave him, he gave to the poor out of love for the martyr. He had completed about four miles of his journey when he started to scratch an itch on his testicle bag with his near hand, and he discovered that those members had also been restored to him, very small indeed but growing bigger, which he even did not refuse to anyone who wanted to feel them.

On his coming to London, he was received with congratulations by Hugh, Bishop of Durham, who would not let him leave him until he had sent a messenger to Bedford to make careful inquiry and had been made certain of the facts.

But even after we had received him in our house [at Canterbury], although he had been preceded by the testimony of very many witnesses, we did not feel satisfied until we heard the substance of the above-written statements confirmed by the letter and testimony of the citizens of Bedford. For they sent letters to us, the contents of which were as follows:

"The burgesses of Bedford to the convent of Canterbury and to all the faithful in Christ, greetings. Be it known to the convent of Canterbury and also to all Catholics that God has worked a wonderful and excellent miracle by the merits of the most holy martyr, Thomas. For it happened that a certain countryman of Weston by the name of Eilward was seized and taken before the viscount of Bedford and knights of the county for a theft valued at only a penny. He was publicly condemned by them and deprived of his eyes and genitals in the presence of clergy, men, and women. The chaplain of St. John of Bedford, to whom the aforesaid countryman confessed [after his mutilation] also testifies to this. And this same is testified by his host, named Eilbrict, in whose house he was afterwards received: namely that he was entirely without eyes or testicles when he was first received in his house. And afterwards, often invoking the merits of St. Thomas the martyr, by an apparition of the aforesaid martyr he was gloriously and miraculously restored to health." ...

Book 4. Chapter 45. Eilwacher of Dover was sailing to lesser Britain. A storm arose and he cast out three anchors but lost all of them through the cables breaking. However, he made it back to land after invoking the martyr. On the return of fair weather he returned with his companions to the sea to seek the anchors, for the place where he had lost them was not far from the land. For three days they searched and found nothing, so one of them said, "Let's also promise to the martyr of Canterbury a wax anchor so that he will give us back our iron ones." All agreed, and straightaway letting down into the water the instrument with which they were searching the bottom, they drew out all of the anchors. So they turned back to England and came to the martyr. They brought to him the gift they had promised. ...

Decorated box designed to hold relics of St. Thomas Becket (c. 1190).
The town of Limoges, from which this box originated in the late twelfth century, became part of the territory ruled by Henry II and Eleanor of Aquitaine with their marriage in 1152. Becket is shown at the altar, being attacked from behind.

Sin, Corruption, and Indulgence

from William Langland, *Piers Plowman* (B-text, c. 1377–81)

Langland's *Piers Plowman* is one of the major English literary texts of the fourteenth century—and also one of the most important historical documents in the overlapping histories of religious and secular developments during the period. The full poem is a long and in many ways a challenging and confusing text. It is framed as a Christian allegory, with characters such as Truth and Reason pronouncing on the ills of the world, and on the way to salvation. An important thread running through the poem is the attempt of an individual soul to seek out the stages that will lead to salvation; each of the various parts of the poem is called a "passus," or "step." The poem also includes powerful elements of social satire, in which many of the ways of the fourteenth-century world are harshly criticized. Chief among these are corrupt religious practices—perhaps most notably the practice of purchasing "indulgences" from the Church. (The principle of an indulgence was that a sacrifice of money, meant to help the Church with its financial obligations to the community, could ensure the forgiveness of the giver's sins.) Langland's text also includes wide-ranging criticisms of the greed and lack of charity that he saw as characterizing the behavior of the rich and privileged, nobles and clergy alike.

Langland did not advocate any revolutionary program to remedy society's ills and injustices; he intended to prick the consciences of the powerful to encourage them to mend their ways and carry out good works, but he did not intend to aid in any overthrow of their authority. Indeed, when it became clear that *Piers Plowman* was providing inspiration to the leaders of the uprising of 1381, Langland revised the poem in ways that made it less inflammatory.

Though Langland lived in London (he is believed to have held a modest position in the church), he eschewed the rhymed style of poetry that Chaucer and other Londoners had come to favor, preferring instead to write alliterative verse in a style reminiscent of that of Old English. (*Piers Plowman* is a key text in what scholars have come to refer to as the "alliterative revival" of the fourteenth century.) *Piers Plowman* has come down to us in many manuscripts, and exists in three versions, known as the A-, B-, and C- texts. The concise A-text and the considerably longer B-text are both more sharply critical of authority than is the C-text, which dates from after the 1381 rebellion (and in which Langland distances himself from the rebels' agenda).

Much as *Piers Plowman* is a central text of late medieval social protest, it is also a religious text and a spiritual allegory. The excerpts below give some sense both of the roots of social protest and of the degree to which what we would see as secular and religious elements are virtually inseparable in a text of this sort.

The first sixteen lines of the first Passus of the poem are provided below in the original as well as in a modernized version. As the selection from Passus 5 suggests, the poem has harsh advice for the common folk as well as for the well-to-do. But the prevailing note of criticism in the poem is of the sort

seen in the excerpt below from Passus 7; these lines
give some sense of the degree to which *Piers Plowman* takes in a broad sweep of the religious and
social life of the fourteenth century.

from PASSUS 1

What this mountaigne bymeneth and the merke dale
And the feld ful of folk, I shal yow faire shewe.
A lovely lady of leere in lynnen yclothed
Cam doun from castel and called me faire,
5   And seide, "Sone, slepestow? Sestow this peple—

How bisie they ben aboute the maze?
The mooste partie of this peple that passeth on this
        erthe,
Have thei worship in this world, thei wilne no bettre;
Of oother hevene than here holde thei no tale."

10   I was afered of hire face, theigh she faire weere,
And seide, "Mercy, madame, what this to mene?"
        "The tour upon the toft," quod she, "Truthe is
            therinne,
And wolde that ye wroughte as his word techeth,
For he is fader of feith and formed yow alle
15   Bothe with fel and with face and yaf yow fyve wittes
For to worshipe hymn therwith while that ye ben here."

What this mountain means, and the dark dale
And the field full of folk[1] I fairly will show.
A lady, lovely of looks, in linen clothed,
Came down from a castle, and called me fairly
And said, "Son, are you sleeping? Do you see these
        people,
How busy they are, all thronging about?
Most of the people that pass their time on earth,

Have honor in this world, and they wish for no better
They don't care about any heaven but the one here
            on earth."
    I was afraid of her face, though she was fair,
And I said, "Mercy, madam, what does this mean?"
        "The tower on the hill," she said, "Truth is therein

And he would like you to do as his word teaches;
For he is Father of Faith, who formed you all
Both with flesh and with face, and gave you five senses
To worship him with, while you are here."

---

[1] The Prologue introduces the narrative as a dream vision, in which
Piers recounts that he has seen a tower on a hilltop, and another in
a valley, and a fair field full of folk between the two:
    A faire field full of folk found I there between,
    Of all manner of men, the mean and the rich …

Passus 5

The king and his knights to the church went
To hear matins of the day, and the Mass after.
Then waked I from my winking, and felt woeful
That I had not slept sounder, and so seen more.
5   But ere I had traveled a furlong, faintness so seized me
That I could not go further on foot, for lack of my
      sleep,
And I sat softly down, and said my belief,
And as I babbled on my beads,[1] they brought me asleep.
      And then saw I much more than I have already told,
For I saw the field full of folk that I before spoke of,
10   And how Reason got ready to preach to the realm,
And with a cross before the king commenced in this way
      to teach.
He proved that these pestilences had to do purely
      with sin,
And the south-west wind on Saturday evening
15   Had plainly to do with pride, and for no point else.
Pear-trees and plum-trees were puffed to the earth
To show you people that you should do better.
Beeches and broad oaks were blown to the ground,
Their tails torn upwards, a dreadful sign
20   That at doomsday deadly sin shall be the sinners'
      undoing.
      Of this matter I may mumble at length
But I will say as I saw, God help me!
How plainly before the people Reason began to preach.
      He told Waster go work as best he could
25   And redeem himself for laziness with some sort of craft.
      And prayed that Pernele take off her costly array
And keep it in her box, in case she might need money
      later.
      Tom Stowe he taught to take two staves
And bring home Phyllis from women's punishment.
30   He warned Wat that his wife was to blame,
Saying that her hat was worth half a mark, but his hood
      cost not even a groat.
      And he bade Batt cut down a bough or even two
With which to beat Betty unless she would work.

from Passus 7

Truth heard what was happening, and sent word to
      Piers
To take his team and to till the earth;
And Truth provided a pardon *a poena et a culpa*[2]
For him, and for his heirs, for evermore after.
5   And told him to stay at home, and plow up his fields,
And those that helped him to plow, to plant, or to sow,
Or any other work that might help Piers–
They too were granted pardon with Piers Plowman.
      Kings and knights that keep Holy Church
10   And rightfully in realms rule over the people
Have pardon to pass through purgatory lightly,
And to join patriarchs and prophets in paradise.
Bishops are most blessed, if they be as they should, …

Merchants had many years to the good,
15   But none were pardoned a *poena et a culpa* by the pope,
For they do not always observe the holy days, as the
      Holy Church teaches, …
Under his secret seal Truth sent them a letter
Saying they should buy boldly what they liked best,
And afterwards sell again, and save their profits
20   To use in helping *maisons Dieu*,[3] and in helping folk in
      misery;
In helping to repair rotten roads, where plainly needed;
And to build up bridges that were broken down;
In helping maidens to marry, or to become nuns;
In helping poor people and prisoners find their food;
25   And helping send scholars to school, or to some other
      craft;
In helping poor religious souls, and in lowering their
      rents …

Now has the Pope power to grant the people
Remission of penance, to pass directly into Heaven:
This is our belief, as lettered men teach us:
30   … I believe loyally (the Lord forbids anything else!)
That pardon, penance, and prayers cause people to be
      saved.

---

[1]   *beads* It is the practice of Roman Catholics to say their prayers to the Virgin Mary on a set of prayer beads called a rosary. The Apostles' Creed, or the "belief," as Piers says, is one of the prayers one recites when one says his or her rosary.

[2]   *a poena et a culpa* Latin: from punishment and from guilt, i.e., absolving the holder of the pardon.

[3]   *maisons Dieu* French: houses of God, i.e., hospitals, houses of charity, etc.

For souls that have sinned the seven deadly sins.
To trust to indulgences—truly I think
Is not so safe for the soul as it is to do well.
35   Therefore I advise all that are rich and
That trust of your treasure …
And especially you masters, mayors, and judges,
Who are held to be wise, and have the world's wealth
Available to purchase your pardons, and the Pope's
    bulls:[1]
40   At the dreadful Doom, when the dead shall arise
And you all will come before Christ, to have it reckoned
How you have led your life, and kept His laws,
And how you behaved day by day, the doom will declare
That however many pardons … of all the friars' orders
45   Promising two-fold indulgence—unless you have
Also good deeds to help you, I rate your patents
And pardons at one pea-pod's value!
Therefore I counsel Christians to cry to God for mercy,
And to Mary His mother to mediate for us,
50   That God grant us grace here, before that we depart,
That we may do such good works, while we are here
That after our death-day Do-well will declare
At the day of Doom that we did as he told us.

from Thomas Wimbleton, Sermon (c. 1388)

The sermon from which the following passages are
taken was preached by Thomas Wimbleton at Paul's
Cross in London; it survives in over a dozen English
(and two Latin) manuscripts.

… As I see, the first question that shall be purposed [to
a new curate or prelate] is this: how hast thou entered?
Who brought thee into this office? Truth other simony?
God or the devil? Grace or money? The flesh or the
spirit?…
    And if we taken heed truly what abominations been
scattered in the church nowadays among priests, we
should well wit[2] that they all cometh nought into the

fold of Christ by Christ's clepynge[3] for the profit but by
other ways to get him worldly wealth; and this is cause
of many errors among the people.… When were [pride,
envy, wrath, and covetousness] so great as they are now,
and so of all other sins? …

The second question that every curate and prelate of
holy church shall answer to is this: how hast thou ruled,
that is to say the souls of the subjects and the goods of
poor men? Give now thine account. First, how hast
thou governed God's folk that was taken thee to keep?
As a [shep]herd or as a hired man that doth all for the
love of his bodily hire? As a father [or] as a wolf that
eateth the sheep and keepeth them nought? …

The third question that this first [curate or prelate] shall
answer to is this: how hast thou lived? What light of
holiness hast thou showed in thy living to the
people?.…Reckon how thou hast lived. As a priest [or]
as a lewd man? As a man or as a beast? It is a wonder
truly how the life of priests is changed. They beith
clothed as knights; they speak as unhonestly as churls,
[or] of winning as merchants; they ride as princes; and
all this that is thus spent is of the goods of poor men
and of Christ's heritages.

Lollardy

One of the earliest movements in the direction of
the Reformation of Christianity was that of John
Wycliffe and the Lollards. Over a century before the
upheavals brought on by Martin Luther, Wycliffe
spoke out strongly against corruption and in favor of
bringing all Christians into more direct contact with
the Word of God. In Wycliffe's view the veneration
of saints and of relics, the drawing of a veil of
mystery around the Bible by refusing to authorize
translations into the vernacular, and the acceptance
of vast levels of wealth and privilege for members of
the clergy were all of a piece—and all deserved to be
brought to an end. Those who followed and
extended Wycliffe's teachings came to be known as
"Lollards"; their "heresies" were ruthlessly stamped
out in the fifteenth century.

---

[1] *Pope's bulls* Declarations by the Pope; specifically in this case,
declarations providing "indulgences," granting pardon for sins in
exchange for money.

[2] *wit* Know.

[3] *clepynge* Calling, bidding.

from Account of the Heresy Trial of Margery Baxter

On April 1, 1429 Johanna Clifland, wife of William Clifland, who lives in the parish of St. Mary the Less in Norwich, being cited, appeared in person before the reverend father and lord in Christ William, by the grace of God Bishop of Norwich [1426–36], holding court in his palace chapel. At the command of the bishop she placed her hand on God's Holy Gospels and swore that she would tell the truth about any and all questions asked of her that concerned matters of faith.

After swearing this oath, Johanna Clifland said that on the Friday [January 28] before the most recent feast of the Purification of the Blessed Mary, Margery Baxter, the wife of William Baxter the wright, recently living at Martham in the diocese of Norwich, was sitting and sewing near the fireplace with the witness in the witness's room. In the presence of the witness and her servants Johanna Grymell and Agnes Bethom, she told the witness and her servants that they should never swear oaths, saying in English: "Dame, beware of the bee, for every bee will sting; and therefore see that you swear neither by God nor by Our Lady nor by any other saint; and if you do the contrary the bee will sting your tongue and poison your soul."

Then the witness said Margery asked her what she did daily in church. The witness told her that as soon as she entered, after kneeling before the Cross it was her habit to say five Our Fathers in honor of the crucifix and the same number of Hail Marys in honor of Blessed Mary, the Mother of Christ. Then Margery scolded her and told the witness, "You act badly by kneeling like that and praying before images in these churches, because God has never been in such a church, and He never has gone forth from heaven nor will He ever. And He will not give or offer you any more merit for the genuflectings, and adorations, and prayers that you do in these churches than a lit candle hidden away under the cover of a baptismal font can give any light to people inside a church at nighttime." …

Next the witness said that the aforesaid Margery told her no child or infant born of Christian parents ought to be baptized in water according to the common custom since such a child had been sufficiently baptized in its mother's womb. So the image-worshipping and idolatry these false and accursed priests do when they dip babies in fonts in churches is done solely to wrench money from people in order to maintain these priests and their concubines.

Next the witness said Margery told her there that the consent of mutual love alone between a man and a woman sufficed to make the sacrament of marriage; no other exchange of words or ceremonies in a church were necessary.

Next she said Margery told her that no faithful man or woman was obliged to fast during Lent, Ember Days, Fridays, the vigils of saints, or other days indicated by the church; and that anyone could eat meat or any other kind of food during these times and on these days; and that on fast days it was better for someone to eat scraps of meat left over from Thursday than to go to the market and run up debts buying fish …

The witness also said Margery asked her and her servant Johanna to come secretly at night to Margery's house, and there they could hear her husband read the law of Christ to them, the law written in a book [i.e., the Bible] which her husband read to her at night; and she said her husband is an excellent teacher of Christianity.

Margery also said that she had spoken with Johanna West, a woman living near the churchyard of St. Mary-in-the-Marsh, about the law of Christ, and that Johanna is on the good road to salvation.

Furthermore, Margery said this to the witness: "Johanna, from your expression it looks like you plan to reveal what I've told you to the bishop." And the witness swore that she wished never to reveal her counsels in this regard unless Margery gave her cause to do so. Then Margery told her: "If you accuse me to the bishop, I'll do to you what I did to this Carmelite friar from Yarmouth who was the wisest friar in the land." The witness asked her what she had done to the friar. Margery answered that she had spoken with the friar, upbraiding him because he begged for his living, and telling him that it wasn't an act of charity to do good to someone or give him aid unless he himself wanted to take off his friar's habit and get behind a plow to work for a living, which would be more pleasing to God than following the way of life of some of these friars. Then the friar asked her whether she had anything else to tell him or teach him. So Margery, as the witness said, explained the Gospels to him in English. After that, the friar left Margery, so the witness said. Later this friar accused Margery of heresy. But Margery, hearing that the friar had denounced her, accused him of wanting to have sex with her, and since she would not give in to him, he accused her of heresy. Margery said this was the reason her husband wanted to kill the friar. Out of fear the friar shut up and left these parts in shame.

Margery also told the witness she had often made false confessions to the Dean of St. Mary-in-the-Fields so that he would think she led a good life. Because of this, he often gave Margery money. Then the witness asked her whether she had confessed all her sins to a priest. Margery told her she had never done harm to any priest, so she had never wanted to confess to a priest or be obedient to any priest, since a priest had no power to absolve anyone from sins; and in fact priests sinned more grievously every day than other people. Margery also said that every man and woman who shared Margery's opinion were good priests, and that the Holy Church exists only wherever all those people were who believed as she did. For that reason, Margery said she was obliged to confess only to God, not to any priest.

Next Margery told the witness that people honor the devils that fell from heaven with Lucifer who, when they fell to earth, entered into the statues standing in churches. They have dwelled in them since then and are still hiding in them, so that people who adore statues are committing idolatry.

Next the witness said Margery informed her that holy water and blessed bread were just trifles with no power, and that every church bell should be pulled down and destroyed, and that all those who set up bells in churches are excommunicated.

Margery also said that even if she were convicted of Lollardy, she shouldn't be burned because she, so the witness said, had and still has a charter of salvation in her womb.

Next Margery said she had won a judgment against the Lord Bishop of Norwich, and Henry Inglese, and the Lord Abbots associated with them.

Next the witness said she had sent Agnes Bethom, her servant, to Margery's house on the Saturday after last Ash Wednesday. Margery wasn't home but Agnes found a kitchen kettle on the fire, and boiling inside it were a piece of salt pork and oat flour—so Agnes reported to the witness.

[Margery confessed on 7 October, 1429. Her sentence included being flogged on four consecutive Sundays as she walked barefoot around her parish church.]

The Persecution of the Jews

The twelfth and thirteenth centuries were tumultuous and difficult times for Jews in Britain. Early Norman kings had encouraged the emigration of Jews from continental Europe, but in the latter part of the twelfth century attacks on Jews on the Continent by crusading Christians became common, and in Britain vicious propaganda against Jews (such as that found in Thomas of Monmouth's *Life and Miracles of St. William of Norwich*) began to be widely disseminated. Physical attacks on Jews (the most horrific of which was the massacre/mass suicide of approximately 150 Jews on 16 March, 1190, described below by Roger of Howden) became widespread in Britain in the late twelfth century. New taxes and restrictions (such as the 1194 Ordnances) began to be placed on Jews, and even more "favorable" developments (such as King John's Charter of 1201 confirming certain Jewish rights) were couched in such terms as to make clear that relations between Christians and Jews would remain entirely on an "us and them" footing. Restrictions became far more extreme with the Ordnances of Henry III, and in 1290 all Jews were expelled from the country by order of Edward I.

from Thomas of Monmouth, *The Life and Miracles of St. William of Norwich* (c. 1173)

When therefore [William] was flourishing in this blessed boyhood of his, and had attained to his eighth year [about 1140], he was entrusted to the skinners to be taught their craft. Gifted with a teachable disposition and bringing industry to bear upon it, in a short time he far surpassed lads of his own age in the craft aforesaid, and he equaled some who had been his teachers. So leaving the country, drawn by a divine urge he betook himself to the city and lodged with a very famous master of that craft, and some time passed away. He was seldom in the country, but was occupied in the city and sedulously gave himself to the practice of his craft, and thus reached his twelfth year.

Now, while he was staying in Norwich, the Jews who were settled there and required their cloaks or their robes or other garments (whether pledged to them, or their own property) to be repaired, preferred him before all other skinners. For [the Jews] esteemed him to be especially fit for their work, either because they had learnt that he was guileless and skillful, or, because attracted to him by their avarice, they thought they could bargain with him for a lower price, Or, as I rather believe, because by the ordering of divine Providence he had been predestined to martyrdom from the beginning of time, and gradually step by step was drawn on, and chosen to be made a mock of and to be put to death by the Jews, in scorn of the Lord's Passion....

For I have learnt from certain Jews, who were afterwards converted to the Christian faith, how that at that time they had planned to do this very thing with some Christian, and in order to carry out their malignant purpose, at the beginning of Lent they had made choice of the boy William, being twelve years of age and a boy of unusual innocence....

Then the boy, like an innocent lamb, was led to the slaughter. He was treated kindly by the Jews at first, and, ignorant of what was being prepared for him, he was kept till the morrow. But on the next day [Tuesday, 21 March], which in that year was the Passover for them, after the singing of the hymns appointed for the day in the synagogue, the chiefs of the Jews.... suddenly seized hold of the boy William as he was having his dinner and in no fear of any treachery, and ill-treated him in various horrible ways. For while some of them held him behind, others opened his mouth and introduced an instrument of torture which is called a teazle [a wooden gag] and, fixing it by straps through both jaws to the back of his neck, they fastened it with a knot as tightly as it could be drawn.

After that, taking a short piece of rope of about the thickness of one's little finger and tying three knots in it at certain distances marked out, they bound round that innocent head with it from the forehead to the back, forcing the middle knot into his forehead and the two others into his temples, the two ends of the rope being most tightly stretched at the back of his head and fastened in a very tight knot. The ends of the rope were then passed round his neck and carried round his throat under his chin, and there they finished off this dreadful engine of torture in a fifth knot.

But not even yet could the cruelty of the torturers be satisfied without adding even more severe pains. Having shaved his head, they stabbed it with countless thorn points, and made the blood come horribly from the wounds they made. And so cruel were they and so eager to inflict pain that it was difficult to say whether they were more cruel or more ingenious in their tortures. For their skill in torturing kept up the strength of their cruelty and ministered arms thereto.

And thus, while these enemies of the Christian name were rioting in the spirit of malignity around the boy, some of those present adjudged him to be fixed to a Cross in mockery of the Lord's Passion, as though they would say: "even as we condemned the Christ to a shameful death, so let us also condemn the Christian, so that, uniting the lord and his servant in a like punishment, we may retort upon themselves the pain of that reproach which they impute to us."

Conspiring, therefore, to accomplish the crime of this great and detestable malice, they next laid their blood-stained hands upon the innocent victim, and having lifted him from the ground and fastened him upon the Cross, they vied with one another in their efforts to make an end of him.

And we, after enquiring into the matter very diligently, did both find the house, and discovered some most certain marks in it of what had been done there....

As a proof of the truth and credibility of the matter we now adduce something which we have heard from the lips of Theobald, who was once a Jew, and afterwards a monk. He verily told us that in the ancient writings of his fathers it was written that the Jews, without the shedding of human blood, could neither obtain their freedom, nor could they ever return to their fatherland. Hence it was laid down by them in ancient times that every year they must sacrifice a Christian in some part of the world to the Most High God in scorn and contempt of Christ....

from Roger Howden, *Chronicle* (1190)

In the same month of March [1190] ... the Jews of the city of York, in number five hundred men, besides women and children, shut themselves up in the tower of York, with the consent of the sheriff, in consequence of their dread of the Christians; but when the sheriff and the constable sought to regain possession of it, the Jews refused to deliver it up. In consequence of this, the people of the said city, and the strangers who had come within the jurisdiction thereof, at the exhortation of the sheriff and the constable, with one consent made an attack upon the Jews.

After they had made assaults upon the tower day and night, the Jews offered the people a large sum of money to allow them to depart with their lives; but this the others refused to receive. Upon this, one skilled in their laws arose and said, "Men of Israel, listen to my advice. It is better that we should kill one another, than fall into the hands of the enemies of our law." Accordingly, all the Jews, both men and women, gave their assent to his advice, and each master of a family, beginning with the chief persons of his household, with a sharp knife first cut the throats of his wife and sons and daughters, and then of all his servants, and lastly his own. Some of them also threw their slain over the walls among the people; while others shut up their slain in the king's house and burned them, as well as the king's houses. Those who had slain the others were afterwards killed by the people. In the meantime, some of the Christians set fire to the Jews' houses, and plundered them; and thus all the Jews in the city of York were destroyed, and all acknowledgments of debts due to them were burnt.

from the Ordinances of the Jews (1194)

All the debts, pledges, mortgages, lands, houses, rents, and possessions of the Jews shall be registered. The Jew who shall conceal any of these shall forfeit to the King his body and the thing concealed, and likewise all his possessions and chattels, neither shall it be lawful to the Jew to recover the thing concealed.

Likewise six or seven places shall be provided in which they shall make all their contracts, and there shall be appointed two lawyers that are Christians and two lawyers that are Jews, and two legal registrars, and before them and the clerks of William of the Church of St. Mary's and William of Chimilli, shall their contracts be made.

And charters shall be made of their contracts by way of indenture. And one part of the indenture shall remain with the Jew, sealed with the seal of him, to whom the money is lent, and the other part shall remain in the common chest: wherein there shall be three locks and keys, whereof the two Christians shall keep one key, and the two Jews another, and the clerks of William of the Church of St. Mary and of William of Chimilli shall keep the third. And moreover, there shall be three seals to it, and those who keep the seals shall put the seals thereto.

Moreover the clerks of the said William and William shall keep a roll of the transcripts of all the charters, and as the charters shall be altered so let the roll be likewise. For every charter there shall be threepence paid, one moiety thereof by the Jews and the other moiety by him to whom the money is lent; whereof the two writers shall have twopence and the keeper of the roll the third.

And from henceforth no contract shall be made with, nor payment, made to, the Jews, nor any alteration made in the charters, except before the said persons or the greater part of them, if all of them cannot be present. And the aforesaid two Christians shall have one roll of the debts or receipts of the payments which from henceforth are to be made to the Jews, and the two Jews one and the keeper of the roll one.

Moreover every Jew shall swear on his Roll, that all his debts and pledges and rents, and all his goods and his possessions, he shall cause to be enrolled, and that he shall conceal nothing as is aforesaid. And if he shall know that anyone shall conceal anything he shall secretly reveal it to the justices sent to them, and that they shall detect, and shew unto them all falsifiers or forgers of the charters and clippers of money, where or when they shall know them, and likewise all false charters.

from the Charter of King John to the Jews (1201)

1. John, by the grace of God, &c. Know that we have granted to all the Jews of England and Normandy to have freely and honourably residence in our land, and to hold all that from us, which they held from King Henry, our father's grandfather, and all that now they reasonably hold in land and fees and mortgages and goods, and that they have all their liberties and customs just as they had them in the time of the aforesaid King Henry, our father's grandfather, better and more quietly and more honourably.

from the Ordinances of Henry III (1253)

The king has provided and decreed ... that no Jew dwell in England unless he do the king service, and that as soon as a Jew shall be born, whether male or female, in some way he shall serve the king. And that there be no communities of the Jews in England save in those places wherein such communities were in the time of the lord King John, the king's father. And that in their synagogues the Jews, one and all, worship in subdued tones according to their rite, so that Christians hear it not. And that all Jews answer to the rector of the parish in which they dwell for all parochial dues belonging to their houses. And that no Christian nurse hereafter suckle or nourish the male child of any Jew, and that no Christian man or woman serve any Jew or Jewess, nor eat with them, nor dwell in their house. And that no Jew or Jewess eat or buy meat in Lent. And that no Jew disparage the Christian faith, nor publicly dispute touching the same. And that no Jew have secret intercourse with any Christian woman, nor any Christian man with a Jewess. And that every Jew wear on his breast a conspicuous badge. And that no Jew enter any church or any chapel save in passing through, nor stay therein to the dishonor of Christ. And that no Jew in any wise hinder another Jew willing to be converted to the Christian faith. And that no Jew be received in any town without the special licence of the king, save in those towns wherein Jews have been wont to dwell.

And the justices appointed to the guardianship of the Jews are commanded to cause these provisions to be carried into effect and straitly kept on pain of forfeiture of the goods of the Jews aforesaid. Witness the king at Westminster on the 31st day of January. By the king and council.

Illustration from *Flores Historianum* (14th century). Three Jews (all depicted with beards, as was customary) are attacked by a soldier.

Edward I's Order (1290)

Edward ... to the treasurer and barons of the exchequer, greeting. Whereas formerly in our Parliament at Westminster on the quinzaine of St. Michael in the third year of our reign, to the honor of God and the profit of the people of our realm, we ordained and decreed that no Jew thenceforth should lend anything at usury to any Christian on lands, rents or other things, but that they should live by their commerce and labor; and the same Jews, afterwards maliciously deliberating among themselves, contriving a worse sort of usury which they called courtesy, have depressed our people aforesaid on all sides under color thereof, the last offense doubling the first; whereby, for their crimes and to the honor of the Crucified, we have caused those Jews to go forth from our realm as traitors: we, wishing to swerve not from our former choice, but rather to follow it, do make totally null and void all manner of penalties and usuries and every sort thereof, which could be demanded by actions by reason of the Jewry from any Christians of our realm for any times whatsoever; wishing that nothing be in any wise demanded from the Christians aforesaid by reason of the debts aforesaid, save only the principal sums which they received from the Jews aforesaid; the amount of which debts we will that the Christians aforesaid verify before you by the oath of three good and lawful men by whom

the truth of the matter may the better be known, and thereafter pay the same to us at terms convenient to them to be fixed by you. And therefore we command you that you cause our said grace so piously granted to be read in the aforesaid exchequer, and to be enrolled on the rolls of the same exchequer, and to be straitly kept, according to the form above noted. . . .

Quem Quaeritis
c. 970

The *Quem Quaeritis* (Latin: "Whom do you seek?") was originally a trope, or an expansive insertion into the standard text of the Mass (in this case, during Easter services). It appears to have originated in the early tenth century, taking the form of an antiphonal song, wherein two groups of the choir on opposite sides of the cathedral nave would sing in a call-and-answer form. With a few lines of rudimentary dialogue the trope dramatized the biblical account of the meeting of the three Marys and the angel at the tomb of Christ on Easter morning. In the earliest version that has come down to us (c. 925), these are taken without embellishment from the Latin text of Luke 24:

> *Quem quaeritis in sepulchro, o Christicolae?*
> *Jesum Nazarenum crucifixum, o caelicolae.*
> *Non est hic, surrexit sicut praedixerat.*
> *Ite, nuntiate quia surrexit de sepulchro.*

> Whom do you seek in the sepulcher, O Christians?
> Jesus of Nazareth who was crucified, O heavenly one.
> He is not here; He is risen, as He said beforehand would happen.
> Go, announce that He has risen from the sepulcher.

Although the ceremony in its most basic form bears little resemblance to a play, it quickly developed into a more overtly theatrical work. Within fifty years, a variant of the *Quem Quaeritis* with substantial "stage directions" was recorded in Bishop Æthelwold of Winchester's *Regularis Concordia* (c. 975), a codification of monastic liturgy in tenth-century England. That text is reproduced below. In Æthelwold's version, four priests act out the play, taking on the roles of the Marys and the angels. The altar of the cathedral is used as a set for the sepulcher, and Æthelwold includes basic costume and properties notes.

⌘ ⌘ ⌘

The Quem Quaeritis[1] Ceremony

from Regularis Concordia of St. Æthelwold[2]

(*When the third lesson of the matins*[3] *is recited, let four brethren*[4] *dress themselves. Let one, wearing an alb,*[5] *enter as if to take part in the service; and let him without being observed approach the place of the sepulcher,*[6] *and, holding a palm in his hand, sit there quietly. While the third responsory is being sung, let the remaining three brethren follow, all of them wearing capes and carrying thuribles*[7] *filled with incense. Then slowly, in the manner of seeking something, let them move toward the place of the sepulchre. These things are to be performed in imitation of the Angel seated on the tomb, and of the women coming with spices to anoint the body of Jesus. Therefore, when the seated angel sees the three women, wandering about as if looking for something, let him begin to sing in a pleasing voice of medium pitch:*)

ANGELS.   Whom do you seek [in the sepulcher, O followers of Christ?]

(*When he has sung this to the end, let the three respond in one voice:*)

MARYS.   Jesus of Nazareth [who was crucified, O celestial one.]

(*He [then says] to them:*)

ANGELS.   He is not here: He is risen, just as He foretold. Go, announce that he is risen from the dead.

(*At the word of his command, let the three turn to the Choir, and say:*)

MARYS.   Alleluia! The Lord is risen.
Today is risen the strong lion, Christ, the Son of God.

(*When this has been said, let the speaker, again seating himself, as if recalling them, sing the anthem.*)

ANGELS.   Come, and see the place [where the Lord was laid. Alleluia!]

(*And saying this, let him rise, and let him lift the veil and show them the place bare of the cross, except for the cloths lying there with which the cross was wrapped. Seeing this, let the women set down the thuribles they carried into the sepulcher, and let them pick up the cloth and spread it out before the eyes of the clergy; and, as if making known that the Lord had risen and was not now wrapped in this linen, let them sing this anthem:*)

ANGELS.   The Lord is risen from the sepulcher
[Who for us hung on the cross. Alleluia!]

(*And let them place the cloth upon the altar. When the anthem has ended let the Prior*[8] *begin the hymn, rejoicing with them at the triumph of our king, who conquered death and arose.*)

We praise you, O God.

(*When this has begun, let the bells be rung in unison.*)

—C. 970

---

[1]   *Quem Quaeritis* Latin: whom do you seek?

[2]   This manuscript dates from Winchester between 965 and 975 CE; it provides liturgical instructions for use in Benedictine monasteries. The *Quem Quaeritis* in this version is not a trope to be inserted into the text of the Mass but rather a ceremony to be performed at the conclusion of the service. Included in square brackets are more expansive versions of the text that are frequently found in other versions. The present text has been translated from the Latin for this anthology.

[3]   *matins* Service preceding the first Mass of the day.

[4]   *brethren* Members of the religious community.

[5]   *alb* Tunic of white cloth reaching to the feet.

[6]   *sepulcher* A permanent or temporary structure prepared in a church for the dramatic burial of the Sacrament on Good Friday. The Holy Sepulcher refers to the cave where Christ was buried outside Jerusalem.

[7]   *thuribles* Containers for incense.

[8]   *Prior* Superior officer of a religious house.

NOAH'S FLOOD
c. 1450

N*oah's Flood* is part of the cycle of biblical pageants from Chester, a northern English town near the Welsh border. As with other biblical plays of the period, not much is known about its author or authors. It is possible that one person wrote all of the Chester cycle; the plays demonstrate a close unity of form and style, which strongly suggests either one author or (perhaps more likely) a thorough revision of existing texts over time. Nevertheless, information about the Chester cycle is incomplete, and the cycle surely developed and changed over the two hundred years it was performed. The surviving manuscripts of the play are copies transcribed in the 1600s, long after it stopped being performed, and may therefore not give fully accurate information about the development of the texts.

The story of Noah, a popular subject in medieval biblical drama, encapsulates a miniature version of the broader narrative of creation, fall, and redemption. The Chester *Noah's Flood* came third in a cycle of 24 extant pageants. The cycle was performed on wagons in the city streets at Whitsun (Pentecost) in May or June, probably because the weather would then be suitable for outdoor performances. Scheduling of such performances differed from one town to another, however; towns such as York, for example, performed their plays eleven days later at the Feast of Corpus Christi.

Each play in the Chester cycle was assigned to a specific trade guild within the town. An existing copy of the Chester Banns, a document presumably read by a town crier to announce the impending performance, indicates that *Noah's Flood* was appropriately assigned to the "waterleaders and drawers of Dee," who drew and carried water from the river Dee, which runs through Chester. Stage directions within the text are unusually descriptive and provide useful information on how the play was staged. For example, they indicate that pictures were used to represent the animals that were brought onto the ark. As in other biblical drama of the period, minor actors at least wore contemporary clothing, rather than being costumed according to a conception of what people of the ancient middle east might have worn. The actor playing God probably appeared in ecclesiastical vestments. The ark would in all probability have looked like a medieval ship.

The story of this pageant departs from the biblical narrative of Noah in several respects, perhaps most notably in the depiction of Noah's wife (who is never given a name). Here, as in many medieval versions of the story, both literary and artistic, she is shown as a strong-willed woman who resists doing her husband's bidding and is reluctant to enter the ark; her resistance contributes both to the pageant's religious lesson and to its dramatic tension.

The play's text is in a "tail-rhyme" form, an eight-line stanza with a uniform rhyming structure and pattern of stressed syllables—a form shared by all the pageants within the Chester cycle.

⌘ ⌘ ⌘

The Third Pageant of Noah's Flood[1]

CHARACTERS:

God/Deus
Noah
Noah's Wife
Sem
Cam
Jaffett
Sem's Wife
Cam's Wife
Jaffett's Wife
The Good Gossips

(*And first in some high place—or in the clouds, if it may be—God speaketh unto Noah standing without[2] the ark with all his family.*)

GOD.   I, God, that all this world have wrought,
Heaven and yearth, and all from nought,
I see my people in deed and thought
Are set fowl in sinne.
5 My goost° shall not lenge° in mone°   spirit / linger / man
That through flesh-liking is my fone°   foe
But till six score years be commen and gone
To looke if they will blynne.°[3]   cease, desist

Man that I made I will distroye,
10 Beast, worm, and fowl to flye;
For on yearth they do me noye,°   vex, annoy
The folk that are thereon.
It harms me so hurtefullye,
The malice that doth now multiplye,

15 That sore it grieves me inwardlye
That ever I made mon.°   man

Therefore Noah, my servant free,
That righteous man art as I see,
A ship, son, thou shalt make thee
20 Of trees dry and light.
Little chambers therein thou make
And binding sliche° also thou take;   ropes
Within and without thou ne slake°   weaken, decrease effort
To annoint[4] it through all thy might.

25 Three hundred cubits[5] it shall be longe
And fifty broad to make it stronge;
Of height sixty. The meete° though   quantity, amount
     fonge;[6]
Thus measure thou it about.
One window work through thy wit;
30 A cubit of length and breadth make it.
Upon the side a door shall shut,
For to come in and out.

Eating-places thou make also
Three, roofed chambers one or too,°   two
35 For with water I think to flow
Mone° that I can make.   man
Destroyed all they world shall be—
Save° thou, thy wife, thy sons three,   except
And their wives also with thee—
40 Shall fall before thy face.

NOAH.   A, lord, I thank thee loud and still
That to me art in such will
And spares me and my household to spill,
As I now smoothly find.
45 Thy bidding, lord, I shall fulfill
Nor never more thee grieve ne gryll,°   irritate, offend
That such grace hath sent me till
Amonges° all mankind.   amongst

---

[1]   The Chester cycle of Mystery plays exists in eight manuscript versions, two of which date from c. 1500 or slightly before. For the present text, spelling and punctuation have been substantially modernized, but alterations that would affect rhythm or rhyme have (with few exceptions) been avoided. Stage directions that appear in the original appear here in parentheses. Some additional stage directions have been added for the sake of clarity; these appear in square brackets.

[2]   *without* Outside.

[3]   *But till ... they will blynne* I will give sixty more years to see if they will turn away from sin.

[4]   *annoint* Rub with oil or grease.

[5]   *cubits* Ancient form of measurement (a cubit is roughly equivalent to the length of a forearm).

[6]   *The meete though fonge* Take the measurement.

Have done, you men and women all.
50 Hye° you, lest this water fall,   *hasten, hurry*
to worche° this ship, chamber and hall,   *work*
as God hath bidden us do.

SEM. Father, I am already browne:°   *tough*
An axe I have, by my crown,
55 As sharp as any in all this town
For to go thereto.

CAM. I have an hatchet wonder keen
To bite well, as may be seen;
A better ground, as I ween,°   *know, believe*
60 Is not in all this town.

JAFFETT. And I can well make a pin
And with this hammer knock it in.
Go we worch° bowte° more din,°   *work / without / noise*
And I am ready bowne.°   *to prepare*

65 NOAH'S WIFE. And we shall bring timber too,
For we mon nothing else do—
Women bynne° weak to underfoe[1]   *being, i.e., are*
Any great travel.°   *travail*

SEM'S WIFE. Here is a good hackstock;°   *chopping block*
70 One this you may hew and knock.
Shall none be idle in this flock,
Ne now may no man fable.°   *weaken*

CAM'S WIFE. And I will go gather slytche,
The ship for to clam° and pitch.°   *smear, daub / fix*
75 Anoint it must be with stitche—
Board, tree, and pin.

JAFETT'S WIFE. And I will gather chips° here   *woodchips*
To make a fire for you in fear,
And for to dighte° your dinner   *prepare*
80 Again you come in.

(*Then Noah beginneth to build the ark.*)

NOAH. Nowe in the name of God I begin
To make the ship that we shall in,

That we may be ready for to swim
At the coming of the flood.
85 These boards I pin here together
To bear us safe from the weather,
That we may row both hither and thither
And safe be from this flood.

Of this tree will I make a mast
90 Tied with gables that will last,
With a seale°-yard for each baste,   *sail*
And each thing in their kynde.°   *place*
With topcastle[2] and bowespreete,[3]
Both cords and ropes I have all meete°   *appropriate, fitting*
95 To sail forth at the next weete°—   *rain storm*
This ship is at an ende.[4]

Wife, in this vessel we shall be kept;
My children and thou, I would ye lept.[5]

NOAH'S WIFE. In faith, Noah, I had as leeve thou slepte.[6]
100 For all thy Frenyshe fare,[7]
I will not do after thy reade.°   *command*

NOAH. Good wife, do now as I thee bid.

NOAH'S WIFE. By Christ, not or° I see more need,   *unless*
Though thou stand all day and stare.

105 NOAH. Lord, that women been crabbed° aye,   *ill-tempered*
And none are meek, I dare well say.
That is well seen by me today
In witness of you each one.
Good wife, let be all this bear
110 That thou makest in this place here,
For all the weene° that thou arte mastere— *knowledge, belief*
And so thou art, by sayncte° John.   *saint*

---

[2] *topcastle* Platform at the head of a ship's mast.

[3] *bowespreete* Boom running out from the stem of a vessel to which stays are fastened.

[4] *This … at an ende* The ship is completed and ready.

[5] *Wife, in this … ye lept* Wife, we (the children, yourself, and me) will be kept in this ship once you have entered it.

[6] *I had as … slepte* I would rather you were sleeping.

[7] *For all thy Frenyshe fare* For all your Frenchified behavior.

---

[1] *underfoe* To have understanding, or skill.

(*Then Noah with all his family shall make a sign as though they wrought upon the ship with diverse instruments. And after that God shall speak to Noah as followeth*:)

DEUS.[1]   Noah, take thou thy meanye°   *family*
   And in the ship hye that ye be;
115 For none so righteous man to me
   Is now on yearth living.
   Of clean beasts with thee thou take
   seven and seven or then thou slake;
   He and she, make to make,
120 Be leeve in that thou bring;

   Of beasts unclean two and two,
   Male and female, bowt moo;[2]
   Of clean fowls seven also,
   The he and she together;
125 Of fowls unclean twayne° and no more,   *two*
   As I of beasts said before.
   That man be saved through my lore,
   Against I send this wedder,°   *weather*

   Of meats that mon° be eaten,   *may*
130 Into the ship look the be getten,
   For that may be no way forgotten.
   And do this all bydeene°   *immediately*
   To sustain man and beasts therein
   Aye till the water cease and blynne.
135 This world is filled full of sin,
   And that is now well seen.

   Seven days bynne yet cominge;
   You shall have space them in to bringe.
   After that, it is my likinge
140 Mankind for to annoy.
   Forty days and forty nights
   Rain shall fall for their unrightes.°   *misdeeds*
   And that I have made through mights
   Now think I to destroy.

145 NOAH.   Lord, at your bidding I am bayne.° *ready, willing*
   Sythen° no other grace will gain,   *since*

---

[1]   *Deus*   Latin: God.

[2]   *bowt moo*   No more.

   It will I fulfill fain,
   For gracious I thee find.
   One hundredth winters and twenty
150 This ship-making tarried have I,
   If through ammendment thy mercy
   Would fall to mankind.

   Have done, ye men and women all;
   Hye you lest this water fall,
155 That each beast were in stall
   And into the ship brought.
   Of clean beasts seven shall be,
   Of unclean two; thus God bade me.
   The flood is nigh, you may well see;
160 Therefore tarry you nought.

SEM.   Sir, here are lions, leopards in;
   Horses, mares, oxen, and swine,
   Geates,° calves, sheep, and kine°   *goats / cows*
   Here sytten thou may see.

165 CAM.   Camels, asses, man may find,
   Buck and doe, hart° and hind.° *male deer, stag / female deer*
   All beasts of all manner of kind
   Here bynne,° as thinketh me.   *been*

JAFETT.   Take here cats, dogs too,
170 Otters and foxes, fullimartes° also;   *polecat*
   Hares hopping gaily can go
   Here have cole[3] for to eat.

NOAH'S WIFE.   And here are bears, wolves set,
   Apes, owls, maremussett,°   *small monkeys*
175 Weasels, squirrels, and ferret;
   Here they eaten their meat.

SEM'S WIFE.   Here are beasts in this house;
   Here cats maken it crowse;°   *lively*
   Here a rotten, here a mouse
180 That standen near together.

CAM'S WIFE.   And here are fowls less and more—
   Hernes,° cranes, and byttoer,°   *herons / bitterns*
   Swans, peacocks—and them before
   Meat for this wedder.

---

[3]   *cole*   Kind of stew, e.g. kale, cabbage, or turnip.

185 JAFETT'S WIFE.   Here are cocks, kites,[1] crows,
    Rooks, ravens, many rows,
    Ducks, curlews, whoever knows,
    Each one in his kind.
    And here are doves, digges,° drakes,   *ducks*
190 Redshanks running through lakes;
    And each fowl that leaden[2] makes
    In this ship man may find.

NOAH.   Wife, come in. Why stands thou there?
    Thou art ever frowarde;° that dare I swear.   *difficult*
195 Come, in God's name; have time it were,
    For fear lest that we drown.

NOAH'S WIFE.   Yes, sir, set up your sail
    And row forth with evell hayle;°[3]   *haul*
    For withowten any fail
200 I will not out of this town.

    But I have my gossips[4] everyechone,°   *everyone*
    One foot further I will not gone.
    They shall not drown, by sancte John,
    And I may save their life.
205 They loved me full well, by Christ.
    But thou wilte let them into thy chiste,°   *chest*
    Elles° row forth, Noah, when thy list   *else*
    And get thee a new wife.

NOAH.   Sem, son, lo thy mother is wraowe;°   *wroth, contrarious*
210 By God, such another I do not know.

SEM.   Father, I shall fetch her in, I trowe,°   *trust*
    Withowten any fail.
    Mother, my father after thee send
    And bids thee into yonder wende.°   *turn, go*
215 Look up and see the wind,
    For we benne ready to sail.

NOAH'S WIFE.   Son, go again to him and say
    I will not come therein today.

NOAH.   Come in, wife, in twenty devils way,
220 Or ells° stand there without.   *else*

CAM.   Shall we all fetch her in?

NOAH.   Yea, son, in Christ's blessing and mine,
    I would ye hyed° you betime°   *hurried / in good time*
    For of this flood I stand in doubt.

225 THE GOOD GOSSIPS.   The flood comes fleeting in full
       fast,
    On every side that spredeth full fare.
    For fear of drowning I am agast;
    Good gossip, let us draw near.

    And let us drink or° we depart,   *ere, before*
230 For ofetymes° we have done so.   *often times*
    For at one draught° thou drink a quart,   *drink*
    And so will I do or° I go.   *ere*

    Here is a pottell[5] full of malnesaye[6] good and strong;
    It will rejoice both heart and tonge.°   *tongue*
235 Though Noah think us never so long,
    Yet we will drink atyte.[7]

JAFETT.   Mother, we pray you all together—
    For we are here, your own childer°—   *children*
    Come into the ship for fear of the wedder,
240 For his love that you bought.

NOAH'S WIFE.   That will I not for all your call
    But° I have my gossips all.   *unless*

SEM.   In faith, mother, yet thou shall,
    Whether thou will or not.

[He forcibly leads her onto the boat, leaving the gossips behind.]

245 NOAH.   Welcome, wife, into this boat.

---

[1]   *kites*   Bird of prey.

[2]   *leaden*   Language of birds, i.e., a birdsong.

[3]   *with evell hayle*   With hard haul.

[4]   *gossips*   In the late medieval period the noun "gossips" was used to refer to godparents, friends, or familiar acquaintances.

[5]   *pottell*   Measure for liquids.

[6]   *malnesaye*   I.e., malmsey, a sweet wine.

[7]   *Though Noah ... atyte*   Noah will not think we have been away long, so long as we drink quickly.

NOAH'S WIFE.   Have thou that for thy note!

[*She takes a swipe at him.*]

NOAH.   Aha, marry, this is hot;
　　It is good for to be still.
　　Ah, children, me think my boat remeeves.°   *removes*
250　Our tarrying here me highly grieves.
　　Over the land the water spreads;
　　God do he as he will.

(*Then they sing, and Noah shall speak again.*)

NOAH.   Ah, great God that arte so good,
　　That worchis° not thy will is wood.°   *work / crazy, mad*
255　Now all this world is one a flood,
　　As I see well in sight.
　　This window I will shut anon,
　　And into my chamber I will gone
　　Till this water, so great one,
260　Be slaked through thy might.

(*Then shall Noah shut the window of the ark, and for a
little space within the boards he shall be silent; and afterward
opening the window and looking round about saying.*)

　　Lord God in majesty
　　That such grace hast granted me
　　Where all was lost, salfe° to be!   *save*
　　Therfore now I am boune°—   *bound*
265　My wife, my children, and my menye—
　　With sacrifice to honour thee
　　Of beasts, fowls, as thou mayest see,
　　And full devotyon.°   *devotion*

GOD.   Noah, to me thou art full able
270　And thy sacrifice acceptable;
　　For I have found thee true and stable,
　　One thee now must I myne.°   *mention, recall*
　　Warry yearth I will no more
　　For man's sins that grieves me sore;
275　For of youth man full yore
　　Has bynne inclined to sin.

　　Ye shall now grow and multiply,
　　And yearth again to edify.

Each beast and fowl that may fly
280　Shall be feared of you.
　　And fish in sea, all that may fleete,°   *swim, scout*
　　Shall sustain you, I thee behett;°   *command, promise*
　　To eat of them ye ne let
　　That clean bynne you mon know.

285　Thereas ye have eaten before
　　Trees and roots since ye were bore,
　　Of clean beasts now, less and more,
　　I give you leave to eat—
　　Save blood and flesh both in fear
290　Of wrauge° dead carrion that is here.   *raw*
　　Eat ye not of that in no manner,
　　For that aye ye shall leave.

　　Manslaughter also aye ye shall flee,
　　For that is not playsante° unto me.   *pleasant*
295　They that sheden blood, he or she,
　　Ought-where amongst mankynde,
　　That blood foul shed shall be
　　And vengeance have, men shall see.
　　Therefore beware all ye,
300　You fall not into that sin.

　　And forward, Noah, with thee I make
　　And all thy seed for thy sake,
　　Of such vengeance for to slake,
　　For now I have my will.
305　Here I behette thee an heeste°   *command*
　　That man, woman, fowl, ne beast
　　With water while this world shall last
　　I will no more spill.

　　My Vow between you and me
310　In the firmament[1] shall be,
　　By very tokeninge° that you may see *meaning, signification*
　　That such vengeance shall cease.
　　The man ne woman shall never[2] more
　　Be wasted by water as hath before;
315　But for sin that greveth me sore,
　　Therefore this vengeance was.

---

[1] *firmament* Arch or vault of heaven.

[2] *The man ... never* Neither man nor woman shall ever.

Where clouds in the welkin° bynne,   *sky, heaven*   And this behett I thee.
That ilk° bow[1] shall be seen,   *same*
In tokeninge that my wrath and teen°   *annoyance* 325   My blessing now I give thee here,
320 Shall never thus worken be.   To thee, Noah, my servant dear,
The string is torned° towards you   *turned*   For vengeance shall no more appear.
And towards me is bent the bow,   And now farewell, my darling dear.
And such wedder shall never show;   —LATE 14TH CENTURY

IN CONTEXT

Biblical Source Material

Noah's Flood supplements Biblical source material, as do most other medieval plays that present Biblical stories. Below is the relevant Biblical text, in the Douay-Rheims version.

from Douay-Rheims Bible, Genesis 6–9

CHAPTER 6

1 And after that men began to be multiplied upon the earth, and daughters were born to them,

2 The sons of God seeing the daughters of men, that they were fair, took to themselves wives of all which they chose.

3 And God said: My spirit shall not remain in man for ever, because he is flesh, and his days shall be a hundred and twenty years.

4 Now giants were upon the earth in those days. For after the sons of God went in to the daughters of men, and they brought forth children, these are the mighty men of old, men of renown.

5 And God seeing that the wickedness of men was great on the earth, and that all the thought of their heart was bent upon evil at all times,

6 It repented him that he had made man on the earth. And being touched inwardly with sorrow of heart,

7 He said: I will destroy man, whom I have created, from the face of the earth, from man even to beasts, from the creeping thing even to the fowls of the air, for it repenteth me that I have made them.

8 But Noe[2] found grace before the Lord.

9 These are the generations of Noe: Noe was a just and perfect man in his generations, he walked with God.

10 And he begot three sons, Sem, Cham, and Japheth.

11 And the earth was corrupted before God, and was filled with iniquity.

12 And when God had seen that the earth was corrupted (for all flesh had corrupted its way upon the earth,)

---

[1] *bow* I.e., rainbow.

[2] *Noe* I.e., Noah.

13   He said to Noe: The end of all flesh is come before me, the earth is filled with iniquity through them, and I will destroy them with the earth.

14   Make thee an ark of timber planks: thou shalt make little rooms in the ark, and thou shalt pitch it within and without.

15   And thus shalt thou make it: The length of the ark shall be three hundred cubits: the breadth of it fifty cubits, and the height of it thirty cubits.

16   Thou shalt make a window in the ark, and in a cubit shalt thou finish the top of it: and the door of the ark thou shalt set in the side: with lower, middle chambers, and third stories shalt thou make it.

17   Behold I will bring the waters of a great flood upon the earth, to destroy all flesh, wherein is the breath of life, under heaven. All things that are in the earth shall be consumed.

18   And I will establish my covenant with thee, and thou shalt enter into the ark, thou and thy sons, and thy wife, and the wives of thy sons with thee.

19   And of every living creature of all flesh, thou shalt bring two of a sort into the ark, that they may live with thee: of the male sex, and the female.

20   Of fowls according to their kind, and of beasts in their kind, and of every thing that creepeth on the earth according to its kind; two of every sort shall go in with thee, that they may live.

21   Thou shalt take unto thee of all food that may be eaten, and thou shalt lay it up with thee: and it shall be food for thee and them.

22   And Noe did all things which God commanded him.

Chapter 7

1   And the Lord said to him: Go in thou and all thy house into the ark: for thee I have seen just before me in this generation.

2   Of all clean beasts take seven and seven, the male and the female.

3   But of the beasts that are unclean two and two, the male and the female. Of the fowls also of the air seven and seven, the male and the female: that seed may be saved upon the face of the whole earth.

4   For yet a while, and after seven days, I will rain upon the earth forty days and forty nights; and I will destroy every substance that I have made, from the face of the earth.

5   And Noe did all things which the Lord had commanded him.

6   And he was six hundred years old, when the waters of the flood overflowed the earth.

7   And Noe went in and his sons, his wife and the wives of his sons with him into the ark, because of the waters of the flood.

8   And of beasts clean and unclean, and of fowls, and of every thing that moveth upon the earth,

9   Two and two went in to Noe into the ark, male and female, as the Lord had commanded Noe.

10   And after the seven days were passed, the waters of the flood overflowed the earth.

11   In the six hundredth year of the life of Noe, in the second month, in the seventeenth day of the month, all the fountains of the great deep were broken up, and the flood gates of heaven were opened:

12   And the rain fell upon the earth forty days and forty nights.

13   In the selfsame day Noe, and Sem, and Cham, and Japheth his sons: his wife, and the three wives of his sons with them, went into the ark:

14   They and every beast according to its kind, and all the cattle in their kind, and every thing that moveth upon the earth according to its kind, and every fowl according to its kind, all birds, and all that fly,

15   Went in to Noe into the ark, two and two of all flesh, wherein was the breath of life.

16   And they that went in, went in male and female of all flesh, as God had commanded him: and the Lord shut him in on the outside.

17   And the flood was forty days upon the earth, and the waters increased, and lifted up the ark on high from the earth.

18   For they overflowed exceedingly: and filled all on the face of the earth: and the ark was carried upon the waters.

19   And the waters prevailed beyond measure upon the earth: and all the high mountains under the whole heaven were covered.

20   The water was fifteen cubits higher than the mountains which it covered.

21   And all flesh was destroyed that moved upon the earth, both of fowl, and of cattle, and of beasts, and of all creeping things that creep upon the earth: and all men.

22   And all things wherein there is the breath of life on the earth, died.

23   And he destroyed all the substance that was upon the earth, from man even to beast, and the creeping things and fowls of the air: and they were destroyed from the earth: and Noe only remained, and they that were with him in the ark.

24   And the waters prevailed upon the earth a hundred and fifty days.

CHAPTER 8

1   And God remembered Noe, and all the living creatures, and all the cattle which were with him in the ark, and brought a wind upon the earth, and the waters were abated.

2   The fountains also of the deep, and the flood gates of heaven were shut up, and the rain from heaven was restrained.

3   And the waters returned from off the earth going and coming: and they began to be abated after a hundred and fifty days.

4   And the ark rested in the seventh month, the seven and twentieth day of the month, upon the mountains of Armenia.

5   And the waters were going and decreasing until the tenth month: for in the tenth month, the first day of the month, the tops of the mountains appeared.

6   And after that forty days were passed, Noe, opening the window of the ark which he had made, sent forth a raven:

7   Which went forth and did not return, till the waters were dried up upon the earth.

8   He sent forth also a dove after him, to see if the waters had now ceased upon the face of the earth.

9   But she, not finding where her foot might rest, returned to him into the ark: for the waters were upon the whole earth: and he put forth his hand, and caught her, and brought her into the ark.

10   And having waited yet seven other days, he again sent forth the dove out of the ark.

11   And she came to him in the evening, carrying a bough of an olive tree, with green leaves, in her mouth. Noe therefore understood that the waters were ceased upon the earth.

12   And he stayed yet other seven days: and he sent forth the dove, which returned not any more unto him.

13   Therefore in the six hundredth and first year, the first month, the first day of the month, the waters were lessened upon the earth, and Noe opening the covering of the ark, looked, and saw that the face of the earth was dried.

14   In the second month, the seven and twentieth day of the month, the earth was dried.

15   And God spoke to Noe, saying:

16   Go out of the ark, thou and thy wife, thy sons, and the wives of thy sons with thee.

17   All living things that are with thee of all flesh, as well in fowls as in beasts, and all creeping things that creep upon the earth, bring out with thee, and go ye upon the earth: increase and multiply upon it.

18   So Noe went out, he and his sons: his wife, and the wives of his sons with him.

19   And all living things, and cattle, and creeping things that creep upon the earth, according to their kinds, went out of the ark.

20   And Noe built an altar unto the Lord: and taking of all cattle and fowls that were clean, offered holocausts upon the altar.

21   And the Lord smelled a sweet savour, and said: I will no more curse the earth for the sake of man: for the imagination and thought of man's heart are prone to evil from his youth: therefore I will no more destroy every living soul as I have done.

22   All the days of the earth, seedtime and harvest, cold and heat, summer and winter, night and day, shall not cease.

CHAPTER 9

1   And God blessed Noe and his sons. And he said to them: Increase and multiply, and fill the earth.

2   And let the fear and dread of you be upon all the beasts of the earth, and upon all the fowls of the air, and all that move upon the earth: all the fishes of the sea are delivered into your hand.

3   And every thing that moveth and liveth shall be meat for you: even as the green herbs have I delivered them all to you:

4   Saving that flesh with blood you shall not eat.

5   For I will require the blood of your lives at the hand of every beast, and at the hand of man, at the hand of every man, and of his brother, will I require the life of man.

6   Whosoever shall shed man's blood, his blood shall be shed: for man was made to the image of God.

7   But increase you and multiply, and go upon the earth, and fill it.

8   Thus also said God to Noe, and to his sons with him,

9   Behold I will establish my covenant with you, and with your seed after you:

10   And with every living soul that is with you, as well in all birds as in cattle and beasts of the earth, that are come forth out of the ark, and in all the beasts of the earth.

11   I will establish my covenant with you, and all flesh shall be no more destroyed with the waters of a flood, neither shall there be from henceforth a flood to waste the earth.

12   And God said: This is the sign of the covenant which I give between me and you, and to every living soul that is with you, for perpetual generations.

13   I will set my bow in the clouds, and it shall be the sign of a covenant between me, and between the earth.

14   And when I shall cover the sky with clouds, my bow shall appear in the clouds:

15   And I will remember my covenant with you, and with every living soul that beareth flesh: and there shall no more be waters of a flood to destroy all flesh.

16   And the bow shall be in the clouds, and I shall see it, and shall remember the everlasting covenant, that was made between God and every living soul of all flesh which is upon the earth.

17   And God said to Noe: This shall be the sign of the covenant which I have established between me and all flesh upon the earth.

18   And the sons of Noe who came out of the ark, were Sem, Cham, and Japheth: and Cham is the father of Chanaan.

19 These three are the sons of Noe: and from these was all mankind spread over the whole earth.

20 And Noe, a husbandman, began to till the ground, and planted a vineyard.

21 And drinking of the wine was made drunk, and was uncovered in his tent.

22 Which when Cham the father of Chanaan had seen, to wit, that his father's nakedness was uncovered, he told it to his two brethren without.

23 But Sem and Japheth put a cloak upon their shoulders, and going backward, covered the nakedness of their father: and their faces were turned away, and they saw not their father's nakedness.

24 And Noe awaking from the wine, when he had learned what his younger son had done to him,

25 He said: Cursed be Chanaan, a servant of servants shall he be unto his brethren.

26 And he said: Blessed be the Lord God of Sem, be Chanaan his servant.

27 May God enlarge Japheth, and may he dwell in the tents of Sem, and Chanaan be his servant.

28 And Noe lived after the flood three hundred and fifty years:

29 And all his days were in the whole nine hundred and fifty years: and he died.

THE WAKEFIELD MASTER
c. 1400 – 1450

Much is unclear about the identity of the "Wakefield Master" and about the group of plays ascribed to this individual. That group of plays is brought together in a manuscript that is believed to date from the mid sixteenth century. Nothing is sure about its origin, but by the seventeenth century it was in the library of a well-to-do Catholic family, the Towneleys of Towneley Hall near Burnley, Lancashire, from which the Towneley manuscript (now in the Huntington Library in San Marino, CA) takes its name. The manuscript includes thirty-two short plays based largely on biblical story material.

In the manuscript the plays appear in a sequence that approximates that of the Bible, beginning with a play depicting the story of the Creation. For that reason the Towneley Plays were long assumed to represent a cycle similar to that of the York and Chester cycles, in which a sequence of pageant plays was performed once every year, with performances beginning early in the day and running until dark, and with each play mounted under the auspices of one of the trade guilds of the town. Largely because the name "Wakefield" appears on the first page of two of the plays, the assumption took root that all thirty-two plays constituted a unified group that had been performed in that town, and the Towneley plays became widely referred to as the "Wakefield Cycle." As recent scholarship has emphasised, however, the thirty-two form a very disparate group. The plays have a variety of sometimes-incompatible staging requirements; several have been borrowed virtually intact from the York cycle of pageant plays; several exhibit inconsistencies suggesting that they were unlikely ever to have been performed as they now appear. It is thus now thought to be entirely possible that the manuscript collection simply represents a group of plays from various sources, assembled in quasi-chronological order. Some have speculated that the collection may have been brought together in one manuscript with a view more to reading than to performance (though marks in some plays suggest a performance history, it is not clear when these were added to the manuscript). It is now regarded as highly improbable that the thirty-two were all performed together as part of a unified cycle, in Wakefield or in any other town.

Within the Towneley Plays, however, are five plays with strong points of similarity: *Noah*, the *First Shepherds' Play*, the *Second Shepherds' Play*, *Herod the Great*, and *The Buffeting of Christ*. A sixth, *The Killing of Abel*, is sometimes also linked with these five, though it is not written in the same stanzaic form as the others. The two shepherds plays and *The Killing of Abel* (unlike other plays in the Towneley manuscript) contain textual allusions to the Wakefield area. The five maintain a strong metrical structure, presented in the manuscript in the form of nine-line stanzas, with a consistent a a a a b c c c b rhyming pattern throughout. The first four manuscript lines also contain rhyming half lines; in the light of this, recent scholarship is in agreement that an appropriate alternative to the way in which the lines are laid out in the manuscript is to read them as forming thirteen-line stanzas, rhymed a b a b a b a b c d d d c. These plays are also acknowledged to be distinguished by their lively characterization—and by the sheer skill of their composition. Since the nineteenth century they have generally been ascribed to a single author, now conventionally referred to as the "Wakefield Master." Here too, however, recent scholarship has challenged old assumptions. While the commonality of all five plays has not been questioned, we have no firm evidence as to authorship. The quotation marks placed around the name "Wakefield Master" are thus to be taken to indicate that the ascription of authorship is the product of convention rather than proven fact. All that can be said with confidence is that there seems clearly to have been a common force involved in the shaping of all five of these plays.

Whether through the medium of a single author or the shaping editorial hand of the compiler, the five plays demonstrate an extensive and sophisticated knowledge of the Bible. It is also possible that the author or editor had some knowledge of continental literature, as the structures suggest some influences from the French comic theater of the time. The plays are written in a northern dialect of Middle English.

The *Second Shepherds' Play* is the best known and most widely read of the English biblical pageant plays. As with all such plays, it seems to have been intended to make biblical stories interesting to a largely illiterate population. It is noteworthy, however, that the play contains a very significant amount of material that has no biblical source. The play interweaves a touching presentation of Christ's nativity (extrapolated from the biblical account) with a farcical plot involving the thief and trickster Mak. The story material that has been added has considerable entertainment value, but it also offers social commentary.

In *Herod the Great*, King Herod orders the slaughter of all male children in Bethlehem under two years of age in an attempt to kill the Christ child, whom he sees as a potential threat. In its dramatization of this Bible story, the play draws on several medieval literary traditions to portray Herod as an arch-villain. Taking a cue from the depiction of Herod in Matthew 2.16, medieval artists often portrayed Herod as a raving madman. (That this tendency was still alive in Shakespeare's time is evidenced by Hamlet's advice to the players to avoid a performance that "out-Herods Herod.") The play also portrays Herod as a Muslim, another medieval literary tradition; in medieval biblical plays, Herod and his cohorts were often costumed as Saracens. For the most part, however, the play makes no distinction between first-century Palestine and fifteenth-century England. Much as *The Second Shepherds' Play*, where characters anachronistically swear by Christ's cross and by Pontius Pilate before they know of the birth of Jesus, Herod here employs knights and receives the gift of medieval European lands.

⌘⌘⌘

The Second Shepherds' Play[1]

CHARACTERS:
First Shepherd
Second Shepherd
Third Shepherd
Mak
Gill
An Angel
Mary

(*Here begins their second.*)

[*A field near Bethlehem. Enter First Shepherd.*]

FIRST SHEPHERD.   Lord! what these weathers are cold!
     And I am ill-happed;°   *poorly clothed*
I am near-hand dold,° so long have I napped;   *numb*
My legs they fold, my fingers are chapped;
It is not as I would, for I am all lapped°   *wrapped*
5   In sorrow.
     In storms and tempest,
     Now in the east, now in the west,
     Woe is him has never rest,
          Mid-day nor morrow.

10   But we seely husbands[2] that walk on the moor,
In faith, we are near-hands out of the door;
No wonder, as it stands, if we be poor,

---

[1] For the present text spelling and punctuation have been substantially modernized from the original Towneley text. The stage directions in Latin in the Towneley text are here translated into English and shown in parentheses. For clarity some other stage directions have been added; these appear in square brackets.

[2] *seely husbands* Poor farm workers.

For the tilth of our lands lies fallow as the floor,[1]
    As ye ken.°   *know*
15 We are so hamed°   *hamstrung*
For-taxed and ramed,[2]
We're made hand-tamed
    With° these gentlery men.°   *by / gentry*

Thus they reave[3] us our rest, Our Lady them wary!° *curse*
20 These men that are lord-fast,[4] they cause the plough tarry.
What men say is for the best, we find it contrary;
Thus are husbands° oppressed, in point to miscarry *farmers*
    In life.
Thus hold they us under,
25 Thus they bring us in blunder;°   *confusion*
It were great wonder,
    And° ever should we thrive.   *if*

For may he get a paint sleeve, or a brooch nowadays,
Woe is him that him grieve, or once again-says![5]
30 Dare no man him reprieve,° what mast'ry he
    makes;   *reprove*
And yet may no man lefe° one word that he says, *believe*
    No letter.
He can make purveyance,[6]
With boast and bragance,
35 And all is through maintenance
    Of men that are greater.[7]

There shall come a swain, as proud as a po,° *peacock*
He must borrow my wain,° my plough also; *wagon*
Then I am full fain° to grant ere he go. *delighted*

---

[1] *the tilth ... floor* I.e., all of our land—the arable land (tilth) as much as the low–lying areas, is lying fallow; no crops are being grown there. During the fifteenth century many landowners were converting farmland to grazing land.

[2] *For-taxed and ramed* Overburdened and oppressed.

[3] *reave* Take away from.

[4] *lord-fast* Attached to lords.

[5] *For ... again-says!* For, if anyone gets a painted sleeve or a brooch (i.e., wears livery) woe to the man who gives grief to or contradicts that person!

[6] *purveyance* The requisition and purchase of provisions, specifically the right of the crown or of a lord to buy supplies for the household at a price set by a purveyor.

[7] *through maintenance ... greater* Through the support of those with greater power.

---

40 Thus live we in pain, anger, and woe,
    By night and day.
He must have if he longed,
If I should forgo it;[8]
I were better be hanged
45   Than once say him nay.

It does me good, as I walk thus by mine own,
Of this world for to talk in manner of moan.[9]
To my sheep will I stalk and hearken anon,
There abide on a balk,° or sit on a stone *ridge*
50   Full soon.
For I trow,° pardie,[10] true men if they be, *trust*
We get more company
    Or° it be noon.   *before*

[Enter Second Shepherd. He does not see the First Shepherd.]

SECOND SHEPHERD. Benste[11] and Dominus! what
    may this bemean?°   *indicate*
55 Why fares this world thus? Oft have we not seen,
Lord, these weathers are spiteous,° and the *nasty*
    winds full keen;
And the frost so hideous they water mine eeyen,° *eyes*
    No lie.
Now in dry, now in wet,
60 Now in snow, now in sleet,
When my shone° freeze to my feet *shoes*
    It is not all easy.

But as far as I ken, or yet as I go,
We seely wed-men dre mekill woe;[12]
65 We have sorrow then and then, it falls° oft so. *happens*
Seely Capel, our hen, both to and fro
    She cackles;
But begins she to croak,

---

[8] *He must ... forgo it* If he has longed for a thing he must have it, even if I have to do without.

[9] *in manner of moan* In a complaining way.

[10] *pardie* By God (a corruption of the French "Pardieu").

[11] *Benste* Bless us (a corruption of the Latin "Benedicte"); *Dominus* Latin: "Lord."

[12] *seely ... woe* We poor married men suffer a great deal.

To groan or to cluck,
70   Woe is him, our cock,
         For he is in the shackles.[1]

These men that are wed have not all their will;
When they are full hard stead,[2] they sigh full
      still;°   *continually*
God wayte° they are led full hard and full ill,   *knows*
75 In bower° nor in bed they say nought
      theretill,°   *bedroom / in reply*
         This tide.°   *time*
My part have I fun—°   *found*
I know my lesson:
Woe is him that is bun°   *bound*
80 For he must abide.°   *stay that way*

But now late in our lives—a marvel to me,
That I think my heart rives° such wonders to see,   *breaks*
What that destiny drives, it should so be!—
Some men will have two wives, and some men three,
85   In store.
Some are woe° that have any;   *sad, woeful*
But so far can I,[3]
Woe is him that has many,
For he feels sore.

[*To the audience.*]

90 But young men, of wooing, for God that you bought,[4]
Be well ware of wedding, and think in your thought:
"Had I wist"° is a thing that serves of nought;   *known*
Mekill still° mourning has wedding home   *much steady*
      brought,
         And griefs,
95 With many a sharp shower,°   *pang*
For thou may catch in an hour
That shall sow° thou full sour°   *grieve / bitterly*
         As long as thou liffys.°   *you live*

For, as ever read I pistill, I have one to my fere[5]
100 As sharp as a thistle, as rough as a brier;
She is browed like a bristle, with a sour-loten°   *looking*
      cheer;
Had she once wet her whistle she could sing full clear
         Her pater-noster.[6]
She is as great as a whall,°   *whale*
105 She has a gallon of gall;
By him that died for us all,°   *i.e., Jesus*
         I would I had run to° I had lost her!   *till*

FIRST SHEPHERD.   God
      Look over the row!° Full deafly ye stand.   *audience*
110 SECOND SHEPHERD.   Yea, the devil in thy maw, so
      tarryand!°[7]   *tarrying*
         Saw thou anywhere of Daw?
FIRST SHEPHERD.   Yea, on a lea[8] land
Heard I him blow;[9] he comes here at hand,
         Not far;
115 Stand still.
SECOND SHEPHERD.   Why?
FIRST SHEPHERD.   For he comes, hope I.
SECOND SHEPHERD.   He will make° us both a lie   *tell*
         But if° we beware.   *unless*

[*Enter Third Shepherd, a boy. He does not see the
others.*]

120 THIRD SHEPHERD.   Christ's cross me speed, and Saint
      Nicholas!
Thereof had I need, it is worse than it was.
Whoso could, take heed, and let the world pass:
It is ever in dread and brekill° as glass,   *brittle*
         And slithes.°   *slides away*
125 This world fared never so,
With marvels more and more,
Now in weal, now in woe,
         And all thing writhes.[10]

---

[1]   *Seely Capel … in shackles* The husband is in servitude to his wife,
who is likened to a silly hen.

[2]   *full hard stead* Hard pressed, stricken by misfortune.

[3]   *so far can I* This much I know.

[4]   *you bought* Redeemed you.

[5]   *as ever … fere* As continually as I read the Epistle, I have one as
my companion.

[6]   *pater-noster* Latin: "Our Father"; the Lord's Prayer.

[7]   *maw … tarryand* Belly, for taking so long.

[8]   *lea* Fallow, unploughed.

[9]   *Heard … blow* I heard him blow (his horn).

[10]   *all thing writhes* Everything keeps turning.

Was never since Noah's flood such floods seen,
130   Winds and rains so rude, and storms so keen;
Some stammered, some stood in doubt, as I
ween;°   *think*
Now God, turn all to good! I say as I mean.
For ponder:
These floods so they drown
135   Both in fields and in town,
And bear all down,
And that is a wonder.

[*He sees the others, but at first does not recognize them.*]

We that walk in the nights, our cattle to keep,
We see sudden sights, when other men sleep.
140   Yet methink my heart lights—I see shrews° peep.   *villains*
Ye are two all-wights!° I will give my sheep   *monsters*
A turn.
But full ill have I meant;
As I walk on this bent,°   *heath*
145   I may lightly repent
My toes if I spurn.[1]

Ah, sir, God you save, and master mine!
A drink fain would I have, and somewhat to dine.

FIRST SHEPHERD.   Christ's curse, my knave, thou art a
lither hind![2]
150   SECOND SHEPHERD.   What, the boy list° rave!   *likes to*

(*To the Third Shepherd.*)

Abide unto sine;°   *later*
We have made it.
Ill thrift° on thy pate!°[3]   *luck / head*

(*To the First Shepherd.*)

Though the shrew° came late,   *rascal*
155   Yet is he in state
To dine, if he had it.[4]
THIRD SHEPHERD.   Such servants as I, that sweats and
swinks,°   *labors, toils*
Eats our bread full dry, and that me forthinks;[5]
We are oft wet and weary when mastermen winks,°   *sleep*
160   Yet comes full lately° both dinners and drinks.   *very slowly*
But naitly°   *thoroughly*
Both our dame and our sire,
When we have run in the mire,°   *muck*
They can nip at our hire,[6]
165   And pay us full lately.

But hear my truth, master: for the fare that ye make,
I shall do thereafter work as I take;[7]
I shall do a little, sir, emang ever lake;[8]
For yet lay my supper never on my stomach
170   In fields.[9]
Whereto should I threap?°   *complain*
With my staff can I leap,
And men say "light cheap
Litherly foryields."[10]

175   FIRST SHEPHERD.   Thou were an ill lad—to ride on
wowing
With a man that had but little of spending—
SECOND SHEPHERD.   Peace, boy, I bade; no more
jangling,°   *chattering*
Or I shall make thee afraid, by the heaven's king,
With thy gauds!°   *pranks*
180   Where are our sheep, boy? We scorn—
THIRD SHEPHERD.   Sir, this same day at morn
I left them in the corn,

---

[1]   *But full ill ... spurn*   The meaning here is obscure; the suggestion
seems to be that a comical penance (of stubbing his toes) is to be
imposed on the shepherd for having taken his fellow shepherds to be
monsters.

[2]   *lither hind*   Wicked farm servant.

[3]   *Abide ... pate*   Wait a while; we have had food already—bad luck
to you.

[4]   *in state ... had it*   Would like to eat, if he had food.

[5]   *me forthinks*   Upsets me.

[6]   *nip at our hire*   Reduce our wages.

[7]   *I shall do ... take*   I will only work if I am being paid for it.

[8]   *emang ever lake*   Keep playing continually.

[9]   *For yet ... fields*   For I have never had such a full stomach that it
weighed me down in the fields.

[10]   *light cheap / Litherly foryields*   Proverbial saying: Low costs yield
low returns, i.e., you get what you pay for.

When they rang Lauds;[1]

They have pasture good—they cannot go wrong.
185 FIRST SHEPHERD.   That is right. By the rood,° these nights are long! °*cross*
Yet I would, ere we yode,° one gave us a song. °*went*
SECOND SHEPHERD.   So I thought as I stood, to mirth us among.[2]
THIRD SHEPHERD.   I grant.
FIRST SHEPHERD.   Let me sing the tenory.° °*tenor*
185 SECOND SHEPHERD.   And I the treble so high.
THIRD SHEPHERD.   Then the mean° falls to me; °*middle part*
Let's see how ye chant.

(*Enter Mak, with a cloak thrown over his smock.*)

MAK.   Now, Lord, for thy names seven, that made both moon and stars,
Well more than I can neven,[3] thy will, Lord, of me tharnys;[4]
190 I am all uneven,° that moves oft my harns;° °*upset / brains*
Now would God I were in heaven, for there weep no bairns° °*children*
So still!° °*incessantly*
FIRST SHEPHERD.   Who is that pipes so poor?° °*cries so wretchedly*
MAK.   Would God ye wist° how I foor!° °*knew / fared*
195 Lo, a man that walks on the moor, And has not all his will![5]

SECOND SHEPHERD.   Mak, where has thou gone? Tell us tidings.
THIRD SHEPHERD.   Is *he* come? Then each one take heed to his thing.[6]

(*Takes his cloak from him.*)

MAK.   What! *Ich*[7] be a yeoman, I tell you, of the king;
200 The self and the some,° sent from a great lording, °*same*
Und *sich*.° °*and such*
Fie on you! Goeth hence!
Out of my presence!
I must have reverence.
205   Why, who be *Ich*?

FIRST SHEPHERD.   Why make ye it so quaint?° °*affected*
Mak, ye do wrong.
SECOND SHEPHERD.   But, Mak, play ye the saint? I trow that ye long.[8]
THIRD SHEPHERD.   I trow the shrew can paynt,[9] the devil might him hang!
MAK.   I shall make complaint, and make you all to thwang[10]
210   At a word.
And tell even how ye doth.[11]
FIRST SHEPHERD.   But, Mak, is that truth? Now take out that southern tooth,[12]
    And set° in a turd! °*put*
215 SECOND SHEPHERD.   Mak, the devil in your eye! A stroke would I lean° you. °*give*
THIRD SHEPHERD.   Mak, know ye not me? By God, I could teen[13] you.

[*Mak now pretends to recognize the shepherds for the first time.*]

MAK.   God look you all three! Methought I had seen you. Ye are a fair company.

---

[1] *Lauds*   "Laud" was the first hour of the Church day, and it ended with the singing of a Psalm of praise (from the Latin for praise, *laus, laudem*).

[2] *to mirth us among*   To have mirth among us.

[3] *neven*   Refer to, especially by name.

[4] *of me tharnys*   Is unclear to me.

[5] *Lo ... will*   Look, I am just a man out walking, who does not know what to do; or, does not have all he wants.

[6] *Then ... thing*   In that case everyone should look out for his belongings.

[7] *Ich*   The use of this word (together with "sich") suggests that Mak is affecting a southern English dialect.

[8] *play ... long*   Are you pretending to be a saint? I believe that's what you long to be.

[9] *paynt*   Feign, deceive.

[10] *thwang*   Be flogged.

[11] *tell ... doth*   I will even tell (the authorities) how you are acting.

[12] *southern tooth*   Southern dialect.

[13] *teen*   Vex, cause physical injury to.

FIRST SHEPHERD.   Can ye now mene you?[1]

220 SECOND SHEPHERD.   Shrew, peep!°   *look out!*
Thus late as thou goes,
What will men suppose?
And thou has an ill noise
　　　Of stealing of sheep.[2]

225 MAK.   And I am true as steel, all men watt!°   *know*
But a sickness I feel, that holds me full hatt°   *hot*
My belly fares not well, it is out of estate.°   *in poor shape*

THIRD SHEPHERD.   Seldom lies the devil dead by the
　　　gate.[3]

MAK.   Therefore
230 Full sore am I and ill,
If I stand stone still;
I eat not a needle
　　　This month and more.

FIRST SHEPHERD.   How fares thy wife? By my hood,
　　　how fares sho?°   *she*

235 MAK.   Lies weltering,° by the rood, by the fire, lo!   *sprawled*
And a house full of brood;° she drinks well, too;   *children*
Ill speed other good that she will do!
　　　But so
Eats as fast as she can,
240 And each year that comes to man,
She brings forth a lakan°   *baby*
　　　And some years two.

But were I now more gracious, and richer by far,
I were° eaten out of house and of harbour;°   *would be / home*
245 Yet is she a foul douce,° if ye come near.   *woman*
There is none that trows nor knows a worse
　　　Than ken I.
Now will ye see what I proffer?
To give all in my coffer
250 To-morn next to offer
　　　Her head-mass penny.[4]

SECOND SHEPHERD.   I know so forwaked[5] is none in
　　　this shire:
I would sleep if I took less to my hire.[6]

THIRD SHEPHERD.   I am cold and naked, and would
　　　have a fire.

255 FIRST SHEPHERD.   I am weary, for-raked,°   *exhausted*
and run in the mire.
　　　Wake thou!

SECOND SHEPHERD.   Nay, I will lie down-by,
For I must sleep, truly.

THIRD SHEPHERD.   As good a man's son was I
260 　　　As any of you.[7]

[*Lies down.*]

But, Mak, come hither! between shall thou lie down.

MAK.   Then might I lett you bedene of that ye would
　　　rowne;[8]
　　　No dread.
From my top to my toe
265 *Manus tuas commendo,*
Pontio Pilate![9]
　　　Christ's cross me speed!

(*Then he rises, while the shepherds are asleep, and says:*)

Now were time for a man that lacks what he would,
To stalk privily then into a fold,°   *sheepfold*
270 And nimbly to work then, and be not too bold,
For he might aby the bargain, if it were told
　　　At the ending.[10]
Now is the time to reyll°   *act quickly*
But he needs good counsel

---

[1] *Can ye now mene you?*   Are you now able to recognize yourself
too?

[2] *And thou … stealing of sheep*   And you have a bad reputation as a
sheep stealer.

[3] *Seldom … gate*   Proverbial: When the devil seems to lie dead, it
is more likely that he is feigning.

[4] *head-mass penny*   Payment for her funeral mass.

[5] *forwaked*   Tired from lack of sleep.

[6] *I would … to my hire*   I would take less wages if I could sleep.

[7] *As good … any of you*   I am just as good as you are (and therefore
just as deserving of a rest).

[8] *lett you … would rowne*   Hinder your whispering round me.

[9] *Manus tuas commendo Pontio Pilate*   Latin: "Into thy hands I
commend (my spirit), Pontius Pilate." Mak misquotes Luke 23.46
("Father, into thy hands I commend my spirit") and substitutes
Pontius Pilate for God.

[10] *he might … ending*   He (who is too bold) may pay a high price for
it in the end.

275 That fain would fare well,
        And has but little spending.[1]

[*Mak casts a spell on the sleeping shepherds.*]

But about you, a circle as round as a moon!
Till I have done that I will, till that it be noon,
That ye lie stone-still, to° that I have done.   *till*
280 And I shall say there-till of good words a fayne:°   *few*
        "On height,
Over your heads my hand I lift,
Out go your eyes, fordo° your sight!"   *lose*
But yet I must make better shift,°   *arrangements*
285   And° it be right.   *if*

[*Shepherds snore. Mak addresses the audience.*]

Lord, what they sleep hard! That may ye all hear.
Was I° never a shepherd, but now will I lere.°   *I was / learn*
If the flock be scared, yet shall I nip° near.   *come*
How! Draw hitherward! Now mends our cheer
290   From sorrow.
A fat sheep, I dare say,
A good fleece, dare I lay.°   *wager*
Eft-whyte° when I may,   *repay*
        But this will I borrow.

[*Carries the sheep to the door of his house.*]

295 How, Gill, art thou in? Get us some light.
WIFE.   Who makes such din this time of the night?
I am set for to spin. I doubt that I might
Rise a penny to win; I shrew them on height!
        So fares
300 A huswiff that has been
To be raced thus between![2]
Here may no note be seen
        For such small chares.°   *chores*

MAK.   Good wife, open the hek!° Sees thou not   *door*
        what I bring?
305 WIFE.   I may let thee draw the sneck.°   *latch*
Ah, come in, my sweeting!
MAK.   Yea, thou there not reck of my long standing![3]
WIFE.   By the naked neck art thou like for° to   *likely*
        hang!
MAK.   Do way!°   *stop that!*
310 I am worthy my meat,
For in a strait° can I get   *tight spot*
More than they that swink and sweat
        All the long day.

Thus it fell to my lot, Gill: I had such grace![4]
315 WIFE.   It were a foul blot to be hanged for the case.
MAK.   I have scaped, Gillot, oft as hard a glace.°   *blow*
WIFE.   But so long goes the pot to the water, men says,
        At last
Comes it home broken.
320 MAK.   Well know I the token,
But let it never be spoken.
        But come and help fast.

I would he were flayn;° I list° well eat: *skinned / wish*
This twelvemonth was I not so fain of one sheep-
        meat.
325 WIFE.   Come they ere he be slain, and hear the sheep
        bleat—
MAK.   Then might I be ta'en: that were a cold sweat!
        Go spar°   *fasten*
The gate door.
WIFE.   Yes, Mak,
330 For and they come at thy back—
MAK.   Then might I buy, fro all the pack,
        The devil of the war![5]

WIFE.   A good bowrde° have I spied, since thou   *trick*
        ken° none: *know*
Here shall we him hide too they be gone,
335 In my cradle abide. Let° me alone,   *leave*

---

[1] *he needs ... spending*   Someone who would like to fare better but
has few resources needs to follow good advice.

[2] *I am set ... between*   I am all in a tizzy. I don't see how I can gain
anything from this; I curse them mightily! This is how it goes for a
housewife who has been interrupted like this!

[3] *Yea ... standing*   Yes, don't let it bother you how long I've been
standing here!

[4] *I had such grace*   I was so blessed.

[5] *Then might ... war*   Then I might receive, from the pack of them,
a hellishly bad experience.

And I shall lie beside in childbed and groan.

MAK.   Thou red°   *ready yourself*

And I shall say thou was lighted°   *delivered*

Of a knave°-child this night.   *male*

340 WIFE.   Now, well is me! Day bright

      That ever I was bred!

This is a good guise and a far cast;°   *clever trick*

Yet a woman avyse° helps at the last!   *advice*

I wote never who spies; again, go thou fast![1]

345 MAK.   But I come ere they rise, else blows a cold blast!

      I will go sleep.

[*Mak returns to the Shepherds.*]

Yet sleeps all this meneye°   *group*

And I shall go stalk privily,°   *stealthily*

As it had never been I

350   That carried their sheep.

[*He lies down among them. The shepherds begin to wake up.*]

FIRST SHEPHERD.   *Resurrex a mortruis!*[2] Have hold my
    hand!

Judas carnas dominus![3] I may not well stand.

My foot sleeps, by Jesus! and I water fastand.

I thought that we laid us full near England.[4]

355 SECOND SHEPHERD.   Ah, yea!

Lord, what, I have slept well!

As fresh as an eel,

As light I me feel

      As leaf on a tree.

360 THIRD SHEPHERD.   Benste be herein! So me quakes,

My heart is out of skin; what so it makes!

Who makes all this din? So my brows blakes

To the door will I win.[5] Hark, fellows, wake!

      We were four:

365 See ye anywhere of Mak now?

FIRST SHEPHERD.   We were up ere thou.

SECOND SHEPHERD.   Man, I give God a vow,

      That yede he nowhere.

THIRD SHEPHERD.   Methought he was lapt in a
    wolfskin.

370 FIRST SHEPHERD.   So are many happed now: namely,
    within.

THIRD SHEPHERD.   When we had long napped,

    methought with a gin°   *trap*

A fat sheep he trapped, but he made no din.

SECOND SHEPHERD.   Be still!

Thy dream makes thee wood;°   *insane*

375 It is but phantom, by the rood.

FIRST SHEPHERD.   Now God turn all to good,

      If it be his will!

[*They turn to wake up Mak.*]

SECOND SHEPHERD.   Rise, Mak, for shame! Thou lies
    right long.

MAK.   Now Christ's holy name be us emang!°   *among*

380 What is this? For Saint James, I may not well go!

I trow I be the same. Ah, my neck has lain wrang°   *wrong*

      Enough,

Mekill thank, since yester-even.°   *yesterday evening*

Now, by Saint Stephen,

385 I was flayed° by a sweven°   *scared / dream*

      My heart out of slough.°   *skin*

I thought Gill began to croak, and travail° full sad, *labor*

Well near at the first cock,° of a young lad   *cock-crow*

For to mend our flock. Then be I never glad;

390 I have tow on my rok[6] more than ever I had.

      Ah, my head!

A house full of young tharms,°   *stomachs*

The devil knock out their harns!

Woe is him has many bairns,

395   And so little bread!

---

[1]   *I wote never … fast* I don't know who may be looking; go back
(to the shepherds) again quickly!

[2]   *Resurrex a mortruis* Garbled Latin: "He has risen from the dead!"

[3]   *Judas carnas dominus* Corrupted Latin: "Judas, lord of the flesh!"

[4]   *I water … England* I have eaten so little that I thought we had
been lying down very close to England.

[5]   *So my brows … will I win* My brows furrow (out of fear at the
commotion) and I will run away.

[6]   *tow on my rok* Flax on my distaff (i.e., trouble).

I must go home, by your leave, to Gill, as I thought.
Pray you: look up my sleeve, that I steal nought:
I am loth you to grieve, or from you take aught.
[*Exits*]

THIRD SHEPHERD.   Go forth; ill might thou cheve.°   *fare*
400   Now would I we sought,
            This morn,
      That we had all our store.[1]
FIRST SHEPHERD.   But I will go before.
      Let us meet.
405   SECOND SHEPHERD.   Where?
THIRD SHEPHERD.   At the crooked thorn.

[*They leave to check on their sheep. The scene shifts to
Mak's house.*]

MAK.   (*Knocking.*) Undo this door! Who is here? How
      long shall I stand?
WIFE.   Who makes such a bere?° Go walk in the   *noise*
      wanyand![2]
MAK.   Ah, Gill, what cheer? It is I, Mak, your
      husband.
410   WIFE.   Then may we see here the devil in a band.°   *noose*
            Sir Guile!
      Lo, he comes with a lote,°   *noise*
      As° he were holden in° the throat.   *as if / held by*
      I may not sit at my note°   *work*
415   A hand-long° while.   *little*

MAK.   Will ye hear what fare she makes to get her a
      gloze?°   *an excuse*
      And does nought but lakys,° and claws° her
      toes.   *be lacking / scratches*
WIFE.   Why, who wanders, who wakes, who comes,
      who goes?
      Who brews, who bakes? What makes me thus hose?
420   And then
      It is sad to behold,
      Now in hot, now in cold—
      Full woeful is the household
            That wants° a woman!   *lacks*

425   But what end hast thou made with the herds,°   *herders*
            Mak?
MAK.   The last word that they said when I turned my
      back:
      They would look that they had their sheep, all the pack.
      I hope they will not be well paid when they their
      sheep lack,
            Per Die!°   *by God*
430   But howso the game goes,
      It's me they will suppose,°   *suspect*
      And make a foul noise,
            And cry out upon me.

      But thou must do as thou hight.°   *promised*
435   WIFE.   I accord me theretill;
      I shall swaddle him right in my cradle.
      If it were a greater sleight,° yet could I help till.   *trick*
      I will lie down straight; come hap me.
MAK.   I will.
440   WIFE.   Behind!
      Come Coll and his marroo,°   *mate*
      They will nip us full narroo.°   *pinch us hard*
MAK.   But I may cry out "Harroo!"°   *help*
      The sheep if they find.

445   WIFE. Hearken, aye, when they call: they will come anon.
      Come and make ready all, and sing by thine own;
      Sing "Lullay!" thou shall, for I must groan,
      And cry out by the wall on Mary and John,
            Full sore.
450   Sing "Lullay" on fast
      When thou hears at the last;
      And but° I play a false cast,   *unless*
            Trust me no more.

[*The shepherds meet in a field.*]

THIRD SHEPHERD.   Ah, Coll, good morn! Why sleeps
      thou not?
455   FIRST SHEPHERD.   Alas, that ever was I born! We have
      a foul blot!
      A fat wether° have we lorn.°   *sheep / lost*
THIRD SHEPHERD.   Marry, Gods forbott!°   *God forbid!*
SECOND SHEPHERD.   Who should do us that scorn?
            That were a foul spot.

---

[1]   *Now would I . . . store*   Now I would (think we should) check, this
morning, that we have all our belongings.

[2]   *wanyand*   Waning of the moon (an unlucky time).

460 FIRST SHEPHERD.   Some shrew.°   *villain*
I have sought with my dogs
All Horbury Shrogs,[1]
And of fifteen hogs°   *young sheep*
    Found I but one ewe.

465 THIRD SHEPHERD.   Now trow me if ye will: by Saint
    Thomas of Kent,[2]
Either Mak or Gill was at that assent!°   *was involved!*
FIRST SHEPHERD.   Peace, man, be still! I saw when he
    went.
Thou slanders him ill; thou ought to repent
    Good speed.°   *speedily*
470 SECOND SHEPHERD.   Now as ever might I the°   *thrive*
If I should even here die,
I would say it were he
    That did that same deed.

THIRD SHEPHERD.   Go we thither, I rede,° and   *advise*
    run on our feet;
475 Shall I never eat bread, the sooth till I wit.[3]
FIRST SHEPHERD.   Nor drink in my head with him till
    I meet.
SECOND SHEPHERD.   I will rest in no stead° till   *place*
    that I him greet.
    My brother,
One thing I hight:°   *promise*
480 Till I see him in sight
Shall I never sleep one night
    There I do another.[4]

[*They approach Mak's house. They hear Gill groaning
and Mak singing a lullaby.*]

THIRD SHEPHERD.   Will ye hear how they hack?[5] Our
    sire list croon.°   *likes to sing*
FIRST SHEPHERD.   Heard I never none crack so clear
    out of tune.

---

[1] *All Horbury Shrogs* All the hedges of Horbury (a town near
Wakefield).

[2] Thomas à Becket (1118?-1170), Archbishop of Canterbury.

[3] *the sooth till I wit* Until I know the truth.

[4] *Shall I … do another* I will never sleep in the same place two
nights in succession.

[5] *hack* To break a note, i.e., sing badly.

485 Call on him.
SECOND SHEPHERD.   Mak! undo your door soon.
MAK.   Who is that spake, as it were noon,
    On loft?°   *loudly*
Who is that, I say?
490 THIRD SHEPHERD.   Good fellows, were it day!

[*Opening the door.*]

MAK.   As far as ye may,
    Good,° speak soft,   *good fellows*

Over a sick woman's head that is at malease;
I had liefer° be dead than she had any disease.   *rather*
495 WIFE.   Go to another stead; I may not well
    quease.°   *breathe*
Each foot that ye tread goes through my nose,
    So hee!°   *loudly*
FIRST SHEPHERD.   Tell us, Mak, if ye may,
    How fare ye, I say?
500 MAK.   But are ye in this town today?
    Now how fare ye?

Ye have run in the mire, and are wet yit?°   *yet*
I shall make you a fire, if ye will sit.
A nurse would I hire—think ye on it?
505 Well quit is my hire—my dream, this is it!—

[*Points to the cradle.*]

    A season.[6]
I have bairns, if ye knew,
Well more than a few;
But we must drink as we brew,
510   And that is but reason.°   *reasonable*

I would ye dined ere ye yode; methink that ye sweat.
SECOND SHEPHERD.   Nay, neither mends our mood,
    drink nor meat.
MAK.   Why, sir, ails you aught but good?[7]

---

[6] *A nurse … season* I would like to hire a nursemaid—what do you
think of the idea? I've got what was coming to me—just what I had
dreamt of—another child every year.

[7] *Why, sir … good?* Sir, does something that is not good trouble
you?

THIRD SHEPHERD.   Yea, our sheep that we get
515 Are stolen as they yode; our loss is great.
MAK.   Sirs, drinks!
      Had I been there,
      Some should have bought it° full sore.   *paid the price*
FIRST SHEPHERD.   Marry, some men trows°   *believe*
            that ye *were*,
520   And that us forthinks.°   *displeases us*

SECOND SHEPHERD.   Mak, some men trows that it
            should be ye.
THIRD SHEPHERD.   Either ye or your spouse; so say we.
MAK.   Now, if ye have suspowse to° of Gill   *suspicion of*
      or of me,
      Come and rip our house, and then may ye see
525   Who had° her.   *took*
      If I any sheep got,
      Either cow or stot—°   *heifer*
      And Gill, my wife, rose not
            Here since she laid her—[1]

530 As I am both true and lele,° to God here I pray, *loyal*
      That this be the first meal that I shall eat this day.
FIRST SHEPHERD.   Mak, as I have zeal, watch out, I say;
      He learned timely to steal, that could not say nay.

[*They begin to search.*]

WIFE.   I swelt!°   *faint*
535 Out, thieves, from my wonys!°   *home*
      Ye come to rob us, for the nonce.°   *on purpose*
MAK.   Hear ye not how she groans?
            Your hearts should melt.

[*They approach the cradle.*]

WIFE.   Out, thieves, from my barn!° Nigh°   *child / approach*
      him not there!
540 MAK.   Wist ye how she had farne,° your hearts *labored*
      would be sore.
      Ye do wrong, I you warn, that thus comes
      before°   *happens in front of*
      To a woman that has farne—but I say no more!

---

[1] *And Gill ... laid her*   And my wife Gill has not gotten up since
she lay down here.

WIFE.   Ah, my middle!
      I pray to God so mild,
545 If ever I you beguiled,
      That I eat this child
            That lies in this cradle.

MAK.   Peace, woman, for God's pain, and cry not so:
      Thou spills thy brain, and makes me full woe.
550 SECOND SHEPHERD.   I trow our sheep be slain. What
            find ye two?
THIRD SHEPHERD.   All work we in vain; as well may
      we go.

[*Reaches into the cradle.*]

            But hatters![2]
      I can find no flesh,
      Hard nor nesh,°   *soft*
555 Salt nor fresh,
            But° two bare platters ...   *except*

[*Peers into cradle.*]

      Whik° cattle like this, tame nor wild,   *live*
      None, as I have bliss, as loud° as he smiled.° *strongly / smelled*
WIFE.   No, so God give me bliss, and give me joy of my
            child!
560 FIRST SHEPHERD.   We have marked amiss; I hold us
            beguiled.
SECOND SHEPHERD.   Sir, done!
      Sir, Our Lady him save!
      Is your child a knave?°   *boy*
MAK.   Any lord might him have,
565   This child, to° his son.   *as*

      When he wakens, he kipps°—what joy to see.   *grips*
THIRD SHEPHERD.   In good time to his hips, and in seel![3]
      But who was his gossips,° so soon ready?   *godparents*
MAK.   So fair fall their lips![4]
570 FIRST SHEPHERD.   (*Aside.*) Hark now, a lie.
MAK.   So God them thank,

---

[2] *But hatters*   An exclamation, "by God's clothing."

[3] *In good time ... in seel*   Good fortune to him, and happiness!

[4] *So fair ... lips*   Blessings on their lips.

Parkin, and Gibbon Waller, I say,
And gentle John Horne, in good fay—°   *faith*
He made all the garray°   *noise*
575   With his great shank.°   *legs*

SECOND SHEPHERD.   Mak, friends will we be, for we
        are all one.
MAK.   [*Aside.*] We! Now I hold for me, for
        mends° get I none.   *amends*
        [*To the Shepherds.*] Farewell all three! [*Aside again.*] All
        glad were ye gone.

[*They leave the house.*]

THIRD SHEPHERD.   Fair words may there be, but love
        is there none
580   This year.
FIRST SHEPHERD.   Gave ye the child anything?
SECOND SHEPHERD.   I trow, not one farthing.
THIRD SHEPHERD.   Fast again will I fling—
        Abide ye me there.

[*Goes back into the house.*]

585   Mak, take it to no grief° if I come to thy bairn. *don't be upset*
MAK.   Nay, thou does me great reprefe,°   *reproof*
        and foul has thou farn.°   *done*
THIRD SHEPHERD.   The child will it not grieve, that
        little day-star.
        Mak, with your leave, let me give your bairn
        But sixpence.
590   MAK.   Nay, do way: he sleeps.
THIRD SHEPHERD.   Methinks he peeps.
MAK.   When he wakens he weeps.
        I pray you go hence.

[*First and Second Shepherds return.*]

THIRD SHEPHERD.   Give me leave him to kiss, and lift
        up the clout.°   *cloth*

[*Lifts the covering.*]

595   What the devil is this? He has a long snout!
FIRST SHEPHERD.   He is marked amiss.[1] We wait ill
        about.
SECOND SHEPHERD.   Ill-spun weft, I wis, ay comes
        foul out.[2]
        Aye, so? [*Recognizes the sheep.*]
        He is like to our sheep!
600   THIRD SHEPHERD.   How, Gib, may I peep?
FIRST SHEPHERD.   I trow, kind° will creep   *nature*
        Where it may not go.°   *walk (go in a forthright way)*

SECOND SHEPHERD.   This was a quaint gaud,°   *cunning prank*
        and a far cast—°   *clever trick*
        It was a high fraud!
605   THIRD SHEPHERD.   Yea, sirs, was't.
        Let burn this bawd, and bind her fast. (*To Gill.*)
        A false skawde° hangs at the last;   *scold*
        So shall thou.
        Will ye see how they swaddle
610   His four feet in the middle?
        Saw I never in a cradle
        A horned lad ere now.

MAK.   Peace, bid I! What, let go your blare!
        I am he that him got, and yond woman him bare.° *bore him*
615   FIRST SHEPHERD.   What devil shall ye hat° Mak? *be called*
        Lo, God, Mak's heir!
SECOND SHEPHERD.   Let be all that. Now God give
        him care,
        I sagh.°   *saw*
WIFE.   A pretty child is he,
620   As sits on a woman's knee;
        A dilly-down[3] par Die,
        To make a man laugh.

THIRD SHEPHERD.   I know him by the ear-mark—that
        is a good token.
MAK.   I tell you, sirs, hark, his nose was broken.
625   Afterwards, he was forspoken.°   *bewitched*
FIRST SHEPHERD.   This is a false work—I would fain
        be wroken:°   *avenged*

---

[1]   *marked amiss* Deformed, misshapen.

[2]   *Ill-spun weft … foul out* Proverbial: I.e., the deformity of the
parents comes out in the offspring.

[3]   *dilly-down* Term of endearment.

Get a weapon!

WIFE.   He was taken by with° elf,   *by*
    I saw it myself;
630   When the clock struck twelve,
            Was he forshapen.°   *deformed*

SECOND SHEPHERD.   Ye two are well feft° same in a
        stead.°   *endowed / together*

FIRST SHEPHERD.   Since they maintain their theft, let's
    do them to dead.

MAK.   If I trespass eft,° gird° off my head!   *again / cut*
635   With you will I be left.

FIRST SHEPHERD.   Sirs, do my rede:° *take my advice*
            For this trespass,
    We will neither ban° nor flyte,°   *curse / quarrel*
    Fight nor chite,°   *chide*
640   But have done as tight,°   *quickly*
            And cast him in canvas.

[*They toss Mak up and down in a sheet, and then leave
his house.*]

FIRST SHEPHERD.   Lord, what! I am sore, in point for
        to brist;°   *burst*
    In faith, I may no more; therefore will I rist.°   *rest*

SECOND SHEPHERD.   As a sheep of seven score he
        weighed in my fist.
645   For to sleep anywhere, methink that I list.

THIRD SHEPHERD.   Now I pray you,
    Lie down on this green.

FIRST SHEPHERD.   On these thieves yet I mene.°   *think*

THIRD SHEPHERD.   Whereto should ye tene?°   *be angry*
650   Do as I say you.

[*he shepherds fall asleep. An angel sings "Glory to God in
the highest"; then let him say:*]

Rise, herdmen kind, for now is he born
Who shall take from the fiend that which Adam had
        lorn:°   *lost*
That warlock to sheynd,° this night is he born.   *destroy*
God is made your friend now at this morn.
655   He behests
    At Bedlam° go see,   *Bethlehem*
    There lies that free°   *noble one*

In a crib full poorly,
        Betwixt two beasts.

660   FIRST SHEPHERD.   This was a quaint stevyn° that ever
        yet I heard.   *voice*
    It is a marvel to nevyn,° thus to be scared.   *report*

SECOND SHEPHERD.   Of God's son of heaven, he
        spake upward.
    All the wood on a leynn,° methought that he   *lighting*
        he gard°   *made*
            Appear.[1]

665   THIRD SHEPHERD.   He spake of a bairn
    In Bedlam, I you warn.°   *tell*

FIRST SHEPHERD.   That betokens yond star;
        Let us seek him there.

SECOND SHEPHERD.   Say, what was his song? Heard ye
        not how he cracked it,
670   Three breves° to a long?   *short notes*

THIRD SHEPHERD.   Yea, marry, he hacked° it.   *sang*
    Was no crochet° wrong, nor nothing that lacked it.   *note*

FIRST SHEPHERD.   For to sing us among, right as he
        knacked it,[2]
            I can.

675   SECOND SHEPHERD.   Let see how ye croon.
    Can ye bark at the moon?

THIRD SHEPHERD.   Hold your tongues; have done!

FIRST SHEPHERD.   Hark after, then.

SECOND SHEPHERD.   To Bedlam he bade that we
        should gang;°   *go*
680   I am full fard° that we tarry too lang.°   *afraid / long*

THIRD SHEPHERD.   Be merry and not sad; of mirth is
        our sang.°   *song*
    Everlasting glad to mede° may we fang°   *reward / get*
            Without noise.

FIRST SHEPHERD.   Hie we thither, forthy,
685   If we be wet and weary,
        To that child and that lady:
            We have it not to lose.

---

[1]   *methought ... Appear*   It seemed to me that he made the whole
wood light up in a flash.

[2]   *knacked it*   Sang it in a lively or ornate manner.

SECOND SHEPHERD.   We find by the prophecy—let be
    your din!—
Of David and Isaiah, and more than I min—°   *mind*
690 They prophesied by clergy, that in a virgin
Should he light° and lie, to slokyn° our sin   *alight / quench*
    And slake it,
    Our kind from woe;
    For Isaiah said so:
695   *Ecce virgo*
        Concipiet[1] a child that is naked.

THIRD SHEPHERD.   Full glad may we be and
    abide° that day,   *wait for*
That Lovely One to see that all mights may.[2]
Lord, well were me for once and for ay,°   *always*
700 Might I kneel on my knee some word for to say
    To that child.
    But the angel said:
    In a crib was he laid,
    He was poorly arrayed,
705   Both mener° and mild.   *poor*

FIRST SHEPHERD.   Patriarchs that have been, and
    prophets beforn,°   *before now*
They desired to have seen this child that is born.
They are gone full clean;° that have they lorn.° *completely / lost*
We shall see him, I ween, ere it be morn,
710   To° a token.   *as a*
    When I see him and feel,
    Then wot I full well
    It is true as steel
        That prophets have spoken:
715 To so poor as we are that he would appear,
First find, and declare by his messenger.
SECOND SHEPHERD.   Go we now, let us fare; the place
    is us near.
THIRD SHEPHERD.   I am ready and yare°—go we in
    fere°   *eager / together*
    To that bright.
720 Lord, if thy wills be,
    We are lewd°, all three;   *unlearned*

Thou grant us somekins° glee,   *some kind of*
    To comfort thy wight.°   *creature*

[*They enter the stable in Bethlehem.*]

FIRST SHEPHERD.   Hail, comely and clean! hail, young
    child!
725 Hail, Maker, as I mean, of° a maiden so mild! *born of*
Thou has waried,° I ween, the warlock so wild,[3] *cursed*
The false guiler° of teyn° now goes he
    beguiled.   *deceiver / suffering*
    Lo, he merries![4]
    Lo, he laughs, my sweeting!
730   A well-fare meeting!
    I have holden my heting—°   *kept my promise*
        Have a bob° of cherries!   *bunch*

SECOND SHEPHERD.   Hail, sovereign saviour, for thou
    has us sought!
Hail, freely foyde° and flower, that all thing *noble child*
    has wrought!
735 Hail, full of favour, that made all of nought!
Hail! I kneel and I cower. A bird have I brought
    To my barn.
Hail, little tiny mop,°   *moppet*
Of our creed thou art crop!°   *harvest*
740 I would drink in thy cup,
    Little day-star!

THIRD SHEPHERD.   Hail, darling dear, full of godhead!
I pray thee be near, when that I have need.
Hail! sweet is thy cheer! My heart would bleed
745 To see thee sit here in so poor weed,° *clothes*
    With no pennies.
Hail! put forth thy dall,°   *hand*
I bring thee but a ball;
Have and play thee withall,
750   And go to the tennis.

MARY.   The Father of Heaven, God omnipotent,
That made all in seven, his son has he sent.
My name couth he neven,° and light° *utter / alight*
    ere he went.

---

[1]   Latin: "Behold, a virgin shall conceive…" (Isaiah 7.14).

[2]   *That Lovely One … mights may*   To see that lovely one that is able
to do all things that can be done.

---

[3]   *the warlock so wild*   I.e., the devil.

[4]   *Lo, he merries!*   Look, he (Christ) is merry.

I conceived him full even, through might, as he meant;
755   And now he is born.
He keep you from woe!
I shall pray him so;
Tell forth as ye go,
   And mind on° this morn.   *remember*

760 FIRST SHEPHERD. Farewell, lady, so fair to behold,
 With thy child on thy knee.
SECOND SHEPHERD.   But he lies full cold.
 Lord, well is me! Now we go, thou behold.

THIRD SHEPHERD. Forsooth, already it seems to be told
765   Full oft.
FIRST SHEPHERD. What grace we have fun!° *found*
SECOND SHEPHERD. Come forth, now have we won.
THIRD SHEPHERD. To sing are we bun—° *bound*
   Let take on loft! [*They exit, singing.*]

(*Here ends the shepherds' pageant.*)
—C. 1400–1450

Opening page, *The Second Shepherds' Play*, Towneley Plays 1F.38. (This item is reproduced by permission of the Huntington Library, San Marino, California.)

IN CONTEXT

Biblical Source Material

The Second Shepherds' Play supplements Biblical source material very extensively. Here is the relevant Biblical text, in the Douay-Rheims version.

from Douay-Rheims Bible, Luke 2.8–21

8   And there were in the same country shepherds watching, and keeping the night watches over their flock.

9   And behold an angel of the Lord stood by them, and the brightness of God shone round about them; and they feared with a great fear.

10   And the angel said to them: Fear not; for, behold, I bring you good tidings of great joy, that shall be to all the people:

11   For, this day, is born to you a Saviour, who is Christ the Lord, in the city of David.

12   And this shall be a sign unto you. You shall find the infant wrapped in swaddling clothes, and laid in a manger.

13   And suddenly there was with the angel a multitude of the heavenly army, praising God, and saying:

14   Glory to God in the highest; and on earth peace to men of good will.

15   And it came to pass, after the angels departed from them into heaven, the shepherds said one to another: Let us go over to Bethlehem, and let us see this word that is come to pass, which the Lord hath shewed to us.

16   And they came with haste; and they found Mary and Joseph, and the infant lying in the manger.

17   And seeing, they understood of the word that had been spoken to them concerning this child.

18   And all that heard, wondered; and at those things that were told them by the shepherds.

19   But Mary kept all these words, pondering them in her heart.

20   And the shepherds returned, glorifying and praising God, for all the things they had heard and seen, as it was told unto them.

21   And after eight days were accomplished, that the child should be circumcised, his name was called JESUS, which was called by the angel, before he was conceived in the womb.

Herod the Great[1]

CHARACTERS

Nuntius
Herod
1 Miles
2 Miles
3 Miles
1 Consultus
2 Consultus
1 Mulier
2 Mulier
3 Mulier

(*Incipit Magnus Herodes.*)[2]

[*Herod's messenger speaks directly to the audience.*]

NUNTIUS.   Most mighty Mahowne° meng   *Mohammed*
   you with mirth!³
  Both of burgh° and of town, by fellys° and by
   firth,°   *country / moor, marsh / forest*
  Both king with crown and barons of brith,°   *birth*
  That radly° will rowne,° many great
   grith°   *quickly / whisper / protection*
5 Shall behapp.°⁴   *happen*
  Take tenderly intent⁵
  What sondys° are sent—   *messages*
  Else harms shall ye hent,°   *receive*
  And lothes you to lap.⁶

10 Herod, the heynd° king—by grace of   *noble, gracious*
   Mahowne—
  Of Jury,° surmonting° sternly with crown *Jewry / excelling*

On life that are living in tower and in town,
Gracius° you greting, commands you be
  bowne°   *graciously / prepared, ready*
At his bidding.
15 Luf him with lewté;°   *loyalty*
  Drede him, that doughty!°   *virtuous, valiant*
  He charges you be ready
  Lowly° at his liking.   *humbly*

What man apon mold° menys him again⁷   *earth*
20 Tytt teyn° shall be told⁸—knight, squire, or swain.
  Be he never so bold, buys he that bargain
  Twelve thousandfold more than I sayn,°   *say*
  May ye trast.°   *trust*
  He° is worthy wonderly,⁹   *Herod*
25 Selcouthly sorry;¹⁰
  For a boy that is borne hereby
  Stands he abast.°   *upset*

A king they him call, and that we deny.
How should it so fall,° great marvel have I. *happen*
30 Therefore overall° shall I make a cry   *everywhere*
  That ye busk° not to brail,° nor *attempt, prepare / brawl*
   like not to lye
  This tide.°   *time*
  Carpys° of no king   *speak*
  But Herod, that lording,
35 Or busk° to your building   *hurry, hasten*
  Your heads for to hide!

He is king of kings, kindly I know,
Chief lord of lordings, chief leader of law.
There watys° on his wings that bold boast
  will blaw:°   *waits / blow*
40 Great dukes down dingys° for his great awe¹¹ *fall*
  And him lowtys.°   *revere*
  Tuskane and Turky,
  All Inde and Italy,

---

¹ **Herod the Great**   For the present text spelling and punctuation have been substantially modernized from the original Towneley manuscript. Stage directions included in the original appear here in parentheses. Some additional stage directions have been added for the sake of clarity; these appear in square brackets.

² *Incipit Magnus Herodes*   Latin: here begins Herod the Great.

³ *meng … mirth*   Make you merry!

⁴ *Both of … behapp*   I.e., the King's messenger is promising protection for virtually everyone.

⁵ *Take … intent*   Pay close attention.

⁶ *And lothes … lap*   And troubles will surround you.

⁷ *menys him again*   Complains against him.

⁸ *Tytt teyn shall be told*   Shall quickly be called a trouble-maker.

⁹ *worthy wonderly*   Marvelously worthy.

¹⁰ *Selcouthly sorry*   Strangely distressed.

¹¹ *There watys … great awe*   There wait under his protective wing those who will boldly proclaim that even great dukes bow down in awe of him.

Cecyll° and Surry°   *Sicily / Syria*
45   Dread him and dowtys.[1]

From Paradise to Padwa to Mount Flascon,
From Egypt to Mantua unto Kemp town,
From Sarceny to Susa to Greece it abowne,°   *above it*
Both Normondy and Norwa° lowtys°   *Norway / bow*
    to his crown.
50   His renown
Can no tounge tell,
From heaven unto hell,
Of him can none spell°   *speak, say*
But his cousin Mahowne.

55   He is the worthiest of all barnes° that are born.   *children*
Fre° men are his thrall,° full teynfully   *free / servants, slaves*
    torn.[2]
Begin he to brail, many men catch scorn!
Obey must we all, or else be ye lorne°   *lost*
At onys.°   *once*
60   Down ding of your knees,
All that him seys!°   *sees*
Displesyd he beys,
And byrkyn° many bonys.°   *breaks / bones*

Here he commys° now, I cry, that lord I of spake!   *comes*
65   Fast afore will I hy,° radly on a rake,   *hasten, hurry*
And welcome him worshipfully, laughing with lake,°   *glee*
As he is most worthy, and kneel for his sake
So low;
Down deruly° to fall,   *promptly*
70   As rank most ryall.°   *royal*
Hail, the worthiest of all!
To thee must I bow.

[*He kneels. King Herod enters accompanied by
retainers.*]

Hail, luf lord! Lo, thy letters have I laid.
I have done I couth° do, and peace have   *could*
    I prayed—
75   Mekill° more therto openly displayed.   *much*
But rumour is raised so, that boldly they brade°   *outburst*

Emangys them:[3]
They carp of a king;
They cease not sich° chattering.   *such*
80   HEROD.   But I shall tame their talking,
And let them go hang them.

Stint,° brodels,° your din°—   *cease / wretches / noise*
    yei, everychon!
I red° that ye harkyn° to° I be gone.   *advise / listen / until*
For if I begin, I break ilka° bone   *each, every*
85   And pull fro the skin the carcass anone,°   *quickly, readily*
Yei, perde!°   *by God!*
Cease all this wonder
And make us no blonder,°   *trouble, disturbance*
For I ryfe° you in sonder°   *tear, split / quickly*
90   Be ye so hardy.

Peace, both young and old, at my bidding, I red!
For I have all in wold:° in me stands life and
    dead.°   *command, power / death*
Who that is so bold, I brane° him through   *brain, hit*
    the head!
Speak not or I have told what I will in this stead.
95   Ye wote° not   *know*
All that I will mefe.°   *do*
Stir not but° ye have lefe;°   *unless / permission*
For if ye do, I clefe
You small as flesh to pot.[4]

100   My mirthes are turned to teyn,° my meekness into
    ire,°   *grief, anger / anger*
And all for one.° I weyn,° within I
    fare° as fire!   *Christ / believe / behave*
May I see him with eyn,° I shall give him his
    hire.°   *eyes / payment*
But I do as I meyn,° I were a full lewde sire   *intend*
In wonys.°   *everywhere*
105   Had I that lad in hand,
As I am king in land
I should with this steel° brand   *i.e., sword*
Byrkyn all his bones.

---

[1]   *Dread him ... dowtys*   Dread and fear him.

[2]   *teynfully torn*   Distressingly injured.

[3]   *Emangys them*   Amongst themselves.

[4]   *For if ye ... to pot*   For if you do, I will cleave (cut) you as small as
flesh for the pot.

My name springs° far and near: the doughtiest,   *extends*
    men me call,

110 That ever ran with spear, a lord and king ryall.

What joy is me to here° a lad to seize my stall!¹   *hear of*

If I this crown may bear, that boy shall buy° for all.   *pay*

I anger.

I wote not what devil me ails.²

115 They teyn me so with tales

That, by Gottys dear nails,

I will peace no langer.³

What, devil! me think I brast° for anger and   *burst*
    for teyn.

I trow° these kings be past that here with me   *believe*
    has been.

120 They promised me full fast or now here to be seen,

For, else I should have cast an other sleght,°   *trick / believe*
    I weyn.°

I tell you

A boy they said they sought,

With offering that they brought.

125 It mefys° my heart right not   *bothers, moves*

To break his neck in two!

But be they past me by, by Mahowne in heaven,

I shall, and that in hy, set all on sex and seven.

Trow ye a king as I will suffer them to
    neven°   *mention, name*

130 Any to have mastery but myself full even?

Nay, leyfe!°   *gladly*

The devil me hang and draw

If I that losell° knaw,°   *scandal / know, recognize*

Bot I gif him a blaw

135 That life I shall him reyfe.°   *take*

For perils,° yit° I would wist° if they   *if / know*
    were gone.

And ye thereof her told, I pray you say
    anone;°   *at once, immediately*

For, and they be so bold, by God that sits in
    trone,°   *throne*

The pain cannot be told that they shall have,
    ilkon,°   *each one*

140 For ire.⁴

Such pains hard° never man tell,   *heard*

For-ugly and for-fell,°   *bitterness*

That Lucifer in hell

Their bones shall all to-tire.

145 1 MILES.⁵   Lord, think not ill if I tell you how they
    are past;

I keep not layn, truly.⁶ Syn° they came by you   *since*
    last,

Another way in hy they sought, and that full fast.

HEROD.   Why, and are they past me by? We,⁷ out! for
    teyn I brast!

We! Fie!

150 Fie! on the devil! Where may I bide,°   *dwell, wait*

But fight for teyn and al to-chide?°   *scold, fight furiously*

Thiefs,° I say ye should have spied   *scoundrels*

And told when they went by.

Ye are knights to trast! Nay, losels ye are, and thieves!

155 I wote I yield my gast,° so sore my heart it   *give / spirit*
    grieves.

2 MILES.   What need you be abast?° There are   *upset*
    no great mischiefs

For these matters to gnast.⁸

3 MILES.   Why put ye such reprefys°   *reproofs*

Without cause?

160 Thus should ye not thrett° us,   *threaten*

Ungainly° to bete° us.   *impurely / beat*

Ye should not rehett° us   *rebuke, scorn*

Without other sawes.°   *sayings*

HEROD.   Fie, losels and liars, lurdans° ilkon!   *rascals*

165 Traitors and well wars!° Knaves, but knights   *worse*
    none!

Had ye been worth your ears, thus had they not gone.

Get I those land-lepers, I break ilka bone.

---

¹ *to seize ... stall*   To seize my throne!

² *I wote ... me ails*   I know not what devil ails me.

³ *by Gottes ... no langer*   By God's dear nails (of the cross) I will no longer have peace.

⁴ *For ire*   Because of my anger.

⁵ *MILES*   Latin: soldier.

⁶ *I keep ... truly*   I will not hide it.

⁷ *We*   An exclamation for attention or emphasis.

⁸ *There are no ... to gnast*   No mischiefs have been so great to cause you to gnash your teeth.

First vengeance
Shall I see on their bones.
170 If ye bide in these wonys
I shall ding° you with stones—   hit
Yei, ditizance doutance![1]

I wote not where I may sit for anger and for teyn.
We have not done all yit, if it be as I weyn.
175 Fie, devil! Now how is it? As long as I have eyn
I think not for to flitt,° but king I will be seyn   flee
Forever.
But stand I to quart,°   health
I tell you my heart:
180 I shall gar° them start,°   make / flinch
Or else trust me never.

1 MILES.   Sir, they went suddenly or° any man wist,   before
Else had met we—yei, perdy! and may ye trist.
2 MILES.   So bold nor so hardy against our
        list°   desire, inclination
185 Was none of that company durst° met me with   dared
        fist,[2]
For ferd.°   fear
3 MILES.   Ill durst they abide,
But ran them to hide.
Might I them have spied,
190 I had made them a berd.[3]

What couth we more do to save your honour?
1 MILES.   We were ready therto, and shall be ilk hour.
HEROD.   Now, syn° it is so, ye shall have favour.   since
Go where ye will go, by town and by tower.
195 Goys° hence! [The soldiers leave.]   go
I have matters to mell°   discuss
With my privy counsel.

[To his attendants.]

Clerks, ye bear the bell;[4]
Ye must me incense.°   enlighten

---

[1] ditizance doutance! Without doubt!

[2] Was none … with fist None of that company dared meet me in
a fistfight.

[3] I had … a berd I would have outwitted them.

[4] ye bear the bell You are the best.

200 One spoke in mine ear a wonderful talking,
And said a maiden should bear another to be king.
Sirs, I pray you inquire in all writing,
In Virgil, in Homer, and all other thing
But legend.[5]
205 Sekys poece-tayllys;[6]
Lefe pistyls and grales;[7]
Mes,° matins, not avails—°   Mass / has no benefit
All these I defend.°   forbid

[They examine various books.]

I pray you tell, heyndly,° now what ye find.   quickly
210 1 CONSULTUS.[8]   Truly, sir, prophecy it is not blind.
We read thus by Isay:[9] He shall be so kinde°   conceived
That a madyn, sothely,° which never sinde,° truly / sinned
Shall him bear.
Virgo concipiet,
215 Natumque pariet.[10]
"Emanuel" is hete,°   he is called
His name for to lere:°   teach

"God is with us," that is for to say.
2 CONSULTUS.   And other says thus, trust me ye may:
220 "Of Bedlem° a gracious Lord shall spray   Bethlehem
That of Jury mightius king shall be ay,
Lord mighty;
And him shall honour
Both king and emperor."[11]
225 HEROD.   Why, and should I to him cower?°
Nay, there thou lies lightly!°   easily, readily

Fie! the devil thee speed, and me, but I drink onys![12]
This has thou done indeed to anger me for the
        nonys.°   occasion

---

[5] But legend Except scripture.

[6] Sekys poece-tayllys Seek tales of poetry.

[7] Lefe pistyls and grales Leave epistles and graduals (antiphons,
hymns).

[8] CONSULTUS Latin: counselor.

[9] Isay Isaiah (see Isaiah 7.14).

[10] Virgo … pariet Latin: A virgin shall conceive and bear a son.

[11] "Of Bedlem … and emperor" Cf. Micah 5.2.

[12] but I drink onys! Unless I have a drink!

And thou, knave, thou thy mede° shall have, by   reward / God's
    Cokys° dear bonus!
230 Thou can not half thy creed.° Out, thiefs, fro   belief
    my wonys!
  Fie, knafys!
  Fie, dottypols,° with your books—   fools, blockheads
  Go cast them in the brooks!
  With sich wiles and crooks
235 My wit away rafys.°   strays, wanders

  Hard I never such a trant,° that a knave so sleight°   trick
  Should come like a saint and refe° me my right.   deprive
  Nay, he shall on-slant; I shall kill him down stright.[1]
  War,° I say, let me pant! Now think I to fight   beware
240 For anger.
  My guts will out thring°   burst, press
  But I this lad hing.°   hang
  Without° I have a venging,°   unless / vengeance
  I may live no langer.

245 Should a carll° in a cave, but of one year age,   peasant
  Thus make me to rafe?
  1 CONSULTUS.   Sir, peace this outrage!
  Away let ye wafe° all such langage.   put
  Your worship to safe, is he ought but a page°   boy
250 Of a year?[2]
  We two shall him teyn°   injure, harm
  With our wits between,°   combined
  That, if ye do as I mean,
  He shall die on a spear.

255 2 CONSULTUS. For dread that he reign, do as we red:
  Throughout Bedlem and ilk other stead
  Make knights ordain° and put unto dead   prepare
  All knave-children of two years bred
  And within.
260 This child may ye spill°   slay, kill
  Thus at your own will.
  HEROD. Now thou says heretill°   on this matter
  A right noble gin!°   scheme

If I live in land good life, as I hope,
265 This dar I thee warand:° to make thee a pope.   warrant
  O, my heart is risand now in a glope!°   wonder, joy
  For this noble tithand° thou shall have a
    drope°   news / drop
  Of my good grace:
  Marks, rents, and pounds,[3]
270 Great castles and grounds;
  Through all sees and sounds
  I give thee the chase.°   hunting rights

  Now will I proceed and take veniance.

[*To a messenger.*]

  All the flower of knighthood call to legeance,°   allegiance
275 Bewshere,[4] I thee bid; it may thee avance.
  NUNTIUS. Lord, I shall me speed and bring, perchaunce,
  To thy sight. (*He goes to summon the soldiers.*)
  Hark, knights, I you bring
  Here new tithing:
280 Unto Herod king
  Haste with all your might,

  In all the haste that ye may; in armour full bright,
  In your best array, look that ye be
    dight.°   equipped, prepared
  1 MILES. Why, should we fray?°   attack
285 2 MILES.   This is not all right.
  3 MILES. Sirs, withoutten delay I dread that we fight.
  NUNTIUS. I pray you,
  As fast as ye may
  Come to him this day.
290 1 MILES. What, in our best array?
  NUNTIUS. Yei, sirs, I say you.

  2 MILES. Somewhat is in hand, whatever it mean.
  3 MILES. Tarry° not for to stand, there or we   delay
    have been.

(*They go to Herod.*)

---

[1] *he shall ... down stright* He shall come to grief; I will kill him immediately.

[2] *Your worship ... a year?* Saving your worship (i.e., begging your pardon; excuse me, sir), is he not only a year-old boy?

[3] *Marks ... pounds* Monies.

[4] *Bewshere* Beau sire (i.e., Good sir).

NUNTIUS.   King Herod all-weldand,° well be   *all-ruling*
    ye seen!

295   Your knights are comand° in armour full sheen   *coming*
    At your will.

1 MILES.   Hail, doughtiest° of all!   *strongest*
    We are comen at your call
    For to do what we shall

300   Your lust° to fulfill.   *desire, wish*

HEROD.   Welcome, lordingys, iwis,° both great   *truly*
    and small.
    The cause now is this that I send for you all:
    A lad, a knave, born is that should be king ryall;
    But I kill him and his, I wote I brast my gall.

305   Therefore, sirs,
    Veniance shall ye take
    All for that lad sake;
    And men I shall you make
    Where ye come aywhere,[1] sirs.

310   To Bedlem look ye go, and all the coste° about.   *country*
    All knave children ye slo°—and, lords, ye shall be
      stout°—   *slay / fierce*
    Of years if they be two and within.° Of all that
      rout,°   *under / crowd*
    On life leave none of tho that lies in swedill-clowte,[2]
    I red you.

315   Spare no kin's blood,
    Let all run on flood.
    If women wax woode,°   *grow angry*
    I warn you, sirs, to speed° you.   *hurry*

Hence, now go your way, that ye were thore.°   *there*

320   2 MILES.   I wote we make a fray; but I will go before.
3 MILES.   A, think, sirs, I say: I mon wet like a boar.[3]
1 MILES.   Set me before, ay good enough for a score.[4]
    Hail, heyndly!
    We shall for your sake

325   Make a dulfull lake.°   *painful sport*

HEROD.   Now if ye me well wrake,
    Ye shall find me friendly.

[*The soldiers continue on their way.*]

2 MILES.   Go ye now till our noytt,° and   *work, profit*
    handle them well.
3 MILES.   I shall pay them on the cote,[5] begin I to
    reyll.°   *riot*

[*A woman comes toward the soldiers with her child.*]

330   1 MILES.   Hark, fellows! ye dote. Yonder comes
    unceyll.°   *misfortune*
    I hold here a grote° she likes me not well   *wager*
    By we part.[6]

[*To the woman, mockingly.*]

Dame, think it not ill,
    Thy knave° if I kill.   *son*

335   1 MULIER.[7]   What, thief, agans° my will?   *against*
    Lord, keep him in qwarte!°   *good health*

[*The woman is held by the soldiers, but struggles.*]

1 MILES.   Abide° now, abide. No farther thou goes.   *stop*
1 MULIER.   Peace, thief! Shall I chide and make here a
    nose?°   *noise*
1 MILES.   I shall reyfe thee[8] thy pride. Kill we these
    boyse!°   *boys*
340   1 MULIER.   Tyd may betide,[9] keep well thy nose,
    False thief! [*She hits the soldier.*]
    Have on loft on thy hode![10]
1 MILES.   What, whore, art thou woode?

[*He kills the child.*]

---

1   *Where ye … aywhere*   Wherever you go, anywhere.

2   *On life … swedill-clowte*   Leave none of those who lie in swaddling clothes alive.

3   *I mon … boar*   I wet (my tusks, in blood) like a boar.

4   *Set me … score*   Put me in front, I'm as skillful as twenty (men).

5   *I shall … the cote*   I will beat them.

6   *By we part*   By the time we leave.

7   *MULIER*   Latin: woman.

8   *reyfe thee*   Take away from you.

9   *Tyd may betide*   Time brings what it will.

10   *Have on … hode*   Have a hit on your head!

1 MULIER.   Out, alas, my childs blood!
345 Out, for reprefe!°   *shame*

Alas for shame and sin! Alas that I was born!
Of weeping who may blin° to see her child
    forlorn?°   *cease / forsaken*
My comfort and my kin, my son thus al to-torn!
Veniance for this sin I cry, both evyn° and morn!   *evening*
350 2 MILES.   Well done.

[*A second woman comes toward the soldiers with her child.*]

Com hedyr, thou old stry:°   *hag*
That lad of thine shall die.
2 MULIER.   Mercy, lord, I cry!
It is mine own dear son.

355 2 MILES.   No mercy thou mefe. It mends° thee   *profits*
    not, Mawd.
2 MULIER.   Then thy scalp shall I cleave! List thou be
    clawed?[1]

[*She tries to fight off the soldier.*]

Lefe,° lefe, now bylefe!°   *leave / stop*
2 MILES.   Peasse, bid I, bawd!°   *prostitute*
2 MULIER.   Fie, fie, for reprefe! Fie, full of frawde—
360 No man!
Have at thy tabard,°   *knight's overcoat*
Harlot and holard:°   *whoremonger*
Thou shall not be sparde!
I cry and I ban!°   *swear*

[*He kills the child.*]

365 Out, murder man, I say, strang traitor and thief!
Out, alas, and waloway,° my child that was me   *misery*
    lefe!
My love, my blood, my play,° that never   *joy, happiness*
    did man grief!
Alas, alas this day, I would my hart should clefe
    In sonder!
370 Veniance I cry and call

On Herod and his knights all—
Veniance, Lord, upon them fall,
And mekill warldys wonder!

3 MILES.   This is well-wrought gere°   *made / business, cause*
    that ever may be.

[*A third woman comes toward the soldiers.*]

375 Comes hederward° here! Ye need not to flee.   *hither*
3 MULIER.   Will ye do any dere° to my child   *harm*
    and me?
3 MILES.   He shall die, I thee swear. His heart blood
    shall thou see.
3 MULIER.   God forbede! [*He kills the child.*]
Thief, thou sheds my childs blood!
380 Out, I cry! I go near wood!
Alas, my heart is all on flood
To see my child thus bleed!

By God, thou shall aby° this dede that   *pay, suffer for*
    thou has done.
3 MILES.   I red° thee not, stry, by son and by   *tell / complaint, moan*
    moyn.°
385 3 MULIER.   Have at thee, say I! Take thee ther a
    foyn!°   *wound*

(*She attacks him.*)

Out on thee, I cry! Have at thy groyn°   *nose, snout*
Anothere!
This kepe I in store.
3 MILES.   Peasse now, no more!
390 3 MULIER.   I cry and I rore,
Out on thee, mans mordere!°   *murderer*

Alas, my babe, mine innocent, my fleshly
    get!° For sorrow   *offspring*
That God me dearly sent, of bales° who may me   *sorrow, grief / defend*
    borrow?°
Thy body is all to-rent! I cry, both even and morrow,
395 Veniance for thy blood thus spent: "Out," I cry, and
    "horow"![2]

---

1 *List thou … clawed* Does it please you to be clawed?

2 *"horow!"* Help (a cry of distress).

1 MILES.   Go lightly!°   *quickly*
Get out of this wonys,
Ye trattys,° all at onys,   *hags*
Or by Cokys dear bones
400 I make you go wightly!°   *quickly*

[he soldiers force the women to leave.]

They are flayd° now, I wote; they will not abide.   *frightened*
2 MILES.   Let us run foot-hot—now would I we
   hide°—   *hurry*
And tell of this lot,° how we have betide.   *fortune, occurrence*
3 MILES.   Thou can do thy note;° that have   *duty, work*
   I aspide.
405 Go forth now,
Tell thou Herod our tale.
For all our avail,
I tell you, saunce° fail,   *without*
He will us allow.
410 1 MILES.   I am best of you all, and ever has been;
The devil have my soul but I be first seen!
It sits me to call my lord, as I wene.
2 MILES.   What needs thee to brawl? Be not so keen
In this anger.
415 I shall say thou did best—
Save myself, as I gest.°   *thought, believed*
1 MILES.   We! that is most honest.
3 MILES.   Go, tarry no langer.

[The soldiers go to report to Herod.]

1 MILES.   Hail, Herod, our king! Full glad may ye be.
420 Good tithing we bring. Harkyn now to me:
We have made riding throughout Jure.°   *Jewry*
Well wit ye one thing: that murdered have we
Many thousands.
2 MILES.   I held them full hot;°   *severely*
425 I paid them on the cote.[1]
Their dammys,° I wote,   *mothers*
Never binds them in bandys.°   *swaddling clothes*

3 MILES.   Had ye seen how I fared when I came among
   them!

There was none that I spared, but laid on and
   dang° them.   *hit, struck*
430 I am worthy of reward. Where I was among them,
I stood and I stared. No pity to hang them
Had I.
HEROD.   Now, by mighty Mahowne,
That is good of renown,
435 If I bear this crown
Ye shall have a lady

Ilkon to him laid,° and wed at his will.   *presented*
1 MILES.   So have ye long saide—do somwhat
   thertill!°   *for that matter*
2 MILES.   And I was never flayed, for good ne for ill.
440 3 MILES.   Ye might hold you well paid°   *satisfied, pleased*
   our lust to fulfill,
Thus think me,
With treasure untold,
If it like that ye wold[2]
Both silver and gold
445 To give us great plenty.

HEROD.   As I am king crowned, I think it good right.
There goes none on ground that has such a wight.[3]
A hundred thousand pound is good wage for a knight;
Of pennies good and round, now may ye go light
450 With store.°   *plenty, abundance*
And ye knights of ours
Shall have castles and towers,
Both to you and to yours,
For now and evermore.

455 1 MILES.   Was never none borne, by downs° ne by
   dales,°   *hills / valleys*
Nor yit us beforne, that had such avalys.°   *benefits, allowances*
2 MILES.   We have castles and corne, much gold in
   our malys.°   *wallets*
3 MILES.   It will never be worn,° without any   *wasted*
   tales.
Hail, heyndly!
460 Hail, lord, hail, king!

---

[1] *I paid … cote* I gave it to them hard.

[2] *If it … wold* If it pleases you.

[3] *wight* Soul, i.e., person; here, refers to the service the knight has
given—no one on earth had such a servant.

We are forth founding.[1]
HEROD.   Now Mahowne he you bring
Where he is lord friendly!

[*The soldiers exit.*]

Now in peace may I stand—I thank thee,
      Mahowne—
465 And give of my land that longs to my crown.

[*To the audience.*]

Draw therefore nearhand,° both of burgh and   near
      of town:
Marks, ilkon, a thousand, when I am
      bowne,°   prepared, ready
Shall ye have.
I shall be full fain°   happy, glad
470 To give that I sayn.
Wait when I come again,
And then may ye crave.°   demand it
I set by no good, now my heart is at ease,
That I shed so mekill blood. Peace, all my riches!
475 For to see this flode from the foot to the knees
Mefys nothing my mode;° I laugh that I wheeze.   mood
A, Mahowne,
So light is my soul
That all of sugar is my gall![2]
480 I may do what I shall,
And bear up my crown.

I was castyn° in care, so frightly afraid!   cast, tossed
But I there not despair, for low is he laid
That I most dread are,° so have I him
      flayed.°   before / tortured
485 And else wonder where—and so many strayed
In the strete—
That one should be harmeles°   unharmed

And skape away, hafles,°   helpless
Where so many childes
490 There balys° cannot bete.°   harms / mend

A hundred thousand, I watt, and forty are slain,
And four thousand. Therat me ought to be fain;
Such a murder on a flat° shall never be again.   field, meadow
Had I had but one bat° at that lurdan   blow
495 So young,
It should have been spoken
How I had me wrokyn,
Were I dead and rotten,
With many a tongue.

500 Thus shall I teach knaves ensampyll° to take, example
In their wits that raves, such master° to
      make.°   authority / claim
All wantones wafys!° no language ye crak!°   avoid / boast
No sufferan you savys;[3] your necks shall I shak
In sonder!
505 No king ye on call
But on Herod the ryall,
Or else many one shall
Upon your bodys wonder.

For if I hear it spoken when I come again,
510 Your brains bese broken. Therefore, be ye bain.° ready
Nothing bese unlokyn;° it shall be so plain.   explained
Begin I to rokyn, I think all disdain
For-daunche.°   fastidious
Sirs, this is my counsel:
515 Bese not too cruel.
But adieu!—to the devil!
I can no more Franch.° (*Exit.*)   French

(*Explicit Magnus Herodes.*)[4]

---

[1] *forth founding* Hurrying forth.
[2] *That all ... my gall* That my anger is turned to sugar (sweetness).
[3] *All wantones ... you savys* Avoid all insolence! Do not boast! No sovereign will save you.
[4] *Explicit Magnus Herodes* Latin: Here ends Herod the Great.

=====

In Context

Biblical Source Material

Herod the Great supplements Biblical source material, as do other mystery plays. Here is the relevant Biblical text, in the Douay-Rheims version.

from Douay-Rheims Bible

Matthew 2

1　When Jesus therefore was born in Bethlehem of Juda, in the days of King Herod, behold, there came wise men from the east to Jerusalem.

2　Saying, Where is he that is born King of the Jews? For we have seen his star in the east, and are come to adore him.

3　And King Herod hearing this, was troubled, and all Jerusalem with him.

4　And assembling together all the chief priests and the scribes of the people, he inquired of them where Christ should be born.

5　But they said to him: In Bethlehem of Juda. For so it is written by the prophet:

6　And thou Bethlehem the land of Juda art not the least among the princes of Juda: for out of thee shall come forth the captain that shall rule my people Israel.

7　Then Herod, privately calling the wise men, learned diligently of them the time of the star which appeared to them;

8　And sending them into Bethlehem, said: Go and diligently inquire after the child, and when you have found him, bring me word again, that I also may come to adore him.

9　Who having heard the King, went their way; and behold the star which they had seen in the east, went before them, until it came and stood over where the child was.

10　And seeing the star they rejoiced with exceeding great joy.

11　And entering into the house, they found the child with Mary his mother, and falling down they adored him; and opening their treasures, they offered him gifts; gold, frankincense, and myrrh.

12　And having received an answer in sleep that they should not return to Herod, they went back another way into their country.

13   And after they were departed, behold an angel of the Lord appeared in sleep to Joseph, saying: Arise, and take the child and his mother, and fly into Egypt: and be there until I shall tell thee. For it will come to pass that Herod will seek the child to destroy him.

14   Who arose, and took the child and his mother by night, and retired into Egypt: and he was there until the death of Herod:

15   That it might be fulfilled which the Lord spoke by the prophet, saying: Out of Egypt have I called my son.

16   Then Herod perceiving that he was deluded by the wise men, was exceeding angry; and sending killed all the men children that were in Bethlehem, and in all the borders thereof, from two years old and under, according to the time which he had diligently inquired of the wise men.

17   Then was fulfilled that which was spoken by Jeremias the prophet, saying:

18   A voice in Rama was heard, lamentation and great mourning; Rachel bewailing her children, and would not be comforted, because they are not.

19   But when Herod was dead, behold an angel of the Lord appeared in sleep to Joseph in Egypt,

20   Saying: Arise, and take the child and his mother, and go into the land of Israel. For they are dead that sought the life of the child.

21   Who arose, and took the child and his mother, and came into the land of Israel.

22   But hearing that Archelaus reigned in Judea in the room of Herod his father, he was afraid to go thither: and being warned in sleep retired into the quarters of Galilee.

23   And coming he dwelt in a city called Nazareth: that it might be fulfilled which was said by prophets: That he shall be called a Nazarene.

THE SERVICE FOR REPRESENTING ADAM

The *Jeu d'Adam* (*Play*, or *Game of Adam*; in Latin: *Ordo Repraesentationis Ade*, or *Service for Representing Adam*) is a twelfth-century dramatic representation of the stories of the Biblical Temptation and Fall, of Cain and Abel, and of a succession of prophets who herald the coming of Christ. It is one of the oldest surviving dramas to make extensive use of the Anglo-Norman vernacular, and it marks a shift from earlier liturgical texts written and performed exclusively in Latin. Most estimates place the play's composition in the third quarter of the twelfth century, making it roughly contemporary with both the Fleury playbook (which contains ten liturgical plays that dramatize Biblical events named for the French monastery at which the plays are assumed to have been written), and other more secular Anglo-Norman dramas (such as *La Seinte Resureccion*, or *Holy Resurrection*) that were designed to be performed outside an ecclesiastical context.

The artistic flair the *Jeu d'Adam* brings to its liturgical material grows out of a larger medieval dramatic tradition. As early as the ninth century the celebration of the Mass itself involved elements of spectacle, with vestments, processions and responsories (chants sung during services) lending a dramatic air to liturgical proceedings. The ritual of Mass grew in both scope and elaboration until the distinction between church service and the dramatic embellishment of liturgical subjects began to blur. The *Jeu d'Adam* is not liturgical, but it is based on the experience of the liturgy; it draws its inspiration from Biblical texts and sermons, but it was performed outside of churches and was independent of any particular service. The play was staged in England and France, but possibly first composed in England, where French, the official court language, was widely understood.

The drama might have been performed during Advent, Lent, or Christmas. The actors were likely clerics, who would have understood not just the Anglo-Norman dialogue, but also the Latin choral, costume, and stage directions. These guidelines, or *didascalia*, are quite specific, providing explicit instructions about how the actors should modulate their voices when speaking, where they should direct their gaze, and what gestures they ought to make in order to convey the particular emotion of the scene. The *Jeu d'Adam* would probably have been staged on and around the steps of the church, with the church doors symbolizing the gates of heaven, the upper steps standing in for Paradise, and the lower steps representing worldly existence on earth. Hell would be found in the *platea,* the staging area at the bottom of the stairs, encircled by spectators. The audience would be close enough to reach out and touch the devil and his minions as they raced around in their elaborate costumes.

The author of the play is unknown, but it seems safe to assume that he was a priest or monk. The play is extant only in a relatively careless copy, MS. 927 of the Bibliothèque Municipale de Tours, which contains a miscellany of works including liturgical dramas, hymns, songs, and poems. The play ends with Nebuchadnezzer's account of his fiery vision, but the text is truncated, and its abrupt ending has led to speculation about the original conclusion of the play. Some have wondered if the final scene might explicitly link the Old and New Testaments or perhaps dramatize Christ's harrowing of Hell. Whatever finale was originally conceived, it seems likely that the last scene would typologically echo the first, since the ultimate aim of the play was clearly to encourage the audience to accept that only through Christ could they hope to redeem the consequences of both Adam's and their own sin.

⌘⌘⌘

The Service for Representing Adam[1]

DRAMATIS PERSONAE

Adam
Eve
Figure
Devil
Responsory
Cain
Abel
Isaiah
Jew
Responsory of the King's Ministers
Nebuchadnezzar

Let Paradise be constructed in a prominently high place; let curtains and silken hangings be placed around it at such a height that those persons who will be in Paradise can be seen from the shoulders upwards; let sweet-smelling flowers and foliage be planted; within let there be various trees, and fruits hanging on them, so that the place may seem as delightful as possible. Then let our Saviour come, clothed in a dalmatic,[2] and let Adam [and Eve] be stationed before him. Let Adam be robed in a red tunic, Eve in a woman's white garment with a wimple[3] of white silk; and let them both stand before the Figure [of God]—Adam somewhat nearer, with peaceful countenance, Eve on the other hand not quite sufficiently humble. And let this Adam be well coached when he must give answers, lest in answering he should be either too hasty or too slow. Nor him alone, but let all persons be coached thus, so that they may speak in an orderly manner and make gestures appropriate to the things of which they speak; and, in their verses, let them neither add nor subtract a syllable, but pronounce them all steadil-

y, and speak those things that are to be spoken in their due order. Whoever will mention the name of Paradise, let him look in its direction and point it out with his hand. Then let the lesson begin:

In the beginning God created the heavens and the earth.

(When this is finished let the choir sing.)

RESPONSORY.   And the Lord God formed [man].

(When this is finished let the Figure [of God] say:)

Adam! *(Who must answer:)* Sire?
FIGURE.   I have formed you
5   Of loam° of the earth.   clay, mud
ADAM.   I know it well.
FIGURE.   I have formed you in my likeness,
*** 4

In my image I have made you of earth.
10   You must never make war against me.
ADAM.   I will not; but I will believe You,
I will obey my Creator.
FIGURE.   I have given you a worthy companion:
Your wife, Eve by name.
15   She is your wife and partner;
You ought to be entirely faithful to her.
Love her, and let her love you,
If you would both be mine.
Let her be subject to your commandment,
20   And both of you to my wish.
I formed her from your side;
Born of you, she is no stranger.
I fashioned her from your body;
From you she issued,° not from outside.   was born
25   Govern her by reason.
Let no dissension come between you,
But great love and mutual obedience:
Such is the law of marriage.

(To Eve)

Now I will speak to you, Eve.
30   Be heedful, do not take this lightly:

---

[1]   *The Service for Representing Adam*   Translated by David Bevington (copyright © David Bevington, 1975) from the Latin *Ordo Repraesentationis Adae*. Stage directions that appear in the original appear here in parentheses; where stage directions or other material not in the original text has been added for clarity, the added text appears in square brackets.

[2]   *dalmatic*   Ecclesiastical garment with a slit on either side, and with wide sleeves, worn in the Western Church by deacons and bishops on certain occasions.

[3]   *wimple*   Head-dress worn by women, covering the head, chin, neck, and sides of the face.

[4]   ***   Line missing from the original text.

If you wish to do my will,
Cherish goodness in your heart.
Love and honor me as your Creator,
And acknowledge me your Lord.
35 To serve me devote your care,
All your might and all your mind.
Love Adam, and hold him dear.
He is your husband, and you his wife.
To him be obedient at all times,
40 Do not stray from his discipline.
Serve and love him with willing spirit,
For that is the law of marriage.
If you do well as his helpmeet,°   *helpmate*
I will place you with him in glory.
45 EVE.   Sire, I will do according to your pleasure;
I do not wish to stray from it.
I will acknowledge you as sovereign,
Him as my partner and stronger than I.
I will always be faithful to him;
50 From me he will have good counsel.
Your pleasure, your service
I will perform, Sire, in every way.

(*Then let the Figure call Adam nearer and say to him more intently:*)

Listen, Adam, and hear my judgment.
I have formed you; now I will give you this gift:
55 You may live forever, if you obey my teaching;
You may remain healthy, and not feel illness.
You will neither hunger nor thirst for need,
Feel neither heat nor cold.
You will dwell in joy, and never leave,
60 And in this pleasant state you will not taste sadness.
You will spend all your life in joy;
You will live forever, your life will not be short.
I say this to you, and wish that Eve attend;°   *listen, consider*
If she doesn't listen, there will be trouble.
65 Take dominion over all the earth,
Birds, beasts, and other riches.
Let those who envy you be held in slight regard,
For all the world will be obedient to you.
Both good and evil are in your power;
70 He who has such a choice is not bound to a stake.
Hold all in balance, weigh things equally.

Believe in my counsel, be true to me.
Leave the evil, and hold yourself to the good;
Love your Lord, and keep with Him;
75 Do not forsake my counsel for another.
If you do this, you will be without sin.
ADAM.   Great thanks I give for your kindness,
You who created me and give me such bounty
As to place good and evil in my power.
80 I will bestow my will in serving You.
You are my Sire, I am your handiwork;
You give me shape, I am of your making.
My will can never be so stubborn
But that all my care will be to serve You.

(*Then let the Figure point out Paradise to Adam with his hand, saying:*)

85 Adam!
ADAM.   Sire?
FIGURE.   I will tell you my advice.
Do you see this garden?
ADAM.   What is it called?
90 FIGURE.   Paradise.
ADAM.   How beautiful it is!
FIGURE.   I planted it and laid it out.
He who will remain in it will be my friend.
I charge you to remain and guard it.

(*Then he will send them into Paradise, saying:*)

95 I set you both therein.
ADAM.   And can we stay?
FIGURE.   For your entire life, you need fear nothing here;
You can neither die nor fall sick.

(*Let the choir sing.*)

RESPONSORY.   And the Lord God took the man.

(*Then the Figure will stretch forth his hand toward Paradise, saying:*)

100 I will tell you the nature of this garden:
You will find no lack of any delight.
There is no earthly good a creature might desire

That each cannot find to his own measure.
Here woman will receive from man no anger,
105 Nor man from woman have shame or fear.
Man is no sinner for begetting children,
Nor does woman experience pain in bearing them.
You will live forever, thus you will have a wonderful
        existence here;
Your age can never alter.
110 Death you will never fear, nor can it ever harm you.
I do not wish you to leave; here you must make your
        dwelling.

(*Let the choir sing.*)

RESPONSORY. The Lord God said to Adam.

(*Then let the Figure point out to Adam the trees of
Paradise, saying:*)

Of all this fruit you may eat for your pleasure:

(*And let him show him the forbidden tree and its fruit,
saying:*)

This I forbid you, do not take your enjoyment of this
        other one.
115 If you eat of it, you will experience death at once;
You will lose my love, change your fortune into bad.
ADAM. I will keep° all Your commandment.   observe
Neither I nor Eve will disobey in anything.
If for one sole fruit such an abode is lost,
120 It would be right for me to be thrown out to the wind.
If for one apple I forsake Your love,
Throughout my life, whether deliberately or foolishly,
Judge him to be a traitor
Who so perjures and betrays his Lord.

(*Then let the Figure go to the church,*[1] *and let Adam and
Eve walk about, virtuously taking delight in Paradise.
Meantime let devils run to and fro through the platea,*[2]
making appropriate gestures; and let them come, one after

---

[1] *church* I.e., God's heavenly residence, spatially represented by the
church portals behind Paradise at the top of the church steps.

[2] *platea* Open acting area at the foot of the steps, near the
spectators.

*the other, close to Paradise, showing Eve the forbidden
fruit, as if tempting her to eat it. Then let the devil come to
Adam and say to him:*)

125 How are you doing, Adam?
ADAM.   I live in great delight.
DEVIL. Are you well?
ADAM.   I feel nothing that annoys me.
DEVIL. Things could be better.
130 ADAM.   I don't know how.
DEVIL. Would you like to know?
ADAM.   I'd like that!
DEVIL. I know how.
ADAM.   And what does that matter to me?
135 DEVIL. Why wouldn't it matter?
ADAM.   It's of no benefit to me.
DEVIL. It will benefit you.
ADAM.   I don't know when.
DEVIL. I won't hurry to tell you, then.
140 ADAM. Come on, tell me.
DEVIL.   I won't,
Until I see you weary of begging.
ADAM. I don't need to know this thing.
DEVIL. You don't deserve to be well off.
145 You have a good thing that you don't know how to
        enjoy.
ADAM. How is that?
DEVIL.   Would you like to hear?
I'll tell you confidentially.
ADAM. [I'll listen,] surely.
150 DEVIL. Listen, Adam, pay attention to me.
This will be to your advantage.
ADAM.   I consent to that.
DEVIL. Will you believe me?
ADAM.   Yes, very well.
155 DEVIL. In everything?
ADAM.   Everything except one thing.
DEVIL. What thing?
ADAM.   I'll tell you:
I will not offend my Maker.
160 DEVIL. Do you fear Him that much?
ADAM.   Yes, indeed,
I love and fear him.
DEVIL.   That's foolish.
What can he do to you?

165 ADAM.　　　　　　　Both good and evil.
　DEVIL.　You're starting on a very foolish business,
　　To fear so much that evil can come to you.
　　Aren't you in glory? You cannot die.
　ADAM.　God said to me that I shall die
170 　When I transgress° His commandment.　　　　　*disobey*
　DEVIL.　What is this great transgression?
　　I'd like to hear this right off.
　ADAM.　I will tell you quite frankly.
　　He gave me one commandment:
175 　Of all the fruits of Paradise
　　I may eat—so He taught me—
　　Except one only; that one is forbidden.
　　That one I will not touch with my hands.
　DEVIL.　Which one is that?

(*Then let Adam raise his hand and point out to him the
forbidden fruit, saying:*)

180 ADAM.　　　　　　Do you see there?
　　That one has been forbidden to me.
　DEVIL.　Do you know why?
　ADAM.　　　　　I? No, indeed.
　DEVIL.　I'll tell you the reason.
185 　He doesn't care at all about the other fruit,

(*And let him point out to him the forbidden fruit with his
hand, saying to Adam:*)

　　Except for that one which hangs on high.
　　That is the fruit of knowledge:
　　It gives the understanding to know everything.
　　If you eat it, you will benefit from it.
190 ADAM.　How?
　DEVIL.　　　You'll see.
　　At once your eyes will be opened;
　　Everything to come will be revealed to you;
　　You will be able to do whatever you desire.
195 　It will bestow many blessings upon you:
　　Eat it, and you'll prosper.
　　You'll have nothing to fear from your God;
　　Instead, you will be His peer in everything.
　　This is why He has seen fit to refuse you.
200 　Will you trust me? Taste of the fruit.
　ADAM.　I won't do it.

　DEVIL.　[*Ironically.*] Well, listen to this pleasant news!
　　Won't you do it?
　ADAM.　　　　　No.
205 DEVIL.　　　　　How stupid you are!
　　You will remember these words again.

(*Then let the devil withdraw; and he will go to the other
demons, and make a foray through the platea; and, after a
short delay, cheerful and rejoicing, he will return to the
tempting of Adam, and say to him:*)

　Adam, how are you doing? Will you change your mind?
　Are you still having foolish ideas?
　I meant to tell you the other day,
210 God has made you His beneficiary,
　He put you here to eat this fruit.
　Have you then any other pleasures?
　ADAM.　Yes, I lack for nothing.
　DEVIL.　Don't you aspire to anything higher?
215 You can certainly consider yourself fortunate
　When God has made you His gardener!
　God has made you keeper of His garden;
　Won't you look for other pleasures?
　Did He create you solely for material appetite?
220 Didn't He wish to bestow any other honor on you?
　Listen, Adam, pay attention to me:
　I will counsel you in faith
　How you can be without a master,
　And the equal of your Creator.
225 I'll tell you the whole truth:
　If you eat of the apple

(*Then he will raise his hand toward Paradise.*)

　You will reign in majesty.
　You can share omnipotence with God.
　ADAM.　Get away from here.
230 DEVIL.　　　　　What did you say, Adam?
　ADAM.　Get away from here! You are Satan.
　　You give evil counsel.
　DEVIL.　　　　　I? How is that?
　ADAM.　You would deliver me into torment,
235 Set me at odds with my Lord,
　　Remove me from joy, put me in sadness.
　　I won't trust you. Get away from here!

Don't ever be so audacious
As to come into my presence.
240   You are a traitor and without grace.

*(Then, sadly and with downcast countenance, he will
withdraw from Adam and go to the gates of hell, and hold
a conference with the other demons. Thereafter he will
make a foray among the people. Thereupon he will draw
near to Paradise, on the side where Eve is, and with a
joyful countenance, fawningly, he addresses Eve as follows:)*

DEVIL.   Eve, I have come to you.
EVE.   Tell me, Satan, why?
DEVIL.   I want to seek your profit, your honor.
EVE.   May God grant it!
245   DEVIL.   Don't be afraid.
For a long time I have known
All the secrets of Paradise.
One part of them I'll tell you.
EVE.   Begin, and I will listen.
250   DEVIL.   Will you listen to me?
EVE.   I'll do so, all right,
Nor anger you in any way.
DEVIL.   You'll keep a secret?
EVE.   Yes, by my faith.
255   DEVIL.   Will it be revealed?
EVE.   Certainly not by me.
DEVIL.   I will put me in your trust.
I wish no further assurance from you.
EVE.   You can certainly trust my word.
260   DEVIL.   You have been to a good school!—
I have seen Adam, but he is too much of a fool.
EVE.   He's a little hard.°   obstinate
DEVIL.   He will be soft.
He is harder than fire!
265   EVE.   He is very noble.
DEVIL.   On the contrary, he's servile.
He lacks the will to look after his best interests.
He ought to do so at least for you.
You are a delicate and tender thing,
270   And fresher than the rose;
You are whiter than crystal,
Than snow that falls on ice in the valley.
The Creator has made an ill-matched pair:
You are too tender, and he too hard.

275   But notwithstanding you are wiser;
Your mind has discovered great wisdom.
For this reason it is good to approach you.
I wish to speak with you.
EVE.   Speak truthfully, then.
280   DEVIL.   Let no one know of it.
EVE.   Who should know?
DEVIL.   Not even Adam.
EVE.   Certainly not by me.
DEVIL.   I will tell you, and you listen to me.
285   There is no one in this business but us two
And Adam over there, who doesn't hear us.
EVE.   Speak louder, he won't know anything of it.
DEVIL.   I'll acquaint you with a great plot
Laid against you in this garden.
290   The fruit God gave you
Has scarcely any goodness in it;
That one He so vehemently forbade you
Has extraordinary virtue.
In it there is the gift of life,
295   Of power and dominion,
Of knowing all things, good and evil.
EVE.   What taste does it have?
DEVIL.   Heavenly!
To your fair body, to your face
300   This fortunate event would be so well suited
That you would become mistress of the world,
Of the firmament° and of the deep,   *sky, heavens*
And know everything to come,
So that you would become the wise ruler of all things.
305   EVE.   Is the fruit of such a nature?
DEVIL.   Yes, truly.

*(Then Eve will carefully inspect the forbidden fruit, and,
after having considered it for a long while, she will say:)*

It does me good just to look at it.
DEVIL.   What will happen if you eat it?
EVE.   How should I know?
310   DEVIL.   Won't you believe me?
Take it first, and give it to Adam.
At once you will possess the crown of heaven.
You will be the equal of the Creator;
He won't be able to hide secrets from you.
315   As soon as you have eaten of the fruit,

At once your hearts will be transformed.
With God you will be, without fail,
Of equal goodness, equal might.
Taste of the fruit.
320 EVE.   I intend to.
DEVIL.   Don't trust Adam.
EVE.   I'll do it [later].
DEVIL.   When?
EVE.   … Let me [wait]
325 Until Adam is asleep.
DEVIL.   Eat, it, don't be doubtful!
To delay would be childish.

(*Then let the devil withdraw from Eve, and he will go to
hell. Adam will come to Eve, acting annoyed because the
devil has spoken with her, and he will say to her*:)

Tell me, wife, what was that evil Satan
Asking you about? What did he want from you?
330 EVE.   He talked to me about our advancement.
ADAM.   Don't believe the traitor! —
Yes, he is a traitor.
EVE.   I know it perfectly well.
ADAM.   How do you know?
335 EVE.   Because I have tried it out.
What's wrong with his seeing me?
[ADAM.]   He'll make you change your mind.
EVE.   No he won't, because I will believe nothing
Until I've tested him.
340 Adam.   Don't let him come near you,
For he's a fellow of very bad faith.
He wanted to betray his Sovereign
And set himself in place of Him who is highest.
I do not want a scoundrel who has done such things
345 To have access to you.

(*Then a serpent, artfully constructed, arises alongside the
trunk of the forbidden tree. Eve will incline her ear near to
it, as if hearkening to its counsel. Hereupon Eve will accept
the apple, and offer it to Adam. But he will not accept it
yet, and Eve will say to him*:)

Eat, Adam. You don't know what it is.
Let us take this good thing that is at hand for us.
ADAM.   Is it so good?

EVE.   You will know soon,
350 But you can't know until you've tasted.
ADAM.   I'm fearful of it.
EVE.   Stop being afraid!
ADAM.   I won't do it.
EVE.   You delay out of cowardice.
355 ADAM.   I'll take it.
EVE.   Eat. Take it!
By it you will know both good and evil.
I will eat some first.
ADAM.   And I afterwards.
360 EVE.   Promise?

(*Then Eve will eat part of the apple, and say to Adam*:)

I've tasted it. My God, what flavor!
I've never savored such sweetness.
What a taste this apple has!
ADAM.   Like what?
365 EVE.   Like no mortal taste.
Now my eyes see so clearly
I am like the allpowerful God.
I know all that has been and is to come;
I am complete master of everything.
370 Eat, Adam, don't hesitate.
You will take it in a lucky hour.

(*Then Adam will take the apple from Eve's hand, saying*:)

I'll trust you in this. You are my partner.
EVE.   Eat. Don't be fearful.

(*Then let Adam eat part of the apple. When he has eaten he
will recognize his sin at once, and will bend over so that he
cannot be seen by the people. And he will strip off his festive
garments, and will put on poor clothes sewn together with
fig leaves, and, manifesting exceedingly great sorrow he will
begin his lamentation*:)

Alas, sinful wretch, what have I done?
375 Now I am dead without escape.
Without remedy I am dead,
So evil has my fortune fallen.
My fortune has changed for the worse:
Once it was auspicious, now it is harsh.

380 I have forsaken my Creator
Through the counsel of a wicked wife.
Alas, sinful one, what shall I do?
Upon my Creator how can I look?
How can I look upon my Creator
385 Whom I have forsaken through my folly?
Never have I made such a bad bargain.
Now I know what it is to sin.
O Death, why do you let me live?
Why is the world not rid of me?
390 Why do I still encumber° the world?   *burden*
I must experience the depths of hell.
In hell will be my dwelling,
Until the coming of one who can save me.
Thus in hell I will lead my life.
395 Whence will help come to me there?
Whence will rescue come to me there?
Who will draw me away from such sorrow?
Why did I do wrong to my Lord?
Now there is no one that should be my friend.
400 There will be no one that can avail at all.
I am lost without fail.
I have sinned so against my Lord,
I can enter no plea against Him,
For I am in the wrong, He in the right.
405 My God, what a horrible plight I'm in!
Who henceforth will remember me?
For I have sinned against the King of Glory.
Against the King of Heaven I have sinned so
That I have not the slightest claim upon Him.
410 No friend have I, or neighbor,
Who might rescue me from my accusation at last.
And whom shall I beseech to aid me,
When my own wife has betrayed me,
She whom God gave me as partner?
415 She has given me evil counsel.
Oh, Eve!

(*Then he will look at Eve his wife, and say:*)

           Alas, foolhardy wife!
In an evil hour were you born of me!
If only that rib had been burned
420 Which has brought me to this evil pass!
If only the rib had been consumed in fire

Which has caused me such strife!
When He drew that rib from me,
Why didn't He burn it, and kill me?
425 The rib has betrayed the whole body,
Injured and maltreated it.
I don't know what to say or do.
If grace does not come to me from heaven,
I can never be rescued from pain,
430 Such is the evil that torments me.
Ah, Eve! Evil the hour—
Such terrible torment overwhelms me—
When you became my companion!
Now I am dead by your counsel.
435 By your counsel I am reduced to evil fortune,
Brought low from great height.
I will be redeemed thence by no mortal,
None save God in his majesty.
What do I say, unhappy one? Why have I named him?
440 He help me? I have angered him.
None will ever aid me
Except the Son who will come forth from Mary.
I don't know where to turn
Since we have not kept faith with God.
445 Then let all be as it please God:
No alternative except to die.

(*Then let the choir begin.*)

RESPONSORY. While God walked [in the garden of
     Paradise].

(*When this has been said, the Figure will come wearing a
stole and will walk in Paradise, looking around as if
seeking to know where Adam is. But Adam and Eve will
hide in a corner of Paradise, as if knowing how wretched
they are; and the Figure will say:*)

Adam, where are you?

(*Then both will rise, standing before the Figure, and yet
not fully upright, but, through shame for their sin,
somewhat bent forward and extremely sad; and let [Adam]
answer:*)

ADAM.   I am here, reverend Sire.

450 I hid myself from your wrath;
And because I was completely naked
I thus concealed myself here.
FIGURE. What have you done? How have you gone
astray?
Who has drawn you away from your goodness?
455 What have you done? Why are you ashamed?
How will I settle accounts with you now?
Until recently you had nothing
Of which you ought to be ashamed;
Now I see you downcast and mournful.
460 They enjoy themselves ill who live thus.
ADAM. I am so ashamed, Sire, before You
*** [1]

FIGURE.   And why?
ADAM.   Such great shame entwines my body
465 That I dare not look You in the face.
FIGURE. Why have you transgressed my prohibition?
Have you gained anything?
You are my servant, and I your Lord.
ADAM. I cannot deny it.
470 FIGURE. I created you in my own likeness;
Why have you transgressed my commandment?
I shaped you after my own image;
Why have you done me this outrage?
You paid no attention to my prohibition;
475 Deliberately you transgressed it.
You ate the fruit which I told you
I had forbidden you.
Did you think by this to be my equal?
I didn't think you would joke this way.

(*Then Adam will stretch out his hand toward the Figure,
then toward Eve, saying*:)

480 The woman you gave me,
She first committed this trespass:
She gave it to me, and I ate.
Now, I see, it has turned to woe.
I meddled rashly to eat this;
485 I have transgressed through my wife.
FIGURE. You trusted your wife more than me.
You ate the fruit without my permission.
Now I will render you the following recompense:

The earth will be cursed
490 Where you will wish to sow your grain.
It will fail to bear fruit,
It is cursed beneath your hand;
You will cultivate it in vain.
It will deny its fruit to you;
495 It will yield you thorns and thistles.
It will change whatever you sow;
It will be cursed, as punishment to you.
With grievous toil, with great exertion
You will have to eat your bread.
500 In great torment and sweat
You will live night and day.

(*Then the Figure will turn toward Eve, and with a
threatening countenance say to her*:)

And you, Eve, wicked woman,
You began to make war against me:
You held my commandments in light regard.
505 EVE. The wicked serpent deceived me.
FIGURE. Through him did you think to become my equal?
Have you learned how to prophesy well?
Formerly you held sovereignty
Over all living things;
510 How quickly you've lost that!
Now I see you sad and dejected;
Have you gained or lost?
I will render you your just desert,
I will give you this for your service:
515 Misfortune will afflict you in every way.
In sorrow you will bring forth children,
And in pain they will live all their lives.
Your children will be born in sorrow,
And will end their days in great anguish.
520 To such hardship, to such shame
You have brought both yourself and your lineage.
All those who will issue from you
Will deplore your sin.

(*And Eve will answer, saying*:)

I have sinned, it was by my folly.
525 For one apple I will suffer great shame thus,
Because I have placed myself and my lineage in pain.

---

[1] *** A space here appears in the original.

A small gain yields me a heavy toll in sorrow.
If I have sinned, it was no great marvel,
Whereas the deceiving serpent betrayed me.
530 Much he knows of evil; he certainly isn't innocent like
    a lamb.
Anyone who follows his advice is put in evil plight.
I took the apple; now I know I acted foolishly
Against Your prohibition; in that I behaved wickedly.
Evilly I tasted it; now I am hated by You.
535 For a little fruit I must lose my life.

(*Then the Figure will threaten the serpent, saying*:)

And you, serpent, be accursed!
From you I will recover my full right.
Upon your belly you shall go
All the days of your life.
540 Dust will be your daily food
In the wood, in field, on heath.
Woman will detest you;
Forever she will be an evil neighbor to you.
You will lie in wait for her heel,
545 She will pluck you by the head.
She will strike your head such a blow
That it will cause you great hardship.
She will carefully figure out
How she can be revenged on you.
550 You meddled evilly in her company;
She will bow your head.
A root will spring from her
Who will confound all your powers.

(*Then the Figure will drive them forth from Paradise,
saying*:)

Now get out of Paradise.
555 You have made an unhappy change of residence.
On earth you will have your dwelling;
You have no claim on Paradise.
You have nothing that is your due here.
Out you will go, without remedy.
560 You have nothing here to claim through judgment.
Now take some other dwelling.
Depart from bliss;
Hunger and weariness will not fail you,

Nor sorrow and pain,
565 Every day of the week.
On earth you will have an unhappy sojourn;°   *stay*
Then you will finally die;
After you have tasted death,
You will come to hell without remission.
570 Here in hell exile will afflict your bodies,
Peril daunt your souls.
Satan will have you in his power.
There is no man who could aid you:
By whom could you be rescued,
575 If I do not take pity on you?

(*Let the choir sing.*)

RESPONSORY.   In the sweat of your face.

(*Meanwhile an angel will come dressed in white, bearing
a flaming sword in his hand, whom the Figure will station
at the gate of Paradise and will say to him*:)

Guard Paradise well for me
So that this outlaw may not enter there;
That he may not have the power or dominion
580 To touch the fruit of life.
With this flaming sword
Bar him the way.

(*When they are outside Paradise, as though sad and
confused they will be bowed down to the ground, bent over
to their ankles, and the Figure will point at them with his
hand, his face turned toward Paradise. And the choir will
begin.*)

RESPONSORY.   Behold, Adam is become as one [of us].

(*When this is done, the Figure will return to the church.
Then Adam will have a spade and Eve a rake, and they
will begin to till the ground, and sow wheat in it. After
they have sown, they will go and sit for a while in a certain
place, as if worn out by their work, and mournfully they
will often look back at Paradise, beating their breasts.
Meanwhile the devil will come and plant thorns and
thistles in their cultivated fields, and withdraw. When
Adam and Eve come to their fields and see the thorns and*

*thistles that have sprung up, stricken with violent grief they
will throw themselves down on the earth, and, remaining
there, will strike their breasts and their thighs, manifesting
their sorrow with their gestures. And [Adam] will begin his
lamentation:)*

Alas, woe is me, how evil was that hour
585   In which my sins overwhelmed me,
In which I forsook the Lord whom all adore!
Whom shall I ever implore to help me?

*(Here let Adam look back at Paradise, and he will raise
both his arms toward it, and, devoutly bowing his head,
will say:)*

O Paradise, how sweet to dwell there!
Garden of glory, what a beautiful sight you make!
590   I am thrown out for my sin, in truth;
I have lost all hope of return.
I dwelt therein, yet didn't know how to enjoy it;
I believed advice that caused me to leave it too quickly.
Now I repent; it is fitting that I am angry.
595   It is too late; my sighs avail nothing.
Where was my understanding? What became of my
        memory,
That for Satan I forsook the King of Glory?
Now I suffer for it, and have lost my self-esteem.
My sin will be written down in history.

*(Then he will lift up his hand against Eve, who will have
been moved away a short distance from him, and, moving
his head with great indignation, will say to her:)*

600   O wicked woman, full of treason,
How quickly you cast me into perdition
When you banished my understanding and reason!
Now I repent, I cannot have pardon.
Despondent Eve, how inclined you were to evil,
605   When you believed so quickly the counsel of the viper!
Through you I am dead, thus I have lost life;
Your sin will be written in the book.
Do you see the signs of terrible confusion?
The earth senses our curse:
610   We sowed corn, now thistles thrive.

*** [1]
You see the beginning of our misery;
Great is our sorrow, but greater awaits us.
We will be led to hell in heaviness;
615   No pain nor torment will be spared us.
Wretched Eve, what do you think of this?
You have won this, it has been given you for your dowry.
Nevermore can you bring man felicity,
But will be forever contrary to reason.
620   All those who will come hereafter, of our lineage,
Will feel the weight of your misdeed.
You have sinned; all those are condemned by it.
Only much later will He come by whom this will be
        changed.

(Then let Eve answer Adam:)

Adam, dear lord, you have blamed me much,
625   Reviled and reproached my villainy.
If I have sinned, I suffer the weight of it.
I am guilty; I will be judged by God.
I have sinned greatly toward God and you;
My sin will long be reviled.
630   My guilt is great, my sins afflict me.
Wretched me, I have lacked all goodness!
I have no grounds whereby to defend myself against God,
That He should not find me a guilty sinner.
Pardon me, for I cannot make amends!
635   If I could, I would offer a sacrifice.
Sinner, unhappy, wretched,
For my misdeed I am overcome with shame toward God.
Take me, Death, do not permit me to live!
I am in peril, and cannot reach the shore.
640   The wicked serpent, the evil viper,
Made me eat the apple of misfortune.
I gave it to you; I thought it for the best,
And I led you into sin, for which I can't reproach you.
Why wasn't I obedient to the Creator?
645   Why, my lord, didn't I hold to your teaching?
You sinned, but I was the root of it.
For our malady, the cure is a long one.
My sin, my grave misdoing,
Our progeny will pay dearly for.

---

[1]   *** A space appears here in the original.

650 The fruit was sweet, the pain is hard.
It was evil to eat; ours will be the guilt.
Notwithstanding, in God is my hope.
There will be full reconciliation for this sin:
God will tend me His grace and His favor;
655 He will rescue us from hell by His might.

(*Then the devil will come, and three or four devils with
him, carrying in their hands chains and iron fetters, which
they will put on the necks of Adam and Eve. And certain
ones will push them, others drag them to hell; still other
devils will be close beside hell waiting for them as they
come, and among themselves they will make a great
dancing and jubilation over their damnation; and each of
these other devils will point at them as they come, and will
take them and put them into hell. And therein they will
cause a great smoke to arise, and they will shout to one
another in hell, rejoicing, and they will bang together their
pots and caldrons, so that they may be heard outside. And
after a short interval, the devils will issue forth, scattering
across the platea; certain of them, however, will remain in
hell.*

*Then Cain and Abel will come. Let Cain be dressed in red
garments, Abel in white, and they will cultivate ground
that has been made ready.*

*And when he has rested from his labor for a time, let Abel
speak to his brother Cain agreeably and amicably, saying to
him:*)

Brother Cain, we are two kinsmen
And sons of the first of men:
That was Adam, our mother was named Eve.
In serving God let us not be churlish.
660 Let us be at all times obedient to the Creator;
Let us so serve that we will win back His love,
Which our parents lost by their folly.
May there be steadfast love between us two!
So let us serve God that it will please Him always;
665 Pay Him his due, let nothing be held back.
If with willing heart we will obey Him
Our souls will have nothing to fear.
Let us pay His tithes and all that is justly His due,

First-fruits, offerings, gifts, sacrifice;
670 If covetousness impels us to hold back,
We will be lost in hell, without recourse.
Between us two let there be great love;
Let there be neither envy nor dissension.
Why should there be strife between us two?
675 The entire earth has been surrendered to us.

(*Then Cain will look at his brother Abel as if mocking
him, and he will say to him:*)

Dear brother Abel, you certainly know how to preach,
How to lay out and present your arguments!
If anyone paid attention to your notions,
In a few days he wouldn't have much left to give.
680 This giving of tithes has never suited me, anyway.
With your belongings you can do your good deeds,
And with mine I'll follow my own inclination.
You won't be damned by my misdeed.
Nature teaches us to love one another;
685 Between us two let's not have any dissimulation.
Whichever of us two starts an argument,
Let him pay dearly for it, for it is right that one should
complain of this.

(*Again let Abel speak to his brother Cain, who will answer
more mildly than usual; Abel will say:*)

Cain, dear brother, listen to me.
CAIN. Gladly. Listen to what?
690 ABEL. Something to your benefit.
CAIN.   So much the better.
ABEL. Don't rebel against God.
Don't be proud toward Him,
I'm warning you.
695 CAIN.   That's what I want.
ABEL. Believe my advice. Let us make offering
To the Lord God, to please Him.
If He is reconciled toward us,
Sin will not afflict us,
700 Nor sadness come upon us.
It is beneficial to secure His love.
Let us sacrifice at His altar
Such a gift as He would be pleased to look upon.

Let us pray to Him that He give us his love
705   And defend us from evil, night and day.

(*Then Cain will answer as if Abel's counsel has pleased
him, saying*:)

Dear brother Abel, you have said well;
You have written this sermon effectively,
And I'll heed it diligently.
Let us make offering, as is right.
710   What will you offer?
ABEL.   A lamb,
The best and fairest
That I can find in the fold.
This I'll offer, none other;
715   And I will offer him incense.
Now I've told you all my intent.
What will you offer?
CAIN.   Some of my wheat,
Such as God has given me.
720   ABEL. Your very best?
CAIN.   Certainly not.
From that I'm going to make bread for tonight.
ABEL. Such offering is not acceptable
        *** [1]
725   CAIN.   That's nonsense.
ABEL. You are a rich man, and have many cattle.
CAIN. Granted.
ABEL. Why don't you count the number of head
And give a tenth of the total?
730   Thus you will make offering to God's very self,
Sacrifice to Him wholeheartedly;
That way you'll receive a fine reward.
Will you do this?
CAIN.   You're crazy.
735   *** [2]
Of ten, there'll only be nine left!
This advice isn't worth an egg.
Let's make offering, each for himself
What he thinks good.
740   ABEL.   So be it.

_____
[1] *** A space appears here in the original.

[2] *** A space here appears in the original.

(*Then they will go to two great stones that have been
readied for the purpose. One stone will have been set at a
distance from the other so that, when the Figure appears,
the stone of Abel will be on his right hand, the stone of
Cain on his left.*

*Abel will offer his lamb and incense, from which smoke
will arise. Cain will offer a handful of his harvest.
Appearing accordingly, the Figure will bless Abel's gift but
disdain that of Cain. Wherefore, after the oblation,[3] Cain
will make a savage face against Abel; and, when their
oblations have been completed, they will go to their own
places. Then Cain will come to Abel, seeking cunningly to
lead him forth in order to kill him, and will say to him:*)

Dear brother Abel, let us depart.
ABEL.   Why?
CAIN.   To refresh our bodies
And to inspect our labor,
745   To see how the crops have grown, and whether they're
        in flower.
Then we'll go to the meadows;
We will feel refreshed afterwards.
ABEL. I'll go with you, wherever you wish.
CAIN. Come on, then; you'll do well by it.
750   ABEL. You are my elder brother;
I'll follow your wishes.
CAIN. Go ahead, I'll follow after
With unhurried steps, very leisurely.

(*Then they will both go to a place apart and, as it were,
secret, where Cain, like a madman, will rush upon Abel
wishing to kill him, and say to him:*)

Abel, you die.
755   ABEL.   For what?
CAIN. I will be avenged on you.
ABEL. Have I done wrong?
CAIN.   Yes, wrong enough!
You're a proven traitor.
760   ABEL. I certainly am not.
CAIN.   Do you deny it?
ABEL. I've never even thought of committing treason.

_____
[3] *oblation* Offering or sacrifice.

CAIN. You've done it already.

ABEL. Me? How?

765 CAIN. You'll know soon.

ABEL. I don't understand.

CAIN. I'll make you understand plenty soon enough.

ABEL. You can't prove anything, truthfully.

CAIN. The proof is here.

770 ABEL. God will help me.

CAIN. I'll kill you!

ABEL. God will know it.

(*Then Cain will lift up a menacing right hand against him, saying:*)

Look here at this proof.

ABEL. In God is all my trust.

775 CAIN. He won't be of much use to you against me.

ABEL. He could stop you, all right, if He wanted.

CAIN. He can't save [you] from death.

ABEL. He does with me according to His pleasure in
everything.

CAIN. Do you want to hear why I'm killing you?

780 ABEL. Tell me.

CAIN. I'll tell you:
You make yourself too much God's favorite.
Because of you He has rejected me entirely.
Because of you He refused my offering.

785 Do you think I won't pay you back for this?
I'll give you this reward for it:
You'll lie dead today on the sand.

ABEL. If you kill me, that will be wrong.
God will avenge my death on you.

790 I haven't wronged [you], God knows it well;
I haven't slandered you to Him in anything.
On the contrary, I told you to do such deeds
That you would be deserving of His peace:
Render to Him his due,

795 Tithes, first-fruits, oblations—
Thereby you could have His love.
You didn't do this, now you're angry.
God is true; he who serves Him
Spends his time wisely, and loses nothing by it.

800 CAIN. You've talked too much. Now you're going to die.

ABEL. Brother, what are you saying? You led me here;
I came here trusting in you.

CAIN. Trust won't help you.
I'm going to kill you. I defy you!

805 ABEL. I pray God to give me mercy!

(*Then Abel will kneel to the east. And he will have a pot
concealed in his garments, which Cain will strike violently,
as though killing Abel. Abel will lie prostrate as though
dead. The choir will sing.*)

RESPONSORY. Where is Abel, your brother?

(*Meantime the Figure will come forth from the church to
Cain, and, when the choir has finished the responsory, he
will say to him [Cain] as though very angry:*)

Cain, where is your brother Abel?
Have you entered into rebellion?
You have begun to strive against me.

810 Now show me your brother alive.

CAIN. How should I know, Lord, where he's gone,
Whether at home or in his fields?
Why should I find him? I am not his keeper.

FIGURE. What have you done with him? Where have
815 you put him?
I know perfectly well, you have killed him.
His blood cries out to me of it;
The cry has come to me in heaven.
You have committed a grave felony;

820 You will be cursed for it all your life.
Forever you will bear a curse;
For such a misdeed, such is the reward.
Yet I desire not that any man kill you,
But that you endure your life in sorrow.

825 Whoever will kill Cain
Will pay a sevenfold penalty.
Your brother died in my faith;
Your penance will be grave.

(*Then the Figure will return to the church. The devils,
coming forth, will lead Cain to hell, beating him often.
They will lead Abel away more gently.*)

(*Then the prophets will be made ready, one by one, in a
concealed place, as appropriate to them. Let the lesson be
read in the choir.*)

You, I say, I do summon before a tribunal, O Jews.[1]

(*And let the prophets be called by name; and, when they come forward, let them proceed with dignity and announce their prophecies clearly and distinctly. Accordingly Abraham will come first, an old man with a very long beard, dressed in ample garments; and when he has sat on a bench for a little time, let him begin his prophecy in a loud voice:*)

830   Your seed will possess the gates of their enemies, and in [your] seed will all the nations [of the earth] be blessed.

I am Abraham, such is my name.
Now listen to my entire message:
Let him who has good hope in God
835   Hold to his faith and his trust.
He who will have firm faith in God,
God will be with him, this I know through personal
        experience:
He tested me, I did His pleasure;
Well I accomplished His will.
840   I would have killed my own son for Him,
But by Him I was told not to.
I would have offered him for a sacrifice;
God turned me from it, in His justice.
God has promised me—and true indeed it will be—
845   Another such heir will come of my lineage
Who will conquer all his enemies;
Thus strong and mighty will he be.
He will hold their gates in his hands,
And their castles; he will be no serf.
850   Such a man will issue from my seed,
Who will commute our sentence of damnation,
And by whom the world will be ransomed.
Adam will be delivered from his pain;
The peoples of every nation
855   Will receive benison° through him.[2]   *blessing*

(*When these things have been said, and after a brief interval, the devils will come and lead Abraham to hell.*)

(*Then Moses will come, bearing a rod in his right hand and the tablets in his left. When he has sat, let him say his prophecy:*)

God will raise up a prophet from among your brethren; you shall hearken to him as if to me.

That which I tell you, I saw through God:
From our own brethren, from our law
860   God will raise up a man.
He will be a prophet, and the summit of wisdom;
He will know all heaven's secrets;
You ought to believe him more than me.

(*Thereupon he will be led to hell by the devil. Similarly with all the prophets [throughout the play].*)

(*Then Aaron will come, in bishop's apparel, bearing in his hands a rod having flowers and fruit; being seated, let him say:*)

"This is the branch bearing the flower
865   Which gives the perfume of salvation.
The sweet fruit of this branch
Will expiate the sorrow of our death."
This rod,[3] implanted,
Can blossom and bear fruit.
870   Such a rod will come from my lineage
Who will be Satan's nemesis,
Who, without fleshly birth,
Will bear man's nature.
This is the fruit of salvation,
875   Who will release Adam from prison.

(*After him let David approach, royally accoutred and wearing a diadem, and let him say:*)

Truth has sprung out of the earth, and justice has looked down from heaven. For the Lord will give goodness, and our earth will yield her fruit.

---

[1] *You, I say ... Jews* The opening of the pseudo-Augustinian *Sermo contra Judeos, Paganos, et Arianos*, a popular Christmas sermon that inspired the *Ordo Prophetarum* or "Procession of Prophets" in the liturgical drama and supplied the structure for the concluding action in this play.

[2] *I am Abraham ... through him* For Abraham's prophecy see Genesis 12.17–18.

[3] *This rod* See Numbers 17.1–8 for the Biblical account of the blossoming rod.

Out of the earth truth shall arise,
880 And justice, from divine majesty.
God will give us goodness,
Our earth will yield her fruit;
Of her increase she will give her bread,
Which will save the sons of Eve.
885 This will be the Lord of all the earth,
This one will bring peace, end war.[1]

(*Then let Solomon come forward, with the same
adornments as those in which David advanced, except that
he should seem younger; and, being seated, let him say:*)

Being ministers of God's kingdom, you have not judged
rightly, nor kept the law of justice, nor walked according
to the will of God. [Terribly] and swiftly will He appear
890 to you, because a most severe judgment shall befall those
who rule. For to the lowly, mercy is granted.

O Jews, God gave you his law,
But you have not borne Him faith.
He made you custodians of His kingdom,
895 You were well established;
You have not judged justly,
Your verdict was against God.
You have not done His will;
Your iniquity was very great.
900 All you have done will be made manifest;
Extremely harsh vengeance will be visited
On those who were the most high:
They will take a fearful fall.
God will have pity on the lowly:
905 He will make them very happy.
This prophecy will be fulfilled
When the Son of God dies for us.
Those who are ministers of the law
Will kill Him, out of faithlessness.
910 Against all justice and reason
They will put Him on the Cross like a thief.
For this they will lose their ruling authority
That they used to have from Him, during His lifetime.
From great height they will be humbled;
915 Well may they bewail their unhappy state.

He will have pity of poor Adam,
And deliver him from sin.[2]

(*After him Balaam will come, an old man dressed in ample
garments, sitting on an ass. And he will come into the
midst, and, seated on the ass's back, will speak his prophecy.*)

A star shall rise out of Jacob, and a sceptre shall spring
up from Israel, and shall strike the chiefs of Moab, and
920 shall waste all the children of Seth.

From Jacob a star will rise,
Red with the fire of heaven,
And a sceptre will spring up from Israel
Which will overthrow [the chiefs of] Moab
925 And will abase their pride;
For Christ will rise out of Israel,
And He will be that shining star.
All things will be illumined by Him.
His faithful ones He will safely lead,
930 His enemies He will all confound.[3]

(*Thereafter let Daniel approach, young in years, but old in
his dress. And when he has seated himself, let him speak his
prophecy, stretching out his hand toward those to whom he
speaks:*)

When the holy of holies comes, your anointing will
cease.

To you, O Jews, I deliver my sermon,
You who are excessively wicked toward God.
935 When the greatest of all the saints appears—
Of whom you will experience great misfortune—
Then your anointing will cease;
You won't be able to claim it any longer.
By this greatest of saints, I mean Christ,
940 He who wishes His people to gain eternal life through
Him;
For them He will come to earth.
Your tribe will wage terrible war on Him,

[1] *Truth ... end war* See Psalms 85.11–12 for David's prophecy.

[2] *O Jews ... from sin* See the apocryphal wisdom of Solomon 6.5–7.

[3] *From Jacob ... all confound* For Balaam's prophecy see Numbers 24.17.

Will subject Him to His Passion;
On this account they will lose their anointing.
945 Neither bishop nor king will have power;
Thus their law will perish through their means.

(After him Habakkuk will come, an old man. And, sitting down, when he begins his prophecy, he will lift up his hands toward the church; manifesting wonder and fear, let him say:)

O Lord, I have heard your speech and was afraid; I have contemplated your works and feared greatly. Between two beasts you will become known.

950 I have heard strange tidings concerning God:
I am most troubled in my mind about it.
I have considered this sign so intently
That great fear agitates my heart.
Between two beasts He will be recognized;
955 By all the world He will be feared.
He of whom I have such great wonder
Will be pointed out by a star;
Shepherds will find Him in a crib
That will be carved out of dry stone,
960 Where beasts will eat hay.
Then He will reveal Himself to kings;
The star will lead the kings there;
All three will bear offerings.[1]

(Then Jeremiah will enter, bearing a scroll in his hand; and let him say:)

Hear the Word of the Lord, all you men of Judaea, that
965 enter in at these gates to worship the Lord.

(And with his hand he will point to the doors of the church.)

Thus says the Lord of Hosts, the God of Israel: Make your ways and your doings good, and I will dwell with you in this place.

Hear the Holy Word of God,
970 All you who are of His doctrine,

The mighty lineage of righteous Judaea,
You who are of His household.
By this door you will enter
To adore our Lord.
975 The Lord of Hosts summons you,
The God of Israel, from heaven on high:
Make good your ways,
Let them be straight as furrows,
And let your hearts be pure,
980 That no shame may come to you;
Let your endeavors be good,
Free of wickedness.
If you do thus, God will come,
Will dwell with you;
985 The Son of God, the glorious one,
Will come down to earth for your sake;
He will be among you as mortal man,
The Lord, the celestial one.
He will release Adam from prison,
990 Giving His own body as ransom.[2]

(After him Isaiah will come, bearing a book in his hand, dressed in an ample cloak. And let him speak his prophecy.)

And there shall come forth a rod out of the root of Jesse, and a flower shall rise up out of his root, and the spirit of the Lord shall rest upon it.

Now I will tell you a marvelous thing:
995 From Jesse's root will come forth
A rod, which will bear a flower
Worthy of great honor.
The Holy Spirit will enclose it,
Will rest upon this flower.[3]

(Then somebody from the synagogue will rise up, disputing with Isaiah, and will say to him:)

1000 Now answer me, Sir Isaiah:
Is this a fable, or prophecy?
What is this you've said?
Did you invent it, or is it written?
You've been sleeping, you dreamed it.

---

[1] *I have heard … offerings* See Habakkuk 3.2.

[2] *Thus says … ransom* See Jeremiah 7.2–3.

[3] *Now I will tell … flower* See Isaiah 11.1–2.

1005 Is this serious or a joke?
ISAIAH. This is not fable; on the contrary, it's all true.
JEW. Make us see this truth, then.
ISAIAH. What I have spoken is prophecy.
JEW. Written in a book?
1010 ISAIAH.   Yes, the book of life.
I did not dream it; I saw it.
JEW. How?
ISAIAH.   By God's grace.
JEW. You seem like an old dotard to me;
1015 Your mind is addled.
You appear to me to be senile.
You know well enough how to look in a mirror:
Now look at this hand for me, and tell

(*Then he will show him his hand.*)

If my heart is sick or healthy.
1020 ISAIAH. You have the disease of wickedness,
From which you will never recover in your life.
JEW. Am I sick, then?
ISAIAH.   Yes, of error.
JEW. When will I get better?
1025 ISAIAH.   Never.
JEW. Now begin your soothsaying.°   *prophesying*
ISAIAH. What I say will not be untrue.
JEW. Now tell your vision again,
If it was a rod, or a stick,
1030 And what will be born from its flower.
We will take you for our master,
And this generation
Will hearken to your teaching.
ISAIAH. Then listen to this great wonder.
1035 Never has our listening heard anything so magnificent;
Never has anything so fabulous been heard
Since this world began:

Behold a virgin shall conceive in her womb and bear
a son, and His name shall be called Emmanuel.

1040 The time is near, it is not far,
It will not delay, it is at hand,

That a virgin shall conceive
And as a virgin shall bear a son.
He will have the name Emmanuel.[1]
1045 Saint Gabriel will be the messenger.
The maid will be the Virgin Mary;
Thus she will carry the fruit of life,
Jesus, our Saviour,
Who will recover Adam from his great sorrow
1050 And put him again in Paradise.
This that I speak to you, I learned from God.
And this will be fully accomplished, in truth,
And you ought to put your hope in it.

(*Then Nebuchadnezzar will come, adorned like a king.*)

Did we not cast three youths, bound, into the fire?
1055 RESPONSORY OF THE KING'S MINISTERS. True, O king.
NEBUCHADNEZZAR. Lo, I see four men loose, walking
in the midst of the fire, and they have no hurt, and the
form of the fourth is like the Son of God.

Hear a wondrous great miracle—
1060 No living man has heard the like—
Which I witnessed, of the three youths
Who were cast into the burning fire.
The fire was very hot and fierce,
And the flame bright and searing;
1065 The three youths rejoiced greatly
There where they were, in the burning fire.
They sang a verse so beautiful
It seemed the angels were in heaven.
When I looked there, thus I saw the fourth
1070 Who gave them very great comfort.
His face shone so resplendently
He seemed the Son of mighty God.[2]
…

—12TH CENTURY

---

[1] *Then listen … Emmanuel* See Isaiah 7.14.

[2] *Lo … mighty God* See Daniel 3.24–25.

Mankind

*M*ankind is one of only a handful of extant "morality plays"—a form that became popular in England between 1400 and 1550, at roughly the same period as the surviving biblical pageant plays. "Morality play" is not a medieval term, but rather a term of convenience first applied to this genre in the eighteenth century. The morality play is a secular form, and unlike the cycle plays it does not tell stories from the Bible or about the lives of the saints. Most morality plays, however, have an overtly religious message and tone. Morality plays may well have developed out of the "Pater Noster" ("Our Father") prayer and its dramatic derivatives, the Pater Noster play, of which no texts have survived. These plays apparently focused on what were known as the seven cardinal virtues (prudence, justice, temperance, fortitude, faith, hope, and charity) and the seven deadly sins (pride, envy, anger, greed, gluttony, lust, sloth), and depicted life as a *psychomachia*, or constant struggle between good and evil within the human soul. The topic of the war between virtue and sin was also favored by popular preachers of the time, which encouraged its entrance into general public discourse. Linked to this focus on vice and virtue was an increasing interest in allegory as an artistic form, as well as a heightened attention to questions of death and the afterlife within the Christian thought of the time. The morality play was one artistic result of the convergence of these interests.

Mankind can be reliably dated to the reign of Edward IV (1465–70) because of its mention of Edward and of the new coins issued in the period. The play was probably performed near Cambridge, as it alludes to villages in the area and the linguistic forms preserved in the manuscript of *Mankind* are consistent with an East Anglian dialect.

Like other morality plays, *Mankind* is an allegorical drama with a universal human character as its protagonist and with a focused moral purpose. The play's central story involves the temptation of Mankind, the play's main character, by the Vices (Mischief, along with Nought, Nowadays, and New Guise), as well as Titivillus (in Christian tradition, one of Satan's demons). These Vices are portrayed as both physically and verbally playful, in contrast to Mercy, with his more reserved behavior and ornate, Latinate language.

Mankind is distinctive among morality plays in its energetic theatricality and its clever use of language. It is unique among extant morality plays in its incorporation of a direct fundraising appeal by the players: during the play the performance is stopped until the audience is able to provide enough money to lure the devil Titivillus into appearing onstage. Formal differences in the play's stanzas distinguish between different sorts of speakers. The Vices speak in eight-line stanzas, the Virtue Mercy in four-line stanzas. When Mankind succumbs to temptation his speeches are patterned like those of the Vices; when he inclines towards virtue they are patterned like those of Mercy.

Little is known of the early performance history of morality plays such as *Mankind*; we do not know, for example, if they were frequently staged by guilds in a manner similar to that of much biblical drama of the period. In the sixteenth century we know that morality plays were sometimes performed by troupes of itinerant players. With the development in the late sixteenth century of more permanent performance spaces and of companies of players sponsored by patrons, the old form of morality play died out. Nevertheless, the form survived in its influence on later drama, most notably in the Seven Deadly Sins segment of Christopher Marlowe's *Doctor Faustus* (1588).

⌘ ⌘ ⌘

Mankind[1]

DRAMATIS PERSONAE

Mankind
Mercy
Titivillus[2]
Mischief
New-Guise
Nowadays
Nought

(*Enter Mercy.*)

MERCY. The very founder and beginner of our first creation,
Among us sinful wretches He oweth to be magnified,
That for our disobedience He had none indignation
To send His own son to be torn and crucified.

5   Our obsequious service to Him should be applied,
Where He was Lorde of all and made all thing of nought,
For the sinful sinner to had him revived,
And, for his redemption, set His own Son at nought.

  It may be said and verified: mankind was dere bought.[3]
10 By the pitious death of Jhesu he had his remedy.
He was purged of his defawte,° that wretchedly   *default, sin*
  had wrought,
By His glorious Passion, that blissyde° lavatory.°   *blessed / purifier*
O soverence, I beseech yow° your conditions to rectify,   *you*
And with humility and reverence to have a remotion
15 To this blissyde prince that our nature doth glorify,
That ye may be participable of His retribution.

I have be° the very mean° for your restitution.   *been / means*
Mercy is my name, that mournith° for your offence   *mourns*
Divert not yowrsilffe° in time of temptation,   *yourself*
20 That ye may be acceptable to God at your going hence.
The great mercy of God, that is of most preemminence,
By meditation of Our Lady, that is ever
  habundaunte°   *abundant, generous*
To the sinful creature that will repent his necligence.° *negligence*
I pray God, at your most need, that mercy be your
  defendawnte.°   *defendant*
25 In good works I avise° yow, soverence,° to   *advise / masters*
  be perseveraunte°   *perseverant*
To purify your sowlys,° that they be not corrupt;   *souls*
For your gostly° enmy° will make his   *spiritual / enemy*
  avaunte,°   *boast*
Your good conditions if he may interrupt.

  O ye soverens that sit, and ye brothern that stand right up,
30 Prick not your felicites in things transitory!
Behold not the earth, but lift your eye up!
See how the head the members daily do magnify.
Who is the head, forsoth, I shall yow certify:
I mean our Saviour, that was likynnyde° to a lamb; *likened*
35 And His saints be the members that daily He doth satisfy
With the precious rever° that runnith° from His *river / runs*
  womb.

  There is none such food, by water nor by londe,° *land*
So precious, so glorious, so needful to our entent;
For it hath dissolved mankind from the bitter bond
40 Of the mortal enmye,° that venomous serpent— *enemy*
From the which God preserve yow all at the Last Judgement!
For sekirly° there shall be a strait° *surely / strict, rigorous*
  examination:
The corn shall be saved, the chaffe[4] shall be brente.° *burned*
I beseech yow heartily, have this in premeditation.

(*Enter Mischief.*)

45 MISCHIEF. I beseech yow heartily, leave your calculation!
Leave your chaffe, leave your corn, leave your
  daliacion!°   *idle, frivolous talk*
Your wit is little, your head is mekyll,° ye   *large*
  are full of predication.°   *preaching*

---

[1] *Mankind* In the present text, spelling and punctuation have been substantially modernized from the original in accordance with the practice of this anthology. Where stage directions are from the original text, they appear in parentheses. Some additional stage directions are here added for the sake of clarity; these appear in square brackets. The play survives in a single text, Folger Shakespeare Library MS Va. 354.

[2] *Titivillus* Traditionally, the name of a devil whose role was to record idle words spoken in churches and any Latin errors committed by priests, and store them in a bag for use as evidence against the speakers on Judgment Day; cf. Matthew 12.36.

[3] *dere bought* Dearly redeemed.

[4] *chaffe* Husks of corn, i.e., grain.

But, sir, I pray you this question to clarify:
Misse-masche, driff-draff,[1]

50 Some was corn and some was chaffe,
My dame said my name was Raffe;
On-schett° your lock and take an   *un-shut, open*
    halpenye.°   *halfpenny*

MERCY. Why come ye hither, brother? Ye were not desired.
MISCHIEF. For a winter corn-thresher, sir, I have hired,
55 And ye said the corn should be saved and the chaff
    should be feryde.°   *burned*
And he provith° nay, as it schewth° by this verse: *proves*
"*Corn servit bredibus, chaffe horsibus, straw firybusque.*"[2]
This is as much to say, to your lewd understanding,
As: the corn shall serve to bread at the next baking;
60 "*Chaff horsibus,*" *et reliqua,*[3]
The chaff to horse shall be good provente;°   *food*
When a man is for-colde,° the straw may   *very cold*
    be brent,
And so forth, *et cetera.*

MERCY. Avoid, good brother! Ye ben° culpable   *are*
65 To interrupt thus my talking delectable.
MISCHIEF. Sir, I have nother° horse nor sadle,   *neither*
Therefore I may not ride.
MERCY. Hie° yow forth on foot, brother,   *hurry, hasten*
    in God's name!
MISCHIEF. I say, sir, I am come hedyr° to make   *hither*
    yow game.
70 Yet bade ye me not go out in the devil's name,
And I will abide.

MERCY. [*Here there is a break in the manuscript; a leaf is
missing. Evidently Mischief exits during the missing section
and New-Guise, Nowadays and Nought up the banter, with
the first two exhorting Nought to dance in a more lively
fashion.*]

NEW-GUISE. And how, minstrels, play the common trace!
Lay on with thy ballys° till his belly   *bellows (pipes)*
    breste!°   *bursts, breaks*

---

[1] *Misse-masche, driff-draff* Sing-song nonsense.

[2] *Corn … firybusque* Mock Latin: corn serves for bread, chaff for horses, straw for fires.

[3] *et reliqua* Latin: and the rest.

NOUGHT. I put case I break my neck: how than?
75 NEW-GUISE. I give no force, by Saint Anne!
NOWADAYS. Leppe° about lively! Thou art a   *leap*
    wight° man.   *active, agile*
Let us be merry while we be here.
NOUGHT. Shall I break my neck to schew yow sport?
NOWADAYS. Therefore ever beware of thy report.
80 NOUGHT. I beschrew° ye all! Here is a shrewd sort.   *curse*
Have thereat, then, with a merry cheer!

(*Here they daunce. Mercy seyth:*)

MERCY. Do way! do way this revel, sirs, do way!
NOWADAYS. Do way, good Adam, do way?
This is no part of thy play.
85 NOUGHT. Yis, mary, I pray yow, for I love not this revelling.
Come forth, good fader,° I yow pray!   *father*
By a little ye may assay.
Anon, off with your clothes, if ye will play.
Go to! for I have had a praty° scottlinge.°   *pretty / caper*

90 MERCY. Nay, brother, I will not dance.
NEW-GUISE. If ye will, sir, my brother will make yow to
    prance.
NOWADAYS. With all my heart, sir, if I may yow
    avaunce.°   *assist, help*
Ye may assay° by a little trace.   *try*
NOUGHT. Yea, sir, will ye do well?
95 Trace not with them, by my counsel,
For I have traced somewhat too fell—
I tell you it is a narow space!

But sir, I trow, of us three I heard yow speak.
NEW-GUISE. Christ's curse had ye therefore! for I was in
    sleep.
100 NOWADAYS. And I had the cup in my hand, ready to
    go to mete.°   *dine, eat*
Therefore, sir, curtly great yow well.
MERCY. Few words, few and well set!
NEW-GUISE. Sir, it is the new guise and the new
    jett:°   *fashion, style*
Many words, and schortely° set—   *shortly, curtly*
105 This is the new guise, every dele.°   *bit, thing*

MERCY. Lady, help! How wretches delight in their
    simple ways!

NOWADAYS.   Say nought again the new guise nowadays!
   Thou shall find us shrews at all assays.°   trials
   Beware, ye may soon like a bofett!°   blow, strike
110 MERCY.   He was well occupied that brought yow
         brether!°   brother
   NOUGHT.   I harde° yow call "New-Guise, Nowadays,   heard
         Nought," all these three together.
   If ye say that I lie, I shall make yow to slither:°   fall
   Lo, take yow here a trepett!° (*Trips him.*)   trip

   MERCY.   Say me yowr names. I know yow not.
115 NEW-GUISE.   New-Guise, I.
   NOWADAYS.   I, Nowadays.
   NOUGHT.   I, Nought.
   MERCY.   By Jhesu Crist, that me dere bought,
   Ye betray many men.
120 NEW-GUISE.   Betray? Nay, nay, sir, nay, nay!
   We make them both fresh and gay.
   But of your name, sir, I yow pray,
   That we may yow ken.°   know

   MERCY.   "Mercy" is my name by denomination.
125 I conceive ye have but a little favour in my communication.
   NEW-GUISE.   Ey, ey, your body is full of English Latin!
   I am aferde° it will brest.   afraid, scared
   "Pravo te,"[1] quod° the bocher° onto me   said / butcher
   When I stale° a leg a mutton.   stole
130 NOWADAYS.   Ye are a strong cunning clerk;
   I pray yow heartily, worshipful clerk,
   To have this English made in Latin:

   "I have eaten a dish-full of curds,
   And I have schetun°[2] your mouth full of turds."—   shitten
135 Now, open your satchel with Latin words
   And say me this in clerical manner!
   Also, I have a wife—her name is Rachel—
   Betwix° her and me was a great battle,   between
   And fain of yow I would here tell
140 Who was the most master.

   NOUGHT.   Thy wife Rachel, I dare lay twenty lise.[3]

NOWADAYS.   Who spake° to thee, foll?° Thou art   spoke / fool
      not wise.
   Go and do that longith° to thine office: belonging, fitting
   Osculare fundamentum![4]
145 NOUGHT.   Lo, master, lo, here is a pardon belly-
         mett°—   satisfying
   It is granted of Pope Pocket:
   If ye will putt your nose in his wife's sokett,°   hole, i.e., vagina
   Ye shall have forty days of pardon.

   MERCY.   This idle language ye shall repent!
150 Out of this place I would ye went.
   NEW-GUISE.   Go we hence all three with one assent.
   My fadyr is irke° of our eloquence;   irked, annoyed
   Therefore I will no longer tarry.
   God bring yow, master, and blissyde Mary,
155 To the number of the demonical friary![5]

   NOWADAYS.   Come wind, cum rain,
   Though I come never again.
   The devil put out both your eyn!°   eyes
   Fellows, go we hence tight.
160 NOUGHT.   Go we hence, a devil way!
   Here is the door, here is the way. (*To Mercy.*)
   Farewell, gentle Jaffrey,
   I pray God give yow good night!

(*Exiant simul. Cantent.*)[6]

   MERCY.   Thankyde be God we have a fayer deliverance[7]
165 Of these three onthrifty° guests!   worthless
   They know full little what is their ordinance.
   I preve,° by reason, they be worse than beasts: prove

   A best° doth after his natural institution;   beast
   Ye may conceive, by their disport and behaviour,
170 Their joy and delight is in derision
   Of their own Christ, to His dishonour.

---

[1]   *Pravo te*   Latin: I curse you.

[2]   *schetun*   To defile with excrement, to deceive.

[3]   *lise*   I.e., lis. An obsolete abbreviation, li, libra for pound; i.e., the wager here is twenty pounds.

[4]   *Osculare fundamentum*   Latin: Kiss my ass!

[5]   A line is missing to complete the stanza.

[6]   *Exiant … cantent*   Latin: Let them all go out together. Let them sing.

[7]   *a fayer deliverance*   Good riddance.

This condition of living, it is prejudicially—
Beware thereof! It is worse than any felony or treason.
How may it be excused before the Justice of all,
175   When for every idle word we must yield a reason?

They have great ease; therefore they will take no thought.
But how then, when the angel of heaven shall blow
     the trumpe°   *trumpet*
And say to the transgressors that wickedly hath wrought:
"Come forth onto your judge, and yield your account"?

180   Then shall I, Mercy, begin sore to weep.
Nother° comfort nor counsel there shall none be had,   *neither*
But such as they have sown, such shall they reap.
They be wanton now, but then shall they be sad.

The good new guise nowadays I will not disallow;
185   I discommend the vicious guise. I pray have me excused,
I need not to speak of it; your reason will tell it yow.
Take that is to be taken, and leave that is to be refused.

(*Enter Mankind, carrying a spade.*)

MANKIND.   Of the earth and of the clay we have our
     propagation.
By the providence of God thus be we derivatt°—   *derived*
190   To whose mercy I recommend this whole congregation.
I hope, onto His bliss ye be all predestinatt!°   *predestined*

Every man, for his degree, I trust shall be
     participatt,°   *a participant*
If we will mortify our carnal condition
And our voluntary desires, that ever be
     pervercionatt°—   *perverse*
195   To renounce them, and yield us under God's provision.

My name is "Mankind." I have my composition
Of a body and of a soul, of condition contrary—
Betwix them tweyn° is a great division.   *of the two*
He that should be subject, now he hath the victory.

200   This is to me a lamentable story,
To see my flesh of my soul to have governance.
Where the good-wife is master, the goodman may be sorry.
I may both syth° and sob; this is a pituose°
     remembrance.   *sigh / piteous*

O thou my soul, so sotyll° in thy substance,   *subtle*
.   .   .   .
205   Alas, what was thy fortune and thy chance
To be associat° with my flesh, that stinking   *associated*
     dungehill?

Lady, help! Soverens, it doth my soul much ill
To see the flesh prosperous, and the soul trodden under foot.
I shall go to yonder man, and assay him I will.
210   I trust of gostly solace he will be my bote.°   *help*

(*He kneels in front of Mercy.*)

All hail, semely father, ye be welcome to this house!
Of the very wisdom ye have participation.
My body with my soul is ever querilous;
I pray yow, for sent charity, of your supportation!

215   I beseech yow heartily of your gostly comfort.
I am unstedfast in living; my name is "Mankind."
My gostly enmy, the devil, will have a great disport,
In sinful guiding if he may see me end.

MERCY.   Christ send yow good comfort! Ye be welcome,
     my friend.
220   Stand up on your feet. I pray yow, arise.
My name is "Mercy." Ye be to me full
     hende;°   *courteous, gracious*
To eschew vice I will yow avise.

MANKIND.   O Mercy, of all grace and virtue ye are the well!
I have heard tell, of right worshipful clerks,[1]
225   Ye be approximate to God and near of his counsel;
He hath institute you above all his works.

O, your lovely words to my soul are sweeter then honey!
MERCY.   The temptation of the flesh ye must resist
     like a man,
For there is ever a battle betwix the soul and the body:
230   *Vita hominis est militia super terram.*[2]

---

[1]   *clerks* Scholars.

[2]   *Vita hominis … terram* Latin: The life of man on Earth is a battle; see Job 7.1.

Oppress your gostly enmy and be Christ's own knight!
Be never a coward again your adversary:
If ye will be crowned, ye must needs fight.
Intend well, and God will be yow adjutory.°   *helper*

235 Remember, my friend, the time of continuance:
So help me God, it is but a cherry time!¹
Spend it well. Serve God with heart's affiance.°   *trust, loyalty*
Distemper not your brain with good ale nor with wine.

"Measure is treasure"; I forbid yow not the use.
240 Measure yourself ever. Beware of excess.
The superfluous guise I will that ye refuse;
When nature is sufficed, anon that ye cease.

If a man have an horse, and keep him not too high,
He may then rule him at his own desire;
245 If he be fed over-well he will disobey
And, in happe,° cast his master in the   *perhaps*
      mire.°   *swamp, bog*

*(New-Guise, Nowadays, and Nought, who have been
listening in on the conversation, now begin to speak. They
remain hidden from Mercy and Mankind.)*

NEW-GUISE. Ye say true, sir; ye are no faitour:° *liar, cheat*
I have fed my wife so well till she is my master!
I have a great wound on my head, lo! and thereon
    leyth° a plaster;   *lies*
250 And another there I piss my peson.°   *pease*
And my wife were your horse, she would yow all to-
    banne.°   *curse*
Ye feed your horse in measure; ye are a wise man!
I trow, and ye were the king's palfrey-man
A good horse should be gesunne.°   *scarce*

255 MANKIND. Where speaks this fellow? Will he not come
    near?
MERCY. All too soon, my brother, I fear me, for yow.
He was here right now—by him that bought me dere!—
With other of his fellows. They kan° much sorrow *know*
They will be here right soon, if I ought depart.
260 Think on my doctrine! It shall be your defence.

Learn while I am here; set my words in heart.

Within a short space I must needs hence.²

NOWADAYS. (*Unseen.*) The sooner the lever, and it be
    even anon!³
I trow your name is "Do-little," ye be so long fro° home*from*

265 If ye would go hence, we shall come everychon,° *everyone*
Mo° then a good sort. Ye have leave, I dare well say; *more*
When ye will, go forth your way.
Men have little deynte° of your play   *joy, pleasure*
Because ye make no sport.

270 NOUGHT. (*Unseen.*) Your potage° shall be for-cold, sir. *soup*
    When will ye go dine?
I have seen a man lost twenty nobles in as little time—
Yet it was not I, by Saint Quentin!
For I was never worth a potful a wortys° sithyn° *cabbage / since*
    I was born.
My name is "Nought." I love well to make merry!
275 I have be sethen° with the common tapster⁴ of Bury *before*
And played so long the fool that I am even very weary—
Yet shall I be there again to-morn.

MERCY. (*To Mankind.*) I have much care for yow, my
    own friend.
Your enmys will be here anon; they make their avaunte.
280 Think well in your heart: your name is "Mankind";
Be not unkind to God, I pray yow! Be his servant.

Be steadfast in condition; see ye be not variant.
Lose not through folly that is bought so dere!
God will prove yow soon; and, if that ye be constant,
285 Of his bliss perpetual ye shall be partner.

Ye may not have your intent at your first desire.
See the great patience of Job in tribulation:
Like as the smith trieth ern in the fire,⁵
So was he tried by God's visitation.

---

¹ *but a cherry time* A brief time, i.e., the duration of a cherry harvest is brief.

² *needs hence* Depart.

³ *The sooner … even anon!* The sooner the better, even if it were right now!

⁴ *tapster* Proprietor of a drinking house.

⁵ *trieth ern in the fire* Tries (refines, purifies) iron in the fire.

290 He was of your nature and of your fragility.
Follow the steps of him, my own sweet son,
And say, as he said, in your trouble and adversity:
"*Dominus dedit, Dominus abstulit; sicut sibi placuit, ita
    factum est; sit nomen Domini benedictum.*"[1]

Moreover, in special I give yow in charge:
295 Beware of New-Guise, Nowadays, and Nought!
Nice° in their array, in language they be large.   *extravagant*
To pervert your conditions, all their means shall be sought.

Good son, intromitt° not yourself in their company!   *intermix*
They heard not a mass this twelmonyth,°   *twelve-month, year*
    I dare well say.
300 Give them none audience; they will tell yow many a lie.
Do truly your labour, and keep your holy day.

Beware of Titivillus—for he lesith° no way—   *loses*
That goth° invisible and will not be seen.   *goes*
He will ronde° in your ear, and cast a net before   *whisper*
    your eye.
305 He is worst of them all, God let him never then!

If ye displease God, ask mercy anon,
Else Mischief will be ready to brace yow in his bridle.
Kiss me now, my dear darling. God shield yow from
    your fon!°   *foes*
Do truly your labour, and be never idle.
310 The blessing of God be with yow and with all these
    worshipful men!   (*Exit.*)
MANKIND.   Amen, for saint charity, amen!

Now, blessed be Jhesu! My soul is well saciatt°   *satisfied*
With the mellifluous° doctrine of this   *sweet, honeyed*
    worshipful man.
The rebellion of my flesh, now it is
    superatt,°   *suppressed, conquered*
315 Thanking be God of the coming that I came.

Here will I sit, and tityll° in this paper   *write*
The incomparable astat° of my   *estate, nature*
    promicion.° (*Writes.*)   *promise*

(*To the audience.*) Worshipful soverence, I have written
    here
The glorious remembrance of my noble condition.

320 To have remorse and memory of myself thus written it is,
To defend me from all superstitious charms:
"*Memento, homo, quod cinis es, et in cinerem reverteris.*"[2]

(*He points to his chest.*)

Lo, I bear on my breast the badge of mine arms.

(*New-Guise comes forward.*)

NEW-GUISE.   The weather is cold. God send us good fires!
325 "*Cum sancto sanctus eris, et cum perverso perverteris.*"
"*Ecce quam bonum et quam jocundum,*" quod the devil
    to the friars,
"*Habitare fratres in unum.*"[3]

MANKIND.   I hear a fellow speak. With him I will not
    mell.°   *speak, meddle*
This earth, with my spade, I shall assay to delve.
330 To eschew idleness I do it mine own self.
I pray God send it His fusion!° (*Digs.*)   *plenty, abundance*

(*Nowadays and Nought come forward through the audience.*)

NOWADAYS.   Make room, sirs, for we have be long!
We will come give yow a Cristemes song.

NOUGHT.   Now I pray all the yemandry°   *yeomanry*
    that is here
335 To sing with us, with a merry cheer!

(*He sings each line; New-Guise and Nowadays encourage the
members of the audience to sing along in response.*)

It is written with a coal, it is written with a coal,

___

[1]   *Dominus dedit … Domini benedictum*   Latin: The Lord gave, and
the Lord has taken away; as it was pleasing to him, so it was done;
blessed by the name of the Lord. See Job 1.21.

[2]   *Momento … reverteris*   Latin: Remember man, that you are dust,
and to dust you will return; see Job 34.15.

[3]   *Cum sancto … unum*   Latin: With the holy you will show yourself
holy, and with the wicked you will show yourself wicked (Psalms 18.
25–26); "Behold, how good and how pleasant it is … for the
brethren to dwell together in unity" (Psalms 133.1).

NEW-GUISE *and* NOWADAYS.   It is written with a coal,
   it is written with a coal,

NOUGHT.   He that schitith° with his hole, he   *shits*
   that schitith with his hole,

NEW-GUISE, NOWADAYS.   He that schitith with his
   hole, he that schitith with his hole,

340 NOUGHT.   But° he wipe his arse clean, but he   *unless*
   wipe his arse clean,

NEW-GUISE, NOWADAYS.   But he wipe his arse clean,
   but he wipe his arse clean,

NOUGHT.   On his breche° it shall be seen, on his breche
   it shall be seen,   *breeches*

NEW-GUISE, NOWADAYS.   On his breche it shall be seen, on
   his breche it shall be seen.

(*Cantant omnes*:)[1]

Hoylyke, holyke, holyke! holyke, holyke, holyke!

345 NEW-GUISE.   Ey, Mankind, God speed yow with your spade!
   I shall tell yow of a marriage:
   I would your mouth and his arse, that this made,
   Were married junctly° together.   *jointly*

MANKIND.   Hey yow hence, fellows, with bredinge!° *reproach*

350 Leave your derision and your japing!°   *mocking*
   I must needs labour—it is my living.

NOWADAYS.   What, sir? We came but late hither.
   Shall all this corn grow here
   That ye shall have the next year?

355 If it be so, corn had need be dear,
   Else ye shall have a poor life.

NOUGHT.   Alas, good fadere, this labour
   fretith° yow to the bone!   *frets, i.e., devours*
   But, for your crop I take great mone:°   *complaint*
   Ye shall never spend it alone!

360 I shall assay to get yow a wife.

How many acres suppose ye here, by estimation?

NEW-GUISE.   Ey, how ye turn the earth up and down!
   I have be in my days in many good town,
   Yet saw I never such another tilling.

365 MANKIND.   Why stand ye idle? It is pity that ye were born!

NOWADAYS.   We shall bargain with yow, and nother
   mock nor scorn:

Take a good cart in harvest, and load it with your corn,
And what shall we give yow for the levinge?°   *crop*

NOUGHT.   He is a good stark labourer—he would fain
   do well!

370 He hath met with the good man Mercy, in a shrewd sell!
For all this, he may have many a hungry meal.
Yit, will ye se? He is politic:°   *prudent, careful*
Here shall be good corn—he may not miss it.
If he will have rain, he may over-piss it;[2]
375 And if he will have compost, he may over-bless it
A little with his arse, like.

MANKIND.   Go and do your labour—God let yow never
   the!°—   *thrive, prosper*
   Or with my spade I shall yow ding,° by the holy *hit, strike*
   Trinity!
   Have ye none other man to mock but ever me?
380 Ye would have me of your set?
   Hie yow forth lively, for hence I will yow driffe!° *drive*

(*He hits them with his spade.*)

NEW-GUISE.   Alas, my jewels!° I shall be   *testicles*
   schent[3] of my wife!

NOWADAYS.   Alas, and I am like never for to thrive,
   I have such a buffett!

385 MANKIND.   Hence I say, New-Guise, Nowadays, and Nought!
   It was said beforn,° all the means should be sought *before*
   To pervert my conditions and bring me to nought.
   Hence, thieves! Ye have made many a lesinge.° *deception, lie*

NOUGHT.   Marred I was for cold, but now am I warm!
390 Ye are evill-avisyde,° sir, for ye have done harm, *ill-advised*
   By Cokkys° body sacred, I have such a pain in my arm *God's*
   I may not change a man a farthing!°   *quarter penny*

(*New-Guise, Nowadays and Nought begin to leave. Mankind
kneels down.*)

MANKIND.   Now I thank God, kneeling on my knee.
   Blessed be His name! He is of high degree.
395 By the subsidy of His grace that He hath sent me,

---

1 *Cantant omnes* Latin: all sing.

2 *over-piss it* Piss over it.

3 *schent* Free of; i.e., I shall lose my wife.

Three of mine enmys I have put to flight. (*He holds up the
    spade.*)
Yet this instrument, soverens, is not made to defend.
David seyth, "*Nec in hasta, nec in gladio, salvat Dominus.*"[1]
NOUGHT.   (*As he is leaving.*) No, mary, I beschrew yow,
    it is *in spadibus!*[2]
400 Therefore Christ's curse come on your hedibus,°   *head*
To send yow less might!

(*Exiant.*)

MANKIND. I promitt yow, these fellows will no more
    come here;
For some of them, certainly, were somewhat too near!
My fadyr Mercy avisyde me to be of a good cheer
405 And again my enmys manly for to fight.

I shall convict them, I hope, everychon.
Yet I say amiss; I do it not alone:
With the help of the grace of God, I resist my fon°   *foes*
And their malicious heart.
410 With my spade I will depart, my worshipful soverence,
And live ever with labour, to correct my insolence.
I shall go fett° corn for my lande. I pray yow of   *fetch*
    patience;
Right soon I shall revert.°   *return*

(*He exits. Enter Mischief.*)

MISCHIEF. Alas, alas, that ever I was wrought!
415 Alas the will, I am worse then nought!
Sithyn I was here, by Him that me bought,
I am utterly undone.
I, Mischief, was here at the beginning of the game,
And argued with Mercy—God give him shame!
420 He hath taught Mankind, while I have be vain,
To fight manly again his fon.

For with his spade, that was his weapon,
New-Guise, Nowadays, and Nought hath he all
    to-betyn—°   *beaten*

I have great pity to see them weeping.
425 Will ye list?° I here them cry. (*Clamant.*)[3]   *listen*

(*New-Guise, Nowadays, and Nought re-enter, crying.
Mischief addresses them.*)

Alas, alas, come hither! I shall be your
    borow.°   *protector, guardian*
Alack, alack! *Vene, vene!*° Come hither, with sorrow!   *come*
Peace, fair babies! Ye shall have an apple—tomorrow.
Why grete° ye so, why?   *weep*

430 NEW-GUISE. Alas, master, alas, my privite!°   *private parts*
MISCHIEF. A, where? Alacke, fair babe, ba° me!   *kiss*
Abide! Too soon I shall it see.
NOWADAYS. Here, here, see my head, good master!
MISCHIEF. Lady, help! Silly darling, *vene, vene!*[4]
435 I shall help thee of thy pain:
I shall smite off thy head and set it on again.
NOUGHT. By Our Lady, sir, a fair plaster!

Will ye off with his head? It is a shrewd charm!
As for me, I have none harm—
440 I were lothe to forbear mine arm.
Ye play: *In nomine patris*,[5] chop!
NEW-GUISE. Ye shall not chop my jewels, and I may.
NOWADAYS. Ye, Christ's cross! Will ye smight my head away?
There, where, on and on? Out! Ye shall not assay—
445 I might well be called a fop.°   *fool*

MISCHIEF. I can chop it off and make it again.
NEW-GUISE. I had a shrewd *recumbentibus*,° *knockdown blow*
    but I feel no pain.
NOWADAYS. And my head is all save and whole again.—
Now, touching the matter of Mankind,
450 Let us have an interleccion,° sithen ye be   *consultation*
    come hither.
It were good to have an end.

MISCHIEF. How, how? A minstrel! Know ye any ought?

---

[1] *Nec in ... Dominus* Latin: Not by the spear or sword does the
lord save; see 1 Samuel 17.47.

[2] *in spadibus!* In spades!

[3] *Clamant* Latin: they cry.

[4] *vene, vene!* Latin: come, come!

[5] *In nomine patris* Latin: in the name of the Father.

NOUGHT.   I kan pipe in a Walsingham[1] whistle, I, Nought,
Nought.
MISCHIEF.   Blow a piece, and thou shall bring him in
with a flute.

(*Nought starts to play the pipe. A voice comes from offstage.*)

455 TITIVILLUS.   I come, with my legs under me!
MISCHIEF.   How, New-Guise, Nowadays, hark or I go:
When our heads were together, I spoke of *si dedero*.[2]
NEW-GUISE.   Ye, go thy way, we shall gather money onto—
Else there shall no man him see.

(*To the audience.*)

460 Now gostly° to our purpose, worshipful soverence.   *devoutly*
We intend to gather money, if it please your negligence,
For a man with a head that is of great omnipotence—
NOWADAYS.   Keep your tayll,° in goodness I pray   *tally*
yow, good brother!
He is a worshipful man, sirs, saving your reverence.
465 He lovith no groats, nor pence of two-pence:
Give us rede reyallys,°[3] if ye will see his   *ready royals*
abominable presence.
NEW-GUISE.   Not so! Ye that mow° not pay the   *may*
ton, pay the tother.°   *other*

(*They begin to take up a collection from the audience.*)

At the good-man of this house first we will assay.
God bless yow, master! Ye say us ill, yet ye will not say "nay."
470 Let us go by and by, and do them pay.
Ye pay all alike. Well mut ye fare!4

(*When they finish taking up the collection they return to the stage.*)

NOUGHT.   I say, New-Guise, Nowadays, *Estis vos pecuniatus?*[5]

I have cried a fayer will,[6] I beschrew your patus!°   *heads*

(*Nowadays turns to call in Titivillus.*)

NOWADAYS.   *Ita vere, magister,*[7] come forth now your
gatus!°   *gate*
475 He is a goodly man, sirs; make space, and beware!

(*Enter Titivillus, arrayed as a devil with a net in his hand.
He addresses the audience.*)

TITIVILLUS.   *Ego sum dominantium dominus,*[8] and my
name is Titivillus.
Ye that have good horse, to yow I say "*caveatis*":°   *Latin: beware*
Here is an able fellowship to trise° hem°   *snatch / them*
out at your gatis!°   *gates*
Ego probo sic:[9]

(*Loquitur ad [10] New-Guise.*)

480 Sir New-Guise, lend me a penny.
NEW-GUISE.   I have a great purse, sir, but I have no money:
By the mass, I fail two farthings of an halpeny.
Yet had I ten pound this night that was.

TITIVILLUS.   (*Loquitur ad Nowadays.*) What is in thy purse?
Thou art a stout villain.
485 NOWADAYS.   The devil have the qwitt!° I am a clean
gendeman.   *reward*
I pray God I be never worse storyde°   *supplied, provided for*
then I am.
It shall be otherwise, I hope, or this night pass.
TITIVILLUS.   (*Loquitur ad Nought.*) Hark now, I say,
thou hast many a penny.
NOUGHT.   *Non nobis, domine, non nobis,*[11] by Saint Deny![12]
490 The devil may dance in my purse for any penny;
It is as clean as a bird's arse.

---

1 *Walsingham*   Town in Norfolk.

2 *si dedero*   Latin: if I give something, i.e., I expect something
(payment in return).

3 *He lovith … reyallys*   Groats, "pence of two pence," and "Ready
Royals" were worth 4 pence, 2 pence, and 10 shillings, respectively.

4 *Well mut ye fare!*   Good luck to you!

5 *Estis … pecuniatus?*   Latin: Are you wealthy?

6 *fayer will*   Fair while.

7 *Ita … magister*   Latin: Truly then, master.

8 *Ego sum … dominus*   Latin: I am Lord of Lords.

9 *Ego probo sic*   Latin: I show it thus.

10 *loquitur ad*   Latin: He speaks to.

11 *Non nobis … nobis*   Latin: Not to us, O Lord, not to us; Cf.
Psalms 115.1.

12 *Saint Deny*   Saint Denis is the patron saint of France.

TITIVILLUS.   (*To the audience.*) Now I say yet again, "*caveatis*":
Here is an able fellowship to trise hem out of your gatis!—
(*To the three rogues.*) Now I say, New-Guise, Nowadays,
and Nought,

495   Go and search the country: anon that it be sought,
Some here, some there, what if ye may catch ought.° *anything*

If ye fail of horse, take what ye may else.
NEW-GUISE.   Then speak to Mankind for the
recumbentibus[1] of my jewels!
NOWADAYS.   Remember my broken head in the
worship of the five vowels.
500   NOUGHT.   Yea, good sir, and the siatica° in my arm! *sciatica*
TITIVILLUS.   I know full well what Mankind did to yow;
Mischief hath informed me of all the matter
thorow.°   *thoroughly*
I shall venge° your quarrel, I make God a vow.   *avenge*
Forth, and espy where ye may do harm!
505   Take William Fyde,[2] if ye will have any mo.°   *more*
I say, New-Guise, whethere art thou avisyde to go?[3]

NEW-GUISE.   First I shall begin at Master Huntington
of Sawston.
Fro thens[4] I shall go to William Thurlay of
Hauston,°   *Hauxton*
And so forth to Picharde of Trumpington—
510   I will keep me to these three.
NOWADAYS.   I shall go to Williham Bakere of Walton,
To Richerde Bollman of Gayton.
I shall spare Master Woode of Fullburn—
He is a "*noli me tangere.*"[5]

515   NOUGHT.   I shall go to William Patrike of Massingham;
I shall spare Master Alington of Bottisham,
And Hamonde of Swoffeham,
For dread of "*in manus tuas,* qweke!"[6]

---

[1]   *recumbentibus* Heavy blow.

[2]   Greg Walker notes that the names in this, and the following
exchanges, were most likely prominent local personalities in the area
where the play was meant to be performed.

[3]   *whethere art … to go?* Where are you thinking of going?

[4]   *Fro thens* From there.

[5]   *noli me tangere* Latin: Touch me not.

[6]   *in manus tuas* Latin: Into your hands (the last words spoken by
Christ on the Cross); see Luke 23.46; *qweke* Sound of a neck
breaking.

Fellows, come forth and go we hence together.
520   NEW-GUISE.   Sith we shall go, let us be well ware°   *aware*
wither.
If we may be take, we come no more hither.
Let us con° well our neck verse, that we have   *know, learn*
not a cheke.°   *disaster*

TITIVILLUS.   Go your way, a devil way, go your way all!
I bless yow with my left hand—foul yow befall!
525   Come again, I warn, as soon as I yow call,
And bring your avantage° into   *advantage (i.e., spoils, booty)*
this place.

(*Exeunt. Manet Titivillus.*[7])

To speak with Mankind I will tarry here this tide,°   *time*
And assay his good purpose for to set aside.
The good man Mercy shall no longer be his guide.
530   I shall make him to dance another trace!

Ever I go invisible—it is my jett—
And before his eye thus I will hang my net
To blench° his sight. I hope to have his   *blind*
fote-mett!°   *take his measure*
To irk him of his labour I shall make a frame:
535   This board shall be hid under the earth
prevely.°   *privately, secretly*

(*Titivillus hides a board beneath a thin covering of earth in
Mankind's field.*)

His spade shall enter, I hope, onredily!° *unreadily, with difficulty*
By then he hath assayde, he shall be very angry
And lose his patience—pain of shame.
I shall menge° his corn with drawke and with durnell;[8] *mix*
540   It shall not be like to sow nor to sell.
Yonder he commith. I pray of counsel.
He shall wene° grace were wane!°   *believe / gone*

(*Enter Mankind, carrying a heavy sack.*)

MANKIND.   Now God, of his mercy, send us of his
sonde!°   *message*

---

[7]   *Manet Titivillus* Latin: Titivillus remains.

[8]   *drawke … durnell* Types of weeds.

I have brought seed here to sow with my land.
545   Qwhill° I over-dylve° it, here it shall stand.   *while / dig*

(*He sets the sack down, and Titivillus walks away with it
while Mankind starts to dig.*)

In nomine Patris et Filii et Spiritus Sancti,[1] now I will begin.

(*His spade strikes Titivillus' board in the earth.*)

This land is so hard it makith me unlusty° and   *tired*
     irke!°   *angry*
I shall sow my corn at venture, and let God work.

(*He turns to get his sack of grain.*)

Alas, my corn is lost! Here is a foul work!
550   I see well, by tilling little shall I win.

(*He throws down the spade.*)

Here I give up my spade, for now and forever!
To occupy my body I will not put me in dever.[2]

(*Here Titivillus goeth out with the spade.*)

I will here my evensong here, or I dissever.°   *depart*
This place I assing° as for my kirke;°   *assign / church*
555   Here, in my kerke,° I kneel on my knees.   *church*

(*Prays, using beads.*)[3]

Pater noster, qui es in caelis.[4]
TITIVILLUS.   (*Returning.*) I promise you, I have no lead
     on my heels![5]
I am here again to make this fellow irke.

Qwhist!° Peace! I shall go to his ear and   *quiet*
     tittle° therein.   *whisper*

(*He whispers in Mankind's ear.*)

560   A short prayer thirlith° heaven. Of thy   *pierces*
     prayer blin.°   *cease*
Thou art holier then ever was any of thy kin.
Arise and avent thee!° Nature compels.   *relieve yourself*

(*Mankind gets up.*)

MANKIND.   (*To the audience.*) I will into this yard,
     soverens, and come again soon.
For dread of the cholic, and eke° of the stone,[6]   *also*
565   I will go do that needs must be done.
My beads shall be here for whosummever° will else.   *whoever*

(*Exiat.*) (*Leaving his prayer beads.*)

TITIVILLUS.   Mankind was busy in his prayer, yet I did him
     arise;
He is conveyde°—by Christ!—from his   *removed, relieved*
     divine service.
Whithe is he, trow ye? Iwisse,° I am wonder wise: *certainly*
570   I have sent him forth to shit lesinges.
If ye have any silver, in happe° pure brass,   *or perhaps*
Take a little powder of Parish° and cast over his face,   *Paris*
And even in the howll-flight° let him pass.   *owl-flight, (i.e., the dark)*
Titivillus can learn yow many praty° things!   *pretty*

575   I trow Mankind will come again soon,
Or else, I fear me, evensong will be done!
His beads shall be trisyde° aside, and that anon.   *tossed, thrown*
Ye shall a good sport, if ye will abide:
Mankind cummith° again—well fare he!   *comes*
580   I shall answer him *ad omnia quare.*[7]
There shall be set abroche° a clerical matter.   *raised*
I hope of his purpose to set him aside.

(*Re-enter Mankind.*)

---

[1]   *In nominee ... Sancti* Latin: In the name of the Father, and the
Son, and the Holy Spirit.

[2]   *I will not ... dever* I will not endeavor.

[3]   *beads* Rosary beads. Each bead on the rosary represents a specific
prayer.

[4]   *Pater noster ... caelis* Latin: Our Father who art in Heaven (the
opening of the Lord's Prayer).

[5]   *no lead on my heels* I.e., I move quickly.

---

[6]   *stone* Kidney-stone.

[7]   *ad omnia quare* Latin: At every why (i.e., question).

MANKIND.   Evensong hath be in the saying, I trow, a fair
　　　while!
　　I am irk of it. It is too long, by one mile.
585　Do way! I will no more so oft° over the church-stile;   *often*
　　Be as be may, I shall do another.
　　Of labour and prayer, I am near irk of both;
　　I will no more of it, though Mercy be wroth.
　　My head is very heavy, I tell yow, forsooth.
590　I shall sleep full my belly, and he were my brother.

(Sleeps.)

TITIVILLUS.   (*To the audience*.) And ever ye did, for me
　　　keep now your silence!
　　Not a word, I charge yow, pain of forty pens!
　　A praty game shall be showed yow, or ye go hence.
　　Ye may hear him snore—he is sad asleep.
595　Qwhist! Peace! The devil is dead, I shall go round in his ear.

(He whispers in Mankind's ear.)

　　Alas, Mankind, alas, Mercy stown° a mare!   *stolen*
　　He is run away fro his master, there wot° no man   *knows*
　　　where.
　　Moreover, he stole both a horse and a nete!°   *ox, cow*

　　But yet I heard say he broke his neck as he rode in France;
600　But I think he ridith° on the gallows, to learn for to dance,   *rideth*
　　Because of his theft—that is his governance!
　　Trust no more on him: he is a married man.
　　Mekill° sorrow with thy spade beforn thou hast   *much*
　　　wrought;
　　Arise and ask mercy of New-Guise, Nowadays, and Nought.
605　They can avise thee for the best. Let their good will be sought;
　　And thy own wife brethell,° and take thee a   *betray*
　　　lemman.°   *mistress*

　　(*To the audience*.) For-well, everychon, for I have done
　　　my game,
　　For I have brought Mankind to mischief and to shame!

(Exit Titivillus. Mankind wakes up.)

MANKIND.   Whope! who! Mercy hath broken his
　　　nekekicher,° avows,   *neck*
610　Or he hangith by the neck high up on the gallows!

Adieu, fair masters, I will hast me to the ale-house
And speak with New-Guise, Nowadays, and Nought,
And get me a lemman with a smattringe° face.   *kissable*

*(New-Guise runs in, a broken noose hanging around his
neck.)*

NEW-GUISE.   (*To the audience*.) Make space, for
　　　Cokkys° body sacred, make space!   *God's*
615　A ha, well over-ron, Gode give him evil grace!
　　We were near Saint Patrick's Way, by Him that me bought;

　　I was twitched by the neck—the game was begun!
　　A grace was, the halter brast° asunder: *Ecce signum!*[1]   *burst*
　　The half is about my neck. We had a near run!
620　"Beware," quod the good-wife when she smote off
　　　her husband's head, "beware!"
　　Mischief is a convict, for he could° his neck-verse.   *knew*
　　My body gave a swing when I hinge° upon the   *hung*
　　　casse.°   *gallow*
　　Alas, he will hang such a lighly man and a ferse°   *fierce*
　　For stealing of an horse—I pray God give him care!

625　Do way° this halter! What devil doth Mankind   *take off*
　　　here, with sorrow?
　　Alas, how my neck is sore, I make avowe!°   *swear*
MANKIND.   Ye be welcome, New-Guise. Sir, what cheer
　　　with yow?
NEW-GUISE.   Well, sir; I have no cause to mourn.
MANKIND.   What was that about your neck, so God you
　　　amend?[2]
630 NEW-GUISE.   In faith, Saint Audrey's holy bend.°   *band, necklace*
　　I have a little dishes,° as it please God to send,   *disease*
　　With a running ring-worm.

*(Enter Nowadays, carrying a number of articles belonging to
the church.)*

NOWADAYS.   Stand a-rom,° I pray thee, brother   *stand back*
　　　mine!
　　I have laboured all this night. When shall we go dine?
635　A church here-beside° shall pay for ale, bread,   *close by*
　　　and wine:

---

[1]   *Ecce signum!*   Latin: Behold the proof/the sign!

[2]   *so God you amend*   God help you.

Lo, here is stuff will serve.
NEW-GUISE.   Now, by the holy Mary, thou art better
    marchande° then I!   *merchant*

(*Enter Nought.*)

NOUGHT.   Avante, knaves, let me go by!
    I cannot get, and I should starve!

(*Enter Mischief, carrying fetters.*)

640 MISCHIEF.   Here cummith a man of arms! Why stand
    ye so still?
    Of murder and manslaughter I have my belly-fill.
NOWADAYS.   What, Mischief, have ye been in prison? And it
    be your will,
    Me semith[1] ye have scored a pair of fetters.
MISCHIEF.   I was chained by the arms—lo, I have them here.
645 The chains I brast asunder, and killed the jailer,
    Yea, and his fair wife halsyde° in a corner—   *embraced*
    A, how sweetly I kissed the sweet mouth of hers!

    When I had do,° I was mine own butler: *done*
    I brought away with me both dish and dublere.°   *plate, platter*
650 Here is anow for me. Be of good cheer!

(*He passes round refreshment and proposes a toast.*)

    Yet well fare the new chesaunce![2]
MANKIND.   (*Kneeling.*) I ask mercy of New-Guise,
    Nowadays, and Nought.
    Once with my spade I remember that I fought;
    I will make yow amends if I hurt yow ought,
655 Or did any grievance.

NEW-GUISE.   What a devil liketh thee to be of this
    disposition?[3]
MANKIND.   I dreamt Mercy was hange°—   *hanged*
    this was my vision—
    And that to yow three I should have recourse and remotion.
    Now I pray yow heartily of your good will:
660 I cry yow mercy of all that I did amiss.

[1] *Me semith*   It seems to me that.
[2] *Yet well … new chesaunce!*   Good luck to the new trade!
[3] *liketh thee … disposition*   Makes you act this way.

NOWADAYS.   (*Aside.*) I say, New-Guise, Nought:
    Titivillus made all this;
    As sekyr° as God is in heaven, so it is!   *sure*
NOUGHT.   (*To Mankind.*) Stand up on your feet! Why
    stand ye so still?

NEW-GUISE.   Master Mischief, we will yow exhort
665 Mankind's name in your book for to report.
MISCHIEF.   I will not so; I will set a court.
    Nowadays, make proclamation,
    And do it *sub forma juris*,[4] dastarde!°   *idiot*
NOWADAYS.   Oy-yt, oy-yit, oyet!° All manner of   *oyez*
    men and common women
670 To the court of Mischief othere° come or sen!°   *either / send*
    Mankind shall return; he is one of our men.
MISCHIEF.   Nought, come forth. Thou shall be steward.

NEW-GUISE.   Master Mischief, his side gown may be sold;
    He may have a jacket thereof, and money told.
675 MANKIND.   I will do for the best, so I have no cold.

(*He takes off his gown reluctantly.*)

    Hold, I pray yow, and take it with yow,
    And let me have it again in any wise.°   *way*

(*Nought scribit.*)[5]

NEW-GUISE.   I promitt yow a fresh jacket, after the new
    guise.
MANKIND.   Go and do that longith to your office,
680 And spare that ye mow!

(*New-Guise exits, taking Mankind's coat. Nought approaches
Mischief.*)

NOUGHT.   Hold, master Mischief, and read this!
MISCHIEF.   Here is (*Reads.*) "*Blottibus in blottis,
Blottorum blottibus istis.*"[6]
    I beshrew your ears, a fair hand!
685 NOWADAYS.   Yea, it is a good running fist;[7]

[4] *sub forma juris*   Latin: In legal form.
[5] *scribit*   Latin: writes.
[6] *Blottibus … istis*   Nonsense Latin, implying blotted writing.
[7] *running fist*   Cursive hand.

Such a hand may not be mist.

NOUGHT.   I should have done better, had I wist.°   *known*

MISCHIEF.   Take heed, sirs, it stoude you on hande:[1]

(*Reads.*)

"*Curia tenta generalis,*[2]

690   In a place there good ale is,

Anno regni regitalis

Edwardi nullateni,[3]

On yestern day,° in Feverere,° the year   *yesterday / February*

    passeth fully;

As Nought hath written—here is our Tully[4]—

695   *Anno regni regis nulli.*"[5]

NOWADAYS.   What how, New-Guise, thou makest much

    tarrying!

That jacket shall not be worth a farthing.

(*New-Guise returns through the audience, carrying Mankind's coat, now cut smaller.*)

NEW-GUISE.   (*To the audience.*) Out of my way, sirs, for

    dread of fighting!

Lo, here is a feet° taill, light to leap about!   *suitable*

700 NOUGHT.   It is not schapyn° worth a morsel   *shaped*

    of bread!

There is too much cloth—it weighs as any lead.

I shall go and mend it, else I will lose my head.

Make space, sirs, let me go out!

(*He exits, carrying Mankind's coat.*)

MISCHIEF.   Mankind, come hither—God send yow the

    goute!

705 Ye shall go to all the good fellows in the country about,

Onto the good-wife when the good-man° is out.   *husband*

"I will," say ye.

MANKIND.   I will, sir.

NEW-GUISE.   There arn° but six deadly sins;   *are*

    lechery is non,°   *not one*

710 As it may be verified by us brethellys° everychon.   *wretches*

Ye shall go rob, steal, and kill as fast as ye may gon.

"I will," say ye.

MANKIND.   I will, sir.

NOWADAYS.   On Sundays, on the morow early

    betime,°   *in the morning*

715 Ye shall with us to the ale-house early to go dine,

And forbear mass and matins, hours and prime.[6]

"I will," say ye.

MANKIND.   I will, sir.

MISCHIEF.   Ye must have by your side a long *da pacem,*[7]

720 As true men ride by the way, for to onbrace° them.   *cut, carve*

Take their money, cut their throats! Thus

    overface° them.   *overcome, overwhelm*

"I will," say ye.

MANKIND.   I will, sir.

(*Nought returns, carrying Mankind's coat. It has now been cut down even further.*)

NOUGHT.   Here is a jolly jacket! How say ye?

725 NEW-GUISE.   It is a good jacket of fence° for a   *defence*

    man's body!

(*They put it on Mankind.*)

Hay, dog! hay, whoppe! whoc! Go your way lightly!

Ye are well made for to run.

(*Mercy enters from the other side.*)

MISCHIEF.   Tidings, tidings! I have aspied one.

Hence with your stuff; fast we were gone!

730 I beshrew the last shall come to his home.

(*Dicant omnes:*)[8]

ALL.   Amen!

---

[1]   *it stoude … hande*   It concerns you.

[2]   *Curia … generalis*   Latin: The general court having been held.

[3]   *Anno regni … nullateni*   Latin: In the regnal year of King Edward the Nothing.

[4]   *Tully*   Marcus Tullius Cicero (106 BCE–43 CE), known variously as "Cicero" and as "Tully," and renowned as an orator and thinker.

[5]   *Anno regni … nulli*   Latin: In the regnal year of no one.

[6]   *mass … prime*   All terms for Christian services. Prime was the earliest of the several "hours" or short religious recitations that were supposed to be performed each day.

[7]   *da pacem*   Latin: peace-maker, i.e., a dagger.

[8]   *Dicant omnes*   Latin: Let all say.

MERCY.   What, how, Mankind, flee that fellowship, I
    yow pray!

MANKIND.   I shall speak with thee another time—to-
    morn, or the next day.

We shall go forth together, to keep my faders
    yer-day.°   *death anniversary*

735 A tapster, a tapster! Stow,° statt,° stow!   *come / slut*

MISCHIEF.   A mischief go with! Here I have a foul fall.

Hence, away fro me, or I shall beschitte° yow all.   *shit on*

NEW-GUISE.   What, how, hustler, hustler, lend us a football!

Whoppe, whow! a-now, a-now, a-now, a-now!

(The three exit, taking Mankind.)

740 MERCY.   My mind is dispersed,° my body   *distracted*
    trembleth as the aspen leaf!

The tears should trickledown by my cheeks, were not your
    reverence.

It were to me solace,[1] the cruel visitation of death!

Without rude behaviour, I cannot express this
    inconvenience.

Weeping, sythinge,° and sobbing were my   *sighing*
    sufficience;

745 All natural nutriment to me as caren is odibull.[2]

My inwarde affliction yeldith° me tedious unto   *makes*
    your presence.

I cannot bear it evenly° that Mankind is so   *calmly*
    flexible!°   *malleable*

Man un-kind, wherever thou be! For, all this world was
    not apprehensible

To discharge thine original offence, thraldam,°   *slavery*
    and captivity,

750 Till God's own well-beloved Son was obedient and passible.

Every drop of his blood was shed to purge thine iniquity.

I discommend and disallow thine often
    mutability!°   *changeability*

To every creature thou art dispectuose°   *despicable*
    and odible.°   *odious*

Why art thou so on-curtess,° so inconsiderate?   *uncourteous*
    Alas, woe is me!

755 As the fane° that turnith with the wind,   *weathervane*
    so thou art convertible.

---

[1] *It were to me solace*   It would be a comfort to me.

[2] *to me as … odibull*   Is odious as carrion to me.

In trust is treason; thy promise is not credible.

Thy perversiose° ingratitude I cannot rehearse!   *perverse*

To God and to all the holy court of heaven thou art
    despectible,°   *despicable*

As a noble versifier makith mention in this verse:

760 "*Lex et natura, Cristus et omnia jura*
    Damnant ingratum; lugent eum fore natum."[3]

O good Lady and Mother of Mercy, have pity and
    compassion

Of the wretchedness of Mankind, that is so wanton and
    so frail!

Let Mercy exceed Justice, dear Mother! Admit this
    supplication:

765 Equity to be leyde onparty,[4] and Mercy to prevail.

To sensual living is reproveable that is nowadays,

As by the comprehence of this matter it may be specified.

New-Guise, Nowadays, Nought, with their
    allectuose° ways   *alluring*

They have perverted Mankind, my sweet son, I have
    well espied.

770 A, with these cursed caitiffs,° and I may,[5] he shall   *wretches*
    not long endure!

I, Mercy, his father gostly, will proceed forth and do my
    propyrté.°   *task*

Lady, help! This manner of living is a detestible pleasure.

Vanitas vanitatum,[6] all is but a vanity.

Mercy shall never be convicte° of his oncurtes   *conquered*
    condition;

775 With weeping tears, by night and by day, I will go, and
    never cease.

Shall I not find him? Yes, I hope. Now God be my
    protection!

(He calls.) My predilecte° son, where be ye?   *beloved*
    Mankind, *ubi es?*[7]

---

[3] *Lex et natura … fore natum*   Latin: Law and nature, Christ and
all justice damn the ingrate, they lament that he was born.

[4] *leyde onparty*   Set aside.

[5] *and I may*   If I have my way.

[6] *Vanitas vanitatum*   Latin: Vanity of vanities. See Ecclesiastes.

[7] *Ubi es?*   Latin: Where are you?

(*He exits, calling "Ubi es?" Enter Mischief.*)

MISCHIEF.   My prepotent fadere, when ye sup, sup out
    your mess!
Ye are all too gloried in your terms—ye make many a
    less.°   *lie*

780 Will ye here? He crieth ever "Mankind, *ubi es?*"

(*Enter New-Guise. Nowadays and Nought follow a few
moments later.*)

NEW-GUISE.   Hic,° hic, hic, hic, hic, hic, hic, hic!   *Latin: here*
That is to say, here, here, here, ny° dead in the   *nearly*
    cryke!°   *creek*
If ye will have him, go and syke,° syke, syke!   *seek*
Syke not over-long, for losing of your mind.

785 NOWADAYS.   If ye will have Mankind—how, *Domine,*
    Domine, Dominus![1]—
Ye must speak to the schrive° for a *cape corpus,*[2]   *sheriff*
Else ye must be fain to return with *non est inventus.*[3]
How say ye, sir? My bolt is schett.°   *shot*
NOUGHT.   I am doing of my nedingys;[4] beware how ye
    schott!
790 Fy, fy, fy! I have foul arrayed° my foot.   *foully covered*
Be wise for shooting with your takyllys,° for,   *equipment*
    God wott,
My foot is foully over-schett.

MISCHIEF.   A parliament, a parliament! Come forth,
    Nought, behind;
A counsel belive!° I am aferde° Mercy will   *quickly / afraid*
    him find.
795 How say ye? And what say ye? How shall we do with
    Mankind?
NEW-GUISE.   Tush, a fly's wing![5] Will ye do well?
He wenith° Mercy were hung for stealing of a mare.   *thinks*
Mischief, go say to him that Mercy sekith everywhere:
He will hang himself, I undertake, for fear.
800 MISCHIEF.   I assent thereto. It is wittily said, and well.

---

[1] *Domine, Domine, Dominus!*   Latin: Lord, Lord, Our Lord.

[2] *cape corpus*   An order to move him. Latin: literally, take his body.

[3] *non est inventus*   Latin: He is not found.

[4] *of my nedingys*   Something necessary.

[5] *a fly's wing*   I.e., a trifling matter.

NOWADAYS.   Qwippe it in° thy coat; anon it   *whip it under*
    were done!
Now, Saint Gabriel's modyr° save the clothes°   *mother / shoes*
    of thy schon!°[6]
All the books in the world, if they had be undone,
Could not a cownselde° us bett.°   *counsel / better*

(*Hic exit Mischief.*) (*He returns with Mankind, now in
despair.*)

805 MISCHIEF.   How, Mankind, come and speak with Mercy!
    He is here fast by.
MANKIND.   A roppe, a rope, a rope! I am not worthy.
MISCHIEF.   Anon, anon, anon! I have it here ready,
    With a tree also that I have get.

(*They prepare a gallows.*)

Hold the tree, Nowadays; Nought, take hede, and be wise!
810 NEW-GUISE.   Lo, Mankind, do as I do: this is thy new guise.
    Give the rope just to thy neck, this is mine avise.°   *advice*

(*New-Guise demonstrates how the noose works. Mercy enters.*)

MISCHIEF.   Help thyself, Nought! Lo, Mercy is here!
He skarith° us with a bales; we may no longer tarry!   *scares*

(*They exit. New-Guise forgets about the noose he has been
demonstrating and begins to hang himself.*)

NEW-GUISE.   Qweke, qweke, qweke! Alas, my throat!
    I beschrew yow, mary!
815 A, Mercy, Christ's coppyde° curse go with you   *abundant*
    —and Saint Davy!
Alas, my wesant!° Ye were somewhat too near.   *throat*

(*They return and rescue New-Guise.*) (*Exiant.*)
(*Mankind falls, despairing.*)

MERCY.   Arise, my precious redempt son! Ye be to me full
    dear.—
He is so timerouse,° me semith his vital   *frightened*
    sprit° doth expire.   *spirit*

---

[6] *Saint … thy schon*   May the mother of Saint Gabriel save the
leather of your shoes (a proverbial expression of thanks).

MANKIND. Alas, I have be° so bestially disposed   *been*
    I dare not appear!

820 To see your solayciose° face I am nor worthy to   *comforting*
    desire.

MERCY. Your criminose complaint[1] woundeth my
    heart as a lance!

Dispose yourself meekly to ask mercy, and I will assent.

Yield me neither gold nor treasure, but your humble
    obeisiance[2]—

The voluntary subjection of your heart—and I am content.

825 MANKIND. What, ask mercy yet once again? Alas, it
    were a vile petition!

Ever to offend and ever to ask mercy, it is a
    puerility.°   *childish thing*

It is so abominable to rehearse my iterat transgression,[3]

I am not worthy to have mercy by no possibility.

MERCY. O Mankind, my singler° solace,   *unique*
    this is a lamentable excuse!

830 The dolorous° tears of my heart, how they   *sorrowful*
    begin to a-mownt!°   *gather*

O pirssid° Jhesu, help thou this sinfull sinner   *pierced*
    to redouce!°   *be led back*

Nam haec est mutatio dexterae Excelsi: vertit impios, et
    non sunt.[4]

Arise and ask mercy, Mankind, and be associate to me.

Thy death shall be my heaviness. Alas, tis pity it should
    be thus!

835 Thy obstinacy will exclude thee fro the glorious perpetuity.

Yet, for my love, ope° thy lips and say "*Miserere mei,*   *open*
Deus!"[5]

MANKIND. The egall° justice of God will   *equal*
    not permit such a sinful wretch

To be revived and restored again; it were impossible.

---

[1] *criminose complaint* Confession of guilt.

[2] *obeisiance* Obedience.

[3] *iterat transgression* Repeated sin.

[4] *Nam haec ... et non sunt* Latin: For this is the change of the right
hand of the Most High; He overthrows the wicked, and they are no
more. See Psalms 77.10 and Proverbs 12.7.

[5] *Miserere mei, Deus!* Latin: Have mercy on me, God!

MERCY. The justice of God will as I will, as himself
    doth preach:

840 *Nolo mortem peccatoris, inquit,*[6] if he will be
    reducible.°   *recoverable*

MANKIND. Than mercy, good Mercy! What is a man
    without mercy?

Little is our part of paradise, where mercy ne were.°   *is not*

Good Mercy, excuse the inevitable objection of my
    gostly enmy.

The proverb seyth, "The truth tryeth° the self." Alas,   *tests*
    I have much care!

845 MERCY. God will not make yow privy unto his Last
    Judgement.

Justice and equity shall be fortified,° I will not deny;   *strong*

Truth may not so cruelly proceed in his straight argument

But that Mercy shall rule the matter, without
    controversy.°   *doubt*

Arise now, and go with me in this deambulatorye.°   *cloister*

850 Incline your capacity; my doctrine is convenient.

Sin not in hope of mercy! That is a crime notary.°   *notorious*

To trust overmuch in a prince, it is not expedient.

In hope, when ye sin, ye think to have mercy: beware
    of that aventure!°   *approach*

The good Lord said to the lecherous woman of
    Chanane°—   *Canaan*

855 The holy Gospel is the autorite,° as we read in   *authority*
    Scripture—

"*Vade, et iam amplius noli peccare.*"[7]

Christ preserved this sinful woman taken in avowtry;°   *adultery*

He said to her these words, "Go and sin no more."

So to yow: "Go, and sin no more." Beware of vain
    confidence of mercy!

860 Offend not a prince on trust of his favour, as I said before.

If ye feel yourself trapped in the snare of your gostly enmy,

Ask mercy anon;° beware of the continuance!   *at once*

While a wound is fresh, it is proved curable by surgery,

That, if it proceed overlong, it is cause of great grievance.

---

[6] *Nolo mortem ... inquit* Latin: I do not wish the sinner's death, he
said; cf. Ezekiel 33.1.

[7] *Vade ... noli peccare* Latin: Go, and sin no more.

MANKIND.   To ask mercy and to have, this is a liberal[1]
    possession.

Shall this expeditious petition ever be allowed, as ye have
    insight?[2]

MERCY.   In this present life, mercy is plenty,°   *readily available*
    till death maketh his division.

But, whan ye be go,° *usque ad minimum*   *gone*
    quadrantem[3] ye shall reckon your right.

Ask mercy, and have, while the body with the soul
    hath his annexion;°   *is united*

870 If ye tarry till your decease, ye may hap of your desire to miss.

Be repentant here! Trust not the hour of death. Think
    on this lesson:

Ecce nunc tempus acceptabile, ecce nunc dies salutis.[4]

All the virtue in the world if ye might comprehend,

Your merits were not premiabyll to° the   *deserving of*
    bliss above—

875 Not to the least joy of heaven, of your proper effort to ascend.

With mercy, ye may. I tell yow no fable; Scripture doth
    prove.

MANKIND.   O Mercy, my suavius° solas° and   *sweet / sole*
    singular recreatory,°   *restorer*

My predelect° special! Ye are worthy to have my love.   *beloved*

For, without desert and means supplicatory,

880 Ye be compacient° to my inexcusable   *compassionate*
    reprove.°   *shame*

A, it swemith° my heart to think how unwisely   *grieves*
    I have wrought!

Titivillus, that goeth invisible, hing° his net   *hung*
    before my eye,

And by his fantastical visions sediciously sought,°   *led*

To New-Guise, Nowadayis, Nowght caused me to obey.

885 MERCY.   Mankind, ye were oblivious of my doctrine
    monitory:°   *warning*

I said before, Titivillus would assay yow a bronte.°   *attack you*

Beware fro hensforth of his fables delusory!°   *deceitful*

The proverb seyth: "*Jacula praestita minus laedunt.*"[5]

Ye have three adversaries and he is master of hem all:

890 That is to say, the Devil, the World, the Flesh and the
    Fell.°   *skin*

The New-Guise, Nowadayis, Nowgth, the "World"
    we may hem call;

And properly Titivillus signifeth the Fiend of hell;

The Flesh—that is the unclean concupiscence of your body.

These be your three gostly enemies, in whom ye have
    put your confidence.

895 They brought yow to Mischief, to conclude your
    temporal glory—

As it hath be showed before this worshipful audience.

Remember how ready I was to help yow;
    fro sweche° I was not dangerous.   *from such*

Wherefore, good son, abstain fro sin evermore after this!

Ye may both save and spill your soul, that is so precious;

900 *Libere welle, libere nolle*[6] God may not deny, iwis.°   *certainly*

Beware of Titivillus with his net, and of all his envious will,

Of your sinful delectation that grieveth your gostly substance.

Your body is your enmy. Let him not have his will!

Take your leave whan ye will—God send yow good
    perseverance!

905 MANKIND.   Sith I shall depart, bless me, fader, here then I go.

God send us all plenty of his great mercy!

MERCY.   *Dominus custodit te ab omni malo!*[7]

In nomine Patris, et Filii, et Spiritus Sancti.[8] *Amen.*

(*Hic exit Mankind.*)

(*To the audience.*) Worshipful soverens, I have do my
    property:°   *done my work*

---

[1] *liberal* Freely and generously given.

[2] *Shall this ... insight* So far as you can judge, will this hasty
request be granted?

[3] *usque ad ... quadrantem* Latin: Unto the smallest farthing.

[4] *Ecce nunc ... dies salutis* Latin: Behold, now is the accepted time,
now is the day of salvation. See Corinthians 6.2.

[5] *Jacula ... laedunt* Latin: Familiar darts sting less.

[6] *Libere ... nolle* Latin: Freely to will, freely not to.

[7] *Dominus ... malo!* Latin: The Lord shall preserve thee from all
evil. See Psalms 121.7.

[8] *In nomine ... Sancti* Latin: In the name of the Father, and the
Son, and the Holy Spirit.